Psychology suggests pathways that invite us to discover. These pathways offer some clear guideposts, many intriguing choices, and even a sense of mystery. A few pathways are relatively orderly and well disciplined; others are rich with sensory experience. Some pathways may look well traveled and familiar, but others offer doors that open into areas never visited before. Please join me in exploring the diverse pathways that characterize psychology.

Margaret W. Matlin

Psychology

Margaret W. Matlin

State University of New York, Geneseo

Harcourt Brace College Publishers

Fort Worth   Philadelphia   San Diego
New York   Orlando   Austin   San Antonio
Toronto   Montreal   London   Sydney   Tokyo

Publisher	*Ted Buchholz*
Acquisitions Editor	*Eve Howard*
Developmental Editor	*John Haley*
Project Editor	*Catherine Townsend*
Production Manager	*Kathleen Ferguson*
Art & Design Supervisor	*John Ritland*
Cover Design	*Nancy Turner*
Text Design	*DUO Design Group*
Compositor	*Syntax International*

Cover Photo: Negley Paint Company, Shertz, Texas
Interior Design by: Chumney Associates
Photo: Bob Shimer, Hedrich-Blessing
Chapter 16 Opener: The William Nathaniel Banks garden from "Gardens of Georgia",
Richard Moore photographer

LIBRARY OF CONGRESS CATALOGING-IN-PUBLICATION DATA

Matlin, Margaret W.
    Psychology/Margaret W. Matlin.
        p. cm.
    Includes bibliographical references and index.
    ISBN 0-03-029508-4
    1. Psychology.
I. Title.
BF121.M415   1992
150—dc20
91-27211
CIP

Address for Editorial Correspondence
Harcourt Brace Jovanovich, Publishers, 301 Commerce Street, Suite 3700, Fort Worth,
TX 76102

Address for Orders
Harcourt Brace Jovanovich, Publishers, 6277 Sea Harbor Drive, Orlando, FL 32887
1-800-782-4479, or 1-800-433-0001 (in Florida)

Printed in the United States of America

3 4 5   063   9 8 7 6 5 4 3

To Beth and Sally Matlin
and all other college students who care about people
and want to learn more about them.

Preface

Psychology is a supremely fascinating discipline that spans topics as diverse as a single cortical neuron and international peacemaking. Its research methods range from highly controlled laboratory studies to lengthy, unstructured interviews. Some psychological phenomena are well understood, but many remain mysterious or paradoxical. Psychology attempts to explain why some people risk their lives for the welfare of complete strangers, yet others murder their own family members. Even our theoretical approaches emphasize diversity in how psychologists view human beings.

The challenge for an author of an introductory psychology textbook is to synthesize this variety, to present the material in a clear, interesting fashion that is guided by the principles of human memory, to encourage students to appreciate scientific methods, and to capture the diversity of human experience in the 1990s.

Goals

As I prepared to write this textbook, I clarified several important goals. I had used five different textbooks in teaching several thousand students. Each book had its strengths, but no book fulfilled all the requirements that seemed essential in an ideal textbook for the 1990s. Accordingly, I wrote this book with four major objectives in mind.

1. *To synthesize the broad range of knowledge about psychology.* I have written four other textbooks: *Human Experimental Psychology*, *Sensation and Perception*, *Cognition*, and *Psychology of Women*. My background in such disparate areas provides an unusually broad perspective about the discipline of psychology. This perspective enables me to point out relationships between topics that might initially seem unrelated. Students can benefit from a textbook that clarifies how certain phenomena covered within a chapter are interrelated.

   In addition, *Psychology* emphasizes consistent patterns in psychological processes. For example, in the social psychology of stereotypes, people are guided by heuristics similar to those used in visual perception and in cognitive tasks. The text also synthesizes both classic and extremely current resources. Finally, I have stressed three important themes that weave through the 19 chapters of the book, providing even further cohesiveness.

2. *To present complex topics in an interesting, clear, and well-organized fashion.* Research in human memory demonstrates that material is more memorable when it is high in imagery, so I have included numerous examples supplied by my students and from my own experience. (Student reviewers responded especially enthusiastically to the use of examples.) Both professors and students have praised the clarity of my previous textbooks, and I have made every effort to maintain that standard.

   In addition, research in human memory emphasizes the importance of organization. Accordingly, every chapter is organized into two to five sections, each followed by a section summary to encourage integration before beginning the next section. Within each section, I often review what we have discussed and preview what we will cover next. The textbook also features numerous pedagogical aids (see pages 16–17). Some authors assume that these student-oriented features are important only for lower level students. I would argue that *all* students profit from these features. The clear majority of my students at SUNY Geneseo ranked in the top 10% of their high school classes. Nevertheless, they confirm that they appreciate such features as section summaries, mnemonic tips, and pronunciation guides.

Finally, research on the self-reference effect in memory has demonstrated that people retain material better if they relate it to their own experience. An important objective in writing *Psychology* was to encourage students to think about their own psychological processes—from saccadic eye movements to the fundamental attribution error. Typically, they have taken these processes for granted prior to a course in psychology. In many cases, I include a demonstration to make the phenomenon more memorable; other times, I urge students to recall relevant experiences.

3. *To emphasize research methodology.* The excitement of psychological research lured me away from a biology major when I was a college freshman, and I later received my PhD in experimental psychology. Furthermore, I wrote my first textbook in experimental psychology. A separate chapter on research methods seems especially important in the 1990s. Chapter 2 discusses methodological issues, which are also emphasized throughout the book. The specific facts of psychology may be substantially different 20 years from now. However, students who have developed the ability to analyze a study critically will be able to evaluate new research and to question studies that were not appropriately conducted. Furthermore, this textbook should encourage students to apply the principles of research methods to their own experiences. Students need to learn that critical thinking skills need not be confined to formal research.

4. *To convey the variety and diversity of human experience.* My expertise in the psychology of women has sensitized me to the invisibility of many groups of people in current textbooks. In contrast, the biological drawings in this textbook do not depict only White male skulls, issues of gender are integrated throughout, elderly people are described in substantial detail, and the experiences of people of color are frequently addressed. In the 1990s, a psychology textbook especially benefits from a multicultural approach that admires and respects diversity.

Features

Consistent with my goals, I have developed some important features that students and professors have appreciated in my other textbooks:

1. Three straightforward themes are emphasized throughout the book:
   - Humans are extremely competent; their performance is generally rapid and accurate, and most errors can be traced to strategies that are typically adaptive.
   - Humans differ widely from one another; as a consequence, people often respond differently to the same stimulus situation.
   - Human behavior is complex; most psychological phenomena are caused by multiple factors.

2. Section summaries occur at frequent intervals throughout the chapters, encouraging integration of material before proceeding to a new topic.

3. Demonstrations or informal experiments encourage students to illustrate a well-known study or important principle, making the material more memorable.

4. New terms are shown in boldface type, with a definition included in the same sentence; these terms also appear at the end of each chapter so that students can test themselves, and they also are listed with definitions in the glossary at the end of the book.

5. An in-depth section examining recent research on a selected topic is featured in chapters 2 through 19. This feature is an important mechanism for achieving depth as well as breadth in an introductory psychology textbook. In addition, it provides an opportunity to emphasize research methodology.

6. A set of review questions encourages students to consolidate their knowledge, apply the information to real-life events, and test the adequacy of their learning.

7. A list of recommended readings, appropriate for introductory psychology students, provides resources for students who want additional information on topics related to the chapter material.

Supplementary Materials

My editors and I agreed that ancillary material developed for other introductory psychology textbooks is often written hastily, with little or no opportunity to coordinate the separate volumes. Therefore, we began to work on these projects almost two years before the textbook was scheduled to be published. The authors have exchanged material with each other so that some questions from the Study Guide could be included in the Test-Item File, so that the same learning objectives could be emphasized in the Instructor's Manual and the Study Guide, and so forth. I thoroughly admire the three ancillary authors who worked on these projects!

Instructor's Manual *(by Lori R. Van Wallendael and Margaret W. Matlin)*

The co-author of the Instructor's Manual is an enthusiastic and well-read faculty member at the University of North Carolina at Charlotte. Dr. Van Wallendael drew from her experience in teaching both classic and highly current topics in introductory psychology to produce an exceptional set of lecture ideas. I supplied her with additional current articles and material that was omitted from the text because of space limitations. She also developed some wonderful classroom demonstrations that she found helpful in her own introductory psychology classes. Finally, we both previewed dozens of psychology films, because we were convinced that instructors would find our own evaluative summaries more helpful than the capsule summaries supplied by the film companies.

Study Guide *(by Drew C. Appleby and Margaret W. Matlin)*

Drew Appleby teaches at Marian College in Indiana, and he is well known for numerous activities focusing on the teaching of psychology. Dr. Appleby's sensitivity to students and his mastery of the subject matter pervade the Study Guide. We decided to organize the exercises in the Study Guide so that in each section, students attempt the easiest task first (matching), next a related task (fill-in-the-blank), and then the task most similar to the one that would appear on their in-class examinations (multiple choice). Each section ends with thought projects that encourage students to contemplate and answer more broad-ranging questions.

We emphasized an organization by sections so that students could read a section in the textbook and then immediately work on that same material in the Study Guide. Each chapter in the Study Guide ends with a crossword puzzle, a feature that has been demonstrated to help students master course material.

Test-Item File *(by Susan D. Lonborg and Margaret W. Matlin)*
Susan Lonborg, the West Coast member of our writing team, teaches courses such as counseling psychology and human sexuality at Central Washington University. She had provided such exceptionally thoughtful critiques of my book when she served as a reviewer that we knew we wanted her to write one of the ancillaries. The Test-Item File includes approximately 150 items for each chapter, and it emphasizes conceptual questions and applied questions that require synthesis and application. It also includes factual questions that test the acquisition of basic information.

Other Teaching Aids
The *ExaMaster* Computerized Test Bank is available in IBM or Macintosh format.

EasyTest lets you create a test from a single screen. It will construct a test using the questions you have chosen from the database, or it will randomly select questions according to your specifications.

FullTest allows you to select questions as you preview them on screen; edit existing questions; add your own questions; add or edit graphics (IBM version only); link related questions, instructions, and graphics; randomly select questions from a wide range of criteria; create your own criteria on two open keys; block specific questions from random selection; print up to 99 different versions of the same test and answer sheet.

RequesTest lets you order tests that conform to your criteria. Call 1-800-447-9457, and HBJ will compile the tests and either mail or fax them to you within 48 hours.

Our gradebook program, *ExamRecord*, is free with ExaMaster software. Exam-Record lets you record, curve, graph, and print your students' grades.

The HBJ *Video Library* offers six video sources to supplement Margaret Matlin's *Psychology*: The Discovering Psychology Telecourse; the teaching video modules from the Discovering Psychology Telecourse; modules from PBS' "The Brain" series; CBS' "60 Minutes" segments; PBS' "The Mind" series; PBS' "The Seasons of Life;" and an additional video featuring five broad areas of research.

The *Whole Psychology Catalog* contains valuable experimental exercises, questionnaires, lecture outlines, and visual aids.

Acknowledgments
One of the pleasures of writing a preface is the opportunity to praise and thank the dozens of people who have helped create and refine a textbook. Holt, Rinehart and Winston (now Harcourt Brace Jovanovich) had been my publisher for three previous textbooks, and I knew they would continue to do well with this larger-scale project. Even so, I was pleasantly surprised at the impressive skill of these team members. My gratitude goes to Eve Howard, psychology editor, for her

superb help in clarifying the goals of the book and providing feedback throughout many months of writing; I admire her expertise and good judgment. John Haley stepped into the job of developmental editor and excelled in the art of tactful suggestions, mastery of writing style, and coordinating the complexities of professional reviews, photo packages, and ancillaries. I really appreciate his intelligence and appropriate attention to detail. Thanks are also due to Cathy Townsend and Kathleen Ferguson for their efficient orchestration of the production process; they were wonderful about making certain that proofs and art work could be sent to me at the earliest possible dates, which facilitated the timely production of the book. In addition, John Ritland deserves a special thank you for his exceptional work on the textbook's design; he managed to translate pedagogical goals into a clear and beautifully functional layout. Linda Webster did a superbly efficient and professional job on the glossary and the indexes. Other people who merit my thanks include Susan Arellano, Susan Driscoll, and Anne Heller, who worked with me in the early stages of the book, Marty Levick for his photo research, and Carol Donner for her superb biological artwork. Finally, Page Sanders and Michael Alread deserve my compliments for their hard work on the brochures and numerous other components of marketing.

Numerous psychologists deserve praise for their suggestions, comments on style and content, and lists of additional references. These reviewers and consultants helped me write a much more accurate and clearly written textbook than I could have managed on my own.

I am deeply indebted to

Lauren Alloy, *Temple University*

Donna Alexander-Redmayne, *Antelope Valley College*

Anne Anastasi, *Fordham University*

Joel Aronoff, *Michigan State University*

Frank Bagrash, *California State University at Fullerton*

Johnston Beach, *United States Military Academy*

Kayla Bernheim, *Livingston County Mental Health Center*

Galen Bodenhausen, *Michigan State University*

John Bonvillian, *University of Virginia*

Scott Borelli, *Boston University*

Robert Bornstein, *Miami (Ohio) University*

Charles Brewer, *Furman University*

William Calhoun, *University of Tennessee at Knoxville*

John Caruso, *Southeast Massachusetts University*

Patricia Chavez y Marquez, *Antelope Valley College*

Eve Clark, *Stanford University*

Francis Coletti, *United States Military Academy*

Kim Dolgin, *Ohio Wesleyan University*

Michael Domjan, *University of Texas at Austin*

Claire Etaugh, *Bradley University*

Leslie Fisher, *Cleveland State University*

Morton Friedman, *University of California at Los Angeles*

Laurel Furumoto, *Wellesley College*

Betty Gaines, *Midland College*

Richard Gibbons, *Iowa State University*

Jean Giebenhain, *College of St. Thomas*

Margaret Gittis, *Youngstown State University*

Robert Guttentag, *University of North Carolina at Greensboro*

Richard Griggs, *University of Florida*

Maury Haraway, *Northeast Louisiana University*

Lewis Harvey, *University of Colorado at Boulder*

Douglas Herrmann, *National Institute of Mental Health*

Winfred Hill, *Northwestern University*

Lyllian Hix, *Houston Community College System*

Margaret Intons-Peterson, *Indiana University at Bloomington*

Alice M. Isen, *Cornell University*

W. Jake Jacobs, *University of Arizona*

Valerie James-Aldridge, *University of Texas, Pan American*

James Jones, *University of Delaware*

Rick Kasschau, *University of Houston*

Daniel Kimble, *University of Oregon*

Alfred Kornfeld, *Eastern Connecticut State University*

John Kounias, *Tufts University*

Terry Knapp, *University of Nevada at Las Vegas*

James Knight, *Humboldt State University*

Michael Knight, *Central State University*

Robert Levy, *Indiana State University*

Susan Lonborg, *Central Washington University*

Kurt Mahoney, *Mesa Community College*

Barton Mann, *University of North Carolina at Chapel Hill*

Deborah McDonald, *New Mexico State University*

Elizabeth McDonel, *University of Alabama*

Linda Musun-Miller, *University of Central Arkansas*

Tibor Palfai, *Syracuse University*

Harold Pashler, *University of California at San Diego*

David Payne, *State University of New York at Binghamton*

James Pennebaker, *Southern Methodist University*

E. Jerry Phares, *Kansas State University*

Edward Rinalducci, *University of Central Florida*

Laurie Rotando, *Westchester County Community College*

Kenneth Rusiniak, *Eastern Michigan University*

James Ryan, *University of Wisconsin at La Crosse*

Edward Sadalla, *Arizona State University*

David Sanders, *Oregon State University*

Warren Street, *Central Washington University*

Ross Thompson, *University of Nebraska at Lincoln*

Lori Van Wallendael, *University of North Carolina at Charlotte*

Michael Vitiello, *University of Washington*

Mary Roth Walsh, *University of Lowell*

Wilse Webb, *University of Florida.*

Susan Krauss Whitbourne, *University of Massachusetts at Amherst*

My thanks also go to my superb student reviewers, who conscientiously read the manuscript, commenting on the clarity of the text, noting inconsistencies, and providing additional examples. I was truly impressed with their expertise, their diligence, and their honesty.

Amy Bolger   **Matthew Prichard**
Jonathan Blumenthal   **Heather Wallach**
Sheryl Mileo   **Martin Williams**
Claudia Militello

In addition, many colleagues, students, and friends supplied examples, ideas, information, and references. I thank Charles Brewer, Ganie DeHart, Karen Duffy, Lisa Elliot, Frederick Fidura, Tina Folmsbee, John Fox, Lori Gardinier, Becky Glass, Walter Harding, Amy Holm, Eve Howard, Patricia Keith-Spiegel, Maria Kountz, Mary Kroll, Peter Muzzonigro, Barbara Nodine, Lynn Offerman, Paul Olczak, Robert Owens, Catherine Perna, Cathleen Quinn, George Rebok, Ramon Rocha, Lanna Ruddy, Donna Shapiro, M. Shelton Smith, John Sparrow, Maura Thompson, Leonore Tiefer, Gail Walker, Helen S. White, Edward Whitson, Rodney Williams, and Melvyn Yessenow. Thanks also to Drew Appleby for all the useful suggestions he offered while reading the manuscript in preparing the study guide. Mary Roth Walsh deserves my deep gratitude for providing references, suggestions, and interesting points of view on numerous issues throughout the textbook.

Many other people have helped in various phases of the preparation of this book. Mary Lou Perry, Shirley Thompson, and Constance Ellis provided countless services that allowed me to devote more time to writing. Several students— Karen Marie Gibson, Andrea Iwanowski, Angela Jause, Leslie Lauer, and Eileen

Stepien—were exemplary in tracking down references, photocopying material, and checking the accuracy of my bibliography. In addition, three members of the Milne Library staff at the State University of New York at Geneseo provided superb expertise and assistance: Judith Bushnell, Paula Henry, and Harriet Sleggs. Ron Pretzer provided the majority of the setup photos, demonstrating his professional competence in photographing students, sparklers, classrooms, and a wide assortment of bizarre objects. Louise Wadsworth also deserves praise for her wonderful photographs of children.

My last, most enthusiastic acknowledgment goes to the members of my family. Thanks to my daughters, Beth and Sally, for providing examples, posing for photographs, acting as guinea pigs in the development of some demonstrations, and also for being wonderful human beings who inspire me to write for students like themselves. To my husband, Arnie, I give my deepest thanks for his technical expertise and suggestions, but more importantly for his love, his committed encouragement, and his spectacular sense of humor. My parents deserve my final note of appreciation: Thanks to Helen White for encouraging my enthusiasm for learning and my love of language, and to Donald White for encouraging my enjoyment of science and for providing a model of a professional who is truly excited about his work.

Margaret W. Matlin

About the Author

Margaret W. Matlin received her BA in psychology from Stanford University and her MA and PhD in experimental psychology from the University of Michigan. She holds the title of Distinguished Teaching Professor at State University of New York at Geneseo, where she has taught courses since 1971 in general psychology, experimental psychology, statistics, sensation and perception, cognitive psychology, human memory, human development, conflict resolution, and the psychology of women. In 1977, she received the State University of New York's Chancellor's Award for Excellence in Teaching, and in 1985 she was awarded the American Psychological Association Teaching of Psychology Award in the 4-year college and university division. Her previous books include *The Pollyanna Principle: Selectivity in Language, Memory, and Thought*; *Human Experimental Psychology*; *Sensation and Perception* (currently in its third edition); *Cognition* (currently in its second edition); and *Psychology of Women* (second edition in preparation). Her husband, Arnie, is a pediatrician, and her daughters, Beth and Sally, attend Wheelock College and Stanford University.

Contents in Brief

Contents

Psychology

CHAPTER

1

**Introducing
Psychology**

One summer on an airplane ride to a psychology convention, I found myself seated next to a friendly looking teenager. As the plane prepared for departure, I closed the convention booklet I had been reading and she glanced over at its title, *American Psychological Association*. "So, you're a psychologist?" she inquired. I admitted I was. "Do you study, you know, dogs and how they drool when a bell rings?" I smiled and answered that my interests tended more toward humans. "So you study people with problems?" was her reply. She seemed somewhat surprised when I explained my fascination with more everyday psychological processes such as human memory, vision, and gender stereotypes.

It is true that psychologists do study drooling dogs and problem-plagued people, and this textbook certainly discusses these topics. However, a larger portion of the book explores how normal people perceive, think, experience emotions, and interact socially. For instance, why can you remember the name of your best friend from fifth grade better than the name of the person to whom you were introduced 14 seconds ago? Why does your heart beat faster when you just missed being hit by a car? Why do you blame your tardiness on the traffic, rather than a basic tendency toward being late, yet you listen suspiciously when a friend offers the same explanation? You will see in this textbook that the scope of psychology is enormously broad, including topics that range from physiological studies of nerve cells to social-psychology studies on large crowds of people.

Psychology can be defined as the scientific study of behavior and mental processes. Let us examine the components of that definition. *Scientific study* means that psychologists use systematic, well-organized methods to learn about psychological processes. As we emphasize later in this chapter and in more detail in chapter 2, psychologists do not gather their data by casual speculation. Instead, they use a variety of more careful methods that include experiments as well as objective observation. *Behavior* means physical actions that can be seen or heard, such as touching or speaking aloud. But psychology also includes *mental processes*, which cannot be seen or heard. These mental processes include perceiving, dreaming, remembering, and making decisions.

Psychologists differ with respect to the goals they emphasize. These goals include the following:

1. *describing* behaviors and mental processes, based on careful, systematic observation;

2. *explaining* why these behaviors and mental processes occurred;

3. *predicting* future events on the basis of past events; and

4. *changing* behaviors and mental processes so that they are more appropriate.

In general, research psychologists focus on the first three goals. In contrast, **applied psychologists** have received training in these three areas, but they are more concerned with *changing* both actions and thoughts.

Let us clarify these different goals with an example of psychologists who study children's aggression. Some psychologists *describe* children's aggressive behavior in a classroom. Others *explain* why children are more aggressive after watching a violent movie. Still others might try to *predict* how aggressive each child will be in first grade, based on his or her aggressiveness as a kindergartener. Finally, applied psychologists would attempt to *change* the children's behavior, reducing their level of aggression. In summary, a single psychology topic can be explored from a wide diversity of perspectives.

This diversity of perspectives also characterizes the history of psychology. This chapter begins with an overview of the different theoretical approaches that psychologists have adopted in their scientific study of behavior and mental processes. After this survey of psychology's past, a section on psychology's present looks at the current theoretical approaches, as well as the profession of psychology. Next we consider three important themes that recur throughout this book and can help you appreciate some underlying consistencies in psychology. The final section includes tips on how to use this book most effectively.

Psychology's Past

Psychology is simultaneously very old and very new. Greek philosophers such as Plato and Aristotle speculated about human nature more than 2,000 years ago. In the 17th century, European philosophers such as John Locke and René Descartes argued about whether we are born with certain abilities, or whether we must acquire them through experience. So, psychology is very old when we consider the number of centuries that people have contemplated psychological ideas.

These early thinkers used an "armchair approach," reasoning and speculating about the nature of psychology without scientific study. Suppose you were to sit in your own chair and speculate about whether you were born with the ability to hear the difference between two similar speech sounds. You *might* reach the correct answer, but the armchair approach often provides misleading answers. For instance, try Demonstration 1.1, which asks you to evaluate some popular sayings that were devised using the armchair approach and casual observation.

Demonstration 1.1

Evaluating Popular Sayings

Below are nine popular sayings. Each of these sayings has been examined by psychologists. Read each saying and decide whether you think the psychological evidence supports or does not support the saying. Write *true* or *false* in front of the saying. Turn to the end of the chapter to find what current researchers have concluded.

_____ 1. Misery loves company.
_____ 2. Spare the rod and spoil the child.
_____ 3. The squeaky wheel gets the grease.
_____ 4. Actions speak louder than words.
_____ 5. Beauty is only skin deep.
_____ 6. Cry and you cry alone.
_____ 7. Marry in haste, repent at leisure.
_____ 8. Familiarity breeds contempt.
_____ 9. He who lives by the sword dies by the sword.

In contrast to the armchair approach, psychologists in recent years have depended upon **empirical evidence**, the kind of scientific evidence obtained by careful observation or experimentation. As you saw in Demonstration 1.1, empirical evidence—gathered by research psychologists—frequently contradicts our intuitions.

When we consider the history of *empirical psychology*, then psychology is very new, particularly in comparison with other sciences. For example, the Italian physicist Galileo (1564–1642) introduced the telescope into astronomy and used it to discover the changing phases of Venus and the moons of Jupiter more than three centuries ago (Haugeland, 1985). Interestingly, scientists had long ago developed more effective methods to explore distant planets than to investigate ourselves. In fact, the history of empirical psychology began in 1879, just a little more than a century ago, with the German psychologist Wilhelm Wundt. We begin our history of psychology with the founding of his laboratory.

Wilhelm Wundt

Wilhelm Wundt, the founder of academic psychology.

Wilhelm Wundt (pronounced "*Vill*-helm Voont"; 1832–1920) is usually considered to be the founder of empirical psychology. In 1879, Wundt created the first institute for research in experimental psychology at the University of Leipzig, Germany. For the first time in history, students in this new discipline could conduct psychological research. In the 1990s, we are so accustomed to psychology as an academic subject that we need to remind ourselves that psychology courses were not available prior to Wundt's era (Schlesinger, 1985).

Wundt argued that psychology had been progressing slowly because it relied on casual armchair speculation (Blumenthal, 1975). Wundt preferred more formal, careful methodology. For example, some of his research involved **introspection**, that is, observing one's own psychological reactions. Wundt insisted that introspection be conducted in a rigorous fashion, following careful training in standardized techniques for introspection. Wundt's approach, developed more fully by his students, was called **structuralism**, because it examined the structure of the mind and the organization of the basic elements of sensations, feelings, and images.

One reason that Wundt is so important in the history of psychology is that he was impressively productive as a researcher. In roughly 50 years of work, he published about 500 research papers and books, producing about 60,000 printed pages (Gardner, 1985; Schlesinger, 1985). His interests ranged widely and included memory, language, emotion, abnormal psychology, religion, history, and art (Blumenthal, 1975).

Let us consider a typical Wundt study, one on memory. For a fraction of a second, Wundt presented to trained observers a set of letters such as this:

```
r   v   n   e
w   o   z   g
m   b   t   u
```

Wundt found that most observers could report no more than six letters, yet they claimed they *saw* more (Wundt, 1912/1973). It seemed that the additional letters slipped away from memory in the process of recalling them. As you will see in chapter 7, this fragile, fleeting characteristic of memory was explored again half a century later in an important study. This topic is now called sensory memory (Sperling, 1960). Impressively, the basic phenomenon was initially described by psychology's first systematic researcher.

Wundt deserves credit not only for his findings, but also for his methods. For example, he emphasized the importance of **replications**, or studies in which a phenomenon is tested several times, often under different conditions. For instance, the study with the letters could be repeated several times, using a different group of participants and a different set of letters each time.

Finally, Wundt influenced psychology by training other psychologists. Students flocked from around the world to study with him, and he eventually sponsored 186 PhD dissertations in psychology (Hearst, 1979).

William James

American psychologists at the end of the 19th century were more influenced by William James (1842–1910) than by Wilhelm Wundt. James preferred a more informal approach, emphasizing the kinds of questions we encounter in daily life. He wrote extensively about **consciousness**, which we now define as our awareness of the environment and ourselves (chapter 5). James also developed an influential theory that explained emotional reactions in terms of our perception of physiological responses (chapter 12).

William James, the first major American psychologist.

James was deeply impressed with the theories of evolution proposed by biologist Charles Darwin. James believed that psychological processes had evolved in the same fashion as other human processes. He was particularly interested in the evolution and functions of consciousness, and he wondered how consciousness helps human beings. This emphasis on the functions of psychological processes inspired the name for James's approach to psychology: functionalism. **Functionalism** is the view that psychological processes are adaptive; they allow humans to survive and to adapt sucessfully to their surroundings.

Whereas Wundt was known for his laboratory, James was known for his textbooks. For several decades, American psychology students read either the two-volume *Principles of Psychology* (1890) or the shorter version, *Psychology, Briefer Course* (1892). Professors referred to the longer version as "James," and they nicknamed the shorter version "Jimmy" (Hilgard, 1987). A century later, psychologists still admire these important books.

Many of James's ideas seem remarkably modern. For example, he emphasized that the human mind is active and inquiring, a view still current today (Matlin, 1989). James also suggested that humans have two different kinds of memory. As chapter 7 will note, this proposal was reemphasized nearly 80 years later (Atkinson & Shiffrin, 1968).

American Psychology in the Early 20th Century

A number of Wundt's students left Germany for the United States. Some of them, such as Edward Titchener, continued in Wundt's tradition. Titchener founded a psychology laboratory at Cornell University and further developed the introspection technique. But other students developed their own, different agendas. G. Stanley Hall, at Johns Hopkins University, founded the American Psychological Association and created the first psychology journal, *American Journal of Psychology*. Figure 1.1 describes eight men and women who made important early contributions to psychology in the United States.

One of these psychologists, John B. Watson, initiated a major new force in psychology known as behaviorism. **Behaviorism** is an approach to psychology that stresses the study of observable behavior, instead of hidden mental processes.

John B. Watson (1878–1958) had originally conducted research in animal psychology. He admired the objective research that could be conducted on observable behaviors of animals. In contrast, he found little value in studying consciousness or using introspective techniques. As he wrote in an early article,

Psychology as the behaviorist views it is a purely objective experimental branch of natural science. Its theoretical goal is the prediction and control of behavior. Introspection forms no essential part of its methods, nor is the scientific value of its data dependent upon the readiness with which they lend themselves to interpretation in terms of consciousness. (Watson, 1913, p. 158)

Behaviorism was extremely appealing to American psychologists. People in the United States have always been known for their practicality; in fact, it is considered a national trait (O'Donnell, 1985; Schnaitter, 1987). American psychology was eager for some practical applications, and behaviorism provided some appealing answers. Wundt's introspection technique and James's ideas about the nature of consciousness and emotions were both important in developing *theories* about psychology, but neither emphasized observable behavior.

Another reason for the appeal of behaviorism in the United States is that its founders were American, not German. The anti-German feelings increased even

Figure 1.1
Early U.S. psychologists.

William James (1842–1910). First American psychologist; author of influential textbooks; theorist on emotions and consciousness.

G. Stanley Hall (1844–1924). Student of Wundt; founder of American Psychological Association.

Christine Ladd-Franklin (1847–1930). Taught at Johns Hopkins and Columbia; formulated a theory of color vision.

Mary Whiton Calkins (1863–1930). Student of James; pioneer in memory research; first woman president of American Psychological Association.

Edward Bradford Titchener (1867–1927). Student of Wundt; developed introspection techniques in the United States; taught at Cornell.

Margaret Floy Washburn (1871–1939). First woman to receive a PhD in psychology; wrote a book on animal behavior that foreshadowed behaviorism.

Edward Lee Thorndike (1874–1949). Student of James; investigated trial-and-error animal learning.

John B. Watson (1878–1958). Founder of behaviorism, which influenced U.S. psychology for over 50 years.

further during World War I (Baars, 1986). As a consequence, Wilhelm Wundt did *not* have a fan club in the United States during that period.

The behaviorists' emphasis on observable behavior led them to reject any terms referring to mental events, such as *idea, thought,* or *mental image.* (In the early 1970s, I had an office partner who was a strict behaviorist; he shuddered visibly whenever I would say, "I think that. . . .") Early behaviorists classified thinking as simply a form of speech. Presumably, tiny movements of the tongue (an observable behavior) could be detected with the appropriate equipment. Behaviorists argued that vague, invisible constructs such as *thought* were simply unnecessary.

Behaviorism dominated psychology in the United States from the 1920s through the 1960s. As one author wrote, "If you were to knock on the door of an academic psychologist's office in the 1930s, the chances were better than nine out of ten that you would be answered by a behaviorist" (Schlesinger, 1985, p. 13). Thus, American research psychology in the early 20th century rejected unobservable mental processes, consciousness, and introspection. Instead, psychologists embraced the behaviorist approach, which examined only observable behavior.

European Psychology in the Early 20th Century

Behaviorism may have captivated Americans, but it had no loyal following in Europe. Instead, European psychology in the early part of this century was influenced by three new psychological approaches: Gestalt psychology, the psychoanalytic approach of Sigmund Freud, and the early cognitive psychology approach.

The Gestalt (pronounced "Geh-*shtahlt*") approach originated in Germany at the beginning of the 20th century. According to the **Gestalt approach**, we perceive objects as well-organized, whole structures, instead of separated, isolated parts. Gestalt psychologists stressed that our ability to see shapes and patterns is determined by subtle relationships among the parts. For instance, consider the square shown in Figure 1.2. This object looks well organized; it seems to be a complete figure, a cohesive square, rather than four isolated lines. The Gestalt psychologists had an important impact on research in visual perception (chapter 4), and they also conducted influential research in problem solving (chapter 8).

Europe's most important contribution to psychology came from Sigmund Freud (1856–1939), an Austrian physician. Freud was specifically interested in neurology and psychological problems. He argued that people are driven by sexual urges, a view that was not warmly greeted when it was first introduced during the straitlaced Victorian period. In addition, Freud emphasized that human behavior is motivated by the unconscious—by thoughts and desires far below the level of conscious awareness. In the late 19th and early 20th century, however, European psychologists were being trained in Wundt's laboratory. Wundt encouraged them to report on *conscious* experiences, and the unconscious had no place in Wundt's research program.

Freud's emphasis on sexuality and the unconscious meant that he entered the game with two strikes against him. Nevertheless, Freud's theories eventually gained widespread popularity among therapists. As is emphasized later in this chapter, the psychoanalytic approach of Sigmund Freud has probably been the most influential force in the history of clinical psychology.

However, psychoanalytic theory did not have a major impact on *research* psychology, either in the United States or Europe. As is stressed later in this book, most of Freud's theory was difficult to test empirically. Instead, early researchers in the United States favored behaviorism, and researchers in Europe favored Wundt's approach, the Gestalt approach, or else a new option called the cognitive psychology approach.

Figure 1.2
According to Gestalt psychologists, this square forms a well-organized, complete figure.

Jean Piaget, whose theory of children's thinking helped shape current ideas about developmental psychology.

The cognitive psychology approach emphasizes mental processes, and its best known European advocate was Jean Piaget (pronounced "Zhohn Pea-ah-zhay"). Piaget was a Swiss psychologist whose ideas about children helped shape our knowledge about the development of thinking. Piaget proposed that even young babies think, though their thoughts are connected with their senses and their body movements. He argued that the nature of thinking changes during childhood, becoming much more abstract and complex. Chapter 10 explores Piaget's theories on children's cognitive development in some detail.

From psychology's early beginnings in Wundt's laboratory in Germany, the discipline developed and diversified. By the 1930s, the field included behaviorists in the United States, many of Wundt's students scattered throughout Europe, therapists practicing psychoanalysis in the Freudian tradition, Gestalt psychologists investigating the organization of perception, and cognitive psychologists exploring human thought processes.

Section Summary: Psychology's Past

- ■ **Psychology, or the scientific study of behavior and mental processes, was first studied systematically by Wundt, who emphasized careful research techniques.**
- ■ **James, an American, examined human consciousness and wrote influential textbooks.**
- ■ **Behaviorism soon dominated American psychology; this approach emphasized research on observable behaviors.**
- ■ **Meanwhile, the early 20th-century European trends included the Gestalt approach, Freud's psychoanalytic approach, and the cognitive approach.**

Psychology Today

As we complete the second half of this century, some of the earlier approaches have lost their strong support, though they have influenced contemporary approaches. For instance, Wundt's emphasis on careful research is still current. Both Wundt's and James's ideas about mental processes helped inspire modern cognitive psychology. In addition, every perception textbook discusses the Gestalt principles of shape perception. Let us now turn our attention to contemporary psychology.

Five Contemporary Approaches in Psychology

The first page of this book emphasized the broad scope of psychology, from microscopic nerve cells to large crowds of people. In fact, psychology spans the enormous distance between **biology**, which examines the structure and functions of living things, and **sociology**, which examines how groups and institutions function in society. It would be impossible for one single approach to inspire researchers as diverse as a physiological psychologist interested in the nerve cells within the eye and a social psychologist interested in stereotypes about race. Five approaches dominate contemporary psychology. We explore them in the same order as they are covered in more detail in the later chapters of the book. As Table 1.1 shows, the physiological approach is introduced in the chapter on the biological basis of behavior, behaviorism dominates the learning chapter, and the cognitive approach first enters in the memory chapter. The psychoanalytic and humanistic approaches are more concerned with personality and psychotherapy, so they take leading roles toward the end of the book.

Table 1.1   *Chapters in the Textbook Emphasizing the Five Major Current Approaches in Psychology*

	THE CURRENT APPROACHES				
	Physiological	**Behaviorist**	**Cognitive**	**Psychoanalytic**	**Humanistic**
Ch. 3: The Biological Basis of Behavior	+				
Ch. 4: Sensation and Perception	+				
Ch. 6: Learning		+			
Ch. 7: Memory			+		
Ch. 8: Thinking			+		
Ch. 9: Language and Conversation			+		
Ch. 10: Development in Infancy and Childhood			+		
Ch. 11: Development From Adolescence Through Old Age			+	+	
Ch. 12: Motivation and Emotion	+		+		
Ch. 13: Personality			+	+	+
Ch. 14: Assessing Intelligence and Personality			+		
Ch. 15: Psychological Disorders	+	+	+	+	
Ch. 16: Treating Psychological Disorders	+	+	+	+	+
Ch. 17: Social Cognition			+		
Ch. 19: Health Psychology	+	+	+		

Note: The omitted chapters do not cover psychological approaches in detail.

The Physiological Approach   In recent decades, an increasing number of psychologists have used physiological methods to explore behavior and mental processes. This **physiological approach** proposes that each behavior, emotion, and thought is caused by a physical event in the brain or other parts of the nervous system.

The physiological approach is really a method of attacking a research question, rather than a theoretical framework. Chapter 3 introduces you to some of the research techniques used in the physiological approach. For example, researchers can examine a person who has an unusual disorder, in order to increase our knowledge of human behavior. Consider a young man who was accidentally stabbed through his nostril—into the brain. He now has a very specific problem: He cannot learn any new material. Research with this man has helped clarify the functions of a very specific area of the brain. Other physiological techniques include electrical stimulation of a region of the brain, recording of signals from the brain, and the study of genetic defects.

During the last decade, a new field called neuroscience has emerged. **Neuroscience** is an interdisciplinary field that combines the efforts of psychologists, biologists, biochemists, and medical researchers; neuroscience examines the structure and function of the nervous system.

The Behaviorist Approach   As we discussed earlier, the behaviorist approach, which was initiated by John Watson, emphasizes observable behavior. The area of modern psychology that has been most significantly influenced by the behaviorist approach is learning. Chapter 6 discusses how rewards and punishments influence both animal and human learning. In addition, behavioral approaches are used in treating many psychological disorders (chapter 16).

One of behaviorism's most important contributions concerns research methods. Behaviorists insisted that psychological concepts must be precisely defined and that responses must be objectively measured. These contributions were adopted by those who favor the cognitive approach, one of the most popular contemporary approaches.

The Cognitive Approach   Earlier, we noted the origins of the cognitive approach in the work of Wundt, James, and Piaget. However, America's emphasis on behaviorism prevented researchers from paying much attention to hidden mental processes during the period from about 1920 to the late 1960s.

The **cognitive approach** focuses on unobservable mental processes involved in perceiving, remembering, thinking, and understanding. For instance, as your eyes race across this page, you can perceive meaningful letters, rather than a clutter of random squiggles. You can also remember the meaning of words. You can think about related concepts (for instance, why strict behaviorists would oppose a cognitive approach). And you can understand ideas (for instance, why the behaviorists' emphasis on objective measurement is important). Researchers in cognitive psychology find a challenge in creating precise definitions for invisible mental processes (e.g., *mental image*) and devising methods for measuring these processes objectively.

The cognitive approach differs from the earlier behaviorist approach not only with respect to its emphasis on unobservable processes, but also in its view of humans. The early behaviorists viewed humans as passive organisms who waited for an appropriate stimulus from the environment before they responded. In contrast, the cognitive approach argues that people are eager to acquire information; we continually search for new developments. Our previous knowledge and beliefs help to guide this search. For example, if two strangers had walked into your high school English class, you would have been eager to find out why they were there. After class, you would question the teacher, because previous knowledge informs you that the teacher would know more about such matters than would other students.

Your previous knowledge and beliefs also influence what you remember. For instance, suppose your English teacher had read a passage from Shakespeare, and you were asked to recall it later. The version you remembered was likely to be closer to the modern-day English, with which you are familiar. In summary, the cognitive approach insists that the mind is not a sponge, passively absorbing information from the environment. Instead, you actively seek information and your cognitive processes transform that information.

Why did many American psychologists shift their loyalty from behaviorism to cognitive psychology? Some reasons include the following:

1. Psychologists were discovering that it was difficult to explain complex human behavior using only the terms from behavioral learning theory. For instance, behaviorist approaches have difficulty handling the complexity of language's structure or the organization of memory.

2. Jean Piaget's theories of human development had won the respect of child psychologists and educators.

3. Perhaps most important, the information-processing approach was developed. According to the information-processing approach, incoming information is selected, combined with previous information, and rearranged in various ways. Essentially, then, the human brain operates like a very sophisticated computer (Evans, 1983). Currently, the information-processing approach is such an important part of cognitive psychology that the two terms are often used interchangeably.

Excitement about the cognitive approach grew rapidly, so by about 1970, most researchers interested in memory, language, and thinking had adopted this new approach. In fact, the period between the late 1960s and the early 1970s is often called the "cognitive revolution" (Baars, 1986). The cognitive approach was soon applied to other areas, such as motivation, personality, and psychotherapy. In each case, theorists emphasized the importance of people's thoughts and how the human mind could manipulate, transform, and even distort these thoughts. As Table 1.1 illustrates, the cognitive approach now forms an important part of most chapters in this textbook.

The Psychoanalytic Approach   Although the cognitive approach is extremely popular with researchers, most students enrolled in introductory psychology courses are probably more familiar with Freud's psychoanalytic approach. (For example, high school health courses typically require students to memorize many Freudian terms, such as *id* and *regression*.) The psychoanalytic approach is easily the most influential theory of personality disorders, and even therapists who favor other approaches have received substantial training in psychoanalytic theory. Terms such as *unconscious*, *ego*, and *repression* are so common in our everyday vocabulary that we may forget that they originated with psychoanalytic theory.

Sigmund Freud, the founder of psychoanalytic theory.

The **psychoanalytic approach** emphasizes three central points: (1) childhood experiences determine adult personality, (2) unconscious mental processes influence everyday behavior, and (3) conflict underlies most human behavior.

As discussed earlier, Sigmund Freud developed the psychoanalytic approach in Austria at the beginning of the 20th century. Chapter 13 (Personality) describes the development of this theory as well as Freud's explanation of both normal and abnormal personality development. Chapter 16 (Psychotherapy) examines the psychoanalytic approach to the treatment of psychological disorders. In addition, chapter 11 (Development From Adolescence Through Old Age) explores a theory of identity development proposed by Erik Erikson, one of the most prominent psychologists who were guided by Freud's ideas.

The Humanistic Approach   We have seen that behaviorism developed out of a dissatisfaction with Wundt's and James's approaches, and the cognitive approach developed out of a dissatisfaction with the behaviorist approach. Similarly, the humanistic approach developed out of a dissatisfaction with the two major theories that dominated the first half of the 20th century, the psychoanalytic and behaviorist approaches. American psychologists, such as Carl Rogers and Abraham Maslow, argued that the psychoanalytic approach to personality and psychological disorders focused on the "sick" side of human beings. Furthermore, they pointed out that behaviorism only examined simple behaviors. They preferred a theory that emphasized the more positive human qualities as well as more complex and noble human goals.

Carl Rogers, a major humanistic theorist.

The **humanistic approach** stresses that humans have enormous potential for personal growth. They have the ability to care deeply for other people and to establish meaningful, productive lives for themselves. Chapter 13 (Personality) examines Carl Rogers's person-centered approach to personality and psychotherapy, as well as Abraham Maslow's theory that people seek self-actualization, or fulfillment of their true potential.

Psychology in the 1990s   In this chapter we first traced the early origins of psychology, from Wundt's efforts to transform the discipline into an empirical science and James's views of human consciousness, through the founding of behaviorism in the United States and the development of Gestalt, psychoanalytic, and cognitive approaches in Europe. Then we examined five current perspectives: the physiological, behaviorist, cognitive, psychoanalytic, and humanistic approaches. This overview makes it clear that psychologists have not been inspired throughout their history by one all-encompassing theory, one single truth.

Abraham Maslow, a major humanistic theorist.

When Wilhelm Wundt decided to conduct research on human behavior and mental processes, no one handed him a statement about the best way to proceed. He began at a logical starting point, by asking people to report on their own psychological processes and by conducting some basic experiments. Behaviorists emphasized visible behavior rather than hidden mental processes, and they advanced the discipline by stressing that concepts should be precisely defined and that responses should be measured objectively. Cognitive psychologists then adopted this emphasis on precise definitions and objective measurement, and they applied these techniques to the measurement of mental processes. Viewpoints in research psychology continue to change, each new approach attempting to improve upon the previous approaches.

Similarly, the viewpoints on the treatment of psychological disorders have continued to change. It is safe to say that few therapists uphold every word that Sigmund Freud ever wrote. Also, most therapists acknowledge that some psychological disorders can be partly traced to a physiological problem, so that drug therapy may be helpful. Most therapists would also see the value of some behaviorist techniques that are based on learning theory and cognitive techniques designed to change inappropriate thought patterns, as well as humanistic listening techniques. Thus, a therapist may have a strong preference for one of the five approaches, but borrow techniques from the other four. The complexity of human psychology requires a complex approach in treating disorders, rather than strict loyalty to just one approach.

Professions in Psychology

We have emphasized the diversity in the goals of psychology as well as the historical and current approaches to psychology. This diversity also characterizes the professional specialties within psychology. Let us first discuss four representative specialties that emphasize basic research and then consider three applied specialties that emphasize practical applications of psychological knowledge.

Biological psychologists, also called neuropsychologists or physiological psychologists, examine how genetic factors, the brain, the nervous system, and other biological factors influence behavior.

Experimental psychologists conduct research on topics such as perception, learning, memory, thinking, language, motivation, and emotion.

A biological psychologist at a sleep clinic fastens on electrodes to learn more about this young girl's sleep disorders.

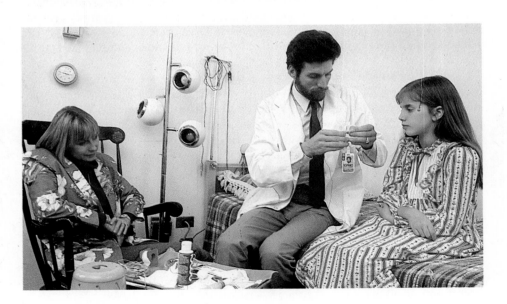

Developmental psychologists examine development throughout the life span. Most developmental psychologists specialize in one part of the life span, such as childhood or old age.

Personality psychologists investigate how people are influenced by relatively stable inner factors. Their research focuses on how people differ from one another.

Two important applied specialties in psychology are concerned with helping people who have psychological problems. **Clinical psychologists** assess and treat people with psychological disorders. On the basis of interviews and psychological tests, they suggest a diagnosis of the problem. Then they provide either individual or group psychotherapy. Counseling psychologists represent a profession that is growing in importance. Like clinical psychologists, **counseling psychologists** assess and treat people, but their clients are likely to have less severe problems. Some counseling psychologists provide marriage or career counseling; others work in college mental health clinics.

Incidentally, many people confuse clinical and counseling psychologists with a group of medical professionals known as psychiatrists. **Psychiatrists** receive training in medicine, rather than psychology, and their medical orientation emphasizes treating certain disorders with medication. Thus, psychiatrists are *not* psychologists.

The other major profession in applied psychology—besides clinical and counseling psychology—is industrial/organizational psychology. **Industrial/organizational psychologists** focus on human behavior in business and industry. Some may help organizations hire and train employees; others study the work setting, with the goal of improving work productivity, morale, and job satisfaction. Still others measure consumer attitudes toward a company's products.

We have looked at a variety of research and applied professions within psychology. You may be curious, however, about some of the characteristics of professional psychologists. According to current statistics, 67% of all bachelor's degrees and 53% of all PhD degrees in psychology are currently awarded to women (Howard et al., 1986; Women's Programs Office, 1988). Thus, the status of women in psychology has changed considerably since the beginning of the century, when Harvard University refused to grant a PhD to Mary Whiton Calkins—even though William James proclaimed her to be his brightest student (Russo, 1983; Scarborough & Furumoto, 1987).

According to recent statistics, Black students receive about 7% of all bachelor's degrees, and Hispanic students receive about 4%. Of PhD degrees, 3% are awarded to Blacks and 3% to Hispanics (Kohout, 1990). The history of Black and Hispanic psychologists has been traced by Guthrie (1976). A prominent early Black psychologist was Gilbert Haven Jones, who received his PhD degree in Germany in 1901. J. Henry Alston, shown in Figure 1.3, was the first Black American to publish research in a major psychology journal. His 1920 paper examined the perception of heat and cold, a topic mentioned in chapter 4. Black and Hispanic psychologists have been particularly active researchers in the area of minority children's scores on psychological tests, a topic examined in chapter 14. For instance, Jorge Sanchez, shown in Figure 1.4, was one of the first to discuss how the tests produced biased scores for Mexican-American children (Guthrie, 1976).

In the 1990s, several programs have been developed to encourage minority students to pursue graduate degrees. For example, the Minority Fellowship Program, sponsored by the American Psychological Association, offers financial assistance for training in research, the neurosciences, and clinical psychology.

The diversity of psychology is illustrated in the variety of theoretical approaches and professions. However, underlying this diversity is a unified concern. All psychologists—whether they are biological, experimental, developmental, per-

Dr. George Rebok, a developmental psychologist, is a leading researcher in the study of Alzheimer's disease.

Dr. Maria Kountz is a clinical psychologist who teaches at Beaver College in Glenside, Pennsylvania, and counsels clients who have personal problems.

Industrial/organizational psychologists study human behavior in the workplace. Dr. Lynn Offermann, pictured above, specializes in the study of leadership, social influence processes, and team building.

sonality, or clinical psychologists—are concerned with the scientific study of behavior and mental processes. Three themes that can be traced throughout many diverse topics within psychology are explored in the next section.

Figure 1.3
J. Henry Alston, the first Black psychologist to publish a paper in a major psychology journal.

Figure 1.4
Jorge Sanchez, an early critic of intelligence tests that were biased against minority groups.

> ### Section Summary: Psychology Today
>
> - The physiological approach to psychology proposes that all behaviors and mental processes correspond to physical events in the brain and other parts of the nervous system.
> - The behaviorist approach, emphasizing observable behavior, provides important contributions to learning theory and psychotherapy.
> - The cognitive approach focuses on unobservable mental processes and emphasizes that people actively search for new information.
> - The psychoanalytic approach, which stresses the importance of childhood experiences, unconscious mental processes, and conflict, produced the most influential theory of personality disorders.
> - The humanistic approach emphasizes humans' enormous potential for personal growth.
> - Viewpoints in both research psychology and therapy continue to change in the 1990s.
> - Some professions in psychology emphasize research (including biological, experimental, developmental, and personality psychologists) whereas others emphasize applications (including clinical, counseling, and industrial/organizational psychologists).

Three Important Themes in Psychology

In preparing this textbook, I asked myself the following question: Suppose that students who had read this textbook were asked—10 years later—to list several main points they recalled from the book. What points would I want them to remember? Three themes that recur throughout psychology seem most important. These themes are neither sophisticated nor earth-shattering. Instead, they are very straightforward. In many cases, the themes will be pointed out in future chapters. Keep these themes in mind as you read the textbook, and try to identify examples of the themes, even when they are not specifically noted.

Theme 1: Humans Are Extremely Competent

You have had many years of experience as a human being. However, it is likely you do not fully appreciate the talents that you and other humans share. For instance, suppose you answer the telephone and the speaker says, "Is this Max's Pizza Parlor?" You manage to decode the stream of sounds effortlessly, understand the speaker's question, and answer—equally effortlessly—"No, I'm sorry, but you have the wrong number." This accomplishment may not sound particularly impressive unless you realize that no computer can analyze language and respond appropriately with even a fraction of your own degree of competence.

The theme that humans are skilled is first introduced in chapter 3 when we discuss the biological underpinnings of behavior. Here we see that the human nervous system permits information to travel quickly, and the brain features numerous specialized parts that perform specific functions. Our miraculous talents can be traced to our miraculous nervous system.

This theme also occurs frequently throughout the chapter on sensation and perception, particularly in the discussion of vision and hearing. However, the theme is most prominent in the three chapters on human cognition—memory, thinking, and language. Naturally, humans occasionally make errors. However, in many cases, these errors can be traced to a general strategy that usually produces correct responses, in a minimum amount of time. Thus, even our errors tend to be "smart mistakes." By the time you have completed the textbook, you should no longer be so casual about your mental abilities.

Theme 2: Humans Differ Widely From One Another

We noted earlier that one of the goals of psychologists is to predict behavior. However, humans differ so impressively from one another that prediction is often difficult. Consider, in contrast, how relatively easy it is to make predictions in some other disciplines. For example, if I take a tablespoon of vinegar and add it to a tablespoon of baking soda, I can predict that the mixture will foam and produce a fizzing noise. In fact, I tried that three times, each with a different kind of vinegar, and the results were boringly predictable. Each time, the mixture foamed and fizzed. In psychology, however, predictions cannot be made with the same accuracy. I can take one student, add a lecture on visual perception, and that student will foam and fizz with excitement. Another student, similar from all outward appearances, may fall asleep and begin to snore loudly. The individual differences among students—or any other humans—mean that they often respond in different ways to the same identical stimulus.

Students in any classroom—like any group of humans—display individual differences.

Individual differences make clear-cut results more difficult to obtain in psychological research. For instance, suppose that a group of researchers wants to test a new method of improving memory. Students perform one memory task, then they are told how to use the new memory-improvement method, and then they perform a second memory task. Compared to the first task, some students' scores improve, some decline, and some remain the same—demonstrating substantial individual differences. The researchers must determine whether the two sets of scores are substantially different from each other, compared to the individual differences.

Researchers in some areas of psychology consider individual differences to be a nuisance, a factor that decreases their chances of obtaining significant experimental results. However, researchers in other areas—particularly in the psychology of personality—concentrate specifically on studying these individual differences. Personality researchers examine the factors that produce these individual differences. One psychologist's garbage is another psychologist's favorite dish.

Theme 3: Human Behavior Is Complex

When we examine the factors that influence human behavior, we seldom identify just one important factor. For example, suppose that researchers are trying to determine why 10-year-olds perform better on a memory test than 6-year-olds. They are likely to find that the explanation is complex and involves many factors. One factor may be that the older children are more familiar with the vocabulary. Another factor may be that the older children are more likely to figure out relationships between words on the list and remember the words in clusters. Still another factor may be that the older children are more aware that they need to figure out a memorization strategy, whereas the younger children do not believe they need to make a special effort to coax the words into memory. In short, most behavior is caused by multiple factors.

Furthermore, this complexity theme also operates when we try to figure out why two kinds of behavior are related to each other. For instance, in chapter 6, we see that the amount of violent television a child watches is related to that child's aggressive behavior. Three different factors probably account for this relationship: (1) Watching violent television encourages children to act aggressively; (2) Aggressive children like to watch violent television programs; and (3) The kind of family that allows children to watch violent television tends to allow children to act aggressively. A single explanation is not sufficient.

The theme that human behavior is complex should encourage you to be suspicious of simple one-factor explanations. For example, suppose you read that when fathers are emotionally cold and unresponsive, their daughters tend to develop eating disorders. Remember that many factors, other than the father's emotional tone, are likely to be responsible. (Furthermore, the individual differences theme should encourage you to speculate that emotional unresponsiveness may promote an eating disorder in some young women, but have no effect on some other young women.)

If human behavior were less competent, if individual differences were smaller, and if explanations could be simple, this textbook would be very short. We would have all the answers, researchers would be unemployed, and there would be no need for therapists or other applied psychologists. However, the reality is that humans are amazingly competent, so we need to explain all their different talents. Humans also differ enormously, so we need to realize that people may respond differently to the same stimulus, and we need to explain these individual differences. Finally, human behavior is complex, and it is difficult to unravel the explanations for behavior. Psychologists have probably learned more about behavior and mental processes in the last 30 years than in the previous 3,000. Still, we do not yet have all the answers, and in fact we have not even asked all the interesting questions.

Section Summary: Three Important Themes in Psychology

- **Theme 1 states that humans are extremely competent.**
- **Theme 2 states that humans differ widely from one another.**
- **Theme 3 states that human behavior is complex.**

How to Use This Book

Psychology includes several features to help you understand, learn, and remember the material. This section tells you how to use these features most effectively.

Notice that each chapter begins with an outline. Before reading a new chapter, inspect the outline and try to understand the structure of the topic. For instance, on page 21, notice that chapter 2 is divided into three sections: The Major Research Methods, Research Issues, and Analyzing the Data.

An important feature of this textbook is a summary at the end of each of the major sections in a chapter, rather than at the end of the entire chapter. These section summaries allow you to review the material frequently and to master relatively short topics before moving on to new areas. When you reach the end of a section, test yourself to see whether you can remember the important points. Then read the section summary and notice which items you forgot or remembered incorrectly. Then test yourself again and recheck your accuracy. Some students find that they like to read only one section at a time, check themselves on the section summary, and then take a break. Then when they return to the textbook, they find it helpful to review previous section summaries before beginning the new material.

As you read the chapters, note that I have included many examples of psychological principles. Research on memory has demonstrated that people remember material better when it is illustrated with examples. It is also helpful to think of examples from your own experience. For instance, the section on short-term memory in chapter 7 points out that memory is often fragile—an item you just heard can disappear from memory if your attention is distracted. When you read a statement like this, try to determine whether it matches your own experiences. Pause and try to recall some specific examples. Psychologists have found that one of the most effective methods of enhancing recall is to ask people to relate the material to themselves (e.g., Rogers et al., 1977). You have lived with yourself for many years now, so take advantage of your experience.

This textbook also includes informal experiments labeled *demonstrations*. You have already had a chance to try a demonstration on page 3. Each demonstration can be done quickly and usually requires no special equipment. In most cases, you can perform the demonstrations by yourself. These demonstrations should also help to make the material more concrete and easy to remember. More tips on improving memory are discussed throughout chapter 7.

Notice, also, that new terms appear in boldface type (for example, **psychology**). A definition is included in the same sentence as the term so that you do not need to search an entire paragraph to determine the term's meaning. Each of these terms also appears in the glossary at the end of the book and in the index. If your professor uses a psychology term during a lecture, and you cannot recall its meaning, check the glossary for a brief definition, or look in the index to find where the topic is discussed in more detail. A phonetic pronunciation is provided where a new term or a person's name (like Wilhelm Wundt) does not have an obvious pronunciation. (The accented syllable will appear in italics.)

Chapters 2 through 19 each contain an *in depth* section, which examines recent research on a selected topic relevant to the chapter. These sections look closely at the research methods and the results of studies on a topic that is currently intriguing psychologists.

A set of review questions can be found at the end of each chapter. Many review questions ask you to apply your knowledge to a practical problem. Other review questions encourage you to integrate information from several parts of a chapter. Prior to an exam, you may find it helpful to read all the section summaries in a chapter, then try to answer the review questions.

A list of new terms is included at the end of each chapter. You can study these new terms by trying to supply a definition and—where relevant—an example for each new term. You can monitor your accuracy by checking either the glossary or the pages of the textbook.

The final feature of each chapter is a list of recommended readings. This list can supply you with resources if you want to write a paper on a particular topic or if an area interests you. In general, I included books, chapters, and articles that provide more than a general overview of a topic but are not overly technical.

The major point of this section is that psychological principles can be used to help you master psychology. By actively thinking about the material and reviewing it systematically, you will find that you can remember more of the important concepts of psychology.

REVIEW QUESTIONS

1. Suppose you are describing your college courses to a high school student. Based on this chapter, how would you define psychology? Describe the four goals of psychology to this imaginary student. Make up an example of research or an applied project that a psychologist could conduct for each of those four goals.

2. What is the armchair approach to psychology? Why does it differ from the approach that relies on empirical evidence? Which of these two approaches would the behaviorists be likely to favor?

3. Wilhelm Wundt is often considered the founder of modern-day psychology. What did he study and what contributions did he make to psychology?

4. Three important eras in American research psychology have been the psychology of William James, the behaviorist movement, and the cognitive revolution. Describe each of these eras, and contrast them with respect to their emphasis on observable behavior versus mental processes.

5. Before beginning this chapter, what had you heard about Sigmund Freud's theory? Does that information match what you have read in the textbook? Why or why not?

6. What does the cognitive psychology approach emphasize? What are its early origins in European psychology, and why did its popularity rise later in the century? What is the humanistic approach, and how did it come about?

7. Describe the five current psychology approaches: physiological, behaviorist, cognitive, psychoanalytic, and humanistic. If you were to pursue a career in psychology or in an area related to psychology, which of these approaches would you be likely to find most useful? Which approach(es) would be most relevant for a physician? a classroom teacher? a businessperson? a social worker?

8. Contrast the view of human beings that is provided by those who favor the behaviorist, cognitive, psychoanalytic, and humanistic approaches. Which approach or approaches do you find most consistent with your own view of humans?

9. Imagine that a number of psychologists from a variety of specialty areas in psychology have gathered together for a conference on aggression. Each of the following will be presenting a paper on his or her work related to aggression: a biological psychologist, an experimental psychologist, a developmental psychologist, a personality psychologist, a clinical psychologist, and an industrial/ organizational psychologist. Make up a sample paper topic for each of these six psychologists.

10. What are the three themes presented near the end of the chapter? Explain each of them, and provide your own example for each one.

NEW TERMS

psychology	neuroscience
applied psychologists	cognitive approach
empirical evidence	information-processing approach
introspection	psychoanalytic approach
structuralism	humanistic approach
replications	biological psychologists
consciousness	experimental psychologists
functionalism	developmental psychologists
behaviorism	personality psychologists
Gestalt approach	clinical psychologists
biology	counseling psychologists
sociology	psychiatrists
physiological approach	industrial/organizational psychologists

ANSWERS TO DEMONSTRATIONS

Demonstration 1.1.

1. True—Depressed people are more likely to seek emotional support from others than are people who are not depressed.
2. False—Children who are severely punished when young are more likely to develop psychological problems in adulthood than are those whose parents "spared the rod."
3. True—When management students were asked to decide the salary levels of various job candidates, they awarded higher salaries to the applicants who had requested higher salaries.
4. True—When students watched videotapes of people whose self-descriptions conflicted with their actual behavior on characteristics such as "shy" and "friendly," their judgments were influenced much more strongly by what the people did than what they said.
5. False—Attractive people turn out to have higher self-esteem and to be better treated than less attractive people. (We discuss the issue of physical attractiveness in detail in chapter 2.)
6. True—Students who had talked on the phone to depressed people are not interested in spending time with these people, compared to students who had talked to nondepressed people.
7. True—People who marry young or after just a short courtship are more likely to seek a divorce later on, in comparison to those who marry after age 20 or after a long courtship.
8. False—In a variety of studies, people have indicated their preference for items (such as words, symbols, and photos) that they have seen frequently.
9. True—If we transform the ancient sword into the modern handgun, the saying has clear support; gunshot deaths are much more likely to occur in homes where a gun is kept, and guns are more likely to kill a resident than an intruder, by a ratio of about 350 to 1. (*Sources:* Jordan, 1989; Kohn, 1988.)

RECOMMENDED READINGS

Guthrie, R. V. (1976). *Even the rat was white: A historical view of psychology.* New York: Harper & Row. The title of the book refers to psychology's early neglect of racial and ethnic minorities; this book helps to correct this neglect, especially by presenting biographies of pioneering Black psychologists.

Hilgard, E. R. (1987). *Psychology in America: A historical survey.* San Diego, CA: Harcourt Brace Jovanovich. Written by a researcher who made contributions to many areas of psychology, this textbook provides an in-depth history of American psychology and includes biographies of dozens of important psychologists.

Scarborough, E., & Furumoto, L. (1987). *Untold lives: The first generation of American women psychologists.* New York: Columbia University Press. This fascinating book includes chapter-long biographies of several early women psychologists, including Calkins, Washburn, and Ladd-Franklin, shorter portraits of other women, and an analysis of the forces that limited women's academic achievements at the beginning of this century.

Wertheimer, M. (1987). *A brief history of psychology* (3rd ed.). New York: Holt, Rinehart and Winston. This overview of psychology's history covers the pre-Wundt period, includes chapters on Wundt and James, and traces psychology to the present.

Woods, P. J. (1987). *Is psychology the major for you? Planning for your undergraduate years.* Washington, DC: American Psychological Association. Students interested in psychology should consider buying their own copies of this book because it contains useful information on deciding whether to major in psychology, preparing for careers, applying for jobs, and applying for graduate school. To order a copy, send a check for $11.95 (which includes postage and handling) to: Order Department, American Psychological Association, 1400 North Uhle Street, Arlington, VA 22201.

CHAPTER

2

**Research Methods
In Psychology**

Several years ago, my introductory psychology class was discussing how praise can shape behavior more effectively than criticism or punishment. One student recalled an example of his high school football coach, who roused the spirits of team members during halftime by praising them and pointing out their strong points during the first half of the game. Even when the team was losing, the coach always had something complimentary to say. The student speculated that his team played better during the second half because the coach had provided such effective reinforcement.

This student made an informal observation about the relationship between praise and performance. How could we test this speculation more scientifically? One way would be to enlist a large number of football coaches in an experiment. We could assign them to one of two groups. One group would hear a presentation on the effects of praise on performance; the coaches would be encouraged to outline a plan for praising their team members during halftime for their effort and aggressiveness, for making use of the opposing team's mistakes, and so forth. The other group would hear a different, irrevelant presentation, perhaps a talk on new developments in sports medicine. We could then gather data on team performance for the two groups of coaches. Specifically, we could assess performance during the second half of the games, measuring the number of yards gained, first downs, and number of interceptions.

This psychology student speculated that reinforcement could influence football performance. You have undoubtedly had your own speculations about human thoughts, emotions, and behavior. Do people study harder in the courses they enjoy? Does weather influence our mood? What is the best way to help a friend stop smoking? Do people eat more when they are with friends or alone? Questions like these have also intrigued psychologists.

Psychological research and everyday speculation do not really differ with respect to the type of questions asked. Instead, they differ in the approach to the problem. Everyday speculation typically uses a single test of a question and informal observation. In contrast, psychological research uses repeated tests and formal, systematic observation. As a consequence, the conclusions reached in everyday life are necessarily tentative and ambiguous, whereas the conclusions reached in psychological research can be much firmer.

A background in psychology research methods can help you understand why psychologists take certain precautions in conducting a study (for instance, why an ideal study on football performance requires at least two groups, instead of just one). This chapter therefore provides background information to help you analyze critically the material in the remainder of the book.

An understanding of methods can also help you become a more critical consumer of advertisements and summaries of psychology studies, often found in the popular media. For instance, a recent newspaper article summarized a study in which 92% of adolescent women with eating disorders described their relationship with their fathers as "distant." After reading this chapter, you should be able to ask critical questions about such a study. For instance, what percentage of adolescent women *without* eating disorders would report distant relationships with their fathers? Maybe the relationships are not really distant, but the young women perceive them inaccurately. Furthermore, the article implies that distant fathers produce daughters with eating disorders, but could it also be possible that the daughters' unusual behavior alienates the fathers?

Finally, an appreciation of research methods can help you think more clearly about your own behavior and make more rational decisions (Wood, 1984). For example, suppose you study conscientiously for a biology exam, arranging for eight hours of sleep the night before, and you receive a C+. For the next exam, you study less and sleep less, receiving a B. Can you conclude that you will receive an even higher score on the third exam by studying and sleeping even less? After reading this chapter, you should be on the lookout for alternative explanations of relationships. (For instance, the second exam might have been easier, or you may have become more accustomed to the instructor's exams.)

This chapter begins by exploring several major research methods. The second section includes some important research issues, such as the problem of measuring behavioral responses, the issue of avoiding biases in psychological studies, and social and ethical aspects of psychological research. The final section provides a brief overview of data analysis, which considers how psychologists summarize the data they collect from their studies and how they draw conclusions based on these data.

The Major Research Methods

Psychology research is based on the scientific method. The **scientific method** consists of four basic steps:

1. Identify the research problem.

2. Design and conduct a study.

3. Examine the data.

4. Communicate the results.

Psychologists use six major methods to explore behavior; each method takes a different approach to the steps of the scientific method, and each has its strengths and weaknesses. By combining several different approaches, researchers can achieve a much more complete picture of psychological processes. For instance, the experimental method is especially useful for determining the cause of a particular behavior. In contrast, the naturalistic observation method tells little about causes, but it is valuable when examining how people and animals behave in their normal lives.

The six methods also differ with respect to the amount of control the researchers can exercise when they conduct their studies. In experimental studies, researchers can control what the participants see, hear, and do. In naturalistic observation, those who are being studied control their own behavior; the researcher simply observes.

The Experimental Method

The experimental method is the most effective way to identify a cause-and-effect relationship. In an **experiment**, researchers systematically manipulate a variable under controlled conditions and observe how the participants respond. For example, researchers who are interested in the effect of noise on children's arithmetic performance could systematically manipulate (or change) the amount of noise children hear while working on arithmetic problems. Perhaps half of the children work in a quiet room, and the other half work in a room with a moderately loud noise level, provided by a tape recorder just outside the door.

In an experiment, researchers manipulate one variable (e.g., noise) and they hold constant the variables not being tested (e.g., children's age and ability level). If behavior changes when only that manipulated experimental variable is changed, then the researchers can conclude that a cause-and-effect relationship exists (e.g., between noise and arithmetic performance).

Independent and Dependent Variables   The first step in designing an experiment is to state a hypothesis. A **hypothesis** is a tentative explanation, a statement of what you expect to happen if certain conditions are true. A hypothesis can be stated in an "if . . . then" format: *If* certain conditions are true, *then* certain things will happen. For example:

If | **loud noise is present** | **then** | **arithmetic performance is less accurate.**

A hypothesis tells what relationship a researcher expects to find between an independent variable and a dependent variable. The **independent variable** is the variable that the experimenters manipulate. They decide how much of that variable to present to the participant. The independent variable is described in the *if* part of the "if . . . then" statement of the hypothesis. In the previous example, the independent variable is the amount of noise presented to the participants.

The **dependent variable** concerns the responses that the participants make; it is a measure of their behavior. The dependent variable is described in the *then* part of the "if . . . then" statement of the hypothesis. In the example, the dependent variable is the arithmetic performance of the children, which would probably be measured by counting the number of problems answered correctly.

You can remember the two kinds of variables by noting that the dependent variable *depends* upon the value of the independent variable. For example, the arithmetic performance (the dependent variable) *depends* upon the noise level (the independent variable). Table 2.1 shows several other examples of independent and dependent variables.

Experimental and Control Conditions   In an experiment, the researcher must arrange to test at least two conditions that are specified by the independent variable. In the simplest example of the noise experiment, we could test one group of children in a "no-noise" condition and a second group in a "noise" condition. In other words, one group, the **control condition**, is left unchanged; the children receive no special treatment. The second group, the **experimental condition**, is changed in some way. A particular variable is present in the experimental condition that is absent in the control condition. (In this study, noise is either present or absent.)

Most of the experiments described in this book involve more than just two conditions. The noise study could compare four conditions: a no-noise control and three experimental conditions (low, medium, and high noise). However, all experiments require some kind of comparison between conditions. If you have only one condition, you do not have an experiment, and you cannot draw conclusions.

Consider why conclusions cannot be drawn from just a single condition. You have probably read advertisements for so-called subliminal tapes. Each tape recording presumably contains positive messages, spoken so softly that they cannot be consciously heard. Instead, the listener hears only soothing music or natural sounds, such as gentle winds or ocean waves. The ads claim, however, that

Table 2.1   *Examples of Independent and Dependent Variables*

HYPOTHESIS	INDEPENDENT VARIABLE	DEPENDENT VARIABLE
1. If prison guards treat inmates courteously . . . then inmates will comply better with prison rules.	Nature of guards' communications (courteous vs. rude)	Extent of compliance with rules (e.g., absence of forbidden items)
2. If people consume caffeine prior to bedtime . . . then they will take longer to fall asleep.	Caffeine dose (present or absent)	Amount of time taken to fall asleep
3. If residents in a nursing home can control aspects of their lives . . . then they will be healthier.	Personal control (e.g., allowed to decide about room decorations vs. no input in decision)	Health measures (e.g., number of serious illnesses)
4. If students learn Spanish vocabulary words by creating vivid mental images . . . then they will learn the words better.	Learning method (mental images vs. no special instructions)	Score on a vocabulary test

Note: Hypotheses are often stated in formats that do not use the words *if* and *then*. For example, Hypothesis 1 could appear as *Inmates comply better with prison rules when prison guards treat them courteously.* To identify the independent and dependent variables, simply reword the hypothesis in an *if . . . then* format.

the subconcious mind responds to the hidden messages and that these messages will transform your life. Each ad features testimonials from people about their weight loss, improved self-image, increased memory, better sex life, and other life transformations. One testimonial on weight loss reads,

> I have lost 15 pounds without too much effort using your [weight control] tape. To say I'm extremely pleased is putting it mildly. Thank you so much for making this help available.

Intrigued by these ads, I wrote to seven companies that offered subliminal tapes. In each case, I requested information on experimental studies that contrasted the performance of experimental and control groups. So far, no company has replied. It is likely that the companies never tested the tapes experimentally. As a result, we read the testimonials, and their enthusiasm convinces us that the tapes work miracles.

However, suppose that one company decides to test the weight loss tape using a single condition. In this single condition, everyone listens to the tape, complete with the subliminal message. Suppose, as well, that 80% of the people report at least some weight loss. The problem is that we do not know what percentage of people in a control condition—who never listened to any tapes—would have reported at least some weight loss. Without a comparison condition, we cannot draw conclusions.

Let us sketch the basic design for an experiment to test the effects of the tape. People could be assigned to either the control condition (no tape) or the experimental condition (tape with "subliminal" message). The participants would be weighed, given the necessary instructions, and then weighed again several weeks later. If the people in the experimental group lost substantially more weight than those in the control group, we could conclude—tentatively—that the tapes might have caused the effect. Proper controls allow researchers to draw cause-and-effect conclusions that are inappropriate when the control groups are absent.

Confounding Variables   A **confounding variable** is any variable—other than the independent variable—that is not equivalent in all conditions. Confounding variables can cause researchers to draw incorrect conclusions. Suppose that at the beginning of the weight loss study, the people in the "subliminal" condition were,

This student is listening to a subliminal tape while he studies. However, we do not have research evidence that these tapes are effective.

on the average, 45 pounds overweight, whereas people in the other conditions were an average of 25 pounds overweight. Original weight would be a confounding variable. If people in the "subliminal" condition showed greater loss, this advantage might really be traceable to the fact that it is easier for someone who is 45 pounds overweight to lose a large number of pounds than it is for someone who is only 25 pounds overweight. That is, the "subliminal" messages may have been irrelevant.

How can researchers guard against confounding variables? One common method uses random assignment. As the name implies, **random assignment** means that people are assigned to experimental groups using a system—such as a coin toss—which ensures that everybody has an equal chance of being assigned to any one group. If the number of participants in the study is sufficiently large, then random assignment usually guarantees that the various groups will be reasonably similar with respect to important characteristics.

If researchers use a technique such as random assignment to eliminate confounding variables, we can say that they have a **well-controlled study**. With a well-controlled study, we can feel more confident about drawing cause-and-effect conclusions in an experiment.

An Example of an Experiment   Consider an experiment by David Olds and his colleagues that has important implications for the lives of young children (Olds, 1988; Olds et al., 1986). These researchers were concerned about the children born to economically disadvantaged, unwed teenage mothers in a rural region of upstate New York. Their hypothesis was: "If young mothers participate in a special intervention program, they will improve the way they raise their babies during infancy."

Young mothers were randomly assigned to either a control group or an experimental group. The researchers checked the characteristics of the group and found them to be equivalent on important variables such as age, education, and pregnancy risk. Thus, important confounding variables could be eliminated.

The mothers in the control group received no special services during pregnancy or after the child was born. In contrast, mothers in the experimental group were visited by a nurse an average of 9 times during pregnancy and 18 times during the first 10 months after the baby was born. During these visits, the nurses discussed infant development and the importance of involving family members and friends in child care. Their approach emphasized the strengths of these women and their potential to be good mothers.

When the infants were 10 months old, the researchers observed both the mothers and their babies. Figure 2.1 shows some of these results. As you can see, mothers in the experimental condition were less likely to restrict or punish their infants, and they were more likely to provide appropriate play material. However, some other measures showed no differences. For instance, a statistical analysis of the data on crying showed no important differences between babies in the experimental and control conditions. Looking at a large number of dependent variables, we can conclude that the intervention improved some aspects of child rearing, though other aspects were not affected.

We have examined the experimental method, in which researchers manipulate a variable and observe how the participants respond. If the conditions in an experiment are carefully controlled and confounding variables are avoided, the researchers can conclude that a change in the independent variable *caused* a change in the dependent variable. (For instance, a change in the care given to teenage mothers caused a change in their treatment of their babies.)

The experimental method has one clear advantage over other approaches: It is the only method in which we can firmly draw cause-and-effect conclusions.

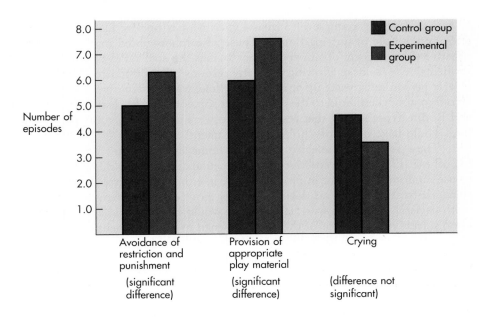

Figure 2.1
A comparison of experimental and control groups on selected behavioral measures.

In several other methods, alternative explanations prevent researchers from concluding that the independent variable is causally related to the dependent variable. In still other methods, the goal is to observe, rather than to interpret the cause of behavior.

The strength of the experimental method—its control over the important variables—is also its weakness. That is, a situation in which all the variables are carefully controlled is not a normal, natural situation. As a result, we may have difficulty generalizing to the real world from what we observe in an experiment (Locke, 1986). This criticism is especially true of experiments conducted in a psychology laboratory; it is not as true of experiments conducted in the field, such as the study on the teenage mothers.

Let us turn now to the studies in which the experimenter has less control. These studies are particularly useful in explaining how people and animals behave in their normal lives. In addition, we often need to use one of these other methods when it is impossible to assign people randomly to groups or to manipulate the independent variable.

The Quasi-Experiment

The prefix *quasi-* means "resembling" or "sort of," as in the word *quasi-official*. Similarly, a **quasi-experiment** resembles an experiment, but it does not meet all the criteria of a full-fledged experiment. The most important criterion that quasi-experiments lack is random assignment to groups. In an experiment, a coin toss or some other random system can be used to decide which person belongs in which group (for instance, which teenage mothers are assigned to the experimental group and which to the control group).

However, ethical or practical reasons often prevent random assignment. Consider a study about sibling jealousy and whether such jealousy was influenced by the older child's presence at the birth of the younger sibling (DelGiudice, 1986). The researcher certainly could not randomly assign these families to the present-at-birth or absent-at-birth conditions. Instead, the family and the older sibling needed to make that decision. Thus, the participants assigned themselves to one of the two conditions. (Incidentally, the results showed no difference between the two conditions in sibling jealousy.)

An excellent example of a quasi-experiment is one by Langer and Rodin (1976) on people in nursing homes. These researchers noted that an important negative characteristic of nursing homes is that the staff takes control over the residents' lives, seldom allowing them any responsibility or choices. Typically, an elderly person must wake up at a specified time, watch the movies that he or she is told to watch, and hold to the routine that someone else has established. Langer and Rodin hypothesized that residents who were given more control over their lives would have better psychological adjustment.

These researchers selected a nursing home in which they could test their hypothesis. From the perspective of experimental design, it would have been ideal to use random assignment in placing people in either the control group (with the standard treatment and no decision-making power) or the experimental group (with decision-making power). However, it would be impractical to have half of the residents on each floor of the home assigned to one treatment group and half to another. And it would be unethical to move the residents so that they could live in the randomly assigned location. Instead, one floor in the home was selected as the control condition, and the other was selected as the experimental condition. The nursing home staff filled out questionnaires about the personal characteristics of the residents before the study began, and the researchers found that the two groups were roughly equivalent before the experimental manipulation.

The independent variable in Langer and Rodin's study was the type of communication given to the residents in a group meeting. The residents of one floor (experimental condition) were told that the residents themselves should be responsible for decisions about movie selections, room arrangement, visiting, and so forth. They were also given a small plant as a gift, which they were told to care for as they wished. The residents of the other floor (control condition) were told that the staff should be responsible for all decisions. They, too, were given a small plant, but they were told that a staff member would take care of it for them. The control group therefore had substantially less control over their lives and possessions.

After 3 weeks, the staff members were asked to complete questionnaires about all the residents. Compared to people in the control group, the residents in the experimental group showed much greater improvement in their activity level, alertness, and general happiness. The members of the experimental group were also much more likely to participate in nursing home social activities. Moreover, in a follow-up 18 months later, only 15% of the experimental group members had died, in contrast to 30% of the control group (Rodin & Langer, 1977). Thus, the study has important theoretical implications about the importance of personal responsibility, as well as practical implications for the management of nursing homes.

Quasi-experiments are also ideal when researchers want to determine whether a new program works in a school, or whether a new policy would be helpful in a factory. In these real-life situations (unlike the psychology laboratory), we typically cannot assign people at random to conditions; they already belong to a preformed group. However, by obtaining the appropriate measures before the study begins, we can determine whether the groups are somewhat similar. Then we can manipulate the independent variable and draw tentative conclusions. Clearly, however, when researchers report the findings of a quasi-experiment, they need to mention potential confounding variables.

An experimental study has shown that residents of a nursing home are more active, alert, and happy—and they live longer—when they are encouraged to be responsible for themselves.

Correlational Research

In **correlational research**, psychologists try to determine if two variables or measures are related. They obtain two measures on each person (or situation) and try to establish whether there is a systematic pattern in the data. Correlational research involves neither random assignment to groups nor the manipulation of variables. Researchers do not intentionally *change* anything, though they may administer a test to gather necessary data.

After obtaining measures on the group that is being studied, the researchers can calculate a statistic called the **correlation coefficient**, which is a number that can range between -1.00 and $+1.00$. Correlation coefficient is often symbolized as r (e.g., $r = +.28$).

Correlations allow researchers to make predictions about future behavior, based on past behavior. (You may recall that one of the goals of psychology, mentioned in chapter 1, is to predict behavior.) When there is a strong correlation between two variables of behavior (that is, the r is close to either $+1.00$ or -1.00), we can predict future behavior quite accurately on the basis of past behavior. In contrast, when there is a weak correlation (that is, the r is close to zero), predictions are not accurate. We know, for example, that there is a moderately strong correlation between grades in high school (Variable 1) and grades in college (Variable 2). On the basis of high school grades, an administrator can predict students' college grades with a moderate degree of accuracy.

Kinds of Correlations   Correlational research can yield a positive correlation, a zero correlation, or a negative correlation. Consider a **positive correlation**, which means that people who receive a high number on Variable A also receive a high number on Variable B. Furthermore, people who receive a low number on Variable A also receive a low number on Variable B.

A correlation coefficient will be $+1.00$ if there is an absolutely perfect, direct relationship between the two variables. However, in psychology, we seldom find correlations of $+1.00$. As emphasized by one of our themes, behavior is too complex, and too many other factors can contaminate the relationship. We are more likely to find correlations closer to zero than to $+1.00$, indicating weak but positive correlations. The chapters on personality and assessment contain many examples of weak, positive correlations. (Incidentally, you will see many examples of "naked" correlations, unadorned by $+$ and $-$ signs; a correlation such as .47 is positive *unless* it is preceded by a $-$ sign.)

Figure 2.2 shows an example of a positive correlation. This figure is based on 20 students' scores on my first and second examinations one semester. As you can see, students who receive high scores on one measure tend to receive high scores on the other measure, and low scores on one measure are associated with low scores on the other measure.

Correlations whose values are close to zero (e.g., $-.06$, .00, and $+.09$) are zero correlations. A **zero correlation** indicates no substantial relationship between

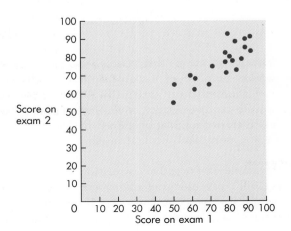

Figure 2.2
An example of a positive correlation between students' scores on exam 1 and their scores on exam 2. Each dot represents one student.

Figure 2.3
An example of a zero correlation; phase of the moon is not correlated with the number of admissions to psychiatric hospitals. (Hypothetical data, consistent with findings of Rotton & Kelly, 1985)

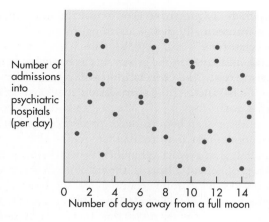

the two variables. Consider an example of a zero correlation—one that might surprise you. Some people believe that the full moon brings forth peculiar behavior. For instance, a lawyer friend of mine claims that whenever she receives numerous phone calls about robberies and murders—rather than more ordinary legal cases—her calendar consistently indicates that the moon has been full. (In fact, the word *lunacy* is based on the Latin word for moon, *luna.*) I am sorry to disappoint you, but a comprehensive study by Rotton and Kelly (1985) indicated a zero correlation between phases of the moon and several different measures of "lunacy," such as murders, other criminal offenses, and admissions to mental hospitals. Figure 2.3 shows a typical example of no relationship between two variables.

Figure 2.4
An example of a negative correlation between each person's psychological adjustment and awareness of his or her own faults. (Hypothetical data, consistent with findings of Taylor & Brown, 1988)

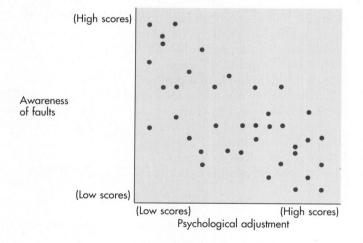

A **negative correlation** means that people who receive a high number on Variable A receive a *low* number on Variable B. People with a low number on Variable A receive a *high* number on Variable B. A correlation coefficient will be −1.00 if there is an absolutely perfect, inverse relationship between the two variables. Again, however, perfect relationships (whether positive or negative) are extremely rare. We are more likely to find negative correlations closer to zero than to −1.00.

Consider an example of a negative correlation in Figure 2.4. According to Taylor and Brown (1988), psychological adjustment is *negatively* correlated with awareness of one's faults. Thus, people who are very well adjusted are likely to be fairly unaware of personal faults. On the other hand, people who are poorly adjusted are likely to be fairly aware of their faults. (Incidentally, these results seem to contradict common sense.)

Figure 2.5 provides some guidelines for interpreting correlation coefficients, both strong or weak and negative or positive. It is important to emphasize that the strength of the correlation coefficient depends upon how far that number is from .00. Thus, −.60 is just as strong a correlation as +.60. The + and − signs indicate whether the correlation is positive or negative, not whether it is strong or weak.

Strong negative correlation	Moderate negative correlation	Weak negative correlation	Zero correlation	Weak positive correlation	Moderate positive correlation	Strong positive correlation

−1.00 −.90 −.80 −.70 −.60 −.50 −.40 −.30 −.20 −.10 0 +.10 +.20 +.30 +.40 +.50 +.60 +.70 +.80 +.90 +1.00

Figure 2.5
Interpreting the strengths of various correlation coefficients.

Interpreting Correlations Correlational research is useful when psychologists want to determine whether two variables are related to each other and when random assignment and manipulation of variables are not possible. For example, Taylor and Brown (1988) could not possibly assign people at random to the adjusted and maladjusted groups. ("OK, Sam, you're in the adjusted group. Tough luck, Joe, get over here in the maladjusted group.") Nor could they actively manipulate variables. ("OK, Sam, here's what I'm going to do to make your life better. And Joe, here's how I'll make your life miserable.") Instead, researchers using correlations must study the characteristics that people bring with them to the study.

A correlational study tells us whether or not two variables are related. However, it is difficult—and often impossible—to determine *why* they are related, when we only have correlational information.

For example, consider a study by Newport and her colleagues (1977). These researchers were interested in the relationship between parents' speech and their children's speech. As part of the study, they discovered a positive correlation ($r = +.62$) between the number of times a mother identified an object and the size of her child's vocabulary. In other words, a mother who frequently identified objects (e.g., "That's your mouth" or "There's a kitty") was likely to have a child with a large vocabulary. A mother who seldom identified objects was likely to have a child with a more limited vocabulary.

These researchers pointed out, however, that it is impossible to identify which of these factors was the *cause* and which was the *effect*. Consider these options:

1. A mother's speech influences her child's speech; the more the mother teaches, the more the child learns.

2. The child's vocabulary level shapes the mother's language. A bright child with a large vocabulary stimulates the mother to point out many new objects, whereas a mother does not want to overwhelm a slower child.

In reality, both options are probably correct, as shown in Figure 2.6.

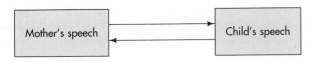

Figure 2.6
The correlation between a mother's speech and her child's speech probably has at least two possible interpretations.

The phrase "Correlation is not necessarily causation" is important when we discuss the interpretation of correlations. Just because two factors go together, we cannot conclude that one actually causes the other. It *may* be that Factor A causes Factor B. But perhaps Factor B causes Factor A. Finally, a third factor (perhaps not yet identified) may cause both A and B. In the language example, the correlation may be traceable to a third variable such as family intelligence. An intelligent mother is likely to enjoy teaching her youngster. Because a mother's intelligence is correlated with her child's intelligence, an intelligent mother is likely to have an intelligent child. This intelligent child will probably have a better-than-average vocabulary.

Consider this example in which a correlation can be completely explained by a third variable. Some years ago, research on motorcycle accidents revealed that the number of accidents was highly correlated with the number of tattoos the riders had (Martin, 1977). How can we interpret this correlation? Do people cheer themselves up after an accident by hustling over to the nearest tattoo parlor? (A → B) On the other hand, do motorcycle riders gaze at their tattoos—rather than the road—so that they crash their motorcycles? (A ← B) Wouldn't it be more reasonable to propose that a factor (such as risk taking) that encourages people to drive dangerously would also encourage them to get a tattoo?

In summary, then, the correlational method allows us to discover whether variables are related to each other. This advantage is particularly helpful in real-life settings where an experiment would be impossible. However, a major disadvantage of correlational research is that we cannot draw the firm cause-and-effect conclusions that an experiment permits. Correlational research does generate cause-and-effect *hypotheses* that can be tested later, using the experimental method.

The Survey Method

A headline in a recent newspaper claims, "Poll says top daydream in United States is to be rich." The article, which describes a survey of 1,992 people, reported that 49% of the respondents checked "being rich" as their favorite daydream. In addition, 29% selected "a better job." The least frequent fantasy was "being elected to political office," chosen by only 4%.

In the **survey method**, a researcher selects a large group of people and asks them questions about their behaviors or thoughts. Typically, the researchers also collect **demographic information** about the characteristics often used to classify people, such as sex, age, marital status, race, education, and so forth (Sudman & Bradburn, 1982).

When survey results have been collected for many years, we can determine whether the responses have changed systematically across the years. For instance, Figure 2.7 shows the trend since 1976 in the percentage of college students who

Figure 2.7
Reasons noted as very important in deciding to go to college. (Based on American Council on Education, 1988)

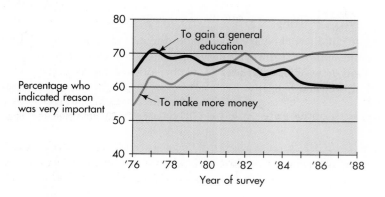

selected "to gain a general education" and "to make more money" in answering the question about important reasons for attending college (Astin et al., 1988). You will note, incidentally, that this emphasis on money corresponds to the number-one daydream reported in the newspaper survey.

We discussed earlier that this chapter should encourage you to adopt a critical attitude toward the psychological research reported in the media. Some common problems in surveys include these:

1. The sample studied in a survey may not be typical of the entire population, a point we return to shortly.

2. People may distort their answers to make themselves appear more positive (Mishler, 1986).

3. People may not recall information accurately (Loftus et al., 1985). For instance, in a survey assessing whether Americans have been the victims of crime, respondents may forget to report some minor incidents.

The survey produces valuable descriptive information. The results may also be useful in a correlational study. For instance, researchers could determine whether the relationship between a student's family income and the endorsement of the goal "to make more money" involves a positive, zero, or negative correlation. (What would you guess?) Keep in mind, however, that the survey method typically cannot be used to determine the causes of human behavior.

In-Depth Interviews and Case Studies

So far, we have discussed methods in which the ideal researcher remains distant, uninvolved, and neutral. Researchers meet the participants briefly (if at all) and interact with them minimally. Some theorists argue, however, that these methods have their limitations (e.g., Gergen, 1988; Jack, 1988; McHugh et al., 1986). They point out that interviews and case studies provide essential information about human behavior, thought, and emotion.

An **in-depth interview** requires the interviewer to gather answers to open-ended questions, often over a period of many hours or days. For example, Belenky and her colleagues (1986) questioned 135 women, one at a time, for 2 to 5 hours each. The interview focused on these women's thoughts about knowledge. Some women thought that all information from "experts" was trustworthy; others relied more on their own knowledge and sense of what was correct.

In-depth interviews often require the interviewer to achieve warmth and rapport with participants (Benmayor, 1987). For instance, Alvarez (1987) would have learned relatively little about the Black Puerto Rican woman she interviewed if she had not been fluent in Spanish and if she had not grown close to the woman during previous meetings. In this excerpt from the interview, the woman shared her thoughts about child rearing:

> I brought my children up in the 20th century. I wasn't too free with them but neither was I too strict. . . . I raised them without having to fight, without having to hit them . . . and with my daughters little by little I went on explaining to them about sex because, you know, it's not good to live in ignorance. (p. 60, translated from Spanish)

A **case study** is an in-depth description and analysis of a single person (Shaughnessy & Zechmeister, 1990). The data in a case study typically include an interview, observation, and test scores. Most often, the individual selected for a case study is highly unusual (Bromley, 1986). For instance, Curtiss (1977) reports a case study on Genie, whose parents kept her locked in a small bedroom, most often harnessed to a potty chair. For almost 14 years, Genie never heard any language except her father's swearing. Curtiss's study specifically focused on Genie's language development, which evolved slowly after Genie's "release" and never achieved the richness of normal language. For example, here is an interchange between Genie and her foster mother, when Genie was 18:

> **Genie**:   At school is washing car.
>
> **Mother**:   Whose car did you wash?
>
> **Genie**:   People car.
>
> **Mother**:   How many cars did you wash?
>
> **Genie**:   Two car. (Curtiss, 1977, p. 28)

Both the in-depth interview and the case study provide a much fuller appreciation of an individual than any other methods. A skillfully conducted study helps us understand what it is like to live inside someone else's skin. Naturally, however, the researchers do not claim that their findings hold true of all people— or even many people. Nor do they claim that we can draw cause-and-effect conclusions from the observations. It should be mentioned, too, that interviews and case studies are also useful in providing ideas that can be explored further using other research methods.

Naturalistic Observation

One of the goals of psychology discussed in chapter 1 is to describe behavior. Naturalistic observation is especially appropriate for this goal. As the name implies,

Table 2.2   *Comparing Psychological Research Methods*

METHOD	ADVANTAGES	DISADVANTAGES
Experiment	1. Can control potentially confounding variables. 2. Can draw cause-and-effect conclusions.	1. May be difficult to generalize to real-world settings.
Quasi-Experiment	1. Can study behavior in real-world settings. 2. Can draw tentative cause-and-effect conclusions.	1. Cannot control confounding variables as well as in an experiment. 2. Cause-and-effect conclusions are not as firm as with experimental method.
Correlation	1. Can study behavior in real-world settings. 2. Can determine whether two variables are related.	1. Cannot draw cause-and-effect conclusions.
Surveys	1. Can obtain descriptive information about large groups of people. 2. Provides data for use in studies using other methods.	1. Results may be biased because of atypical sample, overly positive answers, and inaccurate recall. 2. Cannot draw cause-and-effect conclusions.
Case Study and In-Depth Interview	1. Provides in-depth information on individuals. 2. Provides ideas for further research.	1. Cannot generalize the results to other individuals. 2. Cannot draw cause-and-effect conclusions.
Naturalistic Observation	1. Provides information about people and animals in real-world settings. 2. Provides ideas for further research and data for use in studies using other methods.	1. Cannot draw cause-and-effect conclusions.

naturalistic observation involves systematic observing and recording in a natural setting (Shaughnessy & Zechmeister, 1990; Weick, 1985). Researchers often use naturalistic observation as a first step in a research project to identify variables that would be worthwhile studying with one of the other research techniques.

A second function of naturalistic observation is to gather descriptive information about the typical behavior of people or animals. For instance, one hard-working researcher in the late 1800s decided to determine what bees did in their daily lives and whether the complimentary phrase "busy bee" was truly appropriate. He systematically tagged a series of bees and observed them carefully. No single bee ever worked more than $3\frac{1}{2}$ hours a day. Instead, the lazy little slouches spent most of their time doing nothing (Hubbell, 1988).

A third function of naturalistic observation is to provide data for use with another technique, such as the experimental method, the quasi-experiment, or the correlational method. For example, Dunn and Shatz (1989) observed young children at home with their mothers and older siblings, for 2 hours each. They recorded each child's conversations, focusing on the number of times the child intruded upon a remark made to someone else. The researchers then used the correlational method to determine that the age of a child was positively correlated with the number of intrusions he or she made.

We have noted that naturalistic observation is used in generating research ideas, gathering descriptive information, and providing data for other studies. In all cases, however, a hallmark of this method is that behavior is observed (and not manipulated) in natural settings.

Comparing the Methods

Table 2.2 lists the six research methods we have discussed, together with each method's advantages and disadvantages. Clearly, some questions can be more readily answered with one method than with others. However, in the 1990s, psychologists are increasingly likely to favor a multimethod approach, using several different research techniques.

Section Summary: The Major Research Methods

- In the experimental method, researchers manipulate variables and observe how the participants respond; conditions are carefully controlled, and participants are randomly assigned to conditions.
- Quasi-experiments are used when random assignment is impossible, but variables can still be manipulated with this method.
- Correlational research establishes whether two variables are related; correlations can be positive, zero, or negative. Correlations cannot tell us which variable is the cause and which is the effect.
- The survey method is used to collect information about the behaviors and thoughts of a relatively large group of people.
- An in-depth interview requires extensive questioning of the research participants, often after the interviewer achieves rapport; a case study also typically includes an interview, observation, and psychological testing.
- In naturalistic observation, the researcher observes people or animals in their natural setting.
- Each research method has its strengths and weaknesses, and many questions can be answered best by combining several research methods.

Research Issues

We have examined six research methods commonly used in psychology, and we noted some problems associated with each one. However, some potential problems are more general; they are not found with just one of the six methods. In this section, we consider these more general research issues, which include sampling, measuring responses, assessing age differences, and avoiding biases. We also discuss social and ethical aspects of research. This section on research issues concludes with an in-depth discussion of research on physical attractiveness, in which we consider how several different research methods have approached the important topic of personal appearance.

Sampling

"Four out of five doctors recommend Blatz cough syrup," proclaims the television advertisement. I hope you are skeptical about ads like these and wonder which doctors they chose for their "research." How many were asked? How were they chosen? Would they be likely to have a biased viewpoint? Perhaps they questioned only five doctors: Dr. John Blatz, Dr. Maria Blatz, Dr. Phil Blatz, Dr. Suzanne Blatz (all of whom swore they loved it) . . . and Dr. Chris Blatz, who always *was* the honest sort.

When researchers want to test a hypothesis, they must select participants for the study. We seldom have the resources to study an entire population (for instance, all humans living in the Western Hemisphere). Instead, we select some members from that population, called a **sample**, with the intention of discovering something about the population from which the sample was drawn (Kidder & Judd, 1986). For instance, the study on Americans' top daydream, mentioned in the discussion on surveys, examined a sample of 1,992 people, rather than all members of the population.

When you read articles about psychology research, either in psychology journals and textbooks or in the popular media, be sure to note sample size. You can trust an experiment conducted on 100 people more than an experiment conducted on 8. And you would trust the Blatz cough syrup ad more if you knew that the sample size was 1,000 than if it was only 5—especially if the 5 were all Blatzes! Sample size is therefore an important criterion in judging a study.

A second important criterion relevant to sampling is that the participants should be randomly chosen. In a **random sample**, every member of the population has an equal chance of being chosen. When a sample is random, the characteristics of the sample are likely to be similar to the characteristics of the population. In contrast, in a **biased sample**, every member of the population does not have an equal chance of being chosen. For instance, in the Blatz cough syrup example, people whose last name was *Blatz* had a much higher chance of being selected than people with other last names.

It is important that the sample be similar to the population because eventually we want to be able to generalize our findings to the population from which the sample was selected. For example, from the information about the daydreams of 1,992 people, we want to say something more general about the American people.

One of the most famous cases of a biased sample—where the sample was not similar to the general population—occurred during the presidential campaign of 1936 (Snodgrass et al., 1985). A magazine called *Literary Digest* conducted a poll, based on more than 2 million responses, and predicted that the Republican candidate Alf Landon would win. Do you remember President Landon? In actuality, Franklin D. Roosevelt won that election, receiving close to two thirds of the popular vote.

The problem was that the *Digest* had a biased sample, because the sample was selected from telephone directories and lists of *Digest* subscribers. The sample had overrepresented wealthy people, who could afford telephones and magazine subscriptions during the Depression era . . . and who tend to vote Republican. The sample was not representative of the population of Americans who actually cast votes in that election.

Unbiased samples are particularly important in surveys when we want to assess the views of a large population. However, sampling is also important when we use other research methods and then want to make general statements about the results. We can only generalize the results to people similar to our sample. For instance, the research by Olds (1988) reported results on White unwed mothers—very few Blacks live in the Appalachian region he studied. Appropriately, his discussion cautioned against generalizing the findings to Black or urban populations.

Measuring Responses

Psychologists are typically concerned with hidden mental processes such as memory, anxiety, and attitudes. For each psychological concept they study, psychologists construct an **operational definition**, that is, a precise definition that specifies exactly how the concept is to be measured. For example, a consumer psychologist who wants to assess the public's response to a new kind of cracker might select an operational definition, "number of crackers eaten in a 10-minute period by a panel of testers." The advantages of operational definitions are that they allow us to understand exactly how a variable was measured and they permit other researchers to replicate a study using the same system of measurement.

Let us consider three representative approaches to measuring responses, in other words, three different classes of operational definitions. These include self-report, behavioral measures, and physiological measures. As you will see, the conclusions that researchers draw from their study often depend on the operational definitions they choose. This point will be illustrated with examples from the research on gender differences and similarities in empathy. (Empathy involves feeling the same emotion as another person is feeling. Thus, a person who is empathic can hear a friend tell about the death of a favorite relative and experience the same feelings of sadness, loneliness, and loss that the friend feels.)

Self-Report   When researchers use **self-report** to assess psychological processes, they ask participants to report their own thoughts, emotions, behaviors, or intentions. Commonly, self-reports are measured with a rating scale, such as the one shown in Demonstration 2.1. The rating scale allows us to capture a hidden process such as empathy or anger or happiness and represent it with a concrete number. The numbers can then be analyzed statistically, as the next section of this chapter illustrates. In many cases, self-report is the most useful measure of people's subjective experience.

An important drawback to self-reports is that people are likely to give biased answers. People may report that they are much more noble, normal, and nice than they truly are. We would like the response measure to reflect reality. However, when we try to measure reality, the measurement process often intrudes on people's normal responses, giving us a distorted, rose-colored view of reality.

One kind of bias in self-reports is that people often tend to respond the way they believe they are *supposed* to respond. According to a common stereotype, women are supposed to show empathy, whereas men are supposed to remain cool and objective. The research on empathy indeed shows a substantial gender difference in self-reported empathy. In a review of the research, Eisenberg and Lennon

Demonstration 2.1

Gender Comparisons

Assemble 10 index cards and one blank envelope, and go to a location with a large number of males and females. (If you live in a coed dorm, you are all set.) Approach five females and five males individually and ask if they have a spare moment. Explain that you are conducting an informal survey. Hand everybody an index card, and ask them to rate themselves on a scale where 1 = "not at all" and 7 = "very much." Then explain that the item you would like them to rate themselves on is "I tend to get emo-tionally involved in a friend's problems." Everyone should simply supply a number from 1 to 7, and then indicate F for females and M for males. Stress that they should not write their name on the card but should place it face down in the envelope. When you have collected all 10 responses, figure out an average score for females by adding up the scores for the five female respondents and dividing by 5. Repeat the process for the male respondents. Are the two averages substantially different from each other?

(1983) found that women consistently rated themselves higher than did men on self-report questions such as the one in Demonstration 2.1, "I tend to get emo-tionally involved in a friend's problems." One semester, I asked students in my introductory class to rate themselves on this question on a slip of paper, indicating their gender but omitting their name. The average man rated himself 4.0, whereas the average woman rated herself 5.0. (The maximum score was 7.0.)

Do these self-reports reflect reality, or are they biased, drifting in the direction of the popular stereotypes about "appropriate" behavior for women and men? Unfortunately, we cannot peel away a person's scalp, look at a little dial on the brain, and discover that the *true* empathy rating (unbiased by stereotypes) is really a 3. However, two other methods for measuring responses may seem more ap-pealing: behavioral and physiological measures.

Behavioral Measures   **Behavioral measures** objectively record people's observ-able behavior. For instance, as we see in the part of chapter 14 on personality assessment, psychologists who want to measure a person's aggressive tendencies might use naturalistic observation, recording the number of aggressive acts per-formed in a specified time. They might argue that these measures would be more objective and less biased than the person's self-report about aggressive tendencies.

Of course, if individuals know they are being observed, their behavior could be just as biased a reflection of reality as any self-report. Furthermore, behavioral measures cannot be used in research on some invisible mental processes. How would you obtain behavioral measures on people's daydreams? Sitting and watch-ing them will not inform you that their number-one daydream is to be wealthy.

One kind of behavioral measure assesses nonverbal behavior, for instance, facial expression. In a study of children's empathy, boys and girls listened to a tape recording of an infant crying. Measuring facial expression, the researchers found no gender differences in empathy (Eisenberg & Lennon, 1983).

Physiological Measures   A third option in measuring psychological processes is to obtain **physiological measures**, which are objective recordings of physiological states, assessed, for example, by heart rate, breathing rate, perspiration rate, and brain activity. We examine some of these physiological measures in chapter 3 on the biological basis of behavior, in chapter 5 on dreams, and in chapter 12 on emotions.

Physiological measures provide objective numbers that are unlikely to be distorted by the desire to look good. The problem, however, is that the body only has a limited number of ways of responding, and many different emotions can produce the same response. Suppose, for instance, that a man's palms start to sweat (as measured by an index called the electrodermal response). That physiological response could reflect increased excitement, anxiety, or sexual arousal. Which one should we choose? A physiological measure simply tells us we have more sweat—the sweat droplets do not appear with little labels identifying which emotion generated them.

Let us return to the question of gender differences and similarities in empathy. According to Eisenberg and Lennon (1983), researchers have obtained a variety of physiological measures on people watching an adult being shocked or an infant crying. Physiological measures such as heart rate, pulse, and blood pressure show no gender differences in empathy.

One physiological measure of psychological processes is called the electrodermal response. When you perspire more, your skin changes its electrical conductivity, as registered by this machine.

Conclusions About Response Measurement Approaches   You have learned that self-reports may be biased, that behavioral measures cannot be gathered for some psychological processes, and that it is often difficult to interpret the origin of physiological measures. Should psychology researchers just pack up and go home? Obviously not. It is true that no flawless response measure exists, just as no flawless research method exists. However, we can obtain a clearer picture of reality when research on a particular topic is conducted with a variety of response measures. In the case of empathy, for instance, the fact that gender differences appear in self-report—but evaporate when measured behaviorally or physiologically—should make you suspicious. It is likely that men and women are reasonably similar in their empathic reactions, and that their self-reports are distorted to match the stereotype that women *should* be empathic and men *should* be emotionally uninvolved.

Assessing Age Differences

So far in this section on research issues, we have addressed the problems of sampling and response measurement, which are general concerns in most psychological research. Now consider a more specific problem, one that is critical in the two chapters on developmental psychology: How should we study age differences?

When we investigate how children, adolescents, and adults develop, we often want to compare people of different ages. For instance, a study on the development of children's attitudes toward politics might examine whether the attitudes of 8-year-olds, 10-year-olds, and 12-year-olds differ. The problem with the age variable, however, is that we cannot randomly assign people to different age categories. Most 30-year-olds would object to being transformed into 50-year-olds—even if we had the technology to do so.

Developmental psychologists typically use one of two methods of assessing age differences. In the **cross-sectional method**, researchers test individuals of different ages at the same time. For instance, next Tuesday, a researcher might select samples of children who are 8, 10, and 12 years old to question them about their political attitudes. Alternatively, in the **longitudinal method**, researchers select one group of individuals who are the same age, and they retest them periodically. For instance, a researcher might select a sample of 8-year-old children and retest this same group when they are 10 and then 12 years old. (In other words, it would take at least 4 years to complete the study.)

In the longitudinal method, a researcher follows a group of people (all the same age) as they grow older. For example, these students could be tested again two and four years later.

Each of these two methods has advantages and disadvantages. Because neither method uses random assignment, both can be plagued by confounding variables, though the methods differ in the kinds of confounding variables that infect them. For instance, the longitudinal method can be confounded by time of measurement. Suppose that researchers measured the political attitudes of 8-year-olds in 1987 and returned to test these same children in 1989. They might find that the 10-year-olds were much more negative about politics and politicians than they were two years before. Should the researchers propose that children undergo a transformation in their thinking when they are about 9 years old? The researchers would be wise to look for alternative hypotheses. For instance, at the first time of measurement, in 1987, fewer politicians resigned because of unsavory dealings than at the second time of measurement, in 1989.

The cross-sectional method has a different set of confounding variables. For instance, suppose that researchers would like to determine whether 30-year-olds, 45-year-olds, and 60-year-olds differ in their intellectual functioning. They administer intelligence tests, using three groups of people of the appropriate age. The results indicate a distinct drop in the older groups. Is it all downhill after 30, with intelligence inevitably decreasing? The confounding variable in this case is that each group was born in a different era. The three groups differ in their educational experiences. Many more of the 30-year-olds would have attended college, in comparison to 45- and 60-year-olds. Their higher scores could perhaps be traced to having had greater intellectual stimulation. In fact, cross-sectional research frequently shows a decrease in intellectual performance after age 30. In contrast, longitudinal research, tracing the same group of individuals across time (and therefore controlling for factors such as college attendance) shows little change in intellectual performance up to the age of 60 (Baltes & Kliegl, 1989).

In the best of all worlds, researchers would use methods combining the cross-sectional and longitudinal approaches. In fact, formal techniques have been developed that combine the two approaches (e.g., Baltes, 1973; Schaie, 1965). Furthermore, when we can contrast the results of two approaches, we learn more than with either method alone. For instance, in the research on intellectual performance, we learned that lack of education—and not age-related decline—may explain why older people received lower test scores.

Avoiding Gender and Racial Biases

Many parts of this chapter discuss biases that can creep into psychological research and distort the results. For example, a biased sample will not provide an accurate picture of the population, and a biased self-report will not provide an accurate picture of an individual's true reactions. Confounding variables, such as amount of education, can lead to a biased picture of age-related changes in intelligence. One of psychology's goals is to discover how psychological processes operate, and these biases can lead us to incorrect conclusions.

Biased studies can be especially harmful when the results are used to discriminate against certain groups of people. For instance, at the beginning of this century, people from certain ethnic groups received low scores on intelligence tests, and these data were used to restrict the immigration of people from these groups. The confounding variable here was familiarity with the English language and American culture.

Biases can operate at any stage of the research process, from the formulation of the hypothesis, to designing and performing the study, to interpreting the data, to communicating the findings (Cannon et al., 1988; Halpern, 1986; Matlin, 1987). For instance, participants should be carefully selected to avoid confounding variables. If we want to study the mental health of men and women, we should compare men who are employed with women who are employed. If we compared employed men with nonemployed women, employment status would be an important confounding variable, especially because nonemployed women are more likely than employed women to have psychological problems (McHugh et al., 1986; Warr & Parry, 1982). Any gender difference might therefore be traceable to the confounding variable of employment. Furthermore, a study on racial differences in child rearing should control for social class, an important potential confounding variable.

Biases can also enter when the researchers interpret their data and write summaries of their results. One common mistake, for example, is that researchers are likely to report any gender differences their study may have demonstrated. In contrast, if they find no gender differences, they yawn and fail to report this finding; they think gender similarities are boring. You can anticipate the problem that arises: Psychology journals will end up with many published articles noting gender differences, and the gender similarities will be underrepresented (Denmark et al., 1988; Matlin, 1987).

A second mistake researchers make when they write their research summaries is to magnify group differences. For instance, an author might write, "Although only 35% of Blacks responded that . . . fully 39% of Whites. . . ." The words "only" and "fully" seem so different that the reader may fail to appreciate that the groups differ by only 4%.

The previous examples on bias have focused on gender and race. However, researchers should guard against all kinds of biases and assumptions about social class, disability, age, and sexual orientation—as well as gender and race. Whenever biases favor one group, they may harm another group, limiting the group members' potential for achievement and life satisfaction.

Social Aspects of Research

Whenever people interact, they have the possibility of influencing one another. Chapters 17 and 18 examine these social interactions in some detail. However, we need to keep in mind that psychological research often requires social interactions between the researchers and the participants. During these interactions, researchers may convey certain expectations, and participants may develop certain expectations. Both sets of expectations may influence the outcome of a study, leading the researchers astray in their search for accurate information about psychological processes.

Experimenter Expectations.   The term **experimenter bias** means that researchers' biases and expectations can influence the results of a study. The major researcher in this area is Robert Rosenthal. He found, for example, that research assistants who expected a group of laboratory rats to be exceptionally bright actually obtained exceptional performance from these animals, compared to assistants who expected their rats to be slow learners. Furthermore, elementary school teachers who expected certain students to be bright actually obtained better performance from these students, relative to other students of similar ability (Rosenthal, 1968, 1973).

Rosenthal's (1976) review of relevant studies showed that experimenter bias operated in about one third of those studies. In other words, experimenter bias does not always influence people's responses. Still, it operates often enough for us to be concerned that significant results in a study may be due to the researchers' expectations.

Participants' Expectations   The participants—as well as the experimenters—develop expectations about what is supposed to happen in a research study. Students who enter a psychology lab to participate in a study often wonder what the study is *really* about. "What is under that box?" "Are we being watched through that funny-looking mirror?" "The professor said it was about memory, but I wonder if it really is. . . ." Humans seldom sit passively, waiting to be studied by psychologists. Instead, they actively consider alternative hunches, searching for clues about the true purpose of the study.

The clues that the participants discover are called the **demand characteristics** (Orne, 1962). Demand characteristics include rumors they hear about the study, the description supplied when they signed up to participate, the activities of the researchers, and the laboratory setting itself. All of these clues are called demand characteristics because the participants believe that these clues *demand* certain responses. For instance, suppose that you have gathered information about a study that suggests the researchers want to see whether people will conform to the opinion of the majority. The clues *demand* that you conform. Now you might decide to cooperate, or you might decide not to—but the point is that you developed certain expectations. These expectations may influence how you respond and may therefore change the nature of the results. People may behave the way they *think* they should behave, instead of behaving naturally. In short, bias can intrude, based on the expectations of either the researchers or the participants.

Demand characteristics are the clues that the research participants discover about the nature of the study. In this case, an important source of demand characteristics is the piece of equipment being pointed out by the researcher.

Ethical Aspects of Research

Psychologists study living creatures. We need to make certain that we do not harm these creatures in the process of learning more about them. In recent decades, the American Psychological Association and government agencies have developed ethical principles and regulations that specify how people and animals should be treated in psychological research (American Psychological Association, 1982; Ceci et al., 1985; Stanley et al., 1987). Table 2.3 lists some of the ethical principles concerning human participants.

As you can see, some principles outline how participants must be recruited ethically. For example, the participants must be given a full description of the study (see item 1); any physical dangers should be noted in this description. Participants also have the right to say "No, thanks" at any point during the study (see item 2). Let us examine the remaining items in more detail and then consider the ethical treatment of animals in psychological research.

Avoiding Potential Harm   Any experiment that is likely to cause permanent harm must be avoided. When researchers need to study physical pain in an experiment,

Table 2.3   *Some of the APA Ethical Principles for Research With Human Participants (American Psychological Association, 1982)*

1. The researcher must inform participants about all aspects of the research that are likely to influence their decision to participate in the study.

2. Participants must have the freedom to say that they do not wish to participate in a research project; they may also withdraw from the research at any time.

3. The researcher must protect participants from physical and mental harm.

4. If deception is necessary, researchers must determine whether its use is justifiable; participants must be told about any deception after completing the study.

5. Information obtained on participants must be kept confidential, and researchers must be sensitive about invading the privacy of the participants.

they should participate in the experiment themselves before testing any participants. They must also check their equipment frequently, to make certain that it is functioning properly.

Researchers must avoid mental harm as well as physical harm. For example, a study that encourages low self-esteem in participants would be ethically questionable. Fortunately, psychologists' current awareness of ethical principles, as well as governmental regulations, make it highly unlikely that you will ever participate in a study involving physical or mental harm.

Avoiding Unnecessary Deception   The relationship between the researcher and the participants should be based on openness and honesty. Whenever possible, deception must be avoided. Unfortunately, this rule was sometimes violated in previous decades. For instance, in a study described by Warwick (1975), a researcher recorded information about gay men by passing as gay at private gatherings. He noted people's license plates and then traced the car owners through the police. Later, he went to the men's homes to interview them. Note that this unethical study violated every one of the current-day principles listed in Table 2.3.

In some studies, however, modest deception is necessary. If researchers describe precisely what will happen during a study, the demand characteristics will distort the results and make them meaningless. For example, consider a study on perceptual attention in which participants are told to pay attention to the sentences presented via earphone to their right ear. Later, they are tested on these sentences, as well as on other sentences presented to their left (unattended) ear. If they had been told initially that they would be tested on these other sentences, their attention would have certainly shifted, and the results would be useless.

An important part of any psychological research is debriefing. Proper **debriefing** requires telling the participants afterward about the purpose of the study, the nature of the anticipated results, and any deceptions used. The purpose of debriefing is partly educational; if people donate their time to a project, they deserve to learn something from the experience. If deception was used, the debriefing also identifies any false information. Researchers must also be certain that participants' questions have been answered and that all of their concerns have been addressed.

Ensuring Privacy   Privacy means that people can decide for themselves whether they want to share their feelings, thoughts, and personal information with others. Thus, participants must feel free to say that they do not choose to answer personal questions on a survey, for example. Any personal information should also be kept confidential, rather than being shared with other people. Data should also be gathered anonymously, so that the researchers cannot identify which person supplied which data.

We have seen that human subjects should be treated humanely in psychological research, avoiding physical harm, mental harm, unnecessary deception, and invasion of privacy. Try Demonstration 2.2 to discover your own ideas about ethical issues in psychology. Then we turn our attention from human participants to animals.

Ensuring the Ethical Treatment of Animals   Popular media suggest that psychologists routinely mistreat animals in their research. Fortunately, these accusations are seldom true.

Consider one animal rights organization, Mobilization for Animals (1984). They distributed a pamphlet describing research in which animals received intense, inescapable electric shock, in which they were intentionally starved to death, and in which their limbs were mutilated. However, a survey of journal articles published in the major animal-research journals discovered that none of the claims were found true in any of the 608 articles published during a 5-year span (Coile & Miller, 1984).

Biologists have studied animals to understand and develop treatment for diseases such as Parkinson's disease, diabetes, and acquired immunodeficiency syndrome (AIDS). Psychologists have studied animals to establish the basic prin-

---

Demonstration 2.2

Ethical Issues in Psychological Research

Each of the following paragraphs describes a research study that was actually conducted. After reading them, rank all in terms of their compliance with ethical standards discussed in this section. Give a ranking of *1* to the most ethical study and a ranking of *6* to the one you consider least ethical. It should be stressed that the clear majority of psychological research complies with all ethical principles; most cases cited here are unusual ones presented to ethics review committees.

_____ A. A researcher wanted to create a realistic experiment, so he told participants that they were being hired for a semipermanent job. At the end of the day, they were told it was only an experiment. One person had turned down other jobs because of this job.

_____ B. A professor asked her students to do her a favor by staying after class to fill out a brief questionnaire. She added that the task was voluntary, but when one of the students began to leave, she said, "Well, I'm certainly glad the *rest* of you are willing to help me out."

_____ C. Students are given a list of paired words to memorize. Afterward, their recall is tested. The researcher then announces, "Now we'll go on to something else," and instructs them to solve simple jigsaw puzzles. Fifteen minutes later, the students are again asked to recall the pairs, even though they had been led to believe they would not be tested further on this material.

_____ D. As part of a study, students completed a "life-goals inventory" and a "graduate school potential test." The researcher then informs some of them that the test results indicated that they are not graduate school material. One student decides to give up her goal of graduate work in English. The researcher later informed them that the purpose of the research was to see whether life goals would be clarified by discouraging or encouraging evaluations.

_____ E. An experimenter gave research participants an insoluble task to perform. He assured them that the task could be solved, intending to make them angry.

_____ F. Students participating in a survey about cheating are told that they should not write their names on the survey so that the results could be kept confidential. However, the questionnaire includes many demographic questions, asking students to supply their gender, major, year, and so forth. After turning in the questionnaire, several students worry that the information may allow them to be identified.

Check page 54 to see how a professional psychologist answered this demonstration.

Sources: American Psychological Association, 1973; Faden et al., 1986; Keith-Spiegel & Koocher, 1985.

ciples of learning (chapter 6). Animals have also been used in such research areas as the relationship between stress and disease, the treatment of eating disorders, and the effect of noise on hearing loss (Miller, 1985). We often hear people say that scientists should be trying harder to find a cure for AIDS or that they should be conducting more research on drug addiction (Feeney, 1987). It is not clear how such research could progress without experiments on animals. Should a potentially helpful new AIDS treatment be administered to humans without first testing on animals?

Obviously, research animals should be well treated, and all unnecessary pain must be avoided. Ultimately, you need to decide for yourself whether you support animal research. You may truly believe that human lives should not have priority over animal lives, and you may conscientiously avoid eating meat or wearing leather products. Or you may agree with most psychologists, who maintain that no animals should suffer needlessly, but that animal research is justified in answering some important questions.

The ethical standards for research on animals specify that all animals should be well treated, avoiding unnecessary pain.

○ ○

In Depth: Research on Physical Attractiveness

Be honest: Can you truthfully say that when you meet a person for the first time, you pay no attention to physical attractiveness? If your self-report is honest, you will probably admit that personal appearances do affect your judgment. You have probably heard the terms *racism* and *sexism*, referring to discrimination on the basis of race and gender. This section examines another form of discrimination, popularly called *looksism*, or discrimination on the basis of personal appearance (Freedman, 1986).

One of the first demonstrations of the importance of physical attractiveness was a study in which Karen Dion and her colleagues (1972) asked college students to make judgments about other young adults who differed in attractiveness. The results showed that physically attractive people were judged to have more socially desirable personalities than less attractive people. In other words, it seems that "what is beautiful is good" (Dion, 1986). This effect extends to different ethnic groups and to judgments of individuals from different age groups. For instance, in one study, Black, White, and Mexican-American students thought that cute babies from all three ethnic groups would be more likely than less attractive babies to be happy, well behaved, and smart (Stephan & Langlois, 1984).

People judge that cute babies are more likely than less attractive babies to be happy, well behaved, and smart.

In this in-depth discussion, we consider several studies that illustrate how different research methods approach a psychological question. We first discuss an experiment, then a study that combines naturalistic observation and correlational research, and finally an in-depth interview.

Experimental Method Can our first impressions of a person's attractiveness shape that person's future behavior? Mark Snyder, Elizabeth Tanke, and Ellen Berscheid (1977) were interested in this question, but they faced a problem. To eliminate confounding variables, they would have to assign people randomly to either an "attractive" or an "unattractive" condition—ordinarily an impossible task. Let us see how Snyder and his colleagues solved this problem.

Female and male undergraduates at the University of Minnesota volunteered to participate in a study of "the processes by which people become acquainted with each other." They were scheduled in male-female pairs. The pairs were unacquainted and never actually met face to face during the study—they conversed only by telephone. Each member of the pair completed a background questionnaire about academic major, high school attended, and so forth, and the form was given to the conversational partner. In addition, each male student received a snapshot, with the explanation that it was a photo of his partner. In reality, however, the photo showed either an attractive or unattractive female student from another college. (Attractiveness was operationally defined as the average rating supplied by 20 other college-age men, using a 10-point rating scale.) This procedure allowed each male-female pair to be randomly assigned to either an "attractive female" or an "unattractive female" condition. After receiving the photo and the background information, each man rated his partner with adjectives describing physical attractiveness, intelligence, friendliness, sensitivity, enthusiasm, and so forth, to assess initial impressions.

Each pair then conversed for 10 minutes, using microphones and headphones; these conversations were tape-recorded. The dependent variable that most interested the researchers was the nature of the female's interactions. Would the women whose partners thought they were attractive actually start to talk in a more friendly, socially skilled manner?

Each of the tape recordings was rated by a different sample of student judges, who were not told about the perceived physical attractiveness of the women on the tapes. They heard only the tapes of the women's voices, and they judged each woman on the basis of adjectives mentioned earlier, as well as questions such as "How much is she enjoying herself?" These student judges rated the conversations of the presumably attractive women as being more poised, sexually warm, and outgoing. As the authors point out, "What had initially been reality in the minds of the men had now become reality in the behavior of the women with whom they had interacted . . ." (p. 661). The independent variable (perceived attractiveness of a conversational partner) did indeed have a significant influence on the dependent variable (conversational behavior of the partner). To some extent, we become what people expect us to be.

Combining Naturalistic Observation and Correlational Research   The experiment by Snyder and his colleagues demonstrated the importance of attractiveness, using an experiment in the laboratory. But what happens in real life? Are people really treated differently if they are attractive?

Research by Gregory Smith (1985) combines naturalistic observation with correlational methods to provide some interesting answers with young children. Smith studied middle-class White preschoolers between the ages of 2 years, 9 months, and 5 years, 7 months. Using naturalistic observation, he recorded the behavior of each child in the preschool classroom for a 5-minute session on 5 separate days. In particular, he recorded how other children treated this child. Were the other children prosocial—helping, patting, and praising the target child? Were these other children physically aggressive—hitting, pushing, or kicking this child?

The next step was to establish whether these naturalistic observations about behavior toward a child were correlated with that child's attractiveness. As an operational definition of attractiveness, Smith asked college students to rate each child, based on a photograph of the child's face.

Interestingly, attractiveness was correlated with the way little girls were treated, but not little boys. Specifically, the more attractive little girls tended to receive more prosocial treatment; the correlation was $+.73$. Furthermore, the more attractive little girls also tended to receive less physical aggression; the correlation was $-.41$. In other words, cute little girls get helped more and hit less. How about the little boys? For them, physical attractiveness was not related to either prosocial behavior ($r = +.05$) or physical aggression ($r = +.03$). Figure 2.8 shows the actual data in Smith's study, which is especially interesting because it illustrates one positive correlation, one negative correlation, and two zero correlations. Notice that attractiveness matters more for little girls than for little boys,

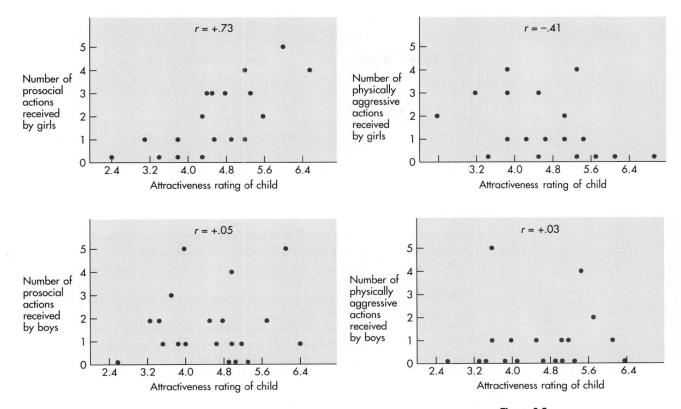

Figure 2.8
Smith's (1985) attractiveness study.

(upper left) The relationship between attractiveness and prosocial treatment for girls.

(upper right) The relationship between attractiveness and physically aggressive treatment for girls.

(lower left) The relationship between attractiveness and prosocial treatment for boys.

(lower right) The relationship between attractiveness and physically aggressive treatment for boys.

consistent with the greater emphasis on attractiveness for females of all ages (Freedman, 1986).

The previous discussion of the correlational method emphasized that we cannot identify causes and effects in a correlation. In the case of attractiveness and prosocial behavior in little girls, for instance, it is likely that a major part of the correlation can be traced to the fact that a pretty face elicits kind behavior from other people (A → B). However, it is also possible that kind behavior produces smiles and self-confidence in a little girl, and so she looks especially attractive in a photograph.

In-Depth Interviews   So far, it seems that beauty brings benefits, at least to females. However, the interview approach suggests that the relationship is more complex. For instance, Hatfield and Sprecher (1986) interviewed several people who noted that looks can backfire. Here is a short excerpt from one professional woman they interviewed:

> Here's something that happened to me recently: I was elected to be on an important state committee—a 30-member committee, all men. But I was nominated in a devastating way. An important committee member stood up and announced in front of everyone, "We have to have Audry on the committee—she's the prettiest thing here." I was stunned! Shocked! I couldn't say anything. I wasn't prepared for such a statement. . . . We were all there because we had professional credentials. After getting over my initial astonishment, my reaction was to get very, very angry. (pp. 66–67)

In summary, from the experimental method, we can learn that looks can influence how people behave—when confounding variables have been removed. The correlational method, drawing on data gathered from naturalistic observation, identifies the relationship between attractiveness and the way people are treated in a real-life setting. Finally, in-depth interviews help complete the picture, illustrating that good looks may sometimes distract other people from an individual's professional competence.

Section Summary: Research Issues

- A sample should be sufficiently large and unbiased.
- Responses can be assessed by methods such as self-report, behavioral measures, and physiological measures; each method has its advantages and disadvantages.
- Age differences can be assessed using the cross-sectional or longitudinal method; again, each has its advantages and disadvantages.
- Researchers must guard against gender, racial, and other biases at every step in the research process.
- Two social factors, experimenter bias and demand characteristics, can distort research results.
- Ethical treatment requires ethical recruitment of participants, the avoidance of potential harm or unnecessary deception, the guarantee of privacy, and the proper treatment of animals.
- A research issue, such as attractiveness, is best investigated by combining several different research approaches.

Analyzing the Data

Suppose that you tried Demonstration 2.1, asking five women and five men to rate themselves between 1 and 7 on the statement "I tend to get emotionally involved in a friend's problems." Suppose that the ratings you gathered are the data shown in Table 2.4. What do these numbers mean? Researchers who want to convey their findings to other psychologists would find it awkward to write, "The five women gave ratings of 4, 5, 5, 5, and 6, whereas the five men gave ratings of 2, 4, 4, 4, and 6." And the situation would become preposterous if you tested dozens of people, rather than just 10.

Researchers have developed standardized, efficient methods for describing their data that avoid listing every individual person's score. They have also developed standardized methods for drawing conclusions about their data. These methods allow them to determine whether the differences between groups or the relationships between variables are significant. Let us first discuss how researchers describe data and then consider how they draw conclusions. Appendix A provides more detailed information about statistics, with an emphasis on statistical formulas and calculations.

Descriptive Statistics: Describing the Data

In any group of data, two of the most important features you would like to know are some measure of central tendency ("What is the typical score?") and a measure of variability ("Are the other scores clustered closely around the typical score, or are they more spread out?") These **descriptive statistics** allow us to summarize data in a brief, useful form that other researchers can easily interpret.

Central Tendency   **Central tendency** is a measure of the most typical, characteristic score. For instance, for the men's scores in Table 2.4, what is the number that best captures the men's ratings? (The name makes sense if you realize that all other numbers have a *tendency* to cluster toward some *central* number.) There are three ways of measuring central tendency.

Table 2.4   *Calculating the Mean, Median, and Mode*

Imagine that you tried Demonstration 2.1 and gathered the following data on men's and women's empathy:

Women: 4   5   5   5   6
Men: 2   4   4   4   6

1. Calculate the **mean** for each group:

For the women $= \dfrac{4 + 5 + 5 + 5 + 6}{5} = \dfrac{25}{5} = 5.0$

For the men $= \dfrac{2 + 4 + 4 + 4 + 6}{5} = \dfrac{20}{5} = 4.0$

2. Calculate the **median** for each group:

For the women $= 4 \quad 5 \quad ⑤ \quad 5 \quad 6$ 5 is the score in the middle

For the men $= 2 \quad 4 \quad ④ \quad 4 \quad 6$ 4 is the score in the middle

3. Calculate the **mode** for each group:

For the women $= 4 \quad \boxed{5 \quad 5 \quad 5} \quad 6$ 5 is the most frequent score

For the men $= 2 \quad \boxed{4 \quad 4 \quad 4} \quad 6$ 4 is the most frequent score

---

1. The **mean** is the simple average of all scores, obtained by adding all the scores together and dividing by the number of scores. For the women, we perform this calculation:

$$\dfrac{4 + 5 + 5 + 5 + 6}{5}$$
←——— **Add together all scores.**
←——— **Divide by 5, the number of scores.**

The mean for the women is 5.0, whereas a similar calculation for the men yields a mean of 4.0. The mean is usually the most valuable measure of central tendency, because it is used when we want to draw conclusions about the data (as shown in the discussion of inferential statistics and in appendix A).

2. The **median** is the score that falls precisely in the middle of a distribution of scores. (The word *median* sounds like *middle*.) To calculate a median, arrange the scores in order from lowest to highest and identify the score in the middle, with half the scores above and half the scores below. For the data in Table 2.4, the median for the women is 5, and the median for the men is 4.

The median is an especially useful measure of central tendency when a small number of scores lie extremely far from the mean. Table 2.5 is an example showing people's incomes. Notice that the median income, $19,000, is closer to the majority of scores than is the mean income, $27,111. The single high score, $100,000, produced an enormous distortion in the mean, but not in the median.

3. The **mode** is the score that occurs most often in a group of scores. The mode can be established by simply inspecting the data and noting which number appears most frequently. For the data in Table 2.4, the mode is 5 for the women and 4 for the men. (Incidentally, in our examples, the mean, median, and mode are the same in each distribution, an unusual occurrence in most studies.)

Table 2.5   *The Median Is Sometimes a More Representative Measure of Central Tendency Than Is the Mean*

Annual income of 9 employees of the Blatz Corporation:

$15,000 $16,000 $16,000 $17,000 $19,000 $20,000 $20,000 $21,000 $100,000

Mean income for Blatz Corporation employees: $27,111 (Note that the mean is greatly increased by the one extremely high income.)

Median income for Blatz Corporation employees: $19,000 (Note that the median is *not* greatly increased by the one extremely high income.)

Variability   Once we know a measure of central tendency such as the mean, we have some feeling for the data. However, these central tendency measures can only tell us where the center of the data lies—not the extent to which the scores are spread out. Measures of **variability** give us a feeling for the extent to which the scores differ from one another.

An example can illustrate why we need information about variability—as well as central tendency—to convey an adequate statistical picture of the data. Suppose that Dr. Ted Schwartz teaches introductory psychology at two different colleges. Class A and Class B each have 40 students. He grades the first examination and calculates that the mean number of items correct is 35 (out of 50) for each of the two classes. In addition, he calculates that the median for each class is also 35, and the mode is 35 as well. For each class he constructs a **histogram**, a graph in which the data are arranged so that they show the frequency of each score (Figure 2.9).

Although the three measures of central tendency are identical for the two classes, a glance at the histograms suggests that Class A shows greater variability, with the scores widely scattered. In contrast, the scores in Class B are clustered close to the mean. Information about the variability of test scores could be very useful to Dr. Schwartz. With Class A, Dr. Schwartz may need to give extra help to people receiving low scores, and he might contemplate special enrichment material for the outstanding students. In contrast, he knows that if he aims his lectures at the average students in Class B, the level will be easy enough for the poor students and challenging enough for the good students, because of the low variability.

Figure 2.9
Examples of variability.

(left) The histogram for Class A (hypothetical data).

(right) The histogram for Class B (hypothetical data).

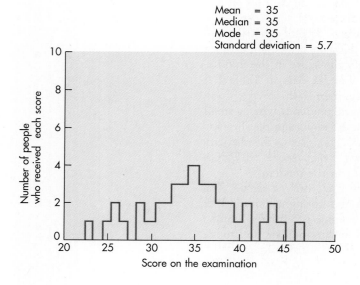

Mean   = 35
Median = 35
Mode   = 35
Standard deviation = 5.7

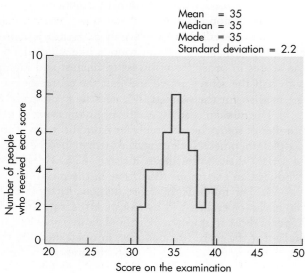

Mean   = 35
Median = 35
Mode   = 35
Standard deviation = 2.2

Let us consider two ways of measuring variability:

1. The **range** is the difference between the highest and the lowest scores. Class A's scores are spread between 23 and 47, so the range is 24 (that is, 47 minus 23). Class B's scores, in contrast, have a range of only 8 (39 minus 31). The range gives us a very quick estimate of variability in the scores.

2. The **standard deviation** is the more commonly used measure, and it is based on how far each score deviates from the mean. Psychologists use the standard deviation when they want to draw conclusions about their data, for instance, to see whether they have an important difference between two groups. It takes much longer to calculate the standard deviation than to calculate the range. (The formula is shown in appendix A.) However, the standard deviation gives a much more complete picture of the variability than does the range, because the standard deviation takes into account the specific value of *every* number in the distribution, not just the highest and the lowest. A calculation for the two distributions in Figure 2.9 shows that the standard deviation is 5.7 for Class A, but only 2.2 for Class B. As you might imagine, larger standard deviations indicate greater variability.

Inferential Statistics: Drawing Conclusions About the Data

So far, we have only discussed descriptive statistics, which describe a distribution's central tendency and variability. When psychologists conduct experiments, quasi-experiments, and correlational research, they want to draw conclusions. They use **inferential statistics** to draw these conclusions. In everyday language, an inference is a conclusion based on evidence. For instance, from a toddler's tear-stained face, you might make the inference that the child had been crying. Our everyday inferences are very casual. In contrast, inferential statistics provide a formal procedure for using data to test for **statistical significance**, that is, whether the findings are likely to be due to chance alone, or whether the differences are major.

Let us return to the example of men's and women's self-ratings on the statement "I tend to get emotionally involved in a friend's problems." One semester, the 41 men in my class supplied a mean rating of 4.05, whereas the 100 women supplied a mean rating of 5.03. Inferential statistics allowed me to decide if the difference between those two means—roughly 1 point on the rating scale—was statistically significant.

A single point on a rating scale might not seem to merit a statistical analysis. However, when comparing two groups statistically, we need to consider three factors:

1. the size of the difference between the two means (a large difference is more likely to produce a statistically significant difference);

2. the size of the standard deviations (small standard deviations are more likely to produce a statistically significant difference);

3. the number of people tested (large numbers are more likely to produce a statistically significant difference).

In the case of this comparison, the standard deviations were fairly small and the number of people tested was fairly large, so it seemed likely that a 1-point difference might be important.

An analysis that uses inferential statistics tells us how likely it is that the results we obtained could have occurred by chance alone. Suppose, for instance, that the analysis told us that a difference of 1 point or larger would be likely to occur by chance about 50% of the time, that is, with a probability (p) of .50. We would respond with a yawn—that difference is certainly not worth any excitement. However, if a difference of that size occurred by chance only 10% of the time

($p = .10$), we might become somewhat more excited . . . but would we have reason to become *very* excited? By tradition, psychologists have agreed that they are willing to say that a finding is statistically significant if it is likely to occur by chance alone less than 5% of the time, which is symbolized as $p < .05$. In other words, this is the formal boundary between what are considered to be ho-hum results and a major difference that we would be likely to duplicate if we repeated the study.

In the case of men's and women's responses to the question about emotional involvement, a statistical analysis showed that a 1-point difference between the groups (with 141 participants and the specified standard deviations) would be likely to occur less than 1 time in 10,000 ($p < .0001$). This is far less than .05, so we can conclude that the difference is statistically significant.

Statistical analyses allow us to compare two or more groups, to see if they are different. They also allow us to analyze correlational data, to determine whether the relationship between two variables is statistically significant.

We need to distinguish between statistical and practical significance. **Practical significance** means that the results have some important, practical implications for the real world. A study may therefore demonstrate statistical significance but not practical significance. For instance, in one study examining gender differences in mathematics performance, 440,000 high school students were tested. The results demonstrated a statistically significant gender difference, with male students performing better. However, an inspection of the means for the test scores indicated that the difference was $\frac{6}{10}$ of 1 point. It is hard to imagine how roughly half a point difference could have practical significance—any important implications for the way people should treat male and female students in the real world (Fox et al., 1979).

Let us consider one final issue in inferential statistics. Suppose that several clinical psychologists are interested in the treatment of phobias, which are intense, irrational fears of particular objects (e.g., snakes). They have systematically examined all the articles published in psychology journals to determine whether Therapy A or Therapy B is most effective in treating phobias. In all, 9 studies favor Therapy A, 4 favor Therapy B, and 3 show no difference. What should the researchers conclude? If they simply tally the outcomes, Therapy A seems preferable, but not consistently so.

A new technique called meta-analysis has revolutionized the way in which psychologists draw conclusions when the previously published psychology articles show conflicting results (Green & Hall, 1984). **Meta-analysis** is a systematic statistical method for synthesizing the results from numerous studies on a given topic (Hyde, 1986a). This method statistically combines the results from all these studies, yielding a single number that tells us whether a particular factor has an overall effect on behavior. For instance, a meta-analysis comparing Therapy A with Therapy B might tell us that Therapy A was preferable (especially if the 9 positive studies had larger numbers of participants and more statistically significant results than the 4 negative studies and 3 neutral studies). Meta-analysis will be mentioned several times throughout the book, for example, in the discussion of intellectual abilities, psychological therapy, and social psychology.

Data analysis is important in all sciences. It is particularly critical in psychology because most psychological research yields numbers. Because humans vary so much from one another and because behavior is so complex, a casual inspection of these data seldom allows us to draw a clear-cut conclusion. Instead, psychologists must calculate descriptive statistics, which portray the data's central tendency and variability, and inferential statistics, which provide a systematic method for drawing conclusions about statistical significance.

Section Summary: *Analyzing the Data*

- Central tendency can be measured by the mean, median, and mode.
- Variability can be measured by the range and the standard deviation.
- Inferential statistics provide a formal procedure for testing statistical significance and drawing conclusions; meta-analysis allows us to draw conclusions about a large number of separate studies.

REVIEW QUESTIONS

1. Name and briefly describe each of the six major research methods, listing their advantages and disadvantages. Then think of an example of a study that could be conducted using each of the six methods.

2. Suppose that you are interested in the factors that influence college students' performance on examinations, and—with their consent—you would like to collect data on your classmates' performance on their first examination in introductory psychology; these scores therefore provide one variable for your study. Describe how you could use the experimental, the quasi-experimental, and the correlational methods to conduct three different studies on this topic.

3. Suppose that you are interested in the topic of abused children. Describe how you could use the correlational, survey, case study, and naturalistic observation methods to conduct four different studies on this topic.

4. Dr. Mayra Lopez is a clinical psychologist who would like to test a new method of helping clients overcome snake phobia. How might she assess the dependent variable—that is, people's responses to snakes both before and after therapy—using each of the three methods of measuring responses discussed in the second section of the chapter?

5. What does the phrase "correlation is not necessarily causation" mean? Suppose you read that a significant positive correlation exists between teenagers' preferences for heavy-metal rock music and their juvenile delinquency tendencies. What three explanations could you provide for this correlation?

6. Suppose you read in a magazine written for nonprofessionals who are interested in psychology that a survey has been conducted. This survey appeared in an issue of the magazine, and readers were invited to return the survey, which concerned whether people are prejudiced against those who have experienced psychological disorders. How might the sample be biased, and why should the magazine article be cautious about its generalizations?

7. Dr. Ralph Bradburn is an applied psychologist who has been hired to determine attitudes toward the automatic-teller service at a large bank. The bank's executives speculate that as people grow older, they grow more skeptical about interacting with machines, such as the automatic-teller service. Dr. Bradburn decides to assess attitudes toward machines, using a cross-sectional approach and asking for volunteers from various age groups. Describe at least two problems with this study.

8. Analyze the experiment on attractiveness by Snyder and his colleagues from the standpoint of social aspects of the experiment, specifically experimenter bias and demand characteristics.

9. In one of the most frequently quoted studies in psychology, local citizens volunteered for a "learning" experiment, in which they were told to shock another person, the "learner," whenever he made a mistake. This person actually received no shock, but pretaped screams from the other room sounded as if he were being hurt. When the volunteers said they wanted to discontinue the study, they were told that they must continue (Milgram, 1963, 1965). What criticisms could you offer about ethical aspects of this study if it were to be proposed in the 1990s?

10. Psychologists try to discover accurate factual information about psychological processes. Name as many factors and biases as you can recall from this chapter that would interfere with the discovery of accurate results.

NEW TERMS

scientific method	biased sample
experiment	operational definition
hypothesis	self-report
independent variable	behavioral measures
dependent variable	physiological measures
control condition	cross-sectional method
experimental condition	longitudinal method
confounding variable	experimenter bias
random assignment	demand characteristics
well-controlled study	debriefing
quasi-experiment	descriptive statistics
correlational research	central tendency
correlation coefficient	mean
positive correlation	median
zero correlation	mode
negative correlation	variability
survey method	histogram
demographic information	range
in-depth interview	standard deviation
case study	inferential statistics
naturalistic observation	statistical significance
sample	practical significance
random sample	meta-analysis

ANSWERS TO DEMONSTRATIONS

Demonstration 2.2. Dr. Patricia Keith-Spiegel, an expert in psychological ethics, was invited to provide her assessment of the ethics of these six episodes. She responded,

> Although I would want more information about each of these studies before making definitive ratings, I have ranked the studies on the basis of their potential for harms and wrongs as a consequence of participation. Studies C (rated first, or least objectionable) and E (rated third) may create momentary upsets among some participants, assuming that they will be "debriefed" *promptly* after the experimental trial. Study E is the more unsettling of the two because the attempt to elicit an *uncomfortable* emotion was purposeful and willful. Neither study appears, on the basis of the

information given, to be a particularly significant piece of work, nor do we know if any attempt was made to study the phenomenon of interest in a way that did not involve deception. Two of the conditions that should pertain in order to justify the use of deception techniques are (1) the research should hold out the prospect for important findings, and (2) all other alternatives to deception should be carefully considered and ruled out as unfeasible.

Study F (rated second) is judged as only somewhat objectionable as opposed to a serious violation of the participant's rights to confidentiality. (I am assuming that the researchers were simply insensitive to the possibility that participants might fret because of the delicate subject of the survey and that the researchers have no intention of identifying anyone.)

Study B (rated fourth) illustrates the ethical infraction of coercion; that is, a professor places students over which she holds some power (i.e., the assignment of a grade) in a position where full voluntary consent is not possible. This concern is proven out when she ridicules a student for exercising the right to refuse participation.

Studies A (rated fifth) and D (rated sixth) are of greatest concern because the potential for wrong and harm to participants is high. Study A illustrates a harm that actually materialized. The more typical participant in Study A probably lost a day of life that might have been spent in more meaningful and productive ways otherwise and endured some degree of disappointment. Study D is rated as the most reprehensible because trusting students, most of whom are struggling with their decisions about their futures and feeling vulnerable about them, are given bogus feedback that could deflate their self-confidence. Had the researchers "debriefed" within an hour after inflicting the deception, little harm would probably have been done (although one always wonders what happens to the trust of deceived participants toward psychologists!). The most unsettling element of Study D is that considerable time was purposely allowed to pass before the researchers "came clean" with the students. The students had the time to fret, to possibly begin to doubt themselves, to become confused. Here is also an instance where debriefing the participants does not necessarily "disabuse" them. That is, even when the students learn that it was all "just research," that does not necessarily restore them to their former senses of self. (Keith-Spiegel, 1990)

In summary, Dr. Keith-Spiegel's rankings are as follows: A. 5; B. 4; C. 1; D. 6; E. 3; and F. 2.

RECOMMENDED READINGS

American Psychological Association. (1982). *Ethical principles in the conduct of research with human participants.* Washington, DC: Author. This handbook outlines the important ethical issues in research with humans, providing examples of unethical studies.

Christensen, L. B. (1988). *Experimental methodology* (4th ed.). Boston: Allyn & Bacon. This textbook provides a very readable overview, with primary emphasis on the experimental method, but it also includes chapters on special topics such as quasi-experimental design and ethics.

Kidder, L. H., & Judd, C. M. (1986). *Research methods in social relations* (5th ed.). New York: Holt, Rinehart and Winston. This textbook focuses primarily on social psychology examples, including material on all six methods but more detail on questionnaires and applied research than the other textbooks listed here.

Shaughnessy, J. J., & Zechmeister, E. B. (1990). *Research methods in psychology* (2nd ed.). New York: McGraw-Hill. Intended for middle-level undergraduates, this textbook provides good coverage of all six research methods, though it provides somewhat more detail on the experiment.

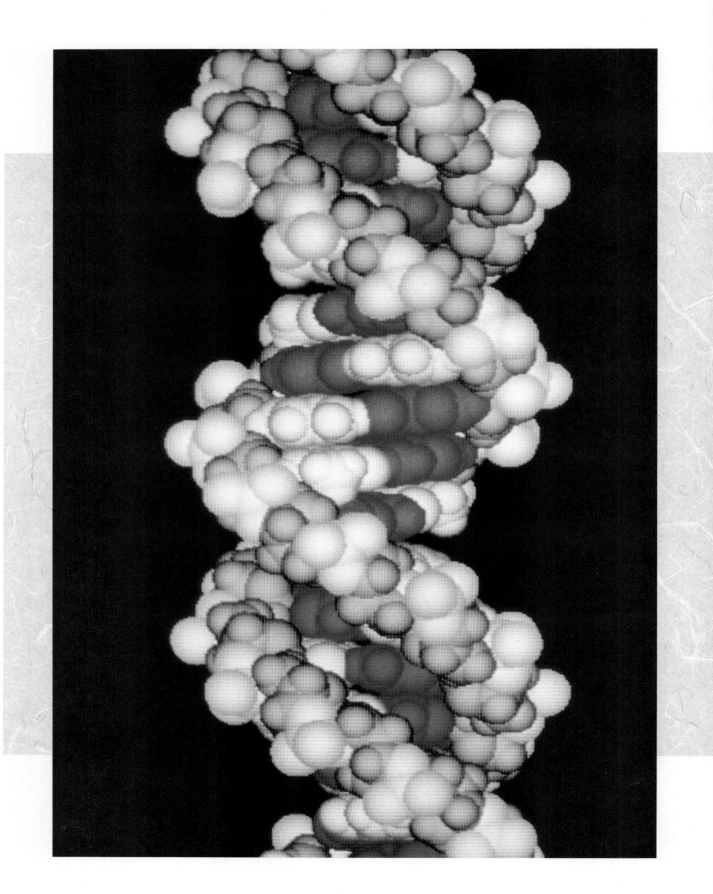

CHAPTER

3

The Biological Basis
of Behavior

The human body features several sophisticated communication systems, which we explore in this chapter. For example, when your professor lectures, the message is received by the receptors in the ear and changed into a form that can move through the auditory nerve. That message is relayed to a region on the left side of your brain. Next, the material is processed. Then another message is conveyed down to your fingers, directing them to make the appropriate tiny squiggles in your notebook. Your brain and the rest of the nervous system are designed to perform quickly and accurately in conveying messages.

Your body also includes another route for sending messages at a more leisurely rate—the endocrine system. This chapter provides an overview of how the endocrine system sends hormone messages through the bloodstream. The chapter concludes with a summary of genetics, the most complex message system of all. We will see that 46 microscopic chromosomes capture the complete genetic formula for producing a new human being.

Introduction to the Nervous System

The Neuron

The **neuron** is a cell that is specialized to process, store, and transmit information throughout your body. No one knows for certain how many neurons the human brain contains. However, one well-educated guess is about 100 billion (or, in its more impressive form, 100,000,000,000) (Hubel, 1979; Soper & Rosenthal, 1988; Thompson, 1985).

Figure 3.1
A schematic drawing of a neuron.

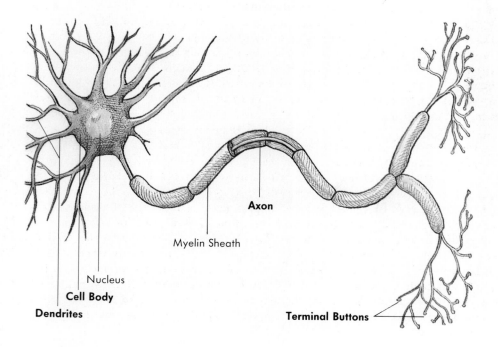

Axon

Myelin Sheath

Nucleus

Cell Body

Dendrites

Terminal Buttons

Neurons come in many sizes and shapes, depending on their function in the nervous system. Figure 3.1 shows one representative neuron, drawn schematically to show the important parts: the dendrites, cell body, and axon. Figure 3.2 is a photograph of actual neurons, greatly magnified so that you can appreciate its structure. Let us discuss some of the features of a typical neuron.

The **dendrites** of a neuron are slender, branched fibers that carry neural impulses in the direction of the cell body in a neuron. The name *dendrite* comes from the Greek word for tree, and if you use your imagination, you can indeed see a tree-like structure in the dendrites. The greater the area of the dendrites, the more information they can receive from other neurons (Kalat, 1988).

The prominent central structure in Figure 3.1 is the **cell body**, the area of the neuron that stores the cell nucleus, as well as other structures that help the cell function properly. However, keep in mind that Figures 3.1 and 3.2 show greatly enlarged neurons. Even though the cell body looks relatively large in these illustrations, the cell bodies found in mammals are usually less than 0.1 mm in diameter, barely visible to the human eye (Kalat, 1988).

Finally, notice the long fiber in the middle of Figure 3.1, called the *axon*. The **axon** carries information away from the cell body, toward other neurons. In some neurons, the axon can reach a length of nearly 1 meter (Kimble, 1988). (Incidentally, it may be helpful to remember that the neural impulses travel through the structures in the neuron in reverse alphabetical order: <u>d</u>endrite, <u>c</u>ell <u>b</u>ody, <u>a</u>xon.)

The conduction of nerve signals involves a complex interaction of chemical substances and electrical signals. An inactive neuron contains an excess of negatively charged ions (i.e., atoms and molecules) inside its cell membrane. However, when the dendrite is stimulated, the cell membrane opens up its miniature channels, allowing positively charged ions to flow inward. As a consequence, the cell's charge becomes depolarized (less negative) for a fraction of a second. The depolarization spreads down the dendrite and into the cell body.

A single one of these electrical signals is usually not sufficiently strong to be transmitted to an adjacent neuron. A structure within the cell body combines all these weak signals. When the total input of these signals exceeds a certain threshold, then depolarization occurs at the axon membrane. This brief change in the electrical charge of an axon is called an **action potential**. This electrical signal then flows rapidly down to the end of the axon.

An important characteristic of action potentials is that they follow an all-or-none law. That is, if the total input is greater than the threshold, an action potential occurs, and the impulse is transmitted. If the total input is less than the threshold, there is no action potential. The nervous system does not allow any partial action potentials.

A feature that aids the transmission of neural messages is that the larger axons in the nervous system are coated with an insulating material called the **myelin sheath**, which is part fat and part protein. The myelin sheath helps the action potential travel faster and farther along the axon. It also helps insulate the axon from other nearby axons. Without the myelin sheath, the messages in neighboring axons might become scrambled with each other. Obviously, a sophisticated message system must avoid scrambled communications.

All the fine qualities of the neuron would be wasted if there was no way for neurons to communicate with one another. Clearly, neurons must connect to other neurons. The location at which the axon of one neuron connects with the dendrite of a neighboring neuron is called the **synapse**. Turn back to Figure 3.1 and notice the knobs located at the far end of the axon; these knobs are called **terminal buttons**. Figure 3.3 shows a highly magnified view of several of these terminal buttons.

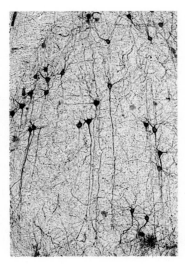

Figure 3.2
A photograph of neurons from a rat's cerebral cortex.

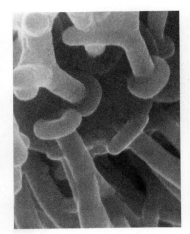

Figure 3.3
An electromicrograph of several terminal buttons (magnified 11,250 times their normal size). (Lewis, Everhart, & Zeevi, 1969)

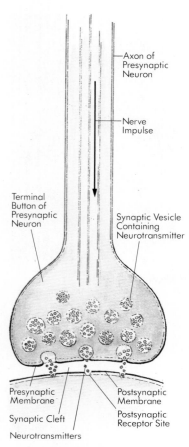

—Axon of
Presynaptic
Neuron

—Nerve
Impulse

Terminal
Button of
Presynaptic
Neuron

Synaptic Vesicle
Containing
Neurotransmitter

Presynaptic
Membrane

Postsynaptic
Membrane

Synaptic Cleft

Postsynaptic
Receptor Site

Neurotransmitters

Dendrite of
Postsynaptic Neuron

Figure 3.4
A schematic diagram of a synapse.

Early researchers thought that the terminal buttons from one axon rested directly on the dendrite of the adjoining axon. However, with more refined microscopic techniques, researchers learned that the synapse actually contains a narrow space between adjacent neurons, called the **synaptic cleft**.

How does the electrical message from one neuron leap across the synaptic cleft to reach the neighboring neuron? In the great majority of brain synapses, the mechanism is chemical (Thompson, 1985). Figure 3.4 shows a schematic diagram of one of the 10 trillion synapses in the brain. As you can see, the electrical signal is conducted down the axon to the terminal button. The arrival of this electrical signal triggers the release of **neurotransmitters**, which are chemical substances stored in many tiny vesicles (containers) in the terminal button. Each vesicle dumps the entire contents of its pouch into the synaptic cleft, and these chemicals spread across the channel to the receptor neurons on the other side. Let us examine these neurotransmitters in more detail, because they figure prominently in later chapters.

Neurotransmitters

The neurotransmitter released at a synapse will either excite or inhibit the receptor neuron on the other side of the synaptic cleft. Synapses, therefore, may be either excitatory or inhibitory. When an **excitatory synapse** is triggered by an action potential, it releases a neurotransmitter that excites the receptor neuron on the other side of the synaptic cleft. In contrast, when an **inhibitory synapse** is triggered by an action potential, it releases a neurotransmitter that inhibits the receptor neuron on the other side of the synaptic cleft. As a consequence, this second neuron is less likely to produce an action potential.

One well-studied neurotransmitter is **acetylcholine**, abbreviated **ACh**. ACh is found in synapses in the brain, where it is important in a variety of functions such as arousal, attention, memory, aggression, sexuality, and thirst (Panksepp, 1986). ACh can also be found at the junction between neurons and muscle fibers, where it acts as an excitatory neurotransmitter.

Several powerful poisons are deadly because of their influence on ACh production. For example, the poisonous bite of a black widow spider is effective because it produces a flood of ACh from the terminal buttons into the synapses between the neurons and the muscle fibers. This excess release of ACh produces violent muscle contractions and—frequently—death. Our very survival therefore depends upon the vesicles releasing the right amount of ACh, neither too much nor too little.

Whereas ACh acts as an excitatory neurotransmitter for muscle fibers, **dopamine** can act as an inhibitory neurotransmitter. Perhaps you know someone with **Parkinson's disease**, which involves symptoms such as tremors of the hands and difficulty walking (Dakof & Mendelsohn, 1986). Parkinson's disease has been traced to a deficit in dopamine production, caused by a deterioration in the neurons in the part of the brain that releases this neurotransmitter. One drug used to treat Parkinson's disease is L-DOPA, a substance that the body converts into dopamine, thereby replenishing its supply.

There are several dozen other neurotransmitters, in addition to ACh and dopamine, and new neurotransmitters seem to be discovered each year (Bridgeman, 1988). However, we need to trace the actions of these neurotransmitters on the other side of the synaptic cleft.

It takes about 50 microseconds (one 20 thousandth of a second) for a neurotransmitter to reach the dendrite on the other side of the cleft. Once the neurotransmitter is on the other side, it interacts with specialized membranes. These membranes contain gates that are "guarded" by protein molecules. In much the same fashion as a key opens a lock, the neurotransmitter enters the membrane by moving the protein molecule aside and fitting neatly into the keyhole.

When the neurotransmitter attaches itself in position onto the dendrite on the other side of the synaptic cleft, the electrical balance in the dendrite is upset. In an excitatory synapse, this imbalance usually produces an action potential in the axon of this second neuron. Figure 3.5 summarizes the stages in synaptic transmission.

Besides neurotransmitters, other chemical substances called neuromodulators also act at the synapse. As the name suggests, **neuromodulators** modify neuronal activity, either increasing or decreasing it. They operate more slowly and indirectly than neurotransmitters (Kimble, 1988; Panksepp, 1986). One important category of neuromodulators is the endorphins. **Endorphins** are chemicals that occur naturally in the brain; when they are released, endorphins decrease a person's sensitivity to pain.

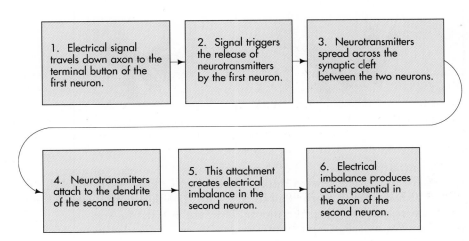

Figure 3.5
The stages in synaptic transmission.

Another important category of neuromodulators includes drugs used to treat psychological disorders. Almost every drug used in psychiatry acts by increasing or decreasing neuronal activity at the synapse (Snyder, 1985). We return to further discussion of neuromodulators when we examine pain perception (chapter 4) and medications in psychotherapy (chapter 16).

The Reflex Arc

We have discussed the isolated neuron, and then we saw how messages can be transmitted between two neurons. But what can two neurons accomplish? Impressively, a simple reflex requires only two neurons.

In a **reflex arc**, the neuronal message travels between a sensory neuron and a motor neuron. One example of a reflex arc is the familiar knee jerk, in which the sensory neuron registers the sensation of touch, and the motor neuron signals the muscle to move. Demonstration 3.1 illustrates this reflex. This is a very rapid reflex, requiring about $\frac{1}{20}$ second between the time the tendon is tapped and the beginning of the leg kick. The knee-jerk reflex is particularly rapid because the message does not need to travel to the brain; the synapse between the two neurons is located in the spinal cord. Figure 3.6 is a schematic diagram of the two-neuron reflex, illustrating both the sensory neuron (the one that is stimulated when the knee is struck) and the motor neuron (the one that causes the muscle in your leg to contract).

Demonstration 3.1

Comparing a Reflex With a Voluntary Action

A. Put pillows on a chair until the seat is high enough for a person's legs to dangle freely, and invite a friend to sit down. With your fingertips, locate the soft area just down from the kneecap. Take a ruler, and gently strike its edge against the soft region. You may need to adjust the exact area you strike and the strength with which you strike. You will know you have succeeded when your friend's leg shoots forward instantaneously,

demonstrating the knee-jerk reflex.

B. Have your friend sit in the same position. Instruct your friend to kick his or her leg as fast as possible after you have touched it. Then wait about 30 seconds, and quickly touch your friend's leg in the same soft region below the kneecap. Notice how long it requires to execute this voluntary action (Carlson, 1986).

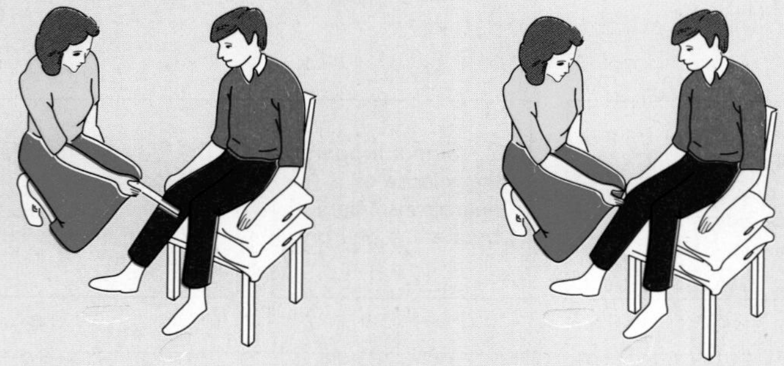

In contrast, the second part of Demonstration 3.1 involves a voluntary action, rather than a reflex. The sensory information—that the knee has been touched—needs to be transmitted all the way to the brain. The decision to respond must then be processed, and then the motor information must be transmitted back down to the leg muscle. Granted, this process does not require as much time as reading *War and Peace*. However, the fastest voluntary action takes up to five times as long as a reflex (Kimble, 1988).

Most reflexes require more than two neurons. Consider the withdrawal reflex, which involves three kinds of neurons. Notice the third kind, the interneuron, in Figure 3.7. As you can see, the interneuron is located in the spinal cord. As its name suggests, it is located between two neurons, the sensory neuron and the motor neuron. I will not include a demonstration urging you to torment your friends by holding a burning match next to their fingers or placing thumbtacks under their feet. However, the next time you touch a burning object and your hand withdraws rapidly, you will demonstrate the withdrawal reflex.

Figure 3.6
(left) A diagram of a reflex involving two neurons, such as a knee jerk reflex.

Figure 3.7
(right) A diagram of a reflex involving three neurons, such as a withdrawal reflex.

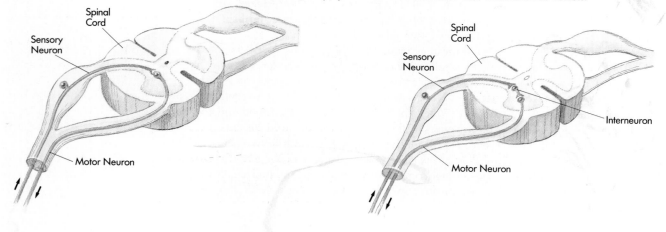

The Divisions of the Nervous System

Let us place these neurons in context throughout the human body. Figure 3.8 shows the various divisions of the nervous system; note that the major distinction is between the central and peripheral nervous systems. Place a paper clip on this page so that you can turn to it readily when you read about the components of the nervous system. Most of this chapter involves the central nervous system, specifically the brain. However, we begin with the peripheral nervous system, the division of the nervous system that psychologists are less likely to study. Nevertheless, this system is still important enough to keep you alive until you finish reading the end of this sentence.

The Peripheral Nervous System　　The word *peripheral* refers to things that are not central. Peripheral vision, for example, involves the edges of your visual field, rather than the central part. Similarly, the **peripheral nervous system** consists of everything in the nervous system except the brain and spinal cord. The peripheral nervous system transmits messages from the sensory receptors to the **central nervous system** (that is, the spinal cord and brain), and it also transmits messages back out from the central nervous system to the muscles and glands.

　　The peripheral nervous system is further divided into two parts, the somatic division and the autonomic division. The **somatic division** consists of the sensory and motor neurons that control the voluntary muscles. You use this somatic division when you scratch your nose, chew gum, or perform any other voluntary action. Your friend also used the somatic division of the peripheral nervous system in part B of Demonstration 3.1.

　　In contrast, the **autonomic division** helps control the glands, blood vessels, and internal organs such as the intestines and the heart. The autonomic nervous

Figure 3.8
The divisions of the nervous system.

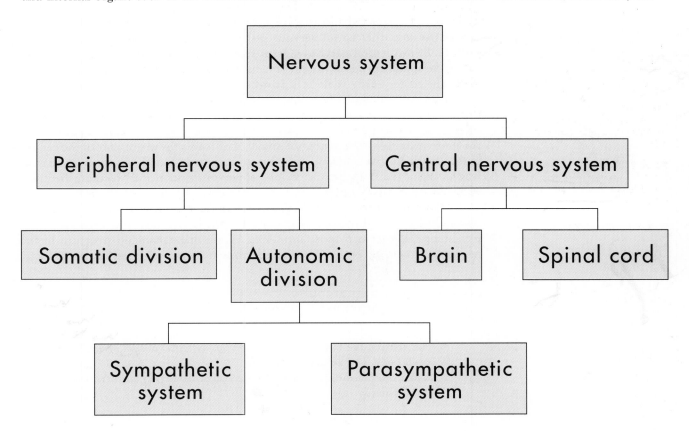

system usually works automatically; unlike the actions in the somatic division, you do not need to decide to make your heart beat for the next 60 seconds. You can remember the name *autonomic* because it resembles the word *automatic*.

The autonomic division is further divided into two parts, the sympathetic nervous system and the parasympathetic nervous system. These two systems usually work in opposition to each other, with both of them providing neurons for each of the glands, blood vessels, and internal organs in the autonomic division.

The **sympathetic system** prepares the body for action. It secretes adrenaline to increase your heart rate, and it dilates the pupils of your eye. It makes you sweat, and it makes you blush. The sympathetic neurons also connect with hair follicles and with tiny arteries in the skin. The next time you find yourself in a frightening situation, notice how your heart beats faster, your pupils grow wide, and you sweat and blush. Furthermore, people say that when they are frightened, their "hair stands on end." Humans cannot demonstrate this feature of the sympathetic system as dramatically as an alley cat does, but you might notice tiny goosebumps.

The **parasympathetic system** works in just the opposite fashion; it slows down your body functions and conserves energy. For example, the parasympathetic system slows your heartbeat and constricts your pupils. (Incidentally, it may be helpful to remember that the sympathetic system spends energy; the parasympathetic system preserves it.) Working together, these two systems ensure that your body maintains its balance. Immediately after a frightening experience, the sympathetic system is dominant. Soon after, however, the body's alarm system alerts the parasympathetic system to relax the functions and bring the body back to normal. The impressive coordination of these two systems is an important example of one of the themes of this book, that humans are well designed to function in their environments.

The Central Nervous System   Let us turn now to the other major division of the nervous system, the central nervous system. As Figure 3.8 shows, the two components of the central nervous system are the brain and the spinal cord.

The **spinal cord** is a column of neurons that runs from the base of the brain, down the center of the back. It is protected by a series of bones, just as the brain is protected by the skull. The spinal cord is the oldest part of the central nervous system, both in terms of evolution and in terms of the development of the embryo prior to birth (Bridgeman, 1988). Its organization is similar for all vertebrates. For the more primitive vertebrates, the spinal cord forms the major part of the central nervous system. For humans, it performs more basic functions, providing a gateway for signals to and from the peripheral nervous system and executing the kinds of reflexes discussed earlier.

It would be impossible to function without the various parts of the peripheral nervous system, and damage to the spinal cord is certainly disabling. However, psychologists are much more interested in the one remaining structure in the nervous system: the brain. We consider that in the next section of this chapter.

Section Summary: Introduction to the Nervous System

- **The neuron, the basic unit in the nervous system, consists of dendrites, a cell body, and an axon.**
- **A neuron transmits its message to nearby neurons via neurotransmitters at the synapse.**

- ■ Neurotransmitters can be excitatory; for example, acetylcholine (ACh) is a neurotransmitter that plays an important role in attention, memory, and sexuality.
- ■ Neurotransmitters can also be inhibitory; for example, dopamine is a neurotransmitter involved in motor movement, and Parkinson's disease involves dopamine deficiency.
- ■ The reflex arc requires two or more neurons and does not require processing by the brain. Examples are the knee-jerk reflex (two neurons) and the withdrawal reflex (three neurons).
- ■ The nervous system has two components: the peripheral nervous system and the central nervous system.
- ■ The peripheral nervous system is divided into two components: the somatic division (which involves voluntary action) and the autonomic division (which controls glands, blood vessels, and internal organs). The two subdivisions of the autonomic nervous system are the sympathetic and the parasympathetic nervous systems, which usually work in opposition to each other.
- ■ The central nervous system has two components: the spinal cord, a column of neurons running downward from the base of the brain, and the brain itself.

The Brain

Your brain looks somewhat like a 3-pound lump of leftover lukewarm oatmeal. Its texture is very soft and jellylike. In fact, it is so fragile that researchers find it nearly impossible to handle a fresh brain from a recently deceased human without damaging it (Carlson, 1986). Figure 3.9 shows a preserved version of this not-very-impressive-looking structure.

Yet the human brain is the most complicated object known (Coen, 1985). The brain never rests, even when we are asleep. The various chemical and electrical systems in the brain are in a perpetual state of change. Some writers say that the brain is like a computer, but the analogy is not entirely accurate. The brain is

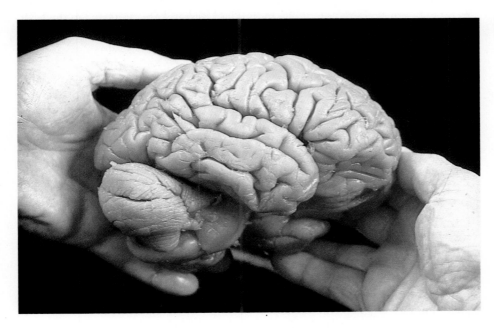

Figure 3.9
The human brain.

more complex than the computers that have been developed so far, and computers cannot grow or change (Ornstein & Thompson, 1984).

People have attempted to understand the brain for thousands of years. The ancient Greek philosophers thought that the brain served as a radiator, essentially performing the mundane task of cooling the blood. In the 18th century, an anatomist from Vienna named Franz Joseph Gall proposed an elaborate scheme of regional specialization. He argued that the shape and size of a person's skull could be used to determine the amount of brain tissue lying underneath. For example, a person with a bulge at the top back portion of the head might have unusually high self-esteem, whereas bulging eyes revealed a fantastic memory.

Of course, this theory was wrong, and the scientific community thought that this approach was so ridiculous that it resisted accepting the genuine evidence for regional specialization that began to emerge at the end of the 19th century (Blakemore, 1985). As we see in this section, many aspects of human feeling and cognitive processes are localized in particular, specialized regions of the brain. For example, an important early brain researcher named Paul Broca (1861) discovered that language could be impaired when highly specific regions of the brain had been damaged (Geschwind, 1985).

In this section of the chapter, we begin by examining some of the methods researchers have used in studying the brain. The next topic is the various regions of the brain, followed by a discussion of hemispheric specialization. The final topics are brain damage and Alzheimer's disease.

Brain Research Methods

If the brain is the most complicated object we know, how can researchers explore it? Researchers in the interdisciplinary field of neuroscience have examined both the structure and the function of the brain. Their techniques include methods as diverse as recording messages from a single neuron and observing a human with a normal brain.

Case Study   As you may recall from the previous chapter, a **case study** is a careful in-depth examination of one individual. Researchers interested in the brain have advocated using the case study method with brain-damaged people in order to better understand the functioning of people with normal brains.

Consider the case of a man known by his initials, N.A., who had joined the Air Force after a year of junior college. His roommate was playing with a miniature fencing foil when N.A. turned suddenly toward him and was stabbed through the right nostril, a thrust that was deep enough to penetrate the brain. He lost consciousness temporarily, and he also showed some temporary paralysis. Twenty years later, when tested by Squire (1987), he was found to have a high intelligence quotient (IQ) and the ability to carry on normal conversations. However, N.A. has a very specific deficit: He cannot learn new material. He loses track of his belongings, forgets what he has done, and forgets the people he has visited. His mother, who lives nearby, prepares meals for him. However, he often forgets that the meals are in the refrigerator, and he goes out to a restaurant instead. He forgets to take his medication, and he forgets to refill his prescriptions. He stubbornly refuses to keep reminder notes, saying that these notes would operate like crutches that would prevent him from exercising his memory. The destruction of a small portion of N.A.'s brain has had an impact on his entire life.

The case study technique can provide some valuable clues to the mechanisms underlying a deficit in behavior (Heilman & Valenstein, 1985). However, there are some important drawbacks. For example, it is difficult to generalize to other people on the basis of just one patient. In addition, a person is unlikely to have damage in only one specific area of the brain, so it may be difficult to untangle the various symptoms and trace them to the appropriate parts of the brain (Hannay, 1986). Furthermore, people with disorders often compensate for their deficits after a short time, which is fortunate for these people, but difficult for the researchers. Thus, researchers use other additional techniques to learn more about the brain.

Lesion Production　　A **lesion** is a wound or disruption of the brain. Lesions can be produced in laboratory animals to confirm some suspicions about the functions of brain structures. (In contrast, the previous section on case studies discussed brain lesions that occur by accident in humans.)

The reasoning behind the lesion technique is that researchers can figure out which kind of behavior is missing in an animal once an area of its brain has been destroyed; that part of the brain may be responsible for the missing behavior. For example, if an animal can no longer see after a region of the brain has been destroyed, we can conclude that this region plays some role in vision. However, Carlson (1986) notes that we must interpret the results very carefully. For example, on what basis does the researcher conclude that the animal is blind? Perhaps it bumps into objects or fails to run toward a light signaling food. Maybe the researcher should conclude that the lesion produced a deficit in motor coordination, not a deficit in vision.

Brain Stimulation　　Researchers can also examine the brain by electrically stimulating a localized region. When **electrical stimulation** is used, the researcher places a small electrode in a specific location of the brain and delivers a weak electrical current. For example, a neurosurgeon may want to operate on a patient with severe epilepsy in order to remove the portion of the brain that causes the seizures. Prior to surgery, the neurosurgeon identifies the suspicious region of the brain (typically using EEG, which we discuss shortly). Then the patient receives a local anesthetic so that he or she can be conscious during surgery but experience no pain. A piece of the skull is then temporarily removed, and the neurosurgeon delivers electrical stimulation in the vicinity of the suspicious region. The purpose of this investigation is to identify the functions of the brain tissue in this region so that surgery can be conducted without disrupting areas that are important for normal functioning. For example, stimulation of one region might disrupt memory, whereas stimulation in another region might cause a tingling in the mouth. The neurosurgeon would leave these areas intact. Figure 3.10 shows

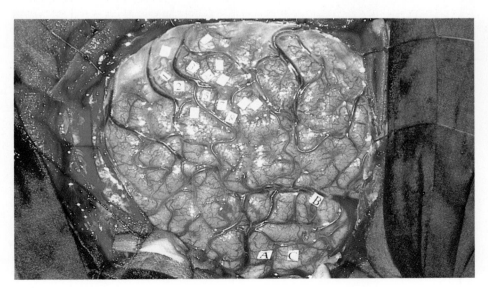

Figure 3.10
The brain stimulation technique. The numbered tags mark responses from stimulation of the sensory and motor cortex. The lettered tags indicate epileptic abnormality on the electrical recording of the cortex to guide surgical removal. (Reprinted with permission of neurosurgeon Dr. William Feindel, Montreal Neurological Institute)

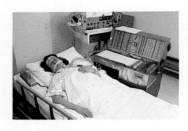

Figure 3.11
An example of the EEG technique: The electrical message from the neurons beneath the electrodes on this person's scalp is being recorded on the graph paper.

this procedure. Naturally, brain stimulation techniques help people with serious neurological disorders, but they also provide a useful map of the brain's functions (Carlson, 1986; Penfield & Jasper, 1954).

Brain Recording   Several methods can be used to record signals from the brain. You have probably heard of EEG, which is the abbreviation for **electroencephalography**. In the **EEG** technique, electrodes are placed on the scalp. The electrical message from the thousands of neurons beneath the electrodes are then recorded on graph paper, as Figure 3.11 shows. As we will see in chapter 5, the EEG has provided useful information about brain activity when people are awake versus sleeping. The EEG can also locate major abnormalities in the brain.

By itself, however, the EEG cannot provide the kind of precise information that researchers need about brain activity. After all, an EEG "listens" to thousands of neurons. Researchers can obtain more precise recordings of brain activity by inserting a tiny electrode next to (or even into) a single neuron, a method called the **single-cell recording technique**. As we see in the next chapter, a researcher can insert an electrode into a neuron of a monkey's visual cortex. By presenting a variety of stimuli, the researchers can determine the kind of visual pattern that produces the most vigorous electrical activity from the neuron.

Imaging Techniques   Three new techniques have been devised to provide a picture of the living human brain. All three use computers to combine a series of images of the brain. These techniques are useful for researchers, and they are also invaluable in diagnosing the part of the brain that might be affected by head injury or a disease such as multiple sclerosis. All three are known by their initials: CAT scans, PET scans, and MRI.

A **computerized axial tomography**, or **CAT scan**, passes X-ray beams through the head from a variety of angles, plotting a two-dimensional picture that resembles a horizontal "slice" through the brain. Then the patient's head is moved either up or down, and a second picture is plotted from this new position. Eventually an entire series of pictures is assembled.

A **positron emission tomography**, or **PET scan**, traces the chemical activity of various parts of the living brain (Jacobson, 1988). A tiny amount of a radioactive

Figure 3.12
PET scans of normal people performing different types of tasks. Red indicates the highest level of cell activity; purple indicates the lowest rate. Five tasks are illustrated.

Visual: Participants open their eyes and look at a visual screen. This activates the visual center (arrows).

Auditory: Participants listen to music and language, which activates the right and left auditory cortex (arrows).

Cognitive: Participants count backward from 100 by 7's. This activates the frontal cortex (arrows).

Memory: Participants are asked to recall previously learned facts. This activates small structures called the hippocampus (arrows).

Motor: Participants touch their fingers to the thumb of the right hand. This activates the left motor cortex (slanted arrow) and supplementary motor cortex (vertical arrow).

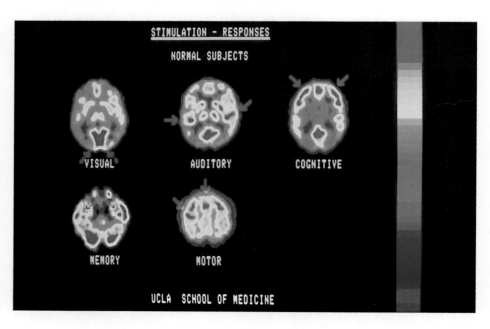

chemical is injected into the brain, and the active cells in the brain temporarily accumulate this chemical. A machine similar to a CAT scanner then passes beams of X rays through the head.

The PET scan is useful in tracking psychological disorders. For example, a man with an emotional disorder had a PET scan showing high cell activity when he was in a very cheerful mood, but low cell activity when he was severely depressed (Kalat, 1988). Figure 3.12 shows PET scans of normal people who were asked to perform various tasks while the PET scan was taken.

The newest imaging technique is **magnetic resonance imaging** or **MRI**; this technique is similar to a CAT scan. However, instead of an X ray, it passes a strong (but harmless) magnetic field through a patient's head. The MRI scanner picks up radiation from hydrogen molecules, which are present in different concentrations in different tissues. This technique provides a picture of a "slice" of the human brain, and it is particularly useful for detecting lesions in the central nervous system (Regenbogen, personal communication, 1988).

All of these methods are proving useful in increasing our understanding of the brain, although much more remains to be discovered. These methods have allowed researchers to identify the structure and function of parts of the brain that we examine in the next section, as well as the biological processes involved in each of the areas investigated in the remainder of this book.

Regions of the Human Brain

If you check back to Figure 3.8, you will notice the label, "brain." Now we need to verbally dissect this astonishing structure to examine its components. Figure 3.13 provides an overview of the brain's organization so that you can appreciate how the parts fit into the overall structure. Figure 3.14 shows a schematic diagram of these structures so that you can see their anatomic arrangement.

The Hindbrain   The **hindbrain** is located in the bottom portion of the brain, and it consists of several important parts. The **medulla** can be found just above the spinal cord. It can be considered to be a larger, fancier extension of the spinal cord. The medulla is important in several basic functions; for example, it controls

Figure 3.13
The major structures in the brain.

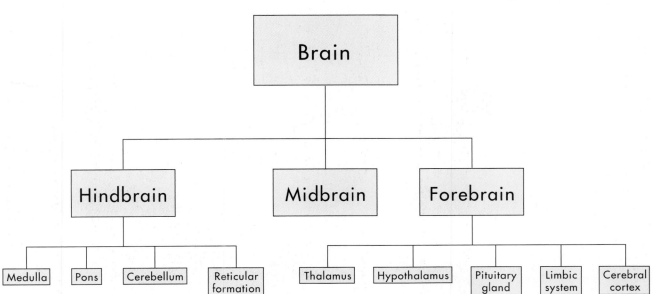

The cerebellum is important in the control of this dancer's motor movements.

breathing and heart rate. The medulla is also involved in coughing and sneezing. The me*dulla* sounds rather *dull*, but you could not survive without it.

The **pons** is a bulging structure located above the medulla. The word *pons* means bridge. As Figure 3.14 shows, it does not look much like a bridge, but it serves the function of a bridge, because it connects the lower brain regions with the higher brain regions. It also helps regulate facial expression.

The **cerebellum** looks like a miniature version of the entire brain, tacked on at the rear of the brain. The cerebellum is one of the oldest structures in the history of the nervous system in higher animals (Thompson, 1985). It is well developed in fish, birds, and lower mammals. The cerebellum occupies a much larger percentage of total brain space in your pet cat's brain than in your own brain. Unfortunately, researchers still do not have a clear idea of the functions of the cerebellum, though it certainly contributes to the control of movement (Stein, 1985). It is also important in maintaining balance and in learning motor tasks (Ornstein & Thompson, 1984).

Figure 3.14
A schematic view of the human brain.

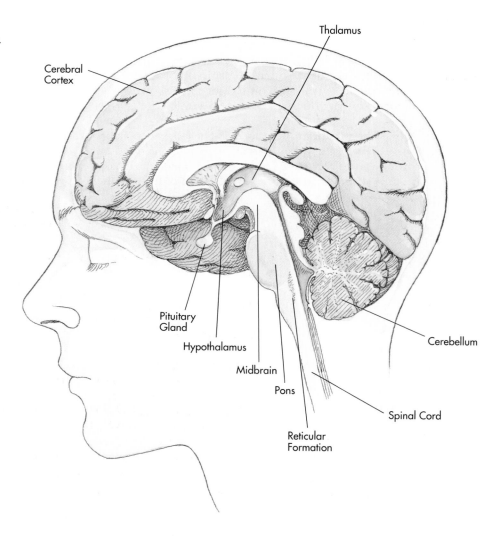

Finally, notice the structure called the **reticular formation**, which runs up from the hindbrain, through to the midbrain. Axons from the reticular formation even reach upward into the cerebral cortex at the top of the brain. This structure is important in attention (a topic in chapter 4) and in sleep (chapter 5) as well as in simple learning tasks (McGinty & Szymusiak, 1988).

The Midbrain The **midbrain** continues upward from the pons portion of the hindbrain. All the signals that pass between the spinal cord and the forebrain must pass through this structure. Furthermore, visual information passes through the midbrain on its route from the eyes to its ultimate destination in the cortex region of the forebrain.

Before we approach the more complex forebrain region, let us review where we have been. The hindbrain controls some basic functions such as breathing and heart rate (the medulla), it connects the lower and the higher brain regions (the pons), it controls movement (the cerebellum), and it is important in attention,

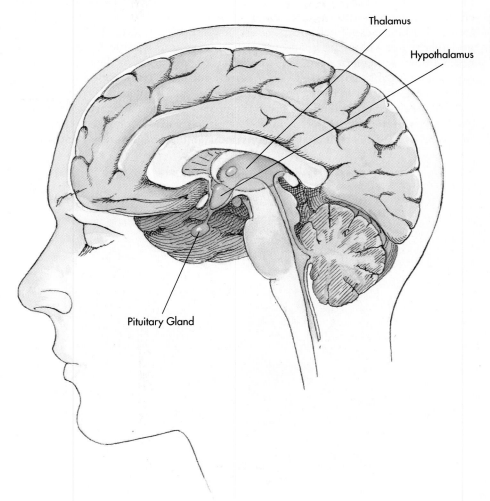

Thalamus

Hypothalamus

Pituitary Gland

Figure 3.15
Three structures in the forebrain: the thalamus, the hypothalamus, and the pituitary gland.

sleep, and learning (the reticular formation). The midbrain serves as an important relay station for information traveling to the forebrain. You could not survive without your hindbrain and your midbrain, but it is the forebrain that is most important in perception, thought, and social behavior—those aspects of human life most relevant to psychology.

The Forebrain   In humans, the **forebrain** is the largest part of the brain. The cerebral cortex is the structure that interests us the most, but several other parts of the forebrain are also critical in human behavior.

1. The **thalamus** looks like two eggs resting side by side. Nearly all the information from the senses passes through the thalamus on its route from the sensory receptors to the cerebral cortex. (The one exception is smell, which sends its signals on a more direct route.) The thalamus is not merely a way station along the route to the cortex, however. Instead, information is organized and transformed in the thalamus. As we see in the next chapter, vision and the other senses are impressively complex. In order to read this sentence, the information registered by your visual sensory receptors must travel a complex route and be reorganized several times by structures such as the thalamus. The thalamus is shown in Figure 3.15.

2. The **hypothalamus** lies just below the thalamus (the prefix *hypo* means *under*). This relatively small structure controls the autonomic nervous system, which you may recall is the part of the nervous system responsible for the glands, blood vessels, and internal organs. The hypothalamus features several distinct clusters of neurons that regulate different kinds of motivated behavior such as eating, drinking, sexual behavior, aggression, and activity level. This structure is no larger than a kidney bean, and yet each of its regions is critically important to normal functioning. For example, stimulation of one region of the hypothalamus causes an animal to gorge itself—even after a full meal. Stimulation of a nearby region causes it to stop eating entirely (McGinty & Szymusiak, 1988).

3. The **pituitary gland** is a hormone-producing gland attached by a stalk to the bottom part of the hypothalamus. The pituitary gland is not technically part of the brain, but it is regulated by the hypothalamus. The pituitary gland has the

Figure 3.16
The structures in the limbic system.

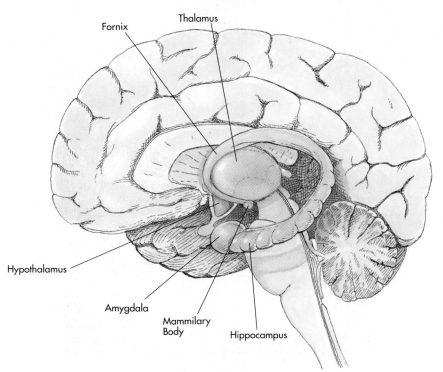

starring role in the section of this chapter concerned with hormones, because it not only manufactures its own hormones but also regulates the other hormonal glands in the body.

4. The **limbic system** consists of several related structures, such as the hippocampus and the amygdala. Figure 3.16 shows some of the structures included in the limbic system. The limbic system is classified as a system because the structures are connected with each other and they perform similar functions.

The limbic system helps regulate the emotions, and it is also critical in some aspects of memory and thought. For example, one case study described a man with severe epilepsy. To try to control the disabling seizures, the surgeons removed his hippocampus. Following surgery, he was reasonably accurate in recalling old memories. However, it was nearly impossible for him to form and recall memories for events occurring after his surgery (Gazzaniga, 1986; Milner et al., 1968).

5. The **cerebral cortex** is the outer surface of the two cerebral hemispheres of the brain; it processes all perceptions and complex thoughts. In the evolutionary history of vertebrate animals, the cerebral cortex is the most recently developed structure. A goldfish has no cortex, and a snake's cortex is very primitive. In contrast, about three fourths of all the cells in the human brain are found in the cortex (Schneider & Tarshis, 1986).

The entire cerebral cortex is only as thick as the covering on this textbook, but it is elaborately folded rather than smooth. (Turn back to Figure 3.9 to appreciate this folded structure.) If the cerebral cortex could be smoothed and flattened, the total area would be about the size of the screen on a 21-inch television. However, this folding is probably necessary so that the extensive structure of the cortex could be packed into a box the size of a human skull (Hubel & Wiesel, 1979).

Figure 3.17 shows another view of the brain, looking down from above. Once again, appreciate the wrinkled walnutlike appearance. This view also highlights the fact that there are two cerebral hemispheres. Although these two half brains look nearly identical, we will see that they perform somewhat different functions. There are also sharp boundaries between the regions of the brain (Kaas, 1987). Figure 3.17 points out three regions visible from an overhead position.

Let us change our viewpoint. Looking at the left side of the brain in the schematic drawing in Figure 3.18, you can see all four regions of the cerebral cortex. Researchers have used techniques such as brain stimulation to identify the functions of the different parts of the brain shown in Figure 3.18.

We start this tour of the cerebral cortex with the **occipital lobe**, at the back of the head. The most important part of this region of the brain is the visual

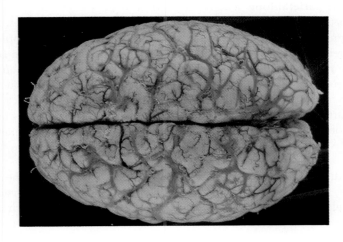

Figure 3.17
The cerebral cortex (as seen from overhead).

Figure 3.18
A schematic drawing of the cerebral
cortex, as seen from the side.

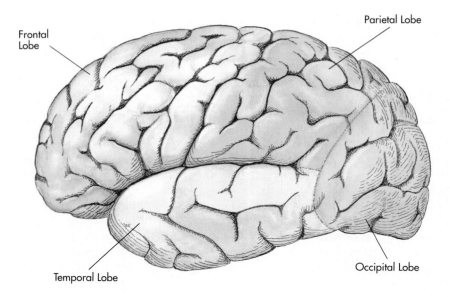

Frontal
Lobe

Parietal Lobe

Temporal Lobe

Occipital Lobe

cortex. As you see in chapter 4, information travels from the receptors in the eyes, through the thalamus, to the visual cortex. If you place the palm of your hand just above your neck, the visual cortex lies right in front of your hand. One important feature of the visual cortex is its spatial arrangement. Specifically, the pattern of information on the retina (the receptors at the rear inner surface of the eyeball) corresponds fairly closely to the pattern of information on part of the visual cortex; this correspondence is called a **retinotopic arrangement**. Try Demonstration 3.2 to appreciate this retinotopic arrangement.

As Demonstration 3.2 points out, there are some distortions in the correspondence between the retina and the visual cortex. Nevertheless, this correspondence was close enough to inspire Dobelle and his colleagues (1974) to try to design special equipment for the blind. They arranged electrodes in a particular shape on top of a blind man's visual cortex. He reported "seeing" the geometric shape that corresponded to the pattern of stimulation from the electrode. These researchers had hoped that this kind of system could be used to restore some aspects of vision to people with defective retinas whose visual cortexes could work correctly if they received appropriate stimuli. However, the tissue in the cortex was damaged when electrical stimulation was used on a long-term basis. Therefore, direct stimulation of the cortex cannot substitute for normal vision.

Moving upward from the occipital lobe (which contains the visual cortex), we reach the **parietal lobe**. The front portion of the parietal lobe is the somatosensory cortex, the portion of the cortex that handles the skin senses. Take a moment to appreciate these senses, though we discuss them more completely in the next chapter. Right now, your right hand may be touching a page of this textbook, you may feel a slight pressure from the watch on your wrist, and the room temperature may seem slightly cold. In addition to sensations of touch and temperature, you may also feel pain in one part of your body, muscle tension in another part, and an itch somewhere else. Each of these skin senses will be registered on your somatosensory cortex. As Figure 3.19b illustrates, the skin on certain parts of your body (such as your lips) receives more than its fair share of the cortex, a fact we also noticed for the visual cortex.

The discussion of the visual cortex noted that the areas of the retina with the clearest vision correspond to the largest areas on the visual cortex. There is a similar relationship for the somatosensory cortex. The lips, which correspond to the largest area on the somatosensory cortex, are very sensitive to touch. For

The Spatial Arrangement in the Visual Cortex

Stand in front of a full-length mirror. An image of yourself is now being registered on the retina, at the back of each eye. We could make a map illustrating how each point on the retina is represented on the visual cortex. When you look at a road map, you see that Illinois is closer to Michigan than it is to California. This road map therefore corresponds to geographic reality. Similarly, when you look at yourself in this mirror, the map on your visual cortex represents your left eyebrow as being closer to your left eye than it is to your feet. This visual-cortex map is therefore similar to the pattern of stimulation on your retina.

However, do not take this retinotopic arrangement too literally because many fac-

tors make this representation less than perfect. For example, about half of the neurons in the visual cortex receive information from the very small portion in the central part of your retina. This is the part of the retina in which vision is crisp and clear. If you look in the mirror at your chin, for instance, you will see your chin very clearly. At this moment, your chin is taking up far more than its fair share of your visual cortex. If you maintain your gaze on your chin, note that the part of your body below your waist becomes increasingly blurry. Your knees and toes occupy only a small part of the visual cortex.

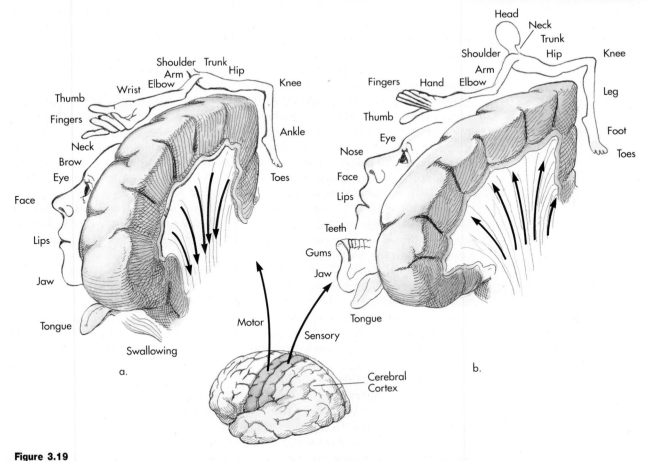

Figure 3.19
A portion of the left cortex: (a) A diagram of the regions of the motor cortex that control various body parts. The size of each body part corresponds to the amount of space on the cortex that controls each body part. (b) A diagram of the regions of the somatosensory cortex that receives signals from various body parts. The size of each body part corresponds to the amount of space on the cortex that receives signals from that body part. (After Penfield & Rasmussen, 1950)

example, if you hold two index cards so that they are just barely separated, and you touch their corners to your lips, you can easily tell that there are two distinct surfaces. If you hold the cards in the same position to touch your knee, it seems as if there is just one thick surface. In both vision and touch, greater space on the cortex allows for more precise perceptions.

Moving farther forward to the **frontal lobe**, we find that an important area here is the motor cortex. The cells in this region control voluntary movements for different parts of the body. Figure 3.19a shows the motor cortex, with the parts of the body it controls. As you will notice, this figure resembles Figure 3.19b. The parts of the body that correspond to the largest parts on the motor cortex tend to be the parts that humans use the most. We use our fingers often, and we make very precise movements with them (notice the precise movements you make with your pen to differentiate the handwritten letter *a* from the letter *v*). Without special training, you could never do this with your toes (which correspond to a relatively small part of the motor cortex).

As you can see, large parts of the motor cortex are also devoted to the lips and tongue, which humans use to make very precise discriminations when they talk. Notice how your tongue makes only a slight adjustment inside your mouth to turn *save* into *shave* or *tip* into *chip*. It is fortunate that you are blessed with a structure as agile as your tongue to make these important motor movements. Think how slurred your speech would be if your mouth contained a less precise body part, such as your knee or your elbow!

The motor cortex is the part of the frontal lobe that is best understood. The function of the rest of the frontal lobe is somewhat of a mystery. People whose frontal lobe is injured in an accident can manage quite well in most circumstances. Their deficits are often difficult to pinpoint. For example, they may not plan ahead carefully, or they may not think through the consequences of their actions. I know a man who experienced frontal lobe injury who now asks inappropriate questions at the wrong time during a group discussion. Thus, the frontal lobe appears to be responsible for the kinds of higher mental functions that make humans into socially sensitive beings who have long-range goals.

The last part of the cerebral cortex is the **temporal lobes**, which are located on the sides of the head. (You can remember that the temporal lobes are near the temples of your forehead.) The temporal lobes contain the auditory cortex, which processes information about sounds, speech, and music.

For more than 130 years, researchers have been using the case study technique to link specific regions of the brain with specific language functions. For example, a person whose brain has been damaged in a region near the front of the auditory cortex will produce little speech, and these words will be uttered with great effort. "Go New York Sunday" would be a typical sentence. A person whose brain has been damaged in a nearby area will speak rapidly, producing sentences with normal grammatical structure. This person's sentences lack precision and meaningful content. When asked a question about the weather, this person might respond, "It's like it was on the other one when they had the water." In contrast, the person with the other disorder would probably have replied simply "rainy" (Geschwind, 1985).

We have identified several important structures throughout the four lobes of the cerebral cortex. At this point you may have the impression that each tiny pinpoint of the cortex can be identified with one specific behavioral function. However, the brain does not reveal its secrets that easily, and numerous mysteries remain. For example, brain damage in some areas of the frontal lobe often produces no major deficits in behavior (Stuss & Benson, 1984). There are large regions of the cortex that simply do not respond to electrical stimulation. Students in introductory psychology classes often assume that psychologists have already answered all the interesting questions about the origins of behavior. With the cerebral cortex, however, there are probably more uncharted territories than there are on the globe.

Furthermore, structures in the brain perform more than one function. For example, we discussed how the reticular formation—located in the relatively primitive hindbrain area—is important in processes as different from each other as sleep and learning. Furthermore, most psychological processes require the participation of more than one portion of the brain. In the next chapter, for example, we consider in detail the eye movements used in reading and driving, which are called saccadic eye movements. They do not seem particularly complicated, yet researchers have determined that saccadic eye movements require the cooperation of many structures in the brain, including part of the midbrain, a region of the cerebral cortex, and probably additional structures that have not yet been identified (Goldberg & Bruce, 1986).

This discussion should remind you of the theme that most human behaviors have more than one explanation—more than one cause. Naturally, this complexity presents a challenge to introductory psychology students, who must try to make sense out of this complexity. It is clear that the human nervous system did not evolve into a neat, orderly set of organs, each with only a single, well-defined function. Evolution did not have as its goal a brain whose structures would be easy for introductory psychology students to memorize. Instead, evolution has produced a brain that is amazingly skillful in performing a wide variety of tasks both quickly and accurately. The speed and accuracy of human behavior, as you will recall, is itself another theme of this textbook.

We have examined techniques for research on the brain, as well as the structure of the brain. Now let us turn to an important question concerning the brain and its functions: Do the two hemispheres of the brain operate similarly?

Do the Right and Left Hemispheres Function Differently?

Turn back to Figure 3.17 and notice that the cerebral cortex is divided into two hemispheres. As we see in this section, these two hemispheres have somewhat different functions, though we should not exaggerate these differences. We can learn about hemispheric differences from people who have had a special operation called the split-brain procedure and also from more subtle observations on normal humans with intact brains.

The Split-Brain Procedure   The normal brain features a bridge between the two hemispheres, called the **corpus callosum**, which is a thick bundle of about 800,000 nerve fibers (Trevarthen, 1987). The corpus callosum permits communication between the two hemispheres, so a message received in the one hemisphere can be quickly transmitted to the other hemisphere. Figure 3.20 shows where the corpus callosum is located.

During the 1960s, a group of researchers—which included psychologists Roger Sperry and Michael Gazzaniga—began to explore what happens when the corpus callosum is cut, literally producing a split brain. They examined people who had such disabling epilepsy that a seizure beginning in one hemisphere would spread across the corpus callosum to the other hemisphere. Encouraged by earlier research on cats and monkeys, these researchers hoped they could reduce the intensity of seizures by cutting the corpus callosum that linked the two hemispheres.

Operations on a small number of people with severe epilepsy have typically been very successful. The split-brain patients usually experience fewer, less severe epileptic seizures. Furthermore, they seem to behave normally in their daily lives. However, research in the laboratory revealed deficits—which we will consider

Figure 3.20
An overhead view of the corpus callosum dissected indicating how it joins the two hemispheres together.

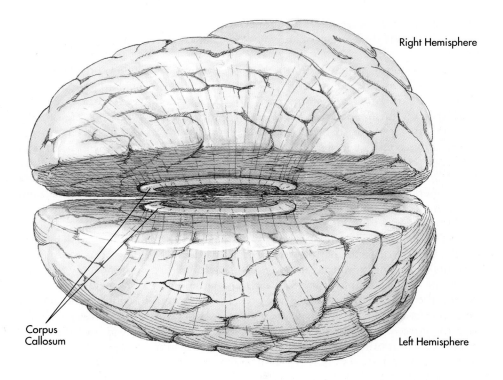

Right Hemisphere

Corpus
Callosum

Left Hemisphere

shortly—and allowed us to see how each hemisphere functions when separated from the other hemisphere.

To understand this research, you need to know how the brain is "wired." If you were to look straight ahead, everything that appears in your left visual field would be registered in the *right* side of your visual cortex. In contrast, everything that appears to the right would be registered in the *left* side of your visual cortex.

In the normal brain, information about an object in the left visual field (and therefore the right hemisphere) can be shared with the left hemisphere; the signal quickly travels across the corpus callosum. Imagine what would happen if the bridge in Figure 3.20 had been cut. Information in the left visual field would still reach the right hemisphere. However, it could not travel across to the left hemisphere. (A person with a split brain could register this object in the left hemisphere only by turning his or her head until the object was included in the right visual field, something that can be done very easily in daily life.)

In the laboratory, researchers asked the split-brain patients to sit at a table and gaze straight ahead (Sperry, 1982; Gazzaniga & LeDoux, 1978). Then the researchers presented a photo of an object, perhaps a spoon, to the right visual field (i.e., the left hemisphere). The patients had no difficulty identifying the object (see Figure 3.21a). These results confirmed researchers' strong suspicions that the left hemisphere is primarily responsible for language.

Now let us consider what happens when the same photo of the spoon was presented to the left visual field (i.e., the right hemisphere). When asked what they had seen, patients typically replied "nothing" (Figure 3.21b). Here, the information about the spoon is sent to the right hemisphere, where it is "trapped." In a person with a normal brain, that information could travel across the corpus callosum to the "verbal" left hemisphere, and the person could easily say "spoon." However, in a person with a split brain, the right hemisphere apparently does not possess the verbal skills to identify the spoon.

The right hemisphere may be mute, but it is not helpless, as Figure 3.21c shows. In this second left-visual field condition, patients were asked to reach

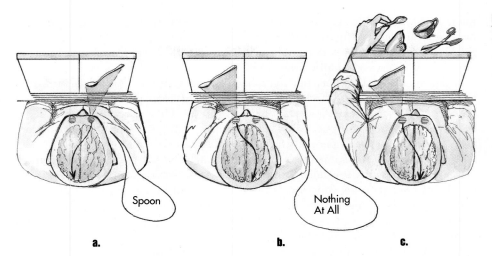

Figure 3.21
Testing a split-brain patient.

Spoon

Nothing
At All

a.   b.   c.

behind the screen with their left hand and identify by touch the object that had been presented on the screen. As you can see, the patient correctly grasps the spoon. These results confirmed researchers' strong suspicions that the right hemisphere is skilled in identifying spatial information, such as the shapes of objects. With the help of the left hand (also controlled by the right hemisphere), it was easy to identify the spoon-shaped object.

In his review of many studies, Gazzaniga (1983) concluded that the split-brain research illustrated a clear-cut difference between the two hemispheres. This kind of hemispheric specialization (with the left hemisphere being more competent on language tasks and the right hemisphere being more competent on spatial tasks) is known as **lateralization**. Now let us consider what research on people with normal brains can tell us about hemispheric differences.

Research on People With Intact Brains   Fewer than 100 people with split brains have been studied for lateralization effects. Unless you are one of those rare people, you may be wondering if lateralization has any relevance to your brain. As it turns out, research on people with normal communication between the hemispheres reveals some important differences between the left and the right hemispheres. However, we should be cautious about exaggerating those differences.

Research on people with intact brains shows increased brain wave activity, metabolism, and blood flow in the left hemisphere when a person is speaking. In contrast, these same measures show increased activity in the right hemisphere when a person performs certain perceptual tasks (Springer & Deutsch, 1985). However, the differences are not overwhelming; in most cases, the less active hemisphere is simply responding at a lower level.

Another way of studying lateralization involves dichotic (pronounced die-*kot*-ick) listening. In the **dichotic listening technique**, people wear earphones that present two different simultaneous messages, one to each ear. These dichotic listening studies have demonstrated that most listeners perceive the right-ear message more accurately. Reviewing the evidence, Geffen and Quinn (1984) conclude that the left hemisphere is specialized for processing the difference between speech sounds. Furthermore, when messages are presented to the left ear, some of the information is lost during the journey through the right hemisphere, across the corpus callosum, and into the left hemisphere.

We have been singing the praises of the left hemisphere. What can the right hemisphere do? As one psychologist pointed out, the right hemisphere was once regarded as "swampland," but it now has the status of prime real estate (Searle-

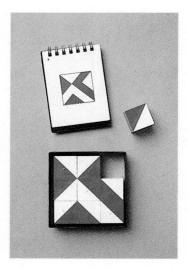

When people are asked to construct this block design out of these blocks, the task primarily requires right-brain activity.

man, 1988). Levy (1983) points out that the right hemisphere must be important, because brains are costly in terms of glucose and oxygen consumption. Evolution could not produce such a large right hemisphere if it were destined simply to occupy space in the right half of the skull!

As mentioned earlier, the right hemisphere seems to specialize in spatial tasks. For example, people who have damaged right hemispheres sometimes find it difficult to discriminate between two visual stimuli. They also have trouble filling in the missing parts of a puzzle and—in extreme cases—they cannot discriminate any differences between people's faces (Corballis, 1983).

Table 3.1 shows some of the tasks for which the left and right hemisphere are at least somewhat specialized. It is important, however, to remember that the two hemispheres do *not* function as two independent brains. For example, when you read a story, the left hemisphere translates the written words into their appropriate sounds, figures out grammatical relationships in the sentences, and notes the relations among word concepts. Your right hemisphere decodes the visual information, figures out the story structure, and appreciates the story's humorous and emotional aspects. Similarly, both hemispheres are important in tasks involving creativity or logic (Levy, 1985).

We must conclude that both hemispheres are capable of performing most tasks, but one hemisphere is usually much faster and more accurate (Allen, 1983). As Levy (1985) concludes, "Normal people have not half a brain nor two brains but one gloriously differentiated brain, with each hemisphere contributing its specialized abilities" (p. 44).

Brain Disorders

According to one estimate, 8 million people in the United States receive head injuries each year, and this head injury produces brain damage in approximately 400,000 individuals (Peterson, 1980). Another source of brain damage is a **stroke**, a disorder in which a blood clot closes an artery and prevents the artery from supplying oxygen to an area of the brain. Strokes are seldom found in young people. However, every year 1% of all people in their 60s experience a stroke (Kalat, 1988). Brain damage is also produced by tumors, bacteria and viruses, and drugs.

Some people recover at least partially from damage to the nervous system. For example, neurons in the peripheral nervous system do show an impressive ability to grow after they have been injured (Marshall, 1984). However, the brain

Table 3.1   *Some Tasks on Which One of the Hemispheres Shows Superiority*

TASK	LEFT HEMISPHERE	RIGHT HEMISPHERE
Vision	Translation of letters into sounds	Recognition of faces
Hearing	Language sounds	Nonlanguage sounds; music
Memory	Verbal memory	Visual memory
Language	Grammar	Humor, emotional content
Mathematics	Arithmetic	Geometry
Problem solving	Problems to be solved, analytically	Problems to be solved, holistically
Complex tasks	Tasks to be performed, one part at a time	Tasks to be performed, all parts simultaneously

Sources: Kolb & Whishaw, 1985; Levy, 1985; Tucker & Williamson, 1984.

cannot recover by manufacturing new neurons. Even if the brain could make new neurons, how would they establish the correct connections with other neurons that make up the complex network of the brain?

To some extent, the brain demonstrates **plasticity**; that is, when one region of the brain is damaged, another region may eventually take over some of the functions originally performed by the damaged portion (Cotman & Nieto-Sampedro, 1982). Furthermore, a person who has experienced brain damage can sometimes learn to make better use of skills that were impaired but not completely destroyed (Kalat, 1988). Figure 3.22 shows a hospital therapist helping a stroke victim work with an interactive computer to aid recovery.

Fortunately, the body also has several other mechanisms for recovering from brain damage. For example, specialized cells in the nervous system remove most of the damaged tissue as well as the toxic substances generated by this dead tissue. Sometimes the nervous system rallies to the relief of a brain-damaged area by activating synapses that were previously silent and by sprouting new branches from the nearby undamaged axons (Kalat, 1988).

Unfortunately, the brain does not always regain functioning in its damaged parts. Let us conclude this section on the brain by considering a disorder that is currently considered irreversible: Alzheimer's disease.

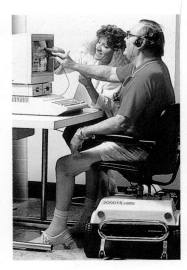

Figure 3.22
A hospital therapist working with a stroke victim.

○ ○

In Depth: Alzheimer's Disease

This year, several hundred thousand Americans will begin to lose their ability to remember simple things. They will not recall whether they turned off the oven or whether they let the cat out. It will become difficult for them to recall the names of common objects. They will no longer be able to balance a checkbook (Wurtman, 1984). Nevertheless, these people may look healthy to a casual observer. Most of these people are elderly, though their symptoms are not caused by normal aging. They have a specific disorder called **Alzheimer's disease**, which is a severe mental and emotional decline, accompanied by changes in the structure and function of the brain (Kimble, 1988).

According to one estimate, approximately 1 million Americans suffer from incapacitating Alzheimer's disease (U.S. Congress, 1987). Because of the increasing life span, it is estimated that about 5 million U.S. citizens will be affected by Alzheimer's disease by the year 2040—unless a prevention or cure can be discovered before then.

Unfortunately, no biochemical test can reliably identify Alzheimer's disease (Katzman, 1987). Instead, physicians make a diagnosis on the basis of medical history, physical examination, and EEG or one of the imaging techniques discussed earlier—CAT scanning, PET scanning, or MRI (Agbayewa, 1986; Duara et al., 1986; Erkinjuntti et al., 1987). The accuracy of diagnosis may be as high as 90% if the examination also includes a battery of psychological tests (U.S. Congress, 1987). Demonstration 3.3 includes some of the items from one of these psychological tests.

Let us look in more detail at some of the symptoms of Alzheimer's disease. Then we turn to the physiological changes that the disease produces.

Symptoms   Perhaps the most prominent symptom of Alzheimer's disease is decreased memory, particularly for events that occurred very recently. For example, an elderly person may turn on the stove and forget about it just minutes later. Surprisingly, however, memory for childhood events may be excellent (Kimble, 1988). (Item 4 in Demonstration 3.3 helps to assess memory difficulties.)

Demonstration 3.3

The Mini-Mental State Examination

The following items have been selected from the Mini-Mental State Examination, one of the tests that is frequently used to help diagnose Alzheimer's disease. Imagine that an elderly relative is living in your home. Read over these items and try to form a concrete impression of a person who would *not* be able to answer these questions correctly. Try to imagine a conversation between this person and yourself. Try to picture how this person would have difficulty performing even the simplest of household chores. Alzheimer's disease is now the major reason that an elderly person is admitted to a nursing home; Alzheimer's disease is so disabling that its victims require constant care (Katzman, 1986).

1. What is the year?

2. What is the season?
3. Can you tell me where we are right now? For instance, what city are we in?
4. I am going to name three objects. After I have said them, I want you to repeat them. Remember what they are because I am going to ask you to name them again in a few minutes. Please repeat the three items for me: "apple" . . . "table" . . . "penny" . . .
5. (show wristwatch) What is this called?
6. I am going to give you a piece of paper. When I do, take the paper in your right hand, fold the paper in half with both hands, and put the paper down on your lap.
7. Write any complete sentence on that piece of paper for me.

Source: Adapted from Folstein et al., 1985.

Another serious problem is the deterioration of language skills. The names of common objects may no longer be available. (For example, a person with Alzheimer's disease may be unable to identify a wristwatch.) Alzheimer's victims may no longer be able to read or write coherently. Figure 3.23 shows two sentences produced by Alzheimer's patients who were asked to write a complete sentence.

Alzheimer's patients also have difficulty with spatial locations. For example, they may get lost, even in familiar environments (Hostetler, 1988). They also have difficulty representing spatial relationships. Figure 3.24 shows a man who was previously employed as a graphic artist and is now an Alzheimer's patient. Notice that when he was asked to copy the design of the hand and the circle, he counted the fingers incorrectly, drew the hand too small, and misplaced the fingernails.

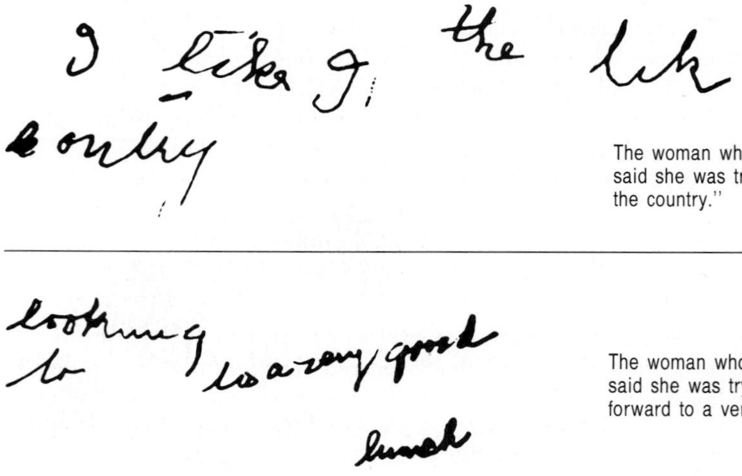

Figure 3.23
Sentences produced by Alzheimer's patients who were instructed to write a complete sentence.

The woman who wrote this sentence said she was trying to write, "I like the country."

The woman who wrote this sentence said she was trying to write "looking forward to a very good lunch."

Figure 3.24
This man, previously employed in a profession that required excellent spatial-relationships ability, now suffers from Alzheimer's disease. When asked to copy the figure on the top, he produced the distorted version on the bottom.

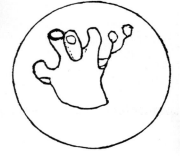

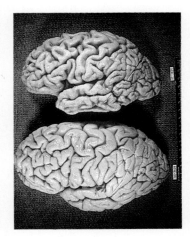

People with Alzheimer's disease may also experience mood problems and other psychological disorders resembling the kinds of abnormalities we examine in chapter 15. For example, they may be depressed and irritable. Some may have hallucinations or delusions (i.e., holding false beliefs despite clear contradictory evidence).

In contemplating these symptoms, keep in mind that the disease lasts for many years and that many Alzheimer's sufferers are essentially helpless. The average Alzheimer's patient suffers for about 8 years between the first onset of symptoms and the time of death. Symptoms can last as long as 25 years. We take our human cognitive abilities for granted; *of course*, we can remember, speak, and know who and where we are. Unfortunately, then, people with Alzheimer's disease live a substantial portion of their lives without some of these basic abilities.

Neurological Changes Caused by Alzheimer's Disease   Alzheimer's disease causes profound changes in the human brain. One of the major changes is a dramatic loss of neurons, especially in the cortex and in the hippocampus portion of the limbic system. (The hippocampus plays an important role in memory.) Figure 3.25 compares a normal brain with the brain of a patient who had Alzheimer's disease. Note that the visual cortex (at the right side of each figure) is relatively intact, but the remaining cortex has shrunk substantially.

Even the neurons that remain may show degeneration. For example, many of the dendrites on a cortical neuron may be destroyed. It is likely that these dendrites are important in cortical activities such as memory and thinking (Kimble, 1988).

Alzheimer's involves not only the disappearance of normal neurons in the brain, but also the development of abnormal structures in the cortex and the hippocampus. Two common abnormalities are neurofibrillary tangles, a tangled web of tiny neural threads, and amyloid plaques, clumps of protein that form around the remnants of degenerated nerve cells (Selkoe, 1986). Presumably these structures interfere with neural transmitting.

In addition, Alzheimer's patients show a decreased production of a substance that is critical in the production of the important neurotransmitter acetylcholine

Figure 3.25
Examples of the brain of a person who had Alzheimer's disease (upper) and a normal brain (lower).

(Katzman, 1986). As you may recall, ACh is important in functions such as attention, memory, sexuality, and thirst.

We have seen that Alzheimer's disease involves serious disruptions in thought processes and major changes in the structures and chemistry of the brain. But what *causes* Alzheimer's disease? Some possibilities include a genetic explanation, an abnormal-protein theory, and a blood-flow model. Unfortunately, there is no clear-cut favorite among the many competing theories (Katzman, 1986; Wurtman, 1985). Furthermore, although there are occasional reports that medications may be temporarily helpful, drugs are primarily useful in simply relieving symptoms such as depression or sleep disorders (Katzman, 1986; Summers et al., 1986). At present, then, Alzheimer's disease remains one of the most serious threats to the health and well-being of thousands of people in this country.

○ ○

Section Summary: The Brain

- Some of the methods used in brain research include the case study, lesion production, brain stimulation, brain recording (EEG and the single-cell recording technique), and imaging techniques (CAT scanning, PET scanning, and MRI).
- The hindbrain includes the medulla, the pons, the cerebellum, and the reticular formation; this region helps regulate basic functions such as breathing, body movement, and sleep.
- Signals pass through the midbrain on the way to the forebrain. The forebrain includes the thalamus, the hypothalamus, the pituitary gland, and the limbic system (all structures critical in relaying information and regulating hormone production, motivation, and emotion). The forebrain also includes the cerebral cortex, which is responsible for vision, the skin senses, motor movements, hearing, and all complex thought processes.
- The right and left hemispheres of the brain are somewhat different in their functions (with the left hemisphere more competent at language skills and the right hemisphere more competent at spatial skills), but the differences should not be exaggerated.
- The causes of brain disorders include head injury, strokes, and tumors; the brain often demonstrates plasticity in recovering from brain damage.
- Alzheimer's disease is a common disorder among elderly people; its symptoms include severe deterioration of memory, language skills, spatial abilities, and psychological adjustment; neurological changes include loss and degeneration of neurons, the development of abnormal structures, and decreased amounts of acetylcholine (ACh).

The Endocrine System

So far, this chapter has concentrated on the nervous system, a complicated communication network in which information travels through your body in just a fraction of a second. The nervous system provides jet-plane type service for messages. Now let us turn to the system that more closely resembles the leisurely pace of a gondola in the Venice canals—the endocrine system.

The **endocrine system** is a system of glands that release their chemicals into the bloodstream. The nervous system has its own independent communication network provided by the neurons. The endocrine system, in contrast, is cleverly and economically designed to spread its messages through the bloodstream. The chemicals released by the endocrine system are called **hormones**. They circulate through all parts of the bloodstream, yet they influence only specific target organs. For example, when a newborn baby sucks on the mother's nipple, **oxytocin** is released from the pituitary gland in the mother, which is illustrated in Figure 3.26. The oxytocin may travel through regions as distant as the mother's earlobe and her big toe, but it will primarily influence the cells in the breast ducts where the milk is stored, releasing the flow of milk.

Note two important characteristics of this oxytocin example: (1) There is a delay of many seconds between the time when the hormone is released and the time of the milk flow, a much longer delay than those found in the nervous system; and (2) many functions in the endocrine system are very cleverly designed so that the hormone is released only when it is needed. It would be inefficient and unpleasant for a nursing mother to be producing a constant drip of oxytocin so that her milk flowed all the time. Instead, milk is produced only when her baby sucks on the nipple (Eiger & Olds, 1987).

The most important gland in the endocrine system is the pituitary gland; its role in breastfeeding is just one of its many functions. This structure, dangling from the base of the hypothalamus, is about the size of a pea. Part of the **pituitary**

When this baby sucks on the mother's nipple, oxytocin is released, stimulating the flow of milk inside the mother's breast.

Figure 3.26
Some of the more important endocrine glands in the human body.

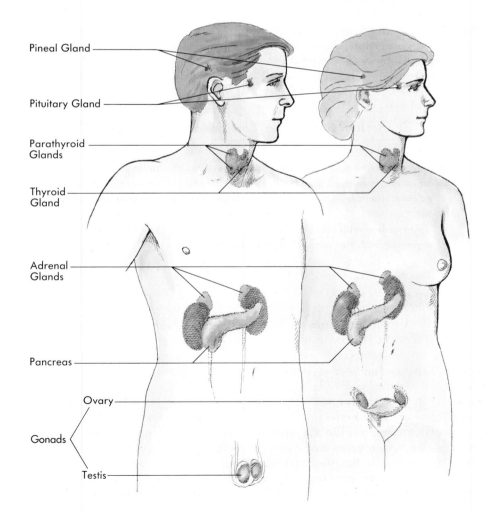

Pineal Gland

Pituitary Gland

Parathyroid Glands

Thyroid Gland

Adrenal Glands

Pancreas

Ovary

Gonads

Testis

gland contains neurons, which receive neural messages from the brain; a different part of the pituitary receives hormonal messages from the brain. When those hormonal messages are received, the pituitary responds by releasing its own hormones. One important chemical it releases is called growth hormone. If too little growth hormone is released during childhood, the child will become a midget. If too much growth hormone is released, the child will become a giant.

The impressive pituitary gland does not merely release hormones, however. As it happens, these hormones influence the hormone production of other endocrine glands. One pituitary hormone influences the **thyroid gland**, a gland producing its own hormone that is important in regulating the body's metabolism (see Figure 3.26).

A second pituitary hormone stimulates the **adrenal glands**, which are two lumpy structures perched on the top of the kidneys. The adrenal glands produce several dozen kinds of hormones. These hormones perform critical tasks such as regulating the concentration of minerals in the body and regulating the concentration of sugar in the blood. The adrenal glands also produce sex hormones, such as androgen hormones. **Androgen hormones** are the hormones that produce changes in males during early prenatal development, guiding the development of the male reproductive system. Another hormone produced by the adrenal glands is **adrenaline**, which encourages the sympathetic portion of the autonomic nervous system. Adrenaline is released when someone jumps out at you from a dark street, and your heart starts pounding vigorously.

A third kind of gland stimulated by the pituitary is the **gonads**, or sex glands. As Figure 3.26 shows, the gonads are the testes in males and the ovaries in females. Like the adrenal glands, the gonads produce a variety of hormones that are crucial in sexual development and reproduction. Let us turn now to genetics, an important component of reproduction.

Section Summary: The Endocrine System

- The endocrine system releases hormones into the bloodstream.
- The most important gland in the endocrine system is the pituitary, which releases hormones that encourage other endocrine glands to produce hormones.
- Three other endocrine glands (all stimulated by the pituitary) are the thyroid gland, the adrenal glands, and the gonads.

Genetics

So far, this chapter has emphasized two of the three themes of the textbook. We have seen that the biological underpinnings of behavior are complex, with even simple behaviors requiring the cooperation of many regions of the brain. We have also seen that the nervous system and the endocrine system allow us to function well in our assigned task of being human. However, this chapter has not yet even hinted at the third theme, individual differences. Clearly, this section on genetics has important implications for the variation among humans.

Furthermore, genetics must be mentioned in this chapter because it was the information in your genes that controlled your development from a single-celled creature into a fully functioning adult. Thus, genes are responsible for the fact that your knee jerks in response to an appropriate tap and the fact that your adrenal glands squirt adrenaline in response to a fearful situation.

We discuss genetics at several points throughout this textbook. The chapter on infant and child development examines genetics in connection with both pre-natal development and children's personality. In the chapter on assessment and intelligence, we learn that genetic studies help psychologists determine the extent to which intelligence is inherited. The chapter on psychological disorders, points out that depression and other disorders are at least partly inherited (Henderson, 1982; Loehlin et al., 1988). To provide a basis for these future topics, we need to discuss three aspects of genetics: genes and chromosomes, methods for studying the genetic basis of behavior, and the nature-nurture question.

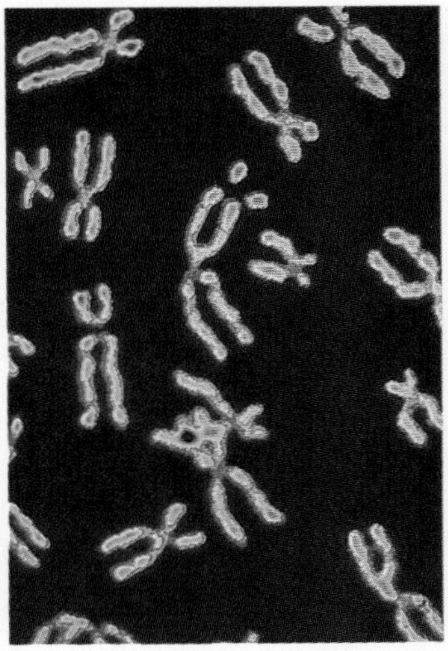

Genes and Chromosomes

Genes are the basic units of heredity. In humans, the genes are located on 23 pairs of **chromosomes**. In virtually every cell in your body, you have 46 chro-mosomes carrying the genetic information that had a critical role in making you into yourself. One set of 23 chromosomes was contributed by your father; the other set came from your mother.

It is not clear why we humans have precisely 23 pairs of chromosomes. One primitive species of worm has only one pair of chromosomes, but a type of one-celled marine organism has about 800 pairs (Davis & Solomon, 1986). Figure 3.27 shows several chromosome pairs.

As you may know, one of the 23 pairs of chromosomes determined whether you would be male or female; this pair is called the **sex chromosomes**. Females have a pair of sex chromosomes called X chromosomes (symbolized XX). Males have one sex chromosome called X and one called Y (symbolized XY). That Y chromosome is much smaller than the X chromosome. It is ironic that a char-acteristic that most humans consider to be extremely important—whether you are male or female—is determined by just one chromosome pair. As we discuss issues related to gender differences and gender stereotypes in later chapters, keep in mind that all this controversy can be traced to the sex chromosomes, which are so tiny that they must be magnified hundreds of times before they are visible.

Studying the Genetic Basis of Behavior

Researchers interested in genetics have devised a variety of methods for under-standing more about the relationship between genetics and behavior. These tech-niques include the investigation of genetic abnormalities, twin studies, and adoption studies.

Genetic Abnormalities   Several characteristic, genetic abnormalities are related to abilities and behavior. For example, people with **Down syndrome** have an extra chromosome added to the 21st pair. People with Down syndrome usually have round faces and small folds of skin across the inner edges of the eyes (see Figure 3.28). Down syndrome children are typically retarded; when interacting with other people, they are often friendly and cheerful.

Furthermore, some psychological disorders now appear to have a genetic origin. For example, the amyloid plaques that are an important component of Alzheimer's disease have their gene coding on one of the arms of the 21st chro-mosome (Loehlin et al., 1988; Tanzi et al., 1987).

Twin Studies   Jerry Level and Mark Newman are identical twins who were sep-arated at birth. When they were finally reunited, the two middle-aged bachelors discovered that they shared an uncanny number of peculiar characteristics. Both were compulsive flirts, and both were raucously good humored. They both liked

Figure 3.27
Human chromosomes (greatly magnified).

Figure 3.28
A child with Down syndrome.

beer and drank the same brand. Both drank from the bottle, with the little finger extended underneath the bottom of the bottle. Both were volunteer fire fighters (Bouchard & Segal, 1989; Rosen, 1987). Studies of other pairs of identical twins who were reared apart have yielded some intriguing observations about a potential genetic basis for human characteristics.

More often, however, researchers compare **identical twins** (who came from a single fertilized egg and are genetically identical) with **fraternal twins** (who came from two separate eggs and are thus no more genetically similar than two siblings). These comparisons of identical and fraternal twins are called **twin studies**. In most studies, identical twins are more similar to each other than are fraternal twins (e.g., Bouchard & McGee, 1981).

We discuss these studies in the chapter on intelligence, but let us pause to consider a problem with these findings. It is tempting to conclude that the greater genetic similarity in the case of the identical twins explains their greater psychological similarity. Again, though, consider an alternative hypothesis: Perhaps parents and other people treat identical twins quite similarly, because they look so similar. In contrast, two fraternal twins might be treated differently . . . perhaps one is more attractive, or more athletic, or more intelligent. Twin studies can provide some useful information, but we have to keep in mind that identical twins are not only more genetically similar to each other, but they also are likely to receive more similar environmental treatment.

Adoption Studies   Researchers interested in the influence of genetics on human behavior can examine people with genetic abnormalities, or they can compare identical and fraternal twins. They can also perform **adoption studies** to determine whether adopted children are more like their biological parents (who contribute genes) or their adoptive parents (who contribute a home environment). In some cases, adopted children are more likely to resemble their biological parents than their adoptive parents. For example, children whose biological parents are alcoholic are at risk for becoming alcoholics themselves, even if they are reared by adoptive parents who are not alcoholics (Vaillant & Milofsky, 1982).

Both twin studies and adoption studies assess the relative contribution of genes and environment to human behavior. These studies provide important

The identical twins on the left probably behave quite similarly. In contrast, the fraternal twins on the right will probably behave quite differently from one another when they reach adolescence. Is this because the identical twins are more similar genetically or because they were treated more similarly by other people?

information for a long-standing controversy in psychology known as the nature-nurture question.

The Nature-Nurture Question

Stop reading for a moment and try to identify two friends who differ tremendously on a psychological characteristic. One friend, for example, may be extremely outgoing, whereas your other friend wins the prize for "most likely to blend into the wallpaper." How would you explain the difference between these two people? Is it determined by differences in the genes they inherited from their parents, that is, by their **nature**? Alternatively, is the difference between the two determined by differences in the way they were reared, that is, by their **nurture**? Notice why it is difficult to draw a simple conclusion; the issue is complex. For example, you may be tempted to attribute the difference to genetics by noting that the parents of the outgoing friend are themselves very outgoing. Perhaps they passed on the relevant genes to their child. However, another explanation is that outgoing parents are likely to raise (or nurture) their children in an outgoing fashion.

We raise the nature-nurture question at several points throughout this book, because it is a major theme in psychological research. You will see that psychologists cannot provide a clear-cut "It's all nature" or "It's all nurture" response. Furthermore, you will see that an even more important determinant of a person's current behavior is neither nature nor nurture, but the current situation. (For example, even your outgoing friend can be subdued in some situations.)

An important concept in the nature-nurture debate is heritability. **Heritability** is the extent to which the variation in some characteristic can be traced to differences in heredity as opposed to differences in environment (Kallat, 1988). This numerical figure can vary between zero and 1.00. A heritability figure near zero indicates that little of the variation can be traced to heredity. In contrast, a heritability figure near 1.00 indicates that almost all of the variation can be traced to heredity. For example, studies suggest that the heritability for intelligence is between .50 and .70 (DeFries et al., 1987; Loehlin et al., 1988; Plomin, 1990). It is important to stress, however, that this heritability figure can vary substantially, depending on the populations that are studied, the environments in which they were reared, and the way they are tested.

Our exploration of the biological basis of behavior has covered the structures and functions of the nervous system, the endocrine system, and genetics. You have learned how electrical impulses travel throughout the nervous system, how hormones ooze out of endocrine glands, and how tiny structures called genes carry information related to psychological characteristics. We must now move beyond the biological level and consider how people experience the world through sensation and perception.

> ### Section Summary: Genetics

- Humans have 23 pairs of chromosomes, each of which contains a number of gene pairs.
- Techniques for studying the genetic basis of behavior include the study of genetic abnormalities (e.g., Down syndrome), twin studies, and adoption studies.
- The nature-nurture question considers the extent to which differences in psychological characteristics can be traced to nature (genetics) versus nurture (rearing); heritability is a measure that assesses the relative contribution provided by genetics.

REVIEW QUESTIONS

1. In the discussion of the nervous system, the brain, and the endocrine system, some of the reactions that were described are chemical, whereas others are electrical. List which reactions belong to each of these two categories.

2. Draw a representative neuron. Label the following structures on that neuron: dendrites, cell body, axon, myelin, synapse, and terminal buttons.

3. What is a neurotransmitter? List as many neurotransmitters as you can recall, and specify their relationship to several neurological disorders: poisoning from a black widow spider, Parkinson's disease, and Alzheimer's disease. Finally, describe how neurotransmitters perform in the synaptic cleft.

4. An important figure in this chapter outlined the divisions of the nervous system. Try to reproduce Figure 3.8, being certain to include the following terms in your diagram: autonomic division, central nervous system, sympathetic system, brain, spinal cord, peripheral nervous system, somatic division, parasympathetic system, and (at the top of the diagram) the nervous system. Then try to recall some recent activity that required the use of each of these portions of the nervous system.

5. Suppose that researchers wanted to know more about the way that visual stimuli are processed in the brain. List each of the brain research methods described in this chapter and speculate how each could be used to provide information about vision.

6. It is likely that you know someone who has had neurosurgery to remove a tumor in the brain or someone whose physician requested one of the three imaging techniques following a head injury, a stroke, or a serious disease. Describe in as much detail as possible the way these medical procedures are performed.

7. Figure 3.13 is a diagram of the organization of the brain. Try to reproduce as many of the listed organs as you can recall, listing the structures under the heading of hindbrain, midbrain, and forebrain. Then consult Figure 3.13 to complete your diagram. Using a different-colored pen, jot down notes about the functions performed by each of these structures. Try to notice which of these structures have similar functions, and try to identify overall differences between the functions of the three major regions of the brain.

8. Imagine that a friend has just discovered that an elderly relative has been diagnosed as having Alzheimer's disease. What kind of information could you supply about the general nature of the disease, its symptoms, and its neurological changes?

9. How does the endocrine system work? Why is the pituitary gland so important? Finally, describe the other glands discussed in this chapter.

10. Imagine that a high school freshman whom you know needs a quick overview of genetics. Summarize the information from the last part of the chapter, being sure to include genes and chromosomes, genetic research methods, and the nature-nurture issue. Illustrate the nature-nurture issue with your own example.

NEW TERMS

neuron

dendrites

cell body

axon

action potentials

myelin sheath

synapse

terminal buttons

synaptic cleft

neurotransmitters

excitatory synapse

inhibitory synapse

acetylcholine (ACh)

dopamine

Parkinson's disease

neuromodulators

endorphins

reflex arc

peripheral nervous system

central nervous system

somatic division

autonomic division

sympathetic system

parasympathetic system

spinal cord

case study

lesion

electrical stimulation

electroencephalogram (EEG)

single-cell recording technique

computerized axial tomography (CAT scanning)

positron emission tomography (PET scanning)

magnetic resonance imaging (MRI)

hindbrain

medulla

pons

cerebellum

reticular formation

midbrain

forebrain

thalamus

hypothalamus

pituitary gland

limbic system

cerebral cortex

occipital lobe

retinotopic arrangement

parietal lobe

frontal lobe

temporal lobes

corpus callosum

lateralization

dichotic listening task

stroke

plasticity

Alzheimer's disease

endocrine system

hormones

oxytocin

thyroid gland

adrenal glands

androgen hormones

adrenaline

gonads

genes

chromosomes

sex chromosomes

Down syndrome

identical twins

fraternal twins

twin studies

adoption studies

nature

nurture

heritability

RECOMMENDED READINGS

Carlson, N. R. (1986). *Physiology of behavior* (3rd ed.). Boston: Allyn & Bacon. Carlson's book is more advanced and longer than the other two textbooks listed here; it has a particularly strong chapter on research methods.

Kalat, J. W. (1988). *Biological psychology* (3rd ed.). Belmont: Wadsworth. Kalat's textbook includes interesting chapters on sexual behavior and genetics; it also contains some superb color photos of structures in the nervous system.

Kimble, D. P. (1988). *Biological psychology*. New York: Holt, Rinehart and Winston. This clear, well-illustrated textbook includes chapters on brain development and brain disorders.

U.S. Congress, Office of Technology Assessment. (1987). *Losing a million minds: Confronting the tragedy of Alzheimer's disease and other dementias.* Washington, DC: U.S. Government Printing Office. This government document reviews the literature on Alzheimer's disease, including information on the social consequences of the disease, as well as its neurological basis.

**Sensation and
Perception**

Right now, you are actively sensing and perceiving. Your eyes are racing across this page, registering little lines, dots, and squiggles that will be transformed into meaningful sentences. If you look up from your book, you will encounter a rich assortment of objects that have different shapes and colors. You also perceive that some objects are nearby, whereas others out your window seem miles away. Simultaneously, your auditory system may be tracking a screeching automobile, a familiar song on the stereo next door, or fragments of a conversation in the hallway. Your skin senses may detect room temperature, the mild pain of too-tight shoes, or the pressure of your chair against your back. A trip to the dining room can activate an equally rich variety of taste and smell experiences. During every waking moment, you are constantly sensing and perceiving.

Sensation refers to the immediate, basic experiences that simple stimuli generate. **Perception** requires the interpretation of those basic sensations; perception involves organization and meaning. Suppose that a friend plays a note on the piano. The loudness and pitch of that note are *sensations*. However, if you hear the first five notes and recognize that they form a melody, rather than random sounds, you experience a *perception*. In reality, the distinction between sensation and perception is not clear-cut. How complex can a stimulus become before it crosses the boundary into perception? How much interpretation is required before sensation wanders into the territory of perception? Psychologists concede that the boundary between these two terms is blurred.

People usually take sensation and perception for granted. After all, it requires so little effort to see, hear, touch, smell, and taste. You open your eyes and see pencils, trucks, and petunias. You open your mouth, insert a spoonful of food, and taste frozen yogurt, a cheeseburger, or a chicken enchilada. These processes that seem so commonplace have intrigued psychologists. How are the qualities of objects—for example, the flower in Figure 4.1—recreated inside your head? The picture lies an arm's length in front of you, yet the flower's color, shape, and features are conveyed to your cortex so that you experience a reasonably accurate, well-organized representation of the flower.

This chapter explores how we achieve accurate, well-organized perceptions. An important prelude to that exploration is an understanding of how sensations are measured—an area known as psychophysics.

Psychophysics

How can we measure how the world appears? Sensation is a private activity. A person who decides to watch you engage in sensory processes soon grows bored, because there is so little visible activity. **Psychophysics** is an area of psychology that examines the relationship between physical stimuli and people's psychological reactions to those stimuli. Suppose two trombone players play a C on their instruments, and Joe's C is slightly higher than Carlos's C. That is, the two *physical* stimuli differ slightly. Will their conductor be able to discriminate between the two tones, indicating that they are *psychologically* different?

Figure 4.1
In perception, the qualities of an object (for example, of this photograph of a rose) are recreated inside your head.

A typical study in psychophysics might assess people's psychological reactions to a faint tone. The intensity of that physical stimulus—that faint tone—can be measured precisely in units devised by physicists. Measuring people's psychological reactions is more challenging. For more than a century, researchers have been devising psychophysical methods for converting these private psychological reactions into objective numbers. These numbers inform us about human sensory ability, and they also provide objective measures for research in perception.

Basically, psychophysicists ask two kinds of questions: (1) Can people detect this low-intensity stimulus? (2) Can people discriminate between these two similar stimuli? Let us consider these questions separately.

Detection

Suppose that you are tasting a fruit punch at a party. Is that subtle flavor some kind of alcohol? Or suppose that you look across the street at the home of a neighbor who is away on vacation. Is that a faint light in their dining room? These two situations involve detection. In **detection** studies, the psychologist provides low-intensity stimuli and records whether people report them. The psychologist can study detection using either of two major approaches to detection: the classical psychophysics approach or the signal detection theory approach.

The Classical Psychophysics Approach   The goal of the classical psychophysics approach to detection is to establish a threshold. A **detection threshold** is the smallest amount of energy required for the observer to report the stimulus on half (50%) of the trials. For example, if researchers want to measure the detection threshold for light, they must establish how intense the light must be for the observers to say, "I see it" half the time and "I don't see it" half the time.

Just how sensitive are the senses? Table 4.1 shows examples of some very impressive detection thresholds. However, do not conclude that psychophysicists spend their work hours dropping bee wings on people's cheeks. They are more likely to use carefully calibrated hairlike fibers to assess detection thresholds for touch.

Table 4.1   *Several Approximate Detection Threshold Values*

SENSORY PROCESS	APPROXIMATE DETECTION THRESHOLD
Vision	A candle flame seen at 30 miles on a dark clear night.
Hearing	The tick of a watch at 20 feet under quiet conditions.
Touch	The wing of a bee falling on your cheek from a distance of $\frac{1}{2}$ inch.
Smell	One drop of perfume diffused into the entire volume of a three-room apartment.
Taste	One teaspoon of sugar in 2 gallons of water.

Source: Adapted from Galantar, 1962. Used with permission.

The Signal Detection Theory Approach   The more current approach to detection argues that we cannot locate an absolute threshold, such that the stimulus is perceived above that boundary and not perceived below that boundary (Gescheider, 1985; Luce & Krumhansl, 1988). For example, the likelihood of your hearing a faint whisper depends upon whether you are listening in a quiet restaurant or in a rock concert. The likelihood also depends on your expectations and motivation.

A student, Bruce Edington, provided a good example of how our responses depend on expectations. Bruce had applied for a job, and the manager had stressed that Bruce could expect a phone call between 3:30 and 4:00 on a particular afternoon. Within that 30-minute period, Bruce was convinced that he heard the phone start to ring two or three times. His "I hear it" responses were more common than in other circumstances because of (1) the high probability that the phone should actually ring during that period and (2) the important benefits of answering the phone if it did ring, in contrast to the major drawbacks of not answering the phone. Bruce's story provides an excellent example of how our expectancies influence the probability of saying "I detect this stimulus."

In contrast to the classical psychophysics approach, **signal detection theory** stresses the importance of the observer's **criterion**—or willingness to say "I detect the stimulus"—when the observer is uncertain about whether the stimulus has been presented. Bruce Edington had a lenient criterion when he was waiting for the phone call. In fact, he probably would have answered the phone if the doorbell rang! Two common determinants of the criterion are (1) the probability that the stimulus will occur and (2) the benefits and drawbacks associated with making the particular response. In Bruce's case, these two factors conspired to send him running to the phone when no stimulus had occurred.

The important contribution of signal detection theory to psychophysics is that it reminds us of the variability within each human. We are not rigid "detection machines" who consistently report "I perceive it" whenever a stimulus reaches a specific intensity. Instead, our knowledge of the situation determines whether or not we perceive a particular stimulus.

Discrimination

We have seen that one major psychophysical talent we have involves detecting a stimulus. Another psychophysical task we often perform is to discriminate between two similar stimuli. In **discrimination** studies, the experimenter presents two stimuli and assesses how different these stimuli must be in order for the observer to report "These two are distinguishably different." Consider some discrimination tasks people perform every day. Is the blue stripe in this shirt the same color as the blue in these pants, or is it a bit greener? Does this chicken recipe have the same amount of lime as the one in the Afrilanka Restaurant, or

Signal detection theory predicts that expectations and motivations of this air traffic controller will influence the likelihood of her detecting a particular signal in this display.

is it more sour? Is the tone played by the first clarinetist the same as the tone played by the second clarinetist?

Classical research on discrimination tasks produced an important concept, the just-noticeable difference. As the name implies, the experimenter changes the physical stimulus until a **just-noticeable difference** (or **jnd**) is produced. For instance, suppose that 60 candles are burning in one room. If we light just one more candle, bringing the total to 61, researchers have found that we can create a just noticeable difference.

Suppose, however, that we start with 120 candles. Can people discriminate between the light in that room and light in a room in which 121 candles are lit? After all, we have added the same one candle to make the room brighter. However, pioneering researchers in psychophysics discovered that when we start with more intense stimuli, we need to make a larger adjustment before the change is noticeable. When we start with 120 candles, for example, we need to light *two* more candles to create a just-noticeable difference.

One early researcher, Ernst Weber (pronounced *Vay*-bur) noticed that if we take the change in intensity required to produce a just-noticeable difference and divide it by the original intensity, we obtain a constant number; this relationship is known as **Weber's law**. Stated mathematically, the formula for Weber's law is

$$\frac{\Delta I}{I} = k$$

In this formula, I is the intensity of the original stimulus, ΔI is the amount the stimulus must be changed to produce a jnd, and k is a number that is constant for a particular task. This constant number k is $\frac{1}{60}$ for noticing the change in visual brightness (for example, $\frac{2}{120} = \frac{1}{60}$).

This constant, k, has different values for different perceptual tasks. For instance, we are not very sensitive to changes in the intensity of a smell; k is usually about $\frac{1}{4}$ for smell. In contrast, we are spectacular in judging changes in the pitch of a tone; k is about $\frac{1}{333}$ for judging tones (Engen, 1971). At a band concert, the first and second clarinetists should produce tones that differ by less than this fraction, or the audience will be able to perceive they are not playing the same tone. A wide variety of studies on vision, hearing, and other senses have demonstrated that Weber's law is reasonably accurate in predicting sensory discrimination.

Demonstration 4.1

An Illustration of Weber's Law

You can illustrate how Weber's law works for the perception of heaviness by locating three quarters, two envelopes of the same size, and a pair of your own shoes. Place one quarter in one of the envelopes and place the other two quarters in the second envelope. With your right hand, lift one envelope and put it down. Then, also with your right hand, lift the second envelope and put it down. The second envelope should feel substantially heavier; this difference is easy to discriminate.

Now insert one envelope into one of your shoes and the other envelope into your second shoe. With your right hand, lift one at a time. You are not likely to be able to discriminate the difference between the two weights. When you start with a more intense stimulus (in the case of an envelope in a shoe, a *heavier* stimulus), you would need to make a larger adjustment before the change is noticeable (based on Coren & Ward, 1989).

Try noticing some applications of Weber's law. For example, you are likely to notice a 5-pound weight loss on a slender friend, but a plumper friend might need to lose 10 pounds for the loss to be noticeable. Or perhaps you have observed that people complain about a 20¢ increase in the cost of a hamburger. However, they would never notice a 20¢ increase in the cost of an automobile tire! As a final demonstration of Weber's law, try Demonstration 4.1.

Psychophysics is a useful tool for assessing people's private perceptual responses, and for converting those private responses into numbers. These numbers are useful in research in sensation and perception. However, the detection thresholds and some of the discrimination thresholds also illustrate the theme that humans are endowed with extremely impressive equipment which allows them to function accurately and efficiently.

Section Summary: Psychophysics

- Sensation refers to the immediate experiences generated by simple stimuli, whereas perception involves additional organization and meaning. The boundary between the terms is blurred.
- Psychophysics investigates the relationship between physical stimuli and psychological reactions.
- Two approaches to detection involve the classical psychophysical approach and signal detection theory, which points out that expectations and motivations influence an observer's criterion.
- In research on discrimination, Weber's law notes that there is a predictable relationship between the amount the stimulus must be changed to be noticeably different and the size of the original stimulus.

Vision

Stop and think about your perceptual experiences at this very moment. You may be aware of sound, touch, smell, and taste, but it is probably sight that is most noticeable. This extraordinarily rich sense supplies us with knowledge (for example, you just read about Weber's law); social information (for example, whether your friend's face is smiling or scowling); entertainment (for example, movies, music videos, and art galleries); and information necessary for survival (for example, warning signs). Just as vision dominates our perceptual experiences, it has dominated the research in sensation and perception. As a result, we know far more about visual stimuli, sensory processing, and complex perceptual phenomena in vision than we know about the other senses. Let us begin with an introduction to the visual system.

The Visual System

The human eye is about the size of a large olive, yet it performs an impressive variety of tasks with remarkable accuracy and efficiency. The eye processes information about shape, color, texture, and distance—even though it is less than 2 inches in diameter.

The visual stimulus that initiates this impressive variety of tasks is light. Light is one form of electromagnetic radiation. Electromagnetic radiation includes all forms of waves that are produced by electrically charged particles. Therefore, a star in the Big Dipper, which is 90 light-years away, generates electrically charged particles. Ultimately, that stimulus produces physiological changes in the light

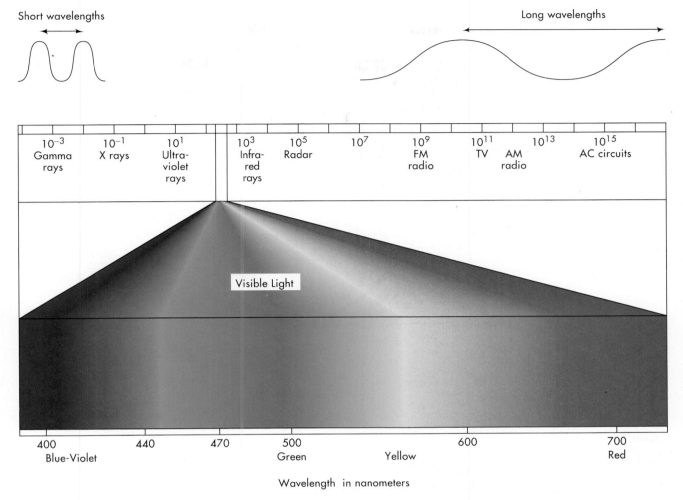

Short wavelengths

Long wavelengths

| 10^{-3} Gamma rays | 10^{-1} X rays | 10^1 Ultra-violet rays | 10^3 Infra-red rays | 10^5 Radar | 10^7 | 10^9 FM radio | 10^{11} TV | AM radio | 10^{13} | 10^{15} AC circuits |

Visible Light

| 400 Blue-Violet | 440 | 470 | 500 Green | Yellow | 600 | 700 Red |

Wavelength in nanometers

Figure 4.2
The electromagnetic spectrum.

receptors in your eyes, enabling you to see a distinct pinpoint of light in the clear night sky.

Figure 4.2 shows that humans see only a small part of the electromagnetic radiation spectrum. We cannot see the shorter ultraviolet rays that tan our skin or the longer infrared rays or radio waves.

Light travels in waves, and **wavelength** is the distance between two peaks in these waves. This distance is measured in nanometers (abbreviated nm), which equal 1 billionth of a meter. We see light in the wavelength range between about 400 nm and 700 nm.

Wavelength is a characteristic of light that helps to determine the **hue** or color of a visual stimulus. The height of the light wave, or **amplitude**, is the characteristic that determines the **brightness** of a visual stimulus. Thus, the wavelengths in a bright sky-blue color are relatively close together and tall, whereas the wavelengths in a dark shade of red are relatively far apart and short.

The Anatomy of the Eye   Figure 4.3 illustrates the major structures of the eye. The **cornea** is a clear membrane with a curved structure that helps to bend light rays when they enter the eye. Just behind the cornea is the **iris**, a ring of muscles that gives your eyes a color ranging from pale blue to dark brown. The tiny muscles within the iris contract and dilate to change the amount of light that enters the eye. The opening in the center of the iris is called the **pupil**.

Figure 4.3
Inside the human eye.

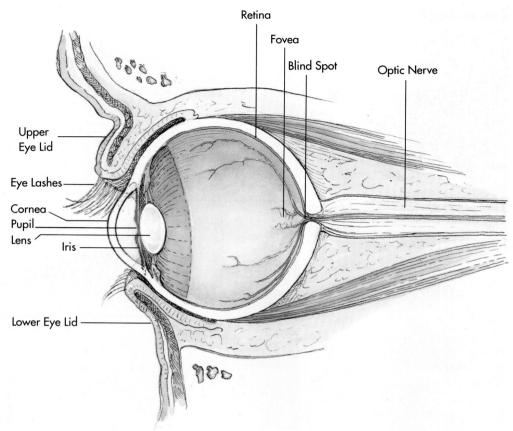

Figure 4.4
A diagram of the kinds of cells in the retina.

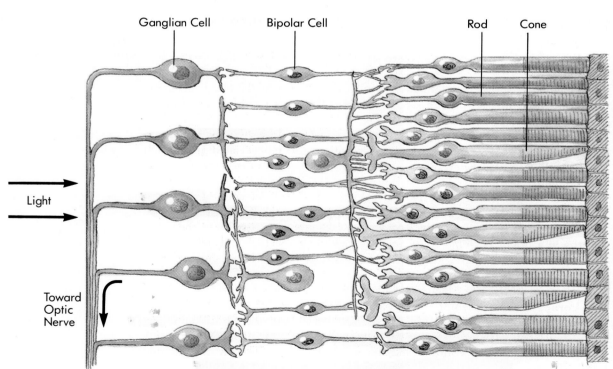

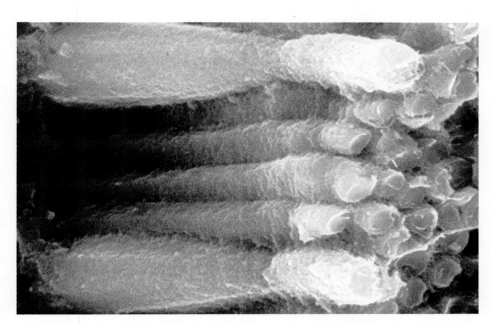

An enlarged photograph of rods and cones, as shown by an electron microscope. Note that the cylinder-shaped structures are rods and the tapered structures are cones.

Directly behind the iris and the pupil is the **lens**, which changes shape to focus on objects that are nearby or far away. The lens completes the process begun by the cornea of bending the light rays so that they gather in focus at a point on or near the retina, at the back of the eye.

The **retina** absorbs light rays and converts them into a form that can be transmitted by the neurons. The retina is a vitally important part of the eye, yet it is only as thick as a page in this book. Notice the tiny region of the retina called the **fovea**, an area in which vision is the sharpest. We discuss why this area is especially significant when we consider eye movements in reading.

Cells in the Retina   Figure 4.4 shows four different kinds of retinal cells that all have a critical function in converting light into sight.

The two kinds of cells that respond to light are called cones and rods. **Cones** are responsible for color vision, and they operate best in well-lit conditions. **Rods** handle black-and-white vision; they are not sensitive to the different colors of the spectrum. However, when the lighting is poor, rods function better than cones.

These two kinds of cells also differ in their distribution throughout the retina. Cones are concentrated primarily in the fovea; rods are found mostly outside the fovea. There are only about 6 million cones, but there are about 125 million rods (Pugh, 1988).

The structure of the retina illustrates the theme that humans are remarkably well equipped to function in their environment. Rather than having only one kind of light receptor that would be required to perform a variety of tasks in a variety of different conditions, we have two specialized receptors; each excels in its own area. When you inspected the photograph of the rose in Figure 4.1, your cones were active in transmitting color information in a well-lit situation. In contrast, rods are active when you stargaze at night. Rods are highly sensitive in detecting faint spots of light under poor illumination.

The cones and rods convert light into electrical activity at the cell membrane, a process called **transduction**. This electrical message is received by the **bipolar cells** and passed on to the next level in visual processing—the ganglion cells. The **ganglion cells** collect information from the bipolar cells and bring it farther toward the brain.

The Blind Spot

Close your right eye and use your left eye to look at the X. Gradually move this page toward your eye and then away. Keep the distance in the range of 5 to 15 inches, and do not let your focus drift away from the X. At some point, you will reach a distance at which the butterfly seems to disappear. At this distance, the butterfly is falling on your blind spot. However, in daily life you are usually unaware of the blind spot for two reasons: (1) The left eye usually picks up something that the right eye misses, and (2) the human visual system spontaneously tends to complete an object in which a part is missing.

×

The entire retina contains only about 1 million ganglion cells. Because the retina has about 6 million cones and 125 million rods, many receptor cells must share each ganglion cell. On the retina—as in life itself—the sharing is far from equal. The cones receive more than their share. In the foveal region of the retina, which is rich with cones, a typical ganglion cell might receive information from fewer than 10 cones. When a cone-rich area of the retina examines an intricate picture, most of the tiny details will be passed on to the ganglion cells. In contrast, in the rod-rich edge of the retina, a ganglion cell might receive information from

Figure 4.5
The visual pathway from the eye to the brain.

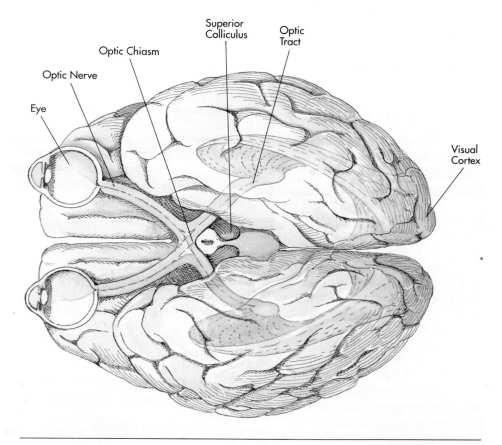

Optic Chiasm

Superior Colliculus

Optic Tract

Optic Nerve

Eye

Visual Cortex

100 rods. Suppose that region of the retina was exposed to a pattern of narrow black-and-white stripes. The rods might pick up that detailed information about black and white, but the information would all converge on a single ganglion, resulting in a blurry gray. An important implication of this unequal sharing of ganglion cells is that vision is sharper in the cone-rich fovea than in the rod-rich edges.

Figure 4.4 also shows how the axons of the ganglion cells gather together. This collection of ganglion-cell axons is called the optic nerve. The **optic nerve**, which is nearly the same diameter as your little finger, travels out of the eye and onward to higher levels of visual processing. Turn back to Figure 4.3 to notice that the location where the optic nerve leaves the retina is called the **blind spot**. Neither rods nor cones inhabit the blind spot, so you cannot see anything that reaches this part of the retina. Try Demonstration 4.2 to experience your own blind spot.

From the Eye to the Brain   Figure 4.5 illustrates how information travels in its route to the cerebral cortex. You can see how the optic nerves come together at a location called the **optic chiasm**. At this point, the ganglion-cell ends split and regroup. As a consequence, everything that was originally registered on the left side of each retina ends up traveling toward the left side of the brain; everything from the right side of the retinas travels toward the right side. As you might guess, this complicated partial crossover arrangement accomplishes something important for the human visual system. We have **binocular vision**; our two eyes work together and we have partially overlapping fields of view. An object on your left is registered on both your right and left retinas. However, information about that object will end up on the same side of your brain, where that information can be combined.

Those ganglion cells that originated in the retina and traveled through the optic chiasm eventually stop at the thalamus. New neurons then travel from the thalamus to the **visual cortex**, the outer part of the brain that is concerned with vision. The visual cortex is located at the back of your brain, just above your neck.

How do the cells in the cortex operate? Researchers in neuroscience have uncovered important information about the structure and function of the visual cortex. Much of this research has used the single-cell recording technique discussed in chapter 3. Two prominent researchers, David Hubel and Torsten Wiesel (1965, 1979), inserted a tiny electrode into an animal's visual cortex in order to record action potentials from individual cells. They systematically presented a series of visual stimuli to the specific region of the retina that was thought to be monitored by the cortex cell. For each stimulus, they recorded the response rate. Then they moved on to another cell and another set of stimuli.

Hubel and Wiesel discovered that the cells in the visual cortex were extremely specialized with respect to the kind of visual stimulus that provoked the highest response rate. For example, some cells have been called **feature detectors** because they respond to very specific features located in a more complex stimulus. For example, one particular neuron might produce a sudden burst of activity only when a vertical line is presented. Another neuron may require a horizontal line, and yet another "prefers" a line tilted 15 degrees. Other neurons in different parts of the visual cortex respond most to moving objects rather than to objects that remain stationary. Still other neurons are so picky that they might respond energetically only if a right angle containing lines of certain lengths moved diagonally upward and toward the right (Lennie, 1980).

Neurons in even more sophisticated areas of the visual cortex respond only to complex visual patterns. In one research project, Charles Gross and his colleagues at Harvard University were using the single-cell recording technique in a monkey (Thompson, 1985). They presented the customary variety of visual stimuli—lights, bars, and other simple stimuli. The neuron in this particular area failed to respond to the stimuli, and so the researchers decided to move on to another cell. One of the experimenters bid that cell a symbolic farewell by waving his hand in front of the monkey's eye. The cell immediately began to fire rapidly to the moving hand! The excited researchers then cut out a variety of hand-shaped stimuli and waved them in front of the monkey's eye. This cell proved to respond most excitedly to a hand shaped like a monkey's paw.

As we have toured the visual system, we have seen that the cells in the first step of visual processing—the rods and the cones—require only a small amount of light to respond. Within the visual cortex, however, the cells become increasingly finicky, until they respond only to selected stimuli containing certain contours and movement patterns. Later in the chapter, we examine the distinctive-features approach to shape perception, which argues that this information about lines, angles, and contours is essential in helping us recognize shapes such as letters of the alphabet.

Color Vision

An artist I know once decided to add blue food coloring to the creamed corn to be served at dinner. She thought it would add visual interest to a meal that might otherwise look confined to the yellowish 620-nm portion of the visible spectrum. Her father refused to eat the corn; the violation of his expectations about color was simply too overwhelming. Color seems to be a critical part of an object's identity, and people object when such a crucial feature is altered.

In the history of research on color vision, most of the early studies were inspired by a debate between supporters of two different theories of color vision (Haber, 1985a). This conflict has been resolved peacefully. Researchers now conclude that both theories are correct, but they apply to different regions of the visual processing system.

The **trichromatic theory** of color vision points out that there are three kinds of cones, each sensitive to light from a different portion of the spectrum. This theory was originally proposed in the 1800s by an English physician named Thomas Young and a German physiologist named Hermann von Helmholtz. About a century later, researchers began to uncover physiological evidence that the visual system indeed does contain three kinds of cones (Dartnall, Bowmaker, & Mollon, 1983; Rushton, 1958). One kind of cone is most sensitive to short wavelengths (in the 450-nm range), another to medium wavelengths (in the 550-nm range), and a third to long wavelengths (in the 600-nm range). By combining different stimulation levels from each of these three kinds of cones, the visual system can produce the wide variety of perceptions we experience in our daily lives.

Trichromatic theory explains how we see the various colors of the spectrum, but it leaves some questions unanswered. For example, why is it that we can perceive a greenish blue but not a yellowish blue? Also, how can we explain **chromatic adaptation**, a phenomenon illustrated in Demonstration 4.3, in which prolonged exposure to yellow produces blue, and prolonged exposure to green produces red?

Ewald Hering, a German physician, developed the opponent-process theory in the late 1800s to account for color phenomena such as impossible color combinations and color afterimages. The current interpretation of color vision is that trichromatic theory explains how the cones gather color information. This information is then passed on to the ganglion cells, which operate in an opponent-process fashion.

A Color Afterimage

Set a sheet of plain white paper to the side of the picture below. Stare at the picture for 30 to 40 seconds, being certain not to move your eyes. Quickly transfer your gaze to the white paper and notice the afterimage. You can blink several times to preserve the afterimage.

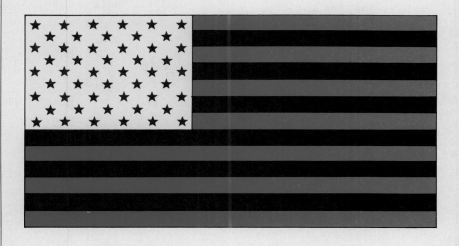

According to current color perception explanations, **opponent-process theory** specifies that a ganglion cell responds by increasing its activity when one color is present and decreasing its activity when another color is present. For example, one cell will increase activity when exposed to yellow colors and decrease it when exposed to blue colors. A different cell will increase activity when exposed to blue and decrease it when exposed to yellow. Thus, this set of cells works in an opposing, or mirror-image, fashion. A second opponent system works the same way for red and green. A third opponent system responds to light and dark. All of these opponent processes occur at the ganglion level, before the electrical stimulation leaves the retina.

Let us see how opponent-process theory explains the two-color phenomena discussed earlier. You cannot see a yellowish blue because the cell that increases its activity to yellow will decrease its activity to blue and vice versa. (Similarly, you cannot see a greenish red.) You saw a blue background for the stars because prolonged viewing of yellow produced chromatic adaptation, weakening the yellow response and leaving its opponent color—blue—relatively strong. (Similarly, prolonged staring at the green stripes will leave the opponent color—red—relatively strong.)

For some of you reading this section, the discussion about color phenomena may not match your personal experience. It is possible that you have a color deficiency. Although color deficiencies are relatively rare in females, about 5% of males have a color deficiency. Try Demonstration 4.4, which is a typical item in a much more extensive test for color deficiencies.

Incidentally, note that the appropriate term is *color deficiency*. The term *color blindness* is inaccurate because most of the people affected do see some colors. Only a very small number of people see no color at all. Their perceptual world is similar to your world on a dark night—everything is simply a different shade of gray (Hurvich, 1981).

Demonstration 4.4

An Example of an Item From a Color-Deficiency Test

Find a location in which the lighting is a little less bright than you normally would use for reading. Examine the test item below. What numbers do you see? The answer ap-pears at the end of the chapter. This item tests for sensitivity to deep reds. A complete test of color deficiencies would include a large number of items in each of many colors.

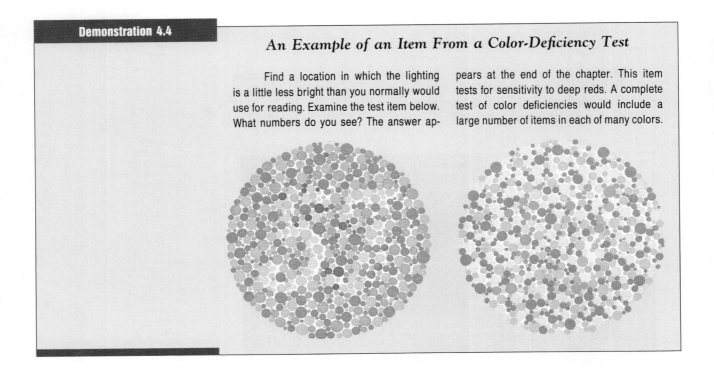

Basic Visual Functions

We have seen that the visual system can extract information about an object's shape and color. In addition, the visual system can appreciate fine details, and it can adapt to a wide variety of lighting conditions. The eyes also can move in ways you may not have previously appreciated.

Acuity   Suppose that you are walking in an isolated area, and you spot a shape in the distance—is it a person or a bush? Does the dot on the horizon represent one tree or two trees close together? Is there a yellow spot—perhaps a yellow flower—next to the birch tree? These all represent acuity tasks. **Visual acuity** is the ability to see precise details in a scene. Because visual acuity tests are easy to administer, they represent the standard method of measuring visual ability (Olzak & Thomas, 1986). People differ from one another on numerous perceptual tasks. However, we are most aware of differences in visual acuity, because people with poor acuity need corrective lenses. Table 4.2 describes three common kinds of focusing disorders that influence acuity—nearsightedness, farsightedness, and as-tigmatism—as well as some other visual problems.

What does it mean to have 20/40 vision on an acuity test? Usually this kind of score is obtained by asking an observer to read an eye chart that has rows of letters ranging from large to small, standing at a distance 20 feet away from the chart. If you can read the letters that a person with normal vision can read at 20 feet, then you have 20/20 vision. Suppose you must stand closer—say, 10 feet away—to read those same letters. Then you have 10/20 vision. It is customarily doubled, however, because numbers below 20 are not typically used. Your vision would therefore be called 20/40 vision. A person whose vision with corrective lenses is poorer than 20/200 is considered legally blind (Landers, 1988).

Dark Adaptation   You have probably had an experience like this: In the middle of a sunny afternoon, you enter a movie theater. The movie has already started, and you grope your way through the theater, reaching for what you hope is the

Table 4.2   *Some Common Visual Disorders*

FOCUSING DISORDERS
- Nearsightedness. If the eyeball is too long or the lens of the eye is too thick, the images of objects are focused in front of the retina. Nearsighted people can only see objects clearly if they are *nearby.*
- Farsightedness. If the eyeball is too short or the lens of the eye is too thin, the images of objects are focused at a point behind the retina. Farsighted people can only see objects clearly if they are *far away.*
- Astigmatism. People with astigmatism have a cornea that is not perfectly curved; some areas have more curvature than other areas. As a result, some regions will appear blurry.

DISORDERS INVOLVING EYE COORDINATION
- Strabismus, or "cross-eye." This disorder occurs when the muscles of the two eyes do not work together. As a result, an object's image does not fall on corresponding parts of the right and left retina. This disorder should be corrected in early childhood to allow the development of proper binocular vision. The disorder occurs in about 3% of the population (Sanders, 1986).
- Stereoblindness. If strabismus is not corrected, stereoblindness develops. With this disorder, people cannot use the depth information from binocular vision as a depth cue (to be discussed later).

DISORDERS OF THE LENS AND RETINA
- Cataracts. When the lens loses its transparency and becomes too cloudy, light cannot pass through to the retina. Most cataracts occur in older people (Vaughan & Asbury, 1986). The lens of the eye can be surgically removed, and a substitute lens can be implanted, or special contact lenses or eyeglasses can be worn.
- Diabetic retinopathy. Blindness can occur in people who have had severe diabetes for many years. It occurs because fluid leaks out from the thickened blood vessels that supply the retina.

OTHER DISORDERS
- Corneal damage. An object can scratch the cornea or become lodged in the cornea. Anyone with corneal damage should immediately receive medical care. Otherwise, disease germs could enter, potentially destroying the cornea within 24 hours (Vaughan & Asbury, 1986).
- Glaucoma. The fluids inside the eyeball normally maintain the eye's characteristic shape. However, in glaucoma, there is extra fluid within the eye, causing too much pressure and potentially causing deterioration of the ganglion cells in the retina and the optic nerve. People over the age of 40 should be tested periodically for glaucoma to avoid these severe problems.

back of an empty seat, rather than someone's shoulder. (My grandfather was once asked whether he had known the woman who had sat on him in a dark theater. Thinking fast, he replied that he did not know her name, but he could identify her nationality: She was a Laplander.)

The darkened theater experience is one example of **dark adaptation**; your eyes adjust and become more sensitive as you remain in the dark. As you have discovered, your sensitivity increases tremendously after just 10 minutes. Dark adaptation allows us to extend the range of light levels in which the visual system can function. The illumination from the bright noon sun is about 100 million times as intense as the illumination from the moon (Hood & Finkelstein, 1986). Nonetheless, the visual system is so superbly designed that we can function in both kinds of illumination, as well as in the vast intermediate region.

How can we explain dark adaptation? Consistent with the theme that humans are complicated, most human processes and behaviors have more than one explanation. Three mechanisms help account for dark adaptation: (1) The pupils dilate to let more light pass through. (2) Dark-adapted rods contain a greater amount of the special chemical that determines sensitivity (Pugh, 1988). (3) Neurons beyond the level of the rods must play an important role, though the details of their action are unclear (Green & Powers, 1982).

○ ○

In Depth: Eye Movements

We have seen that the retina records both the orientation of lines and the color of stimuli, and the visual system ensures both acuity and proper functioning in a wide variety of illuminations. The flexibility of your visual system is even further enhanced by eye movements. Your eyes are not locked in a fixed position. Instead, you can follow the flight of a bird using smooth pursuit eye movements. You can move your eyes inward to focus on the tip of your nose. Your eyes even make tiny involuntary movements when you stare at an object for a long time. However, the most common kind of eye movement involves the rapid little jumps your eyes make when you read, drive, or inspect the various parts of a picture. Let us examine this kind of eye movement in detail.

Your eyes follow the flight of a bird with smooth pursuit movements.

Saccadic Eye Movements   The most common kind of eye movement is saccadic movement (pronounced suh-*kaad*-dick). **Saccadic movement** refers to the rapid movement of the eye from one location to the next. Figure 4.3 illustrated the fovea, which is the region of the retina with the highest acuity. Saccadic movements are necessary to bring the fovea into position over the object you want to see most clearly. To help you appreciate saccadic movement, try Demonstration 4.5.

Saccadic movement differs from the eye movement we use to pursue the path of a seagull or a baseball because saccadic movement is jerky. Saccadic movement is also more rapid—the eye can move through a 60-degree arc in just $\frac{1}{10}$ second (Hallett, 1986). Surprisingly, even relatively large saccadic movements do not tire the eye substantially (Fuchs & Binder, 1983).

Psychologists know the most about the saccadic movements used in reading. For example, researchers know that:

1. The size of the average saccadic movement is 5 to 10 letters (McConkie & Zola, 1984).

2. The eye avoids blank regions and words that offer little information, such as *the* or *an* (Balota et al., 1985; McConkie & Zola, 1984).

3. The size of the saccade will be shorter if the following word in the sentence is either misspelled or long (McConkie & Zola, 1984).

The Perceptual Span   Psychologists also have examined the **perceptual span**, which is the region seen when the eye pauses after a saccadic movement. Think for a moment how you might measure this perceptual span. Could you simply ask people to report what they saw, that is, how many letters they could clearly perceive? The problem with this approach is one we often encounter in psychology: People often do not have access to their mental processes. In this case, they may not be able to report accurately on their perceptions.

Researchers in the area of eye movements had difficulty measuring perceptual span objectively. In recent years this difficulty was overcome by a creative method called the **gaze-contingent paradigm**: The reader's eyes are tracked as he or she reads material displayed on a screen, and the text display is carefully altered as the person continues reading. The researchers can replace letters in certain parts of the text. Suppose that the sentence you are now reading were displayed on a screen. The researchers could, for example, keep all the letters intact that are 10 letters to the right and 10 letters to the left of the letter on which you are focusing. Outside of this region, the passage collapses into gibberish. Naturally, if the researchers replace letters that are too close to the word you are reading, you

Saccadic Eye Movements

Glance over at the opposite page and select a word in the middle of the column. Focus on that specific word, and notice how the letters are increasingly fuzzy in the words that are farther from your target word. (If you cannot explain why, check the discussion of rods and cones in the retina.)

Now start to read the entire sentence. Are you aware that your eye is advancing across the page in small, jerky leaps? Try to read the next sentences by letting your eyes roll smoothly across the page. You will probably find that your eyes can indeed move smoothly, but you do not seem to be perceiving the words.

would make too many errors or slow your reading rate. The goal of the gaze-contingent paradigm is to determine how many letters can be replaced without altering a person's reading pattern.

Underwood and McConkie (1985) established that the typical reader has a perceptual span that includes four letters to the left of the focus point and eight letters to the right. In other words, as long as that region remained intact, people could read normally. When letters within that region were replaced, people's reading patterns were altered. Table 4.3 illustrates this perceptual span.

Notice that this perceptual span is clearly lopsided. There are only four positions to the left, whereas there are eight to the right. This lopsidedness makes sense for readers of English and other left-to-right languages; we do not need to monitor what we have already seen, but we need to know what to expect in the material we will soon be reading. Interestingly, readers of Hebrew have perceptual spans that are lopsided in the opposite direction, with more positions to the left than to the right (Pollatsek et al., 1981). This reversed lopsidedness is entirely appropriate because Hebrew is read from right to left.

The information about saccadic movements provides clear evidence for the theme that humans are well equipped for functioning in their environment. The design of the eye provides a small region of the retina with high visual acuity. If your eyes remained in a fixed position above a page of text, you could never read beyond the third word. Fortunately, the visual system solves this problem by allowing your eyes to jump across the page. However, we have seen that the eye does not make random jumps; for example, it avoids certain useless regions of the text. Furthermore, we have noted that the perceptual span, which follows each saccadic movement, allows us to see where we are going more clearly than where we have been.

Table 4.3 *The Perceptual Span*

Unaltered text:	The gaze-contingent paradigm was used to study . . . ↑
Text with a very narrow unaltered region:	Sxf oklm qontinpvyg jdfbvkip exw dwma uy bvqwr . . . ↑
Text with an unaltered region that is just barely legible:	Sxf oklm-contingent pdfbvkip exw dwma up bvqwr . . . ↑

Note: The arrow indicates the letter on which the reader is focusing.

○ ○

Shape Perception

We have examined many of the visual system's capabilities. The visual system can process information about color, it can see fine details in a scene (acuity), it can function in both bright sunlight and pale moonlight, and it can execute several different kinds of specialized movements.

You have read only part of the story, however, because now we move into the topics more commonly associated with perception than with sensation. These topics include the perception of shape, motion, distance, constancy, and illusion.

If you lacked shape perception, your visual world would consist of random patches of light and dark, a disorderly mass of colored and uncolored fragments. If you look up from your book, however, you will notice that your visual world contains objects that have distinct borders and clear-cut shapes. Pattern and organization appear in even the messiest of rooms, and we are able to recognize objects—a lamp, a psychology professor, and a letter of the alphabet. Two important aspects of shape perception are organization and pattern recognition.

Organization   If you look out a nearby window, you will appreciate that the visual world is organized. An automobile seems to form a distinct shape against the background of the parking lot, and the lamppost does not blend into the grass beneath it. One important component of the organization in our perceptual worlds is called the **figure-ground relationship**. When two areas share a common boundary (e.g., the contour of the automobile and the parking lot that surrounds it), the figure is the distinct shape with clearly defined edges. The ground is simply the part that is left over, forming the background in the scene. Take a moment to glance through some of the pictures in this textbook, noting the relationship between the figure and the ground.

In the section on history in the first chapter of this book, you were introduced to the Gestalt approach, which was prominent in Europe in the first decades of this century (Hochberg, 1988). According to the **Gestalt approach**, we perceive objects as well-organized, whole structures, instead of separate, isolated parts. The Gestalt psychologists stressed that our ability to see shape and pattern is determined by subtle interrelationships among the parts (Greene, 1985).

Edgar Rubin (1915/1958), a Gestalt psychologist from Denmark, reached several conclusions about the figure-ground relationship:

1. The figure has a definite shape, whereas the ground seems shapeless. Notice the clear shape of the seagull on page 108, for example, in contrast to the shapeless sky.

2. The ground seems to continue behind the figure. For example, you *know* that there is sky behind that seagull.

3. The figure seems closer to the viewer, with a clear location in space. In contrast, the ground seems farther away; it lacks a clear location. In the seagull picture, for example, the sky is clearly farther away from you.

In almost all cases, the figure-ground relationship is clear-cut. Occasionally, however, the relationship is ambiguous, often because an artist has created it that way. Figure 4.6 is an example of an ambiguous figure-ground relationship, drawn by the Dutch artist M. C. Escher. Notice that in the middle region, the birds and the fish take turns becoming figure and ground.

We discriminate figure from ground, imposing one important kind of organization on our visual experience. In addition, we organize visual stimuli into

Figure 4.6
An etching by M.C. Escher, illustrating ambiguous figure-ground relationship.

patterns and groups. The Gestalt psychologists developed several laws of grouping to describe why certain objects seem to go together, instead of remaining isolated and independent:

1. The **law of proximity** (or law of nearness) states that objects near each other tend to be perceived as a unit.

2. The **law of similarity** states that objects similar to each other tend to be seen as a unit.

3. The **law of good continuation** states that we tend to perceive smooth, continuous lines, rather than discontinuous fragments.

4. The **law of closure** states that a figure with a gap will be perceived as a closed, intact figure.

Each of these laws is illustrated in Figure 4.7.

Pattern Recognition   How do we recognize patterns? It seems so simple, because we recognize them every second we are awake. As you read, you recognize the letters in a word, and then you recognize the word itself. A tall, slender configuration—wearing a moustache, plaid shirt, and ragged jeans—approaches; you recognize him as Henry, the student who sits near you in your political science class. You can recognize a familiar person in countless situations, whether he or

Figure 4.7
The Gestalt laws of grouping.

(upper left) The law of proximity. You perceive this arrangement of desks in terms of vertical columns, rather than horizontal rows, because you group items together that are near each other.

(upper right) The law of similarity. You group this arrangement in terms of horizontal rows, grouping together the cats on this wrapping paper because they are facing the same direction.

(lower left) The law of good continuation. You see the design on this plaid shirt in terms of straight, continuous lines, rather than lines that form right-angle zigzags.

(lower right) The law of closure. You see the left-hand border of this greeting card as a closed, intact edge, even though it is interrupted by the leaf that the dove is carrying.

she is near or far, standing or sitting, laughing or crying, in sunshine or in shadow (Corballis, 1988).

Psychologists acknowledge that it is a major challenge to explain how we manage to recognize objects so readily. There are two major theories of pattern recognition. Pattern recognition is such a major achievement that we need more than one explanation.

The distinctive-features approach, developed by Eleanor Gibson, focuses on how we identify letters of the alphabet. Gibson (1969) argues that we differentiate between letters on the basis of **distinctive features**, which are characteristics such as straight versus curved lines. Thus, the letter *E* has four straight lines, whereas the letter *O* has none. We recognize the letter *C* because it is the only curved letter with an opening at the side that is also symmetrical. The distinctive-features approach to pattern perception is based on feature detectors, those neurons in the visual cortex that are sensitive to lines, angles, and contours.

According to the second major theory, **prototype-matching theory**, we store abstract, idealized patterns, or **prototypes**, in memory. When we see a particular object, we compare it with this prototype. If it matches, we recognize and identify the pattern. If Henry from your political science class shaved his moustache, you would still recognize him because that stimulus pattern matches your prototype closely enough.

In the section on signal detection theory, we saw that expectations and prior knowledge influence the probability of saying, "Yes, I perceive the stimulus." Similarly, pattern recognition also depends upon expectations and prior knowledge, as well as sensory activity. Psychologists acknowledge that pattern recognition depends upon both bottom-up and top-down processing.

Bottom-up processing depends on the information from the senses at the bottom (or most basic) level of perception. The stimulus is registered on the retina, and the rods, the cones, and other neurons begin to produce bursts of electrical activity, which ultimately reach the visual cortex. However, bottom-up processing will not be sufficient for you to recognize Henry; top-down processing is also necessary.

Top-down processing emphasizes the importance of the observers' concepts, expectations, and prior knowledge—the kind of information stored at the top (or highest level) of perception. Part of the reason you recognize Henry when you see him is that you expect to see him in certain places. Out of context—in your hometown hardware store—he would be more difficult to recognize.

Some of the most convincing evidence for top-down processing comes from research on letter recognition. According to the **word-superiority effect**, we perceive letters better when they appear in words than when they appear in strings of unrelated letters (Taylor & Taylor, 1983). For example, suppose you are looking at a sequence of blurry letters. It is easier to recognize the letter *A* when you see it in the word *THAT* than when you see it in the unpronounceable, meaningless nonword *TTAH* (Chastain, 1986; Reicher, 1969). The surrounding letters in the word *THAT* provide a context that facilitates the recognition of each of the letters. If the word-superiority effect (and, more generally, top-down processing) did not operate, you would not be able to read so quickly and so accurately. In fact, you would probably still be reading the first chapter of this book!

Motion Perception

Our discussion of perception has emphasized shapes that are static—a letter frozen on a textbook page or a row of fish immobilized in an etching. But you glance up from your textbook to a world that is rich with motion. Consider a basketball game, for example. You perceive players running and jumping, balls soaring and bouncing, and spectators waving their arms and leaping to their feet.

Motion perception is a basic skill. Even primitive animals and insects such as the fly have excellent motion perception (Johansson, 1985; Ullman, 1983). In recent years, some of the most interesting discoveries about motion perception involve **biological motion**, which is the pattern of movement exhibited by people and other living things. Gunnar Johansson, a Swedish psychologist, attached small flashlight bulbs to the major joints of a male colleague, as shown in Figure 4.8. Johansson made a movie of this man as he moved around the darkened room. Johansson then showed the movie to groups of observers who were asked to interpret the pattern of lights. Even though there were only 12 tiny lights, the observers could readily tell the difference between walking and jogging movements.

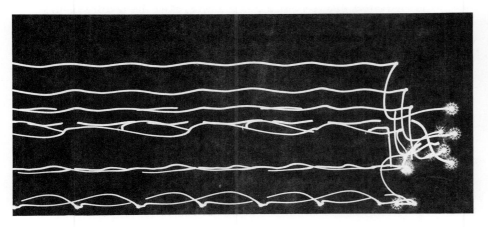

Figure 4.8
To illustrate biological motion, a man wears flashlight bulbs at his joints, and a film is made of his movements. In this particular photo, the camera shutter was kept open for several seconds and the lights trace paths in the picture. He was initially sitting in a chair at the right with one leg swung over the other. Then he stood up and walked across the floor to the left.

When the man pretended to limp, the observers spotted the change in body movement (Johansson, 1975; Johansson et al., 1980). Other researchers have discovered that observers watching a pattern of lights can distinguish a female walker from a male walker (Cutting, 1983). Observers can also tell whether a person is preparing to throw an object 6 feet or 30 feet (Runeson & Frykholm, 1983).

Biological motion is complicated to describe mathematically, yet it is easy for our visual system to process (Johansson, 1985). We are so quick and so accurate in identifying various kinds of biological motion that researchers have proposed that some neurons may be specially organized to decode and interpret the motion of other living organisms (Johansson, 1985).

Distance Perception

Except for reading, most of our visual activity requires looking at objects that are solid rather than flat, or examining pictures or television screens, which try to capture depth and distance. Let us move into the third dimension to consider distance perception.

A major challenge for psychologists interested in perception is to explain how we are able to know that an object has depth, as well as height and width, and how we can appreciate that an eraser is closer to us than the chalkboard. After all, the retina can only register height and width; the chalkboard is not represented as being *deeper* into the surface of the retina in comparison with the eraser.

There is no single explanation for depth perception. In fact, most perception textbooks list at least a dozen (e.g., Coren & Ward, 1989; Goldstein, 1989; Matlin & Foley, 1992). You can probably guess by this point in the book that any process which occurs so automatically and so accurately is likely to be facilitated by a variety of factors.

Some of these sources of information about distance are **monocular**—they can be seen with just one eye. These monocular factors, which are illustrated in Figures 4.9 and 4.10, include the following:

Figure 4.9
It is easy to see distance in this photo because it provides information about relative size, overlap, texture gradient, and linear perspective.

1. *Relative size:* If two similar objects appear together, we judge the one that occupies more space on the retina to be closer to us. (Notice the relative size of the arches in Figure 4.9.)

2. *Overlap:* When one object overlaps another, we judge the completely visible object to be closer than the partly covered object.

3. *Texture gradient:* The texture of surfaces becomes denser as the distance increases. Although this is an important factor in distance perception, its value has only recently been acknowledged (Gibson, 1979; Hagen, 1985). Notice, for example, how the texture of the rocks in Figure 4.10 is much more tightly packed and dense toward the horizon. (To appreciate texture gradient, turn the picture upside down and notice how the texture looks bizarre.)

4. *Linear perspective:* Parallel lines appear to meet in the distance, as you probably learned in art class.

5. *Atmospheric perspective:* Distant objects often look blurry and bluish. Notice in Figure 4.10 how the distant hills look grayish blue.

Other information about depth requires two eyes. The most important of these binocular factors is binocular disparity. Your eyes are about 3 inches apart, a distance that guarantees that each eye receives a slightly different view of any object. The difference between the two retinal images of an object is known as

Figure 4.10
In this photo, distance is conveyed by relative size, texture gradient, and atmospheric perspective.

binocular disparity. Your eyes are so sensitive to binocular disparity that they can detect different views that correspond to one thousandth of a millimeter when registered on the retina (Yellott, 1981). As Demonstration 4.6 illustrates, binocular disparity is smaller for faraway objects. As a consequence, binocular disparity conveys useful information about distance.

Binocular information is clearly useful in depth perception, and people are substantially more accurate when they have information from both eyes than when they have only monocular information (Foley, 1980, 1985). Take a moment to review the "Disorders Involving Eye Coordination" listed earlier in Table 4.2 to appreciate more fully why these disorders should not be treated casually.

Constancy

When you move around in the world, you approach objects and then move away. However, the telephone does not seem to grow in size as you run to answer it. The image of a bus on your retina grows larger as it approaches you, yet you know it really does not change its size. As Figure 4.11 shows, the textbook assumes a different shape on your retina when you view it from a different angle; it projects a trapezoid shape, rather than a rectangle. Still, you know it did not *really* change its shape. The phenomenon described in these examples is **constancy**, which is the tendency for qualities of objects (such as size and shape) to seem to stay the same, despite changes in the way we view the objects.

Size constancy means that an object seems to stay the same size despite changes in the distance between the viewer and the object. One reason that size constancy operates is that we are familiar with an object's customary size. You know how big a bus is, so even when it is two blocks away, you know that it is customarily large. Another explanation for size constancy is that we take distance

Demonstration 4.6

Binocular Disparity

Sit in a location where you are directly in front of a small visual stimulus (e.g., a doorknob) about 8 feet away. Hold your left index finger 6 inches away from your eyes and your right index finger at arm's length. Line up both fingers so that they are in a straight line between your eyes and the visual stimulus. Close your left eye and open your right eye. Then close your right eye and open your left eye. Notice how your left finger, which is closer to your head, appears to jump a large distance, relative to that visual stim-

ulus, depending upon which eye is used to view the scene. In contrast, your right finger appears to move a much smaller distance.

This demonstration illustrates that each eye sees an object from a different angle. In the case of a nearby object (e.g., your left finger), there is a larger difference between each eye's view of the object. In the case of a faraway object (e.g., your right finger), there is a smaller difference between each eye's view of the object. That is, the binocular disparity is smaller.

Figure 4.11
This textbook seems to maintain its rectangular shape, even though it would project a trapezoidal shape onto your retina if you were to view it from the angle shown in the photo on the right.

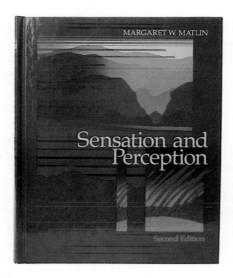

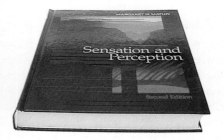

into account when we see an object (Rock, 1983). Without being consciously aware of the process, we figure out an object's true size. Even animals seem to use this principle, so it cannot involve complicated, conscious calculations (Gogel, 1977).

An important American theorist, James J. Gibson (1959), argued that perception is much more direct. We do not need to perform any calculations—conscious or unconscious—because the environment is rich with information. For example, you know the size of an object by comparing it to the texture of the surrounding area. If this textbook were placed on a tile floor, it would just about cover one linoleum tile, whether you viewed it from a distance of 3 feet or 30 feet. Tile, grass, strands of yarn in a carpet, and other kinds of background textures all provide a kind of yardstick against which we can preserve size constancy.

Other kinds of constancy are also demonstrated by the visual system. **Shape constancy** means that an object seems to stay the same shape, despite changes in its orientation toward the viewer. A compact disc does not distort itself into an oval when we view it from an angle; we know it remains round. Shape constancy is even stronger when shapes appear in the context of meaningful clutter—such as a messy office desk—rather than when the shapes are shown against a clean background (Lappin & Preble, 1975).

In addition, our visual system demonstrates **lightness constancy**; that is, an object seems to stay the same lightness in spite of changes in the amount of light falling on it. A pair of black shoes continues to look black in the bright sun, although these shoes may reflect more light than the white pages of this textbook if you were reading the book in a dimly lit corner. The visual system acknowledges that black shoes are dark, relative to other lighter objects in the scene.

One last important constancy is **color constancy**. We tend to see the hue of an object as staying the same in spite of changes in the color of the light falling on it. Thus, a blue shirt seems to stay about the same color whether we view it in the bright daylight, in artificial light, or even under a green light bulb.

Notice how the constancies simplify our perceptual world. We can count on objects to remain the same, even when we change the circumstances in which we view those objects. Imagine what a nightmare we would face otherwise! Objects would grow and shrink, stretch into uncharacteristic shapes, become light and dark, and assume unexpected colors. Perhaps a major movie producer will adopt this nightmarish idea. Coming soon to a theater near you—*A World Without Constancies!*

Illusions

An **illusion** is an incorrect perception. Figure 4.12 shows the most famous visual illusion—the Müller-Lyer illusion. The two lines in this illusion are really the same length. However, the "wings outward" version looks about 25% longer than the "wings inward" version. There are probably several factors that make the wings outward version look longer. One of the most likely explanations is that people judge the wings outward version to be longer because the eyes move a longer distance to perceive the entire figure. When our eyes move a longer distance, we tend to perceive that the figure is longer (Coren, 1981).

One of the themes of this textbook is that individual differences among humans are large. In the case of visual illusions, some people may perceive a large difference between the two versions of the Müller-Lyer, whereas others may perceive them to be reasonably similar. Coren and Porac (1987) investigated individual differences in susceptibility to visual illusions, and they found a negative correlation between a person's spatial ability and susceptibility to the Müller-Lyer and other illusions. Figure 4.13 is similar to the kinds of items that measure spatial ability. A person who receives a high score on this spatial ability test tends to be *less* susceptible to the illusions. (The two versions of the Müller-Lyer illusion would look fairly similar, for example.) A person who is skilled at separating the

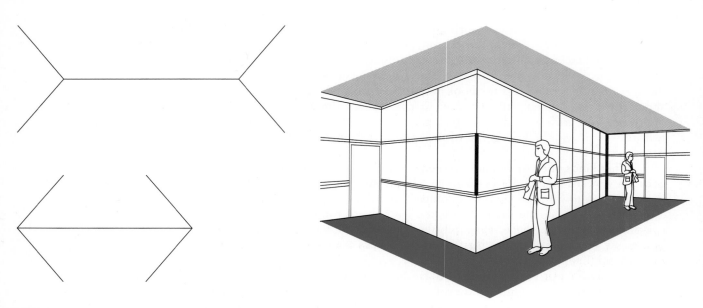

Figure 4.12
Müller-Lyer illusion.

(left) Classic Müller-Lyer illusion.

(right) In this variant of the classic Müller-Lyer illusion, compare the length of the two dark vertical lines. The additional distance cues make the illusion even stronger.

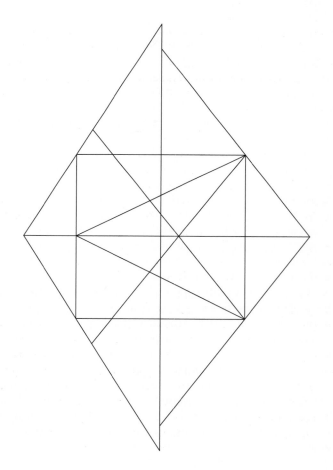

Figure 4.13
A figure similar to those measuring spatial ability; participants would be asked to locate the letter *M* in this figure. (The *M* can be rotated clockwise or counterclockwise.)

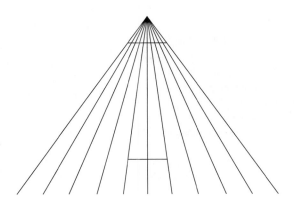

Figure 4.14
The Ponzo illusion.

letter M out from all the other irrelevant lines in Figure 4.13 would also be able to ignore the irrelevant "wings" and focus purely on line length in the Müller-Lyer illusion.

Figure 4.14 shows the Ponzo illusion. The bar on the top looks longer in this illusion, and perhaps you can figure out why. We interpret the converging set of 11 lines as conveying linear perspective: The top of the figure definitely seems farther away. Therefore, the horizontal bar that appears in the "distant" part of the figure must also be farther away. The rules of constancy tell us that we must take distance into account in judging the size of an object, so we judge that "distant" bar to be larger. This explanation for the Ponzo illusion and others that contain strong depth cues is called the **theory of misapplied constancy** (Gillam, 1980).

Our susceptibility to illusions seems to contradict the theme that humans are extremely competent and accurate. However, this theme also noted that many of our errors can be traced to strategies that usually produce correct responses. In most cases, cues suggesting linear perspective *do* correspond to a real world in which the point of convergence is more distant. It is therefore a "smart mistake" to see depth in Figure 4.14.

Why do psychologists study visual illusions? One reason is that they are intriguing and fun. We typically perceive the objects in the world so accurately that we find ourselves puzzled when we make mistakes. A second reason is that the study of illusions may help us understand the underlying perceptual processes (Westheimer, 1988). If the visual system makes consistent mistakes, we can draw conclusions about how visual information is sorted as it passes from the retina to the cortex. In the case of the Ponzo illusion, we learn that perceivers conclude that one part of a figure is farther away than another, given only minimal distance cues. We also see in the chapters on memory and cognition that our occasional errors help psychologists to identify some general principles of how people think.

A final reason for studying illusions is that they can have practical applications. For example, consider the Poggendorf illusion shown in Demonstration 4.7. In the Poggendorf illusion, a line disappears at an angle behind a solid figure. It appears on the other side of the figure at a position that seems inappropriate. In 1965, the Poggendorf illusion was responsible for a tragic plane crash (Coren & Girgus, 1978). Two airplanes were about to land in the New York City area. A cloud formation was between them, and the Poggendorf illusion created the perception that they were heading directly toward each other (similar to the line on the left and the bottom line on the right in Demonstration 4.7). Quickly, the two pilots changed their paths to correct what seemed to be an error. The planes collided. Four people died and 49 others were injured . . . and only an illusion was to blame.

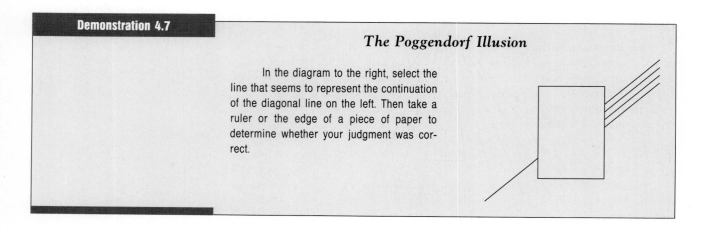

Demonstration 4.7

The Poggendorf Illusion

In the diagram to the right, select the line that seems to represent the continuation of the diagonal line on the left. Then take a ruler or the edge of a piece of paper to determine whether your judgment was correct.

Section Summary: Vision

- The retina of the eye absorbs light rays via the cones and the rods. Light is converted to electrical messages, which are passed on to other cells in the retina, ultimately reaching the visual cortex.
- We perceive color because of two processes: (1) The three kinds of cones are sensitive to different portions of the spectrum, and (2) pairs of cells at the ganglion level of the retina work in an opponent-process fashion.
- Two important features of vision are visual acuity and dark adaptation. In addition, the eye can make different kinds of movements, such as the saccadic movement used in reading.
- The figure-ground relationship and the Gestalt laws of grouping help us perceive shapes.
- Two leading theories of pattern recognition are distinctive-features theory and prototype-matching theory; top-down processing also facilitates pattern recognition.
- Humans can readily recognize biological motion and can identify subtle differences in motion.
- We perceive distance and depth because of a variety of monocular factors such as overlap and texture gradient and because of binocular disparity.
- The visual system demonstrates constancy; an object's important qualities seem to stay the same, even when we view that object from different distances and angles and in different lighting conditions.
- Illusions are incorrect perceptions that help psychologists to identify important consistencies in visual processing.

The Other Perceptual Systems

Vision is certainly the most prominent of our perceptual abilities. However, think what you would experience if all your other perceptual systems were absent and vision were your only source of information about the outside world. Without hearing, you would miss the cry of "fire" that could save your life, and you would certainly wish you could participate in conversations. Without touch and the other skin senses, you would expose yourself to objects that are harmfully hot and heavy—objects that your warning systems usually help you to avoid. Without the sense of smell, you would walk into rooms filled with smoke or poisonous gases. Without taste, you might not be motivated to eat.

Hearing

This section begins with an overview of the nature of sound and the characteristics of the auditory system. We then consider two theories of pitch perception. The last part of this section investigates four qualities of sound perception. We save the important topic of speech perception for the chapter on language and communication. Furthermore, we consider the recent research on infants' astonishing speech perception skills in chapter 10.

The Nature of Sound   I live in a house in the woods, a location that you might suspect would be nearly soundless. However, when I close my eyes and concentrate on hearing, I am amazed at the variety of sounds. I can hear the light rain on the roof and the surrounding trees, the heating system humming, the ice-cube maker in the refrigerator noisily depositing a dozen cubes, and my chair squeaking conspicuously. Each of these widely different sounds is caused by tiny disturbances in air pressure called **sound waves**. The air pressure rapidly compresses and expands as the sound waves travel to your eardrum, causing it to move slightly. The perception of these successive pressure changes is called **sound**.

It is amazing that the movement of invisible air molecules is strong enough to produce hearing. However, your auditory system is so exquisitely sensitive that you can hear something when your eardrum moves just 1 billionth of a centimeter (Green, 1976).

One important attribute of sound is **frequency**, which is the number of cycles a sound wave completes in 1 second. If you strike middle C on the piano, you produce a sound wave that vibrates up and down 262 times each second. Another important attribute of sound is **amplitude**, or the size of the change in pressure created by the sound wave. As we discuss in more detail later, the physical quality of frequency is roughly equivalent to the psychological experience of *pitch*, whereas amplitude is roughly equivalent to *loudness*.

The Auditory System   These sound waves need to be transformed into neural messages, and the auditory system is neatly designed to accomplish this. As Figure

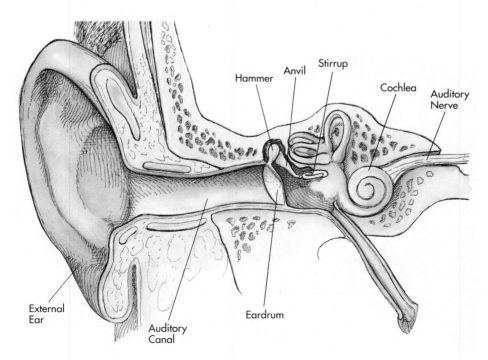

Figure 4.15
The anatomy of the ear.

4.15 illustrates, sound enters the **auditory canal**, the tube running inward from the outer ear. The sound waves bounce against the **eardrum**, which is a thin membrane that vibrates in sequence with the sound waves.

Resting on the other side of the eardrum are three small bones in the middle ear, which an imaginative early anatomist named the hammer, the anvil, and the stirrup. These bones are the smallest ones in the human body, but they have an important function. Sound waves travel through air to the middle ear, but liquid is on the other side of the middle ear. Sound waves cannot travel easily from the air into the liquid. Fortunately, the perceptual system is superbly constructed so that these three bones partly compensate for this problem by magnifying the pressure on the inner ear.

The most important structure in the inner ear is the cochlea (pronounced *coke*-lee-uh). The **cochlea** is a bony, fluid-filled coil that contains the auditory receptors. (The cochlea is therefore equivalent to the retina in vision.) The receptors for hearing are called the **hair cells**. They are embedded in a part of the cochlea called the **basilar membrane** and are illustrated in greatly magnified form in Figure 4.16.

Pressure from the stirrup on the cochlea causes waves in the fluid within the cochlea. These waves produce a vibration in the membrane on which the hair cells sit. When those hair cells are stimulated, they send electrical impulses through their neurons, and the auditory nerve picks up these impulses. The vibrating of air molecules, the pounding of a miniature hammer, the sloshing of liquid in the cochlea, and the stimulation of microscopic hairs are all complex actions that are necessary to convert sound into a form that the auditory nerve can receive.

The **auditory nerve** is a bundle of neurons that carries information from the inner ear toward higher levels of processing. Along the way, information passes through several structures, including a part of the thalamus near the location where visual information also passes. The information eventually travels to the **auditory cortex**, which is located in a deep groove on each side of the surface of the brain. Because this location is so inaccessible, studying the auditory cortex is difficult; we know less about the auditory cortex than we do about the visual cortex (Brugge & Reale, 1985). The auditory cortex is relatively large in humans, probably because speech and language are more developed in humans than in other animals (Kiang & Peake, 1988).

Figure 4.16
Photograph of hair cells embedded in the basilar membrane (greatly magnified).

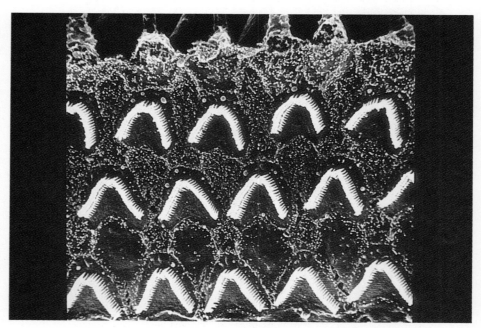

How the Auditory System Registers Frequency   When we discussed color vision, we examined two theories of color vision that were once considered incompatible. We now know that both theories are correct. Similarly, the history of research on hearing once featured a battle between two theories about the mechanism used by the auditory system to register frequency. If you play the lowest note on the piano, you perceive a different pitch than if you played that highest note. But how does the complex auditory system manage to record these differences? Researchers now conclude that the two important theories are both correct; together they explain how the auditory system processes the frequency of a sound wave.

According to **place theory**, each frequency of vibration produces a vibration in a particular *place* on the basilar membrane. (Remember that the basilar membrane contains the hair cells, which are the receptors in the auditory system.) A very low tone causes the greatest vibration in the part of the basilar membrane that is farthest away from the stirrup; a very high tone causes the greatest vibration farther toward the stirrup. Imagine yourself running your finger along the keys of the piano, from the lowest notes to the highest notes. Initially, the ripple would be largest at the far end of the basilar membrane, and the hair cells resting on that part of the membrane would produce rapid electrical discharges. By the end of your demonstration, the hair cells closer to the stirrup would be most active.

Place theory emphasizes the location of the vibration, whereas frequency theory emphasizes how often the membrane vibrates. More specifically, **frequency theory** states that the entire basilar membrane vibrates at the same frequency as the tone that is sounded. Thus, if the frequency of the stimulus is 400 cycles per second, the basilar membrane responds by vibrating at a rate of 400 cycles per second.

Figure 4.17 shows how the two theories are actually compatible. As you can see, frequency theory accounts mostly for low- and middle-frequency ranges. Place theory accounts mostly for middle- and upper-frequency ranges. Notice that the middle range is particularly well cared for. The speech sounds, which are so important in our social interactions, fall in this middle range. This does not seem to be a coincidence. As Kiang and Peake (1988) note:

> Each organism responds to sounds in ways appropriate for survival in its ecological niche. Humans use hearing to monitor the environment, to locate sound sources, to identify sound generators, and, most importantly for a social animal, to communicate with others. . . . (p. 277)

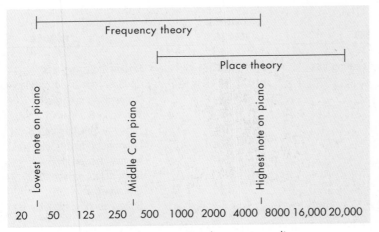

Figure 4.17
Frequency theory and place theory operate in partly overlapping ranges.

Hearing Disabilities   About 13 million people in the United States are hearing impaired (Moore, 1977). One kind of impairment is called **conduction deafness**; it involves problems in either the outer or the middle ear. As the name suggests, the auditory system has difficulty conducting sounds. A hearing aid is typically useful for a person with conduction deafness.

The other kind of impairment is called **nerve deafness**; it involves problems in the inner ear—specifically, in the cochlea or auditory nerve. People who work with extremely noisy equipment or listen to loud music for an extended period of time—without protection—may experience nerve deafness.

A simple hearing aid cannot help someone with complete nerve deafness. The hearing aid could *conduct* the sound waves, but the receptors and the auditory nerve could not transmit the message. Some people with complete nerve deafness are able to use a device called a cochlear implant (Lidke, 1988). The **cochlear implant** consists of a number of electrodes implanted into the bone behind one ear. The electrodes respond to sounds by stimulating the auditory nerve fibers.

People who are fitted with the cochlear implant find it challenging at first to translate the stimulation into meaningful sounds. One middle-aged man had been deaf for 16 years. After the cochlear implant surgery, he said, "At first when I heard people talk, it was mostly garble. I would describe the sound as bubbles— a sort of 'bloop, bloop.' But finally the words started making sense" (Lidke, 1988, p. 12). In his case, 22 electrodes were performing the work done by 20,000 nerve endings in a hearing person. The cochlear implant certainly offers some hope for a small number of hearing-impaired people, but its inadequacies make us appreciate even more the normal human cochlea.

Characteristics of Sound   The four most important characteristics of sound are pitch, loudness, timbre, and localization. Let us consider these features.

1. **Pitch** is the psychological reaction that corresponds to the physical characteristic of frequency. The highest note on a piccolo has a frequency of about 3,700 cycles per second. The pitch of that note is much higher than the pitch of the lowest note on the bass tuba, which has a frequency of only 39 cycles per second.

2. **Loudness** is the psychological reaction that corresponds to the physical characteristic of amplitude; loudness is measured in decibels, abbreviated dB. Table 4.4 shows some representative sounds of different amplitudes. At present,

Table 4.4   *Some Representative Amplitudes of Everyday Noises, as Measured by the Decibel Scale of Loudness*

LEVEL	LOUDNESS (DECIBELS)	EXAMPLE
Substantial hearing loss	180	Rocket launching pad
	160	Loudest rock band on record
Intolerable	140	Jet airplane taking off
	120	Very loud thunder
Very noisy	100	Heavy automobile traffic
Loud	80	Loud music from radio
Moderate	60	Normal conversation
Faint	40	Quiet neighborhood
	20	Soft whisper
Very faint	0	Softest sound detectable by human ear

The tones produced by these orchestra members differ not only in pitch and loudness, but also in timbre.

government regulations insist that workers cannot be exposed to more than a 90-dB sound level for 8 hours a day (Kryter, 1985). However, people expose themselves to much louder sounds as a form of entertainment. For example, Hartman (1982) found that the sound level at the two discos near his college averaged about 125 dB. One third of the college students who regularly visited these discos showed substantial hearing loss.

3. **Timbre** (pronounced *tam*-burr) refers to sound quality. You are certainly familiar with the two previous characteristics, pitch and loudness, but the term *timbre* may be unfamiliar. The squeaky brakes on your friend's car may produce a sound that exactly matches the pitch and loudness of a tone produced by the finest soprano in the Metropolitan Opera Company. However, these two sounds differ in timbre. You can immediately recognize voices on the telephone that are identical in pitch and loudness, again because they differ in timbre.

If pitch is related to frequency and loudness is related to amplitude, what physical feature of sound corresponds to timbre? The answer is tone complexity. Some sounds are composed of a small number of sound waves; the timbre of these sounds is pure and clean. (Consider the timbre of a tone played by a professional flutist, for example.) Other sounds consist of many sound waves combined; the timbre of these is richer and less crisp-sounding. (Consider the timbre of a violin or a guitar.) Timbre involves qualities such as richness, mellowness, and brightness (Evans, 1982).

4. **Localization** refers to our ability to determine the direction from which a sound is coming. When you hear water dripping, you can locate the appropriate faucet. When your alarm rings in the early morning hours, your arm reaches out in (approximately) the correct direction. How do we manage to localize sound? The hair cells in the ear can register the physical characteristics of sound such as frequency, amplitude, and complexity. However, hair cells cannot code that the alarm is ringing near your right shoulder rather than near your left knee (Oldfield & Parker, 1986).

In the section on vision, we saw the usefulness of binocular vision: It is easier to figure out where objects are located because we have two eyes. Similarly, it is easier to figure out where a sound comes from because we have two ears. The major factor in explaining sound localization is that your ears are about 6

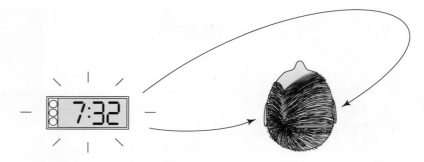

inches apart. As a consequence, they receive somewhat different stimuli. As Figure 4.18 shows, the ringing of the alarm clock reaches your left ear before it reaches your right ear. In addition, your head creates a barrier, so the amplitude of the sound is somewhat lower when it reaches your right ear. These two factors and other sources of information about a sound's location enable us to locate a sound within 1 degree of its true location (Matlin & Foley, 1992; Phillips & Brugge, 1985).

Now try Demonstration 4.8 to illustrate your accuracy in localizing sounds. Then pause for a moment to appreciate the variety of sounds around you, and how your auditory system manages to process the sound of someone typing next door, a car horn honking out in the street, or your yellow highlighter squeaking as it marks passages in this book.

Touch and the Other Skin Senses

The largest sensory system you own is your skin. It has more than 2 square yards of receptive surfaces, dwarfing the relatively small receptive surfaces of the retina and the basilar membrane. However, we appreciate the skin senses much less than vision or hearing. The skin senses warn you that you must go around a large object, rather than through it, that another object could cause tissue damage, and that the outdoor temperature is dangerously cold. Thus, the skin senses include touch, pain, and temperature perception. Let us consider the first two of these in more detail.

Touch   We experience both passive and active touch. In **passive touch**, an object is placed on the skin. Try Demonstration 4.9 to illustrate passive touch. As you may recall, the detection threshold is the boundary where a stimulus is reported half the time. When researchers systematically measure detection thresholds for passive touch, they discover that the parts of the body differ in their sensitivity to touch. For example, people are more sensitive on their faces than on the bottom of their big toes (Weinstein, 1968).

Demonstration 4.8

Sound Localization

Locate an object that makes a distinctive above-threshold noise (e.g., a dripping faucet, a ticking clock, or a distant radio). This object should be located in a room that is uniformly lit. If one part of the room is brighter than other parts, you may rely on visual cues to locate the object. Once you have selected the object, stand several feet away, plug your ears with your fingers, close your eyes, and turn around several times until you are not certain which direction you are facing. Then stop and point to the source of the sound as quickly as possible. How accurate were you?

Thresholds for Passive Touch

Pull just one hair from your head. Hold it about 1 inch from the end, and press it against your cheek. This sensation will probably be above threshold. Now stroke it on the palm of your hand and on the back side of your hand. Are these skin surfaces as sensitive as your cheek? Then try your big toe, a very *insensitive* region. Notice that the threshold for passive touch depends upon the area of skin that is being stimulated.

All skin surfaces—including your big toe as well as your face—show adaptation. In **adaptation**, the perceived intensity of a repeated stimulus decreases over time. For example, are you aware of the pressure of your watch against your wrist? The wristband is depressing your skin's surface just as much as it was when you slipped the watch on this morning. However, touch adaptation guarantees that you will stop noticing touch after a few moments of mild constant pressure.

In passive touch, people wait to be prodded or poked by objects. In contrast, **active touch** occurs when people actively explore objects. At this moment, for example, you may be rubbing your finger along the edge of a desk. In about 2 minutes, you will be actively running your fingers along the right margin of this book, preparing to turn the page. Try to pay more attention to the ways you use active touch and the variety of sensory impressions you receive. Unaided by vision, you can fasten a zipper, search through a backpack, and turn off an alarm clock.

We also use active touch to identify objects. For example, researchers have discovered that we are much more accurate in identifying the shape of cookie cutters when we can use our fingers to explore them, rather than relying simply on passive touch (Gibson, 1962; Heller, 1984).

Pain   It is no challenge to persuade people that we need vision, hearing, and touch. You may wonder why we need pain. Some people cannot feel pain, and you might envy them at first. However, consider some of Sternbach's (1968, 1978) descriptions. Children who are born with pain insensitivity have bitten off their tongue and fingers by mistake. Adults may be unable to detect a ruptured appendix or cancer in time to seek adequate treatment. One woman died from damage to her spine; she had not made the usual kinds of posture adjustments we routinely make when our muscles begin to ache.

Pain is often puzzling. Consider the following observations:

1. People who have had an arm or leg amputated continue to feel pain in the missing limb, even though no pain receptors are stimulated (Rivlin & Gravelle, 1984).

2. A soldier in World War II reported intense pain when a bullet nicked his forehead, yet he felt nothing some time later when his leg was torn off (Wallis, 1984).

3. Sometimes patients receive a **placebo**, an inactive substance such as a sugar pill, which they believe to be a medication. Nevertheless, the placebo relieves the pain substantially (Critelli & Neumann, 1984).

These examples illustrate that pain perception involves more than the stimulation of pain receptors. Pain requires not only a physiological explanation but

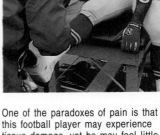

One of the paradoxes of pain is that this football player may experience tissue damage, yet he may feel little pain.

also a psychological explanation (Melzack, 1986). The most widely accepted explanation of pain is Ronald Melzack and Patrick Wall's **gate-control theory**, which proposes that pain messages ordinarily pass through a gate in the spinal cord on their route to the brain. When the gate is open, we experience pain. However, the brain can send messages to the spinal cord, indicating that the gate should be closed. If the gate is closed, pain messages are blocked from reaching the brain. As a consequence, we feel no pain (Melzack, 1986; Melzack & Wall, 1965). For example, the brain's messages probably helped to block pain perception when the soldier's leg was torn off. Gate-control theory illustrates how top-down processing, discussed in connection with visual pattern perception, can also influence pain perception.

Chapter 3 discussed endorphins, chemicals that occur naturally in the brain and decrease a person's sensitivity to pain. It seems likely that these endorphins may play an important role in the gate-control mechanism, though the specifics are not yet known. Researchers have discovered, however, that psychological stress triggers the release of endorphins, which makes painful stimuli seem less intense (Coren & Ward, 1989; Lewis et al., 1984).

In this section on the skin senses, we have seen that our perceptual processes provide us with the ability to experience the pressure of touch as well as the ability to *stop* noticing it. They also allow us to recognize objects by their shape. These perceptual processes also cause us to feel pain in some circumstances but to stop feeling it in other situations. Once again, we see that humans are well equipped to interact with their environment.

Smell

Smell may be the most mysterious of the senses (Gesteland, 1978). Of all the research in perception, only 2% of journal articles examine smell (Teghtsoonian, 1983). One reason that smell suffers such neglect is that it is difficult to classify the stimuli for smell. We can describe visual and auditory stimuli in terms of characteristics such as wave frequency and amplitude. But how can we describe smelly stimuli? We cannot translate the fragrance of chocolate chip cookies or the stench of an ancient tuna sandwich into wavelengths. With odorous stimuli, we must settle for qualitative descriptors such as spicy, minty, and citruslike.

In the last section, you learned about adaptation to touch. Similarly, we often experience adaptation to odors. Have you ever walked into a locker room, permeated with the odor of dozens of sweaty bodies? The odor was initially strong, yet after a few minutes you no longer noticed it. In fact, you may appreciate adaptation only if you leave the room and return at a later point. The perceived intensity of an odor decreases substantially during adaptation. Within 1 minute, the perceived intensity has dropped to only 30% of its original level (Cain, 1988).

In learning how people differ substantially from one another, we have discussed visual and auditory disorders, two sources of individual differences. We also mentioned a less common disorder—insensitivity to pain. A corresponding disorder in the perception of odors is called **anosmia**, an insensitivity to smell caused by drug reactions, certain illnesses, and concussions (Jafek et al., 1988; Monmaney, 1987). In fact, 1 in 15 victims of head trauma wakes up to an odorless world. However, even people without anosmia show a wide range of sensitivity to smell. Individual differences are in the range of 20 to 1 (Rabin & Cain, 1986). In other words, if the people in your introductory psychology class were tested for their threshold to one odorous substance, the "worst smeller" in the class might require a 1% concentration of the substance to detect it. In contrast, the "best smeller" might require a much weaker concentration—only 0.05%—to detect it.

The current research on the perception of odors tends to fall into two categories: (1) recognition of odors and (2) applied research. Let us look at these two areas.

I have used an interesting demonstration in my classroom to test odor recognition. Students are asked to sniff and identify the contents of several opaque jars. There are always several odors that produce a pained expression on my students' faces. The odors aren't dangerous, but they are annoyingly puzzling. Carbon paper and pencil shavings are particularly likely to elicit this pained expression. This ability to recognize that an odor is familiar combined with the inability to identify its name is called the **tip-of-the-nose phenomenon** (Lawless & Engen, 1977). It is similar to the more common tip-of-the-tongue phenomenon in which you know the word for which you are searching, yet that word remains perched on the tip of the tongue, refusing to leap forth.

Research on odor identification has demonstrated that some odors can be recognized easily; coffee, paint, and chocolate pose no challenge. In contrast, fewer than 20% of the participants in one study were able to identify correctly odors such as cigar, cat feces, ham, and sawdust (Desor & Beauchamp, 1974).

People are reasonably accurate in recognizing other humans by their odors. In this research, people are asked to wear a T-shirt for one day. Then participants in the experiment sniff these dirty T-shirts and try to identify the wearer. College students can recognize their own odors fairly well (Russell, 1976). Furthermore, mothers can recognize which T-shirts were worn by their children, even when these children are 2-day-old newborns (Porter, Cernoch, & McLaughlin, 1983; Porter & Moore, 1981).

Another group of researchers in smell perception are concerned with practical applications. One profitable application of smell perception is the development of perfumes (Brady, 1982; Moskowitz, 1978). Each year Americans spend billions of dollars on perfume. The scent strips inserted in magazine advertisements cost $35,000 more to produce than standard advertisements, but they boost perfume sales substantially (Gibbs, 1988).

Scent strips are often inserted in magazines in order to increase perfume sales.

Other applied research in smell perception sounds less glamorous, yet it has important implications for our health. For example, what concentration of cigarette smoke is unacceptable to people sitting in a room with a smoker (Cain, 1987; Cain et al., 1987a)? Other research focuses on protecting workers from toxic or explosive gases that have no odor. How much of a harmless but easy-to-detect odor needs to be added to those gases for workers to be able to smell a gas leak (Cain et al, 1987b; Cain & Turk, 1985)?

Let us now move on to the last of the perceptual systems—taste. As we will note, smell and taste help to create the experience of flavor.

Taste

Taste is actually a limited term. In fact, **taste** refers only to the perceptions that result when substances make contact with the special receptors in the mouth (Bartoshuk, 1971). When psychologists use the word *taste* correctly, they are referring only to perceptions such as sweet or salty.

Flavor, a much broader term, includes smell, touch, and pain—in addition to taste. If you have eaten a bowl of spicy chili, the flavor included impressions such as the pungent smell of onion and cumin seed, the creamy smooth texture of an exploded bean on your tongue, and the distinct pain from the chili pepper.

One of the most important taste phenomena is taste adaptation. You take a first sip of lemonade, and it is so sour that your lips instantly pucker. After a few sips, though, the drink is more tolerable; the sourness has apparently decreased. Notice that taste adaptation is similar to the adaptation to touch and

Figure 4.19
Adaptation to a specific taste, and subsequent recovery.

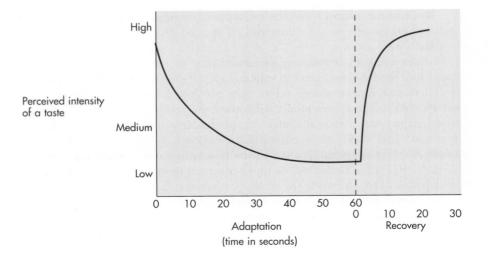

Perceived intensity of a taste

High

Medium

Low

0   10   20   30   40   50   60
Adaptation
(time in seconds)

0   10   20   30
Recovery

A. K. Das is a professional tea taster in Assam, India. However, he does not simply judge the *taste* of a tea. He also assesses the color and texture of the dry tea leaves, as well as the color and fragrance of the tea liquid.

odors we have already discussed. That is, the perceived intensity of a repeated stimulus decreases over time. As Figure 4.19 shows, the perceived intensity of a taste decreases quickly. After about half a minute of sipping, the lemonade does not taste nearly as sour as the first mouthful. Notice that people recover rapidly from adaptation, however. If you stop drinking the lemonade for just half a minute and then take another sip, your lips will pucker again.

The most important application of taste is in the area of food technology. A new breakfast cereal must be judged on qualities such as sweetness, crispiness, and aroma before it reaches the consumers. Flavor enhancement is a new branch of food technology that contributes to medical therapy. For example, a man who was recovering from surgery had a craving for mashed potatoes that clearly could not be satisfied by the intravenous feeding required during the postoperative period. Dr. Susan Schiffman, a prominent researcher in the area of flavor and taste, was able to supply him with a powder that smelled and tasted exactly like mashed potatoes yet dissolved completely on the tongue (Blackburn, 1988). Schiffman has also helped to develop powders and sprays with flavors such as peanut butter and jelly, pizza, and—one surgical patient's request—southern boiled fatback and green beans. These flavor enhancers can also be helpful in treating obesity and in encouraging elderly people to eat. Some elderly people have decreased taste sensitivity, and they eat less, because the food seems so boringly bland. In contrast, Schiffman found that elderly people at a retirement home ate more beef when its flavor had been boosted by a beef flavor enhancer. If the fashion magazines are filled with scent strips from luxury perfumes, what can we expect from the gourmet food magazines of the future? Will *Bon Appétit* have flavor strips for well-aged Camembert cheese? Will *Gourmet* reek with Peking duck flavor enhancer?

Section Summary: The Other Perceptual Systems

■ In hearing, the auditory system transforms sound waves into neural messages. Vibrations are transmitted to hair-cell receptors in the cochlea that register the frequency of a sound by means of both the place on the basilar membrane that vibrates and the frequency with which the membrane vibrates.

■ Two different hearing disabilities are conduction deafness and nerve deafness.

- Four characteristics of sound perception are pitch, loudness, timbre, and localization.
- Research on touch shows that the different parts of the body vary in their sensitivity to touch and that we show adaptation to touch after repeated stimulation. Furthermore, identifying objects with active touch is easier than with passive touch.
- Pain requires a psychological explanation in addition to a physiological explanation, because higher level, top-down factors influence pain perception.
- People show adaptation to odors, and individual differences in sensitivity to odors are large. Some odors are difficult to identify, but people are reasonably accurate in recognizing other humans by their odors.
- Taste is a more limited term than flavor. People show adaptation to tastes. Flavor enhancers are helpful in medical therapy.

Attention

You have probably discovered that paying complete attention to several stimuli at the same time is impossible. If you are listening to the conversation of two students seated behind you in your psychology course, you cannot attend to what your professor is saying. **Attention** means a concentration of mental activity. Attention is relevant to perception because if we concentrate our mental activity on one perceptual task, we may not be able to perceive a second perceptual stimulus simultaneously. This section of the chapter examines three components of attention: divided attention, selective attention, and search.

Divided Attention

In **divided attention**, people try to distribute their attention among two or more competing tasks. One example of divided attention is trying to listen simultaneously to a conversation and your professor. Another example, with even more competing tasks, occurred when you first learned to drive. Remember what it was like to pull out of a parking space for the first time? You had to simultaneously watch the traffic, determine that you had the correct gear, notice how close your fenders were to the cars on each side, and regulate the accelerator. If your driving instructor was talking at the same time, the divided-attention task probably became almost overwhelming!

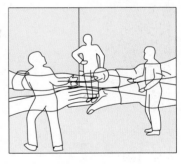

Figure 4.20
Outline tracings of the divided-attention task studied by Neisser and Becklen (1975).

Consider a laboratory version of a divided-attention situation. Neisser and Becklen (1975) asked participants to watch a television screen. As Figure 4.20 shows, the screen displayed two different kinds of games taking place simultaneously. One was a hand-slapping game that you may have played when you were younger. The participants were instructed to press a switch with their right hand whenever one player successfully slapped the other's hands. In the other game shown on the television screen, three men moved around a room, passing the ball to one another. The participants were told to press a switch with their left hand whenever the ball was passed from one player to another. Neisser and Becklen found that the participants had no trouble following one game at a time. However, when the participants were required to monitor both games simultaneously, their performance deteriorated. In fact, they made eight times as many errors in the divided-attention task in contrast to the error rate when monitoring only one game.

When you first began to drive, your experience may have resembled the divided-attention situation of the participants in Neisser and Becklen's study. It is not difficult to watch the traffic, just as it is not difficult to monitor a hand-slapping game. The challenge comes when you must perform another perceptual task simultaneously. After several years of driving experience, however, you can perform complex driving maneuvers and also listen to the radio and talk with a friend at the same time.

Divided attention is difficult in the initial stages of learning, but practice usually makes perfect (Hirst et al., 1980). For example, college students in one experiment learned to read stories to themselves while simultaneously categorizing words that were read to them (e.g., writing down the category ANIMAL when they heard the word DOG) (Spelke et al., 1976). In another study, an experienced typist was able to recite nursery rhymes while typing a different passage at high speed (Shaffer, 1975). You may want to try reciting "Little Bo-Peep" while typing a paragraph from this textbook. Unless you have been a professional typist for several years, either your speed or your accuracy will suffer on this divided-attention task.

Selective Attention

In **selective attention**, people who listen to several simultaneous messages are instructed to focus attention on one message and ignore the others. Therefore, divided attention and selective attention both involve several simultaneous tasks. However, divided attention requires you to pay attention to everything. In contrast, selective attention requires you to pay attention to only one task.

Think of some selective-attention situations you have recently faced. Maybe you tried to listen to the news while conversations elsewhere in the room threatened to distract you. At a party, you may have concentrated on hearing one conversation rather than on several other simultaneous messages. If you are conscientiously attending to one message, you will notice little about other messages presented at the same time.

In the laboratory, selective attention is often studied in a **dichotic listening task**; listeners are instructed to repeat a message presented to one ear while ignoring a different message presented to the other ear. The research generally shows that if the message in the attended ear is spoken quickly, people may not even notice whether the message in the unattended ear is in English or German (Cherry, 1953). However, in some circumstances, people do notice characteristics of the unattended message (Johnston & Dark, 1986). For example, when sexually explicit words are presented to the unattended ear, college students notice these words and are not as accurate in monitoring the primary message (Nielsen & Sarason, 1981).

Try noticing your own attention patterns. Which divided-attention tasks are easy and which ones seem impossible? When can you notice characteristics of the message you are supposed to be ignoring in a selective-attention task? Does a selective-attention task suddenly become a divided-attention task when you find that you want to monitor *two* interesting conversations?

Search

When you search for something, you focus your attention on locating specific stimuli. Try Demonstration 4.10 and decide which of the two search tasks was easier. From the research of Anne Treisman and her colleagues, we know that search can involve either of two kinds of attention (Treisman, 1986; Treisman & Gelade, 1980; Treisman & Gormican, 1988). In one kind of search, called **preattentive processing**, you automatically register the features in a display of objects. For example, in part A of Demonstration 4.10, you used preattentive processing, because the blue figure seemed to "pop out" almost effortlessly. In this low-level kind of attention, we pay attention only to such isolated features as "blue."

Preattentive Processing Versus Focused Attention

Cover the two designs below before you read further.

A. In this part of the demonstration, see how long it takes you to locate the blue figure. Remove the cover from the left-hand design and find the blue figure.

B. Now see how long it takes you to locate the blue X in the other design. Remove the cover and find the blue X.

Which of these involved preattentive processing, and which involved focused attention?

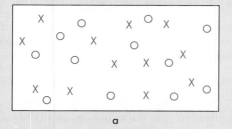

a

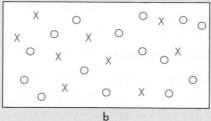

b

The second, more complicated kind of search, called **focused attention**, requires processing objects one at a time. In part B, you used focused attention and examined each of the objects in the box. The blue X did not simply "pop out" from the display. As you can imagine, focused attention is relatively time consuming. Notice how you use focused attention when searching a telephone directory for a friend's name, for you must skim through each of the names on the list.

In part B of the demonstration, you searched for an object on the basis of both color and shape. In general, it is more effective to search for color than for shape (Bundesen & Pedersen, 1983; Rayner, 1978). If you cannot find your car in a crowded parking lot, keep that advice in mind.

Researchers have also discovered that it is easier to search for a target when the irrelevant items look different from the target (Eriksen & Schultz, 1979). Locating a kindergarten teacher is easier when he or she is standing with students, rather than in the midst of the faculty lounge with all the other teachers.

In this chapter, we have examined how stimuli from the outside world are registered on our sensory receptors and how that sensory information is processed by our perceptual systems. However, perceptual information does not remain trapped and neglected in the human cortex. Instead, that information is used as we experience states of consciousness (chapter 5) and as we learn, remember, and think (chapters 6 through 8).

Section Summary: Attention

- In divided-attention situations, people have difficulty performing two tasks simultaneously; however, practice improves the accuracy.
- In selective-attention situations, people who pay complete attention to one task typically notice little about the unattended message.
- The two kinds of search are the relatively automatic preattentive processing and the more time-consuming focused attention.

1. Describe a recent situation you encountered that involved detection. How could someone measure a detection threshold in this situation, using the classical psychophysical approach? What factors would determine your criterion, as analyzed by signal detection theory? Now describe a recent situation that involved discrimination; discuss how the concept of just noticeable differences applies here.

2. Imagine that you are waiting for an elevator. Suddenly you see the light above the door turn green, and a bell rings simultaneously. Your elevator has arrived. Trace how these two stimuli—one visual and one auditory—would be processed, beginning with the receptors and ending at the cortex.

3. Vision and hearing share a number of similarities. For example, color perception and pitch perception each have two explanations to account for their operation. Describe as many other similarities as you can recall.

4. What factors provide information about an object's distance in vision? What factors provide information about the distance of an auditory stimulus?

5. The section on shape perception emphasized that the figure-ground relationship and the Gestalt laws of grouping impose organization on visual stimuli. Discuss these two topics, listing the Gestalt laws. Now apply each of these principles to auditory stimuli: How is our hearing organized?

6. Suppose you know a reading teacher. How would you summarize for him or her what you know about perceptual aspects of reading, especially eye movements and pattern recognition?

7. In the section on shape perception, we argued that perception involves both bottom-up and top-down perception. Describe these two approaches, and discuss how they could be applied to signal detection theory, shape perception, and pain perception.

8. The concept of adaptation was discussed in connection with touch, smell, and taste. Describe these three topics, providing an example of each from your recent experience.

9. Throughout this chapter, we discussed perceptual disorders and individual differences. Describe as many as you can recall.

10. Question 9 involved the theme of individual differences. Now find evidence in this chapter for each of the other two themes: (a) Humans are remarkably well equipped to function in their environment, and (b) Human behavior is so complex that it usually has more than one explanation or cause.

NEW TERMS

sensation	Weber's law	retina
perception	wavelength	fovea
psychophysics	hue	cones
detection	amplitude (vision)	rods
detection threshold	brightness	transduction
signal detection theory	cornea	bipolar cells
criterion	iris	ganglion cells
discrimination	pupil	optic nerve
just-noticeable difference (jnd)	lens	blind spot

optic chiasm
binocular vision
visual cortex
feature detectors
trichromatic theory
chromatic adaptation
opponent-process theory
visual acuity
dark adaptation
saccadic movement
perceptual span
gaze-contingent paradigm
figure-ground relationship
Gestalt approach
law of proximity
law of similarity
law of good continuation
law of closure
distinctive features
prototype-matching theory
prototypes
bottom-up processing
top-down processing

word-superiority effect
biological motion
monocular
binocular disparity
constancy
size constancy
shape constancy
lightness constancy
color constancy
illusion
theory of misapplied constancy
sound waves
sounds
frequency
amplitude (hearing)
auditory canal
eardrum
cochlea
hair cells
basilar membrane
auditory nerve
auditory cortex
place theory

frequency theory
conduction deafness
nerve deafness
cochlear implant
pitch
loudness
timbre
localization
passive touch
adaptation
active touch
placebo
gate-control theory
anosmia
tip-of-the-nose phenomenon
taste
flavor
attention
divided attention
selective attention
dichotic listening task
preattentive processing
focused attention

ANSWERS TO DEMONSTRATIONS

Demonstration 4-4.   57, 15

RECOMMENDED READINGS

Coren, S., & Girgus, J. S. (1978). *Seeing is deceiving: The psychology of visual illusions.* Hillsdale, NJ: Erlbaum. This clearly written book emphasizes that illusions are a normal part of the perceptual processes; it also contains numerous examples of interesting illusions.

Coren, S., & Ward, L. M. (1989). *Sensation & perception* (3rd ed.). Orlando: Academic Press. This upper-level book provides a complete overview of the topic, including chapters on individual differences in perception as well as the role of experience in perception.

Goldstein, E. B. (1989). *Sensation and perception* (3rd ed.). Belmont, CA: Wadsworth. Goldstein's textbook is especially strong in the area of sensation; it also includes a wealth of intriguing illustrations.

Matlin, M. W., & Foley, H. (1992). *Sensation and perception* (3rd ed.). Boston, MA: Allyn & Bacon. This textbook emphasizes cognitive processes in perception, and it contains many examples of applications in professions and in everyday life.

**States of
Consciousness**

Right now you are probably experiencing normal waking consciousness. You may be methodically reading this chapter, taking in the words on this page and relating them to your previous ideas about consciousness. Or you may be daydreaming, your mind straying away from the topic of consciousness . . . toward next Friday's plans. Within the next 24 hours, you will enter another state of consciousness, when you sleep and dream. It is also possible that you have experienced other states of consciousness if you have tried certain drugs, hypnosis, or meditation.

Consciousness is your awareness of external and internal stimuli. For example, you are conscious of the words on this page. Perhaps you are also conscious of other external stimuli, such as a telephone ringing nearby. In addition, consciousness includes awareness of internal stimuli—perhaps you are thinking about hunger pangs. These internal stimuli can also include your thoughts—perhaps you are thinking that consciousness appears to be more complex than you had originally believed.

The term *consciousness* is related to the term *attention*, which was introduced in the last part of chapter 4. In fact, selective attention is the cognitive process that restricts the amount of information that enters consciousness. The prominent American psychologist William James (1890) wrote that attention serves as the searchlight of consciousness. Attention therefore searches the environment, admitting only selected stimuli into consciousness and ignoring all others.

The popularity of consciousness has fluctuated dramatically in the last century. William James included a chapter on consciousness as part of his important psychology textbook (James, 1890). Several decades later, the behaviorists dominated psychology. They did not believe that consciousness was an appropriate topic for scientific study because it is difficult to observe or measure. As a result, consciousness had essentially vanished from the psychological scene by the middle of this century (Hearnshaw, 1987; Hilgard, 1986).

By the late 1960s, however, psychologists began to be persuaded by the research and theories of cognitive psychology. Consciousness re-emerged, and it is currently a very acceptable topic for research. In fact, it might even be considered a trendy area. An influential cognitive psychologist named Howard Gardner recently proposed that consciousness is likely to become one of the most important topics of the future (Gardner, 1988).

Let us begin our discussion of states of consciousness by first considering normal waking consciousness, which occupies the major part of our lives.

Normal Waking Consciousness

Most of this textbook focuses on our normal waking state. When you use memory, cognition, or language, you are awake and conscious. Your social interactions also involve normal waking consciousness.

Active and Passive Modes of Consciousness

One of the most prominent theorists on consciousness, Ernest Hilgard, has distinguished between two basic kinds of waking consciousness (Hilgard, 1980). The **active mode of consciousness** involves planning, making decisions, and acting upon these decisions. The active mode of consciousness makes up the major part of your mental life, because you are often planning. The planning may involve long-range goals ("Should I major in psychology?"). It also may involve short-range goals ("Should I read the definition of consciousness one more time?").

You are particularly likely to use this active mode of consciousness when you acquire new knowledge and behavior. You are probably no longer conscious about putting your foot on the brake in response to a red light, but you certainly used the active mode of consciousness when you were first learning to drive. You are also highly likely to use the active mode of consciousness when you make judgments and choices, for example in planning a career. The active mode of consciousness is also important when automatic processing fails. For example, an experienced driver may have been driving for half an hour without really being conscious of the task. However, one glimpse of a police car in the rear view mirror is a sufficient warning to shift to the active mode of consciousness.

In contrast, the **passive mode of consciousness** includes a less focused awareness of the environment. It also includes the kind of artistic experience in which you are the receiver rather than the performer, for example, when you are listening to music but not actively analyzing it. The passive mode of consciousness also includes daydreaming.

In a **daydream**, you shift your attention away from external stimuli toward internal events and fantasies. The average college student daydreams approximately $1\frac{1}{2}$ hours each day (Kunzendorf et al., 1983). As you daydream, your mind constantly shifts from one thought to another. You may take a brief side trip into your own imagery and memory as you listen to a lecture or read a book (Klinger, 1987). For example, when I mentioned the topic of learning to drive, you may have briefly shifted your thoughts to some incident that occurred when you were a beginning driver. Daydreams may also be unrelated to ongoing stimuli. Does an image ever pop into your head—perhaps a scene from your childhood or a fanciful picture—that has no connection with your current activities?

Consistent with the theme of individual differences, you can guess that people differ tremendously in their daydreaming patterns. For instance, some students report that they never daydream, whereas others say they daydream 10 hours each day. Daydreaming is related to three other topics we consider later in the chapter. Specifically, people who report a large number of hours spent daydreaming are also likely to report that they sleep relatively few hours each night. Also, people who report having unpleasant daydreams are likely to say that they have nightmares and difficulty sleeping. Finally, daydreamers are somewhat more responsive than other individuals to suggestions during hypnosis (Kunzendorf et al., 1983; Starker, 1985).

Are there racial differences in the content of daydreams? Giambra (1982) selected Black and White participants, matched on important variables such as education, income, and age. Everyone completed a questionnaire about the frequency of different kinds of daydreams. Figure 5.1 shows five representative items. Notice that the racial differences are not significant on the first three of these factors. However, Blacks tended to have more achievement-oriented daydreams, presumably indicating that they were more concerned about success. They also had more hostile daydreams, which Giambra suggests might be traceable to hostile treatment from White people. In general, however, Giambra's study revealed that the daydreams of Blacks and Whites are fairly similar.

Consciousness About Higher Mental Processes

Are you aware of your thought processes? That is, can you accurately assess how you remembered something or why you came up with the solution to a particular problem? This issue of consciousness about our cognitions has provoked a con-

Figure 5.1
Some representative topics and characteristics of daydreams of Blacks and Whites. (Based on Giambra, 1982)

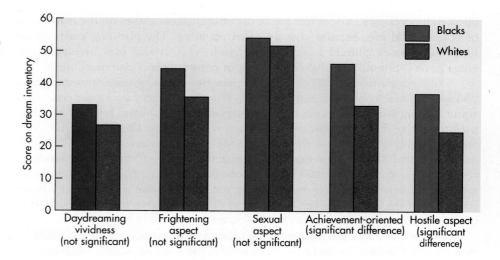

troversy among psychologists. For example, consider this question: "What is your mother's maiden name?" Now answer a second question, "How did you arrive at the answer to the first question?" The name probably leapt swiftly into your consciousness, yet you probably found that you could not explain your thought processes. The name simply seemed to "pop" into memory (Miller, 1962).

As Nisbett and Wilson (1977) argued, we often have little direct access to our thought processes. We may be completely conscious of the *products* of our higher mental activities (for instance, your mother's maiden name), but we are usually not conscious of the *process* that created the product (for example, how you retrieved that information from memory). "The sorting, sifting, and shuffling that preceded the recollection seem to be hidden from us" (Lyons, 1986, p. 101).

However, we can be conscious of other, more leisurely thought processes. If you are searching for somebody's name that is on the tip of your tongue, you can trace your progress as you coax that name out of hiding. Perhaps you first realized the first letter of the name, then another name it sounded like, and then its number of syllables. In addition, people seem to have access to consciousness when they report their thought processes about creative projects, such as writing poetry (Perkins, 1981). In short, then, some mental processes are available to consciousness, whereas others remain hidden and relatively mysterious.

Section Summary: Normal Waking Consciousness

- ■ The topic of consciousness, or awareness of external and internal stimuli, has fluctuated greatly in popularity throughout the history of psychology.
- ■ The active mode of consciousness involves planning, making decisions, and responding to those decisions.
- ■ The passive mode of consciousness includes daydreaming; daydreaming patterns are related to sleep patterns, nightmares, and hypnotic susceptibility.
- ■ We seem to have only limited access to some of our thought processes, yet we are apparently conscious of some more leisurely mental activities.

Sleeping and Dreaming

If you live to the age of 75, you will spend close to 25 of those years asleep. Even though you spend about one third of your lifetime sleeping, it is unlikely that you will discuss sleep in detail in any other college course. Only 53 professors in the United States are listed as offering a course in the psychology of sleep (College Marketing Group, 1988, Fall).

Sleep is defined as a state of unresponsiveness from which we can be aroused relatively easily (Oswald, 1987a). People may be unresponsive when they are asleep, but the brain is far from passive. In fact, recordings from the brains of sleeping animals demonstrate that the overall level of neuron activity is just as great during sleep as during the waking state (Kimble, 1988).

Of course, body movement is greatly reduced during sleep. The modern artist Andy Warhol made a 6-hour movie called *Sleep*, which simply showed a man sleeping for 6 hours. Not surprisingly, the movie did not break any box office records.

Let us begin our exploration of sleep by looking at the sleeping-and-waking cycle. Other topics include variations in sleep patterns, stages of sleep, sleep deprivation, the function of sleep, and insomnia. In the final part of this section, we see that dreams provide further evidence for the active nature of sleep.

Circadian Rhythms

Your daily life repeats itself in regular cycles everyday, with each cycle including both a sleeping and a waking period. These cycles are called circadian rhythms, based on the Latin *circa dies*, meaning "about a day." Therefore, a **circadian rhythm** is one that has a cycle lasting approximately 24 hours.

Part of the reason you maintain a 24-hour cycle is that your world is filled with reminders about time. Clocks and watches remind you of the precise time of day. The position of the sun and the outdoor temperature give approximate time clues. Mealtimes offer still further clues that help you maintain that 24-hour schedule. All of these clues that encourage you to adopt a 24-hour cycle are known as **zeitgebers** (pronounced "*tsite*-gay-burs"), a German word for "time givers."

Free-Running. What would happen if we were deprived of zeitgebers? Would we still obey an internal biological clock, or would our circadian rhythms run haywire? To answer this question, researchers have asked volunteers to live for several weeks in isolation from zeitgebers. They give up their watches, radios, televisions, and telephones and live for several weeks in a place where sunlight cannot penetrate. Typical locations include underground caves in the United States and in the Swiss Alps, as well as specially constructed apartments. The research staff who work with these volunteers are instructed not to wear watches and to avoid time-related greetings such as "good morning" and "good night."

In a typical study, the volunteers initially keep to a rigid, predetermined schedule. They go to sleep at midnight and are wakened by the staff at 8 a.m. (Coleman, 1986). After 20 days of this routine, the rules change. The volunteers are free to decide when to go to sleep and when to awake.

If humans were perfectly circadian, they would continue to maintain that midnight-to-8 a.m. schedule, a 24-hour cycle, even without zeitgebers. However, nearly all people show the same pattern: On the first night, they go to sleep at 1 a.m. and sleep until 9 a.m. On each subsequent night, they fall asleep about one hour later; they also arise about one hour later each subsequent morning. This natural tendency to adopt a *25-hour* cycle, one hour later each day, is known as **free-running**. Because of this free-running tendency, volunteers request their scrambled eggs for breakfast at 8 p.m. after about 12 days without zeitgebers.

Disrupted Circadian Rhythms. In the 20th century, Americans are likely to experience two sources of disruption to their circadian rhythms: shift schedules and jet lag. In both cases, sleep patterns and performance during waking hours are likely to deteriorate.

Consider the train crash described by Coleman (1986). At 4:45 in the morning, the engineer and the head brakeman had both fallen asleep. Their 115-car train was speeding down a hill on the same tracks as another freight train; they had slept through the flashing yellow signals 20 miles earlier. They awoke too late to stop their train, and two people on the other train were killed. Just 9 days earlier, five crew members were killed in a train accident at 3:55 a.m. As it turns out, 3 a.m. is the lowest point in the body's cycle of alertness. The workers on these trains had been obeying their biological clocks, rather than the more fragile clocks imposed by their work schedules.

About 20% of workers in the United States are on **shift schedules**, in which they must work during the normal sleeping hours (Moorcroft, 1987). As a consequence, they sleep fewer hours, and they wake up more often during sleep. In fact, a review of all the studies conducted on shift work concluded that 62% of shift workers complained about sleep disturbances, in contrast to 20% of day workers (Coleman, 1986). It makes sense that they have difficulty sleeping during the day, because the rest of the world is scheduled to be particularly active then . . . telephones ring, automobiles honk, and children squabble. Furthermore, like the sleeping crew members in the train crash, shift workers fall asleep on the job. In one survey, more than half of the shift workers admitted to falling asleep at work on a regular basis (Coleman, 1986). In many cases, these brief naps may be harmless. However, an unannounced late-night inspection of a nuclear plant found 5 of the 13 employees asleep—a report that did not amuse nearby residents.

Jet travel is another very effective way to disrupt circadian rhythms. One summer, I traveled to Sydney, Australia. When I arrived, it was 2 p.m. on a Sunday in Australia, but it was 11 p.m. on Saturday in New York. It took several days for me to adjust my internal clock. **Jet lag** is the term for the disturbances in body rhythm caused by lengthy journeys involving time-zone changes. In contrast, travelers do not experience jet lag when they fly in a north-south direction, without changing any time zones (Gregory, 1987).

It is daytime in this airport, but these jet passengers are still operating according to biological clocks established in their own countries.

Variations in Sleep Patterns

You may be wondering about individual differences in the circadian rhythms that encourage us to maintain regular sleep-wake schedules. You may have one friend who seems to thrive on 4 hours of sleep each night, whereas another requires at least 9. You may do your best thinking at 9 o'clock in the morning, yet your best friend would not dare sign up for a class that meets before noon.

Amount of Sleep.   In one case study, a 70-year-old woman averaged 67 minutes of sleep each night (Meddis et al., 1973). She showed no signs of fatigue, and she was puzzled that other people wasted so much time sleeping. According to statistics, the average American adult sleeps 7 to 8 hours a night, with 85% sleeping in the broader range of 6 to 9 hours a night. Try Demonstration 5.1 to determine whether these averages hold true for your acquaintances.

Look at your data on Demonstration 5.1 and see if you can detect any major personality differences between your friends who thrive on just a few hours of sleep and those whose sleep patterns approach Rip Van Winkle's. In general, researchers have not found many systematic differences between habitual short and long sleepers (Mendelson, 1987; Webb, 1982). However, contrary to what we might expect, people who require little sleep actually seem to be somewhat more energetic and alert during the day than those who require more sleep (Hicks & Guista, 1982). Age has a significant influence on sleep. Newborns sleep about 15 hours a day, and elderly people sleep about 6 (Kimble, 1988).

If you have a pet cat, you are aware that species differ in their sleep requirements. Cats spend most of their lives asleep, and they are not embarrassed about

Demonstration 5.1

Individual Differences in Amount of Sleep

Ask 10 or more friends to estimate how much they sleep each night. Specifically, ask them the average time at which they went to bed during the last week, as well as the average time at which they awoke. Do almost all of them fall within the range of 6 to 9 hours? Also, ask them how many times a week they take naps. Researchers have determined that most college students take naps, providing about 3 hours of additional sleep each week (Evans et al., 1977; Webb, 1982).

dozing during the day. Figure 5.2 shows some typical figures for a variety of mammals.

Owls and Larks Individual differences is one of the themes of this textbook, and we have seen that people differ in the amount of sleep they require. However, another important way in which their sleep patterns differ is in the timing of their sleep . . . that is, whether they are owls or larks. Look back at the data you collected in Demonstration 5.1, and you will probably find one friend who goes to sleep at 10:30, whereas another considers 1 a.m. to be an early bedtime.

Only about 10% of the population can be categorized as extreme larks—who go to sleep early and function best in the morning—or extreme owls—who go to sleep late and function best at nighttime. The rest of us function somewhere in the middle (Coleman, 1986). Try Demonstration 5.2 for an estimate of where you fit on the owl and lark test.

Extreme larks find that their performance peaks in the early morning and falls off as evening approaches; they have great difficulty adjusting to shift work, jet lag, and any change in schedule. Extreme owls, in contrast, work best at night and have relatively little difficulty adjusting to new schedules (Coleman, 1986).

Stages of Sleep

We need to take a closer look at sleep itself, focusing on the different stages within a night's sleep. Sleep consists of five different phases, each with a different kind of brain activity.

Figure 5.2
Average sleep time of mammals during each 24-hour period.

The Owl and Lark Questionnaire

Try this shortened version of a questionnaire designed by Horne and Ostberg (1976) to test whether you are a morning person or an evening person. For items 1, 2, and 10, circle the appropriate number below the scale to indicate the range of times that best answers the question. For the remaining items, note the number next to the box you have checked.

Now add up all the points. Check this table for an estimate of where you fall on the Owl-Lark scale.

	SCORE
Definitely Lark Type	35–43
Moderately Lark Type	30–34
Neither Type	23–29
Moderately Owl Type	18–22
Definitely Owl Type	10–17

1. Considering only your own "feeling best" rhythm, at what time would you get up if you were entirely free to plan your day?

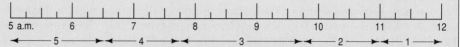

2. Considering only your own "feeling best" rhythm, at what time would you go to bed if you were entirely free to plan your evening?

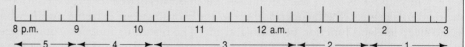

3. If there is a specific time at which you have to get up in the morning, to what extent are you dependent on being woken up by an alarm clock?

Not at all dependent . . . . ☐ 4
Slightly dependent . . . . ☐ 3
Fairly dependent . . . . ☐ 2
Very dependent . . . . ☐ 1

4. Assuming adequate environmental conditions, how easy do you find getting up in the mornings?

Not at all easy . . . . ☐ 1
Not very easy . . . . ☐ 2
Fairly easy . . . . ☐ 3
Very easy . . . . ☐ 4

5. How alert do you feel during the first half hour after having woken in the mornings?

Not at all alert . . . . ☐ 1
Slightly alert . . . . ☐ 2
Fairly alert . . . . ☐ 3
Very alert . . . . ☐ 4

6. How is your appetite during the first half hour after having woken in the mornings?

Very poor . . . . ☐ 1
Fairly poor . . . . ☐ 2
Fairly good . . . . ☐ 3
Very good . . . . ☐ 4

7. During the first half hour after having woken in the morning, how tired do you feel?

Very tired . . . . ☐ 1
Fairly tired . . . . ☐ 2
Fairly refreshed . . . . ☐ 3
Very refreshed . . . . ☐ 4

8. When you have no commitments the next day, at what time do you go to bed compared to your usual bedtime?

Seldom or never later . . . . ☐ 4
Less than one hour later . . . . ☐ 3
1-2 hours later . . . . ☐ 2
More than two hours later . . . . ☐ 1

9. You have decided to engage in some physical exercise.   A friend suggests that you do this one hour twice a week and the best time for him is between 7 and 8 a.m. Bearing in mind nothing else but your own "feeling best" rhythm how do you think you would perform?

Would be in good form . . . . ☐ 4
Would be in reasonable form . . . . ☐ 3
Would find it difficult . . . . ☐ 2
Would find it very difficult . . . . ☐ 1

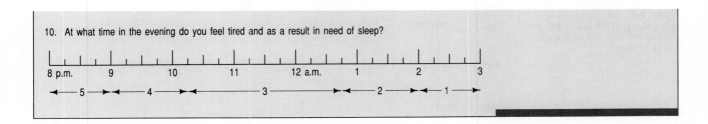

10. At what time in the evening do you feel tired and as a result in need of sleep?

8 p.m.   9   10   11   12 a.m.   1   2   3

◄——— 5 ———►◄——— 4 ———►◄——————— 3 ———————►◄——— 2 ———►◄— 1 —►

To study sleep, researchers cannot casually stroll into volunteers' houses, perch on a chair near the bed, and watch these somewhat self-conscious folks begin to snooze. Instead, research must be conducted in a sleep laboratory. Sleep labs are usually located in a sleep clinic. They consist of several bedrooms next to an observation room.

Imagine that you have volunteered to participate in a sleep experiment. You have just arrived at the lab and have introduced yourself to the researchers—and because you have just finished reading about circadian rhythms, you realize that these people certainly qualify as shift workers. You get yourself ready for bed, and then the researchers tape the electrodes of an electroencephalogram onto your scalp (and, fortunately, you remember reading in chapter 3 how the EEG measures electrical activity in the brain). In addition, the researchers fasten on additional electrodes to measure your eye movements and your muscle tension (see Figure 5.3). They may also measure your breathing rate, your heart rate, and your level of genital arousal.

Figure 5.3
A person prepared for a night's sleep in a sleep laboratory.

How well do you suspect you would sleep in this strange setting, feeling as if you have more strings attached to yourself than a marionette? Researchers are aware that the first night of sleep in the lab is bound to be abnormal, so they typically ignore any data collected at this time (Carlson, 1986).

The following night, though, the sleep project begins in earnest, and the researchers start to collect various measures. When you first climb into bed, you will probably be awake and alert for a few minutes. Your EEG will show mostly **beta waves**, which are rapid brain waves at the frequency of at least 14 per second. Then you close your eyes and relax, and the EEG begins to show a pattern of **alpha waves**, which occur at the slower frequency of 8 to 12 per second. Notice the difference between these two brain-wave patterns in Figure 5.4.

Soon after, you begin to drift from a pleasant drowsiness into the stages of sleep.

In **Stage 1 sleep**, the EEG records small, irregular brain waves. You are drifting into a light sleep. You can be readily awakened from Stage 1 sleep.

In **Stage 2 sleep**, the EEG shows very rapid bursts of activity known as sleep spindles. If a sleep researcher sneezed next door, you probably would not hear it.

In **Stage 3 sleep**, your EEG begins to show a few delta waves, at the very slow frequency of about 2 per second. Your breathing slows substantially, and your muscles are completely relaxed.

In **Stage 4 sleep**, the EEG now shows almost exclusively delta waves. You are now in deep sleep. The researchers could probably wander into your room without waking you.

These four stages of sleep do not tell the complete story, however. You do not simply drift downward into deep sleep after you crawl into bed, and drift upward into light sleep as morning approaches. Instead, you spend the first 30 to 45 minutes progressing from Stage 1 to Stage 4, and the next 30 to 45 minutes reversing the direction, back up to Stage 1.

At this point you enter a different kind of sleep called rapid eye movement, or REM sleep. During **REM sleep**, your eyes move rapidly beneath your closed

Figure 5.4
EEG patterns of the two stages prior to sleep, the four non-REM stages, and REM sleep.

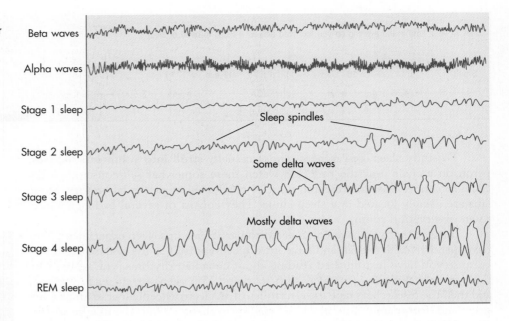

eyelids, giving this stage its name. The EEG shows long sections in which there are rapid brain waves, similar to the waves in Stage 1. Your heart beats rapidly and you breathe quickly and irregularly. Your genitals are likely to show arousal—vaginal congestion and moisture in females and erections in males.

REM sleep is also associated with dreaming. About 90% of people who are awakened during REM sleep report that they have just had a vivid dream (Coleman, 1986). We discuss dreams more extensively later in this chapter.

Each night, you cycle about four times through the various stages, with each cycle lasting about 90 to 100 minutes. A typical night is illustrated in Figure 5.5.

The brain's activity, as revealed by EEGs, is related to the stages of sleep. But what parts of the brain regulate sleep? No single sleep center has been identified in the brain, but several seem to work together. As chapter 3 mentioned, the reticular formation in the hindbrain has an important role. When the reticular formation receives electrical stimulation, a sleeping person wakes up. Furthermore, damage to the reticular formation will produce prolonged sleep (Kalat, 1988). REM sleep requires the cooperation of several brain structures. Researchers do not yet have all the answers, but the current candidates include the reticular formation in the hindbrain and the thalamus and the cerebral cortex in the forebrain (see Figure 3.14).

Sleep Deprivation

In 1959, a disc jockey named Peter Tripp stayed awake for 200 hours. Researchers carefully monitored his physiological measures and recorded his EEG patterns. After about 4 days—halfway through his no-sleep marathon—he began to hallucinate that one of the researchers was wearing a suit of crawling worms. After the 200-hour ordeal, Tripp went to sleep. He owed his body about 60 hours of sleep, yet he slept for just 13 hours (Evans, 1983).

Studies on sleep deprivation show that people typically have difficulty focusing their eyes, and they show some loss of strength. During sleep deprivation, they may become depressed, irritable, and demanding (Moorcroft, 1987). Young adults are more likely than older adults to show mood changes. In contrast, older adults are more likely than young adults to become inattentive; for example, they

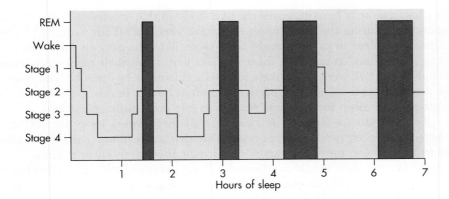

Figure 5.5
A typical sleeper's pattern of normal sleep. Note that there are four stages of sleep and that the maroon-colored bars represent REM sleep.

may find it difficult to search for particular letters on a sheet containing many different letters (Webb, 1985).

Surprisingly, some skills are not consistently influenced by modest sleep deprivation (Meddis, 1982). Webb (1982) found that people's memory was not harmed by 2 nights without sleep. However, Webb only studied memory for one-syllable words, and not—for example—memory for material in introductory psychology textbooks. I am certainly not recommending sleep deprivation before your next exam.

Surprisingly, people who have experienced sleep deprivation rarely suffer from any lasting aftereffects (Horne, 1988). The current world-record holder for sleeplessness in the *Guinness Book of World Records*, Maureen Weston, reportedly outlasted everyone else in a rocking-chair marathon. She went sleepless for nearly 19 days, yet she experienced no lasting aftereffects (Coleman, 1986). These observations bring us quite naturally to our next topic: Does sleep serve a purpose?

Why Do We Sleep?

We have seen throughout this book that a particular human behavior is likely to have more than one explanation. Because sleep is a behavior that we perform for 7 or 8 hours each day, it seems reasonable to expect that we have more than one reason for sleeping. Two of the most likely reasons are that sleep is restorative and that sleep is adaptive.

The Restorative Function   Sleep as a restorative process is an idea that is literally thousands of years old. The Greek philosopher Aristotle, for instance, proposed that some substance builds up during the day, and the nightly sleep rids our body of these poisons. However, researchers have not identified specific "negative" substances eliminated during sleep.

In contrast, researchers have found that the body does manufacture useful substances when we are asleep. Specifically, growth hormone secretions are at their maximum during slow-wave sleep. Furthermore, brain-protein synthesis is at its maximum during REM sleep (Anch et al., 1988).

Researchers have also found that people who have performed vigorous physical activities—such as running a marathon—sleep longer afterward. They are particularly likely to have more of the delta-wave sleep associated with sleep Stages 3 and 4 (Shapiro, 1982). This relationship implies that greater exertion requires more time for the body to be restored to normal.

The Adaptive Function   Another possibility emphasizes the evolutionary purpose of sleep (Moorcroft, 1989; Webb, 1988). The specific pattern of sleep developed by each species may have increased the likelihood of that species' survival. "Non-responding" during the dark hours may have been useful for humans. Those humans who slept in caves at night were more likely to pass on their genes to future generations. In contrast, those humans who spent their nights wandering around in the dark were more likely to have accidents or be eaten by wild beasts. The mechanisms for sleep may persist in modern human brains, even though we no longer need sleep for the same reasons as our prehistoric ancestors.

So, why do we sleep? It is clear that all the answers have not yet been gathered. However, two important reasons are that we sleep to restore our bodies and to keep us (or, more accurately, our distant ancestors) out of trouble.

So far, we have emphasized normal sleep patterns. Millions of people in this country, however, do not enjoy a normal night's sleep, followed by sleep-free daytime activities. There are more than 60 different sleep disorders (Williams & Karacan, 1985). We focus specifically on those disorders involving insomnia.

○ ○

In Depth: Insomnia

Insomnia is a term referring to difficulty in falling asleep and/or remaining asleep. The more formal term for these sleeping problems is **Disorders of Initiating and Maintaining Sleep**, or **DIMS**. Like most sleep researchers, however, we use the more familiar name, insomnia (Hopson, 1986; Trinder, 1988).

About 35% of adults complain about insomnia in any given year, and it is a persistent problem for about 15% to 30% of the population (Fredrickson, 1987). In the words of one of the most famous of sleep researchers, "If we include all of its forms, insomnia is probably the most common medical complaint in the world" (Dement, 1986, p. 43).

Who is most likely to suffer from insomnia? In general, older people have more problems than younger people, and women have more problems than men. People who are widowed, divorced, or separated are more likely than married or single people to report insomnia (Coleman, 1986). Insomnia is also more common among people with psychological problems. Although, as we just noted, between 15% and 30% of the general population complains about insomnia, that same figure is between 50% and 80% for psychiatric patients (Fredrickson, 1987; Williams & Karacan, 1985).

Varieties of Insomnia   Researchers have identified six kinds of insomnia:

1. Transient insomnia is something almost everybody has experienced; sleeplessness lasts only a few days, and it is triggered by factors such as a major college exam or a fight with the boss. Transient insomnia does not need any special attention. However, the five chronic or long-term insomnias often do require medical attention.

2. In stress-conditioned or learned insomnia, people are extremely anxious about whether they will sleep well. Ironically, the harder they try to fall asleep, the worse their insomnia becomes. Through a history of conditioning they have come to associate their beds with tossing and turning, sleepless nights, and anxiety about performing well the next day. People who suffer from learned insomnia can usually be successfully treated in about 5 weeks by encouraging them to worry less and to substitute a more positive approach to sleep (Reynolds, 1986).

3. Psychiatric insomnia, as the name suggests, is caused by psychiatric disorders such as depression and anxiety. A test discussed in chapter 13 called the

Minnesota Multiphasic Personality Inventory (MMPI) shows that these insomniacs differ from normal sleepers on the test scales that measure anxiety, worry, depression, concern about body symptoms, and feelings of inferiority (Freedman & Sattler, 1982; Levin, Bertelson, & Lacks, 1984). In most cases, treating the psychological problem will eventually help the insomnia problem (Coleman, 1986).

4. Physiological insomnia (also known as insomnia secondary to medical illness) can be traced to physical complaints that prevent people from falling asleep and staying asleep. Elderly people are particularly likely to have medical problems such as Alzheimer's disease (which we discussed in depth in chapter 3), arthritis, and other painful symptoms that keep them from sleeping properly. When the medical problem is treated, sleep patterns often improve (Reynolds, 1986).

5. Poor sleep habits, another source of insomnia, include drinking too much coffee, sleeping in noisy environments, and alcoholism. Ironically, another major source of insomnia is a reliance on sleeping pills. Both alcohol and sleeping pills tend to produce shallow, disrupted sleep, abnormal REM sleep, and early-morning waking. Sadly, about 90% of elderly people living in institutions currently receive sleeping pills. These pills probably do more harm than good (Hopson, 1986; Reynolds, 1986; Scharf & Brown, 1986).

6. Subjective insomnia occurs when a person complains of insomnia, yet there is no evidence of objective sleep disturbance. A typical person with subjective insomnia may sleep for 7 or 8 hours in the laboratory (measured objectively by an EEG). Nevertheless, this person may complain in the morning, "I had no sleep at all." When the sleep researcher points out that the sleep pattern was indeed normal, some subjective insomniacs are relieved, and they stop worrying. Others, however, are convinced that the researchers made a mistake . . . maybe they were looking at someone else's sleep record by mistake! One Saudi Arabian woman, for instance, was convinced that the researchers had tricked her by exchanging sleep recordings, as part of a plot to deport her from the United States (Coleman, 1986). A proper diagnosis for subjective insomnia requires several nights in a sleep lab during which a person complains consistently of sleeplessness—despite objective evidence of normal sleep. Researchers currently estimate that only 10% or fewer insomniacs can be classified as having subjective insomnia (Coleman, 1986; Trinder, 1988).

We have discussed a number of factors that produce insomnia. It is important to remember, however, that most insomnia cannot be traced to a single cause. Like most of human behavior, insomnia typically has more than one explanation.

Treating Insomnia   If you know someone who suffers from insomnia—or if the description of insomnia seems all too personally familiar to you—here are some precautions (Buchholz, 1988; Coleman, 1986; Hoch & Reynolds, 1986; Reynolds, 1986):

1. Do not read or do work in bed; keep the bed as a powerful stimulus to sleep.

2. Go to bed only when you are sleepy, and get up at a regular time.

3. Do not lie in bed thinking or worrying. Get up and do something boring until you are sleepy. Some people find it helpful to describe their worries briefly on a sheet of paper.

4. Once you are in bed, relax your muscles and imagine yourself in a soothing setting, perhaps lying on the beach with a warm sun, gentle breezes, and the the restful sound of waves (Moorcroft, 1989).

5. Omit caffeine and alcohol for several hours prior to bedtime.

6. Schedule any exercise at least 2 hours before bedtime.

7. Avoid long-term use of sleeping pills.

8. Improve your sleeping environment; make sure that the room is quiet, dark, and the correct temperature.

9. If all else fails, contact one of the hundreds of sleep centers throughout the United States. A list of centers, as well as brochures on various sleep disorders, is available from the National Sleep Disorders Foundation, 122 South Robertson Boulevard, Suite 201, Los Angeles, CA 90048.

○ ○

Dreaming

In our dreams, we depart from the constraints we experience in our daytime, conscious thought. Even our daydreams are realistic and sedate, in contrast to some of our dreams. Some dreams are so different from ordinary awareness that they were once thought to be caused by the visitation of alien beings (Oswald, 1987b). Figures 5.6 and 5.7 show two representations of these visitations.

As mentioned before, most dreaming is associated with REM sleep. For example, about 90% of people who are awakened during REM sleep will report that they were experiencing a vivid dream (Coleman, 1986). The non-REM sleep

Figure 5.6
"A Maiden's Dream" by Lorenzo Lotto.

Figure 5.7
"Nightmare" by Henry Fuseli.

associated with Stages 1 through 4 seems to involve a different kind of mental activity. In a classic study, Foulkes (1962) asked people who had just awakened, "What was passing through your mind?" People who had been in one of the stages of non-REM sleep usually reported that they were thinking. In contrast, those who had been in REM sleep usually reported a more vivid, emotional, storylike episode.

In the chapter on the biological basis of behavior, we discussed how the two hemispheres of the brain perform somewhat different kinds of mental activity. The kind of thinking involved in our dreams seems to depend primarily upon our more verbal left hemispheres. The right hemisphere may help to construct some of the visual features of the images in our dreams, but it is primarily the left hemisphere that creates the plots of our dreams (Antrobus, 1987).

We spend 5% to 10% of our lives dreaming (Coleman, 1986). However, we recall only a small portion of those dreams. Some people claim that they never dream. Researchers, however, maintain that everyone dreams; some people simply never remember their dreams. Try Demonstration 5.3 to see whether you can recall your dreams.

The Content of Dreams   What do people dream about? In your dreams, you may fly above the rooftops or climb the walls of your living room, though dreams are often duller than might be supposed. The environmental circumstances can influence the content of dreams. For instance, dreams that people report after investigators wake them up in their own homes are typically more aggressive, friendly, sexual, and success-and-failure oriented than the dreams produced in sleep labs (Oswald, 1987b).

Are there gender differences in dream content? Calvin Hall and his colleagues (1982) collected dream reports from students enrolled in psychology classes at the University of Richmond. The dreams were categorized according to their content. Some of the results are shown in Figure 5.8. As you can see, males were somewhat more likely to feature male characters. Their dreams were typically somewhat more aggressive, and they contained a greater number of weapons. However,

---

Demonstration 5.3

A Dream Journal

Try keeping a dream journal for the next month. Arrange your schedule so that you can lie in bed for a few minutes after awaking in the morning. During this time, lie quietly and relaxed, trying to reconstruct what you have been dreaming about. Once you have identified a fragment, see if you can reconstruct any other details. Keep a pad near your bed, and record as much detail as you can (or as time will allow).

Students who keep dream journals have reported that these additional hints aid their dream recall:

1. Before you go to sleep, tell yourself, "I want to remember all of my dreams. It will be easy to remember them when I wake up in the morning."
2. When you wake up, lie quietly and review your dream in a relaxed fashion. Let your mind flow freely, rather than chasing down specific details.
3. After reviewing the dream, write it down, leaving blanks where there are gaps in your memory.
4. Review what you have written, adding any new information that you recall.
5. Try to recall your emotional reaction during the dream; this effort may bring forth other memories of the dream content.

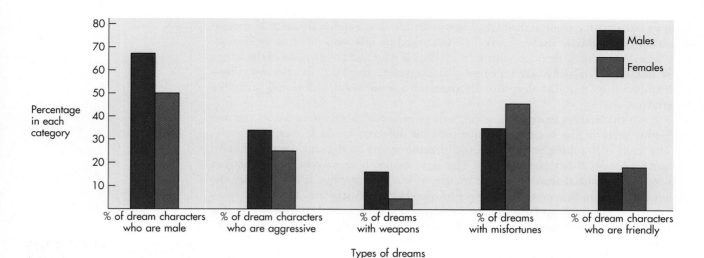

Figure 5.8
Comparing the content of males' and females' dreams. (Based on Hall et al., 1982)

misfortunes were equally likely in men's and women's dreams, and men and women were equally likely to encounter friendly people in their dreams. Yes, women's dreams are slightly different from men's dreams, but the two genders seem to live in largely overlapping dream worlds.

A **nightmare** is a dream that occurs during REM sleep, in which a series of events produces anxiety (Oswald, 1987b). Nightmares usually occur during the end of the sleep period. If sleepers awake quickly from their nightmares, they may be aware that they are unable to move. Our muscles are somewhat paralyzed during REM sleep, yet we are unaware of this paralysis during normal dreaming.

Is the content of your dreams related to the thoughts you had during the previous day? In one study, the content of people's dreams was found to be related to their thoughts as they lay resting and awake immediately before sleep (Rados & Cartwright, 1982). However, the authors point out a problem with the methods of the experiment, related to a concept we discussed in the research methods chapter (chapter 2). The participants in this study were directly questioned about their thoughts during the presleep period. This questioning may have created an experimental demand, so that the participants could have guessed that the experimenter wanted them to report similar dreams. (However, it is difficult to imagine how else the experiments could have gathered the presleep thoughts.)

Can the content of our dreams be modified? Sometimes a telephone ringing while a person is dreaming can change the plot of the dream. However, external stimuli are not incorported into dreams in any consistent fashion (Lavie & Hobson, 1986). Thus, the stimuli from the outside world that figure so prominently during waking consciousness have minimal influence on our dream experiences.

A small portion of people experience **lucid dreaming**; they know they are dreaming and have the sense that they are conscious (Covello, 1984). During these experiences, consciousness seems divided into a dreaming component and a more detached observational component. For example, a British woman reported that she had recurrent dreams of a disastrous telegram. Every time this dream occurred, she would merely remind herself that she was dreaming and shift the plot of her dream (Galvin, 1982). Lucid dreamers can therefore modify the content of their dreams more readily than the rest of us.

Research on lucid dreaming is beginning to blossom (Foulkes, 1990). Laboratory research has established, for example, that lucid dreaming is not simply an intrusion of wakefulness during sleep (Gackenbach & LaBerge, 1988). However, much of the current work on lucid dreaming relies on the self-report of people sleeping in their own homes, unsubstantiated by EEGs to confirm that they were truly dreaming. As noted in chapter 2 and earlier in the current chapter, we cannot necessarily trust self-reports about consciousness (Foulkes, 1990).

Why Do We Dream?   Sigmund Freud's influential theory is examined more thoroughly in later chapters. Freud was one of the first investigators to legitimize the study of dreams. His work, *The Interpretation of Dreams*, sold very few copies when it was published in 1900, yet it eventually provided the first major dream theory of this century (Coleman, 1986).

For Freud, dreams provided access to the unconscious. All our sexual and aggressive impulses were disguised in our dreams. Thus, every dream could be decoded into its true meaning. One person's dream about a tunnel represented a vagina, whereas another person's dream about a banana represented a penis. An analyst could uncover these hidden messages and provide awareness to the dreamer. As you can imagine, hypotheses about symbolism in dreams cannot be readily tested.

A different view of the function of dreams is expressed in the **activation-synthesis hypothesis,** which proposes that the cerebral cortex produces dreams in order to make sense out of the haphazard pattern of signals it receives from the hindbrain. Thus, for example, the hindbrain may send signals to the part of the brain that controls balance, and the cortex "dreams up" an episode about falling. Because the signals arrive at random locations, the dream will have a random, incoherent structure (Hobson, 1988; Hobson & McCarley, 1977).

At this point, answers to the question "Why do we dream?" are largely speculative. It is not clear whether they symbolically represent our embarrassing impulses or whether they are the brain's attempt to make a patchwork quilt out of unrelated neural signals. In any event, both explanations point out that the mind is not simply resting comfortably during sleep. Our muscles may be relatively peaceful, yet our cortex is working overtime.

Sleep researchers have not determined whether our dreams are symbolic or whether they represent the brain's attempt to interpret random signals.

Section Summary: *Sleeping and Dreaming*

- ■ We maintain circadian rhythms partly because of zeitgebers and partly because of our internal clocks; without zeitgebers, we would run on a 25-hour clock.
- ■ Shift schedules and jet lag interrupt the normal circadian rhythms, leading to disrupted sleep and poorer work performance.
- ■ There are wide ranges in the number of hours of sleep that people (and animals) require as well as the time of day at which they function best.
- ■ When people go to sleep, they drift from light sleep (Stage 1) through deep sleep (Stage 4); a different kind of sleep is called REM sleep, when most dreaming occurs.
- ■ Sleep deprivation causes some temporary problems, such as decreased attention and mood changes, but there are no major aftereffects.
- ■ Two theories on why humans need sleep are that sleep is restorative and that it is adaptive.
- ■ Insomnia, a common sleep disorder, has several different origins; in one kind of insomnia, called subjective insomnia, people believe that they have insomnia, though they do in fact sleep.
- ■ Everyone dreams, though people may not recall these dreams; lucid dreamers are people who are aware that they are dreaming.
- ■ Two theories of dreams are that dreams are symbolic and that they make sense out of haphazard cortical stimulation.

Drugs That Influence Consciousness

This chapter began by examining normal waking consciousness, which included both the active mode of consciousness (the focused kind of thought processes) and the passive mode of consciousness (which includes daydreams). Then we explored sleeping and dreaming, a different state of consciousness that involves less body activity, less coherent thoughts, and even different patterns in the brain's electrical activity. However, these states of consciousness occur quite naturally as part of everyday life. Now we consider how consciousness can be altered when people consume certain kinds of mind-altering drugs.

Psychoactive drugs are chemical substances that influence the brain, altering consciousness and producing psychological changes. Psychoactive drugs usually work via the neurotransmitters. As we noted in chapter 3, neurotransmitters are chemical substances stored in the axons; they carry neurological messages across to neighboring neurons. Psychoactive drugs typically increase or decrease the availability of neurotransmitters, or they may even compete with these neurotransmitters.

In many cases, frequent use of a psychoactive drug can produce **tolerance**; increasing amounts of the drug are required to produce the same effect. Habitual users who stop taking the psychoactive drug may experience **withdrawal symptoms**, undesirable effects of discontinued drug use that include nausea, vomiting, abdominal cramps, and muscle spasms. **Addiction** is a physical dependence in which continued use of a psychoactive drug is necessary to prevent withdrawal symptoms.

Psychoactive drugs include illegal drugs such as LSD and cocaine. Psychoactive drugs also include the nicotine in a package of cigarettes, the caffeine in a cup of coffee, and the alcohol in the holiday eggnog. Still, these legal drugs alter consciousness and cause as much harm as those illegal substances. In this chapter we will consider three categories of psychoactive drugs: the depressants such as alcohol, the stimulants such as nicotine and caffeine, and the hallucinogens such as LSD and marijuana.

Depressants

Depressants are drugs that depress central nervous system functioning. These substances reduce pain and tension, and they slow down a person's thinking and actions. The depressants include tranquilizers such as Valium and barbiturates such as Seconal. These depressants are prescription drugs used to treat psychological disorders, and we discuss them in the chapter on psychological therapy (chapter 16).

Another important class of depressants is the **opiates**, which include drugs such as morphine and heroin. These drugs relieve pain, imitating the action of endorphins (chapter 4). Injections of opiates can create a blissful feeling and a decrease in anxiety. When habitual users stop taking an opiate, they often experience severe withdrawal symptoms.

Alcohol is the most familiar of the depressants. Let us consider this potentially very dangerous drug in more detail. Alcohol is often misunderstood. For example, many people assume that it is a stimulant. They claim that alcohol makes a shy person more "stimulated" and outgoing. However, alcohol is actually a depressant. It slows down the rate of impulses through the central nervous system. Alcohol also depresses (or slows the functioning of) parts of the cortex that keep people from performing actions they know are inappropriate. Thus, alcohol acts as a disinhibitor, which explains why shy people may seem to lose some inhibitions after a few drinks. With increasing doses of alcohol, the brain's activity becomes increasingly depressed. People talk with slurred speech, they lose their coordination when they walk, and they fall asleep.

Alcohol problems are common in the United States. Between 11% and 16% of the population is estimated to have alcohol-related problems. The cost of alcoholism—in terms of treatment, loss of productivity, and property damage— is more than $110 billion each year (Gallant, 1987; Kamerow et al., 1986).

Alcohol also causes deaths. The drinkers themselves can die from a single lethal dose; each year, a number of college students die in this fashion. Intoxicated people also die in accidents, and chronic alcoholics die from the long-term damage (Bowden, 1990). People who have been drinking also kill others. Alcohol is involved in 65% of murders and 40% of motor vehicle deaths (Kent, 1990; Salisbury, 1990). As I wrote this chapter, for instance, a local courtroom case involved a man accused of killing a driver education instructor and four students in a daytime drunk-driving incident. Ironically, one of those students had been president of the school's Students Against Drunk Driving organization.

Drunk-driving accidents kill about 22,000 people each year.

Alcoholism also has a devastating effect on the families of alcoholics. It is involved in 65% of spouse beatings and 55% of physical child abuse cases. Children are significantly more likely to have psychological problems if a parent is an alcoholic, though it is important to stress that these problems are not inevitable (Kent, 1990; West & Prinz, 1987). It is also important to stress that these data are based on quasi-experimental and correlational research, so we cannot claim with certainty that alcohol *causes* all these problems.

One active area of research on alcohol's effects concerns the consumption of more moderate amounts of alcohol. In chapter 2, you learned that the participants' expectations can influence the dependent variable. To what extent do drinkers' expectations about the effects of alcohol actually influence their behavior?

A special research design can be used to sort out the effects of the drug itself, as opposed to the effects of people's expectations about how they *should* behave. This design, called the **balanced-placebo design**, consists of four groups of participants, half of whom expect that they will be drinking alcohol and half of whom do not. Furthermore, half of the participants actually do receive alcohol and half do not (see Table 5.1). This kind of design allows researchers to discover the situations in which alcohol influences behavior. For example, it is possible that alcohol makes people uncoordinated only when they think that they are drinking alcohol (condition 1), but it has no effect when they think their beverage contains no alcohol (condition 2).

Jay Hull and Charles Bond (1986) located a total of 36 experiments that use the balanced-placebo design. They then conducted a meta-analysis. (As described in chapter 2, this analysis allows researchers to combine statistically the results of numerous studies in order to draw overall conclusions about the effects of one or more independent variables.) These researchers concluded that alcohol *consumption* had a significant effect on nonsocial behavior. Specifically, it impaired memory and motor behavior, and it improved mood. These three effects occurred

Table 5.1   *The Balanced-Placebo Design to Test the Effects of Alcohol*

| | | EXPECTED BEVERAGE CONTENT | |
		Alcohol	**No Alcohol**
True Beverage Contents	Alcohol	Condition 1	Condition 2
	No Alcohol	Condition 3	Condition 4

whether or not people thought they were drinking alcohol. (In other words, condition 1 and condition 2 in Table 5.1 were similar.) Surprisingly, however, alcohol had little effect on social behavior. It did not make people feel more sexually aroused, and it did not significantly increase aggression.

How did alcohol *expectation* affect behavior? That is, do people who think that the orange juice contains vodka actually behave differently from those who think they are drinking straight orange juice? People who thought they were drinking alcohol were no more likely to experience impaired memory or motor behavior or improved mood. In contrast, those who thought they were drinking alcohol were more likely to report an increase in sexual arousal. (Expectation did not influence the third variable, aggression.)

Let us apply these conclusions. Suppose that a young man has opened a bottle of vodka and consumed several ounces of it. The physiological effects of the alcohol cause him to forget, to act uncoordinated, and to feel happy. Because he knows he has consumed alcohol, he also reports feeling more sexually aroused; expectancy rather than alcohol itself causes this increase in sexual arousal.

Americans have mixed feelings about alcohol; they acknowledge its dangers, yet they associate alcohol with good times. A congressman was once asked to explain his attitude toward whiskey. His reply captures this ambivalence:

> If you mean the demon drink that poisons the mind, pollutes the body, desecrates family life and inflames sinners, then I'm against it. But if you mean the elixir of Christmas cheer, the shield against winter chill, the taxable potion that puts needed funds into public coffers to comfort little crippled children, then I'm for it. This is my position, and I will not compromise. (Lender & Martin, 1982, p. 169)

Unfortunately, however, too many people seem to feel invulnerable to the harmful consequences of this drug. Business executives, government officials, family members, classmates, and regrettably even some of you reading this book will have your lives altered by the effects of alcohol.

Stimulants

Stimulants, as the name implies, are chemicals that increase central nervous system functioning. They appear to work by increasing the release of neurotransmitters such as dopamine in the cortex and the reticular activating system (Dusek & Girdano, 1987). They include caffeine, nicotine, the amphetamines, and cocaine.

Caffeine is the stimulant found in coffee, tea, and some soft drinks. This particular stimulant increases your metabolism, creating a highly awake state. Your heart will probably start to pound faster, and your blood pressure may increase. Caffeine may seem innocent, yet the caffeine in 20 cups of coffee could be lethal if consumed all at once (Dusek & Girdano, 1987).

Next to caffeine, nicotine is the stimulant that is most widely used in the United States. As you know, nicotine is found in cigarettes and other tobacco products. It is clear that nicotine is addicting. A heavy smoker will try to maintain a high level of nicotine by reaching for a cigarette first thing in the morning and continuing to smoke regularly throughout the day (Orford, 1985).

Cigarette smoking is the largest single preventable cause of early death and disability. Smoking has such harmful health consequences that we discuss these consequences—as well as smoking cessation and smoking prevention programs— in the health psychology chapter (chapter 19).

Amphetamines, such as Dexedrine, stimulate both the central nervous system and the sympathetic branch in the autonomic nervous system. These illegal, highly addicting drugs produce an increase in heart rate and blood pressure. Amphetamine users report a feeling of happiness, and other people are likely to notice that users are more talkative and jumpy. Amphetamines can produce irritability and anxiety, and they also interfere with sleep. Some students, disregarding the harmful effects of amphetamines, take these drugs to help them to resist sleep for an all-night study session prior to an examination. However, when they actually take the exam, they are likely to discover that they have difficulty paying attention. In addition, their judgment, problem-solving ability, and accuracy are likely to be impaired (Dusek & Girdano, 1987).

Cocaine is an even more potent stimulant. Sigmund Freud was initially convinced that cocaine could cure nearly all human disorders. Later, however, he discovered its harmful side effects (McKim, 1986). Cocaine creates a feeling of excitement, but large doses and repeated use can lead to anxiety, hallucinations, insomnia, and aggressive behavior. In some cases, even a relatively small dose can lead to cardiac arrest and death. Individual differences in addictive tendencies are large. Apparently some cocaine users seem to be able to control its use; most, however, increase their use and can become addicted (Dusek & Girdano, 1987; Fisher et al., 1987; Washton & Gold, 1987). Obviously, the risks of cocaine use are enormous, and no researchers endorse using this potentially deadly drug.

Crack is a powerful, extremely addictive new form of cocaine. When smoked, its active ingredients travel swiftly to the brain. Crack also produces more medical complications and more psychological disorders than cocaine. For example, crack users experience more disordered thinking and suicidal inclinations, and they are more likely to be violently aggressive (Honer et al., 1987).

Hallucinogens

Hallucinogens are chemical substances that alter people's perceptions of reality and may cause vivid hallucinations. Hallucinogens include several synthetic drugs, such as LSD and PCP, as well as substances extracted from plants, such as marijuana.

LSD, or lysergic acid diethylamide, is an extremely powerful hallucinogen; a tiny speck can alter consciousness within an hour. Shortly after taking LSD, a person typically becomes extremely emotional, with intense laughing or crying. The shapes and colors of objects in the room soon look altered. The LSD user may experience synesthesia, a crossing of the sense responses in which people seem to hear colors and see sounds. Figure 5.9 shows drawings made by one man after taking LSD. Less often, users experience hallucinations. They may report that they see religious figures or enchanted places. LSD clearly impairs cognitive processes, because a person who has taken LSD has difficulty concentrating, appears confused, and refuses to perform simple intellectual tasks. LSD users may also experience intense panic, which can require medical attention.

PCP, or phencyclidine piperidine, is often known by its street name, angel dust. PCP has complex properties: It can be a stimulant, a depressant, a hallucinogen, and a painkiller—all at the same time. The most common effect is that PCP users feel depersonalized, as if they are separated from the people and objects around them. Time seems to slow down, motor coordination decreases, speech becomes senseless, and users may experience hallucinations. PCP users may also feel invulnerable, leading them to take risks and to commit violent acts (Dusek & Girdano, 1987).

Marijuana is considered to be a minor hallucinogen. It is derived from the flowers and leaves of a weed called *Cannabis sativa*. Like other hallucinogens, marijuana alters the perception of sights, sounds, and touch. People who use marijuana every day claim that it encourages them to contemplate and increase

Figure 5.9
Drawings after taking LSD.

a. No effect (20 minutes after first dose).

b. Some alterations in perception (25 minutes after second dose).

c. Most intense effects (2 hours and 45 minutes after first dose).

d. The drug is beginning to wear off (after 5 hours and 45 minutes).

e. Effects are nearly gone (after 8 hours).

a.

b.

c.

d.

e.

their self-understanding. However, a study of regular users showed that they often avoided thinking about the pain they had experienced in their childhood, and they failed to see how they were partially responsible for their current failures in interpersonal relationships (Hendin et al., 1987). Marijuana impairs some kinds of cognitive activities, such as reading comprehension, memory, and arithmetic (Dusek & Girdano, 1987; Miller & Branconnier, 1983).

People who use marijuana regularly tend to have poor academic performance, and they are more likely to commit theft and vandalism (Dusek & Girdano, 1987). However, as you can probably guess, it is difficult to know how to interpret these findings because they are based on correlations. Does marijuana *cause* these problems? Alternatively, are people who have academic and delinquency problems more likely than problem-free people to begin to use marijuana regularly? In other words, people are not randomly assigned to the marijuana users and nonusers groups. Still, caution seems essential until we know more about its long-term effects.

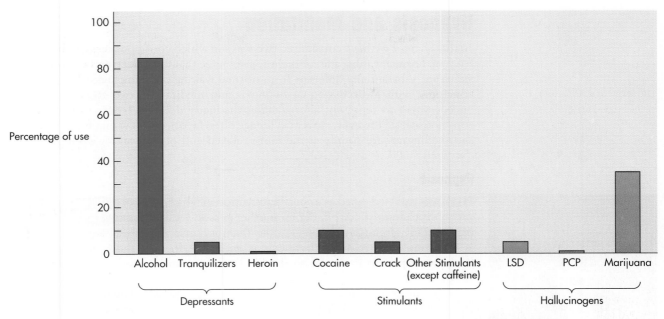

Figure 5.10
Drug use among people aged 18–22.

Psychoactive Drug Use

Figure 5.10 shows some current data about drug use in college students. Alcohol clearly tops the list, followed by marijuana. A substantial percentage of students have also tried cocaine and other stimulants.

From time to time, we hear about proposals to legalize certain currently illegal drugs. Those who favor the legalization of marijuana, for example, argue that marijuana is no more likely than alcohol or tobacco to harm individuals or promote crime. Those who oppose legalization argue that greater availability of these drugs would move us even further toward an addictive society (Bales, 1988). Another argument against legalization is that decades of research were required to accumulate evidence about the dangers of cigarettes. We simply do not have comparable research about the potential dangers of marijuana and other psychoactive drugs. Many medications produce harmful side effects that are not discovered until decades after they have become widely used. Consequently, it is both foolish and dangerous to be casual about using any drugs that alter consciousness.

Section Summary: Drugs That Influence Consciousness

- The most common depressant, alcohol, influences memory, motor behavior, and mood; when people believe they have consumed alcohol (even if they have not), they report being more sexually aroused.
- Stimulants include caffeine, nicotine, the amphetamines, and cocaine; they increase central nervous system functioning.
- Hallucinogens such as LSD, PCP, and marijuana alter people's perceptions, memory, and other cognitive abilities.

Hypnosis and Meditation

In this chapter we have considered two ways in which consciousness can be altered from its normal waking state. Psychologists agree that both sleep and drug-induced states are substantially different from normal waking consciousness. This chapter concludes with a discussion of hypnosis and meditation, two topics that were once thought to represent altered states distinctly different from normal waking consciousness. However, current evidence often favors the view that both hypnosis and meditation are simply at the more relaxed end of the waking state.

Hypnosis

Hypnosis can be defined as a social interaction in which one person—the subject—responds to suggestions offered by another person—the hypnotist; these responses may include alterations in perception, memory, and action (Kihlstrom, 1985). It is important to stress that hypnosis is *not* sleep. In fact, the EEG record of a hypnotized person is similar to the EEG of a person in a waking state (Wester, 1986).

In one of my classes, I asked students to describe how they thought hypnosis was induced in adult subjects. A few thought that the subject would be required to stare at an object hanging from a chain, which swung slowly back and forth. Others thought that subjects were instructed to gaze into the hypnotist's eyes, and they mentioned cartoon representations of flashing stars and pinwheels shooting out from hypnotists' eyes. Nothing that exotic or supernatural is necessary, however. Instead, the hypnotist simply encourages the subjects to relax. Speaking slowly and soothingly, the hypnotist tells the subjects that their eyes will become heavy and will eventually close by themselves (Bowers, 1984).

Deeply hypnotized people report very unusual sensations. They say that they feel very relaxed, but some say that their bodies feel light and others report they feel heavy. Some report floating, some sinking (Bowers, 1976). They report that their arms can rise up into the air on their own, in response to the hypnotist's suggestion. In response to other suggestions from the hypnotist, people may report that a mosquito is buzzing around their legs, that their arms are immobile, and that ammonia smells like an expensive perfume (Balthazard & Woody, 1985). Incidentally, it is important to emphasize that "stage hypnotists"—who use hypnosis for entertaining a crowd rather than research or therapy—count on their subjects to cooperate and fake some of the suggestions. Thus, the volunteer who apparently believes he is Frank Sinatra crooning "Strangers in the Night" is probably an extravert who does not want to disappoint the audience (Barber, 1986).

The first hypnotist was Franz Anton Mesmer, an Austrian physician who claimed to have magnetic powers. In 18th-century Paris, he quickly gained fame by encouraging people into trancelike states, as shown in Figure 5.11. Unfortunately for Mesmer, the king of France appointed a commission to investigate this new technique. (Ben Franklin, who was the ambassador to France at this time, was included in the team.) The royal commission ultimately concluded that hypnotism was a hoax (Bowers, 1976). As a consequence, hypnotism lost its popularity for many years. However, in the 1960s, American researchers revived interest in hypnotism, arguing that it was either an altered state or an example of social role playing, but not a hoax. Let us begin by looking at several hypnotic phenomena. We then consider two important theories of hypnosis.

Specific Hypnotic Phenomena   Part of the reason that hypnosis is so intriguing is that hypnotized people *seem* to behave quite differently from people in the

The hypnotist encourages his subject to relax, so that her eyes close automatically.

Figure 5.11
Franz Anton Mesmer (1734–1815), the first hypnotist.

normal waking state. We discuss five kinds of behavior evidenced by people under hypnosis. First, however, try Demonstration 5.4.

1. *Suggestibility.* Hypnotized people are likely to respond to suggestions from the hypnotist. For example, the hypnotist may suggest that the subjects' hands are slowly being drawn closer and closer together. The subjects respond, their hands gradually approaching each other. A casual observer might conclude that these subjects are consciously obeying a request. However, the subjects often report that they felt their hands drawing together automatically and involuntarily (Bowers, 1984).

The hypnotist may give the subject instructions under hypnosis that are to be carried out after returning to the conscious waking state; this phenomenon is called **posthypnotic suggestion.** The hypnotist typically also instructs the subject not to recall anything about the hypnosis session after leaving the hypnotic state; this phenomenon is called **posthypnotic amnesia.** Suppose, for example, that the hypnotist instructs a hypnotized man that he must scratch his head when he hears a whistle, soon after returning to the waking state. The hypnotist also tells this man that he will recall nothing about these instructions. After leaving the hypnotic state, the man hears a whistle and immediately begins to scratch himself. When asked why he is scratching, the man simply replies, "I had a sudden itch."

2. *Perceptual effects.* Subjects can be encouraged to perceive objects that are not present (**positive hallucinations**). They can also be encouraged *not* to see objects that are present (**negative hallucinations**). For example, a hypnotized woman may be encouraged to "see" a mosquito buzzing around her head. She may also be encouraged to believe that a nearby chair is invisible.

Several studies, however, suggest that the sensory information is still processed by the brain in the case of negative hallucinations. For example, one group of researchers studied the Ponzo illusion (Figure 5.12a) and induced the negative hallucination that the slanted lines on each side would disappear. Subjects were then instructed to judge the relative length of the two horizontal lines. If the two slanted lines were truly invisible, subjects should report that the horizontal lines

---

Demonstration 5.4

Beliefs About Hypnosis

Take a moment to consider how you have been exposed to the topic of hypnosis before reading about it in this chapter. Have you read about it in newspapers, magazines, novels, or other textbooks? Has hypnosis been shown on television programs, or have you heard it mentioned in movies? Have you discussed hypnotism with your friends, or has it been a topic in any previous course? Finally, have you seen a stage hypnotist perform?

Based on the information from all these sources, complete the following questionnaire by answering "true" or "false."

1. When a hypnotist tells subjects that their hands will draw together, they may report that their hands do seem to come together automatically.

2. When the hypnotist instructs subjects that they will be unable to see a visual stimulus, that stimulus becomes truly invisible.

3. If a woman is hypnotized during childbirth, her labor pains can be reduced.

4. Hypnosis increases the accuracy of a person's memory about forgotten events.

5. Under hypnosis, people are more likely to "recall" events that never really occurred.

6. Under hypnosis, people can be "regressed" so they act exactly the way they did when they were younger.

The answers can be found at the end of the chapter.

Figure 5.12
The Ponzo illusion (left) and same horizontal lines without the slanted framing lines (right).

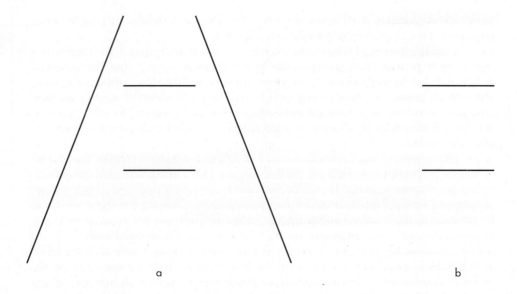

a   b

are equally long, because they should see only the two lines in Figure 5.12b. In fact, they reported that the top line was longer, indicating that their visual systems were still processing the slanted lines. Thus, those mysterious lines were registered in the subjects' visual systems, even though they were not conscious of them (Miller et al., 1973).

One of the most practical applications of hypnosis is a second perceptual effect, reduced pain under hypnosis. In childbirth, for instance, hypnotic instructions can reduce labor pains and also shorten the duration of labor. Or consider the data for people suffering from severe burns. The hypnotic suggestion that the patient feels cool and comfortable can substantially reduce the pain and also the number of times patients request narcotic medications (Ewin, 1986; Kihlstrom, 1985; Venn, 1986). In chapter 4, we noted that pain requires a psychological explanation as well as a physiological explanation. From the research on hypnosis, we have additional evidence that thoughts and suggestions influence how much pain we feel.

3. *Memory.*   You have probably seen a Grade-B movie plot that goes something like this . . . the Sweet Young Thing has been a witness to a blood-curdling murder, yet she cannot remember what the murderer looked like. Enter the hypnotist. You remember him, the one with the flashing stars and pinwheels shooting out from his eyes? "Look deep into my eyes," he chants. The S.Y.T. looks deep into his eyes, and her eyes go blank and dreamy. Then she suddenly shouts, "I now remember it as clear as day! He had black oily hair, slicked back behind his ears, piercing black eyes, and a wart on his left nostril, just above a drooping mustache." Then they track down the villain, who is promptly brought to justice.

You may be disappointed to learn that the research on hypnotically improved memory is nowhere near as convincing as the late-night plot. In fact, in one study, hypnosis was no more effective in retrieving "lost" memories than was a more standard cognitive technique, for example, urging the person to try to recall the context in which the event occurred (Geiselman et al., 1985). Looking over a large number of studies, Smith (1983) concluded, "Controlled laboratory studies have consistently failed to demonstrate any hypnotic memory improvement" (p. 387).

A major problem with "hypnotically refreshed" memory is **confabulation**; a hypnotized subject may simply make up an item in memory to replace one that he or she cannot retrieve. In one study, for instance, Dwyan and Bowers (1983) presented 60 pictures of common objects. Then the participants in the study were encouraged to remember as many pictures as they could, over a period of 7 days. By this time, the typical subject had recalled 38 of the 60 items. Then came the critical test: Would hypnosis bring forth more memories than standard instructions? Half of the participants were then hypnotized and told to relax, focusing all their attention on the pictures they had seen a week ago. The other half were simply told to relax and focus attention on the pictures; they were not hypnotized.

As Figure 5.13 shows, the hypnotized people recalled more than twice as many items that had not previously been mentioned, in contrast to the control group. However, if you look closely, you will see that most of these items were incorrect. That is, they were not on the original list. In fact, the ratio of correct to incorrect items is similar for the hypnotized and the control groups. Hypnotized people may simply be less cautious about reporting items as true memories. Occasionally, they will report something they actually saw, but they are more likely to simply manufacture a memory.

Occasionally, newspapers report the successful use of hypnosis to solve a criminal case. In one impressive case, schoolchildren on a bus had been kidnapped, and the driver recalled very little of this stressful event. Under hypnosis, the driver recalled the license plate numbers of the kidnappers. Admittedly, this is a convincing story, yet Smith (1983) reminds us of a rule we stressed in chapter 2: Where was the control group? How do we know it was the hypnosis that was effective, rather than a relaxing atmosphere and the encouragement for the bus driver to try to reinstate the context at the time of the kidnapping? We really have no evidence that hypnosis per se encouraged the additional recall.

The research on hypnosis and the discovery of the confabulation effect have had an important impact on the use of hypnosis in the courtroom. Specifically, the American Medical Association has recommended that witnesses who have been previously hypnotized should not give courtroom testimony (Orne, 1986). In short, hypnosis is not a magical key that unlocks the unconscious and reveals buried memories.

4. *Age regression.*   In **age regression**, a hypnotized person is given suggestions to reexperience an event that occurred at an earlier age and to act like and feel like a child of that particular age. Like the concept of hypnotically refreshed memory, the concept of age regression seems very dramatic. It is impressive, for example, to watch a 40-year-old begin to print like a kindergartener. However, careful examination almost always shows that people may *report* the experience of being a child is convincingly realistic but that the actions are not really childlike.

Consider the hypnotized subject who was regressed to age 6. He wrote with childlike printing—but perfect spelling—"I am conducting a psychological ex-

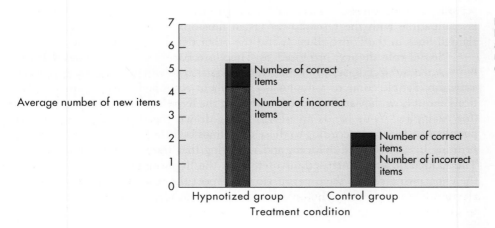

Figure 5.13
New items "recalled" by hypnotized and control groups. Note that the majority of each are incorrect. (Based on Dwyan & Bowers, 1983)

periment which will assess my psychological capacity" (Orne, 1951). Reviewing 60 years of research on age regression, Nash (1987) concludes, "There is no evidence for a literal reinstatement of childhood functioning during hypnotic-age-regression procedures" (p. 42).

5. *The hidden observer.*   Try to picture this experiment: A hypnotized student thrusts her arm into icy water, keeping it there for a full minute. She has been previously instructed that the experience will not be painful. Every few seconds, she rates her pain on a 0 to 10 scale, and she calls out very low numbers. Elbow deep in frigid water, she mysteriously seems to feel no pain. However, she has been told that her other hand has access to a part of her consciousness that is hidden from her hypnotized self. This hand presses a key to indicate that the icy bath is indeed excruciatingly painful. According to this **hidden-observer phenomenon**, the two parts of unconsciousness are separate from each other, with one part apparently hypnotized and the other hidden part being more rational (Hilgard et al., 1975). In the words of one hypnotized person:

> The hidden observer seemed like my real self when I'm out of hypnosis, only more objective. When I'm in hypnosis, I'm imagining, letting myself pretend, but somewhere the hidden observer knows what's really going on. (Hilgard, 1986, p. 209)

Notice that the hidden-observer phenomenon is somewhat like the topic of lucid dreaming, discussed earlier in the chapter. It is as if one part of consciousness enters an altered state, but the other part looks on, from a detached and objective standpoint. Lucid dreaming is rare, but the hidden-observer phenomenon is relatively common. Between 50% and 90% of highly hypnotizable subjects report a hidden-observer experience (Kilstrom, 1985; Zamansky & Bartis, 1985).

Theories of Hypnosis   We have seen that hypnotized people often behave differently from people in the normal waking state, though the differences may not be as dramatic as the media suggest. People report that they obey the hypnotist's instructions involuntarily, they report that objects are no longer seen (though visual-illusion studies demonstrate that they are), and they report they feel no pain (though hidden-observer studies suggest they do). Hypnosis does not enhance memory substantially, and hypnosis does not produce realistic age regression. How can we explain these results? Two theories have been particularly important: neodissociation theory and social role theory.

Neodissociation theory, proposed by Ernest Hilgard (1986), stresses that hypnosis produces a dissociation or division in consciousness, so that behaviors, thoughts, and feelings operate independently—as if there are two different channels. This theory is compatible with the hidden-observer phenomenon of two separate consciousnesses, one feeling pain and the other denying it. Similarly, it is compatible with the research on visual illusions; one channel processes the slanted lines in the Ponzo illusion and the other denies that they exist.

Social role theory, proposed by Theodore Barber (1979), stresses that the hypnotized subject is simply acting out a social role consistent with the social situation. People come to a hypnosis experiment equipped with certain expectations about how they are supposed to act, and the hypnotist also gives instructions (for example, "Your hands are slowly being drawn together . . ."). Hypnotized people therefore act according to these guidelines by bringing their arms together, printing like 6-year-old children, and reporting that the ice bath is not painful. The hidden-observer instructions merely let the hypnotized subjects know that the experimenter gives them permission to report the pain that they have felt all along (Kihlstrom, 1985). Thus, Barber believes that hypnosis does not represent

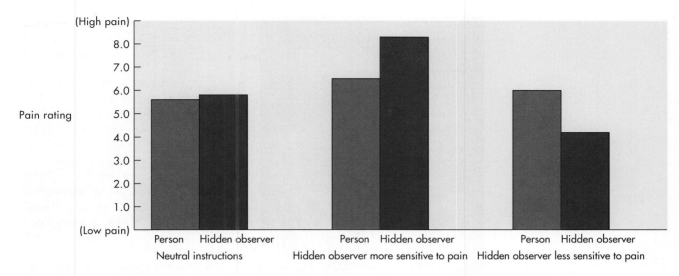

Figure 5.14
Instructions influence whether the hidden observer is more or less sensitive to pain. (Based on Spanos et al., 1983)

a special state of consciousness. Instead, hypnosis represents an unusual social situation in which the hypnotized subjects know that they must act compliant, obeying the demand characteristics of the situation.

It is clear that social role theory can explain some aspects of hypnosis. For example, when the hypnotist tell hypnotized subjects that the hidden observer is particularly sensitive to pain, they report more pain in the "hidden-observer" channel than in the "person" channel. As Figure 5.14 shows, however, the results are just the opposite when people are told that the hidden observer is *insensitive* to pain (Spanos et al., 1983). People's expectations about how they are supposed to behave therefore influence their hypnotic responses.

But does social role theory explain all of the hypnotic effects, or just many of them? Alternatively, does hypnosis produce an altered state of consciousness—as Hilgard suggests—with one part of the mind transformed and the other part cool and rational? I wish the answer were clear-cut. Unfortunately, it would be dishonest to provide a definite "yes" or "no" answer to these questions until the research is more conclusive.

Meditation

Meditation is a group of techniques that attempt to focus attention and to avoid rambling or worried thoughts (Shapiro, 1984). Some meditation techniques focus on body movement, as in the case of the Sufi whirling dervishes shown in Figure 5.15. Other techniques, such as the one shown in Figure 5.16, emphasize that the meditator should be motionless and passive.

Some meditation techniques encourage people to focus their concentration on an external object. For instance, Deikman (1966) encouraged people to focus upon a blue vase. They each reported that their perception of the vase shifted, often to a deeper, more intense blue. Others said that the vase seemed to change shape or size. One person reported feelings of merging with the vase, "as though it were almost part of me." It may be useful at this point to recall the social roles explanation of hypnosis and apply it to meditation. Imagine yourself seated in front of a vase, after receiving instructions about meditation techniques. Would you really feel comfortable reporting to the meditation instructor—after many minutes of staring at that vase—"No, it was blue when I started and blue when I finished"?

Figure 5.15
The Sufi whirling dervishes claim that they enter an altered state of consciousness through an energetic, twirling dance.

Figure 5.16
A different kind of meditative technique is said to produce an altered state of consciousness through quiet meditation.

People who are enthusiastic about meditation claim that it can be helpful in reducing arousal. A comprehensive article by David Holmes (1984) is not very optimistic about these effects, however. Holmes objects to most of the research about meditation on the grounds of methodological flaws. For example, many reports are case studies, which offer intriguing reports of individuals' experiences. Because case studies never include a control group, we cannot conclude that they demonstrate the effectiveness of meditation. Many other studies compare people's arousal levels under meditation with their arousal levels while sitting quietly. However, these studies offer no evidence that meditation is any more effective than instructions to rest and relax.

A third group of studies contrasts an experimental group, instructed to meditate, with a control group, instructed to rest. Unfortunately for meditation enthusiasts, there is no substantial evidence that meditation reduces physiological arousal. For example, breathing rate, blood pressure, and heart rate did not show any consistent significant differences.

Some have claimed that people who practice meditation are better able to control their arousal when they are in a threatening situation. In a typical study, a meditation condition was compared with a condition in which people were trained to relax their muscles as well as with a control condition receiving no treatment (Boswell & Murray, 1979). In this experiment, people then took a difficult IQ test and were lead to believe that they had performed poorly on the test. When the stress levels were then measured, researchers found no significant differences among the conditions. In some other research, relaxation therapy was even found to be more effective than meditation (Holmes, 1984).

Holmes has offered clear-cut evidence that meditation does not change objective measures of arousal; the body does not seem to be substantially changed. It is possible that people subjectively feel as if they have entered a different state of consciousness, just as they subjectively report that their hands are being automatically pulled together in a hypnosis experiment. Can we accept subjective reports as sufficient proof that people have entered an altered state? Most psychologists would require some change in an observable measure—and not simply self-report—before they acknowledge that meditation differs from the normal waking state.

Section Summary: Hypnosis and Meditation

- Hypnotized people may respond to the hypnotist's suggestions and experience visual hallucinations and reduced pain, but their memory is not substantially improved, nor do they show convincing age regression; many report the hidden-observer phenomenon.
- Two major theories of hypnosis are neodissociation theory and social role theory.
- Meditation does not substantially reduce physiological arousal or control arousal in threatening situations.

REVIEW QUESTIONS

1. What is consciousness? Briefly describe the major topics in this chapter, noting which seem to involve major changes from the active mode of consciousness and which may not differ substantially from this "standard" state.

2. How do daydreams differ from dreams that occur during sleep? What factors are related to the amount of time people spend daydreaming?

3. Several parts of this chapter examined people's insights into their mental processes. Discuss this issue with respect to these topics: (a) consciousness about higher mental processes, (b) lucid dreaming, and (c) the hidden-observer phenomenon.

4. One of the main points in the section on sleep was that sleep is an active process. Discuss this concept, being sure to mention (a) EEGs, (b) body movement, and (c) dreams.

5. How do zeitgebers help us maintain circadian rhythms? How are the concepts of free-running, shift schedules, and jet lag relevant to circadian rhythms? In describing these concepts, be sure to think of an example of each.

6. Imagine that a high school student you know is intrigued with the topic of sleep and asks you that inevitable question, "Why do we sleep?" Summarize the major reasons, as clearly as possible. Suppose that the second question is "Why do we dream?" Again, summarize the major explanations.

7. Suppose that an elderly person you know has difficulty falling asleep. List as many of the different kinds of insomnia as you can remember, and propose some suggestions for how to reduce the problem.

8. What are the three major kinds of psychoactive drugs described in this chapter? For each of these, make a list of some general physical and psychological effects that they produce. We discussed expectancy effects in connection with alcohol. How might expectancy effects be relevant for some of the other drugs?

9. Describe each of the hypnotic phenomena that were discussed in this chapter. Then contrast the two theories of hypnosis and describe how each of these theories of hypnosis would explain the various hypnotic phenomena.

10. From what you have read and heard prior to reading this chapter, would you have concluded that hypnosis and meditation were substantially different from the normal waking state? If your opinion on these topics has changed since reading this chapter, what information helped to change your mind?

NEW TERMS

consciousness
active mode of consciousness
passive mode of consciousness
daydream
sleep
circadian rhythm
zeitgebers
free-running
shift schedules
jet lag
beta waves
alpha waves
Stage 1 sleep
Stage 2 sleep
Stage 3 sleep
Stage 4 sleep
REM sleep
insomnia
Disorders of Initiating and Maintaining Sleep (DIMS)
nightmare
lucid dreaming
activation-synthesis hypothesis

psychoactive drugs
tolerance
withdrawal symptoms
addiction
depressants
opiates
balanced-placebo design
stimulants
hallucinogens
hypnosis
posthypnotic suggestion
posthypnotic amnesia
positive hallucinations
negative hallucinations
confabulation
age regression
hidden-observer phenomenon
neodissociation theory
social role theory
meditation

ANSWERS TO DEMONSTRATIONS

Demonstration 5.4   1. T;   2. F;   3. T;   4. F;   5. T;   6. F

RECOMMENDED READINGS

Coleman, R. M. (1986). *Wide awake at 3:00 a.m.* New York: Freeman. An expert on sleep disorders, Richard Coleman provides a very readable perspective on biological clocks, sleep, and sleep disturbances.

Dusek, D. E., & Girdano, D. A. (1987). *Drugs: A factual account* (4th ed.). New York: Random House. These authors include chapters on alcohol, marijuana, hallucinogens, stimulants, and smoking, with background information on biological mechanisms of psychoactive drugs written at a level that introductory students will find appropriate.

Horne, J. A. (1988). *Why we sleep: The functions of sleep in humans and other mammals.* Oxford: Oxford University Press. This more-advanced-level book on sleep offers a clear summary of sleep deprivation and theories and research on sleep.

Kihlstrom, J. F. (1985). Hypnosis. *Annual Review of Psychology, 36,* 385–418. Kihlstrom's chapter provides an excellent overview of hypnotic phenomena, theories, and individual differences in hypnotizability.

CHAPTER

6

Learning

It is the Fourth of July, and the King family is gathering at the county park for their annual family reunion. A psychologist interested in perception might analyze what they see, hear, and taste. A psychologist interested in states of consciousness would note that Uncle Alex appears to be in Stage 2 sleep, and Uncle Joe's beer consumption has brought him to a different state of consciousness. A psychologist interested in learning, however, would focus on the mechanisms by which the behavior of each family member had changed.

For instance, Grandpa is playing with 10-month-old Johnny, and they are enjoying Johnny's favorite jack-in-the-box, which plays "Pop Goes the Weasel." Johnny and Grandpa both jump prematurely at the notes just before Jack actually pops out of the box (classical conditioning). At another table, Aunt Millie has changed the topic of conversation from the upcoming presidential election, a topic that prompted pained expressions from her more conservative relatives, to baseball, a topic that restores their smiles (operant conditioning). At a third table, 2-year-old Vanessa is playing patty-cake, clapping her hands enthusiastically with her grandmother (observational learning). In fact, not a minute will pass during this family reunion without at least one family member demonstrating one of the three kinds of learning we discuss in this chapter.

Psychologists define **learning** as a relatively permanent change in behavior or knowledge due to experience. We need to consider the elements of this definition in more detail. First, notice that the definition uses the word *change*, rather than *improvement*, because learning can involve misconduct as well as socially appropriate behavior. This change involves not only our outward behavior but also our knowledge. (Little Vanessa might know how to have a temper tantrum by watching her older brother, even if she never demonstrates this behavior.) Finally, the phrase "due to experience" is necessary in order to eliminate many other kinds of changed behavior that are not considered learning. For example, drugs, injury, disease, and maturation all produce changes in behavior; however, none of these changes involve learning (Chance, 1988).

Learning is essential to humans because it allows us to change and acquire a complex set of sophisticated skills. To appreciate the importance of learning, imagine that you had an identical twin who was raised since birth with no opportunities to learn. Reared in a barren room, your twin never learned to speak, to read, to form emotional relationships, or to explore the world. Imagine this twin in your shoes right now and visualize this person trying to live your life for the next 24 hours. We often fail to acknowledge the importance of learning unless we imagine life without it.

This chapter explores three basic and important kinds of learning, each illustrating a relatively permanent change in behavior or knowledge that can be traced to experience. The first topic is classical conditioning, a topic that is more complex than it initially appears. In the section on operant conditioning, we consider how rewards and punishments influence behavior. Finally, we discuss how people learn by watching others, in the section on observational learning.

Classical Conditioning

In **classical conditioning**, we learn that certain stimuli in the environment are predictive of certain events. Let us consider an example. Eight-month-old Billy and his family have just moved to a new home. Billy is quietly playing in the bedroom when a gust of wind makes the wind chimes jingle. An instant later, the wind blows Billy's bedroom door shut with a resounding bang. Startled, little Billy flinches and then screams vigorously. This startled reaction is a natural, unlearned response.

The next morning, Billy is lying in his crib when the wind once again jingles the chimes, followed by another loud bang from the bedroom door. Billy is likely to learn that there is a predictive relationship in his environment. That is, the jingling of the wind chimes predicts that the door will slam loudly. After several similar experiences, Billy may begin to flinch and scream as soon as the wind chimes jingle.

In classical conditioning—prior to any learning—an unconditioned stimulus elicits an unconditioned response. The **unconditioned stimulus** is defined as the stimulus in classical conditioning that elicits an unlearned response. The **unconditioned response** is defined as an unlearned response to a stimulus.

In our previous example, the loud noise from the slamming door can be labeled as an unconditioned stimulus, and the startled reaction can be labeled as an unconditioned response (Figure 6.1). The wind chimes (conditioned stimulus) initially produce no reaction. However, they become a reliable predictor for the loud noise. The chimes soon produce a conditioned response of flinching and screaming, even before the door actually slams.

During learning, the organism learns that there is a reliable, predictable relationship between the conditioned stimulus (for instance, the wind chimes) and the unconditioned stimulus (for instance, the door slamming). When classical conditioning has taken place, the conditioned stimulus now elicits a conditioned response. The **conditioned stimulus** is defined as the stimulus that is predictive of the unconditioned stimulus. (That is, the jingling of wind chimes is predictive

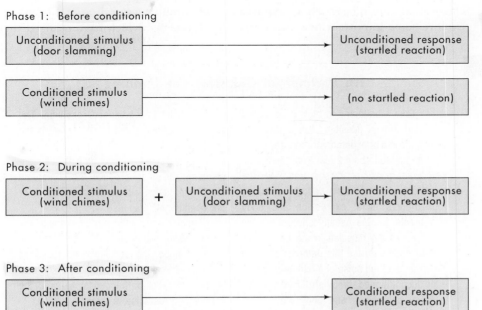

Figure 6.1
An example of classical conditioning.

of a slamming door.) The **conditioned response** is defined as the response that is elicited by the conditioned stimulus.

Take a few minutes to review these four terms and learn them, because they are used throughout this section. Students often find it helpful to keep in mind that *unconditioned* refers to stimuli and responses that do not require learning; this reaction occurs spontaneously. The other two terms, *conditioned* stimuli and responses, require conditioning; this reaction occurs after the learning experience.

Try applying these terms to a different example. Let us assume that you enjoy eating meat and that the taste of steak makes your mouth water. One summer day, you smell the smoke from a neighbor's charcoal fire. Your mouth immediately begins to water, even though you never get an opportunity to taste the meat. Identify the unconditioned stimulus, the unconditioned response, the conditioned stimulus, and the conditioned response. Then try an example of classical conditioning in Demonstration 6.1, which also contains the answer to the barbecued steak question.

Classical conditioning can produce extremely powerful reactions. For example, Leo (1985) describes how a Latin American refugee who had fled to Canada froze in terror when a well-wisher presented him with a gift basket. The basket contained two pineapples, a welcome gift for most people. However, before fleeing his native country, this refugee had been forced to watch as a military guard hacked several prisoners to death with a machete, then calmly carved up a ripe pineapple—without wiping the blade—and ate the bloodstained slices.

Classical conditioning was traditionally considered to be a low-level, automatic kind of learning. In fact, critics typically claimed that classical conditioning was "all spit and twitches" because researchers usually examined salivary responses and reflexes involving muscle movement. In the last 30 years, that view has changed. Classical conditioning may indeed be simpler than many other kinds of learning. However, it often involves memory processes. Furthermore, conditioning involves more than the simple pairing of the conditioned stimulus with the unconditioned stimulus. Even classical conditioning exemplifies our theme of the complexity of psychological processes.

In order to understand classical conditioning more fully, let us first discuss two well-known early studies and then examine the important components of classical conditioning, such as acquisition and stimulus generalization. Then we explore some important new theoretical developments, which have changed the

---

Demonstration 6.1

An Example of Classical Conditioning

Take a balloon and blow it up until it is as inflated as possible. Ask a friend to participate in a brief demonstration, and stand with the balloon about 2 feet from the friend. Take a sharp pair of scissors and move the point toward the inflated balloon, watching your friend's facial expression and body movements. People usually shut their eyes and contract the muscles in the upper part of their bodies during this demonstration. In this case, the loud noise of a balloon popping is the unconditioned stimulus, and the changes in facial expression and body movements represent the unconditioned response. The sight of a balloon about to be popped is the conditioned stimulus (often predictive of a popping noise), which through classical conditioning comes to produce the change in facial expression and body movements, or the conditioned response.

Incidentally, in the earlier example, the unconditioned stimulus is the flavor of meat on the tongue, the unconditioned response is mouth-watering, the conditioned stimulus is the aroma of barbecued steak, and the conditioned response is mouth-watering.

way that psychologists view classical conditioning. The final part of this section looks at some applications.

Two Well-Known Studies in Classical Conditioning

Pavlov's Conditioned Salivation Experiment   It is often intriguing to contemplate how the history of any discipline might have been completely different if an early researcher had been somewhat less curious or less persistent. For example, what might have happened if the Russian physiologist, Ivan Pavlov, had continued to study dogs' digestive systems, rather than making a detour when he observed an interesting psychological phenomenon?

In 1904, Pavlov had received a Nobel prize for his research on physiology. Some of his work used a procedure that measured the production of saliva. Not surprisingly, when meat powder was placed in a dog's mouth, its saliva production increased. However, Pavlov observed that the mere *sight* of food caused an increase in saliva production. More intriguing still, saliva production increased at the mere sight of the experimenter. Even the sound of the experimenter's footsteps elicited salivation.

Pavlov prided himself on being an objective scientist. In fact, the workers in his laboratory were fined if they used any subjective, nonphysiological language (Hergenhahn, 1988). His decision to pursue research on psychological determinants of salivation was therefore a difficult one.

Figure 6.2 shows the experimental equipment used in Pavlov's (1927) classic study on classical conditioning. Notice that the tube running from the dog's cheek allowed the saliva drip to be recorded on the cylinder at the left of the diagram.

The three critical phases of Pavlov's experiment are shown in Figure 6.3. Before conditioning had begun, the unconditioned stimulus (meat powder) produced an unconditioned response (salivation). Pavlov had selected the sound of a bell to serve as the conditioned stimulus. Before conditioning, the bell produced no salivation. Instead the dog simply oriented by looking in the direction of the sound.

Pen Recording on Cylinder

Figure 6.2
The experimental setup for Pavlov's research on classical conditioning, showing saliva tube and harness. (This type of animal research is no longer conducted.)

Figure 6.3
Classical conditioning in Pavlov's study.

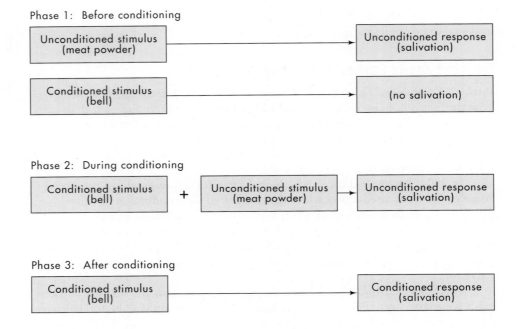

Phase 1: Before conditioning

Unconditioned stimulus (meat powder) → Unconditioned response (salivation)

Conditioned stimulus (bell) → (no salivation)

Phase 2: During conditioning

Conditioned stimulus (bell) + Unconditioned stimulus (meat powder) → Unconditioned response (salivation)

Phase 3: After conditioning

Conditioned stimulus (bell) → Conditioned response (salivation)

During conditioning, the conditioned stimulus (the bell) was followed by the unconditioned stimulus (the meat powder), which continued to produce the unconditioned response (salivation). The conditioned stimulus and the unconditioned stimulus were paired together in this fashion for several trials.

After a number of conditioning trials, Pavlov discovered that the sound of the bell was sufficient to produce salivation. The meat powder did not need to be presented at all. Similarly, a baby may flinch and scream when the wind chimes jingle—the door does not need to slam—and your friends may tense their muscles when the balloon grows dangerously large, even though it has not yet popped.

Watson and Rayner's Conditioned Fear Study   Another famous study was conducted in the United States by John Watson and Rosalie Rayner (1920). These researchers tested an 11-month-old baby named Albert, who showed no fear of animals prior to testing. However, he showed a clear-cut fear reaction whenever a researcher made a loud noise by striking a hammer against a large steel bar located immediately behind Albert's back. (The noise therefore served as the unconditioned stimulus, and the fear reaction was the unconditioned response.)

Watson and Rayner used a white rat as a conditioned stimulus. Whenever Albert reached out to touch the rat, the hammer clanged loudly against the steel bar. After seven pairings of the rat and the noise, Albert cried and avoided the rat, even when the loud noise was no longer delivered. Watson and Rayner concluded that a fear could be learned through conditioning.

Although this study is easily one of the most famous in psychology, it was not one of the best. For instance, Harris (1979) points out a major ethical problem with the study. Watson knew a month in advance that Albert's mother planned to remove him from the research project. Nevertheless, Watson did not decondition the child to make certain that he had no remaining fear of rats. Watson's study would be unacceptable by today's ethical standards. Research participants should not experience unnecessary discomfort or harm. Albert certainly experienced discomfort from the loud noise, and he may have experienced harm if he continued to fear rats after the experiment had ended.

Components of Classical Conditioning

Now that we have discussed several examples, let us examine some components of classical conditioning more closely. You will see that once conditioning has been acquired, it can be applied in some new circumstances (stimulus generalization)—but not all (stimulus discrimination). Furthermore, a conditioned response can be eliminated (extinction), though it may return again (spontaneous recovery). This section therefore helps you appreciate some of the complexities of classical conditioning; this form of learning involves more than the acquisition of a single conditioned response that remains unchanged throughout a lifetime.

Acquisition　**Acquisition** involves learning a new response. In classical conditioning, acquisition involves producing a conditioned response to a conditioned stimulus. Figure 6.4 shows a typical acquisition curve. As you can see, at the beginning of testing, the conditioned stimulus does not elicit the conditioned response. For example, Pavlov's dogs did not initially salivate when the bell rang. During the first few trials, however, the strength of the conditioned response grows rapidly. Later in the testing session, the increase in the strength of the conditioned response is more gradual.

Figure 6.4 shows a fairly leisurely acquisition rate, in which many trials are necessary for the conditioned response to reach its maximum strength. You can probably think of many exceptions to this pattern—cases that require only a single pairing of the conditioned stimulus and the unconditioned stimulus. The Latin American exile mentioned earlier in the chapter acquired his fear of pineapples from a single barbaric act. Recently, my family and I were driving together and had stopped at an intersection, with our flasher indicating a left-hand turn. An inattentive driver rear-ended us, causing some injuries and demolishing our car. For weeks afterward, we all experienced anxiety whenever we were stopped at an intersection and a car approached quickly from the rear. No repeated pairings were necessary; we had learned this anxiety in a single trial. In classical conditioning, acquisition can be rapid—even immediate—when the unconditioned stimulus is intense.

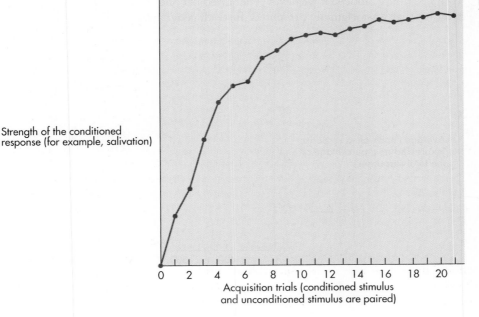

Strength of the conditioned response (for example, salivation)

Acquisition trials (conditioned stimulus and unconditioned stimulus are paired)

Figure 6.4
The acquisition of a conditioned response (typical data).

The blinking red light on top of an ambulance is a conditioned stimulus for most people, because the unconditioned stimulus (the siren) with which it is associated produces an unconditioned response (your heart beats faster).

Most people show some stimulus generalization to the blinking yellow light on the top of a tow truck.

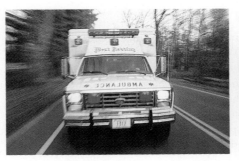

Stimulus Generalization   The car that rear-ended us was large, old, and beige. However, our fear of cars approaching from the rear was not limited to just this kind of car. I suspect that a large old *gray* car would have produced a substantial anxiety response during the month after the accident. My heart might have beaten somewhat faster even if a brand-new red sports car had approached too quickly. We showed **stimulus generalization**, which is the tendency for stimuli other than the original conditioned stimulus to produce the conditioned response (Pearce, 1987).

As you might expect, new stimuli that are highly similar to the conditioned stimulus are more likely than dissimilar stimuli to produce the conditioned response. For example, Figure 6.5 shows data from rabbits that had been conditioned to blink their eyes to a particular tone with a frequency of 1200 Hz (that is, a pitch slightly more than two octaves above middle C). Conditioning was produced by presenting a brief puff of air to the eye, immediately after the tone had been sounded. When the rabbits were tested later, the largest number of conditioned responses was produced by the original tone, 1200 Hz. However, other tones produced some conditioned responses as well. For instance, a tone of 800 Hz (3 notes lower on the piano) produced a substantial response rate, and even a tone of 400 Hz (11 notes lower on the piano) produced some conditioned responses.

Stimulus generalization is useful, both for animals and for humans. After all, classical conditioning involves learning predictive relationships. Our learning would be limited indeed if we never generalized beyond the exact same conditioned stimulus that was originally presented. Instead, generalization allows us to predict

Figure 6.5
Stimulus generalization for a rabbit conditioned with a tone of 1200 Hz frequency. (Based on Liu, 1971)

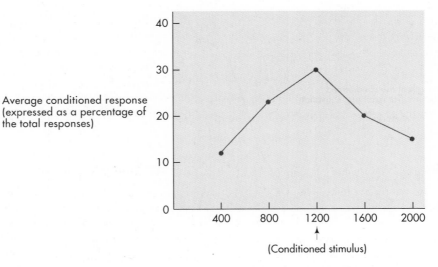

what is likely to happen in new situations. Suppose that a child eats salmon, and the proteins in the salmon produce a strong allergic reaction. The child passes out, has difficulty breathing, and must be brought to the hospital emergency room. Learning should generalize to other fish that look like salmon, in order to avoid further life-threatening episodes. Stimulus generalization is an example of the theme that organisms are well equipped to function in their environments.

Stimulus Discrimination   It is easy to see how stimulus generalization could be carried too far. If people generalized to every new stimulus that somewhat resembled the conditioned stimulus, they would often react inappropriately. Therefore, organisms need to differentiate between similar stimuli, through a process called **stimulus discrimination.** For example, a person who is allergic to fish that have backbones and fins must learn that he or she is not allergic to shellfish. Thus, stimulus generalization and stimulus discrimination work together. Stimulus generalization ensures that we expand our learning beyond the immediate conditioned stimulus. However, stimulus discrimination operates to guarantee that we do not generalize too broadly or inappropriately.

Extinction   Suppose that a dog has learned to salivate to a bell, and then the bell is presented repeatedly *without* the meat powder. Would the dog continue to drool? Pavlov reported that after only five or six trials without meat powder, the dogs no longer produced saliva when the bell was sounded. This gradual weakening and disappearance of a conditioned response is known as **extinction**. Several months after our car accident, for example, my heart no longer pounds when a car approaches from behind.

In general, then, extinction allows us to stop responding when a conditioned stimulus is no longer predictive of an unconditioned stimulus. For example, there is no strong predictive relationship between *car approaching from behind* and *car crashes*. It is likely that I can live the rest of my life without another car approaching from behind and producing a car crash. Therefore, it is not useful for me to remember this relationship.

Spontaneous Recovery   When a period of time has passed following extinction, and the conditioned stimulus is presented once more, the conditioned response may temporarily reappear; this phenomenon is called **spontaneous recovery**. For example, in Figure 6.6, a rabbit has learned to blink (conditioned response) in response to a tone (conditioned stimulus) that is predictive of a puff of air (unconditioned stimulus). Figure 6.6 shows acquisition of this conditioned response over a 12-day period. During the next 8 days, the tone is no longer followed by the puff of air, and extinction occurs. A 4-day rest period follows next, and then the tone is presented, once again, on the next day. The right-hand side of Figure 6.6 shows spontaneous recovery. Notice that the conditioned stimulus produces a substantial conditioned response. However, if the conditioned stimulus continues to be presented without the unconditioned stimulus, extinction will occur once again.

Recent Theoretical Developments in Classical Conditioning

Thirty years ago, psychologists thought that they understood classical conditioning fairly well. After all, what could possibly be complicated about drooling dogs or blinking rabbits? The typical introductory psychology textbook defined classical conditioning as a process in which an unconditioned stimulus is repeatedly paired with a conditioned stimulus, until the conditioned stimulus comes to elicit a response without the presentation of the unconditioned stimulus. We now know

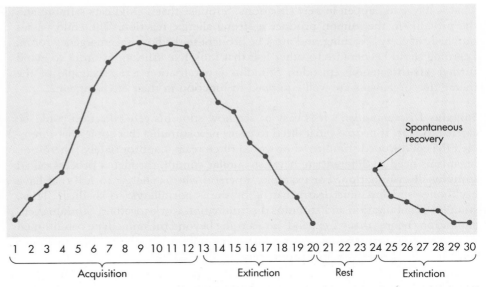

Strength of the conditioned response

1 2 3 4 5 6 7 8 9 10 11 12 13 14 15 16 17 18 19 20 21 22 23 24 25 26 27 28 29 30

Acquisition   Extinction   Rest   Extinction

Spontaneous recovery

Figure 6.6
Acquisition, extinction, and spontaneous recovery of a conditioned response (typical results).

that this definition is incorrect (Rescorla, 1988; Rescorla & Holland, 1982). Let us examine some of the major problems with the earlier views on conditioning and then discuss the implications of these findings for the contemporary ideas about this topic.

1. Classical conditioning does not necessarily require repeated pairings between the conditioned stimulus and the unconditioned stimulus. As we discussed earlier in connection with traumatizing experiences like the Latin American refugee and the pineapple, a single trial may be sufficient to develop a conditioned response.

2. The earlier view stated that learning would occur whenever a neutral, conditioned stimulus was followed by an unconditioned stimulus. That is, contiguity or simple pairing between the conditioned stimulus and the unconditioned stimulus was sufficient to produce learning. We now know that contiguity is *not* sufficient. Let us consider an experiment that demonstrates why simple contiguity is not enough.

Robert Rescorla (1968) studied classical conditioning in rats, using a tone as the conditioned stimulus and a shock as the unconditioned stimulus. He suspected that learning would not occur unless the tone consistently predicted the shock. Situation 1 in Figure 6.7 shows a predictive relationship between the tone and the shock. That is, the shock never occurred except when the tone had been sounded.

In situation 2, however, Rescorla added some extra unconditioned stimuli. That is, rats received additional shocks when the tone was *not* presented. In both cases, there is contiguity between the conditioned stimulus and the unconditioned stimulus; the tone is always presented with shock. Both situations also have an identical number of pairings. However, only situation 1 has a *predictive relationship* between the tone and the shock. Try placing yourself in the position of the rat and figure out whether you would learn to fear the tone in situation 2. The tone is always followed by shocks, but extra shocks are thrown in without the forewarning of the tone. Or imagine Billy and the wind chimes example from the beginning of this section; would Billy react to the chimes if the door often slammed when the chimes did not jingle?

In fact, Rescorla found that the two situations produced different learning patterns. As he had suspected, conditioning occurred in situation 1 but not in situation 2. Simple contiguity is *not* enough. The tone must also provide information about whether the shock will occur. Experiments such as Rescorla's en-

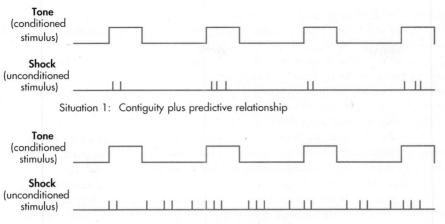

Tone
(conditioned
stimulus)

Shock
(unconditioned
stimulus)

Situation 1: Contiguity plus predictive relationship

Tone
(conditioned
stimulus)

Shock
(unconditioned
stimulus)

Situation 2: Contiguity *without* predictive relationship

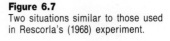

Figure 6.7
Two situations similar to those used
in Rescorla's (1968) experiment.

couraged psychologists to revise their definition of classical conditioning to emphasize *predictive relationships*, rather than simple contiguity (Rescorla, 1988).

3. The earlier view stressed that any perceivable stimulus could function as a conditioned stimulus. However, research by John Garcia and his colleagues demonstrated that some associations are much more readily learned than others (Garcia, 1984; Garcia et al., 1972; Garcia & Koelling, 1966). These studies examined the effects of radiation on laboratory rats. Radiation (an unconditioned stimulus) produces nausea (an unconditioned response). The research examined **taste aversion**, or the development of an intense dislike for a food through conditioning.

Garcia and Koelling (1966) found that classical conditioning could be established when sweet-tasting water was paired with radiation. After a single trial in which they experienced nausea, rats learned to avoid the sweet-tasting water. In a second condition, bright, noisy water (that is, water accompanied by flashing lights and loud noises) was paired with radiation. No conditioning occurred; the rats did not learn to avoid the water.

The startling observation in these studies is that *taste* could be readily conditioned to nausea, whereas *sight* and *sound* could not. It seems that the nervous system of mammals has developed through evolution so that certain associations are learned more easily than others. In the case of rats, the nervous system is "biased" to remember the taste of foods that are associated with nausea. Because sight and sound are typically not related to nausea, they cannot serve as effective conditioned stimuli for nausea.

This built-in bias, which ensures that some relationships between stimuli and responses will be learned more readily than others, is called **biological preparedness**. The concept of biological preparedness altered the traditional view of classical conditioning by demonstrating that stimuli are *not* created equal. Depending upon the kind of conditioning to be acquired, some stimuli are easier to learn than others.

4. The earlier view emphasized that classical conditioning could only occur when the conditioned stimulus came *immediately* before the unconditioned stimulus. In Pavlov's classic study, for example, the sound of the buzzer was immediately followed by the meat powder. In many cases, conditioning requires this split-second timing. However, more recent research points out that conditioning can occur even when there is a delay between the conditioned stimulus and the unconditioned stimulus.

Once again, the most convincing research involves taste aversion, but this time with humans. When cancer patients eat food that has a distinctive flavor—

Biological preparedness explains why coyotes can easily acquire taste aversion. In one program, ranchers placed a nausea-producing substance on lamb carcasses. Coyotes that ate this meat avoided killing lambs in the future.

followed by X rays or medication that causes nausea and vomiting—the patients show taste aversion. That is, they avoid the distinctively flavored food in the future (Flaherty, 1985).

Taste aversion studies have demonstrated, though, that associations can be formed between the distinctive flavor and the X rays or drugs, even though they may be separated in time by several hours (Revusky, 1971). Thus, split-second timing between the conditioned stimulus and unconditioned stimulus is *not* an absolute requirement for conditioning.

We should note that taste-aversion learning is not expected from the viewpoint of classical conditioning theory. However, it does make perfect biological sense and it provides further testimony that organisms are well adapted to their environments. In their natural habitats, animals learn to avoid poisonous foods, and most poisons have delayed symptoms. It is difficult, however, to explain *how* taste aversion can operate with such long intervals between the two stimuli. One current interpretation is that the conditioned stimulus (the food) is somehow represented in memory throughout that long delay period (Rescorla & Holland, 1982). It is not difficult to imagine memory for a particular food lasting 3 or 4 hours in adult humans. Admittedly, however, it is more challenging to explain long-term memory in a rat.

In short, classical conditioning can occur without repeated pairings. Predictability is the essential feature, some stimuli produce better conditioning than others, and two stimuli do not need to occur within minutes of each other.

Classical conditioning may be one of the simplest kinds of learning that any organism can demonstrate. However, the recent research illustrates that even this relatively simple learning is much more sophisticated than psychologists had originally suspected. Consistent with an important theme of this book, psychological processes are complicated. The essence of classical conditioning is not simple pairing, but predictive relationships.

Applications of Classical Conditioning

There are a number of important applications of classical conditioning. Let us begin by exploring a solution to the taste aversion problem in cancer patients. Then we see how conditioning explains some of the effects of heroin overdoses. Applications in psychotherapy are considered in chapter 16.

Taste Aversion   Ilene Bernstein and her colleagues have examined how taste aversion develops in young cancer patients. It seemed that children who were receiving chemotherapy often developed an intense dislike for the particular food they had eaten prior to chemotherapy. To explore the problem more thoroughly, she tested whether children would develop conditioned taste aversion to a new flavor of ice cream, which she labeled "Mapletoff." Half of the children, who were between the ages of 2 and 16, were given a serving of Mapletoff ice cream prior to chemotherapy with a drug that causes nausea and vomiting. The other half of the children served as a control group. They received similar drug treatment, but no Mapletoff beforehand.

Two to 4 weeks later, the children were given a choice: They could either eat Mapletoff ice cream or play with a game. Only 21% of the children who had eaten Mapletoff prior to chemotherapy chose to eat the ice cream, in contrast to 67% of the children who had no previous experience with the Mapletoff (Bernstein, 1978). Clearly, a large number of children in the experimental group had been conditioned to dislike the Mapletoff flavor.

Table 6.1	*Setup for the Broberg and Bernstein (1987) Study on Conditioned Taste Aversion*		
Experimental Group:	Meal	LifeSaver	Chemotherapy
Control Group:	Meal	(nothing)	Chemotherapy

Conditioned taste aversion creates nutritional problems, especially because taste aversion is typically strongest for meat and other sources of protein (Midkiff & Bernstein, 1985). Cancer patients need to eat, and they need their chemotherapy. How can the dilemma be solved? We saw in an earlier section that the problem is not solved by waiting several hours after eating before giving the drug.

Broberg and Bernstein (1987) devised a clever answer. Conditioned taste aversion is especially likely to develop for unfamiliar tastes. (After all, a familiar food such as a pancake is likely to have a long history of positive associations.) Therefore, these researchers gave children an unusual flavor of LifeSavers candy to eat immediately after the meal. Children in the experimental condition were given either root-beer-flavored or coconut-flavored LifeSavers. Children in the control group received no LifeSavers. All were then given chemotherapy (see Table 6.1).

Later testing showed that the children who had received the LifeSavers were more positive about eating the kinds of food that had been included in the earlier meal. In contrast, the control-group children were more likely to have developed taste aversions. It seems that the LifeSavers had served as a scapegoat for the first group, protecting the more nutritious food from acquiring taste aversions.

Conditioning and the Effects of Heroin   In the previous chapter, we discussed psychoactive drugs, including opiate drugs such as heroin. As you may know, heroin users often develop a tolerance for the drug. With repeated drug experience, they require more and more of the drug to produce the original effect. Part of this tolerance is physiologically based, but part now appears to be caused by classical conditioning.

Classical conditioning is relevant for heroin users, because environmental cues become associated with the unconditioned stimulus. An addicted person is likely to inject the drug in a familiar room, using a familiar ritual. Thus, the needle itself and various features of the room are likely to become conditioned stimuli. However, in the case of heroin, it happens that the conditioned stimuli and the unconditioned stimulus actually produce opposite effects. For example, the conditioned stimuli (such as the room) increase the breathing rate, whereas the unconditioned stimulus (heroin) decreases the breathing rate. When a drug user injects heroin in a familiar setting, these two effects counteract each other, resulting in a normal breathing rate.

Can you anticipate what would happen when a drug addict uses heroin in an unfamiliar setting? These new surroundings will not elicit the conditioned response that normally counteracts some of the effects of heroin. Heroin is therefore more powerful than normal and more likely to produce a strong reaction. For example, breathing rate will decrease but not be balanced by the typical increase in breathing rate caused by conditioning. In fact, researchers have discovered that heroin addicts receiving emergency treatment for an overdose usually report that they had injected only a normal dose. However, 70% had injected the drug in an unfamiliar setting (Siegel, 1984). Classical conditioning may therefore account for a large proportion of deaths from heroin overdoses.

The needle, the table, and other objects in this room may become conditioned stimuli for this heroin user.

> ### Section Summary: Classical Conditioning

- In a famous study, Pavlov paired a bell (conditioned stimulus) with meat powder (unconditioned stimulus) until the sound of the bell produced salivation (conditioned response) even when the meat powder was no longer presented. Similarly, Watson and Rayner conditioned a fear of rats in a baby by pairing the rat with a loud noise.
- Five important components of classical conditioning are acquisition, stimulus generalization, stimulus discrimination, extinction, and spontaneous recovery.
- The current theory about classical conditioning points out that conditioning does not require repeated pairings of the conditioned stimulus and the unconditioned stimulus, that predictive relationships are essential, that some stimuli can be conditioned more readily than others, and that the conditioned stimulus and unconditioned stimulus can be separated by several hours.
- Applications of classical conditioning include taste aversion and drug overdose problems.

Operant Conditioning

We have seen that classical conditioning can explain why we drool at the smell of burning charcoal and why our heart pounds harder when we see a flashing signal on an ambulance. Classical conditioning is important in accounting for some emotional reactions. However, it cannot explain how your dog learned to sit up and beg for a bone or why you are reading this textbook right now, rather than watching television or socializing with your friends. We need to turn to a second kind of conditioning to explain these behaviors.

Operant conditioning, or **instrumental conditioning**, involves learning to make a response because it produces a rewarding effect. That rewarding effect may be a bone (in the case of your dog) or a good test grade (in the case of reading a

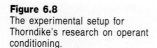

Figure 6.8
The experimental setup for Thorndike's research on operant conditioning.

textbook). In operant conditioning, the important association is between the response and whatever happens afterward (Rescorla, 1987). Operant conditioning also involves learning when *not* to make a response. You will not repeat a joke that produced only an embarrassed silence, and after one painful experience with an electrified fence, a steer will avoid leaning against the fence.

Before we describe operant conditioning in more detail, it is important to distinguish between classical and operant conditioning. Classical conditioning involves adjustments to events (specifically, conditioned and unconditioned stimuli) over which we have no control. In contrast, operant conditioning involves adjustment to situations in which our actions determine what happens to us (Domjan, personal communication, 1989). Recall that the unconditioned responses in classical conditioning are typically involuntary and reflexlike. A loud noise elicits a fear response, and meat powder elicits salivation. However, the responses in operant conditioning are spontaneously emitted. You can choose whether to read a textbook, and your dog sits up by choice—not by reflex.

Let us begin by examining two well-known studies demonstrating operant conditioning. Then we consider the important components of operant conditioning, as well as new developments in the area. Our final section explores some applications.

Two Well-Known Studies in Operant Conditioning

Thorndike's Puzzle Box   Even before Pavlov investigated salivating dogs, the American psychologist Edward L. Thorndike (1898) examined puzzle-solving cats. He placed a hungry cat inside a special cage, equipped with a door that could be lifted when the cat stepped on a lever (Figure 6.8). The cat could escape from the box and receive a food reward.

The cats did not show any systematic strategies in trying to escape from the puzzle box. Instead, they would scramble around the cage until they accidentally stepped on the lever. In fact, a typical cat might require 40 trials before it mastered the art of quickly pressing the lever, then escaping through the door. Notice that the operant learning required in Thorndike's puzzle box demands that the animal perform some voluntary action to receive a reward (Leahey & Harris, 1985).

Skinner's Conditioning Research   The prominent contemporary behaviorist B. F. Skinner (1904–1990) designed a useful learning chamber for animals. It contains either a lever that can be pressed or a location that can be pecked to receive a food reward. Figure 6.9 shows a pigeon pecking a key located inside a small hole. A food pellet will then drop into the tray below. Meanwhile, the apparatus will record the number of times the pigeon pecks the key. This record provides a clear picture of the rate of learning, and it allows researchers to examine how a particular variable affects behavior. For example, they could examine how pecking rate can be influenced by the rate at which the pigeon receives food (e.g., every trial versus every tenth trial).

Components of Operant Conditioning

Now let us explore the important components of operant conditioning. We begin with an overview of reinforcement and punishment and then consider other characteristics such as shaping, the discriminative stimulus, and extinction.

Reinforcement and Punishment   Last semester, I wrote on a student's midterm exam that I liked her use of a vivid example in one of her essays. On the next exam, every paragraph overflowed with vivid examples. My reinforcement had

Figure 6.9
The experimental setup for Skinner's research on operant conditioning.

Table 6.2   *Reinforcement and Punishment*

| | TWO KINDS OF STIMULI | |
	Positive	Negative
Add something	Positive reinforcement	Punishment
Take away something	Punishment	Negative reinforcement

encouraged her to perform a particular activity more often. In contrast, a student who plagiarized a paper in a different course received a failing grade. The punishment—I hope—will encourage this student not to plagiarize.

We have two ways of offering reinforcement and two ways of providing punishment. Table 6.2 illustrates the four possibilities. As you can see, **positive reinforcement** involves adding something positive to the situation after the correct response has been made. For example, a swimming coach may praise a beginning swimmer for demonstrating good breathing technique when swimming the length of the pool.

In **negative reinforcement**, something negative is taken away or avoided. For example, when you sit down to drive a car and you fasten your seat belt, the unpleasant sound of the seat-belt buzzer is removed. Negative reinforcement seems particularly difficult to understand because we often associate the word *negative* with something bad or punishing. It may be helpful to emphasize the upbeat word *reinforcement* in the phrase "negative *reinforcement*."

Positive and negative reinforcement have similar consequences; they strengthen or reinforce the behavior they follow and increase the chances that the behavior will occur again. Thus, positive reinforcement from the swimming coach should increase the probability of good breathing techniques, and negative reinforcement from the cessation of the seat-belt buzzer should increase the probability of fastening the seat belt.

Punishment can occur in two ways: We can add something negative or take away something positive (Skinner, 1953). In the classroom, an example of adding something negative would be a teacher who assigns extra homework when the class is unruly. The teacher could also administer the other kind of punishment, taking away something positive, by telling the students that their unruly behavior will be punished by cancelling the Halloween party.

Punishment tends to decrease the probability of the response that it follows, making that response less likely in the future. Thus, a teacher who tries either of these two kinds of punishment may decrease the probability of unruly classroom behavior. Try Demonstration 6.2 to make sure you understand the concepts of reinforcement and punishment; the answers are on p. 205.

The Punishment Dilemma   Let us discuss punishment in more detail. Few aspects of learning theory or child rearing inspire as much controversy as the use of punishment (Axelrod, 1983; Schwartz, 1989). Nevertheless, punishment is frequently used in one form or another. For example, naturalistic observation of elementary and junior high school teachers has revealed that they yell at students at the rate of one scolding every 2 minutes (Schwartz, 1984; Van Houten & Doleys, 1983). Here are some of the problems with punishment.

1. Punishment may decrease the frequency of an inappropriate behavior, but it does not automatically increase the frequency of the behavior we want. A father may swat his daughter for saying something rude to the neighbor, and she might utter fewer rude remarks in the future. However, she does not learn what remarks *are* appropriate.

Understanding Negative Reinforcement

The following quiz tests your mastery of the concept of negative reinforcement:

1. Is negative reinforcement used to increase or decrease behavior?
2. Do people usually look forward to negative reinforcement?
3. Do you think teachers should avoid using negative reinforcement?
4. Which of the following is an example of negative reinforcement? (You can select more than one.)
   a. Because you talked back, you will have to stay after school.
   b. You will have to stay after school until you clean your desk.
   c. If you do all of your reading assignments without bothering other students, I will not have to call your parents.
   d. Because you scored lower than 80% on this test, you will be required to submit a final paper.
   e. If you submit all of your remaining weekly assignments on time, you may toss out your lowest quiz grade.
5. In terms of its effects on students' behavior, is negative reinforcement more similar to punishment or positive reinforcement?

Source: Based on Tauber, 1988.

2. In order to deliver punishment, the punisher must pay attention to the offender. This attention may in fact be reinforcing—precisely the opposite of the desired effect. A teacher who spends a full 2 minutes lecturing Spike, the class bully, may find that attention reinforces him for his previous aggressive behavior. In the future, Spike may be even more likely to brutalize his classmates (Serbin & O'Leary, 1975).

3. Punishment provides a model of aggressive behavior, via observational learning (to be discussed in the next section). The person who is being punished learns that aggression is a way to solve problems. The research on child abuse provides a tragic example of how people learn to imitate an aggressive model. This research has noted that many people—though certainly not all—who were abused as children will grow up to be abusing parents (Strauss & Gelles, 1980; Widom, 1989).

Realistically, however, we are not likely to eliminate punishment. Every parent, teacher, or pet owner sometimes feels that some sort of punishment is necessary. Learning theorist Barry Schwartz (1989) suggests that if you must punish, the delay between response and punishment should be as short as possible. It is not effective to threaten, "You just wait until your father gets home!" Furthermore, punishment should be consistent. It is not effective to punish cheating today but allow the child to cheat without punishment tomorrow.

A better alternative to punishment is to reinforce a response that is incompatible with the undesired response. If you want children to be less aggressive, praise them when they are interacting in a friendly fashion. This technique requires more thought than does punishment, but it is more likely to produce long-term behavior change (Skinner, 1971, 1988a).

I recall learning as an undergraduate student about the virtues of reinforcing incompatible responses, but I was never fully convinced until about 10 years later. We had invited a family from a nearby city to join us for brunch. We had not met the two sons, Roy and Reginald, but we expected a pleasant morning because they were about the same age as our preschool daughters. The doorbell rang, we opened the door, and the older boy greeted us, "I am a lion and I'm going to tear your house apart." Apparently he was speaking for his younger brother as well, because the two proceeded to rip apart books, scatter toys everywhere, and intimidate our daughters. Every few minutes, a parent would mutter, "Stop that, Roy" or "Don't do that, Reginald." The parents may have intended these remarks as punishment, but they were ineffective.

At one point, though, we looked over to see that Roy, Reginald, and our daughters were quietly talking and playing tea party. My husband commented, "My goodness, you are all playing so nicely together now! That's wonderful!" Roy and Reginald looked up and their jaws dropped with astonishment. Their mother remarked, "They're not used to praise." Now I am not going to claim that their behavior during the rest of the morning qualified them for the Children of the Month Award, but they were noticeably nicer for the rest of the visit. They had been reinforced for pleasant social interactions, and these responses are incompatible with antisocial behavior.

Shaping   Imagine a 6-year-old boy learning to swim. His teacher has asked him to try the basic crawl for the first time. The boy's legs are bent, his arms are awkward, and his head protrudes too far out of the water. Still, the teacher shouts an encouraging, "Good, keep it up." By the end of the lesson, the teacher would require a more refined technique before praising the swimmer. If the boy later trains for the swim team, he would have to be much better before earning reinforcement. Teachers, parents, and other people who want to encourage a particular behavior are likely to use shaping. **Shaping** is the systematic reinforcement of gradual improvements in the desired behavior.

Shaping is a valuable tool because it encourages the learner to acquire a new behavior relatively quickly. A rat in a learning chamber does not spontaneously stroll over to the lever, rise up on its hind paws, and deftly press the lever . . . on the first try. Instead, the experimenter first delivers a food reinforcement when the rat is in the general vicinity of the lever. Then the criterion is made more strict—to earn the food, the rat must lift its paw in the vicinity of the lever. Ultimately, the experimenter reinforces only those responses in which the rat completely depresses the lever (see Figure 6.10). Thus, both the swimmer and the lever-pressing rat are reinforced for gradual improvements in performance.

Figure 6.10
At the end of shaping, the rat must completely depress the lever with its paw in order to receive the pellet of food.

Schedules of Reinforcement   Think about how operant learning applies to your own life. How often do you receive reinforcement for good behavior or correct responses? Unless you are a very fortunate person, your answer is, "Not very often." In operant learning, the term **continuous reinforcement schedule** applies to situations in which the subject is reinforced on every correct trial. Candy and beverage machines usually reinforce the user according to a continuous reinforcement schedule. Every time you insert the appropriate coins, you should be rewarded by receiving food or drink. However, in our everyday lives, it is difficult to think of examples of situations in which we are continuously reinforced by other human beings for appropriate behavior.

In everyday life, we are much more likely to receive reinforcement sporadically. As opposed to a continuous reinforcement schedule, **partial reinforcement** (or intermittent reinforcement) gives reinforcement only part of the time. Table 6.3 shows the four most common kinds of partial reinforcement, which we now examine.

1. In a **fixed-ratio schedule**, reinforcement is given after a fixed number of responses have been made. For example, Dee's Doughnut Shop in Canandaigua, New York, keeps a tally of its patrons' doughnut purchases. After I accumulate 12 tally marks, I will be rewarded with a dozen free doughnuts.

2. In a **fixed-interval schedule**, reinforcement is given for the first correct response made after the specified period of time has passed. For example, the

Table 6.3 *Four Common Partial Reinforcement Schedules*

		REINFORCEMENT DEPENDS UPON	
		Number of Responses	Passage of Time
Reinforcement is	Regular Irregular	Fixed Ratio Variable Ratio	Fixed Interval Variable Interval

U.S. Postal Service has most of us on a fixed-interval schedule for checking our mailboxes. I wait 24 hours after the last mail delivery, and the first time I check my mailbox after that fixed interval, I am reinforced with mail. If I were to check after only 23 hours, however, my mail-seeking responses would be unreinforced.

3. In a **variable-ratio schedule**, reinforcement is given after a varying number of responses have been made. For example, consider a rat pressing a bar for a food pellet, which it receives on the average every 5 bar presses. The first pellet may come after 2 presses, the next after 7 presses, and the next after 6, averaging out to 1 pellet for each 5 responses $\left(\frac{2 + 7 + 6}{3} = 5\right)$. However, unlike in the fixed-interval schedule, the rat never knows exactly when the pellet is coming. Similarly, gamblers who play the slot machines are placed on a variable-ratio schedule, though they usually are not reinforced at the average rate of every fifth trial!

4. In a **variable-interval schedule**, reinforcement is given for the first response made after a varying period of time has passed. For example, someone who hails a cab every morning may have a 3-minute wait on Monday, a 12-minute wait on Tuesday, and a 9-minute wait on Wednesday, averaging out to an 8-minute wait.

The different schedules of reinforcement produce different response patterns. For instance, response rates are higher under ratio schedules, because reinforcement is tied to the number of responses. Furthermore, variable schedules produce a steadier rate of responding. Wouldn't you study more regularly if you did not know which day a weekly quiz would be given than if you could expect a quiz every Friday?

Secondary Reinforcers When learning researchers reinforce a hungry rat with a pellet of food for pressing a lever, they are delivering a primary reinforcer. A **primary reinforcer** is a reinforcer that can satisfy a basic biological need, most likely food or water. Most of human behavior, however, is controlled by **secondary reinforcers**, which are reinforcers that do not satisfy a basic biological need but acquire their rewarding power by association with another established reinforcer.

For example, many learning chambers are designed so that they make a clicking noise as they release a pellet of food. The animal associates that click with the primary reinforcer, food. Soon, the clicking sound serves as a secondary reinforcer. Try to think of the things that are most reinforcing to you—perhaps money, praise from someone you admire, or a good grade. It is hard to argue that a good grade satisfies a basic biological need. Instead, it is a secondary reinforcer.

The Discriminative Stimulus We have been discussing how and when reinforcement can be delivered in an operant conditioning study. An important function of reinforcement is to form a relationship between (1) stimuli associated with the learning environment and (2) the particular response that is being examined. For

Gambling is a good example of a variable-ratio schedule of reinforcement. Research has shown that many compulsive gamblers experienced one big win at some point in their early gambling.

For this child, winning an award serves as a secondary reinforcer.

example, a pigeon in a learning chamber may learn that only when a yellow button is lit up (the stimulus) will its pecking (response) be rewarded. If the button is not lit up, the pigeon could peck incessantly without producing a morsel of food. In this example, the yellow button is serving as a discriminative stimulus. A **discriminative stimulus** is a stimulus signaling that a response will be reinforced.

Ellen Reese (1986) provides an example from human behavior. In our culture, the behavior of dishwashing leads to social reinforcement. If you wash dishes at a friend's house, you usually receive praise. However, you would not be praised if you removed *clean* dishes from the cabinet and washed them. Your dishwashing behavior—no matter how magnificent—would not be reinforced. Dishwashing leads to reinforcement only in the presence of *dirty* dishes, because dirty dishes in this example serve as the discriminative stimulus. Similarly, you learn that shouting at the top of your lungs is reinforced when the discriminative stimulus is a political rally, but not in church or at an elegant dinner.

Extinction   You are familiar with the term *extinction* from classical conditioning. When the conditioned stimulus is presented repeatedly without the unconditioned stimulus, the conditioned response gradually weakens and disappears, producing extinction. In operant conditioning, extinction occurs when an organism repeatedly makes a response without reinforcement. You are certainly familiar with extinction if you have ever inserted coins into a pay phone and received no dial tone. After two or three unsuccessful attempts, any sane person *should* show extinction!

An important principle of learning is that both people and animals show rapid extinction if they have previously received continuous reinforcement, rather than partial reinforcement. Suppose you have a car that has always started reliably. For two years now, you have turned the key in the ignition, and 100% of the time you have been reinforced by the comforting purr of the motor. With this continuous reinforcement schedule, you will extinguish very quickly if you turn the key several times one morning and discover no reinforcing purr. In contrast, suppose you have a car that occasionally starts on the first turn of the key, but it often does not start until two, three, or even six attempts. With this partial reinforcement schedule, you will resist extinction. You are likely to keep turning that key, praying for reinforcement, and you are likely to wear out the battery before you extinguish. Figure 6.11 compares the extinction patterns under continuous reinforcement versus partial reinforcement.

Figure 6.11
During extinction, the response rate drops much more rapidly when animals have previously had continuous reinforcement than when they have had partial reinforcement (typical results).

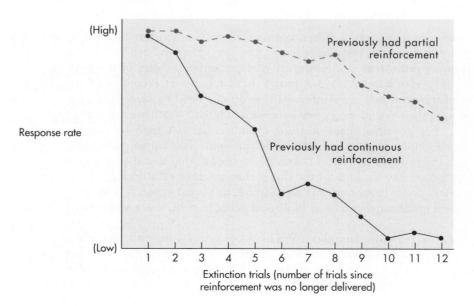

The principle of slow extinction with partial reinforcement helps us understand the extraordinary persistence of some individuals. Maybe an uncle of yours keeps trying out for a part in the local theater productions because once—4 years ago—he was rewarded with a small part. Musicians, athletes, and painters all keep working, lured by the hope that the next attempt may bring them reinforcement. Or consider a toddler in her crib whose parents sometimes (but not always) let her out of bed at night when she has cried for a long time. She is likely to keep crying, lured by the hope that the next heart-wrenching sob may win her freedom.

A Detailed Example of Operant Conditioning   Let us review these components of operant conditioning by applying them to an example. Imagine that you are a fourth-grade student who has decided to play the clarinet in the school band. Your band teacher may give you positive reinforcement for producing a particular note on your instrument ("That's very good!") or negative reinforcement ("You've done your scales right this time, so you won't have to do any more scales this morning."). If you do not practice at home, your parents may deliver punishment of the "adding something negative" variety ("Why don't you ever practice? Do you think we have money to throw away on a clarinet?"). Alternatively, they may use punishment of the "taking away something positive" variety ("You won't get your allowance this week.").

Skilled music teachers (and skilled parents) emphasize reinforcement more than punishment. A good teacher would praise you for improvement in tone, rhythm, and accuracy. Punishment for improper techniques or wrong notes should be used sparingly and should be delivered soon after the mistake has been made.

This teacher would also use shaping. A beginning student would receive praise for producing even the most primitive squawk, but a few days later would be required to produce a decent open G. By high school, however, this same student would have to play a passable rendition of Mozart's clarinet concerto to win reinforcement.

Music teachers cannot use continuous reinforcement, praising their students for every correct note or every correct passage. Instead, they use some kind of partial reinforcement, most likely variable ratio. However, some teachers may reinforce half of the responses, on the average, whereas others might reinforce an average of only once every 30th response or once every 12th lesson.

The notes and the notations in the student's music book would serve as discriminative stimuli. The student receives praise for playing a perfect B flat, only when a B flat is written on the page. A spectacular loud fortissimo wins no smiles if the passage is marked pianissimo.

It is hard to imagine how primary reinforcers could be associated with clarinet playing. Would a parent withhold food when a child does not practice? In contrast, the secondary reinforcers are numerous: receiving praise from the teacher, parents, and Uncle Len; receiving a high rating in solo competitions; being selected as first chair of the first clarinet section; and earning the "Outstanding Music Student" award at the end of the year. However, the critical secondary reinforcement comes from the student listening and hearing that the playing sounds appropriate. In fact, the major task of a music teacher is to encourage students to identify how the music should sound. Indeed, the teacher must turn good sound into a powerful secondary reinforcer (Domjan, personal communication, 1989).

Unfortunately, however, many students experience extinction. An incompetent teacher may not provide reinforcement, parents may not deliver praise, or the student may no longer experience reinforcement in the form of self-satisfaction. Other, different behaviors—perhaps playing football or being a cheerleader—may win more social reinforcement from other students. Without any reinforcement, the student is not likely to continue playing the instrument.

New Developments in Operant Conditioning

In the first part of the chapter, we saw that the major new developments in classical conditioning concern the relationship between the conditioned stimulus and the unconditioned stimulus. With respect to operant conditioning, two major new developments concern the nature of reinforcement and the learning abilities of animals.

The Nature of Reinforcement   Early theories of operant conditioning argued that reinforcement worked for physiological reasons. A rat, deprived of food, pressed a lever to deliver pellets of food. The food reduced its hunger drive, "stamping in" the behavior of pressing the lever (Domjan & Burkhard, 1986).

In recent decades, however, ideas about reinforcement have changed. Many theorists now propose that reinforcement's primary function is to reorganize behavior. In an important experiment, J. E. R. Staddon and Virginia Simmelhag (1971) delivered a food reward to pigeons every 15 seconds. Earlier research had suggested that a reinforcement not tied to any specific response from the pigeon would simply reinforce whatever activity the pigeon happened to be doing at the time (Skinner, 1948). In the early training sessions, Staddon and Simmelhag found a wide variety of behaviors; the pigeons bobbed their heads and flapped their wings, apparently connecting these behaviors with the reinforcement. However, after 20 sessions, the pigeons were most often seen pecking at the wall near the food dispenser at the time the reinforcement was to be delivered. Thus, organisms initially show variability, but reinforcement limits this variability. With further experience, both animals and people select behaviors that seem to increase their chances for success (Domjan, 1987).

Let us return to the example of the hard-to-start car to see how reinforcement reorganizes behavior. Suppose that you slide into the car seat, cross your fingers, sit up straight, and jiggle the key in the ignition before turning the key, and it starts. On future trials, you are most likely to repeat the behavior associated with the ignition—jiggling the key—rather than crossing your fingers or sitting up straight, even if none of the behaviors actually help start the car (Domjan & Burkhard, 1986). In summary, current theorists propose that reinforcement reorganizes behavior, changing what we choose to do.

Operant Conditioning Abilities of Animals   Even before Charles Darwin proposed his theory of evolution, scientists wondered about the limits of animal intelligence. Darwin's theory prompted them to study animal learning as a way of tracing the roots of human intelligence (Domjan, 1987). Some researchers, for example, have investigated whether humans differ from other animals in their patterns of operant conditioning. In general, humans tend to perform the same as rats, pigeons, and other animals when they must learn a task that involves avoiding punishment. However, humans perform somewhat differently from other animals with respect to certain schedules of reinforcement (Higgins & Morris, 1984). Humans may behave differently because they can describe patterns verbally. For example, even 8-year-olds who are on a fixed-interval schedule of reinforcement can verbalize a rule to themselves, "I don't have to do anything until five minutes have passed, and then I'd better start working."

Other researchers have tried to determine the upper limits of animals' intelligence. For example, in chapter 9 we note the moderate success of researchers who have taught chimpanzees to communicate via sign language. Some have also demonstrated that pigeons can acquire subtle concepts (Herrnstein, 1984; Roitblat, 1987). Consider a study in which pigeons acquired the concept of *tree* by watching a series of slides (Herrnstein et al., 1976). About half of the slides were pictures

Figure 6.12
In the research of R. J. Herrnstein, pigeons are able to distinguish a variety of trees from pictures of irrelevant items.

of trees—sometimes a part of a tree, sometimes one tree, and sometimes a forest. When a picture of a tree was presented, the pigeon could peck at a key and receive a food pellet. Pecking when the other pictures were present earned no pellet. After a number of training sessions, a new set of pictures was presented as a test. The pigeons were highly accurate in discriminating trees from nontrees (see Figure 6.12). This kind of achievement makes us wonder whether the term "birdbrain" is really more a compliment than an insult!

Other researchers, however, have emphasized that there are limits to what an animal can learn. That is, animals may seem smart in learning some tasks that are compatible with their natural abilities and slow-witted on other tasks that do not match these natural abilities (Gould & Marler, 1987). Furthermore, according to the **instinctive drift principle**, when an animal is engaged in operant conditioning, its behavior will drift in the direction of instinctive behaviors related to the task it is learning (Bailey & Bailey, 1980; Breland & Breland, 1961).

For example, Keller and Marian Breland trained about 6,000 animals belonging to 38 species, including animals as exotic as reindeer, porpoises, and whales. In one case, they began to train a raccoon to pick up a single coin and to deposit that coin in a piggy bank. This kind of animal act might be interesting at a zoo or other tourist attraction. However, the Brelands found that the raccoon refused to let go of the coin. Instead, it would clutch it firmly or rub coins together for several minutes in a miserly fashion that resembled Mr. Scrooge, rather than a thrifty piggy-bank user. Pigs also refused to learn how to "save money." Instead, they would drop the money on the way to the "bank," then root around for it, toss it up in the air, and drop it again. Both animals showed instinctive drift, because raccoons instinctively manipulate objects, as Figure 6.13 illustrates, and pigs instinctively root around for food. Thus, there are biological constraints that limit the extent to which animals can master operant learning tasks.

Figure 6.13
Because raccoons instinctively handle objects, it is difficult to teach them to perform a trick in which they must release the objects; this is an example of instinctive drift.

Applications of Operant Conditioning

Operant conditioning has produced some interesting and important practical applications. Let us examine two applications: computer-assisted instruction and behavior modification techniques.

Computer-Assisted Instruction   In **computer-assisted instruction (CAI)**, students learn at their own rate, using computers that are programmed to deliver individualized instruction. Information is presented in small chunks, and the students master a relatively easy chunk before proceeding to a somewhat more difficult topic. Students receive immediate feedback about whether each response is correct or incorrect. Furthermore, fast learners can complete the lessons at a more rapid rate, rather than experiencing boredom as they wait for the rest of the class to master a concept. Programs can also be designed to give extra review if a student's answers indicate weakness in a particular area. CAI can be used not only in the classroom but in teaching employees new skills and information.

These students are learning spelling with computer-assisted instruction.

B. F. Skinner enthusiastically supported the way CAI could make use of operant learning principles. He expressed dismay that educators have not made more use of this technique (Skinner, 1987, 1988b). It is clearly effective; in one study, eighth graders completed a full year of algebra in half a year and retained more material than control-group students a year later. Also, CAI excels at delivering personal attention to students, beyond what a teacher could provide to a classroom of 25 pupils. However, schools are obviously reluctant to pay for expensive new equipment. In addition, there is often a time lag between a scientific discovery and its implementation.

Behavior Modification   The application of operant learning that has achieved the most attention is **behavior modification**, which is the systematic use of techniques from learning theory to change human behavior. One researcher described how he used behavior modification to change his own behavior in eating less sugar, flossing his teeth, exercising, decreasing the number of critical remarks he made toward others, and increasing the amount of writing he accomplished (Malott, 1986).

There are several important steps in a behavior modification program, whether you want to modify your own behavior or the behavior of others (Michael, 1985):

1. Define the problem in behavioral terms that are concrete (for example, describe actions rather than thoughts or wishes).

2. Figure out how to measure the relevant behavior in a consistent manner (for example, in terms of the number of times you avoided dessert in a week).

3. Take a baseline measure, which indicates the response rate before you begin the behavior modification program. (For example, you may have avoided dessert once last week.)

4. Figure out reinforcements or punishments for the behavior, and carry them out, still measuring your response rate. (For example, you may reinforce yourself by buying a magazine you enjoy for every 7 days you successfully avoid dessert.)

5. If the program is going well, continue. If it is not, try changing the reinforcement or punishment.

An important tool in behavior modification is called a token economy. In a **token economy**, good behavior is reinforced by a token or symbol, and the tokens can be accumulated and exchanged for a reinforcer (Cooper, Heron, & Heward, 1987). For example, Skinner (1988b) described how a sixth-grade teacher successfully applied a token economy in her classroom. She handed out a card (a token) every time a student finished a homework or classroom assignment. Students wrote their names on each card and placed them in a jar. At the end of the week, she drew one card at random, awarding the lottery prize—perhaps a small pocket radio—to the winner. Her students showed a dramatic improvement in the number of assignments they completed. At little cost, she saved herself from the professional burnout that teachers often experience. Token economies have been widely applied in classrooms, on psychiatric wards, with elderly people, and with young children (Kazdin, 1982).

Behavior modification programs have been used extensively in a variety of settings. For instance, this chapter has used many examples of teachers applying learning principles. A large portion of educational psychology is concerned with behavior modification programs in the classroom (e.g., Rosser & Nicholson, 1984).

Applying the Principles of Behavior Modification

Identify one specific behavior of yours that you would like to change. Perhaps you would like to spend more time studying a particular course, or you wish you snacked less between meals, or you think you should make fewer sarcastic comments. Select a behavior that occurs (or should occur) several times each day. Following Michael's (1985) outline of behavior modification,

1. Define the problem in terms of concrete behavioral terms that are specific, rather than general.
2. Determine how you will measure this behavior consistently. Construct a tally sheet that you can carry with you to record the number of responses made each day.

3. For 1 week, take a baseline measure before you begin with rewards.
4. Identify an appealing reward. (We will avoid punishment and negative reinforcement for the purposes of this demonstration.) The reward might be something small you can enjoy often, or something large, for which you will accumulate tokens (e.g., check marks) over a period of time. Begin the program and record your behavior for 2 weeks.
5. If the program is going well, continue. (You may wish to alter the schedule of reinforcement, however.) If it is not going well, reassess and try to find a more attractive reward.

In chapter 16, we discuss some important applications of behavior modification in therapy for psychological disorders.

Many businesses have also learned the value of behavior modification. These programs have significantly improved company productivity, sales volume, worker safety, and employee-management relations. Behavior modification programs have also decreased tardiness, theft by employees, and shoplifting. Usually the programs include reinforcers such as praise from supervisors, pay bonuses, time off, and mention in the company newsletter (Martin & Pear, 1983).

Now that you have been introduced to the basic principles of operant conditioning and behavior modification, try Demonstration 6.3.

In a behavior modification program in an industrial setting, praise can act as a reinforcer.

Section Summary: Operant Conditioning

- Two important studies in operant conditioning involved cats learning how to escape from a puzzle box (Thorndike) and animals pressing a lever to receive a food reward (Skinner).
- In operant conditioning, a response is followed by positive reinforcement, negative reinforcement, punishment, or—in the case of extinction—nothing. In general, it is better to reinforce a response that is incompatible with an undesired response, rather than to administer punishment.
- Other important components of operant conditioning are shaping, schedules of reinforcement, the discriminative stimulus, secondary reinforcers, and extinction.
- The more recent view of reinforcement is that it reorganizes behavior, rather than operating at a physiological level.
- Research on animals shows their impressive learning capacity, though it may be limited by instinctive drift.
- Operant conditioning has been applied in computer-assisted instruction and behavior modification.

Observational Learning

So far we have seen how classical and operant conditioning can explain how we acquire fears, and how reinforcement and punishment account for learning important skills. Throughout these discussions, we have emphasized broader applications of both classical and operant conditioning. Nevertheless, many of your daily actions cannot be explained by even the most liberal interpretation of conditioning approaches. Classical and operant conditioning are especially limited in accounting for the rapid acquisition of *new* behaviors.

Consider, for example, your very first attempt at driving. You knew exactly where to insert the key and exactly where to place your hands on the steering wheel. Or consider how someone learns to split firewood with an ax; how can this fairly complex sequence of actions be explained by a trial-and-error approach? Of course, operant conditioning is helpful in explaining how you perfect your skills and how you maintain them. However, neither classical conditioning nor operant conditioning can account for the speed and accuracy with which you acquire a behavior that you have never previously attempted.

To account for numerous human accomplishments—especially those performed for the first time—we need to consider the third major kind of learning; observational learning. In **observational learning**, we learn new behaviors by watching and imitating the behavior of others. Observational learning is also known as **modeling** because the learner imitates a model. It is also called **social learning** because learning occurs in a social situation by watching other people.

Let us first discuss the classic research on observational learning. Then we consider the important components of observational learning. Next, an in-depth section discusses television violence and aggression. We end with a brief overview of applications of observational learning.

Well-Known Research in Observational Learning

In the most widely cited research in observational learning, children watched adults as they behaved aggressively with a large inflated toy doll. Throughout a series of studies, Albert Bandura and his colleagues examined whether the children would imitate the adult models (Bandura et al., 1961, 1963). In a typical session, a nursery school child works busily on a picture. Then an adult in a different part of the room approaches a Bobo doll, an inflatable clownlike toy that is weighted on the bottom so that it pops back up whenever it is knocked down. For about 10 minutes, this adult brutalizes Bobo, hitting it with a hammer, knocking it down, and sitting on it. The adult accompanies these aggressive actions with remarks such as, "Kick him" and "Sock him in the nose."

The child is then led into a second room, filled with numerous enticing toys. However, the child is told that the toys are being saved for other children, a comment guaranteed to arouse frustration. Finally, the child is brought to a third room, containing several toys and—you guessed it—a Bobo doll. Bandura and his colleagues watched through hidden windows and noted the children's behavior.

The children who had been exposed to the violent model were likely to beat up on Bobo, even repeating the same phrases and mimicking the identical aggressive actions. In contrast, other children who had not observed a violent adult model were much less likely to treat Bobo aggressively. Children showed this observational learning, whether they directly observed the aggressive adult or viewed the aggression in a film. Notice that observational learning is involved because these particular aggressive behaviors were performed for the first time.

Bandura's original research demonstrated that children would show observational learning, even when neither the adult nor the child received reinforcement. Later research, often using the same kind of Bobo doll, showed that the likelihood of imitation is influenced by whether the adult model is rewarded or punished for being aggressive.

In one study, Mary Rosekrans and Willard Hartup (1967) had preschool children watch an adult model playing with toys. She sometimes beat the Bobo doll with a hammer, and she also poked a fork into handmade clay figures. As in earlier research, she made hostile comments such as, "Wham, bam, I'll knock your head off" and "Punch him, punch him, punch his legs full of holes." These aggressive actions were followed by one of two reactions from another adult: (1) In the reinforcement condition, the adult praised the aggressive model with remarks such as, "Good for you! I guess you really fixed him that time." (2) In the punishment condition, the adult scolded the model with remarks such as, "Now look what you've done, you've ruined it." After watching the model's aggressive actions and seeing her behavior either reinforced or punished, the children in the two conditions were then allowed to play with the same toys. A third group of children, who had not seen an aggressive model, also played with the toys.

As Figure 6.14 shows, those who had watched an aggressive model being reinforced were much more aggressive than children in the other two groups. Notice, then, that children do not blindly imitate a model's actions. Instead, they mimic the actions most carefully only when the model receives praise and approval from others.

Components of Observational Learning

We have seen that people can acquire certain behaviors even without reinforcement. However, we have also seen that reinforcement of the model influences the likelihood that an observer will perform a certain behavior. Let us now discuss some additional useful terminology in observational learning.

An important concept in observational learning is **vicarious reinforcement**, which occurs when the model receives reinforcement. (You may be familiar with the concept of vicarious pleasure, which occurs when a person derives pleasure from someone else's happiness.) Thus, when the children saw the adult receive praise for poking the clay figure, they themselves experienced vicarious reinforcement. Similarly, **vicarious punishment** occurs when the model receives punishment (Bandura, 1986).

Bandura also stresses that people can experience **intrinsic reinforcement**, an internalized sense of satisfaction at performing well. You may be singing in

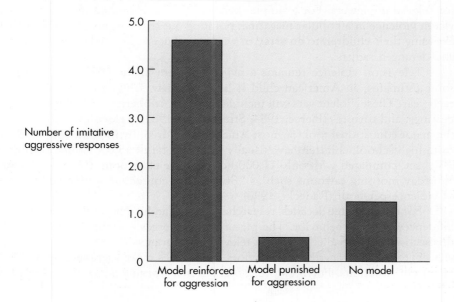

Figure 6.14
Imitative aggressive responses, as a function of whether observers had seen the model being reinforced or punished or had seen no model. (Based on data from Rosekrans & Hartup, 1967)

Figure 6.15
This young boy and girl are likely to have acquired their body language by observational learning.

the shower, knowing that your voice cannot be heard, and feel proud of your mellow tone on a high note. Alternatively, **intrinsic punishment** occurs when you scold yourself for poor performance. If you receive a low score on a section of the study guide for this chapter, you are likely to experience intrinsic punishment, even though no one else will see your score.

Bandura's recent additions to observational learning theory reflect the current emphasis on cognitive psychology (Bandura, 1986). In particular, he emphasizes that a learner observing a model does *not* acquire a perfectly accurate, blow-by-blow replica of the model's behavior. A child who watches an adult attacking a Bobo doll acquires, instead, a **schema** or generalized idea that captures the important components, but not every exact detail. The child's performance will contain many important components but will not be an exact duplicate of every gesture or comment made by the adult. In the next chapter, we discuss further implications of schemas in memory.

Psychologists believe that observational learning theory is particularly effective in explaining social behavior. For example, children may learn many gender-stereotyped behaviors by imitating models, either people they know or characters on television programs (Matlin, 1987; Mischel, 1966). A little girl may learn that she is supposed to act helpless in an emergency, for example. I recently watched a Saturday morning cartoon in which the only female was a mother who fainted during an interplanetary crisis. (Her preteen son came to the rescue and saved the world.)

Vicarious reinforcement is also influential in explaining social behavior. For example, a boy may watch a football hero receiving cheers and admiration from the fans. A junior high girl may experience intrinsic reinforcement as she practices a demure, "feminine" smile in the mirror. Observational learning accounts for the difference in body language shown by the girl and the boy in Figure 6.15.

○ ○

In Depth: Television Violence and Observational Learning

The early research on observational learning showed that children become more aggressive after watching a violent model. Children are even willing to imitate violence that is depicted on film; the violence does not need to occur "live," in the same room as the viewer.

Psychologists quickly realized that these studies had important implications for television viewers. For example, Bandura (1963) addressed the issue of television violence in a popular magazine, pointing out that parents were unwittingly exposing their children to an array of wild gun slingers, hopped-up psychopaths, and deranged sadists.

Television violence remains a major problem in the 1990s. According to some estimates, an American child is likely to view 3,000 episodes of violence each year. These violent acts will include murders, robberies, bombings, assaults, beatings, and tortures (Pierce, 1984; Strasburger, 1985). Television is likely to be the major educational tool for most American children. By the time they graduate from high school, children have usually spent a total of 15,000 hours in front of a TV set, compared with only 11,000 hours in the classroom. By recent counts, Saturday morning cartoons such as "Superman" contain an average of 122 acts of violence per hour (Radecki, 1990).

For the last three decades, researchers have examined how television violence influences viewers' behavior. The picture that emerges is complex. As we see in this section, a steady diet of violent television programs does not inevitably cause viewers to perform aggressive behaviors, but it does make aggression more likely in certain situations. Furthermore, observational learning is not the only mechanism that encourages a relationship between television violence and aggressive behavior.

An examination of the relationship between television violence and aggression is especially useful in an introductory psychology textbook because it allows us to compare several research methods: the experiment, the quasi-experiment, and the correlational technique. We introduced these research methods in chapter 2, and this section provides an opportunity to review them.

The Experimental Method　　In the **experimental method**, the researchers manipulate the independent variable to determine its effects on the dependent variable, that is, the behavior of the participants in the experiment. In research on television violence, the independent variable is typically the kind of television show they watch or the amount of violent television they watch. The dependent variable is some measure of their aggressive behavior or aggressive tendencies.

In a typical study using the experimental method, Atkin (1983) varied the kind of television show that was presented to 10- to 13-year-old girls and boys. Three groups of students watched a 6-minute TV news program containing news stories and commercials. This program was identical for all three groups, except for a critical 15-second portion. In this brief portion, the no-violence control group saw a nonviolent commercial for a movie. In the fantasy violence condition, a 15-second scene showed college students slugging each other in a violent classroom argument; the scene was described as part of an upcoming movie. In the realistic violence condition, the same violent fight was presented as an actual news event, a fight that broke out in a college classroom as a result of a disagreement over politics.

After watching one of the three versions of the program, the children filled out a questionnaire that was designed to measure how they would be likely to respond to aggression. For example, if another child punched them without reason, would they be more likely to strike back or walk away? A series of two-choice questions like this yielded a score for each child that indicated his or her tendency to respond aggressively (the dependent variable).

Figure 6.16 shows how children in the three conditions scored on this measure. As you can see, the no-violence group received the lowest scores. Those who thought that the violence was part of a movie (fantasy violence) scored substantially higher. The group who thought that the episode had really happened (realistic violence) scored even higher. Their aggression scores were nearly 50% greater than those who had seen no violence in the news program.

The advantage of the experimental method is that it allows the experimenter to control the study rigorously. For example, Atkin was able to assign students

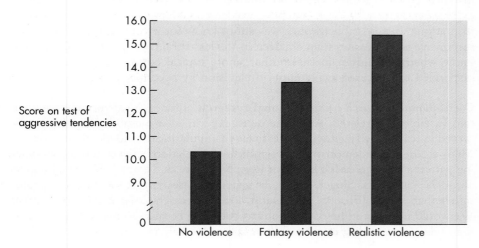

Figure 6.16
The influence of the kind of television violence children watched on their score on a test of aggressive tendencies. (Based on data from Atkin, 1983)

to the three groups on a random basis. He was able to control the nature of the three television programs, so that they differed only with respect to that one critical segment; there were no confounding variables. Finally, the children's aggressive tendencies could be measured in a well-controlled laboratory setting, free from the kinds of distractions and complications that abound in real-life settings. (For example, if Atkin had measured their aggressive behavior in their usual classrooms, their behavior could have been influenced by other children, the teacher, and the ongoing activity in the classroom, all of which are factors that would "muddy" the relationship between the independent and the dependent variable.)

However, the disadvantage of the experimental method is that it is difficult to generalize from the clean, pure results obtained in the laboratory to the messiness of real-life settings. We do not know whether the relationship between the kind of TV program and the children's aggressive tendencies really would hold true in real life. It is for this reason that researchers need to conduct quasi-experiments and correlational research, as well as laboratory experiments.

The Quasi-Experimental Method   In a **quasi-experiment**, the researchers cannot randomly assign participants to different groups. Instead, they locate a situation in which groups already exist that differ substantially from each other. For example, Joy, Kimball, and Zabrack (1986) located a town in a remote part of Canada that had no television prior to 1974, when one station was made available. This town therefore experienced a *change* in television-viewing patterns. In contrast, a second town had one station available both before and after 1974. A third town had four stations available both before and after 1974. Notice that these last two towns did not experience a change in television-viewing patterns.

Figure 6.17 shows the increase in the number of physically aggressive responses, between 1973 and 1974, made by children in the three towns. When television was introduced to children in the first town, they showed a large increase in aggression. In contrast, children in the other two towns experienced no change in television availability during that same time period, and they did not dramatically change their aggressive behavior.

This quasi-experiment shows us that introducing television to a community had a real-life impact on the children's aggressive tendencies. However, keep in mind that the experimenters did not randomly assign the children to the three community groups, and therefore the three groups may have differed substantially to begin with. These researchers discovered from census figures that the towns were identical in population size and income level, but it seems likely that they would have differed in some characteristics not measurable in a census. For instance, children in the remote community may have been more likely to have a "frontier attitude." They may have welcomed adventures and aggressive confrontations. It is possible (though we cannot know for sure) that they were more responsive to aggression than children in the less rural communities. We do not know whether children in these other, more typical communities would have responded to increased availability of television by becoming more aggressive.

Correlational Research   **Correlational research** attempts to determine whether two variables are related. As in the quasi-experimental method, behavior is observed in real-life settings, without actively manipulating the independent variable. Many studies have demonstrated a significant correlation between television-viewing patterns and aggressive behavior (e.g., McIntyre & Teevan, 1972; McLeod et al., 1972; Singer & Singer, 1981). In general, these correlations are moderate, rather than strong (Eron & Huesmann, 1987; Friedrich-Cofer & Huston, 1986). We would not expect the correlations to be strong because so many factors other than television viewing could influence aggressive behavior in children.

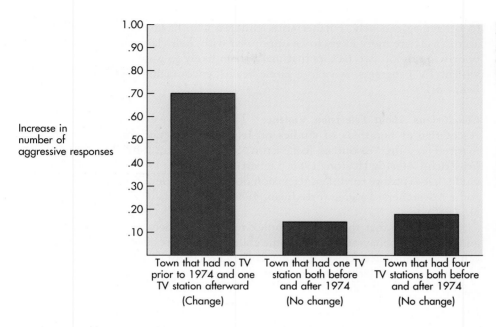

Figure 6.17
The increase in the number of aggressive responses, as a function of change in television availability. (Based on data from Joy et al., 1986)

Correlational studies present two major problems. As discussed in chapter 2, it is possible that some "third variable" is really responsible for the apparent relationship between the two variables examined by the researchers. In our example, for instance, the amount of violent television a child watches is correlated with his or her aggressive behavior. However, that relationship may really be traceable to a third variable, the characteristics of the child's parents. Specifically, the kind of parents who prohibit their children from watching violent TV shows are also likely to discourage aggressive behavior in their children. Fortunately, statistical techniques can be used to determine whether a correlation between television-viewing patterns and aggressive behavior still exists when we have taken some of these possible "third variables" into account. In general, the studies show that the correlation does remain significant (e.g., Liebert & Sprafkin, 1988; McLeod et al., 1972; Singer et al., 1984).

A second major problem with correlational studies is known as the "directionality problem." As chapter 2 discussed, when two variables are correlated, we do not know whether Variable A caused Variable B or whether Variable B caused Variable A. (In fact, *both* explanations can be correct.) With reference to the television violence issue, here are two explanations.

1. Children who watch more violent television are more likely to learn aggressive behavior and therefore more likely to behave aggressively in social situations. (Television violence causes aggressive behavior.)

2. Children who are naturally aggressive tend to like to watch violent programs on television, whereas less aggressive children prefer non-violent programs. (Aggressive behavior causes viewing of television violence.)

Extensive research on television violence and aggression in five different countries suggests that both of these explanations of the correlation are correct. Once again, psychological processes require complex explanations. L. Rowell Huesmann and Leonard Eron (1986) arranged for children between the ages of 6 and 11 to be studied over a 2-year period in Australia, Finland, Poland, Israel, and the United States. Their analysis of the results led them to conclude that children who watch violent TV programs extensively are more likely to learn how

This child may have learned his aggressive behavior from watching violent television, but he also may have been more likely to watch violent television because he was more aggressive than other children.

to behave aggressively. Furthermore, children who have learned how to behave aggressively are more likely to be unpopular with their classmates and to perform poorly in school, two factors that make them likely to watch even more of these violent TV programs. A vicious circle begins, encouraging even more aggressive behavior.

Conclusions About Television Violence   The studies we have examined are representative of hundreds of studies on television violence that have been summarized in other resources (e.g., Eron & Huesmann, 1987; Freedman, 1984; Friedrich-Cofer & Huston, 1986; Liebert & Sprafkin, 1988). Most studies conclude that exposure to violent television does increase viewer's aggression, though some researchers disagree (Freedman, 1984, 1986; Potts et al., 1986; Sprafkin et al., 1987).

It is clear that there is a complex relationship between television viewing and aggressive behavior, because some children are more affected by violence than others. For instance, Heath and her colleagues (1986) concluded that television violence is particularly dangerous for children who have been abused (who see aggression modeled in their daily lives, in addition to television violence). In contrast, children with little real contact with violence may not be as likely to learn aggressive behavior from television. These conclusions are clearly consistent with our theme of individual differences.

It is also clear that several different mechanisms account for the relationship between television violence and aggressive behavior. We have focused on observational learning, the tendency for children to imitate aggressive models. Consistent with the theme of the complexity of human behavior, we need to consider additional influential factors such as vicarious reinforcement, the excitatory effect of television, and the activation of other related aggressive thoughts (Berkowitz, 1984; Huesmann et al., 1983).

If you would like more information about television violence, you can write to The National Coalition on Television Violence (P.O. Box 2157, Champaign, IL, 61820) or Stop War Toys Campaign (P.O. Box 1093, Norwich, CT, 06360).

○ ○

Applications of Observational Learning

In the section on operant conditioning, we discussed carefully developed applications in computer-assisted instruction and behavior modification. Both of these approaches are useful in classroom teaching. Clearly, observational learning also has numerous applications in teaching. For example, students learn how to pronounce French words and how to play football, in large part by observational learning. And their teachers learned how to teach, with observational learning once again playing an important role. Two other areas in which observational learning has been applied are in health psychology and clinical psychology.

Health Psychology   Many children are fearful about visits to the dentist or— quite understandably—surgery in a hospital. Craig (1978) used observational learning to help children overcome their fear of dental visits. In this study, children in one group watched a film in which a model was initially fearful but controlled his fear, receiving verbal praise and a toy at the end of the dental session. These children were much less anxious and disruptive when they visited the dentist than children in a control group who had not seen the film. Similarly, Melamed and Siegel (1975) found that children who had watched a film about a boy's experience with surgery were much less anxious than children in a control group. In this experiment, the dependent variable, anxiety, was assessed by all three methods discussed in chapter 2: self-report, physiological measures, and behavioral measures.

Clinical Psychology   In an important application in clinical psychology, Ladd and Mize (1983) reported that children with behavior problems can be helped by social-skills training. In this technique, children observe the social behaviors of adults and children their own age, or else models in a video presentation. This kind of program can be helpful, for instance, in encouraging a socially isolated preschooler to interact well with other children.

Observational learning is also important in the origins and treatment of **phobic disorders**, which are intense fears that have no rational basis (Domjan & Burkhard, 1986). At one point, many theorists believed that phobic disorders were caused by classical conditioning. For example, someone might develop a snake phobia following a snake bite, producing an extreme fear of the sight of snakes. However, most people with phobias cannot recall a traumatic conditioning event to account for their fears (Barlow, 1988).

Instead, a major component of phobia acquisition seems to come from observational learning. In a series of studies, laboratory-reared monkeys learned to fear snakes. Prior to learning, these young monkeys showed no fear of snakes. Then they were introduced to their parents, who had been reared in the wild. The young monkeys watched as their parents reacted fearfully to real and toy snakes. After brief observation periods, the offspring avoided and appeared afraid of snakes in much the same fashion that their parents had demonstrated (Cook et al., 1985; Mineka et al., 1984). Phobias seem to arise when we watch someone being afraid, rather than when we experience pain directly. Many therapists now help people overcome their phobias by encouraging them to watch movies of a person dealing competently with the feared animal and showing no apparent signs of anxiety. Thus, observational learning can help people eliminate phobias.

In this chapter, we have examined three kinds of learning: classical conditioning, operant conditioning, and observational learning. Each of these approaches to learning presents an important mechanism for changing human behavior and acquiring new skills. However, you have learned many facts and changed many behaviors in the brief time since you began to read this chapter, and only a portion of these changes can be traced to the kinds of learning we examined. As a human, you also have the capacity to change because of your memory capacity, your cognitive skills, and your language ability. We examine these topics in the next three chapters.

Section Summary: *Observational Learning*

- ■ The classic research on observational learning, conducted by Bandura, involved children watching and imitating an adult's aggressive behavior toward a Bobo doll.
- ■ Important components of observational learning include vicarious reinforcement and punishment, intrinsic reinforcement and punishment, and the acquisition of schemas.
- ■ Research on the relationship between television violence and aggressive behavior has used the experimental, quasi-experimental, and correlational methods. Most research shows a moderate relationship between TV violence and aggression, though the relationship is complex and many mechanisms in addition to observational learning play an important role.
- ■ Observational learning has applications in education, health psychology, and clinical psychology.

1. Suppose that you are driving along the road and you spot a pothole imme-diately in front of you. As soon as you see it, your body automatically tightens and you flinch, in preparation for the jolt. Explain how classical conditioning accounts for your reaction. Be sure to use the appropriate terms from this chapter.

2. Try to recall Pavlov's experiment. Make diagrams of the unconditioned stim-ulus, the conditioned stimulus, and the responses in three phases: (a) before conditioning, (b) during conditioning, and (c) after conditioning. First check Figure 6.3 to see if your diagrams are correct. Then do the same exercise for the Watson and Rayner experiment with Albert and the white rat. Finally, describe, with respect to Albert and the rat, how the terms *stimulus general-ization, stimulus discrimination, extinction,* and *spontaneous recovery* could operate.

3. Suppose that you know a high school student whose notes from a beginning psychology class state that classical conditioning involves the repeated pairing of the unconditioned stimulus and the conditioned stimulus. Describe several problems with this definition. Be sure to provide evidence that pairing (con-tiguity) is not sufficient.

4. How would the three kinds of learning discussed in this chapter be useful in clinical and health psychology? Give a specific example for classical condi-tioning, operant conditioning, and observational learning.

5. How do classical and operant conditioning differ? Describe how Thorndike's and Skinner's classic research differs from the situations studied by Pavlov and Watson and Rayner.

6. Imagine that you are babysitting for a child who makes Bart Simpson look angelic. Describe how you could use positive reinforcement, negative rein-forcement, and punishment (both kinds) to improve the child's behavior. Discuss some of the problems with punishment.

7. Think of examples that you have encountered in college of each of the five schedules of reinforcement you learned about in this chapter. Also identify several examples of shaping. Finally, think of examples of discriminative stimuli and secondary reinforcers in your college education.

8. Imagine that you are teaching elementary school and you have decided to begin a behavior modification program to encourage students to perform more accurately on their in-class arithmetic assignments. Describe how you would design this program. At some point, mention each of these terms: reinforcement, schedule of reinforcement, shaping, and token economy.

9. Describe how observational learning helped you learn a particular sport or hobby you enjoy. Mention whether reinforcement was important in your acquisition of this skill. If so, what kind of reinforcement operated?

10. Describe the three research methods that were discussed in the in-depth section on television violence and aggression. Did the information in this section match or disagree with your previous thoughts on the issue of TV violence?

NEW TERMS

learning	unconditioned response	acquisition
classical conditioning	conditioned stimulus	stimulus generalization
unconditioned stimulus	conditioned response	stimulus discrimination

extinction
spontaneous recovery
taste aversion
biological preparedness
operant conditioning
instrumental conditioning
positive reinforcement
negative reinforcement
punishment
shaping
continuous reinforcement
    schedule
partial reinforcement

fixed-ratio schedule
fixed-interval schedule
variable-ratio schedule
variable-interval schedule
primary reinforcer
secondary reinforcer
discriminative stimulus
instinctive drift principle
computer-assisted
    instruction (CAI)
behavior modification
token economy

observational learning
modeling
social learning
vicarious reinforcement
vicarious punishment
intrinsic reinforcement
intrinsic punishment
schema
experimental method
quasi-experiment
correlational research
phobic disorder

ANSWERS TO DEMONSTRATIONS

Demonstration 6.2 1. increase; 2. yes; 3. no; 4. b, c and e; 5. positive reinforcement.

RECOMMENDED READINGS

Cooper, J. D., Heron, T. E., & Heward, W. L. (1987). *Applied behavior analysis.* Columbus, OH: Merrill. This book supplies valuable details on how to implement a behavior modification program. For example, it includes separate chapters on shaping, extinction, and token economies, as well as many examples and discussion of relevant research.

Domjan, M., & Burkhard, B. (1986). *The principles of learning and behavior* (2nd ed.). Monterey, CA: Brooks/Cole. This intermediate-level textbook provides a clear discussion of the details of classical and operant conditioning, with an additional chapter on animal cognition.

Hergenhahn, B. R. (1988). *An introduction to theories of learning* (3rd ed.). Englewood Cliffs, NJ: Prentice Hall. Hergenhahn's textbook focuses on the history of learning theories; separate chapters are devoted to theorists such as Pavlov, Thorndike, Skinner, Bandura, and other cognitive learning theorists.

Liebert, R. M., & Sprafkin, J. (1988). *The early window* (3rd ed.). Elmsford, NY: Pergamon. Here is an excellent, comprehensive review of the literature on television violence. It also discusses other controversial aspects of television, such as how television advertising influences children.

Schwartz, B. (1989). *Psychology of learning and behavior* (3rd ed.). New York: Norton. Schwartz's textbook provides a sophisticated, advanced-level discussion of classical and operant conditioning; it also includes chapters on modern behavior theory and on the interaction between classical and operant conditioning.

Skinner, B. F. (1953). *Science and human behavior.* New York: Macmillan. This classic overview of learning theory, written by the most prominent learning theorist of recent years, discusses such topics as punishment, emotion, and self-control.

Memory

What would happen if your memory were suddenly to disappear, right in the middle of this paragraph? You would not be able to remember your own name. You would look in the mirror and see a stranger staring back. You would not remember that mirrors are supposed to reflect the viewer. In fact, you would not even recall how to walk over to the mirror. Finally, you could not even read this far in the paragraph, because you would be unable to recognize any letters or understand the meaning of any words.

Memory involves storing information over time. This information can be stored for less than a second or as long as your lifetime. For example, memory is involved when you must store the beginning of a word (perhaps *mem-*) until you hear the end of the word (*-ory*). Memory is also involved when you recall the name of your favorite toy when you were a toddler.

Our memory ability both astounds and depresses us. For example, you can probably recall the name of your best friend in third grade, though you may not have thought about this person in years. On the other hand, you have probably been introduced to people whose name you have forgotten 5 seconds later.

Intriguingly, however, we are more likely to pay attention to our memory failures than our memory successes (Lachman et al., 1979). We become flustered when we make a special trip to another part of the house, only to forget why we went there in the first place. However, we do not congratulate ourselves for remembering who the first person was to study classical conditioning, where a friend keeps his chainsaw, and whether the koala is a bear or a marsupial.

It is particularly impressive that our memory is so accurate, because an item must surmount three obstacles to be remembered: acquisition, storage, and retrieval. During **acquisition**, the first stage, we perceive the item and record its important features. During **storage**, the second stage, we hold the information in memory for later use—perhaps less than 1 second, perhaps 17 years. During **retrieval**, the third stage, we successfully locate the item and use it.

In 1968, Atkinson and Shiffrin proposed an extremely influential model of memory. A simplified version of this model appears in Figure 7.1. In the late 1960s, the new area of cognitive psychology was just emerging. Many psychologists considered information-processing approaches such as Atkinson and Shiffrin's to be more useful than the behaviorist principles of learning theory.

As you can see, this model has three components. Information first enters **sensory memory**, which is a storage system that records information from the senses with reasonable accuracy. The capacity of sensory memory is relatively large, but its duration is less than 2 seconds. A fraction of the material from sensory memory then passes on to short-term memory. **Short-term memory (STM)** contains only the small amount of material we are currently using. Memories in STM are fragile, and they can be lost from memory within about 30 seconds unless they are somehow repeated or rehearsed. According to the model, information finally can pass from short-term memory to long-term memory. **Long-term memory (LTM)** has an enormous capacity. It stores memories that are decades old, as well as memories that arrived a few minutes ago. These memories are much more permanent than those in sensory memory and short-term memory.

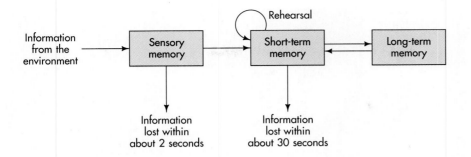

Figure 7.1
A simplified version of Atkinson and Shiffrin's model of memory.

It is important to stress that this model does *not* imply that you have three boxes in your brain or that these three stages occur in different locations within your cerebral cortex. Furthermore, many psychologists believe that the distinction between short-term memory and long-term memory is more blurry than Atkinson and Shiffrin originally envisioned (e.g., Ellis, 1987) or that other models are more useful (e.g., Craik & Lockhart, 1972). Let us discuss these three kinds of memory and then, in the last portion of the chapter, discuss methods for improving memory.

Sensory Memory

Sensory memory holds information for a brief period after the physical stimulus is no longer available. It holds information in raw form, rather than changing it or making it more meaningful. Try Demonstration 7.1 to see several examples of sensory memory.

Why do we need sensory memory? Sensory memory has two major purposes. First, we need to keep an accurate record of the physical stimulus for a brief time while we select the most important stimuli for further processing. In chapter 4 you learned that humans cannot pay attention to all stimuli at the same time. Consider the rich variety of stimuli that are entertaining your senses at this very moment. You can see the words on the page in front of you as well as other details surrounding your book—your hands, perhaps a desk, a notebook, and a lamp. Maybe you hear the squeak of your marker as you underline an important point. You also may hear faint music in the background. Perhaps your other senses are rapidly accumulating information about the room temperature, the scratchiness of your sweater, the aroma from the cafeteria, and the stale taste of cinnamon gum. Of course, the environment in which you are studying is probably simple compared to the overwhelming stimulation of a busy city scene. In any

Demonstration 7.1

Examples of Sensory Memory

Iconic (visual) memory. Take a flashlight into a dark room and turn it on. Swing your wrist around in a circular motion, shining the flashlight onto a distant wall. If your motion is quick enough, you will see a complete circle. Your visual sensory memory stores the beginning of the circle while you examine the end.

Echoic (auditory) memory. With your hand, beat a quick rhythm on the desk. Can you still hear the echo after the beating is finished?

Sensory memory for touch. Rub the palm of your hand quickly along the horizontal edge of your desk. Can you still feel the sharp edge, even after your hand is off the desk?

On a busy street, an amazing variety of stimuli enter sensory memory.

setting, your sensory memory briefly records this rich stimulation. Then you pay attention to only a fraction of the information in this recording.

A second reason we need sensory memory is that these stimuli that are bombarding your senses are constantly and rapidly changing. Consider what happens when your professor asks the question, "Why do we need sensory memory?" The *wh* sound has completely disappeared by the time you hear the word *memory*. Still, you need to retain information about the pitch of the voice at the beginning of the sentence to compare it with the pitch information at the end of the sentence. The rising pitch in the professor's voice allows you to conclude that this sentence was a question.

Atkinson and Shiffrin (1968) suggested that we could have sensory memory for all the senses discussed in chapter 4—vision, hearing, smell, taste, and the skin senses. However, researchers have primarily concentrated on vision (iconic memory) and hearing (echoic memory).

Iconic Memory

Iconic memory allows you to see a trace of a visual stimulus for a brief moment after it has disappeared.

Visual sensory memory is called **iconic memory** (pronounced eye-*conn*-ick). The investigation of iconic memory is challenging, because it is so fragile that it usually fades before we finish measuring it. For example, glance as quickly as possible at the chart of letters in Figure 7.2, and then immediately try to recall as many letters as possible. You are likely to recall only four or five letters from that chart. However, didn't it seem that you registered more than you were able to report? Perhaps it seemed that you processed about 10 items, but many of these appeared to fade during the brief time it required to report the first four or five letters. However, people's introspective reports are not sufficient to establish the quantitative characteristics of sensory memory.

A young graduate student named George Sperling (1960) figured out a clever way to estimate the true capacity of iconic memory. Previous researchers had used the whole-report technique, requiring participants in their experiments to list all the letters they had seen (as you just did). In contrast, Sperling devised a **partial-report technique**, which requires participants to report only a specified portion of the display. Sperling presented a tone to indicate which line of the chart was to be reported. Specifically, a high tone indicated that the listener should report

1.

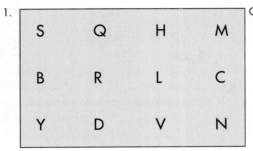

Chart flashes on for 1/20 second

Figure 7.2
Order of events in Sperling's (1960) study.

2.   Tone (high, medium, low) indicates which line must be reported

3.   S   Q   H   Person reports three letters from the indicated row

the top row, a middle tone indicated the middle row, and a low tone indicated the bottom row.

Imagine that you are a participant in Sperling's experiment. As Figure 7.2 shows, the chart flashes on for a fraction of a second. Then a high tone sounds, indicating that you should report as much as possible from the top line. Notice that you had no clue, when you were actually seeing the chart, as to which line you would be asked to recall. Therefore, we can assume that if you had reported three letters from the top line (perhaps S Q H), you also could have reported three letters from either the middle or the bottom row—if those had been requested instead of the top row. To estimate the total number of items in iconic memory, we can multiply by 3 the number of items correct on any one line.

Sperling discovered that people recalled an average of slightly more than 3 items for one line when the partial-report technique was used. Therefore, he estimated that iconic memory holds between 9 and 10 items. However, the image of these 9 or 10 items fades so rapidly that a person using the whole-report technique could report only 4 or 5 of them before the remaining items disappeared from iconic memory.

By delaying the signal tone just half a second, however, Sperling discovered that people stored only an estimated 4 to 5 items. In other words, iconic memory fades so rapidly that it has vanished in less than a second, and recall deteriorates to the same unspectacular level as in the whole-report technique. Figure 7.3 shows the results for both immediate and delayed recall.

Cognitive psychologists were extremely interested in Sperling's results. Since then, hundreds of experiments have been conducted on iconic memory, using a wide variety of research procedures. They typically demonstrate that items remain in iconic memory for less than half a second after the physical stimulus has disappeared (Long, 1980; van der Heijden, 1981).

We do not yet know where iconic memory is located. Some researchers argue that it is located in the rods, the visual receptors that are sensitive to black-and-white stimuli, which we discussed in chapter 4 (e.g., Long & Beaton, 1982; Sakitt, 1976). However, iconic memory also stores information about *color*, so cone receptors must be involved in iconic memory too (Adelson, 1978; Banks & Barber, 1977). Most psychologists believe that iconic memory operates at a higher level of visual processing, rather than being limited to the receptors of the eye. A few psychologists have questioned the very existence of iconic memory (e.g., Haber, 1983; 1985b). However, the majority argue that there is clear research evidence supporting this briefest form of visual memory (summarized by G. R. Loftus, 1985).

Figure 7.3
Number of letters reported, as a function of method (partial-report vs. whole-report) and delay since exposure of chart.

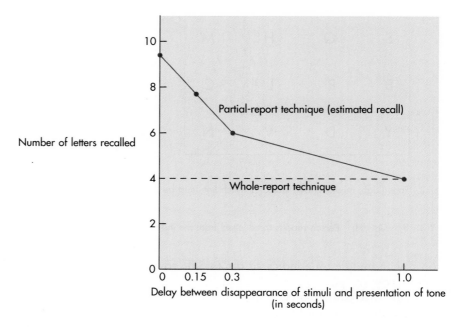

Number of letters recalled

Partial-report technique (estimated recall)

Whole-report technique

Delay between disappearance of stimuli and presentation of tone
(in seconds)

Echoic Memory

Auditory sensory memory is called **echoic memory**. The name *echoic memory* is particularly appropriate, because at times it seems that a sound echoes briefly inside your head. Have you ever noticed that your professor's words seem to reverberate inside your head for a few moments after they have been spoken? Fortunately, this internal echoing allows you to hold the sounds in sensory memory, process them, and write them down a second or two later.

An important demonstration of echoic memory was modeled after Sperling's (1960) partial-report technique. We have discussed Sperling's use of an auditory signal to indicate which part of the visual stimulus was to be reported. Darwin, Turvey, and Crowder (1972) neatly reversed Sperling's study by using a visual signal to indicate which part of the auditory stimulus was to be reported from echoic memory.

Darwin and his colleagues used headphones to present three different auditory messages to the participants. Figure 7.4 shows how this was done. One series of items (J 4 T) was presented to a person's right ear. A second series of items (A 5 2) was presented to the left ear. A third series of items (3 M Z) was presented in such a way that it appeared to come from the middle. All three series were presented at the same time. After hearing all three, people were shown a visual cue on a screen that indicated which of the three series they should report.

These researchers found that the partial-report technique allowed people to report a larger estimated number of items than with the whole-report technique, in which people tried to report all nine items. These results are similar to Sperling's results for iconic memory. Thus, sensory memory stores items for a brief time—so brief that this memory disappears before people can list all its items.

This study also pointed out some differences between the two kinds of sensory memory. Specifically, the capacity of echoic memory seems to be about 5 items, which is considerably fewer than the 9 to 10 items in iconic memory. However, echoic memory lasts about 2 seconds (Crowder, 1982; Darwin et al., 1972)—about four times as long as iconic memory. This information matches our daily experience. Finding everyday examples of iconic memory is difficult because it fades before we are aware it is operating. In contrast, it is easy to think of

Echoic memory guarantees that these students will be able to hear this professor's words echoing in their heads, so that they can take notes after the auditory stimulus has disappeared.

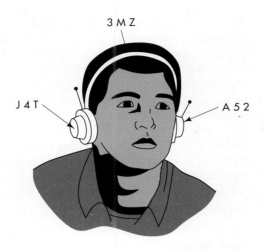

3 M Z

J 4 T

A 5 2

Figure 7.4
A person participating in an echoic
memory study.

examples of echoic memory. After the clock in a bell tower has struck, does it still seem to reverberate in your head? When a friend has spoken and you were not really paying attention, can you reconstruct his words if you immediately "listen" to the echo?

Section Summary: Sensory Memory

■ Atkinson and Shiffrin proposed a model of memory that included sensory memory, short-term memory, and long-term memory.

■ Sensory memory holds information in unprocessed form for a brief period.

■ Iconic memory, originally assessed by Sperling's partial-report technique, holds 9 to 10 visual items for about half a second.

■ Echoic memory holds about 5 auditory items for about 2 seconds.

Short-Term Memory

You have probably had an experience like this. You are standing at a pay telephone, looking up a phone number. You find the number, repeat it to yourself, and close the phone book. You take out the coins, insert them, and raise your finger to dial. Amazingly, you cannot remember it. The first digits were 243, and there was a 5 somewhere, but you have no idea what the other numbers were! They quickly deserted your short-term memory.

As mentioned earlier, only a handful of items will make their way from sensory memory into short-term memory. In fact, only the material to which we pay attention will be transferred to STM. For example, you probably did not pay attention to the street sounds when you were locating the phone number, so they vanished from echoic memory without being transferred to STM. Furthermore, memories stored in STM can be lost within about 30 seconds unless they are somehow repeated. While you were locating the coins, inserting them, and beginning to dial, your attention was directed away from the phone number, and you did not repeat it. Less than a minute later, those numbers have departed.

At this point, you might be wondering how our occasionally poor performance in short-term memory can be reconciled with the theme that humans are extraordinarily competent in adapting to their environment. First of all, keep in mind that we notice our failures more than our successes. Start noticing how often your short-term memory successfully preserves information long enough for you to use it. Secondly, there may be some advantages to forgetting. Would you really want your memory to be cluttered with the phone number of your best friend in fifth grade or the cost of a pack of gum you bought last year? In general, short-term memory retains information long enough for us to deal with it. However, short-term memory also allows us to forget when we no longer find the information useful.

Short-term memory is sometimes called **working memory** because it handles the material we are currently working with, rather than the items we did not pay attention to in sensory memory or the items stored away in long-term memory (Baddeley, 1986). Let us now consider some characteristics of short-term memory, including encoding, duration, and capacity.

Encoding in Short-Term Memory

Encoding involves transforming sensory stimuli into a form that can be placed in memory. For instance, turn back to the diagram of a neuron (Figure 3.1). Look over this diagram and try to remember it. You will probably discover that you are constructing a mental picture of this neuron and trying to connect each of the terms with the appropriate structure. You are working at encoding, because you are transforming those squiggly lines and those letters into something that can be stored in your memory.

Type of Processing   You can encode sensory stimuli using either effortful or automatic processing. When you use **effortful processing**, you make a deliberate attempt to place something in memory. You use effortful processing when you meet someone new and repeat this person's name to yourself or try to remember it by thinking of others with the same first name.

In contrast, **automatic processing** occurs when no deliberate effort is required to place something into memory. For example, can you recall *where* on the page that diagram of the neuron appeared? You encoded the diagram's location, even though you made no effort to memorize this information. We are especially likely to use automatic processing to record information about spatial location, time, and number of occurrences (Hasher & Zacks, 1979, 1984).

In general, we are more aware of memory items that are acquired with effortful processing rather than automatic processing (Cowan, 1988). You *know* that the diagram of the neuron has been committed to memory. In contrast, you probably did not realize that you knew about the diagram's location until I asked you.

Storage Form   Just as information can be encoded using either effortful or automatic processing, it can also be stored in several different forms. Suppose, for example, that you have just looked up a term in the index of a textbook, and you have learned that it is mentioned on pages 20, 42, and 68. How do you keep these page numbers in your short-term memory until you can locate them? Do you encode them in terms of the way they sound, the way they look, or some aspect of their meaning?

It probably seems that you encoded the page numbers in terms of their sound. Perhaps you can even "hear" yourself repeating "twenty, forty-two, sixty-eight." The experimental evidence strongly supports an acoustic code—that is, storage in terms of an item's sound (Wickelgren, 1965; Yu et al., 1985).

In one representative study, Wickelgren presented people with a tape recording of an eight-item list consisting of four letters and four digits in random order. A typical item might be *4NF92GZ8*. As soon as the list was presented, people tried to recall it. Wickelgren was particularly interested in the kinds of substitutions people made. For example, if they did not recall the Z, what did they substitute in its place? He found that they tended to insert an item that was acoustically similar. For example, instead of Z, they might substitute a B, C, D, E, G, P, T, or V, all letters with the "ee" sound. Furthermore, if they substituted a number for Z, it would most likely be the similar-sounding number 3.

The tendency to encode information acoustically in STM is so strong that we are even likely to use an acoustical encoding when the material is presented visually (as in the example of the index pages) as well as when it is presented in spoken form, as in Wickelgren's study (Salamé & Baddeley, 1982). However, not all information in short-term memory *must* be encoded acoustically. It can be encoded visually, in terms of the way the stimulus looks (e.g., Frick, 1988; Posner & Keele, 1967). For instance, you encoded the diagram of the neuron visually, rather than acoustically. Short-term memory also can be encoded in terms of meaning (Wickens et al., 1976). In summary, then, the encoding in short-term memory is primarily in terms of sound. However, humans can be flexible; they also can store information in STM in terms of the way it looks or what it means.

The Duration of Short-Term Memory

How long does material last in short-term memory before it is forgotten? An approach that answered this question can be called the Brown/Peterson & Peterson technique, after a British psychologist, John Brown (1958), and two American psychologists, Lloyd Peterson and Margaret Peterson (1959), who independently devised similar methods of assessing short-term memory.

Peterson and Peterson asked people to study a series of stimuli, each stimulus consisting of just three unrelated letters of the alphabet. The participant saw a single stimulus, then counted backward by threes for a short period, and then tried to recall those three letters. For the first few trials, performance was reasonably accurate. Figure 7.5 shows typical results after a large number of trials, each time with a different triad of letters. Notice that recall was only 80% accurate for these three letters a mere 3 seconds after they had been presented. With just an 18-second delay, recall had plummeted to close to zero. Keep in mind that people were counting backward during the delay period, and this task apparently prevented them from rehearsing or repeating the items silently to themselves. Unless information can somehow be repeated in short-term memory, it can be lost in less than 20 seconds.

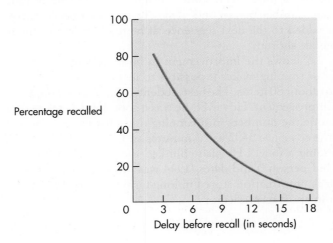

Figure 7.5
Percentage of letters recalled with the Brown/Peterson and Peterson technique (typical results after a large number of previous recall trials with different stimuli).

The Size of Short-Term Memory

You have little trouble remembering a 4-digit street address, such as 2614, for a short period. However, a standard 7-digit phone number (346-3421) is more challenging. If you add on an area code to make the phone number 10 digits (212-346-3421), it is unlikely that you would remember the entire number correctly.

In 1956, George Miller wrote a very influential article called "The Magical Number Seven, Plus or Minus Two: Some Limits on Our Capacity for Processing Information." Miller proposed that we cannot keep many items in short-term memory at one time. In particular, he suggested that people can remember about seven items (give or take two), or between five and nine items.

Miller used the term **chunk** to describe the basic unit in short-term memory. Thus, we can say that short-term memory holds about seven chunks. A chunk can be a single number or a single letter, because people can remember roughly seven numbers or letters if they are in random order.

However, numbers and letters can often be organized into larger units. For example, you may know that the New York City area code is 212 and that all the phone numbers at a particular college begin with the same numbers—346. If 212 forms one chunk and 346 forms another chunk, then the entire phone number, 212-346-3421, really has only six chunks. It may be within your memory span.

Suppose that you need to remember a list of items, perhaps some things to bring upstairs from the basement. How long does that list need to be before it is worthwhile to organize it into chunks? MacGregor (1987) has estimated that when you must recall about four items, both organized and unorganized memory are equally efficient. However, when the number of items in short-term memory reaches five, people who know how to use their memory efficiently will find it useful to group some of the information into chunks.

Miller's original article argued that the memory span was about the same size, whether the items to be stored were numbers or words, and whether these items were encoded acoustically, visually, or in terms of meaning. More recent research concludes that the nature of the material really does have an influence on the size of the memory span. Specifically, the size of the memory span is largest for numbers, intermediate for letters, and smallest for words. Also, we remember more items if they can be encoded acoustically than if they can only be encoded visually or in terms of meaning (Frick, 1988; Zhang & Simon, 1985).

We also know that practice can increase the number of items stored in short-term memory. A group of researchers trained two male college students for many months (Ericsson & Chase, 1982; Ericsson et al., 1980). Both students had average memory abilities and average intelligence for college students. For about an hour a day, 3 to 5 days a week, each student listened to numbers in random order at the rate of one number per second. If he recalled a sequence correctly, an extra number was added to the next sequence. If he made an error, the next sequence was one number shorter.

Figure 7.6 shows the improvement in both students' memory. As you can see, continuous training makes it possible to increase the number of items stored in memory to about 80 items. The best student, S.F., received no special instruction in memory improvement. However, he was a good long-distance runner and soon began to encode the numbers into running times for various races. For example, he recalled the sequence 3492 as "3 minutes and 49.2 seconds, near world-record time for running a mile." He also chunked the numbers into ages ("89.3 years old, a very old person") and dates (1944 was "near the end of World War II"). In other words, information stored in long-term memory was used to recode this information in short-term memory.

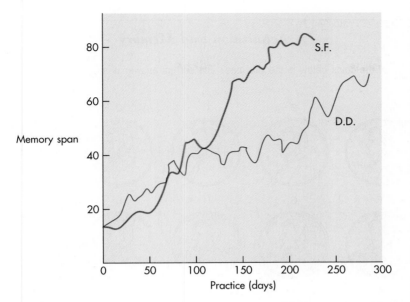

Figure 7.6
Memory span for two people, as a
function of the number of days of
practice. (Based on Ericsson & Chase,
1982)

These researchers later trained a second long-distance runner, D.D., to use S.F.'s memory technique (Ericsson & Chase, 1982). Figure 7.6 shows his performance with this technique, which is impressive, though not quite as remarkable as S.F.'s. These outstanding accomplishments emphasize the importance of prior experience, practice, and the availability of meaningful associations. With these advantages, the size of each chunk can be increased. Under ideal conditions, we can store an impressive number of items in short-term memory.

Section Summary: Short-Term Memory

- Memories stored in short-term memory can be lost within about 30 seconds unless they are repeated.
- Material can be encoded into short-term memory using effortful or automatic processing; it is most often encoded acoustically, though other forms are possible.
- Research using the Brown/Peterson & Peterson technique has demonstrated that material in short-term memory can be easily forgotten.
- In general, short-term memory holds about seven items, though its capacity depends on the nature of the items, type of encoding, and practice.

Long-Term Memory

We have been discussing the fragility of sensory memory and short-term memory. All too often, information that we want to retain for a brief period will disappear from memory. In contrast, material in long-term memory can be extremely resistant to forgetting.

Take a moment to contemplate the information stored in long-term memory. For example, think about how you learned you had been accepted into the college you now attend. Can you remember what you were wearing when you opened the acceptance letter? Although you may recall trivial details like these, your long-term memory often falters on unexpected occasions. For example, try remembering

Demonstration 7.2

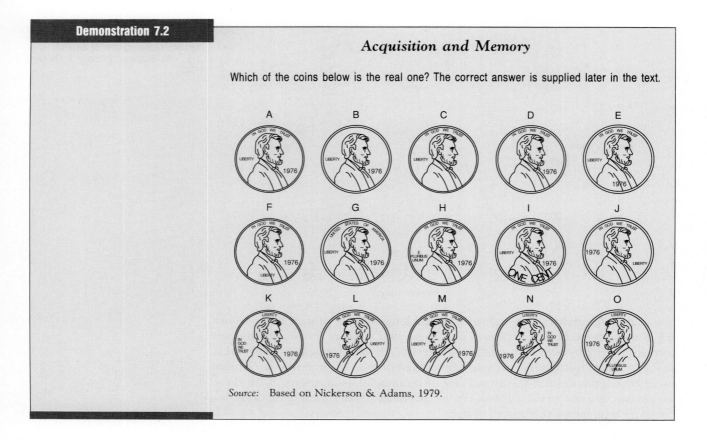

Acquisition and Memory

Which of the coins below is the real one? The correct answer is supplied later in the text.

Source: Based on Nickerson & Adams, 1979.

what courses you are currently taking. If you are like my psychology advisees, you will recall several courses quite easily, but there is an embarrassingly long pause before the name of the last course emerges. (Incidentally, try Demonstration 7.2 at this point.)

In this section, we see how long-term memories are acquired, stored, retrieved, and forgotten. We end by discussing the biological underpinnings of these memories. Throughout this section, we see that our long-term memory usually serves us well. We typically remember general, important ideas quite accurately, though we may forget small details. In addition, long-term memory is carefully structured. This structure generally improves our accuracy, though it can sometimes lead to errors.

Acquisition in Long-Term Memory

In the next 24 hours, you will acquire hundreds of facts, images, and miscellaneous bits of information. How likely will you be to recall these items at a later time? Three factors associated with acquisition—usefulness, depth of processing, and encoding specificity—all influence the likelihood of recall.

Usefulness   Did you select the correct coin in Demonstration 7.2? In a study by Nickerson and Adams (1979), less than half of the participants correctly chose coin A. Furthermore, people perform abysmally when asked to draw from memory the head and tail of coins. For example, only a third of people correctly draw Lincoln facing to the right (Rubin & Kontis, 1983).

Why isn't this kind of information acquired in long-term memory? As you may have figured out, we do not need to know which way Lincoln is facing to spend that penny. You would have no trouble identifying the color of a penny or telling the difference between a penny and all other coins. After all, this information *is* important when you hand coins to the clerk. It is important to consider why memory works the way it does (Bruce, 1985). The reason why we fail to remember the details of a penny—even though we have handled thousands of pennies throughout our lifetime—is that we do not need to bother with this trivia. Why should we cram our cerebral cortex with details about coins when we could be acquiring and storing more interesting, useful information?

Depth of Processing   Before reading further, try Demonstration 7.3 to illustrate how memory performance is influenced by the way we process items during acquisition. In 1972, Craik and Lockhart proposed that psychologists should not focus on the distinction between short-term memory and long-term memory that Atkinson and Shiffrin (1968) had emphasized. Craik and Lockhart argued that we should stress, instead, **depth of processing**, or the method people use to mentally process stimuli. When you see a list of words, you can use a shallow kind of processing that involves judgments about the appearance of the letters in the words or the sound of the words. Alternatively, you can use a deeper, more complex kind of processing, involving judgments about whether a word's meaning is appropriate for a particular sentence.

Depth of Processing

Read each of the following questions and answer "yes" or "no" with respect to the word that follows. As soon as you are done, cover the words.

1. Is the word in capital letters? — BOOK
2. Would the word fit the sentence: "I saw a _____ in a pond"? — duck
3. Does the word rhyme with BLUE? — safe
4. Would the word fit the sentence: "The girl walked down the _____"? — house
5. Does the word rhyme with FREIGHT? — WEIGHT
6. Is the word in small letters? — snow
7. Would the word fit the sentence: "The _____ was reading a book"? — STUDENT
8. Does the word rhyme with TYPE? — color
9. Is the word in capital letters? — flower
10. Would the word fit the sentence: "Last spring we saw a _____"? — robin
11. Does the word rhyme with SMALL? — HALL
12. Is the word in small letters? — TREE
13. Would the word fit the sentence: "My _____ is six feet tall"? — TEXTBOOK
14. Does the word rhyme with BOOK? — look
15. Is the word in capital letters? — FOX

Now, without looking back over the words, try to remember as many of them as possible. Count the number correct for each of the three kinds of tasks: physical appearance (letter size), sound (rhyming), or meaning ("Would the word fit the sentence"). On which task was your memory most accurate?

In Demonstration 7.3, you were probably more accurate in recalling the words that you had processed at a deep level, in terms of their meaning. When Craik (1977) tried a longer, more elaborate version of this demonstration, he found the results shown in Figure 7.7. As you can see, words that had been processed in terms of meaning were recalled much more accurately than words processed in terms of sound, and more than four times as accurately as words processed in terms of physical appearance.

Deep levels of processing promote recall because of two factors, distinctiveness and elaboration (Craik & Lockhart, 1986). Distinctiveness describes the extent to which one particular memory is different from the other memories in the system. Suppose that you want to remember the word *tennis*. If you perform deep processing on that word, you might come up with an encoding that includes the name of your tennis partner from the gym course last semester, an image of a tennis court, your plans for playing more tennis next summer, and the brand name on your tennis racket. This encoding is probably distinctive, because it differs from any other memory trace. An encoding that is distinctly different from other items will be especially memorable.

The second factor that operates with deep levels of processing is elaboration, which involves rich processing in terms of meaning (Anderson & Reder, 1979; Cohen et al., 1986). When you processed the word *duck* in Demonstration 7.3, for example, you might have thought about the fact that a duck is a bird, that it has feathers, that you have seen ducks on ponds, and many other possible associations. The encoding in terms of meaning encouraged rich processing. In contrast, if the instructions had asked whether the word *duck* was printed in capital letters, you would simply answer yes or no. Extensive elaboration would be unlikely.

The deepest, most effective way of processing stimuli is in terms of your own experience—a phenomenon called the **self-reference effect**. Suppose that you are asked to look at a list of adjectives and decide whether each word could be applied to yourself. When people study words using these self-reference instructions, they recall about twice as many items as when they process words in terms of meaning (Klein & Kihlstrom, 1986; Rogers et al., 1977). This self-reference effect operates not only for college students but also for young children and elderly adults (Halpin et al., 1984; Rogers, 1983).

Consider this representative study on the self-reference effect. College students read a story about a fictional character's senior year in high school. Students

Figure 7.7
Effects of depth of processing on memory. (Based on Craik, 1977)

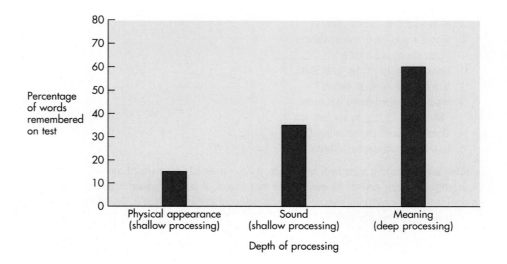

in the self-reference condition were instructed to note the similarities and dissimilarities between their own experiences as high school seniors and those of the fictional student. In contrast, students in the control condition were instructed to note the major ideas in the story. The results showed that students in the self-reference condition later recalled a significantly greater number of items (Reeder et al., 1987).

There is an important practical application for this research on depth of encoding. When you are reading a textbook or reviewing your class notes, try to process the material as deeply as possible. Think about what you are reading, and try to give it meaning by rephrasing a section in your own words. In many cases in a psychology course, you can take advantage of the self-reference effect. When you read about the limits of short-term memory, for example, try to think of examples where you were holding so many items in STM that it seemed that adding a new item would bump an old item into oblivion. At the end of this chapter, we discuss memory improvement techniques. As you will see, many of these are effective because they promote deeper, more distinctive, and more elaborate processing. In contrast, consider the kind of shallow processing in which your eyes drift across the words, and you are suddenly aware that you have not really thought about what you have read. This superficial processing is nearly useless.

Encoding Specificity   You have certainly had an experience like this. You are in the bedroom and realize that you need something from the kitchen. Once you are in the kitchen, however, you have no idea why you went there. Without the context in which you encoded the item you wanted, you cannot retrieve this memory. You return to the bedroom, filled with context cues, and you immediately remember what you wanted.

This example illustrates the **encoding specificity principle**, which states that recall is better if the retrieval context is like the encoding context (Begg & White, 1985; Eich, 1985; Tulving, 1983). In contrast, forgetting is more likely when the two contexts do not match.

The encoding specificity principle predicts that recall will be greatest when testing conditions duplicate learning conditions. Smith and his co-workers (1978)

If this student is using a deep level of processing, her recall will be much better than if she is only using superficial processing.

showed that environmental factors are a critical part of the testing conditions. In one experiment, they asked people to learn material in two very different settings. On one day they learned words in a windowless room with a large blackboard and no cabinets, and the experimenter was formally dressed in a coat and tie. On another day they learned a different set of words in a smaller room with two windows, located in a different section of the campus, with the experimenter dressed in a flannel shirt and jeans. On the third day, people were tested on both word lists. Half of the participants took the test in the windowless room with the formal experimenter, and half took it in the room with windows and the informal experimenter.

The results showed that performance was much better for material that had originally been learned in the same setting. People tested in the same context recalled an average of 14 words, whereas people tested in a different context recalled an average of only 9 words. Thus, if the word *swan* had been learned in the windowless room, it was recalled better in that room than in the room with windows.

The encoding specificity principle has some practical applications for study strategies. Specifically, your performance on tests should be better if your encoding context matches your retrieval context at the time of testing. After you have reviewed the material that will be on an examination, study it further in the same way you will be tested. For example, if you know that you will be tested by an essay exam, try constructing and answering your own essay questions. If you will be tested by fill-in-the-blank items, quiz yourself by constructing and answering fragments such as "The three components of Atkinson and Shiffrin's model are _____ " and "The principle that recall is better if the retrieval context is like the encoding context is called _____ ."

Also try to see if you can match the encoding environment with the retrieval environment whenever possible, to maximize performance. A student once came to my office to take a makeup examination, and she hesitantly asked whether she could take the exam in the regular classroom rather than in my office. When I asked her why, she answered that things in the classroom might help her to remember the answers. Informally, she must have been aware of the value of encoding specificity.

This section has emphasized the importance of acquisition, a part of memory that is often ignored. However, if an item is not properly encoded, it will not enter long-term memory. You cannot possibly recall something that was never there initially. Thus, you will increase your chances of recall if an item is important, if you process it deeply, and if you encode it in a fashion consistent with the way you will be asked to recall it.

Autobiographical Memory

Autobiographical memory is memory for events from your own life (Groninger & Groninger, 1984). This area of research has become increasingly popular because of the current emphasis on ecological validity (Bruce, 1985). **Ecological validity** means that results obtained in research should be generalizable to real-life settings (Cohen, 1989). Laboratory research often produces findings that are useful for everyday memory (Banaji & Crowder, 1989). However, it is easier to generalize research in which people recall life events than when they learn lists of meaningless nonsense words. In this section on autobiographical memory we discuss three topics: eyewitness testimony, flashbulb memory, and prospective memory.

Eyewitness Testimony   In 1979, a Catholic priest awaited trial for several armed robberies in Delaware. Seven witnesses had identified him as the "gentleman

Figure 7.8
Father Bernard Pagano (left), who was almost convicted of armed robbery, and the real criminal, Ronald Clouser (right).

bandit," referring to the polite manners and elegant clothes that the robber had worn. During the trial, many witnesses identified the priest as the one who had committed the robberies. Suddenly, however, the trial was halted in a sequence of events resembling a soap opera plot. Another man had confessed to the robberies (Rodgers, 1982). Figure 7.8 shows the innocent priest and the real criminal, Ronald Clouser, who certainly do not appear to be identical twins.

Reports such as this one have been accumulating for nearly a century, leading psychologists to question the reliability of eyewitness testimony. Although our long-term memory serves us very well in most aspects of daily life, the research on eyewitness testimony demonstrates that we are not very accurate in remembering details about an event that lasted a few seconds and occurred some time ago. Our memory is good, but it cannot be expected to be as accurate as a videotape recorder.

Elizabeth Loftus and her colleagues have identified another important source of inaccuracy in eyewitness testimony. After people witness an event, someone may supply misleading information. This misleading postevent information may bias their recall.

In an important experiment, Loftus, Miller, and Burns (1978) showed a series of slides to participants in their study. In this sequence, a sports car stopped at an intersection, and then it turned and hit a pedestrian. Half of the participants saw a slide with a yield sign at the intersection; the other half saw a stop sign. Twenty minutes to 1 week after the slides had been shown, the participants answered questions about the details of the accident. A critical question contained information that was either consistent with a detail in the original slide series or else did not mention the detail. For example, some people who had originally seen the yield sign were asked, "Did another car pass the red Datsun while it was stopped at the yield sign?" (consistent). Other people were asked the same question with the word *stop* substituted for *yield* (inconsistent). For still other people, the sign was not mentioned (neutral).

After a delay of 20 minutes to 1 week, participants were shown two slides, one with a stop sign and one with a yield sign. They were asked to identify which

Figure 7.9
The effect of type of information and delay on proportion of correct answers. (Loftus et al., 1978)

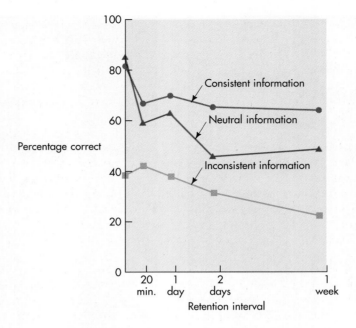

slide they had originally seen. As Figure 7.9 shows, people who had received inconsistent information were substantially less accurate than people in the other two conditions. Loftus and her co-authors concluded that the misleading postevent information had actually altered the details of the slide show that had been stored in memory.

Studies like this one make psychologists suspicious that eyewitnesses in real courtroom cases may suffer from similar inaccuracies if they hear additional information after witnessing the original event. Some researchers are not so pessimistic about these inaccuracies (e.g., Zaragoza et al., 1987). Nevertheless, jury members ought to be skeptical when they listen to eyewitness reports. By one estimate, 8,500 wrongful convictions are made each year in the United States, with perhaps half of them traceable to faulty eyewitness testimony (Loftus, 1986).

Flashbulb Memory   Can you recall what you were doing on January 16, 1991, when you learned that the United States had begun the air war against Iraq? People often have very vivid memories of a situation in which they first learned of a surprising and emotionally arousing event, a phenomenon called **flashbulb memory**.

My clearest flashbulb memory, like most of my generation, is of learning that President John Kennedy had been shot. I was a sophomore at Stanford University, just ready for a midday class in German. I had entered the classroom from the right, and I was just about to sit down at a long table on the right-hand side of the classroom. The sun was streaming in from the left. There was only one other person seated in the classroom, a blond fellow named Dewey. He turned around and said, "Did you hear that President Kennedy has been shot?" I also recall my reaction and the reactions of others as they entered the classroom. Kennedy was shot about 30 years ago, yet trivial details about the news of it are stunningly clear to many people today. You can probably think of personal events in your own life that triggered flashbulb memories—the death of a relative, a piece of important good news, or an amazing surprise.

People are most likely to recall certain characteristics in their flashbulb memory such as where they were, what ongoing event was interrupted by the news, and the person who gave them the news. However, this flashbulb memory is not as accurate as a photograph in which a true flashbulb has been fired (Brown & Kulik, 1977). We also know that people who have strong emotional reactions tend to have more elaborate memories for the event (Heuer & Reisberg, 1990). If you know someone who was devastated by the Reagan assassination attempt in 1981, that person's flashbulb memory of the event will be particularly detailed (Pillemer, 1984).

Prospective Memory   The term **prospective memory** means remembering to do things. When you remember to do something, you use your memory just as extensively as when you remember something from the past. Prospective memory requires remembering both what to do and actually doing it (Cohen, 1989). However, until recently, psychologists have ignored prospective memory. Instead, they have focused on **retrospective memory**, or recall for previously learned information (Harris, 1984; Meacham & Leiman, 1982).

Why is prospective memory so difficult? Why do you have difficulty remembering to take the cake out of the oven, remembering to note the mileage at the end of a trip, or remembering to send a birthday card to your grandfather next week? The task itself is usually very simple—it is not hard to address a card and put it in the mailbox. The difficulty with prospective memory is that you cannot perform that action right now. Successful remembering depends upon recalling to do that action at a later point (Reason, 1984).

One intriguing aspect of prospective memory is absentmindedness. Have you ever reminded yourself to pick up a bag of apples while pushing your cart down the fruit aisle, and then arrived home to find that you never managed to put the bag in your cart? Absentminded behavior is particularly likely in highly familiar surroundings when you are performing tasks automatically. You may have found yourself pouring coffee into the sugar bowl or throwing a check into a wastebasket (Cohen, 1989). These slips are also more likely to occur if you are preoccupied or feeling time pressure (Reason, 1984; Reason & Mycielska, 1982).

Research on prospective memory shows that people are more likely to remember to do something if they are supplied with some kind of reminder, such as a colored tag (Meacham, 1982). My own prospective memory has improved since a friend told me to switch my ring to my right hand whenever I need to remember to do something.

○ ○

In Depth: Reality Monitoring

The research on remembering to do things, or prospective memory, uncovered one kind of absentmindedness that we have not yet discussed. That is, people sometimes confuse the memory of actually doing something with the memory of merely imagining they did it (Johnson & Raye, 1981). For example, you may have clearly remembered giving a book to a friend, yet later you find it in your room.

It should be easy to distinguish between real actions (giving the book to a friend) and imagined actions (thinking about giving the book to a friend). However, it is often difficult to make this kind of decision. For example, Anderson (1984) found that people had trouble remembering whether they had really traced a pen along an outline or whether they had simply imagined themselves doing it.

The mental processes we use when we try to determine the source of events— real or imagined—are called **reality monitoring**. Marcia Johnson, of Princeton University, has been the primary researcher and theorist in the area of reality monitoring. Johnson and her colleague Carol Raye (1981) developed a model for

This photographer is engaging in memory monitoring—trying to recall whether he already added the starter to the developer solution.

how people decide whether a memory source is external (i.e., the event really happened) or internal (i.e., the event was derived from their own imagination and thought).

Specifically, they theorized that

1. You decide that a memory is from an *external* source if it is rich in details and required little cognitive effort.

2. You decide that a memory is from an *internal* source if it lacks details and required great cognitive effort.

Suppose that you are trying to recall whether you took an antibiotic that was prescribed for an illness. You inspect your memory and realize you can readily "see" the pill in your hand and "feel" the glass of water at your lips; the memory is rich with detail. Furthermore, you cannot recall any of the cognitive effort that would have been required in constructing a mental image of taking the pill. In this case, you are likely to conclude that the memory is from an external source; it really happened.

Marcia Johnson and her colleagues Tracey Kahan and Carol Raye (1984) decided to study the recall of dreams. Their study is particularly interesting because we discussed dream recall in chapter 5 and because it is a good example of autobiographical memory, the topic in the previous section.

Johnson and her colleagues studied pairs of people who lived together and who reported dreaming frequently. Each night before bed, the participants opened an envelope that contained instructions about the kind of report they should make the next morning. Let us discuss two of the instruction conditions:

1. Report the dream you actually had (if any) when you wake up tomorrow morning.

2. Read this brief description of someone else's dream (the description was enclosed) and invent a more complete dream story. Then report this story when you wake up tomorrow morning.

This phase of the experiment continued for 2 weeks, and participants tape-recorded their recall each morning. In addition, they listened to their roommate's reports. Then, 2 weeks after the end of the first phase, they came into the laboratory. Here they were shown one-sentence summaries of each of the real dreams and invented dreams, as well as some summaries of dreams that neither person had experienced before. They were asked to identify the source of the description. Was it their own dream or story (internal)? Was it their roommate's, which they had overheard (external)? Or was it entirely new and unfamiliar? They were asked to respond as quickly as possible.

Figure 7.10 shows how accurate people were in identifying an item's source, as a function of whether it was a real dream or an invented dream, and whether it was originally their own or their roommate's. Notice that when people made judgments about material provided by their partner, the percentage correct was similar for the real dream and the invented dream. However, when it was their own material, they were much more accurate for the invented dream than for the real dream. About 60% of the time, they guessed correctly about the source of the invented dream. In contrast, they guessed correctly for the real dreams only about 40% of the time. Astonishingly, they could not correctly identify whether it was their own dream, their roommate's dream, or something unfamiliar!

Why should we be so puzzled about the source of our very own dream? Why do we think it might be our roommate's, which we overheard (external), rather than our own (internal)? Remember that one clue used in reality monitoring

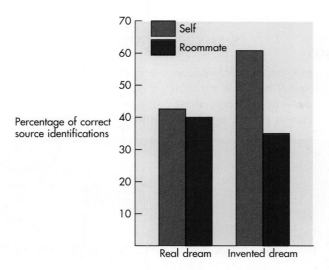

Figure 7.10
Performance on reality-monitoring task, as a function of type of material (real dream or invented dream) and whether the material was originally supplied by self or roommate. (Adapted from Johnson et al., 1984)

is whether that particular item required much cognitive work. Now a dream is not much work; it drifts in uninvited and "happens." In fact, it is hard to think of any internal-source memory that requires less effort. It requires so little work that it is easy to think we simply perceived it, overhearing a roommate's dream. However, it requires more cognitive work to invent a dream; we have to weave the fragments together into a coherent story. A person seeing a summary of an item might recall, for instance, that it was hard to weave together the fragments he or she was given about a grandfather and a political discussion. If the task required this much work, the memory must have an internal source.

The study on dream recall, like most, focused on the methods that adults use to monitor reality and decide whether something actually occurred (external) or whether they imagined it (internal). Other research has investigated children's reality monitoring. Although children are impressively accurate on some kinds of reality monitoring tasks, they have trouble distinguishing what they actually did from what they imagined doing (Foley & Johnson, 1985; Johnson & Foley, 1984; Lindsay & Johnson, 1987). For example, after a child I know had participated in an imaginary trip to the moon at school, she claimed that she had really visited the moon. For children, the boundary between reality and imagination is frequently indistinct.

Schemas and Memory

Take a moment to recall the sequence of events during the last time you went to a fast-food restaurant. You entered the restaurant, stood in line while inspecting the list of options above the counter, told the cashier what you wanted, paid, and received your food. Then you took your tray to a table, ate the food, discarded the waste, and left the restaurant. It is likely that you have visited fast-food restaurants often enough to develop a general idea for the events that will happen and the order in which they will occur. In other words, you have developed a **schema** (pronounced *skee*-muh), or a generalized idea about objects, people, and events that are encountered frequently. You have also developed a schema for "first day of a college course," "attending a concert," and "making a telephone call."

We notice the common features of each of these events through repeated experience with similar kinds of activities (Barclay, 1986). We do not need to

Demonstration 7.4

Schemas and Memory

After reading these instructions, cover them and the rest of the text in this demonstration so that only the picture shows. Present the picture to a friend, with the instructions, "Look at this picture of a psychologist's office for a brief time." Half a minute later, close the book and ask your friend to list everything that was in the room.

Source: Based on Brewer & Treyens, 1981.

remember precise details about much of our daily life (did the ticket taker at the concert stand on the right or the left?). Instead, we take advantage of schemas. They allow us to process large amounts of material, because we can summarize the many regularities in our lives. Schemas provide structure for memory.

Schemas operate at several stages of the memory process. For example, schemas help to determine what items are acquired in memory. Consider a study by Brewer and Treyens (1981). Participants in this study waited, one at a time, in the room pictured in Demonstration 7.4. The experimenter explained that this was his office, and he needed to check the laboratory to see if the previous person had completed the experiment. After 35 seconds, the experimenter asked the participant to move to a nearby room. Here, each person was given a surprise test: Recall everything in the room in which he or she had waited.

Schemas and Memory for Stories

Part 1

Read each sentence below, count to five, answer the question, and go on to the next sentence.

SENTENCE	QUESTION
The girl broke the window on the porch.	Broke what?
The tree in the front yard shaded the man who was smoking his pipe.	Where?
The cat, running from the barking dog, jumped on the table.	From what?
The tree was tall.	Was what?
The cat running from the dog jumped on the table.	Where?
The girl who lives next door broke the window on the porch.	Lives where?
The scared cat was running from the barking dog.	What was?
The girl lives next door.	Who does?
The tree shaded the man who was smoking his pipe.	What did?
The scared cat jumped on the table.	What did?
The girl who lives next door broke the large window.	Broke what?
The man was smoking his pipe.	Who was?
The large window was on the porch.	Where?
The tall tree was in the front yard.	What was?
The cat jumped on the table.	Where?
The tall tree in the front yard shaded the man.	Did what?
The dog was barking.	Was what?
The window was large.	What was?

Part 2

Cover the preceding sentences. Now read each of the following sentences and decide whether it is a sentence from the list in part 1.

1. The girl who lives next door broke the window.   (old _____, new _____)
2. The tree was in the front yard.   (old _____, new _____)
3. The scared cat, running from the barking dog, jumped on the table.   (old _____, new _____)
4. The window was on the porch.   (old _____, new _____)
5. The tree in the front yard shaded the man.   (old _____, new _____)
6. The cat was running from the dog.   (old _____, new _____)
7. The tall tree shaded the man who was smoking his pipe.   (old _____, new _____)
8. The scared cat was running from the dog.   (old _____, new _____)
9. The girl who lives next door broke the large window on the porch.   (old _____, new _____)
10. The tall tree shaded the girl who broke the window.   (old _____, new _____)
11. The cat was running from the barking dog.   (old _____, new _____)
12. The girl broke the large window.   (old _____, new _____)
13. The scared cat ran from the barking dog that jumped on the table.   (old _____, new _____)
14. The girl broke the large window on the porch.   (old _____, new _____)
15. The scared cat which broke the window on the porch climbed the tree.   (old _____, new _____)
16. The tall tree in the front yard shaded the man who was smoking his pipe.   (old _____, new _____)

Source: Based on Jenkins, 1974.

The results showed that people were likely to recall objects consistent with the "office schema." Nearly everyone remembered the desk, the chair next to the desk, and the wall. However, few recalled the wine bottle, the coffeepot, and the picnic basket. These items were not consistent with the office schema, so they were not acquired in memory.

In addition, some people remembered items that were *not* in the room. Many remembered books, though none had been in sight. (Check your friend's list from Demonstration 7.4—did he or she mention books?) This supplying of schema-consistent items shows that schemas also operate when we try to reconstruct a memory. We supply educated guesses that are consistent with the schema. In contrast, your friend probably did not invent items that were inconsistent with the office schema, such as a hair dryer, a tree, or a hot air balloon.

Schemas also operate when we hear a story and store its meaning. Try Demonstration 7.5, a simplified version of a study by Bransford and Franks (1971). How many sentences did you think you recognized in the second half?

Bransford and Franks asked the participants in their study to listen to sentences that belonged to several different stories. Then they took a recognition test that contained only new sentences, many of which were combinations of the earlier sentences. Nonetheless, people were convinced that they had seen these exact sentences before. A sentence such as "The tall tree in the front yard shaded the man who was smoking his pipe" was consistent with the schema they had developed for this particular story. It seems that people gather information together from individual sentences to construct a schema. People think that they have previously seen a sentence that combines all these ideas. Once the sentences have been fused in memory in the form of a schema, they cannot untangle them into their original components and recall those components word for word.

However, people are not likely to say that they recognize a sentence that is inconsistent with the schema. You probably did not check "old" for test item 10, "The tall tree shaded the girl who broke the window."

We briefly discussed the concept of a schema in the last chapter, because Bandura (1986) claims that people store schemas about behaviors that they will later imitate. They do not store precisely accurate images of every little action. Thus, we see that modern learning theory (chapter 6) is related to current ideas about human memory (chapter 7).

The concept of schemas is also closely related to an important principle that we emphasize in the chapter on thinking (chapter 8). Specifically, we see that many thought processes are governed by heuristics. **Heuristics** are rules-of-thumb that are generally accurate. The use of schemas is one example of a heuristic. That is, it is an effective rule-of-thumb to use a schema to organize your memory of an object or an event. In general, schemas will help you to acquire the important memories, reconstruct the appropriate missing items, and organize isolated sentences into a story. Consistent with one of our themes, our memory usually functions well. However, if we depend too heavily on a heuristic, we can make mistakes. We make mistakes, for example, when we depend too heavily on the office schema and fail to notice what is unique about this particular office.

Retrieval

Take a moment to think about all the information you have stored in your long-term memory. You have stored memories of people you have not seen in years, information about songs that left the Top 40 list long ago, ideas about events that occurred when you were in first grade, and a wealth of general information about vocabulary. With this incredibly large storehouse of memories, it is amazing that you can manage to retrieve any specific piece of information—such as the name of your second grade teacher. Three important topics to be considered in this section include the length of time that material can be stored prior to retrieval, how retrieval can be measured, and what happens when retrieval fails.

Permastore   Several years ago, my family and I traveled to Spain. It had been close to 30 years since my high school Spanish courses, but I was amazed at how much I could recall. Admittedly, my verbs were flawed in the past tense, and I startled a Spanish child with my question about the fairy tale "Goldilocks and the Three Eyes (*Ojos*)" rather than "Goldilocks and the Three Bears (*Osos*)." Still, it was comforting to know that long-term memory was so durable.

Harry Bahrick (1984) examined very long term memory with nearly 800 participants who had studied Spanish in high school or college courses. The interval between acquisition and retrieval ranged from 0 to 50 years. Even 50 years later, people recalled about 40% of the vocabulary, idioms, and grammar they had originally learned. Bahrick proposed the name **permastore** to refer to this relatively permanent, very long term form of memory. The astonishing durability of permastore contrasts markedly with the fragility of material in both sensory and short-term memory.

Retrieval Measurement   Your experience with examinations has probably taught you that your retrieval accuracy depends on how you are tested. A **recall** test asks you to reproduce the information that you learned earlier. A recall question testing this chapter might ask, "A generalized idea about objects and events that are encountered frequently is called a(n)_____."

Recognition is usually an easier task. In **recognition**, people select the correct answer from several alternatives. For example, that recall question could be converted into a recognition task by offering several possible answers: (a) short-term memory; (b) phoneme; (c) schema; (d) semantic memory. A multiple-choice test is one example of a recognition task. Another kind of recognition task asks you whether an item is old or new, as in Demonstration 7.5.

Tip-of-the-Tongue Experience   You have certainly had an experience like this. You are trying to remember the name of a sporting goods store, because you want to call to see how late it is open. You are squirming with impatience because you cannot quite recall it . . . it is somebody's last name, it is three syllables long, and the first letter is in the middle of the alphabet, maybe a J. This is an example of the **tip-of-the-tongue experience**, the sensation you have when you are confident that you know the word for which you are searching, yet you cannot recall it.

A classic study on the tip-of-the-tongue experience was conducted by Brown and McNeill (1966). These researchers challenged people by giving them the definition for an uncommon English word, such as "The green-colored matter found in plants" or "The art of speaking in such a way that the voice seems to come from another place." Sometimes people immediately supplied the appropriate word, and other times they were confident that they did not know it. However, in some cases, the definition produced a tip-of-the-tongue state. Brown and McNeill wrote that this state felt like being on the brink of a sneeze—an accurate description.

People who were in the midst of a tip-of-the-tongue experience were asked to provide words that resembled the target word in terms of sound. When the target word was *sampan*, for example, people provided these similar-sounding words: *Saipan, Siam, Cheyenne, sarong, sanching,* and *symphoon.* These similar-sounding words were indeed very similar to the target words. They matched the target's number of syllables 48% of the time and its first letter 49% of the time.

The tip-of-the-tongue phenomenon demonstrates that, even when we cannot recall the target word for which we are searching, we do have some knowledge of the way the word sounds. The phenomenon also demonstrates that there is structure in memory. The word *chlorophyll* is not simply thrown into memory with *banana* or *jinx*. Instead, it is stored so that it is closely identified with other similar-sounding words (maybe *chlorine* and *cholesterol*), and *ventriloquist* is associated with similar-sounding words such as *ventilate*.

Incidentally, when you are attacked by a tip-of-the-tongue experience, you may think to yourself that you cannot recall the target word, but you probably could recognize it. Researchers have demonstrated that this impression is correct (Hart, 1965; Nelson et al., 1986). In contrast, if you think you have no clue about the answer, you are unlikely to choose the correct response on a multiple-choice test. Thus, even if we cannot retrieve a particular memory, we know something about that memory. We know what it sounds like and we know whether or not we could recognize it in a list of alternatives.

Theories of Forgetting

What is the name of the early psychologist who tested cats in puzzle boxes? Who is the psychologist who has been the primary investigator of reality monitoring? It is possible that one or both of these names seem to have escaped your memory—they will not even approach the tip of your tongue. Let us consider several theories of forgetting in long-term memory.

Decay   Psychologists who support the **decay** position say that each item in memory decays spontaneously as time passes. Several days after you originally saw Thorndike's name, that memory will fade and perhaps even disappear completely—unless you have somehow reviewed it. Decay theory matches many of our personal experiences. When you are trying to recall something you had meant to tell a friend, doesn't it seem that this particular memory has faded entirely?

A basic problem with decay theory involves the physical explanation for that decay; no biochemical or structural changes have been identified (Solso, 1991). Decay theory is also overly simple. The process of forgetting does not resemble a giant eraser, methodically making all memories more pale. If decay were the only factor operating, we could not explain why flashbulb memories are so resistant to forgetting, why we so easily forget someone's last name, and why it is difficult to forget how to ride a bike, even if it has been years since last trying it.

Interference   A second approach, **interference** theory, states that forgetting occurs because other items get in the way of the information you want to remember. That is, other items cause interference.

Two kinds of interference are illustrated in Figure 7.11. Suppose that you studied Spanish for several years in high school, and then you began to learn French in college. In **proactive interference**, old memories work in a forward direction to interfere with new memories. Specifically, you would have difficulty remembering the new French word *chien*, because the old Spanish word *perro* would get in the way.

In **retroactive interference**, new memories work in a backward direction to interfere with old memories. You would have difficulty recalling the old Spanish word *perro*, because the new French word *chien* would get in the way. (Incidentally, one way to remember these two kinds of interference is to note that *pro*gress means moving forward, whereas *retro*spect means looking backward.)

Try to think of examples of proactive and retroactive interference. For instance, when you are familiar with a particular car, have you ever driven a different car and experienced proactive interference as you try to remember where the light switch is on this new car? If you become accustomed to the new car, however, you will find that retroactive interference will operate. You will forget

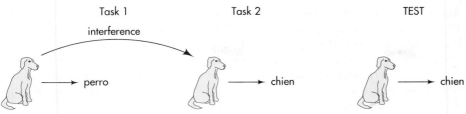

A. In proactive interference, words that are learned in Task 1 interfere when you try to recall words learned in Task 2.

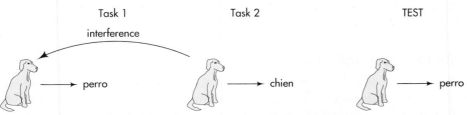

B. In retroactive interference, words that are learned in Task 2 interfere when you try to recall words learned in Task 1.

Figure 7.11
Examples of proactive and retroactive interference.

details about the car you drove originally. Both decay and interference are important sources of forgetting (Mensink & Raaijmakers, 1988; Reitman, 1974).

Retrieval Failure   Recently, I told a friend that one of the best movies I had ever seen was *The Official Story*. He replied that he had never seen it. "I'm sure you've seen it," I urged. "There's this incredible scene when Norma Aleandro is listening to her friend's description of how she had been tortured." Again, my friend returned a blank look. "OK, it's the film where this schoolteacher slowly realizes that her adopted daughter was probably the child of a woman murdered by the Argentinian military. . . . " The light dawned: "Oh, the film from Argentina! Why didn't you say so?"

You have probably experienced similar frustrations in which an item remains stubbornly buried until the right cue coaxes it forth. This third explanation of forgetting is called **retrieval failure**; it specifies that memory failures occur when the proper retrieval cues are not available. For my friend, the title of a movie, the name of the actress, and a memorable scene could not function as proper retrieval cues, though the name of the country in which it took place immediately prompted recall.

Earlier in the chapter we discussed two topics related to retrieval failure. In the section on acquisition, we discussed the encoding specificity principle. (In case you are currently experiencing retrieval failure, this section discussed how people recalled a greater number of words if they learned them in the same room in which they were tested.) Furthermore, the tip-of-the-tongue phenomenon occurs when the retrieval process breaks down.

Research on retrieval failure has demonstrated that if the sound of a word is emphasized during encoding, retrieval failure is likely to occur when meaning—rather than sound—is emphasized during retrieval. For example, as part of a study, people learned words by focusing on their sound: A word such as *hail* was preceded by the question, "Does it rhyme with pail?" Later, retrieval was poor when the hint emphasized meaning (e.g., "It's associated with snow") but excellent when the hint emphasized sound (e.g., "It rhymes with *bail*"). However, if meaning was emphasized during encoding, meaning provided the best retrieval cues (Fisher & Craik, 1977).

Motivated Forgetting   A friend of mine who is a financial consultant told me that he sometimes forgets to return phone calls—especially phone calls to unpleasant people. In **motivated forgetting**, people forget unpleasant memories, such as how poorly they did on an exam or how rude they were to an old friend (Davis & Schwartz, 1987). Memory researchers since the early 1900s have demonstrated that we do indeed remember pleasant events better than unpleasant ones (Matlin & Stang, 1978).

In summary, then, we forget because of decay, interference, retrieval failure, and motivated forgetting. You will recall from chapter 3 that head trauma, strokes, and Alzheimer's disease can also produce forgetting. Consistent with a theme of the book, the forgetting process is complex enough to require several different explanations.

The Biological Basis of Memory

You have just read the definition for motivated forgetting. Let us assume that you processed this definition at a deep level, so that you have ensured that it will be stored in long-term memory. What parts of the brain are involved in forming and storing memories, and what chemical changes take place at the level of the synapse?

The Anatomy of Memory   At the age of 27, a man known by the initials H.M. underwent neurosurgery. H.M. had been suffering from life-threatening epilepsy, and the surgeon removed selected parts of both temporal lobes of the cortex (see Figure 3.18) and portions of the hippocampus, a structure in the limbic system (see Figure 3.16). The surgery was successful in controlling H.M.'s epileptic seizures. However, the operation had an unexpected side effect that made him the most famous neurology patient of all times. Mysteriously, H.M. could accurately recall events that happened before his surgery, but he could not remember what had happened since then (Milner, 1970; Scoville & Milner, 1957).

For example, H.M.'s family moved several months after the surgery. When he was questioned 1 year after the move, he had not yet learned his new address. He could not recall the names of people he saw every day. He might read a magazine article on one day and not recognize that he had read the same article on the three previous days.

H.M. could retain some items in his short-term memory for several minutes, as Milner (1970) describes:

> Thus he was able to retain the number 584 for at least 15 minutes, by continuously working out elaborate mnemonic schemes. When asked how he had been able to retain the number for so long, he replied: "It's easy. You just remember 8, subtract it from 17, and it leaves 9. Divide 9 in half and you get 5 and 4, and there you are: 584. Easy." (p. 37)

However, a minute later, H.M. could not recall either the number or the elaborate memory device. In fact, he could not even recall that the examiner had given him a number to remember! H.M. is one of a few humans who truly has a memory like a sieve; his long-term memory seems to retain no new information. Surprisingly, though, his speech and his intelligence remain normal. You might be able to talk with H.M. for several minutes before noticing that anything was wrong with his memory.

H.M.'s case is important because it was the first study to demonstrate that human memory could be disrupted by surgery on very specific parts of the brain. Specifically, this research has shown that the hippocampus is somehow important in storing or retrieving new memories. Further research has identified other important brain structures that help store memories, such as the amygdala, which is another part of the limbic system (Mishkin & Appenzeller, 1987; Squire, 1986).

In some cases, memory can be traced to a *very* specific location in the brain. For example, McCormick and Thompson (1984) studied classical conditioning of the eyeblink reflex in rabbits, and they managed to identify a location within the cerebellum that controlled this memory. (See Figure 3.14 for the location of the cerebellum in humans.) When they destroyed a portion of the cerebellum that was no bigger than a grain of sand, the conditioned response was lost and could not be relearned.

It is unlikely, however, that human memories can be traced to such specific locations. Human memory is so complicated that memory storage and retrieval cannot be limited to just one brain structure (Berman, 1986). Furthermore, most human memory involves the cerebral cortex—that thin outer layer of your brain (Squire, 1987). However, the specific way in which the cortex contributes to human memory remains a mystery.

The Biochemistry of Memory   Even if we could point to a very specific location in the brain and state that this location stored some specific memory, we would still have to answer another question. What changes occur at the level of the neuron, once some fact is stored in memory? These changes could include changes in the cell structure at the axon and the dendrite on either side of the synapse (the narrow gaps between two neurons). One promising hypothesis is that calcium plays an important role by increasing the number of receptors for a specific neurotransmitter. (As chapter 3 described, neurotransmitters are the chemicals that flow between two neurons.) This process would produce a relatively permanent change in the structure of the neuron, so it could account for the relative permanence of long-term memories (Lynch, 1986; Lynch & Baudry, 1984).

It is clear that neurotransmitters are vitally important in memory. In the discussion of Alzheimer's disease in chapter 3, we pointed out that Alzheimer's patients have decreased amounts of the neurotransmitter called acetylcholine. Furthermore, when monkeys are given a drug that increases the action of acetylcholine, they perform better than normal on recognition memory tests. When they are given another drug that blocks the action of acetylcholine, they perform worse than normal (Mishkin & Appenzeller, 1987).

We have extensive information about the factors that influence memory, as well as the way we use memory in our daily lives. However, the biological explanations of memory remain mysterious. In the words of two prominent researchers in the field, the present work on the biology of memory has only mapped a rough landscape for future exploration (Mishkin & Appenzeller, 1987).

Section Summary: Long-Term Memory

- In general, an item is more likely to be acquired in long-term memory if it is useful and if it has been deeply processed; recall is more likely if the retrieval context resembles the encoding context.
- Eyewitnesses may recall events incorrectly if they have heard other information prior to recall. Other examples of autobiographical memory include flashbulb memory and prospective memory.
- We seem to decide whether an event really happened or whether we imagined it by concluding that it happened if it is rich in details and required little cognitive effort, but we only imagined it if it lacks details and required great cognitive effort.

- Schemas generally improve our memory for events that happen frequently; however, if we rely on them too heavily, we can make mistakes.
- Permastore is a term used to refer to relatively permanent material stored for many years; we typically remember more on a recognition test than on a recall test; sometimes when we try to retrieve a word, we have a tip-of-the-tongue experience, where we retrieve similar-sounding words.
- We forget because of decay, interference, retrieval failure, and motivated forgetting.
- The hippocampus, amygdala, cerebellum, and cortex are involved in memory; memory storage seems to involve changes in the structures of the neuron parts near the synapse, and neurotransmitters are also important.

Improving Your Memory

Our investigation of memory has emphasized the fragility of sensory memory, the limited capacity of short-term memory, and the complexity of long-term memory. Now we shift from description to application. Your memory has excellent potential; how can you improve it?

We have mentioned several points already. First, you cannot remember something if it never enters memory. If you want to remember something—whether it is the details on a penny or someone's name—pay attention to it. Then be certain that you use a deep level of processing when you try to learn the material. You have probably had the occasional experience of discovering that your eyes have moved across several pages of text, yet you have no idea what you have read. That extremely shallow kind of processing will not trap any information in long-term memory. Instead try to think about the meaning of what you read, and rephrase a passage in your own words. Better still, remember the self-reference effect and see if you can relate the material to your own experiences.

Another suggestion for improving memory comes from the encoding specificity principle. As mentioned earlier, you should try to study material in the same fashion in which you will be tested.

Let us look at some other principles of memory improvement as well as some specific mnemonics (pronounced ni-*mon*-icks, with a silent *m*). **Mnemonics** is the use of a strategy to help memory. As you can see, the memory improvement techniques can be grouped into five categories: practice, imagery, organization (all methods relying on cognitive processes), external mnemonics, and also more general approaches.

Practice

As simple minded as it sounds, one way to improve memory is to increase your practice time—merely spend longer learning the material, no matter what technique you prefer. Each semester some of my introductory psychology students come in to ask for help after receiving a low grade on an exam. One of my first questions is, "How long did you spend studying?" An amazing number will provide an answer such as, "Well, I read every chapter and I looked over my notes." Except for a few lucky people, most students cannot master the material with only one exposure to the textbook and one review of lecture notes. Instead, they must read through the material two or three times, each time practicing the retrieval of information. (For example, what is the definition of *mnemonics*?)

The **total time hypothesis** states that the amount you learn depends on the total amount of time you practice (Baddeley, 1982). However, it would not be very effective to spend 3 extra hours studying for an exam if you spent those 3 hours letting your eyes simply drift across the pages of your textbook and notebook. It also would not be very effective to simply rehearse the material, repeating it over word for word. If you have resolved to improve your test performance, spend more time studying; however, study wisely and use the mnemonic devices discussed in this section. (Incidentally, try Demonstration 7.6 before you read further.)

Demonstration 7.6

Instructions and Memory

Learn the following list of pairs by repeating the members of each pair several times. For example, if the pair is CAT-WINDOW, say over and over to yourself, "CAT-WINDOW, CAT-WINDOW, CAT-WINDOW." Just repeat the words, and do not use any other study method. Allow yourself one minute for this list.

CUSTARD-LUMBER
JAIL-CLOWN
ENVELOPE-SLIPPER
SHEEPSKIN-CANDLE
FRECKLES-APPLE
HAMMER-STAR

IVY-MOTHER
LIZARD-PAPER
SCISSORS-BEAR
CANDY-MOUNTAIN
BOOK-PAINT
TREE-OCEAN

Now, try to recall as many responses as possible. Cover up the pairs above.

ENVELOPE _____
FRECKLES _____
TREE _____
CANDY _____
SCISSORS _____
CUSTARD _____

JAIL _____
IVY _____
SHEEPSKIN _____
BOOK _____
LIZARD _____
HAMMER _____

Learn the following list of pairs by visualizing a mental picture in which the two objects in each pair are in some kind of vivid interaction. For example, if the pair is CAT-WINDOW, you might make up a picture of a cat jumping through a closed window, with the glass shattering all about. Just make up a picture and do not use any other study method. Allow yourself one minute for this list.

SOAP-MERMAID
FOOTBALL-LAKE
PENCIL-LETTUCE
CAR-HONEY
CANDLE-DANCER
DANDELION-FLEA

MIRROR-RABBIT
HOUSE-DIAMOND
LAMB-MOON
BREAD-GLASS
LIPS-MONKEY
DOLLAR-ELEPHANT

Now, try to recall as many responses as possible. Cover up the pairs above.

CANDLE _____
DANDELION _____
BREAD _____
MIRROR _____
LAMB _____
FOOTBALL _____

DOLLAR _____
CAR _____
LIPS _____
PENCIL _____
SOAP _____
HOUSE _____

Now, count the number of correct responses on each list. Did you recall a greater number of words with the imagery instructions?

Another important rule about practice is that it is best to distribute your practice throughout several study sessions; this rule is called the **distribution of practice effect**. In contrast, you will remember less material if you mass your learning into a single session (Baddeley, 1982). I intentionally divided each of the chapters in this textbook into two to five sections to encourage you to take advantage of the distribution of practice effect. As chapter 1 suggested, read one section of a chapter and then take a break. After the break, check the section summary on the part you have just read. Then continue with another section. Also, when you are reviewing before a test, spread your study sessions across several days. Do not try to master it all on one day.

The principle of distribution of practice also applies to material you want to remember years from now. Bahrick and Hall (1991) found that people recalled substantially more material from courses such as mathematics if their training in that subject had been spread out over many years, rather than condensed into a shorter period of time.

Imagery

Imagery refers to mental representations of objects. Visual and auditory images are most common, but we can also have images for the other sensory systems. The characteristics of these mental images are discussed in the next chapter, but now we focus on the ways imagery can help your memory. For example, in Demonstration 7.6, were you more accurate when you constructed a visual image in part 2 than when you simply rehearsed the pairs in part 1?

This demonstration is a simplified version of a study by Bower and Winzenz (1970). Participants in one of their conditions repeated the pairs silently to themselves, whereas participants in the imagery condition tried to construct a mental image linking the two words in vivid interaction. Each group saw 15 pairs. When they were tested, people in the repetition condition recalled an average of 5.2 items. In contrast, people in the imagery condition recalled 12.7 items—more than twice as many.

Many popularized articles about memory will urge you to create a bizarre image. For instance, they might suggest that you learn the pair *dollar-elephant* by visualizing an elephant walking into a store with a dollar in its trunk. As it turns out, bizarre images are no more memorable than other more plausible images. The important point is that the items you want to connect should interact with each other (Kroll et al., 1986). For example, *dollar-elephant* could be remembered with the mental image of an elephant stepping on a dollar bill. This is another example of a point made in chapter 1; research often contradicts common sense. It does not really help to concoct a bizarre image, even though bizarre images might *seem* useful.

The key-word method is one kind of mnemonic that relies on imagery. It is particularly useful when you want to link two items together and one of those items is not an English word. Let us say that you are learning Italian, and you want to remember that *roccia* means *cliff*. From the Italian word, *roccia*, you could derive a similar-sounding English key word, *roach*. Then picture a cockroach about to fall off a cliff, as in Figure 7.12. Thus, the **key-word method** uses visual imagery to link a key-word with another word. When Scruggs and his colleagues (1986) told fourth and fifth graders how to use this technique, they found that students improved their learning of Italian vocabulary by about 50%.

The key-word method can also be used to learn people's names, although it requires some effort. However, the time investment is worthwhile, because undergraduates complain that they forget people's names more than anything else (Crovitz & Daniel, 1984). The key-word method has even been used to help those with Alzheimer's disease learn people's names (Hill et al., 1987).

ROCCIA (ROACH)   CLIFF

Figure 7.12
Key-word representation of
roccia = cliff.

Another useful mnemonic based on imagery is the method of loci (pronounced *low*-sigh). The **method of loci** instructs people to associate items to be learned with a series of physical locations. For instance, in your home you might identify several noticeable places, or loci, such as the driveway, inside the garage, the front door, the coat closet, and the kitchen sink. Let us say you need to remember a shopping list that includes hot dogs, cat food, tomatoes, bananas, and orange juice. You could make up an image for each of these items and imagine each in one of those home locations. For instance, picture giant *hot dogs* rolling down the *driveway*, a monstrous *cat eating food* in the *garage*, ripe *tomatoes* splattering all over the *front door*, bunches of *bananas* swinging in the *closet*, and a huge vat of *orange juice* gurgling down the *kitchen sink* (Bower, 1970). Then when you enter the supermarket, mentally walk the route from the driveway to the kitchen sink, recalling the items in order.

The method sounds unlikely, but does it work? In one study, people who had used the method-of-loci technique recalled about twice as many items as people in a control group when both groups were tested 5 weeks after the original learning (Groninger, 1971). Anschutz and her co-authors (1985) found that the method of loci was also helpful for elderly adults when they actually went shopping in a grocery store.

This section has emphasized that visual imagery is a powerful mnemonic. It is valuable when you simply want to link two English words together. Furthermore, the key-word method can help you learn foreign language vocabulary as well as people's names. Finally, you can use the method of loci to learn a list of items.

Organization

In the book *Your Memory: A User's Guide*, Alan Baddeley (1982) points out that long-term memory is like a huge library. Unless the information is stored in it in an organized fashion, you will not be able to retrieve an item when you need it. Organization can help in two ways. First, it structures the material you are learning, so that when you recall a fragment, the rest of the material is also accessible. Second, organization relates the newly learned material to your previous knowledge, providing a structured body of information.

Figure 7.13
The first-letter mnemonics "Every
Good Boy Does Fine" and FACE help
beginning music students learn to
read music.

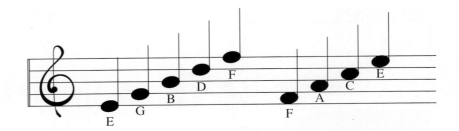

One of the most effective ways to organize material is to construct a hierarchy. A **hierarchy** is a system in which items are arranged in a series of classes, from the most general to the most specific. For instance, Figure 3.8 showed how the divisions of the nervous system can be arranged in a hierarchy. Hierarchies encourage learners to arrange items in an orderly system that can boost recall over 200% (Bower et al., 1969).

A popular mnemonic that makes use of organization is the first-letter technique (Herrmann, 1991). Maybe a piano teacher taught you that the notes which fall on the lines in a musical selection can be remembered by taking the first letters of the sentence, "Every Good Boy Does Fine," and the notes that fall between the lines spell FACE. Perhaps you have even constructed your own mnemonic when faced with memorizing trigonometry formulas, chemical symbols, or lists of presidents. For instance, my daughter prepared for part of a high school history test by constructing a first-letter mnemonic for the first presidents of the United States: "What Are Julie and Margaret Making? A July Volleyball Hunt."

External Mnemonics

What would you do if you wanted to remember 10 things you needed to do before leaving on a trip? Unless they suddenly outlawed paper, you would probably write down a list. In other words, you would be likely to use an external mnemonic rather than one of the internal mnemonics we have been discussing.

When students are asked how often they actually use various memory aids, they report that they frequently rely on reminder notes, shopping lists, and calendars. Many times, they ask someone else to remind them, although they suspect this method is not very reliable (Harris, 1980; Intons-Peterson & Fournier, 1986). In general, students report that they tend to use external memory aids more often than internal aids for prospective memory tasks (for example, remembering to bring a pencil for a test) and for spatial rather than verbal tasks (for example, remembering information from a map).

General Approaches

If you really want to improve your memory, do not assume that the haphazard use of a single mnemonic will transform your memory performance. Instead, it is critical to make comprehensive use of a variety of strategies (Ellis, 1987).

It is also critical to develop your **metamemory**, or your knowledge and awareness about your own memory. When you try out a mnemonic, ask yourself whether this device seems to be working. As we have stressed repeatedly, people differ tremendously from one another. Imagery may work for your best friend, but not for you. Monitor your memory. If you think you know a particular list of items, test yourself and see whether your performance matches your expectations. In general, good students are better than poor students at predicting

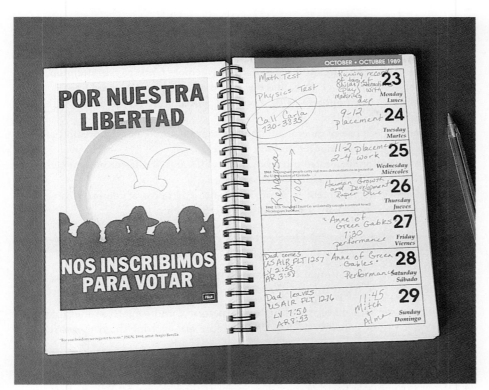

A calendar is an example of an external mnemonic.

performance on psychology tests. Poor students tend to be overly confident (Maki & Berry, 1984; Zechmeister et al., 1986).

After you have taken your next exam, review the questions. If there were any parts on which your recall was excellent, can you reconstruct what study technique you used to master them? Overall, did your study strategy work, or should you try something different?

Within the last decade, several psychologists have criticized the mnemonics approach to memory improvement. They have argued that we cannot find just one solution for all memory problems. For instance, Wilson (1984, 1987) works with people with severe memory disorders. In addition to general memory training, she recommends focusing on specific tasks. For example, she worked with one man who had suffered from a stroke and needed training on four specific memory problems: remembering his daily timetable, people's names, a shopping list, and geographic routes.

It is clear that there is no simple, improve-your-memory-overnight answer to memory problems. Herrmann (1991) stresses that people who seriously want to improve their memories must adopt a complete approach to memory improvement. Pay attention to your physical and mental condition. Keep a memory diary so that you can assess your general memory behavior. Figure out ways you can change your social behavior to help your memory. For example, can you make conversation to "buy time" while you gather information to help you remember some critical fact? Try to develop a wide variety of memory manipulations. No one technique, for instance, will guarantee that you will manage to remember the names of everyone you meet. In addition to using the key-word technique, you might try repeating the name aloud as soon as you are introduced. Then ask the person a question, using his or her name. Also, try to figure out whom the person looks like. Memory improvement must involve the development of a flexible repertoire of techniques.

Section Summary: Improving Your Memory

- The chapter has already discussed several memory hints: paying attention, deep levels of processing, and the encoding specificity principle.
- Memory also improves with increased amounts of practice and with distributed practice.
- Imagery is a useful mnemonic; the key-word method and the method of loci are two mnemonics that use imagery.
- Organization facilitates retrieval; hierarchies and first-letter mnemonics are two kinds of organizational strategies.
- Memory improvement is most successful if it takes a comprehensive approach, especially if it emphasizes metamemory.

REVIEW QUESTIONS

1. Explain why sensory memory is necessary in both vision and hearing. Give some examples from everyday activities. Why is it difficult to measure?

2. Compare sensory memory, short-term memory, and long-term memory with respect to their capacity and duration. How are each of them measured?

3. What would happen if sensory memory retained everything you perceived and nothing ever disappeared from short-term memory?

4. What is the major form of encoding in short-term memory? What other kinds of encoding can be used? Give examples of each kind. From what you know about long-term memory, what kinds of encoding take place there?

5. Organization was mentioned in connection with both short-term memory and the improvement of memory (primarily long-term memory). Why is organization effective in each case? Think of recent examples of when you have used organization in a memory task.

6. What principle does each of these examples of memory illustrate? (a) You cannot remember the words to a song you learned in high school, but they come flooding back when you find your old radio. (b) You cannot recall whether the seeds in an apple have the sharp ends pointing toward or away from the stem. (c) You were searching a friend's term paper for typographical errors, and you cannot recall much of the paper's contents.

7. Long-term memory is relatively permanent, yet we still forget. What are the four theories of forgetting, and what does the study on eyewitness testimony and postevent information suggest about the permanence of long-term memory?

8. Think about several prospective memory tasks you are likely to face in the next few days. What internal and external mnemonics would increase your chances of remembering these tasks?

9. Let us suppose you had a fight with a friend. One particular remark emerges in your thoughts, but did your friend really say it or did you imagine it? How would you resolve this dilemma, according to reality monitoring? Let us suppose you conclude your friend did not make that remark. How might schemas explain your belief that you heard it?

10. Think of as many mnemonics as you can, and select a portion of this chapter to learn using each of these mnemonics. How is metamemory relevant to your activities as you use these mnemonics?

NEW TERMS

memory	depth of processing	decay
acquisition	self-reference effect	interference
storage	encoding specificity principle	proactive interference
retrieval	autobiographical memory	retroactive interference
sensory memory	ecological validity	retrieval failure
short-term memory (STM)	flashbulb memory	motivated forgetting
long-term memory (LTM)	prospective memory	mnemonics
iconic memory	retrospective memory	total time hypothesis
partial-report technique	reality monitoring	distribution of practice effect
echoic memory	schema	imagery
working memory	heuristics	key-word method
encoding	permastore	method of loci
effortful processing	recall	hierarchy
automatic processing	recognition	metamemory
chunk	tip-of-the-tongue experience	

RECOMMENDED READINGS

Cohen, G. (1989). *Memory in the real world*. Hillsdale, NJ: Erlbaum. This clearly written book provides an overview of the developing research in everyday memory, including coverage of absentmindedness, prospective memory, reality monitoring, memory for people, and autobiographical memory.

Ellis, H. C. (1987). Recent developments in human memory. In V. P. Makosky (Ed.), *G. Stanley Hall Lecture Series* (Vol. 7, pp. 161–206). Washington, DC: American Psychological Association. Ellis wrote this chapter for people who teach introductory psychology; it contains an excellent overview of memory at an intermediate level.

Herrmann, D. J. (1991). *Super memory*. Emmaus, PA: Rodale Press. Herrmann's book includes a systematic approach to memory improvement, featuring the assessment of one's own memory and a fascinating section called "How to remember the 100 things you're most likely to forget."

Johnson, M. K., & Hasher, L. (1987). Human learning and memory. *Annual Review of Psychology, 38,* 631–668. This chapter provides an advanced-level overview of recent research on memory.

Matlin, M. W. (1989). *Cognition* (2nd ed.). New York: Holt, Rinehart, and Winston. Several chapters in this intermediate-level textbook are relevant to memory, including sections on sensory memory, memory theories, short-term memory, long-term memory, and schemata.

Wells, G. L., & Loftus, E. F. (Eds.). (1984). *Eyewitness testimony*. New York: Cambridge University Press. Here is a good resource if you want more information on eyewitness testimony. It covers issues such as face memory, "earwitnesses," factors influencing accuracy, and expert testimony.

Thinking

Think about it: How would you define *thinking*? It is difficult to find a satisfying definition for *thinking*, but examples are easy to locate.

1. You are visiting a college campus for the first time, and someone told you how to get from the admissions office to the student union. Now you need to return to the admissions office. You use *mental imagery* to reconstruct your original route and help you retrace your steps.

2. You are writing a paper on an O. Henry short story for English, and you need to figure out whether O. Henry best represents the Romantic or the Modern period. You use *concepts* to decide that his emphasis on emotionality, madness, and death allows you to categorize him as a Romanticist.

3. You have arrived back at your dormitory with take-out food from your favorite Chinese restaurant, only to discover that they forgot to include any plastic utensils—not even chopsticks. The cafeteria, usually a good source of silverware, is closed. You use *problem solving* to realize that a never-used shoehorn could be used to consume your Kung Pao chicken.

4. You are standing on a corner in New York City when a well-dressed gentleman apologizes for bothering you, but his pocket has been picked, including his train ticket back to Connecticut. Could you give him enough money to buy a ticket? You use *decision making* to conclude that he is probably one of those small-time con artists you have read about, rather than a person who deserves your compassion.

All these examples—mental imagery, concepts, problem solving, and decision making—demonstrate thinking. In **thinking**, we manipulate our mental representations to reach a conclusion.

Thinking is one aspect of cognition, or mental activities. **Cognition** involves the acquisition, storage, retrieval, and use of knowledge. The sensation and perception chapter focused on how our perceptual systems acquire knowledge, and the memory chapter emphasized the storage and retrieval of that knowledge. The current chapter emphasizes the *use* of knowledge, and we explore how humans combine, manipulate, and transform that stored knowledge during thinking. When we form a mental image of a geographic area, for example, we combine isolated images. When we form concepts, we note relationships between individual items. When we solve problems, we combine isolated factors to help us reach a goal. And when we make decisions, we combine information from different sources to help us make a choice or a judgment. In each case, then, we demonstrate our impressive ability to synthesize and use information.

Throughout this chapter, we emphasize top-down processing. As discussed in the chapter on sensation and perception, **top-down processing** emphasizes the importance of our concepts, expectations, and prior knowledge. Naturally, thinking also requires **bottom-up processing**, which depends on the information from the senses. For example, when we solve a math problem, we perceive numbers or geometric shapes. However, we also depend upon prior knowledge and strategies. As we have noted in previous chapters, this kind of top-down processing usually encourages both speed and accuracy, though it also produces occasional "smart mistakes." Let us now consider four important components of thinking, each of which requires the manipulation of mental representations as well as top-down processing.

Mental Imagery

Imagine a large pink pig wearing a tuxedo and a top hat, fastening ice skates around its two rear legs and skating gracefully across a frozen pond until it comes to a crack in the ice where it falls through dramatically, plunging deep into a tub of chocolate fudge ice cream concealed below the surface. Presumably, you never saw this happen. However, you have little difficulty constructing this event using mental imagery. **Mental imagery** refers to mental representations of things that are not physically present. Unlike a perceptual image, a mental image is not produced by stimulating the sensory receptors (for example, the rods and the cones of the eye). You can have mental images of events, such as swimming in the ocean, or objects, such as the cover on this textbook. Mental images represent events and objects that we merely imagine as well as those we have actually experienced.

Most people report having imagery. In one survey, McKellar (1972) discovered that 97% of adults reported visual imagery, 93% auditory imagery (for example, imagine you hear your favorite song), 74% motor imagery (imagine yourself scratching your left earlobe), 70% touch (imagine stroking a wet dog), 67% taste (imagine eating a warm chocolate chip cookie), and 66% smell (imagine the smell of a skunk). Incidentally, the fact that about one third of the population lacks imagery for some of these sensory experiences provides additional evidence for the theme of individual differences.

The first part of this section on imagery explores the characteristics of mental images (primarily visual images). The second part is an in-depth investigation of cognitive maps, those mental representations of physical space that we use to find our way from one location to another.

Characteristics of Mental Images

Take a moment to construct a mental image of the cover of this textbook. Now contemplate how that particular image could be stored. Is it stored in a picturelike form, so that it resembles the experience you have when you actually look at the textbook cover and stimulate the receptors in your retina? This is the view of theorists who claim that information is stored in analog codes. An **analog code** is a representation that closely resembles the physical object (Kosslyn, 1980; Shepard, 1978). Psychologists who favor analog codes argue that mental imagery resembles perceptual experience.

However, psychologists who favor the **propositional viewpoint** argue that we store information in terms of abstract descriptions. These descriptions can then be used to generate a mental image (Pylyshyn, 1978, 1984). For example, these theorists would argue that you store an abstract description of your textbook

Mental Rotations

Which of these pairs of objects are the same, and which are different?

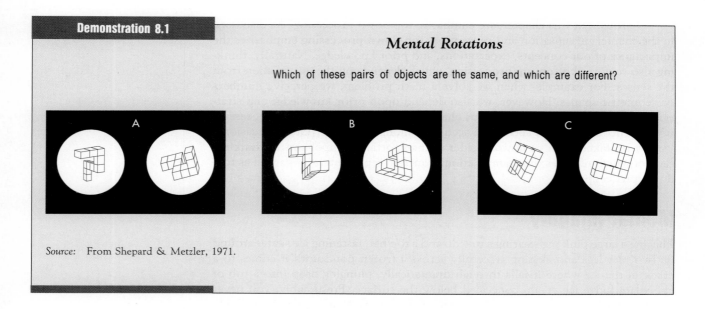

Source: From Shepard & Metzler, 1971.

cover and could use that description to create an image. The controversy between the two approaches has not been resolved, but we will see that some important evidence supports the analog approach.

How can we find out whether a mental image is stored in analog form or in propositional form? In fact, how can we discover anything about the characteristics of mental images, since they cannot be readily observed? After all, you can watch a rat pressing a bar, but what could you hope to learn by watching someone construct a mental image? We could ask people to introspect about their mental images and use these introspections to discover the characteristics of mental images. However, as noted in chapter 5, people often do not have conscious access to their mental processes. Your description of how you constructed a mental image may not accurately capture what you did (Nisbett & Wilson, 1977; Pinker, 1985).

The research on mental imagery took a giant step forward when Roger Shepard had an unusual half-dream on November 16, 1968. He was just emerging from sleep on that morning when he visualized a three-dimensional structure magically rotating in space. This vivid image inspired a carefully controlled study on mental imagery (Cooper & Shepard, 1984; Shepard, 1978). Let us examine this research on the rotation of mental images. Then we discuss the size of mental images as well as some of their other important characteristics.

Rotating Mental Images   Try Demonstration 8.1, which is based on the study inspired by Shepard's dream. Notice that in the first pair of designs (A), the left-hand figure can be converted into the right-hand figure by keeping the figure flat on the page like a picture and rotating it clockwise. Suddenly, the two figures match up, and you reply "same." The middle pair (B), however, requires a rotation in the third dimension. You may, for example, take the two-block "arm" that is jutting out toward you and push it over to the left and away from you. Suddenly, again, figures match up, and you reply "same." In the case of the pair on the right (C), all attempts to match the figures fail, and you conclude "different."

Roger Shepard and his colleague Jacqueline Metzler (1971) asked eight observers to judge 1,600 pairs of line drawings like these and to indicate whether the figures were the same or different. In each case, the experimenters measured the amount of time required for a decision.

As Figure 8.1 shows, the reaction time was strongly influenced by the amount of rotation required to line a figure up with its mate. It takes much longer to rotate a figure 180 degrees than to rotate it a mere 20 degrees. However—surprisingly—reaction times were similar for picture-plane rotations (as in pair A) and for third-dimension rotations (as in pair B).

The Shepard and Metzler study provides support for the analog view of mental imagery. Consistent with that approach, the operations we perform on mental images are similar to the operations we would perform on the actual physical objects. If you were holding two objects in your hands, trying to decide whether they were the same, it would take longer to rotate an object 180 degrees than to rotate it 20 degrees. However, rotating an object clockwise or counterclockwise in a picture plane would take the same amount of time as rotation in the third dimension.

The theme of individual differences reveals itself once more in the research on mental images. For instance, people who receive low scores on tests of spatial ability take about twice as long to rotate an object mentally, in comparison with people with high scores (Just & Carpenter, 1985).

Imagery and Size   Imagine an elephant standing next to a rabbit. Now answer this question: Does a rabbit have a beak? Next imagine a fly standing next to a rabbit. Now answer this question: Does a rabbit have an eyebrow?

Questions like these were part of a carefully planned series of experiments by a major researcher in imagery, Stephen Kosslyn. Kosslyn (1975) wanted to discover whether it would take longer to judge small images than to judge large images. There was a potential problem, however: How could he control the size of someone's mental images? Kosslyn figured that a mental image of an elephant next to a rabbit would force people to imagine a relatively small rabbit. In contrast, a mental image of a fly next to a rabbit would produce a relatively large rabbit.

When you see real-life pictures of animals, you can see all the details quite clearly on a large picture. On the other hand, details are squeezed so close together on a small picture that it is difficult to make judgments about them. If this same rule for real-life pictures also holds true for the pictures in our head, then people should make judgments more quickly with a large mental image (as in a rabbit next to a fly) than with a small mental image (as in a rabbit next to an elephant). Kosslyn's results supported his prediction. Judgments were an average of 0.21 second faster with a large mental image than with a small mental image. This difference was substantial, given the small amount of time required to make these judgments. Once again, we make judgments about mental images the same way we make judgments about an actual picture.

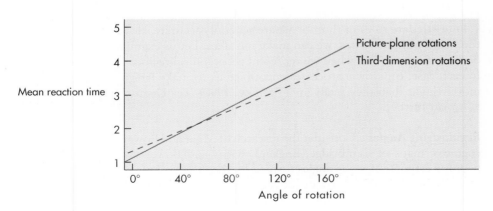

Figure 8.1
Reaction time for deciding that pairs of figures are the same, as a function of the angle of rotation and the nature of the rotation. (Based on Shepard & Metzler, 1971)

Does this woman have a mole on her face? It takes longer to make a judgment when the picture is small, rather than big. Similarly, it takes longer to make a judgment for a small mental image.

Other Characteristics of Mental Images   We have seen that our mental images resemble physical objects with respect to the way they can be rotated and with respect to their size. Other investigations have shown similarities between mental images and physical objects in the way we make judgments about angles and shape (e.g., Paivio, 1978; Shepard & Chipman, 1970). In addition, a mental image can interfere with perceiving another stimulus, the same way perception of a physical object can interfere (Segal & Fusela, 1970). In short, our cognitive system typically treats mental images much like the physical objects they represent, a view that is consistent with the analog approach to visual images. Now let us consider how visual imagery is used when we represent geographic regions in the form of cognitive maps.

○ ○

In Depth: Cognitive Maps

A **cognitive map** is a mental representation of the world as you believe it to be (Gärling et al., 1985). Researchers have discovered that people use several important heuristics when they construct cognitive maps. As discussed in chapter 7, **heuristics** are rules-of-thumb that are generally accurate. However, if we depend too heavily on heuristics, we can make mistakes. Let us examine three systematic distortions that occur when we represent geographical regions in a cognitive map. In each case, top-down processes encourage us to make irregular regions appear more regular than they really are (Tversky, 1990). Try Demonstration 8.2 before you read further.

Regularizing Angles   Consider the research of Moar and Bower (1983) on people's cognitive maps of Cambridge, England. Moar and Bower wanted to determine people's estimates for the angles formed by the intersections of two streets. They were particularly interested in the angle estimates for sets of three streets that formed large triangles within the city of Cambridge. In each case, the authors

Mental Maps

Answer the following questions about pairs of cities:

1. Is Reno, Nevada, to the east or west of San Diego, California?

2. Is Rome, Italy, to the north or south of Philadelphia?

described a particular intersection and asked participants to draw the angle between the two streets at that intersection. Each intersection was drawn on a separate sheet of paper.

The participants showed a clear tendency to regularize the angles so that they were closer to a 90-degree angle. For example, Figure 8.2 shows how three streets formed a triangle that contained real angles of 67, 63, and 50 degrees. You can see that these same angles were estimated to be 84, 78, and 88 degrees.

In all, seven of the nine angles were significantly biased in the direction of a 90-degree angle. Notice the problem, however. The angles in a triangle are supposed to add up to 180 degrees. Unfortunately, the angles in people's cognitive maps do not necessarily sum to 180 degrees. In this particular example, for instance, the angles total 250 degrees.

This systematic distortion can be explained by the heuristic that when two roads meet, they typically form a 90-degree angle. It is easier to represent and remember angles in a mental map as being closer to 90 degrees than they really are. Heuristics allow us to simplify, but sometimes simplification produces errors. You may recall from the discussion of schemata and memory that we tend to store a schema rather than a precise version that accurately represents all the little details. A schema for an office, as we saw in Demonstration 7.4, is a simplification that produces errors. Similarly, the simplification "all street angles are close to 90 degrees" also produces errors.

Rotation and Alignment   In Demonstration 8.2, which city did you guess was farther west, San Diego, California, or Reno, Nevada? If you are like most people—

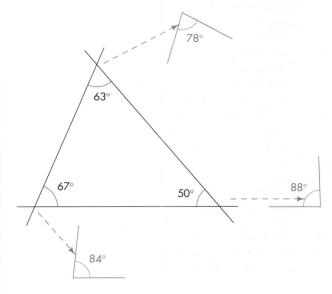

Figure 8.2
A triangle formed by three streets in Cambridge (shown in black). The mental maps for those angles are shown in red. Note that on the mental maps, the angles are closer to 90 degrees.

Figure 8.3
Actual location of four cities in
cognitive map studies.

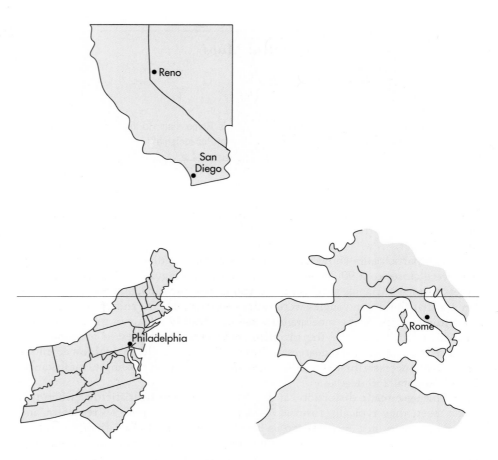

as well as the participants in a study by Stevens and Coupe (1978)—the question
seems ridiculously easy. Of course San Diego is farther west, because California
is west of Nevada. As Figure 8.3 shows, Reno is actually west of San Diego and
Rome is north of Philadelphia.

Barbara Tversky (1981) argues that we use two kinds of heuristics in cognitive
mapping because it is difficult to orient and anchor geographic regions that have
irregular shapes. Therefore we adopt heuristics to facilitate encoding and retrieval
of the orientations and locations of these regions.

One of these heuristics involves rotation. According to the **rotation heuristic**,
figures that are slightly tilted will be remembered as being either more vertical or
horizontal than they really are. For example, the state of California will be recalled
as being more vertical than it really is. If your mental map suffers from this
distortion, San Diego would indeed be west of Reno.

Let us look at the research on the rotation heuristic. Tversky (1981) studied
people's mental maps for the geographic region of the San Francisco Bay area.
The map of California in Figure 8.3 shows how the coastline clearly slants, rather
than having a simple vertical orientation. However, 69% of students attending a
Bay area college in this region showed evidence of the rotation heuristic. In their
mental maps, the coastline was rotated in a more north-south direction than is
true on a geographically correct map. It is worth pointing out, incidentally, that
not everyone fell victim to the rotation heuristic; approximately one third of
students represented the region accurately.

So far we have examined two heuristics used with mental maps: regularization
of angles and rotation. A third heuristic is alignment. According to the **alignment**

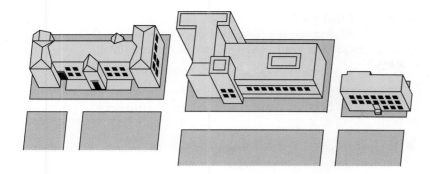

Figure 8.4
The alignment heuristic will operate so that these three buildings are remembered as being lined up in a straight row.

heuristic, figures will be remembered as being more lined up than they really are. For example, Figure 8.4 shows three buildings on my college campus. My mental map represents these buildings as being lined up in a straight row, but the photo clearly shows that the building on the right is in front and the building on the left is in the back. I have fallen victim to the alignment heuristic.

Let us look at the research on alignment. Tversky (1981) presented pairs of cities to students, who were asked to select which member of each pair was north (or east). For example, one of those pairs was Rome-Philadelphia. As Figure 8.3 showed, Rome is actually north of Philadelphia. However, because of the alignment heuristic, people tend to line up the United States and Europe so that they are in the same latitude. Because we know that Rome is in southern Europe and Philadelphia is at the north end of the United States, we conclude—incorrectly— that Philadelphia is north of Rome.

The results indicated that the students showed a consistent tendency to use the alignment heuristic. For example, 78% judged Philadelphia to be north of Rome, and 12% judged they were the same latitude. Only 10% correctly answered that Rome was north of Philadelphia. On all eight pairs tested, an average of 66% supplied the incorrect answer.

The rotation and alignment heuristics may initially sound similar. However, the rotation heuristic involves rotating a single building, country, or other figure in a clockwise or counterclockwise fashion so that its border is oriented in a nearly north-south or east-west direction. Alignment involves lining up a number of buildings, countries, or figures in a straight row. Both heuristics are similar, however, because they encourage us to construct cognitive maps that are more orderly than they should be (see Figure 8.5).

The three heuristics we have examined—regularization of angles, rotation, and alignment—all encourage us to simplify our environment and represent it as more regular than it really is. In general, these heuristics make sense, because our cities tend to have right angles, pictures are generally hung on walls in a vertical orientation rather than at a slant, and houses are typically lined up evenly along the streets. However, when we rely too strongly on these heuristics, we miss the

Figure 8.5
The rotation and alignment heuristics.

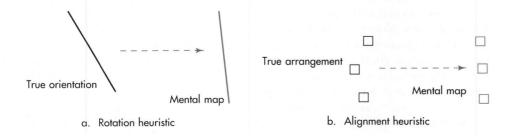

a. Rotation heuristic   b. Alignment heuristic

important details that make things unique. That angle at the intersection is really 70 degrees, not 90 degrees; that coastline does not run exactly north-south; and those continents are not really arranged in a horizontal line.

○ ○

Section Summary: Mental Imagery

- It takes longer to rotate a figure mentally 180 degrees rather than 20 degrees, just as it takes longer to rotate a physical object a greater distance.
- It takes longer to make judgments about small mental images than about large ones, just as it takes longer to make judgments about small physical objects.
- The data on rotation, size, and other attributes tend to support an analog view of mental imagery.
- Our cognitive maps are more regular than the actual geographical environment, because we use the heuristics of angle regularization, rotation, and alignment.

Concepts

A **concept** is a category of objects, ideas, and events that share the same properties. We use concepts whenever we group similar items together. You might use the concept *round* to refer to the way in which a golf ball, a pizza, and a doll's head are similar, as is illustrated on the telephone book cover in Figure 8.6. Whereas the previous section on mental imagery focused on the mental manipulation of spatial arrangements, this section on concepts focuses on the mental manipulation of the properties of items in order to appreciate their similarities.

Notice how you use conceptual grouping to organize your own life. For example, look at the books on your bookshelf. If you have more than one shelf of books, you probably made some effort to group similar items together, for example, by subject matter. If you have a collection of tapes or CDs, think about how you have grouped together similar recordings. Any collection—whether it is books, recordings, clothes, or items in a grocery store—quickly becomes overwhelming unless you organize it according to concepts.

Our tendency to group similar items together serves several functions, in addition to making it easier to find things. For example, concepts allow economy in memory (Sokal, 1977). By grouping items together into a concept, we can remember the attributes of the concept rather than each individual object or event. In chapter 7, we discussed the advantages and disadvantages of schemas, which are similar to concepts. If you have a schema or concept for an office, you will not need to remember the specifics of this particular office. The discussion of heuristics in cognitive maps noted that we categorize 60-degree angles as "essentially 90 degrees." Concepts simplify our lives, though they can lead to oversimplification.

Concepts also allow us to relate objects and events that are similar. Without concepts, each object or event would be unique. Thinking and generalization would be impossible (Johnson-Laird & Wason, 1977). For example, without concepts, that apple you might be about to eat would simply be a unique, lonely object. By using the concept *apple*, you can relate this object to all others in the apple category and know how to respond to this particular apple.

For many decades, psychologists focused on the way humans form concepts about abstract geometric shapes. More recently, attention has shifted to natural concepts or categories.

Figure 8.6
This telephone book cover illustrates examples of the concept *round*.

Eleanor Rosch (1973, 1978) was one of the first to argue that psychologists should focus on **natural concepts**, which are concepts such as birds, fruits, and vehicles that we encounter in our everyday life. She argued that natural concepts are organized according to **prototypes**, or best examples of a concept. Table 8.1 shows three natural concepts, with the prototypes at the top of the list and the nonprototypes at the bottom. Let us consider some of the characteristics of prototypes that researchers have identified.

Supplying Prototypes as Examples

One characteristic of prototypes is that they are supplied more often than non-prototypes as examples of a concept (Mervis et al., 1976). If you were asked to name some birds, you would probably supply examples such as *robin*, *sparrow*, and *pigeon*. You would be unlikely to list *albatross*, *penguin*, and *ostrich*. Not all birds are created equal, and a robin is a "better," more prototypical bird than an ostrich. Because it is a prototype, it is often supplied as an example.

Learning Concepts Based on Prototypes

People learn new concepts quickly if these concepts are naturally structured—that is, organized around a prototype. In contrast, learning is slow when concepts are organized around a nonprototype. When Rosch (1973) examined how people learned color concepts, she needed to find a group of people who did not have a complicated preestablished system of color terms, as we have in English. She chose members of the Dani tribe in New Guinea, who have only two color terms in their vocabulary, roughly equivalent to *light* and *dark*.

For a bank robbery, a gun is an example of a prototype weapon. A lobster is an example of a nonprototype weapon.

Table 8.1   *Prototype Rankings for Words in Three Categories*

Item	Vehicle	Vegetable	Clothing
1	Car	Peas	Pants
2	Truck	Carrots	Shirt
3	Bus	String beans	Dress
4	Motorcycle	Spinach	Skirt
5	Train	Broccoli	Jacket
6	Trolley car	Asparagus	Coat
7	Bicycle	Corn	Sweater
8	Airplane	Cauliflower	Underwear
9	Boat	Brussel sprouts	Socks
10	Tractor	Lettuce	Pajamas
11	Cart	Beets	Bathing suit
12	Wheelchair	Tomato	Shoes
13	Tank	Lima beans	Vest
14	Raft	Eggplant	Tie
15	Sled	Onion	Mittens
16	Horse	Potato	Hat
17	Blimp	Yam	Apron
18	Skates	Mushroom	Purse
19	Wheelbarrow	Pumpkin	Wristwatch
20	Elevator	Rice	Necklace

Source: Based on Rosch & Mervis, 1975.

Some of the participants in the study learned concepts that were based on prototypes. Eight prototypical colors (e.g., a pure blue color) were selected. Eight categories were then constructed, based on those prototypical colors, by selecting two additional colors from the color spectrum, one on each side of the prototype. For example, one category might consist of a pure blue color (the prototype), a blue color tending slightly toward green, and a blue color tending slightly toward purple. This category would correspond to the natural category we would call *blue*. It is naturally structured because it is based on a prototypical color.

Other participants in Rosch's study learned concepts that were based on nonprototypes; these eight colors were selected from regions of the color chart that have no common name in English (e.g., a reddish brown). For example, one category might consist of the reddish brown color (the nonprototype), a reddish brown with more red added, and reddish brown with more brown added. This category is unnaturally structured.

Participants in both conditions then learned the concepts. They saw the colors as stimuli and were asked to supply the same response to all members of the same category. They kept trying until they could give the correct response to all 24 colors. As you can see in Figure 8.7, learning was much faster for concepts based on prototypes.

Substituting Prototypes for Concept Names

Try Demonstration 8.3 before you read further. Rosch (1977) discovered that prototypes can be easily substituted for the name of a concept. However, when a nonprototype is substituted, the resulting sentence is bizarre. Check over your responses in Demonstration 8.3. It is definitely surreal to have 20 penguins sitting on telephone wires. Sentences 3, 6, 9, 12, 15, and 18 involved nonprototypes and therefore probably seemed more bizarre than those involving prototypes. When a prototype is substituted for the name of a concept (for example, *birds*) the resulting sentence seems normal.

The research on natural concepts tells us something important about the way humans form concepts about items they encounter in everyday life. Specifically, some items included in a concept have special privileges. These prototypical items are typically supplied as examples of a concept; they are likely to be learned quickly; and they can readily be substituted for the name of a concept. In contrast, nonprototypical items are underprivileged. A penguin is not a full-fledged bird, and an olive is a feeble fruit.

Figure 8.7
Average numbers of error per trial for concepts based on prototypes and nonprototypes. (After Rosch, 1973)

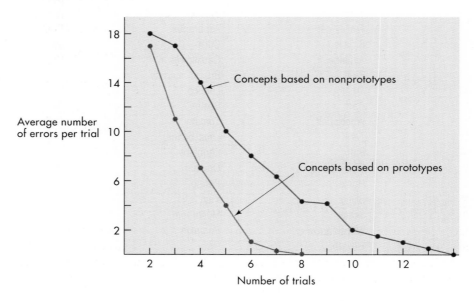

Substituting Prototypes and Nonprototypes in Sentences

Examine each of the sentences below and rate them as to how normal or how bizarre each one seems to you. Use this scale:

```
1     2     3     4     5     6     7
Normal                        Bizarre
```

1. Twenty birds sat on a telephone wire outside my window.
2. Twenty robins sat on a telephone wire outside my window.
3. Twenty penguins sat on a telephone wire outside my window.
4. One of my favorite desserts is fruit pie.
5. One of my favorite desserts is apple pie.
6. One of my favorite desserts is olive pie.
7. How can I go to the fair without a vehicle?
8. How can I go to the fair without a truck?
9. How can I go to the fair without an elevator?
10. The robbers had many weapons.
11. The robbers had many guns.
12. The robbers had many bricks.
13. We like to watch sports on television.
14. We like to watch baseball on television.
15. We like to watch sunbathing on television.
16. The men's wear department had a sale on clothing.
17. The men's wear department had a sale on pants.
18. The men's wear department had a sale on canes.

Think about the way you use prototypes. For example, which instructor is the prototypical faculty member on your campus? Which one is the nonprototype—the one who wins the prize for "looks least like a faculty member"? You even have prototypes and nonprototypes for concepts that are very specialized (Barsalou, 1983). Consider the concept "things to take on a camping trip." A flashlight would be a highly prototypical example, whereas a basketball would be nonprototypical.

Section Summary: Concepts

- Concepts allow us to group similar items together, though they may lead to oversimplification.
- Natural concepts seem to be organized on the basis of prototypes, or best examples.
- Prototypes are different from nonprototypes because they are frequently supplied as category examples, because concepts based on prototypes are easily learned, and because prototypes can substitute for a concept's name in a sentence.

Problem Solving and Creativity

Celia has a problem. She and her roommates, Jennie and Susan, share a phone, and she paid last month's bill. Jennie paid her back, but she lost the itemized list of calls. Susan's father will send Celia a check to cover Susan's calls, but he wants to see that itemized list. How can Celia get reimbursed?

Bob has a problem. Someone stole his human development textbook, and he cannot afford to buy a new one. All the other students in the class will be using their books to study for this Thursday's exam. How can he manage to obtain a book? As in other cognitive tasks, mental manipulation is required, and information must be combined to solve a problem.

We use **problem solving** when we want to reach a certain goal, and that goal is not readily available. In these two examples, for instance, the phone bill and the book are not available. In our interpersonal relationships as well as our occupations in this high-technology society, problem solving is a major human activity (Lesgold, 1988). In this section, we discuss problem understanding, problem-solving strategies, and barriers to problem solving. Our last topic is creativity, a special kind of problem solving.

Understanding the Problem

When you understand a problem, you construct a mental representation of its important parts (Greeno, 1977). You pay attention to the important information and ignore the irrelevant clutter that could distract you from the goal. For example, if you pay attention, the following problem proposed by Halpern (1989) is an easy one:

> Suppose you are a bus driver. On the first stop you pick up 6 men and 2 women. At the second stop 2 men leave and 1 woman boards the bus. At the third stop 2 men leave and 1 woman boards the bus. At the third stop 1 man leaves and 2 women enter the bus. At the fourth stop 3 men get on and 3 women get off. At the fifth stop 2 men get off, 3 men get on, 1 woman gets off, and 2 women get on. What is the bus driver's name? (p. 392)

Many complicated problems become much simpler if you first devise some kind of external representation (Mayer, 1988; Sternberg, 1986). Let us consider several kinds of external representations. (Incidentally, if you still do not understand the bus problem, read the first sentence more carefully.)

Symbols   Sometimes the most effective way to represent a problem is to use symbols, as you learned to do in high school algebra. The major problem is learning to translate words into symbols. During this translation process, students may oversimplify the problem statements. For instance, if the problem reads "the rate in still water is 12 miles per hour more than the rate of the current," college

---

Demonstration 8.4

Representing Problems

Read the information and answer the question at the bottom of the page. (The answer is at the end of the chapter.)

Five people are in a hospital. Each one has only one disease, and each has a different disease. Each one occupies a separate room; the room numbers are 101–105.

1. The person with asthma is in Room 101.
2. Ms. Jones has heart disease.
3. Ms. Green is in Room 105.
4. Ms. Smith has tuberculosis.
5. The woman with mononucleosis is in Room 104.
6. Ms. Thomas is in Room 101.
7. Ms. Smith is in Room 102.
8. One of the patients, other than Ms. Anderson, has gall bladder disease.

What disease does Ms. Anderson have and in what room is she?

students frequently represent the statement in a simpler form, such as "the rate in still water is 12 miles per hour" (Mayer, 1982, 1985). Obviously, a problem cannot be correctly solved if the symbol was not correctly translated.

Matrices   A **matrix** is a chart that represents all possible combinations, and it is an excellent way to keep track of items, particularly when the problem is complex. Schwartz (1971) found that people solving "whodunit" problems such as the one in Demonstration 8.4 were more likely to reach a correct solution if they used a matrix like the one in the answer to the demonstration, at the end of the chapter.

Other Methods   The method of representation that works best quite naturally depends upon the nature of the problem. Symbols and matrices are not always useful. Sometimes a simple list is best. A graph or a diagram can be used to solve a problem that is largely spatial. A visual image is often helpful, as my plumber once discovered when she was trying to fix my humidifier and needed a round metallic part. She represented the problem by trying to visualize this part and then determined where else she had seen an object like this—on an old lamp in her basement.

Problem-Solving Strategies

Once you have represented the problem, you can pursue a variety of strategies in solving it. Some methods are very time consuming, but they always produce an answer—maybe immediately and maybe several years later. Other methods require less time, but they may not produce a solution.

Algorithms   An **algorithm** is a method that always produces a solution to a problem sooner or later. An income tax form is one example of an algorithm; following the steps precisely always produces a solution. An algorithm that is useful for other problems is a systematic random search, in which you try out all possible answers. Suppose that your watch is missing and you know that it must be somewhere in your room. You could start with the back left-hand corner and systematically search every cubic inch of the room, moving from left to right and up and down. You will find your watch, but this strategy is inefficient and unsophisticated because it considers all possibilities, even the unlikely ones (Newell & Simon, 1972).

Algorithms are useful, but we are more likely to use heuristics—those rules-of-thumb mentioned in connection with memory and cognitive maps. In problem solving, heuristics are selective searches that examine only the options most likely to produce a solution. There is no point in searching the empty air for your watch, and it is unlikely that your watch is on the top shelf of the bookcase. Heuristics, unlike algorithms, do not guarantee a solution, but they do make a solution very likely. In your search for your watch, you might adopt a two-step heuristic, "First I'll look where I usually put it, and then I'll search all the flat surfaces." Let us consider two problem-solving strategies that use heuristics.

Means-Ends Analysis   In a **means-ends analysis**, the problem solver divides the problem into a number of subproblems, or smaller problems. Each of these subproblems is solved by assessing the difference between the original situation and the goal, and then reducing that difference. In other words, you figure out which "ends" you want and then determine what "means" you will use to reach those ends. For example, the student with the stolen textbook, mentioned at the beginning of this section, might decide to borrow a textbook from a student who took the course last semester. The problem can then be divided into several

The Hobbits-and-Orcs Problem

Try solving this problem. (The answer is at the end of the chapter.)

Three Hobbits and three Orcs arrive at a riverbank, and they all wish to cross onto the other side. Fortunately, there is a boat, but unfortunately, the boat can only hold two creatures at one time. Also, there is another problem. Orcs are vicious creatures,

and whenever there are more Orcs than Hobbits on one side of the river, the Orcs will immediately attack the Hobbits and eat them up. Consequently, you should be certain that you never leave more Orcs than Hobbits on any riverbank. How should the problem be solved? (It must be added that the Orcs, though vicious, can be trusted to bring the boat back!)

subproblems: (1) make a list of friends and friends of friends who took the course last semester, (2) contact these people, and (3) pick up the book.

Try the Hobbits-and-Orcs problem in Demonstration 8.5. This demonstration illustrates a problem with the means-ends approach. Sometimes the correct solution to a problem depends upon temporarily increasing—rather than reducing—the difference between the original situation and the goal. It is painful to move anybody *backward* across the river to where they originally began (Gilhooly, 1982; Thomas, 1974).

In real life, as in Hobbits-and-Orcs problems, the best way to move forward is sometimes to move backward temporarily. Suppose that you are writing a paper and you thought you had successfully solved one subproblem, locating the relevant resources. You are now working on the second subproblem, reading the resources, and you realize that the topic is too narrow. You have to move backward to an earlier stage and locate additional resources before you move forward again.

Means-ends analysis has been examined with a computer simulation approach. In **computer simulation**, a researcher writes a computer program that will perform the task using the same strategies that a human would. For example, a researcher might try to write a program for the Hobbits-and-Orcs problem. This program would make some false starts, just as you did on Demonstration 8.5. The program should be no better at solving the problem than a human would be, but it also should be no worse.

The researcher tests the program by having it solve a problem and noting whether the steps it takes match the steps that humans typically take in solving the problem. The computer simulation approach forces the theorist to be clear and unambiguous about the components of the theory (Gilhooly, 1982).

Allen Newell and Nobel prize winner Herbert Simon developed a computer program called **General Problem Solver**, or GPS, a program whose basic strategy is means-ends analysis (Newell & Simon, 1972). The goal of the General Problem Solver is not simply to solve problems in the most efficient way, but to mimic the processes that normal humans use when they tackle these problems (Gardner, 1985). The GPS was based on information that was gathered from sessions in which people tried to solve a variety of problems and described their thoughts out loud as they worked on the problems.

The General Problem Solver used several different methods that people typically try. For example, it was programmed to compare the situation at the beginning of the problem with the final goal of the problem, and to try to reduce this difference by pursuing a secondary goal that was similar to the final goal. The GPS could solve transport problems like the Hobbits-and-Orcs problem, letter-number codes, and some trigonometry problems. However, the generality of the

GPS was not as great as psychologists had originally hoped, so more sophisticated and flexible computer programs have been devised (Gardner, 1985; Waldrop, 1988).

Analogy   In an **analogy**, we use a solution to an earlier problem to help solve a new one. As with the means-ends approach, the analogy heuristic usually—but not always—produces a correct solution. Analogies are useful in mathematics. For example, in geometry you probably learned to see the similarity between a problem in a homework assignment and a geometry proof in your textbook. Keep in mind, however, that a heuristic can produce an error. For instance, that textbook proof may be similar to your homework problem only through the first few steps.

In algebra, you probably used the analogy approach to classify an algebra problem into one of the standard categories, such as river-current, work, and number problems. Hinsley and his colleagues (1977) found that people required very little information before they uncovered the analogy with another problem.

> For example, after hearing the three words, "A river steamer . . ." from a river current problem, one subject said, "It's going to be one of those river things with upstream, downstream, and still water. You're going to compare times upstream and downstream. . . ." (p. 97)

Unfortunately, people are often reluctant to transfer what they learned previously when they solve new kinds of problems (Mayer, 1988). After solving one river-current problem, they may fail to use the same strategies on a similar problem 15 minutes later. Even when people do see the similarity and try to substitute new numbers for the numbers in the previous problem, they often make a mistake. They make fewer mistakes if teachers encourage them to construct a table that lists the important variables in both the previous and the new problem, so that the components of the analogy are clearly specified (Reed et al., 1985).

In summary, the analogy strategy is often useful. However, problem solvers may fail to detect the analogy, and they also may make errors in interpreting it.

Barriers to Problem Solving

Try Demonstration 8.6 before you read this section. Two important barriers to problem solving are functional fixedness and mental set. In both cases, old ideas persist and inhibit the development of new ones.

Functional fixedness means that the function we assign to an object tends to remain fixed or stable. Successful problem solving often requires overcoming functional fixedness. For instance, I remember an imaginative high school student

---

Demonstration 8.6

Duncker's Candle Problem

Imagine you are in a room that contains only the material shown in this picture. You must find a way to attach the candle to the wall of this room so that it burns properly and wax does not drip on the floor. The solution appears at the end of the chapter.

who had accidentally torn the hem of her skirt in a classroom, and no one had a pin. She borrowed the teacher's stapler and stapled the skirt. Most of us confine a stapler's function to attaching papers together. This student realized a stapler could also attach fabrics.

The Duncker candle problem is the classic study on functional fixedness (Duncker, 1945). People typically think of the matchbox as simply a container for matches. Because its function seems fixed, they do not initially see that it can also take on the function of "candle holder" (Weisberg & Suls, 1973).

Functional fixedness describes a characteristic of objects in problem solving. A related concept, *mental set*, describes a characteristic of people when they solve problems. With a **mental set**, problem solvers keep using the same solution they have used in previous problems, even though there may be easier ways of approaching the problem. For instance, you are familiar with the kind of number puzzles in which you try to figure out the pattern that explains why a sequence of numbers has a particular order. Try figuring out why these numbers are arranged in the following order: 8, 5, 4, 9, 1, 7, 6, 3, 2, 0.

Functional fixedness and mental sets both demonstrate that mistakes in cognitive processing are usually rational. In general, objects in our world have fixed functions. We typically use a shoehorn to help a foot slip into a shoe, and we typically use a spoon to help food slip into our mouths. The strategy of using one tool for one task and another tool for another task is generally wise because each was specifically designed for its own task. Functional fixedness occurs, however, when we apply that strategy too rigidly and fail to realize that a clean shoehorn makes a suitable spoon, in a pinch.

Similarly, it is also a wise strategy to apply the knowledge you learned in earlier problems when solving the present problem. (After all, that is the basis of the analogy strategy.) However, in the case of mental sets, we apply the past-experience strategy too rigidly and fail to notice more effective solutions. For instance, we might solve a number-series problem by trying to determine whether there is a consistent difference between two adjacent numbers. You could have solved the problem, however, by thinking of other ways of ordering items, such as alphabetical order (*eight*, *five*, *four*, *nine* . . .).

Creativity

Creativity involves finding a solution to an open-ended task in a way that is both unusual and useful (Hennessey & Amabile, 1984). According to this definition, a solution can be unusual—even one of a kind—and still not qualify as being creative. For example, the 19th-century essayist Charles Lamb noted that one way to roast a pig would be to put it into a house and then burn down the house. Yes, it is an unusual solution, but it does not meet the usefulness criterion. Similarly, a friend of mine who knew I liked both chocolate and garlic brought a plate of chocolate-covered garlic cloves to a dessert potluck. The dish was certainly unique, but since only two people had the courage to try this dessert, it probably would not be considered useful.

Think of a person you know whom you consider to be creative. Most people—experts included—associate creativity with creative solutions to problems, responses on creativity tests, scientific explanations, and music or the visual arts (Tardif & Sternberg, 1988). However, people also can be creative in making up a pun, having a dream, or designing a new building (Perkins, 1981).

Measuring Creativity   Psychologists and educators have designed numerous tests of creativity (Mansfield & Busse, 1981). Two of the most popular are illustrated in Demonstration 8.7.

People usually associate creativity with music, art, and science, but the striking design of the Sydney Opera House is another example of creativity.

Two Tests of Creativity

1. The Divergent Production Test measures people's ability to think of a wide variety of responses to a question. Try some representative items.
   a. To the right are four shapes. Combine them to make each of the following objects: a face, a lamp, a piece of playground equipment, a tree. Each shape may be used once, many times, or not at all in forming each object. Each shape may be expanded or shrunk to any size.
   b. Suppose that people reached their final height at age 2, and so normal adult height was less than 3 feet. In a 1-minute period, list as many consequences as possible that would result from this change.
   c. Many words begin with an L and end with an N. List as many words as possible, in a 1-minute period, that have the form L _____ N. (You can insert as many letters as you wish between the L and the N.)

2. The Remote Associates Test measures people's ability to see the relationships between ideas that are remote from each other. For each set of three words, try to think of a fourth word that is related to all three words. For example, the words ROUGH, RESISTANCE, and BEER suggest the word DRAFT, because of the phrases ROUGH DRAFT, DRAFT RESISTANCE, and DRAFT BEER. (The answers are at the end of the chapter.)
   a. FOOD   CATCHER   HOT
   b. TUG   GRAVY   SPEED
   c. ARM   COAL   PEACH
   d. TYPE   GHOST   STORY
   e. COUNTRY   GOLF   SANDWICH

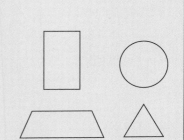

The Divergent Production Tests and the Remote Associates Test, like other measures of creativity, have some potential to predict which people will be creative outside of laboratory testing situations, in school and in work settings. However, the correlations with real-life creativity are not particularly strong (Mumford & Gustafson, 1988; Nickerson et al., 1985). Take a moment to think about a work setting with which you are familiar, and consider several reasons why these creativity tests are not strongly correlated with on-the-job creativity.

People who score high on creativity tests also tend to score high on intelligence tests (Sternberg & Davidson, 1982). Still, some people are highly intelligent but not very creative. Sternberg (1988) describes one student admitted to a graduate program with outstanding scores on the GRE (the Graduate Record Exam, a test for college seniors resembling the SATs that many high school seniors take); close to a 4.0 average as an undergraduate; and superb letters of recommendation. However, she lacked the creativity to do well in research. In contrast, another student was admitted to the same program with relatively low GRE scores and only average grades as an undergraduate. She turned out to be one of the most creative researchers in the program. In other words, creativity overlaps with intelligence, but the two are certainly not identical (Perkins, 1988; Sternberg, 1988).

Creativity and Evaluation   One of the most important discoveries about creativity in recent decades is that it can be inhibited if people know they are going to be evaluated (Amabile, 1983; Hennessey & Amabile, 1984). In a typical experiment, college students were told to compose a poem. Half were told that the experimenter was simply interested in their handwriting, rather than the content of the poem. These students therefore did not expect to be evaluated on their creativity. The other half of the students were told that the experimenter was interested in the

Figure 8.8
The influence of evaluation expectation and working condition on creativity. (Based on Amabile, 1983)

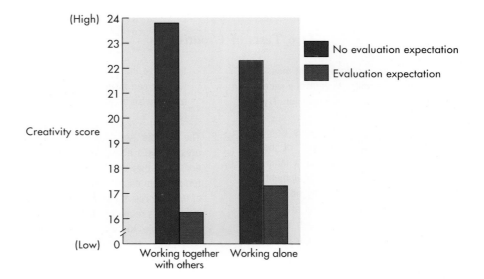

poem's content, and they would receive a copy of the judges' evaluations. In other words, these students knew they would be evaluated.

Each of the poems was judged by people who were poets. As you can see from Figure 8.8, the creativity scores were much higher for students who had no expectation that their poetry would be judged. In contrast, creativity was inhibited when students thought that someone would be judging their poetry. Figure 8.8 shows that creativity was consistently inhibited by concern about evaluation— whether people worked in a group or by themselves.

There are some significant implications from Amabile's research. For instance, our educational system evaluates children. Even elementary students know that the teacher will be judging their artwork, poems, stories, and other creative efforts. This expectation of evaluation is likely to reduce their creativity (Ryan, 1984). How can we design education so that children's creativity is allowed to blossom, in a system where teachers are expected to provide evaluations?

Section Summary: Problem Solving and Creativity

- A problem is often easier to understand if you can construct an external representation using devices like symbols or matrices.
- The algorithm strategy in problem solving consistently produces a solution, but it can be inefficient; heuristics such as a means-ends analysis or an analogy are typically more useful.
- Two barriers to problem solving are functional fixedness and mental set; in both cases, old ideas inhibit the development of new solutions.
- It is difficult to predict creative potential accurately on the basis of creativity tests.
- The expectation of evaluation can inhibit creative performance.

Decision Making

Every day you make dozens of decisions. Is Court Street likely to have more traffic than Main Street at 8 o'clock in the morning? Would the course in human development be more interesting if you signed up for Dr. Lopez's class or Dr. Hasting's? How long will it take to read the rest of this chapter?

Decision making requires you to make a choice about the likelihood of uncertain events. It can occur in situations when you make predictions about the future, select among two or more alternatives, and make estimates about frequency when you have scanty evidence. In decision making, we often lack clear-cut rules that outline how to make the best decision. Decision making, like other cognitive tasks, requires us to combine, manipulate, and transform our stored knowledge.

When we have no rules or step-by-step procedures to use in decision making, we tend to rely on heuristics. As you know, heuristics are rules-of-thumb, or strategies that are likely to produce a correct solution. Heuristics are typically very useful, especially because they help us to simplify the overwhelming amount of information we could potentially consider when we need to make a decision (Hogarth, 1987). The problem arises, however, because we fail to appreciate that heuristics have their limitations. Even good rules-of-thumb should be applied with caution.

Throughout this section, we discuss studies that point out errors in decision making. However, these errors should not lead you to conclude that humans are limited, foolish creatures (Crandall, 1984). Instead, consider the similarity between errors in decision making and errors in perception, that is, illusions (Nisbett & Ross, 1980). Figure 4.14 illustrates the Ponzo illusion. The major explanation for this illusion is the theory of misapplied constancy, which states that we take the constancy rule (one that we *should* use in most circumstances) and apply it inappropriately. Similarly, we make errors in decision making when we take these normally useful heuristics and apply them inappropriately.

In this section on decision making, we look at three important heuristics: availability, representativeness, and anchoring and adjustment. Then we examine how decision making can be influenced by the way a question is asked or framed.

Availability

Suppose that someone asks you whether your college has more biology majors or geology majors. Presumably, you have not memorized the enrollment statistics. Therefore, you would be likely to answer the question in terms of the relative number of people in these two majors whose names come to mind. You can easily retrieve the names of biology majors ("Sara, Lucia, Chi-Ming . . . ") because your memory has stored the names of dozens of people in this major. However, you can think of only one person's name in geology. Because examples of biology majors were easy to retrieve, you conclude that there are more of them at your college. In this case, making a decision based on the number of examples that come to mind could be a fairly reliable way to answer the question.

We use the **availability heuristic** whenever we estimate frequency or probability in terms of how easy it is to think of examples of something (Tversky & Kahneman, 1973). When deciding which major is more popular, for instance, it is easier to think of examples of biology majors than geology majors. The availability heuristic is useful, insofar as the availability (or ease with which examples are remembered) is correlated with true, objective frequency. However, as you will see, there are other factors that influence memory retrieval but are *not* correlated with objective frequency.

Try Demonstration 8.8 on page 266 before you read further.

One factor that influences memory retrieval is recency. In general we can recall an event better if it happened yesterday, rather than a year ago. For example, you can probably recall the details about the latest world crisis more clearly than the details of the 1991 war with Iraq.

Demonstration 8.8

Familiarity and Availability

Cover up the instructions at the bottom of the box and do not be tempted to read them. Then read this list of authors' names. Finally, cover up this list, turn the book upside down, and read the remaining instructions.

Louisa May Alcott
Alice Walker
John Dickson Carr
Laura Ingalls Wilder
Thomas Hughes
Jack Lindsay
Edward George Lytton
Margaret Mitchell
Michael Drayton
Henry Vaughan
Edith Wharton
Richard Watson Gilder
Judith Krantz
Agatha Christie

Robert Lovett
Pearl Buck
Virginia Woolf
Judy Blume
George Nathan
Allan Nevins
Henry Crabb Robinson
Jane Austen
Joseph Lincoln
Emily Brontë
Arthur Hutchinson
James Hunt
Erica Jong
Brian Hooker
Harriet Beecher Stowe

Now, be sure to cover up the names in the list. Estimate whether there are more men or women on this list. You cannot answer "about the same."

Recency also influences judgments about natural hazards. People rush to buy earthquake insurance immediately after an earthquake. However, the purchase rate drops steadily thereafter, as the earthquake fades into history (Slovic et al., 1982). Thus, people judge an event as being more likely to happen if it has happened recently. Their judgment is based on the availability heuristic, that is, how easily examples of earthquakes can be recalled. If an earthquake happened a few days ago, it is easy to recall an example, and therefore an earthquake seems likely.

Familiarity is a second factor that influences memory retrieval. It also distorts frequency judgments in the same way that recency distorts these judgments. Specifically, we are likely to recall items better if they are familiar, rather than unfamiliar. For instance, in Demonstration 8.8 I selected 14 names of well-known women authors and 15 names of not very familiar men authors. It is likely that those more familiar women's names were more easily remembered, and so you estimated that there were more women's names on the list than men's names. In other words, availability was more influenced by familiarity than by true frequency.

This demonstration was a modification of a study by Tversky and Kahneman (1973), who presented people with lists of 39 names. A typical list might contain 19 names of famous women and 20 names of less famous men. After hearing the list, they were asked to judge whether the list contained more men's names or more women's names. About 80% of the participants mistakenly guessed that the group with the most famous, familiar names was the more frequent, even though it was objectively less frequent.

Representativeness

Representativeness is probably the most important of the decision-making heuristics (Nisbett et al., 1983). Let us consider an example before defining the term formally. Suppose that you have a normal penny with both a head (H) and a tail (T). You toss it six times. Which seems like the more typical outcome: (a) H H H H H H; (b) H H H T T T; or (c) H T T H H T? Most people select the last option. After all, you know that a coin tossed six times is likely to come up heads three times and tails three times. It would be much less likely to come up heads all six times in your sample. Furthermore, you know that coin tossing should produce heads and tails in random order. Option *b*, H H H T T T, has the right number of heads and tails, but it does not look very random. The last option, H T T H H T, looks like the most typical, representative outcome.

When you use the **representativeness heuristic**, you decide whether the sample you are judging matches the appropriate prototype (Pitz & Sachs, 1984). For instance, a sample of coin tosses should have 50% heads and no systematic order in the pattern of heads and tails.

When people make decisions about the relative frequency of different samples, such as coin tosses, they often seem to be unaware of the true probabilities (Kahneman & Tversky, 1972). For example, the *specific* sequence H T T H H T is no more likely to occur than the *specific* sequence H H H H H H. However, we do not consider the true probabilities. Instead, we base our decision on representativeness.

It is important to stress that representativeness usually leads to the correct choice in everyday decisions. For example, suppose you were asked which of the following samples of IQs would be more likely: (1) 100, 100, 100, 100, 100, or (2) 140, 140, 140, 140, 140. You would appropriately select the first option because the sample mean of 100 matches the mean of 100 in the population, and there are more IQs of 100 than IQs of 140 in the population. Representativeness is generally a useful heuristic that produces wise decision making. However, when we overuse it, we can make incorrect decisions.

Consider another example in which it is tempting to misuse the representativeness heuristic. Suppose that you are working at a survey research institute and you are checking over some questionnaires filled out by a random sample of adult men in the United States (Beyth-Maron & Dekel, 1985). One of the respondents, who listed his height as more than 6 feet 5 inches, was sloppy when

Would you guess that this man is a poet or a successful businessman? If you focus on representativeness, rather than base rate, you would respond "poet." However, he is the successful owner of a music store in Geneseo, New York.

Demonstration 8.9

The Conjunction Error

Read the following paragraph:

Linda is 31 years old, single, and outspoken. She majored in philosophy. As a student, she was deeply concerned with issues of discrimination and social justice, and also participated in antinuclear demonstrations.

Now rank the following options in terms of their likelihood in describing Linda. Give a ranking of 1 to the most likely option and a ranking of 8 to the least likely option.

_____ 1. Linda is a teacher in elementary school.

_____ 2. Linda is active in the feminist movement.

_____ 3. Linda works in a bookstore and takes Yoga classes.

_____ 4. Linda is a bank teller.

_____ 5. Linda is a psychiatric social worker.

_____ 6. Linda is a member of the League of Women Voters.

_____ 7. Linda is a bank teller and is active in the feminist movement.

_____ 8. Linda is an insurance salesperson.

he answered the question about his profession. It is not clear whether he circled "bank president" or the next profession in the list, "basketball player (NBA)." You must code the response: Which profession would you choose?

Most people would decide that someone this tall would have to be a basketball player. (In my introductory psychology class one semester, 71% chose this answer.) After all, an extremely tall person is more representative of professional basketball players than of bank presidents. But let us examine the flaw in that decision. Consider how many more bank presidents there are than basketball players. There may be roughly 300 NBA players and 15,000 bank presidents (Beyth-Maron & Derek, 1985). Perhaps 60% of basketball players (about 180) are taller than 6 feet 5 inches. Perhaps only 2% of bank presidents are taller than 6 feet 5 inches, but with so many more of them, about 300 bank presidents are in this category.

People make mistakes in decisions like this because they are impressed by the representativeness heuristic—an extremely tall person matches the prototype of a basketball player. Unfortunately, they ignore the base rate, or the proportion in the population (Kahneman & Tversky, 1973).

Try Demonstration 8.9 before you read further. Now look at your answers, specifically numbers 4 and 7. Which did you think was more likely, "Linda is a bank teller" or "Linda is a bank teller and is active in the feminist movement"?

When Tversky and Kahneman (1983) presented problems like these, students answered that Linda was much more likely to be a bank teller who is active in the feminist movement. Students studying for their PhDs in decision making—who had several advanced courses in probability—were just as likely to make this mistake as undergraduates who had little mathematical background.

Let us see why this decision was incorrect. Which is more likely, that someone is a psychology major or that this person is a psychology major at a college in New York? Whenever we add a restriction, such as "at a college in New York," we decrease the probability because we are eliminating some people. There are more bank tellers in this country than there are bank tellers active in the feminist movement—because we have eliminated the group of bank tellers who are not active in the feminist movement (see Figure 8.9). Statistically, the probability of any two events (such as "bank teller and feminist") occurring together cannot be greater than the probability of either one of those events occurring alone (such as "bank teller"). However, people commit the **conjunction fallacy**: They judge the probability of the conjunction (two events occurring together) to be greater than the probability of one event.

The conjunction fallacy can be traced to the representativeness heuristic. The characteristic "feminist" is very representative of someone who is single, outspoken, a philosophy major, concerned about social justice, and an antinuclear activist. A person with these characteristics does not seem likely to become a bank teller, but she seems highly likely to be a feminist. By adding the extra detail of "feminist" to "bank teller," we have actually decreased the number of people in the group. However, we have increased the believability of the description. The description is now more representative, so we decide that it is more likely.

The tendency to misuse the representativeness heuristic suggests that you should pause whenever you are about to decide which of two options is more likely. One option may sound much more attractive because the description is so very representative, or typical. However, before selecting this option, be sure you have paid sufficient attention to base rates and other important information.

Anchoring and Adjustment

When we make an estimate, we often begin by guessing a first approximation—an anchor—and then make adjustments to that number on the basis of additional

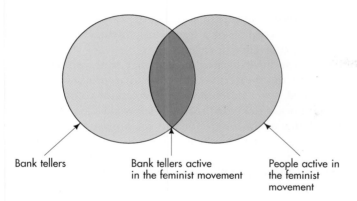

Bank tellers   Bank tellers active   People active in
                    in the feminist movement   the feminist
                                                movement

Figure 8.9
A diagram showing the relationship between the sets described in Demonstration 8-9.

information; this strategy is called the **anchoring and adjustment heuristic**. Like the two other heuristics we have examined, this heuristic often leads to a reasonable answer. However, people typically rely too heavily on the anchor, and their adjustments are usually too small (Slovic et al., 1974; Tversky & Kahneman, 1982).

Consider a study in which people were asked to estimate various quantities (Tversky & Kahneman, 1974). A typical question asked participants to estimate the percentage of African countries in the United Nations. Before requesting the reply, the experimenters spun a wheel while the participants watched. At random, the wheel selected a number between 0 and 100. The participants were asked to indicate whether their answer to the question was higher or lower than the selected number, and to supply an estimate.

Even though the selected number had been chosen completely at random, it still acted as an anchor for people's estimates. For example, if the wheel had stopped on 10, people estimated that 25% of the African countries were in the United Nations. If the wheel had stopped on 65, people estimated 45%. In other words, a number that had no real relationship to the question had served as an anchor for the response. People made adjustments from this number, in the direction of the correct answer. However, these adjustments were typically far too small.

Keep the anchoring and adjustment heuristic in mind when you next need to estimate a quantity. Provide an educated guess as a first anchor. Then make adjustments from that anchor, based on other information. However, urge yourself to make appropriately large adjustments. Suppose, for instance, that you are trying to figure out how many bottles of soda pop to order for a party, to which about 12 people will come. You bought 12 bottles for 6 people last February, so twice that, or 24, would be a first approximation, or anchor. But now it is July, and people are likely to be thirstier. You are serving spicy Buffalo-style chicken wings, so people need to soothe their tongues, and the party is likely to last longer. If you rely too strongly on the anchor, you are sure to run short. Keep in mind that each of those new pieces of information requires a substantial adjustment upward from that original anchor. You had better double your original estimate.

Decision Frames

We have seen that when people make decisions, they use three heuristics that are generally helpful. They make estimates on the basis of the ease with which they can recall examples (availability). They decide which option is more likely on the basis of similarity to a prototype (representativeness). They estimate quantity by selecting an anchor and then making adjustments. In each case, however, people often use a heuristic when it is not appropriate, and they underestimate the importance of other relevant information. In the case of **decision frames**, people are influenced by the wording of a question, and they again underestimate the importance of other relevant information.

Imagine that you have decided to see a play, and you have paid $10 for the ticket. As you enter the theater, you discover that you have lost the ticket. The office did not record ticket purchases, so you cannot recover the ticket. Would you pay $10 for another ticket for the play? Now change the scenario somewhat. Imagine, instead, that you have decided to see a play, and you plan to pay $10 for the ticket. As you enter the theater, you discover that you have lost a $10 bill. Would you still pay $10 for the ticket for the play?

In both cases, the amount of money involved is $10, yet the decision frame is different for these two problems. We seem to organize our expenses into separate mental accounts. In the first example, buying a second ticket to the play seems to raise the ticket price to $20—perhaps more than we want to spend. When Kahneman and Tversky (1984) asked participants in their study, only 46% said that they would pay $10 for another ticket. In contrast, in the second example, we do not tally the lost $10 bill in the same account. We view this loss as being generally irrelevant to the ticket. In fact, 88% of the participants in Kahneman and Tversky's study said that they would purchase the ticket in this second condition.

If we only considered mathematics when we made a decision, we would see that the two examples are identical. However, we are distracted by the wording of the question, or the context in which it appears. The framing effect is just as persistent as the famous Müller-Lyer illusion you saw in Figure 4.12. You know that the lines are supposed to be the same length, just as you know that the $10 ticket loss equals the $10 bill loss. In both cases, however, the frame (either geometric or verbal) influences the interpretation.

This information on framing should encourage you to analyze whether a decision you are making is inappropriately influenced by the question's wording. Researchers have discovered many applications of decision frames in various professions. For instance, credit card companies found that customers preferred the phrase *cash discount*, rather than *credit card surcharge*—even though the money was the same (Thaler, 1980). Furthermore, when people were asked to narrow the pool of applicants for a job, they eliminated more applicants when they were told to accept the most suitable applicants than when they were told to reject the least suitable applicants (Huber et al., 1987).

The framing of a decision is even important in life-and-death decisions. In one study, people were told about two options for treating someone's lung cancer. The surgical option was described as having a lower survival rate over the short term but a higher survival rate over the long term, in contrast to the nonsurgical option. When the options were presented in terms of *living*, 84% of the participants said they preferred surgery. When the options were presented in terms of *dying*, 56% preferred surgery. It is clear that physicians who offer options to patients can influence patients' choices by the language frame in which the question is presented (McNeil et al., 1982; Payne, 1985). The next chapter explores the importance of language and conversations in the broader context of human interactions.

Section Summary: Decision Making

■ **In the availability heuristic, people estimate frequency in terms of how easy it is to think of examples. This heuristic is usually accurate, but it can be distorted by recency or familiarity.**

- In the representativeness heuristic, people make decisions on the basis of whether the sample they are judging matches the appropriate prototype. This heuristic is usually accurate, but people often downplay the base rate or fall victim to the conjunction fallacy.
- In the anchoring and adjustment heuristic, people typically rely too heavily on the anchor and make inadequate adjustments on the basis of additional information.
- In making a decision, people are often influenced by the decision frame, or wording of a question.

REVIEW QUESTIONS

1. An important theme running throughout this chapter is that people tend to simplify and to use a small number of general rules when they are faced with a cognitive task. Explain how people use heuristics in mental maps, problem solving, and decision making. Then explain how the fourth topic—concept formation—is itself a form of simplification.

2. In what ways do people treat mental images the same as they treat physical objects? Discuss the research evidence on this issue that supports the analog code approach to mental images.

3. With respect to mental imagery, predict what will happen in each of these situations: (a) You are trying to remember whether your friend parts his hair on the left or the right, and you have constructed a small mental image, rather than a large one. (b) You are trying to reconstruct an accident at a corner where the two roads meet at a 75-degree angle. (c) You are drawing a map for a friend, based on your recall of a route—one town is not quite north of the other, and the road connecting them is tilted about 20 degrees from vertical.

4. At the beginning of the chapter, we noted that thinking involves the manipulation or use of knowledge. Describe how each of the four topics in this chapter uses knowledge, and illustrate each topic with an example from your recent experience.

5. Think of a prototype for the category *household pet*, and then think of a nonprototype. Compare these two items with respect to whether they would be supplied as examples of a concept and whether they could substitute for the name of a concept in a sentence.

6. Think about the last time you lost something that you needed. Describe how you might have used each of the following problem-solving strategies in locating the object: the algorithm of a systematic random search, means-ends analysis, and analogy.

7. The section on problem solving discussed methods of representing a problem. Think of a problem that would be represented most effectively by each of the following methods: symbols, matrices, graphs, and visual images.

8. The analogy method of problem solving suggests that we should find similar situations in our past experiences. Why do the problem-solving barriers suggest that we should not rely too heavily on our past experiences? How does creativity relate to the idea that we should not rely too heavily on previous solutions to problems?

9. Which decision-making heuristic does each of the following examples illustrate? (a) You try to estimate how long it will take you to read a chapter in

another textbook, based on the fastest rate at which you have read a chapter in this textbook. (b) You see a bearded professor wearing a rather weird jacket, and you decide he is a member of the art department (which has 5 members) rather than a member of one of the science departments (which have a total of 40 members). (c) Someone asks you how common amnesia is, and you say it is quite common, based on your recall of recent soap opera plots.

10. According to an old saying, you can view a pitcher as being either half full or half empty. Why is this saying relevant to decision frames? Summarize some of the information about decision frames.

NEW TERMS

thinking	alignment heuristic	analogy
cognition	concept	functional fixedness
top-down processing	natural concepts	mental set
bottom-up processing	prototypes	creativity
mental imagery	problem solving	decision making
analog code	matrix	availability heuristic
propositional viewpoint	algorithm	representativeness heuristic
cognitive map	means-ends analysis	conjunction fallacy
heuristics	computer simulation	anchoring and adjustment heuristic
rotation heuristic	General Problem Solver (GPS)	decision frames

ANSWERS TO DEMONSTRATIONS

Demonstration 8.4   Ms. Anderson has mononucleosis, and she is in Room 104. To solve this problem, you can set up a matrix with the names of the patients and the room numbers listed. Then read through the list of statements. In three cases, we find out which patient is in which room; this information allows us to place the word *yes* (indicated in red) in three locations in the matrix, and to eliminate these rooms and these people from the "still uncertain" list. (A blue check indicates we have taken care of these rooms and people.) We can also note the disease (in green) where appropriate.

	(asthma)			(mono-nucleosis)	
	101	102	103	104	105
Anderson	✔	✔			✔
(heart disease) Jones	✔	✔			✔
(gall bladder?) Green	✔	✔	✔	✔	yes
(tuberculosis) Smith	✔	yes	✔	✔	✔
(gall bladder?) Thomas	yes	✔	✔	✔	✔

Because Ms. Jones has heart disease, she cannot be the patient with mononucleosis in Room 104; she must be in Room 103. Therefore, Ms. Anderson must be the patient with mononucleosis in Room 104.

Demonstration 8.5   In the Hobbits-and-Orcs problem, let us let R represent the right bank and L represent the left bank. Here are the steps in the solution:

1. Move 2 Orcs, R to L.
2. Move 1 Orc, L to R.
3. Move 2 Orcs, R to L.
4. Move 1 Orc, L to R.
5. Move 2 Hobbits, R to L.
6. Move 1 Orc, 1 Hobbit, L to R.
7. Move 2 Hobbits, R to L.
8. Move 1 Orc, L to R.
9. Move 2 Orcs, R to L.
10. Move 1 Orc, L to R.
11. Move 2 Orcs, R to L.

Demonstration 8.6

The solution to Demonstration 8.6 involves attaching part of the matchbox to the wall, then melting some wax to attach the candle to the platform.

Demonstration 8.7   a. DOG;   b. BOAT;   c. PIT;   d. WRITER;   e. CLUB.

RECOMMENDED READINGS

Best, J. B. (1989). *Cognitive psychology* (2nd ed.). St. Paul, MN: West. Best's textbook includes chapters or sections on concepts and problem solving, and his chapter on artificial intelligence will be particularly interesting to students who want more information on this growing emphasis in cognitive psychology.

Hogarth, R. (1987). *Judgement and choice* (2nd ed.). Chichester, England: Wiley. In addition to information about decision-making heuristics, this mid-level book discusses topics such as the role of memory in decision making and aids to decision making.

Kosslyn, S. M. (1983). *Ghosts in the mind's machine: Creating and using images in the brain.* New York: Norton. Kosslyn's book is written for a fairly sophisticated but nonpsychologist audience. It is one of the most readable summaries of the analog position on mental imagery.

Levine, M. (1988). *Effective problem solving.* Englewood Cliffs, NJ: Prentice Hall. This "how-to" book has some practical suggestions about problem solving. It also includes a section on interpersonal problem solving.

Matlin, M. W. (1989). *Cognition* (2nd ed.). New York: Holt, Rinehart & Winston. This textbook includes chapters on imagery, problem solving, and decision making, as well as a section on concepts.

9

Language and Conversation

Imagine life without language. In fact, imagine only the next 24 hours without words or conversation. You could not read any books or attend any lectures. Television, radio and most forms of entertainment would be eliminated. And what would your life be like without conversation? A colleague who was drafted and sent to Vietnam recalls discussions with his army friends about the possibility of war injuries. Which human ability seemed most precious—sight or mobility, for example? In fact, he concluded that the ability to sit and have a conversation with someone—to enjoy language—seemed most important (Beach, personal communication, 1989).

As George Miller (1981) has pointed out, the capacity for language has made human culture possible. Language enables this big-brained, loudmouthed, featherless species to create artistic and scientific innovations and to interact with each other in extremely complex ways.

Language is an astonishing accomplishment. To understand and produce speech, we must activate our perceptual skills ("Did the speaker say *bear* or *pear*?" "Is that scrawled signature *Tim* or *Tom*?) Indeed, all our cognitive skills are necessary, because language depends upon memory, imagery, concepts, problem solving, and decision making. Language requires memory and thinking—the topics of the last two chapters, yet it is also the most social of our cognitive activities. We can remember, form concepts, solve problems, and make decisions when we are by ourselves. In contrast, we generally use language in social settings, and our knowledge of the social world helps us interpret the language we hear and select the words we speak. Therefore, this chapter foreshadows the social interactions we examine more closely at the end of this book.

This chapter is divided into three sections: understanding language, producing language, and language and thinking. The important topic of language development is examined in the next chapter.

Understanding Language

When we understand language, we hear a set of noises or look at an arrangement of scribbles and somehow manage to make sense of them, using our knowledge about sounds, letters, words, language rules, and information about the world. An important part of understanding spoken language is speech perception. Other topics in this section include understanding and meaning, and reading.

Speech Perception

You have turned on the television and the soap opera hero has just said, "But I really love you, Felicia. . . . " That wiggling of the tongue, contortion of the lips, and throbbing of the larynx produced complex sound vibrations that eventually reached the receptors in your ears (and persumably Felicia's as well). Your auditory system manages to translate these vibrations into a string of sounds that you perceive to be speech.

The speech perception process is extremely complex (Goldstein, 1989; Matlin & Foley, 1992). However, most of us generally pay little conscious attention to this process. Instead, we usually concentrate on the message. We notice greetings, warnings, questions, and statements, but we fail to notice the language that is used to deliver this information (Darwin, 1976).

Bottom-Up and Top-Down Processing   In chapter 4, we discussed how visual shape perception depends on both bottom-up and top-down processing. **Bottom-up processing** begins with information from the sensory receptors, in other words, at the bottom (or lowest level) of perception. **Top-down processing** emphasizes how perception is shaped by observers' concepts, expectations, and prior knowledge—in other words, the kind of information stored at the top (or highest level) of perception. Thus, you recognize yourself in the mirror partly because the rods and cones in your retina are gathering information about hair color, facial shape, and skin complexion (bottom-up). But your prior knowledge informs you that you are the most likely person to appear in that mirror (top-down).

Speech perception, like visual shape perception, is guided by both bottom-up and top-down perception. You recognize each **phoneme** (or basic unit of speech, such as the sounds *th*, *a*, and *t* in the word *that*) partly because the receptors in your cochlea gather precise information about pitch and other characteristics of the sound (bottom-up). However, your concepts, expectations, and prior knowledge are also critically important. If someone says, "The dentist told the girl to brush her tee___," your top-down processing skills are scarcely challenged. The context of the sentence as well as the context of the word fragment *tee-* assure you that the missing phoneme is *th* rather than *b*, *m*, or *z* (Massaro, 1987).

Humans are so skilled at top-down perception that they sometimes believe they hear a phoneme that is truly missing, an effect known as **phoneme restoration**. In a classic experiment, Warren and Warren (1970) played three sentences for the listeners in their study. These sentences were identical with one exception: A different word was spliced onto the end of each sentence. In each case, a coughing sound was inserted in the location indicated by the asterisk:

1. It was found that the *eel was on the axle.

2. It was found that the *eel was on the shoe.

3. It was found that the *eel was on the orange.

These researchers found that the listeners reported hearing different words, as a function of the context. The "word" *eel* was heard as *wheel* in the first sentence, *heel* in the second, and *peel* in the third.

Phonemic restoration is a kind of illusion. People think that they hear a phoneme, even though the correct sound vibrations never reach their ears (Warren, 1984). Additional experiments have confirmed that top-down processing encourages us to "hear" a phoneme or even a word that is not there (Cooper et al., 1985; Huttenlocher & Goodman, 1987; Samuel & Ressler, 1986).

We are so tolerant of missing sounds and mispronunciations in sentences that we often fail to notice children's highly inaccurate pronunciations. For instance, one of my students recalled singing a Christmas carol in which the shepherds "washed their socks by night" instead of "watched their flocks by night." Another remembered a carol that began "O come all ye hateful: Joy, Phil, and their trumpet." Adults typically tolerate these mispronunciations because their top-down processing encourages them to hear what their expectations predict.

Word Boundaries   Have you ever overheard a conversation in a language that you do not know? The words seem to run together in a continuous stream, with no boundaries between them. However, when you hear your native language, you hear distinct words. When you read, you see white spaces clearly identifying the boundaries between words. When you listen, the "white spaces" seem almost as distinct.

In most cases, however, the actual spoken language does not have any clear-cut pauses to mark the boundaries. In fact, researchers have discovered that English speakers use an actual physical event—such as a pause—to mark a word boundary less than 40% of the time (Cole & Jakimik, 1980). Listeners are quite remarkable in using the speech rhythms and their stored knowledge to figure out what sounds are grouped together (Cutler, 1987).

Most of the time, top-down processing—aided by our stored knowledge—produces a correct interpretation when the word boundaries are unclear. However, as we often saw in the previous chapter on thinking, heuristics that usually work can sometimes produce an error. Consider the grandmother who heard a line from a Beatles song. She was more familiar with illness than with hallucinogenic experiences, and so she heard "the girl with colitis goes by" rather than "the girl with kaleidoscope eyes" (Safire, 1979). Thus, relying too heavily on expectations—rather than the auditory stimulus—can produce errors.

Understanding and Meaning

When we understand language, we do much more than perceive phonemes and identify the boundaries between words. We also decode the meaning of the language we hear. We identify meaning in word fragments, in concepts, and in larger units.

Morphemes   A **morpheme** is the smallest language unit that has meaning. A morpheme can be a fragment of a word, as long as it conveys meaning. Thus, the fragments *un-*, *-est*, *-s*, and *-ly* are all morphemes because each of these suggests meaning (e.g., *un*easy, tall*est*, textbook*s*, and slow*ly*). A morpheme can also be an entire word, such as *the*, *small*, and *language*. Notice, then, that the word *unfriendly* contains three morphemes, or meaning units.

Conceptual Meaning   Psychologists and others interested in language find it challenging to describe how humans store conceptual meaning in memory. For example, think about the meaning of the concept *apple*. In your many years of experience with apples, you know the characteristics of apples, you know several varieties of apples, and you know that *apple* belongs to the larger category of *fruit*. (We discussed this last characteristic under the topic of natural concepts in the previous chapter.)

One theory of meaning called a **network model** proposes that concepts are organized in memory in a netlike pattern, with many interconnections. The meaning of a particular concept, such as *apple*, depends upon the concepts to which it is connected (Collins & Loftus, 1975). Figure 9.1 shows what one person's network structure might look like. Keep in mind that each of these concepts in this figure has its own individual network structure. Try imagining a network of associations surrounding the concepts *nutritious*, *red*, and *fruit*. Clearly, the representation of meaning in memory is both rich and complex.

According to the network model, when the name of a concept is mentioned, that particular location becomes activated. In addition, the activation spreads to the nearby terms, much like dropping a rock into a pool of water (Wessells, 1982). So when you hear the word *apple*, all its important characteristics are activated in your memory. Now let us consider larger units of meaning, beyond individual concepts.

Interpreting Strings of Words   Suppose that the weather forecaster says, "It will be colder on Tuesday, with possible snow flurries developing Tuesday night."

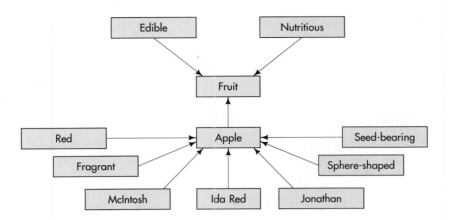

Figure 9.1
An example of a network structure for the concept *apple*.

According to the most widely accepted view of language comprehension, you divide that sentence into constituents, rather than analyze the sentence one word at a time. A **constituent** is a group of words that seems to belong together as a unit. Typically, a constituent contains more than one word but less than an entire sentence (Clark & Clark, 1977). In the case of the weather forecaster's message, you would probably divide that sentence into two major parts, with the comma as the dividing line. Each of those major parts could be divided into smaller constituents (for example, "It will be colder"). Listeners seem to extract the gist or general meaning, from each constituent group of words, rather than analyze a sentence on a word-by-word basis.

Listeners develop a variety of heuristics for identifying constituents (Clark & Clark, 1977; Kimball, 1973). For example, when you hear the word *with* in the forecaster's report, you know that a noun must eventually come. Listeners also rely on word parts, such as *-er*, *-y*, and *-ly* to indicate the part of speech of a word. Thus, *-er* words are usually nouns, whereas *-y* words are usually adjectives and *-ly* words are usually adverbs.

As adult speakers, you are so skilled at identifying constituent structure that you can perform this operation on sentences that are close to nonsense. Consider these lines from Lewis Carroll's poem "Jabberwocky":

> *Twas brillig, and the slithy toves*
> *did gyre and gimble in the wabe:*

Words such as *and* and *the* help us to divide the sentence and identify *wabe* as a noun. The word part *-s* suggests that *toves* is either a noun or a verb. Once again, we use heuristics, or rules-of-thumb, to help us solve the language puzzle.

Surface Structure and Deep Structure   The theorist Noam Chomsky (1957, 1965) changed our view of language when he proposed that listeners have the ability to understand the abstract relationships underlying the strings of words they actually hear. His model distinguished between a sentence's surface structure and its deep structure. **Surface structure** is represented by the words that are actually spoken or written. In contrast, **deep structure** is the underlying, more abstract representation of the sentence.

Two sentences may have different surface structures but similar deep structures, as in the following sentences:

> *The student read the book.*

> *The book was read by the student.*

Two sentences can also have identical surface structure but different deep structures, as in the ambiguous sentence,

The police must stop drinking after midnight.

The meaning of this sentence seems to flip back and forth between its two different deep structures. It is difficult to keep both meanings in mind simultaneously (Miller, 1981).

Chomsky devised rules to describe how listeners transform surface structure into deep structure, and how speakers transform the deep structure they wish to express into the specific words they utter. Currently, most psychologists support Chomsky's notion of the distinction between surface and deep structure, though they are less likely to support some of his more specific predictions (Garnham, 1985; Prideaux, 1985; Tartter, 1986).

Reading

College students spend much of their college years reading. You read not only textbooks, but notices on bulletin boards, subtitles in foreign movies, and the list of ingredients on cereal cartons. By now, reading seems automatic, something you can take for granted.

Reading skills are remarkable, however, once you stop to analyze them. In order to read, your eyes must move forward in saccadic movements (see chapter 4) to identify the letters in each word. (The recognition of letters was also discussed in chapter 4, in the section on shape perception.) You must also recognize the words you are reading and figure out the meaning of unfamiliar words. Furthermore, you can accomplish all these tasks at the rate of several hundred words each minute. Reading is another excellent example of our theme that humans are extremely competent creatures.

Word Recognition   As you are reading this sentence to yourself, how do you actually recognize the words? Some little squiggles decorate this page, interrupted by white spaces. How do those squiggles bring you to a word's meaning? According to current theory, you can recognize some words directly from the printed words.

Demonstration 9.1

Figuring Out the Meaning of a Word From Context

Read the paragraph below. Then define, as precisely as possible, the two words that are italicized.

Two ill-dressed people—the one a tired woman of middle years and the other a tense young man—sat around a fire where the common meal was almost ready. The mother, Tanith, peered at her son through the *oam* of the bubbling stew. It had been a long time since his last *ceilidh* and Tobar had changed greatly; where once he had seemed all legs and clumsy joints, he now was well-formed and in control of his hard, young body. As they ate, Tobar told of his past year, recreating for Tanith how he had wandered long and far in his quest to gain the skills he would need to be permitted to rejoin the company. Then all too soon, their brief *ceilidh* over, Tobar walked over to touch his mother's arm and quickly left.

Source: Based on Sternberg & Powell, 1983.

That is, you can look at a large number of common words, such as *ball*, and that visual pattern allows you to locate information about *ball*'s meaning in your memory.

However, unusual or infrequent words take a slower route. A difficult or unfamiliar word such as *nonphonologically* or *pseudowords* will first be translated from the ink marks on the page to a sound code, before locating that word's meaning. (Think about it: Doesn't it seem that you heard yourself pronouncing these words and sounding them out as you read them?) According to this **dual-encoding model**, a word's meaning is accessed directly from the printed page, in the case of a common word; however, meaning is accessed indirectly—through a sound route—in the case of an uncommon word (Foss, 1988).

Discovering the Meaning of an Unknown Word   Suppose that you had never previously seen the word *accessed* as it was used in the previous sentence. How could you, nevertheless, find out what this new word meant? Sternberg and Powell's (1983) theory emphasizes that people exploit a rich variety of context cues. Try Demonstration 9.1 before you read further.

Sternberg and Powell argue that some of the useful context cues to discovering the meaning of a new word (X) include the following:

1. When X occurs;

2. Where X occurs;

3. What emotion X arouses;

4. The actions X can perform;

5. The physical properties of X.

Consider the sentence

At dawn, the *blen* arose on the horizon and shone brightly.

The phrase at dawn tells us when the *blen* arose. The words *arose* and *shone* describe its actions, and *on the horizon* provides an important cue about where it occurs. With all these different cues, it is easy for an experienced reader to understand that the nonsense word *blen* stands for *sun*.

To test their theory about context cues, Sternberg and Powell (1983) asked high school students to read passages such as the one in Demonstration 9.1. Then the students provided a definition for each of the italicized words in the passage (for instance, *oam* and *ceilidh*). Three trained raters judged the quality of each definition, providing a "definition goodness" score for each word. Powell herself then examined each passage and counted the number of context cues available for each word. The results showed a strong positive correlation between the two measures; words that appear in a rich context of different cues are likely to be more accurately defined by readers. (Incidentally, *oam* means steam, and a *ceilidh* is a visit.) Thus, top-down processing aids the understanding of unfamiliar words, just as it facilitates the perception of speech sounds.

Section Summary: Understanding Language

■ Speech perception is guided by both bottom-up and top-down perception; the phonemic restoration effect demonstrates the importance of top-down perception.

■ Listeners easily perceive word boundaries, even when there are no clear-cut pauses indicating those boundaries.

■ According to one theory of meaning, the network model, concepts are organized in memory in an interconnecting netlike pattern.

■ People seem to extract meaning from language by analyzing constituents—rather than isolated words—and they use a variety of heuristics to identify those constituents; language can be viewed in terms of both its surface structure and its deep structure.

■ When they read, people access a common word's meaning directly and an uncommon word's meaning indirectly, through sounding it out; they rely on many context cues to determine the meaning of an unknown word.

Producing Language

It is amazing that we manage to understand speech, but it is even more astonishing that we can produce it. After all, language is constantly innovative. We continually produce sentences that no one has ever uttered previously in the history of the English language (Chomsky, 1988). For instance, as I was writing the last sentence, my daughter phoned, and her first sentence had certainly never been produced before: "Mom, I need to know the name of the director and the date of the movie *The Return of Martin Guerre* for my history of the family paper, and I figured you'd be able to find that out faster than any library."

In order to produce language, we must first construct a thought, a general idea that must be conveyed. That thought must then be arranged into constituents. Then, the tongue, lips, and other vocal apparatus need to move appropriately (Carroll, 1986). We begin this section on language production with an overview of how people plan speech. We spend more time, however, on the social aspects of language production. We will also discuss bilingualism, nonverbal communication, and the ape-language controversy.

Speech Planning

When you are about to talk, you have some general idea about what you would like to express. You may want to discuss tomorrow's exam, a song on the radio, or an upcoming election. The next time you begin a sentence, think about the planning process. Before you begin, have you (1) selected the subject, but not the verb, (2) selected both the subject and the verb, or (3) selected the subject completely but the verb only partially? In general, research with people who speak English supports the last alternative (Lindsley, 1975). That is, we begin to talk once we know the subject of our statement and we have a general idea of the verb. However, we do not need to select the exact verb before we begin the sentence.

Some kinds of speech require more effort and planning. For example, imagine that you and your psychology instructor are having a conversation about some topic you have studied recently. You would need to remember information and think about the topic; you would also construct innovative sentences. Beattie (1983) found that in this kind of setting, people typically alternated between hesitant and fluent phases. During the planning phase, people speak haltingly and slowly. During the fluent phase, they are rewarded for their earlier planning, and the words flow more easily.

In our more casual conversations, we require fewer pauses, and we produce well-practiced phrases such as "Hello" and "How are you." When people tell familiar stories, they usually plan more than one sentence at a time (Harris & Coltheart, 1986; Holmes, 1984).

The Linearization Problem　　When you speak, you may have a general thought you want to express, or a mental image that needs to be conveyed verbally. These rather shapeless ideas need to be translated into a statement that is linear, with one word following after another in a line. This dilemma is called the **linearization problem** (Bock, 1987; Foss, 1988). Try noticing how linearization usually occurs without effort. Occasionally, however, it may be a struggle. Have you ever wanted to convey an idea, and everything needs to be said at the very beginning?

Psychologists and other researchers interested in language have begun to tackle the linearization problem. We know, for instance, that when people need to list two or more items, they generally place short words before long ones, pleasant words before unpleasant, and prototypes before nonprototypes (Kelly et al., 1986; Matlin & Stang, 1978; Pinker & Birdsong, 1979).

Speech Errors　　The speech we produce is usually well formed (Bock, 1987). However, our everyday conversation often differs from perfect English. Notice how people often pause in the middle of a sentence. They may start a new sentence before finishing the previous one, because the statement had been poorly planned. They also use extra words such as *oh* and *um*.

One kind of speech error is a **slip of the tongue**, an error in which sounds are rearranged between two or more different words. There are three basic kinds of slips of the tongue (Dell, 1986):

1. Sound errors occur when sounds in nearby words are exchanged (e.g., *Snow flurries → flow snurries*).

2. Morpheme errors occur when morphemes (those small, meaningful units in language, such as *-ly* or *in-*) are exchanged in nearby words (e.g., *Self-destruct instruction → self-instruct destruction*).

3. Word errors occur when words are exchanged (e.g., *Writing a letter to my mother → writing a mother to my letter*).

According to a recent theory of slips of the tongue, a speaker who is planning a sentence will construct a representation of that sentence at the word level (Dell, 1986). As we noted at the beginning of this section, the speaker selects many words in a sentence before beginning to pronounce the first word in that sentence. These selected words activate the sounds that are linked with them. In most cases, we speak the most highly activated sound, and this sound is usually correct. However, a sound may be activated by several different words, producing an unusually high activation level. That highly activated sound might burst forth at the wrong time in the sentence. For example, consider this tongue twister:

She sells seashells.

You are likely to say *sheashells*, because the *sh* sound is so highly activated by the *sh* in *she* and *shells*. Table 9.1 shows some of the slips of the tongue that my students produced when they were asked to keep records of their errors.

This section has explored how speakers plan a sentence, molding ideas into a linear sequence (though occasionally making speech errors). However, speech is typically designed to communicate with other humans. Let us therefore consider these social components of language.

Social Aspects of Language

Most language has a social function. Yes, you occasionally talk to yourself or write yourself reminder notes. However, the major reason you talk is to share

Table 9.1   *Some Typical Slips-of-the-Tongue*

SPEECH ERROR	WHAT WAS INTENDED
"Porking at York Landing"	"Parking at York Landing"
"I was gabberflasted."	"I was flabbergasted."
"I wish there was a refrigerator in this light."	"I wish there was a light in this refrigerator."
"Go lump in a jake."	"Go jump in a lake."
"I need to send an aunt to my card."	"I need to send a card to my aunt."
"The shun comes shining through."	"The sun comes shining through."
"My daughter was a real sumbthucker."	"My daughter was a real thumbsucker."
"I got my tang tongueled."	"I got my tongue tangled."

information with others. Think about what you have said so far today. You may have requested, informed, persuaded, and complimented. We direct our words to other people, and our goal is to affect the people with whom we are talking.

Herbert Clark (1985) proposes that conversation is like a complicated dance. Speakers do not simply utter words aloud and expect to be understood. Instead, they consider their conversational partners, make numerous assumptions about those partners, and design their language appropriately. This complicated dance involves precise coordination. They need to coordinate turn taking and their understanding of ambiguous terms. Just as dancers need to know whether their partners are familiar with certain dance steps, speakers need to know whether their conversational partners have the appropriate background knowledge (Harris et al., 1980).

This section on the **pragmatics**, or social aspects of language, begins with a discussion of how speakers attend to their listeners' background knowledge. We also consider conversational interactions and politeness, emphasizing that language is the most social of our cognitive activities.

Listeners' Background Knowledge   Speakers are typically conscientious and concerned about their listeners. They use simplified language in speaking with children or with people who are not familiar with the language the speakers are using. When communication seems unsuccessful, speakers replace difficult words and phrases with easier ones (Cutler, 1987; Valian & Wales, 1976).

Speakers usually assume that listeners have appropriate background knowledge about a conversational topic. For example, we noted in chapter 7 that people develop a schema, or generalized idea, about objects and events that are encountered frequently, such as attending a concert. Speakers count on their listeners' schemas to "fill in the blanks." For instance, you might say to a friend, *I went to the concert last night, but then I lost my ticket stub and someone was sitting in my seat.* You are counting on your friend to know that

1. You enter a concert auditorium by presenting a ticket.

2. The ticket taker tears your ticket, returning the stub to you.

3. The stub, in assigned-seat concerts, lists your seat number.

4. That seat number corresponds to a chair in the auditorium.

5. Each seat should be assigned to only one person.

6. Two people cannot sit in the same seat simultaneously.

7. A problem arose last night.

Two people participating in a conversation assume that they share similar schemas and background knowledge.

We also count on our listeners to share background knowledge about people and objects in our culture. For example, if you say, *Lisa skipped all the way home from school*, you can count on your listener to conclude that Lisa is a female child. In terms of the network model discussed in connection with word meaning, your listener's network surrounding the name *Lisa* includes the concept *female*. The networks surrounding *skipping* and *school* both include the concept *child*. Thus, speakers and listeners have an easier time engaging in a conversational dance because they have similar background knowledge and—equally important—because they *know* that they both share this knowledge.

Conversational Interactions   Imagine that Cindy is calling a hair salon to make an appointment with the woman who last cut her hair, though she cannot remember the woman's name. Cindy and the receptionist will perform a short dance as they try to make certain that they are speaking about the same person:

> **Cindy:**   She's short, about five feet two inches.
>
> **Receptionist:**   Oh, maybe you mean Marilyn. She has short brown wavy hair.
>
> **Cindy:**   Yes, that's right, and glasses? And she went to Puerto Rico last summer?
>
> **Receptionist:**   Yes, that's Marilyn Peters.
>
> **Cindy:**   Yes, that name sounds right.

Notice what happens in this conversational interaction. Both partners put in extra effort together to make certain that they agree they are referring to the same person. Even total strangers collaborate. An important feature of conversational interaction is that the participants check, question, and confirm. That part of the conversation is ended only when both are certain that they are talking about the same person and have established common ground.

Researchers have examined how this collaboration process operates when people work together to arrange complex figures. Demonstration 9.2 is a modification of this study by Clark and Wilkes-Gibbs (1986).

Collaborating to Establish Common Ground

For this demonstration, you need to make two photocopies of these figures. Then locate two volunteers and a watch that can measure time in seconds. Cut the figures apart, keeping each sheet's figures in a separate pile and making certain the dot is at the top of each figure. Appoint one person to be the "director"; this person should arrange the figures in random order in two rows of six figures each. This person's task is to describe the first figure in enough detail so that the "matcher" is able to identify that figure and place it in position 1 in front of him or her. (Neither person should be able to see the other's figures.) The goal is for the matcher to place all 12 figures in the same order as the director's figures. They may use any kind of verbal descriptions they choose, but no gestures or imitation of body position. Record how long it takes them to reach their goal, and then make sure that the figures do match up. Ask them to try the game two more times, with the same person serving as director. Record the times again, and note whether the time decreases on the second and third trials; are they increasingly efficient in establishing common ground? Do they tend to develop a standard vocabulary (e.g., "the ice skater") to refer to a given figure?

The participants in the study played this game for six trials. (Each trial consisted of arranging all 12 figures in order.) On the first trial, the director required nearly four turns to describe a figure and make certain that the matcher understood the reference. However, as Figure 9.2 shows, the director and the matcher soon developed a mutual shorthand. Just as two dancers become more skilled at coordinating their motor movements as they practice together, conversational partners become more skilled in communicating efficiently.

Another characteristic of conversational interactions is that they should obey certain established rules. One rule is that the speakers are supposed to alternate. Speakers do not talk at the same time, and they do not typically pause leisurely in the middle of the conversation.

Notice how telephone conversations have a specified format, including alternation. The answerer must speak first, but only briefly. The person who called must then provide identification and expect a brief acknowledgment before proceeding. There is also a specified etiquette to closing a conversation. Obviously, "I'll let you go" is an accepted phrase, but "What's up?" is not (Jacobs, 1985). It may take numerous alternations to wind down a conversation. Polite adults do not simply fling a "good-bye" into a random pause in the interchange. A typical ending might be this:

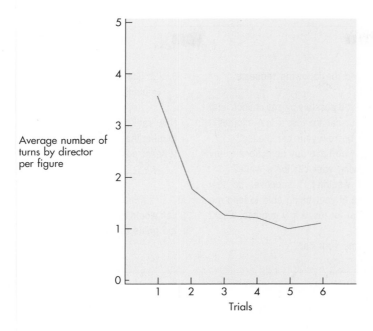

Figure 9.2
Average number of turns that directors took on each figure, as a function of trial number. (From Clark and Wilkes-Gibbs, 1986)

Average number of turns by director per figure

Trials

A: Well, I've got to study for my test tomorrow.

B: OK. I won't keep you, but it was good to talk to you.

A: You, too. Maybe we'll have lunch together some time.

B: Yeah, can I call you this weekend?

A: Sure. Take care now, OK?

B: Yeah. 'Bye now.

A: Bye-bye!

Typically, the leave-taking portion of the conversation involves either specific or vague plans for contact in the future (Clark, 1985).

Politeness   When I was about 10 years old, I accompanied my younger sister to the home of her best friend, Carol, where we planned to have lunch. After we had finished our sandwiches, Carol's mother served thick slices of cake to my sister and Carol, unintentionally forgetting me. I struggled to formulate a request that was as polite as possible. Then I adopted a mournful expression and said, "Does the cake taste good, Carol?" From the perspective of a 10-year-old, my request had reached the heights of diplomacy. From my perspective as an adult, decades later, the choice of words was comical.

Language researchers believe that "politeness means putting things in such a way as to take account of the feelings of the other person" (R. Brown, 1988, p. 749). Try Demonstration 9.3, which focuses on different degrees of politeness, before you read further.

Did your answers to Demonstration 9.3 reveal that more polite requests are almost always longer? In a book on politeness, Penelope Brown and Stephen Levinson (1987) order those statements (from most to least polite): 4, 1, 3, 6, 2, 5. They argue that when people want to be polite, their statements are more complicated and indirect. When they want to make a polite request, they typically begin with small talk, irrelevant to the request, and then they word their question in a fashion that leaves an escape option. Consider, how you might approach a professor for a letter of recommendation. After some preliminary small talk, you

Demonstration 9.3

Politeness

Read the following requests:

1. Could you possibly by any chance lend me your car for just a few minutes?
2. May I borrow your car please?
3. Would you have any objections to my borrowing your car for a while?
4. There wouldn't, I suppose, be any chance of your being able to lend me your car for just a few minutes, would there?
5. Lend me your car.

6. I'd like to borrow your car, if you wouldn't mind.

Now rank these requests from most polite (putting that item's number in the first blank) to least polite:

___ ___ ___ ___ ___ ___

Finally, decide which of those items you would *never* use because they are either too polite or too rude.

might ask, "I wonder if you know me well enough to write a letter of recommendation?" You reason that any professor who would not write an enthusiastic letter could claim that he or she does not know you well.

Politeness depends upon context, however. Consider how differently this request would be interpreted by a next-door neighbor you met only once and one you know well: "I don't suppose I could possibly ask you for a cup of flour, could I?" (Brown & Levinson, p. 142). Too much politeness from a good friend can seem bizarre.

Until now, you may not have spent much time worrying about precisely how you attempt to convey politness in your requests. As we noted in the chapter on consciousness, people are often unaware of their higher mental processes. In most cases, we do not consciously plot how we will be polite in our conversational interactions (Brown & Levinson, 1987). We may be aware that various phrases vary in politeness only when we need to make a major request (such as a letter of recommendation) or when the rules of politeness have been seriously violated. Politeness usually comes as easily to our lips as phonemes do. Otherwise, we would still be lost in thought at the breakfast table, wondering whether to say "Would you mind passing the salt?" or "Please pass the salt."

Bilingualism

So far, our language examples have been confined to English. However, as we approach the 21st century, the United States is quickly acquiring a large bilingual population. For example, Figure 9.3 shows a notice that the New England Telephone Company sent to its Boston patrons.

What can we conclude about bilingualism? What are the myths, and what are the realities? Although the early research was pessimistic, the more recent studies suggest that people who are fluent in two languages actually have an *advantage* over those who only speak English. Researchers have drawn several conclusions (Braine, 1987; Cummins, 1987; Diaz, 1983; Fantini, 1985; Hakuta, 1986, 1987; Johnson & Newport, 1989; Palij & Homel, 1987).

1. In general, bilinguals have more insight into the properties of language and more flexible thinking in problem solving, perhaps traceable to their awareness that a concept can be expressed in more than one way.

Research demonstrates that bilinguals may have more insights about the nature of language than people who speak only one language.

Figure 9.3
A notice sent to Boston residents by a telephone company. The languages on the notice are English, Portuguese, Spanish, Vietnamese, French, Chinese, and Cambodian.

What You Should Know About Automatic Dialing Services.

This is an important notice. Please have it translated.

Este é um aviso importante. Queira mandá-lo traduzir.

Este es un aviso importante. Sírvase mandarlo traducir.

ĐÂY LÀ MỘT BẢN THÔNG CÁO QUAN TRỌNG XIN VUI LÒNG CHO DỊCH LẠI THÔNG CÁO ẤY

Ceci est important. Veuillez faire traduire.

本通知很重要。请将之译成中文。

នេះគឺជាដំណឹងល្អ សូមមេត្តាបកប្រែជូនផង

2. Children who grow up in homes where two languages are spoken may confuse them initially, but they rapidly learn to separate the two languages.

3. Knowledge acquired in one language can be transferred easily to the other language.

4. There are tremendous individual differences in the rate at which people acquire a second language, consistent with one theme of this book. The variation can be traced to personality factors as well as differences in verbal ability.

5. Children who acquire a second language at an early age have better accents in that language than those who learn the second language during adulthood. In addition, their mastery of grammar in their second language may be superior (Johnson & Newport, 1989). For example, Koreans and Chinese who learned English during childhood were better than those who learned English as adults when both groups were asked to identify whether sentences were correct or incorrect (e.g., "Yesterday the hunter shoots a deer.").

In chapter 17 we consider how stereotypes provide biases against minority groups, whose original language was not English. These stereotypes have become exaggerated as some regions of the country have adopted "English only" legislation. Unfortunately, those attitudes do not reflect the research that bilingualism may actually offer an advantage by encouraging greater cognitive flexibility.

Nonverbal Communication

So far, we have only considered verbal language. However, people communicate with each other in many different ways. They can transmit messages by words, by tone of voice, by body movement, and by facial expression. The term **nonverbal communication** refers to all human communications that do not involve words (Dittmann, 1987; Webbink, 1986). In other words, there is more to conversation than a written transcript captures.

Try saying the sentence "I'm really happy you got the job" with great enthusiasm and positive emotion, consistent with the verbal message. Now try

A major part of meaning is conveyed by nonverbal communication, rather than by words.

saying those same words with sarcasm and bitterness. Notice how your tone of voice, hand movements, posture, rate of speaking, and facial expression all change dramatically. As it turns out, nonverbal behavior is often as important as actual words in conveying meaning in a social setting. According to some estimates, between 60% and 70% of meaning is conveyed nonverbally (Burgoon, 1985).

Nonverbal communication includes a large number of varied behaviors, such as the following (Burgoon, 1985; Patterson, 1983; Webbink, 1986):

1. **Paralanguage**, or the use of vocal cues other than the words themselves, such as voice tone, pitch, pauses, and inflection of the voice;

2. **Gestures**, or hand movements that accompany speech;

3. Body orientation or posture;

4. Body movement, such as squirming or playing with a watchband;

5. Interpersonal distance;

6. Touch;

7. Eye behavior, such as the direction of gaze;

8. Facial expression.

In chapter 12, we discuss some of these nonverbal behaviors, especially facial expression, when we discuss how emotion is conveyed and interpreted. In the current chapter, however, we are more concerned with conveying meaning. Let us look specifically at gestures and at nonverbal regulation of conversation.

Gestures   One kind of gesture is called an emblem. An **emblem** is a nonverbal action that is clearly understood by most members of a culture. Each emblem can be translated into a verbal phrase (Deaux & Wrightsman, 1988; McNeill, 1985). Two examples are a wave of the hand in greeting, and the first finger pointing to the side of the head, moving in small circles, indicating that a person is crazy. Try thinking of the emblems for the following phrases: "It stinks," "killing yourself," "stop," "be quiet," "I don't want to hear it," and "come here." Even though you can readily think of a dozen other emblems, middle-class Americans have a smaller number of emblems than most other groups, probably fewer than 100 (Ekman, 1976). (Try Demonstration 9.4 to see how many you can think of.)

One other common kind of gesture is an illustrator. An **illustrator** is a nonverbal action that accompanies speech and quite literally provides an illustration. For example, you might indicate by raising one arm high over your head and bending your hand, "He was a *very* tall man." A surgeon describing an operation might use illustrators to indicate making incisions and sutures. If you are not allowed to use illustrators, for example in a telephone conversation, you will use a greater number of words to describe something (Graham & Heywood, 1975).

Nonverbal Regulation of Conversation   Earlier in this chapter, we discussed conversational characteristics such as turn talking, as well as the verbal formats for beginning and ending conversations. Nonverbal communication is also important in regulating a conversation.

Turn taking often depends as much on paralanguage and other nonverbal cues as on the actual words that are spoken (Deaux & Wrightsman, 1988; Duncan & Fiske, 1977). If you want to keep talking, even when your conversational partner wants to intrude, you will probably talk louder and faster, eliminating any pauses. The person who wants to interrupt may use sounds such as "ah" and "er" as well as shifting his or her posture. If you decide to stop talking and let your partner begin, you are likely to indicate your decision by reducing your pitch and loudness, slowing your last word, relaxing your hand position, and glancing at the partner (Cappella, 1985).

Similarly, you use characteristic nonverbal behaviors to begin and end a conversation. Suppose that you and a friend are approaching each other on your college campus. Your eyes meet, and you nod or wave from a distance. However, you do not continue to gaze as you approach. (In fact, if you have some distance to walk before meeting, you will probably find some excuse to interrupt eye contact. It is simply impossible to keep gazing continuously for nearly a minute!) During the last seconds, however, you renew eye contact, smile, and maybe shake hands or touch each other. Then when you want to end the interaction, you will interrupt eye contact, change body positions, lean forward, and nod your head. You will wait for your conversational partner to match some of these actions before saying goodbye (Webbink, 1986).

The Ape-Language Controversy

Few research questions in the history of science have produced as much controversy as the ape-language debate (Savage-Rumbaugh, 1986). Can chimps communicate the way we humans do?

Demonstration 9.4

Recognizing Emblems

Make a list of as many emblems as you can recall. (For the sake of decency, eliminate the R-rated and the X-rated ones.) Keep working on this list, adding to it whenever you think of a new one, until you have a list of 20 items. Then ask a friend to try to decode your emblems. In each case, do not provide any context or circumstances in which the emblem is likely to be used. Also, do not use any accompanying words. Simply perform one gesture at a time and see whether your friend can guess the appropriate meaning. You may wish to compare your list with others in the class. Working together, can you all identify close to 100 emblems?

Which of these two people would encourage you to end a conversation quickly, by the use of nonverbal communication?

Washoe makes the sign for "doll."

The first reports were clearly pessimistic. For example, Hayes (1951) tried to teach a chimpanzee to pronounce English words. After 6 years of continuous training, the chimp could say only *cup, mama,* and *papa.*

However, it is not really fair to use pronunciation as a measure of the chimp's language ability. After all, chimps are physically unable to pronounce many of the sounds in human speech (Roitblat, 1987). In the late 1960s, researchers began to work with concrete symbols and sign language, rather than speech sounds. For instance, Beatrice Gardner and Allen Gardner (1975) taught five chimpanzees to use American Sign Language. Their first subject, Washoe, learned more than 100 signs, and she also combined signs into simple sentences. For example, when seeing a small rubber doll in her drinking cup, she signed, "Baby in my drink."

Additional researchers taught their chimpanzees artificial languages, in which plastic chips or geometric symbols represent words (Marx, 1980; Savage-Rumbaugh, 1986). For example, a chimp named Lana learned to string a series of symbols together to form a request. A typical request would be "Please machine make music," indicated by pressing the appropriate symbols on a computer. Although Lana also learned to make numerous other requests, her comprehension abilities were relatively limited (Rumbaugh, 1988).

Another somewhat pessimistic account of chimpanzees' linguistic abilities came from Terrace (1979). Terrace had tried to teach sign language to a chimp called Nim Chimpsky (named after the linguist who discussed surface and deep structure, Noam Chomsky). Terrace and his co-workers raised Nim from the age of 2 weeks to 4 years, and Nim learned about 125 symbols. Still, Terrace (1979, 1981) argued that Nim's language was substantially inferior to children's language, which might include 3,000 words by age 4. Here are some of Terrace's arguments:

1. Nim's statements were typically shorter than children's. Also, Nim's longest statements showed much more repetition than children's language, as in his 16-sign command, "Give orange me give eat orange me eat orange give me eat orange give me you" (Terrace, 1981, p. 101).

2. Only 12% of Nim's statements were spontaneous, rather than being prompted by his teacher's signs. In contrast, about 80% of children's statements are spontaneous.

3. Nim frequently interrupted his teachers' signs, whereas children do not. We have discussed how humans use verbal and nonverbal behaviors to regulate turn taking. Chimps apparently cannot master these subtle pragmatic rules of language (Savage-Rumbaugh, 1986).

However, Nim may have been taught in less than ideal circumstances. He had about 60 different trainers, many of whom were not fluent in sign language. Nim was raised in a classroom environment that was much less interesting than Washoe's homelike setting. Dull environments might not inspire conversation (Fouts, 1987). More recently, there have been some fascinating new developments in chimp language learning. For instance, Washoe and three other chimps taught Washoe's adopted son 55 different signs without the aid of human teachers (Fouts, 1987).

What can we conclude? Apes survive in the wild perfectly well without signing to each other (Miller, 1981). Under the right conditions and with tremendous effort, they can acquire a vocabulary that is dwarfed by a young child's word mastery. Apes primarily communicate about their physical needs, not about psychophysics, religion, or 17th-century British poetry. Not even the most enthusiastic supporter of ape language would argue that animals can convey the rich and varied thoughts that we humans take for granted (Premack, 1983).

Still, an evolutionary perspective suggests that our nearest animal relatives, the apes, must have at least some language potential (Savage & Rumbaugh, 1977). It seems safe to conclude that apes can learn a basic vocabulary of signs referring to concrete concepts. However, they cannot master complex grammar or verb tenses. They cannot discuss abstract concepts or contemplate the nature of language. Even a bright chimp like Washoe could not discuss whether apes can master language. Ape language is more sophisticated than we would have guessed in the 1950s when the first chimp struggled to pronounce *cup*. However, ape language clearly cannot match the fluency, flexibility, and complexity of human language.

Section Summary: Producing Language

- In general, people have selected the subject of their sentence, but not the verb, when they begin to say that sentence; in formulating the sentence, they face the linearization problem.
- According to one theory about slips of the tongue, errors occur when overly activated sounds burst forth at an inappropriate time.
- Speakers take their listeners' knowledge into account.
- People interacting in a conversation actively work to establish common ground, ensuring that they are referring to the same person or thing.
- Conversations have specified formats, such as an alternation pattern, and characteristic conversational beginnings and endings.
- In general, polite statements are long and indirect, compared with less polite statements; they also offer the listener an opportunity to escape from the request.
- Bilingualism offers some cognitive advantages over fluency in only one language; individuals differ in the rate of acquisition of a second language.
- Nonverbal behavior is extremely important in conveying meaning, as in the case of emblems and illustrators; nonverbal communication supplements verbal messages in regulating conversational format.
- Apes can master a basic sign-language vocabulary, but not complex grammar or abstract concepts.

Language and Thinking

It is early March and I am looking out at the half-inch coating of snow on the trees. It is the kind of snow that is moist enough to hang together in short ropes as it droops from the branches—certainly not the kind of snow you would contemplate for cross-country skiing or for making snow ice cream. As an English

Benjamin Lee Whorf proposed that Eskimos, who have at least four separate words for snow, would be forced to pay closer attention to the characteristics of snow than English speakers, who have only one word.

speaker, I call this *snow*, but I would also use the word *snow* to refer to the compact slippery stuff I would prefer for cross-country skiing or the light, fluffy ingredient that is essential for a tasty snow ice cream.

Benjamin Lee Whorf, a fire-prevention inspector who was an amateur linguist, raised one of the most intriguing questions about language when he asked whether the language we speak influences our thought processes (Whorf, 1956). For instance, the Eskimo language has at least four separate words for snow, in contrast to only one term in English. Whorf proposed that when Eskimos looked out at the landscape, their language forced them to pay attention to characteristics of snow that English speakers with a smaller "snow vocabulary" would fail to notice.

The **Whorfian hypothesis,** or **linguistic determinism**, states that the structure of language influences the structure of thought. Furthermore, the Whorfian hypothesis argues that a person speaking Language A might carve up the conceptual world differently from a person speaking Language B. For instance, the Eskimo language carves the concept *snow* into four or more pieces, whereas we do not carve it up at all. Because speakers of different language have different ways of carving up their concepts, Whorf argued that they would actually view the world differently.

At present, most language researchers would not argue that the worldview of a German, Japanese, or Spanish speaker is vastly different from the worldview of an English speaker. These researchers might propose, however, that language influences the content of particular thoughts (Matlin, 1985; Steinberg, 1982). Unfortunately, as far as I know, no one has actually compared whether English speakers and Eskimo speakers perceive snow differently. However, two areas that have been investigated are (1) whether color terms influence thoughts about color and (2) whether gender-biased language produces gender-biased thought.

Color Terms

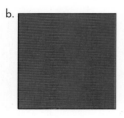

Figure 9.4
People show substantial agreement in labeling the red color on the top; they show little agreement for the green color on the bottom.

Is it easier to remember a color for which we have a readily available name in English? For instance, you would probably call the color on the top in Figure 9.4 "red." English speakers would show substantial agreement about this name. In contrast, reaching agreement about the color on the bottom would be more challenging. I would describe it as "sort of brownish green, like the inside of an avocado that has been exposed to the air for a day." You would probably choose some other phrase. In fact, a dozen of us looking at this color would create a dozen different descriptions.

In the first study to test the Whorfian hypothesis experimentally, Brown and Lenneberg (1954) wanted to see whether language would be related to thinking. For example, would the language used to describe a color (for instance, the extent to which people could agree on a name for a color) be related to some measure of thinking (specifically, how easily the color could be recognized)? Their results confirmed this relationship. Those colors that produced a description with high agreement, such as the red in Figure 9.4, were easier to recognize than colors that produced a description with low agreement, such as old-avocado-insides green. This classic research seemed to provide good evidence that language helped to structure thought. That is, if we have a good, available name for something, we can remember it better and recognize it when we see it again.

However, Eleanor Heider provided a different interpretation of that study. (Her other research on natural concepts and prototypes was described in chapter 8 [Eleanor Rosch, 1973, 1978].) Heider (1972) suspected that colors such as a pure, true red might be easily recognized because they were prototypes, or best examples of a color. The words used to describe the color might be totally irrelevant; some colors are simply "better" than other colors. Heider also suspected that color

Writing Paragraphs

Write a short paragraph of several sentences to elaborate on each of the following sentences:

1. In a large coeducational institution, the average student will feel isolated in his introductory courses. . . .
2. People who live in the United States are often surprisingly ignorant about the geography of other continents. . . .
3. For centuries, man has struggled with the question of life after death. . . .
4. Long before traveling to another country, everyone must make sure that his or her passport is up to date. . . .

This demonstration is discussed in connection with the experiment by Moulton et al. (1978) later in this section.

systems might be universal. That is, perhaps people in all cultures—despite a variety of different languages—might divide up the color spectrum in the same fashion. (For instance, it is possible that the cones in human eyes would process some colors better than others. Possibly a color such as the red in Figure 9.4 would be a prototypical or "best color" in all cultures, no matter what language is spoken.)

Heider conducted some studies with the Dani people of New Guinea, who have only two color names, roughly equivalent to "dark" and "light." In the Dani language, both colors in Figure 9.4 would be described as *dark*, or *mili*. In a memory test, Heider showed that the Dani recognized prototypical colors such as a true red better than nonprototypical colors such as brownish green. Colors considered to be prototypical by English speakers are simply "better," more recognizable colors—even to people who do not honor these prototypical colors with special names.

According to Heider, language cannot account for the differences in thoughts about colors (measured in terms of recognition memory). Instead, our thoughts about color seem to be universal, across many cultures. In the case of color, language does *not* seem to influence thought. Furthermore, Heider explains Brown and Lenneberg's (1954) results—which initially seemed to support the Whorfian hypothesis—by arguing that prototypes are more easily recognized than nonprototypes. (Try Demonstration 9.5 before you read further.) Let us now consider an area in which language does seem to influence thought.

In Depth: Gender-Biased Language

Several years ago, I opened the newspaper and read an article about a home-school counselor at a local elementary school. The (male) counselor was quoted as saying, "When a child sees that he has something in common with me, it's like a miracle the way he opens up." I visualized a troubled boy, feeling relaxed and comfortable with the counselor, sharing his concerns and discussing possible alternatives. But then I wondered what happened to the troubled girls. Had the counselor's choice of the pronoun "he" reflected a greater interest in the problems of male students? Were their problems more conspicuous? Did the troubled girls who visited the counselor rarely have anything in common with the counselor, and therefore rarely opened up? Most important to the Whorfian hypothesis, did the counselor's use of the word "he" tend to limit his thinking so that he directed his services to more boys than girls? Does the language we use tend to bias us toward thinking about males more than females?

Table 9.2   *Examples of Generic-Masculine Terms*

Man	To man (as in, "To man a table at a fair")
He/his/him	Forefathers
Mankind	Caveman
Businessman	Bachelor's degree
The working man	Master craftsman
To fraternize	Middleman
Chairman	Fellow man
Brotherly (as in "Brotherly love")	One-man show

Source: Nilsen et al., 1977.

The problem we are facing involves the **generic masculine**, the use of masculine pronouns and nouns to refer to all human beings—both males and females—instead of males alone. Table 9.2 shows some of these generic masculine terms.

Many people recall being told by their grade school teachers that the word "he" really includes women as well as men. Thus, the sentence, "Each student brought his book" is supposed to refer to both male and female students. Similarly, for many years people in the biology department at my college argued that their course, called Biology of Man, referred to both females and males. (The course title was recently changed to a gender-neutral name, Human Biology.)

In the dictionary, "he" may refer to "he and she," and "man" may refer to "men and women." Are these generic-masculine terms *truly* gender neutral? Alternatively, are generic-masculine terms more likely than gender-neutral terms to produce thoughts about males? Researchers have needed to design creative experiments to answer these questions. After all, how can you measure something as internal and private as "thoughts about gender," when measurement of the dependent variable requires overt responses? Researchers have used a variety of devices for translating these internal thoughts into measurable responses. The research overwhelmingly shows that generic-masculine terms (such as "he") are more likely than gender-neutral terms (such as "he or she" and "they") to produce thoughts oriented toward males (Henley, 1989; Matlin, 1985).

The Research   One study, for example, used picture selection as the dependent variable. Students were asked to search for potential illustrations for a textbook. The results showed that students were more likely to choose all-male pictures when the chapter titles were "Social Man" or "Industrial Man," rather than "Society," "Industrial Life," or other gender-neutral terms (Schneider & Hacker, 1973).

In another study, word usage was the dependent variable. Students were instructed to write stories based on a topic sentence, such as the ones you saw in Demonstration 9.5. Some students saw a sentence such as "In a large coeducational institution, the average student will feel isolated in his introductory courses" (Moulton et al., 1978, p. 1034). Other students were given a similar topic sentence, except that the term "his" was replaced by gender-neutral terms (e.g., "his or her"). In each case, the students wrote a paragraph based on the topic sentence. Then the paragraphs were examined to see whether the students had used female pronouns and female names. Did the generic-masculine language limit people's thinking so that they were less likely to think about women? Check your own responses to see whether your paragraphs in Demonstration 9.5 described males or females.

As you can see from Figure 9.5, people were much more likely to write about females if the pronoun was gender neutral. In contrast, the term "his"

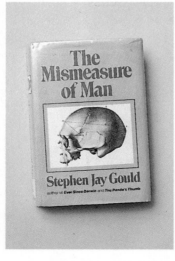

Students reading this book title would be likely to think more often about males than females.

tended to limit thinking; people wrote stories that mentioned women only about one third of the time. The language used in the sentence does influence thought. Specifically, the use of the word "he" calls forth mental images in which males predominate and women are relatively invisible.

Other studies about the generic masculine have used different dependent variables to assess the kinds of thoughts that generic-masculine terms produce. For instance, Martyna (1980) constructed a number of sentences referring to a hypothetical neutral person. A typical item was, "When someone prepares for an exam, he must do some studying." Other variations of that sentence substituted either "they" or "he or she" for the word "he." Students were shown a sentence, accompanied by a picture of someone performing the appropriate activity, in this case, studying. The picture sometimes showed a male and sometimes a female. In each case, the students were asked to decide whether the sentence did or did not apply to the picture; their responses constituted the dependent variable. The results showed that the sentence with the "he" form (generic masculine) was judged not to apply to the picture of the woman in 40% of the trials. When people saw the word "he," they found it disconcerting to see a picture of a woman. Once again, generic-masculine terms like "he" suggest thoughts about men, rather than women.

Many students judge that the sentence "When someone prepares for an exam, he must do some studying" does not apply to this picture.

Some studies also demonstrate that the generic masculine may have important implications for career choices. In one study, students saw a generic-masculine version of a paragraph describing psychologists. They later rated psychology as an unattractive profession for women. In contrast, students who had seen a gender-neutral version gave more favorable ratings (Briere & Lanktree, 1983). Language could therefore influence thought so much that a woman might not contemplate a career that had been described in generic-masculine terms.

Implications of the Research   After examining the studies on gender-biased language, the American Psychological Association adopted a policy that favors gender-neutral language. Some of their suggestions for change are included in Table 9.3.

In later chapters in this textbook, we examine some important biases against females in this culture. For instance, most parents prefer sons as their firstborn child, and they are disappointed when a daughter is born (Hamilton, 1991; Peterson & Peterson, 1973). In the discussion of stereotypes in chapter 17, we examine other negative ideas about women. Gender bias is so complicated that gender-biased language clearly cannot be responsible for all the biases against females.

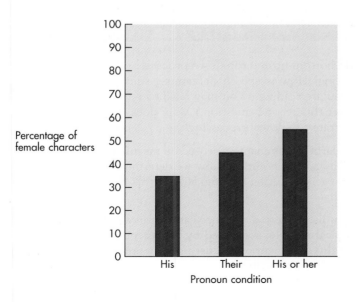

Figure 9.5
Percentage of female characters, as a function of pronoun condition. (Based on Moulton, Robinson, & Elias, 1978)

However, female self-esteem is certainly not improved by using language that omits girls and women (American Psychological Association, 1983; Association for Women in Psychology, 1975).

Table 9.3   *Suggestions for Nonsexist Language*

1. Use the plural form. "Students can monitor their progress" can replace "A student can monitor his progress."
2. Use "his or her" or "her or his," as in the sentence, "A student can monitor her or his progress."
3. Use "you." The sentence "Suppose that you have difficulty recalling your social security number" involves the reader or the listener more than "Suppose that a person has difficulty recalling his social security number"—and it is also less sexist.
4. Reword the sentence to eliminate the pronoun. "The best judge of the value of counseling is usually the client" can replace "The client is usually the best judge of the value of his counseling."

Source: Based on American Psychological Association, 1983, p. 45.

Section Summary: Language and Thinking

■ According to the Whorfian hypothesis, the structure of language influences the structure of thought. Furthermore, because speakers of different languages have different language structures, they should view the world differently.

■ Some early research on color terms suggested that the structure of language seemed to influence thought (specifically recognition). However, later research suggested that these recognition data could be handled by explanations other than the Whorfian hypothesis.

■ Many studies, using a variety of different approaches, have demonstrated that the use of the generic masculine (for instance, ''he'' or ''man'') is more likely to produce thoughts about males, whereas gender-neutral terms are more likely to produce thoughts about both males and females.

REVIEW QUESTIONS

1. How do bottom-up and top-down processes operate when you listen to someone talking? How is speech perception similar to the perception of words when you are reading? (You may need to review pages 112–113 in chapter 4 to answer this second question.) Why does the phonemic restoration effect demonstrate top-down processing?

2. Several parts of this chapter focused on meaning. Describe the network theory of meaning. Then point out how we determine the meaning of an unfamiliar word, especially during reading. How is this last process similar to top-down processing?

3. A person listening to a sentence can figure out much more information than the physical stimulus registered by the receptors in the cochlea. Provide support for this statement by discussing the word-boundary issue and the surface structure-deep structure issue, as well as any other relevant topics.

4. How would the dual-encoding model explain how you are able to understand the meaning of the words you are reading in this question?

5. What are some of the processes involved in planning a sentence? Think about the sentence you produced to answer that question: How was the linearization problem relevant?

6. In order to carry on a conversation, two people must work together and be finely attuned to each other. Explain how the following factors are important in a conversation: background knowledge, collaboration to establish common ground, and politeness.

7. How can people manage to alternate in a conversation? Discuss both verbal and nonverbal aspects. Also discuss how conversations begin and end.

8. From your background on the ape-language controversy, make a list of the ways in which chimp language resembles human language and the ways in which it differs.

9. Two parts of this chapter mentioned languages other than English. Discuss the language skills of bilinguals. Then speculate about the problems that bilinguals might encounter if the Whorfian hypothesis were absolutely correct, and speakers of different languages did carve up the world differently.

10. Suppose that you know a person who always uses generic-masculine terms such as "he" and "men." What information could you tell him or her about the way people interpret these terms? Why is this issue important?

NEW TERMS

bottom-up processing	surface structure	paralanguage
top-down processing	deep structure	gestures
phoneme	dual-encoding model	emblem
phonemic restoration	linearization problem	illustrator
morpheme	slip of the tongue	Whorfian hypothesis
network model	pragmatics	linguistic determinism
constituent	nonverbal communication	generic masculine

RECOMMENDED READINGS

Clark, H. H. (1985). Language use and language users. In G. Lindzey & E. Aronson (Eds.), *Handbook of social psychology* (2nd ed., Vol. 2, pp. 179–231). New York: Random House. This chapter provides a comprehensive, readable overview of social aspects of language production and conversations.

Foss, D. J. (1988). Experimental psycholinguistics. *Annual Review of Psychology, 39,* 301–348. Foss's chapter is an upper-level review of the current research on topics such as word recognition, conversation, reading, and language production.

Hakuta, K. (1986). *Mirror of language: The debate on bilingualism.* New York: Basic. This interesting book provides a well-organized coverage of topics such as childhood bilingualism, how adults learn a second language, and bilingual education.

Knapp, M. L., & Miller, G. R. (Eds.). (1985). *Handbook of interpersonal communication.* Beverly Hills, CA: Sage. This book contains 15 chapters on various aspects of verbal and nonverbal communication, particularly focusing on the social aspects of communication.

**Development in
Infancy and
Childhood**

When my daughter Sally was 4 years old, she brought a music box to me and asked how it worked. I pried open the lid and pointed out the rotating cylinder, with its carefully spaced, protruding knobs. Then I showed her how those knobs struck the little prongs on the other side, producing a melody. She gazed intently at the various structures, prodding them with her finger. I felt a warm glow of pleasure at Sally's growing understanding of objects and the way they worked. And then she asked, "But where does the little man sit to play the piano?" To an adult, music-box melodies have a mechanical explanation. To a 4-year-old, melodies must be produced by a human, even—in the case of a music box—a very tiny human.

Encounters with young children often convince adults that a wide gulf separates their beliefs from our own, and we see evidence of this gulf throughout the chapter. However, in many areas, infants and children are remarkably competent. They have many abilities that a casual observer may not notice. In those areas, infants and adults are somewhat similar.

In this chapter and the next, we focus on human development. **Development** refers to the changes in physical, cognitive, and social abilities that occur throughout the life span.

Three important questions are often asked in connection with human development. We note them now and raise each of them again later in the chapters:

1. **The nature-nurture question**: Can development be primarily explained by nature, or genetics? Alternatively, is development primarily determined by nurture, that is, by learning and experience? For example, does little Rigoberto start to walk at about 12 months because his genes have specified that his muscles, bones, and coordination will be appropriately mature at this age (nature)? On the other hand, does he walk only after he has had enough experience and training (nurture)? The appropriate answer is that development is determined by both nature and nurture, just as the area of a rectangle is determined not simply by its width or its length, but by both in combination (Maccoby, 1990).

2. **The continuity-stages question**: Is development a gradual process, with adults simply having a greater *quantity* of some particular skill? Alternatively, do children and adults differ in the *quality* of their psychological processes? For example, children and adults differ in their mathematics skills. But do adults simply have *more* math skills (continuity), or do they have a *different kind* of math skills (stages)? Although many skills show continuity throughout development, we see evidence for stages in several areas of development.

3. **The stability-change question**: Do people maintain their personal characteristics as they mature from infants into adults (stability)? Alternatively, do infants acquire new characteristics that bear little resemblance to those they had in infancy (change)? For example, did the grumpy boy who sat next to you in second grade mature into a grumpy adult, or has he transformed himself into a smiling, friendly young man? We see in our discussion of infant temperament that there is some stability as infants mature into children. The stability is far from complete, however.

This toddler is just beginning to walk. Should we explain this behavior in terms of nature or nurture?

We consider four aspects of development as we examine infants and children: physical and perceptual development, cognitive development, gender, and personality and social development. In other words, the topics in this chapter are arranged in the same order as those in the textbook itself, beginning with more biological areas and ending with more social areas.

Physical and Perceptual Development

In just 9 months, a barely visible human egg matures into a baby ready to be born. The newborn has remarkably well-developed perceptual abilities, though his or her motor abilities are limited. Compared to a colt that manages to walk shortly after birth, a newborn has little reason to brag. Just a few years later, however, this same baby may run fast enough to escape from parents at a crowded airport and may be able to pry loose the tops from so-called childproof bottles. Let us begin at the beginning.

Prenatal Development

Conception occurs when a sperm cell from the father fertilizes an egg cell (or ovum) from the mother. The fertilized egg begins to divide rapidly and attaches itself to the wall of the uterus.

Before the second month of the **prenatal** (or prebirth) period, the developing human is called an **embryo**. At this stage, the cells continue to divide rapidly and begin to develop specialized functions. For instance, cells that are part of the primitive visual system develop about 3 weeks after conception. At 4 weeks, other cells start to develop into arms and legs. Around 6 weeks, the face starts to form. The embryo begins to look and function like a human.

The **fetal period** begins 2 months after conception and lasts until the baby is born about 7 months later. As you can see from Figure 10.1, the 4-month-old fetus already looks remarkably human, even though it weighs less than half a pound and is only about 6 inches long. Around this time, the mother begins to feel her baby's movements for the first time.

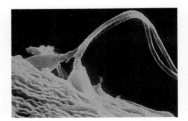

At conception, a sperm cell from the father fertilizes an egg cell from the mother.

Figure 10.1
A fetus 4 months after conception.

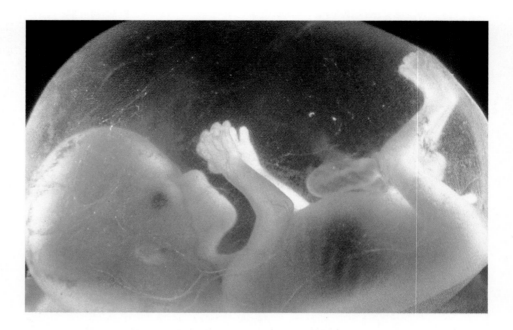

The brain, heart, lungs, and other important organs develop further during the next few months of pregnancy. If the mother gives birth prematurely, seven months after conception, these organs are sufficiently well developed, and the baby is likely to survive (Snow, 1989). During the last 2 months, the fetus's appearance changes little, though it does grow larger.

Hazards of Prenatal Development

Unfortunately, the developing embryo and fetus can be harmed by numerous substances and diseases, as shown in Table 10.1. Let us discuss in more detail two of the most common harmful substances—alcohol and tobacco.

Pregnant women who drink alcohol may not be aware that they could harm their babies significantly. Heavy drinking can produce **fetal alcohol syndrome**, as shown in Figure 10.2. These children are likely to be short, with small heads. You can also see the characteristic facial features, including widely spaced eyes, narrow eye slits, and flattened nose. They are likely to be mentally retarded, apparently from damage to the brain while in the uterus (Tomlinson-Keasey, 1985). Some studies suggest that alcohol is potentially dangerous to the fetus, even in small doses. Therefore, many experts suggest that pregnant women should not consume *any* alcohol (Haynes, 1982).

Women who smoke cigarettes when they are pregnant are likely to give birth prematurely. If they carry their babies to full term, these babies are likely to weigh less than average (Sexton & Hebel, 1984). In fact, women who smoke five or more cigarettes a day are likely to produce babies with retarded growth (Nieburg et al., 1985). As these babies grow older, they are likely to have attention problems and difficulty in reading and arithmetic (Vorhees & Mollnow, 1987).

Sadly, the developing baby can also be harmed if someone else in the house smokes, providing passive exposure to the harmful substances in cigarettes. In one study, a fetus whose father smoked at home faced about two thirds the risk of reduced birth weight as a fetus whose mother smoked (Rubin et al., 1986). Ads like the one in Figure 10.3 should also mention the hazards that other smokers in the home can create for the fetus.

Table 10.1   *Substances and Diseases Harmful to the Developing Fetus*

HARMFUL AGENT	POSSIBLE DANGER
Substances	
Alcohol	Excessive use can produce fetal alcohol syndrome, including small head, retardation, heart defects, growth defects.
Cigarettes	Heavy smoking can lead to premature birth and low-birth-weight babies, possible attention-span and school problems.
Cocaine	Use, particularly in first 3 months, may lead to premature birth and low-birth-weight babies who are less alert and responsive to stimulation.
Marijuana	Heavy use can lead to premature birth and babies with abnormal reactions to stimulation.
Caffeine	High consumption is possibly linked with premature birth and miscarriages.
Aspirin	In large quantities, can produce low-birth-weight infants and prenatal bleeding.
Tranquilizers	Regular use can produce respiratory problems in newborns.
Barbiturates	In large doses, can interfere with baby's breathing.
Diseases	
Rubella (German measles)	Before the 11th week of pregnancy, likely to cause heart defects and deafness in the baby.
Genital herpes	Can cause infant death and blindness.
Acquired Immunodeficiency Syndrome (AIDS)	Can be transmitted to the fetus; infants infected with the virus can be born with facial disorders and growth failure.

Sources: Iosub et al., 1987; Miller et al., 1982; Shaffer, 1989; Snow, 1989; Streissguth et al., 1984; Sullivan-Bolyai et al., 1983; Vorhees & Mollnow, 1987.

Figure 10.2
Fetal alcohol syndrome. This child was photographed at birth, 8 months, and $4\frac{1}{2}$ years. Note short nose, thin upper lip, and widely spaced eyes.

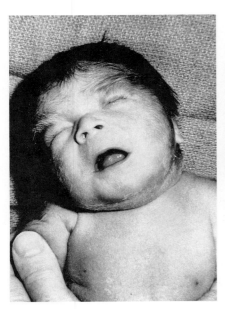
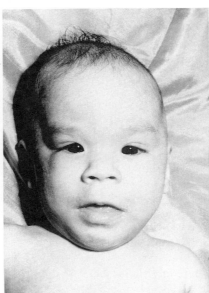
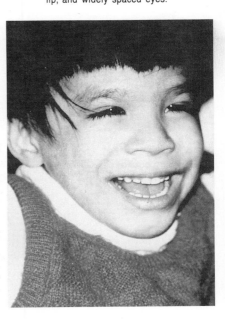

Figure 10.3
A stop smoking ad from the American Cancer Society.

Figure 10.4
Average age and variation for major motor milestones in infancy. (After Frankenburg & Dodds, 1967; Shirley, 1931)

The Neonate

Every term I show a film on childbirth to students in my human development class. At the moment the baby emerges, a student occasionally faints, and many experience tears of joy. If students in a classroom, watching a film, can experience such intense emotions, imagine what the baby's parents must feel!

The baby that emerges does not look much like the newborns in the magazine ads, however. The strenuous trip through the birth canal often leaves babies with a squashed nose and a lopsided head. They are probably red and wrinkled, and more scrawny than the advertisements show. During the **neonatal period**, or first 4 weeks after birth, the babies' features resume their normal shape, and their bodies start to fill out. A major task for the newborns is to master circulation, respiration, digestion, and temperature control. In addition, newborns develop rapidly in both motor and perceptual skills, as we see in the next two sections.

Motor Development

General Trends   Motor development usually follows certain patterns as newborns mature into children. For instance, the **cephalocaudal principle** states that parts of the body near the head (*cephalo* in Greek) develop before the parts near the feet (*caudal* literally means *tail* in Greek). Even prior to birth, the upper part of the fetus becomes active before the bottom part (Hall & Oppenheim, 1987). Newborn babies also have much better head control than leg control.

Furthermore, the **proximodistal principle** states that the parts near the center of the infant's body (*proximo* means *near* in Latin) develop before the more distant parts. For example, babies can control their arm movements earlier than the movements of their more distant wrists or fingers (Snow, 1989).

2 months Raise head to 45 degrees (1.5—4)	2.8 months Roll over (2.5—5)	4 months Sit with support (1.5—4.5)	5.5 months Sit without support (4.5—8)	5.8 months Stand holding on (5—10)

7.6 months Pull self to standing position (6—10)	9.2 months Walk holding on to furniture (7.5—13)	10 months Crawl and creep (7—12)	11.5 months Stand alone (9.5—14)	12.1 months Walk without assistance (11.5—14.5)

Motor Milestones   Figure 10.4 shows some of the important milestones or accomplishments during **infancy**, a period that extends from birth through the first year or year and a half of life. Notice that the chart shows both an average and a range, with the range indicating the 25th to 90th percentiles. It is important to realize that babies do not all leap to their feet and start walking as soon as they reach their first birthday. Instead, most take their first step between $11\frac{1}{2}$ and $14\frac{1}{2}$ months of age. Notice, too, that these figures tell you that one quarter of all babies begin walking before $11\frac{1}{2}$ months, and one tenth after $14\frac{1}{2}$ months. In infancy, as in all of human development, individual differences are strong.

It is also important to appreciate how walking expands an infant's world (Gibson, 1988). A baby too young to walk must be carried from place to place and cannot independently explore. But toddlers can expand their cognitive and social horizons. They can explore new places in the park or shopping mall, and they can wander over to people they would not otherwise meet. Most important, they can *decide* what parts of the world merit further investigation.

Fine Motor Skills   Try Demonstration 10.1 to illustrate another important area of motor development. Your large muscles allow you to sit and walk, but your fine motor skills allow you to write and draw. When you first held a crayon as a toddler, you grabbed it in your fist and moved it primarily by using the muscles in your upper arm (as specified by the proximodistal principle). Then you learned to hold it with your thumb and first two fingers, though most movement was still directed by the upper-arm muscles. Just before you entered kindergarten, you gained fine motor control and could master more precise crayon movements. At this point, too, you had acquired the fine motor skills that would allow you to print letters of the alphabet, an ability that would develop even further throughout elementary school.

Perceptual Development

When babies emerge from 9 months of gestation, they open their eyes for their first view of the world that has become so familiar to us. What do they see? Is it the disorganized "blooming, buzzing confusion," as claimed by America's first psychologist, William James (1890, p. 488)? And what do these newborns experience in the world of sound, touch, smell, and taste?

The systematic investigation of infants' perceptual abilities was virtually nonexistent 35 years ago. In recent decades, however, researchers have become increasingly more skilled at figuring out clever techniques for determining the characteristics of infant perception (Aslin, 1988). As a consequence, psychologists

Demonstration 10.1

The Development of Fine Motor Skills

Take a pen or pencil in the hand that you normally use for writing. Hold it in your fist, with the point facing down. Write your name on a piece of paper, keeping your wrist and fist rigid and using only upper-arm muscles to make movements. Experiment with letters of varying sizes. Next hold your pen or pencil with your thumb and first two fingers, again forcing your shoulder muscles to do as much of the work as possible. Once more, try letters of varying sizes. Finally, for comparison, print your name as you would normally. Notice how you obtain more motor control and produce neater printing with the motor movements used in later development.

are now much more aware of the impressive competence of infants with respect to perceptual abilities.

Vision   As recently as the 1960s, textbooks claimed that newborns were blind at birth (Aslin, 1988). The landmark work of Robert Fantz (1961) showed otherwise. He placed infants inside a special chamber and attached pairs of test objects (e.g., a patch of gray versus a patch of narrow stripes) onto the ceiling above them. Researchers monitored the amount of time the infant spent looking at each of the two objects. If little Jimmy looked significantly longer at the stripes than at the gray patch, then he must be able to tell the difference between the two stimuli. Figure 10.5 shows narrow stripes that a 1-month-old can just barely differentiate from a gray patch. Notice that Fantz designed a way to measure infants' acuity, that is, their ability to see precise details.

Babies are also more skilled in recognizing human faces than was once suspected. Between 1 and 3 months of ages, babies develop the ability to distinguish between parents and strangers (Barrera & Maurer, 1981; Bushnell, 1982). Furthermore, by 7 months of age, they can distinguish between happy and surprised facial expressions (Caron et al., 1982).

Imagine a 7-month-old baby girl crawling rapidly from the upstairs bedroom toward the stairway. She pauses on the top step, looking down on the next step. Can she perceive distance and note that the next step is farther away? Figure 10.6 shows an example of a visual cliff, an apparatus in which the infant is placed between a side that looks shallow and a side that looks deep. Gibson and Walk (1960) found that 6 to 14-month-old babies systematically crawled to the shallow side of the apparatus, avoiding the side that looked deeper and farther away. Using other techniques that involve physiological measures—rather than requiring infants to crawl—researchers discovered that infants as young as 2 months can distinguish between the deep and the shallow sides of a visual cliff (Campos et al., 1970; Hetherington & Parke, 1986). Distance perception receives an additional boost around 4 months of age, when babies begin to use binocular depth information (Aslin, 1988). In distance perception, two eyes are better than one.

Pause for a moment and consider why it is difficult to resolve the nature-nurture question with respect to the issue of distance perception. If a 2-month-old baby boy manages to distinguish between the deep and the shallow side of a visual cliff, it is possible that this ability can be traced to nature; he may have been born with this distance perception, or else his genes specified that distance perception should develop by his second month of life. But it is also possible that nurture plays an important role. By 2 months of age, he has had experience with objects moving closer and farther, so he has learned some of the visual cues that are associated with distance. We would feel more confident that distance perception could be traced to nature if it were demonstrated in a baby who was 5 minutes old, without any real experience in the visual world. However, even the most clever vision researcher has not yet discovered how babies can "tell" us

Figure 10.5
A 1-month old baby can just discriminate the stripes on the left from the gray patch on the right, when both are presented at a distance of 10 inches from the baby's eyes.

Figure 10.6
The visual cliff used by Gibson and Walk (1960) to test distance perception. Notice that the clear glass lies above a surface that appears to be shallow on one side and deep on the other.

what they know about distance perception at this tender age. And we cannot creep inside their head to discover how the world actually looks to them.

In the chapter on sensation and perception, we considered size constancy, which means that an object seems to stay the same size despite changes in the distance between the viewer and the object. Adults know that a teddy bear does not really grow larger as we approach it, but what does an infant perceive? The current belief is that newborns have some primitive form of size constancy, and it may be fairly well developed by about 4 months of age (Aslin & Smith, 1988; Day, 1987). Fortunately, then, young infants experience some stability in their visual world. Teddy bears, bottles, and grandparents do not seem to expand dramatically as infants are moved closer to them and shrink just as dramatically as the distance increases.

Hearing We have seen that young infants are reasonably precocious in their visual abilities. However, they are even more impressive in their hearing abilities, especially in the area of speech perception. For instance, infants as young as 1 month can hear the difference between sounds as similar as *bah* and *pah*. (Try saying these words out loud to appreciate how similar they are.) In fact, by 6 months of age, infants can discriminate between virtually any two phonemes (or basic sounds) used in language (Aslin & Smith, 1988; Eimas et al., 1971).

But that is not all. Six-month-old babies are able to make distinctions between sounds that older infants and adults can no longer make. For instance, babies growing up in English-speaking households can tell the difference between two different kinds of *t* sounds that are important in the Hindi language spoken in India. By the ripe old age of 10 months, however, babies in English-speaking homes can no longer tell the difference between these two sounds (Werker & Tees, 1984).

By the age of 7 months, babies appreciate that when they hear a happy voice, it should be coming from a happy-looking face. Similarly, an angry voice should come from an angry-looking face (Walker-Andrews, 1986). In summary, then, babies are fairly sophisticated in appreciating the subtle properties of speech sounds. These abilities prepare them well to be receptive to the conversations that surround them and to be ready to speak by about 1 year of age—as we see in the section on language development.

By the age of 6 weeks or earlier, the infant can distinguish between the smell of mother and the smell of a stranger.

Other Perceptual Skills   Touch is important in the world of the young infant because it provides contact with other people. Touch is also important in connection with several reflexes. For example, if you touch a baby's cheek on one side of the mouth, the baby's head turns in the direction of the touch. This reflex makes sense, because it allows babies to find a nipple that has slipped to the side of their mouth.

Infants also have a fairly well developed sense of smell. For example, they can smell the difference between mother and a stranger by 6 weeks of age or even earlier (Cernoch & Porter, 1985; Russell, 1976).

Taste buds seem to be functional at birth. Even 1-day-old babies prefer sweet liquids to unflavored water (Desor et al., 1977; Mistretta, 1981). Unfortunately for our later health, we seem to be born with a sweet tooth—even before we really have teeth. This preference for sweet tastes can clearly be traced to a nature explanation, because a 1-day-old has not lived long enough for nurture to influence preferences.

In summary, the material on perception in young humans provides important support for the theme that humans are remarkably well equipped for experiencing the world, even shortly after they are born. In appreciation of these remarkable capacities, researchers often refer to these young humans as "the amazing newborn."

Section Summary: Physical and Perceptual Development

■ Three important issues in connection with human development are the nature-nurture question, the continuity-stages question, and the stability-change question.

■ During prenatal development, the fertilized egg becomes an embryo (during which cells develop specialized functions) and then a fetus (during which further development and growth occur).

■ Potential hazards during prenatal development include harmful substances, such as alcohol, cigarettes, cocaine, marijuana, caffeine, aspirin, tranquilizers, and barbiturates, and diseases, such as rubella, herpes, and AIDS.

■ Two general trends in motor development are the cephalocaudal and proximodistal principles; also, motor milestones vary considerably.

■ Infants have some degree of visual acuity by 1 month of age, depth perception by 2 months, face recognition by 3 months, and size constancy by 4 months.

■ Infants are even more advanced in their hearing than in their vision, particularly in the area of speech perception. Touch sensitivity is evident in certain reflexes. Young infants can also smell the difference between their mother and a stranger at an early age, and they show an early preference for sweet tastes.

Cognitive Development

We have seen that young infants are quite competent with respect to perceptual skills. They can take in stimuli from the outside world and make sense of them. Their perceptual world is not a "blooming, buzzing confusion." Instead, it is reasonably orderly. What can they accomplish with these reasonably orderly perceptions? As we see in this section, they can remember, think, and use language.

Memory

Infancy   One index of memory in infancy is that young babies can remember what their mother looks like, sounds like, and smells like—before they reach the age of 3 months. Infants even show evidence of remembering some sounds from before they were born. In one study, newborns preferred a particular passage from a Dr. Seuss book that their mother read aloud each day during the last 3 months of pregnancy, rather than a similar passage that had never been read (DeCasper & Spence, 1986).

The most extensive program of research on infant memory has been conducted by Carolyn Rovee-Collier and her associates, using the conjugate reinforcement technique. In the **conjugate reinforcement technique**, a mobile is placed above an infant's crib. A ribbon connects the infant's ankle with the mobile, so that his or her kicks make the mobile move (see Figure 10.7). Young infants love this game, and they shriek with delight as their kicking activates the mobile. Memory can be tested by allowing the infant to learn the connection between kicking and mobile movement and then waiting several days before presenting the mobile once again. Will the baby remember to kick? (Note that this memory task uses operant conditioning, a kind of learning we discussed in chapter 6.) Using this technique, Rovee-Collier and her colleagues have shown that a 3-month-old typically remembers how to activate the mobile after a delay as long as 12 days (Rovee-Collier, 1987; Rovee-Collier & Hayne, 1987).

Figure 10.7
The conjugate reinforcement technique, used to test infant memory.

Rovee-Collier and her colleagues also demonstrated that infants are even more sensitive than adults to the encoding specificity principle. As you may recall from the chapter on memory, the encoding specificity principle states that recall is better if the retrieval context is like the encoding context. As an adult, you remember material better if you are tested in the same surroundings in which you originally learned the material. In one study, 3-month-old infants learned the kicking response in cribs lined with one brightly patterned fabric; they were later tested with a different fabric. Infants showed no retention of the kicking response after only a 7-day delay (Rovee-Collier et al., 1985). With infants, a moderate change in the context can lead to complete forgetting.

Childhood   In some respects, children's memories are similar to adults'. For instance, they are somewhat similar in the capacity and duration of their sensory memory, that very brief storage of sights and sounds we discussed in the memory chapter (Engle et al., 1981; Hoving et al., 1978). Their recognition memory is also reasonably accurate (Kail, 1984). If you show children a magazine ad and later ask them to scan some ads to point out the one they saw earlier, they will probably recognize the correct item.

Children have a clear disadvantage on other kinds of memory tasks, however. Consider short-term memory. The average 2-year-old can remember only two items in a row, in contrast to about seven items for 12-year-olds and adults (Dempster, 1981). Long-term memory, as tested by recall rather than recognition, is also relatively poor for young children (Cole et al., 1971; Myers & Perlmutter, 1978).

Why should young children perform so poorly on these memory tasks? One reasonable explanation is that young children have poorly developed metamemory. As discussed in the memory chapter, metamemory is your knowledge and awareness about your own memory. Specifically, young children do not seem to realize that they need to make a special effort or use special memory strategies (Gross, 1985). They think that they will be able to remember a list of items by simply looking at them, without using deep processing.

This girl thinks that she can memorize these objects by merely looking at them. Without deep processing, however, she will remember very little.

As children grow older, however, they become more accurate in predicting their own memory abilities, and they are more aware that they need to *work* to improve their memory (Wellman, 1985; Yussen & Levy, 1975). Their improving metamemory skills make them aware they need to use strategies.

Two of the strategies that children learn to use are rehearsal and organization. **Rehearsal**, or merely repeating the items to be remembered, is not particularly effective, but it is better than nothing. Flavell and his colleagues (1966) watched children's spontaneous lip movements, indicating silent rehearsal, as they learned a list of items. The 10-year-olds in the group were much more likely to use rehearsal than the younger 5- and 7-year-olds.

In the memory chapter, you learned that organization is a valuable memory strategy because it allows you to group similar items together and provide a structure for encoding and recall. In a representative study, Moely and his colleagues (1969) presented children with a series of pictures belonging to categories, perhaps including a hat and a shirt as examples of clothing, a desk and a sofa as examples of furniture, and so forth. Older children were much more likely than younger children to rearrange the pictures. However, young children who were specifically instructed to rearrange the pictures showed an improvement in their recall. Thus, these young children do not spontaneously realize that organization would be a useful strategy, though they do have the ability to organize items and to use organization as a memory aid. In summary, young children have inadequate metamemory skills, so they do not tend to use strategies. Because they do not use strategies, their memory performance suffers.

Thinking: Jean Piaget's Approach

A major force in shaping current knowledge about children's thinking is Piaget. Jean Piaget (pronounced "Zhohn Pea-ah-*zhay*") was a Swiss theoretician interested in child development who lived from 1896 to 1980.

Piaget argued that children are active learners rather than passive "sponges" waiting around to soak up stimuli from the environment. In fact, Piaget's work was probably one of the principal factors that led to the decreased popularity of the stimulus-response behaviorist approach (Gelman, 1983; Ginsburg & Koslowski, 1976).

An important central concept in Piaget's theory can be called meaning-making. **Meaning-making** refers to children's active attempts to make sense out of their world and their experiences (Kuhn, 1984). They try to construct general concepts based on these experiences. For example, children are likely to have seen many examples of a glass filled with liquid, and they construct an idea that the level of liquid in a glass forms a line that is parallel with the bottom of the glass. If you ask them to draw a line to indicate how the liquid would look in a tilted glass, they are likely to draw a line parallel with the bottom of the glass (Figure 10.8). No child has ever *seen* liquid defy the laws of gravity, arranging itself along a slanted surface. Instead, their drawings reflect their meaning-making, or their understanding of the relationship between liquids and glasses.

Piaget proposed two concepts to account for the way humans use and modify stimuli they encounter. In **assimilation**, we deal with these stimuli in terms of our current thought structures. For example, a child seeing a little pony for the first time might call it *doggie*, because *doggie* is a concept that is part of the child's current thought structure. You might find it helpful to remember that in *assimilation*, that child treats the stimulus as if it is *similar* to a familiar concept. Imagine, however, what might happen if children only used assimilation: How would their thought structures grow more complex?

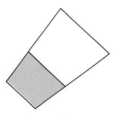

Figure 10.8
When children are shown a drawing of liquid in a glass and asked to draw a line indicating the level when the glass is tilted, they draw a line parallel with the bottom of the glass, as in the figure on the bottom.

Accommodation is the mirror image of assimilation. In **accommodation**, our thought structures change to fit the stimuli we encounter. For example, the previous concept *doggie*—formerly used to refer to medium-sized, hairy, four-legged creatures—might now be broken into two categories, *doggie* and *horsie*.

Throughout this chapter, you have used both assimilation and accommodation. For example, when you read about size constancy in the perceptual development section, you could fit some of this information into your existing concepts (assimilation). However, you also changed your concepts to include the new information that constancy can exist in infants as young as 4 months of age (accommodation).

Piaget described four major periods of human development. With respect to the continuity-stages question discussed at the beginning of this chapter, Piaget clearly voted for "stages." That is, certain periods in cognitive development appear in a fixed order. Each period is necessary for the formation of the period that follows (Piaget, 1983). Furthermore, each period differs qualitatively (in terms of *kind* of thinking) from other periods, rather than simply differing quantitatively (in terms of amount, such as number of correct items). An outline of Piaget's four periods appears in Table 10.2. Let us look at these four periods and then evaluate Piaget's theory in light of current research.

Sensorimotor Period   The term **sensorimotor period** is appropriate, because the infant's major cognitive tasks include sensory activities (such as seeing, hearing, touching, smelling, and tasting) and motor activities (such as kicking, sucking, and reaching). Babies have not yet developed language and symbols, but they can perform some actions. Piaget believes that these actions constitute the very first forms of intelligence. In the first few weeks of life, basic reflexes—such as the sucking reflex—are most important.

At the beginning of the sensorimotor period, infants do not have a sense of **object permanence**, which is the knowledge that an object exists even if it is

Table 10.2   *An Outline of Piaget's Four Periods of Cognitive Development*

PERIOD	APPROXIMATE AGE	DESCRIPTION
Sensorimotor	Birth–2 years	1. The infant interacts with the world through sensory and motor activities. 2. The infant learns that objects exist even when they are not visible.
Preoperational	2–7 years	1. The child represents objects with words and mental images. 2. The child shows egocentrism.
Concrete operational	7–11 years	1. The child demonstrates conservation. 2. The child shows more logical thinking.
Formal operational	11 years through adulthood	1. The person can reason abstractly; concrete objects no longer need to be present. 2. The person can form and test hypotheses.

Source: Ginsburg & Opper, 1988.

Figure 10.9
This infant lacks object permanence. For her, a favorite toy that is hidden beneath the blanket no longer seems to exist.

temporarily out of sight (see Figure 10.9). Toward the end of the sensorimotor period, however, babies become experts at finding a missing object, even when it is moved several times.

Preoperational Period   A critical characteristic of the **preoperational period** is the development of language. The child can now use symbols and words, instead of simple physical actions, to represent thought. Language provides an enormous advantage to children; they can now refer to objects that are not physically present.

Another critical characteristic of the preoperational child is egocentrism. When we use the word *egocentrism* in everyday speech, we imply selfishness. However, Piaget uses **egocentrism** to mean that a child sees the world from only one point of view—his or her own. Little Tanya may annoy her parents by standing directly between them and the television set. *She* can see the program perfectly well; from her point of view, there is no problem. Egocentrism diminishes gradually throughout childhood.

Concrete Operational Period   During the **concrete operational period**, children acquire important mental operations (or mental manipulations) such as conservation. Children who show **conservation** realize that a given quantity stays the same, no matter how its shape or physical arrangement may change. Figure 10.10 shows a preoperational child, who believes that a tall, thin glass contains more milk. She is so impressed by the height of the liquid in the new container that she fails to realize that the other glass is wider—or that the amounts must be equal since nothing was added or subtracted. Children in the concrete operational period acquire conservation, and they can provide these kinds of justifications for their decisions that the amounts are the same. Now try Demonstration 10.2 to test conservation in children.

Children also show more logical thinking during the concrete operational period. For instance, they no longer believe that inanimate objects are alive. One of my students asked children of different ages what their stuffed animals did at night when everyone was asleep. Preoperational Thomas, at 4 years of age, said,

Figure 10.10
A preoperational child fails to show conservation.

The child believes that two similar glasses contain the same amount of liquid.

She watches the liquid being poured from one container to the other.

She indicates that the taller, thinner glass contains more liquid.

"They play, but then go back to sleep when they get tired." Ruth, much more worldly and concrete operational at the age of 7, replied, "My dad says they get up and play, but I don't believe him. They can't do that."

Formal Operational Period   In the concrete operational period, children can reason logically and maturely on many different problems—as long as the problem is physically in front of them. However, they have trouble with more abstract reasoning. During the **formal operational period**, teenagers and adults can think scientifically and systematically. They can solve problems without the help of concrete representation. They can contemplate complex ideas and think flexibly about a variety of problems. In a typical problem, people are asked to determine which of several factors influences the speed of a swinging pendulum. Younger children construct hypotheses haphazardly and test them inadequately. People in the formal operational period, however, systematically vary factors such as the weight of the pendulum, the height from which it is dropped, and the length of the string on which the pendulum dangles. After careful observation, they correctly conclude that the length of the string is the critical factor.

Demonstration 10.2

The Development of Conservation

In this demonstration, you will be examining conservation of liquid and number. First locate one or more children between the ages of 5 and 8. To test conservation of liquid, find two short, wide glasses and one tall, thin glass, similar to the ones shown in Figure 10.10. First pour liquid into the two wide glasses so that the heights of the liquids are similar. Ask the child whether both contain the same amount of liquid or whether one contains more. If the child thinks they are unequal, ask him or her to pour a few drops from one glass to the other to make them equal. Once they appear equal, pour the liquid from one wide glass into one narrow glass, as in Figure 10.10. Now ask whether both contain the same amount of liquid or whether one contains more. Ask the child to explain his or her answer.

Next test conservation of number. Form two rows of 10 pennies each, with both rows similarly spaced (see *a*). Ask the child whether both rows contain the same number of pennies or whether one contains more. Once the child has determined that the rows contain the same number, push the pennies in the bottom row closer together (see *b*). Ask again whether the two rows have the same number or whether one row has more. Finally, ask the child to explain his or her answer.

a. Two horizontal rows, each with 10 pennies, lined up so that the two sets of edges are matching.

b. Two horizontal rows, each with 10 pennies, lined up so that the bottom row is denser.

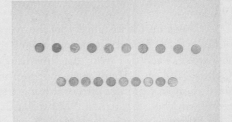

Evaluation of Piaget's Theory   Clearly, Piaget provided an extremely comprehensive and complex theory of cognitive development. No other theorist has proposed such a complete picture of children's thinking. He identified intriguing ideas, such as object permanence and conservation, that no one else had ever investigated. In addition, his theory inspired thousands of studies, which is one indication that psychologists and other researchers have judged his work to be very interesting (Case, 1987).

Nevertheless, Piaget's theory can be criticized in several respects. For example, he did not pay much attention to individual differences (Case, 1987), a theme stressed throughout this textbook.

In general, Piaget was correct about the order in which children master cognitive tasks (Flavell, 1985). Furthermore, researchers agree that children's thinking undergoes a major transformation around 6 or 7 years of age, which corresponds well with the beginning of the concrete operations stage in Piaget's theory (Fischer & Silvern, 1985). However, Piaget sometimes underestimated the cognitive abilities of infants and children. For instance, he misjudged what babies can perceive and remember. New equipment and experimental designs have been used in recent research to show us that infants are remarkably competent (Flavell, 1985). Furthermore, when researchers use simpler, more interesting experimental setups, they can demonstrate that children show conservation at an earlier age than Piaget proposed (Gelman, 1969, 1983). Conservation is more complicated than Piaget described, because it depends on the characteristics of the task.

In summary, Piaget proposed a broad, complex theory of the development of thinking. However, even Piaget underestimated the rich, complicated nature of children's thoughts. The complexity of humans makes it difficult to explain their behavior in any simple, sweeping statements. This theme clearly applies to infants and children, as well as adults.

Language Development

"Mama!" (8 months)

"Hi, Mom!" (1 year, 4 months)

"Don't cry, honey." (1 year, 5 months)

"My grandma gave me this dolly, Cara. My grandma is my mommy's mommy. I have another grandma, too. She's my daddy's mommy. And Aunt Elli is my daddy's sister." (2 years, 9 months)

These selections from the early language of my daughter are typical of the remarkable accomplishment involved in language acquisition. Within a period of 2 to 3 years, all normal children progress from one-word utterances to complex descriptions about relationships. In fact, language acquisition is the most impressive intellectual accomplishment many people ever perform (Miller & Gildea, 1987).

Consider, for instance, that the average 6-year-old has some mastery of about 14,000 words. To acquire a vocabulary this large, children must learn about nine new words each day from the time they start speaking until their sixth birthday (Gelman, 1979). Perhaps even more impressive than the size of children's vocabulary is their expertise in combining these words into phrases that have never been heard before, such as "My dolly dreamed about toys" (2 years, 2 months).

Fortunately, young children have a head start on language. As we saw in the section on speech perception, infants are impressively accomplished at making distinctions between speech sounds. Human infants seem to be biologically "programmed'' to appreciate human speech sounds, an observation consistent with the position discussed earlier (Flavell, 1985; Gibson & Spelke, 1983).

Let us now change our focus from early language perception to early language production. Later in this section we will explore the development of children's grammar, pragmatics, and theories of language acquisition.

Early Language Production   Children's early vocalizations pass through a series of stages. Infants make cooing sounds around 2 months of age. Cooing includes a variety of sounds that typically involve *oo* and are usually made with rounded lips (Carroll, 1986). At 3 to 4 months, babies begin babbling, or making sounds similar to speech. Babbling includes both vowels and consonants, and it sounds more like adult speech.

Children say their first words around the time of their first birthday. By 18 months, they may have a vocabulary of 40 words or more (Bee, 1989; Lamb & Bornstein, 1987). These first words usually refer to objects and events that are familiar and important in their everyday lives. In our culture, these initial words typically refer to family members, animals, vehicles, toys, food and drink, body parts, items of clothing, and household objects (Flavell, 1985).

These early words include many overextensions. An **overextension** is the use of a word to refer to other objects in addition to the appropriate object. Around the age of 2 years, children often show overextensions for common words such as *dog* and *ball*. For example, one child produced the name *dog* for nine species of dog and one toy dog—all appropriate labels. However, he also used *dog* to apply to a bear, a wolf, a fox, a doe, a rhinoceros, a hippopotamus, and a fish—all overextensions (Thomson & Chapman, 1977). Notice, incidentally, that the linguistic term *overextension* corresponds to the Piagetian term *assimilation*.

Grammar   One important aspect of grammar is **syntax**, or the organizational rules for determining word order, sentence organization, and relationships among words (Owens, 1988). Syntax becomes relevant as soon as young children begin combining two words in a single phrase. These two-word sentences typically begin to appear before the child's second birthday (Anisfeld, 1984). Here are some representative first phrases (Clark & Clark, 1977; de Villiers & de Villiers, 1985):

A young child may use *overextension* and call a tomato an apple.

"Push car" (action-object)

"Sit chair" (action-place)

"Daddy pants" (possessor-possessed)

"Baby sleeping" (actor-action)

Notice that these beginning phrases express a wide variety of relationships. Also, the word order in the phrases suggests an early awareness of English word order.

Another characteristic of these sentences is **telegraphic speech**, which includes nouns and verbs but leaves out the extra words such as prepositions and articles that only serve a grammatical function. (The name is derived from a telegram, in which the nonessential words are omitted.) In the examples here, the child expresses only the essential meaning, omitting the extra, less important words.

Pragmatics   As noted in the last chapter, the term *pragmatics* refers to the social aspects of language. Children need to learn what should be said—and what should not be said in certain circumstances. A student in one of my classes described the embarrassment his family felt when a younger brother shouted to an elderly gentleman on his way to the bathroom during a party, "Mommy says to make sure to aim straight so you don't get the seat wet!"

Children also learn to master the markers of courtesy, such as *please* and *may I*. Naturalistic observation in nursery schools has shown that 3- and 4-year-olds frequently use these polite terms to obtain a toy (Garvey, 1984). They also learn how to interpret subtle requests. Children discover, for instance, that a parent's comment, "My, it's noisy in here," is not simply an observation about the ambient decibel level (Flavell, 1985).

Children must also master another pragmatic skill, the art of taking turns in a conversation. Sophisticated turn taking requires each speaker to anticipate when the other person will complete his or her remark, a skill that demands an impressive knowledge of language structure. Two-year-olds have conversational gaps that average about 1.5 seconds, in contrast to gaps of about 0.8 second in adults (McTear, 1985).

We saw that Piaget believed young children have difficulty in taking another person's point of view. However, research on children's language shows that preschoolers are reasonably skilled in adapting their language to their listeners' level of understanding. For example, Shatz and Gelman (1973) found that 4-year-olds modified their speech substantially when the listener was a 2-year-old rather than a peer or an adult. Specifically, the 4-year-olds described a toy to their 2-year-old listeners using short, simple utterances. For instance, one child described a toy dumping station to a younger child:

> I gave you it. You want to have something funny? Put the marbles in here. Put the marbles in here. I'll give you the marbles. Now pour them in here. Go up here. And pour them in here.

To her mother, however, she used less repetition and longer, more complex sentences:

> You put it in here . . . And then push it all the way in, and then you get marbles out here. You'll need gas. It only has enough gas to go to the gas station. It backed in here. That's good. (p. 9)

Children learn language so they can accomplish social goals that are important to them (Rice, 1989). As Marilyn Shatz commented in an interview:

> Children are very impatient to be members of the family, genuine members. They learn very early that speech is the way to realize and maintain contact with other family members and, at the same time, to be taken seriously. A 2-year-old already has the goal of being a person in the family instead of a baby, of being someone to interact linguistically with instead of an object of discussion. (Roşu & Natanson, 1987, p. 5)

This enthusiasm about learning language encourages children to master the words, grammar, and pragmatics of speech.

Theories of Language Acquisition Let us now turn to three important explanations that have been proposed for language acquisition: the learning view, the inborn view, and the cognitive view.

1. *Language is acquired by learning.* According to the behaviorist view, language acquisition can be explained by principles of learning such as the ones you read about in chapter 6. Young children learn to associate certain objects with the sounds of words. They imitate the words and the grammar they hear around them. They receive reinforcement for correct language in the form of smiles, hugs, and the food or other objects they request (Skinner, 1957). Just as a pigeon in an operant conditioning task learns to peck a button to receive a pellet of food, a young child learns to say "cookie" to receive a cookie.

Learning theory sounds logical, and it is clear that learning is important in language acquisition. However, it is equally clear that learning cannot solve all the mysteries. For instance, imitation cannot explain how children manage to produce grammatical forms and novel sentences they have never heard before. What child has heard his parent say, "I holded two mices"? I assure you my daughter never heard her parents say, "My dolly dreamed about toys." Furthermore, operant conditioning theory would suggest that children learn grammar by being rewarded for proper grammatical constructions and punished, in the form of a correction, for improper constructions. However, researchers have noted that

In speaking to his younger brother, this preschooler would use simpler vocabulary and shorter sentences than when speaking with an adult.

parents are eager to correct children for factual errors, but not grammatical errors. Thus, a parent corrects a child for calling a tomato an apple. However, "I holded two mices" elicits no reaction (Brown et al., 1968).

2. *Language is inborn.* According to the inborn view, language development is genetically programmed. In the words of Noam Chomsky, the major supporter of this view,

> Language learning is not really something that the child does; it is something that happens to the child placed in an appropriate environment, much as the child's body grows and matures in a predetermined way when provided with appropriate nutrition and environmental stimulation. (Chomsky, 1988, p. 134)

Some evidence for this view comes from the fact that language tends to appear at roughly the same age in a wide variety of cultures, and the same kinds of meanings are encoded in children's early words and sentences (Rice, 1989; Slobin, 1985). If similar trends occur in widely different learning environments, then humans must be born with a language-making capacity. Naturally, however, this language-making capacity must be combined with learning the rules and specific vocabulary of the language in which the child is reared.

3. *Language depends upon cognition.* According to the cognitive view, language expresses children's current understanding of the world. For instance, we saw in Piaget's theory that children's first thoughts are expressed via sensory and motor activities, in terms of objects and actions on these objects. Similarly, children's first speech concerns these same objects and actions. Furthermore, toddlers begin to say "all gone" about the same time they can solve more complicated object-permanence tasks. Now that they appreciate what "all gone" means, they begin to talk about it (Rice, 1989).

The cognitive view also emphasizes that children are active language learners (Flavell, 1985; Moskowitz, 1978). They continually analyze what they hear, testing hypotheses and trying to fit together the pieces of the language jigsaw puzzle. The child is not simply a pigeon, pressing a button and awaiting a reward, as the learning view suggests. The child is not just a flower, unfolding according to a preordained genetic plan, as the inborn theory suggests. Instead, the child is a junior scientist, actively working to discover the explanations underlying language.

We have stressed repeatedly that language is complicated. You will not be surprised, then, to read that the answer to the language-acquisition question also must be complicated. Children manage to master language because of learning principles, an inborn ability, and an active, problem-solving approach.

Furthermore, the adults who raise children tend to make language acquisition somewhat simpler by adjusting their language when speaking with children. The

Demonstration 10.3

Speaking Motherese

Locate a doll that resembles an infant as closely as possible in features and size. Select a friend who has had experience with children, and ask him or her to imagine that the doll is a niece or nephew who has just arrived for a first visit. Encourage your friend to interact with the baby as he or she normally would. Observe your friend's language for qualities such as pitch, variation in pitch, vocabulary, sentence length, repetition, and intonation. Also observe nonverbal communication. What qualities are different from the language used with adults?

Source of idea: Dr. Ganie DeHart, SUNY Geneseo.

term chosen for this special language intended for children is "motherese"—an unfortunate example of the generic feminine that ignores the fact that fathers also adjust their speech to children. **Motherese** language style has a simple vocabulary, well-formed sentences, many repetitions, a focus on the here and now, and a slow rate of speech (Rice, 1989). Demonstration 10.3 illustrates motherese.

In summary, children acquire language because they are remarkably well equipped. In addition, they can use learning principles to supplement their inborn abilities, and they are active in their pursuit of language. Adults also help to make language acquisition more manageable by adjusting their communication style to accommodate children's linguistic skills.

Section Summary: Cognitive Development

- The conjugate reinforcement technique has been used to show that 3-month-olds can remember an activity up to 12 days and that infants have encoding specificity.
- Children do not differ substantially from adults in their sensory memory or their recognition memory, but their short-term memory and long-term recall memory are clearly inferior.
- Children have poorly developed metamemories, so they do not realize they must use memory strategies to remember something; consequently, their memory performance suffers.
- Piaget's theory stresses that children actively try to make meaning out of their world. He proposed four periods in cognitive development: sensorimotor (when infants gradually acquire object permanence); preoperational (when children develop language but show egocentrism); concrete operational (when they demonstrate conservation and more logical thinking); and formal operational (when they can reason abstractly and test hypotheses).
- Although Piaget's theory has been widely admired, it has been criticized for inattention to individual differences and underestimation of cognitive abilities in some areas.
- Early language development includes cooing and babbling; the first words include many overextensions.
- Children's first phrases express a wide variety of relationships, and they are telegraphic; language acquisition also requires mastery of pragmatic rules, such as polite terms, turn taking, and taking the listener's knowledge into account.
- An explanation of language acquisition needs to be complex, involving learning mechanisms, inborn language ability, a relationship between language and cognition, and parents' adjusting language to their children.

Gender-Role Development

Adults believe that gender is tremendously important. As evidence, consider these two examples:

1. Think about the most likely question to follow the announcement that a baby has been born: "Is it a boy or a girl?" One pair of researchers asked the parents of newborns to telephone friends and relatives to announce their baby's birth (Intons-Peterson & Reddel, 1984). In 80 percent of the cases, the first question concerned the baby's sex. People eventually asked questions about the health of the mother or the baby, but only after they had established whether the baby was female or male.

2. People respond differently to infants, depending upon whether they are perceived to be boys or girls. In one study, college students played with a young infant who was introduced as either Johnny or Jenny (Sidorowicz & Lunney, 1980). In reality, the baby in each condition was a boy on some occasions and a girl on other occasions. Just out of the infant's reach lay some toys, including a miniature football (stereotypically masculine) and a doll (stereotypically feminine). "Johnny" was handed the football about three times more often than the doll. "Jenny" was handed the doll about five times more often than the football.

In another study on responses to infants, people watched a series of videotapes of an infant, who was labeled female half of the time and male half of the time (Condry & Condry, 1976). At one point, the baby cried when a jack-in-the-box opened suddenly. When people thought they were watching a baby girl, they judged that the emotional reaction represented fear. When they thought they were watching a baby boy, they judged that the emotional reaction represented a much more active, less helpless emotion: anger. In reality, however, everyone saw exactly the same video. The labels "female" and "male" had biased people's reactions.

In the previous chapters, we have seen that young children possess impressive talents in perception, memory, thinking, and language. Based on these observations, we might expect children to be knowledgeable at an early age about **gender roles**, which are sets of expectations about appropriate activities for females and males (Katz & Boswell, 1986). Let us first discuss in depth what children believe about gender roles. Then we consider explanations for gender-role development.

○ ○

In Depth: Children's Beliefs About Gender Roles

We have seen that adults hold different beliefs about male and female infants. Do young children share adults' beliefs about the characteristics, occupations, and behaviors of males and females?

Characteristics   Gloria Cowan and Charles Hoffman (1986) studied boys and girls who were either in the $2\frac{1}{2}$- to 3-year-old range or in the $3\frac{1}{2}$- to 4-year-old range. They used the cross-sectional approach, as described in chapter 2, so that these children represented different groups of children who were tested at the same time. (An alternative approach would have been to use the longitudinal approach, following those same $2\frac{1}{2}$- to 3-year-old children 1 year later when they were $3\frac{1}{2}$ to 4 years old.) The children represented a variety of racial, religious, and socioeconomic backgrounds.

The children were shown two pictures of infants. One was actually a baby girl and one a baby boy. (However, in a pretest, different children who were the same age could not guess the infants' sexes accurately.) For example, the infants in Figure 10.11 might be introduced, "This baby is a boy named Tommy [pointing to the baby on the left], and this baby is a girl named Susie [pointing to the baby on the right]." Next the experimenters checked to make certain the children recalled which was the girl and which was the boy. Then the children were asked, "One of these babies is big, and one is little; point to the baby which is big." (The experimenters were careful to reverse the photos on half the trials and also to vary the order of the adjectives.) They also asked children to make decisions about seven other adjective pairs, such as mad-scared, strong-weak, and soft-hard.

The results showed that the children chose a stereotyped response 64% of the time. That is, they tended to say that the boy baby was big, mad, strong, and hard, whereas the girl baby was small, scared, weak, and soft. The results were statistically significant, indicating that even preschoolers have stereotypes about

Figure 10.11
Photos of two infants, similar to those used in Cowan and Hoffman's (1986) study.

gender. However, boys and girls were equally stereotyped. Furthermore, age did not influence the degree of stereotyping.

In a second study, Cowan and Hoffman presented line drawings of a boy and a girl, who were also introduced by name. In this study, 5-year-olds showed stereotyping 77% of the time. By the age of 5, then, children are quite well informed about the characteristics that boys and girls are supposed to have.

Occupations   Children also have strong beliefs about occupations. Mary Trepanier and Jane Romatowski (1985) examined stories written by young boys and girls who ranged in age from 6 to 12. The children were free to choose their own topics and plots for this project. One interesting analysis involved the occupational roles assigned to the female and male characters in the stories. Both boys and girls were more likely to mention an occupation for a male character. About 25% of the male characters had a job mentioned, in comparison to less than 9% of the female characters. These stories therefore reflected a stereotype that work is more important or noteworthy for men than for women. The authors also analyzed the occupations listed by the children. Male characters could be policemen, presidents, detectives, robbers, doctors, and managers. The female characters were generally described as housekeepers, salespeople, and teachers, traditionally feminine occupations.

Behaviors   If children have strong beliefs about appropriate behaviors for males and females, then they would be likely to object when people act inappropriately. In one study, preschool and kindergarten children were asked a number of questions, such as whether it was OK for a boy to wear nail polish to nursery school and whether it was OK for a girl to have a crew cut (Smetana, 1986). The children usually responded that these violations were "bad," and they tended to think that it was more serious for boys to act feminine than for girls to act masculine. These views seem to reflect the attitudes of adults, who also consider it to be more serious when males violate gender stereotypes (Matlin, 1987).

As you might have expected, there are individual differences in children's gender stereotypes. Sometimes, racial or ethnic groups differ in the extent to which they show gender stereotyping. For instance, White children often give more stereotyped responses than Black children. However, Hispanic children do not seem to differ substantially from Anglo children (Bardwell et al., 1986).

Changing Stereotypes   Can we change gender stereotypes, so that children are more flexible in their judgments about what females and males can do? Sometimes it is helpful to expose children to people who perform nonstereotypical roles.

Children can learn to be less stereotyped when they are exposed to people who perform nonstereotypical roles.

For instance, children whose school principals were female tended to be less stereotypical (Paradise & Wall, 1986). Furthermore, children who had read non-stereotypical stories tended to be more flexible. For instance, when schoolchildren read about a boy who took care of a baby, or a girl who parachuted in an emergency situation, they later responded that a variety of activities could be performed by both boys and girls, rather than just boys or just girls (Scott, 1986).

Remember, however, that children—like adults—are complex. In some cases, children may resent a teacher's efforts to change the stereotypes. Unfortunately, some educational programs can backfire. In one case, for instance, ninth grade boys became *more* sexist following a 6-week program on gender stereotypes (Guttentag & Bray, 1977). We will see that many forces contribute to the development of children's stereotypes. To change stereotypes, each of these forces must be modified, and the efforts must continue for years rather than weeks. A complex problem demands a complex solution.

○ ○

Theories of Gender Development

Children believe that males and females differ significantly. Furthermore, a small number of gender differences—such as play patterns—emerge during childhood. Psychologists currently favor three leading theories about the development of gender: social-learning theory, cognitive-developmental theory, and gender-schema theory.

Social-Learning Theory   According to **social-learning theory**, two major mechanisms explain how girls learn to act "feminine" and boys learn to act "masculine": (1) they receive rewards and punishments for their own behavior, and (2) they watch and imitate the behavior of others (Jacklin, 1989; Mischel, 1966). As you can see, this theory resembles the theory that children acquire language by learning.

Social-learning theory sounds plausible. Little Bobby wins smiles for playing with the fire truck, but his parents look horrified when he emerges from the bedroom wearing his sister's ballet costume. Furthermore, the models provided by television show dominant men, solving problems and giving orders, and submissive women, concerned primarily with family and romantic relationships (Gunter, 1986).

However, social-learning explanations cannot be completely responsible for gender typing. For instance, parents have been found to treat their own sons and daughters fairly similarly (Jacklin, 1989). If this is the case, how can we explain the occasional gender differences? Furthermore, children do not consistently prefer to imitate models who are the same sex as they are (Matlin, 1987; Raskin & Israel, 1981). We need to look for additional explanations to supplement the social-learning approach.

Cognitive-Developmental Theory   According to **cognitive-developmental theory**, children's own thought processes are primarily responsible for the development of gender typing. Inspired by the work of Piaget, Lawrence Kohlberg argued that children learn about gender roles in the same way that they learn about other concepts, such as conservation and morality (Kohlberg, 1966; Kohlberg & Ullian, 1974). Like Piaget, Kohlberg emphasized that children actively work to make meaning out of concepts related to gender.

By age 3, children identify themselves as male or female. About a year later, children can accurately classify other people as female or male. However, many 4-year-olds fail to appreciate **gender constancy**, which is the concept that a person's gender stays the same in spite of changes in outward physical appearance. We saw earlier that young children think that the quantity of milk changes when poured from a short, fat glass to a tall, thin glass. Similarly, they believe that a man can become a woman by wearing a dress or carrying a purse, and that a woman can transform herself into a man by cutting her hair very short. In both cases, children are misled by external appearances.

Once children have acquired gender concepts, they begin to show systematic preferences. A child who realizes she is a girl, for example, prefers feminine objects and activities. She may pat only "girl dogs," ignoring the "boy dogs." Research supports this concept of systematic preferences (e.g., Matlin, 1987; Thompson, 1975).

However, cognitive-developmental theory predicts that a boy must know he is a boy before he begins to prefer trucks to dolls, yet little Bobby may prefer his fire truck to Raggedy Ann before he can say whether he is a boy or a girl. The stages do not consistently unfold in the order Kohlberg specified (Jacklin, 1989). Furthermore, the theory does not explain why children target gender as the critical factor in classifying people, objects, and activities. Why not eye color or size?

Gender-Schema Theory **Gender-schema theory** proposes that children use gender as an important schema to structure and guide their view of the world. As the memory chapter noted, a schema is a generalized idea that organizes one's perceptions and thoughts. In our culture, gender is extremely important; as we saw earlier, the first question to new parents usually concerns gender. We also interpret a baby's crying differently, depending upon whether we think the baby is a boy or a girl. According to gender-schema theory, children develop gender schemas, and they learn that the world should be divided into two important categories— male or female (Bem, 1981, 1985; Liben & Signorella, 1987).

Gender-schema theory combines social-learning theory and cognitive-developmental theory. It specifies that gender typing is a learned phenomenon. As children grow up, they learn society's definition of what it means to be female or male. Gender-schema theory also stresses, however, that children's own thought processes encourage gender development. Thus, little Jenny heads for the kitchen center in nursery school because she has been rewarded for domestic activities and because she has seen more women than men in the kitchen. However, she also prefers the baking set because she realizes that she is a girl, and girls should prefer kitchen activities.

At present, gender-schema theory is the dominant explanation for how children acquire gender-related thoughts and behaviors (Jacklin, 1989). A prime advantage of gender-schema theory is its acknowledgment that complex explanations are required to account for the complexity of the way we think about gender and the way in which our actions are influenced by gender. Table 10.3 summarizes the three theories of gender typing examined in this section.

Table 10.3   *The Three Major Theories of Gender Development*

Social-Learning Theory
  Rewards and punishments ⎫
                          ⎬ → Gender-typed behavior
  Observation and imitation ⎭

Cognitive-Developmental Theory
  Child identifies self as female or male → Child prefers same-gender objects/activities → Gender-typed behavior

Gender-Schema Theory
  Culture emphasizes gender → Gender schema → Gender-typed behavior

Gender-schema theory suggests that this little boy learns how to act masculine because he has learned society's definition of masculinity and because his own thoughts encourage the development of gender-stereotyped behavior.

Section Summary: Gender-Role Development

■ Adults stress the importance of gender in their questions to parents of newborns and in their responses to infants.

■ Even young children believe that males and females have different characteristics, and they believe it is inappropriate to act like a member of the other gender.

■ The three leading theories about gender typing include social-learning theory, cognitive-developmental theory, and gender-schema theory.

Personality and Social Development

The general organization of this textbook begins with the biological aspects of behavior and then moves on to cognitive areas; the last part of the book focuses on individual differences and social relationships. Similarly, this chapter began by considering biological aspects of human development, such as motor and perceptual development. Then it moved on to cognitive areas: memory, thinking, and language. The third topic, gender, involved both cognitive development and social relationships. In this last section of the chapter, we consider personality and social development, foreshadowing the chapters in the last part of the book.

An important concept in this section is **socialization**, or the acquisition of motives, values, knowledge, and behavior needed to function adequately in adult society (Maccoby, 1984). In general, psychologists who study personality development and socialization tend to focus on individual differences, or the variation between individuals who are the *same* age. A typical study might examine the personality characteristics of 4-year-olds whose parents have different styles of child rearing. In contrast, psychologists who study cognitive development tend to focus on the performance of children who are *different* ages, as well as explanations for any differences. For instance, a study on children's memory might examine how long-term memory improves between the ages of 5 and 9, and how the increased use of memory strategies can explain this memory improvement. Thus, the research on personality and social development has a different flavor from the research on cognitive development.

It is also important to emphasize how personality and social development depends closely upon all of the processes we have discussed in this chapter. We began by discussing motor development; consider how children who have the ability to walk can increase their social interactions. Toddlers can rush in to see who has arrived at the front door, and they can wander in search of social excitement at the airport, the grocery store, and the playground. When infants perfect their perceptual skills, they can recognize how the important people in their lives look, sound, and smell. Clearly, these perceptual skills are necessary in forming social bonds with parents and siblings.

The development of memory allows children to recall past social events, to form schemas about social situations, and to predict how people will act toward them in the future. As children's thinking matures, their egocentrism declines. If they can take another person's point of view, they are less likely to act selfishly (Maccoby, 1984). As stressed earlier, language development enables children to become true members of a family group, able to share their own ideas and desires.

The development of gender roles also has important implications for personality and social behavior. Children's thoughts about whether they are male or female influence their social behavior. Perhaps more important, children develop gender schemas so that they begin to expect different behavior from the males and females in their lives. They acquire stereotypes, believing that men *should* be more aggressive, strong, and independent.

This section begins by considering infant temperament—the origins of individual differences. We also discuss self-concept, another important component of personality. Our examination of children's social interactions includes relationships with parents, the day-care dilemma, the development of positive social skills, and minority-group children. Our final topic provides an overview of the status of children in contemporary society.

Infant Temperament

The term **temperament** refers to a person's characteristic mood and activity level. Even in infancy, humans differ enormously from one another. For instance, a student in my human development class babysits for two 9-month-olds. One baby smiles continuously, babbles joyfully, and welcomes cuddling. The other baby cries continuously, and his tiny body grows rigid with rage when he is held.

Our knowledge about infant temperament advanced substantially when three researchers—Stella Chess, Alexandar Thomas, and Herbert Birch—launched the New York Longitudinal Study in 1956. These three physicians noticed tremendous variation among the young children they saw in their medical practice. In the 1950s, any deviant behavior—such as continuous crying—was typically blamed on the family, especially the mother (Chess & Thomas, 1986). Some people favored Freudian theory, and others preferred behaviorist learning theory. Both of these approaches emphasized, however, the importance of early *experience*, and who could be more influential in these early experiences than the mother? In contrast to these nurture approaches to infant temperament, Chess, Thomas, and Birch emphasized nature. They stressed that individual differences in temperament are largely inborn and are well established around 10 weeks of age (Thomas & Chess, 1977).

To gather their data, Thomas, Chess, and Birch (1968) conducted extensive interviews with mothers of infants between 2 and 3 months of age. Each infant was rated on nine dimensions of temperament, such as mood, activity level, and attention span. Infants were placed into categories on the basis of these ratings. "Easy" babies were positive in their mood, adaptable to new situations, and regular in their sleep and eating schedules. About 40% of the babies (fortunately!) could be classified as easy. "Difficult" babies, on the other hand, were negative in their mood, intense in their reactions, and not very adaptable. About 10% of the sample was categorized as difficult. "Slow-to-warm-up" babies were more reserved and not very intense in their reaction. (I once went to a carnival with a slow-to-warm-up child whose mother said, "Look how much she enjoys the Ferris wheel!" The child was wearing a barely perceptible smile—for her, a relatively intense reaction.) About 15% of the sample was categorized as slow to warm up. The remaining 35% of the sample did not clearly fit into a single category.

At the beginning of the chapter, we discussed important questions that often arise in developmental psychology. Two of those are relevant to infant temperament. With respect to the nature-nurture question, most of the authorities on infant temperament emphasize the biological underpinnings of temperament (Goldsmith et al., 1987; Kagan, 1989). Characteristics that seem to be inherited include shyness, emotionality, activity level, and attention span (Snow, 1989). However, we cannot neglect nurture completely, because experience does contribute to temperament. For instance, infants develop best when there is goodness-of-fit. When **goodness-of-fit** occurs, the infant's personality matches the opportunities, expectations, and demands of important people in his or her life (Goldsmith et al., 1987). In contrast, if a difficult baby is born to parents who expect their infant to be a cooing, smiling angel, poorness-of-fit occurs.

With respect to the stability-change question, a panel of experts concluded that temperament shows somewhat more stability than most other aspects of behavior (Goldsmith et al., 1987). In the New York Longitudinal Study, for example, Thomas and his co-authors found that 70% of the difficult infants developed behavior problems, in contrast to only 18% of the easy infants (Thomas & Chess, 1986; Thomas, Chess, & Birch, 1968). Other researchers also have found relatively high correlations between infant temperament and adult temperament (Plomin & DeFries, 1985). However, studies typically demonstrate that some people show impressive continuity, whereas others show dramatic changes in their temperament (Thomas & Chess, 1985). In other words, there are individual

This baby's positive mood and other adaptable characteristics allow her to be classified as an easy baby.

differences in the extent to which people retain their individual differences in temperament.

Self-Concept

The **self-concept** is a schema of thoughts and feelings about oneself as an individual. The self-concept begins to develop in infancy. As we see in the next chapter, self-concepts become much more elaborate during adulthood as people contemplate their abilities, priorities, and life goals.

Newborns do not have a sense of self, because they are not aware that they are separate from other people and objects (Snow, 1989). Infants between the ages of 2 to 6 months begin to sense that they are physically separated from mother or other caretakers and that they have different experiences from these other people (Stern, 1985).

An important component of self-concept is self-recognition, which is the ability to recognize your own image (Fogel, 1984). In one study, Lewis and Brooks (1978) unobtrusively placed a spot of rouge on babies' faces, so that they were unaware they had been marked. Then the babies were allowed to look in the mirror. Infants between the ages of 9 and 12 months simply looked in the mirror but showed no distinctive reactions. One quarter of babies in the 15- to 18-month age range and three quarters of babies in the 21- to 24-month age range stared in the mirror and touched the rouge spot on their own face. As if they said, "Hey, that's me!" they acknowledged that the babies with the silly red spots were indeed themselves (Figure 10.12).

The theory of Erik Erikson (1950, 1968) includes one of the most comprehensive accounts of the development of self-concept. Erikson's theory proposed eight stages of development throughout the life cycle. We consider four stages in this chapter and four in the adult development chapter; in that chapter we discuss identity development in more detail.

Erikson suggested that the individual confronts a specific task or dilemma during each of the eight stages. Healthy development is more likely if the individual resolves the tasks successfully. As Table 10.4 shows, the first four stages of development require infants and children to develop trust in others, a sense of independence, ability to plan activities, and a feeling of competence. According to Erikson, these early experiences are critical in determining later development and a positive sense of self.

Figure 10.12
This little girl shows self-recognition; she is touching the spot on her face that corresponds to the red spot on the mirror.

Table 10.4   *Erikson's Theory of Psychosocial Development (Birth Through Childhood)*

STAGE	AGE	PSYCHOSOCIAL TASK	DESCRIPTION OF TASK
1	0–1	Trust versus mistrust	The infant whose needs are met by caretakers develops a sense of trust in others.
2	1–3	Autonomy versus doubt	The toddler tries to learn independence and self-confidence.
3	3–6	Initiative versus guilt	The young child learns to initiate his or her own activities.
4	6–12	Competence versus inferiority	The child tries to develop skill in physical, cognitive, and social areas.

Source: Erikson, 1950, 1968.
Note: A complete list of Erikson's eight psychosocial stages appears in Table 11.2.

Relationships With Parents

Children's first social relationships involve their parents. Let us look at the early attachments that infants develop for their parents. Then we examine how parenting style influences development during childhood.

Early Attachment   **Attachment** is the close emotional bond of affection between an infant and his or her caregivers. At birth, infants are equipped with behaviors that encourage the caregiver to come close. A baby's cry might seem unpleasant, but it usually *does* draw parents nearer. Mary Ainsworth, the major attachment theorist, argues that attachment evolved through natural selection because it yielded a survival advantage. Specifically, attachment increased the chances that an infant would be protected by caregivers (Ainsworth, 1989).

At birth, infants simply cry, with no attempt to direct their cries to any particular person. Several months later, however, they have the perceptual and cognitive abilities to discriminate between people. They may cry or whine when a parent leaves the room (**separation anxiety**). In addition, they may raise their arms toward a parent, but not a stranger (Bretherton, 1985). A few months later, babies begin to crawl, so they can become more active and effective in staying close to the people to whom they feel attachment (Ainsworth, 1989). Attachment becomes even firmer when infants develop object permanence and are aware that mother and father still exist, even when they are not in the same room.

The nature of attachment changes after infancy. Children become less ego-centric, so they begin to understand that their parents can have different motivations and plans that do not necessarily match the child's motivations and plans. They also develop the language skills that allow them to discuss future plans in a more sophisticated fashion. Finally, the ability to walk enables children to wander away from the security of the people to whom they are attached. They can connect with a wider variety of people, including playmates and strangers (Ainsworth, 1989).

As you might expect, some babies have a more positive attachment experience than others. According to the major classification system, babies who show **secure attachment** tend to use the caregiver as a secure base. A baby may wander away from the caregiver for a while to explore the surroundings, usually glancing back from time to time, and returning frequently. In contrast, babies who show **insecure attachment** tend to avoid their caregivers or feel ambivalence toward them. They may also show extreme fear of strangers and become upset when mother leaves the room (Ainsworth, 1979, 1989).

What causes these individual differences in attachment? Characteristics of the parents themselves are often crucial. For instance, securely attached infants in one study were likely to have mothers who were more sensitive to their baby's needs and feelings. These mothers were also more likely to express affection toward them (Smith & Pederson, 1987).

There is also a relationship between attachment patterns and a child's later adjustment. For instance, infants who are securely attached to their caregivers tend to be happier and less frustrated when they are 2 years old, in contrast to insecurely attached infants (Matas et al., 1978; Santrock & Yussen, 1989).

We have seen that sensitive, responsive parents can produce securely attached infants. Furthermore, securely attached infants are likely to be happier, less frustrated toddlers. Let us look at how another dimension of parenting style influences a child's development.

Parenting Styles   Diana Baumrind (1971) proposed that the most effective parents are affectionate, but they provide control when necessary. These **authoritative**

parents respect each child's individuality, they are loving, and they allow children to express their own points of view. However, they have clear-cut standards, which they uphold in a consistent fashion. Baumrind's research in 103 preschool children, raised according to three different parenting styles, demonstrated that these children tended to be self-reliant, competent, content, and socially responsible.

In contrast, **authoritarian parents** demand unquestioning obedience from their children. They punish children forcefully when children do not meet their standards, and they are less likely to be affectionate. Children from authoritarian families tend to be unhappy, distrustful, and ineffective in social interactions. The terms *authoritative* and *authoritarian* sound similar. However, in *authoritative* homes, the parents are firm but caring sources of authority or expertise. The word *authoritarian* is typically associated with a dictatorial person who demands unquestioning obedience.

Finally, **permissive parents** make few demands on their children, allowing them to make their own decisions. Some permissive parents simply do not care what their children do. Other permissive parents are involved in their children's lives but believe that children should be allowed freedom and choice. In one extreme case, a 14-year-old son moved his parents out of their large bedroom suite and claimed it for himself, along with an expensive stereo system and television! You will not be surprised to hear that he has never learned to live according to established rules, and he has few friends (Santrock & Yussen, 1989). In Baumrind's research, the children from permissive families were immature; they had little self-control, and they explored less than children from authoritarian and authoritative families.

In later research, Baumrind (1975) used the longitudinal method to track the nursery school children into adolescence. In general, children from authoritative families still tended to be most socially competent and mature. Children are most likely to thrive when their parents are warm and affectionate, yet expect socially appropriate behavior from their offspring. We have been focusing on parents; what happens when children are cared for during the day by someone other than parents?

The Day-Care Dilemma

In 1988, about two thirds of all women with children under 18 years of age were working outside the home. Furthermore, 51% of mothers with infants returned to employment before the baby's first birthday (National Commission on Working Women, 1989). Statistics like these raise a vitally important question: What is the influence of day care on children?

Unfortunately, this question cannot be answered easily. In fact, the day-care dilemma highlights the theme that humans are extremely complex. Let us assume that hundreds of well-controlled studies had been conducted on this topic (though, regrettably this has *not* yet been done). If we could assemble all these studies, we would probably discover that the influence of day care on children depends upon a wide variety of such variables as the age of the child, the quality of the day-care center, the economic background of the child, and the number of hours each week that the child attends day care. In other words, each of these independent variables—and more—could influence the child's outcome.

Furthermore, the answer to the day-care dilemma would probably depend upon how we chose to measure the dependent variable. It seems likely that day care might have one kind of influence on the child's cognitive development, and a different kind of influence on the child's attachment to parents. Other dependent variables that could be examined would include interactions with peers, emotional maturity, and gender-role beliefs.

In other words, we are not likely to conclude either that "day care is good" or that "day care is bad" for all children in all conditions and all measures of their adjustment. The true picture is undoubtedly very complex. Rather than hundreds of well-controlled studies, we have several dozen, typically with sample sizes of fewer than 100 children. Try to imagine the most complex painting you know, and imagine that several dozen people were each viewing that painting by holding a narrow tube up to one eye, peering out at one small fragment of the painting. Similarly, we can see fragmented insights about day care, but we cannot see the entire picture. Let us now consider some of the findings, concentrating on cognitive development, social relationships, and attachment in infancy.

In general, children who have been in day care are likely to be somewhat advanced in intellectual development, compared with children cared for at home. Specifically, researchers have found that children in day care between the ages of $1\frac{1}{2}$ and 5 receive higher scores on intelligence tests (Clarke-Stewart, 1989; Clarke-Stewart & Fein, 1983). However, home-care children typically catch up once they enter preschool or kindergarten. We can conclude that day care certainly does not harm the cognitive development of young children; it may even be helpful.

The picture is less clear when we consider social development. Children who have participated in day care tend to be more socially skilled. According to some researchers, they show more cooperative behavior and confidence in social inter-actions, and they are more skilled at taking another person's point of view (Howes & Olenick, 1986; Phillips et al., 1987). However, day-care children are somewhat more aggressive and resistant to adult requests (Haskins, 1985; Phillips et al., 1987). The answer to these contradictions may be that day-care children are more likely to think for themselves and want their own way—not that they are maladjusted (Clarke-Stewart, 1989).

The most controversial issue, however, concerns infants' emotional rela-tionships with their mothers. Does day care influence the development of early attachment—that close emotional bond we discussed earlier in this section? Several studies have suggested that there is a small effect. For instance, Clarke-Stewart (1989) reviewed 17 studies that compared home-care and day-care infants with respect to their attachment to their mother. In all, 29% of infants with nonem-

The quality of care is a critical factor in the day-care dilemma. Development is optimal when children can interact often with nurturant adults.

ployed or part-time-work mothers were classified as insecurely attached. In contrast, 36% of infants with full-time-work mothers were classified as insecurely attached. In summary, this analysis revealed a difference of 7% between the two conditions, a difference that was statistically significant.

However, does this 7% difference have any *practical* significance? Should parents contemplate how they arrange their schedules so that their infant is cared for at home by either mother or father rather than in a day-care center? Even Jay Belsky, one of the researchers whose work has revealed more attachment problems in day-care children, suggests that the day-care dilemma is complex (Belsky & Rovine, 1988).

Parents who are considering day-care arrangements clearly should consider the quality of the facility. A crowded room with few toys and an inadequate number of teachers does not promote adequate child care. In contrast, "Children appear to profit from a verbally stimulating environment in which adult caregivers and children are frequently engaged in conversation" (Phillips et al., 1987, p. 542). In the 1990s, people concerned about children need to work together to develop high-quality day-care centers where the caregivers are warm and nurturing and where children can develop cognitively, socially, and emotionally.

Prosocial Behavior

A student in my human development class described her 3-year-old nephew's concern for other family members. When his 6-month-old sister cries, he pats her back until she falls asleep. On several occasions when his mother was sleeping, he climbed into his sister's crib to play with her, so that her crying would not wake their mother. This young boy's compassion for his baby sister and his mother conflicts with Piaget's theory that children are egocentric. It seems that even young children can sometimes view the world from the perspective of another person and realize that a sister needs comforting and a mother needs sleep. Indeed, even preschoolers are capable of understanding others' feelings and being helpful (Eisenberg, 1986).

Prosocial behavior is action that benefits another person. Prosocial behavior can include comforting, cooperation, generosity, sympathizing, and rescuing (Barton, 1986; Zahn-Waxler et al., 1986). How does prosocial behavior develop during childhood? What factors are related—and unrelated—to this positive form of social interaction? Finally, how can prosocial behavior be encouraged?

The Development of Prosocial Behavior Even very young children often show evidence of prosocial behavior. For example, 1-year-olds in a laboratory setting frequently showed concern when an adult pretended to cry (Weston & Main, 1980). When 2-year-olds were observed in their own homes, researchers found that they often shared with adults. These young toddlers also acted nurturantly toward younger siblings, animals, and dolls (Rheingold & Emery, 1986). Two-year-olds also bring objects to someone who seems to be suffering, and they actively try to help (Radke-Yarrow et al., 1983). These efforts to help may reveal some degree of egocentrism, however. If Jimmy sees that Janey is crying, he may run to bring *his* mother, even though Janey's mother is closer.

We might imagine that helping and sharing would increase during early and middle childhood. Surprisingly, however, consistent increases in sharing and helping have *not* been found between the ages of 3 and 9 (Marcus, 1986; Zahn-Waxler et al., 1986). During this developmental period, cognitive skills increase rapidly. The findings on the *lack* of increase in prosocial skills suggests an intriguing question: Do American parents and schoolteachers place too little emphasis on sharing and helping?

Factors Related to Prosocial Behavior   Some cultures value prosocial behavior, whereas others do not. The Hopi Indians of Arizona urge their children to be concerned about everyone's rights and feelings; helpfulness and cooperation are stressed. The Ik, who live in the mountains of Uganda, had a well-established social structure until political changes and technology deprived them of their hunting grounds. Their normal way of life changed so that lying, stealing, and deceit were normal. Parents were no longer compassionate toward their children, and children were not encouraged to be caring and kind (Mussen & Eisenberg-Berg, 1977). The values of one's culture are clearly related to prosocial behavior.

Within a particular culture, however, some families are more likely than others to encourage prosocial behavior. In general, nurturant, prosocial parents are likely to encourage these same qualities in their children. For instance, people who were active in the civil rights movement in the 1950s and 1960s were likely to have parents who had vigorously worked for social causes in previous decades (Mussen & Eisenberg-Berg, 1977).

Biologically based temperamental factors also may influence prosocial behavior (Eisenberg, 1987). Earlier in this section, we discussed how certain temperamental characteristics are relatively stable throughout childhood. Similarly, there are individual differences in responding to another person's distress. One child may respond with intense emotion, whereas another looks away and shows no apparent concern. These styles of responding tend to remain stable into the early school years (Cummings et al., 1986).

According to the stereotype, young girls should be more prosocial than young boys. However, researchers have found little evidence for differences in children's willingness to help other people (Maccoby, 1986; Pelletier-Stiefel et al., 1986). This finding is consistent with the general conclusion that gender differences in actual behavior are typically smaller than our stereotypes suggest (Matlin, 1987).

Encouraging Prosocial Behavior   We have seen that children do not typically grow increasingly prosocial throughout the school years. Assuming that we want children to become caring, helpful individuals, how can we encourage prosocial behavior? An interesting article by Barton (1986) suggests that it is not an easy job. For instance, it is not helpful simply to *instruct* children to share. Children also learn little from simple modeling, the process of imitation we discussed in the learning chapter. Positive reinforcement for prosocial behavior is somewhat more helpful, but it produces an immediate increase in prosocial behavior rather than a long-lasting effect.

Barton concludes that no single method can be particularly effective. Instead, the answer involves combining a variety of techniques. For instance, if Ms. Hernandez wants to increase prosocial behavior in her classroom, she might begin by

---

Demonstration 10.4

Observing Prosocial Behavior

Save this demonstration for the next time you eat at a fast-food restaurant or other setting with many children. Try to note any examples of prosocial behavior in these children, such as helping, comforting, complimenting, and sharing. Also note examples of antisocial behavior, such as aggression, neg- ative comments, and selfishness. How do the two numbers compare? If you find a particularly prosocial or antisocial family group, can you identify any characteristics of the parents that might contribute to the children's behavior?

talking about helpfulness, and later she should model prosocial behavior. On other occasions, she should prompt prosocial behavior, suggesting how children can help their classmates and encouraging them to practice these positive behaviors. Children should be systematically praised for being prosocial.

Prosocial behavior is sufficiently complex that we cannot expect a simple answer to the question, "How can we encourage prosocial behavior?" Long-lasting effects that generalize to a variety of new situations require parents and teachers to be creative. On many different occasions and in many different ways, adults need to act prosocially themselves and encourage children to attend to the needs of others.

Now that you are more familiar with the dimensions of prosocial behavior, try Demonstration 10.4.

Minority-Group Children

The theme of individual difference has been repeated throughout this textbook. When we consider children in different minority groups, it becomes even more clear that children's life experiences can differ widely. Table 10.5 shows the number of Americans in several major ethnic and racial groups.

The largest minority group in the United States is African American, or Black. Blacks account for about 13% of our country's population.

It is difficult to try to characterize Black children. We should not exaggerate the differences between Black and White children, or ignore the variation within each group. However, some evidence shows that Black families place more emphasis than White families on emotions and feelings. They also stress social connectedness, or responsibilities to a family or group, rather than the "rugged individualism" associated with White families. Black families also value high levels of stimulation, preferring action that is lively and energetic (Boykin, 1986; Boykin & Toms, 1985).

Many White Americans assume that prejudice against Blacks ended decades ago and that Black workers may even have an advantage in the job market. However, Blacks still earn lower wages than Whites, even when education and occupation are equivalent. In fact, the average Black college graduate earns less than the average White male high school dropout (Hess et al., 1988). As a consequence of their parents' lower incomes, Black children are more likely to be economically disadvantaged. One half of minority children are raised in poverty, in contrast to one quarter of all U.S. children (Horowitz & O'Brien, 1989).

Table 10.5   *Number of Americans in Major Ethnic/Racial Groups (Estimated)*

ETHNIC/RACIAL GROUP	NUMBER OF PEOPLE
White (non-Hispanic)	190,000,000
Black	31,000,000
Hispanic	21,000,000
Asian	4,000,000
American Indian	1,000,000

Sources: Bureau of the Census, 1984a, 1984b; Garcia & Montgomery, 1990, Spencer, 1989.

Children seem to be aware of such racial cues as skin color, hair texture, and facial features before they reach the age of 3. Minority-group children apparently acquire this knowledge before White children do (Milner, 1983). In one study, kindergartners who were just entering a racially integrated school already preferred children of their own race (Finkelstein & Haskins, 1983). Because racial attitudes are formed before children attend school, members of various racial and ethnic groups tend to stay together without interacting much with classmates from other groups. Even at a school with both Blacks and Whites, children may not have many opportunities for interracial interactions (Shaffer, 1989). White children who are prejudiced before entering school may not have the chance to learn that they can be friends with Black children. As children continue through the kindergarten year, they show even stronger preferences for same-race friends, and the trend becomes stronger still during grade school (Finkelstein & Haskins, 1983; Hartup, 1983).

Hispanic Americans are currently the second largest minority group, and they are expected to be our largest minority by the year 2000 (Vasquez & Barón, 1988). *Hispanic* refers to all people of Spanish descent. They share language, values, and customs. However, a Mexican-American child growing up in a farming region in central California may have very different experiences from a Puerto Rican child growing up in Manhattan.

Chicanos, or Mexican Americans, place high value on the family as the central focus. They emphasize affiliation and the need for warm, supportive relationships (Vasquez & Barón, 1988). Some studies of children's social development reveal that Chicano children show more cooperative behavior at a younger age than Anglo children (Martinez & Mendoza, 1984.)

Asian Americans have often been labeled the "model minority" because of their high education and income levels. For example, adult Asian Americans are twice as likely as White Americans to have graduated from college (Tsai & Uemura, 1988).

Like Hispanics, Asian Americans come from many different countries. Asian Americans include, in order of population, Chinese, Filipinos, Japanese, Vietnamese, Koreans, Asian Indians, and 22 other Asian groups.

Many cultural values of Asian Americans resemble those of middle-class White Americans. For example, both groups emphasize education and achievement for their children. However, Asian Americans typically place more emphasis on family and interpersonal harmony, whereas White Americans stress individuality and independence (Tsai & Uemura, 1988).

Television tends to stereotype people from minority groups, so children receive an inaccurate and unfavorable view. For example, Blacks are underrepresented on many TV shows. In 82% of children's programs, White and minority children never appear together (Barcus, 1983; Liebert & Sprafkin, 1988).

Treatment of Blacks on television has improved somewhat in recent years, but the treatment of other minorities has not changed substantially. For instance, Hispanic Americans fill less than 2% of the roles, although they constitute about 10% of the population. Furthermore, almost all Hispanic TV characters are men; Hispanic women scarcely exist on television. Finally, non-Black minorities are typically portrayed either as villains or as victims of violence (Gerbner et al., 1986; Liebert & Sprafkin, 1988).

When we think about children, we must consider their diversity. They represent a wide variety of racial and ethnic groups whose cultural values and aspirations may differ substantially. Try to visualize a children's Saturday morning TV show that could capture this diversity and portray these children playing with each other and providing viewers with models of prosocial behavior.

The Status of Children in Today's Society

Most of us want to believe that children receive top priority in the United States. However, in an international survey of child health, 21 countries ranked better than the United States in infant mortality rates (Wegman, 1989). Countries such as Spain, France, and Belgium reported fewer infants dying before the age of 1 year. As an index of our concern for school-age children, 19 countries ranked better than the United States in teacher-to-student ratio. However, the United States ranked first in military expenditures (Children's Defense Fund, 1988). Children's welfare does not seem to be our major concern.

Let us consider some of the threats that American children face as we approach the 21st century. Some of these threats were unheard of when you were an infant. For example, 2,525 pediatric cases of acquired immunodeficiency syndrome (AIDS) had been reported by August, 1990 (Moll, 1991). Other infants will die or face serious problems because their mothers used cocaine or other narcotics during pregnancy, an issue we discussed at the beginning of this chapter. The problem of drug use in pregnancy has certainly increased in the last part of this century. Still other children are victims of child abuse and neglect. In 1986, for instance, child protection agencies in the United States reported nearly 2.2 million cases of abuse or neglect. This number represents a 223% increase from 1976 (American Association for Protecting Children, 1987). (Note, incidentally, that this increase can be partly traced to increased availability of agencies and increased incidence of reporting, and not simply to higher rates of child abuse.)

In the section on minority children, we noted that one quarter of all children and one half of minority children are raised in poverty. Let us consider some of the consequences of poverty for children's welfare. One quarter of pregnant women in America receive no prenatal care (Children's Defense Fund, 1988). Only half of children living in families below the poverty level receive Medicaid coverage for medical care (Wise & Meyers, 1988). Thus, many children lack medical care both before and after birth. Furthermore, numerous children are homeless. Families with children now comprise about 28% of homeless people (Alperstein & Arnstein, 1988).

Children in this New York neighborhood represent a variety of ethnic and racial groups.

Figure 10.13
An example of a "hurried child."

Recent estimates show that between 40% and 50% of all children can expect to spend at least 5 years in a single-parent home. Divorce is a potentially traumatic experience that can disrupt virtually all aspects of children's lives. Many children adjust successfully to their new life circumstances, but a substantial number suffer long-term negative effects (Horowitz & O'Brien, 1989; Weitzman & Adair, 1988).

In addition, children's sense of well-being is threatened by violence. Reports of crime and murder crowd the newspaper headlines, and we discussed the high incidence of television violence in chapter 6. Sadly, even young children are aware of the potential for worldwide destruction in the form of nuclear war (Gould et al., 1986; Greenwald & Zeitlin, 1987). Researchers have discovered that elementary school students know more about nuclear war than adults expect. For instance, a first grader was asked "What does nuclear war bring to mind?" She replied:

> The terriblest bomb in the whole world . . . could kill half the state. Some people would have burns but not be dead . . . more wars . . . houses wrecked . . . people would lose food and money . . . refrigerators would go down . . . plants and trees die . . . no food. (Greenwald & Zeitlin, 1987, p. 66)

Others who are concerned about children's well-being point out that we are hurrying young people through childhood. They lament that some regions are urging universal preschool education. Rushed into full-time school settings, 4-year-olds are deprived of playtime, which is valuable for children's overall development (Zigler, 1987). One pediatrician complains that the middle- and upper-class parents in her Manhattan practice enroll their children in a $1,000 cram course to prepare for entrance exams . . . for kindergarten (Rubinstein, 1986). David Elkind (1981), a psychologist well known for his work in Piagetian research, entitled his book *The Hurried Child: Growing Up too Fast too Soon.* Elkind points out Piaget's warning that children should not be pushed, but should be allowed to develop at their own pace. Many American parents, however, want to rush their children through each stage of cognitive development as rapidly as possible.

Americans buy designer jeans for their toddlers, equip them with miniature brief-cases, and supply them with grown-up makeup and hairstyles (Figure 10.13). Elkind urges us not to hurry our children, but to allow them instead their right to be children.

In this chapter, we have seen that young children are miraculous human beings, capable of impressive perceptual, cognitive, and social skills. Yet these miraculous beings face obstacles in the form of disease, deprivation, threat, and premature pushing. Frances Horowitz and Marion O'Brien (1989) conclude a special issue on children in *American Psychologist* with a memorable caution:

> Children are ever the future of a society. Every child who does not function at a level commensurate with his or her possibilities, every child who is destined to make fewer contributions to society than society needs, and every child who does not take his or her place as a productive adult diminishes the power of that society's future. (p. 445)

Section Summary: Personality and Social Development

- Socialization is heavily influenced by the development of motor skills, cognitive skills, and gender roles.
- Temperament shows some stability through infancy and childhood.
- Erik Erikson's theory traces the development of self-concept through stages that emphasize trust, independence, planning, and competence.
- Securely attached infants are likely to have sensitive, affectionate mothers; they tend to become relatively happy toddlers.
- Authoritative parents are more likely than authoritarian or permissive parents to have competent, content, and socially responsible children.
- It is not yet clear exactly what effects day care has on children; it may be helpful for cognitive development, it has some positive and negative effects on social development, and it may be slightly more likely than home care to produce insecure attachment.
- Prosocial behavior can be seen even in 1-year-olds, though it does not seem to increase substantially between the ages of 3 and 9.
- Race is related to the values that families emphasize; television often misrepresents minority individuals.
- Children do not receive top priority in contemporary society; some of the problems they face include AIDS, drug-related disorders, poverty, divorce, violence, and being pushed to grow up too fast.

REVIEW QUESTIONS

1. The introduction to this chapter presented three important issues in developmental psychology: the nature-nurture, continuity-stages, and stability-change questions. Discuss each issue and point out how one or more of these questions is important for each of the following topics: (a) early perceptual skills, (b) cognitive (Piagetian) development, and (c) infant temperament.

2. Briefly trace the course of prenatal development, and then describe the neonate. Suppose you have a pregnant friend; what kinds of precautions would you suggest during her pregnancy?

3. Suppose that your friend has now delivered a healthy baby. What kinds of abilities could you describe that she might expect during the early weeks of life? Mention perceptual skills, memory, cognitive (Piagetian) development, and language.

4. How would a 12-year-old and a 5-year-old differ with respect to sensory memory, short-term memory, and long-term memory (both recall and recognition)? Why could metamemory and memory strategies partially explain some of these differences?

5. The term *egocentrism* was described in the section on the Piagetian approach to cognition. How is egocentrism important in children's thinking? To what extent are children egocentric with respect to the pragmatics of language and their prosocial skills?

6. What are the three major theories of language acquisition and the three major theories of gender typing? Do you see any similarities between the two sets of theories?

7. Part of the definition of socialization emphasized the acquisition of knowledge needed to function in society. Discuss some of the knowledge that young children acquire about gender.

8. We discussed parents at several points throughout this chapter. How are parents relevant in language development, attachment, parenting style, and the current problems children face?

9. What is prosocial behavior, and how does it develop throughout childhood? If you were a third grade teacher, what are some of the ways in which you could encourage prosocial behavior in the children you teach?

10. Imagine that you have been named the director of a newly created national organization, which has been assigned the task of addressing the needs of children in the 1990s. If the funds were generous, what kinds of programs would you initiate to help children and provide support services for them?

NEW TERMS

development	object permanence	self-concept
nature-nurture question	preoperational period	attachment
continuity-stages question	egocentrism	separation anxiety
stability-change question	concrete operational period	secure attachment
prenatal period	conservation	insecure attachment
embryo	formal operational period	authoritative parents
fetal period	overextension	authoritarian parents
fetal alcohol syndrome	syntax	permissive parents
neonatal period	telegraphic speech	prosocial behavior
cephalocaudal principle	motherese	
proximodistal principle	gender roles	
infancy	social-learning theory	
conjugate reinforcement technique	cognitive-developmental theory	
rehearsal	gender constancy	
meaning-making	gender-schema theory	
assimilation	socialization	
accommodation	temperament	
sensorimotor period	goodness-of-fit	

RECOMMENDED READINGS

Ginsburg, H. P., & Opper, S. (1988). *Piaget's theory of intellectual development* (3rd ed.). Englewood Cliffs, NJ: Prentice Hall. This book provides a clear, comprehensive overview of the complex theory of this influential psychologist.

Horowitz, F. D., & O'Brien, M. (Eds.). (1989). Children and their development: Knowledge base, research agenda, and social policy application [Special issue]. *American Psychologist, 44*(2). This special issue contains review articles on a variety of social and cognitive topics as well as articles on the impact of societal problems on children.

Intons-Peterson, M. J. (1988). *Children's concepts of gender*. Norwood, NJ: Ablex. It is difficult to summarize the wealth of information on the development of gender; this book is currently the best available resource.

Owens, R. E., Jr. (1988). *Language development: An introduction* (2nd ed.). Columbus, OH: Merrill. Owens's textbook offers a readable and thorough introduction to language development, including topics such as neurolinguistics, pragmatics, and children's bilingualism.

Snow, C. W. (1989). *Infant development*. Englewood Cliffs, NJ: Prentice Hall. Snow's book might make an appropriate gift for a new parent, because it contains practical information on such topics as health, safety, and nutrition as well as coverage of motor, cognitive, and social development.

**Development from
Adolescence
through Old Age**

During the week that I began to write this chapter, six teenagers attacked a jogger in Central Park. They beat her with a metal pipe, raped her, and left her in a coma. Why would adolescents hurt a complete stranger? Also that week—in another part of New York City—a group of Brooklyn teenagers gathered medical and school supplies to send to their sister city, Bluefields, Nicaragua. The city had been devastated by a hurricane that left only a few buildings standing, and these teenagers were eager to help in the reconstruction process. Why would adolescents help complete strangers? And how could two groups of adolescents—so similar in many respects—respond so differently to other humans?

A 70-year-old woman, once energetic and independent, tells her son that she has nothing to look forward to. She wants to die. A 66-year-old woman who runs an interracial community center says in the film *Acting Our Age*, "I don't think I'll retire from seeking justice and equality as long as I live and I can get one foot in front of another and can raise my voice." Why do these two women differ so conspicuously from each other?

We see that the theme of individual differences underlies most of the topics in this second chapter on human development. As in the previous chapter, we discuss physical and perceptual development, cognitive development, gender, and personality and social development. Our age range includes adolescence (the period between about 12 and the late teens), adulthood (from about 20 to 65), and old age (from about 65 onward).

Physical and Perceptual Development

Physical Changes during Adolescence

Puberty is the period of development in which a young person becomes physically capable of sexual reproduction (Nielsen, 1987). Puberty officially begins when the hypothalamus (Figure 3.14) signals the pituitary gland to begin releasing special hormones. In turn, these hormones cause the adolescent female's ovaries to boost their production of estrogen by 500%. The elevated estrogen levels are responsible for breast development, broadening of the hips, and the beginning of menstruation. Similarly, the hormones from the pituitary cause the adolescent male's testes to boost their production of androgen by about 2000%. The elevated androgen levels are responsible for muscle development, increased body hair, and changes in the vocal cords.

We must stress the tremendous individual differences in the timing of puberty. For instance, breast development in females begins anywhere between 8 and 13 years of age (Brooks-Gunn, 1988).

Menarche and Menstruation   **Menarche** (pronounced "*men*-ar-kee") is the first menstrual period. The average age of menarche in the United States is now about 13, with a typical range between 11 and 14 (Golub, 1983; Warren, 1983).

Children vary impressively in the age at which they reach puberty, as illustrated in this group of elementary-school children.

In the United States today, almost all young women learn something about menstruation from their mothers. Older sisters and other young women, as well as school programs, provide additional information. Fathers are seldom mentioned, however (Brooks-Gunn, 1989). Apparently, menstruation is a taboo conversational topic for fathers and daughters.

Typical symptoms accompanying menstruation include cramps, backache, and swelling (due to water retention). Young women who have just reached menarche are more likely than their mothers to report these symptoms (Stoltzman, 1986; Woods, 1986).

Interestingly, young women who have traditional views about women's roles in society are more likely than nontraditional young women to believe that menstruation is debilitating (Woods, 1986). It should be stressed, however, that researchers have actually found that cognitive skills do not change throughout the menstrual cycle (Asso, 1983; Sommer, 1983). In other words, a teenager should not panic if her period arrives the day before her SATs.

The popular press constructed what Chrisler and Levy (1989) call a "menstrual monster" with propaganda about the premenstrual syndrome. The **premenstrual syndrome**, also called **PMS**, refers to a variety of symptoms that may occur a few days before menstruation; these symptoms may include headaches, swelling, and a variety of psychological reactions such as depression and irritability. However, researchers have discovered that the media's picture was exaggerated. Some women may indeed experience PMS symptoms, but not everyone does. Furthermore, women's moods are more strongly influenced by days of the week than by their menstrual cycle (Englander-Golden et al., 1986; McFarlane et al., 1988). That is, a woman's mood depends more on whether it is Monday or Friday than whether she is premenstrual or postmenstrual.

Puberty in Males   We know relatively little about boys' reactions to body changes in puberty. Researchers have found, however, that pubertal boys rarely receive information from adults or peers about ejaculation (release of semen), and they seldom discuss its occurrence (Brooks-Gunn, 1988; Gaddis & Brooks-Gunn, 1985). Girls receive much more information from their mothers about menstruation.

A book entitled *Changing Bodies, Changing Lives* records two boys' impressions about puberty:

> When I was 14 I went around for about two weeks with this dirty smudge on my upper lip. I kept trying to wash it off, but it wouldn't wash. Then I really looked at it and saw it was a mustache. So I shaved! For the first time.

> All of a sudden I realized my voice was low. On the telephone people started thinking I was my father, not my mother. (Bell, 1980)

Compared with the dramatic body changes in adolescence, the physical changes in adulthood are relatively undramatic. However, these changes can influence self-image.

Physical Changes in Adulthood

As adults grow older, their skin develops wrinkles, and height may decrease. Older adults may still "feel" young, however. They may be confused about their identity when seeing wrinkles and graying hair in the mirror or when others refer to them as that "old lady" or "old man" (Whitbourne, 1985).

Female hormone levels begin decreasing around age 30, and the average woman experiences menopause by age 50. **Menopause** occurs when menstrual periods have stopped for at least a year (Kaufert, 1986). Contrary to many myths, most women do not regret the loss of fertility that accompanies menopause (Datan et al., 1987). Furthermore, menopause itself does not change a woman's perception of her physical health (McKinlay et al., 1987a). Finally, let us dispel that major menopause myth: Researchers have repeatedly demonstrated that menopause is *not* linked with depression (Archer, 1982; Buie, 1988; McKinlay et al., 1987b; Perlmutter & Bart, 1982). Middle age is a stressful time for many women, but factors other than menopause are more important in determining their psychological well-being.

Men may also experience a change during middle age. The **male climacteric** (pronounced "klie-*mack*-terr-ick") includes decreased fertility and decreased frequency of orgasm (Whitbourne, 1986a). About 1 in 20 middle-aged men report symptoms such as fatigue, depression, and general physical complaints (Henker, 1981). However, no relationship exists between male hormone levels and mood. With both women and men, stressful factors—and not hormones—account for mood changes.

Another physical change in adulthood is more important than menopause or the male climacteric: A consistent finding is that older adults have slower reaction times (Whitbourne, 1986a). It seems likely that these slower reaction times can be traced to brain changes that make the central nervous system less able to process many incoming stimuli. Sadly, slower reaction time is one of the causes of the high rate of traffic accidents in elderly people. According to statistics, accident rates are relatively low for drivers between the ages of 45 and 74. However, drivers age 75 and over have an accident rate that is higher than all other groups except 16- to 24-year-olds (Carney, 1989).

Life Expectancy

Figure 11.1 shows the life expectancy for four groups of Americans. As you can see, a White female is about 1.5 times as likely as a Black male to reach the age of 65. The racial difference may be at least partially explained by differences in income, and therefore differences in nutrition and health care. Unfortunately,

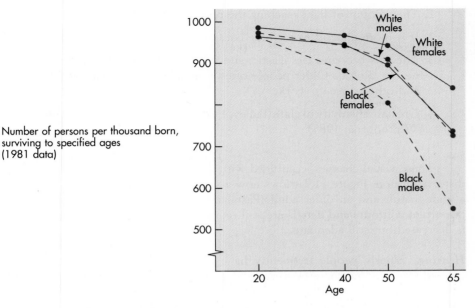

Figure 11.1
The number of persons per thousand born who will survive to each specified age. (Bee, 1987; U.S. Bureau of the Census, 1984)

Mexican Americans and Native Americans have even shorter life expectancies than Blacks (Bee, 1987).

Notice, too, that females are much more likely than males to live to 65, and this gender difference holds true for both Blacks and Whites. Several factors may account for women's longevity (Lewis, 1985):

1. Women are exposed to fewer hazards at work.

2. Women drink less alcohol and smoke less. (However, if trends in smoking continue, women will be *more* likely to die of lung cancer than men, several decades from now.)

3. Women may be more knowledgeable about health care and more likely to visit a doctor.

Perceptual Changes

Before examining perceptual changes during aging, let us discuss a potential methodological problem in studies using elderly people. Suppose that we test a group of college students whose average age is 19 and a group of residents of a nursing home whose average age is 78. Let us suppose that we find that the college students score much higher on a test of speech perception. It would be difficult to attribute the difference in their scores totally to age, because the two groups also differ with respect to several confounding variables.

As we discussed in chapter 2, confounding variables are factors—other than the factor being studied—that are present to different extents in the two groups. For instance, the confounding variables in this example could include health, amount of education, and medications. In unbiased research, the elderly population should be healthy, well educated, and not taking medicines that could alter perception.

Vision   The most significant change in the structure of the eye during aging is the thickening of the lens (shown in Figure 4.3). There are four important consequences of a thickened lens:

1. The amount of light reaching the retina decreases.

2. It is more difficult to see blue colors.

3. The lens becomes less elastic, and it becomes more difficult to see nearby objects. Older people often need special glasses for reading and other close-up work.

4. Greater sensitivity to glare (Bailey, 1986; Koretz & Handelman, 1988; Whitbourne, 1985).

These visual changes, combined with decreased acuity in old age, produce distorted vision. Figure 11.2 shows how a scene at a grocery store might look to a young adult and an older adult (Pastalan, 1982). Notice, however, that most important contours and details are still retained. For most elderly people, vision is decreased but still adequate.

Hearing   Elderly people frequently have increased difficulty in hearing high-pitched tones. Somewhere between 10% and 35% of people over the age of 65 have difficulty perceiving speech sounds, particularly the sounds *z*, *s*, and *ch* (Whitbourne, 1985). Elderly people are likely to hear even less if they try to listen to a lecture in a room that echoes. Telephone conversations are difficult when the connection is faulty. When speaking with an elderly person with a hearing loss, lower the pitch of your voice and eliminate distracting background noises.

The Other Senses   Psychologists are not certain how touch, smell, and taste change as we grow older. One problem is that elderly people vary even more than young adults in their sensitivities (Whitbourne, 1986a). We do know that many elderly people are less sensitive to cold, a problem that can be threatening in cold climates. However, no clear-cut differences exist for pain perception (Corso, 1981; Whitbourne, 1985).

Elderly people are typically less sensitive to odors, though some studies do not show age changes (Stevens & Cain, 1987; Whitbourne, 1985). As a consequence, many elderly people would be less likely than younger people to detect gas leaks and smoke from fires. Many elderly people complain that food is less flavorful, which can present a problem if they avoid nutritious food because it seems bland.

The number of taste buds also decreases as we age. Taste sensitivities sometimes—but not always—decrease during the aging process (Moore et al., 1982; Whitbourne, 1985). Thus, your elderly uncle may oversalt his mashed potatoes.

Although many perceptual processes can change as we grow older, it is crucial to remember the theme of individual differences. You may know elderly people whose perceptual world has changed very little since they were teenagers.

Figure 11.2
Scene at a store, as it would look to a young adult (left) and an older adult (right).

Section Summary: Physical and Perceptual Development

- During puberty, breasts develop in girls and menstruation begins; muscles and body hair develop in boys and their voice changes.
- During menopause, menstrual periods stop for women; male fertility also decreases for middle-aged men. However, mood changes in middle age are not linked to hormonal changes.
- Reaction times are slower for elderly people, contributing to an increased accident rate.
- Whites tend to live longer than Blacks, Mexican Americans, and Native Americans; women tend to live longer than men.
- Visual changes during aging include difficulty seeing nearby objects, sensitivity to glare, and reduced acuity.
- Some—but not all—elderly people experience reduced ability to perceive speech sounds, and decreased sensitivities to cold, odor, and taste.

Because sensitivity to odors and to taste tends to decrease with age, this dinner may not be as flavorful to older people as it is to younger people.

Cognitive Development

Irene Hulicka (1982) shares an illustrative story about the way people judge cognitive errors made by elderly people. A 78-year-old woman served a meal to her guests, and the meal was excellent except that she had used Clorox instead of vinegar in the salad dressing. Her concerned relatives attributed the error to an impaired memory and general intellectual decline, and they discussed placing her in a nursing home. As it turned out, someone else had placed the Clorox in the cupboard where the vinegar was kept. Understandably, she had reached for the wrong bottle, which was similar in size, shape, and color to the vinegar bottle.

Some time later, the same group of people were guests in another home. A young woman in search of hair spray reached into a bathroom cabinet and found a can of the right size and shape. She proceeded to drench her hair with Lysol. In this case, however, no one suggested that the younger woman be institutionalized; they merely teased her about her absentmindedness. Thus, a cognitive error can be interpreted differently, depending upon the age of the person who made the error.

In this section on cognitive development we first consider memory changes during aging. Then we discuss thinking from a Piagetian perspective, as well as performance on other cognitive tasks. Our final topic is moral development.

Memory Changes during Aging

As we grow older, performance on some memory tasks declines, whereas performance on other memory tasks remains stable. For instance, researchers have found little developmental change in the duration of sensory memory (Birren et al., 1983; Kline & Schieber, 1981). In other words, if a teenager and her grandmother are listening to the radio, the speaker's words should persist equally long in their echoic memory. In general, short-term memory is also roughly equivalent for young and elderly adults (Bayles et al., 1987; Rebok, 1987). For example, the teenager and her grandmother should be equally accurate in recalling a phone number mentioned on the radio several seconds after it was announced.

With respect to long-term memory, however, the situation is too complex to draw overall conclusions (Erber, 1982). In general, elderly people perform relatively well when they are tested in terms of recognition, rather than recall (Craik et al., 1987). In other words, a 70-year-old might be just as likely as a 20-

year-old to recognize a name as being familiar, but the 70-year-old would probably be less likely to answer correctly a recall question such as "What was the name of the detective in the movie we saw last week?"

Elderly people perform relatively well on the kind of long-term memory tasks that measure knowledge about world events (e.g., "What was the previous name of Muhammad Ali?") and about their own lives (e.g., "Did you vote in the 1988 presidential election?"). In general, elderly people remember important information (Lachman & Lachman, 1980; Rodgers & Herzog, 1987). For instance, Figure 11.3 shows how elderly people, whose average age was 67, performed just about the same as younger people, whose average age was 40, on questions that tested how well people recalled important information about the day's activities (Sinnott, 1986). However, elderly people do show memory deficits when asked to recall less important information or unrelated sentences (Light & Anderson, 1985; Sinnott, 1986; Zelinski et al., 1984). Thus, the nature of the task and the material influences whether elderly people show deficits in long-term memory.

How do older adults compare with younger adults with respect to meta-memory? In general, elderly people are not very accurate in guessing the total number of items they will recall on a later memory test (Lovelace & Marsh, 1985). Also, elderly people often comment that their memory is not as accurate as it was in previous years (Hulicka, 1982; Lovelace & Twohig, 1984). Try Demonstration 11.1 to see whether your own memory failures match the kinds of failures about which elderly people complain.

Elderly people often realize that they must make certain adjustments to compensate for memory deficits. For instance, healthy, well-educated elderly people in one study reported that they used certain mnemonics more often than they had when they were younger. Specifically, they were more likely to use calendars and shopping lists, and they were more apt to write memos to themselves and put items in a noticeable place (Lovelace & Twohig, 1984).

In summary, elderly people perform relatively well on many kinds of memory tasks, though performance does decline in some areas of long-term memory. Fortunately, many healthy adults learn to adjust by using mnemonics more frequently.

Figure 11.3
Recall for important information as a function of age group and time of testing. (Based on Sinnott, 1986)

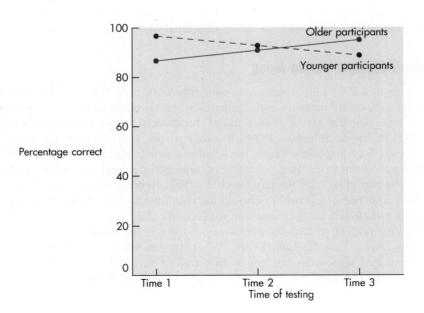

Thinking: Jean Piaget's Approach

In chapter 10, we noted that Jean Piaget's theory of cognitive development proposed a final stage called formal operations. During formal operations, adolescents and older adults can presumably reason abstractly and can test hypotheses systematically (see Table 10.2).

A major question for Piagetian research on adolescents and adults concerns the extent to which adults actually reach the formal operational stage. Many researchers have devised a variety of tasks that measure the ability to reason abstractly and test hypotheses. It seems that Piaget's original descriptions may have been too optimistic. For example, some researchers have concluded that fewer than half of adults have moved beyond concrete operations to formal operations (e.g., Epstein, 1979; King, 1985; Sroufe & Cooper, 1988). Naturally, some tasks are more likely than others to elicit abstract reasoning, and people trained in abstract thinking perform better than untrained people. However, we must conclude that people do not automatically progress from concrete operations to formal operations.

Performance on Other Cognitive Tasks

As we grow older, do we experience a decline in our general cognitive functions? Does your 80-year-old neighbor possess less intelligence than she did as a young adult? Some argue that intellectual functioning inevitably declines in old age, due to physiological changes. However, even those gloomy theorists admit that good health and intellectual stimulation can make the decline less noticeable (Schooler, 1987).

Several theorists argue that some kinds of intelligence decline more than other kinds (Horn & Cattell, 1967). Specifically, they propose that **fluid intelligence**, or the ability to solve new problems, reaches a peak in the late teens and then declines slowly but steadily throughout adulthood. These theorists also propose that **crystallized intelligence**, which involves specific acquired skills such as verbal ability, continues to grow throughout adulthood. In general, research supports the distinction between these two kinds of intelligence and their different paths of development across the life course (Whitbourne, 1986a).

Demonstration 11.1

Common Memory Failures

How often do each of the following memory failures occur for you? Record whether these failures occur (a) at least once a week, (b) occasionally, or (c) never.

_____ 1. Forgetting a word when conversing (e.g., tip of the tongue)

_____ 2. Forgetting why you did something (e.g., going into the kitchen and forgetting why you went).

_____ 3. Forgetting to bring up a point in a conversation.

_____ 4. Forgetting whether you did a particular task.

_____ 5. Forgetting to do a routine task.

_____ 6. Losing your train of thought.

Now compare your responses with those of the elderly people in Lovelace and Twohig's (1984) study, who reported that these memory failures occasionally occurred to them. However, few reported that they happened at least once a week. The only failure that occurred at least weekly for more than 20% of the sample was forgetting a word in a conversation, which was reported by 42%.

It is also important to note that experience can compensate for some kinds of cognitive decline. For instance, a 65-year-old typist actually strikes the keys more slowly than a younger typist; however, the older typist's years of practice compensate for that deficit. In fact, Salthouse (1987) found that typing speeds were similar for older and younger typists.

Let us also dispell that myth that says "you can't teach an old dog new tricks." Many people continue to grow throughout their professional career, and others discover a new profession later in life. For instance, Anna Mary Robertson Moses—better known as Grandma Moses—began painting professionally at the age of 76. Even with this late start, she became our best-known folk artist.

In our discussion of cognitive development we have considered only healthy older adults. However, it is important to remember the characteristics of Alzheimer's disease, discussed in chapter 3. As we noted in that chapter, an estimated 1 million elderly Americans experience severe cognitive and emotional impairment because of this neurological disorder (U.S. Congress, 1987).

Moral Development

Before you read further, try Demonstration 11.2. The "moral dilemma" in this story is one of 11 that Lawrence Kohlberg (1964, 1984) constructed to examine the development of moral thinking. Kohlberg analyzed the reasoning that people used with these moral dilemmas and constructed a stage theory of moral development. In categorizing people's responses, Kohlberg ignored whether people said that Heinz should or should not steal the drug. Instead, Kohlberg focused on the justifications provided. Let us examine each of these stages, together with the justification typical of that stage and a representative answer to the moral dilemma about Heinz.

Stage 1: Reasoning is based on avoiding punishment. For example, Heinz should not steal the drug because he might be sent to jail.

Stage 2: Reasoning is based on self-interest, with the hope that good deeds will be repaid. For example, Heinz should steal the drug because his wife will repay him after she recovers.

Stage 3: Reasoning is based on pleasing others and being a good person. For example, Heinz should steal the drug because his wife will admire him.

Stage 4: Reasoning is based on upholding the law. For example, Heinz should not steal because stealing breaks the law.

Stage 5: Reasoning is based on personal standards and the fact that it is best for society if people obey the law. For example, Heinz should not steal the drug because it is bad for society if people steal whenever they become desperate.

Stage 6: Reasoning is based on personal standards, even if the standards conflict with the law. For example, Heinz should steal the drug because human life should be more important than upholding the law.

In general, the results of studies on Kohlberg-type moral dilemmas show that stage 1 responses are not provided beyond adolescence. Stage 2 responses, the most common category for 10- to 12-year-olds, drop gradually and disappear by about 30 years of age. Stage 3 and 4 reasonings are the most common categories throughout adolescence and young adulthood. In contrast, few supply stage 5 and 6 responses at any point during development (Bee, 1987; Colby et al., 1983).

Is there support for Kohlberg's theory of moral development? In general, people move forward from one stage to the next in the sequence he suggested (Walker et al., 1984). Furthermore, the theory is supported by cross-cultural research in such populations as West German students, rural Guatemalan Indians, Buddhist monks in Tibet, Black Caribbean boys in Honduras, and kibbutz residents in Israel (Snarey, 1985). Also, moral reasoning is related to other attitudes and behavior. For instance, people in the higher levels of moral development are

Moral Judgment

Read the following paragraph and then answer the question.

> In Europe a woman was near death from a special kind of cancer. There was one drug that the doctors thought might save her. It was a form of radium that a druggist in the same town had recently discovered. The drug was expensive to make, but the druggist was charging ten times what the drug cost him to make. He paid $200 for the radium and charged $2,000 for a small dose of the drug. The sick woman's husband, Heinz, went to everyone he knew to borrow the money, but he could only get together $1,000 which is half of what it cost. He told the druggist that his wife was dying and asked him to sell it cheaper or let him pay later. But the druggist said, "No, I discovered the drug, and I am going to make money from it." So Heinz got desperate and broke into the man's store to steal the drug for his wife.

Question: Should Heinz have done this? Why or why not?

Source: Based on Kohlberg, 1969, p. 379.

more likely to be politically liberal and are more competent in dealing constructively with significant losses in their lives, such as the death of a family member (Emler et al., 1983; Lonky et al., 1984).

Carol Gilligan's (1982) book, *In a Different Voice: Psychological Theory and Women's Development*, argues that Kohlberg's theory is too narrow. Specifically, Gilligan notes that Kohlberg was only concerned about justice, which she asserts is a traditionally masculine focus. Gilligan proposed that a comprehensive theory of moral development should also emphasize traditionally feminine concerns such as caring, compassion, and social relationships. Gilligan is correct that these factors are important in moral reasoning. However, we should emphasize that researchers have found that women and men actually respond similarly on tests of moral reasoning (Colby & Kohlberg, 1987; Friedman et al., 1987; Greeno & Maccoby, 1986; Walker, 1984). Therefore, women and men do not live in different moral worlds, with men emphasizing justice and women emphasizing social relations. The psychological similarities between men and women are typically more noteworthy than the differences (Matlin, 1987).

Section Summary: Cognitive Development

- In general, elderly people show little decline in sensory memory, short-term memory, recognition memory, world knowledge, and recall of important information; they are more likely to show long-term-memory deficits for less important information and for unrelated sentences.
- On Piagetian tasks, many adult participants do not perform at the formal operational level.
- In general, fluid intelligence reaches a peak during the late teens and declines during adulthood, whereas crystalized intelligence continues to grow throughout adulthood.
- Kohlberg proposed that moral reasoning develops in six stages, though most adults do not pass through the last two stages; cross-cultural research supports his theory.

Gender in Adolescence and Adulthood

In the last chapter, we inspected children's stereotypes about males and females and then we examined three theories about the development of gender roles. In the current chapter we discuss three activities that are critically important in adolescence and adulthood: work, love relationships, and parenting. As you will see, gender is relevant in all three areas.

Work

Table 11.1 shows a number of occupations, together with the percentage of people in those occupations who are female. As you can see, certain occupations are almost exclusively male (e.g., carpenters, mechanics), whereas others are almost exclusively female (e.g., secretaries, nurses). Gender is clearly related to job choice.

Gender also influences salaries. At present, if we consider only full-time workers in the United States, female workers earn about 65% as much as male workers (Blau & Winkler, 1989). Naturally, some of this pay discrepancy can be traced to the fact that male-dominated jobs pay more than female-dominated jobs. For instance, mechanics are paid more than secretaries. However, pay discrepancies exist even within the same occupations. For example, female clerical workers earn only 66% as much as male clerical workers (Glenn & Feldberg, 1989).

Vocational Decisions Adolescents are frequently asked, "What do you want to be when you grow up?" John responds, "a carpenter or a mechanic" or else "a lawyer or a doctor." He does not answer, "a nurse or a secretary," and he would never dream of responding, "I just want to be a husband and a father." We do not know much about the forces that encourage boys into stereotypically masculine occupations.

Researchers know much more about the way in which young women make their vocational decisions. For instance, it seems that they plan their lives in two stages. During the first stage, most young women rule out high-prestige occupations that require many years of education. They have been trained to value marriage and family more than a career, and they perceive (correctly, as it happens) that men often dislike career-oriented women (Corder & Stephan, 1984).

During the second stage of planning, young women choose a specific occupation from the narrow range of remaining options, even when these options are not appealing. For instance, a study of high school women showed that many

Table 11.1   *Percentage of Workers Who Are Women in Selected Occupations*

OCCUPATION	PERCENTAGE OF WORKERS WHO ARE WOMEN
Carpenters	1
Mechanics	1
Engineers	3
Lawyers	12
Physicians	13
College professors	37
Teachers (elementary, secondary)	71
Nurses	96
Secretaries	99

Sources: Kaufman, 1989; U.S. Department of Labor, 1980.

were planning on clerical jobs, even though they readily admitted that these jobs would be boring (Gaskell, 1985). Incidentally, keep in mind that this model applies to a large number of high school women and may not apply to the selected sample of women who choose to attend college.

Of course, some women do decide to pursue nontraditional careers. For example, in 1987, 37% of American medical students were female. By contrast, in 1967, only 10% of medical students were female (Jonas & Etzel, 1988). Try Demonstration 11.3 to learn which factors tend to predict women's career choices.

Keep in mind the theme of individual differences, however. You may know an ambitious young woman whose ability is not especially high, whose mother has never been employed, and whose father is not supportive of her career plans.

Black adolescent females are more likely than White adolescent females to plan on working outside the home. In one study, 95% of Black high school women had mothers who are employed (Malson, 1983). As one Black student said in an interview,

> I'd never known a woman who stayed home with children . . . I did not know any housewives. That form of life was kind of alien. I did not even know that was possible. When I found out that people actually only stayed home and did nothing but raise children and clean house, I thought it was fascinating . . . I always assumed I'd work and have children. (Malson, 1983, p. 107)

Household Tasks   Another, less visible kind of work is performed at home. Who makes the beds, does the dishes, takes out the garbage, and picks up the socks?

Demonstration 11.3

Women's Career Choices

Think about the most ambitious female student from your high school class—the one you thought was most likely to do well in a male-dominated career. Review the list of factors in the right-hand column, and place a + next to each item that describes this student, in the column labeled "Most ambitious student." Then think of a female student from your high school class who planned a more traditional career. Review the list of factors once more, placing a + in the second column next to each item that describes this second student. When you have finished, count whether there are more + marks for the first student than for the second one.

MOST AMBITIOUS STUDENT	MORE TRADITIONAL STUDENT	FACTORS THAT ARE GENERALLY ASSOCIATED WITH A WOMAN CHOOSING A NONTRADITIONAL CAREER
_____	_____	High ability
_____	_____	Liberated gender-role values
_____	_____	High self-esteem
_____	_____	Highly educated parents
_____	_____	Female role models
_____	_____	Employed mother
_____	_____	Supportive father
_____	_____	Strong academic self-concept
_____	_____	Work experience as adolescent

Source: Based on Betz & Fitzgerald, 1987.

Joseph Pleck's (1985) book, *Working Wives/Working Husbands*, provides some answers. In the most elaborate study, more than 2,000 people kept diaries about how they spent their time during several typical days. Figure 11.4 shows the amount of time that husbands and wives spent on housework, depending on whether the wife worked outside the home. According to this study, employed wives spent about twice as much time on housework and other chores as employed husbands did. Furthermore, the employment status of the wife had little impact on how much time husbands spent on housework. In fact, if their wives were employed, husbands spent only about 2 minutes more each day on housework than if their wives were not employed.

Similarly, a review of eight other studies showed that women spent about three times as many hours on housework as their husbands (Coverman, 1989). It makes sense, then, that 73% of women in another survey complained of having too little leisure, in contrast to 51% of the men (Michaels & Willwerth, 1989).

In this section, we have seen that gender is related to career choice, salaries, and the performance of household chores. Gender also has important implications for romantic relationships.

Love Relationships

Although adults typically believe their work is important, they report that the most important things that happen to them involve other people. For instance, Pleck (1985) found that 49% of men and 56% of women strongly agreed with the statement, "The most important things that happen to me involve my family." In this section, we look at intimate relationships, examining three common options for adults: marriage, gay relationships, and being single.

Marriage   Between 90% and 95% of all Americans marry at least once (Fitzpatrick, 1988). Interestingly, men and women tend to emphasize the same qualities in choosing a partner for a long-term, meaningful relationship: honesty, personality, warmth, sensitivity, and fidelity (Nevid, 1984). We see in chapter 17 that physical attractiveness is important when people first meet. However, it is not as important when people plan lifetime commitments.

Who is more likely to fall head over heels in love, men or women? Most people are surprised to learn that men are more likely than women to receive high scores on a "romanticism scale" (Rubin et al., 1981). Men are more likely to believe in love at first sight, true love lasting forever, and love overcoming the barriers of race and economics.

Figure 11.4
Amount of housework performed each day by wives and husbands as a function of whether wife was employed. (Based on Pleck, 1985)

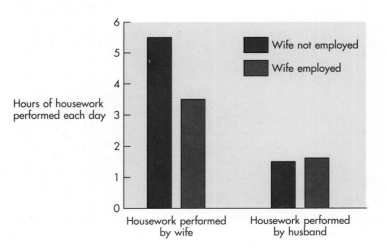

In general, men are also happier with their marriages than women are. For instance, men are more likely than women to say that they would marry the same person again (Rhyne, 1981). In contrast, women are more likely to report that they want more companionship and conversation than they currently receive (Turner, 1981; Turner & Turner, 1982). Surprisingly, though, a wife's marital satisfaction is not strongly correlated with her husband's marital satisfaction (Acitelli & Duck, 1987; Fitzpatrick, 1988; Whitbourne, 1986a).

People usually say that their marriages are happiest during the first years (Hatfield et al., 1984; Turner & Turner, 1982). Marital satisfaction is relatively low among couples with teens living at home, but it often improves again among older couples.

Some estimates project that 40% of all people born in the 1970s who marry will end those marriages with a divorce. Divorce is a traumatic event for most couples, though divorced men tend to show more emotional and physical disturbances than divorced women (Price & McKenry, 1988).

But what about the happily married couples? In a happy marriage, both wife and husband feel that their emotional needs are fulfilled, and each partner enriches the life of the other. Both understand and respect each other, and both are concerned for one another's happiness and welfare (Stinnett et al., 1984; Turner & Helms, 1989). Several of the characteristics that researchers have found to be correlated with happy marriages include the following:

In selecting a partner for a meaningful relationship, both men and women emphasize personal characteristics such as honesty, personality, and warmth.

1. High level of education

2. Good communication

3. Good conflict-resolution skills

4. Good skills in interpreting each other's emotions

5. Both consider their spouse to be their best friend.

6. Each is fairly high in stereotypically feminine traits such as "understanding," "gentle," and "affectionate."

7. Each is high in self-esteem (Antill, 1983; Bee, 1987).

Gay Relationships   A researcher visited the home of a lesbian in California to interview her for a project on lesbians and gay men. The researcher later wrote,

> She was very friendly, interested, talkative, and open. I felt like I was a friend whom she was inviting in to share part of her life. I liked her paintings, her roommate's photographs of the Bay Area, and the warm togetherness of their home. She and her roommate were obviously very much in love. Like most people who have a good, stable, five-year relationship, they seemed comfortable together, sort of part of one another, able to joke, obviously fulfilled in their relationship. They work together, have the same times off from work, do most of their leisure activities together. She is helping her roommate to learn to paint, while her roommate is teaching her about photography. They sent me home with a plateful of cookies, a good symbolic gesture of the kind of welcome and warmth I felt in their home. (Bell & Weinberg, 1978, p. 200)

A **gay person** is attracted to people of the same gender. In general, the terms *gay* and *lesbian* are preferred to the term *homosexual*, which focuses too narrowly on the sexuality of a relationship, rather than the broader psychological and emotional attachments that gay people feel for each other (Owens, personal communication, 1990).

Researchers have found that lesbians and gay men have relationships that are as satisfying as heterosexual relationships.

Research with gay people reveals that between 40% and 75% of lesbians and gay men are currently in a steady relationship (Peplau, 1988). These data clearly refute the stereotype that gay people shun long-lasting relationships. Furthermore, surveys of lesbians, gay men, and heterosexuals have found no significant differences among the three groups on measures of satisfaction with the relationship (Kurdek & Schmitt, 1986; Peplau et al., 1982).

Many heterosexuals think that gay people can change their orientation through counseling and therapy. However, Boddé (1988) consulted 11 experts on gay relationships, and they agreed that gay people are unlikely to change their preferences. In 1973, the American Psychiatric Association decided that homosexuality should no longer be listed as a disorder, so it is not appropriate for therapists to encourage gay people to develop heterosexual preferences.

Therapy can be useful, however, for helping gay people deal with homophobia from other people. **Homophobia** is an irrational, persistent fear and contempt for gay people (Kitzinger, 1987). Homophobia probably exists in your own college community. For example, 55% of gay students at Rutgers University reported that they had been verbally abused on the campus, and 42% said they had been harassed by their roommates (Dodge, 1989).

Many gay couples raise children. Researchers have concluded that children from gay households do not differ from children raised in heterosexual households in important characteristics such as intelligence, general adjustment, development, and gender identity (Cramer, 1986; Pennington, 1987).

It is interesting to imagine how our culture's stereotypes about gay people would be reduced if we placed less emphasis on the gender schema. As we discussed in chapter 10, gender is extremely important in our culture, and we encourage children to believe that males are very different from females. If we placed less emphasis on gender, then we would not be so concerned that a gay person chooses to love someone of the same gender, rather than a person of the other gender.

Being Single   In a study examining attitudes toward single people, Etaugh and Malstrom (1981) discovered that single people were perceived as being less sociable, attractive, and reliable in comparison with other people. Single people often discover that their married friends have strange biases. For instance, one of my single friends told me that a married acquaintance of hers believed that single people were not particularly concerned about saving money for the future. According to this stereotype, single people have only short-range goals and are incapable of planning for their old age.

The number of people who remain single has increased in recent years. For instance, among 25- to 29-year-olds, 25% of females and 38% of males are single (Turner & Helms, 1989).

Single people believe that being single has both advantages and disadvantages. Single women in one study frequently stressed that they valued their independence (Simon, 1987). As one woman responded:

> Am I a "lone ranger," out on the range of life without companionship or help? Sometimes. In fact, often. But, just as often, I am sitting in the lap of family and friendship, drawing on the wisdom, and laughter, and camaraderie that sisters and buddies offer. It seems that I am both people. One of the reasons I never married, despite five reasonable offers, is that I thought it would be much harder in marriage to go back and forth between being that "lone ranger" and being close. (Simon, 1987, p. 37)

A common complaint raised by both single and divorced people is that they feel disadvantaged in settings where others expect everyone to be part of a couple. Some also mention loneliness, though single people are not as lonely as the stereotypes suggest (Cargan & Melko, 1985). In general, single people and married people are similar in their adjustment and life satisfaction (Gigy, 1980).

In this section we looked at three options for adults: marriage, gay relationships, and being single. Each of these options can bring loneliness and frustration, yet each can also bring warm relationships and the opportunity for personal growth. Now let us consider another social relationship that is important in the lives of most adults: being a parent.

Parenthood

A young father finds that he has become much more involved with fatherhood than he had ever anticipated:

> It's been a lot of fun to watch her grow. . . . I just didn't have any idea of what being a father was all about. . . . And, I'm really attached. I find myself thinking about her at work, rushing to the day care center to pick her up, just because every day she learns something new and you just want to see it and kind of share it with her. (Grossman, 1987, p. 89)

A mother of twin daughters comments on how her children have affected her life:

> In many ways the children have brought us together. They have given us a joint *aim* in life. . . . It's worth going on and getting things better and working hard because of the pleasure we can get from the children and what we can do for them. It gives you a reason for doing it all. . . . (Boulton, 1983, p. 60)

For many women and men, parenthood represents a major life transition because they realize they are now responsible for the welfare of a new human being. In general, men and women are similar in their interest in becoming parents (Gerson, 1986). Contrary to the stereotypes, then, men are just as eager as women to become parents.

Clear gender differences exist, however, in the amount of time that mothers and fathers spend with their children. When the mother is not employed outside the home, fathers spend about 20% to 25% as much time in direct interaction with children as mothers spend. When the mother is employed outside the home,

Researchers have discovered that fathers can be as skilled as mothers at taking care of infants.

she naturally spends less time interacting with her children, but fathers do not increase their interaction time (Lamb, 1987).

Women and men also differ in the way they interact with their children. Most of mothers' interactions focus on caretaking, whereas fathers spend a greater percentage of their time in play. Lamb (1987) points out, though, that fathers and mothers are equally competent in taking care of newborns. Women are no better at "mothering" than men are at "fathering." However, mothers spend more time on the job, so they acquire more competence than fathers do. As the baby develops, fathers come to feel less confident about their parenting abilities, and they volunteer less often for caretaking. Thus, the differences between mothering and fathering increase as the babies grow up. Lamb assures us, though, that most fathers who become primary caretakers (for instance, when the mother dies) readily acquire the necessary skills. In short, when the opportunities arise, fathers can demonstrate their "paternal instincts" just as competently as mothers demonstrated their "maternal instincts."

Section Summary: Gender in Adolescence and Adulthood

- Men and women often pursue different careers, and they earn significantly different salaries; adolescent women choose traditional careers perceived to be compatible with a family; women perform substantially more household chores, even when employed.
- Although men and women seek similar qualities in a marriage partner, men tend to be happier with their marriages and to be more disturbed by a divorce than their wives.
- Gay people tend to want long-lasting relationships, and they are as happy with these relationships as heterosexuals; therapy generally does not alter sexual orientation; children raised by gay parents do not differ substantially from children raised in heterosexual homes.
- Although stereotypes portray single people negatively, they tend to be satisfied with their lives.
- Fathers and mothers have similar interests in becoming parents and similar initial skills in parenting, though mothers usually gain more expertise by spending more time in child care.

Personality and Social Development

As we examine personality and social development, it is important to emphasize the theme of individual differences, because these differences increase as people grow older. Think about the vastly different kinds of experiences that a group of 60-year-olds could have encountered in their six decades on Earth. This increased variability during aging is called **individual fanning out**, and it emphasizes that 60-year-olds are more different from one another than 10-year-olds (Neugarten, 1982; Schlossberg, 1984; Sherrod & Brim, 1986).

In this last section of the chapter, we begin with a discussion of self-concept. Our next topic is the stability-change question, one of the three developmental issues introduced in chapter 10. Then we consider interpersonal relationships during adulthood. The other subjects in this section include minority-group adolescents and adults, dealing with death, life satisfaction, and an in-depth discussion of stereotypes about the elderly.

Self-Concept

In chapter 10, we began to explore the term *self-concept*, or the schema of thoughts and feelings about oneself as an individual. Beginning in infancy, children develop a concept of themselves as an individual. Toddlers can recognize themselves in the mirror, and children develop feelings of competence. However, adolescents and adults have a much more differentiated sense of who they are and how they have changed. For instance, a friend named Anne Hardy (personal communication, 1987) reflected on her life.

> At the age of 69, I still don't feel "old," although chronologically, I'm not "young." I think one ages—given reasonable health—as one has been gradually aging in all the years before, very much depending on the quality of life one has built. My interests haven't changed, except that we have the added joy of six grandchildren in our lives. Elderly people are as diverse as young people. Differences between them remain; previous likes and dislikes remain, for the most part. I am still me, "old" or not, though I feel that I have become more understanding, less judgmental, more open to new experiences, still trying to grow as a person.

According to the principle of individual fanning out, 60-year-olds differ more from each other than do 10-year-olds.

Erikson's Psychosocial Approach   In the last chapter, we introduced Erik Erikson's (1950, 1968) theory that people confront a specific task during each of eight stages of development. Table 11.2 reviews the first four stages that describe childhood development and adds the four stages that are important in adolescence and adulthood.

In chapter 10, we discussed Piaget's theory of cognitive development, and in the current chapter we briefly examined Kohlberg's theory of moral development. In chapter 13, we spend some time on Freud's theory of personality development. However, none of these developmental theories matches Erikson's theory with respect to its attention to older adulthood.

Throughout the life course, Erikson argues, individuals struggle with identity development. It seems likely that Erikson focused on identity because of the identity confusion he experienced in his own life. Erikson was born in Germany, shortly after his Danish father abandoned his Jewish mother. Several years later, his mother married a Jewish doctor, and they both raised the young boy in the Jewish faith, under the name Erik Homburger. His Christian friends at school considered him to be Jewish, but his Jewish friends at the temple considered him to be Christian, because he looked very Scandinavian. During adolescence, Erik's family pressured him to study medicine, yet he wanted to become an artist. Eventually, he pursued training in psychoanalysis with Anna Freud, daughter of Sigmund Freud, who was herself a prominent child psychoanalyst. He left Europe for the United States in 1933, changing his last name from Homburger to Erikson. It is clear that Erikson often confronted the question "Who am I?" especially during the first decades of his life.

As Table 11.2 shows, the major task for the adolescent in stage 5 is to struggle with the question "Who am I, and where am I going?" In fact, it was Erikson who gave us a term popular in everyday English: *identity crisis*. Identity issues are particularly relevant for adolescents because of the major physical changes they experience in puberty and the cognitive changes that encourage abstract thought. In addition, they need to make decisions about occupations and education.

If adolescents successfully resolve their identity crisis, they begin to work on the stage 6 tasks during young adulthood. This period is the critical time to develop an intimate relationship with another person. An individual who does not develop intimacy will be overwhelmed by a sense of isolation, according to Erikson. Young adults also struggle with career decisions.

In stage 7, Erikson argues that a major task is child rearing, or attempting to influence the next generation. Generativity may also be expressed by helping other young people or by creative, productive work or volunteer activities that benefit others.

Erikson's stage 8 requires looking back on life's accomplishments. For example, Anne Hardy (personal communication, 1987) reflected about her lifetime, which was devoted to working for racial equality and world peace:

> "This is the way it is" is something we can't settle for. We have to work toward being able to say, "That is the way it *was*, and we have helped to improve it." . . . A Fundamentalist relative asked me recently what I felt about eternity. I answered that for me eternity is being created daily in what I do, how I live vis-à-vis other human beings, what kind of values I gave and continue to give our children so that they in turn would have good values to pass on to their world and their children.

A person who can reminisce about a satisfying life achieves a sense of integrity, according to Erikson. In contrast, a person who has accomplished little develops a sense of despair.

Table 11.2   *Erikson's Theory of Psychosocial Development, From Birth Through Old Age*

STAGE	AGE	PSYCHOSOCIAL TASK	DESCRIPTION OF TASK
1	0–1	Trust versus mistrust	The infant whose needs are met by caretaker develops a sense of trust in others.
2	1–3	Autonomy versus doubt	The toddler tries to learn independence and self-confidence.
3	3–6	Initiative versus guilt	The young child learns to initiate his or her own activities.
4	6–12	Competence versus inferiority	The child tries to develop skill in physical, cognitive, and social areas.
5	12–19	Identity versus role confusion	The adolescent tries out several roles and forms an integrated, single identity.
6	20–40	Intimacy versus isolation	The young adult tries to form close, permanent relationships and to make career commitments.
7	40–65	Generativity versus stagnation	The middle-aged person tries to contribute to the world through family relationships, work productivity, and creativity.
8	65 on	Integrity versus despair	The elderly person thinks back on life, experiencing satisfaction or disappointment.

Source: Erikson, 1950, 1968.

Recent Research on Adult Identity   Let us look at a good example of some of the more recent explorations into the question of adult identity. Susan K. Whitbourne (1986b) examined 94 adults between the ages of 24 and 61 in a book entitled *The Me I Know: A Study of Adult Identity.* In addition to questions about family identity, work identity, and age identity, she also explored people's life values. Demonstration 11.4 is a modification of this portion of the interview.

Whitbourne found that people considered their values to be a major part of their identity. Those whose identities were dominated by family roles described values that focused on doing things for others. Those whose identities were dominated by occupational accomplishments described values that focused on hard work and competence.

Interestingly, Whitbourne did not find major gender differences in this study, a conclusion consistent with the general statement that men and women share similar psychological characteristics (Matlin, 1987). In this sample of adults, women were just as likely as men to stress values such as assertiveness, independence, and competitiveness. Furthermore, the men in Whitbourne's sample were as likely as the women to value love, friendship, selflessness, and helpfulness.

One of the most frequently mentioned values was honesty. In fact, 36 of the 94 respondents specifically mentioned this trait. For them, honesty meant not stealing, cheating, or lying. Some people also noted that they valued the ability to look at the world realistically and honestly. Still others emphasized honesty as a value to be transmitted to one's children or honesty in the workplace. One man reported:

Demonstration 11.4

Important Values during Adulthood

Locate a friend or relative you would feel comfortable interviewing about personal issues. It would be ideal to locate someone at least 50 years old, but a younger person would be satisfactory. Tell this person that you will be conducting an informal interview about important values, and that he or she should feel free not to answer any questions that seem too personal. Each general question is followed by a probe, which you may find useful if your respondent requires clarification or hesitates about an answer.

1. Please describe for me your major values, the principles you try to live your life for.
   PROBE: What is important to you in the way you try to live your life?
2. How strongly do you feel about your values?

PROBE: How important to you is it that you follow this value?
3. How do your values affect the way you feel about yourself as a person?
   PROBE: Do you judge yourself by your values? How do you come out with respect to these values?
4. Do you think your values are changing?
   PROBE: Do you have any questions or doubts about your values?
If yes: 5a. How are they changing?
   PROBE: What is it about your values that is changing?
If no: 5b. Do you think your values are likely to change in the future?
   PROBE: Do you think you will ever have questions about your values in the future?

Source: Based on Whitbourne, 1986b, pp. 245–246.

I place honesty very high, and I just get upset when people lie to me. . . . If you award a contract to the sub-contractor with certain terms and specifications spelled out very clearly, and the sub-contractor tries to cheat, so to speak, substitute with unequal materials or workmanship, that really upsets me very much, and I try to treat people honestly and fairly and be treated the same way. (Whitbourne, 1986b, p. 222)

In addition to honesty, other frequently mentioned values were the Golden Rule, or doing unto others as you would have them do unto you, and trying to get along well with others, even when it required overlooking their faults. In summary, then, Whitbourne's study demonstrated that a critical component of adult identity involved concern for the well-being of other people.

The Stability-Change Question

In chapter 10 we considered the stability-change question when we asked whether infants maintain their personal characteristics as they mature into children. Now we need to consider the same issue in adulthood. The prominent American psychologist, William James, wrote a century ago, "For most of us, by the age of 30, the character has set like plaster, and will never soften again" (James, 1892, p. 124). In other words, James clearly cast his vote for "stability" in the great stability-change debate.

You might vote for "change," however, if you had known Benjamin Carson as an angry high school student and watched his transformation into a neurosurgeon. Ben Carson failed most of his math quizzes as a fifth grader in inner-city Detroit. As a high school student, Ben was known for his violent temper. He would attack anyone who offended him, using a bottle, brick, knife, or any other

Neurosurgeon Ben Carson visiting Andrews University premed students.

handy weapon. One day, in a rage, he thrust a knife at a boy. The boy happened to be wearing a large metal belt buckle, which broke the blade on Ben's knife. Ben instantly realized that he could have killed another person. He ran home, closed himself into the bathroom, and sat on the edge of the tub. He thought and prayed, and then emerged three hours later with his anger gone. The anger never returned, and Ben focused his attention on his school work, achieving an A average in the remainder of high school. He was accepted to Yale University for his undergraduate work and the University of Michigan for medical school. Ben Carson became a neurosurgeon, and later achieved fame for his surgery in separating Siamese twins connected at the head (Woodford, 1989).

Personality Characteristics   Does the research support the stability view of William James or the change view suggested by life transformations such as Ben Carson's? According to one review of the research, the answer depends upon how stability and change are measured (Bengston et al., 1985). For instance, when the studies are *correlational*, they tend to demonstrate that people show considerable stability as they grow older. For example, people who are friendlier than average in high school tend to remain friendlier than average in old age.

However, when the studies measure *average level* of a characteristic, the results are inconsistent. That is, some personality characteristics may stay at the same level as people age; for instance, people do not systematically increase or decrease their anxiety level as they age. On the other hand, other personality characteristics may show a systematic shift as people age; for instance, the average rating on the characteristic "energy level" probably decreases systematically as people grow older.

My mother recently attended the 50th reunion of her high school class in Great Falls, Montana, and her report of the event meshed well with the data on stability versus change. In general, she noted moderate stability in the extent to which people were extraverted or outgoing. The high school senior who had been active in numerous school organizations was now, at 68, the extraverted master of ceremonies for the reunion, whereas the quieter people were still quiet. Of course, the correlation between high school personality and adulthood personality was far from perfect. For instance, the woman who had graduated from a prestigious university, moved to California, and had traveled extensively, had become much more self-confident and outgoing. Another woman, initially similar in self-confidence, had attended the local college and now lived in a small town in Montana; her self-confidence had not changed. Still, consistent with the findings of Bengston, high school extraversion seemed generally correlated with late-adulthood extraversion.

My mother also observed that a second personality characteristic *had* changed, when assessed in terms of average level. This characteristic was the willingness to share personal information and to laugh at oneself. As adolescents, they had been reluctant to talk about themselves and laugh at their foibles; as adults in their 60s, the average level of "sharing and laughing" had increased remarkably.

In short, the conclusions on the stability-change question are complex. Stability is more likely in correlational studies, whereas change and stability are equally likely in average-level studies; the outcome depends upon the characteristic being studied. We can find evidence for both stability and change across the life span (Schlossberg, 1984; Whitbourne, 1986a).

Midlife Crises   An important issue related to the stability-change question is the so-called *midlife crisis*. You have probably read in popular magazines that adults are supposed to experience some kind of major change in their lives in their early 40s. For example, a happily married 39-year-old accountant turns 40 and divorces his wife, deserts his children, and moves to Southern California with a woman 15 years younger.

Several psychologists have proposed theories focusing on a midlife crisis that involves substantial changes in a person's occupation, personal relationships, and values (e.g., Gould, 1978; Levinson et al., 1978; Vaillant, 1977). However, one review of midlife-crisis theories concludes,

> These claims by the authors of the mid-life crises theories are not, however, sufficiently strong to stand up against the increasingly large body of reputable data that challenges the proposition that a mid-life crisis is a typical or developmentally beneficial event in an adult's life. (Whitbourne, 1986a, p. 244)

The concept of a midlife crisis is believable because each of us knows at least one person whose life changed drastically during middle age. Yes, some people do have midlife crises. Others have crises earlier or later. Many more never experience a major life upheaval; their lives have remained stable. We must conclude that individual differences are large with respect to midlife crises, and these major crises certainly are not universal.

Interpersonal Relationships

In chapter 10 we considered the first major interpersonal relationship, attachment to parents. Now we pursue child-parent relationships during adolescence. In the previous section of this chapter, we examined a major interpersonal issue during adolescence and adulthood when we discussed love relationships. Another major interpersonal issue is friendship, our second topic.

Adolescent-Parent Relationships   Perhaps you once read a teen novel that contained a passage like this:

> All the scolding and criticism from her parents was simply too much for 15-year-old Meredith. Tears streaming down her pale cheeks, she tore into her bedroom, slamming

the door behind her slender young legs. She hurled herself onto her bed, sobbing deeply into her lavender pillow. "I hate you, I hate you, I hate you!" she cried to her parents in a voice choked with emotion.

Are the relationships between adolescents and parents as stormy as the popular press would have us believe? It is true that teenagers and their parents quarrel about loud music, hairstyles, and keeping the bedroom neat. These minor conflicts are more frequent than they were during childhood. However, few of these conflicts focus on major problems such as delinquency or drugs. It may surprise you to learn that most teenagers and their parents say they enjoy one another (Offer et al., 1981). In fact, Nielsen (1987) concludes, "Not only is the generation gap an exaggerated notion, but most adolescents and their parents like each other and have relatively few conflicts during adolescence" (p. 357). The stereotype of the rebellious, alienated teenager applies to only a minority of adolescents (Petersen, 1988).

Friendship   Take a moment to think about your definition of a friend. Consider your best friend, and think about how your relationship with this person differs from other relationships you have. Then contemplate some of the friendships you had when you were younger.

The definition of friendship changes as children become adolescents. A 4-year-old emphasizes concrete characteristics, for example, "I like Randy because he has fun toys." A 10-year-old would be more likely to stress mutual activities, for example, "I like Pedro because he's fun to play basketball with."

By adolescence, however, friendships are based on similar characteristics. Adolescents who are 13 or 14 years old mention emotional support and protectiveness. For instance, a good friend must "stick up for you." Adolescents and young adults stress that a friend must be open and honest. (Recall that Whitbourne's study [Whitbourne, 1986b] also emphasized the personal quality of honesty.) Finally, friends are people with whom you can share personal problems and feelings (Nielsen, 1987; Smollar & Youniss, 1982). It seems likely that these deeper friendships can develop only after young people have lost most of their egocentrism—to use Piaget's term—and can appreciate the perspective of another

People who have good interactions with their friends are likely to be more satisfied with their lives.

person. Also, Erikson's approach suggests that truly intimate friendships require that both friends must have resolved their identity crises associated with stage 5 in Erikson's theory.

In adulthood, people usually have three or four interest-related friendships. **Interest-related friendships** are based on similar lifestyles and interests. In contrast, people typically have only one or two close, or deep friends. **Deep friendships** require intimacy and feeling personal closeness, beyond a simple sharing of interests (Bensman & Lilienfeld, 1979; Hayslip & Panek, 1989).

Among retired adults, friendships typically provide more satisfaction than family members do (Larson et al., 1986). The nature of friendships may change as people age, however. A study of friendships between the ages of 18 and 75 showed that in old age, men placed more emphasis on concern and thoughtfulness toward their friends, in contrast to when they were younger. Older women showed more tolerance and less confrontation with their friends than when they were younger (Fox et al., 1985).

Furthermore, life satisfaction seems to be correlated with interaction with friends (Aizenberg & Treas, 1985; Bee, 1987; Hochschild, 1973). As an elderly man concluded in one interview, "Without friends, you're like a book that nobody bothers to pick up. . . ." (Fox et al., 1985, p. 500).

Minority-Group Adolescents and Adults

One reason that it is important to examine minority groups is to dispel racial and ethnic stereotypes. However, in dispelling these stereotypes, we must avoid another error—concluding that racial and ethnic distinctions are irrelevant in the lives of adolescents and adults. That is, we must avoid stereotyping minorities, yet simultaneously attend to the genuine distinctions that exist between members of the White middle class and members of minority groups (Nielsen, 1987; Sue, 1981). In this section, we look at academic achievement, adolescent characteristics, and the status of the elderly members of minority groups.

Academic Achievement   Table 11.3 shows the percentage of high-school students from five groups who continued their education in college. As you can see, the percentages range from 19% for Native Americans to 62% for Asian Americans (Stubbs & Harrison, 1982).

What are some of the factors that encourage academic success for minority-group adolescents? Interviews with successful Black students indicated that parents' encouragement was a primary factor. Parents were often unable to provide much financial help because of low family income, but they had promoted values and study habits that encouraged their children's academic success. Other helpful

Table 11.3   *Percentage of High School Graduates Who Attended College in 1980 by Racial/Ethnic Group*

RACIAL/ETHNIC GROUP	PERCENTAGE ATTENDING COLLEGE
Asian American	62%
Black	38%
White	38%
Hispanic	27%
Native American	19%

Source: Stubbs & Harrison, 1982.

factors were good educational experiences and comments from famous Black athletes that encourage Black students to continue their education (Lee, 1985). Furthermore, Black students whose parents encourage them to develop racial pride and an appreciation of Black heritage tend to receive higher grades than students whose parents rarely mentioned racial issues (Bowman & Howard, 1985).

Asian Americans are often stereotyped as the "ideal minority group" because of their high academic achievement. In general, Asian Americans show more skill in mathematics and science than in verbal areas. As a consequence, they are more likely to pursue careers in engineering, technology, natural sciences, and medicine (Phillips, 1981). However, these interests are certainly not universal. I recall a Chinese-American student commenting that she wanted to major in literature, but her family, her Asian friends, and her White professors all kept nudging her toward science—an area she did not enjoy.

Characteristics of Minority-Group Adolescents In recent years, political changes have encouraged some Black students to raise their self-esteem. In a national sample of Black young people between the ages of 14 and 24, 23% reported that their families had conveyed messages such as "never be ashamed of your color" as well as information about famous Black people. An additional 12% said that their families had emphasized equality via statements such as "Skin color is not a factor in one's worth." Finally, 14% noted that their families had emphasized hard work, self-reliance, and character building (Bowman & Howard, 1985).

At present, political forces have not yet encouraged a strong sense of ethnic identity among Hispanic adolescents. For example, a survey of eighth and ninth graders in Texas showed that they had significantly lower self-esteem than their non-Hispanic classmates (Grossman et al., 1985).

One important concept in Hispanic American cultures is *machismo*. Machismo emphasizes male superiority, but some experts feel that outsiders over-emphasize this facet and pay too little attention to its positive aspects. In Hispanic groups, machismo also includes being trustworthy, revering one's mother and wife or girlfriend, and assuming responsibility for the family's support (Baron, 1981; Hernandez et al., 1976; Nielsen, 1987).

The Status of Minority-Group Elderly By the year 2050, it is estimated that one fifth of all elderly people will be non-White (Myers, 1985). As we will see, minority-group elderly experience some advantages and some disadvantages in comparison with elderly White people.

According to the **multiple-jeopardy hypothesis,** people who are both Black and elderly are particularly handicapped because they experience both prejudice against Blacks and prejudice against elderly persons. With respect to income, the multiple-jeopardy hypothesis is correct. For instance, the income of elderly Blacks has risen less than the income of elderly Whites during recent years (Chen, 1985; Jackson, 1985). Furthermore, 82% of elderly Black women are classified as either poor or near poor (Minkler & Stone, 1985).

However, the multiple-jeopardy hypothesis does not apply to health status for elderly people. For instance, White and Black people have somewhat similar health problems in old age, whereas when we look at health status in *middle* age, Black people are much less healthy than White people (Markides, 1983).

When we consider family support, Black elderly seem to have the advantage over White elderly. According to a review of the literature, elderly Blacks are more likely than elderly Whites to interact with and receive social support from their younger family members (George, 1988). In summary, then, the multiple-jeopardy hypothesis does not extend beyond income to include health and social status. Now let us turn our attention to a topic that is relevant to all elderly people, whether White or minority: awareness of dying.

Studies generally show that elderly Black people are more likely than elderly White people to receive social support from family members.

Dealing with Death

Erik Erikson and his co-authors (1986) interviewed elderly people in preparing their book, *Vital Involvement in Old Age*. One respondent said, "You don't know whether you are going to be here tomorrow or not. Nobody does, of course, but when you are older your chances are more questionable." Many respondents did not hide their fear of death. One person said tremblingly, "On New Year's night, when they drop that ball, I am so glad I lived another year. I don't like to die at all! I am frightfully afraid of death!" (p. 65).

We mentioned earlier that Erikson's stage 8 stressed looking back on one's life; this process is usually prompted by an awareness of death in the near future (Butler, 1963). This **life review** is a special kind of reminiscing about the past in which an older person recalls past experiences and tries to work through them to understand them more thoroughly (Kiernat, 1984; Whitbourne, 1986a). In one study of people between the ages of 58 and 93, Romaniuk (1981) discovered that 56% of the participants had completed a life review and an additional 25% were currently in the process of life review. Only 19% indicated no concern with life review.

What are the thoughts and emotions of someone who is about to die? Some years ago, Elisabeth Kübler-Ross (1969) proposed that people who are terminally ill pass through a series of five distinct stages. The first stage is *denial*; the second, *anger*; the third, *bargaining* (for instance, promising to lead a better life if given more time before dying); the fourth, *depression*; and the fifth, peaceful *acceptance* of death.

Kübler-Ross's pioneering work was useful because it urged physicians and other professionals to pay more attention to the emotional needs of dying patients and their families (Rainey, 1988). However, the research has been criticized for being based too heavily on personal impressions, rather than more concrete data. People do not seem to express these five emotions in any consistent pattern. In fact, depression seems to be the only emotion that is consistently present in dying patients (Bee, 1987; Schneidman, 1980). In the words of one researcher,

I find *no* evidence . . . to support specific stages of dying. Rather, dying patients demonstrate a wide variety of emotions that ebb and flow throughout our entire life as we face conflicts and crises. (Pattison, 1978, p. 141)

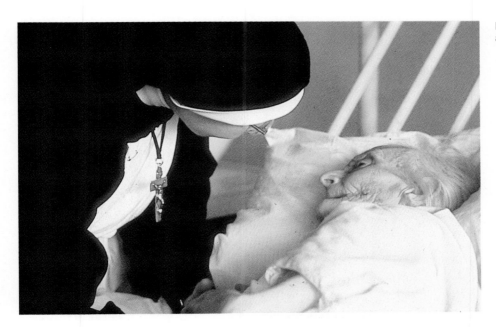

Hospice workers help dying people and their families.

Fortunately, in recent years, the death-education movement has grown stronger. For example, more than 400 psychology and sociology professors currently offer courses on death and dying (College Marketing Group, 1988), and many textbooks and other resources offer both information and practical advice (e.g., Cook & Oltjenbruns, 1989; DeSpelder & Strickland, 1987; Wass et al., 1988). Many people are helped by **hospices**, special organizations in which staff and volunteers aid terminally ill patients and allow them to die with dignity.

Life Satisfaction in Old Age

It would seem that elderly people have many reasons to be unhappy. We have discussed physical changes during the aging process, as well as perceptual and cognitive deficits in old age. Poor health, limited income, the loss of friends and family members, and fear of death could all contribute to a doom and gloom frame of mind.

Amazingly, however, age seems to have little effect on people's sense of well-being or happiness. For instance, a review of 15 studies showed that elderly people were—if anything—slightly higher in self-esteem than younger people (Bengtson et al., 1985). Figure 11.5 illustrates the results of an interesting survey by Palmore

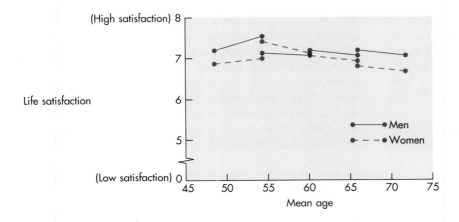

Figure 11.5
Life satisfaction does not depend upon age or gender. (Based on Palmore, 1981)

Elderly people do not differ from young people in their life satisfaction. In this photo, Mary Killips, 100 years old, plays the piano with Rachel Killips, her 2-year-old great granddaughter.

(1981). Each segment on this graph shows the score on a life satisfaction scale at the beginning of the study and the same people's rating 6 years later. As you can see, women do not differ substantially from men in life satisfaction. Furthermore, life satisfaction remains remarkably stable, with no systematic increases or decreases. In short, elderly people manage to overcome several important disadvantages, as well as some negative attitudes we discuss in the next section. Satisfaction with life is not limited to those under 65.

○ ○

In Depth: Attitudes Toward the Elderly

This chapter has probably encouraged you to think about your beliefs and opinions about the elderly. We begin this in-depth section by exploring the media's treatment of the elderly. Then we consider how laypeople and professionals respond to the elderly.

How the Elderly Are Treated in the Media   A student in my introductory psychology course showed me an advertisement for a skin cream, "It's never too late. Then again, it's never too early, either." If we take this ad seriously, we should hand out samples when children sign up for nursery school. Ads make people feel guilty about aging skin and graying hair. Women are told to do something about their sagging bustline, and men are told to buy expensive products to keep from becoming bald.

The Gray Panthers, a political action group concerned about treatment of the elderly, complain that the media show the elderly with blank or expressionless faces (Davis & Davis, 1985). Older adults object to the narrow range of images, and they would like to see elderly people who seem intelligent and well educated (Kaiser & Chandler, 1988).

The elderly are clearly underrepresented in television programs. For example, women over the age of 60 constitute 9% of the U.S. population, but only 3% of the characters on television (Holtzman & Akiyama, 1985; Passuth & Cook, 1985).

 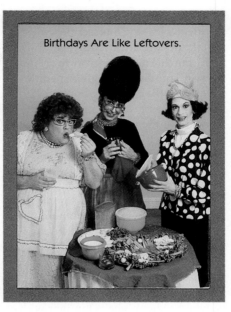

Figure 11.6
Examples of two birthday cards that focus on aging.

The next time you stop by a greeting-card store, check out the birthday cards for adults. The card on the right in Figure 11.6 is representative of a large group of cards that show growing old in a very negative light (Demos & Jache, 1981; Huyck & Duchon, 1986). Even the fairly positive card on the left contains the negative phrase "over the hill." You might also want to monitor the cartoons in magazines and newspapers. One analysis showed that the elderly were frequently depicted as useless, outdated, and isolated (Sheppard, 1981).

In short, elderly people are often missing in the media. When they do appear, they are often portrayed negatively.

Reactions to the Elderly   Robert Butler, the former director of the National Institute on Aging, defined **ageism** as stereotyping and discrimination against the elderly. He wrote that ageism is

> . . . a process of systematic stereotyping and discrimination against people because they are old, just as racism and sexism accomplish this with skin color and gender. Old people are categorized as senile, rigid in thought and manner, old-fashioned in morality and skill. . . . Ageism allows the younger generations to see older people as different from themselves; thus they subtly cease to identify with their elders as human beings. (Butler, 1975, pp. 11–12)

It is important to stress that ageism, like many psychological concepts, is extremely complex. For instance, children are somewhat positive toward elderly people. In one study, Black and White children between the ages of 5 and 13 responded as positively to old adults as to young adults (Mitchell et al., 1985).

In general, however, young adults tend to be negative about the elderly. For example, a review of 43 studies found that 30 comparisons showed more negative reactions toward the elderly than toward younger people, and 11 showed the reverse; 2 showed no difference. A meta-analysis of these studies demonstrated a significant negative bias against the elderly (Kite & Johnson, 1988).

Nevertheless, it is clear that ageism is an overly general term. For instance, younger adults are likely to rate elderly people as being fairly pleasant, even if they provide negative ratings about their competence. Also, younger adults are more positive about specific elderly people than they are about elderly people in general (Kite & Johnson, 1988). As you might expect, people who have had frequent pleasant interactions with elderly people are more likely to report that elderly people are friendly, optimistic, and self-reliant (Knox et al., 1986).

Furthermore, ageism may hurt females more than males. According to the **double standard of aging**, people are more negative about older women than older men (Bell, 1989; Sontag, 1979). For example, in a survey of married people, husbands were much more negative about their wives growing old than wives were about their husbands growing old (Margolin & White, 1987). Finally, Giesen and Datan (1980) asked respondents to describe the problems encountered by people of different ages. They were especially likely to report problems for older women, who were seen as dependent, without a clear purpose in life. Older men were judged to be more competent; for instance, they were perceived as advisors to young people. It is particularly sad that older women are the losers because most elderly people *are* women.

We have discussed attitudes toward the elderly in some detail because they provide an illustration of one of our themes. A simplistic view of ageism would suggest that everyone is guilty of stereotyping and discrimination toward all elderly people. However, reality is more complicated. To predict with any accuracy whether a person holds ageist views, we would need to know how old that person is, whether he or she is familiar with elderly people, what attributes of the elderly are being judged, and whether the elderly people being judged are male or female.

We have been examining how laypeople react to the elderly. What are the attitudes of people who are responsible for their health and welfare? An analysis of speeches in the U.S. Congress revealed numerous stereotypes about elderly people as socially isolated or inadequate as employees (Lubomudrov, 1987). Furthermore, physicians respond differently to elderly people. They are less likely to ask the elderly questions about family problems, and they are more likely to give incomplete answers and explanations (Greene et al., 1987).

Psychologists also have different reactions to older and younger clients. Ray and her colleagues (1987) constructed a paragraph about a depressed woman. On half of the forms, her age was identified as 72; on the other half it was 32. Clinical psychologists were asked how ideal this person would be for their own practice, and how likely the person would be to recover from the depression. As Figure 11.7 shows, psychologists reacted much more favorably toward the younger clients.

One of the most dangerous stereotypes about the elderly is that they are helpless and must depend upon other people. A study of the staff members in

Figure 11.7
Psychologists' ratings of "idealness" and likelihood of recovery, as a function of client's age. (Based on Ray et al., 1987)

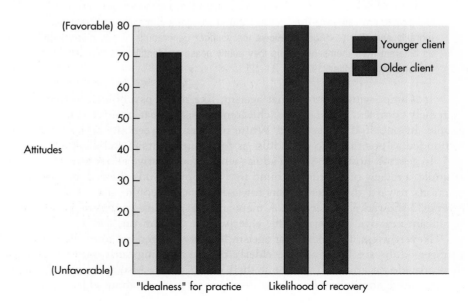

nursing homes showed that those who held the greatest number of stereotypes about the elderly were the most likely to encourage dependence (Kahana & Kiyak, 1984).

People who work with the elderly point out that we must try to eliminate the stereotype that elderly people are passive and helpless. Instead, we should encourage self-determination, so that older people can make their own choices and decide how to control their own lives. As evidence of the importance of self-determination, you may recall the research by Rodin and Langer (1977) discussed in chapter 2. Residents in a nursing home who were encouraged to take responsibility for themselves were rated as happier, more sociable, and more independent. More important, they were likely to live longer than people in a control group who had been treated in the standard fashion, which fosters dependence.

This study is particularly important because it shows how attitudes can influence life satisfaction and even longevity. When younger people in the community or in nursing homes treat the elderly with respect, encouraging them to make their own decisions, elderly people are likely to respond by becoming more independent and—amazingly—by living longer.

Section Summary: Personality and Social Development

- Erikson's theory of identity development proposes that adolescents and adults struggle with identity, intimacy, generativity, and integrity. Whitbourne's more recent research on adult identity emphasizes that values such as honesty form a critical component of identity.
- Studies on adult development show both stability and change in personality; however, researchers find little evidence for a universal midlife crisis.
- In general, adolescents and their parents are reasonably compatible; adolescents are more likely than children to emphasize emotional support in a friendship. In adulthood, life satisfaction is related to interactions with friends.
- Research on minority-group adolescents and adults shows that different racial and ethnic groups differ in college attendance, self-esteem, career choices, work patterns, and support from family members.
- People who are dying do not consistently experience the five stages of dying popularized by Kübler-Ross. Surveys show that elderly people tend to be as satisfied with their lives as younger people.
- Elderly people are often missing from or are represented negatively on TV and in other media.
- Young adults are often negative about the elderly, though there are important exceptions. Politicians, doctors, and psychologists may show ageist tendencies; people who view the elderly as active and self-determining may encourage elderly people to have happier, longer lives.

REVIEW QUESTIONS

1. The theme of individual differences appears many times in this chapter. Try to recall as many examples of this theme as possible, including physical changes at puberty, perceptual changes in aging, moral development, and personality and social development.

2. Elderly people experience some deficits during the aging process, but in other respects, the elderly do not differ substantially from younger adults. Discuss this statement with respect to reaction time, perception, memory, and performance on other cognitive tasks.

3. This chapter frequently discussed myths and stereotypes. Discuss the popular misconceptions—as well as the research—about the following topics: adolescent-parent relationships, midlife crisis, the elderly, gay people, single people, and death and dying.

4. How would you characterize the adolescent with respect to physical development, cognitive processes, career choices, identity development, and interpersonal relationships?

5. Gender is both relevant and irrelevant in the lives of adolescents and adults. Discuss gender differences and similarities in reactions to puberty, life expectancy, moral decisions, work, love relationships, parenting, and adult development. Finally, provide examples of the double standard of aging.

6. What are Erikson's last four stages of psychosocial development? Gather information from the sections on work, love relationships, and death and dying to provide more details on the central tasks in each of these four stages.

7. Race and ethnic group sometimes influence psychological development, but sometimes they have little effect. Discuss this statement in connection with the topics of longevity, adolescent career choice, and attitudes toward the elderly, as well as the topics in the section on minority groups.

8. Try to imagine yourself and several good friends 20 years from now. What would correlational studies on this group of people be likely to reveal about the stability-change issue? How about studies that assess average level of a personality characteristic? What would be suggested by the concept of individual fanning out?

9. We noted how researchers can reach the wrong conclusion if their study includes confounding variables. Explain how a study on life happiness throughout the life span might reach an incorrect conclusion if it failed to control several confounding variables. (It might be useful to begin by listing some possible confounding variables.)

10. What is ageism? How is it revealed in the media? Discuss how laypeople, politicians, doctors, and psychologists demonstrate ageism. Finally, describe how ageism can affect the quality and duration of people's lives.

NEW TERMS

puberty
menarche
premenstrual syndrome (PMS)
menopause
male climacteric
fluid intelligence
crystallized intelligence
gay person
homophobia

individual fanning out
interest-related friendships
deep friendships
multiple-jeopardy hypothesis
life review
hospices
ageism
double standard of aging

RECOMMENDED READINGS

Bee, H. L. (1987). *The journey of adulthood*. New York; Macmillan. Bee's book about adulthood and aging is conversational in tone and is particularly strong in its coverage of social relationships.

Nielsen, L. (1987). *Adolescent psychology*. New York: Holt, Rinehart and Winston. This comprehensive textbook of adolescent development includes a chapter on adolescents from minority cultures.

Petersen, A. C. (1988). Adolescent development. *Annual Review of Psychology, 39,* 583–607. This review chapter includes information on the history of research on adolescence, adolescent adjustment, puberty, and family interactions.

The Gerontologist. Published by the Gerontological Society of America, this journal contains a wide variety of readable articles from various disciplines.

Whitbourne, S. K. (1986a). *Adult development* (2nd ed.). New York: Praeger. Whitbourne's advanced-level textbook is especially strong in its discussion of physical, perceptual, cognitive, and personality changes during aging.

**Motivation and
Emotion**

Ashrita Furman, who manages a health food store in Queens, New York, is listed 11 times in the *Guinness Book of Worlds Records*. For example, he set the record for continuous juggling, keeping three balls in the air for 6 hours, 7 minutes, and 4 seconds. He has also set the record for underwater pogo-stick bouncing; he made 3,647 jumps in 3 hours, 40 minutes—in the Amazon River. He also holds the records for long-distance walking with a full milk bottle balanced on his head (32.9 miles, without a drop spilled) and for continuous somersaulting (12.2 miles).

What motivates Ashrita Furman when many others who manage health food stores would be content to spend their days selling tofu and alfalfa sprouts? The activities are not physically enjoyable. Somersaulting, for instance, made him feel totally dizzy and nauseated. Instead, Ashrita is motivated by the challenge itself. As he commented, "What thrills me is to do something when I'm not even sure it's physically possible" ("Talk of the Town," 1989, p. 26).

Motivation, the first of two topics in this chapter, focuses on *why* people behave in certain ways. Why did you eat a second slice of chocolate fudge cake, when you felt completely full before the first slice? Why does sexual motivation increase for some people when their necks are stroked? And why is Ashrita Furman currently negotiating with the officials in Paris to pogo-stick up the Eiffel Tower?

Motivation is the process of activating behavior, sustaining it, and directing it toward a particular goal. The word *motivation* comes from the Latin word *motivus*, which means *moving*. Motivation moves us to act and accomplish.

The second part of this chapter examines emotion. Both motivation and emotion can move us to act. For instance, angry emotions can prompt us to act aggressively. However, we will see that emotions usually suggest feelings (Buck, 1988). The definition of emotion is complex because it involves three components: cognitive, physiological, and behavioral. Specifically, **emotion** is a subjective experience or feeling that is accompanied by changes in physiological reactions and behavior.

Consider how these three components might operate in a typical emotional situation. You splurged on a plane trip to visit a friend who lives in another part of the country. You arrive at the airport and glance up at the monitor to confirm the departure time. Next to your flight number is a single word: CANCELLED. Your subjective experiences include surprise, anger, and anxiety. Physiological reactions include an increase in heart rate and breathing rate. Behaviorally, your jaw drops, and your forehead wrinkles. You are also likely to search for someone who can tell you what to do next.

Motivation and emotion are intertwined concepts. Intense emotions—either positive or negative—typically accompany motivated behavior. For example, consider how the emotions of anticipation, anger, fear, and joy might be evoked as the members of a basketball team strive for the winning point in the final seconds of the last game of the tournament.

We are often motivated by emotional reactions, even when we know they are irrational. Consider a study by Rozin and his co-authors (1986). College students watched an experimenter open a container of sugar and pour it into two identical bottles. The students were then instructed to take two labels, one marked

Ashrita Furman is listed 11 times in the *Guinness Book of World Records*. Among his records is one for long-distance walking with a full milk bottle balanced on his head.

sugar and one marked *sodium cyanide*, and apply one to each bottle, making their own choice. The students later avoided eating the sugar in the bottle marked with the poisonous label, even though they knew the contents could not be poisonous. A strong emotional reaction—perhaps a blend of fear and disgust—had motivated them to choose the other bottle.

Let us begin by considering the topic of motivation. In the second part of the chapter we explore emotion.

Motivation

We humans frequently search for motives. The scandal newspaper at the supermarket asks why the wealthy hotel-chain owner cheated on her income tax, or why the New Jersey mother sold her infant twins to buy a sports car for her new boyfriend. On a more literary level, consider the questions your English professor might raise in examining a Shakespearean play. Why did Iago want Othello to believe that his wife, Desdemona, had been unfaithful? Why did Richard III murder the young princes, who were the rightful heirs to the throne?

Human behavior is activated by a variety of motives. Some motives are largely biological, emphasizing bodily needs such as hunger, thirst, and excretion. Others are primarily social motives, such as the needs for achievement, affiliation, and nurturance. We cover several motives in other chapters. For example, the sleep motive was discussed in chapter 5, and nurturance was examined in the parenting section of chapter 11. Chapter 17 considers affiliation and love, and chapter 18 discusses aggression.

This chapter explores three representative human motives: hunger, sexuality, and achievement motivation. We begin with the most biological of these topics—hunger—and progress to the most social of the three—achievement motivation. However, we note that even hunger is influenced by social and cognitive factors; clearly this most basic bodily need is influenced by more complex variables than simple nutritive value.

Hunger and Eating

The Roman Emperor Vitellius, not known for his vegetarian habits, had a particular fondness for a stew consisting of flamingo tongues and peacock brains. People in modern-day Southeast Asia savor a fruit called *durian*, which has an odor like very rotten cheese. The food that inspires enthusiastic eating in one person often produces nausea in another. Humans have no simple, universal rules that separate the delightful from the disgusting.

We begin by discussing the biological basis of hunger and eating, and then we consider some external, environmental influences. Our last two topics are obesity and eating disorders.

Biological Factors Regulating Eating   What internal factors trigger hunger and eating? Most people guess that contractions of the empty stomach produce the subjective experience of hunger. However, researchers have established that people report they are hungry even when their stomachs have been removed for medical reasons (Wangensteen & Carlson, 1931). The explanation is more complex, involving regulation by both the brain and body chemistry.

In chapter 3, you learned the hypothalamus is a portion of the brain that regulates eating. Figure 12.1 shows the hypothalamus of a rat, the animal used for much of the research on hunger. The hypothalamus consists of several regions that function differently. Let us look at the early research that presented a neat, straightforward explanation for how the hypothalamus regulates eating. Then we consider more recent research showing that eating—like other psychological processes—is not that simple.

The early research suggested that the **lateral hypothalamus** (or **LH**, located at the side of the hypothalamus) functioned as the "start eating" center. That is, mild electrical stimulation of this region in rats caused them to start eating. Furthermore, when the LH was destroyed in other rats, they refused to eat. In contrast, it seemed that the **ventromedial hypothalamus** (or **VMH**, located toward the center of the hypothalamus) functioned as the "stop eating" center. That is, stimulation of this region caused rats to stop eating. Furthermore, as Figure 12.2 shows, when the VMH was destroyed, rats overate wildly until they doubled or

Figure 12.1
The lateral hypothalamus (LH) and the ventromedial hypothalamus (VMH) in the rat's brain (this picture represents the view you would have if the front half of the rat's brain had been cut away).

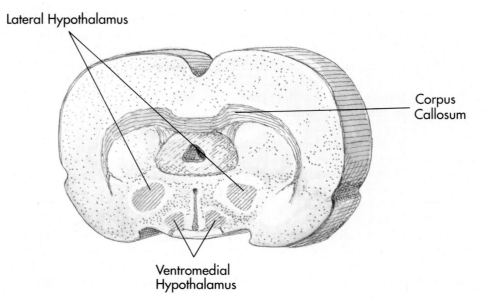

Lateral Hypothalamus

Corpus Callosum

Ventromedial Hypothalamus

tripled their normal weight. Summarizing these studies, one theorist proposed that the LH was the brain's hunger center and the VMH was its fullness center (Stellar, 1954).

However, the true story is more complex than the original theory. For instance, although rats with a destroyed LH refused to eat initially, they could be persuaded to eat eventually if they were first tube-fed and then offered delicacies such as moistened chocolate chip cookies. Thus, rats can start eating even though they lack a lateral hypothalamus (Teitelbaum & Epstein, 1962).

Furthermore, although rats with a destroyed VMH initially ate huge quantities of food, after about 3 weeks they ate only slightly more than normal. In addition, these rats became quite picky about the foods they chose to eat. For example, they rejected food with a bitter taste. Thus, rats that lack a ventromedial hypothalamus can stop eating (Weingarten, 1982).

We can conclude, therefore, that structures in the hypothalamus help regulate hunger and eating. However, these structures do not operate in a simple on-off fashion (Keesey & Powley, 1986; Logue, 1986).

Body chemistry is another biological factor that regulates hunger and eating. For example, the level of glucose is important. **Glucose** is a simple sugar nutrient that provides energy. In general, when the level of glucose in your bloodstream is low, you feel hungry. When the glucose level is high, you feel full. The blood glucose level appears to be monitored by **glucostats**, neurons that are sensitive to glucose levels. Researchers are not certain where these glucostats are located, but it seems likely that the hypothalamus receives messages about glucose levels.

Another important body chemical is **insulin**, which is a hormone secreted by the pancreas. Insulin plays an important role in converting blood glucose into stored fat. As you may know, diabetics lack insulin, and they must receive insulin injections in order to use glucose as a source of energy. Insulin therefore influences hunger *indirectly*, by decreasing glucose levels.

However, researchers have determined that insulin also influences hunger *directly*. In experiments, participants' blood glucose was maintained at a constant level while insulin injections artificially raised the insulin level (Rodin, 1985). People with elevated insulin levels were likely to report feeling hungry and typically ate more food than those with a normal insulin level (Figure 12.3.) Later, we will see how insulin rises when people think about food.

External Factors Regulating Eating

Although hunger and eating can be influenced by physiological factors, our eating habits are also determined by other factors. Obviously, the taste of a food influences how much we eat. However, we learn food preferences in our culture. My parents recall a Mexican geologist who tried to convince them to try a special delicacy of his region, a worm that lived exclusively in the maguey plant. They politely declined. One day they were eating particularly tasty tacos at his home. As my mother took another bite of her taco, a plump deep-fried worm fell to her plate. A moment earlier, the taco had tasted delicious, but once she realized that it contained a culturally forbidden food, she could not contemplate taking another bite.

Our culture determines not only what we eat, but when we eat. Americans tend to eat their evening meal about 6 p.m., whereas residents of Madrid are likely to begin at 10 p.m. Certainly, the stomach, hypothalamus, glucose and insulin do not operate differently in Spain! Instead, learning is an important external factor.

Other external factors that influence eating include the social situation in which we eat. For example, we typically eat more food in the company of others than when we are alone (Zajonc, 1965). Naturally, characteristics of the food are also important. For instance, we eat more food when it appears in many different

Figure 12.2
Destruction of the ventromedial hypothalamus in this animal caused it to eat more, tripling its body weight.

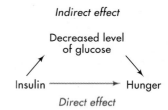

Figure 12.3
The indirect and direct influence of insulin on hunger.

forms. People eat more cooked pasta when they are offered three separate forms of pasta (e.g., separate bowls of spaghetti, macaroni, and bow ties) rather than just a single form (Rolls et al., 1982).

Explanations for Obesity   We have seen that the factors influencing eating are complex, involving both internal and external forces. Similarly, the determinants of obesity are complex, involving much more than simple overeating. Consider a study in which researchers carefully monitored all the food that two 260-pound women consumed. The researchers concluded that these women were maintaining stable body weights on only 1,000 calories per day, the caloric equivalent of just three peanut butter sandwiches (Wooley et al., 1979). When overweight people claim that they really do not eat excessive amounts, they may well be telling the truth.

If food intake cannot fully explain obesity, what can? Three important factors are genetic makeup, set point, and an exaggerated insulin response to the sights and smells of food.

Genetic predisposition makes some people more likely than others to become obese. For instance, Stunkard and his colleagues (1986) studied 540 adults in Denmark who had all been adopted. Their current body weight was closely related to the body weight of their biological parents, but it was not related to the weight of the adoptive parents. In this study, then, nature was more important than nurture in determining whether a person was slender, normal-sized, or overweight. It seems likely that an important inherited factor is metabolic rate. Some people burn up calories more quickly than other people. If your parents have high metabolic rates, it is likely that your rate is also high, and you are not likely to gain weight easily.

A second major explanation for obesity involves the notion called **set point**, a mechanism that seems to keep people at roughly the same weight throughout their adult lives. You probably know some people who try valiantly to lose weight, and with heroic efforts they lose 15 pounds. However, they gain it back several months later, even though they have been eating sensibly ever since the initial weight loss.

According to set-point theory, each person's body has a fixed number of **fat cells**, which are cells that store fat. Fat cells may shrink in size when an overweight person diets, but the number remains constant. Thus, conscientious dieters may decrease the size of their fat cells, but those cells sit around, waiting for the opportunity to swell up again (Sjostrom, 1980). Some researchers propose that the shriveled fat cells send hunger messages to the dieter's brain. As a consequence, dieters are likely to feel that they are continually hungry. To make the situation even worse, when overweight people begin a diet their metabolism often slows down, maintaining body functions by using up fewer calories. Therefore, it is harder to lose weight—and easier to gain it back.

Thus, overweight people may face a losing battle with genetics, set point, fat cells, and metabolism. Some overweight people have an additional handicap because they are particularly sensitive to external cues about eating. Demonstration 12.1 shows some of the characteristics of people who are externals, or people who eat because of the sight and smell of food, as well as other external cues about eating, rather than internal states of hunger. In a series of studies, Judith Rodin (1981, 1985) tested people who varied in their responsiveness to external food cues. These people went for 18 hours without food and then came to Rodin's laboratory at lunchtime. While blood samples were being drawn, researchers brought in a steak and placed it nearby. The steak was still grilling and crackling in the frying pan, providing a rich source of sights, sounds, and smells to remind these hungry people about food.

Demonstration 12.1

Sensitivity to External Cues About Eating

Answer each of the following questions either "yes" or "no."

_____ 1. If you are at a party, and you are standing near a conspicuous bowl of potato chips, do you begin munching them, even though you are not really hungry?

_____ 2. Does an advertisement for food on television send you to the kitchen or other sources of snacks?

_____ 3. When you are in a shopping mall and the unmistakable aroma of chocolate chip cookies assails your senses, do you buy a cookie, even though you have just eaten?

_____ 4. In your home, are you tempted to eat a snack that is in plain view, though you would be safe if it were stored in the refrigerator?

_____ 5. When your watch indicates it is lunchtime, do you automatically go to lunch, even though you had a late breakfast and really are not hungry?

_____ 6. Does the sight of your favorite food make you very hungry and eager to begin eating?

Now count up the number of "yes" responses. In general, people with a large number of "yes" responses are especially sensitive to external eating cues.

Interestingly, thoughts about food tend to produce a rise in insulin level. As mentioned earlier, insulin tends to increase the sensation of hunger. Rodin discovered that people who had high scores for responsiveness to external food cues were likely to have especially large insulin responses when exposed to the grilling steak. That luscious steak sent their insulin levels soaring, making them even hungrier than before. So an overweight person who is sensitive to external food cues frequently feels hungry. Consequently, a person with a genetic predisposition toward obesity, who has a slow metabolism, a large number of fat cells, a high set point—and also has the bad fortune to be responsive to external food cues—finds weight loss especially difficult.

Because obesity is not limited to a single cause, it is not likely that it will have a single cure (Rodin, 1981). Table 12.1 lists some hints that may encourage weight loss.

Eating Disorders A young woman remarked, "When I say I overeat, it may not be what you think. I feel I'm gorging myself when I eat more than one cracker with peanut butter" (Bruch, 1978, p. 3). To save calories, she even avoided licking postage stamps. She has an eating disorder called **anorexia nervosa**, which is characterized by an irrational pursuit of thinness and concern about gaining weight (Sholevar, 1987). Anorexics feel fat, even when they look emaciated. The American Psychiatric Association specifies that a person may be classified as anorexic if body weight is 25% less than specified on standard weight charts and if no known physical illness accounts for the low weight.

About 95% of people with anorexia nervosa are females, and the most common age for this disorder is 12 to 18 (American Psychiatric Association, 1980). However, clinicians need to be aware that men and older people can also become anorexic, even though young women are the most common victims.

It is not clear how anorexia nervosa begins, though the disorder frequently occurs in response to a new situation such as entering college (Bemis, 1978). Depressed mood and anxiety tend to be associated with anorexia (Sholevar, 1987). However, it is difficult to interpret this relationship. Like many correlations, we

People who are very responsive to external food cues are likely to have larger insulin responses when exposed to a grilling steak.

Table 12.1   *Strategies that May Encourage Weight Loss*

1. Substitute low-calorie foods for high-calorie foods (e.g., melon for dessert rather than brownies).
2. Take moderately small portions, and avoid sitting near additional sources of the food.
3. Become aware of situations that encourage you to overeat (e.g., eat-all-you-want buffet restaurants), and arrange to avoid them.
4. Prior to a problem situation that you cannot avoid, plan a coping strategy (e.g., mentally rehearse how you will select only one cookie from a tray, rather than a handful).
5. If you do slip from time to time, do not condemn yourself and abandon your willpower.
6. Set a modest goal for yourself and reward yourself (but not with food!) if you meet that goal.
7. Exercise to use up more calories; exercise also tends to increase your metabolic rate, which will make it easier to keep the weight off.

A bulimic may consume up to 50,000 calories during a single binge-eating episode.

cannot clearly define which is the cause and which is the effect (chapter 2). Do depressed, anxious people develop anorexia? Alternatively, do anorexics become depressed and anxious because of their physiological, starved condition?

Anorexia nervosa is a life-threatening disorder, and 2% to 8% of anorexics die from it (Kreipe et al., 1989). In anorexia, concern about thinness takes priority over maintaining a healthy body. As one parent told me about his anorexic daughter, "She'd rather be dead than fat."

Bulimia (pronounced "boo-*lih*-mee-ah") is characterized by binge eating, or episodes in which people consume huge amounts of foods, sometimes up to 50,000 calories at a time. The food is gobbled down quickly, often with little enjoyment of its taste. During the binge, bulimics are aware that they are eating abnormally and they are afraid that they will not be able to stop eating voluntarily. Some bulimics induce vomiting after a binge, and they may also fast between binges. Like anorexics, bulimics are obsessed about food, eating, and body weight (Hamilton et al., 1984).

It is difficult to know how common bulimia is, because the bingeing is often done secretly and because bulimics may maintain normal body weight. Thus, bulimics are not as noticeable as anorexics. However, some experts estimate that it occurs in more than 10% of a college population (Schlesier-Stropp, 1984). Roughly 90% of its victims are female (Schwartz, 1987). Bulimia is dangerous because it causes intestinal, kidney, and other medical problems, though it is not as life-threatening as anorexia.

For some time, researchers have noticed a correlation between bingeing and dieting. That is, the same people who binge frequently are also likely to place themselves on strict diets when they are not bingeing. Most researchers assumed that bingeing *caused* dieting. However, Polivy and Herman (1985) argue that dieting causes bingeing. In other words, the clear majority of bulimics began restrictive diets *before* they began to binge.

Why should dieters develop bingeing habits? Polivy and Herman (1985) believe that cognitive factors are more important than physiological explanations. Specifically, when dieters temporarily eat too much, they then abandon restraint and begin to eat lustily. In a laboratory study, both dieters and nondieters were required to drink either two high-calorie milkshakes or none at all. Afterward, they were presented with several different kinds of ice cream, and they were encouraged to eat all they wanted.

As Figure 12.4 shows, the dieters actually ate more ice cream after drinking two milkshakes than when they had no milkshake "preload." It is as if the dieters told themselves, "Oh well, those two milkshakes ruined my diet for today . . . I might as well enjoy the ice cream!" This pattern of eating lustily after a high-

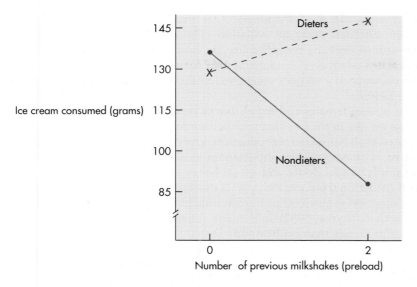

145 — Dieters — ✗

Ice cream consumed (grams)

130
✗
115
100
Nondieters
85

0 2

Number of previous milkshakes (preload)

Figure 12.4
Consumption of ice cream as a function of number of previous milkshakes and body-weight category. (Based on Hibscher & Herman, 1977)

calorie preload is called **counter-regulation**. In contrast, nondieters show normal regulation: They eat more with no preload than after a large preload.

How can dieters avoid becoming bingers? If they slip temporarily, they should not condemn themselves and abandon their sensible eating habits. More helpful still, our society should abandon its glorification of the kind of anorexic models shown in high-fashion magazines—an attitude that encourages young women to starve themselves. In the long run, it is better to be a few pounds overweight than to begin a severely restrictive diet that will encourage binge eating.

Sexuality

Ideas and decisions about sexuality are an important component of many students' daily lives. For example, when students were asked to write about an important current conflict in their lives, one young woman wrote about a controversy that has dominated her relationship with her boyfriend for the last four years:

> The major issue which has always caused conflict in our relationship is sex. He wants to, I don't; but it's not that simple. . . . I just don't feel I am ready, there are things I want to do for myself first, before I get really deeply involved, and, never one to gamble, I don't want to chance anything. Besides, if something went wrong and if, for example, I got pregnant, I would be the one who was stuck. I have other reasons, though not so easily explained; it's a matter of self-esteem. I was raised in a very traditional environment, and I have my own dreams of how things will be. I want to wait until I am married. I know most people don't agree, they believe it is silly and prudish; but it is part of my moral code, something which I feel very strongly about, and something which is part of the many interwoven, inexplicable things which make up my identity.

To discuss the topic of sexuality, we need to consider not only people's moral codes, but also topics as diverse as hormone levels and sexual passion.

We begin this section with a discussion of the biological aspects of sexuality, and next discuss external and cognitive factors that influence sexuality. We then study the sexual response cycle and sexual behavior; in this last section we examine some of the factors that must be considered whenever a person—such as this young woman—is making a decision about a sexual relationship.

Sex Hormones In most mammals other than humans, the level of the female hormone estrogen peaks at ovulation. The elevated hormone level makes the female animal sexually receptive (or "in heat"). In contrast, the male hormone level remains relatively constant and male sexual behavior normally depends more on the presence of a sexually receptive female than on variations in hormone level (Feder, 1984).

In human females and males, hormones are critically important during puberty, as we saw in the last chapter; they are responsible for developing structures that are essential in sexual reproduction, as well as changes in adolescents' bodies. However, hormones are less important in regulating the pattern of sexual behavior. For example, sexual desire and sexual behavior are not significantly higher at the time of ovulation (Harvey, 1987; Williams & Williams, 1982). Similarly, the day-to-day variation in the level of testosterone in males is generally unrelated to their sexual activity (Byrne, 1982). In humans, sexual arousal depends more on external and cognitive cues than on hormone levels.

External and Cognitive Factors Touch is one of the most powerful sources of sexual arousal. A caress, a passionate kiss, or stroking the inside of the thigh . . . people vary in the kind of touch and the location of touch that they find most sexually stimulating.

Touch is an extremely powerful source of sexual arousal.

Humans can also be effectively aroused by visual stimuli, either by the sight of a nude person or by erotic pictures. Research has demonstrated that men and women are similar in their tendency to be aroused by slides and movies showing foreplay and intercourse (Hyde, 1986; Schmidt & Sigusch, 1970). However, we need to be concerned about some potential problems with viewing erotic material. For instance, Weaver and his colleagues (1984) found that men who had viewed a video of attractive nude females in provocative poses were likely to rate their girlfriends as less physically attractive. Furthermore, Malamuth and Check (1985) found that men who frequently read sexually explicit magazines were more likely to believe that women enjoy forced sex—a rape myth that is clearly false. (Incidentally, these results are correlational, and therefore part of the results may be due to personality differences *before* reading the pornographic magazines.)

Touch and visual stimuli can be sexually arousing; however, human imagination and fantasy can create sexual excitement even without the aid of hormonal peaks and external stimuli. A saying captures the importance of cognitive factors: "The brain is our most important erogenous zone." As further evidence, researchers estimate that the majority of cases of sexual dysfunction are psychological, lending additional support to the notion that our thoughts play a critical role in sexual arousal and behavior (Hyde, 1986).

The Sexual Response Cycle Current models of the stages of sexual response emphasize cognitive factors. For example, a model proposed by Zilbergelt and Ellison (1980) stresses that sexual interest or desire precedes four more physiological stages of the sexual response cycle that includes excitement, plateau, orgasm, and resolution (Masters & Johnson, 1966).

During the first stage, called the **excitement phase**, both women and men become sexually excited. (As we just discussed, a variety of stimuli can produce sexual excitement.) Breathing, heart rate, and muscle tension increase. Blood rushes into the genital region, causing erection in a man's penis and swelling in a woman's clitoris, which is the small, very sensitive organ located in front of the vagina.

In the **plateau phase**, the breathing, heart rate, and muscle tension increase even further. In the man, the penis reaches full erection, and fluid may appear at the tip of the penis. This fluid, however, may contain enough sperm to produce conception. In the woman, the lower one third of the vaginal wall becomes engorged with blood, and the clitoris becomes extremely sensitive.

In the **orgasmic phase**, muscles in the pelvic region and the genitals contract rhythmically, producing a pleasurable feeling of sexual release. In addition, the man ejaculates, expelling a milky fluid rich in sperm.

During the final, or **resolution phase**, breathing, heart rate, and muscle tension return to normal. The genitals also gradually return to the size they were prior to excitement.

As you can see from this overview, men and women have somewhat similar sexual responses. This physiological similarity was highlighted in the original research of Masters and Johnson (1966). In addition, men and women have similar psychological reactions to orgasm. Look at Demonstration 12.2 and try to guess whether a man or a woman wrote each description. In one study, people's guesses were no better than chance (Vance & Wagner, 1977). In short, women and men share more similarities than differences—even in the area of sexuality.

So far, our discussion of sexuality has emphasized swelling genitals, heavy breathing, and beating hearts. But sexual behavior is much more complex than the physiological processes might imply. Let us therefore shift our attention to human sexual behavior.

Sexual Behavior   A colleague recalls her graduate school professor saying that anything capable of a great deal of good is also capable of a great deal of harm (Smith, personal communication, 1990). This statement clearly applies to sexuality. A sexual relationship under ideal circumstances can provide intense pleasure and

---

Demonstration 12.2

Psychological Reactions to Orgasm

Each of these descriptions of an orgasm was written by a sexually experienced woman or man. Based on your ideas about gender, try to guess who wrote each passage. Place a W or an M in front of each description. The answers appear at the end of the chapter.

_____ 1. A sudden feeling of lightheadedness followed by an intense feeling of relief and elation. A rush. Intense muscular spasms of the whole body. Sense of euphoria followed by deep peace and relaxation.

_____ 2. To me an orgasmic experience is the most satisfying *pleasure* that I have experienced in relation to any other type of satisfaction or pleasure that I've had which were nonsexually oriented.

_____ 3. It is like turning a water faucet on. You notice the oncoming flow but it can be turned on or off when desired. You feel the valves open and close and the fluid flow. An orgasm makes your head and body tingle.

_____ 4. A build-up of tension which starts to pulsate very fast, and there is a sudden release from the tension and desire to sleep.

_____ 5. It is a pleasant, tension-relieving muscular contraction. It relieves physical tension and mental anticipation.

_____ 6. A release of a very high level of tension, but ordinarily tension is unpleasant whereas the tension before orgasm is far from unpleasant.

_____ 7. An orgasm is a great release of tension with spasmodic reaction at the peak. This is exactly how it feels to me.

_____ 8. A building of tension, sometimes, and frustration until the climax. A *tightening* inside, palpitating rhythm, explosion, and warmth and peace.

Source: From Vance & Wagner, 1977, pp. 207–210.

---

feelings of intimacy. However—as described by the young woman at the beginning of this section—it can lead to loss of self-esteem and worry.

One source of worry and concern, especially in the 1990s, is the spread of sexually transmitted diseases (STDs). Two common ones that have been familiar for several decades are **gonorrhea** (a bacterial disease that infects the genital membranes) and **genital herpes** (a virus that causes bumps and sores in the genital area). However, the most dangerous sexually transmitted disease is **AIDS,** or **acquired immunodeficiency syndrome**, a disease that destroys the body's natural immunity. Once the immune system has been destroyed, diseases such as pneumonia and cancer can take over, leading eventually to death. By the end of 1990, approximately 101,000 people had died of AIDS. By 1993, roughly 200,000 people will be living with AIDS ("The HIV Challenge Continues," 1991). Victims of AIDS are often people who have abused intravenous drugs. Original reports suggested that AIDS was sexually transmitted only between gay men, but we now know that AIDS can also be spread during heterosexual intercourse. Chapter 19 considers AIDS in more detail, in connection with health psychology.

Heterosexual individuals have an additional responsibility; they must make thoughtful and informed decisions about pregnancy. Figure 12.5 shows the pregnancy rates for teenage women, and it contrasts data for U.S. teenagers with those in four other countries. As you can see, the rate in the United States is roughly double the rate in Canada and Sweden. Each pregnant teenager faces a personal struggle, whether she considers an abortion, giving up the child for adoption, or spending the next 20 years raising the child.

Studies have demonstrated that teenagers are amazingly uninformed about important aspects of sexuality (Morrison, 1985). For instance, some believe that they cannot get pregnant the first time they have intercourse. Moreover, even well-informed teenagers (and adults, too) may make an important cognitive error: They believe that the statistics about pregnancy rates without the use of contraceptives apply to *other* people, not to themselves (Morrison, 1985). As Hayes (1987) concludes, numerous factors contribute to the incidence of unplanned pregnancy.

We have noted some of the negative aspects of sexuality. We need to discuss one other unpleasant topic relevant to some relationships—coercive sexual interactions. **Sexual coercion** involves forcing someone to have sex against her (or his) will (Allgeier, 1987).

Figure 12.5
The rate of teenage pregnancies in the United States is substantially greater than the rate in other comparable countries.

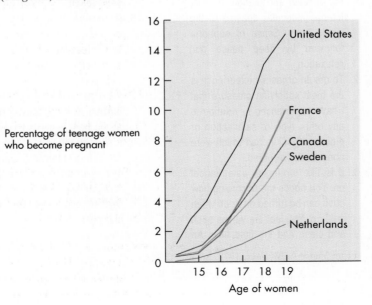

Percentage of teenage women who become pregnant

Age of women

The most extreme example of sexual coercion is **rape**, which is sexual intercourse that is forcibly committed, without consent (Hilberman, 1978). Rape can be committed by a stranger, but data show that people who have been raped are likely to know those who raped them (Katz & Mazur, 1979; Matlin, 1987). Consider the case of a young woman who had four previous dates with a male student at her college. On the fifth date, after fairly intensive sex play, he forced her to have sex, despite her objections. In a survey of college women, one fifth reported that they had been pressured to have sexual intercourse against their will (Koss & Oros, 1982). Unfortunately, most cases of date rape go unreported (Kanin, 1985).

Whereas rape involves physical violence or threatened violence, other kinds of sexual coercion involve different threats, such as "Sleeping with me is the best way to get that promotion." This is an extreme example of **sexual harassment**, or an unwelcome sexual advance, request for sexual favors, or other verbal or physical conduct of a sexual nature (Equal Employment Opportunity Commission, 1980). Table 12.2 lists some examples of rape and sexual harassment.

In coercive relationships, one person has more power than another. In contrast, **consensual sexual interactions** are defined as participation in sexual relationships "by fully informed adults who freely choose to engage in mutual sexual stimulation" (Allgeier, 1987, p. 11). When two mature people respect each other (and when neither feels guilty about the relationship), sexual interactions can offer uniquely positive pleasures. Most of you reading this book will be making—and have made—decisions about sexuality, and no book can make the decision for you. Any decision in the 1990s must take into account the possibilities of both disease and pregnancy. However, as Allgeier (1987, p. 11) writes, "Humans are blessed with a potential capacity for experiencing intense intimacy and

Table 12.2   *Examples of Rape and Sexual Harassment*

Rape
* A college sophomore attends a party, where she meets an attractive male who also seems to be a student. After dancing together for about 15 minutes, he suggests that they go outside to cool off. Once outside, he throws her down, knocks her out, and rapes her.
* A 67-year-old woman answers her door to find a man who says he is from a delivery company. He begins beating her head with a wrench, rapes her, and steals her TV and jewelry.
* A 13-year-old girl leaves her home in the early evening to go to the corner store. A stranger grabs her, forcing her to the ground, and rapes her.

Sexual Harassment
* A woman takes a summer job in a restaurant. Her boss has been patting her and making suggestive comments for about a week, and then he suggests that they go to a motel after work that evening.
* A student at a community college is learning how to use a new machine. The instructor puts his hand on her inner thigh as he explains how to use the machine.
* A student at a university is taking a course required for her major. Last week she needed to talk to the course instructor about her paper, and he seemed too friendly, asking questions she thought were too personal. He asked her to come back today. This time, he says he would like to go to bed with her. She is repulsed by the idea, but she is afraid he may fail her in the course if she declines.

Note: Sexual coercion includes all cases of rape. However, Allgeier's (1987) definition of sexual coercion would exclude cases of sexual harassment that do not involve sexual intercourse, oral sex, or anal sex.
Source: Examples based on Brownmiller, 1975; Burgess & Holmstrom, 1980; Dziech & Weiner, 1984.

connection, not to mention exquisite sensations, in the context of their sexual interactions with one another."

Achievement Motivation

So far, we have discussed motives that have some clearly identified physiological components. The hypothalamus and the levels of glucose and insulin play an important part in our motivation to eat. Biological changes in the genitals underlie the four stages of the sexual response cycle. However, researchers have not developed physiological explanations for achievement motivation.

The **achievement motive** involves meeting personal standards of success, doing better than others, and mastering challenging tasks. Carlos does not try to do well in his college courses because a structure in his brain forces him to study, and Jane does not strive for the salesperson of the month award because of a high level of hormone pulsing through her blood. We discussed the cognitive components of both hunger and sexuality, but the cognitive components of achievement motivation are even more critical. People who are achievers think about doing things well, even when there is no stimulus to excel (McClelland, 1985).

In this section, we begin by examining individual differences in achievement motivation, followed by a discussion of fear of success. We then consider how reward can sometimes decrease achievement-related behavior. Our final topic explores the relationship between achievement motivation and emotion.

Individual Differences in Achievement Motivation   Take a moment to reread the definition of the achievement motive, and think about several friends who are clearly high in this motive. Now think about several other friends who are low in the achievement motive—people who are not particularly interested in success, competition, and mastery. Although achievement motivation is determined by many different factors, our theme of individual differences runs through this entire section.

How do researchers measure these individual differences? Achievement motivation is usually measured with an assessment instrument called the Thematic Apperception Test (TAT), which will be considered in detail in chapter 14. If you were to take the TAT, you would see a series of ambiguous pictures, for instance, a picture of a man daydreaming or a picture of a middle-aged woman with an older woman in the background. You would be asked to tell a brief story about each picture. These stories would presumably express the extent of your motivation to achieve, to affiliate with others, to strive for power, and so forth. With respect to achievement motivation, for instance, a story about a person who wanted to win a sports competition would receive a high rating.

Let us consider some of the characteristics of people who are high in achievement motivation. As we might expect, they are likely to be superior students. Researchers have demonstrated that they perform relatively well on examinations, for instance (Atkinson & Raynor, 1974).

People high in achievement motivation are also extremely persistent. In one study, people were instructed to work on a task that was actually not solvable. The results showed that 47% of the people high in achievement motivation persisted on this impossible task until the time period was over, in contrast to only 2% of people low in achievement motivation (French & Thomas, 1958).

These high achievers also prefer being personally responsible for a project. When they are directly responsible, they can feel satisfaction from a task well done (McClelland, 1985). In contrast, they cannot be very proud of a project where chance alone determines whether they are successful.

Persistence is an important characteristic of people high in achievement motivation.

Individuals with high achievement motivation tend to seek out situations where they can receive feedback on their performance. It is not as appealing if they have no way of determining how well they are doing (McClelland, 1985).

Finally, people high in achievement motivation prefer to work on moderately difficult tasks, ones in which they have a 30% to 50% chance of a successful outcome. They find that these tasks are difficult enough to be interesting. However, they do not enjoy extremely difficult tasks, because the probability of success is too low. Neither do they enjoy extremely easy tasks; they cannot pat themselves on the back for a task with a 95% success rate.

In contrast, people *low* in achievement motivation do not have especially strong preferences about the ideal level of difficulty—sometimes they will choose an easy task, but they are just as likely to choose a difficult task, or one in between. For instance, deCharms and Carpenter (1968) asked fifth and seventh graders to familiarize themselves with some spelling words and then to decide which level of difficulty they preferred for a subsequent spelling test. As you can see from Figure 12.6, the children high in achievement motivation showed a strong preference for moderately difficult tests, but the children low in achievement motivation showed no clear-cut preferences.

Now that you have learned some of the important characteristics of people who are high in achievement motivation, try Demonstration 12.3 to informally assess your own achievement motivation level.

Fear of Success   Now try Demonstration 12.4, because it illustrates fear of success, a factor that can inhibit achievement motivation. **Fear of success** involves worrying that success in competitive achievement situations will lead to unpleasant consequences such as unpopularity. Some bright people face a double bind in achievement situations. They know that if they fail on a task, they will not meet their own standards of performance. On the other hand, they know that if they succeed, they may be rejected for doing too well.

Important early research on fear of success was conducted by Matina Horner (1968, 1972). Her research attracted substantial attention in popular magazines and newspapers because the original studies showed sizable gender differences in fear of success. Specifically, 62% of the women students responded to the "Anne" version by making up a story in which something unfortunate happened to Anne

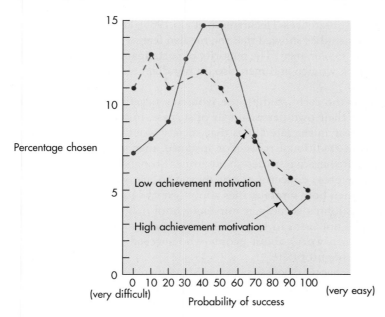

Figure 12.6
The percentage of tasks chosen at each level of difficulty, as a function of achievement motivation. (Based on deCharms & Carpenter, 1968)

Informal Assessment of Achievement Motivation

Naturally, a quick test cannot accurately measure any quality as complex as achievement motivation. However, answer each of the following questions honestly with a "yes" or "no."

_____ 1. Do you enjoy doing tasks well, even when no one tells you to do a good job?

_____ 2. Do you feel great satisfaction in mastering a difficult task that you were not sure could be done?

_____ 3. Is success especially pleasurable when you have competed against other people?

_____ 4. Are you a good student (for instance, were you in the top 10% of your high school class)?

_____ 5. When you are working on a difficult task, do you persist even when you run into roadblocks?

_____ 6. Do you prefer a task for which you have personal responsibility, rather than one where chance plays an important role?

_____ 7. Do you like receiving feedback about how well you are doing when you are working on a project?

_____ 8. When given a choice of several tasks, would you pick one that is moderately difficult, rather than a very difficult or easy task?

In general, people with a large number of "yes" answers tend to be high in achievement motivation, based on previous research (e.g., McClelland, 1985). Keep in mind, however, that overgeneralizations should not be made on the basis of a single, informal quiz.

as the result of her success. (Negative outcomes in the story were interpreted as evidence of fear of success.) In contrast, only 9% of the men wrote stories in which something unpleasant happened to John. Women wrote stories in which Anne was socially rejected or worried about her femininity. Men wrote stories in which John's hard work brought rich rewards and social approval.

However, in the decades since Horner's early work, psychologists have concluded that men and women are similar in their fear of success. The most important reason is that later studies using methods similar to Horner's have failed to find gender differences (Heckhausen et al., 1985; Tresemer, 1977). For instance, a review of 64 studies showed that the median fear of success in women was 49%, in contrast to 45% in men. The majority of participants in the studies were White; however, Black women and men also do not differ substantially in fear of success (Paludi, 1984).

Even in the early studies, the women's negative stories probably did not simply reflect their own personal fear of success. Instead, they probably reflected the realistic fear in the late 1960s that society would be unkind to women who deviated from traditional roles. For instance, men were even more likely than women to write negative stories about Anne (Monahan et al., 1974). Interestingly, people also express concerns about men who are successful in feminine roles. Men and women both wrote stories about fear of success when asked to complete a story about John's success in nursing school (Cherry & Deaux, 1978). Thus, the issue does not seem to be gender differences in fear of success; instead both men and women worry about people who succeed in areas that are considered to be gender inappropriate.

The last chapter discussed women's and men's occupations, noting that men were more likely to be found in high-prestige, high-paying jobs. Many people once

Fear of Success

In this demonstration, you will write a paragraph in response to a sentence which begins that paragraph.

If you are a female, write a paragraph beginning with this sentence: "After first term finals, Anne finds herself at the top of her medical school class. . . ."

If you are a male, write a paragraph beginning with this sentence: "After first term finals, John finds himself at the top of his medical school class. . . ."

thought that these occupational differences could be explained by women's fear of success. However, men and women do not seem to differ substantially in this area. Other people once suggested that occupational differences could be explained by men's greater tendency to say that their success was due to high ability. However, more recent research has shown that men and women are similar in their explanations for their success (Frieze et al., 1982; Gaeddert, 1987; Sohn, 1982). It seems likely that gender stereotypes are more powerful than gender differences in achievement-related areas in explaining women's and men's occupations.

When the research on fear of success began showing gender similarities, most psychologists seemed to lose interest in the general topic of fear of success. However, we need to keep in mind that fear of success can restrict people's accomplishments whether they are female or male. Thus, a college woman may be reluctant to major in engineering because she is afraid her boyfriend will think the field is too masculine. And a high school boy may be reluctant to enter the poetry contest because his friends will tease him if he wins. Educators at all levels need to be sensitive to the ways in which fear of success can limit achievement.

The Paradoxical Effects of Reward on Achievement　As a high school junior, Roger volunteered after school in a facility for profoundly retarded children. He enjoyed helping people who could not accomplish much on their own, and he found it rewarding when, after hours of training, a child finally mastered a task. That summer, the facility was able to pay Roger for his work, when one staff member left suddenly. However, when a permanent replacement was hired, Roger was told

In the 1990s, highly competent women are no more likely than highly competent men to be high in fear of success.

Fear of success is as big an obstacle for a male trying to succeed in a feminine area as it is for a female trying to succeed in a masculine area.

that the funds were no longer available to pay him, but he was welcome to work as a volunteer again. Roger politely declined; he was no longer interested in volunteering. Reward, in the form of a salary, had decreased Roger's original enthusiasm for his work.

The previous sections discussed how fear of success can diminish achievement-related behavior. It is fairly clear how this factor would serve as a barrier. The inhibiting effect of reward is more paradoxical and puzzling, reaffirming the theme of human complexity.

The answer to the paradoxical effect of reward involves **intrinsic motivation**, which is the desire to perform an activity for its own sake. People are likely to do something—and to do it well—when they find it inherently enjoyable (Graef et al., 1983). In contrast, **extrinsic motivation** is the desire to perform an activity because of external rewards.

The problem is that extrinsic motivation can undermine intrinsic motivation. When people are intrinsically motivated to work on a task, and then they are offered an external reward—such as a salary—intrinsic motivation often declines (Deci & Ryan, 1985). For instance, Roger's intrinsic motivation in working with the retarded children probably decreased once he began receiving a salary. Later when the external reward is no longer available (for instance, when Roger could no longer receive a salary), people no longer spontaneously work on the task. Without extrinsic motivation, and with reduced intrinsic motivation, the task is no longer appealing. A simple operant conditioning approach (chapter 6) suggests that reward should increase the probability of performing a task. An appreciation of human complexity, however, shows that reward can backfire.

A classic study by Deci (1971) illustrates how reward can decrease intrinsic motivation. In this experiment, students worked on an interesting puzzle called Soma for each of three sessions. During the first session, both the experimental and the control groups were introduced to the puzzle, and then the experimenter left the students alone for 8 minutes to see how long each group spent spontaneously playing with the puzzle. (Some current popular magazines were also available to read.) During the second session, the experimental manipulation was introduced: Students in the experimental group were told that they would receive

$1 for every correct solution they produced with the Soma puzzle. The students in the control group received no payment. Theoretically, the external reward should decrease intrinsic motivation for the experimental group, but intrinsic motivation should remain high for the control group.

Everyone returned for a third session, for which neither group received pay. Figure 12.7 shows how students in the experimental group showed a substantial decline in the amount of time they spent spontaneously playing with the puzzle, relative to the control group and relative to their own previous time spent with the puzzle. As you can see, the people in the experimental group spent less time in session 3 than in session 1, whereas the people in the control group actually spent more time in session 3 than in session 1. Reward seemed to decrease intrinsic interest in the puzzle for those in the experimental group.

More recent research has shown that some rewards can decrease intrinsic motivation, whereas other rewards can—fortunately—increase it (Deci & Ryan, 1985, 1987). If someone tries to use a *controlling* reward, for instance by offering a concrete reward such as money, intrinsic motivation is likely to decline. In contrast, if he or she uses an *informational* reward, by offering positive feedback that informs you about performance, intrinsic motivation is likely to rise. In other words, teachers are likely to enhance the intrinsic motivation of their students by congratulating them ("Superb essay, John—good organization of the three major themes"). In contrast, giving the top student a $5 award may actually decrease that student's enthusiasm in achievement for its own sake.

The Relationship Between Achievement Motivation and Emotion   At the beginning of the chapter, we noted that emotions often accompany motivation. For example, strong emotions can motivate us to pursue or avoid a goal. Bernard Weiner (1985a) has explored another link between the two topics: Specifically, our explanations for our motivated behavior can produce emotional reactions.

Weiner proposes that the outcome of motivated behavior leads both directly and indirectly to emotions. For example, if you do well on an examination, your direct reaction is positive emotions (e.g., "I am happy."). In addition, however, you make an **attribution**, or causal explanations for your success or failure. If you explain success on an examination by saying that the high score is due to your intelligence and ability, you will indirectly experience a second emotion—pride— in addition to happiness. In contrast, if you explain your success by reminding yourself that you cheated, the second emotion is likely to be guilt (Weiner et al., 1982).

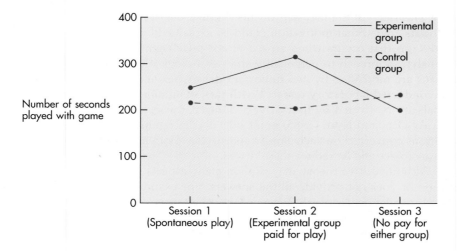

Figure 12.7
The amount of time spent playing with puzzle, as a function of presence or absence of external reward. (Based on Deci, 1971)

Notice how the research on achievement motivation has evolved. The early research in the area identified individual differences and situations that encouraged achievement, including factors such as fear of success that diminish achievement. The studies by Deci and his colleagues shifted the emphasis to cognitive interpretations and intrinsic motivation. Finally, Weiner's work emphasizes cognitive interpretations of achievement and also notes that these interpretations have important emotional consequences.

General Theories of Motivation

We have explored three different kinds of motivation, involving hunger, sexuality, and achievement. We have seen that hunger and sexuality involve some biological factors, but cognitive and social factors are crucial in all three areas. Let us now consider several theoretical approaches to all motivated behavior, not limiting ourselves to the three topics we have discussed. Why do we act? What energizes our behavior, sustains it, and directs it toward a certain goal? We look at five major approaches to motivation. In the next chapter, we will examine a sixth important approach—Maslow's hierarchy of needs—in connection with Maslow's humanistic theory of personality.

Instinct Theories   One of the first approaches proclaimed that motivation could be explained by **instincts**, which are inborn, internal forces that make humans behave in predictable ways. Inspired by Darwin's evolutionary theory, psychologists at the beginning of the century suggested that humans are driven by a set of instincts that operate in the same compelling fashion as for other animals. They proposed that each species was governed by its own specific set of instincts. Ducklings follow their mother, spiders spin their webs, and salmon return to their birthplace to deposit their eggs.

The major proponent of instinct explanations of human behavior was William McDougall (1908). McDougall suggested that human instincts include aggression, reproduction, curiosity, and parental care. Other theorists added their own favorite candidates, and the list of instincts exceeded 2,500 by the mid-1920s (Bernard, 1924). One problem with the instinct approach is the difficulty of constructing firm criteria for behaviors that could be considered instinctive, rather than learned. Furthermore, if we call a behavior an instinct, we merely provide a label, rather than an explanation for why that behavior occurs (Petri, 1986). For those reasons, modern psychologists usually look for other approaches to explain motivation.

Drive Theories   In the first half of this century, two very different kinds of psychologists argued that motivation could be explained by the concept of **drive**, or the tension that occurs when a need is not met. Sigmund Freud, with his psychoanalytic approach to personality and psychological disorders, argued that we humans are motivated by two important drives, sex and aggression. Clark Hull, who conducted laboratory research with rats, maintained that humans and other animals are motivated by four drives—hunger, thirst, sex, and the avoidance of pain. As Deci and Ryan (1985) point out, it is intriguing that two such different traditions converged on such similar approaches. Both argued that internal forces push us to act and to reduce these drives.

Although drive theory may explain many aspects of thirst and hunger motivation, it does not provide all the answers. For example, how would it explain counter-regulation, in which dieters eat more after two milkshakes than after no preload? Neither Hull's nor Freud's approach answers why humans are curious. What kind of drive would explain why you peek through a hole at a construction site or why it is difficult to hand your roommate a postcard without looking to see who sent it? Furthermore, neither approach explains achievement motivation— let alone subtleties such as the paradoxical effect of reward.

In short, drive theory has lost popularity during the second half of this century. Psychologists acknowledge that humans are conscious organisms who think, plan ahead, and figure out how to reach their goals (Geen, 1984).

Opponent-Process Theory   Several years ago, a tightrope walker attracted some notoriety in New York City. On several occasions, he managed secretly to set up a tightrope between two buildings, high above the city streets. Crowds would gather to watch him teeter precariously and then land safely on the adjacent building . . . only to be led off in handcuffs by the New York City police. (As it turns out, tightrope walking between buildings is illegal.) What could possibly motivate such a bizarre activity? Sex, aggression, hunger, thirst? Not really. Avoidance of pain? Certainly not!

Richard Solomon (1980) proposes that the motivation for many behaviors can be explained by **opponent-process theory**, which argues that one emotional state will trigger an opposite emotional state that lasts long after the original emotion has disappeared.

Solomon's opponent-process theory has important applications, particularly in explaining the motivations of people who enjoy risky behavior. For example, the terror of teetering above New York City crosstown traffic triggers an ecstatically positive emotional response . . . an ecstasy that persists while our hero is marched off to jail. Indeed this ecstasy will motivate him to attempt other, similar escapades in the future. Opponent-process theory also proposes that this positive emotional response will grow stronger with each tightrope episode, providing additional motivation for engaging in this unusual activity.

Another interesting area that has been studied in humans is blood donation. As people prepare to give blood for the first time, anxiety produces a negative emotional reaction. This reaction triggers an opposite, positive emotional state as soon as they have donated blood (Piliavin et al., 1982). Each time they donate blood in the future, anxiety diminishes somewhat, and the positive response grows even stronger. As a consequence, the motivation to donate blood increases further.

Opponent-process theory would argue that these skydivers' terror in risking their lives would trigger an extremely positive emotional response.

Robert White—and others who believed that many human activities are intrinsically motivating—have argued that children feel pride in their accomplishments.

At present, most of the research has been conducted on animals, rather than on humans. Therefore, we do not know how generalizable opponent-process theory is to diverse kinds of human motivational behavior (Geen, 1984)

Intrinsic Motivation   In the section on achievement motivation, we discussed how some kinds of reward can decrease intrinsic motivation. However, in that discussion we did not really examine the nature of intrinsic motivation, which is the fourth theoretical approach to motivation to be discussed here.

The concept of intrinsic motivation was originally proposed by Robert White (1959), who argued that many behaviors such as play and exploration do not need to be reinforced in order to be performed. White also argued that people—even young children—have an internal force that encourages them to be competent and effective. For instance, I recall one of my daughters, at age 1, playing with an old footstool that she had turned upside down. She would climb in and beam with pride at her accomplishment; then she would climb out, grinning once again with her sense of mastery. She did not look to her parents for approval. Competent interaction with her environment was its own reward (Deci & Ryan, 1985).

Researchers have discovered that enjoyment in life is correlated with experiencing daily activities as intrinsically motivating. As a math professor once remarked, "I love my work so much that every morning I leave my house and say, 'Just imagine getting paid for something that's so much fun!'" In one study, 107 working men and women rated the extent to which their work was intrinsically motivating, as well as their sense of well-being (Graef et al., 1983). The correlation between intrinsic motivation and happiness was +.28, which was statistically significant.

Try noticing how often you do activities because they are intrinsically motivating, rather than because they reduce some drive or accomplish some goal. Do you look out the window at an interesting sight? When pursuing a word in the dictionary, are you distracted into reading an irrelevant definition (even though you do not expect any reward from knowing the meaning of words such as *peplum*, or *centaury*, or *hendecagon*)? When you see a couple together in a restaurant, do you strain to hear their conversation because you are curious whether they are well acquainted or on their first date? This curiosity cannot be explained by instinct, drive, or opponent-process theory, but—at least for some people—it is intrinsically motivating.

Incentive Theory   We have explored four approaches to motivation that emphasize internal forces within the organism. A person or an animal is motivated to act because of inborn instincts, driving tensions, one emotional state triggering an opposite emotional state, or an internal force that encourages competence and inquiry.

In contrast, **incentive theory** emphasizes how external goals motivate us to respond and to act. We therefore engage in a particular activity so that we can receive a specific reward (Mook, 1987). Similarly, we do not engage in other activities because we wish to avoid an undesirable outcome.

Incentive theory is useful in explaining some aspects of achievement motivation. A student is motivated by the incentive of good grades, an executive is motivated by the incentive of a raise, and a college instructor is motivated by the incentive of a promotion. Incentive theory argues that the probability of engaging in a particular activity depends both on the *expectation* of obtaining a particular goal and the *value* of obtaining that goal. For example, you are likely to study for a biology exam if you expect that studying will lead to a high grade and if that grade is valuable to you.

We have reviewed five general theoretical explanations for motivated behavior. In many areas, several theoretical approaches can be compared. In none of these cases can we conclude that one approach is entirely correct and all other approaches are entirely wrong. In considering human motivation, the complexity of human behavior suggests that the instinct approach is the least useful, and the drive approach is also limited. Opponent-process theory may have applications for some puzzling kinds of behavior. However, most of human motivation seems best explained in terms of more subtle and all-encompassing approaches such as intrinsic motivation and incentive theory.

Section Summary: Motivation

- Hunger is partially regulated by biological factors such as the hypothalamus and levels of glucose and insulin, but external factors such as culture and social setting are also important.
- Explanations for obesity include food intake, genetic makeup, set point, and insulin responses to external cues.
- The eating disorder anorexia nervosa is a life-threatening pursuit of thinness; bulimia, or binge eating, may be encouraged by dieting.
- In human sexuality, external and cognitive cues are more important determinants of arousal than hormones.
- In both women and men, the sexual response cycle includes four phases: excitement, plateau, orgasm, and resolution.
- Important topics concerned with sexual behavior include sexually transmitted diseases (STDs), concern about pregnancy, and sexual coercion, as well as the sense of intimacy and connectedness that are part of consensual sexual interactions.
- People who are high in achievement motivation are likely to be good students who are persistent; they prefer tasks for which they can take personal responsibility and tasks that provide feedback and a moderate level of difficulty.
- Fear of success and certain kinds of reward can diminish achievement-related behavior.
- Five theoretical explanations for motivation include instinct, drive, opponent processes, intrinsic motivation, and incentive theory.

Emotion

Imagine the ending of the opera *Rigoletto* drained of its emotions. Rigoletto is determined to kill the Duke of Mantua, who has seduced Rigoletto's precious daughter, Gilda. In the dark, the hired assassin stabs someone in man's attire. Rigoletto discovers that it is Gilda, instead of the Duke. In the emotion-drained version, he calmly pronounces, "Gosh, we should have checked more carefully." Or consider the soap opera "General Hospital." Frisco has been suffering in a Bulgarian jail for months until his escape. He limps home to Port Charles, only to find his wife, Felicia, about to say "I do" to another man. In the emotion-drained version, Frisco watches the wedding dispassionately and offers congratulations to the newlyweds. Without emotions, our lives would be dominated by cold cognitions, filmed in black and white instead of passionate purple and vibrant turquoise.

As we noted at the beginning of the chapter, the emotions in our daily lives are rich, complicated experiences. These complicated experiences include cognitive, physiological, and behavioral reactions. For instance, try to recall the last time you experienced a particularly positive emotion. Can you reconstruct your cognitive, subjective experience? What were your physiological reactions—can you recall your heart beating faster? Did your behavioral reaction include a change in facial expression, and did you rush to share your good news with someone else?

We begin the discussion of emotion by considering these three components of emotion—cognitive, physiological, and behavioral. (You may recall the three different methods of measuring psychological responses, discussed in chapter 2: self-report—a cognitive assessment, behavioral, and physiological.) Our fourth topic is the classification of emotions, followed by an in-depth examination of the effects of mood on cognitive processes. We end with a discussion of various theories of emotion.

It is important to mention that many of the remaining chapters discuss some aspect of emotion. For instance, chapters 15 and 16 examine mood disorders and therapy for these disorders. Chapters 17 and 18 frequently discuss emotional reactions to other people. Finally, chapter 19 considers the relationship between stress and health.

Cognitive Emotional Reactions

Psychologists can assess physiological reactions with equipment that measures breathing rate and blood pressure, and behavioral reactions can be assessed in terms of facial expressions. But how do they measure people's *thoughts* about their emotions? Psychologists have not devised any perfectly objective measure that can firmly establish whether a person is experiencing joy, sorrow, or embarrassment. Similarly, no perfectly objective measure can establish whether a person is experiencing a particular color of the spectrum—yet perception researchers do not hesitate to investigate color phenomena. Likewise, the absence of objective measures does not block research on emotion, because most psychologists consider people's self-reports to be accurate reflections of their true feelings (Ortony et al., 1988; Scherer, 1986).

Psychologists typically use rating scales to assess cognitive emotional reactions. Examples of research using rating scales appear in the in-depth section of this chapter, as well as in later chapters. These rating scales are also common in the assessment of **subjective well-being**, or a person's current level of happiness or life satisfaction. Psychologists have also devised more than a dozen multiple-item scales of subjective well-being (Diener, 1984).

In general, people's ratings on these scales are positively correlated with their self-esteem and income. However, there is no consistent relationship between subjective well-being and other demographic variables, such as age, gender, race, and education (Diener, 1984).

Let us look more closely at a representative study that used self-report rating scales to assess emotional reactions. Philip Brickman and his co-authors (1978) were intrigued with informal reports, beginning with early Greek philosophers, that happiness is relative. Specifically, people seem to judge their current happiness relative to the level of happiness to which they have become accustomed. As part of the study, these researchers interviewed 22 people who had won between $50,000 and $1 million in the Illinois State Lottery. They also interviewed 58 other people who lived near the winners; these people formed the control group in this quasi-experiment.

One of the most interesting findings involved respondents' ratings of seven everyday activities. On a 6-point pleasantness scale ranging from 0 for "not at all" to 5 for "very much," they assessed how pleasant they found activities such as talking with a friend, hearing a funny joke, and eating breakfast. The lottery winners supplied an average rating of 3.3 for these mundane activities, whereas

the respondents in the control group supplied an average rating of 3.8—which was significantly higher. Winners apparently judged current pleasures relative to that past stupendous pleasure. Compared to winning $400,000, the daily pleasures of friendships, jokes, and scrambled eggs seem pale and drab. For people in the control group, mundane activities continued to be fairly pleasant. In short, this study suggests that happiness is indeed relative.

Physiological Emotional Reactions

In chapter 3 we noted biological reactions to emotional experiences. For example, in a frightening situation, the sympathetic system—within the autonomic nervous system—prepares your body for action. Your heart beats faster, your pupils widen, and you sweat and blush. In contrast, the parasympathetic system restores your body to its normal state, for instance by slowing your heartbeat and constricting your pupils. Let us consider several physiological measures of emotion and then discuss a practical application: Are lie detection tests useful?

Physiological Measures   People who study the biological components of emotion tend to collect certain measures of activity in the autonomic nervous system. These measures include the following (Ekman et al., 1983; Strongman, 1987):

1. Blood pressure and pulse rate, as indexes of general changes in the activity of the heart and the rest of the circulatory system;

2. Temperature of the fingers;

3. The electrodermal response, which measures skin perspiration;

4. Breathing rate; and

5. Muscular tension.

An additional physiological measure can also be obtained on electrical activity in the central nervous system; researchers may obtain an electroencephalogram, or EEG (discussed in chapter 3) as an index of the brain's activity.

Lucille Ball's facial expressions of happiness, disgust, and surprise produce similar heart rate, despite the major differences in the subjective experience of these emotions.

Physiological measures generate such precise-looking numbers that it is tempting to think each emotion might be associated with a unique set of numbers. Perhaps a 10% increase in blood pressure, a 5% decrease in finger temperature, and a 15% increase in the electrodermal response might consistently indicate fear. Unfortunately, however, the situation is more complex.

Some studies indicate that autonomic nervous system activity can distinguish among several emotions, but not all of them. For instance, Ekman and his colleagues (1983) asked professional actors to contract specific muscles in their faces in order to produce facial expressions that were consistent with six different emotions: happy, disgusted, surprised, angry, afraid, and sad. Measurements of heart rate and finger temperature allowed these researchers to distinguish three different subgroups of emotions, indicated in Figure 12.8.

Notice that anger is the only emotion associated with high heart rate and high skin temperature. However, both fear and sadness are associated with high heart rate and low skin temperature. You *feel* different when you are afraid than when you are sad, but your autonomic nervous system responds about the same. Furthermore, three very different emotions—happiness, disgust, and surprise—are all associated with low heart rate. Physiological measures provide some indexes of emotional response, but they cannot adequately discriminate among some emotions that are subjectively very different.

The Debate about Lie Detector Tests   In 1987, a college student named Shama Holleman took a part-time job as a cashier for a New York City department store. After 1 month with a top-notch work record, she was fired. A lie detector test had indicated that she could be a drug dealer. In fact, she was not, and she later received compensation for the false accusation. One year later, in 1988, Congress passed a law forbidding lie detector tests in the screening of most private employees (Gorman, 1989).

A lie detector test, or—more formally—**polygraph examination**, measures physiological changes such as heart rate, breathing, and electrodermal response while a person is asked a carefully structured set of questions. The examiner notes the pattern of autonomic-nervous-system arousal in order to decide whether the person being tested is innocent or guilty (Saxe et al., 1985). Note that the polygraph does not really detect lies, but rather emotional arousal.

An ideal test for truthfulness requires a perfect correspondence between reality and the examiner's conclusion. That is, an innocent person should have minimal arousal of the autonomic nervous system, and the person who examines the polygraph should conclude that he or she is indeed innocent. A guilty person should show strong arousal, and an examination of the polygraph should lead to the conclusion "guilty."

Unfortunately, research on the polygraph exam shows that the correspondence with reality is far from perfect. Consider a representative study by Kleinmuntz

Figure 12.8
A "decision tree" for discriminating emotions, based on research by Ekman and his coauthors (1983).

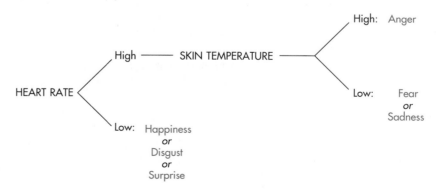

and Szucko (1984). The participants in this research were 50 confessed thieves and 50 innocent people who had been suspected of theft, but had later been cleared because the real thieves had confessed. An ideal polygraph exam would condemn the thieves and declare the innocent people "not guilty." Six people, employed by a polygraph company, were asked to interpret the polygraphs. Table 12.3 shows the results. As you can see, 37% of the innocent people were falsely identified as thieves, and 24% of the thieves were falsely declared innocent.

Other research confirmed the inaccuracy of polygraph tests. In a review of 10 studies, for instance, innocent people were falsely declared guilty between 0% and 75% of the time, and guilty people were falsely declared not guilty between 0% and 24% of the time (Saxe et al., 1985).

Chapter 1 noted that applied psychologists emphasize the practical application of psychological knowledge. The investigation of polygraph testing is an example of how applied psychologists can influence public policy. The studies demonstrated that physiological measures typically showed an unacceptably low correspondence with the innocence of the person being examined (Carroll, 1988; Gudjonsson, 1988). As a consequence, polygraph testing cannot be used when private companies screen potential employees. However, it is still legal to test government employees, armored-car guards, and employees who have access to restricted drugs. Furthermore, some states still permit polygraph data as evidence in court (Gorman, 1989; McCurry, 1989). Fortunately, however, most of you will not need to worry about being unjustly accused of a crime you did not commit—based on the use of a test that is often inaccurate.

Behavioral Emotional Reactions

So far, we have discussed the cognitive and physiological components of emotion. Now we shift to the last component, behavioral reactions. We focus on the most common measure of behavioral reactions, namely, facial expression. Facial expression is one component of nonverbal communication. In chapter 9, our discussion of nonverbal communication concentrated on the way gestures convey specific meaning, as well as the nonverbal regulation of turn taking. In the current section, we emphasize how facial expression can convey emotions. First, however, test your accuracy in interpreting emotional expression by trying Demonstration 12.5.

How correct are we in decoding the emotion expressed in a photograph? In one study, people in the United States were fairly accurate in matching photos with some kinds of emotional labels (Ekman, 1973). Happiness was correctly identified by 97% of the respondents, and surprise was identified by 95%. However, only 67% accurately identified anger. Notice that some behavioral emotional responses can be misinterpreted, just as some physiological responses might be interpreted as happiness, disgust, or surprise, and just as some polygraph tests might confuse the innocent and the guilty. Still, it is impressive that people are

Table 12.3   *Accuracy of Polygraph Judgments*

| | | POLYGRAPH INTERPRETER CONCLUDES | |
		Person Is a Thief	Person Is Innocent
The Truth	Person Is a Thief	76%	24%
	Person Is Innocent	37%	63%

Note: Data represent the averages for six experienced interpreters.
Source: Kleinmuntz & Szucko, 1984.

Demonstration 12.5

Identifying Behavioral Emotional Reactions

Examine the photos and match each one with one of the following six emotions: (1) fear; (2) happiness; (3) anger; (4) disgust; (5) surprise; (6) sadness. The answers appear at the end of the chapter.

reasonably accurate in decoding most emotions, since they must rely only on informal assessment of facial cues—rather than precise physiological measures.

Are Facial Expressions Universal?   Are members of various cultures similar or different in the way they express various emotions? Scientists have debated this question for more than a century. Charles Darwin (1872/1965), for instance, argued that facial expressions are innate behaviors, developed through human evolution. In contrast, anthropologist Margaret Mead (1975) proposed that facial expressions are learned socially, the same as spoken language. As a consequence, an emotion could be conveyed by different facial expressions in different cultures. When you are happy, does nature or nurture explain why the edges of your mouth curl upward?

The answer seems to be that both explanations are correct (Ekman, 1984). That is, immediate, involuntary facial expressions seem to be highly similar across cultures. However, when you must control your facial expressions—for example, in public settings—you tend to display the facial expression prescribed by your specific culture (Argyle, 1988; Ekman, 1984).

These customary regulations about the control of facial expression are called **display rules**. Consider, for instance, the display rule in our culture that males should not cry. One man recalls an early experience in suppressing an emotional expression:

I was in the sixth grade at the time my grandfather died. I remember being called to the office of the school where my mother was on the phone. . . . She told me what had happened and all I said was, "Oh." I went back to class and a friend asked me what happened and I said, "Nothing." I remember wanting very much just to cry and tell everyone what had happened. But a boy doesn't cry in the sixth grade for fear of being called a sissy. So I just went along as if nothing had happened while deep down inside I was very sad and full of tears. (Hochschild, 1983, p. 67)

Let us consider some empirical evidence, first for the universality of facial expressions, and then for culture-specific display rules.

We had noted earlier that people in the United States ranged in average accuracy from a low of 67% to a high of 97% in identifying emotions similar to those in Demonstration 12.5. Ekman (1973) also tested people in Brazil, Chile, Argentina, and Japan. In each country, people were asked to identify the name of the emotion displayed in the photos. Across all four cultures, the average accuracy was 85% for all six emotions. However, the people in those four cultures were all familiar with American television. Was this high level of accuracy simply a reflection of their familiarity with the facial expressions of television stars such as Lucille Ball and John Wayne?

In order to avoid familiarity with American TV, Ekman and Friesen (1971) went to New Guinea to test people who had never been exposed to television. In this study, people were asked to identify each emotion by pointing to the picture that corresponded to each of six stories. For example, researchers tested "sadness" by asking them to point to the picture of the man who just learned that his child had died. As with the other four cultures, the New Guinea residents were highly accurate. Additional research has demonstrated that people in cultures as diverse as Turkey, Estonia, and Japan agreed with people in the United States about the intensity of various emotions (Ekman et al., 1987).

What about the evidence for display rules? In a representative study, Ekman and Friesen (1969) contrasted the immediate and the delayed emotional responses of Americans and Japanese. Each participant in the study watched an extremely unpleasant film about sinus surgery. Each person was seated alone in the room, and the facial expressions were secretly videotaped. The videotapes of the immediate facial expressions were highly similar for people in the two cultures; both groups showed disgust. Later, each person was interviewed about the film. In these delayed responses, the Americans continued to show negative expressions, but the Japanese produced happy faces. An important Japanese display rule is that one should not display negative emotions when an authority is present (Ekman, 1984).

This study and related research suggest that we react to a situation with a facial expression that is reasonably uniform in many cultures. Moments later, however, we assume the facial expression we have learned in our culture: An American boy conceals his sadness with a neutral countenance, and a Japanese man smiles to conceal his disgust.

Cross-cultural research suggests that people in different parts of the world should be reasonably accurate in identifying this emotional reaction as surprise.

Accuracy in Decoding Emotions   As you might imagine, people vary tremendously in their ability to decode emotions. Even within one culture, sensitivity to nonverbal cues ranges widely. Think about someone you know who can sense your sadness when you are barely aware of it yourself. Another acquaintance may spend several hours with you, unaware that you are depressed. This ability to decode emotions can be measured with tests such as Profile of Nonverbal Sensitivity (PONS). This test asks people to identify what is happening in 220 very brief

In our culture, display rules demand that men conceal their sorrow. The man in front is clearly struggling to cover his sadness by trying to look brave.

scenes, using nonverbal cues about the face, body, and tone of voice (Rosenthal, 1976).

Research using tests like the PONS shows that the ability to decode nonverbal cues increases systematically between childhood and adulthood, reaching a maximum between the ages of about 20 and 30 (Hall et al., 1978).

Females tend to be somewhat better than males at decoding nonverbal expressions. Gender differences seem to be largest in judging facial expression, somewhat smaller in judging body posture, and smallest in judging voice cues (Hall, 1984; Hall et al., 1978). These gender differences are found as early as elementary school and have also been observed in other cultures. Psychologists have not discovered a complete explanation for these differences, but one likely possibility is that females are encouraged to pay more attention to nonverbal behavior and that they have greater practice in trying to decipher emotions (Hall, 1984). Keep in mind, though, that gender differences in decoding ability are widespread, but not inevitable. In other words, it is likely that you know women and men who defy the general trend. For example, can you think of a male friend who is better than most female friends at deciphering people's moods?

So far, our discussion of emotion has focused on three components of emotion: our cognitive reactions, physiological responses, and facial expressions. Let us now shift our focus toward several other critical issues in the study of emotions.

The Classification of Emotions

Psychologists often attempt to organize human experiences by introducing a classification system. In chapter 4, for instance, we noted that taste sensations are categorized as sweet, salty, sour, and bitter. In chapter 13, we consider the search for the major personality traits—basic human characteristics such as conscientiousness and emotional stability. Similarly, psychologists interested in emotions have tried to identify the basic human emotions. If we could sort through all the words we use to describe all feelings—from ecstasy to rage—how many distinct categories could we establish?

When you were trying to decipher the emotions illustrated in Demonstration 12.5, the six options were fear, surprise, sadness, disgust, anger, and happiness. Researchers who study cross-cultural facial emotions often use this six-category system (e.g., Ekman, 1973).

Figure 12.9
According to Plutchik's model, emotions can be divided into eight basic categories.

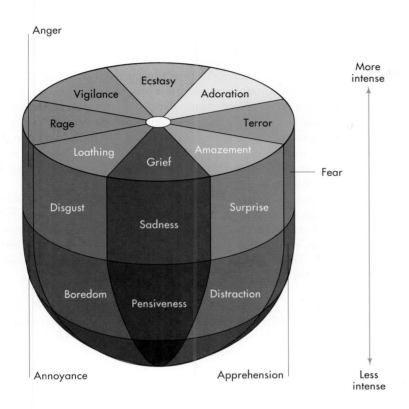

Anger

Ecstasy
Adoration
Vigilance
Rage
Terror
Loathing
Amazement
Grief
Disgust
Surprise
Sadness
Boredom
Distraction
Pensiveness

Fear

More intense

Less intense

Annoyance   Apprehension

Figure 12.10
In Plutchik's three-dimensional model, human emotions vary in intensity as well as type. (Note that anticipation, joy, and acceptance would appear along the back surface of this diagram.)

Other psychologists have included additional terms. For instance, one popular classification system adds two more basic emotions, anticipation and acceptance, and substitutes joy for happiness. Figure 12.9 shows this eight-category model, devised by Robert Plutchik (1980a, 1980b).

The eight basic emotions in Figure 12.9 describe general categories. Each of these emotions can be experienced in several "shades," from vivid to pale. For example, when you are intensely disgusted with something (or someone), you experience loathing. In a much milder form, you experience boredom. Figure 12.10 shows how human emotions vary in intensity, as well as type. This three-dimensional model of emotions provides an interesting method of organizing the richness of human emotions. However, it is important to stress that classification systems such as Plutchik's are based on theorists' intuitions, rather than empirical research (Isen, personal communication, 1990). In fact, this dissatisfaction with the subjectivity of classification systems has led some theorists to reject completely the notion of basic emotions (Ortony & Turner, 1990).

In Depth: The Influence of Positive Emotions on Cognitive Processes

Imagine this scenario. You are on your way to an exam in an English course, and you are wondering what the major essay question will be. You have read short stories by five authors, and your professor typically asks you to find similar themes in your readings. (For instance, on the last exam, you were instructed to discuss how several authors treated the theme of good versus evil.) You are just about to enter the building when you spot a $10 bill half-buried in the leaves. No one else is in sight, so you put the bill in your pocket. Delighted with this modest but unexpected windfall, you sit down to take your exam. Will that positive experience influence your performance on the test? Before we consider the answer to that question, try Demonstration 12.6.

Alice M. Isen of Cornell University has conducted a wide range of studies on the influence of positive emotions on cognitive processes. She and her colleagues have found that a relatively minor manipulation of the independent variable (emotional state) has an important influence on an impressive variety of dependent variables (performance on many cognitive tasks). Isen has found that she did not need to spend $10 to make a research participant happy. A free sample notepad, a dime in the coin return of a public telephone—and even a list of 10 happy words—were each sufficient.

Isen's research makes an interesting topic for an in-depth section because it illustrates an investigator's search for generalizability. Her work has demonstrated that the influence of emotions is not limited to just one kind of cognitive task. Instead, emotions can affect many cognitive processes, which you read about in chapters 7, 8, and 9. These include conceptual organization, memory, concept formation, and problem solving.

Conceptual Organization   In one study, Isen and her colleagues (1985) proposed that positive emotions would influence the way ideas are organized. Specifically, they hypothesized that people in a good mood would be more likely to think of subtle, unusual relationships between ideas.

To test this hypothesis, they distributed booklets containing word associations similar to the ones in Demonstration 12.6. For one third of the participants, the first 10 words were positive. An additional one third saw 10 neutral words, and the final one third saw 10 negative words. For all participants, however, the last 10 words were neutral. In this study, then, the independent variable was manipulated in the first 10 words, and the dependent variable was assessed by the responses to the last 10 words. All participants were instructed to read each word, one at a time, and write down their first association to every word.

The researchers then consulted a book that lists the word associations supplied by 1,000 college students. For instance, the book specified that in response to the stimulus word *house*, 230 people supplied *home* and 3 people supplied

---

Demonstration 12.6

Word Associations

Take out a blank piece of paper and cover the words below. Then take a second blank piece of paper and write the numbers 1 through 20 in a column on the left side of the sheet.

In this demonstration, you will be supplying word associations. When you see a word, write the first response that comes to mind, using the numbered sheet to record each response. Move the blank sheet down the first column of words in the textbook, exposing one word at a time. Respond as quickly as possible, and then move on to the next word. When you are done with the first column, move on to the second column.

1. triumph	11. scissors
2. happy	12. heavy
3. beauty	13. eagle
4. freedom	14. butter
5. tranquil	15. shoes
6. blossom	16. spider
7. friend	17. ocean
8. music	18. doors
9. smile	19. white
10. sunset	20. needle

Now check the end of the chapter to see how to score your responses.

mansion. The relationship between *house* and *home* is obvious, but the relationship between *house* and *mansion* is unusual. By consulting these norms, Isen and her colleagues could assess whether a participant's response was common or unusual.

Figure 12.11 shows the results. As you can see, people supplied a greater number of unusual associations when their first 10 words in the task had been positive than when those first words had been either neutral or negative. Did you supply many unusual associations in Demonstration 12.6, when you had previously responded to positive words?

Thus, this study demonstrated that positive mood increases people's ability to detect subtle or unusual relationships. The study suggests, incidentally, that the positive emotions you experience when you find a $10 bill would encourage you to appreciate subtle relationships among short stories on an English exam. Positive mood has a similar impact on other cognitive tasks.

Memory   Isen, Daubman, and Gorgoglione (1987) showed students either an entertaining cartoon film (positive mood) or a film about statistics (neutral mood). Later, participants heard a 30-word list that included 10 critical words subtly related to the American Revolution (such as *stars, stripes, colony,* and *doodle*). The results of this study showed that people in the positive-mood condition remembered a significantly larger number of these critical words. A likely explanation is that the positive mood encouraged people to see subtle relationships among the words. Furthermore, as you know from chapter 7, recall improves when a list of words is well organized and interrelated.

Concept Formation   Chapter 8 introduced natural concepts, which are the concepts we encounter in the real world. For instance, the concept *vehicle* includes some excellent prototype examples such as *car* and *truck,* as well as some non-prototype examples such as *raft, sled,* and *camel.* At least to North Americans, a camel is a highly unusual means of transportation!

Isen and Daubman (1984) wondered if positive mood might encourage people to broaden their categories and perceive items as being related when the relationship was fairly subtle. First they encouraged positive affect by showing people a comedy film, giving them a free candy bar, or serving refreshments. Similar participants in a control group either saw a neutral film or received no candy or refreshments. Then everyone rated a list of words, judging the extent to which

According to the research of Alice M. Isen and her colleagues, the positive mood of these students should encourage them to detect subtle relationships when they work on cognitive tasks.

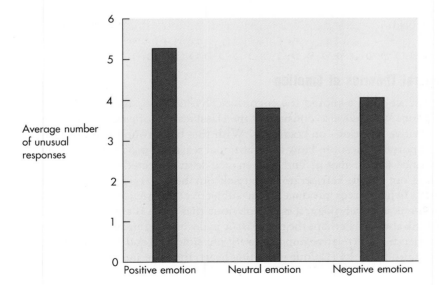

Figure 12.11
The number of unusual responses supplied on a word-association test, as a function of affect condition. (Based on Isen et al., 1985)

each word was a good example of the category. Relative to the control group participants, people in the experimental positive-affect groups were much more generous with their ratings. If you are in a good mood, a camel is a reasonably fine vehicle, a yam is a good example of a vegetable, and a wristwatch is an excellent article of clothing. Once again, positive mood enhances the ability to perceive relationships, even when those relationships are subtle.

Problem Solving   Chapter 8 also examined problem solving and creativity, which is another kind of cognitive task that is influenced by positive affect. In fact, turn back to Duncker's candle problem, illustrated in Demonstration 8.6 (p. 261). Isen, Daubman, and Nowicki (1987) found that people who had viewed a comedy film produced a larger number of acceptable solutions than people who had viewed a neutral film. Positive mood seems to increase the number of ways in which objects can be seen as related to one another.

As Demonstration 8.7 (p. 263) showed, the Remote Associates Test is one measure of creativity. This test requires people to see how words such as *food*, *catcher*, and *hot* are related to each other (in this case, they are all related to the word *dog*). By now, you will not be surprised to learn that people in the positive-affect condition received an average score of 5, whereas people in a neutral-affect control group received an average score of only 3 on the Remote Associates Test. Once again, happy people are more likely to appreciate subtle relationships.

Possible Explanations   Isen and her colleagues have uncovered a large number of cognitive tasks influenced by positive mood—we have looked at just a fraction of them. But *why* does a good mood influence cognitive organization, so that ideas seem more related than they would with a neutral mood? Unfortunately, we do not have a single, simple answer; the answer is undoubtedly complicated.

One possibility is that a positive mood produces a larger number of divergent ideas, creating a richer cognitive context when people try to remember, form a concept, or solve a problem. Another possibility is that positive mood may be more likely to activate the right hemisphere of the brain, which could in turn encourage the appreciation of relationships, rather than isolated perceptions. It is also possible that positive mood influences motivation, encouraging people to set more ambitious goals for themselves (Isen, 1987). Furthermore, positive mood could increase people's self-confidence, making mental processes more flexible (Izard, 1989). Factors such as these may work together to encourage people to process information in a more integrated fashion when they feel delighted with the world.

General Theories of Emotion

So far, we have explored the cognitive, physiological, and behavioral aspects of emotion. We have also considered the classification of emotion and the influence of positive emotions on cognition. With this background, we can now consider an important question: How are emotional reactions produced? You are watching a science fiction movie, and—when you least expected it—the 17-legged alien leaped out of the refrigerator to attack our hero. You experienced terror. But exactly what forces produced that subjective experience of terror? Like many questions in psychology, it is not obvious that there *is* a problem until you start to think about it. Perhaps the major issue in developing an explanation of emotional experience is the relative importance of physiological and cognitive forces. Is your terror produced by (1) your pounding heart, the knot in your digestive tract, and the physiological side effects of your terrified facial expression, or (2) your cognitive processes that assess the situation and choose the label "terror"?

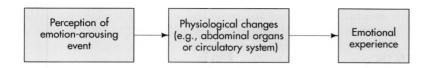

Figure 12.12
The James-Lange theory of emotion.

We begin by considering the James-Lange theory, which emphasizes a physiological explanation; we also note some criticisms of this approach, as well as a modern-day variant. Then we discuss the Schachter-Singer theory, which emphasizes the importance of cognitive labels. Finally, we consider Izard's more complex theory, which argues that cognitive processes are important in some emotional reactions but unnecessary in other emotional reactions.

The James-Lange Theory   William James, the first major American psychologist, explained emotional experiences using a theory that seemed unlikely when he proposed it in 1890. This explanation still seems to contradict most people's common sense. The commonsense explanation of emotions probably runs something like this: When you see the 17-legged alien, you experience terror, and this terror sets off physiological reactions (such as a knot in the stomach or an increase in blood pressure).

James (1890) argued, however, that the commonsense explanation places events in the wrong order. If he were watching the science fiction movie with you, he would claim that the perception of an emotion-arousing event (say, a 17-legged alien) directly produces physiological reactions. These physiological reactions send a message to the brain, producing the emotional experience of terror. As James wrote in his famous psychology textbook,

> Common sense says, we lose our fortune, are sorry and weep; we meet a bear, are frightened and run; we are insulted by a rival, are angry and strike. . . . The more rational statement is that we feel sorry because we cry, angry because we strike, afraid because we tremble, and not that we cry, strike, or tremble, because we are sorry, angry, or fearful as the case may be. (p. 13)

James argued that each emotion is signaled by a specific physiological pattern. He particularly emphasized physiological reactions in the abdominal organs (such as a tense feeling, or "knot in the stomach"). In 1887, a Danish psychologist named Carl Lange (pronounced "*Lang*-eh") suggested a similar theory, but he emphasized physiological reactions in the circulatory system (such as an increase in blood pressure). The **James-Lange theory** therefore proposes that physiological changes are the source of emotional feelings (Figure 12.12).

The Cannon-Bard Theory   Several decades later, a physiologist named Walter Cannon (1927) wrote an article that criticized the James-Lange approach. Among Cannon's complaints were the following:

1. Physiological changes are too slow to be sources of emotional feeling; for instance, we experience many emotional reactions less than a second after exposure to a stimulus, and this delay is too short to be explained by the relatively leisurely responses of the abdominal organs.

2. When physiological changes are induced artificially (for instance, by a hormone), people should experience an emotional reaction, yet in experimental studies, they did not experience a genuine emotion. (They typically made comments such as, "I feel as if I had a great fright, yet I'm really calm.")

Strack and his co-authors (1988) would predict that the young woman should rate the comic pages as being funnier when her lips are in the configuration on the bottom rather than the one on the top.

3. If emotional reactions are produced by physiological sensations, then each emotion should be linked with a unique combination of physiological changes. Cannon pointed out contradictory evidence, consistent with our discussion of this topic in the section on physiological measures.

Cannon and his colleague L. L. Bard proposed their own theory as a substitute for the James-Lange theory (Bard, 1928; Cannon, 1927). According to the **Cannon-Bard theory**, an important mediator in emotional experience is the thalamus, a part of the brain that receives messages from the sensory receptors. The thalamus, in turn, sends separate messages to the autonomic nervous system and to the cortex. As Figure 12.13 shows, you do not have to wait for your stomach to churn before your cortex knows that you are terrified. Instead, both events occur at the same time. For several decades the Cannon-Bard theory was more popular than the James-Lange approach.

The Facial Feedback Hypothesis   Some recent research, however, provides support for the earlier James-Lange approach, though the new approach emphasizes feedback from facial expression, rather than from the abdominal organs and circulatory system. According to the **facial feedback hypothesis**, changes in your facial expression can *cause* changes in your emotional state (Laird, 1984; Zajonc et al., 1989). Thus, your terrified expression when the alien jumps out of the refrigerator encourages you to experience terror.

In a representative study, Strack and his co-authors (1988) asked participants to hold a pen in either their mouth or their teeth. At this point, you may be wondering about the sanity of these researchers. However, if you try holding a pen in your lips (without touching your teeth), you will find that your facial expression is much more grumpy than if you hold a pen in your teeth (without touching your lips). Notice, then, that people adopted nonsmiling or smiling facial expressions without ever hearing any emotional labels like "smile." With the pen still in position, the participants rated a series of cartoons on a scale that ranged from *not at all funny* to *very funny*. Impressively, the people wearing smiles judged the cartoons to be significantly funnier than did the unsmiling people!

In general, the research on facial feedback shows that facial expression has a modest effect on emotional experiences (Matsumoto, 1987). It would be unreasonable to claim that facial feedback is the main factor in all subjective emotions. However, researchers have demonstrated a possible mechanism for this effect: Frowning facial expressions actually restrict the flow of cooled air to areas near the brain, producing an unpleasant emotional experience (Zajonc et al., 1989). It may sound unlikely, but when a photographer tells you to say *cheese*, your mood may actually improve!

The Schachter-Singer Theory   So far, you have heard all about thumping hearts, knotted stomachs, and chilled brains—a variety of ways in which physiological reactions might mediate emotional experiences. It was not until the early 1960s

Figure 12.13
The Cannon-Bard theory of emotion.

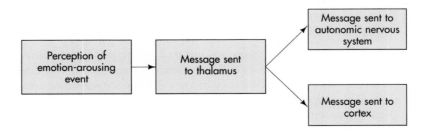

that theorists suggested that cognitive interpretations might be relevant in forming our emotional experiences. Stanley Schachter and Jerome Singer (1962) proposed that these higher mental processes help us label whether we are experiencing joy or terror.

According to the **Schachter-Singer theory**, an emotion-arousing event causes physiological arousal, and you examine the external environment to help you interpret that event. For example, if your heart is pounding, you try to figure out *why*. If a 17-legged alien has suddenly appeared on the movie screen, you interpret your arousal as terror. If a very attractive person has just sat down next to you and is gazing into your eyes, you interpret this arousal very differently! As Figure 12.14 shows, the combination of physiological arousal and a cognitive label produces an emotional experience.

To test their two-factor theory, Schachter and Singer (1962) gave adrenaline injections to college men. As you may recall, adrenaline increases arousal. Imagine that you were a participant in this study, and you had been told that adrenaline causes an increase in heart rate and breathing rate. Now the researchers lead you to another room, where another person (in reality an accomplice of the researchers) is acting strangely. This fellow seems extremely happy, playing basketball with a wad of paper, playing with a hula hoop, and flying paper airplanes. As you watch this very happy person, your heart rate and breathing rate begin to increase. What emotion would you feel? Schachter and Singer found that the participants in this condition felt no major change in their emotions. After all, they could attribute their arousal to the drug. The accomplice's joyfulness did not "rub off." Similarly, participants showed no major change in their emotions in another condition where people—informed about the effects of adrenaline—stayed in a room with a hostile person who complained about the insulting questionnaire he was completing and eventually stamped out of the room.

Now imagine that you were a participant in this study, except you have been told that the injection would cause no effects. Now you find yourself sitting in a room with a person who is either extremely happy (in one condition) or extremely hostile (in another condition). Your heart is pounding, and you are breathing rapidly. How can this be happening? You search around for a cognitive label, some emotional explanation for your reaction. If you are sitting with an airplane-flying optimist, it must be because you are happy. If you are sitting with a complaining pessimist, it must be because you are angry.

Schachter and Singer's complicated experiment—which included many more conditions than described here—did not turn out exactly as their theory had predicted. Furthermore, other research, which included additional precautions, failed to support the Schachter-Singer theory (Marshall & Zimbardo, 1979; Maslach, 1979; Reisenzein, 1983). Thirty years after the original research, theorists are not convinced that physiological arousal is essential for an emotional experience. Furthermore, many believe that people can have emotional experiences without any contribution from cognitive labels or higher mental processes. One such theorist is Carroll Izard, whose approach to emotions concludes this section.

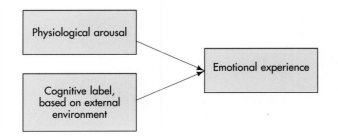

Figure 12.14
The Schachter-Singer theory of emotion.

Izard's Theory   Carroll Izard (pronounced "Ih-*zahrd*") has proposed the richest and most complex approach to emotional experiences. **Izard's theory** suggests that two different kinds of emotion activations are responsible for our feelings. Cognition is not necessary for the first kind of emotional experience, but it is for the second kind.

Imagine that it is late at night, your bedroom is dark, and you have emerged from bed for a drink of water. Suddenly you stub your toe, and you are instantly very angry. The sensation of pain leads *immediately* to anger. You do not need to evaluate the stimuli in the environment, and you do not need to speculate about who could have left the object in your path. In this example, cognition is not necessary.

One source of evidence that cognition is not essential comes from studies with 2-month-old infants. When these infants received their immunizations, Izard and his colleagues (1983) observed that the pain from the shot produced an angry reaction. A cognitive explanation is not appropriate for young infants, who cannot yet interpret or categorize the emotion-arousing event. Izard (1989) proposes that evolution has developed inborn nervous-system pathways for processing certain emotions very efficiently. He notes that these inborn pathways have not been studied as extensively as the pathways involved in learned emotional responses. However, he proposes that the thalamus and the amygdala (see p. 72)—but not the cortex—are the important brain structures in this pathway. The cortex, which is critical in processing the second kind of emotional experience, plays no role in the inborn nervous-system pathway.

Robert Zajonc (pronounced "*Zie*-unce"), at the University of Michigan, also argues that cognition is not essential for all emotional processing. Zajonc (1980; 1984) summarizes research to support his position. In one study, various geometric shapes were presented for an extremely brief exposure—only 1 millisecond. Previous research had established that people prefer stimuli they have seen before, rather than unfamiliar stimuli. In this study, participants preferred the geometric shapes they had previously seen—even when they could not recognize them as being familiar. That is, they liked a stimulus (an emotional reaction) without remembering that it was familiar (a cognitive reaction). We do not always need to think, ponder, and weigh the pros and cons before we claim to like something!

However, cognition is clearly involved in other emotional reactions. Suppose that someone bumps into you on the sidewalk, and your immediate emotional response to the pain is anger. Then you notice that the person is blind. Your

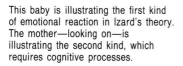

This baby is illustrating the first kind of emotional reaction in Izard's theory. The mother—looking on—is illustrating the second kind, which requires cognitive processes.

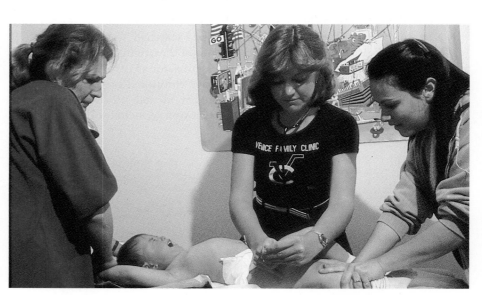

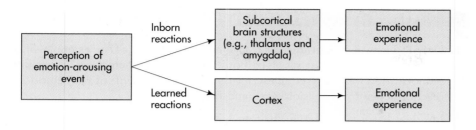

Figure 12.15
Izard's theory of emotion, which proposes two separate routes for the production of emotional experiences.

anger is likely to be replaced by another emotional response—perhaps pity. This more complex emotion cannot be generated by primitive brain structures such as the thalamus or the amygdala. The cortex is required to note that the white cane identifies this person as being blind. The cortex is also required to acknowledge that the accident was not intentional. As Izard (1989) notes, this second kind of emotional reaction requires "numerous cognitive processes, including comparison, matching, appraisal, categorization, imagery, memory, and anticipation" (p. 48). Figure 12.15 illustrates the two pathways for emotional reactions, as proposed in Izard's theory.

Let us briefly review the role of cognition in each of these theories of emotions. In the James-Lange theory, cognitions are not critical in determining the emotional experience; instead, physiological changes are important. Similarly, cognitions are not critical mediators in the Cannon-Bard theory or the facial feedback hypothesis; again, physiology is important. In the Schachter-Singer theory, however, cognitions are essential in interpreting physiological arousal. ("Why is my heart pounding? It must be because I'm terrified by the sudden appearance of the 17-legged alien.") Finally, in Izard's theory, cognitions are important in one kind of emotional reaction, but they are not involved in the more basic emotional reactions demonstrated in infants and in some immediate reactions in adulthood. It seems likely that some variant of Izard's theory will be most useful in explaining the variety and richness of human emotions.

Section Summary: Emotion

- Cognitive emotional reactions are often assessed with rating scales, such as those used to measure subjective well-being or emotional reactions to daily events for people who were lottery winners.
- Each emotion is not uniquely linked to a specific combination of physiological reactions; similarly, the polygraph examination (lie detector test) is not very reliable in separating innocent people from guilty people.
- Immediate, involuntary facial expressions seem to be highly similar across cultures, but display rules—which govern delayed reactions—vary from culture to culture.
- Adults are more sensitive than younger people in interpreting nonverbal cues; females are also somewhat better than males, particularly in judging facial expression.
- Plutchik's system of classifying emotions includes eight categories of emotion, which can differ in their intensity.
- The work of Isen suggests that people are more likely to appreciate subtle relationships on conceptual organization, memory, concept-formation, and problem-solving tasks when they are in a happy mood.
- Five theories of emotion are the James-Lange theory, the Cannon-Bard theory, the facial feedback hypothesis, the Schachter-Singer theory, and Izard's theory.

REVIEW QUESTIONS

1. Define the terms *motivation* and *emotion*. Then think of an example of an episode in your life that involved both motivation and emotion. What kind of motivation was involved? Describe the three components of your emotional reaction (cognitive, physiological, and behavioral).

2. Imagine that it is 6:30 p.m., half an hour past your normal dinnertime, and you are standing in front of a closed bakery shop, admiring the desserts while you wait for a friend to pick you up for dinner. Identify the factors contributing to the sensation that you are hungry.

3. Many parts of the motivation section contrasted external and internal factors and their role in determining motivation. Discuss the importance of both external and internal factors in determining hunger level, obesity, sexual interactions, achievement motivation, and intrinsic motivation.

4. Individual differences are important in many aspects of motivation. Discuss individual differences in body weight, coercive versus consensual sexual interactions, and achievement motivation.

5. Now discuss two important group variables, culture and gender, noting the areas in which these variables are important as well as areas in which they are usually irrelevant. Be sure to include examples from both motivation and emotion.

6. A major portion of the section on emotions emphasized the cognitive, physiological, and behavioral components of emotions. What are the pros and cons of each of these indexes of emotion? Which do you think provides the best index of your own emotions?

7. Suppose that a friend is puzzled about why polygraph examinations are no longer legal in many situations. Describe these tests, their results, and the reason they are not widely used in the 1990s.

8. This chapter discussed the influence of positive affect on cognitive processes. Describe some of the higher mental processes influenced by emotion, and speculate about some of the tasks you perform that could be influenced by emotions. Can you think of any practical applications for these findings?

9. The section on cross-cultural aspects of facial expression discussed immediate facial responses as well as delayed facial responses that are governed by display rules. Which theory of emotions best explains these two kinds of responses?

10. This chapter examined five explanations for motivation and five for emotion. Describe each of these theoretical approaches, indicating which theory or theories are best able to explain a wide variety of motivations and emotions.

NEW TERMS

motivation	set point	orgasmic phase
emotion	fat cells	resolution phase
lateral hypothalamus (LH)	anorexia nervosa	gonorrhea
ventromedial hypothalamus (VMH)	bulimia	genital herpes
glucose	counter-regulation	Acquired Immunodeficiency
glucostats	excitement phase	Syndrome (AIDS)
insulin	plateau phase	sexual coercion

rape	attribution	display rules
sexual harrassment	instincts	James-Lange theory
consensual sexual interactions	drive	Cannon-Bard theory
achievement motive	opponent-process theory	facial feedback hypothesis
fear of success	incentive theory	Schachter-Singer theory
intrinsic motivation	subjective well-being	Izard's theory
extrinsic motivation	polygraph examination	

ANSWERS TO DEMONSTRATIONS

Demonstration 12.2.   1. W;   2. M;   3. W;   4. W;   5. M;   6. M;   7. M;   8. W.

Demonstration 12.5.   1. anger;   2. fear;   3. disgust;   4. surprise;   5. happiness; 6. sadness.

Demonstration 12.6.   The purpose of the first 10 words was to create a happy mood; you do not need to examine your responses to these items. However, inspect your responses to the last 10 words. In each case, I have listed the most common responses. If your response is *not* among the common responses, place a U (for uncommon) next to your response. 11. cut, sharp;   12. light, fat, hard, load, weight;   13. bird, fly;   14. bread, yellow;   15. feet, laces, socks, stockings;   16. web, black, bug, insect, legs;   17. water, blue, deep, sea, waves;   18. windows, house, open, window;   19. black, snow; 20. thread, eye, pin, sew, sharp. Finally, count the number of U marks on your sheet. I constructed these norms so that people who had been in a neutral mood should have an average of one U on a page. If you had a large number of U marks, it is likely that your positive mood inspired you to think more flexibly and provide unusual responses.

RECOMMENDED READINGS

Hyde, J. S. (1990). *Understanding human sexuality* (4th ed.). New York: McGraw-Hill. Janet Hyde, who is well known for her work in the psychology of women, is the author of this comprehensive textbook, which includes chapters on sexual preference and sexual difficulties as well as coverage of physiological and behavioral aspects of sexuality.

Isen, A. M. (1987). Positive affect, cognitive processes, and social behavior. *Advances in Experimental Social Psychology, 20*, 203–253. Isen's chapter summarizes how positive affect influences social behavior, as well as a wide variety of cognitive tasks—including many not discussed here.

Izard, C. E. (1989). The structure and functions of emotions: Implications for cognition, motivation, and personality. In I. S. Cohen (Ed.), *The G. Stanley Hall Lecture Series* (Vol. 9, pp. 37–73). Washington, DC: American Psychological Association. Izard's chapter provides an overview of current issues in research on emotions, including his own theory, facial feedback theory, and the development of emotions in children.

McClelland, D. C. (1985). *Human motivation.* Glenview, IL: Scott, Foresman. This textbook for advanced undergraduates discusses the history of motivational theories but focuses on achievement motivation.

Strongman, K. T. (1987). *The psychology of emotion* (3rd ed.). New York: Wiley. Strongman's book offers a historical overview of theories of emotion for advanced undergraduates; it also includes some information on the role of cognition in emotion, as well as some research on affect and memory not examined here.

13

Personality

You may know someone like Susan. Her half of the dormitory room is spotless. Her desk is immaculate, adorned only by a carefully dusted lamp. The pencils, pens, and markers in the drawer are neatly arranged. Her dresser holds only one photograph, in a pale blue frame that matches her bedspread. Susan's clothes are neatly folded in the dresser drawers and precisely arranged in categories in her closet. You suspect she even polishes her wastebasket. Neatness seems to be a crucial part of Susan's personality.

Personality is a pattern of characteristic feelings, thoughts, and behaviors that persists across time and situations; personality distinguishes one person from another (Phares, 1988). For instance, it seems likely that Susan has always been neat and tidy; neatness persists across time. She probably keeps the work area neat in her work-study job at the library, and her bedroom at home is certainly immaculate as well; neatness persists across situations. Furthermore, Susan's neatness distinguishes her from her roommate, whose idea of a neat room requires only a narrow path through the dirty clothes on the floor; a clean desk means that there is enough space among the dirty coffee cups for one textbook.

In this chapter, we will consider how four personality theories account for individual differences (such as the difference between Susan and her roommate):

1. The **psychoanalytic approach**, which originated with Sigmund Freud, emphasizes childhood experiences and unconscious motivations. A psychoanalytic theorist, for instance, might trace Susan's neatness to her toilet-training experiences.

2. The **social cognitive approach** emphasizes observational learning and the contribution of cognitive factors. A psychologist who favored this approach might speculate that Susan observed and imitated her mother's emphasis on cleanliness.

3. The **trait approach** proposes that human personality should be described in terms of specific, stable personal characteristics, such as shyness or aggressiveness. A trait theorist would not try to explain why Susan is neat. Instead, he or she would try to determine whether Susan's neatness does indeed persist across different situations, and whether neatness is related to other traits, such as promptness.

4. The **humanistic approach** stresses that humans have enormous potential for personal growth. A humanistic theorist would be concerned about whether Susan's excessive neatness prevents her from being spontaneous, and whether it limits the development of her true potential.

Students in my introductory psychology class often wonder why psychologists bother with personality theories. A theory is important, however, because it provides a general framework for understanding individual differences. In addition, each of the four theories that we discuss identifies critical questions that should be answered. Research is therefore more orderly and systematic.

Furthermore, the personality approach we adopt has an important influence on our view of human nature (Rychlak, 1981a). For instance, a person who admires the psychoanalytic view that humans are not rational, but governed by unconscious wishes, would approach the judicial system differently than one who prefers the social cognitive view, which suggests that people commit crimes because models have provided bad examples. Also, a supporter of the psychoanalytic tradition would probably conclude that wars are inevitable, but social cognitive and humanistic theorists would disagree.

In this chapter, we compare the four theoretical approaches on these four dimensions:

1. What is the source of data? Are the data obtained from an expert analyst, from an objective test, or from self-reports? Are the observations based on people in therapy, or from more general populations?

2. What does the theory propose as the cause of behavior? Is the cause internal or external to the person?

3. How comprehensive is the theory? Does it attempt to explain almost all behavior, or does it focus on isolated characteristics and behavior patterns?

4. What is the theory's outlook on human nature? Is it positive, neutral, or negative?

Before beginning, however, we need to discuss two precautions. First, these four theories are not mutually exclusive. In many areas, the theories are complementary, because they focus on different aspects of human personality. It would be a mistake to think that one of these theories must be correct, and all the others must be wrong. Second, human personality is so complex that it cannot be adequately captured even by four different perspectives (Phares, 1988). Theorists from each of these four perspectives have been accumulating information about personality for several decades. Still, we need more decades—and perhaps even new perspectives—to describe human personality adequately.

The Psychoanalytic Approach

The psychoanalytic approach emphasizes three central concepts: (1) childhood experiences determine adult personality; (2) unconscious mental processes influence everyday behavior; and (3) unconscious conflict underlies most of human behavior.

Sigmund Freud, the founder of the psychoanalytic approach, was born in 1856 and grew up in a Jewish family in Vienna, Austria. His training was in medicine, and he was specifically interested in neurology and psychological problems. In his 30s, Freud began a brief collaboration with Josef Breuer, a prominent Viennese physician. Together they developed a method in which patients relieved psychological symptoms by talking about them. The two men had a falling-out several years later, and Freud won acclaim on his own. Freud, in turn, inspired other influential scholars; we consider three of them—Carl Jung, Alfred Adler, and Karen Horney—later in this section.

It is important to stress that Freud's theories were extremely controversial for the end of the 19th century. The Victorian era was known for its straitlaced attitudes toward sexuality, yet Freud argued that people were driven by sexual urges. At that time, too, psychologists favored the views of Wilhelm Wundt, the

Sigmund Freud strolling in the mountains with his daughter Anna Freud (who also became a psychoanalyst).

founder of scientific psychology, which emphasized conscious experience. In contrast, Freud focused on the unconscious. Given this opposition, it is particularly remarkable that Freud's theories eventually gained such prominence.

Approximately a century after Freud's theories gained prominence, we must still acknowledge his influence. His theory has been called "the single most sweeping contribution to the field of personality" (Phares, 1988, p. 75). Another current theorist writes about the scope of Freud's ideas: "Freud is now the standard against which other personality theories must be judged" (Rychlak, 1981a, pp. 14–15).

Even if psychologists abandon Freud—and many have—his influence invades many other areas of life. Phrases such as "Freudian slip" and "unconscious" are part of our routine vocabulary. For example, high school health textbooks have been influenced more by Freud than by any other theorist discussed in this chapter. In these books, terms such as "reaction formation" and "repression" are presented as if they were documented facts, rather than part of a theory.

People in the humanities are particularly enchanted with psychoanalytic approaches. Consider a review of the movie *The Stepfather*. In connection with the movie's teenage daughter, the reviewer writes about

> . . . the elements of desire which fuel the pre-Oedipal and post-Oedipal stages—most particularly masochism, which is associated with pre-Oedipal desires for union with the mother, and sadism, which is linked to post-Oedipal desires for dominance and control. (Erens, 1987–1988, p. 54)

In fact, film journals contain more references to Freudian theory than do current mainstream psychology journals.

Freud's personal history provides evidence that childhood experiences are critical. His father once remarked, after 7-year-old Sigmund had acted foolishly, "The boy will come to nothing" (Freud, 1900/1953, p. 216). Freud spent his lifetime demonstrating that his father's early prediction was incorrect.

We begin this overview of the psychoanalytic approach by considering Freud's basic theories on the structure of personality. We then discuss his methods, his views on defense mechanisms, and the stages of psychosexual development. We end with a discussion of three other psychoanalytic theorists and an evaluation of psychoanalytic theory.

The Structure of Personality

Freud envisioned three basic components to human personality: the id, the ego, and the superego (Freud, 1933/1964). Humans are born with an **id**, which consists of the basic drives and provides both the power and the energy for all human behavior. Freud also maintained that the id lacks moral judgment; it cannot distinguish between good and evil. The id is unconscious, without contacts to the external world.

The **ego**, in contrast, develops to deal with the external world. The ego serves as a mediator between the id and reality. Freud proposed that the ego begins to function about the age of 6 months, when the infant starts to take past experiences into account. The id, with its focus on basic drives, cannot judge which activities are safe and which ones are harmful. Therefore, the ego must allow the id to gratify its desires without being harmed.

So far, we have an irrational id, governed by pleasure, and a cooler, calmer ego, governed by reality. Freud's third personality component is the **superego**, which includes individual personal conscience and ideals. The superego acquires its principles from society. Because Victorian society in Freud's era was stifling and discouraged sexual expression, Freud thought the superego suppressed the sexual impulses.

In Freud's theory, then, the ego acts as supervisor. It must negotiate a compromise between the id's drives and the superego's rules about moral behavior. Finally, the ego must continuously assess reality and ask questions like "Is this possible?" and "Is this safe?"

A description in one textbook may help you remember this trio:

Freudian theory would say that this child's superego prevents her from taking a forbidden cookie.

> Imagine a sex-starved hedonist [the id], a black-frock-coated Puritan minister [the superego], and a totally humorless computer scientist [the ego] chained together and turned loose in the world, and you have a good approximation of what Freud was trying to show us about the personality.
>
> Because they are chained together, the id, ego and superego cannot decide to go their separate ways. They have no alternative but to adjust to one another. And the result, for better or for worse, is the adult human personality. (Geiwitz & Moursund, 1979, p. 27)

Let us discuss how the id, ego, and superego are related to level of awareness. Freud compared the human mind to an iceberg. As in Figure 13.1, the bulk of the iceberg is hidden below the surface of the water. Similarly, most psychic processes are not conscious; they are hidden from the outside world. Freud proposed that the **unconscious** holds thoughts and desires that are far below the level of a person's awareness. The unconscious is similar to the bottom part of the iceberg. Your unconscious may hold a particularly traumatic childhood memory, for example. That traumatic memory is not likely to reach consciousness during normal daily activities, though it may influence your behavior without your being aware of it. Notice in Figure 13.1 that the id is totally unconscious, and parts of the ego and superego are also unconscious.

Moving upward in this iceberg of awareness, Freud proposed that the **preconscious** holds material just slightly below the surface of awareness; this material can be easily retrieved. An example would be the name of your psychology professor. That name was not immediately in your consciousness, though you effortlessly brought it to the surface. Notice in Figure 13.1 that parts of both the ego and superego are preconscious, though the id never rises that near the surface.

Finally, the **conscious** includes everything you are aware of at a particular moment. As noted in chapter 5 on states of consciousness, our conscious experiences refer to our sensory awareness of the environment and of ourselves. At

Figure 13.1
Freud's model of the three structures of the human mind, similar to an iceberg.

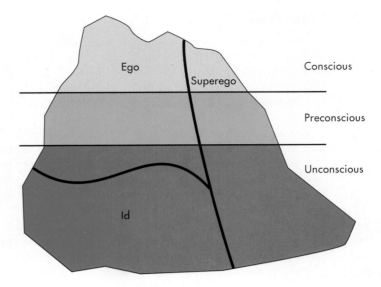

this moment, for instance, your conscious may include the definition for conscious, a sketch of an iceberg, and the thought that you need to buy toothpaste tomorrow. Notice in Figure 13.1 that only the ego and the superego are included in the conscious. However, if the id has a special urge that must be satisfied, it provokes conflicts with the ego and the superego. The id can express itself *indirectly* in the conscious.

Freud's Methods

As a physician, Freud studied people with serious psychological disorders. In traditional psychoanalysis, the patient is seen several times a week, and analysis may last for 2 or 3 years. The patient may lie on a couch, with the analyst sitting in a chair near the patient's head. (You have probably seen the setup in cartoons.) Modern analysts are likely to seat the patient in a chair, however. In all cases, the client is encouraged to relax.

A major psychoanalytic technique is **free association**, in which patients are encouraged to say anything that occurs to them, no matter how silly or irrelevant it may seem to their conscious judgment (Rychlak, 1981b). An analyst may stimulate recall with an open-ended question such as "What is on your mind today?" However, free associations do not need to be rational or tied to the present time. For example, a woman in therapy may suddenly have an image of a perfume bottle. Perhaps this image brings forth a recollection from childhood, such as a fight with a brother near her mother's bureau. Freud felt that free association was one tool that allowed access to the unconscious.

As we noted in the discussion of dreams in chapter 5, Freud believed that the unconscious reveals itself in dreams via symbols. He argued that the ego relaxes its control when we sleep, so the unconscious is more obvious in dreams than in the awake state. A second Freudian method, therefore, was dream analysis. For instance, an analyst may listen to a patient's report of a dream about riding on a bull in an amusement-park carousel, and the analyst may interpret the bull as a symbol of the patient's father. The conscious, remembered story line of a dream is called its **manifest content**. The unconscious, underlying aspects of the dream are called the **latent content.**

A third Freudian method is the interpretation of reactions. For instance, a modern-day analyst worked with a 2-year-old girl who was concerned about broken crayons (Chehrazi, 1986). This analyst interpreted the broken crayons as a symbol of the girl's wish for a penis.

A fourth Freudian method is the interpretation of slips-of-the-tongue. The chapter on language discussed a cognitive interpretation of these slips-of-the-tongue. Freud believed, however, that these slips reveal unconscious thoughts. For instance, suppose that a psychology professor, who is not an admirer of Freud, says, "Let me insult a comment about Freud" rather than "Let me *insert* a comment about Freud." The slip would presumably reveal the professor's true feelings about Freud.

Psychologists trained in experimental research techniques often feel uncomfortable about Freudian methods, which seem so subjective and difficult to verify. For example, how do we know that the little girl with the broken crayons is not simply worried about broken crayons rather than a missing penis? More generally, it is difficult to establish experimentally that any symbol represents a particular personality problem.

Defense Mechanisms

The conflict among the id, the ego, and the superego is central in Freud's theory. Freud proposed that anxiety occurs when the ego fears that it will lose this conflict. The ego protects itself against anxiety by using defense mechanisms. **Defense mechanisms** are normal coping processes that distort reality in the process of reducing anxiety (Holmes, 1984b).

Table 13.1 shows seven of the major defense mechanisms, which Sigmund Freud developed in collaboration with his daughter, Anna. As you read each of these definitions, try to think about the underlying anxiety, how it is channeled into a particular defense mechanism, and how reality is distorted. Notice, too, that in Freudian theory, defense mechanisms can produce some positive outcomes.

Table 13.1   *Freudian Defense Mechanisms*

DEFENSE MECHANISM	DEFINITION	EXAMPLE
Repression	Pushing back unacceptable thoughts into the unconscious.	A rape victim cannot recall the details of the attack.
Regression	Acting in ways characteristic of earlier life stages.	A young adult, anxious on a trip to his parents' home, sits in the corner reading comic books, as he often did in grade school.
Reaction formation	Replacing an anxiety-producing feeling with its exact opposite, typically going overboard.	A man who is anxious about his interest in gay men begins dating women several times a week.
Rationalization	Creating false but believable excuses to justify inappropriate behavior.	A student cheats on an exam, explaining that cheating is legitimate on an unfair examination.
Sublimation	Redirecting forbidden impulses toward a socially desirable goal.	A soldier, who enjoyed his tour in Vietnam, becomes a policeman in a dangerous urban neighborhood.
Displacement	Redirecting emotional feelings (e.g., anger) to a substitute target.	A husband, angry at the way his boss treated him, screams at his wife.
Projection	Attributing your own unacceptable feelings to another person.	An employee at a store, tempted to steal some merchandise, suspects that other employees are stealing.

Sources: D. S. Holmes, 1984; Monte, 1987.
Note: If you would like a mnemonic to help you recall these basic seven defense mechanisms, remember that the first four all begin with the letter *R* (they are actually listed in reverse alphabetical order), and the first letters of the other three (S, D, and P) can be remembered via the phrase "Study Diligently, Please."

Freud proposed that Leonardo da Vinci painted Madonnas as a form of sublimation.

For instance, Freud (1930/1963) argued that the great Italian artist Leonardo da Vinci painted madonnas as a sublimated symbol of his mother. Leonardo had been separated from his mother at a young age, and he longed to be reunited with her. Freud's pessimism about human nature is often revealed in these defense mechanisms, however. For instance, why are you so extraordinarily helpful to your neighbor? According to Freud, your helpfulness may be caused by a reaction formation against the aggressiveness you truly feel toward the neighbor (Wallach & Wallach, 1983). For example, you shovel snow from his sidewalk every morning because unconsciously you want to harm him.

Stages of Psychosexual Development

Freud's research with his patients convinced him that psychological disorders typically begin in childhood. As a result, much of adult personality can be explained by examining important early events.

Freud argued that humans first experience tension in the mouth area, during the oral stage.

Freud argued that at different ages, humans feel tension at different parts of the body, known as **erogenous zones**, and that pleasant stimulation of these zones reduces the tension. The first erogenous zone, the focus of tension for the infant, is the mouth, followed at later ages by the anus, and finally the genitals.

Furthermore, Freud proposed that children experience conflicts between urges in these erogenous zones and the rules of society. Society requires infants to learn to drink from a cup rather than to suck. Society requires toddlers to be toilet trained, and it specifies that children should not masturbate. If a conflict in a particular erogenous zone is not successfully resolved, a person may experience **fixation**, becoming permanently locked in conflict about that erogenous zone. Table 13.2 outlines the five stages of psychosexual development. Let us explore them further.

Table 13.2   *Freud's Five Stages of Psychosexual Development*

AGE	STAGE	DESCRIPTION
0–18 months	Oral stage	Stimulation of the mouth produces pleasure; the baby enjoys sucking, chewing, biting.
18–36 months	Anal stage	Stimulation of the anal region produces pleasure; the toddler experiences conflict over toilet training.
3–6 years	Phallic stage	Self-stimulation of the genitals produces pleasure; the child struggles with sexual feelings about the same-gender parent.
6–puberty	Latency	Sexual feelings are repressed; the child avoids members of the other gender.
Puberty onward	Genital stage	Adolescent or adult has mature sexual feelings and experiences pleasure from sexual relationships with others.

An Overview of the Five Stages   During the **oral stage**, the mouth experiences the most tension. The id tries to reduce this tension by encouraging the child to suck on nipples, thumbs, and pacifiers. A person fixated in the oral stage might be overly demanding or sarcastic (Fenichel, 1945).

In the **anal stage**, the erogenous zone shifts to the anal region. Freud proposed that toddlers experience satisfaction when their anal region is stimulated, for instance by retaining or eliminating feces. Toilet training begins at this stage, and parents begin to insist that the child eliminate feces in the toilet. Conflict arises between the child's id and the new restrictions imposed by society. According to Freud's theory, an unsuccessful resolution of this conflict produces fixation at the anal stage; a person might be too orderly or overly concerned about punctuality.

During the **phallic stage**, the erogenous zone shifts to the sex organs, and the child presumably finds pleasure in masturbation, self-stimulation of the genitals. Freud proposed that boys in the phallic stage experience an Oedipus complex. In the ancient Greek tragedy *Oedipus Rex*, King Oedipus unknowingly kills his father and marries his mother. Similarly, a young boy in the phallic stage presumably has sexual feelings for his mother and hostile feelings for his father.

Freud's explanation of the phallic stage in little girls was not as completely developed (Phares, 1988). However, Freud maintained that little girls experience the Electra complex, named after the Greek legend of Electra, who helped to kill her own mother. A young girl notices that she lacks a penis (experiencing penis envy) and decides that her mother was responsible for castrating her. She therefore develops hostile feelings for her mother while her love of her father grows.

How do children resolve these complexes? Freud proposed that children use a defense mechanism—specifically repression—to push back these unacceptable thoughts. Furthermore, they begin an identification process, in which they take on characteristics of the same-gender parent, and the superego grows stronger. Unsuccessful resolution of the phallic stage, however, can cause a person to be either overly proud or overly timid (Fenichel, 1945).

During the **latency stage**, children's sexual feelings remain in the repressed state in which they were left at the end of the phallic stage. Children are presumably ashamed and disgusted about sexual issues, and so they tend to avoid members of the other gender.

Freud's final stage of psychosexual development is the **genital stage**; during puberty, sexual urges reappear and the genitals once again become an erogenous zone. Freud argued that genital pleasure in the earlier phallic stage comes from self-stimulation. In contrast, genital pleasure during the genital stage arises from sexual relationships with others.

Freud would explain the gender segregation in this classroom as a manifestation of the latency stage, in which children avoid members of the other gender.

Freudian Theory and Women   In the last two decades, moreover, people who support the equality of women and men have argued that Freudian theory misrepresents women (e.g., Lerman, 1986). Freud's writing often refers to female inferiority, which he traces primarily to women's lack of a penis. Freud argued that when young girls notice that they are missing a penis, they "feel themselves heavily handicapped . . . and envy the boy's possession of it" (Freud, 1925/1976, p. 327).

Freud believed that girls cannot experience an Electra conflict that is as intense as boys' Oedipal conflict, because they lack a large, obvious genital organ. Because the conflict is milder, girls identify less strongly with their mothers. As a consequence, their superegos never develop fully. Freud writes, "for women the level of what is ethically normal is different from what it is in men. . . . they show less sense of justice than men" (Freud, 1925/1976, p. 258).

We should note that psychological research has not produced evidence for female's penis envy (Fisher & Greenberg, 1977; Lerman, 1986). In fact, most young girls are unconcerned about genital differences. Some, indeed, are relieved that they lack this anatomical structure. Consider, for instance, the little girl who took a bath with a young male cousin and observed the genital differences in silence. Later, she said softly to her mother, "Isn't it a blessing he doesn't have it on his face?" (Tavris & Offir, 1977, p. 155). Furthermore, as noted in chapter 11, men and women do not differ significantly in their moral development. It is important to remember, however, that Freud was writing in a time when women were considered inferior, so his ideas reflect his own culture and historical context.

Other Psychoanalytic Theorists

Freud has influenced our thinking about personality both directly through his own writing and indirectly through the ideas of his followers. We discuss three of these students: Carl Jung, Alfred Adler, and Karen Horney.

Jung   The Swiss analyst, Carl Jung (pronounced "Yoong") developed an early interest in Sigmund Freud's theory of dreams. Recalling his initial meetings with Freud, Jung wrote, "Freud was the first man of real importance I had encountered. . . . I found him extremely intelligent, shrewd, and altogether remarkable" (Wehr, 1987, p. 96). However, the collaboration between Freud and Jung ended when Jung proposed that Freud had overemphasized sexuality (Jung, 1917/1953).

Jung's theory retained Freud's emphasis on the unconscious, but Jung argued that the unconscious contained two layers. The first layer, or **personal unconscious**, stores material that has been forgotten or repressed. Jung's personal unconscious therefore resembles Freud's notions about the unconscious. However, Jung also proposed a second, deeper layer called the collective unconscious. Jung's **collective unconscious** stores memory fragments from our ancestral past. Jung's theory proposes, then, that all humans share the same collective unconscious. Jung argued that the collective unconscious explains why diverse religions feature similar themes, and why diverse cultures feature similar symbols in their paintings. Figure 13.2, for instance, shows mandalas—or figures with a circular design— from two different countries. The concept of a collective unconscious was greeted more enthusiastically by artists and anthropologists than by psychologists.

Perhaps Jung's most important contribution to psychology was the idea that people could be categorized as either introverts or extraverts. An **introvert** tends to be shy and withdrawn, more oriented toward his or her own internal experience. In contrast, an **extravert** tends to be outgoing, more oriented toward other people and events. Jung's approach was an early forerunner of the trait approach, which we examine in the third section of this chapter.

Adler   Like Jung, Alfred Adler believed that Freud had overemphasized the importance of sexuality in his theory. Instead, Adler's theory emphasized people's striving toward power or superiority. Adler proposed that children feel physically weak and helpless in a world ruled by adults. When parents are either overprotective or neglectful, these feelings of inferiority can develop into an inferiority complex (Adler, 1924). People generally try to compensate in order to overcome these feelings of inferiority. They want to improve themselves and overcome difficulties.

Figure 13.2
These mandalas were painted by artists from two different cultures. The one on the left was made by a psychiatric patient in Western culture, and the one on the right was created by an artist in Tibet. Jung argued that they are similar because we all share the same collective unconscious.

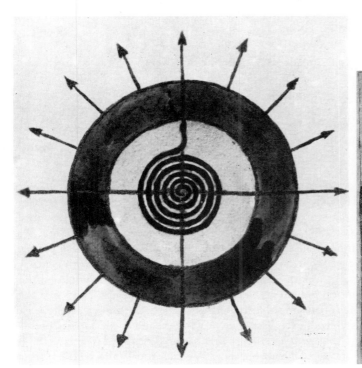

Horney   Karen Horney (pronounced "*Horn*-eye") challenged Freud's theory of penis envy and proposed that women are more likely to envy men's status in society than their genitals (Horney, 1926/1967). Like Adler, Horney proposed that young children feel relatively helpless and threatened. Children develop several strategies to cope with the anxiety generated by this helplessness (Enns, 1989; Horney, 1945):

1. They can move *toward* other people, showing affection or dependency.

2. They can move *against* other people, displaying aggression or hostility.

3. They can move *away from* other people, protecting themselves by withdrawing from relationships.

Horney proposed that normal people balance the three strategies. Psychological disorders develop, however, when one strategy dominates personality.

We have outlined Freud's theory and then summarized the contributions of three theorists who were strongly influenced by Freud. A fourth, Erik Erikson, is perhaps the best known of the theorists influenced by Freud; we discussed his eight stages of psychosocial development in the two chapters on human development. We see further evidence of Freud's influence when we discuss psychotherapy in chapter 16.

Evaluation of the Psychoanalytic Approach

Table 13.3 summarizes four important characteristics of psychoanalytic theory: its source of data, proposed cause of behavior, comprehensiveness, and outlook on humans.

What can we conclude about the psychoanalytic approach roughly a century after it was formulated? By current standards, it has some major problems:

1. *It is difficult to test.*   Psychoanalytic theory emphasizes the unconscious, yet the unconscious rarely expresses itself directly. Therefore, it is difficult to measure. Furthermore, consider the following problem: Suppose that an analyst suspects that a man is pessimistic. Any pessimistic feelings expressed in therapy will be taken as evidence of pessimism. However, any optimistic feelings will also be taken as evidence of pessimism, because these feelings could be a reaction formation against the original pessimism. Some aspects of psychoanalytic theory cannot be disproven, because the theory could predict both a particular characteristic and its opposite (Phares, 1988).

2. *When it is tested, the studies are often inadequate.*   The psychoanalytic approach is criticized for improper methodology. For instance, the observers may be biased, interpreting ambiguous observations so that they are consistent with a particular theory. How do we know that a little girl's concern over broken crayons represents penis envy, when simpler explanations exist? Furthermore, Freud's theory was based on a nonrepresentative sample from a different era. We cannot generalize from a small sample of troubled, well-to-do Viennese people, studied many decades ago, to a variety of cultures at the end of the 20th century.

3. *It is biased against women.*   We noted earlier that Freud maintained that women have inferior moral judgment, clearly a gender bias. He also proposed that women are **masochistic** (pronounced "mass-uh-*kiss*-tick"), deriving pleasure from being mistreated. This view does a disservice to women, and it encourages people to think—incorrectly—that women enjoy being battered or raped (Caplan, 1984).

4. *It is too pessimistic about human nature.*   Wallach and Wallach (1983) argue in their book, *Psychology's Sanction for Selfishness*, that Freudian theory rarely allows

Table 13.3   *A Summary of the Psychoanalytic Approach*

	PSYCHOANALYTIC APPROACH
Source of data	Obtained from expert analyst from people in therapy
Cause of behavior	Internal conflict, unconscious forces, childhood experiences
Comprehensiveness of theory	Very comprehensive
Outlook on humans	Negative

for direct motivations toward what is right or good. As noted in the discussion on defense mechanisms, Freud believed that people are often helpful toward others because of a reaction formation against the aggressiveness they truly feel. They act ethically, because they fear punishment from their superegos. However, the discussion of the development of prosocial behavior in chapter 10 noted that very young children are helpful and kind toward others. Wallach and Wallach point out that humans are basically concerned about others; Freud's explanation was unnecessarily indirect and negative.

We have noted several problems with psychoanalytic theories. Nevertheless, we need to remember that we cannot blame Freud for being unable to predict how humans and their society would behave a century after he developed his theories.

Most important, we must praise Freud for encouraging psychology to explore human emotions and motivations rather than focusing only on thoughts and intellectual reactions. Freud's concept of the unconscious is clearly valuable to many modern psychologists (Erdelyi, 1985). Freud also contributed useful concepts such as anxiety and defense mechanisms. Furthermore, Freud's theory is the most fully developed and comprehensive approach we consider in this chapter. He tried to explain an enormous range of human behavior. Finally, we have to admire Freud's brilliance and persistence in developing a theory so different from the trends of his era.

Section Summary: The Psychoanalytic Approach

- The psychoanalytic approach stresses that human behavior is influenced by childhood experiences, unconscious mental processes, and conflict; Freud's theory was radically controversial when it was first presented. Freud's theory has had a strong impact on both psychology and other disciplines.
- Freud proposed three components of personality: the id, ego, and superego; the id is totally unconscious, whereas the ego and superego each have unconscious, preconscious, and conscious components.
- Psychoanalytic techniques include free association and the interpretation of dreams, reactions, and slips-of-the-tongue.
- Psychoanalytic defense mechanisms include repression, regression, reaction formation, rationalization, sublimation, displacement, and projection; these defense mechanisms distort reality in order to reduce anxiety.
- Freud argued that the erogenous zone shifts throughout development during five stages called oral, anal, phallic, latency, and genital.

■ Other psychoanalytic theorists include Jung, known for his idea of the collective unconscious and his introvert-extravert categories; Adler, known for his work on the inferiority complex; Horney, known for challenging Freud's theory that women have penis envy and for her concept that people can move toward, against, or away from others; and Erikson, whose theories were discussed in earlier chapters.

■ Criticisms of psychoanalytic theory include difficulty in testing it, inadequate studies, its bias against women, and its extreme pessimism. Positive features include its emphasis on emotions, some useful concepts, and its comprehensiveness.

The Social Cognitive Approach

We have been exploring psychoanalytic approaches to personality, which emphasize the importance of feelings and emotions. Those approaches stress that we are often ruled by unconscious forces, childhood experiences, and conflict.

In contrast, the social cognitive approach makes humans seem much more levelheaded and less passionate. This explanation of personality focuses on the way people observe, evaluate, regulate, and think. We may not always make the correct decision, but we are usually rational. Furthermore, we are ruled mostly by conscious forces and relatively recent experiences.

We begin by investigating the origins of this social cognitive approach in behaviorism and learning theory. Then we review the basic concepts of observational learning, an important component of the social cognitive approach. Our next topic is reciprocal influences, the concept that environmental factors, personal factors, and behavior all interact to form a person's personality. Next we consider self-efficacy, the feeling people have that they are competent and effective. Then an in-depth section focuses on the dynamic self-concept. We conclude with an evaluation of the social cognitive approach.

Origins of the Social Cognitive Approach: Behaviorism

The social cognitive approach to personality has its origins in behaviorism. As discussed in chapter 1, behaviorism is an approach to psychology that stresses the study of observable behavior instead of unobservable mental processes. Behaviorists were most influential in the development of learning theory, primarily the operant conditioning we examined in chapter 6. In operant conditioning, reinforcement and punishment are the major determinants of behavior. You do your physics homework, and you are reinforced by good grades on exams, so you continue to do homework in the future. A girl burps at the dinner table, receives chilling glances and negative comments from family members (punishment), so she stops making these noises.

The behaviorist who had the strongest influence on personality theory was B. F. Skinner. Skinner worked primarily with pigeons and rats rather than people. Skinner rejected general theories, preferring to focus instead on research results (Phares, 1988). It is ironic, then, that a person who worked with nonhumans—and did not like theoretical approaches—had such an important impact on human personality theory.

Skinner emphasized that we do not need to talk about the human mind or internal characteristics when we discuss people's personal traits. For instance, if a young man is friendly and outgoing, his behavior can be explained in terms of past and present reinforcement and punishment—that is, strictly external factors. Skinner believed that nothing is achieved by discussing this man's "extraversion trait." To understand the essence of humans, Skinner and other behaviorists

Skinner would propose that we can understand this politician's outgoing behavior by identifying genetic and environmental factors, without discussing internal characteristics.

proposed that we need to examine only genetic factors and the stimuli, reinforcements, and punishments in the environment, not any enduring personal characteristics (Skinner, 1974).

Albert Bandura is one of the major theorists who found Skinner's approach inadequate. Bandura (1986) argues that people learn much more by observational learning than by the trial-and-error learning involved in operant conditioning. Furthermore, Bandura emphasizes that people think about and interpret events. Unlike Skinner, Bandura stresses that the human mind makes an important contribution to personality. Bandura (1986) decided to call his approach social cognitive theory, because it emphasizes the contribution of social factors (e.g., observational learning) and thought (e.g., beliefs about competence) in explaining personality and behavior.

Observational Learning

Let us briefly review observational learning, which was discussed together with classical conditioning and operant conditioning in the chapter on learning. In observational learning, new behaviors are learned by watching and imitating the behavior of others. For instance, a freshman arrives at college and observes other students, who serve as models. Specifically, he learns that it is appropriate to smile (but not too broadly) at the people nearby in the registration line. It is also appropriate to ask other students where they are from and what their major is. The freshman then imitates this behavior. (Incidentally, note that observational learning is more flexible than operant conditioning in explaining these more complex social interactions.)

You may also remember that observational learning does not require us to learn only from live models who are in the same room. We can also learn from symbolic models on television, in movies, and in books. (I know a teenager who became Holden Caulfield for a weekend, after reading *Catcher in the Rye*.) Social cognitive theorists emphasize that we acquire many of our typical ways of responding—our personality characteristics—via observational learning.

Reciprocal Influences

My daughter Sally is outgoing and adventurous. At age 16, she went by herself to Mexico to perfect her Spanish, and she lived with a Mexican family. Sally made dozens of friends, including members of a local band. On her last evening there, her Mexican family and friends arranged a surprise farewell party, and the band played backup while she sang solo on her favorite Latin American song, "Doce Rosas." I picture myself at 16 and marvel at the difference in our personalities. I was not so outgoing, I could never have gone alone to a foreign country, and the option of singing solo in Spanish would have been only slightly less horrifying than walking barefoot on hot coals.

Bandura (1986) has proposed an explanation for the way initial individual differences become even stronger through reciprocal influences. According to the principle of **reciprocal influences**, three factors—personal/cognitive, behavior, and environment—all influence each other (Figure 13.3). For example, a person who is outgoing and friendly, who expects that she will be successful in interpersonal interactions (personal/cognitive), will be likely to introduce herself to strangers and react positively to them (behavior). Furthermore, someone who is outgoing and friendly is likely to seek out social situations rather than sitting in her room (environment). The environment, in turn, promotes even more friendly behavior, more self-confidence, and an even greater expectation for success in interpersonal interactions. In contrast, a shy, withdrawn person will dread interpersonal interactions, avoid strangers, and stay away from social situations. This behavior and the lack of exposure to new environments will encourage the person to become even more withdrawn and to expect future interactions to be unsuccessful.

Skinner's theory proposes that the environment shapes the human. In contrast, Bandura argues that behavior involves more complex processes; indeed, personality, behavior, and environment shape each other in a reciprocal fashion. This more complex approach is necessary to explain the impressive complexity of humans.

Bandura (1982a, 1986) adds another concept to his theory to account for even more complexity. He suggests that the three critical factors can be profoundly altered by chance encounters with people, objects, and events. For instance, Nobel prize winner Herbert Brown (1980) received his PhD in the exotic area of boron-hydride chemistry. How did he choose this field of study? When he received his bachelor's degree during the Depression, his girlfriend gave him a book entitled *The Hydrides of Boron and Silicon*, and Brown grew fascinated with the subject. Why did she select this book? It was the least expensive book ($2.06) in the bookstore, and she was far from wealthy. In fact, if she had been wealthier, Brown might never have received the Nobel prize! Try Demonstration 13.1 to help you appreciate the important role of chance encounters.

Figure 13.3
The principle of reciprocal influences.

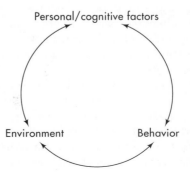

Demonstration 13.1

Chance Encounters

Ask several friends to tell you how they selected the college they now attend. If they have declared a major, ask what factors influenced this decision. Finally, if they are in a love relationship, ask how they happened to meet their particular partner. In each case, try to determine whether chance encounters had any influence.

Self-Efficacy

Let us examine in more detail the personal/cognitive part of Bandura's theory, because this component is most central to personality. Bandura (1982b,1986) believes that the most important personal/cognitive characteristic is self-efficacy. **Self-efficacy** is the feeling people have that they are competent and effective. It is not particularly critical that a person can, in fact, succeed on a particular task. Instead, it is much more important that a person *thinks* he or she can succeed (Cantor & Kihlstrom, 1987). Thus, Bandura emphasizes thoughts and expectations, rather than actual behavior. (Note that Skinner would have emphasized actual behavior rather than thoughts and expectations.) If you are trying to decide whether to try a new dance step in public, the deciding factor is whether you *think* you are a good dancer, not whether you *are* a good dancer!

Research confirms that people with a sense of self-efficacy do indeed manage their lives more successfully. In general, these people tend to be more persistent and more successful in school. They also tend to be less depressed and anxious (Maddux & Stanley, 1986). People who are confident in their abilities typically approach new challenges with optimism. If they are initially unsuccessful, they try a new approach and work harder. In contrast, a person with low self-efficacy usually gives up. (Notice that self-efficacy is related to achievement motivation, discussed in chapter 12.)

Bandura (1986) points out that a sense of self-efficacy is possible because humans have the ability to analyze their varied experiences and to think about their own thought processes. In chapter 7, in connection with memory strategies, and also in chapter 10, in connection with children's memory, we discussed the concept of metamemory, or your knowledge and awareness about your own memory. However, you can think about numerous other personal attributes, in addition to your memory. Consider how often you have evaluated attributes such as athletic ability, academic ability, friendliness, and optimism. When you read the description of self-efficacy, you probably evaluated your own self-efficacy. The thoughts we have about ourselves are the focus of the next section, an in-depth examination of the dynamic self-concept.

○ ○

In Depth: The Dynamic Self-Concept

We have had several opportunities to discuss the notion of *self* in previous chapters. In the memory chapter, the self-reference effect was mentioned; we remember items better if we process them in terms of our own experience. (For instance, you remember the term *reciprocal influences* better if you can think of an example of how that concept applies to your own personality.) In the chapter on infancy and childhood, we discussed self-concept in connection with children recognizing themselves in the mirror and also Erik Erikson's theory on the development of self-concept. In the chapter on adolescence and adulthood, we again examined Erikson's theory and also noted the values that adults consider to be important

This ballplayer's self-concept probably includes thoughts about his athletic ability. If he were to strike out, however, his working self-concept could shift dramatically, though probably briefly.

components of the self-concept. In chapter 15 we examine the self-concept of psychologically depressed people and the disrupted sense of self that accompanies some kinds of anxiety disorders. In psychology in the 1990s, it is difficult to avoid the self-concept!

This in-depth section focuses primarily on the work of Hazel Markus and her coauthors at the University of Michigan. Markus proposes that the major premise of recent research on the self is that the self-concept does not merely *reflect* ongoing behavior, so that your actions shape your thoughts about yourself. Instead, as noted in the discussion of reciprocal influences, the self-concept also *regulates* behavior; your thoughts about yourself shape your behavior. Markus and her colleague Elissa Wurf (1987) use the term **dynamic self-concept** to capture the view that the self-concept is active and forceful. Like any dynamic system, the self-concept is capable of change.

Early researchers in the area of self-concept tended to view the self-concept as unified and unchanging—a single lumplike structure that remained absolutely stable. Now we realize that a person's self-concept is complex; it contains many different dimensions (Markus & Wurf, 1987). Furthermore, at any given moment, some identities that are part of the complete self-concept will be unaccessible.

The **working self-concept** is the self-concept at a particular moment, consisting of all accessible self-knowledge. This working self-concept may shift 5 minutes from now. Thus, a young man who believes that he is attractive and sophisticated may shift his working self-concept (at least temporarily) when he looks in the mirror and discovers a conspicuous strand of spinach decorating one of his front teeth. At a particular moment, your working self-concept may include the knowledge that you are a good conversationalist (perhaps you are encouraging a shy friend, drawing him into a discussion). The knowledge that you are not skilled at sports may not be part of your working self-concept at this moment.

The working self-concept resembles the availability heuristic, discussed in connection with decision making in chapter 8. When we make a decision, we base that decision on information that comes readily to mind, perhaps information from the recent past. In evaluating ourselves and in making decisions, we attend to information in our consciousness. Notice that the social cognitive approach emphasizes consciousness in contrast to Freud's emphasis on the preconscious or the unconscious.

According to Markus and Wurf (1987), the working self-concept shows both stability and change. (You may recall that in the two chapters on human development, we also concluded that personal characteristics show both stability and change.) For instance you know that your self-concept remains fairly stable from one day to the next. In fact, you will resist other people's attempts to modify your self-concept (Greenwald & Pratkanis, 1984). For example, I have a friend whose self-concept has been negative in recent months. I try to remind her about her superb sense of humor, her professional competence, and her conversational skills. She does not seem to hear me; the negative self-concept remains stable.

Yet, as noted earlier, the working self-concept also shows change. For example, a college woman's self-concept is different when she is being asked for a date than when she has just been stood up (Markus & Kunda, 1986). Our immediate social environment makes some attributes available and some temporarily unavailable to our working self-concept.

Research by Markus and Kunda (1986) demonstrates both stability and change in self-concept. These researchers arranged an experiment so that people felt either very similar to or very different from the other participants. In each session of this study, there was one female participant and three female confederates (people instructed to supply specified responses). Each member of the group was asked to evaluate a series of three items, such as three cartoons, reporting which item she preferred. In each case, the actual participant gave her responses first.

In the similarity condition, the three confederates all agreed with the participant 83% of the time. In the uniqueness condition, the three confederates agreed with the participant only 17% of the time. Markus and Kunda reasoned that a participant in the similarity condition would be concerned that she was too much like all the others, which should force thoughts about her unique and special qualities to become more available. In contrast, a participant in the uniqueness condition would be concerned that she was too different, perhaps even bizarre. Thoughts about how she really is similar to other people (rather than abnormal) should become more available.

After performing the evaluation task, the participants were asked to make judgments about themselves. They saw a series of adjectives, and they pressed one button (labeled *me)* if the adjective applied to them. If the adjective did not apply, they pressed the *not me* button. Some of the adjectives were related to similarity to others (e.g., *average, normal*); other adjectives were related to uniqueness (e.g., *original, independent*); and other adjectives were simply irrelevant filler items. Markus and Kunda recorded both the words to which the person pressed the *me* button and the speed with which she made her decisions.

If we consider the word types, the study demonstrates stability in the self-concept. People tended to choose the same number of similarity words, no matter whether their similarity or uniqueness had been emphasized earlier in the session. People in the two groups also tended to choose the same number of uniqueness words. In other words, if a person thinks that she is *normal* and *independent*, she will still apply those words to herself, even after a session in which she was made to look either very similar to others or conspicuously unique.

However, if we consider a more subtle measure—response latency—the study demonstrates change in the self-concept. Figure 13.4 shows how long the participants took to press the button for the words that focused on similarity, such as *average* and *normal*. Participants in the uniqueness condition (whose thoughts about their similarity to others should be temporarily prominent and available) responded quickly that some of those similarity words applied to themselves. These same participants took a relatively long time to decide that other similarity words were in the *not me* category. Can you picture yourself in this condition, anxious to reestablish your similarity to others? You might say to yourself on seeing the word *normal*, "Of course I'm normal!" and quickly press the *me* button. For the word *average*, you might say, "Hmm, let me see. Well, I'm like other people, but I'm not sure I'd call myself average." After a pause, you would press the *not me* button.

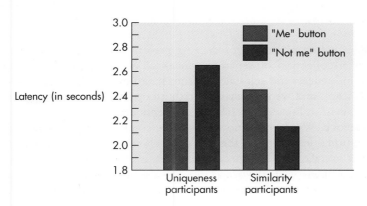

Figure 13.4
Latency, or the amount of time taken to press the button for words focusing on similarity, for participants in both the uniqueness and similarity conditions who pressed either the "me" or the "not me" button. (Markus & Kunda, 1986)

Notice, too, that the participants in the similarity condition responded exactly the opposite. Anxious to reestablish their uniqueness, they paused before accepting any similarity words, reluctant to acknowledge this similarity. They quickly rejected other similarity words.

So, is our self-concept stable or changeable? We must answer, "Both." The actual words we use to describe ourselves remain stable. However, our social experiences can change the speed with which we apply those words to ourselves, because those experiences change the immediate availability of the descriptive words. This study illustrates the importance of including more than one dependent variable in an experiment. If Markus and Kunda had measured just word types or just response latencies, their results would not have captured the rich complexity of self-concepts.

○ ○

Evaluation of the Social Cognitive Approach

Table 13.4 summarizes four important characteristics of the social cognitive approach, contrasting it with the psychoanalytic approach. As you can see, the two approaches differ on all four characteristics. The people on whom the theory is based differ, as do the kind of data collected. The cause of behavior is largely internal in the psychoanalytic approach, whereas both internal and external factors are emphasized in the social cognitive approach. The two approaches differ in their comprehensiveness, an issue we comment on shortly. Finally, the psychoanalytic approach proposes a negative outlook on humans; even their positive behavior may have origins in humans' selfishness and conflict. In contrast, the social cognitive approach proposes a neutral outlook on humans. People can become noble and prosocial, or evil and antisocial, depending upon the models to whom they are exposed. However, no internal tendency forces all people toward either positive or negative behavior.

The social cognitive approach can be criticized for two major reasons:

1. *It is not comprehensive.*   At present, the social cognitive approach is narrower in scope than the psychoanalytic approach. Remember that it grew out of the behaviorist tradition, which focused only on observable behavior. The social cognitive approach has begun to address the importance of thought processes. For instance, Bandura stresses that our thoughts about our competence are often more important than our actual competence. Markus, as well, emphasizes that our thoughts about our self-concepts organize behavior. Still, the social cognitive approach has not integrated unconscious forces into the theory. Also, it has not specifically addressed how personality develops from childhood to adulthood. We may not agree with Freud's theory of psychosexual development, but we can admire him for trying to explain how personality changes as children grow older (Phares, 1988).

2. *It is not an integrated theory.*   At present, the social cognitive approach consists of a collection of separate concepts. We have observational learning, reciprocal influences, and self-efficacy from Bandura. We have Markus's work on the self-concept, and we also have contributions from other social cognitive theorists. However, a loose collection of concepts does not constitute a satisfying, cohesive theory. We do not know how these concepts relate to each other. How do observational learning and the working self-concept influence each other, for example?

The problems with the social cognitive approach, however, certainly will not doom it to failure. It seems likely that researchers will be tackling these two problems in the near future, and they may find some satisfying solutions.

Table 13.4   *A Comparison of the Social Cognitive Approach with the Psychoanalytical Approach*

	PSYCHOANALYTIC APPROACH	SOCIAL COGNITIVE APPROACH
Source of data	Obtained from expert analyst from people in therapy	Obtained from observation of behavior and questionnaire responses from normal people
Cause of behavior	Internal conflict, unconscious forces, childhood experiences	Reciprocal influence of personal/cognitive, behavior, and environment
Comprehensiveness of theory	Very comprehensive	Not very comprehensive
Outlook on humans	Negative	Neutral

A major advantage of the social cognitive approach is that it is testable, partly because the theories are specific rather than general. Hypotheses can be proposed, data can be gathered, and the hypotheses can be accepted or rejected. In contrast, recall that the psychoanalytic approach was frequently too general to be tested. Furthermore, that theory often proposed that a person would show either one characteristic or its exact opposite—a situation that makes testing impossible.

A second major advantage is that the social cognitive approach fits in successfully with the research on other aspects of human experience, specifically the wealth of knowledge that psychologists have gathered on human information processing. Much of this information has been summarized in the chapters on sensation and perception, learning, memory, cognition, and language. The same brain that collects information to make a decision or speak a sentence also manages to form a working self-concept. Of the four approaches to personality considered in this chapter, the social cognitive approach is most compatible with other ongoing research on humans.

Section Summary: The Social Cognitive Approach

- The social cognitive approach grew out of behaviorism, by adding observational learning to classical and operant learning.
- In observational learning, new behaviors are learned by watching and imitating behavior; personality characteristics can be accquired from both live and symbolic models.
- The concept of reciprocal influences proposes that personal/cognitive factors, behavior, and environment all influence each other.
- Another important concept in the social cognitive approach is self-efficacy, or people's feeling that they are competent and effective.
- The working self-concept shows both stability and change.
- Criticisms of the social cognitive approach include that it is neither comprehensive nor well integrated. Positive features include its testability and its compatibility with other research on human information processing.

The Trait Approach

Individual differences have provided an underlying theme throughout this chapter on personality. According to the psychoanalytic approach, the unsuccessful resolution of conflict produces fixation, and a person fixated in the oral stage has different personality characteristics from someone fixated in the anal stage. The social cognitive approach suggests individual differences that can be traced to different observational learning experiences, different patterns of reciprocal influence, and different levels of self-efficacy.

Of the four personality approaches described in this chapter, however, the trait approach focuses most closely on our theme of individual differences. As noted in the introduction to the chapter, the trait approach proposes that personality should be described in terms of specific, stable personality characteristics called traits. Thus, a **trait** is a relatively stable way in which individuals differ from one another (Guilford, 1959).

The trait approach is not particularly concerned with the way these individual differences arise. No trait theory explains *why* Susan should be neat, Sam should be stingy, and Paulette should be habitually late. Instead, the trait approach attempts to describe *how* people differ from each other. People who favor the trait approach tend to ask questions such as: Do people differ significantly on a particular trait? Does this trait remain stable across time, so that a person who is neat at age 5 will also be neat at age 55? Does this trait remain stable across situations, so that a person who is late to work will also be late to social events? Can we condense all traits down to just a small number of trait clusters?

Incidentally, you have already been exposed to some of the research by trait theorists in the developmental chapters, in connection with the stability-change issue, when we noted that traits remain somewhat stable across time. An infant's characteristics tend to be related to his or her characteristics during childhood. Furthermore, a young adult's characteristics tend to remain somewhat stable through later adulthood.

In this section, we first examine two psychologists who developed the trait approach: Gordon Allport and Hans Eysenck. Then we discuss the most widely accepted view of the number of underlying basic traits, followed by the most controversial topic in personality: the person-situation debate. We conclude this section with an evaluation of the trait approach.

Allport's Trait Theory

Gordon Allport (1897–1967) began his undergraduate years at Harvard University with C's and D's on his examinations (Allport, 1967). It is hard to imagine how someone who began so unpromisingly and ended so prominently could have formulated a theory that focused on stability rather than change. However, Bandura's idea of chance encounters helps to explain the change. After graduation, Allport decided to teach at a college in Turkey. After 2 years there and in Europe, he visited his brother, who was living in Vienna, Austria, on the way back to the United States. Allport arranged to pay a visit to Sigmund Freud. (What would have happened if Allport's brother had been living in Salzburg or London instead of Vienna?) Freud invited him into his inner office. Allport wrote,

> He did not speak to me but sat in expectant silence, for me to state my mission. I was not prepared for silence and had to think fast to find a suitable conversational gambit. I told him of an episode on the tram car on my way to his office. A small boy about four years of age had displayed a conspicuous dirt phobia. He kept saying to his mother, "I don't want to sit there . . . don't let that dirty man sit beside me."

To him everything was *schmutzig* [dirty]. His mother was a well-starched *Hausfrau* [housewife], so dominant and purposive looking that I thought the cause and effect apparent.

When I finished my story Freud fixed his kindly therapeutic eyes upon me and said, "And was that little boy you?" Flabbergasted and feeling a bit guilty, I contrived to change the subject. While Freud's misunderstanding of my motivation was amusing, it also started a deep train of thought. (Allport, 1967, p. 8)

This encounter convinced Allport that the psychoanalytic approach plunged too deeply into symbols, producing misinterpretations. He resolved to focus on conscious motives rather than unconscious ones.

Before reading further, try Demonstration 13.2. One of Allport's first research activities was to examine an unabridged dictionary, recording every term that could describe a person (Allport & Odbert, 1936). He located a total of 18,000! After eliminating many that seemed to describe temporary rather than enduring characteristics (e.g., *elated, shamefaced*), he still had a list of more than 3,000 traitlike words—clearly too many to study systematically.

Eventually, Allport (1937, 1961) decided to organize this overwhelming task by proposing three levels of traits:

1. A **cardinal trait** is the one that dominates and shapes a person's behavior. For my daughter Beth, for instance, a single-minded interest in infants and children has shaped her life. At the age of 21 months, she showered affection and tiny gifts on her newborn sister. At 8 years of age, she volunteered as an unpaid parents' helper, and later worked for six summers in day-care centers. She is now studying early childhood education, passionately anticipating running her own day-care center. After a summer experience with children in Latin America, she is helping to raise money for day-care centers in Nicaragua. Perhaps you know someone who is obsessed with becoming wealthy, or another person whose life focus is religion. Allport proposed that these cardinal traits are rare, however. Most of us lack a single theme in our lives.

2. A **central trait** is a general characteristic, found to some degree in every person. These basic building blocks shape much of our behavior, though they are not as overwhelmingly influential as cardinal traits. Some central traits could be honesty (which chapter 11 noted was a dominant theme in adult personality), extraversion, and cheerfulness.

3. A **secondary trait** is a characteristic seen only in certain situations. These must be included to provide a complete picture of human complexity. For instance, some typical secondary traits might include "uncomfortable in large crowds" and "likes to drive sports cars."

Allport argued that a person's pattern of traits determined his or her behavior. No two people are completely identical, and as a result no two people respond completely identically to the same environmental situation. As Allport said, "The same fire that melts the butter hardens the egg" (Allport, 1937, p. 102).

Demonstration 13.2

Listing Traits

Take a blank sheet of paper. In 5 minutes, list as many trait words as you can. Recall that a trait is defined as a relatively stable way in which individuals differ from one another. See if these traits can be organized so that they fall into a small number of clusters. This topic is discussed in connection with the so-called Big Five traits.

For this young woman, an intense interest in infants and children constitutes a cardinal trait.

Eysenck's Biosocial Theory

Hans Eysenck (pronounced "*Eye*-senk") (b. 1916) was born in Germany but left during Hitler's regime, eventually settling in London. Eysenck has been a prolific scientist, publishing approximately 600 journal articles and over 30 books (Corsini, 1984).

Eysenck proposed that three major dimensions account for most of human behavior (Eysenck, 1953, 1975):

1. Introversion versus extraversion is a dimension fairly similar to Jung's categorization of people as either introverts or extraverts. However, Eysenck notes that few perfect introverts or extraverts exist. Instead, a person can be placed anywhere between these two extremes.

2. Stability versus instability refers to a person's general moodiness. A stable person is calm, even-tempered, and reliable. A person who is unstable is moody, touchy, and restless. Again, however, a person can be placed at any point along the stability-instability continuum.

3. Psychoticism, which is present in different degrees in particular personalities, is a psychological disorder. A person at the extreme end of this dimension is solitary and insensitive, showing no loyalty or concern for others.

More than other theorists discussed in this chapter, Eysenck has examined the biological basis of personality. For example, he reported that introverts and extraverts differ in their level of arousal in a specific structure of the brain, the reticular formation (Eysenck, 1970). In general, introverts have higher levels of arousal internally, so they tend to avoid external stimulation. In contrast, extraverts tend to have lower levels of arousal internally, so they tend to seek out external stimulation. On a social occasion, an introvert would back away, whereas an extravert would move into the center of the crowd.

The Search for Basic Trait Dimensions

After decades of searching, trait researchers still disagree about the basic personality trait dimensions. Some propose as many as 16 basic traits, whereas others—such as Eysenck—suggest only 2 or 3 (Mischel, 1986). In other words, all the richness and subtlety contained in Allport and Odbert's (1936) list of more than 3,000 trait words (or your own shorter list in Demonstration 13.2) can be distilled into a much smaller list.

The solution to the number-of-traits question that has attracted the most attention has been called the *Big Five* (Carson, 1989). There is some disagreement about the exact identification of these five basic traits (e.g., Digman & Inouye, 1986; McCrae & Costa, 1985, 1986, 1987; Noller et al., 1987). However, Demonstration 13.3 (p. 446) shows one of the most widely accepted variations. In this demonstration, the **Big Five traits** include extraversion, agreeableness, conscientiousness, emotional stability, and openness to experience. Some researchers are recommending that personality tests based on these five dimensions should be used to supplement the diagnostic tests that clinical psychologists currently use (McCrae & Costa, 1986).

The Person-Situation Debate

A major ongoing controversy in studies examining the trait approach can be called the person-situation debate. Here are the two extreme positions in this debate:

1. *Person:* Each person possesses stable, internal traits that cause him or her to act consistently in a variety of situations.

2. *Situation:* Each person does not possess stable, internal traits. Instead, his or her behavior depends upon the specific characteristics of each situation.

People who support trait theory tend to cluster toward the *person* position. In contrast, behaviorists in the tradition of B. F. Skinner believe that environmental stimuli are far more important. If we can specify the external stimuli in a situation, we can predict how anyone would respond, without needing to discuss any internal characteristics. People who cluster toward the *situation* position might even suggest that we eliminate the personality chapter of introductory textbooks: There is no such thing as personality, only situations. Let us examine this controversy.

Mischel's Position For many decades, personality psychologists had supported the *person* position, particularly because it is consistent with our common sense about personality. Of course there is consistency! Julie is consistently unconcerned about others, whereas Pete is always compassionate. A strong challenge to this position was presented by Walter Mischel (pronounced "Mih-*shell*"), who came from a tradition based on learning theory.

Mischel (1968) examined dozens of previous studies and discovered that the behaviors that are supposed to reflect the same internal trait are only weakly correlated with each other. One such study examined punctuality, or the tendency to be on time. Dudycha (1936) made more than 15,000 observations on college students. He recorded the time that the students arrived for assorted scheduled events, such as classes, appointments, religious services, and entertainment. The average correlation between punctuality for one event and punctuality for another event was only $+.19$, which means that the correlation was very weak. If you know what time Jeanne arrives for a 10 o'clock class, you really cannot predict what time she will arrive for a 2 o'clock appointment.

The Big Five

On the rating scales below, informally assess yourself on three components each of the Big Five traits. (You should keep in mind, however, that any informal demonstration such as this is not intended to provide accurate diagnosis.) In each case, record the number that best describes yourself on each of the rating scales. Then calculate an average score for each of the Big Five traits.

1. **Extraversion**

(Average rating =   )

| 1 | 2 | 3 | 4 | 5 | 6 | 7 |

Sociable	Retiring
Fun-loving	Sober
Affectionate	Reserved

2. **Agreeableness**

(Average rating =   )

| 1 | 2 | 3 | 4 | 5 | 6 | 7 |

Softhearted	Ruthless
Trusting	Suspicious
Helpful	Uncooperative

3. **Conscientious**

(Average rating =   )

| 1 | 2 | 3 | 4 | 5 | 6 | 7 |

Well organized	Disorganized
Careful	Careless
Self-disciplined	Weak-willed

4. **Emotional Stability**

(Average rating =   )

| 1 | 2 | 3 | 4 | 5 | 6 | 7 |

Calm	Worrying
Secure	Insecure
Self-satisfied	Self-pitying

5. **Openness to Experience**

(Average rating =   )

| 1 | 2 | 3 | 4 | 5 | 6 | 7 |

Imaginative	Down-to-earth
Preference for variety	Preference for routine
Independent	Conforming

Source: Based on McCrae & Costa, 1986.

But why do we persist in believing that personality ⸻
sistent across situations? Mischel (1968) proposed that trai⸻
minds of the beholder. If I think that some of my friends ar⸻
punctual and others are characteristically late (and, incidentally, ⸻
this apparent consistency is caused by my own cognitive biases. ⸻
biases is the primacy effect: We tend to maintain our first impression⸻
even if he or she acts very differently on later occasions. Perhaps b⸻
friend Suzanne arrived late and flustered to the dinner party where I first⸻
I have failed to notice that she has been reasonably prompt since then. A⸻
source of bias is that we usually see a person in only a limited set of situat⸻
Perhaps a young man in your high school seemed very friendly and sociable ⸻
you, but you only saw him in situations where he felt comfortable. On a colleg⸻
interview (where you did not see him), he may have been timid and withdrawn.

It is important to stress that Mischel did *not* say that people showed no consistency whatsoever (Mischel, 1979). Yes, we do show some slight consistency from one situation to another, according to Mischel, but the people who know us tend to exaggerate that consistency.

Individual Differences in Consistency   One of the most interesting responses to Mischel's position came from Bem and Allen (1974). These authors asked participants in a study to rate themselves. Specifically, respondents were asked to judge whether they saw themselves as consistent or inconsistent on two traits—friendliness and conscientiousness. The results showed that people who judged themselves as highly consistent on a particular trait did indeed behave consistently in a variety of situations. In fact, the average correlation was an impressive +.57! Furthermore, those who thought they were inconsistent actually showed much less consistency; their average correlation was only +.27. (Incidentally, think about whether you are consistent or inconsistent on these two traits.)

In short, Bem and Allen provided an expansion on one of our themes. Yes, people show individual differences. Furthermore, there are individual differences in the extent to which people consistently demonstrate these individual differences.

Other Factors That Enhance Consistency   We have seen that cross-situational consistency is high for certain traits. The support for traits is not as pessimistic as Mischel (1968) had described. People also show more consistency if we measure the average behavior across several events rather than just a single event (Epstein, 1983; Epstein & O'Brien, 1985). This makes sense. You might be late to class one day, but early four other days. Your *average* punctuality for classes is likely to be fairly strongly correlated with your *average* punctuality for appointments—even if your punctuality on any particular day is only weakly correlated with other measures.

Furthermore, traits can be more easily expressed in some situations than others (Kenrick & Funder, 1988; Schutte et al., 1985). For instance, some situations constrain our behavior, so the traits cannot be easily expressed. At a funeral service, the friendly people will not act much different from the unfriendly people. However, at a picnic, individual differences will be strong. Cross-situational consistency will be higher if we look only at unconstrained situations.

Conclusions About the Person-Situation Debate   As Kenrick and Funder (1988) conclude in their review of the person-situation debate, "As with most controversies, the truth finally appears to lie not in the vivid black or white of either extreme, but somewhere in the less striking gray area" (p. 31). Behavior is probably not as consistent across situations as our intuitions suggest. As noted, we believe

Cross-situational consistency is higher in an unconstrained situation like a picnic, where the situation has less formal structure and individual differences can reveal

people to be somewhat more consistent than they really are because of systematic biases that encourage us to believe in traits. However, some consistency really does exist. Furthermore, in some situations, for some people, and some traits, the consistency can be reasonably high.

In chapter 10, we saw that it was impossible to answer which factor was more important, nature or nurture. Both are important. Similarly, we cannot answer which factor is a better predictor of behavior, person or situation. Again, both are important. If we want to predict how a person will behave, it is helpful to have some measure of his or her internal traits, but it is also necessary to understand the characteristics of the external situation.

Evaluation of the Trait Approach

Table 13.5 summarizes four important characteristics of the trait approach, contrasting it with the other two approaches discussed so far. As you can see, it is very different from the psychoanalytic approach and reasonably similar to the social cognitive approach. In fact, the only major difference is that social cognitive theorists place more emphasis on the environment than do trait theorists.

Like the social cognitive approach, the trait approach can be criticized for two important reasons.

1. *It is not comprehensive.* The trait approach does not even attempt to explain *why* people have certain traits to varying degrees. Because it relies on self-assessment and observation of participants, it also does not attempt to deal with unconscious forces. In fact, the trait approach is the least comprehensive of the four approaches examined in this chapter.

2. *It is not an integrated theory.* In fact, it is probably more realistic to call the trait approach a research technique rather than a theory. The approach produces a wealth of information about people's characteristics, but no comprehensive view of humanity.

We cannot be too critical, however, because the trait approach never aspired to be either comprehensive or integrated. To its credit, it has provided abundant information about internal characteristics, for example, concerning the consistency of personality characteristics.

Table 13.5   *A Comparison of the Trait Approach with the Psychoanalytical and Social Cognitive Approaches*

	PSYCHOANALYTIC APPROACH	SOCIAL COGNITIVE APPROACH	TRAIT APPROACH
Source of data	Obtained from expert analyst from people in therapy	Obtained from observation of behavior and questionnaire responses from normal people	Obtained from observation of normal people and people in therapy
Cause of behavior	Internal conflict, unconscious forces, childhood experiences	Reciprocal influence of personal/cognitive, behavior, and environment	Stable, internal characteristics
Comprehensiveness of theory	Very comprehensive	Not very comprehensive	Not very comprehensive
Outlook on humans	Negative	Neutral	Neutral

Section Summary: The Trait Approach

- Allport proposed three levels of traits: cardinal, central, and secondary; the combination of these traits determines a person's behavior.
- Eysenck proposed that three major dimensions account for most of human behavior: introversion-extraversion; stability-instability; and psychoticism. He also proposed a biological basis for personality.
- The most widely accepted categorization of trait dimensions is known as the Big Five: extraversion, agreeableness, conscientiousness, emotional stability, and openness to experience.
- The resolution to the person-situation debate lies between the two extremes: People have traits that are somewhat consistent across situations, but our cognitive biases make this consistency seem somewhat greater than it really is; when we examine the traits on which people believe their behavior is consistent, when behavior is averaged, and when the situation is not constrained, cross-situational consistency will be higher.
- Trait theory is neither comprehensive nor integrated, but it has produced some worthwhile information about the internal characteristics of personality.

The Humanistic Approach

We began this chapter with an overview of the psychoanalytic perspective, an approach that paints a dismal portrait of human nature. Then we considered the social cognitive and trait approaches, which take a neutral position. In contrast, the humanistic approach is much more optimistic about human goals. This approach argues that people have enormous potential for personal growth. Humanistic psychologists also propose that each of us has subjective experiences that are unique. Even your closest friend cannot fully understand what it is like to be *you*.

The humanistic approach gained prominence in the early 1960s when Rogers (1961) and Maslow (1962) published important books. Many psychologists were dissatisfied with the two current personality theories. On the one hand, there was the psychoanalytic approach, which proposed that human kindness and caring often has its origins in evil impulses. On the other hand, there was the behaviorist approach, which at that time focused on animal research. How could research on rats and pigeons inform us about higher human goals, such as the search for truth and beauty? (In the 1950s, the cognitive social approach had not yet been proposed, and the trait approach is not really a theory.)

Carl Rogers, Abraham Maslow, and others developed the humanistic approach as an alternative to these other two theories, and so humanistic psychology is sometimes called *Third Force psychology*. As you will see, this approach focuses on people's healthy side—in contrast to the psychoanalytic emphasis on our sick side. Furthermore, it concentrates on the whole person, our internal experiences, and our higher goals, in contrast to behaviorism's focus on simple behaviors, external stimuli, and observable responses.

In this section, we examine the ideas of the two most prominent humanistic theorists, Rogers and Maslow. Then we end with an evaluation of the humanistic approach.

Carl Rogers's Person-Centered Approach

Carl Rogers (1902–1987) was born in Illinois and began his professional career working with troubled children, though he later extended his therapy to adults. In his clinical work, he used the term *clients*, because he felt that the standard term *patients* implied that these people were ill. Chapter 16 examines Rogers's approach to behavior disorders, called client-centered therapy. This approach requires the therapist to try to see the world from each client's point of view rather than from the therapist's own framework.

The behaviorist approach emphasizes external stimuli. In contrast, Carl Rogers emphasizes that each of us interprets the same set of stimuli differently. As he wrote,

> The only reality I can possibly know is the world as I perceive and experience it at this moment. The only reality you can possibly know is the world as *you* perceive and experience it at this moment. And the only certainty is that those perceived realities are different. There are as many "real worlds" as there are people! (Rogers, 1980, p. 102)

Self-Actualization   Carl Rogers observed that his clients often used the word *self* in statements such as "I haven't been acting like myself recently." Like later social cognitive theorists such as Hazel Markus, Rogers viewed the self as the key to personality. Rogers proposed that humans continually struggle to define and become their real selves. Rogers used the term **self-actualization** to capture this natural tendency for humans to fulfill their true potential (Rogers, 1963, 1980).

Rogers marveled that this actualizing tendency could persist, even in the most hostile environments. He draws a parallel with a childhood observation:

> I remember that in my boyhood, the bin in which we stored our winter's supply of potatoes was in the basement, several feet below a small window. The conditions were unfavorable, but the potatoes would begin to sprout—pale white sprouts, so unlike the healthy green shoots they sent up when planted in the soil in the spring. But these sad, spindly sprouts would grow 2 or 3 feet in length as they reached toward the distant light of the window. These sprouts were, in their bizarre, futile growth, a sort of desperate expression of the directional tendency I have been describing. They would never become plants, never mature, never fulfill their real potential. But under the most adverse circumstances, they were striving to become. Life would not give up, even if it could not flourish. (Rogers, 1980, p. 118)

Rogers argued that people strive toward growth, even in less-than-favorable surroundings.

Rogers often thought of those potato sprouts when interacting with people on the back wards of large hospitals. The lives of these clients had been terribly warped. Despite unfavorable conditions, Rogers believed that these people were still striving toward growth. Rogers emphasized that this active self-development tendency provided the underlying basis of the person-centered approach.

Personality Development   Carl Rogers did not propose any stages of development, as do the theories of Sigmund Freud or Erik Erikson. He did not believe that people passed through any well-specified series of changes. Instead, he thought that personality development depended upon the way a person is evaluated by others (Phares, 1988).

Rogers proposed that even young children need positive regard, to be highly esteemed by other people. Children also develop a need for positive *self*-regard, to be esteemed by oneself as well as others. A mature, independent person must have positive self-regard.

From his work with clients who had psychological disorders, Rogers found that self-actualizing tendencies were frequently stifled by restricting self-concepts. Specifically, these clients had learned that they had to act in ways that distorted their "true selves" in order to win positive regard from others.

Rogers proposed that most children experience **conditional positive regard**; parents and other important people withhold their love and approval if the child fails to conform to their elders' standards. For instance, parents might award positive regard to their son *only if* he makes the football team. Positive regard is given only in certain conditions. In contrast, positive regard is withheld if the son fails to achieve in athletics or if he succeeds in other areas, such as music or the debate club.

In contrast, Rogers believed that everyone should be given **unconditional positive regard**, or total, genuine love without special conditions or strings attached (Rogers, 1959). Once again, however, the person-centered approach emphasizes the individual's perception of reality. A mother may believe that she is giving unconditional positive regard. It is possible that the child experiences conditional positive regard, and this is the reality that matters to the child (Ross, 1987). In short, children need to feel that the important people in their lives accept them for who they are.

Rogers believed that children need unconditional positive regard.

The research partly supports Rogers's ideas. As you may recall from chapter 10, Diana Baumrind's (1971, 1975) work on parenting styles indicated that parents do make a difference. Authoritarian parents, who demand unquestioning obedience from their children, do tend to produce unhappy, ineffective offspring; these children who clearly lack unconditional positive regard are not likely to experience self-actualization. However, permissive parents, who make few demands and allow children to make their own decisions, produce immature offspring with little self-control. Baumrind found that the most successful parenting style was used by authoritative parents, who were loving but upheld clear-cut standards. Thus, it seems that unconditional positive regard—without clear-cut standards—does not encourage self-actualization. Children need to know that some parental rules will be upheld.

Maslow's Hierarchy of Needs

Abraham Maslow (1908–1970) was born in Brooklyn, New York. As a young psychologist, he was initially attracted to behaviorism. However, when his first child was born, he realized that behaviorism could not account for the miracle of an infant's experience (Phares, 1988). With Carl Rogers and two others, Rollo May and Charlotte Buhler, Maslow founded the American Association of Humanistic Psychology (Lundin, 1984).

Maslow is probably best known for his theoretical exploration of self-actualization, this important tendency to realize our own potential. Maslow theorized that our human motives are arranged in a hierarchy, with the most basic needs at the bottom and the more highly developed needs (esteem needs and—finally—self-actualization needs) at the top (Maslow, 1970).

Figure 13.5 shows **Maslow's hierarchy of needs**, in which each lower need must be satisfied before the next level of need can be addressed. For instance, people whose homes have just been destroyed by a flood will primarily be concerned with physiological and safety needs rather than the more lofty goal of self-actualization. Let us examine the five levels in Maslow's hierarchy, beginning with the most basic level.

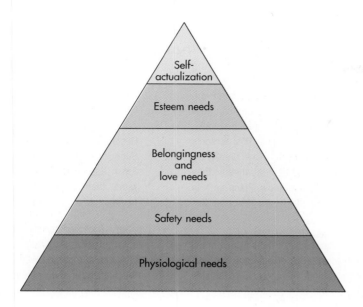

Figure 13.5
Maslow's hierarchy of needs.

1. *Physiological needs:* We need food, water, sleep, and sex. Notice that these needs are also those that motivate lower animals.

2. *Safety needs:* These include the needs for security, protection, and the avoidance of pain.

3. *Belongingness and love needs:* These needs include affiliation with other people, as well as affection, or feeling loved.

4. *Esteem needs:* We also need to respect ourselves and to win the esteem of others. Otherwise, we feel discouraged and inferior, and Maslow proposes that we will not strive for the highest level in the hierarchy.

5. *Self-actualization needs:* A person who has satisfied all the lower needs can seek self-actualization, attempting to reach her or his full potential.

Maslow became particularly intrigued with this highest level, self-actualization, in attempting to understand two of his favorite teachers, anthropologist Ruth Benedict and Gestalt psychologist Max Wertheimer (Maslow, 1971). He saw that they shared many underlying qualities. Later, he began to select other prominent people from both historical and modern times. These were healthy, well-adjusted people who had used their full potential. The list included social worker Jane Addams, presidents Thomas Jefferson and Abraham Lincoln, first lady Eleanor Roosevelt, and physicist Albert Einstein. Demonstration 13.4 encourages you to think about some of the characteristics of self-actualized people.

Evaluation of the Humanistic Approach

Table 13.6 summarizes four important characteristics of the humanistic approach, contrasting it with the other three approaches. As you can see, the humanistic position is distinctive. Data are obtained from self-reports from normal people (in Maslow's work) and people in therapy (in Rogers's work). Behavior is motivated by self-concepts and the tendency to self-actualize. The theory is reasonably comprehensive, more so than the social cognitive or trait approaches. Finally, compared with the other three theories, humanistic psychology proposes a blissfully positive interpretation of human nature.

Pioneer social worker Jane Addams was one of the people Maslow identified as a self-actualizer.

Demonstration 13.4

Qualities of a Self-Actualized Person

Think about someone you know who seems to be a self-actualized person, who has lived up to his or her full potential. (Ideally, this is someone you know personally, so you are more familiar with this person's qualities.) Now read each of the characteristics listed below and decide whether they apply to the person you know. Place an X in front of each one that does describe this person.

_____ An acceptance of himself or herself
_____ An acceptance of other people
_____ Involvement in some cause outside of himself or herself

_____ Very spontaneous in both actions and emotions
_____ Focused on problems and solutions rather than himself or herself
_____ Resists pressures to conform
_____ Superior creativity
_____ Fresh appreciation of other people, rather than stereotyped reactions
_____ Strongly developed set of values

How many of these characteristics apply to your target person? If any did *not* apply, do you think that this person would be even more self-actualized if she or he possessed these qualities?

Source: Based on Maslow, 1968, 1971.

The humanistic approach can be criticized for several reasons:

1. *It relies on subjective experience.* The humanistic approach emphasizes that reality lies in a person's own interpretation of the world. Some people have only a limited ability to express themselves, so their self-reports probably do not reflect their experiences (Phares, 1988). We are therefore left with inadequate data.

2. *The studies are often inadequate.* Both Rogers and Maslow tended to study only a selected sample of the entire population. Specifically, they worked with people who were more intelligent and verbal than average. Humanistic principles may not be applicable to other groups. Furthermore, as Maslow (1971) himself admits, his work on self-actualizing people does not really qualify as *research.* An important criticism of this work, for example, is that his choice of self-actualized people is rather arbitrary. They may have fulfilled their potential in some respects, but not others. Abraham Lincoln had periods of severe depression, for instance, and Eleanor Roosevelt's family relationships were less than ideal. Thus, much of the so-called support for the humanistic approach is too subjective. Even humanistic psychologists point out that important aspects of life, such as the meaningfulness of experience, cannot be adequately studied by traditional research techniques (Rogers, 1985).

3. *It is too selfish.* Both Rogers and Maslow encourage us to focus on self-actualization. However, as Wallach and Wallach (1983) point out in their book, *Psychology's Sanction for Selfishness,* what is good for the self often differs from what is good for other individuals or for the general welfare. By focusing attention on their own personal goals, people can ignore their responsibilities toward others. Our globe is plagued with hundreds of problems. Should issues such as acid rain, homelessness, social justice, and world peace be placed on the back burner while we all concentrate on self-actualization?

4. *It is too optimistic.* As Rogers's colleague and friend Rollo May (1986) observes, many humanistic theorists are overly optimistic. If you glance at today's newspaper, you will probably find little evidence that people are inherently good, striving toward self-actualization. Incidents of suicide, murder, battering, child abuse, and rape have all increased in recent decades. As soon as one global conflict is resolved, another one arises. Rollo May agrees with Rogers that many people perform heroic and prosocial deeds. As he said, following a list of human atrocities,

Table 13.6   *Contrasting the Four Approaches to Personality*

	PSYCHOANALYTIC APPROACH	SOCIAL COGNITIVE APPROACH	TRAIT APPROACH	HUMANISTIC APPROACH
Source of data	Obtained from expert analyst from people in therapy	Obtained from observation of behavior and questionnaire responses from normal people	Obtained from observation of normal people and people in therapy	Obtained from self-reports from normal people and people in therapy
Cause of behavior	Internal conflict, unconscious forces, childhood experiences	Reciprocal influence of personal/cognitive, behavior, and environment	Stable, internal characteristics	Self-concepts, self-actualizing tendencies
Comprehensiveness of theory	Very comprehensive	Not very comprehensive	Not very comprehensive	Fairly comprehensive
Outlook on humans	Negative	Neutral	Neutral	Positive

"I am not arguing that we human beings are only evil. I am arguing that we are bundles of both evil and good potentialities" (May, 1986, p. 17). May's more neutral view of humans seems much more consistent with reality.

Despite these criticisms, humanistic psychology must be praised for its substantial strengths. For instance, the humanistic approach focuses on the present and the future, whereas the psychoanalytic and behaviorist perspectives make us "captives of the past" (Phares, 1988, p. 217). The humanistic approach also deserves credit for pointing out that we humans do not share identical interpretations of reality. Furthermore, this approach offers an integrated view of humans. Each of us is a whole person, rather than a collection of isolated traits.

Finally, humanistic psychologists have been impressively influential. Humanistic principles are being applied in therapy, education, business, and child rearing. A visit to any bookstore illustrates its impact: You will find dozens of self-help books that promise a golden path to self-actualization. Although the names Rogers and Maslow are not as well known as Freud's, the humanistic approach has clearly shaped many aspects of popular psychology.

Section Summary: The Humanistic Approach

- The humanistic approach, emphasizing the potential for personal growth, was formulated as a reaction to the psychoanalytic and behavioral approaches.
- Carl Rogers's person-centered approach emphasizes that people have different perceived realities, that people strive toward self-actualization, and that everyone should be given unconditional positive regard.
- Abraham Maslow's hierarchy of needs proposes that people must fulfill certain needs in order, from physiological, safety, and love, to esteem and self-actualization; he also proposed several characteristics for self-actualized people.
- The humanistic approach can be criticized for its reliance on subjective experience, the inadequacy of the studies, its basic selfishness, and its excessive optimism. Its strengths include its focus on the present and future, its perspective on perceived realities, its integrated view of humans, and its influence on popular psychology.

REVIEW QUESTIONS

1. Imagine that a high school student you know has asked you about the chapter you have just read in your psychology textbook. Define the word *personality* and summarize each of the four theories in one paragraph each.

2. Which of the four theories of personality do you find most appealing? If you had to design your own theory, what features of the other three approaches would you incorporate? In your opinion, are there some aspects of personality that you feel none of the approaches has addressed?

3. Try to reproduce the information in Table 13.6 from memory. Label the columns with the names of the four approaches (psychoanalytic, social cognitive, trait, and humanistic). Label the rows with the four dimensions we considered (source of data, cause of behavior, comprehensiveness, outlook on humans). If there is any missing information, consult Table 13.6.

4. Describe Freud's stages of normal human development. Now compare the following theorists with respect to the way they might explain the origins of abnormal behavior: Freud, Adler, Horney, Skinner, Bandura, Eysenck, and Rogers.

5. Imagine that you are a talk-show host. The two invited guests today are, miraculously, Sigmund Freud and Carl Rogers. How might each of them respond to your questions: (a) Are wars inevitable? (b) Why do people sometimes perform heroic, prosocial acts? (c) What should people strive for in life?

6. Which of the theories you examined deals with the self? Describe how the self is envisioned in those theories, elaborating in particular on Markus's research.

7. Try to imagine a situation in which a person is blocked at the first level of Maslow's hierarchy. Then imagine situations for the second, third, and fourth levels. Where would you locate yourself today in this hierarchy?

8. What is the person-situation debate? Think about a particularly noticeable trait of your best friend. Does this trait seem to persist across situations? What cognitive biases encourage you to believe in its persistence? How would trait theorists respond to someone who proposed that this particular trait would show little stability across situations?

9. Explain the concept of reciprocal influences. Can you identify some way in which this concept could be applied to your own life?

10. How do the four theories compare with respect to the emphasis on internal forces versus external stimuli? Also include behaviorism in this comparison.

NEW TERMS

personality	unconscious
psychoanalytic approach	preconscious
social cognitive approach	conscious
trait approach	free association
humanistic approach	manifest content
id	latent content
ego	defense mechanisms
superego	repression

regression
reaction formation
rationalization
sublimation
displacement
projection
erogenous zones
fixation
oral stage
anal stage
phallic stage
latency stage
genital stage
personal unconscious
collective unconscious
introvert

extravert
masochistic
reciprocal influences
self-efficacy
dynamic self-concept
working self-concept
trait
cardinal trait
central trait
secondary trait
Big Five traits
self-actualization
conditional positive regard
unconditional positive regard
Maslow's hierarchy of needs

RECOMMENDED READINGS

Feist, J. (1990). *Theories of personality* (2nd ed.). Fort Worth: Holt, Rinehart and Winston. Feist's textbook provides a chapter on each of 17 theoretical approaches to personality; the final chapter provides an interesting comparison of the theories.

Kenrick, D. T., & Funder, D. C. (1988). Profiting from controversy: Lessons from the person-situation debate. *American Psychologist, 43*, 23–34. This well-organized article summarizes the theoretical positions and recent research in this controversial area.

Markus, H., & Wurf, E. (1987). The dynamic self-concept: A social psychological perspective. *Annual Review of Psychology, 38*, 299–337. In addition to an overview of Markus's view of the dynamic self-concept, this chapter also examines self-regulation and the impact of self-concept on social interactions.

Phares, E. J. (1988). *Introduction to personality* (2nd ed.). Glenview, IL: Scott, Foresman. Phares's textbook is clear, comprehensive, and interesting in its overview of personality.

Rogers, C. R. (1980). *A way of being.* Boston: Houghton Mifflin. This book contains 15 selected articles, primarily from the 1970s, on both personality and psychotherapy.

Wallach, W. A., & Wallach, L. (1983). *Psychology's sanction for selfishness.* San Francisco: Freeman. I really enjoyed reading this book! It reviews the personality theories, primarily those of Freud, Freud's followers, and the humanistic approaches, pointing out how all major theories encourage us to focus on our own needs and desires, rather than the welfare of others.

14

Assessing
Intelligence and
Personality

You have been tested since the moment you were born. When you were a few minutes old, the person who delivered you probably provided an Apgar score, which is a number between 0 and 10 that assesses a newborn's general health. Some months later, a pediatrician probably assessed your motor and cognitive development with a screening test. Several years later, you may have been tested when you were about to enter school.

The testing intensified once you entered school. At regular intervals, you took standardized intelligence and achievement tests (in addition to the normal quizzes and tests on class material). In high school, you probably spent many hours preparing for and taking the PSATs, the SATs, or the ACTs. Then you probably spent your first hours at college taking tests in writing, foreign language, or mathematics. As your senior year approaches, many of you will sign up for the GREs, LSATs, GMATs, or MCATs if you plan on graduate school or professional degrees in law, business, or medicine. And some of you will be tested on your cognitive ability or personality when you apply for a job.

Because tests are so important in shaping our lives, it is strange that the average high school student is taught much more about trigonometry than about the nature of psychological tests. A **psychological test** is an objective, standardized measure of a sample of behavior. Just as a lab technician makes observations on a small sample of a person's blood, a psychologist collects a small sample of a person's behavior (Anastasi, 1988). For instance, psychologists might test a child's arithmetic problem-solving skills, a pilot's spatial ability, or an employee's achievement motivation.

This chapter will help you understand how we can measure the individual differences in cognitive skills (introduced in chapters 7, 8, and 9) and in personality (chapter 13). As you will see, psychological testing is a challenging topic because we cannot simply peel back a person's scalp and watch all these psychological processes in action (Kail & Pellegrino, 1985). And we cannot peek into someone's ear and assess his or her level of verbal ability or extraversion. Instead, we must study mental processes by looking at people's responses on standardized tests.

Constructing and Evaluating Tests

You have probably seen informal quizzes in newspapers and popular magazines. In several minutes, you can presumably test yourself and find out whether you are a wallflower or the life of a party, a Pollyanna or a pessimist. If you believe the claims of the articles, these quizzes can also assess whether you are a good roommate, a feminist, and a worrywart.

On the surface, these tests look reasonable. For instance, a quiz in *Seventeen* magazine is entitled "Are You a Worrywart?" (Weston, 1985). One question asks,

Right after you pop a letter into the mailbox, you
a. Go on your merry way.
b. Check to make sure it went down.
c. Panic! "Did I stamp it? Was it addressed right?" (p. 48)

Readers assign themselves 1 point for answer *a*, 2 points for *b*, and 3 points for *c*, and they score themselves on each of 11 questions. They key at the bottom of the quiz claims that people with total scores between 26 and 33 points tend to be cautious worrywarts, those between 19 and 25 are well-adjusted people who worry the right amount, and those between 11 and 18 points are too laid-back and apathetic.

Magazine quizzes like the worrywart test differ from the formal tests devised by psychologists in the way they are constructed and evaluated. A proper psychological test has three important properties:

1. *Standardization.* A psychological test is pretested with a large, representative sample of people so that we know, for example, the respondents' average score. (In contrast, the author of the worrywart test probably did not conduct pretesting; the three score categories are probably based on a good hunch, rather than formal testing.)

2. *Reliability.* A psychological test must provide a test taker with roughly the same score each time the test is taken. (In contrast, we do not know whether your score on the worrywart test would be the same tomorrow or much higher or lower.)

3. *Validity.* A psychological test should measure what it is supposed to measure, not some other characteristic. (In contrast, the worrywart test might measure the test taker's desire to appear well adjusted; true worrywarts may be reluctant to choose option *c* because it sounds too bizarre—even though *c* is their true response. The worrywart test would not be valid if it measures "desire to appear well adjusted" rather than worrywart tendencies.)

In this section, we examine standardization, reliability, and validity—the three characteristics of a psychological test. This discussion should convince you that a high-quality psychological test cannot be constructed casually.

Standardization

Suppose that during the freshman orientation at your college you take a test of writing ability, and you receive a score of 29. By itself, your score is meaningless. You cannot tell whether it is high, average, or low. To make this score meaningful, you would need to compare it with a norm or standard.

The test would first need to be administered to a large group of people, who all take the test in situations as uniform as possible. The scores would be meaningless if one group had the instructions read to them, had no time limit, and had the opportunity to ask questions, whereas another group read the instructions to themselves, had only 45 minutes to complete the test, and had no opportunity to ask questions. Thus, the first step in standardizing a test requires the systematic administration of the test under uniform conditions.

A second important step in the standardization of a psychological test involves the determination of **norms**, or established standards of performance on the test. An individual's score on the test becomes meaningful by comparing the score with those standards. For instance, suppose that on the writing ability test on which you received a raw score of 29, the average student received a 20. That information about the norms is useful, because you now know your score was better than average. However, you would also need some normative information about variability. If most people received a score within 3 points of 20—so that the variability on the test was small—your score of 29 would be spectacular. However, if most people received a score within 10 points of 20—so that the

When a test is standardized, it must be administered under uniform conditions.

variability was large—your score of 29 is still good, but not truly spectacular. The norms include information about both the average score and the variability (or, in the statistical terms discussed in chapter 2 and the Appendix, the *mean* and the *standard deviation*).

In summary, then, **standardization** is a process of determining norms on a group of people who have taken a test under uniform conditions.

Reliability

Reliability refers to the consistency of a person's scores. This consistency is established by reexamining the test takers with the same test on two different occasions, or by some other method of measuring the stability of the scores (Anastasi, 1988).

Every test involves some measurement error. Even objective measurements can show variation. If you weigh yourself now and 1 hour from now, your two weights probably will not be identical. However—if the scale is reliable—your weight will be reasonably consistent.

Unfortunately, psychological tests are not as reliable as bathroom scales, because psychological characteristics are more difficult to measure than physical characteristics. Still, reliability is one of the three qualities of a high-quality psychological test.

Three major methods can be used to measure the reliability of a test:

1. In **test-retest reliability**, the same identical test is administered on two occasions, usually one day to several weeks apart. The test-retest reliability is high if each person's score is similar on the two tests.

2. In **split-half reliability**, everybody takes just one test, but the items are split into two halves (often the even-numbered versus the odd-numbered questions). The split-half reliability is high if each person's score is similar on the two halves.

3. In **alternate-form reliability**, two alternate forms of the test are administered, usually one day to several weeks apart. The alternate-form reliability is high if each person's score is similar on the two tests.

In each case, reliability is measured by calculating a statistical measure called a correlation coefficient, or r. As noted in chapter 2, a correlation coefficient tells us whether a person's score on one measure is related to his or her score on another measure. A test is reliable if a person who receives a high score on the first measure also receives a high score on the second measure, and if medium and low scorers also show this same consistency.

An r of 1.00 indicates a perfect correlation, or absolute consistency in the two scores. Psychological tests do not achieve r's of 1.00, because the tests are not perfect and because human behavior is too complex to be absolutely consistent. On the other hand, an r close to .00 indicates absolutely no relationship between the two scores. You might receive a very high score on Measure 1 and a very low score on Measure 2, and a friend might receive a moderately low score on Measure 1 and a moderately high score on Measure 2. Other people who took the test also show no particular pattern in their scores when there is a zero correlation.

Psychologists are extremely satisfied if the reliability is greater than about .85. Many tests have lower reliability. Figure 14.1 shows a test whose alternate-form reliability was calculated to be .72 (moderately high). The tally mark in the top right corner represents a person whose score on Form 1 was between 70 and

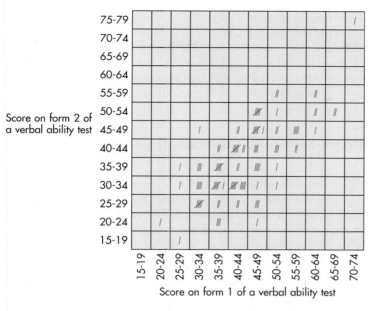

Figure 14.1
Illustration of an alternate-form reliability of .72. (Based on Anastasi, 1988; Anastasi & Drake, 1954)

Score on form 2 of a verbal ability test

Score on form 1 of a verbal ability test

Note: Each tally mark represents one person, who obtained scores on each of two measures.

74, and whose score on Form 2 was between 75 and 79. Although this person's score remained fairly consistent (and so did the scores of many others), notice the exceptions. For example, one person received a good score (between 45 and 49) on Form 1 and a poor score (between 20 and 24) on Form 2. Overall, however, the scores show moderate consistency across the two tests.

Validity

Validity refers to a test's accuracy in measuring what it is supposed to measure. For instance, if a test is a valid measure of intelligence, people's scores on that test should be strongly correlated with their grades in school.

Consider this real-life example of a potentially invalid test. On June 20, 1989, the answer key to the year-end New York State Regents Examination in chemistry was stolen, and the answers were published in the New York *Post*. Most high schools near New York City decided not to administer the test. If they had given the test, it would have been invalid. The test would have measured students' ability to locate and buy the New York *Post*, rather than their knowledge of chemistry. The test would not have measured what it is supposed to measure.

Researchers need to consider the issue of test validity throughout the construction and evaluation of a psychological test (Anastasi, 1986). Psychologists have devised various validation procedures. An ideal validation includes several types of evidence about a test's validity (American Psychological Association, 1985). This chapter considers two approaches, content-related validity and criterion-related validity.

1. **Content validity** refers to a test's ability to cover the complete range of material that it is supposed to cover. If your psychology professor announces that the final examination will be comprehensive, but the exam includes no questions on learning, memory, or thinking, that exam lacks content validity. An exam that covers material that was never assigned in the course would also lack content validity.

2. **Criterion-related validity** refers to a test's ability to predict a person's performance on another measure, that is, an independent criterion. For example, suppose that researchers want to assess criterion-related validity for a test of intelligence. They could measure whether scores on that test are correlated with the number of years of education that each person achieved (Anastasi, 1988).

Section Summary: Constructing and Evaluating Tests

- A psychological test is an objective, standardized measure of a sample of behavior; a good test must be standardized, reliable, and valid.
- Standardization requires the determination of norms on a group of people who have taken a test under uniform conditions.
- Reliability, or consistency, can be measured in terms of test-retest reliability (taking the same test twice), split-half reliability (correlating the two separate halves of a test), and alternate-form reliability (taking two different forms of a test).
- Validity, or a test's ability to measure what it is supposed to measure, can be assessed in terms of content validity (covering the range of material) and criterion-related validity (correlation with an independent criterion).

Assessing Intelligence

Before you read further, try Demonstration 14.1. If you had difficulty in defining the term *intelligence*, you are in good company. Even the earliest survey of experts showed little agreement on a definition of intelligence ("Intelligence and Its Measurement," 1921), and the experts still do not agree, more than 70 years later.

In this book, we define **intelligence** as the capacity to acquire and use knowledge. Intelligence therefore uses a wide range of cognitive skills, including perception, learning, memory, problem solving, and reasoning (Scarr, 1984).

Although experts have difficulty agreeing on a definition of intelligence, they seem to agree quite well about the characteristics of an ideally intelligent person. Table 14.1 shows some of the characteristics that experts think are important. As you can see, some of these characteristics focus on verbal intelligence, whereas others stress problem-solving ability. Interestingly, however, the experts also judge some less academic, more practical characteristics to be important (Sternberg et al., 1981). Furthermore, when Sternberg and his colleagues asked nonexperts about the characteristics of an intelligent person, the nonexperts provided answers that were highly similar to those provided by the experts. Let us now turn our attention to the tests that have been used to measure human intelligence.

Demonstration 14.1

Defining Intelligence

1. In one or two sentences, define the word *intelligence*.
2. Now, instead of a definition, think of the important characteristics of an ideally intelligent person. What kind of qualities would this intelligent person have? Make a list of 10 characteristics that you think would be most descriptive of a highly intelligent person. Then check Table 14.1 for a list of characteristics that experts considered to be very important.

Table 14.1   *Representative Characteristics of an Ideally Intelligent Person, as Judged by Experts in the Field of Intelligence*

Verbal intelligence
  Displays a good vocabulary
  Reads with high comprehension
  Displays curiosity
Problem-solving ability
  Able to apply knowledge to problems at hand
  Makes good decisions
  Poses problems in an optimal way
Practical intelligence
  Sizes up situations well
  Determines how to achieve goals
  Displays awareness of world around him or her

Source: Sternberg et al., 1981.

The History of Intelligence Testing

As far as we know, the first formal intelligence tests were administered in China about 4,000 years ago (Aiken, 1987). The Mandarin emperors screened candidates for government positions, using a series of oral tests.

In the English-speaking world, the first major contribution to intelligence testing came from Sir Francis Galton, a half cousin of the prominent evolutionary theorist, Charles Darwin. From an early age, Galton was preoccupied with the topic of intelligence and giftedness. As he wrote in a letter to his tutor,

> My dear Adele,
>
>   I am four years old and I can read any English book. I can say all the Latin Substantives and Adjectives and active verbs besides 52 lines of Latin poetry. . . . (Pearson, 1914, p. 66)

Galton's enthusiasm for assessing intelligence motivated him to collect measures on more than 9,000 men and women at the 1884 International Health Exhibition in London. These measures included head size, visual acuity, color sense, and reaction time—none of which would be included on a modern intelligence test (Fancher, 1985). Galton's most important contribution to psychology was not his specific measurement techniques, but the *idea* that individual differences in intelligence could be assessed.

Formal Intelligence Testing   The forerunners of modern intelligence tests were constructed by the French psychologist, Alfred Binet (pronounced "Bin-*nay*"). Binet had wide-ranging skills and occupations, having been a lawyer, writer, hypnotist, and experimental psychologist before developing an interest in intelligence testing (Aiken, 1987).

In the early 1900s, the Paris schools were overcrowded, and the minister of public instruction decided to remove the slower learners from the regular classrooms so that they could receive special instruction. The minister appointed a commission to design an appropriate intelligence test, and this commission included Alfred Binet. Binet and his co-workers designed an intelligence scale; Table 14.2 shows some of the tests that were included in the 1911 version of this scale. As you can see, Binet's test items are much more congruent with our current notions of intelligence than were Galton's more physiological measures.

Table 14.2 *Sample Tests from Binet's 1911 Mental Age Scale*

A normal child would be expected to complete these tasks:

Age 3
Point to eyes, nose, and mouth
Repeat a two-digit number
Age 6
Describe the difference between morning and evening
Count 13 pennies
Age 10
Reproduce line drawings from memory
Make up a sentence containing the words *Paris, fortune,* and *stream*

Interestingly, Binet's intelligence scales were greeted with even more enthusiasm in the United States than in Binet's own country (Aiken, 1987). Many of the states had passed laws that required children of "normal" intelligence to attend school until the age of 13 or 14. Thus, they welcomed an intelligence test that could identify children who would not profit from regular classroom instruction. Several researchers translated and modified Binet's scales. One of the most popular of these was constructed by Lewis Terman, working at Stanford University. We discuss this Stanford-Binet Intelligence Scale shortly.

When the United States entered World War I in 1917, the military requested a method of classifying its 1.5 million recruits. Obviously, it would be impossible to test 1.5 million people, one at a time, to decide who should receive officer training, who should be assigned to regular duty, and who should be rejected. Accordingly, army psychologists revised some existing tests so they could be administered in large groups (Samelson, 1987). So began our country's enchantment with intelligence testing and intelligence scores.

This brief history illustrates the saying, "Necessity is the mother of invention." The exploration of intelligence was certainly hastened by the need to devise tests that could sort large numbers of individuals for schools or for the military. Unfortunately, however, the tests were often technically crude, because more effort was spent in administering them than in refining them (Anastasi, 1988). In general, too, the practical applications were emphasized more than the development of theories about intelligence.

Intelligence and Underlying Factors One major theoretical argument dominated the history of intelligence testing: Does intelligence consist of a single core factor or many separate, unrelated abilities? Think about several people you know whom you consider to be extremely intelligent. Are they all intelligent in the same way, or do they have different strengths—perhaps one is highly verbal, another a whiz at math, and another skilled at fixing mechanical things?

This question was addressed by Charles Spearman (1904, 1923) who developed a technique that examines the correlations among many variables in order to identify closely related clusters of variables. When several variables are highly correlated with each other, the researcher concludes that they are all related to the same underlying factor.

Spearman used this technique to investigate intelligence tests. He concluded that all the varied cognitive abilities could be narrowed down to one critical factor—one general mental ability, which he called *g*. Spearman did acknowledge that individuals may excel in certain areas (such as language, mathematics, or mechanical aptitude). Still, he argued that a person who was exceptional in one area was also likely to be strong in other areas.

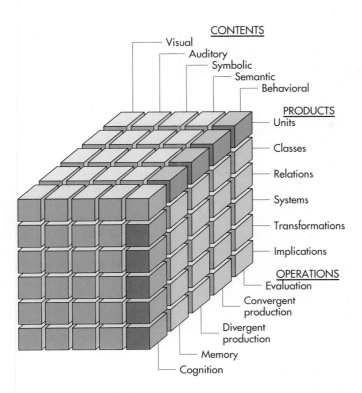

Figure 14.2
J. P. Guilford's model of intellect, consisting of 150 distinct abilities. (Based on Guilford, 1985)

Other psychologists disagreed. They proposed that a person might have exceptional verbal ability, for example, yet receive dismal scores on tests of memory and spatial ability. How many kinds of special abilities could we have? Some argued that intelligence could be divided into a relatively small number of different factors, perhaps seven (Thurstone, 1955). However, J. P. Guilford proposed an influential theory that intelligence consisted of 150 distinct abilities (Guilford, 1967, 1985).

Guilford's model is illustrated in Figure 14.2. According to this model, each of the cubes represents 1 of the 150 possible cognitive abilities that make up intelligence. Let us look at 1 of these 150 cubes, the one that requires divergent thinking (thinking of many different answers), symbolic content (because letters are symbols), and a system (or sentence) as the final product. People's ability on this particular skill could be assessed by asking them to supply as many sentences as possible that fit this set of first letters:

N _____ s _____ d _____ a _____.

A person who could quickly create many sentences such as "Nancy sings difficult arias" and "Never suggest dancing again" would rate high on this particular cognitive ability. Now that leaves only 149 other abilities to explain!

Eventually, Guilford managed to identify and test more than 80 of these individual skills, an impressive achievement. However, other researchers have determined that many of these abilities are too closely correlated with each other to be considered separate, distinct skills (Horn & Knapp, 1973). It is not clear whether there is evidence of a general *g* underlying all intelligent behavior, but we probably do not have as many as 150 isolated cognitive skills.

Current Tests of Intelligence

Let us now consider three of the most popular tests of intellectual skills, the Stanford-Binet test, the Wechsler scales, and the Scholastic Aptitude Test (SAT).

The first two tests are given individually by trained professionals, whereas (as many of you can testify) the SAT is a group test.

Tests of intelligence differ not only in the method of administration, but also with respect to whether they are supposed to measure achievement or aptitude. An **achievement test** is designed to measure current skills, usually based on a formal exposure to a subject area (Anastasi, 1985; Angoff, 1988). For example, you may have taken a standardized achievement test in trigonometry, American history, or a foreign language. Achievement tests therefore measure knowledge in a fairly specific area.

In contrast, an **aptitude test** is supposed to predict future success on the basis of current performance. These tests draw their material from a broader range of human experience, including information gained outside the classroom. Whereas an achievement test focuses backward, on material already learned, an aptitude test focuses forward, on an individual's ability to learn something in the future. However, as you can imagine, the borderline between achievement and aptitude is not perfectly clear-cut. Let us now examine several aptitude tests.

The Stanford-Binet Intelligence Scale   As noted earlier, this test is derived from Alfred Binet's tests. Lewis Terman, working at Stanford University, found that the norms developed in Paris did not apply well to California children. Terman's revised version is called the Stanford-Binet Intelligence Scale. Like all major tests, the Stanford-Binet has been revised many times.

The material used in the current edition of the Stanford-Binet is illustrated in Figure 14.3. As you can see, it contains beads to be strung in a specified order from memory, blocks to be arranged to match a picture, and a unisex, multiethnic child, which young children use for pointing to specified body parts. The test also includes other tasks, such as arithmetic, vocabulary, and memory for sentences (Thorndike et al., 1986).

Performance on tests such as the Stanford-Binet can be scored and transformed into an intelligence quotient. An **intelligence quotient**, or **IQ**, is currently

Figure 14.3
Test material used in the Stanford-Binet Intelligence Scale (fourth ed.).

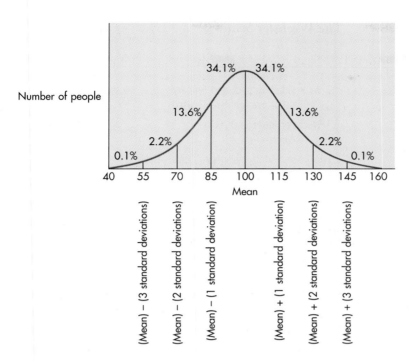

Figure 14.4
The distribution of IQ scores for a
very large sample of people.

computed by assigning a score of 100 to a person whose performance is average
for a particular age group; higher and lower IQ scores are then based on where
a person's score falls in comparison to the average. The scores are assigned so
that 34% (about one third) of the scores fall between 100 and 115, and 34% fall
between 85 and 100 (Figure 14.4). Notice that IQs higher than 145 or lower than
55 are very rare.

The Wechsler Scales   David Wechsler was born in Romania and emigrated to
the United States at the age of 6. As a young adult, he volunteered to help the
army score its intelligence tests during World War I (Fancher, 1985). With this
background, Wechsler decided to construct his own scales. His first task was to
design an intelligence test specifically aimed at adults, because other tests were
modifications of ones designed for children. At present, there are three different
Wechsler tests, each specializing in a particular age range (see Table 14.3).

The Wechsler scales—like the Stanford-Binet—include both verbal and
nonverbal (or performance) questions. Here are some typical items:

1. What does the word *unobtrusive* mean?

2. After you have heard this list of numbers, repeat them in order: 4,
   7, 2, 9, 5, 1, 8, 3.

3. Arrange these five pictures in order so that they tell a story.

4. Assemble these cutouts so that they make a familiar object.

This child is taking the WISC-R.

As with all standardized tests, the reliability and the validity of the Wechsler
scales have been examined extensively. The reliabilities generally range from about
.88 to .98, which is excellent. Validity studies of the Wechsler scales do not
produce such impressive data, though they are adequate. For example, criterion-
related validity research has shown that people in white-collar jobs receive higher
scores on the verbal portion than on the performance portion; in contrast, skilled
workers receive higher scores on the performance portion (Anastasi, 1988). This

Table 14.3   *The Wechsler Scales*

ABBREVIATION	NAME	INTENDED AGE RANGE
WPPSI-R	Wechsler Preschool and Primary Scale of Intelligence—Revised	4–6
WISC-R	Wechsler Intelligence Scale for Children—Revised	6–16
WAIS-R	Wechsler Adult Intelligence Scale—Revised	adults

makes sense, because one would expect the first group to be skilled with words and the second group to be skilled with spatial relationships. Furthermore, IQ scores are correlated about .70 with achievement in elementary school (Rattan & Rattan, 1987). However, we consider some possible problems with the validity of IQ tests later in the chapter when we discuss potential biases in these tests.

The Scholastic Aptitude Test   So far we have looked at tests that are administered individually. In contrast, the Scholastic Aptitude Test (SAT) is a group test; it is designed to measure aptitude for college work. Try Demonstration 14.2 to familiarize yourself with this test, in case you did not take it, or to refresh your memory, in case you did.

The SAT yields separate measures of verbal and mathematical abilities. Its name suggests that it is an aptitude test, yet you can see from Question 3 that it requires some knowledge of geometry. Thus, it really measures past achievement and formal education, as well as aptitude for future work (Linn, 1982; Messick, 1980).

Consumer groups—as well as thousands of students—often ask whether the SATs are truly useful. Can they predict college success? It is true that high school grade point averages (GPAs) are better at predicting college grades. The correlation between high school and college grades is typically about .49. In contrast, the validity of SAT scores is about .38, which is not very impressive. The real value of the SAT scores comes when the data from high school GPA and SAT are combined; together, they are correlated .56 with college grades (Kaplan, 1982). Notice, however, that even this combination does a far-from-perfect job in predicting college success. If you were a college director of admissions, what other information would you gather, and what kinds of additional tests would you construct, so that you could predict college grades with greater accuracy?

The Two Extremes of Intelligence

Turn back to Figure 14.4 and notice the scores on the extreme left and the extreme right of the distribution, because we now direct our attention to retarded and gifted individuals.

Mental Retardation   The essential features of **mental retardation** are (1) intellectual functioning that is significantly below average, (2) difficulty functioning in normal settings, (3) onset prior to age 18 (Grossman, 1983). An IQ below 70 is considered to be "significantly below average," but the examiner must also consider an individual's adaptive functioning before making the diagnosis of mental retardation. Children who receive low scores on standardized intelligence tests but can feed themselves, dress themselves, and show fairly normal motor skills may not be classified as mentally retarded (Grossman, 1983). Table 14.4 shows the four general categories of mental retardation.

The Scholastic Aptitude Test

Answer each of the questions below; they are sample items from the mathematical and verbal portions of the SAT. The answers appear at the end of the chapter.

1. There are 45 students in a certain physics class. If two thirds of the students are boys, and one half of the boys are blue-eyed, how many blue-eyed boys are in the class?
   (A) 15   (B) 30   (C) 34
   (D) 38   (E) 43

2. To which of the following is $\frac{a}{b} - \frac{a}{c}$ equal?

   (A) $\frac{a}{b-c}$ (B) $\frac{1}{b-c}$

   (C) $\frac{1}{bc}$ (D) $\frac{ab-ac}{bc}$

   (E) $\frac{ac-ab}{bc}$

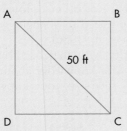

3. In the above figure, the distance from *A* to *C* in the square field *ABCD* is 50 feet. What is the area, in square feet, of field *ABCD*?
   (A) $25\sqrt{2}$ (B) 625   (C) 1,250
   (D) 2,500   (E) 5,000

4. Choose the word or phrase that is most nearly *opposite* in meaning to the word in capital letters.
   LENIENCY:
   (A) wealth   (B) severity
   (C) status   (D) brevity
   (E) defense

5. Choose the word that *best* fits the meaning of the sentence as a whole. To many thoughtful people, the tremendous coverage of sporting events by television stations presents a _____: the instrument which has made us a sports-conscious nation is also the instrument which may destroy amateur and professional athletics in this country.
   (A) nuance   (B) hyperbole
   (C) handicap   (D) paradox
   (E) digression

6. Select the lettered pair that *best* expresses a relationship similar to that expressed in the original pair.
   COMPOSER: SYMPHONY:
   (A) playwright: rehearsal
   (B) actor: comedy
   (C) conductor: orchestra
   (D) director: movie
   (E) poet: sonnet

Table 14.4   *Categories of Mental Retardation*

LEVEL OF RETARDATION	IQ RANGE	NUMBER OF AMERICANS	DESCRIPTION
Mild mental retardation	50–70	4,200,000	May complete sixth grade academic work; in supportive setting, may hold a job.
Moderate mental retardation	35–50	1,200,000	May complete second grade academic work; may hold a job in a sheltered workshop.
Severe mental retardation	20–35	400,000	May learn to talk; often needs help even for simple tasks.
Profound	below 20	200,000	Little or no speech; requires constant help and supervision.

Sources: American Psychiatric Association, 1987; Grossman, 1983; Ruch, 1984.

According to one estimate, 350 known causes of mental retardation have been identified (Spitz, 1986). The causes have traditionally been divided into two general categories, organic and cultural-familial. People with **organic retardation** are retarded because of a genetic disorder (such as the Down syndrome discussed in chapter 3) or physical damage to the brain. This damage can often be traced to an infectious disease or medical complicatons from a premature delivery.

The majority of mentally retarded people have **cultural-familial retardation**; their disorder can be traced to environmental factors rather than a physical or biological reason. People with cultural-familial retardation come from environments that are psychologically, socially, and economically impoverished. In general, their housing, nutrition, and medical care are also inadequate (Grossman, 1983).

Until the mid-1800s, mentally retarded people lived at home. Then the United States established institutions for the retarded. Residents often lived in crowded conditions with little personal attention and no educational programs. In recent decades, however, real progress has been made in establishing smaller, more personalized group homes in the community, where retarded individuals are encouraged to live as independently as possible.

Let us now consider the cognitive components of retardation. Suppose that we want to compare a mentally retarded child with a younger nonretarded child, who received the same raw score on a standard IQ test. How will the two children compare on cognitive tasks? On the Piaget-type tasks discussed in chapter 10 (for example, conservation), the two will probably perform similarly (Zigler & Balla, 1982). However, on the information-processing tasks discussed in chapter 7 and 8 (for instance, memory and concept formation), the nonretarded child will frequently perform better (Weiss et al., 1986). It is not clear why retarded individuals have particular difficulty with some cognitive tasks but not others. However, it seems likely that retardation is complex; it cannot be traced to a single, general cause that produces equal deficits on all tasks (Weiss et al., 1986).

Retarded individuals also seem to have difficulty with metacognition. In earlier chapters, we discussed metamemory, which is your knowledge about your own memory. A more general term, **metacognition**, refers to your knowledge

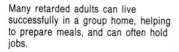

Many retarded adults can live successfully in a group home, helping to prepare meals, and can often hold jobs.

Gifted individuals are particularly exceptional in the kind of planning and organizing required for original projects.

about your cognitive processes. Retarded individuals typically cannot describe or discuss their thought processes. They also have difficulty with a related aspect of metacognition, planning and monitoring their cognitive processes. Nonretarded people can plan how to solve a problem, and they check to see how they are progressing. In general, retarded individuals lack these metacognitive skills (Campione et al., 1982). As a result, they have trouble with long-range projects.

Giftedness   We have no firm cutoff that separates the gifted from other people. We could apply the term *gifted* to people in the top 5% of intelligence, or the top 1% or even 0.1%. However, many school districts with special programs for **the gifted** often select those with IQs over 130, roughly the top 2% (Horowitz & O'Brien, 1986).

We saw that retardation was not defined just in terms of IQ; the definition also included difficulty in functioning normally. Similarly, many theorists and educators emphasize that giftedness involves more than simply a high IQ score. Some argue, for instance, that people who have exceptional creativity, leadership skills, or artistic abilities should also be called gifted. Others propose that people are gifted only if they meet all three of the following criteria: (1) above average ability, (2) creativity, and (3) task commitment, or focused motivation in completing a project (Mönks & Van Boxtel, 1985; Renzulli, 1986).

Gifted children are typically as well adjusted emotionally as children of average intelligence; if anything, they are somewhat better adjusted (Schneider, 1987). However, they may tend to be perfectionists or overly sensitive to criticism (Freeman, 1985).

You saw that retarded individuals have difficulty with metacognition. As you might guess, gifted people tend to be exceptional with respect to metacognition. They seem to be particularly good at planning, organizing, and transferring strategies from one task to another (Jackson & Butterfield, 1986). This understanding of their own thought processes and ability to monitor progress will prove especially useful later on. In life outside of a school setting, success often depends on initiating and pursuing an original idea, rather than simply doing a task that has been assigned.

Group Differences in Intellectual Skills

The topic of group differences in intellectual skills is easily the most controversial in any discussion of intelligence. Professionals and laypeople may argue about whether the SATs really predict college success, or what criteria should be used for the classification of gifted children. However, none of these debates has generated as much heat as the question of whether certain groups differ from others in their cognitive abilities. The two major controversies involve gender and race.

Gender and Cognitive Skills   You may have heard recent discussions about whether women and men differ in their cognitive abilities. The research on this topic suggests that the issue is highly complex, consistent with one of our themes (Linn, 1986). In general, however, the evidence suggests that the similarities between men and women are greater than the differences.

Let us summarize the research in four areas:

1. *General intelligence.*   The items on intelligence tests are usually balanced carefully, so that gender differences rarely appear on IQ tests (McGuinness, 1985). Thus, we cannot evaluate whether men and women differ in general intelligence.

2. *Spatial ability.*   Spatial ability involves skill in perceiving and manipulating shapes and figures. One everyday application of spatial abilitiy is reading a road map. Interestingly, the data contradict a common stereotype; men and women perform similarly on the Standardized Road-Map Test of Direction Sense (Caplan et al., 1985).

Linn and Petersen (1986) used the meta-analysis technique to study gender and spatial ability. As discussed in chapter 2, this procedure statistically combines the results of many different studies in order to produce a single overall statistic. Examining numerous previous studies, they concluded that males and females are similar in their spatial visualization skill, as measured by tests such as one in which people must locate a hidden figure. However, males have a slight advantage on mental rotation tests (see Demonstration 8.1).

3. *Mathematics ability.*   Boys and girls in grades 8 through 12 receive similar scores on the numerical ability part of a standardized test called the Differential Aptitude Test (Feingold, 1988a). However, males score higher on the mathematics section of the SAT and the preliminary version of the SAT, called the PSAT (Benbow, 1988 ; Benbow & Stanley, 1980). You may have read about the controversy regarding these scores, particularly because National Merit Scholarships are awarded on the basis of PSAT scores. Since 1986, only 36% of these scholarship winners have been female (Rosser, 1989).

Nevertheless, females receive higher grades than males for mathematics and science courses in both high school and college (Benbow, 1988; Farmer, 1988; Kimball, 1989). In other words, the research on gender and mathematics shows no gender differences on some measures, whereas other measures favor either males or females. There is no clear-cut evidence for gender differences in mathematics (Hyde et al., 1990).

4. *Verbal ability.*   According to the stereotype, females are superior in their verbal ability, and many previous summaries of this topic agreed with the stereotype. A recent meta-analysis, however, examined 165 different studies, involving a total of 1,418,899 people. Although some verbal skills showed slightly better performance for females, the authors concluded that gender differences in verbal ability are currently so negligible that they can effectively be considered nonexistent (Hyde & Linn, 1988).

In summary, then, the research on gender and cognitive skills reveals similarities rather than differences. As a consequence, you are likely to know women—as well as men—who have superior spatial and mathematical abilities. You are also likely to know men—as well as women—who have superior verbal abilities.

Another consequence of this research concerns the gender differences in occupations, which we discussed in chapter 11. Cognitive gender differences are too small to explain why men and women enter different occupations (Linn, 1986). A more likely explanation involves gender stereotypes, considered in more detail in chapter 17.

Race and Intelligence   In general, studies show that Blacks in the United States score an average of 15 points lower than Whites on a variety of IQ tests (Mackenzie, 1984). It is important to stress, however, that individual differences within each race are very large. For instance, the variation among Blacks or among Whites is much larger than the 15-point difference between the two groups.

In the late 1960s, educational psychologist Arthur Jensen was invited to write an article for the prestigious *Harvard Educational Review*. Jensen was asked to address the topic, "How much can we boost IQ and scholastic achievement?" and his article was to be followed by commentaries from other experts. Because of deadlines, however, the commentaries were postponed to a later issue of the journal (Fancher, 1985). Thus, Jensen's article had a stronger impact than originally intended.

Jensen's article began with the sentence "Compensatory education has been tried and apparently it has failed" (Jensen, 1969, p. 1). The article concluded that programs designed to improve the intelligence of culturally deprived children actually had little or no benefit. Jensen also argued that nature was much more important than nurture, an issue addressed in the next section. This issue, by itself, would not have provoked much controversy, except that Jensen also wrote, "It seems a not unreasonable hypothesis that genetic factors are strongly implicated in the average Negro-white intelligence difference" (p. 82).

The popular press tended to exaggerate and oversimplify Jensen's arguments. For instance, an article in the March 31, 1969, issue of *Newsweek* was entitled "Born Dumb." Whereas Jensen had been vague in some areas, the media implied that he had argued that no amount of extra schooling for Black children could reduce the 15-point IQ gap (Cronbach, 1975). Because Blacks and liberal Whites were particularly sensitive to racial issues in the late 1960s, you can imagine the reaction to these claims (Snyderman & Rothman, 1988).

It is impossible to summarize all the arguments that have been presented both for and against a genetic interpretation of racial differences in IQ. And as Mischel (1986) comments,

> For now, at least, there is no way to answer the question. Indeed, the question itself is meaningless as long as black and white people continue to live in a biased society and hence are exposed to different environments and experiences. (p. 143)

We must remember from the history of the United States that Blacks spent their first 200 years in slavery and the following 120 years frequently deprived of the educational opportunities available to White people. For instance, most slave states declared that it was a criminal offense for slaves to read and write, and it was also a criminal offense for Whites to teach Black people. Angoff (1988) points out that these years of denial have undoubtedly had a long-lasting influence on the educational ambitions of Blacks. As we move toward somewhat greater opportunities for Blacks, the gap on some educational tests has been decreasing (Angoff, 1988; Jones, 1983). However, as we noted in chapter 10, half of Black children still live below the poverty line, in contrast to only one quarter of White children.

Even though we cannot draw conclusions about the explanation for the 15-point IQ gap, let us consider some relevant research that tends to favor an environmental, or nurture explanation for this gap. For example, one research team asked whether Black children, adopted into relatively wealthy White homes, would have relatively high IQs. Scarr and Weinberg (1976) studied children in the Minneapolis, Minnesota, region and found that the average IQ of these adopted children was 106, in contrast to an average IQ of 90 for Black children reared in their own homes in this region. Children raised in upper-middle-class homes, where educational goals are emphasized, tend to have above-average IQs — whether their skin color is Black or White. Environment does make a difference. (Incidentally, as Flynn (1987) has pointed out, this study still underestimates the potential influence of the environment, because the adopted children undoubtedly experienced racism in the world outside their adoptive families.)

In another study, Scarr and her colleagues (1977) examined a different aspect of the race question. If racial background really is a critical determinant of intelligence, then people who have more Black African ancestry should have lower IQs than Blacks with more White ancestry. The research team examined blood samples from the participants, to determine ancestry. The results demonstrated that scores on cognitive tests were *not* related to the relative amount of Black ancestry. In other words, intelligence was not correlated with the genetic/racial factor.

We have seen that one study demonstrated that environment was important, and a second study demonstrated that genetic factors were not important in explaining the race difference in IQ. Other research suggests that the difference can be traced to motivation (C. M. Johnson et al., 1984). In this study, researchers gave IQ tests to Black inner-city children and White middle-class children. Half of the children in each group received tokens as a reward for correct answers, and they were told that the tokens could be exchanged for toys after the test. The other half of each group (the control groups) received no reward. The results showed that the Black children who had been motivated by the possibility of rewards received IQ scores that averaged 13 points higher than the unrewarded Black children. In contrast, reward had no effect for the White children, presumably because White middle-class children were already highly motivated. People in more privileged subcultures learn to try their hardest on an intelligence test.

Many people have argued that IQ tests are aimed at White middle-class vocabulary and culture, so they are biased against minority groups (Scarr, 1984). However, in one study, experts reviewed the test items and eliminated those that seemed biased against minority students. The tests were then rescored. Surprisingly, the gap between majority and minority student scores remained the same (Biachini, 1976). Other studies demonstrated that IQ tests have similar predictive validity for both Black and White students (Oakland & Parmelee, 1985). In other words, these tests predict grades in school equally successfully for both Whites and Blacks. Also, translating the IQ tests into Black-dialect versions does not substantially change scores for inner-city Black children (Kaplan, 1985). Based on current studies, it seems as if test bias may be less important than environmental or motivational factors in explaining the racial differences in IQ scores.

The Nature-Nurture Question

We first raised the nature-nurture question in chapter 3 in connection with genetics. We examined the issue more thoroughly in chapter 10 in connection with the development of children's abilities. The nature-nurture question also underlies the previous topic, racial differences in IQ scores. Let us now focus more specifically on the nature-nurture question in connection with intelligence.

You have probably noticed that intelligence tends to run in families. The three children in the Williams family all graduated at the top of their high school classes, whereas the three children in the Robins family were consistently in the

In many characteristics, children seem to resemble their parents. The athletic skill of these children could be traced to both nature and nurture from their parents.

bottom quarter of their classes. Do your informal observations support the nature or nurture argument? At first, you might be tempted to argue that because these family members are genetically related, "nature" is more important. However, these siblings are also being reared in the same household, by the same parents, so they share—to some extent—the same environment. Should you shift your emphasis to "nurture"? As you could probably guess, the truth lies somewhere in between the two extremes.

Much of the research on the nature-nurture question has been conducted on twins. Identical twins not only look the same, but they share exactly the same genetic makeup. Studies by Bouchard and McGue (1981) have demonstrated that the correlations between the IQ scores for identical twins average .86 when they are reared in the same household; that correlation is remarkably high. When identical twins are reared in separate households (for instance because they were adopted by different families), the correlations average .72. These data tell us two things:

1. Nature is important, because the correlation remains very high, even when the twins have different nurturing experiences.

2. Nurture is important, because the correlation is higher when the twins are raised in the same environment than when they are raised in different environments.

In addition, the correlations between the IQ scores for fraternal twins (whose genetic overlap is the same as for any two siblings, i.e., 50%), reared together, average .60. This correlation is substantially lower than the .86 correlation for identical twins (whose genetic overlap is 100%). These data, then, provide additional evidence that nature is important.

A central concept in the nature-nurture controversy is called heritability. This concept focuses on the variability among all IQ scores, which is impressively large. Specifically, **heritability** estimates how much of the variability found in scores is due to heredity (or nature) and how much is due to environment (or nurture). For instance, you might read the results of a study of urban American high school students that reports a heritability index of .65 on the Stanford-Binet

IQ test. This means that 65% of all the variability in these students' scores can be traced to hereditary factors, whereas 35% can be traced to environmental factors (Anastasi, 1988).

We must stress that heritability is applied to a population, rather than an individual. A heritability index of .65 does *not* imply that Sandra Smith, who participated in the study, can trace 65% of her intelligence to her genetic background and 35% to the environment in which she was raised. At present, most research produces heritability indexes between .50 and .70 (DeFries et al., 1987; Loehlin et al., 1988; Plomin, 1990). In other words, when explaining individual differences in intelligence some studies give equal weight to nature and nurture, whereas others give somewhat more weight to nature.

The Stability-Change Question

Try to recall the names of the smartest people in your fourth grade class. Do you suppose that they are still exceptional? Would the slowest learners still be considered slow? In other words, does intelligence remain stable across the life span? You may recall that we discussed the stability-change question with respect to personality in childhood (chapter 10) and adulthood (chapter 11). Now we apply the same question to intelligence.

In general, intelligence test performance remains fairly stable. For instance, intelligence tests administered at 13 and 18 years of age showed a correlation of .78 (Härnqvist, 1968). Even more impressive, when children between the ages of 2 and $5\frac{1}{2}$ were retested 25 years later, the correlation between the two sets of scores was .59 (Bradway et al., 1958). Naturally, a particular individual's IQ score can change dramatically if his or her environment is sharply altered (for instance by enrollment in a good remedial program). However, the data on IQ tests generally favor stability rather than change.

Suppose that you decide to pursue graduate study, and you take the Graduate Record Examination (GRE). As you might guess, the stability-change question is relevant if you want to predict your score on the GRE. A study of about 23,000 students who took the SAT and then took the GRE General Test 4 or 5 years later showed that the correlations between the two scores were .86 for both the verbal and the mathematical sections (Angoff & Johnson, 1988). These data imply that your GRE scores will probably be fairly similar to your SAT scores. In short, scores on these college-testing exams tend to show the same stability as scores on IQ tests.

Howard Gardner's Theory of Multiple Intelligences

So far, our discussion of intelligence has focused on the development of standardized intelligence tests and controversies arising from the results of these tests. In the last decade, however, researchers interested in intelligence have placed less emphasis on the traditional IQ tests (Gardner, 1986). Theorists such as Howard Gardner and Robert Sternberg (whose approach we consider in the next section) have begun to focus on broader definitions of intelligence and the mental processes we use when we perform intellectual tasks.

Let us first consider Howard Gardner's **theory of multiple intelligences**, which proposes seven different components of intelligence. Gardner argued that the traditional IQ tests assess only three kinds of intelligence:

1. language ability

2. logical-mathematical thinking

3. spatial thinking

This gymnast would excel in Gardner's category of bodily-kinesthetic thinking.

However, Gardner (1983, 1988) argues that we must add four other distinct abilities that are not tapped by the standard tests. These abilities—and an example of a person who excels at them—include the following:

4. musical thinking (e.g., a composer)

5. bodily kinesthetic thinking (e.g., an athlete)

6. interpersonal thinking (e.g., someone with an unusual understanding of other people)

7. intrapersonal thinking (e.g., a person with highly accurate understanding of herself or himself)

Notice, then, that Gardner's work is relevant to the theoretical argument mentioned in the section on the history of intelligence testing: Does intelligence consist of a single core factor or many separate abilities? Gardner would reject Charles Spearman's idea that mental abilities were all influenced by one underlying factor, *g*. However, unlike other participants in that debate, Gardner believes that intelligent behavior also includes skills as diverse as dancing and making a newcomer feel welcome.

Gardner's ideas about multiple intelligences have aroused considerable interest, and they have encouraged us to expand our ideas about the constituents of intelligence. However, critics have argued that the last four components are really talents, rather than intelligences. Furthermore, factor analyses have demonstrated that the various abilities are not as independent as Gardner suggested. For instance, logical-mathematical thinking and spatial thinking tend to be highly correlated (Sternberg, 1985a).

○ ○

In Depth: Robert Sternberg's Triarchic Theory of Intelligence

The traditional research on intelligence focused on individual differences in test scores. Typically, the scores were statistically analyzed to identify which cognitive abilities were related to which other cognitive abilities. This approach to intelligence emphasizes the *products*, or end results of intellectual work.

In contrast, Robert Sternberg focuses more on the *process* of intellectual work. Sternberg's approach emphasizes the information-processing approach discussed in chapters 7, 8, and 9. According to this approach, information is received by the senses, some of this information is selected (while other information is lost), and this information is compared, rearranged, and transformed through a series of cognitive processes.

Like several other psychologists discussed in the section on the history of intelligence testing, Robert Sternberg had a long-standing interest in intelligence tests. As a sixth grader, he had been so terrified when he took an IQ test that he performed miserably and ended up retaking the test with fifth graders. Soon after that, he invented his own intelligence test and even began administering the Stanford-Binet Intelligence Tests to his classmates—until an angry parent complained to the school. Today, Sternberg is one of the most active researchers on the topic of intelligence—no one complains when he administers intelligence tests.

Sternberg (1985b, 1988) developed an approach called the triarchic (pronounced "try-*are*-kick") theory of intelligence. The **triarchic theory of intelligence** specifies that there are three important parts of intelligence: (1) componential intelligence, (2) experiential intelligence, and (3) contextual intelligence. People can excel in one, two, or all three kinds of intelligence.

Componential Intelligence Componential intelligence involves the components (or mental processes) used in thinking. **Componential intelligence** is the branch of Sternberg's theory that corresponds most closely with traditional notions of intelligence, as measured by intelligence tests. You probably know several people who are high in componential intelligence. They score high on tests, and they get good grades in school. However, they may not be outstanding in thinking of new, original ideas or in everyday street-smart intelligence.

Componential intelligence contains three kinds of processes: (1) metacomponents, (2) performance components, and (3) knowledge-acquisition components. The left-hand portion of Table 14.5 lists the three processes within componential intelligence.

Metacomponents are roughly equivalent to *meta*cognition, which we discussed earlier. Metacomponents are the processes that plan, monitor, and evaluate. Consider how these metacomponents work when you are assigned a typical intellectual task, writing a paper. You need to plan your general strategy for the paper, monitor your writing, and evaluate how well the finished paper meets its goals (Sternberg, 1988).

Performance components are the lower-order processes that actually carry out the commands of the metacomponents. When you write a paper, you must assemble the words and sentences onto the pages of the paper. This work is not glamorous, but you cannot hand in a paper without performance components.

Knowledge-acquisition components are the processes we use to figure out how to solve a problem in the first place. The knowledge-aquisition components are crucial in researching a paper. Notice, then, that the satisfactory completion of a paper depends upon all three aspects of componential intelligence.

Experiential Intelligence The second major division within the triarchic theory is experiential intelligence. As the name implies, **experiential intelligence** focuses on how people perform on tasks with which they have either no previous experience or great experience. A person who is high in experiential intelligence can solve a new problem easily, even with no prior experience. For instance, you may have a friend with average grades, who was able to figure out what to do when she lost her passport in Madrid, or how the railroad system operates in Germany,

Table 14.5   *Sternberg's (1985b) Triarchic Theory of Intelligence*

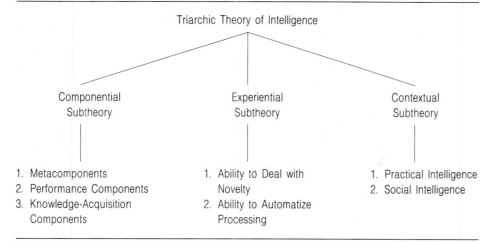

Triarchic Theory of Intelligence

Componential Subtheory	Experiential Subtheory	Contextual Subtheory
1. Metacomponents 2. Performance Components 3. Knowledge-Acquisition Components	1. Ability to Deal with Novelty 2. Ability to Automatize Processing	1. Practical Intelligence 2. Social Intelligence

even though she speaks neither Spanish nor German. She seems to thrive in new, unfamiliar settings.

A person who is high in experiential intelligence also figures out how familiar tasks can be performed more automatically. He or she quickly learns to drive "without thinking," leaving extra cognitive capacities available for other more interesting activities such as listening to music or talking.

Contextual Intelligence   In Sternberg's triarchic theory, the third major kind of intelligence is **contextual intelligence**, or intelligence in everyday life—that is, street smarts. More formally, contextual intelligence requires adapting to, selecting, and shaping one's real-world environment (or *context*).

Part of contextual intelligence is called practical intelligence. This skill involves knowing the pathway to success in your culture. For instance, a student in my college's masters program in psychology several years ago excelled in practical intelligence. Brian's GRE scores were not high, and his grades were good but not exceptional, but Brian knew how to be a graduate student. He mastered the computer and volunteered to help faculty members frustrated with statistical dilemmas. He asked faculty members if they were planning any research projects on which he could collaborate. He read psychology journals and could discuss controversial topics. Brian was accepted into a prestigious PhD program and is now one of the leaders in his specialty area.

Componential intelligence and experiential intelligence can be assessed using tests resembling the standard tests for IQ and creativity. However, the traditional tests do not really measure practical intelligence. Sternberg (1984a, 1985b) therefore developed several tests of practical intelligence, to try to measure people's ability to learn the ropes of their occupations. In one study, for instance, he devised a test for business executives. A typical item on this test required the test taker to rate various work strategies in terms of how useful they would be in the everyday work of a business manager (e.g., "Delegate tasks to competent others whenever possible"). The results showed that the test had predictive validity; people who scored high on the test had significantly higher salaries than those who scored low ($r = .46$).

As you can see from Table 14.5, the last part of contextual intelligence is called social intelligence, or the ability to understand others and interact suc-

Congresswoman Louise Slaughter's social intelligence has won her the admiration of people in her congressional district. Here she is pictured with one of her constituents.

cessfully with them. You certainly know people who have high componential and experiential intelligence, yet they are socially inept. They ask too many questions in class, appearing to be completely unaware that the other students are sighing with impatience and that the professor is not charmed. They offend nearly everyone they talk to, boasting about their accomplishments and failing to notice or consider the feelings of other people. These people are unlikely to be successful in social settings, despite their high IQs.

Evaluation of Sternberg's Theory   At present, the triarchic theory is still being developed. However, Sternberg (1984b) argues that this broader view of intelligence—beyond what the traditional IQ tests measure—will help us explain a greater percentage of the variability in real-world performance. In contrast, Sternberg notes, the traditional tests explain only between 10% and 25% of this variability.

Some experts in the field agree that Sternberg's theory is the most comprehensive view of intelligence yet offered (Tyler, 1984; Yussen, 1984). Others protest that Sternberg failed to provide a good rationale for the exact categories he chose (Baron, 1984). Some also complain that Sternberg never discusses the genetic factors that might underlie these various forms of intelligence (Vernon, 1984).

Sternberg's most important point is that "Intelligence is not a single thing: It comprises a very wide array of cognitive and other skills" (Sternberg, 1984a, p. 286). In the future, we can expect to see further refinements in the tests used to assess the wide variety of skills we call intelligence.

○ ○

Section Summary: Assessing Intelligence

- Both experts and nonexperts believe that an intelligent person has verbal skills, problem-solving ability, and practical intelligence.
- Important figures in the history of intelligence testing include Galton (the first to try to assess intelligence systematically); Binet (who designed a forerunner of current tests); Spearman (who believed that a general mental ability was responsible for all specific abilities); and Guilford (who, in contrast, proposed 150 distinct abilities).
- The Stanford-Binet Intelligence Scale and the three Wechsler Scales must be administered individually, and performance on these tests can be converted to IQ scores; the Scholastic Aptitude Test, a group test, is useful in predicting college success when its scores are combined with high school grades.
- Two general categories of retardation include organic and cultural-familial retardation; retarded people have particular difficulty with some cognitive skills such as metacognition. In contrast, gifted people excel at metacognition.
- The research on gender and cognitive ability reveals more similarities than differences.
- The gap between Whites and Blacks on intelligence tests appears to be due to environmental and motivational factors, more than genetic factors or test bias.
- Both nature and nurture are important determinants of intelligence; present estimates of the heritability index suggest that the two factors are equally important, or perhaps nature may be somewhat more important.

■ IQ scores and SAT/GRE scores show impressive stability over time.

■ Howard Gardner's theory of multiple intelligences proposes that intelligence consists of verbal ability, logical-mathematical thinking, spatial thinking, musical thinking, bodily kinesthetic thinking, interpersonal thinking, and intrapersonal thinking.

■ Sternberg's triarchic theory of intelligence proposes three important parts of intelligence, each subdivided further: componential intelligence, experiential intelligence, and contextual intelligence.

Assessing Personality

Intelligence tests are essential when educators want to assess cognitive abilities and skills. The other major category of psychological tests assesses personality. Psychologists use personality tests for four different purposes (Kleinmuntz, 1975):

1. To aid in the clinical diagnosis of psychological disorders;

2. To counsel people about everyday issues, such as career choice;

3. To select employees, for example, in business and government; and

4. To conduct research, for example, on a specific psychological trait such as extraversion-introversion.

Just as the section on intelligence testing focused on the assessment of the cognitive skills discussed in earlier chapters, this section on personality testing focuses on the assessment of personality characteristics discussed in chapter 13. Recall how that chapter examined four different approaches to personality. As you might imagine, a psychologist's theoretical approach has a major influence on the kind of psychological test he or she favors. Someone who admires Skinner's behavioral approach to personality would be unlikely to ask people to free-associate to an inkblot. Similarly, a supporter of Freud's psychoanalytic approach would be unlikely to conduct a behavioral assessment.

Let us consider three major categories of personality tests: projective tests, self-report inventories, and behavioral assessment. Before reading further, however, try Demonstration 14.3.

Demonstration 14.3

Responding to an Inkblot

Look at the inkblot to the right, which is similar to those on the Rorschach Inkblot Test. Try to describe what the picture looks like and what it could be. Write down your answer. (You do not need to use complete sentences.)

When you have finished your description, go back over it and explain how you arrived at each part of that description. It is important to keep in mind, however, that this is not a true Rorschach Test, and that these tests cannot be interpreted adequately without expert training.

Projective Tests

When psychologists administer **projective tests**, they ask people to respond to a standard set of stimuli that are vague and ambiguous. These stimuli presumably evoke a person's feelings, needs, and personality characteristics. In projective tests, people *project* their psychological reactions onto the test stimuli. The two most common projective tests are the Rorschach and the TAT.

The Rorschach Inkblot Test   As an adolescent, Hermann Rorschach won the nickname "Klex," which is German for *inkblot* (Allison et al., 1988). The name was appropriate, because Rorschach developed his early interest in inkblots into a projective test that is one of the two most frequently used personality tests (Lubin et al., 1984). In the **Rorschach Inkblot Test**, people respond to ambiguous inkblots, and the responses are analyzed for recurring themes, emphases, and emotional characteristics.

The Rorschach consists of 10 inkblots, some colored and some black and white. During the first, or free-association phase, the examiner asks the individual to examine the inkblot and describe it. The examiner records word for word the test taker's reaction. During the second phase, the examiner asks the test taker to describe how he or she arrived at each response (Aiken, 1989). The Rorschach is designed to be administered and interpreted by trained professionals.

Consider how one person responded to a card in the Rorschach Test, shown in Figure 14.5. During the free-association phase, Mrs. T. reported that she saw "two elephants, two itty-bitty elephants . . . fighting over a roach—cockroach—in the middle. . . ." (Allison et al., 1988, p. 203). During the second phase, she elaborated on the elephants, "they both got their—their snozzoolas—[half laughs] or their trunks or whatever you call them wrapped around the cockroach" (p. 203).

The therapists' interpretation of this response focused on Mrs. T.'s defense mechanisms, which attempted to shrink a huge attacking creature into something small and playful. The interpretation also noted her phallic emphasis, because she focused on the elephants' trunks, yet blocked momentarily on the specific name for this penislike body part. As you can see, the Rorschach provides psychoanalytically inclined professionals with a test rich with symbolic possibilities.

Some researchers argue that the Rorschach has reasonably high reliability and validity (Parker et al., 1988). However, the majority of evaluations of the Rorschach conclude that most research indicates only weak reliability and validity (Sundberg, 1990; Walsh & Betz, 1990). An important advantage of the Rorschach, in any event, is that it is an assessment technique that allows a tester to observe a broad segment of a person's behavior while he or she supplies reactions to the inkblot (Walsh & Betz, 1990).

Figure 14.5
The Rorschach Inkblot Test stimulus to which Mrs. T. gave her description of the elephants and the cockroach.

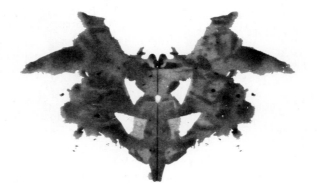

Figure 14.6
An item similar to those that appear
on the Thematic Apperception Test.

The Thematic Apperception Test   The second most popular projective test is called the **Thematic Apperception Test**, or **TAT**. The TAT consists of a series of ambiguous scenes, which the test taker is invited to describe, telling what is happening now, what happened in the past, and what will occur in the future. The TAT was first published by Christina Morgan and Henry Murray in 1935, and many different forms of the TAT are now in use.

Figure 14.6 shows a picture similar to those on the TAT. In responding to a picture like this, one woman wrote,

> This is a woman who has been quite troubled by memories of a mother she was resentful toward. She has feelings of sorrow for the way she treated her mother; her memories of her mother plague her. These feelings seem to be increasing as she grows older and sees her children treating her the same way she treated her mother. She tries to convey this feeling to her own children, but does not succeed in changing their attitudes. She is living her past in the present, because the feeling of sorrow and guilt is reinforced by the way her children are treating her. (Aiken, 1989, p. 364)

The TAT was designed to bring forth unconscious tendencies that a person may be unwilling or unable to reveal, such as difficulties with one's parents. In general, the pictures depict interpersonal relationships. Though the pictures look somewhat unusual, they are more realistic than the abstract shapes in the Rorschach. The test taker presumably projects his or her needs, concerns, and traits onto one or more of the characters in the scene. As you may recall, we discussed the use of the TAT in chapter 12, in connection with achievement motivation.

As with the Rorschach Test, the person administering the test must be professionally trained, asking questions that encourage further clarification without being threatening or suggestive. Training is also necessary for interpreting the results. The examiner cannot simply flip through a test manual to discover the meaning of every sentence uttered by the test taker. The results are often interpreted within a psychoanalytic framework, as with the Rorschach. For instance, when a person omits reference to a gun shown in a TAT picture, the examiner may conclude that he or she tends to repress aggressive impulses. A tendency to introduce figures not shown on the cards may reveal the defense mechanism of projection (Phares, 1988).

Research on the TAT shows that it is sensitive to current motivational and emotional conditions. For instance, people who have been deprived of sleep do tend to tell stories about sleepy people, and people who have experienced recent failure tell stories about unsuccessful story characters (Anastasi, 1988). However, critics are skeptical about whether the test can measure more enduring personality traits (Anastasi, 1988; Mischel, 1986).

Evaluation of Projective Tests   One major advantage to projective tests is that their purpose is disguised: Test takers are seldom aware how their responses will be interpreted (Anastasi, 1988). In contrast, an objective self-report test often has one answer that looks socially acceptable, and test takers may be reluctant to select the other answer—even if it is correct. For instance, a suicidal person may be reluctant to say yes to the question, "Sometimes I think I may kill myself." He or she may be more likely to mention death spontaneously on a projective test, however.

A second, related advantage proposed by psychoanalytically inclined psychologists is that projective tests are more likely than objective tests to tap the unconscious. In contrast, defense mechanisms (such as repression or sublimation) presumably prevent people from supplying true answers to objective tests.

An important disadvantage of projective tests is that they are not as standardized as objective tests. Several alternative scoring systems may be used, and the accuracy depends upon the examiner's professional skill.

Another disadvantage is that the test taker may misunderstand the task, resulting in invalid assessment. For instance, a friend of mine, knowing I was a psychologist, described how he had aced a psychological test. (From his description, it was the TAT.) He thought that he would be awarded a high score for finding a common thread interwoven through all the scenes. Because the first card showed a violin, he painstakingly forced each story to revolve around violins and music. His answers may have revealed creativity or persistence, but I doubt that they really revealed his unconscious personality traits.

Self-Report Tests

When you were reading about the projective tests, with their carefully ambiguous stimuli and their elaborate symbolic interpretations, did you find yourself muttering, "Wouldn't it be simpler just to *ask* them how they feel?" This is the approach of **self-report tests**, which are instruments that instruct people to answer questions about their behaviors, beliefs, and feelings. Let us look at the most widely used personality test, the MMPI, and then evaluate the general status of self-report tests.

The Minnesota Multiphasic Personality Inventory   Several decades ago, the Rorschach test was the most popular personality test. By the mid-1960s, that prime position was occupied by the **Minnesota Multiphasic Personality Inventory (MMPI)**, an objective personality test that assesses personality traits using about 550 personality items (Korchin & Schuldberg, 1981).

In the late 1930s, a psychologist named Starke Hathaway and a psychiatrist named J. R. McKinley began to develop a set of personality scales to be used in diagnosing psychological disorders. They insisted that their test, which ultimately became the MMPI, should be based on research, rather than nonscientific intuitions. They collected about 1,000 questions from their clinical experience, other tests, and textbooks. These items covered a wide range of topics, such as psychological problems, physical symptoms, and attitudes (Butcher & Finn, 1983).

During the next phase of test development, the MMPI was administered to more than 1,500 unhospitalized people, including students and hospital visitors. The MMPI was also administered to more than 800 carefully selected psychiatric patients, representing the major clinical subgroups such as depression and schizophrenia. An item was selected for a particular scale of the MMPI only if the two groups—the normal group and the group with psychological disorders—showed significantly different response patterns. For instance, people with a particular psychological disorder were much more likely than people in the control group to say "true" to the item, "Someone has been trying to poison me." In contrast, an item was rejected if the two groups answered it the same way (for instance, if 61% of one group and 60% of the other group said "true"). It is important to realize that the *content* of the item is irrelevant; the critical point is whether the item discriminates between the normal group and the group with a psychological disorder.

The items on the MMPI are grouped into 10 clinical scales and 3 validity scales. Table 14.6 provides some examples.

More than 8,000 studies have been conducted with the MMPI (Butcher & Finn, 1983). Meta-analyses indicate that the reliability is .84, which is excellent, and the validity is .46, which is satisfactory (Parker et al., 1988). It is important to stress, however, that the MMPI was primarily designed to assess psychological disorders, such as depression and paranoia. Companies that routinely administer the MMPI as part of a job application are therefore using the test inappropriately.

In 1989, a revised form of the MMPI was published. This new MMPI-2 is based on a larger sample of test takers, with members of different races represented in the same ratio as in the general population. The revised version also reworded test items that included gender-biased language or outdated content. However, some psychologists complain that 45% of the sample were college graduates, in contrast to only 17% in the general population, and they are not convinced that the MMPI-2 is a substantial improvement over the "classic" MMPI (Adler, 1989, 1990).

Table 14.6 *Some Examples of Scales from the Minnesota Multiphasic Personality Inventory*

NAME OF SCALE	KIND OF SCALE	DESCRIPTION	HYPOTHETICAL TEST ITEM (answer indicating the disorder is in parentheses)
Depression Scale	Clinical	Derived from patients who show extreme pessimism and feelings of hopelessness.	"I usually feel that life is interesting and worthwhile." (*False*)
Psychopathic Deviate Scale	Clinical	Derived from patients who show extreme disregard for social customs and aggressiveness.	"My activities and interests are often criticized by others." (*True*)
Paranoia Scale	Clinical	Derived from patients who show abnormal suspiciousness or delusions.	"There are evil people trying to influence my mind." (*True*)
Lie Scale	Validity	Measures overly good self-image.	"I smile at everyone I meet." (*True*)

Adapted and reproduced by permission of the publishers. The Minnesota Multiphasic Personality Inventory. Copyright © 1943, renewed 1970 by the University of Minnesota.

Even if some psychologists are not delighted with the revision of the MMPI, this instrument is clearly an important tool for clinical assessment. As Walsh and Betz (1990) conclude, "There is little question that the Minnesota Multiphasic Personality Inventory . . . is the most useful psychological test available in clinical and counseling settings for assessing the degree and nature of emotional upset" (p. 117).

Evaluation of Self-Report Tests   A major advantage of self-report tests, such as the MMPI, is that they can be easily administered, even in large groups. They also can be objectively scored in a standardized fashion; the results do not depend upon the training or personal interpretations of the examiner. They also allow more complete, precise assessments than could be provided by casual observation.

However, one of the advantages also produces an important disadvantage. Because tests such as the MMPI are so easy to administer, they may be used inappropriately—as noted earlier. A second disadvantage was mentioned in the discussion of the advantages of projective tests: It is often easy to guess the socially appropriate answer on a self-report test. The MMPI includes the "lie scale" to assess this tendency to supply socially desirable responses, but most self-report tests do not. We discuss other aspects of self-report tests in the remaining chapters of this textbook. First, however, we need to discuss the third and last method of assessing personality.

Behavioral Assessment

The projective technique assumes that people will project their personality characteristics onto ambiguous stimuli, and the self-report technique asks people to report on certain specific aspects of their personality. In contrast, **behavioral assessment** attempts to measure personality by objectively recording people's observable behavior, as well as environmental conditions.

As the name implies, behavioral assessment is a technique especially favored by behaviorists. After all, behaviorists emphasize people's behavior. They do not believe in unconscious personality characteristics, so they have no use for projective tests. And they do not trust the accuracy of the self-report technique. Instead, they focus on what people *do*, what conditions in the environment preceded this action, and what conditions followed it. Behaviorists pay attention to these environmental conditions because they believe that the external situation is more important than any enduring personal characteristics.

One of the most common methods of behavioral assessment is naturalistic observation (Haynes, 1983). As discussed in chapter 2, naturalistic observation is the systematic recording of behavior in the natural environment, typically by trained observers. These observers first need to define the categories of behavior that they will record, using categories that other observers could easily understand (Martin & Bateson, 1986). For example, researchers who are examining children's aggressive tendencies at summer camp would need to write down their precise definitions of the categories they plan to observe. These categories might include hitting, shoving, and verbal aggression.

Behavioral assessment is not limited to naturalistic observation, however. Researchers can observe the behavior of people in settings other than their natural environment, for instance, in a clinic setting. People can also be asked to assess their own behavior (e.g., smoking, binge eating, bed-wetting). In a typical study, people reported on the number of times they thought about worrisome topics (Emmelkamp & Kwee, 1977). Obviously, these self-assessments might have problems with both reliability and validity (Haynes, 1983; Korchin & Schuldberg, 1981).

It is important to keep in mind that researchers can combine several techniques in trying to obtain a comprehensive view of an individual's personality. For instance, they could administer a TAT and an MMPI, but also record the person's behavior while taking the tests. We discuss further applications of these personality assessment techniques in the chapters on psychological disorders and social psychology.

Section Summary: Assessing Personality

- Projective tests require people to respond to ambiguous stimuli; the two most common projective tests are the Rorschach Inkblot Test and the Thematic Apperception Test; the advantages of these tests include a disguised purpose and the presumed ability to tap the unconscious; disadvantages include lack of standardization and the potential for misunderstanding.
- The most common self-report test is the Minnesota Multiphasic Personality Inventory, now the most popular personality test; the major advantages of self-report tests are that they are easily administered and they are standardized; disadvantages include the frequency of misuse and the tendency to elicit socially appropriate answers.
- Behavioral assessment can be conducted with naturalistic observation as well as observation in other environments and observations provided by the participants themselves.

REVIEW QUESTIONS

1. Imagine you are designing a test to assess the personality dimension of optimism-pessimism. Define the terms *standardization, reliability,* and *validity,* and then describe how you could standardize the test and establish its reliability and validity. (Choose one measure of reliability and one of validity.)

2. Suppose you are taking a test as part of a job application. Why would you want to know whether the test is standardized, reliable, and valid?

3. Suppose you are part of a team that is designing a test for giftedness, which will separate those children who will be enrolled in gifted programs from children enrolled in regular programs. Describe three specific ways of measuring its reliability and two specific ways of assessing its validity. In each case, be as concrete as possible about how you would obtain these measurements.

4. Trace the origins of the current intelligence tests, both in other countries and in the United States. What effect have these tests had on the categorization of mentally retarded individuals?

5. One ongoing controversy in intelligence testing has focused on the number of different kinds of intelligence. Discuss this topic with respect to general mental ability (*g*) versus the proposal that intelligence consists of dozens of different abilities. Also note Gardner's and Sternberg's contributions to this controversy.

6. How are metacognition and metacomponents relevant in mental retardation, giftedness, and Sternberg's theory of intelligence? Speculate why metacogni-

tion should be centrally important in intelligence. (You may want to review chapter 10 on the development of metamemory.)

7. What are the issues in the nature-nurture and stability-change questions? What is the general conclusion on these two issues with respect to intelligence?

8. Name and describe three major parts in Sternberg's triarchic theory of intelligence. Turn back to Table 14.5 to look at the subdivisions within each of these parts. Think of an example of when you had to use each of these seven kinds of intelligence.

9. List and describe the three major categories of personality tests. What kind of personality theorist would most strongly support each of these three kinds of tests? Why?

10. Imagine you are designing a personality test to assess some characteristic of your own choice. Describe this characteristic and then discuss how you could assess it using all three of the kinds of personality tests examined in this chapter.

NEW TERMS

psychological test

norms

standardization

reliability

test-retest reliability

split-half reliability

alternate-form reliability

validity

content validity

criterion-related validity

intelligence

achievement test

aptitude test

intelligence quotient (IQ)

mental retardation

organic retardation

cultural-familial retardation

metacognition

the gifted

heritability

theory of multiple intelligence

triarchic theory of intelligence

componential intelligence

experiential intelligence

contextual intelligence

projective tests

Rorschach Inkblot Test

Thematic Apperception Test (TAT)

self-report tests

Minnesota Multiphasic Personality Inventory (MMPI)

behavioral assessment

ANSWERS TO DEMONSTRATIONS

Demonstration 14.2   1. A;   2. E;   3. C;   4. B;   5. D;   6. E.

RECOMMENDED READINGS

Aiken, L. R. (1989). *Assessment of personality*. Boston: Allyn & Bacon. Lewis Aiken's very readable textbook includes material on test construction, specific self-report inventories, and projective techniques.

Anastasi, A. (1988). *Psychological testing* (6th ed.). New York: Macmillan. Anne Anastasi's textbook is one of psychology's classics; it provides an excellent, in-depth discussion of test construction, social and ethical considerations, and intelligence and personality tests.

Kail, R., & Pellegrino, J. W. (1985). *Human intelligence: Perspectives and prospects.* New York: Freeman. This book inspects intelligence theory at a level appropriate for intermediate students; it contrasts the traditional theories of intelligence with the information-processing approach, Piaget's approach, and more recent perspectives.

Sternberg, R. J. (1988). *The triarchic mind: A new theory of human intelligence.* New York: Viking. Robert Sternberg wrote this book for a more popular audience than his more academically oriented book, *Beyond IQ. The Triarchic Mind* discusses other theories of intelligence and examines the triarchic view in detail, providing applications as well.

Walsh, W. B., & Betz, N. E. (1990). *Tests and assessment* (2nd ed.). Englewood Cliffs, NJ: Prentice Hall. This clearly written textbook provides a good summary of test construction and the assessment of personality, cognitive ability, and career interests. Another interesting topic is the assessment of environment (e.g., the quality of a college's environment).

Psychological Disorders

At 30 years of age, Karen constantly worried about the safety of her four children. On one occasion, she imagined that her son had broken his leg at school. Karen even called the school to see if he had been harmed, but she continued to worry despite reassurances. Specific numbers had acquired a special meaning to Karen, and this preoccupation interfered with her everyday chores. When she went grocery shopping, Karen believed that if she selected the first item on the shelf—such as a box of cereal—then something terrible would certainly happen to her oldest child. Choosing the second, third, or fourth item would similarly doom one of the other children. Furthermore, she felt compelled to smoke four cigarettes in a row to avoid harm to all four children (adapted from Oltmanns et al., 1986).

Debra, at age 22, had an image of herself as a totally useless person. She reported to an interviewer that she felt as if she were "litter" . . . a piece of drifting newspaper that was being blown along the sidewalk and being kicked aside. Debra felt like "excess matter in the universe, unwanted and without value" (adapted from Scarf, 1979).

Rich, who was 26 years old, was removed from an airplane by the airport police when he created a disturbance. When he was brought to the hospital, he claimed he was Jesus Christ and that he could move mountains. His speech was largely incoherent. For instance, he wanted to leave the city "because things happen here I don't approve of. I approve of other things and I don't approve of the other things. And believe me it's worse for them in the end." He also complained that the Devil wanted to kill him and that his food contained "ground-up corpses" (adapted from Carson et al., 1988).

Everyone reading this textbook has at some time worried needlessly about a friend's safety. Everyone has at least occasionally felt depressed. And everyone has uttered a garbled sentence or two. However, Karen, Debra, and Rich have psychological problems that interfere with their normal functioning. Before considering specific psychological problems, let us discuss some general problems in defining and diagnosing mental disorders.

Background on Psychological Disorders

Defining Psychological Disorders

It is obvious that no clear-cut boundary divides psychologically well-adjusted people from those with disorders. However, psychologists often specify that psychological disorders involve behavior that is both infrequent and maladaptive (Gorenstein, 1984). Let us look at these components.

1. *Infrequent.*   A person's thoughts and behaviors are considered disordered if they are statistically rare in the general population. For instance, most people do not claim to be Jesus Christ, and most do not think that the Devil is trying to kill them. However, infrequency cannot be our only criterion, because intellectual geniuses are not classified as disordered, even though they are statistically rare.

Gary Kasparov, a recent world chess champion, plays chess simultaneously with seven humans and one computer. His chess skill is statistically rare, but it would not be considered a disorder because it is not maladaptive.

2. *Maladaptive.* Infrequent behaviors are more likely to be considered abnormal if they are harmful and disabling in an individual's social setting. Geniuses and chess champions are not harmed by their intellectual capacity or their strategies in a chess game. In contrast, Karen's everyday life is hindered by her obsessive-compulsive behavior. Debra's depression interferes with her work and leisure activities. Rich's schizophrenia prevents normal language and thought processes, and it clearly limits his social interactions.

In addition, some psychologists include another characteristic: The thoughts and behaviors should cause emotional distress to oneself. A problem with this criterion arises, however, when we consider certain psychological problems such as antisocial personality disorder, discussed at the end of this chapter. These people cause great harm to other individuals, and yet they feel no remorse or distress. Consequently, the characteristic of emotional distress is not essential in the definition of psychological disorders.

Diagnosing Psychological Disorders

Psychologists have identified the general components of psychological disorders. A second issue is the diagnosis of specific disorders. Typically, a mental health professional first conducts a diagnostic interview, which includes questions about the person's social relationships, psychological functioning, family background, and any previous psychological disorders. The responses to the questions convey useful information, but the diagnostic interview also provides the interviewer with an impression of the individual's general appearance, mood, and cognitive functioning. The interviewer may also administer a psychological test such as the Minnesota Multiphasic Personality Interview (MMPI), discussed in the previous chapter.

The most frequently used resource for classifying psychological disorders is the **Diagnostic and Statistical Manual of Mental Disorders**, or **DSM** (McReynolds, 1989). The first edition was published in 1952. The most recent edition, called the *DSM-III-R* (or third edition, revised) was published in 1987. The *DSM-*

III-R describes 17 major categories of psychological disorders, which include approximately 230 conditions.

The current edition describes specific criteria that must be met before a diagnosis can be assigned. The list of disorders and the criteria change over time to reflect recent research and current beliefs. For example, earlier editions of the *DSM* considered homosexuality to be a disorder. However, mental health professionals now acknowledge that being gay or lesbian does not mean that someone has a psychological problem.

Some professionals object to any diagnostic instrument that tries to specify who is normal and who is not. Consider a well-known study that added to the controversy. Dr. David Rosenhan, a psychologist, asked several other professionals to join him in testing the validity of psychiatric diagnoses. Each person was instructed to arrive at a mental hospital, complaining of just one symptom. In particular, they were to report that they had heard voices during the last 3 weeks that said "empty," "hollow," and "thud." Otherwise, they acted normally and provided accurate information to the hospital staff. Rosenhan (1973) found that all the pseudopatients were admitted to the mental hospital with a diagnosis of schizophrenia—a very serious disorder. They were kept in the hospital an average of 19 days. Furthermore, the hospital staff interpreted the pseudopatients' normal behavior as being abnormal. For instance, when Rosenhan took notes, note taking was considered a symptom of schizophrenia.

Rosenhan's study illustrated that psychiatric personnel have difficulty judging who is really disturbed and who is really normal. The study also demonstrated the effects of psychiatric labeling. Once an individual receives a label indicating a psychological disorder, all subsequent behavior is interpreted in terms of that label. In chapter 17, we see additional examples of how stereotypes can influence people's interpretations of behavior.

As you can imagine, Rosenhan's study provoked debate. Some felt that his results suggested that psychiatric diagnosis was invalid. Others pointed out that the staff at psychiatric hospitals would have been inhumane to turn away anyone who complained about hearing voices (Spitzer, 1975). However, it is safe to say that this study demonstrated that the mental health system has a bias toward an immediate diagnosis of "disordered" rather than "normal." The study may have inspired many psychologists and other mental health professionals to be more cautious in their diagnoses.

Chapter 14 considered the issue of reliability in psychological assessment. An ideal diagnostic system should produce reliable diagnoses, so that two professionals would provide the same diagnosis for an individual. In general, the reliability of the *Diagnostic and Statistical Manual* has been moderately strong, though not close to the ideal reliability of 1.00 (Eysenck et al., 1983).

Approaches to Psychological Disorders

In this chapter, we examine the general categories of psychological disorders listed in Table 15.1. In each of the four sections, we also consider the theoretical explanations for these disorders. We discussed most of these explanations in earlier chapters in this book. The approaches we consider include the following:

1. The *biological approach* explains disorders in terms of brain structure, brain chemistry, genetic factors, hormones, and other biological factors. People who favor this approach argue that psychological problems are comparable to physical problems. Just as an earache has specific biological causes, symptoms, and treatment, the biological approach suggests that disorders such as depression have biological causes, symptoms, and treatments. However, some psychologists protest the "biologicalization" of psychological problems. For example, Carson

Table 15.1   *Psychological Disorders Discussed in Chapter 15*

A. Disorders based on anxiety
  1. Anxiety disorders
    a. Generalized anxiety disorders
    b. Panic disorders and agoraphobia
    c. Phobic disorders
    d. Obsessive-compulsive disorders
  2. Somatoform disorders
    a. Conversion disorder
    b. Hypochondriasis

  3. Dissociative disorders
    a. Amnesia
    b. Fugue
    c. Multiple personality disorder
B. Mood disorders
  1. Major depression
  2. Bipolar disorder
C. Schizophrenic disorders
D. Personality disorders
  1. Antisocial personality disorder
  2. Other personality disorders

(1988) argues that all psychological disorders should not be interpreted in biological terms, as if a person with a disorder is simply a passive victim, with no responsibility for changing his or her condition.

2. The *psychoanalytic approach* argues that psychological disorders arise from conflicts among the three forces: the id (which consists of unconscious instincts), the ego (which serves as mediator between the id and reality), and the superego (which consists of society's moral standards). When the ego fears that it will lose a conflict, it protects itself against anxiety by using defense mechanisms. The exaggerated use of these defense mechanisms produces psychological disorders. Other disorders arise when adult emotional experiences trigger emotions associated with childhood losses. For instance, the death of a spouse might evoke the anger a person once felt toward rejecting parents. Psychoanalytic theorists believe that depression represents anger turned inward against oneself.

3. The *behaviorist approach* looks outward to stimuli and reinforcers in the environment, rather than inward to forces within the individual. Thus, psychological disorders can be explained by a person's learning history. For instance, behaviorists propose that anxiety occurs when a person encounters a stimulus that was previously associated with stressful consequences. Furthermore, behaviorists would suggest that depression is caused by a general decrease in reinforcement (Salinger, 1988a).

4. The *social cognitive approach* emphasizes observational learning, which helps us understand how people can acquire some irrational fears by watching other people's actions (e.g., a child can acquire a fear of spiders by observing a parent's fearful behavior). Additional psychological disorders are caused by inappropriate interpretations of situations, for example, concluding that one low score on an exam indicates general incompetence in all academic endeavors. The social cognitive approach also points out that psychological disorders are related to people's feelings that they are not effective, competent individuals.

5. The *sociocultural approach* examines how social and cultural factors influence mental health. For instance, we will note that schizophrenia is more common in lower social classes. People living in poverty—with inadequate nutrition, poor housing, and the constant threat of crime—experience more stress than people in higher income brackets (Kessler et al., 1985). The sociocultural approach also emphasizes that minority-group members and women are more likely to experience discrimination and low status. As a consequence, psychological disorders are more common in these groups. For instance, we will see that disorders such as phobias and depression occur much more often among women than among men. In short, the sociocultural perspective emphasizes the need to look outside the individual

The sociocultural approach emphasizes that people living in poverty experience more stress, which leads to psychological disorders.

to find the source of psychological disorders. The real villains are poverty and society's discrimination against certain groups of people.

Section Summary: Background on Psychological Disorders

- Psychological disorders involve behavior that is infrequent and maladaptive.
- The diagnosis of a disorder begins with a diagnostic interview; classification of the disorder is typically based on the criteria in the *DSM-III-R*.
- Critics of the diagnosis process object to the general tendency to provide an immediate diagnosis based on inadequate information; however, the *DSM-III-R* has fairly strong reliability.
- Approaches to psychological disorders include the biological approach (abnormalities in the brain's structure and chemistry); the psychoanalytic approach (internal conflicts and defense mechanisms); the behaviorist approach (stimuli, reinforcers, and learning history); the social cognitive approach (observational learning and cognitive factors); and the sociocultural approach (cultural factors and societal inequalities).

Disorders Based on Anxiety

In this section, we consider a variety of disorders related to anxiety. People who experience these disorders usually report being unhappy, and their behavior is maladaptive. These people typically live in the community, however, rather than in a hospital setting. It is estimated that this group of anxiety-based disorders affects between 8% and 15% of adults in the United States (National Institute of Mental Health, 1985). In other words, about 20 million Americans are anxious, unhappy, afraid, and functioning at a level substantially below their potential.

We begin by discussing the most common of these disorders, known simply as anxiety disorders. Then we look briefly at two other categories, the somatoform disorders and the dissociative disorders.

Anxiety Disorders

Try to imagine that you are the student described in the following passage:

> *Usually, I'll be doing something, for instance, one day I had a real mild panic attack just standing around talking to some other people, and they'll mention one word. . . . Immediately when the word or episode or whatever is mentioned . . . I'll just withdraw into myself and start fighting anxiety, going "Well why is talking about math bothering me now? You know, I don't have a test coming up." . . . I try to talk myself out of it . . . which sometimes helps. . . . But generally I'll feel hot and the heat will come and go for up to like a half hour and if it continues I'll start getting nauseated, and the nausea will come and go. And then I get kind of shaking and I can't concentrate on anything. My mind just keeps hoppin' and skipping all around. . . . (Taylor & Arnow, 1988, p. 9)*

Most of us feel anxious from time to time. It is reasonable to feel anxious when facing a test for which you are unprepared, when you are about to go on stage for your first solo musical performance, and when you are worried about the outcome of a friend's surgery. However, when anxiety persists—without any clear explanation—and when that anxiety causes intense suffering, these problems are called **anxiety disorders**. Let us consider four of these disorders: generalized anxiety disorders; panic disorders and agoraphobia; phobic disorders; and obsessive-compulsive disorders.

Generalized Anxiety Disorders   **Generalized anxiety disorders** are characterized by continuous, long-lasting uneasiness and tension. People with this disorder cannot identify a specific cause of their anxiety. They also have physical symptoms such as nausea, dizziness, and muscle tension. A diagnosis of generalized anxiety disorder requires that a person report excessive anxiety about two or more life circumstances (e.g., school work and finances) for at least 6 months (American Psychiatric Association, 1987; Gorman, 1987).

Generalized anxiety disorders clearly disrupt normal thought processes. For instance, 86% of people with these disorders reported difficulty in concentration, and 55% said they were unable to recall important things (Beck et al., 1985). As you can imagine, a person with generalized anxiety disorder would find it difficult to study for an exam, perform well at work, or enjoy a conversation with friends.

Panic Disorders and Agoraphobia   **Panic disorders** are marked by recurrent attacks of overwhelming anxiety that occur suddenly and unexpectedly. Whereas generalized anxiety disorders are continuous, panic disorders involve specific panic attacks that occur without forewarning. Someone in the midst of a panic attack may feel smothering sensations, severe chest pains, and a fear of dying. (In fact, it can often be mistaken for a heart attack.) After several severe panic attacks, people often become very concerned about when their next panic will occur. If they are worried that the panic attack will occur in public, the condition can sometimes lead to agoraphobia (Turner et al., 1986).

Agoraphobia is the fear of being in public places or situations where escape is difficult. People with agoraphobia are afraid of situations such as traveling on a bus, being in a crowd, and leaving their home. About 80% of people with agoraphobia are female (Chambless & Goldstein, 1980). Clearly, agoraphobia is disabling. For example, one woman with this disorder no longer left her house. Even when her husband remained home with her, she continued to be frightened (Fodor, 1982). Or consider this description from an agoraphobic young man in medical school:

> The first lecture of the day is at 9 a.m. and that means . . . facing a crowded lecture theater. I push toward the building, eyes down, conscious of my wet palms. Fortunately there is an aisle seat. My heart leaps when the door is closed. I fear that I will need to leave during the lecture, embarrassing myself as I stumble to the door, but I manage to stay. . . . In the crowded room the atmosphere is stifling. Part of me wants to be outside. I feel blasts of panic anxiety. (Wardman, 1985, pp. 33–34)

Agoraphobics become extremely anxious in places where it is difficult to escape, such as this crowded subway car.

Phobic Disorders   A **phobic disorder** is an excessive fear of a specific object, activity, or situation. This fear is out of proportion to the true danger, and it cannot be eliminated by rational thought. People with phobias realize that their fears are unreasonable (Marks, 1987). They avoid the feared object or situation, even if it means missing a pleasurable activity.

Many phobias involve a specific fear about one kind of object or animal. Common phobias include fears of snakes, insects, spiders, and mice (King et al., 1988). About 95% of people with these phobias are females (Fodor, 1982). Phobias often begin in childhood, and they may lead to a lifetime of planning, in order to avoid the feared object. For example, one woman had a butterfly phobia, which led her to avoid trips to the country. She eventually consulted a therapist when

Common phobias involve fear of snakes, insects, spiders, and mice.

the phobia began to interfere with a relationship with a man who liked to spend weekends in the country (Fodor, 1982).

People who have a social phobia experience excessive fear of social situations. They are afraid that they will do something embarrassing in public. A person with a social phobia may be afraid to speak in front of others—even in a nonthreatening situation. Males and females are equally likely to suffer from social phobias (Fodor, 1982). Notice that the phobias discussed in this section can disrupt one's life. Phobias are not as disabling as agoraphobia, however, where the victim may be unable to leave home.

Obsessive-Compulsive Disorders   Obsessive thoughts and compulsive actions are parts of everyday life for many of us. We check a third time to make certain that an airplane ticket is safe in a pocket. We refuse to eat with a fork that has dropped on a recently cleaned floor, even though it is clear that contamination is unlikely. It is only when these obsessive thoughts become frequent and intense—or when the compulsive rituals begin to interfere with a person's functioning—that the diagnosis of obsessive-compulsive disorder is made (Baer & Jenike, 1986).

Obsessive-compulsive disorders are relatively rare disabling conditions that involve recurrent, time-consuming obsessions and/or compulsions (American Psychiatric Association, 1987; Turner et al., 1985). **Obsessions** are persistent, unwanted thoughts that are unreasonable. Typical obsessions include worry over germs or illness (e.g., worry about becoming infected by shaking someone's hand) and excessive concerns about others (e.g., concern about being responsible for someone's injury).

Obsessions focus on persistent *thoughts*, whereas compulsions focus on persistent *actions*. That is, **compulsions** are repetitive behaviors performed according to certain rules, in response to obsessive thoughts. People with this disorder usually realize that their compulsive behavior is unreasonable. Common compulsions include hand washing, counting, and checking (e.g., checking the location of an object). Karen's behavior, described in the first paragraph of this chapter, is an example of a later stage of an obsessive-compulsive disorder.

Clinicians stress that people with little training in psychology or psychiatry often misuse the terms *obsessive* and *compulsive* (Reed, 1985). In a conversation, a friend may refer to her sister's obsession with golf. Another friend may complain about his roommate's compulsive studying. However, the sister and the roommate probably believe that their behavior is appropriate, that they are acting by conscious choice, and that they enjoy spending time and energy on these activities. In contrast, obsessive-compulsives realize that their behavior is inappropriate; they do not choose to behave in that way, and they do not enjoy it. True obsessive-compulsive disorders are extremely disabling, not simply inconvenient.

Table 15.2 summarizes the four major kinds of anxiety disorders we have discussed so far. Now we consider two other related problems, the somatoform disorders and the dissociative disorders.

Somatoform Disorders

The **somatoform disorders** are anxiety-based problems in which the individual complains about physical illnesses and problems, yet no organic explanation can be found. Notice that the distinctive feature of these somatoform disorders is a concern about one's body. (In contrast, the generalized anxiety disorders, phobias, and obsessive-compulsive disorders—which we have just discussed—did not focus on physical complaints.) The physical symptoms in the somatoform disorders are not intentionally produced; a person with this disorder cannot consciously control which symptoms he or she will experience (American Psychiatric Association, 1987).

Table 15.2   *The Anxiety Disorders*

NAME	DESCRIPTION
a. Generalized anxiety disorders	Continuous, long-lasting uneasiness and tension
b. Panic disorders and agoraphobia	Recurrent attacks of overwhelming anxiety (panic disorder), which often lead to a fear of being in public places (agoraphobia)
c. Phobic disorders	Excessive fear of a specific object, activity, or situation
d. Obsessive-compulsive disorders	Persistent, unwanted, unreasonable thoughts (obsessions) and repetitive behaviors performed according to rules (compulsions)

We look at two kinds of somatoform disorders: conversion disorder and hypochondriasis.

Conversion Disorder   **Conversion disorders** are characterized by a loss in physical functioning of some body part—with no medical explanation for the condition. Conversion disorders are usually triggered by some traumatic event. A person suddenly becomes blind or deaf, or may report complete loss of feeling in one hand.

The *DSM III-R* notes that conversion disorders apparently express a psychological conflict or need (American Psychiatric Association, 1987). Specifically, the *DSM III-R* suggests some purposes that a conversion disorder could serve. For instance, during wartime a soldier might develop a "paralyzed" arm, to avoid firing a gun. A person who is experiencing conflicts about dependency may develop an inability to walk, to prevent a spouse from leaving the marriage.

In earlier eras, people believed that someone could be suddenly "struck blind," and physicians lacked sophisticated equipment to examine the neurological basis for these disorders. Conversion disorders were also fairly common during World Wars I and II, when soldiers with conversion disorders could avoid combat situations (Carson et al., 1988). However, conversion disorders are relatively rare in the 1990s.

Hypochondriasis   The disorder known as **hypochondriasis** involves persistent anxiety about having a serious disease—one that could even be deadly. Hypochondriasis (pronounced "high-poe-konn-*drie*-uh-siss") is typically characterized by numerous physical complaints and a wide variety of problems. Hypochondriacs continually visit the hospital or medical office, yet their physicians report no physical problems. Hypochondriacs are seldom reassured, however, and their anxiety persists.

As you might imagine, people who have had previous experience with a true disease are particularly likely to become hypochondriacs. A man who has had a previous heart attack or a woman whose sister has had breast cancer are alert for even minor physical symptoms. These people *should* be concerned about early indicators of illness. However, hypochondriacs are so excessively worried and preoccupied with illness that the anxiety interferes with normal living.

Dissociative Disorders

The dissociative disorders resemble the somatoform disorders because both are reactions to extreme stress. However, the somatoform disorders involve physical symptoms. In contrast, dissociative disorders involve psychological symptoms. Specifically, the **dissociative disorders** actually split off (or dissociate) a person's

The medicine cabinet of a hypochondriac, who takes many medications for imagined disorders.

This woman, who came to be known as "Jane Doe," suffered from severe dissociative amnesia.

identity, memory, or consciousness. Ordinary people have a sense of who they are. They remember their life events, and they are conscious of their attributes and surroundings. People with dissociative disorders suddenly lose their memory or change their identity. It is important to stress that dissociative disorders are relatively rare, even though the soap operas and tabloid newspapers are over-populated with cases of amnesia and multiple personality.

Amnesia   Dissociative **amnesia** involves forgetting of past experiences, following a stressful event. We all have less than perfect memories, as chapter 7 noted. However, amnesia is characterized by extensive memory loss. The amnesia may be limited to a specific time period surrounding a traumatic episode, or a person may forget his or her entire life history.

An example of this second, less common kind of amnesia is a woman dubbed Jane Doe, who was discovered by a Florida park ranger in 1980. She was incoherent, covered with animal and insect bites, and close to death. She could not recall her name or her past, and she was unable to read or write. An older couple in Illinois was certain that Jane Doe was their daughter, who had opened a store in Florida several years earlier. However, the young woman never recalled her past (Carson et al., 1988).

Fugue   The word *fugue* (pronounced "fewg") is derived from the Latin word for *flight*. The critical features of **fugue** disorders are (1) sudden, unplanned travel away from a familiar location, (2) assumption of a new identity, and (3) inability to recall one's earlier identity. Occasionally, a victim of fugue takes on an entirely new life and a more outgoing personality. More often, a fugue is less dramatic, involving briefer travel and an incomplete new identity.

Fugue disorders typically follow severe stress, such as a natural disaster or a serious quarrel with one's spouse. People usually recover rapidly from fugue disorders. However, they typically recall none of the events that occurred during the fugue period.

Multiple Personality Disorder   The critical feature of amnesia is forgetting, and the critical features of fugue are travel, a new identity, and forgetting the old identity. In contrast, **multiple personality disorders** occur when a person has two or more distinct, well-developed personalities (American Psychiatric Association, 1987). An individual with this disorder may shift from one personality to the other as often as every few minutes . . . or as rarely as every few years. Typically, the personalities are dramatically different from each other. Multiple personality disorder therefore involves a distinctive unawareness of one's other personalities.

Consider the case of Paula, a college student who received A's on the first two exams in a college course but failed to appear for the third exam (Oltmanns et al., 1986). Paula's instructor suggested that she speak with a psychologist after Paula had written an essay about a long-term abusive and incestuous relationship with her father. The psychologist learned that Paula had developed a second personality, named Sherry, when she was in high school, in response to her father's sexual abuse. The psychologist had initially thought that Paula was faking a dramatic set of symptoms to win the sympathy of her family. He later accepted the multiple personality classification, however, because Paula was not knowledgeable about the characteristics of this disorder and because she had no clear motive for *pretending* to have multiple personalities. Paula seemed to experience a genuine disruption of consciousness because when her father became abusive, the studious Paula would "leave" the situation, and irresponsible Sherry would be left to deal with him.

Table 15.3   *The Somatoform Disorders and Dissociative Disorders*

NAME	DESCRIPTION
1. Somatoform Disorders	Physical illness without an organic explanation
a. Conversion disorder	Loss in physical functioning of a body part
b. Hypochondriasis	Persistent anxiety about having a serious disease
2. Dissociative Disorders	Splitting off of a person's identity, memory, or consciousness
a. Amnesia	Forgetting of past experiences
b. Fugue	Sudden travel and adoption of a new identity
c. Multiple personality disorder	Two or more distinct, well-developed personalities

Multiple personality disorders are extremely intriguing, but they are also rare. Some authorities estimate that only between 100 and 300 genuine cases have been reported (Oltmanns et al., 1986), though others propose much higher estimates (Kluft, 1987). Clearly, this disorder represents an unusually severe form of a loss of personal identity. Table 15.3 summarizes the varieties of somatoform disorders and dissociative disorders that we have discussed in this section.

Explaining Disorders Based on Anxiety

We have considered a variety of psychological disorders, each connected with anxiety. Some of these disorders, such as a specific phobia, may have little impact on an individual's life. Others, such as agoraphobia and multiple personality disorder, cause major disruptions in interpersonal relationships, performance at work, and ability to enjoy life. How does anxiety arise, and why does it produce the particular symptoms we have outlined? We now discuss how several of the explanations introduced at the beginning of the chapter account for one or more of the anxiety-based disorders.

The Biological Approach   Some investigators maintain that genetic factors are important in the acquisition of anxiety disorders such as agoraphobia (Andreasen, 1984). For instance, a person is more likely to develop agoraphobia if he or she has a sibling or parent with this disorder than if no close relatives are afflicted (Harris et al., 1983). However, several explanations are possible for these data. Indeed, hereditary factors could be responsible for a mother and daughter both developing agoraphobia. However, it is also likely that the daughter had many opportunities to watch her mother's fearful behavior; the kind of observational learning discussed in chapter 6 could account for the daughter's modeling of her mother's agoraphobia.

It is possible that biological factors may play a role in obsessive-compulsive disorders. For instance, Turner and his colleagues (1985) discuss electroencephalogram (EEG) disorders that have been reported in some obsessive-compulsive people. However, they admit that the abnormalities are not consistent.

In summary, certain studies hint at possible biological underpinnings for some of the disorders we have discussed. However, the evidence is not strong, and psychosocial explanations seem more powerful.

The Psychoanalytic Approach   Sigmund Freud suggested that anxiety can be caused by a variety of events, such as separation from mother or a fear of castration (removal of the genitals). Anxiety is therefore a signal of unconscious fantasies about dangerous situations (Freud, 1909; Taylor & Arnow, 1988). This anxiety stimulates a variety of defense mechanisms. As discussed in chapter 13, defense mechanisms can sometimes be helpful. But psychological disorders result from overusing them. For example, psychoanalytic theorists would suggest that people develop phobias as a defense mechanism, to protect themselves from repressed conflicts that are too painful to confront (Davison & Neale, 1986).

The Social Cognitive Approach   Some time ago, theorists proposed that phobias resulted from classical conditioning. However, as noted in the learning chapter, most people with phobias cannot recall a traumatic conditioning event to account for their fears (Barlow, 1988; Mineka, 1986; Taylor & Arnow, 1988). Instead, those who trace anxiety disorders to learning now favor an observational learning approach.

For example, children learn to be afraid of dentists by modeling their parents' anxious behavior in the dentist's office (Bandura, 1986; Craig, 1978). Furthermore, the children of hypochondriacs model their parents' excessive concern with body ailments (Carson et al., 1988; Kellner, 1985). Disorders are therefore produced by observing inappropriate models (Merluzzi et al., 1986). Children learn not only specific behaviors, but also more generalized schemas and expectations about responding to stressful situations.

Another important social cognitive factor in anxiety disorders is self-efficacy, or the feeling people have that they are competent and effective. Individuals with phobias rate themselves low in self-efficacy; after treatment for the phobia, their self-efficacy rises (Bandura, 1982b; Taylor & Arnow, 1988).

The Sociocultural Approach   We noted earlier that the majority of people with simple phobias and agoraphobia are female. The reason for this finding is not clear, but gender stereotypes probably encourage women to be passive and dependent. Agoraphobic women, for example, are likely to have little experience living on their own. Women are socialized to be dependent on other people, and agoraphobics receive a stronger dose of this message (Fodor, 1982; Padawer & Goldfried, 1984).

We have considered a variety of approaches to the explanation of disorders based on anxiety. At present, however, no single explanation seems ideal (Taylor & Arnow, 1988). Furthermore, psychologists have no clear explanation for why one person develops agoraphobia, whereas another develops hypochondriasis. The only safe conclusion is that an adequate explanation of these disorders must be complex, incorporating perhaps a biological component as well as observational learning, low self-efficacy, and sociocultural factors.

Section Summary: Disorders Based on Anxiety

- Generalized anxiety disorder involves continuous uneasiness and tension, typically accompanied by disrupted thought processes.
- Panic disorders entail recurrent attacks of overwhelming anxiety, which may lead to agoraphobia, or a fear of being in public places where escape is impossible.
- Phobic disorders are characterized by an excessive fear of a specific object, activity, or situation.
- Another kind of anxiety disorder, called obsessive-compulsive disorders, involves persistent, unwanted thoughts (obsessions) and repetitive behaviors based on those obsessions (compulsions).

- The somatoform disorders include conversion disorders, which involve the loss in physical functioning of some body part (with no medical basis), and hypochondriasis, or persistent anxiety about serious diseases.
- The dissociative disorders involve a splitting off of one's identity or memory; they include amnesia (forgetting past experiences), fugue (assuming a new identity following unplanned travel), and multiple personality disorder (developing two or more distinctive personalities).
- An explanation of disorders based on anxiety might involve some biological component, but it probably relies more on psychosocial factors.

Mood Disorders

Sylvia Plath was an American writer whose novel, *The Bell Jar*, is frequently assigned in both literature and psychology of women courses. The novel is largely autobiographical, because it traces its heroine's struggles with depression and suicidal tendencies. In 1963, Plath carefully stuffed towels into the cracks around the kitchen door, and gassed herself in the oven of her stove. The following passage from *The Bell Jar* reveals her experiences with depression:

> I hadn't washed my hair for three weeks. I hadn't slept for seven nights. My mother told me I must have slept, it was impossible not to sleep in all that time, but if I slept, it was with my eyes wide open. . . . The reason I hadn't washed my clothes or my hair was because it seemed so silly. I saw the days of the year stretching ahead like a series of bright, white boxes, and separating one box from another was sleep, like a black shade. Only for me, the long perspective of shades that set off one box from the next had suddenly snapped up, and I could see day after day glaring ahead of me like a white, broad, infinitely desolate avenue. It seemed silly to wash one day when I would only have to wash again the next. It made me tired just to think of it. (Plath, 1971, pp. 142–143)

The primary characteristic of **mood disorders** is persistent, extreme disturbances of mood or emotional state. One kind of mood disorder is called **major depression**, and it is characterized by frequent episodes of intense hopelessness and lowered self-esteem (see Figure 15.1). The other kind of mood disorder is less

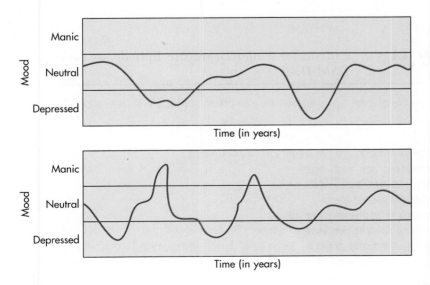

Figure 15.1
Mood patterns for a typical person with major depression (top figure) versus a typical person with bipolar disorder (bottom figure).

common. In **bipolar disorders**, a person sometimes experiences depressive episodes and sometimes experiences mania. **Mania** is an abnormally positive, overexcited state, accompanied by high self-esteem.

We first discuss the general characteristics of major depression, followed by an in-depth examination of the social interactions of depressed people. Then we consider why women are more likely than men to develop depression. After an overview of bipolar disorders, we discuss several theoretical approaches to the explanation of depression.

The Characteristics of Major Depression

From time to time, you have probably felt dissatisfied and discouraged. Most people have occasional periods in which they feel isolated from other people or pessimistic about the future or lacking in energy. Sometimes these episodes can be traced to a specific stressful event, such as the death of a relative or the breakup of a love relationship. In most cases, these discouraged moods improve. However, a substantial number of Americans experience a major depressive episode at some point in their lives. Table 15.4 lists nine criteria for a major depressive episode; note that a diagnosis requires evidence of at least five of these criteria. Researchers estimate that about 10% of men and about 20% of women experience a major depressive episode during their lifetime (Boyd & Weissman, 1981). Later in this section, we look more closely at this gender difference.

Some people with major depression experience only one major depressive episode during their lifetime. However, data indicate that about half of people who have successfully recovered from a major depressive episode will have a relapse within 2 years (Belsher & Costello, 1988).

Depression can be disabling because it influences most aspects of psychological functioning—emotions, cognitive performance, and behavior. Depressed people are also likely to report physical problems, such as indigestion, headaches, dizzy spells, and generalized pain (Beck & Greenberg, 1974; Lewinsohn et al., 1976). As you can imagine, these physical problems are likely to make a person even more depressed. Let us focus, however, on the psychological components of depression.

Emotions   Depressed people describe themselves as feeling apathetic, discouraged, and hopeless (Oltmanns et al., 1986). They tend to have negative feelings about themselves, the world, and the future.

Table 15.4   *Criteria for Major Depressive Episode, as Listed in the DSM-III-R*

At least five of these nine symptoms must be present during a two-week period:

1. depressed mood
2. reduced interest in almost all activities
3. significant weight gain or weight loss, without dieting
4. insomnia or too much sleep
5. too much or too little motor activity
6. fatigue or loss of energy
7. feelings of worthlessness or guilt
8. reduced ability to concentrate or think
9. recurrent thoughts of death

Source: Based on American Psychiatric Association, 1987.

Consider the research of Paula Pietromonaco and Hazel Markus (1985), which is related to Markus's work on self-concept discussed in chapter 13. These authors administered the Beck Depression Inventory to college students; Demonstration 15.1 illustrates several items similar to those on the test. On the basis of scores on this test, people were assigned to either the depressed or the nondepressed group.

As part of the study, people were asked to form a mental image of a specified emotional event. Half of the events were happy (e.g., "your professor praises your paper") and half were sad (e.g., "You overhear someone saying you are selfish"). In each case, the participants rated the clarity of their mental picture of the event.

As you can see from Figure 15.2, the depressed and the nondepressed participants responded similarly to the happy events. However, depressed people visualize a sad event much more vividly than nondepressed people can. For example, they can easily create a clear mental image of other people commenting on their selfishness.

Depressed people are also more likely to report that thoughts about negative emotions emerge automatically in their daily life. For instance, depressed psychiatric patients were likely to report that they often had negative thoughts, such as "I'm no good," "My life is a mess," and "My future is bleak" (Eaves & Rush, 1984).

Demonstration 15.1

Assessing Depression

Think about how you have felt during the last *week*, including today. Carefully inspect each set of statements and circle the number in front of the item that most accurately describes your feelings.

A. 1. I have not felt sad during the past week.
   2. I have felt occasional sadness.
   3. I have felt sad most of the time.
   4. I have felt so sad that it's unbearable.

B. 1. I have never cried during the past week.
   2. I have cried once or twice during the past week.
   3. I have cried often during the past week.
   4. I used to cry often, but now I am so sad I'm beyond crying.

C. 1. Life is about as satisfying as it has been in the past.
   2. I don't enjoy life as much as I used to.
   3. It's hard to find satisfaction with life now.
   4. Everything about my life is dissatisfying.

D. 1. People are just as interesting as they have always been.
   2. People aren't as interesting as they used to be.
   3. Most people aren't interesting to me.
   4. I've lost my interest in other people.

E. 1. I am just as efficient as I've always been.
   2. It's hard to be as efficient as I've been in the past.
   3. I really have to push myself to get things done.
   4. Somehow I can't accomplish anything these days.

G. 1. I am fairly happy with myself.
   2. I feel neutral about myself.
   3. I am disappointed in myself.
   4. I hate myself.

To score your answers, add up all the points. *It is important to stress that this is not a standardized test of depression, and no 6-item test can assess depression accurately.* However, people who are depressed would be likely to receive higher scores on this informal assessment.

Figure 15.2
Vividness of mental image, as a
function of instructions and depressed/
nondepressed status. (Based on
Pietromonaco & Markus, 1985)

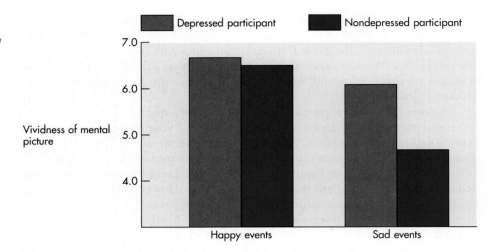

Cognitive Performance   Depressed people differ from nondepressed people in two important cognitive areas. First, depressed people provide different explanations for events in their lives. Second, depressed people perform more poorly on several kinds of cognitive tasks.

Let us look at the explanations that depressed people provide for sad and happy events. Suppose that you received a low score on your first biology examination. Try to think about the attributions you would provide for that poor performance. How would you explain it?

Depressed people are likely to provide explanations that are *internal*; they blame themselves, rather than the external circumstances. They are also likely to provide *stable* explanations, blaming a permanent characteristic, rather than one that is simply temporary. Finally, they are likely to provide *global* explanations, blaming a general tendency that applies to a variety of skills and behaviors rather than a very specific one. If a seriously depressed woman received a low biology score, for example, she might be likely to say, "This just shows how stupid I am—I'm never going to make it through college." In other words, she blames her supposed lack of ability (internal). She presumes her stupidity is long-lasting (stable). And she assumes her stupidity applies to all subjects, not just biology (global).

In contrast to the internal, stable, global attribution patterns that depressed people use to explain their poor performance, nondepressed people show a different pattern. They blame failure on external factors ("That room was too noisy"). Their attributions are also likely to involve unstable causes ("I didn't get enough sleep the night before that test"). And attributions apply only to specific areas ("I may not be great at biology, but I'm doing well in all my other courses").

Many researchers have investigated these intriguing attributional patterns. In fact, Sweeney and his colleagues (1986) managed to locate 104 studies involving about 15,000 participants. They conducted a meta-analysis, statistically combining the results of all these independent studies. The meta-analysis confirmed that an internal, stable, global attributional style regarding negative experiences was indeed characteristic of depressed people.

Depression is related not only to cognitive attributions; it is also related to cognitive performance. For instance, depressed people have difficulty concentrating and paying attention. They also are likely to have difficulty on memory tasks, particularly if they are severely depressed (Johnson & Magaro, 1987). Finally, depressed people are more worried about risks than nondepressed people are (Pietromonaco & Rook, 1987). An important consequence of this decision-making performance is that depressed people are likely to avoid social interactions

Because depressed people are more worried about risks, they tend to avoid social interactions.

that might be somewhat risky. This tendency can lead to further isolation from other people.

Behavior   In addition to emotional and cognitive changes, severely depressed people also show behavioral changes. For instance, their speed of performance decreases (Williams et al., 1988). They show decreased ability to do daily chores, let alone more complex tasks in the workplace.

The most alarming behavioral problem of serious depression is attempted suicide. Before you read further, try to answer the questions in Demonstration 15.2.

Demonstration 15.2

Myths and Realities About Suicide

Decide whether each of the following questions is true or false. Then turn the page to see the answers in Table 15.5.

_____ 1. People who actually talk about suicide are not likely to commit suicide.

_____ 2. People who attempt suicide are likely to have a high family incidence of suicide attempts.

_____ 3. Men are more likely than women to attempt suicide.

_____ 4. Men are more likely than women to actually kill themselves by suicide.

_____ 5. Suicidal people typically give many warnings about suicidal intentions.

_____ 6. Suicidal people are fully intent on dying.

_____ 7. A person who has attempted suicide is likely to have suicidal inclinations forever.

_____ 8. When a person has been severely depressed and the depression begins to lift, the danger of suicide decreases substantially.

_____ 9. Suicide is found just as often among the poor as among the rich.

_____ 10. Unemployed people are more likely to commit suicide.

Table 15.5   *Myths and Realities About Suicide: The Answers to Demonstration 15.2*

1. *False.* About 80% of people who actually commit suicide have discussed their suicidal intentions with someone.
2. *True.* A high family incidence of suicide is found among people who attempt suicide as well as among those who actually kill themselves.
3. *False.* About three times as many women as men attempt suicide.
4. *True.* About three times as many men as women actually kill themselves by suicide.
5. *True.* Research indicates that suicidal people give many clues and warnings about their suicidal intentions.
6. *False.* Most suicidal people are undecided about living or dying. They gamble with death, leaving it to others to save them.
7. *False.* People who want to kill themselves are usually suicidal for a limited period of time.
8. *False.* Suicides are most likely to occur within about 3 months of an improvement, when depressed people have the energy to put their suicide plan into effect.
9. *True.* Suicide is found at roughly the same rate in all levels of society.
10. *True.* Unemployment, financial distress, and other recent lifestyle changes increase the risk of suicide.

Sources: Boyer & Guthrie, 1985; Schneidman, 1980.

According to the statistics, about 200,000 Americans attempt suicide each year, resulting in about 15,000 deaths (Hirschfeld & Davidson, 1988). Even these chilling statistics probably underestimate the incidence of suicide, because many may disguise their suicides to look like accidents. Suicide is relevant to our discussion of depression because researchers estimate that approximately half of the people who attempted suicide were suffering from depression (Boyer & Guthrie, 1985).

This year, some of you reading this book will have a friend or family member who begins to talk about suicide. What should you do? Unfortunately, no simple formula can prevent suicide, but here is some general advice (Farberow, 1974; Shneidman, 1985):

1. *Take the suicide threat seriously.* As noted in the demonstration, people usually do give warnings about suicidal thoughts.

2. *Provide caring support.* Show genuine support for a suicidal person. Even if you know the person only slightly, provide empathy and understanding.

3. *Try to clarify the central problem.* As noted earlier, depressed people have cognitive difficulties. If you can isolate the critical problem, the situation may not seem so overwhelming.

4. *If you think a friend is suicidal, ask direct questions.* Asking "Are you thinking about killing yourself?" will not "put the idea" into your friend's mind.

5. *Suggest alternative actions.* Offer other solutions to the central problem. However, do not adopt a falsely cheerful "everything will just work out" attitude.

6. *Encourage consulting a professional.* Even if you have talked someone out of a suicide attempt, the problem needs further attention. Help the person find a counselor or other professional; offer to go along, if necessary.

7. *The worst thing you can do is nothing.* It is most important to take action and show concern; ignoring the problem is not a helpful solution.

○ ○

In Depth: The Social Interactions of Depressed People

We have considered the general characteristics of depression, including emotional, cognitive, and behavioral components. Now we turn to an in-depth discussion of the way depressed people interact with others, both strangers and close acquaintances.

Relationships With Strangers   How do college students react to a depressed class-mate they have met for the first time? In a study by Stephen Strack and James Coyne (1983), female introductory psychology students completed the Beck Depression Inventory, which contains items similar to those in Demonstration 15.1. On the basis of these scores, the researchers identified 60 nondepressed students, each of whom would carry on a conversation with one other student. These conversational partners were 30 other nondepressed students and 30 depressed students. Each pair of students were told that they were participating in a study about the casual acquaintance process. The experimenter then left the room, and the partners talked for 15 minutes. Then each student went to a different room, and they completed questionnaires.

As Figure 15.3 shows, the students who had spoken with a depressed person rated themselves as much higher in anxiety, depression, and hostility than those who had spoken with a nondepressed person. Those who had spoken with a depressed person were also more likely to say that they did not want to meet with that person again.

A number of similar studies have examined social interactions with depressed people. Although some exceptions have been found, most show that depressed people tend to be rejected (Gurtman, 1986).

What are the depressed people doing that alienates others—even after a short conversation? Unfortunately, researchers do not know exactly what behaviors produce these negative reactions (Coyne et al., 1987). One good possibility is that depressed people are apt to make negative statements about themselves. We saw earlier in this section that negative automatic thoughts are likely to emerge when people are depressed. Research by Jacobson and Anderson (1982) reveals that depressed people are likely to express these negative self-disclosures. These

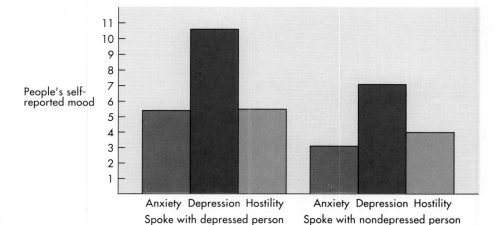

Figure 15.3
People's reactions after speaking with depressed and nondepressed individuals. (Based on Strack & Coyne, 1983)

authors found that depressed people were especially likely to make negative statements about themselves that were unsolicited—that is, their partner had not asked a question for which a negative self-disclosure would be an appropriate answer. For instance, in response to a comment about the rainy weather, a depressed person might say, "I really find I get cranky whenever it rains."

In addition, depressed people seem to be so preoccupied with negative aspects of their own lives that they cannot be successful conversational partners. The chapter on language noted that an important component of the pragmatics of conversation is being a good listener. Unfortunately, depressed people are unlikely to be helpful listeners or offer emotional support to people with whom they interact (Coyne et al., 1987). As you might imagine, this inadequacy hinders a conversation with a stranger, but it has a more important, long-term impact on close relationships.

Interactions in Close Relationships   How do depressed students interact with their roommates? Sue Ann Burchill and William Stiles (1988) used the Beck Depression Inventory to identify depressed and nondepressed college students, who then reported to the psychology lab with their roommates. In the lab, each member of the roommate pair discussed concerns that he or she had about living with the roommate. For the first 10 minutes, one person spoke while the other listened, and the two switched roles for the second 10 minutes.

One interesting observation was that when the depressed students served as listeners, they made an average of only 119 comments, in contrast to 154 comments when the nondepressed students served as listeners. In addition, the roommates of depressed students reported that they spent little waking time together, in contrast to the roommates of nondepressed students. Students also reported that they liked depressed roommates less than nondepressed roommates.

Students who interact with a depressed roommate over a number of months are likely to become somewhat depressed themselves. Mary Howes and her colleagues (1985) tracked new college students who had been assigned to a roommate with whom they were unacquainted. Through screening of Beck Depression Inventory scores, the authors identified some nondepressed students rooming with a nondepressed student and some nondepressed students who were rooming with a depressed student. The Beck Depression Inventory was then administered to all students during the 1st, 5th, and 11th week of school.

As you can see from Figure 15.4, those who were living with nondepressed people continued to receive low scores on the Beck Depression Inventory. In contrast, those who were living with depressed people grew substantially more

Figure 15.4
Average scores on the Beck Depression Index for students who had lived with a depressed or a nondepressed roommate (high scores represent more depression). (Based on Howes et al., 1985)

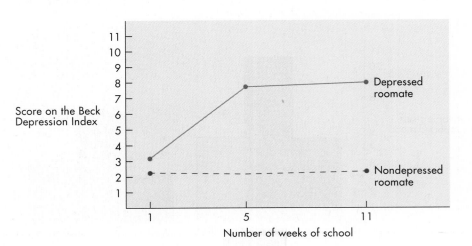

depressed as the term progressed. However, it is not clear whether the students become depressed because they begin to model their depressed roommates' moods and behavior, or because of unhappy interactions with the depressed roommates. Other research has demonstrated that people living with a depressed spouse are also more likely than others to become depressed (Coyne et al., 1987).

In summary, the studies of conversations with strangers as well as relationships with more long-term partners suggest that depressed people have a negative impact on others. This rejection by others seems likely to increase depression still further.

Gender and Depression

According to surveys, women are two to three times as likely as men to show signs of depression (e.g., Norman et al., 1984; Zigler & Glick, 1986). This same ratio holds for both Whites and Blacks in the United States as well as in most other developed countries (Jones et al., 1981; Weissman & Klerman, 1979).

Factors Related to Depression in Women Some characteristics tend to be associated with depression in women. For instance, depression is somewhat more common among divorced women, married women with several young children, women who do not work outside the home, and women who have not had an advanced education (Hammen, 1982; Jack, 1987a; Weissman, 1980).

Personal and social factors, however, are typically more helpful in predicting depression. Before you read further, try Demonstration 15.3.

Research by Schaefer and Burnett (1987) demonstrated that women were significantly more likely to be depressed if their husbands were hostile, detached,

---

Demonstration 15.3

Factors in a Male-Female Romantic Relationship

If you are a female in a romantic relationship with a male, answer the following questions from your point of view. If you are a male in a romantic relationship with a female, try to answer the questions from the female's point of view. Other students may wish to apply this demonstration to a particular male-female relationship with which they are familiar.

Answer each question *yes* or *no*. The answers appear at the end of the chapter.

1. He talks over his problems with me.
2. He is always trying to change me.
3. He respects my opinion.
4. He acts as though I am in the way.
5. He won't take no for an answer when he wants something.
6. He gives me as much freedom as I want.
7. He is always thinking of things that would please me.
8. He argues back no matter what I say.
9. He encourages me to follow my own interests.
10. He makes fun of me.
11. He wants to have the last word on how we spend our time.
12. He lets me make up my own mind.
13. He has a good time with me.
14. He wants to control everything I do.
15. He is happy to go along with my decisions.
16. He says I'm a big problem.

Source: Based on Schaefer & Burnett, 1987.

Women are likely to work at low-paying jobs and are therefore more likely to develop depression, according to one explanation for women's relatively high depression rate.

or overly controlling. Demonstration 15.3 is based on their questionnaire. Furthermore, women tend to be depressed if they derive their identity from other people, rather than from their own accomplishments (Warren & McEachren, 1983).

Why Are Women More Depressed?   Biologically based explanations do not offer satisfactory support for the gender differences in depression rates (Nolen-Hoeksema, 1987, 1990). The gender differences in depression also cannot be traced to therapist bias (Scarf, 1979). Some more likely explanations seem to be the following:

   1. *Women are less likely to find gratification in their lives* (Gove, 1980).   That is, women are depressed because low-paying jobs and housework provide little reward. People tend to be more impressed by someone with a large income than someone who is skilled in taking care of others (Jack, 1987b; Zigler & Glick, 1986).

   2. *Women are more likely to experience learned helplessness.*   The **theory of learned helplessness** proposes that people learn to be helpless when they think that the responses they make are not related to the rewards and punishments they receive (Radloff, 1975; Seligman, 1974). This helplessness leads to depression. According to this explanation, women are less likely than men to find a relationship between their efforts and what happens to them. For example, a woman is more likely than a man to see that the effort she puts into her job is not related to the rewards she receives (e.g., raises or promotions).

   3. *Women may be more likely to worry about their depression, whereas men may be more likely to distract themselves.*   When college students are depressed, women report that they are more likely to think and talk about their feelings. These activities tend to focus attention on the depression, making women even more depressed. In contrast, men are more likely to report that they do something physical or avoid thinking about the depression (Nolen-Hoeksema, 1987). Ignoring one's emotions may produce other problems, but these strategies do tend to distract men from their depressed moods.

   In this section we have looked at the characteristics of depressed people. Like Debra, the woman considered at the beginning of this chapter, depressed people believe they are unworthy—like litter in the universe. In contrast, people with a diagnosis of bipolar disorder may feel as if they are litter today, but next week they may experience such expanded self-esteem that they consider themselves among the most important individuals in the universe.

Bipolar Disorders

As discussed earlier, people with bipolar disorders sometimes experience depressive episodes and sometimes experience mania. The name *bipolar* suggests two poles. Like the two poles of the earth, depression and mania represent opposite ends of the human emotional experience. We have discussed the characteristics of depressive episodes; now let us consider the manic episodes that people with bipolar disorder also experience.

   Consider a track coach named George, who was in the midst of a manic episode when he was admitted to the hospital. George declared that he was the coach of the U.S. Olympic track team, and he offered to hold tryouts for other patients in the hospital. He rapidly paced the halls of the ward and flew into a rage at the slightest irritation. When a staff member blocked his entrance to the nursing station, George threatened to report her to the president of the Olympic committee. He had not slept for 3 days (Oltmanns et al., 1986).

   Less than 1% of the population suffers from bipolar disorders, in contrast to between 10% and 20% for depression (Andreasen, 1984). Some of the important characteristics of the manic episode phase of a bipolar disorder include the following:

1. Inflated self-esteem;

2. Decreased need for sleep;

3. Extreme talkativeness or "pressured speech";

4. Subjective experience that thoughts are racing; and

5. Excessive involvement in activities that are likely to produce painful consequences (American Psychiatric Association, 1987).

During a manic episode, people feel on top of the world. As one man recalled, "I just remember feeling wonderful. . . . Everybody else had a good time. I know they did—we were all laughing until our sides hurt, and tears came running down our faces. Wow—what a time. Yes, I remember everyone else stopping, but I didn't—I couldn't—it was as if I was out of control" (Duke & Nowicki, 1986, p. 213).

Some people with bipolar disorders have such grandiose schemes during a manic episode that they may withdraw their life savings to undertake a project that is bound to fail. Others, however, are more fortunate: Their mania may be expressed as artistic creativity. For instance, Handel composed *The Messiah* in 24 days of a manic episode. Others who are thought to have been manic-depressives include composer Hector Berlioz, playwright Eugene O'Neill, and writers Virginia Woolf and Ernest Hemingway (Leo, 1984).

We know that people in the midst of a manic episode have grandiose self-esteem and are exceedingly optimistic. However, we do not have many details about cognitive processes during mania. Several interesting studies have shown that memory is decreased during the manic state. Also, intriguingly, manic patients show more overinclusive thinking than control-group people . . . they link items together that are only remotely related (Johnson & Magaro, 1987). Do you remember Isen's research discussed in the motivation and emotion chapter? It showed that people in a happy mood were better able to appreciate subtle relationships between items. These two observations are probably connected with each other.

However, manic episodes cannot last forever. The bubble bursts, and mood returns to normal, or it may crash into a depression. The consequences of some manic behavior (e.g., a spending spree) may intensify the depression.

What causes mood disorders, both major depression and bipolar disorder? Why should people develop these disabling disorders that influence so many psychological processes?

Georg Friedrich Handel was a manic-depressive, according to recent analyses.

Explaining Mood Disorders

Earlier, we considered how several theoretical approaches viewed the disorders based on anxiety. Let us now apply some of these approaches to mood disorders.

The Biological Approach   In the last decade, researchers have been enthusiastically examining the biological basis of depression. Every month, the professional journals report the discovery of another biochemical abnormality in depressed patients or another antidepressant medication (Willner, 1985).

Genetic factors seem to influence a person's chances of developing a mood disorder. Consider the genetic studies on twins. When one member of an identical twin pair is diagnosed as having major depression, the other member stands a

65% chance of exhibiting depression. For fraternal twins, who are less genetically similar, the rate drops to 14% (Nurnberger & Gershon, 1982). Bipolar disorders have also been linked with genetic abnormalities (Egeland et al., 1987; Loehlin et al., 1988).

Genes are important because they determine the levels of neurotransmitters in the brain. As chapter 3 discussed, neurotransmitters carry messages between the neurons. Mood disorders often tend to be associated with the levels of several neurotransmitters in the brain. For some time, researchers have known that two neurotransmitters, serotonin and norepinephrine, are related to mood disorders (McNeal & Cimbolic, 1986). To put it simply, depression is related to a deficiency in one or both of these substances, and manic episodes are related to an excess of these substances. Supportive evidence came from studies on animals, as well as drugs given to humans to relieve mood disorders.

However, in the 1990s, we know that the picture is not so simple. For instance, some drugs have been developed that relieve depression but have no effect on norepinephrine or serotonin levels (Carlson, 1986). Thus, there is no simple correspondence between neurotransmitter deficiency and depression. The situation is even more confusing because clinicians suspect there are at least two categories of depression. One category seems to be largely biologically based and responsive to antidepressant medication. The other category may not be biologically based; this kind is more responsive to psychological rather than biological treatment. As a summary of the research concludes, "There may be multiple biochemical as well as psychological pathways to depression" (McNeal & Cimbolic, 1986, p. 372).

The Psychoanalytic Approach   As you will recall, Sigmund Freud emphasized that psychological disorders can be traced to unconscious emotions and childhood experiences. Those who favor a psychoanalytic approach to mood disorders often argue that depression is caused by feelings of anger toward a parent who has died. Similarly, a romantic partner may break off the relationship, triggering emotions

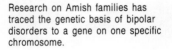

Research on Amish families has traced the genetic basis of bipolar disorders to a gene on one specific chromosome.

and memories of disrupted relationships during childhood. Indeed, researchers have found that depressive episodes often occur after an important relationship has broken up (Barnett & Gotlib, 1988).

However, depression does not develop overnight. It may be that people who are developing depression alienate the people around them, as Coyne's research illustrated. Furthermore, even if the breakup of a relationship does directly *cause* depression, why do we need to trace the blame to childhood experiences? The remaining approaches provide more straightforward explanations.

The Behaviorist Approach   Peter Lewinsohn (1974) argues that learning theory can explain depression. The death or departure of a loved one produces a reduction in rewards. Lewinsohn also emphasizes that depressed people lack the necessary social skills to receive reinforcement from other people. As we already saw in the in-depth section, depressed people often create negative reactions in people with whom they interact. We also saw that others tend to reject and avoid depressed individuals. As a consequence, depressed people often lack social support. They will not be likely to receive rewards in the form of pleasant social interactions.

The Social Cognitive Approach   While some researchers are energetically tracking down biological factors associated with depression, an equal number are examining cognitive factors. A variety of different social cognitive theories have been offered. All of them share one characteristic: They all maintain that depression can be traced to maladaptive cognitive reactions to life events. In other words, depressed people interpret reality differently from nondepressed people, and this cognitive style can cause depression.

One of the social cognitive theories, proposed by Aaron Beck, suggests that some people have negative schemas about themselves and life events (Beck, 1976; Segal, 1988). Whereas most of us have a tendency to view the world through rose-colored glasses, depressed people view the world through mud-colored glasses. Taylor (1989) describes a therapist's story about a woman patient who felt very depressed after seeing a movie. She reported that the movie was extremely sad, and she could relate her life to it. The therapist advised her to select a happier movie on the next occasion. So she selected an upbeat movie. On the next visit, she reported to the therapist that the movie left her very depressed. After all, the happy movie showed her how delightful life could be, and the contrast with her own miserable life had made her more depressed than ever!

According to Beck's view, depressed people exaggerate their problems, ignore the positive events, and misinterpret innocent statements. In short, their beliefs are self-defeating (Beck, 1982). Beck would argue that negative self-schemas cause depression.

A second social cognitive approach argues that one form of depression can be explained in terms of a diathesis-stress model. Some people have a predisposition (or *diathesis*) toward a psychological disorder. When life events provide *stress* to the system, disorders are likely to arise. Thus, the **diathesis-stress model** argues that neither predisposition nor a stressful life event is sufficient by itself to produce a disorder; instead, disorders arise from the combination of both factors.

In the case of depression, this second social cognitive approach argues that certain people have a traitlike tendency toward depression-causing thought patterns (Abramson et al., 1989; Alloy, 1988; Peterson & Seligman, 1985). These people are likely to have the attribution style we discussed earlier. That is, they explain their poor performance in terms of internal, stable, global attribution patterns. Following a poor grade on a test, a person may remark, "This just shows how stupid I am—I'll never make it through college." This traitlike tendency

The diathesis-stress model would propose that this man's depression can be traced to a depression-causing attributional style, in connection with stressful life events.

Seligman argues that people concerned about the welfare of others are less likely to develop depression. In this photo, students in Mississippi are spending their spring break constructing homes for Habitat for Humanity.

may also include an inclination to think that horrible consequences are likely to result from a relatively minor event. When a stressful life event does occur to a person with these thought patterns, this person experiences hopeless depression; things are disastrous, and there is no hope that life will improve.

Notice that this second social cognitive approach helps account for some of the mysteries of depression. You may know some people who endure numerous personal tragedies and still maintain an underlying optimism. For others, a relatively minor stress leaves them hopeless and depressed. Individual differences in cognitive attributional style may account for the individual differences in response to stress.

The Sociocultural Approach   The sociocultural perspective suggests that we look to social pressures—rather than the individual—for explanations of depression. As we saw, women are two to three times more likely than men to develop depression. The sociocultural approach emphasizes that their low status and more limited rewards encourage depression in women.

Life is clearly more stressful for certain groups in the United States. They experience more of the "environmental stresses that are responsible for the higher rates of emotional disturbance among the poor, the powerless, the disenfranchised, and the exploited" (Albee, 1982, p. 1043).

Because of racism, some Blacks, Hispanics, native Americans, and Asian Americans feel a sense of inferiority and reduced self-esteem. In discussing this issue, David Sue and his co-authors (1986) describe a Chinese-American college student named Janet who entered therapy for major depression. She felt worthless and was contemplating suicide; she reported being unable to concentrate. In therapy, she expressed scorn for everything that reminded her of being Chinese. Four months earlier, her Caucasian boyfriend had broken off their relationship because his parents had objected to Janet's race. Janet clearly felt racially inferior.

Our culture's values, in the 1990s, also encourage depression. Martin Seligman, well known for his work on cognitive aspects of depression, has analyzed data from large-scale studies on this disorder. He reported that depression is about 20 times more likely for those born after 1950 than for those born before 1910 (Seligman, 1989). He attributes this increase to our current emphasis on the self. In previous eras people felt strong commitments to their country, their religion, or their family—all larger institutions than the self. Seligman speculates that Americans are currently committed only to buying material possessions and advancing themselves. As a consequence, it is difficult to find meaning in life. Depression can result from this sense of meaninglessness. Seligman offers a clear prescription for depression in the 1990s: We should be less concerned with ourselves and more concerned about the welfare of others and the common good.

Toward an Explanation of Depression   How do all the pieces fit together in explaining depression? It seems likely that several different kinds of depression exist, so that one explanation holds true for some people and a different explanation holds true for others (McNeal & Cimbolic, 1986).

For instance, we saw that some people have a biological predisposition toward depression. For other people, a traitlike pessimistic outlook on life and attributional style combine with stressful life events to bring about depression. Some of these stressful events may be intensified by sociocultural factors.

People who are depressed tend to have disorganized cognitive processes, negative interactions with other people, and negative thought patterns. Each of these three symptoms generates even more life stress. After all, it is stressful to be unable to pay attention, to have other people reject you, and to think that you

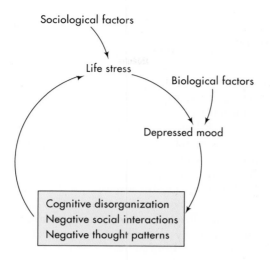

Figure 15.5
In the vicious cycle of depression, the symptoms generate even more depression. For example, sociocultural factors may produce stress, which, in combination with biological factors, can produce a depressed mood. The symptoms of this depressed mood, in turn, create additional stress.

are a terrible person and that poor performance is always your own fault. A vicious cycle begins, in which depression grows steadily worse (see Figure 15.5). As we see in the next chapter, however, this vicious cycle can be interrupted, and depression can be successfully treated.

Section Summary: Mood Disorders

- The characteristics of major depression include apathy and hopelessness; internal, stable, global explanations for poor performance; decreased cognitive functioning; and contemplation of suicide.
- Depressed people are likely to produce negative reactions from other people—either strangers or people in close relationships.
- Women are two to three times more likely than men to develop depression; depression is particularly likely in those who derive their identity from other people, rather than their own accomplishments.
- People with bipolar disorders experience both depressive and manic episodes; during manic episodes, they have inflated self-esteem, talkativeness, racing thoughts, and excessive involvement in activities.
- The explanation for mood disorders is undoubtedly complex, especially because it involves biological factors in some cases; the vicious cycle of depression includes stressful events (often sociocultural in origin) producing a depressed mood. The depressed mood creates disorganization and other negative symptoms that in turn create more stress.

Schizophrenic Disorders

A young woman, diagnosed as schizophrenic and hospitalized at the age of 19, recalled that she first began to hallucinate at the age of 9. In the classroom, she would "see" a troup of elves jumping merrily from desk to desk and then tweaking the teacher's nose. At other times, her desk seemed to behave like a hungry animal, reaching out to bite her dress (Asarnow & Goldstein, 1986).

In the last section, we focused mainly on depression, which primarily involves disordered *emotions*. **Schizophrenia**, in contrast, primarily involves severely disordered *thoughts*, though perceptual, emotional, and social processes may also be disturbed.

Schizophrenia was a term introduced by a Swiss psychiatrist (Bleuler, 1911/ 1950). The name comes from the Greek words for "split mind." Unfortunately, some people assume that schizophrenia really means "split personality." However, multiple personality disorder is a different problem, which we already discussed. In schizophrenia, the mind is split in a different sense, because schizophrenics experience a splitting or disorganization of normal thought processes. In some cases, this disorganization is so extensive that individuals lose contact with reality.

Schizophrenia is much less common than mood disorders. Roughly 1% of the U.S. population develops schizophrenia at some point during their lifetime (American Psychiatric Association, 1987). In contrast, 10% to 20% of the U.S. population experiences a major depressive episode (Boyd & Weissman, 1981). Men and women are equally likely to develop schizophrenia, whereas you will recall that depression is more common in women.

Specific symptoms of schizophrenia vary from person to person. In fact, no single feature is present in every schizophrenic person (Torrey, 1988). Furthermore, every feature found in schizophrenics can also be found in people who have disorders other than schizophrenia (American Psychiatric Association, 1987; Bernheim & Lewine, 1979). It is clear that schizophrenia can be extremely disabling, however, frequently requiring hospitalization. In fact, in one report, 38% of all people admitted to state or county mental hospitals had a primary diagnosis of schizophrenia (Mandersheid et al., 1985).

What are some of the symptoms that make schizophrenia so disabling? What is its pattern of development? Finally, how can we explain this disorder that so profoundly alters an individual's thinking, emotions, and social interactions?

The Characteristics of Schizophrenic Disorders

As we review these symptoms, keep in mind that schizophrenics differ dramatically. Just as psychologically healthy people show a wide range of individual differences, people with schizophrenic disorders are far from uniform. Let us consider some of the more common symptoms, which include attention problems, disorganized thinking, hallucinations, delusions, emotional disturbances, and disrupted social interactions.

Attention Problems   As you saw in chapter 4, normal people can pay selective attention to one message, screening out the stream of other distracting noises, sights, smells, and so on. For instance, as you read this sentence, you can ignore a conversation out in the hallway, the visual clutter that surrounds you, and hundreds of other stimuli that could divert you from your goal of completing this sentence. However, schizophrenics are more easily distracted (Mirsky & Duncan, 1986). One possible explanation is that schizophrenics are generally more aroused than other people, and heightened arousal disrupts tasks that require attention (Gjerde, 1983).

Disorganized Thinking   Just as the schizophrenic's attention may wander from item to item, his or her thinking may wander from topic to topic. It is easiest to appreciate this disorganized thinking by considering the speech patterns of schizophrenics. Before you read further, try Demonstration 15.4.

Notice how Sylvia Frumkin leaps from doctors to makeup to famous people, family members, and Hobbits . . . in just one paragraph. In many cases, the connection between two thoughts is weak (for instance, between the second and third sentences), and sometimes it is nonexistent (for instance, between the third and fourth sentences). Schizophrenics like Sylvia Frumkin do not seem to show any awareness that the topics are unconnected.

Characteristics of Schizophrenic Language

Read the following passage, a recording of a monologue that a schizophrenic woman named Sylvia Frumkin addressed to another woman at a psychiatric center (Sheehan, 1982, p. 72).

I'm a doctor, you know. I don't have a diploma, but I'm a doctor. I'm glad to be a mental patient, because it taught me how to be humble. I use Cover Girl creamy natural makeup. Oral Roberts has been here to visit me. My sister's name is Joyce Frumkin, and I like her. . . . I'm only five foot four and I'm the tallest one in my family. This place is where *Mad* magazine is published. The Nixons make Noxon metal polish. When I was a little girl, I used to sit and tell stories to myself. When I was older, I turned off the sound on the TV set and made up dialogue to go with the shows I watched. The people in Creedmoor are Hobbits. I dictated the Hobbit stories to Tolkien, and he took them all down. I'm the Hobbit. Ask John Denver. He told me I was. I'm the only person who ever got Ringo Starr angry. All the trouble started when my father decided to move from Brooklyn to Queens when I was seven. . . .

Next, read through this passage again, with a pen in hand. Count the number of times there is an abrupt break between two sentences, with no apparent link between them.

Now locate a letter from a relative or friend (or else ask someone to quickly write a page about what has happened recently in his or her life). Again, count the number of times an abrupt break occurs between two sentences. Notice that in Ms. Frumkin's monologue, abrupt breaks are more common than linked sentences. In contrast, your letter probably contains more linked sentences.

Some schizophrenic speech shows more interest in the sound of language than its meaning. Sylvia's reference to Nixon and Noxon is one example. Consider how another schizophrenic patient responded when a psychologist asked about the color of a test item: "Looks like clay. Sounds like gray. Take you for a roll in the hay. Hay day. Mayday" (Chaika, 1985, p. 31).

Just as schizophrenics place unrelated or bizarrely related items next to each other in speech, they may also show the same disorganization in their artistic efforts. For instance, Figure 15.6 shows a painting by a schizophrenic named August Neter. A giant witchlike face is constructed from fields and roads—faces and fields are not usually found together (Arnheim, 1986).

Hallucinations   Schizophrenics often experience **hallucinations**, or strong mental images that seem like they truly occurred. The most common hallucinations are auditory, such as voices coming from outside one's head. The voices may speak directly to the person, or the voices may comment on the person's behavior. Less often, the hallucinations are visual, as in the elves in the girl's report at the beginning of this section. Smells, tastes, and skin-sense hallucinations may also occur.

We have noted before that the distinction between so-called normal behavior and psychological disorders can be blurry. A colleague of mine provided a good example. She is a clinical psychologist, and one of her responsibilities is to test the graduates of a theological seminary, to detemine whether they are psychologically healthy and suitable for the ministry. What should she conclude if a man who is a minister-to-be says that he hears God talking to him? Is this normal, or is it a sign of schizophrenia (Krauthamer, personal communication, 1989)?

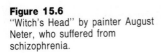

Figure 15.6
"Witch's Head" by painter August Neter, who suffered from schizophrenia.

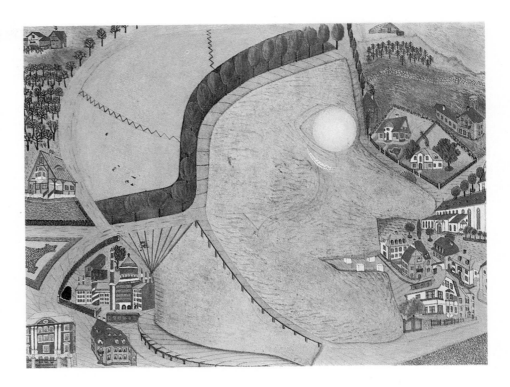

You may recall that the memory chapter discussed Marcia Johnson's work on reality monitoring. When we monitor reality, we try to decide whether something really happened or whether we just imagined it. Interestingly, research on schizophrenics shows that they have more difficulty than normal people in discriminating words they actually said out loud from words they merely *thought* about saying out loud (Harvey, 1985).

Delusions   A **delusion** is a false belief that a person firmly holds, despite any objective evidence. For example, Sylvia Frumkin claimed that she was a doctor one moment, and a Hobbit the next. Some delusions are more long-lasting. For instance, schizophrenics may have persistent beliefs that they are being spied on, or that some external power is placing thoughts in their head.

Emotional Disturbances   Schizophrenics often show **flat affect**, or little sign of either positive or negative emotion. In flat affect, the voice is a monotone, and the face has no expression. Some schizophrenics may also show inappropriate emotion. As a college student, for instance, I accompanied some people from a local psychiatric hospital to a performance of *The Sound of Music*. One man, diagnosed as a schizophrenic, began to laugh out loud at one of the saddest parts of the play, when Maria decides she must leave the family to return to the abbey. Some schizophrenics show inconsistent moods. A person wearing a bland expression may suddenly erupt in a burst of anger.

Social Problems   Schizophrenics usually have trouble with interpersonal relationships (American Psychiatric Association, 1987). Sometimes they are socially withdrawn, as if in their own isolated world. Other schizophrenics may cling to their acquaintances, unaware that too much closeness makes people feel uncomfortable. In general, people with schizophrenia have little experience in the kinds of everyday social skills that normal people take for granted.

Negative and Positive Symptoms This section has emphasized individual differences in the characteristics of schizophrenics. For many years, clinicians have attempted to construct a system of categorizing people with this disorder. One recent system divides the schizophrenic disorders into just two categories, based on whether the individual has more negative symptoms or positive symptoms. **Negative symptoms** mean that a normal human characteristic is missing; negative symptoms include social withdrawal, impoverished speech, and apathy. In contrast, **positive symptoms** mean that certain characteristics are either too strong or bizarre; positive symptoms include hallucinations, delusions, and bizarre behavior (Andreasen, 1982; Crow, 1985). Further research will need to clarify whether this classification system is both reliable and valid.

People hospitalized for schizophrenia tend to be socially withdrawn and isolated.

The Course of Schizophrenia

Schizophrenia typically develops during adolescence or early adulthood, though an onset during childhood or old age is also possible (American Psychiatric Association, 1987; Asarnow & Goldstein, 1986). The disorder usually begins with a clear deterioration that includes social withdrawal, peculiar behavior, or unusual language disturbances. Friends and relatives begin to comment that the individual no longer seems to be the same person as before. Major symptoms that may develop later include incoherent speech, delusions, and hallucinations.

Most schizophrenics do not return to a perfect normal state for the rest of their lives. The prognosis is best, though, for people who are relatively well-adjusted during the most severe period of the disorder (American Psychiatric Association, 1987; Salinger, 1988b). Also, people who have more positive symptoms than negative symptoms have a better prognosis, and their symptoms are more likely to be helped by medication (Crow, 1985).

Although schizophrenics are unlikely to recover completely, some of them can still lead productive lives. Consider, for example, Dr. Frederick Frese, who is a psychologist working with the Ohio Department of Mental Health. After graduating from college, Frese became a Marine Corps officer. However, he found it extremely stressful to work around the atomic weapons. He began to believe

Dr. Frederick Frese, who works with schizophrenic people at the Western Reserve Psychiatric Habilitation Center in Ohio.

that some of his fellow Marines were being controlled through posthypnotic suggestion by the Chinese. After release from the Marines, he recovered long enough to graduate from business school and work successfully with a major company. This work was interrupted by a second acute episode in which he reported the experience of turning into a monkey, a reptile, a worm, and then a single atom at the center of an atom bomb. During a 10-year period, he was hospitalized 9 times.

In the past 13 years, however, Frese has not been rehospitalized. He earned a PhD in psychology and has worked as a psychologist and administrator, primarily helping other schizophrenic people. He still experiences occasional breakdowns, but he has learned to anticipate the symptoms and take time off from his job to work out the problems. Obviously, his personal experience provides valuable insights for his work with schizophrenic clients. His message to many of them is "It was not and is not easy. . . . But if I can do it so can you" (Frese, 1989, p. 5).

Explaining Schizophrenic Disorders

Finding an explanation for schizophrenia is difficult. The symptoms include a wide variety of disorders in attention, thinking, emotions, and social interactions, as well as hallucinations and delusions. Researchers are particularly active in pursuing biological explanations. Psychosocial explanations are also clearly important. However, psychologists have not developed detailed psychoanalytic, behavioral, or cognitive explanations of schizophrenia. We begin by examining biological explanations of schizophrenia and then consider psychological and sociocultural approaches.

Biological Approaches   Three major areas in which biological factors could operate are in genetic transmission of schizophrenia, brain abnormalities, and neurotransmitter abnormalities.

The accumulated research evidence strongly supports a genetic contribution to the development of schizophrenic disorders (Faraone & Tsuang, 1985). For example, a person who has a schizophrenic parent or sibling has about an 8% risk of developing schizophrenia (Gottesman & Shields, 1982; Plomin, 1989). This risk is about eight times greater than the risk for people without any schizophrenic relatives. A large-scale study of twins reported that the genetic component of schizophrenia is larger than the genetic component of several common medical problems such as diabetes, ulcers, and heart disease (Kendler & Robinette, 1983; Loehlin et al., 1988). Perphaps the most famous example of the genetic component of schizophrenia is the Genain quadruplets, shown in Figure 15.7.

Even though the evidence for a genetic basis of schizophrenia is strong, we need to keep in mind two cautions. First, researchers have no evidence for a simple single-gene explanation (Faraone & Tsuang, 1985). Second, genetic transmission certainly does not account for all schizophrenia. In fact, about 90% of schizophrenics do not have a schizophrenic parent. Clearly, a satisfactory explanation of this disorder must focus on nurture as well as nature (Bernheim & Lewine, 1979).

The structure of the brain seems to be somewhat different in schizophrenics. In chapter 3 we discussed new techniques for producing images of the brain, such as magnetic resonance imaging. Using these techniques, researchers have discovered that schizophrenics typically have large ventricles (the hollow, fluid-filled regions in the brain). If the hollow spaces are larger in schizophrenics, then some portions of the brain must be smaller. Researchers suspect deficits in both the temporal and frontal lobes of the cerebral cortex (Andreasen, 1988; Posner, 1988; Suddath et al., 1989). However, it is not yet clear how these deficits translate into abnormal thoughts, emotions, and social interactions.

Figure 15.7
The Genain quadruplets, four sisters with schizophrenia, in a picture taken at their 51st birthday party. (Keep in mind that these sisters shared a similar environment as well as identical genes.)

Finally, neurotransmitter action seems to be different in schizophrenics. In particular, the neurotransmitter called dopamine seems to be more active (Pickar et al., 1984; Wong et al., 1986). One possibility is that the dopamine receptors in the brain are more abundant in schizophrenics than in other people. However, it is likely that the overactive dopamine system simply exaggerates the symptoms of schizophrenia, which are actually caused by some other factor (Carson et al., 1988). As with many explanations for psychological disorders, we do not know whether a biological symptom is a cause or an effect of the disorder.

In short, biological explanations provide some enticing hints. However, none of them provides a satisfying, complete answer to the mystery of schizophrenia.

Psychological Approaches   In general, the standard psychological explanations have not been fully developed to account for the specific disorders found in schizophrenia. Although some theorists have explained schizophrenia in psychoanalytical, behaviorist, and social cognitive frameworks, other more specific explanations are more widely accepted. However, researchers have not discovered a perfect psychological explanation. It seems most likely that psychological factors trigger schizophrenia in people who have a biological predisposition toward the disorder (for example, a genetic history of schizophrenia in the family). Two prominent explanations are the family dynamics approach and the diathesis-stress model.

The family dynamics approach argues that the risk of schizophrenia is greater in families with (1) communication problems or (2) high expressed emotion. In general, researchers have discovered that schizophrenics are somewhat more likely than normal people to grow up in homes where communication is fragmented or muddled (Goldstein, 1984). Children cannot understand what the other family members are saying, and so they create their own private world that encourages schizophrenic thinking.

The family dynamics approach also proposes that a high level of expressed emotion can make schizophrenia more likely if a person is predisposed to this disorder. High **expressed emotion** means that a family member shows highly critical attitudes toward another family member. For example, one parent said to her son that he was "not any benefit to himself or any benefit to society or any benefit to the family situation" (Leff & Vaughn, 1985, p. 41). Interviews with families do show higher expressed emotion in families of schizophrenics (Leff & Vaughan, 1985). It is possible, however, that expressed emotion is the *result* of trying to communicate with a schizophrenic . . . rather than being the direct *cause*.

In the previous section, we considered a diathesis-stress approach to depression. The diathesis-stress approach to schizophrenia argues that schizophrenia is the result of a biological predisposition toward this disorder (diathesis) combined with life stress. This model proposes that someone with a strong biological predisposition (through heredity, brain structure, or neurotransmitters) would develop schizophrenia with only a moderate level of life stress. Someone with a weaker biological predisposition would develop schizophrenia only if life events were extremely stressful. Finally, someone with no biological predisposition would never develop the disorder (Curran & Cirelli, 1988; Gottesman & Shields, 1982). The sociocultural approach emphasizes one important source of this stress.

The Sociocultural Approach   Our discussion of sociocultural approaches to depression focused on gender. In contrast, our discussion of sociocultural approaches to schizophrenia focuses on social class. Specifically, schizophrenia is found more often in lower social classes (Dohrenwend & Dohrenwend, 1974; Zigler & Glick, 1986). Being poor presents long-term stress: You may not have enough money to pay the rent, and the landlord may threaten to sell the building anyway. Also, people who are economically poor often find that their lives are controlled by other people (e.g., unreasonable bosses or unsympathetic people in a welfare office). As a result, they may not have the opportunity to take charge of their lives and effectively cope with stress.

Another possible rationale for the correlation between social class and schizophrenia is called *downward mobility*. That is, people with a severe psychiatric disorder like schizophrenia are unlikely to hold high-paying jobs. As a consequence, they are more likely to drift downward into low-income groups. According to most current theorists, social class is both a cause and an effect of schizophrenia (Zigler & Glick, 1986). Consistent with patterns we have seen throughout this book, the interpretation of correlations usually involves complex explanations.

Section Summary: Schizophrenic Disorders

- Schizophrenic disorders include a wide variety of symptoms that are not found uniformly in all schizophrenics; these disorders include attention problems, disorganized thinking, hallucinations, delusions, emotional disturbances, and problems in social interactions.
- Schizophrenia most often develops during adolescence and early adulthood; full recovery from schizophrenia is not common, but some schizophrenics lead productive lives nonetheless.
- Biological explanations of schizophrenia include the genetic transmission of schizophrenia, brain abnormalities, and dopamine abnormalities.
- The most widely accepted psychological approaches to schizophrenia include the family dynamics explanation of communication problems and high expressed emotion, as well as the diathesis-stress model; sociocultural approaches suggest that individuals in lower social classes experience more stress.

Personality Disorders

In chapter 13, we saw that personality traits are relatively stable ways in which individuals differ from one another. When these traits become inflexible and maladaptive, they are called **personality disorders**. These disorders may prevent normal social interactions, but they do not create the extensive break with reality that we saw, for example, in the discussion of schizophrenia.

DSM-III-R lists 11 different personality disorders. For instance, a person with a dependent personality disorder has extremely low self-esteem and allows other people to make every decision. A person with a narcissistic personality disorder has an inflated sense of self-importance, and expects special treatment from other people. A person with borderline personality is impulsive and unpredictable, with unstable moods and relationships with others. However, these personality disorders have received far less attention than the anxiety disorders, depression, or schizophrenia. The personality disorder that has attracted the most attention is the one causing the most harm to other people, the antisocial personality. Let us first consider its characteristics and then discuss some explanations.

The Characteristics of Antisocial Personality Disorder

Consider the case of Howard, an American soldier who met and married an Englishwoman. When he was discharged from the army, he headed back to the United States—on the day his wife gave birth to their first child. She managed to trace him to New York, and he swore that he would be trustworthy from that day on. The following week, he left for Florida without telling her. When explaining his actions to another person, he said that he had simply forgotten. He had other things to do (Doren, 1987).

As the name implies, **antisocial personality disorders** are characterized by a variety of antisocial behaviors including lying, violence, and other actions that show little concern for the welfare of others. The diagnosis is given only if the person is at least 18 years of age and had similar behavior problems prior to the age of 15 (American Psychiatric Association, 1987).

It is estimated that about 3% of American males have this disorder, in comparison to less than 1% of American females. Thus the gender ratio in this disorder is the reverse of the gender ratio for depression. (It is worth noting that males are also more likely to develop substance abuse problems, including alcoholism; these problems were considered in chapter 5.)

Ted Bundy was attractive and charming, yet he murdered many women, apparently without experiencing guilt. His characteristics are consistent with those of the antisocial personality.

Let us consider some of the more common characteristics of antisocial personality disorder:

1. *Aggressiveness.*   People with antisocial personality disorder often become involved in physical fights. Spouse abuse and child beating are also common.

2. *Lying and deception.*   Antisocial personalities often begin lying during childhood. Some may develop elaborate deceptions. For example, a man named Stephen had been teaching at a small college in Wisconsin, where he had received excellent evaluations from his students. However, school officials later discovered that he had faked his college transcripts and letters of recommendation in order to apply for the position. He apparently had no academic training (Doren, 1987).

3. *Lack of guilt.*   Antisocial personalities typically do not feel guilty about their immoral behavior or the harm it does to other people. As a consequence, they are unlikely to seek therapy. They fail to acknowledge any problem. (Iacono, 1988).

4. *Low tolerance for frustration.*   Most antisocial personalities want pleasures now, without frustrating delays (Millon, 1981). This interest in immediate pleasures may partially explain the observation that antisocial personalities tend to have high rates of alcoholism (Lewis et al., 1985).

5. *Exploitation of others.*   People with antisocial personality disorder are likely to exploit other people. They are often likable, outgoing, and charming. As in the case of Howard, who was mentioned earlier, they often appear sincere when they apologize for wrongdoing. However, they typically continue to exploit the person to whom they have just apologized.

The best publicized examples of antisocial personality disorder are those who come into conflict with the law. However, clinicians who work with this disorder argue that only a minority actually break the laws. As Millon (1981) points out, our competitive society tends to admire aggressive, clever, charming people who may bend the law, although they do not actually break it. The typical antisocial personality is probably more likely to be a successful businessperson than a mass murderer.

Explaining Antisocial Personality Disorder

Some biological explanations have been proposed for antisocial personality disorder. For instance, research suggests that the disorder has a hereditary component (Doren, 1987; Newman et al., 1985). Some speculate that the disorder may be caused by faulty functioning of the limbic system (see Figure 3.16). However, research on the biological underpinnings of antisocial personality disorder is nowhere as extensive as for depression or schizophrenia.

Psychological explanations have also not been fully developed. Psychoanalytic theorists propose that the disorder can be traced to rejecting parents. The child does not acquire the parents' moral values and therefore does not develop conscientious behavior.

Behaviorists argue that antisocial behavior develops when parents do not reinforce children's positive, socially admirable behavior. Those who endorse a social cognitive explanation maintain that children become antisocial when they lack appropriate adult models and when the models they encounter act aggressively (Millon, 1981).

Clinicians agree that this disorder is difficult to explain and also difficult to treat. For instance, one antisocial individual joked with his therapist about the possibility of the death penalty after he committed a series of crimes that included first degree murder. With defiance in his voice, he stated, "They can do what they want with me, but they'll never break me. I'll never surrender to the system" (Doren, 1987, p. 246). Individuals with disorders related to anxiety, those with mood disorders, and schizophrenics appear to be tormented by their disorders.

In contrast, individuals with antisocial personality disorder believe that the rest of the world has a problem, but they do not.

Throughout this chapter, we have examined psychological disorders in which humans become anxious, depressed, disorganized, and antisocial. We have also discussed a variety of explanations for these disorders. However, Lyn Abramson and her co-authors (1989) present an interesting proposal: Perhaps the real mystery is *not* why some humans develop depression and other disabling psychological problems. Instead, the mystery may be that so many people continue to remain competent, caring beings in a world where natural disasters and our fellow humans present so many obstacles to a fulfilling life.

Section Summary: Personality Disorders

- ■ Antisocial personality disorder is the most harmful of the 11 personality disorders; it is more common in men than women.
- ■ Common characteristics of the antisocial personality include aggressiveness, lying, lack of guilt, low frustration tolerance, and exploitation of others.
- ■ Explanations for this disorder include a hereditary component, possible disorders in the limbic system, faulty moral development due to rejecting parents, lack of reinforcement for prosocial behavior, and inappropriate role models.

REVIEW QUESTIONS

1. We discussed the fact that no clear-cut boundary separates people with psychological disorders from those considered normal. Select an example of an anxiety disorder, a somatoform disorder, and a mood disorder and provide an illustration of normal behavior that might be considered somewhat similar to a disorder.

2. Suppose that a neighbor believes that her adolescent child has a psychological disorder. How is a clinician likely to make a diagnosis? What are some possible disadvantages of diagnosing psychological disorders?

3. What is the biological approach to psychological disorders? Describe three major components of this approach, and provide examples of each of these that were discussed in connection with depression and schizophrenia.

4. Describe the sociocultural approach to psychological disorders. If you supported a sociocultural explanation for psychological problems, would you suggest therapy for an individual with a disorder, or would you favor another solution?

5. Make a diagram to indicate the classifications within the anxiety disorders, somatoform disorders, and dissociative disorders. Describe each disorder and try to explain why each of these would affect a person's life—though not as seriously as schizophrenia would.

6. What is the difference between major depression and bipolar disorders? How would each of these disrupt a person's cognitive, emotional, and social behavior?

7. Describe the social interaction patterns of depressed people. How do these interactions fit into the vicious cycle of depression?

8. We noted that women and men differ in the likelihood that they would develop phobias, major depression, and antisocial personality disorder. Review the explanations for the greater likelihood of women developing the first two disorders (adding any ideas of your own) and then speculate about reasons for men's greater likelihood of developing antisocial problems.

9. We noted that schizophrenics experience intense disorganization. Describe how the thought processes, emotional experiences, and social interactions of schizophrenics reveal this disorganization.

10. Describe some of the major characteristics of someone with antisocial personality disorder. Contrast that person with someone who has been diagnosed as having major depression.

NEW TERMS

Diagnostic and Statistical Manual of Mental Disorders (DSM)
anxiety disorders
generalized anxiety disorders
panic disorders
agoraphobia
phobic disorders
obsessive-compulsive disorders
obsessions
compulsions
somatoform disorders
conversion disorders
hypochondriasis
dissociative disorders
amnesia
fugue

multiple personality disorders
mood disorders
major depression
bipolar disorder
mania
theory of learned helplessness
diathesis-stress model
schizophrenia
hallucinations
delusion
flat affect
negative symptoms
positive symptoms
expressed emotion
personality disorders
antisocial personality disorders

ANSWERS TO DEMONSTRATIONS

Demonstration 15.3   Begin with a score of zero, and add one point for a *yes* answer to each of the following items: 2, 4, 5, 8, 10, 11, 14, and 16. Then subtract one point for a *yes* answer to each of the following items: 1, 3, 6, 7, 9, 12, 13, and 15.

In general, scores above zero indicate a relationship that is likely to encourage depression in women, whereas scores below zero indicate a relationship that is less likely to encourage depression.

RECOMMENDED READINGS

American Psychiatric Association. (1987). *Diagnostic and statistical manual of mental disorders* (3rd ed. rev.). Washington, DC: American Psychiatric Association. This manual is clear and well organized, providing descriptions and criteria for each disorder as well as information on its incidence and course of development.

Carson, R. C., Butcher, J. N., & Coleman, J. C. (1988). *Abnormal psychology and modern life* (8th ed.). Glenview, IL: Scott, Foresman. One of the classic textbooks on psychological disorders, this book covers theoretical approaches, the individual disorders, and therapies.

Coyne, J. C., Kahn, J., & Gotlib, I. H. (1987). Depression. In T. Jacob (Ed.), *Family interaction and psychopathology* (pp. 509–533). New York: Plenum. This chapter provides an overview of depression as well as detailed coverage on the social interactions of depressed people.

Taylor, C. B., & Arnow, B. (1988). *The nature and treatment of anxiety disorders.* New York: Free Press. This book reviews theories about anxiety, the specific disorders, and their treatment.

Vonnegut, M. (1975). *The Eden express: A personal account of schizophrenia.* New York: Praeger. This book is a fascinating autobiographical account of a struggle with schizophrenia, written by the son of well-known author Kurt Vonnegut.

Treating Psychological Disorders

According to a recent estimate, about 42 million adults and children in the United States—one in five Americans—are struggling with a psychological disorder (Backer & Richardson, 1989). Among these are people afraid to leave their home, people feeling depressed and useless, and people whose schizophrenia prohibits normal thought processes. This chapter examines how these psychological disorders are currently treated, using both psychological and biological approaches to therapy.

We need to view current therapy within the framework of historical efforts to treat psychological disorders. Evidence from the Stone Age (more than 500,000 years ago) suggests that people treated these disorders by carefully cutting a hole in the skull, as illustrated in Figure 16.1. Presumably, evil spirits trapped within the brain could escape through this opening. In early Greek civilization, psychological problems were thought to be caused by an imbalance in the body's fluids. For example, mania might be treated by draining "excess" blood. During the Middle Ages, people with mental problems were accused of being possessed by the Devil. The remedy—even more extreme than earlier treatments—was to hang them or burn them at the stake.

By the 17th century, the preferred method of treatment was more moderate. People with serious psychological disorders were placed in prisonlike hospitals, typically deprived of adequate food and fresh air. Often, they were chained to the walls.

Following the French Revolution, Philippe Pinel, a physician and director of a Parisian asylum, tried an experiment. He discovered that when patients were treated kindly and provided with better living conditions, their behavior improved dramatically. In the United States, a psychiatrist named Benjamin Rush and a teacher named Dorothea Dix continued Pinel's emphasis on humane treatment.

Figure 16.1
In an ancient procedure called trephining, a hole was cut in the skull to allow evil spirits to escape from the brain.

Still, Rush recommended that physically violent people should be confined to a "tranquilizing chair." This restraining device was replaced by the straitjacket, which in turn became outmoded in the 1950s. By then, researchers had discovered drugs that could provide chemical control for violent outbursts.

As we explore the treatment of psychological disorders in the 1990s throughout this chapter, we note that therapists have developed a variety of psychological approaches. In addition, the pharmacological research begun in the 1950s has evolved into much more sophisticated and effective biological treatments of disorders.

Psychotherapies

At present, there are more than 250 different kinds of psychotherapy, representing such diversity that it is difficult to find a general definition that applies to them all (Corsini, 1989; Parloff, 1987). Usually, however, **psychotherapy** involves verbal interactions between a person with a psychological disorder and someone who has been trained to help correct that disorder. In the words of one therapist,

> All psychotherapies are intended to change people: to make them think differently (cognition), to make them feel differently (affection), and to make them act differently (behavior). Psychotherapy is learning. (Corsini, 1989, p. 5)

Therapy can be provided by people from many different backgrounds, as shown in Table 16.1, with many different theoretical orientations. We focus on the four major psychotherapies: psychoanalytic, behaviorist, cognitive, and humanistic. It is important to emphasize, however, that few therapists in the 1990s would confine themselves to the techniques of just one approach. For example, many behaviorist therapists now include methods borrowed from cognitive ther-

Table 16.1   *Major Professionals Involved in Psychotherapy*

TYPE	DESCRIPTION
Psychiatrists	Physicians with MD degrees who specialize in treating psychological disorders. They can prescribe medication.
Clinical and counseling psychologists	Psychologists with PhD degrees (with more emphasis on research) or PsyD degrees (with more emphasis on applied work). All have been trained to treat psychological disorders.
Psychoanalysts	Usually psychiatrists (though sometimes psychologists) who have received training in the psychoanalytic techniques emphasized by Sigmund Freud and his followers.
Clinical social workers	People who have earned an MSW (Master of Social Work), which usually requires 2 years of study after a bachelor's degree.
Other therapists	People from a wide variety of backgrounds, including pastoral counselors (typically with a religious connection) and psychiatric nurses (with either an RN or a master's degree).

apy. Furthermore, many clients receive drug treatment—a biological approach—in combination with psychotherapy. Thus the boundaries between the different approaches are somewhat flexible.

Despite some flexibility, therapists usually practice a kind of treatment that is consistent with their beliefs about the origin of psychological problems. For instance, someone who believes that problems can be traced to inappropriate learning is likely to favor behaviorist principles in therapy. In contrast, someone who believes that disorders are caused by neurotransmitter imbalances is likely to favor a biological treatment such as medication. Finally, those who support sociocultural explanations—that poverty and discrimination cause psychological problems—favor a more global, community psychology approach, to be discussed in the last part of this chapter.

Psychoanalytic and Psychodynamic Approaches

Psychoanalysis, the therapy technique developed by Sigmund Freud, attempts to resolve problems by making people aware of the conflicts buried in their unconscious. Therapy focuses on unconscious conflicts rather than outward problems. Therefore, the key to psychoanalysis is to use a variety of methods to uncover these buried conflicts, which often developed during childhood. Conscious insight releases the energy previously wasted on the conflict, so that the person can now have a more satisfying life. Let us first examine the classic psychoanalytic concepts, and then we consider some modern developments.

Psychoanalytic Concepts   Classical psychoanalysis requires many years of therapy, with several sessions each week, to allow in-depth probing of the unconscious. Freud originally used hypnosis to encourage the expression of unconscious thoughts, but he discovered that many people could not be hypnotized. He then developed the method of **free association**, in which clients relax and express their thoughts and emotions freely and without censorship. He encouraged relaxation by having clients recline on a couch facing away from the therapist. He also stressed that clients should express any ideas that came to mind, no matter how trivial, silly, or embarrassing they might seem.

A second method Freud developed is **dream analysis**, in which the therapist interprets the hidden meaning of the patient's dreams. Freud argued that the conscious, remembered aspect of a dream (its manifest content) was a distorted version of unconscious sexual or aggressive conflicts (its latent content). The analyst's task is to decode the symbols in the manifest content in order to reveal the latent content to the patient. Freud proposed that both free association and dream analysis could be used to circumvent defense mechanisms such as repression.

Three other psychoanalytic concepts describe important processes that usually occur during psychoanalysis. These are transference, resistance, and insight.

In **transference**, the patient transfers both positive and negative emotional reactions associated with childhood authority figures, directing them toward the therapist. The therapist can encourage transference, using it to reveal feelings toward a parent. For example, a 50-year-old male business executive had been in therapy for a year. Here is a transcript of his interchange with the male therapist:

> **Patient:**   I really don't feel like talking today.
>
> **Analyst:**   (Remains silent for several minutes, then) Perhaps you'd like to talk about why you don't feel like talking.
>
> **Patient:**   There you go again, making demands on me, insisting I do what I just don't feel up to doing. (Pause) Do I always

have to talk here, when I don't feel like it? (Voice becomes angry and petulant) Can't you just get off my back? You don't really give a damn how I feel, do you?

    Analyst: I wonder why you feel I don't care.

    Patient: Because you're always pressuring me to do what I feel I can't do. (Davison & Neale, 1986, p. 479)

This client had been plagued by his feelings of weakness and incompetence, despite his professional success. The analyst had begun to suspect that these feelings originated with the client's childhood experiences with his extremely critical father, who never seemed satisfied with his son's accomplishments. The analyst reasoned from the client's tone of voice and overreaction that the patient had transferred the anger from the father to the analyst. The episode provided a key for the client to reevaluate his childhood fears of expressing anger toward his father.

A second process that frequently occurs during psychoanalysis is **resistance**, which consists of all the conscious and unconscious forces that work against the treatment process. It is stressful to recall unpleasant memories that had previously been unconscious, and this stress provokes resistance. Examples of resistance include refusing to discuss an important topic or protesting that the therapist's interpretation is incorrect. The therapist notes any examples of resistance during therapy, because they provide clues about conflict-laden issues and the activation of defense mechanisms.

A third concept is also important in classical psychoanalysis. The term **insight** refers to the client's awareness of the unconscious conflicts that cause his or her psychological problems. Insight grows gradually during the course of psychoanalysis as the therapist pieces together evidence from free association, dream analysis, transference, and resistance.

Current Psychodynamic Approaches   We have looked at the major psychoanalytic concepts developed by Sigmund Freud. In the 1990s, however, few therapists follow Freud's principles completely. The term **psychodynamic approaches** refers to a variety of approaches descended from Freudian theories, which focus on unconscious mental forces.

Unlike Freud's patients in leisurely turn-of-the-century Vienna, few people seeking therapy today have the time or resources to spend an hour each day in therapy for several years. However, many therapists in the Freudian tradition offer brief psychodynamic therapy. Psychodynamic therapy differs from traditional therapy in several respects (Baker, 1985; Kutash, 1976):

1. Therapy is likely to consist of perhaps 25 sessions, once a week, rather than several years of daily sessions;

2. Rather than Freud's intentionally broad-ranging scope, the therapist and the client might select a more specific, central issue that requires resolution;

3. Psychodynamic approaches place more emphasis on the individual's current social problems than on early childhood experiences;

4. For Freud, insight was sufficient, but modern psychodynamic therapists emphasize the concept **working through**, which refers to the development of new behaviors and emotions following insight (Valenstein, 1985). After understanding the source of the conflict, clients work through their problems by giving up their maladaptive defenses and relating to people in a more mature fashion.

Although psychoanalysis no longer dominates psychotherapy as it did several decades ago, its impact is still substantial (Arlow, 1989). Many psychologists object to Freud's emphasis on the unconscious and on childhood experiences, as well as his failure to emphasize scientific methods. Still, Freud's ideas have had widespread influence on many contemporary therapists.

Behaviorist Approaches

Behaviorist approaches use the principles of learning theory to eliminate undesirable behavior. In other words, behavior therapists apply techniques based on the principles of classical and operant conditioning that we discussed in chapter 6. An important feature of behavior therapy is the explicit specification of treatment goals. (In contrast, therapists who favor psychoanalytic or humanistic approaches would be reluctant to list specific goals.) Let us consider systematic desensitization, based on classical conditioning, as well as some applications of operant conditioning.

Systematic Desensitization   The goal of **systematic desensitization** is to reduce fear or anxiety by substituting a response that is incompatible with anxiety (i.e., relaxation). During the first phase, the therapist and client work together to construct a **fear hierarchy**, with the least anxiety-provoking items at the bottom and the most terrifying items at the top. For example, a student with extreme test anxiety might place at the bottom of the hierarchy, "thinking about an examination that will occur in 3 months." At the top of the hierarchy the student might place "sitting in the exam, looking at a statistics problem" (Gilliland et al., 1984).

The client is then given systematic relaxation training, learning to relax all muscles, while imagining being in a serene, beautiful place. The reasoning behind this technique is that anxiety and relaxation cannot coexist, and relaxation can replace anxiety.

After the client has learned to relax, the therapist presents the item at the bottom of the fear hierarchy. If the client feels anxious, the therapist immediately encourages the beautiful imagery. Gradually, they work their way up the hierarchy. Training can be particularly effective if it involves actual contact with the feared

Systematic desensitization is used to help people overcome their phobia about flying in an airplane. Training is especially effective when it involves contact with the feared object. This program, called SOAR, includes a step in which clients experience a plane flight.

object, rather than just imagining it (Lazarus & Fay, 1984). As you can imagine, systematic desensitization is especially useful in treating phobias.

Operant Conditioning   Systematic desensitization emphasizes classical conditioning. In contrast, other behaviorist techniques use principles from operant conditioning, shaping behavior through rewards and punishments. Consider an example in which an entire ward of a mental hospital adopted a token economy. Chapter 6 described how a token economy reinforces good behavior with tokens, which can be exchanged for a reinforcer. Ayllon and Azrin (1968) rewarded the residents for activities such as combing hair and doing work on the ward. These token rewards could later be exchanged for special activities, such as listening to records and watching movies. Grooming and performing chores both increased so dramatically that other institutions soon adopted token economies. These token economies have been used successfully to treat behavior problems of children in classroom settings, delinquent adolescents, and adults living at home—as well as in institutions (Lazarus & Fay, 1984).

A second operant conditioning technique uses behavioral contracts and records to change unwanted behaviors. The client works together with the therapist on a contract that describes specific goals, and the client keeps a careful record of the relevant behavior. Consider, for example, how this method can be used to treat bulimia, the eating disorder discussed in chapter 12 in which people consume large quantities of food. Kuehnel and Liberman (1986) describe therapy with a bulimic college student named Andrea. The therapist asked her to keep a systematic record of bingeing and vomiting, to provide a baseline measure prior to therapy. Andrea also kept notes about when each episode occurred, to help identify situations that triggered the problem behaviors.

Andrea and the therapist worked out a set of short-term goals. For example, within the first month, she should reduce the vomiting episodes to two times a week from the current level of six times a week. They also established long-term goals that specified the complete elimination of vomiting and the reduction of bingeing to once a month. These goals were to be met by a date 6 months after the beginning of therapy. By the end of the therapy sessions, Andrea had eliminated the problem behaviors. A similar program using behavioral techniques with 14 bulimics demonstrated a better recovery rate than in a control group that had no goal setting or record keeping (Kirkley et al., 1985).

Behaviorists stress that clients should pay particular attention to *when* the problem behavior occurs, because this information provides hints for therapy. For instance, one man who wanted to quit smoking noticed that he was likely to smoke in social settings—while having coffee with friends or when talking on the phone. The behavioral program he worked out allowed him to smoke only in the bathroom (hardly a social setting!). Smoking was no longer pleasurable, and he quit smoking after a month. A follow-up 1 year later revealed he was still not smoking (Martin & Pear, 1983).

If you are intrigued by behaviorist techniques, you may wish to turn back to Demonstration 6.3. This demonstration showed how behavior modification methods can increase or decrease certain behaviors. Keep in mind, however, that behavior therapists have had extensive training. Do not plan a major transformation on your own, or you may be disappointed.

Let us summarize the behaviorist approaches by comparing them with psychodynamic approaches. Psychodynamic therapists proclaim that people are driven by hidden conflicts of which they are unaware. In contrast, behaviorists view people as objective and rational, able to identify their problems (Messer, 1986). Behaviorists focus on the symptom, without searching for what it might symbolize. Finally, behaviorists concentrate on the present, observable behavior, rather than the past history that might have produced the behavior.

One instrumental conditioning technique is record keeping. This therapist is instructing her client about how to keep systematic records on certain targeted behaviors.

Cognitive Approaches

The behaviorist approaches we have discussed emphasize observable behaviors and well-defined problems. In contrast, cognitive approaches emphasize people's thoughts. Specifically, **cognitive therapists** argue that people are plagued by psychological disorders because their thinking is inappropriate or maladaptive; recovery requires a restructuring of the client's thoughts.

In the 1980s and 1990s, cognitive psychology has had a powerful influence on most areas of psychology, including behaviorist approaches. As a result, most behavioral theorists agree that thoughts (as well as stimuli in the environment) can influence behavior, and therapists should target inappropriate thoughts in addition to inappropriate behaviors. Furthermore, most cognitive therapists borrow some of the behaviorist techniques discussed in the previous section. As a consequence, many therapists practice a blend of the two approaches, which can be called **cognitive-behavior therapy**.

The two best known cognitive approaches are Albert Ellis's Rational-Emotive Therapy and Aaron Beck's cognitive therapy. Although their techniques differ, both emphasize **cognitive restructuring**, an approach that emphasizes changing one's maladaptive thought patterns (Golden & Dryden, 1987).

Ellis's Rational-Emotive Therapy   This cognitive approach was founded in 1955 by Albert Ellis, a clinical psychologist practicing in New York City. Ellis originally tried a psychoanalytic approach, but he felt that this technique was not particularly effective or scientifically based (Wiener, 1988). He became increasingly convinced that people's emotions depend upon the way they structure their thoughts. His new approach emphasizes that irrational thoughts cause psychological disorders. Here are several of the unreasonable beliefs he frequently noticed among his clients (Ellis & Harper, 1975):

1. I must have love and approval from the people I care about—at *all* times.

2. I must be thoroughly competent and achieving.

3. When I am frustrated or rejected, it is a major catastrophe.

4. Because something influenced my life in the past, it must continue to dominate my life.

Ellis points out that people create problems for themselves when they go beyond the data at hand and overgeneralize (Dryden & Ellis, 1987). For instance, a man who observes a group of people laughing may infer (without any rational evidence) that they are laughing at him. He may draw other irrational conclusions such as, "They think I am stupid" and "I am an incompetent, rotten person."

Basically, **Rational-Emotive Therapy** (or **RET**) encourages people to examine their beliefs carefully and rationally, to make positive statements about themselves, and to solve problems effectively. Ellis first works with his clients to detect irrational beliefs. These beliefs are likely to contain words such as "should," "must," and "always." Ellis then urges clients to debate their irrational beliefs. Demonstration 16.1 encourages you to debate yourself about an irrational belief that you might have.

Consider how Ellis (1986) used the technique of debating irrational beliefs to help a woman named Jane, who was overly anxious about social interactions. She was extremely shy and felt very incompetent about talking with men. Ellis encouraged Jane to debate several unreasonable beliefs, such as, "Where is it written that I *have to* be interesting and clever?" and "When I don't speak well

Disputing Irrational Beliefs

Take a few minutes to identify a personal belief that you suspect may be irrational. Often, these irrational beliefs are based on the idea that you must be perfect or must satisfy everyone. Here are some examples:

"I must win the approval of everyone in my sorority."

"I must meet my parents' expectations at all times."

"I should receive an A in each of my courses this semester."

Now complete the following questions (based on Ellis, 1979).

1. What irrational belief do you want to dispute and give up? (Describe this belief in some detail.)
2. Can you rationally support this belief?
3. What evidence do you have that this belief is true?
4. What evidence do you have that the belief is false?
5. What are the worst possible things that could actually happen to you if you do not achieve the goal specified in Item 1?
6. What good things could happen or could you make happen if you never achieve the goal specified in Item 1?

Does this technique help you think more flexibly about this particular belief?

and impress people, how does that make me a stupid, inadequate person?" (p. 281).

Jane was also encouraged to construct some positive statements to repeat to herself several times a day, such as "I *can* speak up to others, even when I feel uncomfortable doing so" and "I'm an intelligent person." Finally, Ellis worked with her on strategies for solving practical problems, such as how to meet appropriate men and how to handle job interviews. Notice, then, that Rational-Emotive Therapy can emphasize behaviors as well as cognitions. It encourages people to develop practical skills and changes in behavior, not simply a new way of thinking about the world (Brewin, 1989; Moses, 1989).

Beck's Cognitive Therapy   In chapter 15, our discussion of the social cognitive approach to depression noted Aaron Beck's proposal that depressed people have negative schemas about themselves and life events. **Beck's cognitive therapy** attempts to correct these systematic errors in reasoning, known as cognitive distortions. Some of the reasoning errors that this therapy addresses include the following (Weishaar & Beck, 1987):

1. Drawing a conclusion based on a detail taken out of context, ignoring other relevant information;

2. Overgeneralization, or drawing a general rule from one or just a few isolated incidents and applying the conclusion broadly to unrelated situations;

3. Mental filtering, or dwelling on a negative detail and ignoring the positive side; and

4. "All-or-nothing" thinking, so that experiences must be categorized as either completely good or completely bad, rather than somewhere in between the two extremes.

In many respects, Albert Ellis's and Aaron Beck's approaches have similar goals, so it is easy to confuse them. But Ellis targets a fixed number of specific irrational beliefs, whereas Beck identifies a more general tendency to develop a negative self-schema, so that the client's entire attitude is consistently distorted. The specific methods of the two therapists also differ, with Ellis more likely to instruct and lecture, and Beck more likely to encourage clients to discover and test their irrational beliefs on their own.

Consider how Beck's cognitive therapy helped one young man who was planning to postpone his dream of going to college. He argued that people would consider him stupid if he did not appear completely confident and sure of himself (Weishaar & Beck, 1987). The therapist urged him to design an experiment to test his beliefs. At college registration, he asked several students for directions, for information regarding schedules, and for help with a confusing computerized list. Following the experiment, he reported that every one of the students had been friendly, and they were often as confused as he. In fact, by gathering information with his questions, he was also able to help other lost students. The experiment helped him develop a positive attitude toward college and toward his own abilities. He also learned that his view of reality was quite different from what actually takes place.

A number of studies have demonstrated that cognitive therapy techniques are successful in helping people with severe depression as well as less serious mood disorders treated in college counseling centers (Fösterling, 1985; Hogg & Deffenbacher, 1988; Hollon et al., 1987; Reynolds & Coats, 1986). A meta-analysis that combined the results of 69 studies showed the effectiveness of modifying personal statements. In the method of **self-statement modification**, people are encouraged to replace negative statements about themselves with more positive statements. The average person who used this technique was better adjusted after therapy than 77% of people in a control group (Dush et al., 1983). Thus, self-statement modification does not help everyone, but it is reasonably effective.

Therapists now have their options of about 20 varieties of cognitive therapy, including Ellis's and Beck's approaches (DeAngelis, 1988). Some therapists develop their own techniques compatible with cognitive approaches. For example, Dowrick & Jesdale (1989) make videotapes of depressed clients. In a later session, they play an edited version of the tape, showing only the nondepressed sequences. The mood of the clients improves when they see realistic evidence that they can act competently and present themselves in a positive manner.

To summarize, the cognitive therapies argue that psychological disorders are caused by maladaptive thinking, not by unconscious conflicts (psychoanalytic theory) or inappropriate conditioning (behaviorist approaches). Cognitive therapy focuses on current problems and uses a variety of techniques to encourage clients to think more logically. Now let us turn to the last major category of psychotherapies, the humanistic approach.

Humanistic Approaches

As we discussed in the chapter on personality, the humanistic approach stresses that humans have tremendous potential for personal growth and self-actualization. However, people can run into roadblocks. For example, parents may withhold their love and approval unless a young person conforms to their own standards (conditional positive regard). The goal of **humanistic therapy** is to remove the blocks to personal growth and to help people appreciate their true selves. In this section, we emphasize Carl Rogers's approach but also consider Gestalt therapy; in the 1990s, these two approaches are the most prominent humanistic psychotherapies.

Rogers's Person-Centered Therapy   Several years ago, a survey asked 800 clinical and counseling psychologists to list the psychotherapists they believed to be most influential. Carl Rogers was awarded the first rank, followed by Albert Ellis in the second position and Sigmund Freud in the third (Warga, 1988).

As its name suggests, **person-centered therapy** attempts to focus on the person's own point of view, instead of the therapist's interpretations. Rogers (1986) proposes three conditions that are particularly likely to encourage growth in person-centered therapy:

1. **Congruence**, also known as genuineness or realness; the therapist expresses what he or she genuinely feels, rather than maintaining a formal "I'm the doctor" attitude;

2. **Unconditional positive regard**, or a positive, nonjudgmental attitude toward the client;

3. **Empathic understanding**, or accurate feeling of the client's emotions.

Carl Rogers points out that most institutions in American culture are based on distrust. In education, government, business—and much of religion, psychotherapy, and family life—people are viewed as being incapable of choosing suitable goals. So, the institution sets these goals. In contrast, the person-centered approach is built on trust. After all, this approach maintains that every human has a basic tendency to grow, to develop, and to reach his or her full potential.

In person-centered therapy, the therapist does not lead the client. Instead, therapists act as companions in the clients' search for themselves (Rogers, 1986).

An important tool in person-centered therapy is **active listening**, in which the therapist attempts to understand both the content and the emotion of a client's statement. The therapist then uses **reflection**, or summarizing content and emotion, communicating this summary back to the client. Rogers believes that it is valuable to offer a symbolic mirror that reflects the client's own views. Although active listening originated in person-centered therapy, it is now standard in most other therapeutic approaches.

Now try Demonstration 16.2 (p. 544), which features an example of person-centered therapy.

Gestalt Therapy   Another important humanistic therapy is called Gestalt therapy (pronounced "Geh-*shtalt*"). This approach is usually traced to Fritz Perls (1893–1970), a psychoanalyst who left Nazi-occupied Germany for the United States (Yontef & Simkin, 1989). His years in Germany familiarized him with the Gestalt psychologists whose research on perception and cognitive processes we discussed in chapters 1 and 4. The Gestalt approach to perception, for example, argues that we perceive objects as well-organized, whole structures, rather than separated, isolated parts. Gestalt therapy is somewhat similar because it emphasizes that in healthy humans, the parts are integrated into a whole being. However, the relationship between the classic Gestalt psychologists (who did not emphasize emotions or therapy) and current Gestalt therapists is not very strong (Sherrill, 1986).

The goal of **Gestalt therapy** is for clients to become aware of what they are doing and how they can change themselves, while also learning to accept and value themselves (Yontef & Simkin, 1989). Gestalt therapy emphasizes getting in touch with one's feelings at this very moment. It places less emphasis on thoughts than on feelings, and less emphasis on the past than on the present. In addition, it encourages clients to take responsibility for their own feelings, rather than searching for the historical basis of these reactions.

To help clients appreciate their current feelings, Gestalt therapists urge clients to attend to their posture and gestures. In the following interchange, for example,

---

Demonstration 16.2

Person-Centered Therapy

In the following interview, Carl Rogers interacts with a 28-year-old client named Jim, who had been hospitalized for 19 months with the diagnosis of schizophrenia. Read through the interview once to understand the general method. Then read through again, noting the technique of reflection. During this second reading, pay particular attention to the following: (1) Rogers's congruence (his genuineness, rather than pompous formality); (2) unconditional positive regard; and (3) empathic understanding.

Client: I just ain't no good to nobody, never was, and never will be.

Therapist: Feeling that now, hm? That you're just no good to yourself, no good to anybody. Never will be any good to anybody. Just that you're completely worthless, huh?—Those really are lousy feelings. Just feel that you're no good at all, hm?. . .

Client: I'm gonna take off.

Therapist: You're going to take off? Really run away from here? Is that what you mean? Must be some—what's the—what's the background of that? Can you tell me? Or I guess what I mean more accurately is I know you don't like the place but it must be that something special came up or something?

Client: I just want to run away and die. . . . All day yesterday and all morning I wished I were dead. I even prayed last night that I could die.

Therapist: I think I caught all of that, that—for a couple of days now you've even prayed for that. One way this strikes me is that to live is such an awful thing to you, you just wish you could die, and not live.

[During the following interchange, the two explore Jim's statement about wanting to die, or at least leave the hospital.]

Client: I might go today. Where, I don't know, but I don't care.

Therapist: Just feel that your mind is made up and that you're going to leave. You're just—just going to leave, hm?

Client: (Muttering in discouraged tone) That's why I want to go, 'cause I don't care what happens.

Therapist: Huh?

Client: That's why I want to go, cause I don't care what happens.

Therapist: M-hm, m-hm. That's why you want to go, because you really don't care about yourself. You just don't care what happens. And I guess I'd just like to say—I care about you. And I care what happens. . . . (Jim bursts into tears and unintelligible sobs.)

(Based on Rogers, 1987, pp. 202–205)

the therapist and the client (a 51-year-old woman) are discussing how she feels at this moment.

> **Therapist:**   Just hold that pose for a moment. See if you can get in touch with how you are. [Videotape is again played back.] What is that posture like for you?

> **Client:**   Cold. I've got my feet up like I am starting a race here. I brace myself with my hands, and my head is to the side, like balancing myself.

> **Therapist:**   So, if your posture could talk, what would it say?

> **Client:**   My feet would say I better stay on my toes. . . . I'm hanging onto the chair like it might be a rocky landing. (Simkin et al., 1986, pp. 210–211)

Although person-centered therapy and Gestalt therapy have somewhat different emphases, they both focus on helping people discover their true emotions. Table 16.2 summarizes the four major therapies we have discussed to help clarify their similarities and differences.

Other Psychotherapies

Even when we consider the numerous variations on the four major approaches to psychotherapy, the total is only a portion of the 250 different kinds of psychotherapy presently available. The diversity of these other approaches is impressive. In some, the therapist says and does nothing. In others, people are symbolically rebirthed. Still other approaches treat clients as children, or encourage them to scream, or to meditate quietly (Corsini, 1989). Two general approaches that encompass many of these other psychotherapies are group therapy and family therapy.

Group Therapy   In **group therapy**, the therapist works with an interacting group of 7 or 8 people who have something in common. The therapist usually does not

Table 16.2   *The Four Major Approaches to Treating Psychological Disorders*

	THERAPY APPROACH			
	Psychoanalytic	**Behaviorist**	**Cognitive**	**Humanistic**
1. Psychological component emphasized	Emotions	Behaviors	Thoughts	Emotions
2. Source of the problem	Unresolved conflict buried in unconscious	Inappropriate learning	Maladaptive thinking	Blocking of full development
3. Focus of therapy	Bring conflict to consciousness	Target and correct specific undesirable behaviors	Restructure maladaptive thinking	Discover true emotions and goals
4. Techniques of therapy	Psychoanalysis, using free association and dream analysis	Systematic desensitization and operant techniques	Client conducts "experiments," self-statement modification	Conversations, largely guided by client

Group therapy is helpful for people who share similar problems.

actively direct the conversation, but lets it unfold naturally. The group is encouraged to use its own resources and to develop a sense of belonging and common goals (Meissner, 1988). It should be noted, incidentally, that the traditional psychotherapies can also be conducted in a group setting.

One of the major advantages of group therapy is that it encourages people to realize that others have similar problems—they are not alone. Consider how group therapy can help gay men struggling with the prejudices of a homophobic society (Schwartz & Hartstein, 1986). In group therapy, the men would not need to hide their sexual orientation. They can rapidly identify with the group, yet they can appreciate the diversity of gay lifestyles. Together, they can deal with the fact that they may have internalized some of society's homophobia, feeling somewhat guilty and apologetic, rather than proud of their identity. They can share strategies about dealing with mutual problems, such as relationships with family members or coming out (telling others that they are gay). Group therapy can also be helpful for widows, people with disabling diseases, alcoholics, and people whose relatives have problems. Although many of these groups are most inspired by the humanistic or psychodynamic approaches, they may use some behaviorist or cognitive techniques (Long, 1988).

Family Therapy   As the name implies, **family therapy** considers the entire family—not just one family member—to be the client. According to the family therapy approach, many problems involve disturbed interactions among several family members, rather than just one person (Hazelrigg et al., 1987). Furthermore, the family's dysfunction may reveal itself in the symptoms of one or more family members. Generally, all members of the nuclear family—even younger children—are included in the therapy. The approach and goals of family therapy resemble those of group therapy, except that the family is a preformed group whose members have interacted for many years before coming to therapy (Meissner, 1988).

Consider the case of the Chapin family, who sought family therapy when their 16-year-old son was suspended from school (Taylor, 1986). The therapist met with the parents and their four children to sort out problems that involved not only the one son, but also the husband's resentment about the wife's new job, the wife's overprotectiveness, and the troubled interactions of the children. By the time the Chapins ended their therapy sessions, they were not problem free, but they had resolved the crises and had figured out how to handle future difficulties.

In family therapy, the entire family becomes the client.

Section Summary: Psychotherapies

- Psychoanalysis aims to resolve problems by making people aware of conflicts buried in their unconscious, using techniques such as free association and dream analysis.
- Two processes that often occur in psychoanalysis are transference and resistance; through successful therapy, the client develops insight.
- Modern versions of psychoanalysis, called psychodynamic approaches, usually require less time; they focus on more specific problems.
- Behaviorist approaches try to eliminate undesirable behavior by using the principles of learning, such as systematic desensitization and operant learning techniques.
- The cognitive approaches argue that psychological disorders can be corrected by restructuring the client's maladaptive thoughts; two major approaches are those of Ellis and Beck.

- Albert Ellis's Rational-Emotive Therapy encourages people to examine their beliefs rationally, to make positive statements about themselves, and to solve problems effectively.
- Aaron Beck's cognitive therapy encourages people to discover through real-life experiments that their negative self-schemas are not logical or realistic.
- Humanistic approaches stress that people have tremendous potential for growth and self-actualization, and the blocks to personal growth must be removed.
- Carl Rogers's person-centered therapy attempts to encourage growth and self-discovery; the therapist shows congruence, unconditional positive regard, and empathic understanding; the techniques include active listening and reflection.
- Another humanistic approach is Gestalt therapy, which emphasizes clients' getting in touch with their current feelings.
- Beyond these four major therapies are numerous other approaches, including group therapy and family therapy.

Biological Treatments

We have discussed several psychological approaches to disorders. People recall their dreams, learn new behavior patterns, or devise alternative ways of viewing their lives. In all these approaches, however, the therapists focus attention on thoughts and behaviors. In contrast, biological treatments alter the physiology of the central nervous system. The two most important biological approaches in the 1990s are drug treatment and electroconvulsive therapy.

Drug Treatment

In the late 1940s, a French neurosurgeon named Henri Laborit was searching for a medication to calm his patients prior to anesthesia. A laboratory provided him with chlorpromazine, a sedating antihistamine similar to an ingredient found in many remedies for the common cold. Chlorpromazine proved to be such an effective sedative that Laborit and his colleagues decided to give it to hospitalized people with psychological disorders (Delay & Deniker, 1952; Snyder, 1984). The drug turned out to be especially successful in calming schizophrenics. The success of chlorpromazine inspired the search for other drugs that could relieve psychological disorders. Beginning in the mid-1950s, several hundred thousand hospitalized people received drug treatment. They could now function well enough to leave the straitjackets and padded cells in mental hospitals and return to somewhat normal lives in their communities.

As the name suggests, **drug treatment** involves treating psychological disorders via medication. In chapter 15, we discussed four important disorders: (1) anxiety disorders, (2) depression, (3) bipolar disorder, and (4) schizophrenia. In this section, we examine four drug treatments, each corresponding to one of those disorders: (1) antianxiety drugs, (2) antidepressant drugs, (3) lithium, and (4) antipsychotic drugs.

Antianxiety Drugs **Antianxiety drugs**, often called minor tranquilizers, tend to reduce tension and excitability. Unfortunately, physicians sometimes prescribe these drugs too freely to people who might be better served by determining the source of the anxiety—rather than swallowing a pill to alter their brain chemistry.

In addition, some of these drugs are potentially addictive, and others become less effective when used for several years. They are most useful for the short-term treatment of anxiety, fear, and tension (Baldessarini & Cole, 1988). Furthermore, psychiatrists have found that some kinds of people are more likely than others to benefit from this medication. People who have little sophistication in psychology and are unable to express their unhappiness verbally are likely to show improvement with antianxiety drugs, whereas active, vigorous extraverts are likely to complain about the drug's sedative effects.

Antidepressant Drugs   **Antidepressant drugs** are useful in making a person's mood more positive. For many years, the two major classes of antidepressants were the MAO inhibitors and the tricyclics. These two kinds of medications worked by different mechanisms, but both ultimately bolstered the action of two important neurotransmitters, serotonin and norepinephrine. In recent years, however, the most commonly prescribed antidepressant has been a newer drug named Prozac. Prozac prevents serotonin from being reabsorbed, thereby raising the level of available serotonin.

Antidepressants cannot help everyone who suffers from depression. They are most effective for people who are severely depressed, who have had previous depressive episodes, and whose family history suggests a genetic component (Andreasen, 1984). Furthermore, the drugs work slowly, often requiring 2 to 6 weeks to make a person feel back to normal. Other problems include side effects such as a dry mouth and weight gain, as well as the danger of suicide from an overdose. To be safe, physicians often limit the number of pills they prescribe at one time.

Antidepressants have their drawbacks, and people who take them should be closely monitored, with drug treatment supplemented by psychotherapy. Nonetheless, they have been extremely effective in helping many people function more normally. For example, Joan Nobiling is the program director of a psychiatric rehabilitation program called Operation Friendship; she herself suffers from depression. After she gave a presentation at my college, I asked her to provide a summary of how she felt medication had helped her:

> Medication is a must for me. I find it impossible, no matter how much assistance I receive from family, friends, my psychiatrist, or my self-help method, to function without first having my chemical imbalance "balanced." That's what medications, in my case an MAO inhibitor and Trilafon, an anti-psychotic drug, do for me. Then I'm able to use all of my other supports, and I am able to enjoy living.
>
> It's like someone who's drowning. They have to be able to get their head up from under the water to breathe. Then they can resume swimming. (Nobiling, personal communication, 1989)

Lithium   If you have taken a chemistry course, you might recall an element in the upper left-hand corner of the periodic table called *lithium*—hardly a substance you would expect to find in a psychology course! Nevertheless, **lithium** is very useful in treating bipolar disorder. Like its chemical relative, sodium, lithium is present in the human body. Therapeutic doses of lithium seem to affect all major neurotransmitters, but no comprehensive explanation has been developed to account for exactly *how* lithium works (Lazarus, 1986).

Lithium is typically administered in a hospital initially, so that the level of the drug in the bloodstream can be carefully monitored; an overdose can be toxic, and too little medication is ineffective (Andreasen, 1984). In straightforward cases, a frantically manic person—like the man described in the last chapter who was devising grandiose plans for Olympics tryouts in the hospital ward—can return to normal in several days.

Antipsychotic Drugs   Earlier, we noted Laborit's accidental discovery about chlorpromazine's effectiveness in reducing schizophrenic symptoms. Chlorpromazine

Joan Nobiling, the program director for a community psychiatric rehabilitation group, feels that medication is an essential part of her treatment.

is one of the **antipsychotic drugs**, which reduce symptoms of schizophrenia such as agitation, confusion, delusions, and hallucinations.

Numerous other antipsychotics have been developed since chlorpromazine. In general, the challenge is to find a medication where the **target effects** (or improvement of the major symptoms of a disorder) outweigh the **side effects** (undesirable medical or psychological problems). For example, antipsychotics often produce drowsiness and reduced alertness. A substantial number of people develop a condition called **tardive dyskinesia**, which is characterized by involuntary body movements and abnormal gait in walking (Brown & Funk, 1986). Tragically, this disorder can often be irreversible.

The antipsychotics operate by binding onto the receptors associated with the neurotransmitter dopamine. As a result, dopamine cannot reach the receptors. A reduction in dopamine diminishes the schizophrenic symptoms, but it may increase unwanted motor-movement symptoms.

Antipsychotic medication can have very specific target effects. Consider Miss R., a young woman whose schizophrenic symptoms included hallucinations of hearing the letter A. Just as Hester Prynne was forced to wear the letter A (for adultery) in Hawthorne's *The Scarlet Letter*, Miss R. believed that voices haunted her with the letter A to remind her of her previous sexual activities. With antipsychotic medication, Miss R. reported a 75% reduction in the frequency of hearing the letter A, as well as a reduction in other symptoms such as delusions (Janowsky, 1986).

A middle-of-the-road position seems appropriate for antipsychotics as well as all other drug treatments. In keeping with the theme of individual differences, medication seems to help some people, though drugs are not universally successful. Any drug treatment should be monitored frequently and carefully, noting any side effects. Furthermore, psychologists would strongly argue that any disorder serious enough to be treated medically requires psychological therapy as well.

Electroconvulsive Therapy

We also need to take a moderate position on a second, very different kind of biological treatment—one that may initially sound more barbaric than drug treatment. In **electroconvulsive therapy** (ECT), a person receives a series of electric shocks that produce convulsions, which often relieve the symptoms of severe depression where other treatments have failed.

A person scheduled for ECT is given a sedative and a muscle relaxant to reduce body movements during therapy. Then an electric current, about 100 volts in intensity, is passed through one or both hemispheres of the brain (see Figure 16.2). Treatment is repeated periodically for several weeks. It is important to dispel two common misunderstandings: (1) The modern ECT method is *not* painful—though it may be slightly uncomfortable. (2) The convulsion, rather than the shock, produces the helpful effects. A person who receives ECT awakes with no recall of the experience, and is typically less depressed.

Electroconvulsive therapy is usually reserved only for those whose depression is severe enough that suicide is a real danger. Its advantages are that it works quickly and that it is effective when other approaches have failed (Crowe, 1984). A meta-analysis that statistically combined the results of all English-language publications on ECT has shown that this treatment is substantially more effective than either antidepressants or control-group treatments (Janicak et al., 1985). As a panel organized by the National Institutes of Health concluded, "Not a single controlled study has shown another form of treatment to be superior to ECT in the short-term management of severe depressions" (Holden, 1985, p. 1511).

When treatment is supervised appropriately, physical problems are minimal. One side effect that is often debated is memory loss. ECT does cause temporary disorientation; a typical person will not be able to recall his or her age until perhaps half an hour after treatment (Daniel et al., 1987). In addition, the possibility exists that ECT could produce subtle deficits, especially in the area of autobiographical memory (Weiner, 1984). Weighing the pros and cons, Weiner concludes,

> Given the misery, anguish, and risk of death by suicide, starvation, or debilitation associated with severe depressive illness, for example, it still appears that ECT, at least for the present, must continue to be available. (p. 1)

Table 16.3 summarizes the major biological treatments, that is, the four kinds of drug therapy and electroconvulsive therapy. Note that every one of these

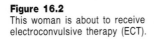

Figure 16.2
This woman is about to receive electroconvulsive therapy (ECT).

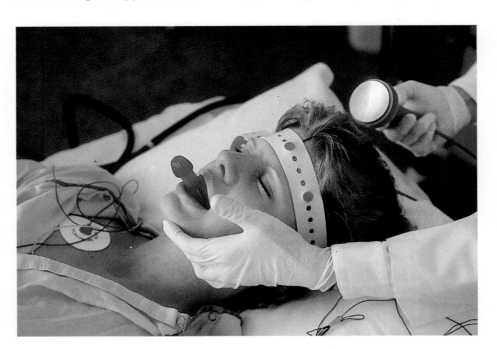

Table 16.3   *Summary of the Biological Treatments*

KIND OF TREATMENT	PSYCHOLOGICAL DISORDER FOR WHICH TREATMENT IS INTENDED	TYPICAL BRAND NAMES	SIDE EFFECTS
I. Drug Treatments			
A. Antianxiety drugs	Anxiety disorders	Valium, Librium, Miltown, Equanil	Potential addiction, reduced effectiveness
B. Antidepressant drugs	Severe depression	MAO inhibitors: Nardil, Parnate, Marplan	Dry mouth, blood pressure disorders if some yeast products are eaten
		Tricyclics: Tofranil, Elavil	Weight gain, dry mouth, danger of suicide from overdose
		Prozac	Headache, upset stomach, nervousness
C. Lithium	Bipolar disorders	Eskalith, Lithobid, Lithonate	Digestive problems; drowsiness and motor problems if dosage is too high
D. Antipsychotics	Schizophrenia	Thorazine (chlorpromazine), Mellaril, Stelazine	Potential tardive dyskinesia, drowsiness, reduced alertness
II. Electroconvulsive therapy (ECT)	Severe depression (with suicidal tendencies)	—	Temporary disorientation; potential loss of some memory

Sources: Andreasen, 1984; Bladessarini & Cole, 1988.

treatments carries a potential risk. In some cases, the risks outweigh the benefits. Especially in the case of severe disorders, however, biological approaches can form the cornerstone of successful treatment. In many cases, they can eliminate symptoms of psychological disorders, making individuals more receptive to psychotherapy. Foreshadowing a point to be emphasized later in the chapter, though, we should note that if people had easy access to services that helped *prevent* psychological disorders, many drug prescriptions and ECT treatments would probably not be necessary.

Section Summary: Biological Treatments

- Antianxiety drugs reduce tension and excitability, but they are often overprescribed.
- Antidepressants are most useful for relieving severe depression in people with a family history of depression.
- Lithium is a chemical element that can prevent or reduce recurrences of episodes of bipolar disorder.
- Antipsychotic drugs diminish schizophrenic symptoms such as agitation, confusion, delusions, and hallucinations.
- Electroconvulsive therapy is used for severely depressed people who are suicidal; the most important drawback is potential memory loss.

Issues in Treating Psychological Disorders

This chapter has emphasized a variety of psychological and biological approaches to the treatment of disorders. Since the 1970s, however, therapists have noted a decline in "sibling rivalry" among competing approaches (London, 1988; Parloff et al., 1986). In fact, many therapists now prefer an eclectic approach. According to a book on eclectic psychotherapy, the **eclectic approach** selects what seems best from a variety of theoretical perspectives (Norcross, 1987). Psychotherapists may integrate two or more psychological approaches.

Furthermore, psychotherapy may be combined with drug therapy, a combination that is most common for people with anxiety disorders, severe depression, or schizophrenia (Silberman, 1987). For example, a survey of clinical psychologists with PhDs revealed that about 80% provided psychotherapy for clients who are also receiving medication (Chiles et al., 1984). In the past, a sharp boundary separated those who preferred psychotherapy from those who preferred drug therapy. However, therapists are now thinking more flexibly about the possible advantages of using both tools (Hersen, 1986).

This final section of the chapter begins by discussing a related question: How can we evaluate psychotherapy to measure its effectiveness? In this section, we also discuss therapy and gender, and therapy with members of minority groups. We will conclude with a discussion of community mental health.

○ ○

In Depth: Evaluating Psychotherapy

Suppose that a friend of yours seems deeply depressed. Should you recommend therapy? So far, you have read about a variety of approaches in treating disorders such as depression, but you might have some doubts. Is it really effective to ask people to explore their hidden conflicts, to learn new behavior patterns, to restructure their thoughts, or to remove the roadblocks to self-actualization? We begin by examining the usefulness of psychotherapy in general, and then we compare the effectiveness of various approaches. In the final section, we will emphasize similarities among the therapies.

Does Psychotherapy Work?   It is easy to ask whether psychotherapy works, but how can we answer that question? We cannot peek inside someone's ear at a dial labeled *Current Mental Health*—and see whether the dial moves upward after therapy. The problem is one introduced in chapter 2 in the discussion of research methods: We need to find an accurate way of measuring a psychological process.

One such method of measurement mentioned in chapter 2 was the self-report. We ask consumers to report how much they like a toothpaste or a television set. Why not use self-report to measure consumer satisfaction with therapy? Several dozen researchers have asked people in both outpatient and hospital settings to indicate how satisfied they were with the psychotherapy they had received. In the typical study, about 75% of the respondents said they were satisfied (Lebow, 1982).

Perhaps you can anticipate problems with this approach. For instance, many people may have failed to respond to the surveys, including those who are too anxious, depressed, or disturbed to be able to fill out a questionnaire. Also, respondents may tend to give socially desirable responses, replying that therapy had been satisfactory. Both of these factors could make the responses more optimistic than reality.

Another problem is that these self-report studies seldom include a control group of people who did not participate in therapy. It is likely that some of the respondents could have shown **spontaneous remission**, that is, recovery without any therapy. Researchers can learn more from a study that compares people who have had psychotherapy with similar people who were assigned to a no-treatment control group. Furthermore, mental health should be measured either by objective tests, like those discussed in chapter 14, or by a trained clinician who does not know whether a person is in the "therapy" or the "no-treatment" condition. These controlled experiments on the effectiveness of psychotherapy are labeled **outcome research**.

The first major analysis of outcome research was conducted by Hans Eysenck (1952), whose trait approach to personality was discussed in chapter 13. Eysenck's surprising conclusion was that psychotherapy was not any more effective than no treatment at all. If other psychologists had agreed with Eysenck, they would have packed up their bags and switched professions . . . and you would not be reading this chapter 40 years later! Numerous critics challenged Eysenck's techniques and conclusions, inspiring more systematic research (Strupp, 1986).

The next landmark in outcome research occurred when Mary Lee Smith and her colleagues applied the meta-analysis technique to summarize the large number of studies that had been conducted (Smith & Glass, 1977; Smith, Glass, & Miller, 1980). In the 1980 study, for instance, they located 475 studies that compared a therapy group with an untreated control condition. On 88% of the comparisons, the therapy groups demonstrated greater improvement than the control groups.

Smith and her colleagues also analyzed the *amount* of improvement demonstrated in the studies. Figure 16.3 shows the distribution of scores for untreated people. As you can see, the distribution for psychotherapy clients is substantially more positive. For instance, the arrow indicates the score received by the average untreated person. (In this distribution, 50% receive a higher score than average, and 50% receive lower than average.) Of the psychotherapy clients, 80% received a score that was more positive than the score of the average untreated person. Psychotherapy does not benefit everyone, a conclusion that must be stressed. However, it is reasonably effective.

Since 1980, other studies and meta-analyses have confirmed that psychotherapy clients typically fare better than no-treatment controls (e.g., Lambert et al., 1986; Shapiro & Shapiro, 1982a). The focus has now changed, however. Researchers no longer ask the question of whether psychotherapy "works." Instead, they are interested in discovering what form of therapy works best, for whom, and under that conditions (Elkin et al., 1985).

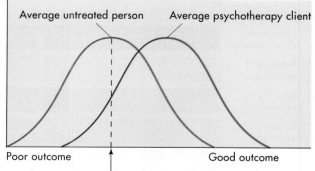

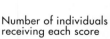

Figure 16.3
A comparison of the average psychotherapy client with the average untreated person. Note that most psychotherapy clients (80%) have an outcome that is more positive than the average untreated person (which is indicated by the arrow).

Which Psychotherapy Works Best?   You can probably guess that it is even trickier to determine which psychotherapy works best than to discover whether psychotherapy is better than no treatment. In this section, we consider answers provided by meta-analysis and by an important large-scale study.

In their first meta-analysis, Smith and Glass (1977) compared several major psychotherapy approaches. Figure 16.4 shows their results, in terms of percentile scores based on the no-treatment control group. Compared to an average score in the 50th percentile for the control group, the average scores for the therapy groups ranged between 60 and 82.

In general, the meta-analytic studies reveal that the behavioral and cognitive approaches are slightly but consistently more helpful than the psychodynamic and humanistic therapies (Lambert et al., 1986; Shapiro & Shapiro, 1982b). It is important to stress, though, that the differences are small. A person should not switch therapists on the basis of these studies alone. There are limitations to the meta-analytic studies, however. In general, they are based on research conducted with college students whose problems are not severe, and the therapists are usually graduate students studying to become professionals, rather than experienced clinicians (Shapiro & Shapiro, 1983). Furthermore, the different kinds of therapists are likely to be treating different kinds of disorders. For example, systematic desensitization is used for very specific phobias, but other therapies address more generalized disorders—which are probably more difficult to correct. Thus, the success of systematic desensitization can partly be traced to a confounding variable.

Irene Elkin and her colleagues (1985, 1989) used a different approach to the question of which psychotherapy works best. Their project is called the National Institute of Mental Health Treatment of Depression Collaborative Research Program (NIMH-TDCRP). The goal of this large-scale study is to compare three therapy techniques frequently used to treat depression, the most common of the serious psychological disorders.

The three treatments Elkin and her co-workers selected were Beck's cognitive therapy (which focuses on restructuring the client's disordered thoughts); interpersonal psychotherapy (which focuses on improving interpersonal relations and clarifying emotional states); and a common antidepressant medication called imipramine. In addition, they included a pill-placebo condition. A **placebo** (pronounced "pluh-*see*-bow") is an inactive substance given to a control group instead

Figure 16.4
The effectiveness of various kinds of psychotherapy, relative to no-treatment control (based on Smith & Glass, 1977). *Note:* Therapeutic approaches are given in the order listed in this chapter. The success of each approach is listed relative to the average for the control group.

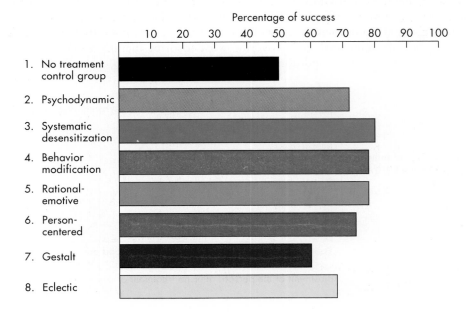

of a medication; the clients may show some spontaneous remission in this condition and may also show improvement because they interact with a supportive, encouraging psychiatrist.

This study differed from previous, more limited studies because it employed 28 experienced therapists—each carefully trained in a therapeutic method—treating clients at three different locations in the United States. A total of 240 patients were randomly assigned to one of the four conditions, providing a well-controlled experiment.

After 16 weeks of treatment, each client was evaluated on several different tests. Let us examine the scores for the Hopkins Rating Scale for Depression (HRSD), an established instrument that measures depressive symptoms. Each client was evaluated on this test by a clinical psychologist who was not aware of the client's treatment condition.

Figure 16.5 shows the results, in terms of the percentage of people in each group whose scores on the HRSD were low enough that they could be considered "recovered." If you look first at those people whose initial depression level was considered less severe, you will see that the four treatment conditions produce similar results; psychotherapy, medication, and a placebo administered by a psychiatrist all produced recovery in about half of the clients. Significant differences emerge, however, for people who were initially severely depressed. The antidepressant medication produced the most impressive recovery, the two psychotherapies were intermediate (and similar to each other in effectiveness), and the placebo condition was least effective. An important additional note is that, after therapy, only about half of all clients were considered "recovered." No current therapy is a cure-all.

Like any interesting study, the research of Elkin and her colleagues raises a number of provocative questions. For example, will these same differences be maintained when the clients are retested after several months or years have passed? Elkin and her colleagues (1989) also speculate about an issue that may have occurred to you: Would the combination of medication and psychotherapy be superior to only medication or only psychotherapy? As in many areas of psychology, we certainly do not have all the answers.

Underlying Similarities in Therapies   We have been focusing on therapeutic differences, but it is important to keep the similarities in mind. All therapies offer support, reassurance, suggestions, and attention from the therapist. In all therapies, self-fulfilling prophecies may operate because clients anticipate that they *should*

Irene Elkin (left) and her co-worker, Tracy Shea (right) examine some of their data from a study comparing therapies.

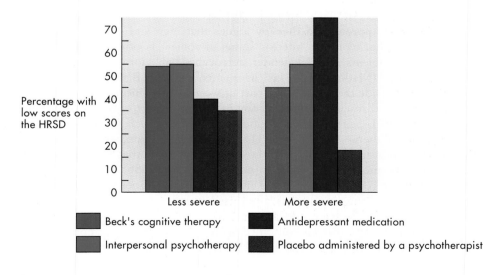

Figure 16.5
Percentage of people considered to be "recovered" because they had low scores on the Hopkins Rating Scale for Depression. Note that the figure separates those whose original condition was less severe from those whose original condition was more severe. Also note the four therapy conditions.

recover. Furthermore, all therapies share a common goal of reducing anxiety and improving the client's functioning and self-efficacy—though their specific routes to competent functioning may differ (Lambert et al., 1986; Strupp, 1986).

In addition, an active ingredient in all therapies is the characteristics of the therapist. Effective therapists of all persuasions are people who are warm, genuine, and caring. Therapists who encourage trust and develop empathy with their clients are more likely to provide successful therapy, no matter which approach they favor (Kokotovic & Tracey, 1990).

○ ○

Therapy and Gender

Before you begin this section, try Demonstration 16.3, which focuses on gender. You may wonder how gender can be relevant in therapy for psychological disorders. Some years ago, the American Psychological Association (1975) sent a questionnaire to therapists, asking them for examples of biased treatment in psychotherapy with women. One respondent answered that she had been dismayed by the treatment given to women at a state hospital. They were urged to go home, be good wives, and pay more attention to cleaning the house—the very problems that had sent them to the hospital in the first place. Others echoed this complaint, that therapists were inclined to emphasize wifely duties rather than women's concerns about employment. Other problems revealed in the survey included therapists who told gender-biased jokes, used demeaning labels for women, and ignored violence toward women. Another problem is therapists who have sexual relationships with their clients—obviously unethical conduct (Pope et al., 1987).

Clearly, therapists should not damage the very people they are hired to help. Furthermore, we need to avoid a double standard in psychotherapy, in which therapeutic treatment depends upon a person's gender. Both men and women deserve to be treated in a nonsexist fashion.

In recent years, an increasing number of therapists have adopted a feminist approach to therapy. First, let us define the term *feminist*, and then we see how this approach is relevant in psychotherapy.

A **feminist** is a woman or man whose beliefs, values, and attitudes reflect a high regard for women as human beings (Hunter College Women's Studies Collective, 1983; Lerman, 1986b). Check over your own answers to Demonstration 16.3. If you have checked a large number of these items, you are a feminist. It is important to emphasize that men can be feminists, if they respect women as much as men.

A **feminist approach to therapy** argues that men and women should be valued equally, that women's inferior status in society is often responsible for psychological problems, and that gender-stereotyped behavior is harmful for both women and men (Matlin, 1987). Just as women can enrich their lives through achievements outside the home—not part of women's traditional role—men can enrich their lives through caring and compassion—not part of men's traditional role (Alpert, 1986).

Traditional therapies emphasize that the therapist is the expert, and the client has much less power. In contrast, feminist therapists argue that the therapist and client should be more nearly equal in power (Howard, 1986). If women clients have subordinate roles in therapy, the situation simply echoes women's inferior status in society. Group therapy is often used to emphasize clients' power and potential for change (Kravetz, 1987).

Feminist therapy can be combined with other approaches. For example, Luepnitz (1988) describes how traditional family therapy often blames women for

In a consciousness-raising group, women discuss their shared problems.

Beliefs about Gender

Read the following statements and place a check mark in front of each statement that you believe is correct. This demonstration is discussed later in the chapter.

_____ 1. If a man and a woman are doing equally well at the same job, they should receive equal pay.

_____ 2. If a man and a woman are doing equally well at the same job and they have been employed an equal number of years, they both should have the same chance of being promoted.

_____ 3. If a man and a woman perform equally well on a college examination, they should receive the same grade.

_____ 4. If a man and a woman perform equally well throughout college and are equivalent on all impor-

tant measures, they should both have the same chance of receiving admission to graduate school.

_____ 5. If a man and a woman perform equally well throughout college and are equivalent on all important measures, they should both have the same chance of being offered a prestigious job.

_____ 6. A man and a woman who are equally well qualified for political office should have an equal chance of being elected.

_____ 7. If a husband and a wife both spend the same number of hours on the job, they should spend the same number of hours on chores in the home.

_____ 8. A man has no right to physically abuse his wife, because she is not his "property."

the family's psychological disorders. She feels that the answer is *not* to start blaming men for children's problems but to help the entire family function better. For example, a therapist could encourage a family to develop greater appreciation for a mother by emphasizing his or her own respect for this woman.

In his presidential address to the American Psychiatric Association, Alan Stone declared, "There can be no new psychology of women that does not require a new psychology of men" (Stone, 1984, p. 14). Feminist therapists encourage us to create new therapy techniques to help both men and women become more fully human.

Therapy and Ethnic Group

The United States is in the process of becoming one of the most ethnically diverse societies in the world. As a consequence, American clinicians need to be sensitive to different values and beliefs when they provide mental health services (Comas-Díaz & Griffith, 1988).

In general, members of minority groups are not as likely as White Americans to use mental health services (Trimble & LaFromboise, 1985; Yamamoto, 1986). Some of the reasons for this underutilization include (1) lack of awareness that mental health clinics exist; (2) shame in talking about personal problems to someone who is not a family member; (3) distrust of therapists, especially White therapists; (4) language barriers; (5) reluctance to recognize that help is necessary; and (6) culturally based preference for nontherapy interventions such as prayer and rituals (Bernheim, personal communication, 1990; Ho, 1987; Sue & Sue, 1985).

In most cases, a member of a minority group is not able to see a therapist of his or her own ethnic background. For example, 180 Native Americans currently hold MAs or PhDs in psychology (and certainly many of them are not clinicians), yet the Native American population is about 1.5 million (LaFromboise, 1988). Most Native Americans who need psychological help will therefore see someone from a different ethnic background. Or consider Hispanics; not many mental health professionals are fluent in Spanish, so language can be a major barrier (Martinez, 1986). To help make the situation more vivid (if your own first language is English), try imagining what it would be like to describe psychological problems to someone who speaks only Spanish. You may know enough Spanish to ask about the weather, but could you describe to a Hispanic therapist how and why you feel depressed? Could you precisely capture the subtleties of anxiety, let alone the terrors of schizophrenia?

Bias Against Ethnic Minorities   Although some research indicates that therapists are not biased in their approach to ethnic minorities, several studies suggest that we need to be concerned (Atkinson, 1985; López, 1989). Consider, for example, an experiment in which White psychiatrists were asked to look at a three-page summary of an interview with a 25-year-old male client with marital and work problems (Geller, 1988). This summary discussed his childhood, his anxiety symptoms, and his present social interactions. In addition, each psychiatrist received one of three additional descriptions (assigned at random): (1) the man was White, with an IQ of 120; (2) the man was Black, with an IQ of 120; and (3) the man was White, with an IQ of 85.

One of the most interesting findings was the psychiatrists' evaluation of the patient's ability to do the work required in psychotherapy. Those who judged the Black, 120-IQ man felt him to be significantly less verbal, competent, introspective, and knowledgeable about psychology, in comparison to those who judge *either* White man, even the one with a reported IQ of only 85. In other words, skin color influenced their judgments about intellectual capacity more than the measured intelligence scores. The psychiatrists were also more likely to recommend drug treatment for the Black man than for either of the White men. It is possible that this bias is at least partially responsible for the fact that Black people are much more likely than White people to be involuntarily committed to a mental institution (Lindsey & Paul, 1989).

Sometimes the assessment process is biased, though the therapist may not intend to be biased. For instance, Mexican-American clients were judged to have more emotional and thought disorders when they were interviewed in English than in Spanish (Martinez, 1986). Also, Puerto Ricans who took the Thematic Apperception Test (TAT) in English were judged to have more serious problems than they really had (Suarez, 1983). As you may recall from chapter 14, the TAT requires people to tell a story about a picture. Pauses and inappropriate word usage are interpreted as evidence of psychological problems on this test—clearly a bias against those not fluent in English.

Treating Ethnic-Minority Clients   We noted many reasons why ethnic-minority people may avoid seeking help. Those who do seek help are likely to search for any evidence of anxiety, rejection, or bias in the therapist (Baker, 1988). Clients who think the therapist is not supportive are not likely to return for another session.

White therapists need to be flexible and eagerly committed to learning more about the culture of their minority-group clients. Several general strategies that have been useful with Native American clients seem appropriate for other groups as well (Bernheim, personal communication, 1990; Miller, 1982; Trimble & LaFromboise, 1985):

1. Search the client's history for strengths that can promote the counseling process;

2. Be aware of any personal biases that might interfere with the counseling relationship;

3. Encourage the client to actively identify and learn skills associated with positive growth;

4. Show empathy, caring, and an appreciation of human potential;

5. Develop interventions that respect the client's cultural values;

6. Do not make assumptions; let the client teach you about his or her culture and values.

Some therapists specifically focus on ethnic group during therapy sessions—though this strategy might backfire when the therapist is not a member of the client's ethnic group. Lillian Comas-Díaz (1988) describes how she approaches ethnicity with her Puerto Rican clients. She frequently uses Carl Rogers's technique of reflection to mirror clients' observations. For example, she might comment, "It is difficult for you to see yourself as Puerto Rican" or "You avoid people from your community because they remind you of being Puerto Rican." On other occasions, she might help clients try to reconstruct their cultural identity and see how it can be integrated with their own personal identity.

Techniques sensitive to culture are currently being developed to help *prevent* psychological disorders, not just treat them. For example, a project in New York City features *cuentos*, or Puerto Rican folktales (Costantino et al., 1986). Forty stories were selected that were judged to express thoughts, feelings, and values of Puerto Rican culture. Some stories stressed themes such as the control of aggression; others emphasized the advantages of waiting for a reward. Mothers and their 5- to 11-year-old children (previously identified as being at risk for psychological problems) read the stories and discussed them during weekly sessions for 20 weeks.

In this example of a *cuento*, or folktale, a daughter is doing her homework and the father is telling a son to do his homework. This *cuento* is designed to address interpersonal relationships, achievement motivation, and delay of gratification.

Dr. Giuseppe Costantino and Migdalia Coubertier discuss a *cuento* with Puerto Rican mothers and their children, with a videotape of the *cuento* in the background.

Figure 16.6 shows the scores on a measure of anxiety, taken 1 year after the therapy had ended. As you can see, the children in the *cuento* condition were substantially better adjusted than those in a treatment group that involved art and play therapy or those in a no-treatment control group.

Psychologists who specialize in cross-cultural issues stress that clinicians should be very sensitive about individual differences (Malgady et al., 1987). For instance, within the Hispanic culture, Mexican Americans differ from Puerto Ricans, who differ from Cubans and other groups. And within each of these smaller groups, one person may be eager to act Anglo American, whereas another wants to maintain traditional values. The goal of therapy should not be to homogenize all clients, but to respect individual differences while encouraging people to develop their human potential.

Community Mental Health

George Albee, a psychologist at the University of Vermont, describes his impressions when a cab driver drove him to a psychiatric hospital in Brooklyn, New York, where Albee was scheduled to give a lecture:

> We drove through long stretches of Bedford-Stuyvesant, which looked a lot like a post-World War II bombed-out city. Buildings were boarded up, or scorched from fires; able-bodied men were passing around bottles in brown paper bags, teenagers who should have been in school were rapping on our cab windows and asking for quarters, teenage prostitutes shared the littered sidewalks with teenage mothers and teenage muggers. In short, we saw the pathology that characterizes this urban monument to an economic system which encourages discrimination, prejudice, involuntary unemployment, and that results in every form of social pathology. (Albee, 1987, p. 37)

Albee had arrived early, so he waited outside for an hour and was astonished to see a series of chauffeur-driven limousines pull up to the hospital entrance. A well-dressed woman emerged from each limousine. Obviously puzzled, Albee questioned one of the chauffeurs. The fellow responded, "Psychoanalysis . . . every day we bring our employers here for their hour-long psychoanalytic session." Albee suddenly realized that he was witnessing a prototype of the problems of the mental health system in the United States.

The irony is that millions of people will never come into contact with a therapist. At the beginning of the chapter, we noted that roughly 42 million adults and children in our country are struggling with a psychological disorder. The major therapies, however, usually offer one-on-one treatment, though some therapy does occur in small groups.

Figure 16.6
Anxiety score of Puerto Rican children, measured 1 year after treatment (based on Costantino et al., 1986). *Note:* high scores indicate better adjustment (less anxiety).

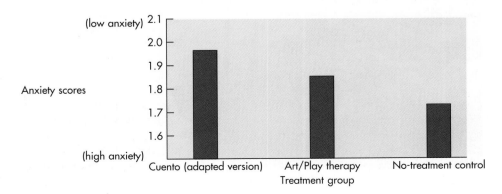

The community psychology approach to psychological disorders emphasizes that our current mental health policy is inadequate. Rather than emphasizing hospitalization or one-on-one daily therapy sessions, the **community psychology approach** focuses on the prevention of psychological disorders as well as treatment in community mental health centers. Let us first consider the issue of preventing psychological disorders. Then we discuss the implications of deinstitutionalization, as well as other options in the community.

Preventing Disorders   As we saw in chapter 15, the sociocultural approach argues that disorders are caused by social and cultural factors. As Albee (1986) emphasizes, disorders are especially likely when people experience poverty and degrading living conditions and when they feel powerless and low in self-esteem. Many psychologists point out that the only effective way to reduce psychological problems is to change society so that all people receive fair treatment and adequate living conditions, and that we should eliminate discrimination on the basis of gender, ethnic group, and other social categories—hardly an easy task! Notice that this approach of blaming society is very different and much more radical than blaming the individual person's biological makeup or past experiences.

Some of the prevention techniques that community psychologists recommend include the following (Albee & Gullotta, 1986; The Commission on the Prevention of Mental-Emotional Disabilities, 1987a):

1. Education, to help groups alter their behavior, learn problem-solving skills, and prepare for changes in their lives;

2. Health care, especially good prenatal nutritional and medical monitoring to reduce the danger of brain damage in the newborn;

3. Promotion of feelings of competency, to enhance self-esteem;

4. Community organization, to try to improve our major institutions.

Only a small portion of the money our country spends on mental health is funneled into prevention. As a result, most projects are small scale, though the results are often encouraging. One typical project is the *cuento* approach with high-risk Puerto Rican children, described earlier. Another program offered a 10-week training program in life-coping skills and stress management to Michigan women on welfare. After training, the women were better at problem solving. They were more likely to take charge of their lives, and they were also less depressed. (The Commission on the Prevention of Mental-Emotional Disabilities, 1987b). Still another prevention program was aimed at grade school children whose parents were recently divorced. In a supportive group atmosphere, children shared feelings, clarified misconceptions about divorce, and learned problem-solving and anger-control skills. These children later showed fewer problem behaviors and less anxiety (Pedro-Carroll & Cowen, 1985).

Will we shift our emphasis from treating the disorder to preventing the disorder? In the late 1970s, public policy seemed to be changing in this direction, but more recent reports are less optimistic (Klerman, 1983; The Commission on the Prevention of Mental-Emotional Disabilities, 1987c).

Problems With Deinstitutionalization   In the 1960s, the mental health system adopted a program of **deinstitutionalization**, or discharging people from mental hospitals into the community. In theory, this policy could be useful because it could return people to the supportive environment of family and friends. Deinstitutionalization could also encourage independence and coping abilities. In practice, however, the policy has not worked. For instance, many people who would have been in a psychiatric hospital are now cared for in a general hospital without a psychiatric unit. As a result, since about 1970, the number of people admitted to hospitals for psychological disorders has actually *increased* by about 60% (Kiesler & Sibulkin, 1987). It is expensive and not particularly effective to treat psychological problems in a general hospital.

A major dilemma is that many people with long-term problems have nowhere to go when they are released from a hospital (either a mental hospital or a general hospital). Ideally, people could turn to support systems in the community, yet the hospital that releases them frequently has no plans whatsoever for follow-up (Torrey, 1988).

Many people discharged from hospitals become homeless. A large-scale survey of over 1,000 clients in a men's shelter in New York estimated that 50% of the people had clear psychological problems (Brown, 1984). An in-depth examination of a smaller sample in Boston placed the estimate at 91% (Bassuk et al., 1984). The stress and instability of homelessness ensure that even relatively problem-free people would develop psychological disorders.

Furthermore, many mentally ill individuals end up in prison. By some estimates, up to 20% of prisoners have serious mental illnesses (Torrey, 1988). Ironically, in this respect many people with psychological disorders now live in conditions similar in spirit to those found in the 17th century, before Philippe Pinel's recommendations to treat patients humanely.

The goal of deinstitutionalization was to provide care for the chronically mentally ill in the community and to help integrate them into the mainstream. Unfortunately, these efforts have failed (Bernheim & Lehman, 1985). The answer is not simply to put these people back into hospitals (Kiesler & Sibulkin, 1987).

Other Options in the Community   The community psychology approach argues that the problem of mental illness is too complicated to be remedied by any one program. Instead, a systematic approach requires a variety of different organizations and services. These include community mental health centers, intermediate care facilities, hotlines, assistance for family members, and organizations for those with long-term mental illnesses.

Ideally, mental health centers should be available in the community to offer emergency services, well-planned outpatient services (so that people could live at home and receive therapy and rehabilitation at the center), and education about preventing psychological disorders. These centers could provide systematic aftercare for people who have been released from a hospital.

Intermediate care facilities should also be available. For instance, in a **halfway house**, people with similar problems who have recently been discharged from a hospital live together in a home (with trained staff) and learn the skills necessary to live independently.

Many communities sponsor a **crisis hotline**, a phone number to call for immediate counseling and comfort. These services are used not only by people who have already been hospitalized for a psychological disorder, but also by others who are experiencing a crisis—for rape victims, battered women, drug abusers, and people considering suicide. Hotline volunteers provide counseling and information about services available in the community.

The families of the mentally ill are another community resource. About two thirds of discharged mental patients return to live with their families (Goldman, 1982). Until recent years, however, families were not counseled; instead, family members were frequently told by psychologists and psychiatrists that they were to blame for the problems in the first place (Lefley, 1989). Consider the stress a family faces when a family member with psychological disorders comes home from the hospital to live with them. Their relative's symptoms may be less dramatic now but are likely to include bizarre speech, self-destructive ideas and behavior,

According to studies, a large number of homeless people have psychological disorders.

social withdrawal, or lack of motivation. The family must figure out how to find services, how to cope with family conflicts, what to tell friends and neighbors, and how to reduce their own guilty feelings (Bernheim, 1989; Bernheim & Lehman, 1985).

These families also live with constant fears. As one parent commented,

> There are no mental vacations. Even when you are physically away from the ill person, you are thinking about her, "Is she all right? Should I call to check? Did she remember to shut off the stove after cooking dinner? Did she wander out in the middle of the night?" (Bernheim et al., 1982, p. 76)

Clearly, families deserve **family consultation**, or supportive family counseling to relieve their own anxieties and help make them more effective in providing for their disabled family member. Many families become involved in an organization called the National Alliance for the Mentally Ill (NAMI), an organization that also welcomes people with psychological disorders as well as other interested people in the community. Members receive support, comfort, and helpful strategies from other families in similar situations (Backer & Richardson, 1989).

A final community resource is the people themselves—those living with psychological disorders. An excellent example of a community resource is Operation Friendship, in Rochester, New York. Operation Friendship is a psychosocial club run by community members who have psychological disorders. As stated in their brochure,

> Our goal is to make *OPERATION FRIENDSHIP* a part of this community where our being present is not based on what is wrong with us, but rather on what we can do to be helpful, to contribute, a place where people believe in our potential to do a better job . . . where opportunities we need come together in one place. (Operation Friendship, 1989)

Two members of a community rehabilitation group talk together at Operation Friendship.

Operation Friendship acknowledges that an important part of therapy is **empowerment**, or developing a sense of self-worth and control over one's own life (Rose & Black, 1985). People help themselves and each other with a variety of services and programs that include meals, trips, courses, self-esteem groups, and assistance in applying for jobs. As one member says, "You can experience something negative on the outside—like not getting the job you applied for—and you can recover like that . . . because you can come here and get support and acceptance, instantly" (Jacobson, 1987, p. 4C).

Section Summary: Issues in Treating Psychological Disorders

- Modern psychotherapy often uses an eclectic approach, in many cases also combining drug treatment with psychotherapy.
- Research on psychotherapy shows that clients are generally satisfied; meta-analyses confirm that psychotherapy clients are typically better adjusted after psychotherapy, compared to controls.
- Meta-analyses comparing psychotherapy approaches show somewhat more positive outcomes for behavioral and cognitive approaches; a large-scale study by Elkin and her colleagues reported that treatment conditions were equally effective for less severely depressed individuals, but for more severely depressed individuals, two psychotherapy conditions were less effective than an antidepressant and more effective than a placebo.
- The feminist approach to therapy argues that men and women should be valued equally and that the therapist and client should have more nearly equal power in therapy sessions.
- Minority-group members are less likely than White Americans to use mental health services, and some (but not all) research shows biases; therapists working with members of minority groups should be alert to their own biases and be sensitive to cultural differences.
- The community mental health approach emphasizes the prevention of disorders, adequate follow-up for people discharged from hospitals, community mental health centers, halfway houses, crisis hotlines, family consultation, and organizations for the mentally ill that encourage empowerment.

REVIEW QUESTIONS

1. In one sentence each, describe how the following approaches explain the origin of psychological disorders: psychological (psychoanalytic, behaviorist, cognitive, and humanistic), biological, and sociocultural.

2. In one sentence each, describe the therapeutic approach that corresponds to each of the theoretical approaches listed in the previous question.

3. Using the information from the beginning and the end of the chapter, trace the history of the treatment of the mentally ill.

4. The quote by Corsini (1989) at the beginning of the chapter emphasized, "Psychotherapy is learning." Precisely what is learned in psychoanalytic, behaviorist, cognitive, humanistic, and family therapy?

5. Focusing on the psychoanalytic approach, describe two techniques that encourage the expression of the unconscious, two important processes that may occur during analysis, and one process that indicates successful psychoanalysis.

6. Suppose that a behaviorist was treating the young man who was afraid to go to college (described in connection with Beck's cognitive therapy). How would a behaviorist use systematic desensitization and operant conditioning techniques to encourage him to register for classes?

7. Suppose that a therapist finds the cognitive and humanistic approaches most appealing. Describe how the approaches of Albert Ellis, Aaron Beck, and Carl Rogers could be integrated in treating someone who suffers from depression.

8. Considering the biological treatments for psychological disorders, what treatment(s) can be used for each of the following problems: (a) severe depression, (b) schizophrenia, (c) bipolar disorders, and (d) anxiety?

9. Suppose that a relative of yours is considering therapy but wonders whether it would be worth the time and money. Based on the in-depth section, what would you reply, and what would you suggest about the specific therapeutic approach to be used?

10. The chapter ends by considering the community mental health approach to mental image. In an ideal society, how would your own community provide services to help prevent psychological disorders and meet the needs of the mentally ill?

NEW TERMS

psychotherapy
psychoanalysis
free association
dream analysis
transference
resistance
insight
psychodynamic approaches
working through
behaviorist approaches
systematic desensitization
fear hierarchy
cognitive therapists
cognitive-behavior therapy
cognitive restructuring
Rational-Emotive Therapy (RET)
Beck's cognitive therapy

self-statement modification
humanistic therapy
person-centered therapy
congruence
unconditional positive regard
empathic understanding
active listening
reflection
Gestalt therapy
group therapy
family therapy
drug treatment
antianxiety drugs
antidepressant drugs
lithium
antipsychotic drugs
target effects

side effects
tardive dyskinesia
electroconvulsive therapy (ECT)
eclectic approach
spontaneous remission
outcome research
placebo
feminist
feminist approach to therapy
community psychology approach
deinstitutionalization
halfway house
crisis hotline
family consultation
empowerment

RECOMMENDED READINGS

Dryden, W., & Golden, W. L. (Eds.). (1987). *Cognitive-behavioural approaches to psychotherapy*. Cambridge, England: Hemisphere. In addition to chapters by Ellis and Beck, this volume discusses behaviorist techniques and additional cognitive approaches.

Garfield, S. L., & Bergin, A. E. (Eds.). (1986). *Handbook of psychotherapy and behavior change* (3rd ed.). New York: Wiley. This handbook contains 19 chapters emphasizing general treatment issues, such as outcome research, therapy with children, and therapist characteristics.

Kutash, I. L., & Wolf, A. (Eds.). (1986). *Psychotherapist's casebook*. San Francisco: Jossey-Bass. This fascinating casebook presents 30 examples of psychological disorders and how they were treated by prominent therapists using approaches discussed in this chapter and others such as transactional analysis, interpersonal psychotherapy, and hypnoanalysis.

Nicholi, A. M., Jr. (Ed.). (1988). *The new Harvard guide to psychiatry*. Cambridge, MA: Harvard University Press. This resource places more emphasis on the medical treatments than do the other three books just noted. It also includes chapters on special populations (e.g., children, retarded people).

Social Cognition

Suppose that you glanced up from your textbook and discovered that all other human beings had suddenly vanished. Try to imagine how your life would be transformed without social relationships and activities. These social interactions are so central that a life in solitude seems grossly distorted and frighteningly bleak.

In the next two chapters, we examine **social psychology**, which focuses on the way that other people influence our thoughts, feelings, and behaviors. This first chapter discusses **social cognition**, how we think about other people and ourselves. For instance, when I began writing this chapter, I thought about a young woman who had bagged my groceries that afternoon. With a cheerful smile on her face, she talked nearly nonstop to me—about how she was planning to skip work for several days, how her mother would react, and whether the boss would care. Her conversation would have been appropriate with a friend or co-worker, but why did she discuss these issues with me—a complete stranger? Days later, I was still struggling to explain her behavior.

In this chapter, we consider attitudes, person perception (including explanations for behavior), stereotypes, and interpersonal attraction. Then in chapter 18 we discuss social influence, or how other people have an impact on group interactions, social-pressure situations, conflict, and altruism. It is important to stress, however, that the topics in the two chapters are closely interrelated. For instance, if we have stereotypes about members of a group, we are more likely to develop conflicts with them and less likely to show altruism.

In reading about social cognition in the present chapter, remember that the human mind struggling to understand social relationships is the same human mind we examined in the chapters on cognition. In those chapters, it was emphasized that humans are typically efficient and accurate in perceiving, remembering, and thinking, and most errors are actually "smart," or logical errors. We also discussed how people perceive objects, remember stories, and think about problems.

The same rules hold when people perceive, remember, and think about other people. We are surrounded by a complex social world, so rich with human interaction that we cannot achieve perfect accuracy in understanding that world. We approach the social world with the same kinds of heuristics we use for stimuli that are not social; these **heuristics**, or rules-of-thumb, are similar to the cognitive shortcuts discussed in earlier chapters. Still, taking everything into account, we are admirably accurate and efficient. As a review of social cognition concluded, "Human perception and cognition are functional and adaptive systems" (Higgins & Bargh, 1987, p. 387).

Attitude and Attitude Change

An **attitude** is an evaluative reaction toward an object, person, institution, or event (Ajzen, 1988). Attitudes can be positive, negative, or neutral. For example, you might have a positive attitude toward a new program for homeless people, a negative attitude toward television violence, and a neutral attitude toward the governor of your state.

Think about an issue that is very important to you, one about which you have a very strong attitude (either positive or negative). Now answer this question:

What were your attitudes on this issue 1 month ago? Were they about the same, or have they changed drastically?

Robert Abelson (1988) examined the stability of attitudes toward four issues that were controversial during the late 1980s: (1) whether abortion should be illegal; (2) whether government welfare programs should be cut; (3) whether the Star Wars weapons system was a good idea; and (4) whether the United States should aid the contras in Nicaragua. In phone interviews, the researchers identified people as having either high conviction (that is, strong attitudes and great concern about an issue) or low conviction on each of the four issues. The respondents provided their attitudes on two occasions, a month apart.

As Figure 17.1 shows, the high-conviction respondents showed strong stability in their beliefs, in contrast to low-conviction people. People who are really convinced that welfare programs should *not* be cut will be likely to be equally convinced a month from now. But if the issue does not seem very important, they are more likely to change their mind during the next month.

Let us now consider three long-standing questions concerning attitudes and attitude change: (1) What is the relationship between attitudes and behavior? (2) What happens when a person's attitudes are inconsistent, as in the case of cognitive dissonance? and (3) What persuasion techniques produce the greatest attitude change?

Do Attitudes Influence Behavior?

More than half a century ago, a psychologist named Richard LaPiere (1934) traveled around the United States with a Chinese couple, eating in restaurants and staying overnight in hotels. Although prejudice against Asians was fairly common during that era, only one establishment refused to serve the couple in their 10,000 miles of travel. Later, LaPiere wrote to these same establishments and asked whether the owners would provide restaurant and hotel services to Asian people. Over 90% responded that they would not. From this study, it seemed that negative attitudes had little influence on actual behavior.

Of course, you can probably think of some reasons why the study was flawed. For instance, the people who actually served the Chinese couple may not have been the same ones who answered LaPiere's letter. However, more recent research has confirmed these early results: Attitudes often have less influence on behavior than we might expect.

Consider a study by Fiske and her co-authors (1983) on the relationship between people's attitudes about nuclear war and their actual behavior. As part

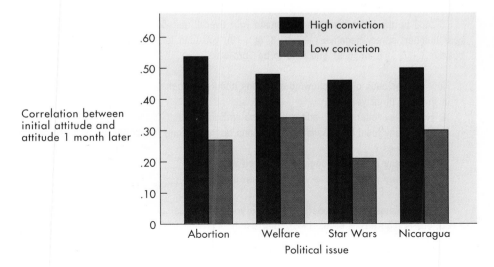

Figure 17.1
Stability of attitudes across time, for high-conviction and low-conviction participants. (Based on Abelson, 1988)

of a larger project, these researchers conducted a telephone survey of Pittsburgh residents. Attitudes toward nuclear war were measured with the first three questions in Demonstration 17.1, and behavior was measured with question 4.

If attitudes have a strong influence on behavior, we would expect that people who had passionate attitudes about nuclear war issues (either pro or con) would *do* something, such as writing letters or signing petitions. However, the correlation between intensity of attitudes and nuclear issue behavior was only +.18, a relationship that is barely statistically significant. If you felt strongly about nuclear war issues in the demonstration, did you also indicate a high level of relevant behavior?

The complexity of human behavior predicts, however, that we would find a less-than-perfect relationship between attitudes and behavior. If your own be-

---

Demonstration 17.1

The Relationship Between Attitudes and Behavior

Answer each of the following questions:

1. What should be the policy of the United States toward the U.S.S.R.? (circle a number)

| −3 | −2 | −1 | 0 | +1 | +2 | +3 |

We should try to   Neutral   We should
reduce tensions   get tougher

2. Do you believe that the development of the atomic bomb was a good thing or a bad thing?

| −3 | −2 | −1 | 0 | +1 | +2 | +3 |

A bad thing   Neutral   A good thing

3. Do you favor a freeze on the production of nuclear weapons?

| −3 | −2 | −1 | 0 | +1 | +2 | +3 |

Yes   Neutral   No

Add up the three numbers to indicate your overall attitude on nuclear war issues. If your number is very negative (−7, −8, or −9), you tend to be "anti-war"; if it is very positive (+7, +8, or +9), you tend to be "pro-war."

4. Now answer each of the following questions about your behavior on nuclear war issues in the past three years:
   a. How many letters-to-the-editor have you written? _____
   b. How many local or national organizations do you belong to (concerned with nuclear war issues)? _____
   c. How many letters to Congress have you written? _____
   d. How many petitions have you signed on this issue? _____

Add up these four numbers to indicate your overall behavior. A total of 0 is typical; 2 or more is high (Fiske et al., 1983). The results of a similar study are discussed above.

If the stimulus situation is ideal, a person with a strong attitude about an issue will show behavior that is consistent with that attitude.

havior did not match your attitudes in the demonstration, can you think of some possible explanations?

We know that the relationship between attitudes and behavior is stronger when the stimulus situation is ideal (Kleinke, 1984). For instance, maybe you would be happy to sign a petition about nuclear war issues, but you have never been in the same room with a relevant petition. Another important factor is knowledge; people who know more about the issues are more likely to show behavior that is consistent with their attitudes (Davidson et al., 1985). Maybe you feel you would like to write a letter to an editor, but you do not feel sufficiently well informed.

Figure 17.2 illustrates how these two other important factors can influence the relationship between attitudes and behavior. In answer to our initial question, "Do attitudes influence behavior?" we must respond, "It depends upon the situation and on the person's knowledge level." We have been examining inconsistencies between attitudes and behaviors; now let us consider what happens when someone holds two inconsistent attitudes.

Cognitive Dissonance

A young woman had decided in high school that she would not apply to any colleges outside of her native New York state. However, the college that offered the best program in her major turned out to be located in Boston—a city obviously outside New York's boundaries. In September, she found herself driving in the

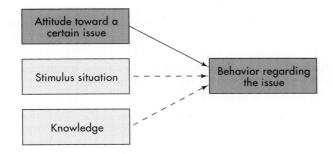

Figure 17.2
The relationship between an attitude toward a certain issue and behavior is also influenced by other factors.

Figure 17.3
Ratings for enjoyment of a boring task, as a function of condition. (Based on Festinger & Carlsmith, 1959)

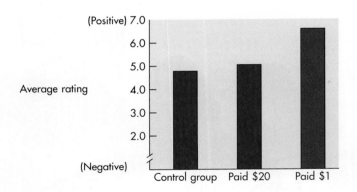

family car to attend school in Boston; her behavior clearly did not match her original attitude.

According to Leon Festinger's classic **theory of cognitive dissonance**, a discrepancy between two inconsistent cognitions produces psychological distress; people will be motivated to reduce this discrepancy or dissonance by changing one of the cognitions (Festinger, 1957). This Boston-bound college student, for example, began to praise Boston's restaurants, sights, and shopping—feeling sorry for her high school classmates who had remained in New York.

In one of the first studies on cognitive dissonance, Festinger and Carlsmith (1959) instructed college students to perform an extremely boring task—turning pegs one quarter of a turn or lining up spools in a tray—for a full hour. This portion of the experiment should produce the attitude, "That was a boring experiment." Then the experimenter offered the participants either $20 or $1 to convince another person that the experiment had been exciting and interesting. (A control group just rested for an equivalent period of time.) Then another experimenter questioned the participants about their attitudes toward the dull tasks.

If you are not already familiar with this experiment, try to guess who liked the experiment best. Reinforcement theory would suggest that the more reinforcement you receive, the better you like the task. Thus, the $20 people should have liked it better than the $1 people. However, the reverse was found: The $1 participants liked it better than those in the other two groups (see Figure 17.3).

Let us see how cognitive dissonance theory accounts for these strange results. Participants are faced with a mismatch between their cognition, "That was a boring experiment," and their cognition, "I have just told someone that it was an exciting experiment." Now the $20 participants could resolve this dissonance quite readily because they had a reason for saying that the experiment was exciting; after all, they had been paid $20 for a few minutes' work. The $1 participants could not use this justification, and so they were forced to modify their attitude toward the experiment so that it was more positive.

Cognitive dissonance theory has generated more than 1,000 research articles and numerous controversies (Cooper & Fazio, 1984; Tesser & Shaffer, 1990). Researchers have discovered, for instance, that people are indeed physiologically aroused when they experience cognitive dissonance (Croyle & Cooper, 1983). They have also learned that attitude change seems to occur only when your behavior violates your own self-concept. For instance, when you do something that harms another person, this behavior violates the self-concept that you are a caring person (Aronson, 1988a). Students in Festinger and Carlsmith's study probably changed their attitude toward the experiment because their deceitful behavior violated their self-concept of honesty.

In a field as ripe with research as cognitive dissonance, someone is certain to propose a different explanation for the results, and Daryl Bem's (1972) theory

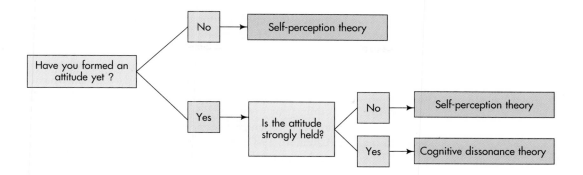

Figure 17.4
Summary of when dissonance theory
and self-perception theory operate.

provides one of the most widely accepted alternatives. Bem's **self-perception theory** proposes that we are not driven by some need within ourselves to be consistent. Instead, we come to know our attitudes by noticing our own observable behaviors. For instance, when Sarah asks John whether he likes movies, he may not have previously evaluated his attitude. Instead, he infers his attitude from his actions, noting that he has seen four movies in the last 2 weeks. He answers that he loves movies.

Do we adjust our attitudes so that they are consistent with each other (dissonance theory), or do we observe our behaviors to know about our attitudes (self-perception theory)? A resolution to the controversy is that the two approaches are actually complementary; they operate in different circumstances. When we behave in a way that clearly contradicts a strongly held attitude, we feel tense and aroused, and we feel forced to change either our interpretation of that behavior or else that strongly held attitude—thus supporting dissonance theory. However, when we behave in a way that *slightly* contradicts an attitude, or when we have not yet formed an attitude, we feel neither tension nor arousal, and self-perception theory operates (Fazio et al., 1977; Tesser & Shaffer, 1990). Figure 17.4 summarizes the resolution of the dissonance theory/self-perception theory debate.

We have seen how people respond to an inconsistency in their attitudes. Now let us see how persuasion can be used to change people's attitudes.

Persuasion

We mentioned earlier that the principles governing normal nonsocial cognitive processes also operate in social contexts. This principle is especially clear in the area of persuasion, where we often employ the kind of heuristics discussed in earlier chapters.

A basic challenge of modern living is that our world is overloaded with information. If you carefully weighed the pros and cons of every decision, you would find yourself at 4 p.m. still trying to decide what to have for breakfast. Instead of identifying and analyzing every relevant piece of information when we make a decision, we often pick out just a few reliable features on which to base our decisions (Cialdini, 1986).

A theory proposed by Petty and Cacioppo (1986a, 1986b) predicts when we carefully consider the issues in a persuasive argument and when we use decision-making shortcuts. Their **elaboration likelihood model** argues that when you are involved in an issue and when you have the ability to analyze a message, you consider it carefully and perform *elaboration*; that is, you relate the message to other ideas and issues. However, when people are not involved or are not able to analyze a message, you are not as sensitive to the quality of the message's argument; you are more likely to use decision-making heuristics.

Think about whether the elaboration likelihood model explains the way you process messages intended to persuade you. I know that when I hear something about an issue I care about deeply, that message captures my attention completely. For instance, several dozen of my friends and relatives have traveled to Central America. When I see an article on Central America, I read every word carefully and relate it to my previous knowledge. However, I am less involved and informed about Eastern Europe. If I read an article about an Eastern European country, I am less likely to process it analytically and more likely to judge its merits by certain rules-of-thumb. (For instance, does the author seem to be a trustworthy expert?) In the interest of "cognitive economy," I take some shortcuts to help my decision making (Chaiken, 1987; DeBono & Harnish, 1988).

It is worth noting, too, that people who are highly involved with an issue are less likely to be persuaded by a message than uninvolved people (Johnson & Eagly, 1989). This finding is consistent with Abelson's research discussed at the beginning of the chapter; when people feel an issue is very important, their attitudes are likely to remain the same 1 month later (Abelson, 1988).

What are the heuristics that people use when someone is trying to persuade them, and they are not sufficiently involved with the issue to analyze the argument carefully? Researchers have identified numerous factors. We will look at five of these factors, three concerning the person who is trying to do the persuading, and two concerning the situation. First, however, be sure you tried Demonstration 17.2.

People are more readily persuaded to change their attitudes when the persuader is an expert. In 1988, Surgeon General C. Everett Koop announced that cigarettes and other tobacco products are addicting, and many Americans were convinced by his message.

Expertise of the Persuader   When an authority speaks, we listen, and we are likely to change our attitude. Words from the expert make us stop searching for additional information, so they represent a heuristic, or shortcut for decision making. For example, an undergraduate student I know is applying to a psychology graduate school. I know a senior faculty member in that department, so I called her to ask which faculty members would be best to work with. Her response—that Dr. X was very supportive whereas Dr. Y was rarely available—was much more persuasive than if it had come from a student or a physics professor. A quotation on a tube of toothpaste is also persuasive: "Tartar Control Crest has been shown to reduce the formation of tartar above the gumline. . . . Council on Dental Therapeutics—American Dental Association."

Social psychology research confirms that expertise is a critical factor in persuasion (e.g., DeBono & Harnish, 1988; Olson & Cal, 1984). The classic study on expertise demonstrated that people were more persuaded by an article about a cure for the common cold when they thought it had appeared in the prestigious *New England Journal of Medicine* rather than a popular family magazine called *Life* (Hovland & Weiss, 1951).

Trustworthiness   An expert is persuasive, but a trustworthy person is even more convincing (McGinnies & Ward, 1980). A trustworthy person is someone who has nothing personal to gain from changing your attitude. For instance, some female faculty members at my college tried for several years to persuade the biology department to change the name of its introductory course from "Biology of Man" to an unbiased name such as "Human Biology." Our efforts were stunningly unsuccessful. Then a man who was a professor in the psychology department— and also a strong feminist—made the same argument, and the name was changed immediately. He was more persuasive, apparently because members of the biology department believed he had no vested interest in a pro-women effort.

Advertisers can establish their trustworthiness by beginning with something mildly negative to gain our trust and then listing the positive features. Of the top five advertising campaigns in the United States, three started with something negative. When Avis Car Rental said, "We're number 2, but we try harder," customers really believed that they would try harder. Or have you ever noticed how a waiter at a restaurant gains your trust for the evening (as well as a larger

Looking at Nonsense Words

Read carefully through this list of nonsense words, pronouncing each one to yourself as you read them.

SARICIK	JANDARA	ZABULON	ENANWAL
JANDARA	BIWOJNI	SARICIK	BIWOJNI
BIWOJNI	JANDARA	ENANWAL	SARICIK
SARICIK	NANSOMA	BIWOJNI	ZABULON
ZABULON	SARICIK	JANDARA	NANSOMA
NANSOMA	JANDARA	SARICIK	JANDARA
JANDARA	SARICIK	BIWOJNI	JANDARA
SARICIK	ZABULON	JANDARA	ZABULON
AFWORBU	SARICIK	SARICIK	JANDARA

Now turn the page and continue the demonstration.

(continued)

tip) by suggesting a less expensive dish than you had ordered? It might seem that the waiter was simply being honest and helpful, but this is actually a standard gimmick for establishing trustworthiness (Cialdini, 1986).

Attractiveness   The in-depth section of chapter 2 emphasized that attractive people have many advantages over less attractive people. It may not be fair, but attractive people are also more effective persuaders (Pallak, 1983; Pallak et al., 1983). The next time you see an advertisement that looks persuasive, try asking yourself whether your reaction would be different if the models were less physically appealing.

We have seen, then, that several characteristics of the persuader cause us to take shortcuts when we are not especially involved in an issue. We tend to be more easily convinced to change our attitudes when the persuader is an expert who is trustworthy and attractive. In the interest of cognitive economy, we do not bother to scrutinize what they actually say. Instead, we use these three heuristics to assess the persuader when we consider whether to change our mind. We also use two heuristics involving the situation: audience response and frequency.

Audience Response   Consider how you might react to an ad for a politician who is addressing a group of cheering supporters. Audience response can be an important heuristic, according to a study by Axsom and his colleagues (1987). These researchers found that people who were highly involved in a controversy were not influenced by the enthusiasm of the audience on a tape recording of a speech. However, people who had low involvement were influenced by the audience. When the tape contained many spontaneous bursts of clapping and cheers of approval, these people were persuaded. They were not persuaded when the audience response consisted of a few tentative hand claps.

Frequency   Return to the ratings you provided in Demonstration 17.2. Calculate your average rating for JANDARA and SARICIK (which you saw 10 times). Also calculate averages for ZABULON and BIWOJNI (5 times), for ENANWAL and NANSOMA (2 times), for CIVADRA and AFWORBU (1 time), and for LOKANTA and KADIRGA (zero times). If you are like the participants in dozens of psychology experiments, you preferred the nonsense words you had seen more frequently (Bornstein, 1989; Zajonc, 1968).

(continued)
As the second part of this demonstration, rate each of the following words. Circle a number to indicate the extent to which this word seems bad or good. The text explains the purpose of this demonstration.

ENANWAL	1	2	3	4	5	6	7
	BAD						GOOD

JANDARA	1	2	3	4	5	6	7
	BAD						GOOD

CIVADRA	1	2	3	4	5	6	7
	BAD						GOOD

LOKANTA	1	2	3	4	5	6	7
	BAD						GOOD

AFWORBU	1	2	3	4	5	6	7
	BAD						GOOD

SARICIK	1	2	3	4	5	6	7
	BAD						GOOD

NANSOMA	1	2	3	4	5	6	7
	BAD						GOOD

BIWOJNI	1	2	3	4	5	6	7
	BAD						GOOD

KADIRGA	1	2	3	4	5	6	7
	BAD						GOOD

ZABULON	1	2	3	4	5	6	7
	BAD						GOOD

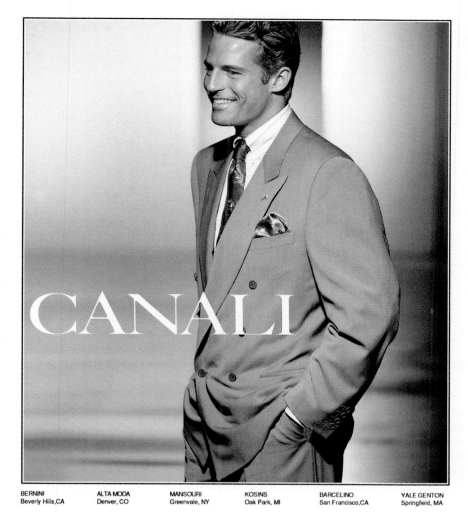

BERNINI
Beverly Hills,CA

ALTA MODA
Denver, CO

MANSOURI
Greenvale, NY

KOSINS
Oak Park, MI

BARCELINO
San Francisco,CA

YALE GENTON
Springfield, MA

SHOW-ROOM CANALI: 9 West 57th Street - Suite 3710 - New York NY 10019 - Ph. (212) 759-6868 - Fax (212) 832-2816

Advertisers use physically appealing models to make their message more convincing. Do we ever see models who look like "real people" in fashion ads?

In 1968, Robert Zajonc (pronounced "*Zeye*-unce") performed a study similar to Demonstration 17.2, exposing these same nonsense words, one at a time, at frequencies ranging from zero to 25 exposures. Figure 17.5 shows the clear-cut results. The phrase **mere exposure effect** refers to this tendency to prefer items (objects, ideas, and people) with which we have had repeated contact.

Think about whether the mere exposure effect can account for any of your preferences. Do you vote for the candidate whose name and face you have seen most often? Do you buy the brand of paper towels your parents had in their home? When we do not care deeply enough about an issue to investigate it completely, we use a simple heuristic: Prefer whatever is most familiar.

You might argue, however, that your responses to Demonstration 17.2 were based at least partially on demand characteristics, or hints from the experimental setup that you were expected to behave in a certain way. A clever study by Mita and his co-authors (1977) minimized demand characteristics, so that the participants were not aware that frequency had been manipulated. Specifically, people in this experiment saw either a photo of themselves (printed the way people see themselves in a mirror) or the same photo reversed (the way other people see them). The participants preferred the mirror-image version—the one with which

Figure 17.5
People rate nonsense words more
positively if they have seen them
frequently. (Zajonc, 1968)

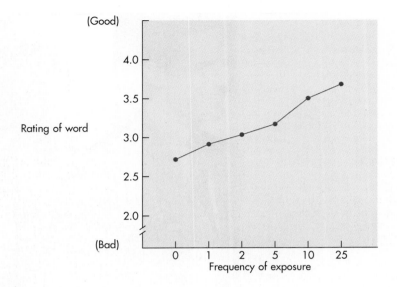

they were most familiar. Their close friends, however, preferred the reversed version—the image they had seen most often.

Summary of Persuasion Factors   We have looked at five factors that can influence whether you will be persuaded to change an attitude. Keep in mind, however, that these three characteristics of persuaders and the two characteristics of the situation will not have much impact if you are strongly involved in an issue or if you choose to examine the issue carefully. For example, suppose that you are strongly opposed to cigarettes—and you have an ongoing campaign to help your friends stop smoking. You are not likely to change your attitude, no matter how expert, trustworthy, or attractive the people appear to be in an ad, no matter what the reaction of an audience might be, and no matter how often you see the ad. However, if the issue does not seem very important or you are too hassled to study the situation carefully, you are likely to use these five heuristics in making the decision.

Section Summary: Attitude and Attitude Change

- Attitudes for which we have high conviction are more likely to remain the same over time.
- Behavior is most likely to match attitudes when the stimulus situation is ideal and when you are knowledgeable about the issue.
- When we hold two contradictory attitudes, we feel aroused, and we change one attitude, consistent with cognitive dissonance theory. However, when we behave in a way slightly different from the attitude or have not yet formed an attitude, we assess our attitude by observing our behavior.
- According to the elaboration likelihood model of persuasion, we consider messages carefully when we are involved in an issue and possess the analytical ability. In other situations, we take cognitive shortcuts by relying on heuristics such as expertise, trustworthiness, attractiveness, audience response, and frequency.

The study by Mira and his coauthors (1977) predicts that you'd prefer the left-hand photo of Dan Rather, because it's oriented the way you usually see him. However, he should prefer the photo on the right, the version he sees in the mirror each morning.

Person Perception

Recently I received a phone call from a friend. She was considering leaving her husband because he had taken money from their bank account, without her knowledge, for some shady business deal that failed. I was astonished. I had only met Bill a few times, but he had seemed caring, intelligent, and considerate. He had changed his infant daughter's diaper, fed her, and played with her enthusiastically—an ideal father! He clearly seemed to love and respect his wife. All this background did not mesh with the new information. And *why* would he do such a thing? I knew things were not great at his work; was it the lure of quick financial gain?

Person perception is the area within social cognition that examines both impression formation and attribution. **Impression formation** involves integrating various pieces of information about a person; in Bill's case, for instance, I tried to integrate traits such as *caring*, *intelligent*, and *considerate* with *deceitful*. **Attribution** involves the explanations we create about the reasons for our own behavior and the behavior of other people. In struggling for possible reasons for Bill's behavior, I focused on attribution.

Impression Formation

Impression formation is absolutely critical in our relationships with others. We constantly form opinions of other people and act on these opinions. If our impressions are not accurate, we often face serious consequences (Cook, 1988). Consider what might happen if John thinks that a potential roommate seems pleasant, but he turns out to be very inconsiderate. Susan might ask for a letter of recommendation from a professor who really turns out to dislike her. Diana and Tony decide to get married, yet neither really assessed the other accurately. Chris accepts a job offer because the head supervisor seems supportive and intelligent, but this person turns out to be incompetent.

When you form impressions of other people, you cannot leisurely interview them and carefully assess all dimensions of their personalities. This approach is so time consuming that if you tried it at the beginning of this term, you would still be interviewing people you met the first day. Our social world is so overloaded with information that you must take mental shortcuts, in the form of schemas. Let us discuss these schemas, and also how the primacy effect and the negativity bias influence impression formation.

Schemas and Impression Formation   In the memory chapter, we introduced a useful concept called schemas. A **schema** is a generalized idea about a frequently encountered object, event, or person. The memory chapter emphasized objects and events; now we focus on the person schema.

A **person schema** consists of selected bits of information about a person, organized into a coherent picture. For instance, your schema for a student you met yesterday might be, "She's the cheerleader type, with blond fluffy hair, an insincere-looking smile, expensive clothes, guys hanging around her . . . a definite airhead." You may have formed this schema after a 30-second conversation. Furthermore, you knit all the diverse pieces of information into a well-organized schema that oversimplifies what you really saw during that conversation. Once again, we see that social cognition involves shortcuts.

A schema is not always accurate. For example, the blond student may be a physics major planning on graduate study, or she might be a talented artist, rather than an airhead. It is likely, however, that your schema will be influenced by both the primacy effect and the negativity bias.

The Primacy Effect   Before you read further, try Demonstration 17.3, which illustrates the primacy effect. Did Jim strike you differently when you read the paragraphs in the reverse order?

Demonstration 17.3

The Primacy Effect

Read the following paragraphs about Jim:

1. Jim left the house to get some stationery. He walked out into the sun-filled street with two of his friends, basking in the sun as he walked. Jim entered the stationery store, which was full of people. Jim talked with an acquaintance while he waited for the clerk to catch his eye. On his way out, he stopped to chat with a school friend who was just coming into the store. Leaving the store, he walked toward school. On his way out he met the young woman to whom he had been introduced the night before. They talked for a short while, and then Jim left for school.

2. After school Jim left the classroom alone. Leaving the school, he started on his long walk home. The street was brilliantly filled with sunshine. Jim walked down the street on the shady side. Coming down the street toward him, he saw the young woman he had met on the previous evening. Jim crossed the street and entered a candy store. The store was crowded with students, and he noticed a few familiar faces. Jim waited quietly until the counterman caught his eye and then gave his order. Taking his drink, he sat down at a side table. When he had finished his drink he went home.

Now describe Jim, noting especially whether he seems to be friendly or shy.

Then, try to clear your head of your current impression of Jim, and read the two paragraphs about Jim in the reverse order, beginning with paragraph 2 and ending with paragraph 1. Does your impression of Jim seem different now?

What is your first impression of each of these students?

The **primacy effect** is the tendency for early information to be considered more important than later information. The primacy effect explains why first impressions are so important.

The section on decision making in chapter 8 (Thinking) introduced a similar effect that operates when we need to make an estimate. We often use the anchoring and adjustment heuristic, by making an initial guess that serves as an anchor, and then making additional adjustments, based on other available information. The anchoring and adjustment heuristic is less than ideal, however, because we often weigh the first guess too heavily, and fail to make large enough adjustments when we learn additional information. Similarly, when you first read the paragraphs in Demonstration 17.3, you formed a first impression based on Jim's three inter-actions with friends in paragraph 1, and you probably did not substantially adjust that first impression when the information in paragraph 2 actually suggested shy, introverted behavior.

Demonstration 17.3 is based on a study by Luchins (1957). People who read paragraph 1 before paragraph 2 judged Jim to be friendly and outgoing, whereas those who read paragraph 2 before paragraph 1 judged him to be shy and intro-verted. No doubt the primacy effect operated in judging people you have met in college, too.

Notice that the primacy effect is further evidence that we tend to simplify our social world. By relying heavily on our first impression, we do not pay close attention to later information. Instead, we devote our attention to the dozens of other social subtleties that confront us. The problem, however, is that oversim-plification can lead to errors in impression formation.

How often do we make these impression-formation errors in everyday life? As Funder (1987) notes, "People by and large do manage to negotiate their social worlds, choose friends, complete transactions, and perform jobs" (p. 83). Un-fortunately, it is difficult to estimate just how often we judge people correctly and how often we make errors. (Think how complicated it would be to follow people around, assessing their perceptions and noting whether they correspond with reality—and how would we measure reality?) However, the primacy effect is helpful if the people we are judging really are consistent—if Joe is shy when we first meet him and if he remains shy in future interactions. In contrast, we will make an error in impression formation if the people we are judging are as inconsistent as Jim was in paragraphs 1 and 2 of the demonstration. As the personality chapter discussed, psychologists are divided on the question of whether people really do have consistent traits and characteristics that are stable across different situations.

In short, we cannot answer how often humans make person-perception errors. However, you *can* increase your accuracy. When you try to assess people, ask yourself whether you are placing too much emphasis on your first impression. Try to minimize the impact of the primacy effect by paying equal attention to more recent information.

Let us now consider an important by-product of the primacy effect, called self-fulfilling prophecy. Consider this example, which I vividly recall from my seventh grade experience at summer camp. On the first day of camp, a girl named Jan immediately impressed all of us with her sense of humor, her athletic ability, and her friendliness. We all tried to sit at Jan's table at mealtime, and she led the singing around the campfire. We elected her to represent us at the camp council during the second week of camp, and she remained our leader for the entire session. In September, I met another student from her school and eagerly asked how Jan was doing. The student looked puzzled at my enthusiasm and asked, "Oh, you mean Jan, the fat girl?" At camp, our first impression of Jan had been extremely positive, and we continued to have high expectations for her; she lived up to those high expectations. Students at her school apparently had a different first impression, so she "became" a different person.

A **self-fulfilling prophecy** operates in situations where your expectations about someone lead him or her to act in ways that confirm your original expectation (Jussim, 1986). In the classroom, for instance, teachers treat students differently, based on their initial expectations, and students tend to live up (or down!) to these expectations (Jussim, 1986; Rosenthal, 1974). Similarly, in chapter 2, we saw that participants in an experiment tend to fulfill the experimenter's expectations (Rosenthal, 1973). We also saw in the in-depth section of that chapter, on physical attractiveness, that women tended to become more socially skilled on the telephone if the men who were their conversational partners had been led to believe that they were physically attractive (Snyder et al., 1977). In summary, one person's thoughts can influence another person's behaviors.

The Negativity Bias   The beginning of this section on person perception mentioned Bill, my friend's husband who is caring, intelligent, considerate . . . and deceitful. An effect called the **negativity bias** predicts that impression formation is more strongly influenced by a person's negative traits than by his or her positive traits.

For some time, researchers have known that people give more weight to negative characteristics. For instance, suppose that you were asked to rate various people on a scale where +10 was likable and −10 was dislikable. You might rate a person described as *kind* by assigning a +7. You might rate someone described as *dishonest* by assigning a −7. How about someone described as *kind and dishonest?* A simple average would yield a rating of zero. However, studies have systematically demonstrated that the negativity bias operates, and people typically supply a rating of about −3 for *kind and dishonest* (Anderson, 1981). Similarly, my present rating of Bill is more influenced by his deceit than by his positive qualities.

According to a current explanation (Skowronski & Carlston, 1987, 1989), when we judge whether people are morally good or bad, we expect good people to be *consistently* good. In contrast, we expect bad people to be sometimes bad and sometimes good. A person who robs a bank (a dishonest act) may have filed an accurate tax form with the IRS (an honest act). A positive quality (such as *kind*) can be characteristic of either good or bad people, so it is not very helpful in our "diagnosis" of a person. In contrast, a negative quality (such as *dishonest*) is characteristic of only bad people; it *is* helpful in the diagnosis. Consequently, we are more influenced by negative traits than by positive traits. In summary, when we form impressions of other people, our schemas are shaped more by initial information than by later information (primacy effect), and they are shaped more by negative information than by positive information (negativity bias).

Attribution

Suppose you read that a famous billionaire has left his wife for a much younger woman. Don't you want to know *why*? Suppose that your best friend suddenly snubs you. Do you search for a rationale? A common human characteristic is to look for attributions, which we defined earlier as the explanations for people's behavior. We do not *always* search for attributions for everyone's behavior, however. It would be too time consuming, and it is not exactly a high-paying job. Nonetheless, we are likely to make attributions when we are not preoccupied with other tasks (Higgins & Bargh, 1987; Weiner, 1985b).

This section focuses primarily on our attributions for the behavior of other people. However, we also make attributions for our own behavior, as we attempt to explain why we received a high grade on a paper, why we were grumpy toward a friend, and why we made a particular mistake. You may recall that we discussed these self-attributions in connection with major depression in chapter 15: Depressed people tend to attribute their poor performance to internal, stable, and global explanations.

In general, when we are searching for attributions for another person's behavior, we make one of two general kinds of attributions (Trope, 1986). A **person attribution** indicates we believe that an internal trait or characteristic—located within the person—was responsible for the behavior. A **situation attribution**, in contrast, indicates we believe that the specific situation—forces located outside the person—was responsible for the behavior. For example, suppose that you see a homeless man. What attribution would you make for his poverty? If you favor a *person attribution*, you believe that he lacks the motivation to get a

How would you explain this person's homelessness? Would you trace his situation to an internal problem, or to a society that does not take care of its members?

proper job. If you favor a *situation attribution*, you blame the economic situation and other external circumstances. Interestingly, Wagstaff (1983) found that politically conservative people tend to supply person attributions for poverty, whereas politically liberal people favor situation attributions. We will consider factors that influence attribution patterns, as well as several consistent biases in attribution. First, however, try Demonstration 17.4 and decide whether each person's behavior merits a person attribution or a situation attribution.

Factors Influencing Attribution Patterns   Harold Kelley, one of the major pioneers in attribution theory, proposed that three factors influence whether we make person or situation attributions. These factors are (1) *consensus*, or whether other people respond the same way as the target person; (2) *distinctiveness*, or whether the target person responds in a unique way to this stimulus, but differently to other stimuli; and (3) *consistency*, or whether the target person responds the same way to this stimulus on most occasions (Kelley, 1967).

As Figure 17.6 shows, people are likely to make a person attribution in cases with low consensus, low distinctiveness, and high consistency. In contrast, they are likely to make a situation attribution in cases with high consensus, high distinctiveness, and high consistency. When McArthur (1972) constructed brief stories like those in Demonstration 17.4 and asked people to select either a person or a situation attribution for each story, she found that stories similar to 2 and 3 were assigned person attributions, whereas stories similar to 1 and 4 were assigned situation attributions. Did your own results agree with hers? Note that the examples in Figure 17.6 are taken from stories 1 and 2.

It is important to stress that the formulas in Figure 17.6 represent heuristics which usually produce a correct attribution. However, like the decision-making heuristics discussed in chapter 8, they can sometimes lead us astray. For instance, it may be that Sue's boss—an eager fund-drive organizer—is considering Sue for a promotion, and the situation forces Sue to contribute. A major reason for her

---

Demonstration 17.4

Attribution Patterns

Read each paragraph and decide whether the person's behavior can be attributed to his or her internal characteristics (person attribution) or to characteristics of the situation or stimulus (situation attribution). For instance, if you read about John thinking that a lecture is boring, you might conclude either that John is easily bored (person attribution) or that the lecture itself is boring (situation attribution).

1. John laughs at the comedian. Almost everyone who hears the comedian laughs at him. John does not laugh at most other comedians. In the past John has almost always laughed at this comedian. (Person attribution or situation attribution?)

2. Sue contributes a large sum of money to an automobile safety fund. Hardly anyone else contributes to the automobile safety fund. Sue contributes to most fundraisers. In the past Sue has almost always contributed to the safety fund. (Person attribution or situation attribution?)

3. George translates the sentence incorrectly. Hardly anyone who translates the sentence translates it incorrectly. George translates most sentences incorrectly. In the past George has almost always translated this sentence incorrectly. (Person attribution or situation attribution?)

4. Chris is afraid of the dog. Almost everyone is afraid of the dog. Chris is not afraid of most other dogs. In the past Chris has almost always been afraid of this dog. (Person attribution or situation attribution?)

The results are discussed in the text (based on McArthur, 1972).

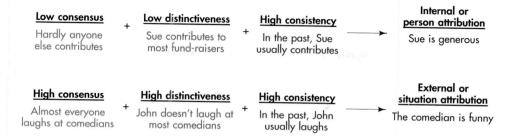

Figure 17.6
Factors influencing attribution. (Based on Kelley, 1967)

contribution is really external, rather than internal. These heuristics encourage us to oversimplify a situation, but they do not promote a systematic bias toward either an internal or an external attribution. However, we are influenced by several systematic biases that do favor either internal or external attribution patterns. Let us consider two of these biases, the fundamental attribution error and the actor-observer bias.

The Fundamental Attribution Error   We are typically surprised when people we know act inconsistently. It is puzzling to see a friend who is normally self-confident seem to stammer and stumble when called on in class. We assume that such a person should remain confident in all situations. In chapter 4 we discussed perceptual constancies, which are our tendencies to see objects as staying the same, despite changes in the way we view the object. Thus, a textbook seems to remain rectangular, even when we view it from an angle. Similarly, we expect constancy in humans; a friend should remain self-confident, even when we view this friend in a new setting (Swann, 1984).

However, the complexity of humans suggests that they will *not* remain constant, but will instead change in response to different situations (unlike a textbook). Unfortunately, however, we humans have biased perceptions. When we try to explain the behavior of other people, we tend to overemphasize the internal, or person attribution. The **fundamental attribution error** refers to the tendency to overestimate the role of internal causes and underestimate the role of external or situation causes (Brehm & Kassin, 1990). This attribution error is called *fundamental* because it is so widespread and basic that it seems to be a fundamental characteristic of social cognition. Another name for this phenomenon is the *correspondence bias*.

Let us consider a representative study. Gilbert and Jones (1986) set up an experiment so that the participants told other people exactly how they were supposed to respond to a set of 14 questions. For instance, the participant might ask, "What do you think of the legalization of marijuana?" and then instruct the person "Press the green button to indicate a liberal response." Half of the participants were supplied with a set of generally liberal responses; the other half had a set of generally conservative responses. In both cases, however, it was clear that the person receiving the questions and answers had absolutely no opportunity to express his or her own personal opinion.

After receiving responses to all 14 questions, the participants were asked to rate their partner on a 15-point scale, with a rating of 1 being most liberal and a rating of 15 being most conservative. On the average, the participants gave a rating of 7.2 to the partners who had been fed the liberal responses and a rating of 9.7 to those who had been fed the conservative responses. This difference was clearly statistically significant. Even though it was obvious that the responders were constrained by the situation, the participants thought the responders really believed the statements they had been forced to make.

A student reported a good example of the fundamental attribution error. An actress in her favorite soap opera had recently won the "best female villain" award and had been scheduled to appear on a morning talk show. The student was astonished to find out that the actress was really a warm, compassionate person—nothing like the character she played on the soap opera! Erroneously, she had attributed the evil deeds to internal forces, rather than the external forces, specifically the script the actress was hired to read on the show.

The Actor-Observer Bias   Before you read further, try Demonstration 17.5, which asks you to make judgments about yourself and a friend.

We saw that the fundamental attribution error leads us to attribute the behavior of other people to internal causes. However, we do not show this same attribution pattern for our own behavior. The **actor-observer bias** is the tendency to attribute our own behavior to external, situational causes, whereas we attribute others' behavior to internal, personal causes (Brehm & Kassin, 1990). That is, we provide different interpretations, depending upon whether we are the actor or someone observing another person. Notice, then, that the actor-observer bias emphasizes that we make the fundamental attribution error in judging others, but not in judging ourselves.

Now check over your responses to Demonstration 17.5. Count up the number of "depends on the situation" responses you supplied for yourself, in contrast to your friend. The actor-observer effect predicts that you will select many "depends on the situation" responses for yourself, because you believe that your behavior can be attributed to situational causes. In contrast, you envision your friend to have much greater "constancy," to be governed by stable, internal traits. Indeed, research similar to this demonstration has supported the actor-observer bias (e.g., Nisbett et al., 1973).

Demonstration 17.5

The Actor-Observer Bias

For each of the following characteristics, rate yourself by checking the item in Column A, the item in Column B, or the final option, "Depends on the situation." Put the letter *M* (for *Myself*) in the appropriate column.

	COLUMN A	COLUMN B	DEPENDS ON THE SITUATION
1.	_____ Serious	_____ Easygoing	_____
2.	_____ Energetic	_____ Relaxed	_____
3.	_____ Realistic	_____ Idealistic	_____
4.	_____ Quiet	_____ Talkative	_____
5.	_____ Cautious	_____ Bold	_____
6.	_____ Uninhibited	_____ Self-controlled	_____
7.	_____ Happy-go-lucky	_____ Conscientious	_____
8.	_____ Future-oriented	_____ Present-oriented	_____
9.	_____ Tough-minded	_____ Sensitive	_____
10.	_____ Calm	_____ Intense	_____
11.	_____ Lenient	_____ Firm	_____
12.	_____ Reserved	_____ Emotionally expressive	_____

Now think about your best friend—someone you know very well. Go through those 12 items once more, this time placing the first and last initials of your best friend in Column A, Column B, or "Depends on the situation."

One likely explanation for the actor-observer bias is that people see themselves as having many different facets to their personality. They believe that they have the capacity to respond differently to different situations because they have so many varied traits—for example, being either serious or easygoing as the situation demands (Sande et al., 1988).

The actor-observer bias is especially noticeable when something bad happens. We tend to manufacture excuses for our own behavior. After all, the act has a negative side, and we would rather blame it on external factors beyond our control, instead of admitting to a personality flaw. In their study of the kinds of excuses people make, Snyder and his colleagues (1983) include categories such as "I couldn't help it" and "It wasn't really me." Another study examined newspaper advice columns ("Ann Landers" and "Dear Abby"). When people described their problems, they tended to blame their own misdeeds on external, situational explanations, whereas they blamed the misdeeds of other people on internal, personal explanations (Schoeneman & Rubanowitz, 1985).

An unfortunate consequence of the actor-observer effect is that we tend to blame the victim in making judgments about other people. Consider the case of Mrs. W., a married middle-aged woman who was raped by a stranger. She resisted to the best of her ability and received a knife wound and a concussion. Despite convincing evidence that there had been a genuine rape, everyone blamed her, including the police, the hospital staff, and even her own husband. For instance, a psychiatrist who saw her bleeding and battered when she was admitted to the hospital asked, "Haven't you really been rushing toward this very thing all your life?" (Russell, 1975).

The actor-observer bias suggests that we should be more forgiving of other people. When a friend does something you consider wrong, ask yourself how you might explain this action if you were in his or her shoes. Could external forces account for the behavior? When something tragic happens to other people, do not automatically begin searching for internal personality flaws that can allow you to conclude, "They got what they deserved."

Throughout this section on person perception, we have noted that people oversimplify their social worlds and make judgments that reflect certain systematic biases. To use a term applied to the perception of objects in chapter 4, we are often governed by top-down processing. Our concepts, expectations, and prior knowledge help us judge people—though they can lead us astray. It is important to emphasize, however, that humans also use bottom-up processing, attending to information in the environment (Higgins & Bargh, 1987). We do pay attention to what we actually see and hear about other people. As a consequence, we are reasonably effective in judging others. However, we can increase our effectiveness by being aware of oversimplification and biases—and by correcting for these tendencies.

Section Summary: Person Perception

- Impression formation, one component of person perception, often involves a person schema; we organize fragments of information about a person into a coherent picture.
- Two biases in impression formation include the primacy effect (with its by-product, self-fulfilling prophecy) and the negativity bias.
- Attribution, a second component of person perception, is largely influenced by three factors: consensus, distinctiveness, and consistency.
- Two biases in attribution include the fundamental attribution error and the actor-observer bias.

Stereotypes, Prejudice, and Discrimination

A student in a wheelchair confides that several grammar school classmates had been told by their parents not to play with her because she was different. A young Black man is chased by White teenagers onto a highway, where he is hit and killed by a passing car. An outstanding woman accountant is denied partnership in her firm, on the grounds that she is not feminine enough; the reason supplied is that she needs a course at charm school and should wear makeup and jewelry. A lesbian woman discovers that someone has thrown a brick—with a dead rat tied to it—through the window of her home.

In this chapter we consider three interconnected concepts related to these examples. A **stereotype** is a structured set of beliefs about the way a group of people think and act (Ashmore & DelBoca, 1979). Stereotypes resemble the schemas we discussed in the previous section. However, stereotypes apply to groups, whereas person schemas apply to individual people. Both stereotypes and schemas involve overactive top-down processing and failure to pay attention to stimulus information. Stereotypes are often negative, though they can be positive. A Mexican-American professor told me, for example, that people often expect him to play the guitar, consistent with their stereotypes about his ethnic group. A Black student revealed that people expect him to be a "natural athlete."

Whereas stereotypes emphasize beliefs (i.e., cognitive reactions), prejudices emphasize attitudes (i.e., evaluative reactions). **Prejudice** is a negative attitude toward a group of people. Notice, then, that prejudice *cannot* be positive. Interestingly, a person who is prejudiced against one group of people that has low status in a culture is also likely to be prejudiced against other low-status groups. Specifically, a study of college students showed that prejudices against Blacks, women, the elderly, and gay people were significantly interrelated (Bierly, 1985).

Whereas prejudice is an attitude, **discrimination** involves action against a person or a group of people. Thus, stereotyped beliefs and prejudiced attitudes often reveal themselves in discriminatory behavior. For example, you may know a person who believes that Black people are lazy (a stereotype), has a negative attitude toward them (prejudice), and would refuse to hire Black people for a job (discrimination).

What kind of stereotypes do you have about these Asian-American students?

We have noted some of these biases in earlier chapters. Chapter 2 addressed looksism, and chapter 11 examined biases against both gay people and the elderly. Biases about gender and race or ethnic group have been discussed in many chapters. People can also have stereotypes, prejudice, and discrimination about religion, social class, and people with disabilities. (Can you think of other categories?)

We begin this section by looking at two of the most common—and most extensively researched—kinds of biases: racism and sexism. An in-depth discussion of the cognitive basis of stereotypes comes next, followed by a summary of stereotypes and self-fulfilling prophecies. We end with somes ideas about overcoming stereotypes and other biases.

Racism

Racism is bias toward certain racial groups; the bias can be revealed in stereotypes, prejudice, or discrimination. Racism occurs when individuals and institutions use power against a racial group considered to be inferior (Jones, 1986).

The United States has had a long and painful history of racism. A major debate at the Constitutional Convention hinged on whether slaves should be counted as people in calculating taxes and representation to Congress. The solution was the "three-fifths compromise." That is, Black slaves counted as three fifths of the value of their White masters (Rothenberg, 1988). Our Constitution no longer contains the three-fifths compromise. However, clear-cut discrimination has been a part of our recent heritage (see Figure 17.7 and Figure 17.8). In the United States, Blacks have consistently experienced the greatest prejudice compared with other races and ethnic groups (Sears, 1988).

In recent years, the Civil Rights Commission no longer sees its mission as enforcing civil rights, and the Equal Employment Opportunity Commission has been less active in enforcing affirmative action cases (Katz & Taylor, 1988). The old-fashioned, obvious forms of bigotry are less prevalent, yet prejudice continues

Figure 17.7
As recently as the 1960s, Black people faced discrimination in public places.

Figure 17.8
During World War II, the U.S. government forced many people of Japanese ancestry to live in relocation camps. This discrimination can be partly traced to racism. In this photo, a man bids farewell to his brother.

in more subtle, indirect ways (Gaertner & Dovidio, 1986). For instance, a Black writer, Patricia Raybon (1989) objects to the biased way in which the news depicts Black Americans:

> This is who I am not. I am not a crack addict. I am not a welfare mother. I am not illiterate. I am not a prostitute. I have never been in jail. My children are not in gangs. My husband doesn't beat me. My home is not a tenement. None of these things defines who I am, nor do they describe the other black people I've known and worked with and loved and befriended over these 40 years of my life. (p. 11)

Sadly, however, television, newspapers, and other media focus on the small number of Blacks who have problems, ignoring the much larger number who are employed and have no experience with drugs, jail, or illegal activities.

Researchers in psychology and sociology call this current racial bias **symbolic racism**, which is the feeling among some White people that Blacks are making inappropriate demands for change (Reid, 1988; Weigel & Howes, 1985). Try Demonstration 17.6, which contains items similar to those included on tests of symbolic racism (Sears, 1988).

An experiment by Frey and Gaertner (1986) examined this modern, relatively subtle form of racism. White female college students were randomly assigned to a condition in which they were led to believe they would be working with a female partner who was either Black or White. This partner was working on a task that was described as either easy or difficult, and during the course of the study, she requested help on the task. How often did the students help? When the task was difficult—so the request for help appeared justified—the students helped Black and White partners equally. However, when the task was easy—so the partner did not seem to be trying hard enough—the White students helped White partners more than twice as often as Black partners (see Figure 17.9). In other words, they did not go out of their way to help Black partners unless the need seemed truly legitimate. When it was more acceptable to say "No," these students showed clear discrimination against Black partners.

Symbolic Racism

Answer true or false to each of the following items, based on your true beliefs about Black people. (Please note that this test is appropriate for Blacks as well as Whites, because Black people can be racist—just as women can be sexist.)

_____ 1. Blacks are getting too demanding in their push for equal rights.

_____ 2. Blacks should not push themselves where they are not wanted.

_____ 3. It is easy to understand the anger of Black people in America.

_____ 4. Over the past few years, the government and news media have shown more respect to Blacks than they deserve.

_____ 5. Over the past few years, Blacks have received more economically than they deserve.

_____ 6. Blacks who receive money from welfare programs really do need the help.

_____ 7. Black people miss out on jobs and promotions because of racial discrimination.

_____ 8. The civil rights people have not pushed fast enough.

Now inspect your answers. Symbolic racism is revealed by true answers to items 1, 2, 4, and 5, and by false answers to items 3, 6, 7, and 8.

Sexism

Sexism is bias toward people on the basis of their gender. A person is sexist who believes that women could not be competent lawyers. A person is also sexist who believes that men could not be competent nursery school teachers. Institutions—as well as individuals—can be sexist. Like racism, this bias can be revealed in stereotypes, prejudice, or discrimination.

Consider the case of sex discrimination that accountant Ann Hopkins brought to court. In 1982, she had established that she was a top-notch accountant at a major accounting firm. She had brought in business worth $25 million, at the top of the 88 candidates proposed for partner status that year. She was also the only woman out of 88 candidates—yet the company did not name her partner. The firm claimed that she lacked interpersonal skills, and they branded her "macho." A sympathetic co-worker suggested that she would improve her chances if she would "walk more femininely, talk more femininely, dress more femininely, wear makeup, have her hair styled, and wear jewelry" (Fiske, 1989, p. 12). In court, Judge Gerhard Gesell ruled that the firm had been guilty of sex discrimination because they had treated a woman with an assertive personality in a different manner from a man with an assertive personality.

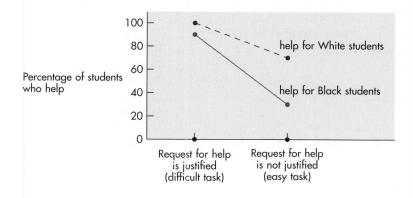

Figure 17.9
When a request for help is justified, White students help Black students just as much as they help other White students. When a request for help is not justified, White students help Black students much less. (Based on Frey & Gaertner, 1986)

Although stereotypes, prejudice, and discrimination are typically most damaging to women, it is important to point out that men can also be victims of sexism. For instance, consider a study by Glick and his colleagues (1988), who asked managers and business professionals to look at some résumés and judge which people they would consider competent enough to actually interview for a job. When the personal characteristics of the job applicant were neutral (rather than stereotypically feminine or masculine), these managers were 27% more likely to interview a male, rather than a female, for a sales management job. For a dental receptionist job, in contrast, a job applicant with neutral characteristics was 59% more likely to be recommended for an interview if the applicant was female, rather than male. Even in the current era, people are more willing to hire a man for a "man's job" and to hire a woman for a "woman's job."

Furthermore, gender stereotypes still thrive as we approach the 21st century. Although some progress has been made, a glance through current magazines will convince you that the media still believe that men should look serious, businesslike, and macho, whereas women should look home-loving, sexy, and submissive (Itzin, 1986; Matlin, 1987).

People are very accurate in identifying the characteristics that are stereotypical of women and men. Try Demonstration 17.7 to test your accuracy in guessing these stereotypes.

However, the problem with stereotypes is that they are often inaccurate. For example, Martin (1987) asked female and male college students to judge whether certain characteristics described themselves. They were also asked to judge whether these same characteristics described male students and female students at their university. If stereotypes are accurate, the students' judgments about male and female students should match their judgments about themselves. However, Martin found that males and females responded quite similarly when judging their own characteristics, but they believed that "typical males" and "typical females" were quite different from each other. For instance, males and females rated themselves similar in independence and hostility, yet they thought that "typical males" were much more independent and hostile than "typical females." Also, they rated themselves similar in "helpfulness" and "gentleness," yet they thought that "typical females" were much more helpful and gentle than "typical males."

Demonstration 17.7

Stereotypes About Women and Men

In this demonstration, you must guess what most college students think about women and men. Put a W in front of those characteristics you think students associate with women more than men, and an M in front of those associated with men more than women. The answers appear at the end of the chapter.

_____ 1. forceful
_____ 2. affectionate
_____ 3. adventurous
_____ 4. aggressive

_____ 5. emotional
_____ 6. gentle
_____ 7. self-confident
_____ 8. rude
_____ 9. submissive
_____ 10. independent
_____ 11. ambitious
_____ 12. appreciative
_____ 13. active
_____ 14. dominant
_____ 15. sensitive
_____ 16. nagging
_____ 17. inventive
_____ 18. sentimental

It seems, then, that gender differences are typically smaller than our stereotypes depict them to be (Deaux & Major, 1987; Matlin, 1987). Unger has called this phenomenon "the illusion of sex differences." She writes, "Men and women are especially alike in their beliefs about their own differences" (Unger, 1979, p. 1086). As in the case of schemas, our stereotypes reveal that we rely too heavily on top-down processing, specifically our beliefs that women and men are different from each other. As a consequence, we do not pay enough attention to bottom-up processing (i.e., actual behavior). If we paid more attention to the actual behavior of women and men, we could appreciate our similarities. The following in-depth section examines how our cognitive processes encourage us to form stereotypes.

○ ○

In Depth: The Cognitive Basis of Stereotypes

For many years, psychologists emphasized the motivational aspects of stereotypes (Deaux, 1985). For example, according to the **scapegoat theory**, people who are frustrated and unhappy about something will choose a relatively powerless group to take the blame for a situation that is not their fault (Aronson, 1988a). According to another motivation-oriented theory, **social identity theory**, we favor the groups to which we belong in order to enhance our self-esteem (Tajfel, 1982; Tajfel & Turner, 1986). Both these approaches argue that stereotypes serve the purpose of boosting our own self-images.

In recent years, however, psychologists have increasingly endorsed the **cognitive approach to stereotypes**, which argues that most stereotypes are a product of normal human thought processes (Bodenhausen & Wyer, 1985). According to David Hamilton (1979), one cognitive process that seems to be characteristic of most humans is the tendency to divide the people we meet into social groups. We separate people into categories such as females versus males, Blacks versus Whites, Catholics versus Protestants versus Jews, and gay people versus heterosexual people. This basic categorization process is a necessary component of stereotyping. We could not have stereotypes of women and men, for example, unless we first made a distinction between them.

Stereotypes help us simplify and organize the world by creating categories in a habitual, automatic fashion. It seems that the primary way we categorize people is on the basis of gender, and we accomplish this categorization with very little thought (Bem, 1981). In fact, after you finish reading this book today, try *not* to pay attention to the gender of the first person you meet. It is very difficult to suppress this tendency to split the world in half, using gender as the great divide. Once we have a stereotype in place (whether it concerns gender, race, or some other attribute), this stereotype often guides the way we cognitively process information. Specifically, it can guide the way we perceive people, make attributions for their behavior, remember them, and evaluate them. Let us look at each of these four processes.

According to the cognitive approach to stereotypes, you would tend to categorize the people in this picture according to characteristics such as gender and race.

Stereotypes and Person Perception   Cognitive psychologists propose that humans are so bombarded with stimuli that we pay attention to some information and ignore other information. We saw earlier that we use a person schema when we perceive one individual person (e.g., a caring, intelligent, considerate husband). Similarly, a stereotype encourages us to pay attention to certain behaviors when we perceive people from a certain group.

For example, John Darley and Paget Gross (1983) conducted an experiment in which one group of participants was led to believe that a 9-year-old White girl

Figure 17.10
Average grade placement for mathematics-test performance, as a function of the participants' beliefs about the child's social class and whether or not they witnessed her performance on the test. (Darley & Gross, 1983)

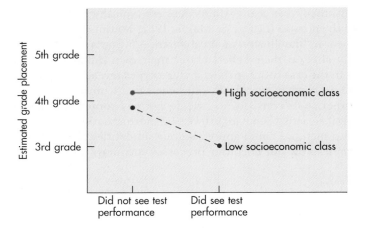

Young people looking at a group of elderly people at a senior citizens' center might conclude that they are all alike, a phenomenon called outgroup homogeneity.

came from a high socioeconomic background, and another similar group was led to believe that she came from a low socioeconomic background. Two other groups also received these differing background stories and then watched a videotape of a girl taking an academic test. Both of these groups actually watched the same videotaped performance, though their expectations were certainly different. All participants were asked to judge the girl's ability level by indicating the grade level appropriate for her performance on tests of liberal arts, reading, and mathematics.

Figure 17.10 shows the results for the mathematics-test estimate. (The other two tests showed similar results.) Notice that when the participants had not witnessed any videotaped performance, social class had little influence on their judgment. When they had watched her performance, however, social class had an important impact. Participants believed that she was working at the fourth grade level if they thought she was upper class, but at the third grade level if they thought she was lower class. The expectations had encouraged people to perceive her behavior very differently in the two conditions. For example, if she were to scratch her head, those who thought she was upper class might have perceived this gesture as a sign of thoughtful contemplation. In contrast, those who thought she was lower class might have perceived this same gesture as a sign that she felt stumped by a question. This selective perception encouraged those who had seen the videotapes to have very different evaluations of the young girl. As David Hamilton (1981) commented about the powerful influence of expectations on perception, "I wouldn't have seen it if I hadn't believed it" (p. 137).

Another way that stereotypes influence person perception is that they encourage us to perceive all members of another group as being similar, a phenomenon known as **outgroup homogeneity**. We perceive members of our own group as diverse and heterogeneous, but people in that other group? "They are all the same!"

In a recent talk, a Black woman poet named Maya Angelou provided a perfect example of outgroup homogeneity. She was describing her close friendship with a White woman. One time this White woman was discussing a Black woman they had both met some time earlier. Maya Angelou could not recall who this woman was, so she asked, "What color was she?" The White friend replied, "But I told you she was Black." Ms. Angelou responded, "Yes, but what color of Black?" To a White person, everybody we compartmentalize as Black is Black, and we fail to appreciate the richness of skin colors between pale tan and rich black.

Psychologists have uncovered evidence of outgroup homogeneity for many different stereotypes (Linville et al., 1986; Quattrone, 1986). For example, White people tend to think that Black people are homogeneous (Linville & Jones, 1980). Young people think that old people are "all the same," whereas old people think that young people are "all the same" (Brewer & Lui, 1984; Linville, 1982). Furthermore, students at two rival universities perceived the students at the other university as being highly homogeneous (Quattrone & Jones, 1980). It seems that we are willing to believe that members of our own group display the kind of individual differences that represent one theme of this textbook, but we deny this same diversity in other groups (Judd & Park, 1988).

Stereotypes and Attribution   A friend recently described an unpleasant incident. She and her husband are both Black, and both received their advanced degrees from prestigious universities. She made an appointment with her son's math teacher to discuss a mediocre grade. The teacher told her that they should not be so worried. "After all," she said, "you and your husband are both overachievers." This teacher failed to acknowledge that the parents' accomplishments were due to high ability, and not just hard work.

A common finding in the research on attribution is that people are more likely to trace a person's success to ability than to other factors if that person is male, rather than female, and White, rather than Black (Matlin, 1987). For instance, in one study, people were asked to assign attributions for successful male and female medical students. The participants tended to say that the male student was successful because he had high ability. In contrast, the female student's success was seldom attributed to ability. Instead, the participants said that the female student had been successful because she was lucky, because the task was easy, or because—the worst news yet—she had cheated on her examinations (Feather & Simon, 1975).

Similarly, in research on race, students read a description of a highly successful banker who was either Black or White, female or male (Yarkin et al., 1982). Students tended to explain the White male's success in terms of his high ability. In contrast, when they made judgments about the White female, the Black male, and the Black female (in other words, all three less prestigious categories), people thought that the most important reasons for success were hard work and luck—but not ability.

Stereotypes and Memory   We have seen that stereotypes can influence perception and attribution; they can also influence memory. Specifically, our stereotypes tend to bias memory so that we remember attributes consistent with those stereotypes (O'Sullivan & Durso, 1984). Consider Cohen's (1981) study of people's stereotypes regarding occupations. People in this study watched a videotape of a woman having a birthday dinner with her husband. If they had been told that the woman was a waitress, people remembered that she was drinking beer during part of the video and that she owned a television. Other people watching the same video were told that the woman worked as a librarian. These people remembered that she wore glasses and that she owned classical records. In general, then, when we are uncertain about something in memory, we tend to "fill in the blanks," consistent with our stereotypes.

It has been stressed throughout this chapter that the cognitive processes operate the same way, whether we think about people, or objects and events. Cohen's results are highly similar to the results of the study by Brewer and Treyens (1981), discussed in the memory chapter. As Demonstration 7.5 illustrated, people who thought they had been in a professor's office tended to recall seeing books, even though none were actually seen. We tend to reconstruct memories that are compatible with our stereotypes and schemas.

Stereotypes and Evaluation   In fifth grade, my teacher divided us at random into two teams for a math contest. I can vividly recall how attractive, intelligent, and nice most of my team members were, compared to the other group. Our tendency to evaluate members of another group more negatively is called **outgroup negativity**, or **ingroup favoritism**.

In one study, Jennifer Crocker and her colleagues (1987) randomly assigned participants to either Group A or Group B by asking them to select a letter (A or B) from a box. The participants then rearranged themselves to sit at either Table A or Table B, and they were instructed not to talk to each other during the study. After several other tasks, all participants rated the members of Group A and the members of Group B. The results showed that people assigned an average rating to their own group of 19.6. The other group received an average rating of 18.0, significantly more negative.

Notice, then, that we humans have become accustomed to categorizing other humans. Even when we cannot categorize on the basis of race, gender, social class, occupation, or other common classification systems, we still seek ways to subdivide people. We may even use a category as clearly arbitrary as a letter of the alphabet randomly drawn from a box. Once we have established a category, we frequently use stereotypes to simplify and bias our perceptions, attributions, memories, and evaluations of other members of our species.

○ ○

Stereotypes and Self-Fulfilling Prophecies

The earlier section on impression formation showed that self-fulfilling prophecies can influence behavior. Individuals often live up to the schemas and expectations that other people have created. Self-fulfilling prophecies also operate in the case of stereotypes; people live up to the schemas and expectancies that other people have created for the group to which they belong. The effects of stereotypes are not confined to the cerebral cortex of the onlooker. Instead, they can guide the behavior of the person who has been stereotyped (Fiske & Taylor, 1991).

Consider a study in which White interviewers interacted with either White or Black people. With Black candidates, the interviewers were less friendly and personal. The interviewers also sat farther away and leaned away from the candidate; in addition, they ended the interview sooner and spoke less smoothly (Word et al., 1974). In a second study, the researchers trained interviewers to imitate either the impersonal interview style used with Black people or the friendly interview style used with White people. Then these interviewers used either the impersonal style or the friendly style with a new set of White students. Those students who had been treated in the impersonal style performed less well. If White interviewers judge Black candidates as less competent than White candidates, part of the blame may lie in the interviewers' own influence on the candidates.

Self-fulfilling prophecies also operate for gender (Deaux & Major, 1987). For instance, women tend to act in a stereotypically feminine fashion when they interact with someone who seems to have traditional views about women (von Baeyer et al., 1981). It seems likely, too, that men might act in a more stereotypically masculine fashion when others expect them to be macho, rather than gentle and compassionate.

It is important to emphasize, however, that we are not always at the mercy of our stereotypes. For example, stereotypes are most likely to operate when we have little stimulus information, so that bottom-up processing is difficult (Lott, 1985; Wright, 1988). Furthermore, people low in prejudice can inhibit the activation of a stereotype, replacing the stereotype with thoughts about equality (Devine, 1989).

In addition, self-fulfilling prophecies do not always influence our behavior. We are not simply marionettes, with other people pulling the strings. Our own self-concepts are usually stronger determinants of behavior than are the expectancies of other people (Swann & Ely, 1984). However, we should be concerned about any instances in which stereotypes bias and oversimplify. And we should also be concerned about any cases where self-fulfilling prophecies keep people from fulfilling their true potential. Now let us consider some ways of reducing stereotypes, prejudice, and discrimination.

Reducing Biases

Any serious attempt to overcome unequal treatment will require major changes in the structure of society and institutions. For example, suppose that a company sincerely wants to incorporate more Blacks into managerial positions. It will not be effective to hire or promote just one Black person. This employee's "solo status" is likely to encourage even more discrimination and racial tension. Researchers have observed that roughly 20% of a group—but not less than two individuals—must have minority status for discrimination to drop substantially (Pettigrew & Martin, 1987).

We saw in the section on attitudes that mere familiarity with a stimulus often encourages more positive attitudes. People concerned with social justice several decades ago thought that desegregation might work because White people and Black people would have more opportunities to interact and become familiar with one another. However, desegregation often failed to change attitudes (Aronson, 1987, 1988a). The problem was that Blacks and Whites usually did not have equal status when they interacted in newly desegregated schools and public places. In rare cases where equal status was ensured—as in public housing—interracial cooperation was much more likely (Deutsch & Collins, 1951).

Elliot Aronson devised a creative method of encouraging equal status in an interracial classroom (Aronson, 1988; Aronson & Osherow, 1980). He and his colleagues visited a newly desegregated school in Austin, Texas, and noticed that one or two students (invariably White Anglos) seemed to have all the answers, whereas the minority students were either incorrect or silent. These researchers then designed the jigsaw technique. In a jigsaw puzzle, all the pieces must fit together in order to complete the picture. Similarly, in a **jigsaw classroom**, all the children must work together to ensure good grades.

In a typical application of the jigsaw classroom, the researchers constructed a six-paragraph biography of a famous publisher, Joseph Pulitzer. One paragraph was then handed to each member of a six-person learning group. Each child therefore learned only one piece of the puzzle, and the children were forced to learn from each other in order to master the complete biography. Consider a representative example of a six-member group that included Carlos, a Mexican-American boy whose second language was English. Initially, the other children were impatient with Carlos's halting English. A classroom assistant pointed out, however, that the other students would need to know information from Carlos's segment to succeed on an exam. The children soon learned that they could learn more from Carlos by paying attention to him and asking him skillful questions. After a couple of weeks, they concluded that Carlos was much smarter than they had originally thought. The Anglo students began to like him, and he began to enjoy school more (Aronson, 1987). With equal status, the children had developed more positive attitudes.

Recall, however, that it was emphasized in the in-depth section that humans seem to have a strong tendency to categorize people into social groups. When we are trapped by our categories, we show mindlessness and fail to pay attention to the true qualities of the people we meet (Langer, 1989). Some degree of categorization is probably inevitable, but we can take steps to reduce stereotypes and other biases (Brehm & Kassin, 1990).

Students can reduce their own stereotypes by focusing on interests they have in common, rather than the categories that separate them.

Keep in mind that stereotypes encourage top-down processing. They are particularly likely to operate when we have too little information about the stimulus to rely on bottom-up processing. The students in Carlos's group, for example, overcame their stereotypes by paying attention to him and noticing his strengths. Indeed, research has demonstrated that discrimination is minimized when members of a less prestigious group are seen as individuals, rather than a single, undifferentiated group (Wilder, 1978).

If you are concerned about reducing some of your own stereotypes, try talking to someone from another social category. Focus on identifying the characteristics you have in common, rather than the categories that separate you. Denise Burden-Patmon (1989), who teaches English classes at Wheelock College, provided a useful example. She found herself standing on a downtown Boston train car next to a young Black male whose dress and mannerisms suggested "problem youth." Most well-educated people would focus upon the boundary that separated themselves from this young man.

However, Burden-Patmon took another approach. She turned to him and asked how he was feeling that day. He was initially shocked, but a wonderful conversation soon developed. It turned out that he had abused drugs and had been in jail, but he responded warmly when he learned she taught English. He revealed that he had written some poetry while in jail, and even began to recite some of it on the train! A mutual appreciation of poetry allowed both of them to conquer an unnecessary category boundary.

Section Summary: Stereotypes, Prejudice, and Discrimination

- A stereotype is a structured set of beliefs, prejudice is a negative attitude, and discrimination involves action; these biases can be based on race, gender, looks, sexual preference, religion, social class, disability status, and other social categories.
- Symbolic racism reveals itself in relatively subtle discrimination, such as refusal to help Black people unless the need seems highly legitimate.
- Sexism, such as refusal to hire or promote on the basis of gender, is more commonly directed against women, though it may also harm men; gender differences are typically smaller than stereotypes suggest.
- The tendency to divide people into social groups is a normal cognitive process; stereotypes can guide the way we perceive people, make attributions for their behavior, remember them, and evaluate them.
- Stereotypes can encourage self-fulfilling prophecies.
- Ideas for reducing biases include increasing the number of minority-group members, encouraging equal status for members of different groups, and paying closer attention to stimulus characteristics in order to encourage bottom-up processing and less reliance on categories.

Interpersonal Attraction

This chapter on social cognition has examined how we think about other people and ourselves. For example, the first section investigated how other people can influence our attitudes. The section on person perception focused on the impressions we form of other people, as well as the attributions we make for their behavior. In the third section, we emphasized the negative aspects of social cognition when we examined systematic biases against groups of people.

In this last section, we consider the positive aspects of social cognition: interpersonal attraction. Even a casual glance around any public area will reveal people clumped together in pairs and groups, rather than people in isolation. The American writer Henry David Thoreau claimed, "I find it wholesome to be alone the greater part of the time. . . . I love to be alone. I never found the companion that was so companionable as solitude" (Thoreau, 1854/1971). But Thoreau holds a minority position; most of us enjoy other people—at least some of the time. In chapter 11, we discussed friendship and love relationships as part of adolescent and adult development. Now we emphasize the social psychological components of interpersonal attraction, paying particular attention to the important determinants of friendship and love.

Friendship

When we hear the word *friendship*, many people think of long, intimate talks in which deep secrets may be revealed. However, the research on actual friendships shows that most friends meet briefly in public places for superficial chats (Duck & Miell, 1986). But what factors determine which people we choose to be our friends? Among the more important are similarity, proximity, and attractiveness.

Similarity   Think about your best friend; why did that friendship develop? It is likely that you and your friend share similar backgrounds, interests, and personal characteristics. You will not be surprised to learn that researchers have also found that similarity is an important determinant of friendship and interpersonal attraction. For example, Gonzales and her colleagues (1983) asked people to complete surveys assessing their own attitudes and social behavior. Each person's responses were used to construct a fake set of responses, which indicated either 0%, 50%, or 100% agreement with his or her own responses. About 2 weeks later, each participant received one of these bogus surveys, with the explanation that it had been completed by another student. Respondents were asked to indicate their personal feelings toward this student, on a scale where the maximum score was 14.

Figure 17.11 shows that the participants were much more positive about highly similar people, in comparison to moderately similar and dissimilar people. When it comes to friendship, opposites certainly do *not* attract!

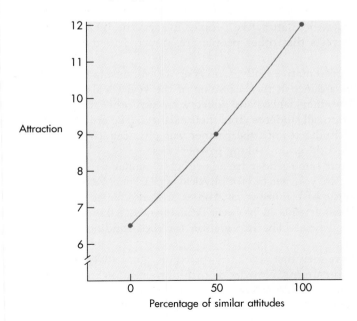

Figure 17.11
The influence of similarity on attraction toward a stranger. (Based on Gonzales et al., 1983)

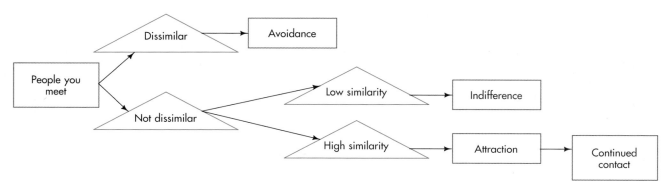

Figure 17.12
The two-step model of attraction.

One interesting explanation of the similarity effect is a two-step model of attraction, which proposes that we first screen out the people very different from ourselves and then seek out very similar people (Byrne et al., 1986; Rosenbaum, 1986). Look at Figure 17.12 and figure out whether it seems to account for your own friendship patterns. For instance, think about several people you have met this year. Were some so dissimilar that you soon avoided them? Then, from the group of others did you later find yourself developing friendships with high-similarity people?

Proximity   Do your closest friends live near you, or are they the ones who happened to sit near you in classes? Is it difficult to maintain a friendship with someone you rarely see anymore? As you saw in the earlier section on persuasion, we like something (or someone) better if we see it more often.

In a classic study of friendship patterns, Festinger and his colleagues (1950) interviewed women who lived in the married students' housing at the Massachusetts Institute of Technology. Couples had been assigned apartments at random, rather than on the basis of prior friendships. When the women were asked to list their three closest friends, about two thirds of the friends lived in the same building. Roughly half of all friends lived on the same floor, and next-door neighbors were especially popular.

Attractiveness   We have seen the powerful effects of attractiveness throughout this book, and most recently in the section on persuasion. As you might expect, we also tend to like attractive people. In fact, the literal meaning of the word *attractive* suggests that other people are attracted to these physically appealing people.

In a representative study, University of Minnesota freshmen were randomly matched for a dance at the beginning of the year (Walster et al., 1966). During the blind date, they danced and talked with each other for about 2 hours. During an intermission, all students rated their partners. The only factor that significantly predicted attitudes toward the partner was physical attractiveness. Both women and men liked the good-looking partners best.

Are your same-gender friends roughly similar to you in attractiveness? In other words, are you *matched* for physical appearance? Feingold (1988b) performed a meta-analysis of a number of studies and discovered that men tended to be similar to their friends in physical attractiveness. However, women showed no matching tendencies. The explanation for these findings is not clear. Can you think of one?

We have seen that similarity, proximity, and attractiveness have an impact on friendship patterns. Now let us turn our attention to that more intense form of interpersonal attraction: love.

Love

In his book *De l'amour*, Stendhal writes, "When you are to see the woman you love in the evening, the expectation of such great happiness makes all the moments that separate you from it unbearable" (Stendhal, 1927, p. 63). In the film, *Out in Suburbia*, a middle-aged lesbian woman says about the woman she loves, "I really realized that I had fallen in love and that all the loving feelings I had ever felt . . . I was feeling, and they were *so* intensified, and it was wonderful . . . it still is!"

This section on love addresses three issues that researchers have examined: What variables predict love relationships? Are there different kinds of love? Finally, what are the characteristics of long-term love relationships?

Factors Related to Love Relationships   To a large extent, the same factors we discussed in connection with friendship are also important in love relationships. Consider similarity, for instance. Dating and married couples tend to be similar in age, race, social class, religion, education, intelligence, and number of siblings. Couples also share similar attitudes, and they are likely to be similar in their tendency to reveal personal information about themselves (Brehm, 1985; Buss, 1985; Hendrick & Hendrick, 1983; Hendrick et al., 1988).

Proximity is also an important factor: We tend to fall in love with people who live nearby. One psychologist writes, "Conceptions of romantic love aside, the 'one and only' typically lives within driving distance: it is naturally easier to become intimate with someone who is close-by" (Buss, 1985, p. 48).

Naturally, attractiveness is also important (Hatfield & Sprecher, 1986). We tend to fall in love with physically appealing people. However, that tendency is modified by a second trend: We also tend to fall in love with people whose attractiveness matches our own. In romantic couples, the attractiveness of the partners is moderately correlated (Feingold, 1988b).

However, attractiveness matters more for sexual relationships than for more permanent partnerships. Nevid (1984) asked students at a large Eastern university to rate on a 5-point scale the degree to which they judged a characteristic to be important. The students provided ratings for both a "purely sexual relationship" and a meaningful, long-term relationship. Table 17.1 shows the five most important characteristics for males judging females and for females judging males. As you will note, men and women emphasize somewhat different characteristics for a sexual relationship, though both focus on physical characteristics.

Notice, however, that men and women are nearly identical in their judgments for meaningful relationships. Both want honesty, personality, fidelity, warmth, and sensitivity or kindness from a partner. These characteristics resemble the 10 ideal qualities identified in a study on couples in a noncollege population: good companion, considerate, honest, affectionate, dependable, intelligent, kind, understanding, interesting to talk to, and loyal (Buss & Barnes, 1986).

We tend to fall in love with people whose attractiveness matches our own.

Table 17.1   *Characteristics That Males and Females Rate as Important for Sexual Relationships and Meaningful Relationships*

	MALES JUDGING FEMALES	FEMALES JUDGING MALES
Sexual relationship	Build/figure	Attractiveness
	Sexuality	Sexuality
	Attractiveness	Warmth
	Facial features	Personality
	Buttocks	Tenderness
Meaningful relationship	Honesty	Honesty
	Personality	Fidelity
	Fidelity	Personality
	Sensitivity	Warmth
	Warmth	Kindness

Source: Nevid, 1984.

As you can see, none of those lists for long-term relationships mention attractiveness. However, perhaps you can anticipate a problem. Looksism operates when we first meet someone. We may reject a person who does not meet our standards of attractiveness. So we do not ever have the opportunity to know— or develop a long-term relationship with—a person who is a good companion, considerate, honest, and otherwise admirable—but not especially attractive.

Different Kinds of Love   Take a moment to think about the various couples you know who love each other. Do they seem to love each other in the same way? Chapter 14 focuses on different kinds of intelligence, such as Robert Sternberg's (1985b) triarchic theory of intelligence. In that theory, Sternberg proposed that intelligence has three important parts—componential, experiential, and contextual intelligence—and that a person could excel in one, two, or all three kinds of intelligence.

Many psychologists are just as eager to categorize love as they are to categorize intelligence. In fact, a theory of love that is currently among the most popular happens to be one proposed by Robert Sternberg (Clark & Reis, 1988; Sternberg, 1986, 1988). He proposes that love, like intelligence, has three important parts. Sternberg's **triangular theory of love** consists of three components: intimacy, passion, and decision/commitment.

Intimacy is the close, connected feeling of warmth in loving relationships. Some important aspects of intimacy include the following (Sternberg & Grajek, 1984):

1. wanting to promote the welfare of the loved one,

2. experiencing happiness with the loved one,

3. having high regard for the loved one,

4. giving and receiving emotional support from the loved one, and

5. valuing the loved one as part of your life.

Passion includes the drives that lead to physical attraction, romance, and sexual relationships. It often creates intense physiological arousal (Hatfield, 1988).

The Passionate Love Scale

Rate each of these items on the scale below to determine whether you are currently experiencing passionate love. If you are not currently in love, think about someone you cared about in the past.

Rating

_____ 1. I would feel despair if _____ left me.

_____ 2. Sometimes I feel I can't control my thoughts; they are obsessively on _____.

_____ 3. I would rather be with _____ than anyone else.

_____ 4. I feel happy when I am doing something to make _____ happy.

_____ 5. I'd get jealous if I thought _____ were falling in love with someone else.

_____ 6. I yearn to know all about _____.

_____ 7. I want _____—physically, emotionally, mentally.

_____ 8. I have an endless appetite for affection from _____.

_____ 9. For me, _____ is the perfect romantic partner.

_____ 10. I sense my body responding when _____ touches me.

Rating Scale:

1	2	3	4	5	6	7	8	9
Not at all true				Moderately true				Definitely true

Source: Hatfield, 1988.

Demonstration 17.8 illustrates a shortened version of a questionnaire, called the Passionate Love Scale (Hatfield, 1988).

The **decision/commitment** component of Sternberg's triangular theory consists of two aspects: (1) a short-term aspect, the decision that you love someone; and (2) the long-term aspect, the commitment to maintain that love.

Figure 17.13 shows how these three components of love form a triangle, with one component at each corner. As in the triarchic theory of intelligence, a person could experience one, two, or all three components. For example, a friend of yours may experience only passion toward his or her partner; this kind of love could be located at the lower left corner of Figure 17.13. Another friend might feel romantic love, or intimacy combined with passion; this kind of love could be located halfway along the line between passion and intimacy. Notice that other love experiences are also possible that involve either one or two components. Located in the center of the triangle is complete love, which combines all three kinds of love.

The triangular theory of love seems to fit our intuitions about loving relationships. In the coming years, researchers will need to test the components of the model to determine whether the data match our intuitions. Let us turn our attention now to enduring love relationships, to see which components of love are most important in these long-term partnerships.

Long-Lasting Love Relationships   Earlier in the chapter, we examined first impressions, which are our initial reactions to strangers. We conclude by looking at the kind of loving partnerships that last for decades.

Figure 17.13
Sternberg's triangular theory of love, with its three components. (Note that the figure also includes three examples, shown in italics.)

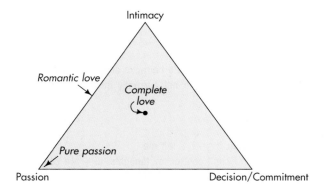

Romantic love

Complete love

Pure passion

Intimacy

Passion

Decision/Commitment

By one estimate, the average duration of a marriage in the United States is 9.4 years—not even one decade (Lauer & Lauer, 1985). Even those marriages that hold together may not be blissful. For instance, married couples tend to use more negative comments toward each other than toward strangers, whereas they direct more positive comments toward strangers than toward each other (Birchler et al., 1975; Byrne & Murnen, 1988). In the learning chapter, you saw that reinforcement is a more effective way to change behavior than punishment (for example, negative comments). Unfortunately, we humans often fail to apply this rule when we interact with people we love.

What are the characteristics of happy couples, who remain deeply in love for many years? Researchers have identified a number of important characteristics (Branden, 1988; Lauer & Lauer, 1985):

1. They tend to express love verbally, and they express their admiration and appreciation for each other.

2. Their partner is their best friend.

3. They regard their relationship as a long-term, important commitment.

According to researchers, couples who have long-lasting relationships tend to express love and affection and enjoy a close friendship.

4. They show physical affection for each other, and they agree about their sex life (though sexuality is typically not the most important aspect of their partnership).

5. They offer each other an emotional support system.

A happy long-term partnership is one that stresses intimacy, commitment, and—in many cases—passion. Couples in love with each other after many decades truly enjoy each other's company. These sentiments are best summarized by a woman who wrote,

> I feel that liking a person in marriage is as important as loving that person. Friends enjoy each other's company. We spend an unusually large amount of time together. We work at the same institution, offices just a few feet apart. But we still have things to do and to say to each other on a positive note after being together through the day. (Lauer & Lauer, 1985, p. 24)

Section Summary: Interpersonal Attraction

- The most important determinants of friendship are similarity, proximity, and—to some extent—attractiveness.
- Love relationships are also determined by similarity, proximity, and attractiveness—though attractiveness matters more for purely sexual relationships than for permanent partnerships.
- Sternberg's triangular theory of love is based on three components: intimacy, passion, and decision/commitment.
- Long-lasting love relationships are based on the expression of love and admiration, friendship, commitment, affection, and support.

REVIEW QUESTIONS

1. Discuss the relationship between attitudes and behavior. Do they tend to be more closely related or less closely related than you would have guessed before reading the chapter? Think of three topics from your own life concerned with attitudes and behavior, and see whether the correspondence between attitudes and behavior depends upon the three factors discussed in Figure 17.2.

2. In what way do dissonance theory and self-perception theory make different predictions about conflicting cognitions? Review Figure 17.4 and describe an incident from your experience that illustrates each theory.

3. Many parts of this chapter emphasized that we humans are overwhelmed by information, and so we use shortcuts, schemas, and heuristics to simplify our social worlds. How is this theme relevant in persuasion, person perception, and stereotypes?

4. What factors influence (a) the likelihood that you will be persuaded, (b) your friendship with another person, and (c) your tendency to love another person? Do you see any similarities among these lists?

5. Why is the primacy effect important in connection with the concept of person schema and self-fulfilling prophecy? Describe similar effects in connection with stereotypes.

6. What three factors influence whether we attribute something to a person or a situation? Describe two biases likely to occur in attribution: the fundamental attribution error and the actor-observer bias. How do attributions operate in the case of stereotypes? How is the actor-observer bias related to another stereotyping effect, outgroup homogeneity?

7. It is likely that at some point you stereotyped someone else on the basis of race, gender, or some other characteristic. Discuss how that stereotyping was promoted by the tendency to categorize. Describe how your stereotype influenced your perceptions, attributions, memory, and evaluations.

8. Review the components of Sternberg's triangular theory of love. Suppose you wanted to devise a similar theory to explain friendship patterns. What components would you choose to explore?

9. This chapter emphasized heuristics and schemas, which characterize top-down processing. Discuss how bottom-up processing can be important as far as (a) the elaboration likelihood model, (b) person-perception accuracy, and (c) our ability to overcome stereotypes.

10. Many students take a psychology course to help them get along with other people. What practical advice have you learned about (a) attitudes, (b) person perception, (c) stereotypes, prejudice, and discrimination, and (d) interpersonal attraction?

NEW TERMS

social psychology	actor-observer bias
social cognition	stereotype
heuristics	prejudice
attitude	discrimination
theory of cognitive dissonance	racism
self-perception theory	symbolic racism
elaboration likelihood model	sexism
mere exposure effect	scapegoat theory
person perception	social identity theory
impression formation	cognitive approach to stereotypes
attribution	outgroup homogeneity
schema	outgroup negativity
person schema	ingroup favoritism
primacy effect	jigsaw classroom
self-fulfilling prophecy	triangular theory of love
negativity bias	intimacy
person attribution	passion
situation attribution	decision/commitment
fundamental attribution error	

ANSWERS TO DEMONSTRATIONS

Demonstration 17.7   Studies by Cowan and Stewart (1977) and Williams and Bennett (1975) have shown that people tend to respond W to numbers 2, 5, 6, 9, 12, 15, 16, and 18 whereas they respond M to numbers 1, 3, 4, 7, 8, 10, 11, 13, 14, and 17.

RECOMMENDED READINGS

Brehm, S. S., & Kassin, S. M. (1990). *Social psychology*. Boston: Houghton Mifflin. This superb textbook is a clearly written overview of the field, with strong coverage of the recent studies; the authors also have a refreshing sense of humor.

Fiske, S. T., & Taylor, S. E. (1991). *Social cognition* (2nd ed.) New York: Random House. This textbook specifically focuses on cognitive aspects of social psychology, including attributions, schemas, person memory, and attitudes.

Katz, P. A., & Taylor, D. A. (Eds.). (1988). *Eliminating racism: Profiles in controversy*. New York: Plenum. Here is a systematic examination of racism, including coverage on symbolic racism, stereotypes, social policy, intergroup conflict, and affirmative action.

Matlin, M. W. (1987). *The psychology of women*. New York: Holt, Rinehart and Winston. My textbook takes a life-span approach to women's lives, from infancy through old age. Stereotypes about gender are discussed throughout the book.

Sternberg, R. J., & Barnes, M. L. (Eds.). (1988). *The psychology of love*. New Haven, CT: Yale University Press. Theories of love are emphasized in this book; prominent researchers also discuss passionate love, romantic love, love in marriage, and other relevant topics.

Social Influence

On January 28, 1986, the space shuttle Challenger exploded shortly after launching. Six astronauts and schoolteacher Christa McAuliffe were killed instantly. Later investigations revealed that engineers had warned NASA administrators about the defective O-rings that had been responsible for the tragedy. However, both NASA and the general public were swept up in the excitement about sending the first civilian into space. An engineer pleaded with a NASA administrator, "I sure wouldn't want to be the person that had to stand in front of a board of inquiry to explain why I launched." Nonetheless, NASA administrators convinced themselves that the show must go on—with tragic results.

In 1969, Mike Wallace of CBS News interviewed a man from an army unit that had massacred hundreds of Vietnamese civilians in the village of My Lai on orders from Lieutenant William Calley. This young man described how he had helped round up about 50 men, women, and children. He reported,

> We made them squat down and Lieutenant Calley came over and said, "you know what to do with them, don't you?" And I said yes. So I took it for granted that he just wanted us to watch them. And he left, and came back about ten or fifteen minutes later and said, "How come you ain't killed them yet?" And I told him that I didn't think you wanted us to kill them, that you just wanted us to guard them. He said, "No. I want them dead." So . . . I started shooting. I poured about four clips into the group. (cited in Milgram, 1974, p. 184)

In 1939, Germany invaded Poland. A 16-year-old Catholic girl named Stefania became deeply concerned about her Jewish friends, and she risked her life to bring food to them in the ghetto area of Warsaw. Eventually, she even built a false ceiling in her small apartment. This space served as a hiding place for 13 Jews for a period of $2\frac{1}{2}$ years. During a traumatic 7-month period, the Germans demanded that Stefania house several German soldiers and nurses in the apartment, yet they never learned about the 13 people in the attic (Fogelman & Wiener, 1985).

In this chapter we explore the influence that people have on each other. We see that people in close-knit groups can encourage each other to make irrational decisions, as in the *Challenger* incident; we act differently in groups than when we are alone. Social pressure can encourage conformity, compliance, and obedience, as in the Vietnamese incident in My Lai. In this chapter we also examine how social forces can encourage conflict and aggression on some occasions and astonishing altruism and kindness on other occasions. We can become the soldier in My Lai, or young Stefania in Warsaw.

The previous chapter emphasized social cognition, or our thoughts about other people. In the current chapter, we emphasize how social situations influence our actions. We consider four topics: (1) group processes; (2) yielding to social pressure; (3) aggression, conflict, and conflict resolution; and (4) altruism. Notice, then, that the first two sections focus on the nature of group interactions, whereas the last two explore how interactions between people can be either negative (aggressive) or positive (altruistic).

Group Processes

According to social psychologists, a **group** is defined as two or more people interacting with each other. Think about a group to which you belong—maybe a social organization, an athletic group, or a group of students who often study together. In your interactions, you depend upon each other and influence each other (Mullen, 1987). Several processes are likely to occur within your group. We discuss how the presence of another person influences performance, how people adopt social roles, how decision making becomes more polarized in a group, and how a group can make unwise decisions in an effort to preserve group harmony.

Social Facilitation

Suppose you have a truly mindless task to accomplish, like washing dishes or raking leaves. Would you finish faster if someone else is nearby or if you are alone? Now suppose that you face a difficult assignment, such as writing an essay about an incomprehensible poem or solving a set of challenging math problems. Would you rather be alone in the room or have someone else present? When you are in a group, other people are nearby, and their presence sometimes helps performance, but sometimes hurts it.

One of the earliest social psychology studies examined how performance is influenced by the presence of other individuals. Norman Triplett (1897–1898) arranged for 40 children to work on a simple task—winding up a fishing reel—either by themselves or working beside other children. Triplett discovered that the children finished faster with other children nearby. However, other later researchers discovered that group settings often produced slower or less competent performance. How could the same variable produce completely opposite results?

In 1965, an intriguing solution was proposed by Robert Zajonc (pronounced "*Zeye*-unce"). In the previous chapter we discussed Zajonc's demonstration that *mere exposure* of a stimulus is enough to make people like it better (Zajonc, 1968). That is, people give positive evaluations to objects and people they have encountered frequently. Zajonc also demonstrated that *mere presence* of another person is enough to change people's performance. Zajonc proposed that we are aroused and energized when another person is around. That person does not need to be talking, working, or doing anything special; mere presence is all that is required.

When we are aroused, we are more likely to produce a dominant response—one that is readily available. Consider what happens when people are asked to give word associations, for instance to the word *house*. When they work on this task by themselves, they tend to provide somewhat unusual associations, such as *hill* or *mansion*. When they work with someone else present in the room, however, they are more likely to produce common or dominant responses, such as *home* (Matlin & Zajonc, 1968).

So how does this tendency to produce a dominant response help us predict whether people perform better alone or in a group? Zajonc (1965) argues that on an easy task, the dominant response is a correct response, so we will perform better and faster in the presence of another person. However, on a difficult task, the dominant response is an error, so we will perform worse and more slowly in the presence of another person (see Figure 18.1). **Social facilitation** is the name of this tendency to do better on easy tasks and worse on difficult tasks when another person is present. It should be noted, incidentally, that this name is only half correct, because *facilitation* occurs only on easy tasks.

Close to 300 studies on the social facilitation effect have now been performed, and the presence of another person has been shown to have an important influence

Figure 18.1
Zajonc's explanation of social
facilitation.

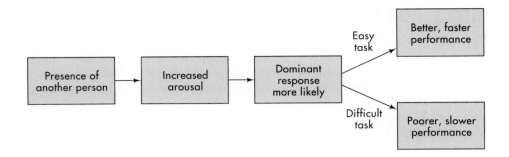

on performance speed (Bond & Titus, 1983). So we can conclude that you will wash dishes and rake leaves quickly with another person nearby. In contrast, for more difficult tasks—such as writing essays or solving math problems—the presence of another person slows your performance speed. Social facilitation has a more modest influence on accuracy, however. With another person present, you are only slightly more accurate on easy tasks and slightly less accurate on difficult tasks.

Social Roles

We have seen that the group can influence an individual simply by supplying other people whose presence increases arousal. However, the group performs another, even more powerful function: It establishes roles for the members of a group. A **role** is a set of rules describing how people in a particular social position ought to behave. Take a moment to think about a group you have belonged to in the past, perhaps your high school graduating class. Certain roles were defined for the class officers, for example. Once elected, these class officers probably began to act more self-important and self-confident. Similarly, if you live in a dormitory, you have noticed that the resident assistants (RAs) occupy certain roles. These students are supposed to act responsible and caring, somewhat more mature than other students. Within your family group, you also occupy certain roles, such as child, sibling, or parent.

One of the most clearly defined sets of roles exists in the prison system. Established policies and unwritten traditions both specify that guards have all the power, and the prisoners must obey. Philip Zimbardo and his colleagues demonstrated the power of these roles when they arranged to have college students play the parts of guards and prisoners in a simulated prison study (Haney et al., 1973; Zimbardo et al., 1973). College men volunteered to participate in this study and—by the flip of a coin—were assigned to either the guard or the prisoner role. The guards were given uniforms, billy clubs, and whistles. They were also told to enforce certain prison rules. In contrast, the prisoners were "arrested" at their homes, "booked" at an actual police station, and driven to "jail"—a prisonlike setup in the Stanford University psychology department basement.

Try to imagine how you would behave if you were assigned the role of either guard or prisoner. In chapter 17, we discussed a study in which people were assigned to either Group A or Group B. Two distinctive groups emerged after a few minutes of sitting at different tables—without any specifically assigned roles (Crocker et al., 1987); what happens when the roles are more clearly defined?

Within a short time, the guards began to act "guardlike." Some tried to be tough but fair, holding strictly to the prison rules. But about a third of them became cruel and abusive. One guard, for instance, placed a prisoner in a small closet overnight for "solitary confinement." They shouted commands, took pleasure in imposing arbitrary rules, and treated the prisoners like animals.

The prisoners and guards readily assumed their roles in Zimbardo's simulated prison experiment.

In contrast, the prisoners quickly became depressed, apathetic, and helpless—or else rebellious and angry. In fact, the situation grew so intolerable that the study had to be abandoned after only 6 days. The line between roles and reality had become too blurry, and it would have been unethical to continue the experiment.[1]

The Zimbardo prison study illustrated that we can take our roles very seriously. Like the self-fulfilling prophecy discussed in chapter 17, we live up to the expectations of other people, and the roles help specify those expectations.

We have seen that a group can influence its members by social facilitation effects and by encouraging members to act out specified roles. A group can also influence the way its members make decisions. Let us consider how a group encourages extreme or polarized decisions and how a closely knit group may fall victim to groupthink.

Group Polarization

Recently, the members of a group at my college called Students for Peace decided to support a nationwide Fast for El Salvador, and 32 of them signed a pledge to go without eating for 1 to 3 days. It was a position that was more extreme than most of them would have taken individually. A couple of months earlier, the College Republicans passed a resolution to petition the student council to stop funding the Students for Peace organization. It, too, was a position that was more extreme than most of them would have taken individually.

Demonstration 18.1 shows an example from a study on a phenomenon called group polarization. In **group polarization**, discussion among the group members produces a more extreme position on a particular issue. Thus, the average position of the Students for Peace on my campus became more liberal, whereas the average position of the College Republicans became more conservative. Notice, then, that *group polarization* means that the whole group adopts a more extreme position after discussion; it does not mean that the attitudes *within* each group become more polarized, with group members more likely to disagree with each other after discussion.

Consider what happened when Myers and Bishop (1970) gathered together groups of relatively prejudiced high school students to discuss racial issues. As Figure 18.2 shows, these students grew even more prejudiced after discussion.

[1] You may wonder whether it was ethical to conduct the experiment in the first place. To help prevent long-term harm to the participants in the prison study, Zimbardo provided extensive debriefing after the study was completed. The participants' responses on subsequent questionnaires indicated that their recovery had been satisfactory (Zimbardo et al., 1972). The research provided valuable information that even encouraged prison reform; still, we need to be concerned that some participants may have experienced psychological harm.

An Item From the Choice Dilemma Questionnaire

Answer this dilemma without discussing it with anyone else.

Mr. J., an American prisoner of war in World War II, has the choice of possible escape with the risk of execution if apprehended, or of continuing to endure the severe privations of the camp.

Imagine that you are advising Mr. J. Here are several probabilities or odds that his escape would succeed. Please check the *lowest* probability of success that you would consider acceptable for an escape to be attempted.

_____ Place a check here if you think Mr. J. should not try to escape, no matter what the probabilities.

_____ The chances are 9 in 10 that the escape would succeed.

_____ The chances are 7 in 10 that the escape would succeed.

_____ The chances are 5 in 10 that the escape would succeed.

_____ The chances are 3 in 10 that the escape would succeed.

_____ The chances are 1 in 10 that the escape would succeed.

Notice whether your response was safe or risky. Wallach and Kogan (1959) found that after discussion with other group members, people tended to shift toward more extreme, risky selections.

Source: Wallach & Kogan, 1959.

Similarly, groups of students who were relatively low in prejudice became even less prejudiced after discussion. Notice, then, that discussion caused each group to adopt a more extreme or polarized position than it had taken initially.

Think about some practical applications of the group polarization effect. Politicians at the Republican National Convention are likely to become more conservative—and politicians at the Democratic National Convention are likely to become more liberal—in comparison to their initial positions. Group polarization also occurs in juries discussing legal cases. And terrorists plot more risky actions when they discuss plans in a group (Brehm & Kassin, 1990; McCauley & Segal, 1987).

Figure 18.2
After discussion with group members, people who initially have positive attitudes toward Black people became even more positive (i.e., less prejudiced), and people who initially have negative attitudes toward Black people became even more negative (i.e., more prejudiced). (Myers & Bishop, 1970)

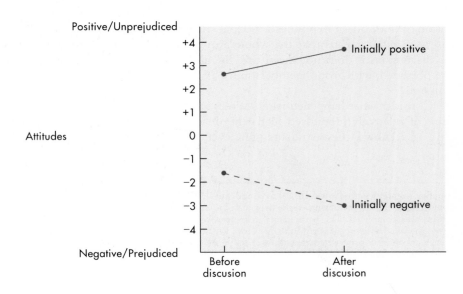

Kennedy and his advisors were influenced by groupthink in 1961 when they decided to invade Cuba. In later major decisions, Kennedy took precautions to minimize groupthink.

Groupthink

In the early 1970s, community leaders in my rural county began meeting to create a regional health center. These people knew each other socially, and they soon became a tightly knit, cohesive group, dedicated to the goal of helping their community. As the project became more elaborate—and more expensive—several physicians and other outsiders tried to warn them to plan a more modest building. However, they decided to construct an elegant, large health center. Several years later, the center went bankrupt.

The health center decision, like the *Challenger* fiasco described at the beginning of the chapter, is an example of groupthink. In a **groupthink** situation, group harmony becomes more important than wise decision making. In the decision-making section of chapter 8, we saw that people often use heuristics—such as availability, representativeness, and anchoring and adjustment—in making decisions. Overwhelmed by the variety of information we should consider in making a decision, we allow our decisions to be guided by a small number of rules-of-thumb. However, when people make decisions in groups, they must consider group processes as well as cognitive information relevant to the decision. When a group is tightly knit and harmonious, the members seem to adopt an unspoken heuristic, "Preserve group harmony by going along uncritically with whatever consensus seems to be emerging" (Janis, 1989, p. 57).

Psychologist Irving Janis (1982, 1989) has examined a number of historic fiascos in which a government leader and his advisors were more concerned about group harmony than wise decisions. Some of these unwise decisions included the British decision to try to appease Hitler in 1938, President Truman's decision to escalate the Korean War in 1950, President Kennedy's decision to invade Cuba in 1961, and President Johnson's decision to intensify the Vietnam War. In the case of Johnson and his advisors, for example, the group ignored abundant evidence that escalation of the war would not defeat the North Vietnamese and would in fact bring disapproval from many U.S. citizens.

Some of the symptoms of groupthink include the following:

1. The illusion of invulnerability, in which group members believe that everything will work out because this group is special and morally superior;

2. Self-censorship, in which group members keep any doubts to themselves;

3. The illusion of unanimity, in which the group opinion seems to be unanimous and unified—partly because of self-censorship; and

4. Direct pressure on dissenters, often suggesting that they are upsetting group harmony.

It is likely that you have belonged to a group or else known about a situation in which groupthink operated. Think about whether these four factors helped push you toward a decision that may have been inappropriate.

How can we prevent groupthink? Janis (1982, 1989) makes several proposals to encourage critical thinking:

1. The leader should present the issue to the group in a neutral manner, without stating his or her preferences;

2. Arrange to spend a block of time surveying any troublesome warning signs;

3. Recommend that group members discuss the issue with people outside the group who seem to support other positions;

4. Encourage two group members to play devil's advocate, arguing as persuasively as possible for another solution to the problem; and

5. Hold a second-chance meeting after reaching the initial decision, to discuss any remaining doubts.

In 1962, President Kennedy was faced with a second crisis about Cuba. U.S. spy planes over Cuba had reported that Soviet nuclear weapons appeared to be aimed at the United States, though the Soviet foreign minister assured us that his country had no such plans. Ultimately, Kennedy resolved the Cuban missile crisis by avoiding groupthink. Specifically, Kennedy decided not to attend all sessions, so other group members were not obliged to follow the leader. He also encouraged each group member to play devil's advocate, challenging any statements that seemed unwise. Furthermore, new advisors were brought in to question the group's policies and make new suggestions. Kennedy's awareness of group processes, combined with efforts to reduce groupthink, may have prevented a nuclear war.

Section Summary: Group Processes

■ According to Zajonc's explanation of social facilitation, the presence of others encourages people to perform better on easy tasks but worse on difficult tasks.

■ People adopt certain roles in a group situation; in Zimbardo's simulated prison study, college men randomly assigned to the role of guard or prisoner soon began to act according to these roles.

■ In group polarization, discussion among the members produces a more extreme position than the members had initially taken as individuals.

■ In tightly knit groups, members emphasize harmony rather than wise decision making; several precautions can encourage more critical thinking, thereby avoiding groupthink.

Yielding to Social Pressure

A student named Jim recalls a time he yielded to social pressure during the autumn before his 10th birthday. It seems that a new boy, Wally, had moved to the neighborhood and several other boys had decided to play a trick on the newcomer. To join the club, they said, Wally had to be buried under leaves. Reluctantly, Jim joined the other boys in heaping leaves upon Wally, who was eager to be initiated into the club—a club that Jim knew did not exist. The boys announced that they would return after 10 minutes to welcome Wally to the club. Of course, they never planned to return, but instead watched from a living room window as Wally emerged from the leaves half an hour later—damp, dirty, and disappointed. Jim wishes he could rewind the video and—resisting the lure of conformity—could say, "Don't do it, Wally!"

Social pressure certainly operated in some of the scenarios we discussed in the first section of this chapter. For instance, social pressure may have compelled some of the gentler guards in the prison study to act more dictatorial. Social pressure may also have encouraged moderate group members toward group polarization and some reluctant members of tightly knit groups to join in groupthink. Now we need to focus more specifically on the nature of social pressure as we examine conformity, compliance, and obedience. We can view these three kinds of social influence along a continuum, with minimum social pressure in the case of conformity and maximum social pressure in the case of obedience (see Figure 18.3). It is important to keep in mind, however, that social pressure can be used to encourage positive social behavior, as well as negative social behavior (Brehm & Kassin, 1990). Thus, the children in Jim's neighborhood could have pressured Jim to go trick-or-treating for UNICEF or help look for a neighbor's lost cat.

Conformity

For several years, people living in California have been asked to conserve water. For instance, a sign in the men's shower room at the University of California at Santa Cruz urged students to save water by turning off the water while soaping up. However, a systematic observation showed that only 6% of the students conformed to the request. Social psychologist Elliot Aronson (1988a) asked several male students to simply act as models by turning off the shower while soaping up. Conformity (in terms of other students conforming to the models and obeying the sign) zoomed up to 67%. Conformity can therefore be used to promote social welfare. Let us look, however, at the classic studies on conformity, which demonstrated less admirable conformity. Then we consider factors influencing conformity.

The Asch Conformity Experiments   **Conformity** can be defined as going along with people's behaviors and attitudes as a result of pressure. In Aronson's shower study, college students conformed with a socially desirable regulation. However, a pioneer social psychologist named Solomon Asch (1952, 1955) demonstrated that college students often conform with a group, even when the group adopts a position that is clearly incorrect.

Imagine that you are a participant in one of Asch's studies. You arrive in the laboratory and learn that the study will require you to state which of three comparison lines matches a nearby fourth line, as shown in Figure 18.4. The

Figure 18.3
The continuum of social influence.
(After Brehm & Kassin, 1990)

Figure 18.4
In Asch's (1955) classic study, participants were asked which of the three lines on the right matched the line on the left.

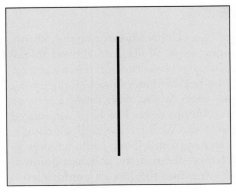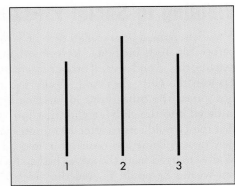

experimenter asks you and several other students to announce your judgments aloud, according to your seating position. The study begins uneventfully, and you begin to wonder about the point of the study. The five people to your right and the one person to your left all supply the same judgments you give.

On the third trial, however, something strange happens. The first five people have all given the wrong answer, selecting a comparison line that is clearly shorter than the standard line. Have you entered the twilight zone? As you may have guessed from this description, all the other participants are confederates who have been hired by the experimenter to supply the wrong answer. In fact, you are the only genuine subject in this study, and the experimenter wants to measure your tendency to show compliance.

When Asch tested 50 subjects, he found that they conformed on 37% of the trials. Consistent with one of the themes of this book, however, Asch noted tremendous individual differences. Of the 50 participants, 14 conformed more than half the time, but 13 never once went along with the group.

Factors Influencing Conformity   How do you think your responses would have been influenced by the number of other people in the group? Asch (1955) found that when only one person provided the wrong answer, the subjects conformed less than 5% of the time. However, as Figure 18.5 shows, conformity rises rapidly as two, three, and four confederates supply the wrong answer. But above four people, additional wrong-answering confederates do not increase conformity. Try

Figure 18.5
The percentage of answers that conform to the wrong answers supplied by the majority depends upon the number of people in that majority. (Asch, 1955)

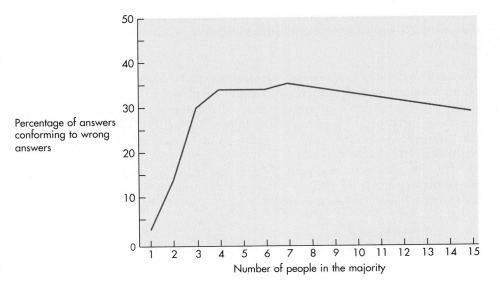

Percentage of answers conforming to wrong answers

Number of people in the majority

Demonstration 18.2, a modification of a study by Milgram and his colleagues (1969), to discover how group size influences conformity.

Personal characteristics of the participants also influence conformity. For instance, people who have a low opinion of themselves are more likely to conform than those who are high in self-esteem (Aronson, 1988a).

How does gender influence conformity? Many—but not all—studies in this area show that women tend to be more easily influenced in an Asch-type conformity study (Becker, 1986; Eagly & Carli, 1981). Eagly (1987) hypothesizes that the presence of other people encourages us to act in a way consistent with our gender roles. Gender roles specify that women should agree with other people, pleasantly preserving harmony. In contrast, gender roles specify that men should be independent, staunchly maintaining their beliefs under pressure from other people. It is important to keep in mind, however, that exceptions always exist; you may know some conforming men and nonconforming women.

Another factor that influences conformity is the presence of a person who continuously expresses a dissenting or minority viewpoint. Consider, a study by Nemeth and Chiles (1988), who asked people to judge the color of various blue slides. Participants in a control condition always judged the slides in isolation. In two experimental conditions, however, the single participant judged the slides along with three confederates. In the "no minority viewpoint" condition, all three confederates correctly said "blue." In the "consistent minority viewpoint" condition, one person consistently—but incorrectly—said "green" on all trials.

In the next phase of the study, three new confederates replaced the previous ones for those in the experimental conditions. Participants then saw a series of red slides, and the confederates consistently supplied the wrong answer by calling out "orange." The dependent variable was the number of "red" responses supplied by the real subjects on 20 trials. As expected, the control subjects showed nearly perfect accuracy. In the "no minority" condition, as shown in Figure 18.6, accuracy was astonishingly low. However, when participants had been exposed to someone who had consistently diverged from the majority, providing a consistent minority viewpoint, they were much more willing to call a red slide "red" during the second phase.

Notice, then, that we are much more likely to remain independent when another person has provided a model for independence at an earlier time—even if that person was *wrong!* Nemeth and her colleagues suggest that when we have been exposed to a persistent minority viewpoint, we tend to think more carefully about issues in the future—rather than simply yielding to pressure from the majority viewpoint. Earlier, we saw that Janis proposed several measures to encourage group members to think critically, rather than succumbing to groupthink.

Demonstration 18.2

The Influence of Group Size on Conformity

Persuade four other people to join you for a brief demonstration. Assemble your group near a classroom or dormitory at least two stories high. One of you should stare persistently at a window on the top floor while the others stand some distance away. Note what percentage of the passersby look upward. Several minutes later, repeat the study with two people staring at the same window, and then—after appropriate intervals—repeat it with three and then four. (You remain behind to record the data.) Milgram and his co-authors (1969) found that conformity among passersby increased from 40% when one person looked up, to nearly 80% with five people looking up at the same window.

Figure 18.6
Number of correct ("red") responses supplied in the second phase of the study, as a function of condition in the first phase. (Based on Nemeth & Chiles, 1988)

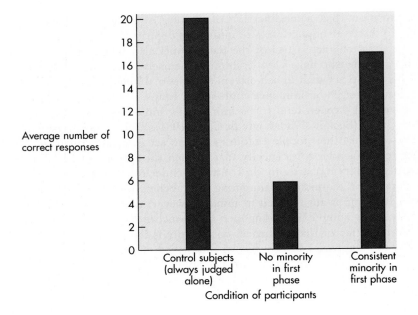

Similarly, the presence of a minority viewpoint seems to encourage us to think more critically before yielding to the dominant opinion (Nemeth, 1986; Nemeth & Staw, 1989).

We have been discussing conformity, the most subtle of the group influence phenomena. Notice that conformity operates through group pressure toward uniformity; no one *tells* you that you must choose Line 1, for instance. We have seen, also, that the pressures to conform are stronger when the group is large or a person has low self-esteem. Furthermore, women are somewhat more likely to conform. Finally, conformity is less likely when a minority consistently disagrees with the majority position.

Compliance

Psychologist Robert Cialdini knows about compliance from firsthand experience. He writes,

> All my life I've been a patsy. For as long as I can recall, I've been an easy mark for the pitches of peddlers, fund raisers, and operators of one sort or another. True, only some of these people have had dishonorable motives. The others—representatives of charitable agencies, for instance—have had the best of intentions. No matter. With personally disquieting frequency, I have always found myself in possession of unwanted magazine subscriptions or tickets to the sanitation workers' ball. (Cialdini, 1988, p. i)

Compliance means going along with a stated request from a person who does not have the specific authority to make you obey. Two terms we have already considered refer to somewhat different phenomena. *Persuasion*, considered in chapter 17, usually refers to attitudes, rather than behavior. *Conformity*, which we just finished discussing, relies upon more subtle group pressures, rather than a stated request. Compliance can be used to encourage appropriate behavior. For instance, in the next chapter we discuss compliance with a physician's instructions not to smoke. However, compliance can also be used to encourage people to buy things they do not need.

Mohandas Gandhi is an example of the power of minority influence. His opposition to British rule in India caused other Indians to question the status quo and ultimately achieve Indian independence.

Robert Cialdini has systematically investigated what he calls "compliance professionals"—that is, salespeople, fund-raisers, and advertisers. To discover more about sales techniques, Cialdini answered newspaper ads for sales trainees and learned how to sell encyclopedias, vacuum cleaners, and dance lessons. Two of the most common compliance techniques he learned are called the foot-in-the-door technique and the door-in-the-face technique.

The Foot-in-the-Door Technique   Have you ever had a friend ask you for a small favor—perhaps to borrow your class notes—and then you later discover that you are doing a much larger favor? If so, your friend has mastered the **foot-in-the-door technique**, a two-step compliance technique in which an influencer achieves compliance with a small request before making a larger request. People who have first said yes to the small favor are more likely to say yes to the larger favor, in contrast to those who were only asked about the larger favor.

Consider a study by Freedman and Fraser (1966). These researchers made telephone calls to 36 phone numbers, selected at random from a telephone directory. The people who answered the phone were asked whether they would answer a short survey as part of a consumer research project, and then the researcher asked eight simple questions such as "What brand of soap do you use in your kitchen sink?" A control group of 36 people were not contacted at this point, so they had no opportunity to perform a small favor. Three days after the experimental group had performed the small favor, people in both groups were contacted about performing a large favor. They were asked to allow five or six men from the consumer research project to spend 2 hours going through their homes, classifying all household products. Of those who had first complied with the small favor, 53% agreed to the large favor. However, of those who were asked only about the large favor, only 22% agreed.

Notice that the name *foot-in-the-door* is appropriate; once the foot is in the door, you soon find yourself inviting the entire salesperson inside, and you are

If this resident allows the salesperson to "put her foot in the door," he may find that a small request will soon become a major purchase.

vulnerable to larger requests. In a book on political psychology, Fischer and Johnson (1986) point out how politicians use this technique:

> The "foot in the door" strategy of initially funding public programs on a low-level basis is an instance of this strategy. The fact that we have already spent hundreds of millions of dollars on the MX, a weapon of dubious military utility, is an advantage to those who favor the MX because they can use this fact to argue against "throwing away" the sunk costs that were paid for by taxpayers' hard-earned dollars. (p. 59)

The Door-in-the-Face Technique   In the comic strip "Calvin and Hobbes," little Calvin asks, "Mom, can I set fire to my mattress?" She replies, "No, Calvin." He then asks, "Can I ride my tricycle on the roof?" "No, Calvin," she again replies. And then Calvin asks the real question, "Then can I have a cookie?" At his tender age, Calvin has already learned the **door-in-the-face technique**, a two-step compliance technique in which an influencer achieves compliance by first making a request that is so large that it is certain to be denied, and then making a smaller, more reasonable request (see Table 18.1).

Table 18-1   *Two Compliance Techniques*

	COMPLIANCE TECHNIQUE	
	Foot-in-the-Door	**Door-in-the-Face**
Order of requests	Small, then large	Large, then small
Research example	"Answer 8 questions"	"Work weekly with juvenile delinquents"
	then	then
	"Let research team into your home"	"Work one day with juvenile delinquents"

To test the door-in-the-face technique, Cialdini and his colleagues (1975) asked one sample of college students for a very large favor—to spend 2 hours each week as a counselor to juvenile delinquents, for a minimum of 2 years. As you might imagine, everybody refused. So then they asked the students if they would be willing to chaperone a group of juvenile delinquents on a day-long trip to the zoo. An impressive 50% said that they would. In contrast, when the researchers asked a similar sample of students for this relatively small favor, without first asking about the large favor, only 17% said yes.

In the section on groupthink, I mentioned a community health center that ultimately went bankrupt. Actually, I was impressed that the backers had been able to raise as much money as they did, but then I learned that the professional fund-raisers had used the door-in-the-face technique. They had learned from community leaders about the professions of each household, and used this information to calculate an outlandishly high donation request. To a family with an estimated income of $35,000, they would say, "We have calculated that a family with your income should contribute about $2,000 over a 3-year period." This family probably would not donate $2,000, but they might actually contribute $500. Without the initial door-in-the-face interaction, however, they probably would have given only $100. Notice, incidentally, that the door-in-the-face technique bears a resemblance to the anchoring-and-adjustment heuristic discussed in chapter 8. People rely heavily on the initial anchor that is supplied to them—in this case $2,000, and they make fairly modest downward adjustments.

Demonstration 18.3

Milgram's Obedience Study

Imagine that you are seated in front of this piece of equipment, which will deliver shock to another participant, who is seated in the next room. Please indicate on the dial how much shock you think you will deliver, if any.

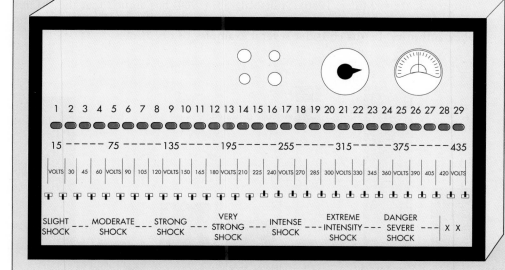

Obedience

So far, we have discussed relatively mild social pressure. A student calls a red slide "orange," consistent with the majority judgment (conformity), or a community member agrees to let a research team into her home (compliance). The third kind of social pressure is much stronger; in **obedience**, a specific command from an authority forces us to change our behavior. Let us first consider the Milgram obedience studies and then discuss some important historical examples of obedience.

Milgram's Obedience Studies   Stanley Milgram's research on obedience is one of the most famous studies in psychology (Sabini, 1986). Try to place yourself in the shoes of one of the participants in these classic studies (Milgram, 1963, 1974). In response to an ad in the local paper, you report to the Yale University psychology department for a study on memory and learning. You meet the experimenter as well as another participant, a pleasant middle-aged man. The two of you draw lots, and you are assigned the role of the teacher, whereas he will be the learner. You are seated in front of an electric-shock generator, and he is strapped into a chair where he will receive electric shock. Your duty is to press a switch and deliver shock whenever he makes a mistake on the learning task. You are further instructed to increase the intensity of shock after each error. Try Demonstration 18.3 on the previous page before you read further.

When Milgram described this study to college students, most claimed that they would stop pressing the lever when it had reached the "strong shock" level, as shown in Figure 18.7. None said that they would deliver beyond the "very strong shock" level. However, when people were actually tested in Milgram's study—and the "learner" groaned and pounded the walls in pain—the majority delivered the full 450 volts of electric shock.

It is important to stress that the "learners" in Milgram's study were really confederates, and they received no actual shock. At the end of the study, the "teachers" were debriefed and assured that the "learners" had felt no pain. However, many psychologists have objected to this study, arguing that the deceit and the mental torment experienced by the participants made the study unethical (e.g., Baumrind, 1964; Miller, 1986). Still, Milgram (1964) has argued that the studies were worthwhile because they provided valuable insights into the way we humans obey authority. Let us consider several examples of obedience.

Figure 18.7
A comparison between estimates of shock people said they would deliver and amount of shock actually delivered by other people. (Based on Milgram, 1974)

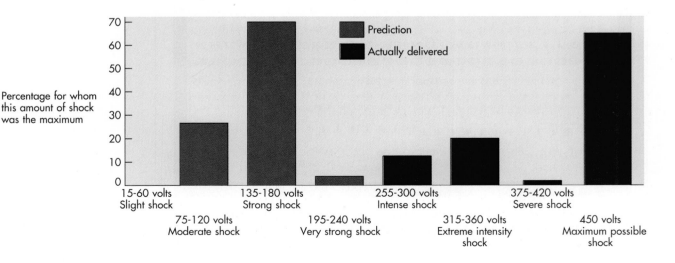

Historical Examples of Obedience Between the years of 1933 and 1945, millions of innocent people were systematically slaughtered by people who were following the commands of Nazi authorities. So-called good citizens built gas chambers and guarded death camps, producing daily quotas of corpses with the same efficiency that would be admirable in the manufacturing of appliances. A single person conceived the plan, but thousands of citizens obeyed his orders (Milgram, 1974).

But blind obedience is not confined to Europe. After all, it was American soldiers like Lieutenant Calley who slaughtered the Vietnamese civilians at My Lai, as we discussed at the beginning of the chapter. Furthermore, Calley and the other soldiers were described as "average American boys." Calley's neighbor stated in *Time* magazine, "He was a wonderful boy, and would do anything for you" ("My Lai: An American tragedy," 1969).

Obedience can even lead people to kill their own children and themselves. In 1978, Reverend Jim Jones led a group of close to 1,000 of his religious followers in Jonestown, Guyana, as they committed mass suicide by drinking a beverage laced with cyanide. He commanded these people, "Please get some medication. Simple. It's simple. There's no convulsions with it. . . . Don't be afraid to die. . . . We must die with dignity" ("The cult of death," 1978).

A tragic example of obedience occurred at Jonestown, Guyana, South America, in 1978 when Reverend Jim Jones convinced hundreds of followers to commit mass suicide.

In each of these three cases, the power of the authority was terrifying. In Nazi Europe, people were killed for defying authority. In Vietnam, soldiers who ignored an order in battle were sometimes executed on the spot ("My Lai: An American tragedy," 1969). And followers of Jim Jones had been mutilated and murdered for failing to obey orders (Osherow, 1988).

However, we frequently obey authorities because of reasons other than fear of personal harm. After all, the Yale University psychology department was unlikely to mutilate a participant for failing to deliver the specified shock. One reason we obey—rather than protest—is simple embarrassment. It is awkward to say, "No, I refuse." Another reason is based on our earlier discussion; our role as subordinates encourages us to obey military leaders and experimenters, even when we are wrongfully hurting other people. A third reason is that authorities typically use the foot-in-the-door technique. For instance, the researcher began by specifying mild shock. Gradually, the situation became more serious, but by then, the participants were entrapped (Ross, 1988).

A final reason we obey is that we are all sometimes guilty of mindlessness, or failure to think through all the consequences of obedience (Langer, 1989). Recall Nemeth and Chiles's (1988) study, when one consistent dissenter encouraged participants to resist conformity. Without the dissenter, participants continued to say that the red slides were orange. When we find ourselves confronted by an illegal or inhumane command, we need to evaluate the situation critically and determine whether we can resist an immoral authority.

Section Summary: Yielding to Social Pressure

- **In the Asch conformity experiments, people often conformed to the majority position, even when it was incorrect; conformity is greater with a large group asserting the majority position, and it is lower when people have been previously exposed to a dissenting minority viewpoint.**
- **Two effective compliance methods are the foot-in-the-door technique (small request followed by large) and the door-in-the-face technique (large request followed by small).**

■ In Milgram's obedience studies, participants usually obeyed an authority's instructions to deliver painful shock to another person; historical
examples of obedience include obeying Nazi officials, the My Lai mas-
sacre, and the Jonestown mass suicide.

Aggression, Conflict, and Conflict Resolution

In April 1989, a band of teenagers roam Central Park in New York City. They
beat an elderly Hispanic man and a middle-aged White man until they are unconscious. They attack a young woman jogger with a metal pipe, hit her in the
face with a brick, rape her, and leave her for dead (Stone, 1989).

In November 1989, government troops in El Salvador torture and kill six
Jesuit priests. One of them, Ignacio Martín-Baró, was the head of the psychology
department at the University of Central America. Ironically, Martín-Baró was a
social psychologist whose research areas were the psychological effects of torture
and the influence of war on children (Bazar, 1990).

In addition to startling, newsworthy acts of aggression such as these, we
encounter more ordinary aggression and conflict in our daily lives. A fight breaks
out during a hockey game. A friend reveals that her boyfriend beat her up last
night. Your roommate refuses to turn the radio down when you are trying to
study. It is no challenge to compile a list of everyday aggressions.

We begin this section by considering several explanations of aggression, and
then we discuss the subject of aggression and gender. Our next two topics are
conflict escalation and an in-depth discussion of interpersonal conflict resolution.
We conclude with an overview of international peacemaking.

Explaining Aggression

Before you read further, test your own beliefs about aggression by trying Demonstration 18.4. **Aggression** is physical or verbal behavior that is intended to hurt
someone (Myers, 1990). However, defining aggression is much easier than explaining it. Let us consider several explanations, beginning with one that has little
support from the psychological research.

Is There an Aggression Instinct?   Nobel prizewinner Konrad Lorenz contends that
all animals—including humans—have a "fighting instinct" (Lorenz, 1974). In other
words, we do not need to learn to be aggressive, because we are born with a
predisposition toward violence. However, the majority of psychologists now reject
this instinctive position.

In May 1986, 20 scientists from 12 different countries gathered in Seville,
Spain, to draft a document called the Seville Statement. The **Seville Statement**
asserts that it is scientifically incorrect to say that we have an inborn, genetic
tendency to be aggressive or that evolution has favored aggressive members of
our species. The document, which was endorsed by organizations such as the
American Psychological Association and the American Anthropological Association, includes the following passage:

> The fact that warfare has changed so rapidly over time indicates that it is a product
> of culture. Its biological connection is primarily through language, which makes possible
> the coordination of groups, the transmission of technology, and the use of tools. War
> is biologically possible, but it is not inevitable, as evidenced by its variation in
> occurrence and nature over time and space. There are cultures which have not
> engaged in war for centuries, and there are cultures which have engaged in war

Beliefs About Aggression

Answer each of the following questions with a T (true) or an F (false). The answers appear at the end of the chapter.

_____ 1. Aggression is caused by a simple, inborn drive.

_____ 2. Humans are the only animals that often kill members of their own species.

_____ 3. Humans are instinctively aggressive.

_____ 4. Research has demonstrated that men are consistently more aggressive than women.

_____ 5. The aggressive instinct can be controlled by participating in substitute activities, such as watching football games and violent movies.

_____ 6. If children are allowed to play aggressively, they will get it out of their system and be better adjusted in the long run.

_____ 7. Extreme acts of violence, such as child and spouse abuse, are typically committed by people with psychological disorders.

_____ 8. War is an expression of our aggression instinct.

Source: Based on Aronson, 1988a; Goldstein, 1989; Groebel & Hinde, 1989a.

frequently at some times and not at others. (Adams, 1990, pp. 1167–1168; Groebel & Hinde, 1989b, pp. xiv–xv)

Observational Learning   In chapter 6, we discussed experimental, quasi-experimental, and correlational research on television violence. It is evident from these studies that many children become more aggressive after they observe violent programs. However, it is also clear that some children manage to remain gentle and considerate, despite the horrors they have seen on the family TV set. A child who observes violence is not condemned to a life of crime.

Let us consider a related question. What happens when adults view violent pornography? Surveys of pornographic violence reveal that sexual aggressors are typically portrayed in a positive fashion, and they are seldom punished for their actions (Check & Malamuth, 1986; Palys, 1986). We should not be surprised to learn, then, that both college and noncollege men who are exposed to pornography are more likely than other men to believe the myth that women enjoy rape (Check, 1984; Malamuth & Check, 1985). Furthermore, men who saw a movie containing sexually violent episodes are more likely than men in a control group to approve of wife battering (Malamuth, 1987; Malamuth & Check, 1981). Finally, men who have seen a sexually violent movie are less likely to sympathize with a rape victim when they serve as jury members in a reenacted rape trial.[2] That is, they are more

Men who have seen sexually violent movies are more likely to believe the myth that women enjoy rape and that rape victims are not seriously hurt by the rape incident.

---

[2] Many students wonder about the ethics of presenting sexually violent material to people who then become less sympathetic to victims of rape. It is important to stress that researchers in this area must provide appropriate debriefing about the reality of rape. A study by Malamuth and Check (1984) provided reassuring evidence that debriefing can correct the rape myths. In this study, students read stories that included a rape scene, and later they were debriefed about the true horror of rape. Ten days later an apparently unrelated "public survey" was administered, and students who had read the stories about rape and then received debriefing were *less* accepting of rape myths than were a group of control students. Clearly, however, the debriefing must be carefully worded and persuasively delivered.

likely to believe that a victim's injury was not very severe, and they are more likely to consider her a worthless person (Donnerstein & Linz, 1984). As a review of the literature concludes,

> . . . some forms of pornography, under some conditions, promote certain antisocial attitudes and behavior. Specifically, we should be most concerned about the detrimental effects of exposure to violent images in pornography and elsewhere, particularly material that portrays the myth that women enjoy or in some way benefit from rape, torture, or other forms of sexual violence. (Donnerstein et al., 1987, p. 171)

The Influence of Frustration   Observational learning explains how people might learn certain aggressive actions. However, it does not clarify *when* people will actually perform these aggressive acts. Several decades ago, John Dollard and his co-authors suggested that people are most likely to act aggressively when they are frustrated (Dollard et al., 1939). These writers argued that frustration inevitably produced aggression.

More recent research has modified that position. We now know that the *interpretation* of frustration is important. For example, an aggressive reaction is more probable if the frustration can be traced to an identifiable source, such as a rival (Groebel & Hinde, 1989a). Aggression is also more probable when the frustration arouses negative emotions (Berkowitz, 1989). Try to recall a time when you were recently frustrated. Were you more likely to react aggressively if you could identify the villain and if you were seething with anger? In short, frustration does not inevitably lead to aggression, but certain kinds of frustrations can make us seek revenge.

Aggression and Gender

According to the stereotype, men are ready to fight and eager to insult, whereas women are much more submissive. Research on gender differences in aggression shows that women and men are more similar than you might suspect. One survey of the literature showed that only about one third of the research studies found men to be significantly more aggressive than women (Eagly, 1987).

Gender differences tend to be larger in studies of children, rather than adults (Hyde, 1986b). Gender differences are also larger when aggression causes physical injury or pain, rather than psychological harm (Eagly & Steffen, 1986). Men are therefore more likely than women to shock somebody, but men and women are equally likely to deliver insults.

It is not clear why males tend to be more aggressive. We certainly see more men modeling aggression in the media. Women are also more likely to feel guilty or anxious about aggression, in contrast to men, and these feelings may inhibit aggressive actions (Frodi et al., 1977). Gender differences in physical strength may also be a contributing factor.

We need to stress, too, that gender differences are relatively small when we examine interactions with strangers. However, men are much more likely than women to injure their spouses severely in episodes of domestic violence (Eagly, 1987; Straus et al., 1980). A woman in one of my classes vividly described how her ex-husband tracked her down in her new apartment and hurled her through the bedroom wall. Ironically, people who accept the myth that men are inevitably more violent may believe—erroneously—that men are biologically incapable of controlling their tempers.

Conflict Escalation

Let us consider a topic closely related to aggression, called conflict. **Conflict** is an interpersonal process that occurs when the actions of one party interfere with the actions of another party (Kelley, 1986). Conflict can occur between two people (you and a rival, for instance), between two groups (e.g., a company's executives and its union members), or between two nations (a glance at the daily newspaper provides many examples of international conflict). Obviously, the dynamics change somewhat when we consider nations, rather than individuals, but many of the same elements can be found in all conflicts.

Notice that we can have conflict without much aggression. For example, you and a friend may be in conflict and refuse to speak to each other. However, conflict usually involves either verbal or physical aggression.

Conflict analysts describe three approaches to a conflict. In a **lose-lose approach**, both parties will suffer a net loss. War is certainly the best example of a lose-lose approach. Even the winner in a war will lose more in terms of human suffering than any positive outcome the war was supposed to accomplish.

Most competitive sports are examples of a **win-lose approach**, in which one player's win is balanced by the other player's loss. Most competitive situations in business also involve a win-lose situation.

However, in a **win-win approach**, both parties gain by cooperating. Here, there are only winners, and no losers. A good example of a win-win approach to conflict occurred several years ago in Southern California. Two neighborhoods located next to each other had experienced increasing violence at their mutual boundary. The conflict was heightened because one neighborhood had mostly Chicano residents, whereas the other neighborhood had mostly gay male residents. Fortunately, some of the residents decided to do something about the violence and planned a street fair for everyone. The fair became an annual event, and the project, known as Sunset Junction Neighborhood Alliance, provided many opportunities for members of the two groups to plan and work together, rather than in conflict (Rebecca, personal communication, 1983). Clearly, a win-win approach favors successful conflict resolution, whereas conflict escalation is more likely with either a lose-lose or a win-lose approach (Deutsch & Shichman, 1986; Heitler, 1990).

We tend to think that conflict is inevitably wrong and unproductive. However, some nonaggressive conflict can be helpful, assuming that people enter the conflict with a win-win approach. For instance, groupthink occurs because the group members want to avoid conflict at all cost. Also, conflict often nourishes social change. What would happen if civil rights reformers were routinely stifled? Would we have wheelchair access to public places if people with disabilities systematically kept their needs quiet? Conflict can also be a creative force that benefits both sides (Pettit et al., 1985). A conflict between the sales and production divisions of a company may be resolved by designing a better product, or one that can be manufactured at a lower cost.

Let us consider several factors that tend to fuel a conflict and encourage the parties to adopt either a lose-lose or a win-lose approach. These factors include issues proliferation, threats, attributional errors, and enemy images.

Issues Proliferation   Often, a conflict starts small, but then each party adds additional grievances, which were not part of the original problem (DeMott, 1987). The tendency for parties in a conflict to increase the number of controversial topics is called **issues proliferation**. Two roommates in conflict over an insulting remark may suddenly start dragging in each other's annoying habits and other long-forgotten injustices. Whenever you hear yourself saying, "And another thing . . ." in the midst of a conflict, you know you are a victim of issues proliferation. A more narrowly focused conflict is easier to resolve.

Threats   We are particularly tempted to make threats in the early phases of a contact, when the opponent is not yet viewed as an enemy, but merely someone interfering with our goals. We may think it is less violent to threaten someone, rather than simply to attack (DeMott, 1987). A young child may say, "If you don't get off that slide, I'm going to punch you in the nose." Threat invites escalation, because the person who receives the threat does not want to appear to be a coward by stepping off the slide at that moment. This person is therefore likely to become more stubborn.

Attributional Errors   In the previous chapter, we examined attributional biases and errors we make in trying to explain the actions of other people. Politicians make these same errors when they try to explain the actions of other nations in international conflicts. For example, Pruitt and Rubin (1986) provide some example from the conflict between the United States and the Soviet Union in the 1980s. When the Soviets invaded Afghanistan, U.S. politicians attributed this action to a stable, internal characteristic of Soviet policymakers, their presumed tendency to take over other countries. We invested billions of dollars in additional military resources as a result of this perceived threat. However, another highly plausible interpretation is that the Soviet Union was simply trying to keep the Communist government from disintegrating, and the action was prompted by a specific external situation.

    The truth is that the actions of others are often ambiguous. In conflict situations, however, we tend to supply negative motivations to our rivals. Someone with whom you have been quarreling for months does a favor for you, and you find yourself asking, "I wonder what she wants from me?" Ironically, you interpreted her positive action as *proof* that she is more evil than you had originally thought. If you find yourself in this situation, try several more charitable attributions!

Enemy Images   Try Demonstration 18.5 before you read further. This demonstration is related to **enemy images**, or the tendency for us to see ourselves as good and peace-loving, and our enemies as evil, aggressive, and warlike. The enemies, however, also have an image of us. Whereas they see *themselves* as good and peace-loving, they see *us* as evil, aggressive, and warlike (Moyer, 1985). Reality is usually ambiguous; we both have our peace-loving and aggressive sides. However, as we saw in the previous chapter, our cognitive processes encourage outgroup negativity, or the tendency to react negatively to people in a different group.

Demonstration 18.5

Enemy Images

Read the following quotation and try to identify which leader of which country made this statement, and who the enemy is that is described in the passage.

" . . . aiming at the exclusive domination of the world, lost in corruption, of deep-rooted hatred toward us, hostile to liberty wherever it endeavours to show its head, and the eternal disturber of the peace of the world."

(The answer is discussed later in the text.)

One of the first to notice the intriguing symmetry of enemy images was Urie Bronfenbrenner, an American psychologist who spoke fluent Russian and interviewed Soviet citizens at the end of the 1950s, when Americans were especially negative about the Soviets. Gradually, he realized "that the Russians' distorted picture of us was curiously similar to our view of them—a mirror image" (Bronfenbrenner, 1961, pp. 45–46). For example, they thought of Americans as the aggressors, that our government exploits the people, and that our government cannot be trusted.

These enemy images distort reality and heighten conflict between nations. We may even recreate history so that it is consistent with our enemy image. For example, a substantial number of Americans believe that the Soviet Union fought *against* the United States—rather than on the same side—during World War II. They also mistakenly believe that the Soviets—rather than the United States—first invented the atomic bomb (Silverstein, 1989).

The irony is that the enemy keeps changing (Stone & Schaffner, 1988). For example, did you guess that the quotation in Demonstration 18.5 was from Thomas Jefferson, one of our most intelligent and respected presidents? The enemy here was Great Britain, whom we no longer consider to be an "eternal disturber of the peace of the world." Figure 18.8 shows enemy images of Germany and Japan during previous world wars; both of these images conflict with our current images.

Enemy images help escalate conflict because they encourage us to think of our adversaries as evil, rather than as people who share the same kinds of strengths and weaknesses we ourselves have. Consider the rival team at a sports event; do enemy images encourage you to see them as evil and immoral?

Successful conflict resolution is more likely if we avoid issues proliferation, threats, attributional errors, and enemy images. Let us consider some other techniques of resolving interpersonal conflicts, and then we briefly discuss international peacemaking.

Figure 18.8
The two enemy images from previous eras in the United States: the Germans in World War I (left) and the Japanese in World War II (right). (Keen, 1986)

○ ○

In Depth: Interpersonal Conflict Resolution

Jerry and his best friend Ron have a conflict. They had planned to go fishing next Sunday, and Jerry had really been looking forward to the chance to get off campus. However, one of Ron's professors announced a quiz next Monday. With all his other exams and papers, Ron knows he will not be able to find the time to study for this quiz if he spends all day Sunday at the lake. He says he needs to stay home. No doubt you have also experienced some kind of interpersonal conflict in the past week—or even in the past few minutes. How can we take a win-win approach to these conflicts and end up with a solution that makes everybody happier?

It is helpful to consider your options in a conflict situation. Dean Pruitt and Jeffrey Rubin (1986) diagram four possibilities, as illustrated in Figure 18.9. This **dual concern model** suggests that our choices depend upon the relative strength of concern about both our own welfare and the welfare of the person with whom we are in conflict.

If Jerry used the dual concern model to analyze his conflict with Ron, he would find he had four options. The two friends could choose inaction, with Jerry staying home and fuming while Ron studies. Jerry could yield, telling Ron he knows exams should take precedence. Jerry could also contend that Ron should stick to his promise. Or the two friends could problem solve and come up with a solution that benefits both. For example, they could drive out to the lake together, and Ron can study in a quiet, pleasant setting while Jerry fishes. Later, they can enjoy the fish dinner together. Both students' interests will be satisfied, and the friendship will not be strained.

Successful problem solving depends upon finding **perceived common ground**, or the likelihood of finding an alternative that satisfies both parties' wishes (Pruitt & Rubin, 1986). A number of conditions contribute to this perceived common ground:

1. Faith in your own problem-solving ability, instead of an attitude that conflict is inevitable.

2. Momentum, or prior success in resolving earlier phases of a conflict. It is sometimes helpful to build momentum by scheduling easier issues early on in a conflict-resolution session.

3. The perception that the other person is ready to solve the problem. (Note that enemy images would discourage this viewpoint.)

4. Trust, or the perception that the other person is concerned about your welfare.

5. Contact and communication, where both parties have equal status. This point is related to our discussion of the jigsaw classroom in the previous chapter; discrimination and stereotyping are more likely if one party has more status than the other.

Steps in Creative Problem Solving   We can specify five steps in resolving problems creatively (Pruitt & Rubin, 1986):

Step 1: *Ask whether a conflict of interest really exists.* As the previous chapter and part of this chapter have emphasized, people often misperceive reality. You may have a false impression about

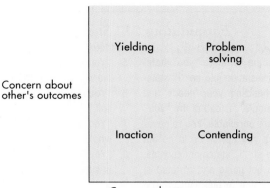

Figure 18.9
Pruitt and Rubin's (1986) dual concern model.

the other person's interests or you may believe that the other person's actions are more costly or unreasonable than they truly are.

Step 2: *Analyze your own interests and start with high aspirations.* Keep in mind that you may have to be flexible about how you obtain your goals and that you might have to modify them at a later point.

Step 3: *Find a way to reconcile both parties' aspirations by identifying an integrative solution.* Several possibilities include (a) finding a way to expand the resource that is in short supply, such as time or money; (b) one person gets what he or she wants and the other person gets another reward of equal value; (c) you each concede on issues of low priority to yourself and high priority to the other person; (d) you both create a new option that satisfies the desires of both people.

Step 4: *If no solution has been found, lower your aspirations and search some more.* Discard your low-priority interests, and search some more until reaching an agreement.

Step 5: *Discuss any unfinished business.* For instance, devise a contingency plan to be used if the solution does not work (DeMott, 1987).

Attitudes and Skills During Problem Solving Keep several cautions in mind as you resolve your conflict. For example, recall from the in-depth section in chapter 12 that thought processes are more flexible when your emotions are positive. Find a pleasant setting for your conversation, and maintain an optimistic outlook. Emphasize the positive, including those issues upon which you agree.

One of the most useful skills in creative problem solving is effective listening. Work on focusing on what the other person is saying, rather than on the response you plan to make (Heitler, 1990). It is helpful to focus on what is *right* in the speaker's statements, not what is wrong. Try to see the situation from the other person's viewpoint. It may help to pretend that you are the other person and imagine how the situation feels from his or her perspective (DeMott, 1987).

In addition to listening, you need to develop the skill of presenting your own position effectively. One useful strategy is to present your statements from the "I" standpoint, rather than the "you" perspective. This orientation makes your wishes more clear, and it avoids threatening, accusatory remarks. For example, notice how negative this "you" statement sounds: "You ignore me. You

Demonstration 18.6

Formulating "I" Statements

For each of the following "you" statements, create a translation into an "I" statement form, emphasizing your needs and emotions. For example, instead of the "you" statement, "You are unreliable. You're never ready when I pick you up for us to go out together," provide an "I" statement such as, "I feel anxious to get going and irritated at the delay when I come to pick you up and you're not ready" (Heitler, 1990).

1. "You were late again, and we won't make it to the meeting on time."
2. "You didn't call me last night, and you promised you would."
3. "You leave your part of the room in such a mess."
4. "You always make plans at the last moment, and then I'm not free to go with you."

5. "You always ask to borrow my notes the night before the exam."
6. "You're always talking about yourself."
7. "You went to the party and spent the whole time with other people."
8. "You aren't doing your share, and this is supposed to be a group project."
9. "But you promised we would go to that concert!"

The last part of this exercise is the most challenging. The next time you find yourself about to make a "you" statement, pause a moment, think about this demonstration, and convert it into an "I" statement.

never take time to do things with me." Notice how much more appealing this "I" statement is: "I would like more time with you. I would love to arrange a plan to get together, maybe for lunch or dinner, or to watch the football game" (Heitler, 1990, p. 304). Demonstration 18.6 gives you practice in converting "you" statements to "I" statements.

○ ○

International Peacemaking

In recent years, researchers have argued that conflicts between individuals, groups, communities, and nations all share certain basic similarities, and the same conflict-resolution principles can be used in many superficially different disputes. When we consider peacemaking between nations, of course, the stakes are infinitely higher. The issue is no longer "What are Jerry and Ron going to do about the fishing trip, but "What is the fate of the Earth and all its inhabitants?"

As I write this chapter, rapport between the United States and the Soviet Union appears to be reasonably stable, but other conflicts are escalating. Our annual military budget far exceeds federal spending on either education or health care. Even if we were to reduce our number of military weapons to perhaps 5% of their current level, we could still wipe out civilization on this planet. For example, even *one* of our nuclear-armed submarines has the potential to devastate every major city in the Soviet Union (White, 1988). With nuclear weapons, the cost of an error is nearly unimaginable. As Plous (1985) writes,

Our species has been evolving for a quarter of a million years. Today through the use of thermonuclear weapons, that evolution can be arrested in less time than it

In the 1990s, the United States has so many nuclear weapons that they represent roughly 200,000 times the force of the nuclear bomb that destroyed Hiroshima in World War II.

takes to mow an average-sized lawn. American Pershing 2 missiles deployed in West Germany can reach the Soviet Union in six minutes—less time than it took the United States government to discover that its nuclear alerts in June of 1980 were false alarms. (p. 363)

A major problem with large-scale international conflicts is that high levels of tension can produce cognitive rigidity, and the political leaders may have difficulty conceiving of new alternatives and options (Deutsch, 1983).

One technique of conflict resolution that is especially useful in international peacemaking is called GRIT. **GRIT, or Graduated and Reciprocated Initiatives in Tension Reduction**, consists of a series of steps in which a party announces a step it will take to reduce tension, the party actually takes the step, and then the party states its expectation for some kind of reciprocation. If the other party reciprocates, the first party starts another round of these initiatives (Deutsch & Shichman, 1986; Osgood, 1962).

An advantage of GRIT is that one small gesture of conciliation creates a more positive atmosphere that can encourage trust. One of the best international applications of GRIT occurred in 1963, when President Kennedy decided to try to de-escalate conflict with the Soviet Union. It was only a few months after the Cuban missile crisis (discussed in connection with groupthink). Kennedy announced that the United States would stop all nuclear tests in the atmosphere in an effort to reduce tension, and it would not resume testing unless some other nation did. The Soviet Union responded by announcing that they would halt production of its strategic bombers. Several other reciprocal gestures continued throughout the next few months, with one of the most important accomplishments being a permanent ban on open-air testing of nuclear weapons (DeMott, 1987).

Unfortunately, this period of reduced international tension ended when the United States became involved in Vietnam, introducing a new source of tension. However, the successful de-escalation is one example of the value of GRIT in both international and small-scale conflict (Lindskold, 1978, 1985).

Section Summary: Aggression, Conflict, and Conflict Resolution

- Aggression is not based on an "aggression instinct"; instead, factors such as observational learning and frustration are important.
- About one third of studies show males to be more aggressive than females, and the differences are larger with children than adults and with physical rather than verbal aggression.
- Conflict escalates with a lose-lose or a win-lose approach, and it also increases when the parties in a conflict employ issues proliferation, threats, attributional errors, and enemy images.
- Interpersonal conflict resolution is facilitated by a five-step approach to creative problem solving; a solution is also more likely when the two parties adopt an optimistic outlook, effective listening techniques, and "I" statements.
- International peacemaking strategies, including GRIT (Graduated and Reciprocated Initiatives in Tension Reduction), are essential if we are to avoid devastating wars.

Altruism

Nancy Pocock, at age 78, is holding a vigil to keep a young man from being deported to Ethiopia, where he would probably be killed by those who killed his parents and tortured his brother. She has helped hundreds of people in similar predicaments, people who faced almost certain death if they returned to the countries from which they had fled. When asked when she would stop her political work, she replied, "What's the point of retiring? As long as I'm able to do something I'm going to be doing it" (Atkinson, 1989, p. 37).

Thomas Guinzburg, the former president of a publishing company, has made a deal with 77 junior high students in Brooklyn. If they can graduate from high school, he will pay their way through college or vocational school. He has also convinced 150 others to join him in helping inner-city students plan their futures (Webb, 1989).

Jim Good is known as "Jaime Bueno" to the people in his community in Paiwas, Nicaragua, where he has helped women set up a carpentry cooperative. He has lived on subsistence wages for many years now, and recently he donated part of his meager salary to help buy a hearing aid for a 10-year-old deaf girl in the community.

These three individuals all exemplify **altruism**, which is defined as concern and help for other people, expecting nothing in return (Myers, 1990). Altruistic people are devoted to others, rather than their own self-interests. Altruism is one kind of prosocial behavior. As we discussed in the chapter on child development, prosocial behavior is action that benefits another person.

Altruism is puzzling for theorists who argue that behavior can be explained by reinforcements—because it is difficult to explain why people would help others without concrete reinforcement (Shaver, 1987). Let us begin by discussing why people are altruistic. Then we consider the bystander effect, altruism and gender, and factors affecting altruism.

Explaining Altruism

Why should we help someone else in a situation where that person is in no position to return the favor at a later time? Try to think how you might answer that question, based on your own experiences with altruism.

Thomas Guinzburg and some of the students whose college education he will sponsor.

Jim Good, with one of the children he is helping in Central America.

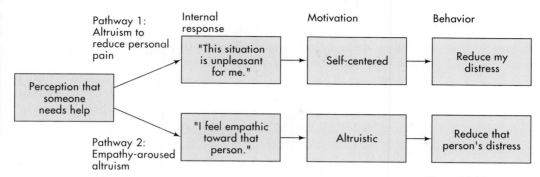

Figure 18.10
Two pathways for altruism. (Based on Batson, 1987)

One possibility is that when we see someone in distress, it is unpleasant and annoying. The best way to get rid of that unpleasant feeling is to help that person (Hoffman, 1981). In other words, altruism really does have a selfish component; we want to avoid personal pain.

Another possibility is that we have learned since childhood that we are supposed to help someone in distress. We would feel both guilty and ashamed if we failed to help. Notice, then, that this explanation—like the first one—traces altruism to the selfish motive of wanting to avoid personal pain.

A psychologist named C. Daniel Batson agrees that altruism can sometimes be selfishly motivated (Batson, 1987, 1990). Figure 18.10 shows this possibility at the top of the diagram. However, Batson argues that in some conditions we take on the perspective of the person who needs help, and then our altruism is guided by a genuine desire to reduce that person's suffering. The bottom of Figure 18.10 illustrates this less selfish route to altruism.

Let us consider in more detail Batson's explanation, which is based on empathy. **Empathy** is an emotional experience that involves a subjective grasp of another person's feelings or experiences (Brothers, 1989). Thus, you may feel empathy for a child whose parents have been killed in an automobile accident. According to Batson's **empathy-arousal hypothesis**, empathy has the power to motivate altruism.

From previous research, we know that people are more likely to perform altruistic and other prosocial actions when they experience empathy (e.g., Eisenberg & Miller, 1987). It makes sense that we are more eager to help people if we can experience some of the same emotions they are feeling. However, Batson and his colleagues have demonstrated that we are likely to help someone with whom we empathize, even when we have the option of escaping the situation and avoiding the unpleasantness and annoyance of seeing someone suffer.

Imagine yourself in a representative study. You have been told that you will be paired with another student, named Elaine, and she will be receiving electric shocks while she performs a task. Your job is to observe. On closed-circuit TV you hear Elaine tell how she was thrown from a horse onto an electric fence, as a child, and these shocks remind her of that trauma. The experimenter then asks you whether you would be willing to trade places. Batson and his colleagues (1981) led half of the participants to believe that their own interests and values were very similar to Elaine's (high-empathy condition) by showing them Elaine's responses to a questionnaire. Her responses were constructed to match their own previous responses quite closely. The other half of the participants were shown a questionnaire in which Elaine's responses were very different from their own (low-empathy condition). A second variable in this study was difficulty of escape. In the easy-escape condition, people were told they could leave after viewing two trials in which Elaine suffered. In the difficult-escape condition, people could either watch Elaine suffer for 10 trials, or switch places.

Figure 18.11 shows the results. Notice that when empathy is low and escape is easy, people leave the experiment, and few are altruistic. When empathy is low and escape is difficult, people often trade places with Elaine, apparently to reduce the unpleasant feeling of watching someone else's pain (consistent with the first explanation of altruism). However, notice that when empathy is high, people seem to feel genuine compassion for Elaine. Consistent with Batson's hypothesis, when empathy is aroused, people are highly likely to be altruistic—even when they have the option of an easy escape. As Batson (1990) argues, we humans do have the capacity to improve others' welfare for their sake, and not simply for our own selfish reasons.

The Bystander Effect

We have discussed one puzzling aspect of altruism, that people help others even when they receive no tangible reinforcements. A second mystery is why people sometimes *fail* to help, even when they know someone is in danger.

This puzzle was first brought to public attention in 1964. Catherine ("Kitty") Genovese was walking toward her apartment building at 3:20 in the morning. A man stabbed her, and she screamed, "Oh, my God, he stabbed me! Please help me! Please help me!" The man left briefly, then returned to attack her a second time. She shouted, "I'm dying! I'm dying." He drove away this time, but was soon back. This last time, he stabbed her again and then raped her (Dowd, 1984; Shear, 1989).

The murder of Catherine Genovese was certainly sadistic, but it was not the sadism that concerned both psychologists and the general public. Instead, the puzzle was that 38 neighbors heard or saw at least part of the crime—18 witnessed all three attacks—and *none* summoned the police until more than half an hour after the initial attack. This apparent apathy is now called the **bystander effect**, an effect in which the presence of other people inhibits helpfulness.

After hearing about the remarkable apathy of these bystanders, Bibb Latané and John Darley (1970) decided to study this phenomenon in the laboratory. Specifically, each participant in the study was led to a small room, where he or

Figure 18.11
Percentage of people who help a needy person, as a function of level of empathy and difficulty of escape. (Based on Batson et al., 1981)

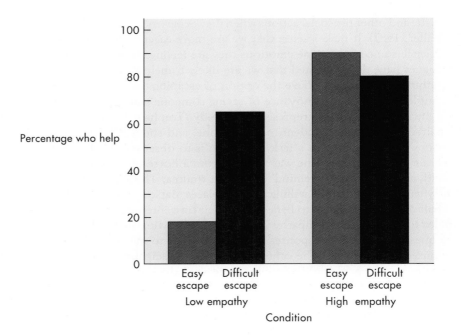

she was instructed to discuss personal problems through an intercom system, presumably with one, two, or five other people in nearby rooms. After an uneventful beginning, one person mentioned that he had a seizure disorder. Soon afterward, he began to stutter badly and then cry out that he was having a seizure. Latané and Darley observed how many participants rushed out to help the young man.

They discovered that all the participants who thought they were in a two-person group rushed out to try to get help. However, when people thought they were in a six-person group, only 62% left their room at some point. Those who left also took significantly longer to do so than in the two-person group. When people think they are part of a large group, no individual person feels responsible for helping, an effect called **diffusion of responsibility**. Notice that the term makes sense, as if the responsibility for altruism has been diffused, or spread across a large number of people. In a public setting, we look around and see inaction; each of us is therefore likely to mimic this inaction.

After 10 years of research on the bystander effect, Latané and Nida (1981) examined dozens of studies that had been conducted in a variety of laboratory and real-life settings. They concluded that when other people are nearby—and they do not communicate with each other—individuals are significantly less likely to be helpful. Altruism is therefore influenced by group size. Let us see how gender is related to altruism, and then we consider other factors that can increase or decrease altruism.

According to the bystander effect, a person is less likely to help someone in need if other people are around.

Altruism and Gender

Try to create a mental picture of somebody being altruistic and helpful to another person. Is that altruistic person male or female? As it happens, we have two different stereotypes about altruism and gender. On the one hand, women are expected to place the needs of other people—especially family members—before their own. They are also supposed to care about the emotions of other people and to be nurturant toward those who need help. On the other hand, men are supposed to be helpful in the heroic sense, placing their own life in danger to save others (Eagly, 1987). This kind of altruism can be directed toward family members, but men are also expected to be altruistic toward strangers.

When Alice Eagly decided to perform meta-analyses on studies of helping behavior, she discovered that social psychologists rarely studied how people help family members and friends (Eagly, 1987; Eagly & Crowley, 1986). Thus, she could only investigate the kind of helpfulness at which men are supposed to excel.

The analysis of helping behavior did indeed show that men tended to be more helpful toward strangers. However, as in the case of her meta-analysis on aggression, Eagly found that the gender differences in helping were very inconsistent across studies. Some showed no gender differences, yet others showed men to be much more helpful. Men were found to be more helpful than women in the presence of an audience, but men and women were similar when no one else was present. Furthermore, men were found to be more helpful when the task was something that was specifically more dangerous for women than for men, such as picking up a hitchhiker. In contrast, men and women were similar when the task was equally safe for men and women, such as answering a stranger who asked, "Excuse me, could you tell me what time it is?" Eagly's studies therefore allow us to conclude that men are more likely to help strangers in situations that seem unsafe for women or situations with an audience watching. However, in most other helping situations, men and women are more similar than different. This theme has been repeated throughout the textbook, and this chapter has provided evidence of gender similarities in conformity, aggression, and altruism.

Factors Affecting Altruism

We have seen that altruism is influenced by the number of bystanders and also—in some circumstances—by gender. Let us consider some other factors that influence altruism:

1. Altruism first requires the realization that help is necessary; clearly, if we are unaware of a crisis, we cannot offer our help.

2. Altruism is more likely when people are in a good mood (Dovidio, 1984). Isen's research, discussed in chapter 12, indicated that people in a good mood perform better on cognitive tasks. Happy people also seem to be more likely to consider positive, altruistic activities (Isen & Simonds, 1978).

3. Altruism is more likely when people are not in a rush, hurrying off to other pressing duties (Darley & Batson, 1973).

4. Altruism is more likely if you have seen another person serving as

---

Demonstration 18.7

Testing Altruism

This test is a shortened version of the self-report altruism scale, devised by Rushton and his colleagues (1981). In each case, indicate how often you have performed each action.

	Never	Once	More than once	Often	Very often
	0	1	2	3	4
1. I have given directions to a stranger.	___	___	___	___	___
2. I have given money to a stranger who needed it (or asked me for it).	___	___	___	___	___
3. I have done volunteer work for a charity.	___	___	___	___	___
4. I have given money to a charity.	___	___	___	___	___
5. I have helped carry a stranger's belongings (books, parcels, etc.).	___	___	___	___	___
6. I have delayed an elevator and held the door open for a stranger.	___	___	___	___	___
7. I have pointed out a clerk's error (in a bank, at the supermarket) in undercharging me for an item.	___	___	___	___	___
8. I have helped a classmate whom I did not know that well with a homework assignment when my knowledge was greater than his or hers.	___	___	___	___	___
9. I have helped an acquaintance to move households.	___	___	___	___	___
10. I have offered my seat on a bus or train to a stranger who was standing.	___	___	___	___	___

When you have completed the items, calculate your score by adding together the numbers at the top that correspond to your answers. The maximum score on this version of the altruism scale would be 40 points.

a model for altruistic behavior. For instance, you are more likely to donate blood if you have just seen someone else volunteer (Rushton & Campbell, 1977).

5. Altruism is more likely in a rural or suburban area than in a city (Steblay, 1987).

These five factors describe situational variables or personal characteristics (such as mood or time pressure) that change over time. One of the themes of this book is individual differences, however. Are some people simply more altruistic than others? To test your own altruistic tendencies, try Demonstration 18.7.

One of the most interesting studies of altruism was conducted by Samuel and Pearl Oliner (1988). They interviewed more than 700 people who had rescued Jews in Nazi Europe during World War II. These were people like Stefania, described at the beginning of the chapter, who risked their own lives to help others—even total strangers. The Oliners found that the characteristic that most distinguished these rescuers from those who had not been rescuers was that they reported a strong sense of empathy and feeling of attachment to other people, including people they did not know. Notice, then, that these findings are compatible with Batson's empathy-arousal hypothesis.

The Oliners found that altruistic people were likely to come from families who used reasoning to teach children why some behaviors were inappropriate. As children, they were often encouraged to think about the consequences of their actions for other people, a technique that seems likely to encourage empathy. The parents themselves served as models of altruistic behavior. Children were also encouraged to ignore social class, race, and religion in choosing their friends. As a consequence, these same children grew into adults who could appreciate the similarities that bind all humans to each other. They were less likely to emphasize the kinds of boundaries that separate "us" from "them." In the previous chapter, we saw how discrimination could be reduced by overcoming boundaries. The Oliners' study emphasizes how the ability to overcome boundaries can also produce empathy and altruism toward all humankind.

Section Summary: Altruism

■ We can be altruistic for basically selfish reasons (either by reducing the unpleasantness of seeing someone in distress or because their distress makes us feel guilty), but less selfish altruism can also be aroused by empathy.

■ According to the bystander effect, the presence of other people inhibits helpfulness, through diffusion of responsibility.

■ Men are more likely than women to help strangers when an audience is present or when the task is especially dangerous for women, but in other situations, men and women are equally helpful.

■ Factors that encourage altruism include a realization that help is necessary, a good mood, no time pressure, viewing an altruistic model, and a rural or suburban setting; altruistic people are also more likely to come from families who encouraged their children to think about other people and overcome boundaries between people.

REVIEW QUESTIONS

1. How can being in a group influence a person's performance? In answering this question, be sure to discuss social facilitation, social roles, group polarization, groupthink, conformity, and the bystander effect.

2. Some of the material in this chapter is related to the discussion of social cognition in the previous chapter. Discuss how social cognition (e.g., self-fulfilling prophecy, the cognitive basis of stereotyping) is related to social roles, attributional errors, enemy images, and any other topics you believe to be relevant.

3. From your own experience in group settings, try to recall any examples you have experienced of group polarization, groupthink, or conformity. Have you ever experienced any evidence of how a minority viewpoint can keep others from complying with a majority viewpoint?

4. We noted that conformity, compliance, and obedience can be placed along a line with respect to increasing social pressure. Discuss how those social pressures are relevant in each case, and then show how each of those three kinds of pressure could be used by someone to encourage altruistic behavior.

5. Discuss the possible explanations for both aggression and altruism, and try to make a synthesis of the explanations by assuming that aggression and altruism are roughly the opposite of each other.

6. We discussed gender at four places throughout this chapter: conformity, aggression, pornography, and altruism. Summarize the conclusions in these four areas.

7. Think about a personal conflict situation you recently faced, and explain how you could have used the win-win, win-lose, or lose-lose approach. Relate each of those possibilities to the options in Pruitt and Rubin's dual concern model.

8. Using either the conflict example in the previous question or another conflict you are facing, outline how you could help increase the perceived common ground. What five steps could you take in problem solving, and what attitudes and skills might be useful? Finally, how could you use GRIT to begin resolving this conflict?

9. The section on international peacemaking emphasized the GRIT model. However, much of the material in the section on interpersonal conflict resolution is also relevant for international peacemaking. Imagine that you are advising the leaders of two countries that are currently in conflict. What kinds of advice would be relevant for them?

10. Based on what you know about altruism, describe all the factors that increase the likelihood of altruism. In other words, if you were in a situation where you needed help, describe the characteristics of the setting and the helper that would be likely to predict high altruism.

NEW TERMS

group	conformity
social facilitation	compliance
role	foot-in-the-door technique
group polarization	door-in-the-face technique
groupthink	obedience

aggression
Seville Statement
conflict
lose-lose approach
win-lose approach
win-win approach
issues proliferation
enemy images
dual concern model

perceived common ground
GRIT (Graduated and Reciprocated
    Initiatives in Tension Reduction)
altruism
empathy
empathy-arousal hypothesis
bystander effect
diffusion of responsibility

ANSWERS TO DEMONSTRATIONS

Demonstration 18.4   1. F; 2. T; 3. F; 4. F; 5. F; 6. F; 7. F; 8. F.

RECOMMENDED READINGS

Aron, A., & Aron, E. N. (1989). *The heart of social psychology: A backstage view of a passionate science* (2nd ed.). Lexington, MA: Heath. Here is a fascinating book that explores how social psychology researchers devised their theories and research programs.

Aronson, E. (Ed.). (1988). *Readings about the social animal* (5th ed.). New York: Freeman. Included in this volume are many of the classic articles on social pressure, roles, aggression, and altruism.

Cialdini, R. B. (1988). *Influence: Science and practice* (2nd ed.). Glenview, IL: Scott, Foresman. This fascinating book discusses compliance, obedience, and other aspects of social influence.

Myers, D. G. (1990). *Social psychology* (3rd ed.). New York: McGraw-Hill. Myers's popular undergraduate textbook is especially strong in its coverage of conflict and peacemaking, and it also contains solid discussions of the other topics summarized in chapter 18.

Pruitt, D. G., & Rubin, J. Z. (1986). *Social conflict*. New York: Random House. This textbook contains clear descriptions of the origins, escalation, and resolution of conflicts.

Health Psychology

Cindy is a college student who is feeling extremely stressed this semester. Her parents were divorced last summer, and her father will not pay for college. Cindy is currently working two jobs, in addition to attending college full time. One month ago, Cindy's mother was hospitalized for major depression, so Cindy had to miss a chemistry exam and drive 4 hours to consult with the psychiatrist. On the way back, her car broke down.

Norman Mailer (1984) writes in a novel about a 12-year struggle to quit smoking. He had given up cigarettes, "once for a year, once for nine months, once for four months. Over and over again I gave them up, a hundred times over the years, but always I went back. For in my dreams, sooner or later I struck a match, brought flame to the lip, then took in all my hunger for existence with the first puff" (p. 4).

Ryan White died from AIDS the week I began this chapter. The 18-year-old was a hemophiliac who contracted AIDS from contaminated blood products. His case made the news early in his illness when people in his Indiana hometown scorned him and prevented him from attending school.

A student struggling with stress, a man addicted to smoking, and a teenager dying of AIDS are all relevant to health psychology, an important area of applied psychology. (As noted in chapter 1, applied psychology emphasizes practical applications of psychological research.) **Health psychology** attempts to understand behaviors that promote and damage people's health, using psychological methods (Pomerleau & Rodin, 1986). A broader term, **behavioral medicine**, refers to an interdisciplinary field that combines knowledge of psychology, sociology, and anthropology (the behavioral sciences) with information from medicine and biology.

Both health psychology and behavioral medicine are gaining attention in the 1990s as we realize the large number of fatal diseases that have a psychological component. When people died in the 1890s in the United States, the leading causes were infectious diseases such as pneumonia and tuberculosis. In contrast, when we die in the 1990s, the leading causes are heart disease, cancer, lung disease, and other ailments that can be partly traced to psychological factors such as stress, cigarette smoking, and improper diet (Krantz et al., 1985).

A chapter on health psychology provides an appropriate conclusion to a general psychology textbook, because so many diverse research areas can be applied to this topic (Goldstein & Krasner, 1987). For example, information from cognitive psychology can help us understand how people remember to take their medicine, how they make decisions about medical problems, and how they discuss their health with their physicians (e.g., DiMatteo, 1985; Pomerleau & Rodin, 1986).

In this chapter, however, we focus more on emotional, personality, and social psychology aspects of health psychology. For example, in the section on stress and coping, we see how stressful emotional experiences are often linked with serious illnesses, and how they can even alter the immune system that protects your body from infectious diseases. The second section of this chapter emphasizes individual differences in health; it targets three personality characteristics that are correlated with health, and it also examines how ethnicity and social class as well as gender are related to health. The last two sections explore two health issues that are especially crucial at the end of the 20th century: AIDS and cigarette smoking. These two topics may initially seem to have little in common. However, in both cases, risky behavior can be life-threatening. In both cases, too, social psychologists need to work together with educators and health psychologists in developing effective methods to help people change their attitudes and their behavior.

Stress and Coping

How would you define *stress*? You may find that it is easier to list examples of stress than to define this elusive concept. The problem is that a definition of stress needs to emphasize both the unpleasant situation that produces stress and also a person's reaction to that situation. Here is one definition that is both useful and precise: **Stress** is the result of an interaction between a person and the environment, in which the person believes the situation to be overwhelming and dangerous to his or her well-being (Lazarus & Folkman, 1984).

Keep in mind, however, that people vary tremendously in their reactions to the same event, consistent with a theme of the book. For example, you have probably attended weddings where the bride and groom look panic-stricken. At other weddings, the couple seems relaxed and joyful; they do not perceive the situation to be stressful. We use our cognitive processes to interpret and evaluate whether situations are stressful (Lazarus & Folkman, 1984; Peterson & Neufield, 1987).

One of the first people to popularize the concept of stress was a physician named Hans Selye (1956). He called his model of stress the **general adaptation syndrome**, or **GAS**, and it consists of three stages of response to stressful situations. As Figure 19.1 shows, the unpleasant situation that produces the stress is called the **stressor**. The general adaptation syndrome includes three phases:

1. In the **alarm phase**, the organism prepares for action. As discussed in previous chapters, the sympathetic division of the nervous system becomes activated in response to stress.

2. In the **resistance phase**, the organism tries to cope with the stressor by releasing stress hormones. In addition, blood pressure, heart rate, respiration, and body temperature all increase. Toward the end of the resistance phase, however, the activity of the sympathetic system declines, whereas the activity of the parasympathetic system increases.

People differ in their reactions to the same event. This couple is enjoying the celebration, but others might perceive the event as stressful.

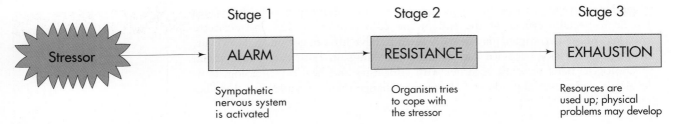

Stage 1   Stage 2   Stage 3

Stressor → ALARM → RESISTANCE → EXHAUSTION

Sympathetic
nervous system
is activated

Organism tries
to cope with
the stressor

Resources are
used up; physical
problems may develop

Figure 19.1
Hans Selye's general adaptation
syndrome (GAS) model of response to
stress.

3. The **exhaustion phase** occurs if the stressor persists. The activity of the sympathetic system declines further still, and now the parasympathetic system is dominant. When the organism uses up the available resources, physical problems and illness are likely to develop.

Selye's model provides a helpful explanation for the way in which stressful events in the environment can influence the development of diseases (Krantz et al., 1985). In this chapter, we examine other components of stress, first by discussing several important sources of stress. Our second major topic is the effects of stress. Finally, we consider methods of coping with stress.

Sources of Stress

If you were to make a list of all the sources of stress that you, your family, and your friends have faced, that entire list of items could be divided into three major categories: catastrophes, important life events, and daily hassles.

Catastrophes   A catastrophe is a large-scale disaster that affects numerous people and causes extensive damage. Catastrophes include major earthquakes, hurricanes, nuclear accidents, and widespread war. In 1980, for example, some residents of Washington State experienced a catastrophe when the volcano Mount Saint Helens erupted, spewing thick layers of ash throughout the community of Othello. A study revealed clear-cut evidence of a disaster stress reaction. For instance, the stress influenced the mental health of residents; cases of psychological disorders more than tripled in the period after the eruption. However, the disaster also influenced physical health. Stress-aggravated illnesses tripled, and emergency room visits increased by 21%. Furthermore, the death rate increased by 19% in comparison to the same period in the previous year (Adams & Adams, 1984). In terms of Selye's model, many community residents had moved beyond the resistance phase of stage 2, and physical health problems developed or intensified in the exhaustion phase of stage 3.

Important Life Events   A second category of stressors are major life events. The first large-scale investigation of this form of stress and physical health was conducted by Holmes and Rahe (1967). These two researchers asked several hundred adults to rate various life events, indicating how much readjustment each event required. They were asked to assign "getting married" an arbitrary value of 50. On this Social Readjustment Rating Scale, death of a spouse received an average rating of 100, divorce received a 73, and trouble with the boss received a 23. Demonstration 19.1 illustrates a version of this scale that is more appropriate for most undergraduates.

Several studies have shown that people with increased scores on the Social Readjustment Rating Scale are likely to develop physical illness, such as diabetes, multiple sclerosis, and heart disease (Garrity & Marx, 1979; Holmes & Masuda, 1974; Krantz et al., 1985). One explanation of this correlation is that stressful life events *cause* physical illness. However, you learned in chapter 2 to be skeptical

The Student Stress Scale

This scale is an adaptation of Holmes and Rahe's (1967) Social Readjustment Rating Scale. In general, students who receive higher total scores on this scale would be more likely to experience health problems.

EVENT	VALUE
Death of a close family member	100
Death of a close friend	73
Divorce between parents	65
Major personal injury	63
Marriage	58
Failing an important course	45
Pregnancy	45
Outstanding personal achievement	36
First term in college	35
Change in social activities	29
Change of college	24
Minor traffic violations	20

about cause-and-effect conclusions in studies using the correlation method. Another possibility is that physical illness causes stressful life events. For instance, frequent absences from work may cause trouble with the boss. In addition, both the stressful life events and illness scales are often measured by self-report, which may introduce systematic biases, as well as memory errors (Schroeder & Costa, 1984).

In general, the more carefully controlled studies on the Social Readjustment Rating Scale tend to show correlations between life events and physical illness that range between .20 and .35. In other words, these stressful life events have a moderate—but not overwhelmingly strong—influence on illness (Maddi et al., 1987). It is important to note that we would not expect these two factors to be strongly correlated because of individual differences in response to the same presumably stressful event. For example, one person might be devastated when parents announce a divorce, whereas another might believe that a divorce was a wise decision, given the circumstances.

Daily Hassles   Think for a moment about the days when you feel most stressed. A student I know described a miserable day that included an unreasonable biology test, a car that refused to start, getting stuck in a friend's snowy driveway, and rushing from school to rehearsal for a play. Are these daily hassles better predictors of health than those more major life events?

Table 19.1 shows the 10 kinds of hassles listed most often by a sample of middle-aged adults (Kanner et al., 1981). Studies on stress often show that the accumulation of numerous daily annoyances is a better predictor of future illness than a scale that only counts the major life events (DeLongis et al., 1982; Eckenrode, 1984; Lazarus, 1984).

Stress in the workplace is an important issue for industrial psychologists. As you can imagine, people frequently complain about the daily hassles that plague

Table 19.1   *Ten Most Frequent Hassles, as Listed by Middle-Aged Adults*

HASSLE	% OF TIMES CHECKED
1. Concerns about weight	52
2. Health of a family member	48
3. Rising prices of common goods	44
4. Home maintenance	43
5. Too many things to do	39
6. Misplacing or losing things	38
7. Yard work or outside home maintenance	38
8. Property, investment, or taxes	37
9. Crime	37
10. Physical appearance	36

Source: Kanner et al., 1981.

them at work. A representative study argues that job stress arises when an employee's personal characteristics do not match the characteristics of the job. Tom Schmidt may be a bright, friendly man, but his job may demand different kinds of strengths and skills. Chemers and his colleagues (1985) studied university administrators and found that administrators whose personality characteristics matched their job characteristics had significantly fewer health problems. They also missed fewer days from work, compared to those administrators whose characteristics did not match their job characteristics.

We have been discussing how catastrophes, major life events, and the more minor daily hassles create a kind of stress that encourages physical illness. Two cautions are necessary, however. First, individual differences in the way people interpret and handle stress may be even more important than these environmental events (Depue & Monroe, 1986). Individual differences will be addressed in the second section of this chapter. Second, the relationship between stress and illness is moderately strong, but the correlation is far from perfect. Please do not assume that every cold or every heart attack can be traced to stress!

The Effects of Stress

You have probably noticed that stress has complicated effects on your functioning. If stress only made your stomach churn or only made you angry, we would not spend one third of a chapter on this topic. However, stress can disrupt behaviors, cognitive processes, emotions, and physiological activities.

Mild stress can actually *improve* your behavior in some cases. If you are an athlete, you may have noticed that performance is better when you feel some stress, rather than complete relaxation. With severe stress, however, behavior may be paralyzed. After an automobile accident, for instance, people are likely to remain nearly immobile for a few moments.

It will not surprise you to learn that stress can impair your cognitive abilities, especially on difficult tasks. For instance, competition, or an audience, or a cash incentive for good performance can cause you to choke under pressure. It seems that when you are pressured to perform well, the stress shifts your attention to the way you are performing, rather than the performance outcome. Your performance suffers because you are distracted and self-conscious (Baumeister, 1984). Under pressure, thoughts irrelevant to the task may intrude (Sarason, 1984).

In some cases, such as this high school play, performance actually improves under mild stress.

During a difficult test, for example, you may find yourself thinking, "Why is everyone leaving? I bet they all know the answers, and I'm still stumped by the questions on the third page." This kind of cognitive interference keeps you from answering the questions effectively.

Stress also disrupts emotions. (We focused on emotional psychological disorders in chapter 15.) Stressful life events, such as the death of a spouse or a serious accident, produced depressed feelings (e.g., feeling blue, lonely, and worried about things) in more than 90% of people who were surveyed (Horowitz et al., 1980). More than 90% also reported feelings of anxiety, such as tension or nervousness.

Physiological stress responses are the last category of the effects of stress. Someone leaps out at you from the dark, or your car skids across the ice, and your body automatically prepares itself for the emergency. The sympathetic system secretes adrenaline, which increases your heart rate and dilates the pupils in your eyes. Your saliva and mucus dry up, leaving wider air passages to your lungs— and a noticeably drier mouth. You are also likely to perspire heavily, a response that cools your energized body.

In addition to these immediate physiological effects, long-term stress can also suppress the immune system. The **immune system** protects the body from bacteria, viruses, cancer cells, and other dangers (Pomerleau & Rodin, 1986). Research in both the laboratory and in naturalistic settings has shown that stressors can decrease the number of lymphocytes, which are the white blood cells that attack the invading bacteria and other harmful agents. For example, studies have demonstrated that lymphocyte production is decreased after the death of a spouse (Schleifer et al., 1983). Additional research has shown that stress influences other aspects of the immune system. For instance, students in dental school had lower levels of antibodies in their saliva during exam time than during vacations (Jemmott et al., 1983; Jemmott & Locke, 1984). Now you know why the lead in your high school musical came down with laryngitis just before opening night!

Coping With Stress

Coping refers to the thoughts and behaviors we use to handle stress or anticipated stress. Studies on methods of coping with stress emphasize wide individual differences (Rodin & Salovey, 1989). Think about some stressful event that you and your friends have experienced, and try to recall the variety of coping strategies you all used. This theme of individual differences was emphasized for me last year. Two of my friends became widows; both husbands had died of cancer. One woman asked her husband's friends to conduct the memorial service, because she knew she would find it too stressful to speak. Another friend organized the service herself, greeting all who attended with warmth and strength. As she buried the urn with his ashes in her backyard, she smiled and said, "Well, I'm burying Sam here for now, but if I move, I'll just dig him up and bury him again." Both women had been equally close to their husbands, but they responded in very different ways to the stressful event.

Arthur Stone and John Neale (1984) gave a questionnaire on coping strategies to 60 married couples. Table 19.2 shows their responses. Notice that direct action is the most common response, but several other coping strategies were also popular. These researchers also discovered some gender differences, with men somewhat more likely than women to take direct action, and somewhat less likely to choose emotional expression and social support.

Methods of coping with stress can be divided into two major categories, problem-focused coping and emotion-focused coping (Lazarus & Folkman, 1984). **Problem-focused coping** includes strategies used to solve problems as well as strategies that change a person's own thoughts. These strategies focus on changing the problem that is creating the stress. In contrast, **emotion-focused coping** is directed at regulating emotional responses to the problem. Let us first look at problem-focused coping and then consider several different kinds of emotion-focused coping.

Problem-Focused Coping   We saw in Stone and Neale's (1984) study that direct action is a popular coping response. If you find yourself in a stressful situation, you try to define the problem, generate several possible solutions, and determine the costs and benefits of each alternative. You then select among these alternatives, and move forward. We have discussed this kind of approach in the problem-solving section of the chapter on thinking, as well as in the conflict-resolution section of chapter 18. This approach is directed outward, toward the problem that exists out there in the world.

In addition, problem-focused coping can also be directed inward. You can reduce stress by cognitive adjustments such as shifting your level of aspiration. A student whose grades are clearly inadequate for medical school may decide to

Table 19.2   *Frequency With Which Adults Use Various Coping Strategies*

COPING STRATEGY	FREQUENCY OF USE (%)
1. Diverting attention away from the problem	26
2. Trying to see the problem in a different light	24
3. Doing something to solve the problem (direct action)	46
4. Expressing emotion	25
5. Accepting the problem	30
6. Seeking social support	14
7. Doing something relaxing	17
8. Seeking religious comfort	6
9. Other	7

Source: Based on Stone & Neale, 1984.

become a biology teacher, for example. Another student whose best friend has been deceitful can decide to become less involved in that friendship. These internal coping strategies are called **cognitive reappraisals** (Lazarus & Folkman, 1984).

Both kinds of problem-focused coping are more likely when we think that conditions and interpretations can actually be changed. When we believe that nothing can be done about a stressful situation, we are likely to try emotion-focused forms of coping, such as denial and seeking support from other helpful people.

Denial   Recently a student told me that she spent her high school years believing that her family was perfect. Only now does she realize that she had been using denial to avoid thinking about her father's alcoholism. When reality is simply too unpleasant, we may deny that the problem exists. **Denial** is the refusal to recognize the reality of a traumatic situation (Goldberger, 1983).

Several decades ago, psychologists thought that denial was maladaptive, because it interfered with the accurate perception of reality. However, we now realize that some denial may be adaptive immediately after an event, though high levels of denial several months to a year after the trauma are often harmful (Janoff-Bulman & Timko, 1987; Suls & Fletcher, 1985).

Why can denial be adaptive? According to Horowitz (1983), short-term denial prevents us from being overwhelmed with panic. Denial allows us to process new information in tolerable doses. For instance, the survivors of Hiroshima's atomic bombing would probably have developed severe psychological disorders if they had not used denial to avoid contemplating the widespread death and destruction (Lifton, 1967).

Seeking Social Support   We saw in Table 19.2 that some people cope with stress by seeking support from other people. Our family and friends can provide emotional reassurance, boost our self-esteem, and express their caring concern. Several large-scale studies confirm that social support does make a difference. People are less likely to die at an early age if they have a large number of high-quality social relationships (e.g., House et al., 1988). Social support also helps people cope with a variety of stress-related illnesses (Compas, 1987; DeLongis et al., 1988; Hobfoll, 1988; Schulz & Decker, 1985).

Short-term denial can sometimes be adaptive. These victims of the October 1989 earthquake in San Francisco could have developed psychological disorders if they did not show some denial in the hours following this disaster.

Social support helps people cope with stress-related illnesses.

Social support is effective because it serves as a buffer that protects people from the harmful influence of stressful events (Cohen & Wills, 1985). Consider a study by Silver and her colleagues (1983) on adult women who had been incest victims during their childhood. One of the most helpful factors in the current adjustment of these women was having at least one person in whom the victims could confide about the incest experience.

People who discuss their traumatic experiences with others may actually improve the functioning of their immune system. James Pennebaker and his co-authors (1988) asked healthy undergraduates to write about either superficial topics (control group) or traumatic experiences (experimental group) during a 4-day period. Measurement of the immune system showed that lymphocytes were more responsive in those students who had discussed their traumatic experiences. Impressively, the experimental group also showed a drop in the number of visits to the health center, relative to the control group (Figure 19.2). Thus, one reason for the effectiveness of social support may be that these supportive people encourage us to discuss our personal problems.

Other Coping Strategies   Some resources on stress reduction recommend aerobic exercise, especially because it tends to relieve depression (Martinsen, 1987; McCann & Holmes, 1984; Rice, 1987). Exercise seems to promote both psychological and physical changes that reduce stress. In addition, people often report that their muscles feel less tense and they feel more tranquil after they have finished exercising (Everly, 1989).

Another stress-management strategy is relaxation (Benson, 1975; Rice, 1987). Several factors encourage effective relaxation: a quiet setting; a mental device—such as a word to be repeated—that focuses your attention; a comfortable position; and a passive attitude that calmly redirects attention toward relaxation if your mind wanders toward stressful topics.

Maybe you have read claims from celebrities who have cured assorted stress-related illnesses by laughing their way to health. In fact, laughter does have a modest influence in buffering or reducing stress (Hall & Goldstein, 1986; Lefcourt & Martin, 1986; Nezu et al., 1988). However, be skeptical about any claims that seem simplistic. Stress is too complex to be easily reduced by a single technique.

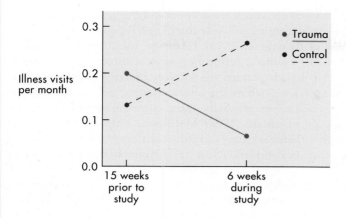

Figure 19.2
Average number of health center visits
for students in an experimental group
who discussed a traumatic event and
for students in a control group.
(Pennebaker et al., 1988)

Section Summary: Stress and Coping

- Selye's general adaptation syndrome (GAS) model of stress includes three stages: alarm, resistance, and exhaustion.
- Stress-related illnesses increase after catastrophes, and these illnesses are also somewhat correlated with important life events; minor daily hassles also contribute significantly to stress-related health problems.
- Stress can impair behavior and thinking, disrupt emotions, alter physiological functions, and suppress the immune system.
- Problem-focused coping includes problem solving and cognitive adjustments; emotion-focused coping includes denial and seeking support from other people.

Psychosocial Factors Related to Health and Illness

When we considered sources of stress in the previous section, we examined forces in the environment that are related to stress and illness. The eruption of a volcano, the death of a family member, and countless daily hassles all predict health disorders. However, we also need to consider individual differences. These more internal factors may be just as important as external forces. We first consider three personality characteristics, and then discuss two social categories: ethnic group and gender.

Type A Behavior Pattern

The Type A behavior pattern is a personality characteristic that was once considered to be strongly related to heart disease, though it is no longer considered to be as crucial. You have probably heard about Type A and Type B behavior patterns. The **Type A behavior pattern (TABP)** includes characteristics such as ambitiousness, aggressiveness, competitiveness, and impatience. Type A people speak rapidly and work quickly, and they are likely to respond to hassles with irritation and hostility (Rosenman, 1990). In contrast, people with Type B behavior pattern lack those Type A characteristics. Type B people rarely have time urgency, and they are seldom impatient or hostile. For example, a Type B woman I know discovered 3 weeks after the switch to daylight savings time that her watch had been an hour off—she was simply unconcerned about time.

About 20 years ago, both researchers and the general public were convinced that Type A people were more likely than Type B people to develop heart disease (e.g., Friedman & Rosenman, 1974). However, the current conclusions are much more cautious. For example, researchers now acknowledge that paper-and-pencil tests of Type A behavior pattern are not very effective in predicting heart disease. A structured interview—where the interviewer records speech patterns, gestures, and facial expression—is generally more accurate in predicting heart disease (Booth-Kewley & Friedman, 1987; Matthews, 1988; Thoresen & Low, 1990). Consistent with a theme of this book, the relationship between Type A behavior and heart disease is complex. (Now try Demonstration 19.2 before you read further.)

Furthermore, researchers have determined that only certain aspects of the Type A behavior pattern are likely to lead to heart disease. Time urgency and ambitiousness now seem fairly innocent. Instead, the hostility and anger components—which only some Type A people have—are more closely related to heart problems. Demonstration 19.2 provided an informal assessment of your own hostility tendencies. Naturally, no informal 10-item test can provide a good assessment of a characteristic as complex as hostility. Still, a high score on this demonstration may encourage you to rethink how you deal with other people—for the sake of your own health and also the well-being of others.

Physicians have speculated about the relationship between hostility and heart disease for several centuries. For instance, John Hunter was a pioneer researcher in cardiology who noticed that he developed heart difficulties after intense conflicts with his colleagues. He died suddenly in 1793 following a heated argument with another physician. A colleague who was present at the time observed, "In silent rage . . . he gave a deep groan and fell down dead" (DeBakey & Gotto, 1977; Dembroski & MacDougall, 1985).

In a representative study on hostility and heart disease, 255 medical students completed the Minnesota Multiphasic Personality Inventory (MMPI), a popular test discussed in Chapter 14. The scores on the hostility subscale of the MMPI

Demonstration 19.2

Assessing Hostility

The following items are similar to those items from the MMPI which Barefoot and his colleagues (1983) used to assess hostility. In front of each item, write T if the statement is true and F if the statement is false. Check your responses against the key at the end of the chapter.

_____ 1. When someone does something wrong, I feel obligated to do something wrong in return.

_____ 2. Many times I've been in the position of taking orders from someone less competent than myself.

_____ 3. Most people are so incompetent that they need a lot of argument to help them see the truth.

_____ 4. My relatives tend to think highly of me.

_____ 5. People usually understand my way of doing things.

_____ 6. It seems perfectly fair to take advantage of people if the opportunity is just sitting there.

_____ 7. I make friends with people because they are likely to be useful to me.

_____ 8. I often find that people let me down.

_____ 9. Even when people are rude to me, I try to be gentle in return.

_____ 10. I usually try to cover up my poor opinion of a person so that he or she never knows how I feel.

The most dangerous component of the Type A behavior pattern may actually be hostility.

were significantly related to the incidence of coronary heart disease 25 years later (Barefoot et al., 1983). Those with high hostility scores were five times as likely as those with low hostility scores to develop heart disease. Not every study demonstrates a significant effect, though the most carefully designed studies are likely to show a relationship. Hostile people probably tend to expect the worst from others, an expectation that provokes unfriendliness from them. A vicious cycle begins, producing stress and conflict. In addition, hostile people may be more physiologically aroused than others, creating additional stress for the endocrine and immune systems (Williams et al., 1985).

As we move toward the 21st century, we may gather additional information. At present, however, it seems likely that people who simply look at their watches and figure out how to accomplish more work in less time do not run an enormous risk of heart disease. However, people who scream at their secretaries and who appear to be eternally angry may be more likely to develop heart problems.

Type A behavior pattern and its related characteristic, hostility, have been the personality attributes that have received the most research attention. However, two other personality characteristics are becoming increasingly prominent. Let us first consider psychological control and then examine explanatory style in more detail.

Psychological Control

A student described a disturbing experience she had several years ago while working in a nursing home. She had befriended a woman patient who had been a psychiatrist prior to her decision to move to a nursing home. (She was from Germany, with no family in this country, and had decided that this move would be wisest for an elderly person.) Since this student planned to be a psychologist, she enjoyed her conversations with the psychiatrist, who provided useful information about Freudian theory as well as remarks about how the nurses' treatment of other residents was likely to make those people feel helpless. After a 2-month absence from the nursing home, the student returned and sought out the psychiatrist. Astonishingly, the psychiatrist no longer recognized the student, and she no longer talked. The elderly woman looked transformed. She had been well dressed and carefully groomed. Now her dresses were improperly buttoned and her hair was disheveled. The nursing home records showed no evidence of a stroke or other organic reason for her decline.

In chapters 2 and 11, we discussed how nursing homes can take away people's sense of psychological control, which seems to produce a decline in physical health. In those chapters, we discussed an important study by Judith Rodin and Ellen Langer (1977). This study showed that when residents of a nursing home were encouraged to make decisions about their lives and establish a sense of control over their own activities, they were happier and they lived longer.

A sense of control is especially critical for elderly people. In nursing homes and in everyday life, well-meaning people may try to help with tasks that the elderly people have previously done on their own. As a result, elderly people may feel ineffective and less in control (Rodin, 1986).

How could a sense of control influence health? According to Rodin (1986) an increased sense of control makes stress less harmful. In addition, people who have control over their lives are less likely to report physical symptoms than those who feel little control. Furthermore, people high in control take better care of themselves. That is, they read articles about healthy habits, they ask questions when they visit their physicians, and they follow the advice these physicians give them.

The research on sense of control suggests some hints for health care providers. For example, an elderly man living at home should be encouraged to work out his own schedule for taking his medicine at regular intervals, rather than adopting an arbitrary schedule imposed by the physician. Everyone should be encouraged to ask questions and discover more about their illnesses. Clearly, nursing homes should allow residents to make decisions about entertainment, room arrangement, and visiting. If we provide people with more control, they may actually be able to extend their lives.

In Depth: Explanatory Style

A third personality characteristic that is related to health involves the explanations we supply for the events in our lives. Before reading further, try Demonstration 19.3, which is a modified version of the Attributional Style Questionnaire. The **Attributional Style Questionnaire** (ASQ) measures people's explanations for the causes of good and bad events. As we discussed in connection with the cognitive characteristics of depressed people, people differ in their explanatory style. When they contemplate bad events—such as the first episode in Demonstration 19.3—some people use a pessimistic explanatory style. An unhappy event has an internal cause ("It's my fault"); a stable cause ("It will always be this way"); and a global cause ("It's this way in many different situations"). In contrast, people with an optimistic explanatory style explain an unhappy event in terms of an external

Table 19.3   *The Explanatory Style of Optimists and Pessimists*

	PESSIMISTS	OPTIMISTS
Unhappy events	Internal, stable, global	External, unstable, specific
Happy events	External, unstable, specific	Internal, stable, global

cause ("It's his fault"); an unstable cause ("It won't happen tomorrow"); and a specific cause ("It's just in this one area"). When explaining *happy* events, however, a pessimistic explanatory style explains these events as having external, unstable, and specific causes; in contrast, an optimistic explanatory style selects internal, stable, and global causes (Table 19.3).

We focus once again on explanatory style because it is related not only to depression, but also to illness patterns. We examine several studies, including one on contemporary college students, one on baseball players, and a longitudinal one on people who were college students in the 1940s.

Measuring Explanatory Style

Try to vividly imagine yourself in each of the two following situations. If the situation really did happen to you, what do you feel would have caused it? Please select the *major* cause if this event happened to you. Read each situation, write one cause in the blank, and answer three questions about the cause.

1. Suppose that you meet a friend who acts hostilely toward you.

   Cause _____

   (a) Is this cause due to something about you or something about the other person or the circumstances? (Circle the appropriate number on the rating scale.)

1	2	3	4	5	6	7

   other person/　　　　　　me
   circumstances

   (b) In the future will this cause again be present?

1	2	3	4	5	6	7

   no　　　　　　　　　　yes

   (c) Is the cause something that just influences this situation, or does it also influence other areas of your life?

1	2	3	4	5	6	7

   this situation　　　many areas

2. Suppose you do a project that is highly praised.

   Cause _____

   (a) Is this cause due to something about you or something about the other person or the circumstances?

1	2	3	4	5	6	7

   other person/　　　　　　me
   circumstances

   (b) In the future will this cause again be present?

1	2	3	4	5	6	7

   no　　　　　　　　　　yes

   (c) Is the cause something that just influences this situation, or does it also influence other areas of your life?

1	2	3	4	5	6	7

   this situation　　　many areas

Source: Based on Peterson et al., 1982.

Contemporary College Students and Illness Patterns Christopher Peterson and Martin Seligman (1987) asked college students to complete a version of the ASQ that was similar to Demonstration 19.3, except that it contained 24 bad events. (With 24 items, the test-retest reliabilities for each of the three dimensions are reasonably high, with r's between .70 and .85.) Each participant also listed all the illnesses he or she had experienced during the previous month. One month later, they again completed the illness measure. One year later, they reported the number of visits they had made to a physician for diagnosis or treatment of an illness.

How was explanatory style related to illness? The first component—whether the explanation was internal or external—was not associated with later illness. However, a score derived by adding stability and globality together was predictive. That is, people with an optimistic explanatory style (with bad events attributed to unstable, specific causes) reported fewer illnesses and fewer visits to a physician.

If you have developed a healthy skepticism, you might criticize this study. After all, it is possible that people who are frequently sick develop a negative explanatory style. Also, people who are depressed might tend to over-report illnesses, and we know from chapter 15 that depressed people have negative explanatory styles. However, Peterson and Seligman (1987) addressed these concerns by statistically subtracting for number of illnesses reported at the first session and for depression level assessed at the first session. Explanatory style was still significantly correlated with illness reports 1 month later ($r = .22$) and doctor visits 1 year later ($r = .23$). Note, however, that the correlations are statistically significant but moderately low.

Baseball Hall of Fame Members One problem with the ASQ assessment technique is that the participant must be alive in order to take this test. Peterson and Seligman did not let a trivial problem like being dead interfere with conducting a study on members of the Baseball Hall of Fame. Instead, they created a new assessment method called the content analysis of verbatim explanation (or CAVE) technique. The CAVE technique analyzes documents such as letters or diary entries. In the case of baseball players, it analyzes their quotations in the sports pages. Participants therefore do not need to be alive to participate in a study, but they need to leave their words behind when they die.

Peterson and Seligman (1987) selected 94 members of the Baseball Hall of Fame who were active players between 1900 and 1950. Then they combed the sports pages of major newspapers during baseball seasons from 1900 to 1950, searching for quotes that included a causal explanation for a good or a bad event. Independent judges, who were unaware of details about the study, then rated the quotes for internality, stability, and globality. In addition, these researchers recorded the age at which the baseball player had died (or his age at the time of the study).

Impressively, players who supplied internal, stable, and global explanations for bad events lived shorter lives ($r = .26$). Explanations for good events produced an even stronger correlation—which led Peterson and Seligman to wish they had included good events in their college-student study. That is, players who supplied external, unstable, and specific explanations for good events lived shorter lives ($r = .45$). Two members of the Hall of Fame who had very different explanatory styles are pictured in Figure 19.3.

Longitudinal Study of Illness Patterns Christopher Peterson, Martin Seligman, and George Vaillant (1988) used the CAVE technique to assess participants in a study of students who attended Harvard University during the 1940s. Participants in this study included only the healthiest and the most academically successful

 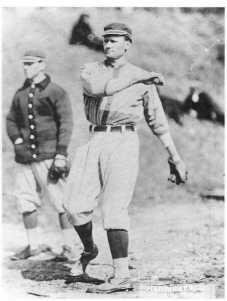

Figure 19.3
Explanatory style and longevity.

(left) Zack Wheat had a highly optimistic (external, unstable, specific) pattern for explaining his success. He remarked, "I'm a better hitter than I used to be because my strength has improved and my experience has improved." He died at the age of 83.

(right) Walter Johnson had a highly pessimistic (internal, stable, global) pattern for explaining his failure late in his career. He remarked, "I can't depend on myself to pitch well. I'm growing old. I have had my day." He died at the age of 59.

students. Peterson and his colleagues focused on the responses that these men gave to open-ended questionnaires completed in 1946, which asked about difficult wartime experiences. In particular, they searched for descriptions of bad events that were accompanied by a causal explanation. Once more, judges rated each cause according to its internality, stability, and globality. Fortunately, each man's physician had also provided a health rating at 5-year intervals.

Peterson and his colleagues added the internal, stable, and global subscales together to create a single explanatory-style score. They then calculated correlations between these scores and the measures of physical health, after first statistically subtracting for each man's initial physical and mental health. Table 19.4 shows the correlation between negative explanatory style and poor physical health, at ages 30 to 60. Clearly, explanatory style is not related to health when the men were younger; nearly all the men were healthy then. However, by the age of 45, health becomes more variable and psychological factors begin to play an important role.

Let us consider two clear-cut examples from this study. At age 25, one man with an optimistic explanatory style reported an unhappy event that had occurred

Table 19.4   *Correlations Between Negative Explanatory Style and Poor Physical Health*

AGE	CORRELATION (r)
30	.04
35	.03
40	.13
45	.37
50	.18
55	.22
60	.25

Source: Based on Peterson et al., 1988.

in the military: He had shared confidential information with another person, and an officer had reprimanded him. This man reported, however, that he had not been at fault, and the officer had not bothered to get all the facts. (In other words, this man's style was external, unstable, and specific.) This man was rated in the healthiest category at age 55. Another man at age 25 wrote, "I cannot seem to decide firmly on a career . . . this may be an unwillingness to face reality" (p. 25). Note that this pessimistic explanatory style is internal, stable, and global. This man had died before the age of 55. Naturally, however, not all of the comparisons were this clear-cut, particularly because the highest correlation was .37. Nonetheless, explanatory style is moderately correlated with physical health.

Why Does Explanatory Style Influence Health?   Several alternative pathways could account for the relationship between explanatory style and illness (Peterson & Seligman, 1987; Peterson et al., 1988):

1. A pessimistic explanatory style may affect the immune system, similar to the way stress operates.

2. People with pessimistic explanatory styles may become passive when faced with disease; they may avoid seeking medical advice or avoid following it.

3. People with pessimistic explanatory styles may neglect their health and not obtain adequate sleep, nutrition, or exercise.

4. People with pessimistic explanatory styles may not be good problem solvers; they do not tackle a problem that could become a crisis.

Explanatory style is also related to sense of control, the characteristic described in the previous section. In addition, explanatory style is probably correlated with overall optimistic mood, a factor that is also correlated with reduced stress and better health (Scheier & Carver, 1987; Scheier et al., 1986). It also seems reasonable to assume that people with optimistic explanatory styles are lower in hostility, which is the poisonous component of Type A behavior pattern. Clearly, personality researchers need to identify the components shared by all these measures that are most strongly related to health. Let us now turn toward other psychosocial characteristics related to health, specifically ethnicity/social class and gender.

Ethnicity and Social Class

Ethnicity and social class are relevant to health psychology because members of some racial and ethnic groups in our country are more susceptible to certain physical illnesses. For instance, Blacks are more likely than Whites to die of cancer. Blacks and Hispanics also have a higher incidence of AIDS (Rodin & Salovey, 1989).

One of the most striking health differences between the races is that high blood pressure (hypertension) is about twice as common among Blacks as compared to Whites. By some estimates, Blacks are between 6 and 15 times more likely than Whites to die of diseases related to hypertension (Gentry, 1985; Thompson, 1980). Possible explanations for the differences include genetic make-up and diet.

Unfortunately, many studies on racial and ethnic differences are confounded with socioeconomic class. In the United States, economically disadvantaged people do not have the same access to health care that the upper classes enjoy (Rodin

& Salovey, 1989; Taylor, 1986). People from lower social classes are less likely to have a personal physician, and more likely to receive treatment in clinics. Health care is lower in quality when you see a different physician on each visit. In addition, clinics are not likely to encourage a sense of control or optimistic explanatory style.

Ethnic background has an additional influence on health care: We also need to consider the attitudes of immigrants toward the physician in the United States. By some estimates, about 600,000 legal immigrants arrive each year, primarily from Asia and Latin America (Kraut, 1990). A recent article in the *Journal of the American Medical Association* urged U.S. physicians to be sensitive to cultural differences. For example, 10,000 refugees from the Hmong tribe in Laos have settled in Minnesota. The Hmong often prefer to seek care from shamans, ritual healers from the Southeast Asian tradition. U.S. physicians can learn to coordinate their care with traditional healing methods. A child with an ear infection might therefore take an antimicrobial medicine prescribed by an American doctor, as well as an herbal concoction recommended by the shaman. Such herbal medicines may indeed have healing properties. In addition, it is especially important to respect cultural beliefs because psychological factors—as we have seen—can influence the immune system and other health factors.

Health care for immigrants may be more effective when people seek traditional healing customs in addition to standard U.S. medical care. In this photo, a man purchases items from a *botanica*, an herbal stall in Mexican culture, which sells herbs, potions, and roots intended to help the users improve their health.

Gender

Currently, the average woman lives about 7 years longer than the average man. Men are more likely to develop cancer in the respiratory or digestive systems; women are more likely to develop breast cancer (Cleary, 1987; Travis, 1988).

Gender differences in heart disease have attracted the most attention. Men are roughly twice as likely as women to develop heart disease (Travis, 1988). The gender difference in heart disease does not seem to be due to hormonal differences or the heart's response to stressors (Polefrone & Manuck, 1987). In response to stress, however, higher levels of adrenaline are released in males than in females (Rodin & Salovey, 1989). It is possible that this adrenaline response has long-term consequences for heart disease.

It is also possible that personality characteristics might explain the gender differences in heart disease. For example, in a study of male and female accountants, men had significantly higher Type A scores (Bedeian et al., 1990). It would also be interesting to see whether hostility scores show significant gender differences. We do know, however, that men and women receive similar scores on the Attributional Style Questionnaire (Peterson & Villanova, 1988).

One factor that may benefit women's health is that they are more likely than men to visit a physician (Verbrugge, 1985). Women are also more likely than men to assign a high rating to the importance of health (Rodin & Salovey, 1989). Perhaps women are more likely to consult physicians during the early stages of disease, before it becomes disabling or fatal. In any event, the explanation for these gender differences in health attitudes is not clear.

How does employment influence the incidence of heart disease in women and men? A survey conducted by Haynes and Feinleib (1980) shows some interesting contrasts. As you can see in Figure 19.4, women employed in white-collar positions were roughly equal to nonemployed women in the incidence of heart disease. Women in clerical and sales jobs had a much higher rate, whereas blue-collar women were intermediate. Notice the very different pattern for men; the incidence of heart disease was highest for white-collar occupations and lowest for clerical and sales jobs. Can you think of any explanation for this contrast?

What happens when men and women occupy highly similar positions? One study examined high-ranking employees of the federal government. In highly demanding occupations, women still had a health advantage over men, but the

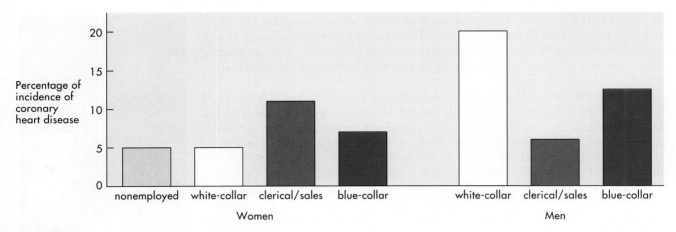

Figure 19.4
Incidence of coronary heart disease for middle-aged men and women, as a function of occupation. (Based on Haynes & Feinleib, 1980)

gender differences were substantially reduced (Detre et al., 1987). Of course, it is difficult to conclude whether women in these demanding occupations experienced more stress, or whether women with certain personality and health characteristics are particularly attracted to these positions.

In summary, no single factor accounts for the gender differences in health. The explanation probably includes physiological, personality, health habits, and occupational differences.

Section Summary: Psychosocial Factors Related to Health and Illness

---

■ Type A behavior pattern predicts heart disease primarily when assessed in a structured interview; furthermore, the most dangerous component of Type A behavior may be hostility.

■ A sense of personal control is particularly important for the health of older people.

■ People with an optimistic explanatory style (e.g., external, unstable, specific causes for bad events) have fewer illnesses as college students; studies of baseball players and men attending college in the 1940s also show greater longevity for those with an optimistic explanatory style.

■ Members of some racial and ethnic groups are more likely than Whites to develop certain diseases, but in many cases these differences are confounded with social class.

■ Women live longer than men, a gender difference that may be traceable to differences in the adrenaline response, personality characteristics, health habits, and employment.

Acquired Immunodeficiency Syndrome (AIDS)

We began this chapter with a discussion of stress, a topic related to emotion that contributes to many health problems. We then considered how health is associated with three personality characteristics, as well as racial or ethnic background and gender. In the last two sections of the chapter, we discuss two health hazards that are critically important in the 1990s: AIDS and smoking.

To a large extent we have no control over the way we die. As I began to write this chapter, our community was mourning the death of four people whose car was crushed by a truck with faulty brakes as these co-workers drove back from lunch. The irony of AIDS and smoking is that we *can* control whether we have unsafe sex or share needles with someone who might have AIDS. We also have the potential to avoid smoking. Nonetheless, thousands of people court suicide every day by engaging in risky behavior. Health psychologists are challenged to find methods that can motivate people to change their risky behavior and to use social psychology techniques to support these behavior changes. Let us begin with a discussion of AIDS and then consider smoking in the final section.

Acquired immunodeficiency syndrome, or **AIDS**, is a viral disease that is spread by infected blood, semen, or vaginal secretions. By the end of 1990, approximately 101,000 people had died of AIDS and by 1993, roughly 200,000 people will be living with AIDS ("The HIV Challenge Continues," 1991).

AIDS is an important topic in health psychology because the disease is spread primarily by high-risk behavior. At present, no medicine can prevent or cure AIDS. Therefore, the primary method of halting AIDS is through education and behavior change (Chang et al., 1990). Our overview of AIDS begins with some background information and then discusses psychological aspects of AIDS and AIDS prevention.

Medical Aspects of AIDS

AIDS is triggered by a virus called **human immunodeficiency virus (HIV)**, which has the potential to destroy part of the immune system. In particular, HIV invades white blood cells called T-helper lymphocytes. Inside these lymphocytes, the HIV replicates itself. As it replicates, it destroys these lymphocytes—the very lymphocytes that help fight diseases in people who are not infected with HIV. When a lymphocyte is destroyed, many HIV viruses are released, and each can infect a new lymphocyte.

People infected with HIV may have no symptoms and may not realize that they are infected. This HIV-positive stage may last for 5 years or more (O'Keeffe et al., 1990). Unfortunately, even during this inactive period, a person can pass the disease on to others.

Some of the early signs of AIDS include unexplained weight loss, night sweats, frequent diarrhea, fatigue, unexplained fevers, and persistent infections. Later, the individual usually develops severe cancers or infections. A common kind of cancer in people with AIDS is Kaposi's sarcoma, a cancer that harms the cells inside certain small blood vessels. It may occur internally, or it may be visible on the skin, where it produces blue or purple discolorations. In addition, people with AIDS frequently develop an infectious disease called *Pneumocystis carinii* pneumonia, a disease that is particularly deadly for people whose immune system no longer works properly (Hall, 1988).

Transmission of AIDS

As the advertisement in Figure 19.5 illustrates, anyone can get AIDS who engages in risky behavior with an infected person. Unfortunately, it is often impossible to tell whether a person is infected. Therefore, any contact with blood, semen, or vaginal secretions is potentially dangerous unless you are certain that these secretions could not possibly be infected with the AIDS virus.

AIDS does not discriminate.

Anyone can get AIDS from sexual contact or sharing needles with an infected person. **Call 1-800-541-AIDS**
But we know how to prevent AIDS. Learn how to protect yourself.
New York State Health Department

Figure 19.5
This advertisement stresses that no population is immune from AIDS.

People who currently carry the greatest risk of developing AIDS include the following:

1. Intravenous (IV) drug users. In the fall of 1987, IV drug users became the most common category of reported risk (Rango & Rampolla, 1990).

2. Gay and bisexual males who have had anal intercourse without condom protection. (It is important to note, incidentally, that lesbian women are at low risk for AIDS as the result of sexual contact.)

3. Women who have had heterosexual contact with infected men.

4. Men who have had heterosexual contact with infected women.

5. Babies born to infected women. More than 600 cases of pediatric AIDS were reported during the 1980s (Rango & Rampolla, 1990).

In all these cases, AIDS is spread via blood, semen, or vaginal secretions. In other body fluids—such as saliva, tears, sweat, and urine—the AIDS virus is in low concentrations. In fact, the concentration is so low that exposure to these fluids does not appear to be dangerous (Batchelor, 1988). Furthermore, you cannot get AIDS by standing near someone with the disease or from a toilet seat.

Psychological Symptoms in AIDS

AIDS can produce psychological symptoms. Some symptoms are produced by direct effects on the nervous system, and some are caused by the stress of living with a deadly disease.

HIV can have several direct effects on the central nervous system. When lymphocytes have been infected with HIV, they secrete substances that change the levels of certain brain chemicals. Furthermore, proteins in the HIV itself can change the functioning of the pituitary and adrenal glands. AIDS may also alter the functioning of dopamine, an important neurotransmitter (Hall, 1988). It is not surprising, then, that people with AIDS often report cognitive problems, such as difficulty remembering and paying attention (Adler, 1989).

Other psychological consequences include pain, reduced energy level, and altered body image—each of which can clearly influence a person's self-image.

Naturally, people with AIDS are often blamed for their own disease, and they are perceived as placing others at risk. You have probably heard about people who have been fired, denied housing, and faced discrimination because they had AIDS. For instance, in Florida, three young brothers tested positive for HIV, and their family's home was burned down (Robinson, 1987). Combined with the knowledge that death is almost inevitable, these stressors are likely to exceed the coping abilities of most people (Herek & Glunt, 1988; Namir et al., 1987). Understandably, research on people with AIDS shows that they are more likely than control populations to report anxiety, depression, and anger (Kelly & St. Lawrence, 1988).

According to research, people with AIDS who take an active approach to life are likely to be relatively well adjusted. Volunteering at an AIDS office such as this one might promote psychological adjustment.

Some people respond to a diagnosis of AIDS with denial (Taylor, 1991a). Those who deny that they have AIDS are not likely to take precautions against infecting other people. As a consequence, the disease is spread even further.

What is the most effective way to cope with the terror of having AIDS? In general, people who use active coping strategies—rather than denial—are likely to have the highest self-esteem and the least depression (Namir et al., 1987). Some of these active strategies include talking to people, increasing physical exercise, and becoming involved in AIDS-related political activities. As we saw earlier, social support is extremely useful when people are trying to cope with stressful situations.

AIDS-Prevention Programs

At present, we have no cure for AIDS. Health psychologists who focus on AIDS therefore face a variety of different challenges. They must deal with the psychological needs of people with AIDS and address the problem of biases and stereotypes about people with AIDS. In addition, they often attend to the psychological needs of family members, partners, and those who take care of individuals with AIDS.

Another priority for health psychologists is designing programs to educate people about AIDS and to help prevent AIDS. An underlying problem in many of these programs is one that was raised in chapter 17: Many times, attitudes are not related to behavior. People know that the consequences of high-risk behavior can be deadly, and they certainly have negative *attitudes* about the possibility of acquiring AIDS. However, their *behavior* may still be risky. Education has persuaded an impressive number of people to avoid AIDS risks. Still, the success rate is far from satisfactory. AIDS prevention requires further reduction in high-risk sexual behavior and IV drug abuse.

High-Risk Sexual Behavior   First, the good news: Sexually active men are much more likely than a decade ago to report using condoms, which reduce the risk of AIDS transmission. For example, in a 9-year study of Black and White teenagers who were sexually active, the reported use of condoms increased from about 20% to about 60%. Now, the bad news: These data suggest that at least one third of sexually active young men are *not* using condoms.

Clearly, the increase in the reported use of "safe sex" has been remarkable in some areas of the United States. For example, gay men in a San Francisco study were 27 times more likely to report practicing safe sex in 1985 than in 1978 (Doll et al., 1987). It is important to stress a potential problem with all these self-report data, however; people may be reluctant to admit they are practicing unsafe sex. As a consequence, the true percentage of people who use condoms is undoubtedly lower.

It is likely that you learned about AIDS risks in high school. A national survey found that 87% of responding school districts had curricula dealing with

Media campaigns have produced effective ads like this one, encouraging AIDS prevention.

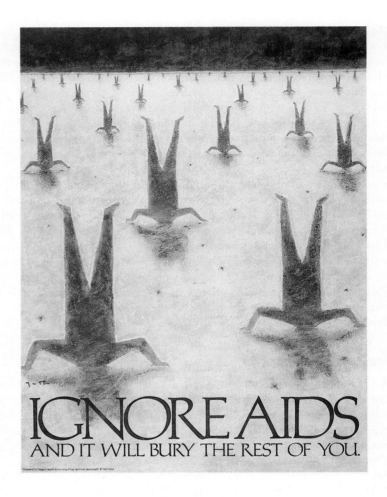

IGNORE AIDS
AND IT WILL BURY THE REST OF YOU.

AIDS. Almost all of these educational programs covered the risks of intercourse in spreading AIDS. Most also emphasized that abstinence is the best way to prevent AIDS (Ruder et al., 1990). Some effective ads on safe sex have also appeared in the media. Still, our nation needs to be more creative in persuading sexually active men and women to convert their *knowledge* about AIDS risks into less risky *behavior*.

High-Risk IV Drug Abuse We have known for decades that IV drug abuse is highly risky. However, those risks increased with the spread of AIDS. Now, an injection of a mind-altering drug can also include an injection of the AIDS virus.

Research indicates that many IV drug users report that they have changed their behaviors to reduce the risk of AIDS (Des Jarlais & Friedman, 1988). For example, in one study, 14% of IV drug users said that they shared needles, in contrast to 46% in 1984 (Harris et al., 1990). However, the participants in this study were extremely promiscuous, and they seldom used condoms during intercourse. As a consequence, AIDS-infected drug abusers are likely to spread the disease to their sexual partners.

At present, our country has more than 1 million IV drug abusers (Pelosi, 1988). Most drug abusers are unlikely to think extensively about future plans, including the risks of developing AIDS. Unfortunately, people who do not think about the future are not likely to worry about health issues and change their high-risk behaviors. At present, the prospect for changing the health habits of IV drug abusers appears dismal.

Section Summary: Acquired Immunodeficiency Syndrome (AIDS)

- ■ AIDS is triggered by HIV, which destroys part of the immune system; the symptoms include weight loss, fatigue, cancer, and pneumonia.
- ■ AIDS is most likely when a person is an IV drug user, or when a person engages in unprotected intercourse with an infected person; AIDS is *not* spread by casual contact.
- ■ AIDS can directly affect the central nervous system; other psychological effects include changes in self-image and increased anxiety, depression, and anger.
- ■ High-risk sexual behavior and IV practices have decreased substantially, and most schools offer AIDS-education programs; nevertheless, many people still engage in high-risk behavior.

Smoking

Cigarette smoking is the largest preventable cause of death in the United States (Feuerstein et al., 1986). Health psychologists are interested in the issue of smoking, especially because they need to explain why a habit so clearly dangerous as smoking should be so difficult to overcome.

At present, 29% of adults in the United States smoke (Toufexis, 1989). Both race and gender influence smoking rates. For instance, a 1985 survey showed that 35% of Blacks smoked, in contrast to 29% of Whites (Fiore et al., 1989). That survey also showed that 34% of men smoked, in contrast to 28% of women. However, the smoking rate is decreasing faster for men than for women. As a consequence, by the year 2000, the United States will probably have more women than men smokers (Pierce et al., 1989).

In addition, you can see from Figure 19.6 that educational status has an impact on smoking. Notice how college graduates are much less likely to smoke than those with less education (Pierce et al., 1989). One likely explanation for these effects of education is that college-educated people are more oriented toward future plans, so they are less likely to engage in an activity that will impair their future health (Schelling, 1989).

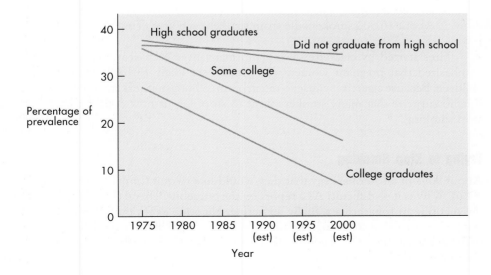

Figure 19.6
The prevalence of smoking as a function of educational status beweeen 1975 and the year 2000. (Pierce et al., 1989)

Let us begin by noting some of the health consequences of smoking. Then we consider the success of efforts to stop smoking, as well as some smoking-prevention programs.

Health Consequences of Smoking

According to recent estimates, about 390,000 deaths each year can be traced to tobacco (Toufexis, 1989). As some have noted with irony, the tobacco industry is the only business that regularly kills its best customers. Another way of presenting the data is that a 25-year-old male who smokes one pack each day shortens his life by an average of 5 years. If he smokes two packs each day, he shortens his life by an average of 8 years (Fielding, 1985a). The total cost in health care expenses and loss of productivity that result from smoking is about $60 billion each year, based on 1984 dollars (Silvis & Perry, 1987).

Here are some of the health hazards that produce illness and early death in smokers:

1. *Lung cancer.* In 1984, approximately 131,000 people died from lung cancer. The average male smoker is 22 times as likely to die from lung cancer as a nonsmoker. Furthermore, lung cancer is quickly replacing breast cancer as the leading cause of cancer deaths in American women (Fielding, 1985a; Toufexis, 1989). However, ex-smokers who have not smoked for 5 years reduce their chances of dying from lung cancer by about 60%.

2. *Other lung diseases.* Cigarette smokers are also much more likely to develop diseases such as emphysema, which harm the lung tissue and make breathing more difficult.

3. *Other cancers.* Smokers also develop cancers in regions of the body other than the lung. Smokers are more likely to develop cancer of the larynx, the mouth, the esophagus, the bladder, the pancreas, the kidney, and—in women—the cervix (Fielding, 1985a).

4. *Heart disease.* About 225,000 deaths each year from heart disease can be traced to cigarette smoking (Fielding, 1985a). However, people who have not smoked in 10 years run a risk of heart disease that is no greater than for nonsmokers.

5. *Strokes.* Smoking also increases the chances of dying from a stroke. About 26,500 smokers die from strokes each year (Toufexis, 1989).

Fires started by cigarettes also claim many lives each year, and chapter 10 emphasized that pregnant women who smoke are likely to harm their unborn children. Because cigarettes cause so much harm to both smokers and their families, it is no surprise that many smokers want to stop. Let us now consider efforts to stop smoking.

Trying to Stop Smoking

About 90% of all smokers say that they would like to quit (Imperato & Mitchell, 1986). Why is it so difficult? As a report by the Surgeon General (1988) concluded, the nicotine in tobacco is actually addicting. Nicotine alters mood and acts as a reinforcer for using tobacco. The nicotine causes a physical dependence, similar to drugs such as heroin and cocaine that were discussed in chapter 5. When people try to stop smoking, they experience withdrawal symptoms.

An increasing number of businesses and public places have no-smoking policies.

External forces also make it difficult to stop smoking. It is harder to break the habit if your friends, other students, or the people at work smoke. With increasing numbers of colleges, public places, and worksites adopting no-smoking policies, however, the environment may be more encouraging for those who want to stop smoking (Biener et al., 1989).

Another external barrier to giving up cigarettes is the tobacco industry, which spends billions of dollars every year on advertisements (Davis, 1987). These ads—showing smokers surrounded by friends, enjoying life to the fullest—are aimed at winning over the nonsmokers and keeping the smokers addicted. The advertising companies are clearly aware of the factors we discussed in chapter 17 that persuade potential buyers.

Some people are able to quit smoking on their own, without a formal stop-smoking program. An article that examined self-quitters in six U.S. cities showed that between 2% and 7% of people who decided to stop smoking had smoked not a single puff a year later (Cohen et al., 1989). Those who smoked less than a pack each day were more than twice as likely to be successful as were heavier smokers. The smoker who finally gives up cigarettes forever averages six previous unsuccessful attempts to quit (Silvis & Perry, 1987).

One way or another, about 41 million people have managed to quit smoking (Surgeon General, 1988). One group of people who are particularly likely to quit smoking are those who have recently suffered a heart attack (Jeffery, 1989; Weinstein, 1989). Perhaps the decision-making heuristic of availability works for these people (chapter 8). A vivid example of a recent life-threatening trauma comes readily to mind when they are tempted to smoke.

Health psychologists believe that physicians should take the opportunity during routine physical exams to advise smokers about the health risks of smoking. They should also give their patients appropriate literature and ask for their concrete plans for giving up cigarettes (Raw, 1986). Chapter 17 discussed how expertise and trustworthiness of the persuader are both important factors in persuasion, so physicians should have the potential to persuade. They could be especially persuasive if they heighten their patients' cognitive dissonance, so that the patients appreciate the discrepancy between their beliefs—smoking is harmful—and their actions of continuing to smoke.

Smoking-cessation programs vary in their approach and effectiveness (Fielding, 1985b). Often, they use behavioral or cognitive-behavioral techniques. One approach uses contracts that require the smoker to deposit money with the program's staff member, to be returned only if the smoker successfully gives up cigarettes. Most programs require smokers to keep smoking diaries, to become more aware of the situations where smoking is most likely. We discussed some of these applications of operant conditioning in chapter 16.

An important application of classical conditioning is **aversive conditioning**, in which an unwanted behavior such as smoking is associated with something extremely negative. For example, a therapist might encourage a smoker to associate smoking with negative thoughts by asking him or her to imagine this scene:

> You are sitting at your desk. . . . There is a pack of cigarettes to your right. . . . You start to reach for your cigarettes. You get a nauseous feeling in your stomach. You begin to feel sick to your stomach, as if you are about to vomit. You touch the pack of cigarettes and bitter spit comes into your mouth. . . . As you are about to put the cigarette into your mouth, you puke all over the pack of cigarettes. The cigarette in your hand is very soggy and full of green vomit. There is a stink coming from the vomit. . . . (Cautela, 1971, p. 113)

An increasing number of business organizations are sponsoring smoking-cessation programs for their employees. An important advantage of these groups is that they create peer group pressure, which encourages people not to smoke. In one program, for instance, both the company and employees collected reward money that was distributed to those who stopped smoking. At the 6-month follow-up, close to 90% of the participants had successfully stopped smoking (Stachnik & Stoffelmayr, 1983).

The most effective way to overcome smoking is one that attempts more than one approach. These should include antismoking messages from the media, specific recommendations from physicians, and enrollment in a smoking-cessation program—ideally one that encourages social pressure against smoking (Taylor, 1986).

Smoking-Prevention Programs

Even the most successful approach—or combination of approaches—is not particularly effective in helping people stop smoking. Instead, most health psychologists encourage the development of programs to prevent people from starting an addiction to cigarettes. These efforts need to be addressed to young children, because most users acquire the habit in their early teens. Furthermore, people who do not become regular smokers during the teen years are not likely to begin smoking later in life (Silvis & Perry, 1987).

Any program directed at preventing smoking should stress that only a minority of teenagers and adults smoke. A study by Leventhal and his co-authors (1987) revealed that a group of eighth graders estimated that 53% of their peers smoked, when in reality "only" 23% did so. These students may inaccurately feel that they are in the minority if they do *not* smoke, and they need to know that the majority is on their side.

A team of social psychologists developed a smoking-prevention program based on some of the principles we have discussed in this textbook. These researchers developed a series of films in which students served as narrators as well as actors in simulated scenes in which they were being urged by friends to try smoking. These films were supplemented by color posters with captions such as

"YOU can resist social pressures to smoke." The quasi-experimental method was used, assigning junior high schools to either the experimental or the control group. One year later, the smoking rate in the experimental group was one half the rate of the control group (Evans et al., 1981).

Another smoking-prevention program chose popular high school students to act as role models for junior high students. The older students led six classroom sessions that included learning how to respond appropriately to cigarette advertisements. For example, they viewed an advertisement implying that women who smoked one brand of cigarettes were "liberated." The students were encouraged to make comments such as, "She's not really liberated if she is hooked on tobacco." Two years later, 7% of the experimental group were smokers, in contrast to 19% in a similar control group (McAlister et al., 1980).

Perhaps even more important than these isolated programs would be a more broad-based approach that trains young people to take their lives and their health more seriously. When adolescents are enrolled in programs designed to help their self-esteem and coping skills, they become more oriented toward future plans (Taylor, 1986). As we noted at the beginning of this section, people who think about the future are more concerned about staying healthy and avoiding activities that would jeopardize their longevity.

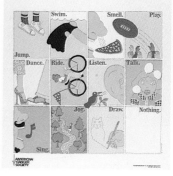

The American Cancer Society has developed effective no-smoking ads aimed at teenagers.

Section Summary: Smoking

- Cigarette smoking is lower among Whites and college-educated people; the health consequences of smoking include lung cancer, other lung diseases, other cancers, coronary heart disease, and strokes.
- Because smoking is addicting, it is difficult to stop; helpful tactics include physicians' advice, programs that include cognitive-behavioral techniques, and groups that create peer pressure for not smoking.
- Smoking-prevention programs should be aimed at young people, providing films or discussion with teenagers acting as role models.

REVIEW QUESTIONS

1. This question helps you review parts of the entire text. Make a list of the 18 previous chapter titles. Then skim this health psychology chapter, jotting notes next to each chapter title wherever you see a relevant application.

2. Try to recall a recent time when you experienced stress. Relate that experience to Selye's general adaptation syndrome model. Which of the three major categories of sources of stress seems most relevant to that situation?

3. Keeping in mind that same stressful period, describe how stress influenced your behavior, cognitive processes, emotions, and physiological activities. What coping strategies did you use? Did your own experiences match the descriptions in this chapter?

4. The section on stress describes how stress affects the immune system. What happens to the immune system in AIDS, and how might AIDS victims' coping reactions have some influence (perhaps not large) on the course of their disease?

5. Suppose that a middle-aged relative tells you that he has read that people who are always "on the go" and time-conscious are more likely to die of heart attacks. How would you explain the current findings?

6. The section on psychological control emphasized that control may actually influence longevity. Think about an elderly relative or neighbor you know, and list some of the ways in which this person could have greater personal control over life events. Describe some of the theories for how control actually might influence longevity.

7. In Demonstration 19.3, you rated your explanatory style. Relate your own style to Seligman's findings and note how you explain both positive and negative events. Which of the explanations for Seligman's results do you find most compelling?

8. How are gender and ethnicity/social class relevant in (a) patterns of coping with stress; (b) health and illness; and (c) likelihood of getting AIDS? Finally, a talk by Schelling (1989) noted that a good way to remember what kind of people have shown the greatest decrease in smoking in recent years is "Those people who wear neckties to work." What did he mean?

9. Imagine that you have been appointed head of a state education committee on teaching health issues to junior high students. What techniques would you use to encourage health-conscious lifestyles? What kind of media approaches would you use to supplement the school program?

10. In both the section on AIDS and the section on smoking, we discussed how people persist in high-risk behaviors, even though they know these activities are dangerous. How are the topics of AIDS and smoking related, and how are they different?

NEW TERMS

health psychology

behavioral medicine

stress

general adaptation syndrome (GAS)

stressor

alarm phase

resistance phase

exhaustion phase

immune system

coping

problem-focused coping

emotion-focused coping

cognitive reappraisals

denial

Type A behavior pattern (TABP)

Attributional Style Questionnaire

acquired immunodeficiency syndrome (AIDS)

human immunodeficiency virus (HIV)

aversive conditioning

ANSWERS TO DEMONSTRATIONS

Demonstration 19.2   Give yourself 1 point for every T response you provided for these items: 1, 2, 3, 6, 7, and 8. Give yourself an additional point for every F response you provided for these items: 4, 5, 9, and 10. In general, those with higher scores tend to be higher in hostility.

RECOMMENDED READINGS

Backer, T. E., Batchelor, W. F., Jones, J. M., & Mays, V. M. (Eds.). (1988). Psychology and AIDS [Special issue]. *American Psychologist, 43*(11). This journal issue includes an overview of the illness itself as well as discussion of AIDS prevention and discrimination against people with AIDS.

Pennebaker, J. W. (1990). *Opening up: The healing power of confiding in others.* New York: Morrow. This clearly written book by one of the major researchers in health psychology discusses the research on how confiding our traumas can have psychological and health benefits.

Rodin, J., & Salovey, P. (1989). Health psychology. *Annual Review of Psychology, 40,* 533–579. This chapter provides an overview of recent topics in health psychology, including cognitive activities related to health, demographic variables, stress, cancer, and chronic heart disease.

Strube, M. J. (Ed.). (1990). Type A behavior [Special issue]. *Journal of Social Behavior and Personality, 5*(1). In addition to covering the research on Type A behavior pattern (and hostility) and health, this journal article also discusses other correlates of TABP.

Taylor, S. E. (1991). *Health psychology* (2nd ed.). New York: Random House. Taylor's popular health psychology textbook covers the topics in this chapter as well as alcoholism, obesity, treating the patient, controlling pain, and managing terminal illnesses.

APPENDIX

Statistical Procedures and Calculations

The research methods chapter (chapter 2) provided on overview of statistics. You learned about descriptive statistics, specifically central tendency and variability, as well as inferential statistics. This information was essential background information for the research discussed throughout the textbook.

For many of you, this course in introductory psychology will be your only exposure to statistical methods. Therefore you may want to know a few more details about statistical procedures and calculations. Consider several examples of situations where statistics might be useful for you:

1. You may pursue a career in sales, and you want to construct a frequency distribution to show how many pieces of equipment were sold in each of the stores to which you supply your products.

2. You may become a grade school teacher, and you want to know how to interpret the percentile scores that are listed for your students on their last standardized test.

3. You may become a physician, and you might be concerned about a woman with bulimia. Her weight is about average for her height, but you are concerned about the variability in her weight during the daily weigh-ins; you want to calculate the standard deviation for these weights.

Let us consider frequency distributions, percentiles, and standard deviations. This information also provides a brief overview of these topics for those of you who will take a statistics course. (Most psychology majors are required to take a statistics course; it is also a frequent requirement for majors in sociology, political science, mathematics, and biology.)

Constructing a Frequency Distribution

A **frequency distribution** is a summary of data that shows how often each score occurs. To construct a frequency distribution, divide your entire range of scores into equal intervals and tally the number of scores that fall in each interval.

Suppose, for example, that you are a businessperson who wants to construct a frequency distribution of the number of your company's television sets sold last week in each of the 60 stores in your district. First, construct a table like Table A.1.

A frequency distribution allows you to summarize a large amount of data into one tidy table. However, you may want to represent these data in a figure that provides a more visual representation. You might therefore choose to construct a **histogram**, which is a graphic representation of a frequency distribution, with the height of each bar representing how often each score occurs. Figure A.1 is a histogram of the data in Table A.1. Many people feel that they can comprehend the general trend in their data more quickly by looking at a histogram than by consulting a less visual frequency distribution that is presented in table form.

Percentiles

You have probably encountered the terms *percentile score* or *percentile rank* if you took a standardized test such as the Scholastic Aptitude Test (SAT) when you were applying for college. For example, if you took the SAT in November of 1988, a score of 600 on the verbal portion was listed as the 92nd percentile. A **percentile score** indicates the percentage of people who received scores below your own score. In this

Table A.1 *Frequency Distribution of the Number of Television Sets Sold in February 1992 in Each of 60 District Stores*

INTERVAL	NUMBER OF STORES IN EACH INTERVAL
0–4	4
5–9	8
10–14	7
15–19	9
20–24	14
25–29	10
30–34	6
35–39	2

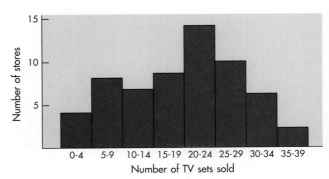

Figure A.1
A histogram of the frequency distribution in Table A.1, illustrating the number of television sets sold in 1 week in each of 60 district stores.

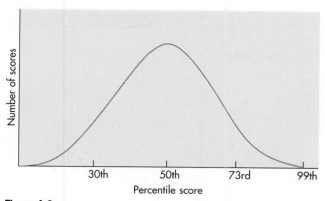

Figure A.2
Examples of percentile scores. (*Note: 30th percentile* means that 30% of the test takers received scores lower than this particular score.)

case, if you received a percentile score of 92, it would mean that 92% of the people who took the test received a score lower than you did. A percentile score is useful because it allows you to understand where your score falls relative to other scores.

Percentile scores are especially important in education. Suppose that you are a fourth grade teacher who is trying to figure out why one of your students, Gordon, is doing poorly in mathematics. You consult Gordon's records and discover that his raw score on the mathematics portion of a standardized test from last year is 27. A raw score, by itself, is meaningless. You have no hint about whether a 27 is low, medium, or high.

Most standardized tests therefore list a percentile score next to the raw score. Suppose that Gordon's percentile score is 73. You would then know that Gordon scored higher than 73% of students; his performance on that test was clearly above average. You would conclude that Gordon seems to have the skill to perform the work. You might suspect a motivational problem or a specific learning disability associated with a particular kind of mathematical skill.

Note, incidentally, that a student cannot obtain a percentile score of 100. That score would mean the student scored higher than 100% of students, including himself or herself—a logical impossibility! Instead, an extremely high raw score is often assigned a percentile score of 99+. For example, in November 1988, a verbal SAT score of 750 to 800 was assigned a percentile score of 99+. Also, note that a percentile score of 50 means that a student has received a score that is at the median of the distribution. As discussed in chapter 2, the **median** is the score that falls precisely in the middle of a distribution of scores. Figure A.2 illustrates several percentile scores.

Standard Deviations

As we discussed in chapter 2, a **standard deviation** is a measure of **variability**, or the extent to which scores differ from one another. Variability can be easily measured in terms of **range**, or the difference between the highest and lowest scores in a distribution. However, the range takes only *two* scores into account. Psychologists are more likely to measure variability in terms of the standard deviation, which uses *all* scores

in calculating the spread-outedness of these scores. As noted in chapter 2, the standard deviation is based on the distance of each score from the mean. Turn back to Figure 2.9 to contrast a distribution, whose standard deviation is 5.7 with a second distribution, whose standard deviation is only 2.2.

Let us suppose that you are a physician who is monitoring a young woman with bulimia. You are particularly concerned about the fact that her weight seems to vary too much from one day to the next. She reports to your office on six consecutive days and you record her weight each time:

123   125   122   125   130   125

To calculate the standard deviation, follow these steps:

1. Calculate the mean of these scores.

$$
\begin{array}{r}
123 \\
125 \\
122 \\
125 \\
130 \\
\underline{125} \\
750
\end{array}
$$

$$
\begin{array}{r}
125 \\
6\overline{)750}
\end{array}
\qquad \text{Mean (symbolized } \overline{X}\text{)} = 125
$$

2. Subtract the mean from each of your scores. Check your accuracy; the sum of these new deviation scores should equal zero.

Score	Mean		Deviation score
123	− 125	=	−2
125	− 125	=	0
122	− 125	=	−3
125	− 125	=	0
130	− 125	=	+5
125	− 125	=	0
			0 ✓

3. Take each of those deviation scores, square it, and add together these squared deviation scores.

Deviation score	Squared Deviation score	
−2	$(-2)^2$	= 4
0	$(0)^2$	= 0
−3	$(-3)^2$	= 9
0	$(0)^2$	= 0
+5	$(+5)^2$	= 25
0	$(0)^2$	= 0

Sum of the squared deviation scores   38

4. Divide the sum of the deviation scores by the number of observations you made.

$$
\begin{array}{r}
6.3 \\
6\overline{)38}
\end{array}
$$

5. Take the square root of the number you calculated in step 4.

$$\sqrt{6.3} = 2.5$$

This figure equals the standard deviation of your scores.

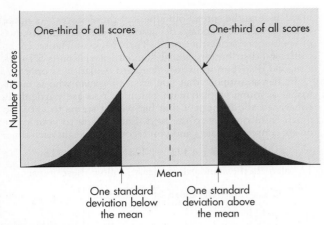

Figure A.3
A distribution of scores, showing the mean and points one standard deviation above and below the mean.

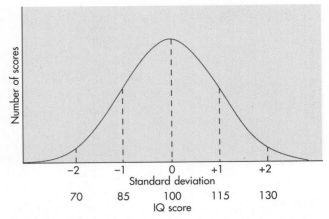

Figure A.4
The distribution of scores on an IQ test showing scores one and two standard deviations away from the mean. (*Note:* Roughly two thirds—68%—of IQ scores lie within one standard deviation of the mean; 95% of IQ scores lie within two standard deviations of the mean.)

Writing out the formula in words, the entire equation becomes:

$$\text{Standard deviation} = \sqrt{\frac{\text{Sum of (deviations)}^2}{\text{Number of scores}}}$$

It is important to remember that large standard deviations indicate greater variability in the scores. Suppose, for example, that you were to calculate a standard deviation of 2.5 for a bulimic woman's weight measurements, prior to the beginning of therapy. Suppose that the standard deviation of her weight measurements, taken after several months of therapy, was 1.1. You could therefore conclude that her newer set of weight measurements was less variable. (However, you would actually need to test your data statistically to determine whether that decrease had been statistically significant.)

The term *standard deviation* is conceptually more difficult than a term such as *mean* or *range*. It is easy to see how both *mean* and *range* are related to the actual scores in the distribution. In contrast, it is difficult to look at the weight scores listed earlier and appreciate how the standard deviation of 2.8 relates to those scores. One helpful point that makes *standard deviation* seem more concrete is this: When you have a large number of scores in a typical distribution, 68% of the scores lie within one standard deviation of each side of the mean. That is, roughly one third of all scores lie between the mean and a point one standard deviation *above* the mean. Roughly one third of all scores lie between the mean and a point one standard deviation *below* the mean. The remaining one third of all scores lie outside these boundaries, either above or below. Figure A.3 shows this general principle. (Note, incidentally, that in the case of the hypothetical bulimic woman, one third of her weight scores lie outside of the interval 125 ± 2.8.)

Let us also relate standard deviations to IQ scores, because most of you are familiar with the kind of scores that are typical on intelligence tests. On many IQ tests, the size of the standard deviation is 15. This means that about 68% of IQ scores should lie within one standard deviation of each side of the mean. If the mean is 100, then 68% of people should receive scores between 85 and 115. Figure A.4 notes, also, that 95% of all scores lie within two standard deviations of each side of the mean, or between IQ scores of 70 and 130.

Finally, I should stress that most psychologists use computers to calculate the majority of statistical measures. When you need to calculate the standard deviation for five scores, as we did earlier, it is no major challenge to figure out a standard deviation by hand. However, the process quickly becomes cumbersome as you increase the number of scores. With the aid of a statistical package for the computer, psychologists simply enter all the scores in a distribution. The printout supplies a variety of useful information, such as the mean, median, frequency distribution, histogram, and standard deviation.

NEW TERMS

frequency distribution
histogram
percentile score
standard deviation
variability
range

A guide has been provided for words whose pronunciation may be ambiguous; the accented syllable is indicated by italics.

Accommodation Piaget's concept proposing that humans change their thought structures to fit the stimuli they encounter.

Acetylcholine (ACh) In the nervous system, a neurotransmitter found in synapses in the brain, where it is important in a variety of functions such as arousal, attention, memory, aggression, sexual arousal, and thirst. ACh can also be found at the junction between neurons and muscle fibers, where it acts as an excitatory neurotransmitter.

Achievement motive Motivation involving meeting personal standards of success, doing better than others, and mastering challenging tasks.

Achievement test Test designed to measure current skills, usually based on a formal exposure to a subject area.

Acquired immunodeficiency syndrome (AIDS) Sexually transmitted viral disease—spread by infected blood, semen, or vaginal secretions—that destroys the body's natural immunity to diseases. Once the immune system has been destroyed, diseases such as pneumonia and cancer can take over, leading eventually to death.

Acquisition In general, learning a new response or new material. In classical conditioning, acquisition involves producing a conditioned response to a conditioned stimulus. Pertaining to memory, acquisition is the first stage of remembering in which we perceive the item and record its important features.

Action potential A brief change in the electrical charge of an axon.

Activation-synthesis hypothesis Hypothesis about the function of dreams proposing that the cerebral cortex produces dreams in order to make sense out of the haphazard pattern of signals it receives from the hindbrain.

Active listening In person-centered therapy, technique by which the therapist attempts to understand both the content and the emotion of a client's statement.

Active mode of consciousness Type of waking consciousness involving planning, making decisions, and acting upon these decisions.

Active touch Touch perception in which we actively explore and touch objects.

Actor-observer bias Tendency to attribute our own behavior to external, situational causes, whereas we attribute others' behavior to internal, personal causes.

Adaptation Phenomenon in which the perceived intensity of a repeated stimulus decreases over time. For example, touch adaptation guarantees that we stop noticing touch after a few moments of mild constant pressure.

Addiction Physical dependence in which continued use of a psychoactive drug is necessary to prevent withdrawal symptoms.

Adoption studies Studies to determine whether adopted children are more like their biological parents (who contribute genes) or their adoptive parents (who contribute a home environment).

Adrenal glands Two structures on top of the kidneys that produce several dozen kinds of hormones, including sex hormones, adrenaline, and hormones that regulate the concentration of minerals in the body and the concentration of sugar in the blood.

Adrenaline Hormone that encourages the sympathetic portion of the autonomic nervous system.

Age regression During hypnosis, a hypnotized person is given suggestions to reexperience an event that occurred at an earlier age and to act like and feel like a person of that particular age.

Ageism Stereotyping and discrimination against the elderly.

Aggression Physical or verbal behavior that is intended to hurt someone.

Agoraphobia Type of anxiety disorder involving fear of being in public places or situations where escape is difficult.

Alarm phase First phase of the general adaptation syndrome (response to stress) during which the organism prepares for action.

Algorithm In problem solving, a method that always produces a solution to a problem sooner or later.

Alignment heuristic Rule-of-thumb stating that figures will be remembered as being more lined up than they really are.

Alpha waves During relaxation states, brain waves occurring at the frequency of 8 to 12 per second.

Alternate-form reliability Method for measuring the reliability of a test in which two alternate forms of the test are administered, usually 1 day to several weeks apart. The alternate-form reliability is high if each person's score is similar on the two tests.

Altruism Concern and help for other people, expecting nothing in return. Altruism is one kind of prosocial behavior.

Alzheimer's disease Illness manifested by severe mental and emotional decline, accompanied by changes in the structure and function of the brain.

Amnesia Psychological disorder involving forgetting past experiences following a stressful event. The amnesia may be limited to a specific time period surrounding a traumatic episode, or a person may forget his or her entire life history.

Amplitude In vision, the height of the light wave; amplitude is related to the brightness of a visual stimulus. In audition, the size of the change in pressure created by the sound wave; amplitude is related to the loudness of an auditory stimulus.

Anal stage One of the stages of psychosexual development during which the erogenous zone shifts to the anal region. Freud proposed that toddlers experience satisfaction when their anal region is stimulated, for instance by retaining or eliminating feces.

Analog code   Mental representation that closely resembles the physical object. Mental images may be stored in analog codes.

Analogy   Problem-solving strategy in which we use a solution to an earlier problem to help solve a new one.

Anchoring and adjustment heuristic
Strategy for making an estimate in which people begin by guessing a first approximation—an anchor—and then make adjustments to that number on the basis of additional information. Typically, people rely too heavily on the anchor, and their adjustments are too small.

Androgen hormones   Hormones that produce changes in males during early prenatal development, guiding the development of the male reproductive system.

Anorexia nervosa   Eating disorder that is characterized by an irrational pursuit of thinness and concern about gaining weight. The American Psychiatric Association specifies that a person may be classified as anorexic if body weight is 25% less than specified on standard weight charts and if no known physical illness accounts for the low weight.

Anosmia   Insensitivity to smell caused by drug reactions, certain illnesses, and concussions.

Antianxiety drugs   Drugs designed to reduce tension and excitability; often called minor tranquilizers.

Antidepressant drugs   Drugs designed to make a person's mood more positive. Examples include the MAO inhibitors, the tricyclics, and Prozac.

Antipsychotic drugs   Drugs that reduce the symptoms of schizophrenia such as agitation, confusion, delusions, and hallucinations.

Antisocial personality disorders
Psychological disorders characterized by a variety of antisocial behaviors, including lying, violence, and other actions that show little concern for the welfare of others.

Anxiety disorders   Anxiety that persists—without any clear explanation—and that causes intense suffering. Four types of anxiety disorders are generalized anxiety disorders, panic disorders and agoraphobia, phobic disorders, and obsessive-compulsive disorders.

Aptitude test   Test designed to predict future success on the basis of current performance. Aptitude tests draw their material from a broad range of

human experience, including information gained outside the classroom.

Assimilation   Piaget's concept proposing that humans use and modify stimuli they encounter in terms of their current thought structure.

Attachment   Close emotional bond of affection between infant and caregivers.

Attention   Concentration of mental activity.

Attitude   Evaluative reaction toward an object, person, institution, or event.

Attribution   In person perception, the explanation we create about the reasons for our own behavior and the behavior of other people. Attributions often involve causal explanations for success or failure.

Attributional Style Questionnaire (ASQ)
Questionnaire that measures people's explanations for the causes of good and bad events.

Auditory canal   Tube running inward from the outer ear, through which sound enters.

Auditory cortex   Portion of the cortex located in a groove on the temporal lobe of the cortex that is responsible for higher levels of auditory processing.

Auditory nerve   Bundle of neurons that carries information from the inner ear toward higher levels of auditory processing.

Authoritarian parents   Parenting style in which parents demand unquestioning obedience from their children, punish children forcefully when children do not meet their standards, and are less likely to be affectionate with their children.

Authoritative parents   Effective parenting style in which parents are affectionate but provide control when necessary. Parents respect each child's individuality, they are loving, and they allow children to express their own points of view. However, they have clear-cut standards, which they uphold in a consistent fashion.

Autobiographical memory   Memory for events from a person's own life.

Automatic processing   Placing material into memory with no deliberate effort.

Autonomic division   In the nervous system, the division that helps control the glands, blood vessels, and internal organs such as the intestines and the

heart. The autonomic nervous system usually works automatically, unlike the somatic division.

Availability heuristic   Rule-of-thumb used when we estimate frequency or probability in terms of how easy it is to think of examples of something.

Aversive conditioning   Conditioning in which an unwanted behavior, such as smoking, is associated with something extremely negative.

Axon   In the nervous system, the long fiber that carries information away from the cell body toward other neurons.

Balanced-placebo design   Research design consisting of four groups of participants, half of whom expect that they will be doing something (e.g., drinking alcohol) and half of whom do not. Furthermore, half of the participants actually do receive something (e.g., alcohol) and half receive a placebo. This research design is used to sort out the effects of the variable itself (e.g., alcohol), as opposed to the effects of people's expectations about how they *should* behave.

Basilar membrane   Membrane on the base of the organ of Corti in the inner ear, which contains hair cells (the receptors for hearing).

Beck's cognitive therapy   Therapy that attempts to correct systematic errors in reasoning, known as cognitive distortions.

Behavior modification   The systematic use of techniques from learning theory to change human behavior.

Behavioral assessment   The measurement of personality by objectively recording people's observable behavior, as well as environmental conditions.

Behavioral measures   In a research study, measurement that objectively records people's observable behavior.

Behavioral medicine   Interdisciplinary field that combines knowledge of psychology, sociology, and anthropology with information from medicine and biology.

Behaviorism   Approach to psychology that stresses the study of observable behavior, instead of hidden mental processes.

Behaviorist approaches   In psychotherapy, the approaches that use the principles of learning theory (classical and operant conditioning) to eliminate undesirable behavior. An important feature of behavior therapy is the explicit specification of treatment goals.

Beta waves   During waking states, rapid brain waves at the frequency of at least 14 per second.

Biased sample   In a research study, a sample in which every member of the population does not have an equal chance of being chosen.

Big Five traits   In personality research, the five most important personality traits, including extraversion, agreeableness, conscientiousness, emotional stability, and openness to experience.

Binocular disparity   In vision, source of distance information provided by two eyes that present slightly different views of the world.

Binocular vision   Characteristic of the human visual system based on our two eyes working together and having partially overlapping fields of view.

Biological motion   In motion perception, the pattern of movement exhibited by people and other living things.

Biological preparedness   Built-in bias ensuring that some relationships between stimuli and responses will be learned more readily than others.

Biological psychologists   Psychologists, also called neuropsychologists or physiological psychologists, who examine how genetic factors, the brain, the nervous system, and other biological factors influence behavior.

Biology   Scientific discipline that examines the structure and functions of living things.

Bipolar cells   In the eye, cells that receive the electrical message converted from light by the rods and cones; the bipolar cells then pass this electrical message on to the ganglion cells.

Bipolar disorder   Mood disorder in which a person sometimes experiences depressive episodes and sometimes experiences mania.

Blind spot   In the eye, the location where the optic nerve leaves the retina. Neither rods nor cones inhabit the blind spot, so a person cannot see anything that reaches this part of the retina.

Bottom-up processing   In perception, processing that depends on the information from the senses at the bottom (or most basic) level of perception, with sensory information flowing from this low level upward to the higher, more cognitive levels.

Brightness   The quality of a visual stimulus, which is determined by the height or amplitude of a light wave; psychological reaction corresponding to the intensity of light waves.

Bulimia   (boo-*lih*-mee-ah) Eating disorder characterized by binge eating, or episodes in which people consume huge amounts of food. Some bulimics also induce vomiting after a binge, and they may also fast between binges.

Bystander effect   Apparent apathy and inaction in the face of a crisis, in which the presence of other people inhibits helpfulness.

Cannon-Bard theory   Early theory of emotion in which the thalamus is an important mediator in emotional experience; this theory was proposed in place of the James-Lange theory, which emphasized the importance of physiological change.

Cardinal trait   Personality trait that dominates and shapes behavior.

Case study   Research method that is an in-depth description and analysis of a single person. The data typically include an interview, observation, and test scores; most often, the individual selected for a case study is highly unusual.

Cell body   In the nervous system, the area of the neuron that stores the cell nucleus, as well as other structures that help the cell function properly.

Central nervous system   Portion of nervous system that includes the spinal cord and brain.

Central tendency   Statistical measure of the most typical, characteristic score (for example, mean, median, or mode).

Central trait   In Allport's theory, a general characteristic, found to some degree in every person, such as honesty, extraversion, and cheerfulness.

Cephalocaudal principle   Principle of motor development stating that parts of the body near the head (*cephalo* in Greek) develop before the parts near the feet (*caudal* literally means *tail* in Greek).

Cerebellum   A structure located at the rear of the brain. Researchers do not have a clear idea of the functions of the cerebellum, though it contributes to controlling movement, maintaining balance, and learning motor tasks.

Cerebral cortex   Outer surface of the two cerebral hemispheres of the brain; it processes all perceptions and complex thoughts.

Chromatic adaptation   Visual phenomenon in which prolonged exposure to yellow produces blue and prolonged exposure to green produces red.

Chromosomes   Structures carrying genetic information in virtually every cell of the body. In humans, the genes are located on 23 pairs of chromosomes.

Chunk   Basic unit in short-term memory.

Circadian rhythm   Daily cycle lasting approximately 24 hours, with each cycle including both a sleeping and a waking period.

Classical conditioning   Conditioning in which we learn that certain stimuli in the environment are predictive of certain events.

Clinical psychologists   Psychologists who assess and treat people with psychological disorders. On the basis of an interview and psychological tests, clinical psychologists provide a diagnosis of the problem followed by either individual or group psychotherapy.

Cochlea   Bony, fluid-filled coil in the ear that contains the auditory receptors.

Cochlear implant   For people with complete nerve deafness, a device that consists of a number of electrodes implanted into the bone behind one ear. The electrodes respond to sounds by stimulating the auditory nerve fibers.

Cognition   Mental activities involving the acquisition, storage, retrieval, and use of knowledge.

Cognitive approach   Approach that focuses on unobservable mental processes involved in perceiving, remembering, thinking, and understanding.

Cognitive approach to stereotypes   Approach stating that most stereotypes are a product of normal human thought processes, such as categorization.

Cognitive-behavior therapy   Psychotherapy that combines both cognitive and behaviorist techniques to target inappropriate thoughts as well as inappropriate behaviors.

Cognitive-developmental theory   Theory of gender development stating that children's own thought processes are primarily responsible for the development of gender typing.

Cognitive map Mental map that represents the world as a person believes it to be.

Cognitive reappraisals Problem-focused coping strategies that attempt to reduce stress by internal cognitive adjustments, such as shifting one's level of aspiration.

Cognitive restructuring Therapeutic approach that emphasizes changing one's inappropriate thought patterns.

Cognitive therapists Therapists who argue that people are plagued by psychological disorders because their thinking is inappropriate or maladaptive; recovery requires a restructuring of the client's thoughts.

Collective unconscious According to Jung, the second, deeper layer of the unconscious that stores memory fragments from our ancestral past. All humans share the same collective unconscious.

Color constancy Phenomenon by which the hue of an object stays the same in spite of changes in the color of light falling on it.

Community psychology approach Approach to psychotherapy that emphasizes the prevention of psychological disorders, as well as treatment in community mental health centers.

Compliance Going along with a stated request from someone who does not have the specific authority to make you obey.

Componential intelligence According to Sternberg, the type of intelligence that involves the components (or mental processes) used in thinking. Componential intelligence contains three kinds of processes: (1) metacomponents, (2) performance components, and (3) knowledge-acquisition components.

Compulsions Repetitive behaviors performed according to certain rules, in response to obsessive thoughts. Common compulsions include hand washing, checking, and counting.

Computer-assisted instruction (CAI) Instructional technique in which students learn at their own rate, using computers that are programmed to deliver individualized instruction. Information is presented in small chunks, and learners receive immediate feedback about whether each response is correct or incorrect.

Computer simulation Writing a computer program that will perform the task using the same strategies that a human would, such as in research on problem solving.

Computerized axial tomography (CAT scan) Imaging technique used to provide a picture of the living human brain by passing X-ray beams through the head from a variety of angles.

Concept Category of objects, ideas, and events that share the same properties. We use concepts whenever we group similar items together.

Concrete operational period One of Piaget's four periods of human development, during which children acquire important mental operations, such as conservation, and show more logical thinking.

Conditional positive regard According to Rogers, the situation in which positive regard is given only in certain conditions; moreover, parents and other important people withhold their love and approval if the child fails to conform to their own standards.

Conditioned response In classical conditioning, the response that is elicited by the conditioned stimulus.

Conditioned stimulus In classical conditioning, the stimulus that is predictive of the unconditioned stimulus.

Conduction deafness Type of deafness that involves problems in conducting the sound stimulus, occurring in either the external ear or the middle ear.

Cones Photoreceptors used for color vision under well-lit conditions.

Confabulation Major problem with "hypnotically refreshed" memory, in which a hypnotized subject may simply make up an item in memory to replace one that he or she cannot retrieve.

Conflict Interpersonal process that occurs when the actions of one party interfere with the actions of another party.

Conformity Going along with people's behaviors and attitudes as a result of group pressure.

Confounding variable In an experiment, any variable—other than the independent variable—that is not equivalent in all conditions.

Congruence In person-centered therapy, the therapist's positive, non-judgmental attitude toward the client.

Conjugate reinforcement technique In research on infant memory, a mobile is placed above an infant's crib with a ribbon connecting the infant's ankle with the mobile, so that his or her kicks make the mobile move. Memory can be tested by allowing

the infant to learn the connection between kicking and mobile movement and then waiting several days before presenting the mobile once again.

Conjunction fallacy Mistake in decision making in which people judge the probability of the conjunction (two events occurring together) to be greater than the probability of one single event.

Conscious In psychoanalytic theory, the conscious includes everything you are aware of at a particular moment. Our conscious experiences refer to our sensory awareness of the environment and of ourselves.

Consciousness Awareness of the environment and ourselves, both external and internal stimuli.

Consensual sexual interactions Participation in sexual relationships by fully informed adults who freely choose to engage in mutual sexual stimulation.

Conservation According to Piaget, the mental operation by which children realize that a given quantity stays the same, no matter how its shape or physical arrangement may change.

Constancy Tendency for qualities of objects (such as size and shape) to seem to stay the same, despite changes in the way we view the objects.

Constituent Group of words that seem to belong together as a unit. Typically, a constituent contains more than one word but less than an entire sentence.

Content validity In testing, a test's ability to cover the complete range of material that it is supposed to cover.

Contextual intelligence According to Sternberg, a type of everyday intelligence or street smarts. Contextual intelligence requires adapting to, selecting, and shaping our real-world environment.

Continuity-stages question Is development a gradual process, with adults simply having a greater *quantity* of some particular skill? Alternatively, do children and adults differ in the *quality* of their psychological processes? Although many skills show continuity throughout development, there is evidence for stages in several areas of development.

Continuous reinforcement schedule In operant learning, situations in which the subject is reinforced on every correct trial.

Control condition In an experiment, the group that is left unchanged; in contrast to the experimental condition, they receive no special treatment.

Conversion disorders Psychological disorders characterized by a loss in physical functioning of some body part—with no medical explanation for the condition. Conversion disorders are usually triggered by some traumatic event.

Coping Thoughts and behaviors we use to handle stress or anticipated stress.

Cornea In the eye, the clear membrane just in front of the iris, with a curved structure that helps to bend light rays when they enter the eye.

Corpus callosum Bridge between the two hemispheres of the brain; a thick bundle of about 800,000 nerve fibers that permits communication between the two hemispheres.

Correlational coefficient In correlational research, a statistic (symbolized as *r*) that can range between −1.00 and +1.00. A strong correlation between two variables (that is, the *r* is close to either +1.00 or −1.00) indicates that two variables are closely related.

Correlational research Research in which psychologists try to determine if two variables or measures are related. In correlational research, behavior can be observed in real-life settings, with neither random assignment to groups nor the manipulation of independent variables.

Counseling psychologists Psychologists who assess and treat people; their clients are likely to have less severe psychological problems than those treated by clinical psychologists. Some provide marriage or career counseling; others work in college mental health clinics.

Counter-regulation For dieters, the pattern of eating lustily after a high-calorie preload.

Creativity Approach to finding a solution to an open-ended task in a way that is both unusual and useful.

Crisis hotline Community service that provides a phone number to call for immediate counseling and comfort. These services are available for people with psychological disorders and for others who are experiencing a crisis, including rape victims, battered women, drug abusers, and people considering suicide.

Criterion In signal detection theory, the observer's willingness to say "I detect the stimulus" when the observer is uncertain about whether the stimulus has been presented. Two common determinants of the criterion are (1) the probability that the stimulus will occur and (2) the benefits and drawbacks associated with making the particular response.

Criterion-related validity In testing, a test's ability to predict a person's performance on another measure (i.e., an independent criterion).

Cross-sectional method Research method used by developmental psychologists in which researchers test individuals of different ages at the same time.

Crystallized intelligence Mental ability that involves specific acquired skills such as verbal ability. Crystallized intelligence continues to grow throughout adulthood.

Cultural-familial retardation Mental retardation caused by environmental factors; these environments are psychologically, socially, and economically impoverished.

Dark adaptation Increase in sensitivity that occurs as the eyes remain in the dark.

Daydream Shift in attention away from external stimuli toward internal events and fantasies.

Debriefing In a research study, telling the participants afterward about the purpose of the study, the nature of the anticipated results, and any deceptions used.

Decay Theory stating that each item in memory decays spontaneously as time passes.

Decision/commitment Component of Sternberg's triangular theory of love, which consists of two aspects: (1) a short-term aspect, the decision that you love someone; and (2) the long-term aspect, the commitment to maintain that love.

Decision frames In decision making, the situation in which we are influenced by the wording of a question while downplaying the importance of other relevant information.

Decision making Cognitive task that requires making a choice about the likelihood of uncertain events. It can occur in situations when people make predictions about the future, select among two or more alternatives, and make estimates about frequency when only scanty evidence is available.

Deep friendships Friendships that require intimacy and feeling personal closeness, beyond a simple sharing of interests.

Deep structure Pertaining to sentence structure, the underlying, more abstract representation of the sentence.

Defense mechanisms Normal coping processes that distort reality in the process of reducing anxiety.

Deinstitutionalization Program adopted by the mental health system to discharge people from mental hospitals into the community. In theory, this policy could be useful because it could return people to the supportive environment of family and friends and encourage independence and coping abilities. In practice, the policy has created problems.

Delusion False belief that a person firmly holds, despite any objective evidence.

Demand characteristics In a research study, the clues discovered by participants about the purpose of the study, including rumors they hear about the study, the description supplied when they signed up to participate, the activities of the researchers, and the laboratory setting itself.

Demographic information Characteristics often used to classify people, such as gender, age, marital status, race, education, and so forth.

Dendrites In the nervous system, the slender, branched fibers that carry neural impulses in the direction of the cell body in a neuron.

Denial Refusal to recognize the reality of a traumatic situation.

Dependent variable In an experiment, the variable that concerns the responses the participants make; it is a measure of their behavior.

Depressants Psychoactive drugs that depress central nervous system functioning. These substances reduce pain and tension, and slow down thinking and actions. The depressants include tranquilizers, barbiturates, opiates, and alcohol.

Depth of processing Method we use to mentally process stimuli; deep processing makes material more memorable than shallow processing.

Descriptive statistics Statistics that provide some measure of central tendency ("What is the typical score?") and variability ("Are the other scores clustered closely around the typical score, or are they more spread out?")

Detection In detection studies, the psychologist provides low-intensity stimuli and records whether people report them. Two major approaches to detection are the classical psychophysics approach and the signal detection theory approach.

Detection threshold   In the classical psychophysics approach, the smallest amount of energy required for the observer to report the stimulus on half (50%) of the trials.

Development   Changes in physical, cognitive, and social abilities that occur throughout the life span.

Developmental psychologists Psychologists who examine development throughout the life span.

Diagnostic and Statistical Manual of Mental Disorders (DSM)   Manual for classifying psychological disorders, currently containing descriptions of 17 major categories of disorders and 230 conditions. The current revised third edition describes specific criteria that must be met before a diagnosis can be assigned.

Diathesis-stress model   Model stating that neither predisposition (diathesis) nor a stressful life event is sufficient by itself to produce a psychological disorder; instead, a disorder arises from the combination of both factors.

Dichotic listening task   (die-*kott*-ick) Task in which listeners are instructed to repeat a message presented to one ear while ignoring a different message presented to the other ear.

Diffusion of responsibility   Effect of being a part of a large group; it produces the situation in which no single person feels responsible for helping.

Discrimination   In psychophysics, the smallest amount that a stimulus must be changed to be perceived as just noticeably different.

Discrimination   In social psychology, discrimination involves action against a person or a group of people.

Discriminative stimulus   In operant learning, a stimulus signaling that a response will be reinforced.

Disorders of Initiating and Maintaining Sleep (DIMS)   Formal term for insomnia, or difficulty in falling asleep and/or remaining asleep.

Displacement   Defense mechanism that involves redirecting emotional feelings (e.g., anger) to a substitute target.

Display rules   Customary regulations prescribed by specific cultures about the control of facial expressions in public settings. For instance, a display rule in our culture says that males should not cry.

Dissociative disorders   Psychological disorder involving the splitting off (or dissociating) of a person's identity, memory, or consciousness.

Distinctive features   In visual perception, characteristics of letters, and other stimuli such as straight versus curved lines.

Distribution of practice effect   Pertaining to memory improvement, rule indicating that it is best to distribute practice throughout several study sessions.

Divided attention   Situation in which attention is distributed among more than one of the competing sources.

Door-in-the-face technique   Two-step compliance technique in which an influencer achieves compliance by first making a request that is so large it is certain to be denied, and then making a smaller, more reasonable request.

Dopamine   In the nervous system, an inhibitory neurotransmitter for muscle fibers.

Double standard of aging   Phenomenon of people being more negative toward older women than older men.

Down syndrome   Genetic abnormality involving an extra chromosome added to the 21st pair of chromosomes. People with Down syndrome usually have round faces and small folds of skin across the inner edges of the eyes. Although typically retarded, Down syndrome children are often friendly and cheerful.

Dream analysis   Psychoanalytic technique in which the therapist interprets the hidden meaning of the client's dream. Freud argued that the conscious, remembered aspect of a dream (its manifest content) was a distorted version of unconscious sexual or aggressive conflicts (its latent content).

Drive   In motivation, tension that occurs when a need is not met.

Drug treatment   Treatment of psychological disorders via medication.

Dual concern model   In conflict resolution, a model suggesting that our choices depend upon the relative strength of concern about both our own welfare and the welfare of the person with whom we are in conflict.

Dual-encoding model   In word recognition, the phenomenon by which a word's meaning is accessed directly from the printed page, in the case of a common word; however, meaning is accessed indirectly—through a sound route—in the case of an uncommon word.

Dynamic self-concept   View that the self-concept is active and forceful, capable of change.

Eardrum   Thin membrane that vibrates in sequence with the sound waves.

Echoic memory   Auditory sensory memory, which is so fragile that it usually fades within 2 seconds.

Eclectic approach   Approach to psychotherapy that selects what seems best from a variety of theoretical perspectives.

Ecological validity   A principle stating that results obtained in research should be generalizable to real-life settings.

Effortful processing   Deliberate attempt to place something in memory.

Ego   In psychoanalytic theory, the component of the personality that deals with the external world. The ego serves as a mediator between the id and reality.

Egocentrism   According to Piaget, the phenomenon of a child seeing the world from only one point of view— his or her own.

Elaboration likelihood model   Model arguing that when people are involved in an issue and when they have the ability to analyze a message, they consider it carefully and perform elaboration; that is, they relate the message to other ideas and issues. However, when people are not involved or are not able to analyze a message, they will not be as sensitive to the quality of the message's argument; they are more likely to use decision-making heuristics.

Electrical stimulation   Method for mapping brain function in which the researcher places a small electrode in a specific location of the brain and delivers a weak electrical current to identify the functions of the brain tissue in this region.

Electroconvulsive therapy (ECT)   During this treatment, a person receives a series of electric shocks that produce convulsions, which often relieve the symptoms of severe depression where other treatments have failed.

Electroencephalography (EEG) Technique in which electrodes are placed on the scalp, and the electrical message from the thousands of neurons beneath the electrodes are then recorded on graph paper. The EEG provides information about brain activity, and it can also locate major abnormalities in the brain.

Emblem A gesture that is clearly understood by most members of a culture. Each emblem can be translated into a verbal phrase.

Embryo The developing human during the first 2 months of prenatal development after conception.

Emotion Subjective experience or feeling that is accompanied by changes in physiological reactions and behavior.

Emotion-focused coping Method of coping with stress that is directed at regulating emotional responses to the problem.

Empathic understanding In person-centered therapy, the therapist's accurate feeling of the client's emotions.

Empathy Emotional experience that involves a subjective grasp of another person's feelings or experiences.

Empathy-arousal hypothesis Hypothesis stating that empathy has the power to motivate altruism.

Empirical evidence Scientific evidence obtained by careful observation or experimentation.

Empowerment Development of a sense of self-worth and control over one's own life.

Encoding Pertaining to short-term memory, the process of transforming sensory stimuli into a form that can be placed in memory.

Encoding specificity principle Principle stating that recall is better if the retrieval context is like the encoding context.

Endocrine system System of glands that release their chemicals (hormones) into the bloodstream.

Endorphins In the nervous system, chemicals that occur naturally in the brain that, when released, decrease a person's sensitivity to pain.

Enemy images Tendency for us to see ourselves as good and peace-loving and to see our enemies as evil, aggressive, and warlike.

Erogenous zones In psychoanalytic theory, parts of the body in which humans feel tension; pleasant stimulation of these erogenous zones reduces the tension. In the first erogenous zone, the focus of tension for the infant is the mouth, followed by the anus, and finally the genitals.

Excitatory synapse In the nervous system, a synapse triggered by an action potential that releases a neurotransmitter, which excites the receptor neuron on the other side of the synaptic cleft.

Excitement phase Phase of the sexual response cycle, during which both men and women become sexually excited. Breathing, heart rate, and muscle tension increase. Blood rushes into the genital region, causing erection in a man's penis and swelling in a woman's clitoris.

Exhaustion phase Third phase of the general adaptation syndrome (response to stress) that occurs if the stressor persists. When the organism uses up the available resources, physical problems and illness are likely to develop.

Experiential intelligence According to Sternberg, the type of intelligence that focuses on how people perform on tasks with which they have either little or no previous experience, or else great experience.

Experiment Research design in which researchers systematically manipulate a variable under controlled conditions and observe how the participants respond; participants are randomly assigned to two groups. The experimental method is the most effective way to identify a cause-and-effect relationship.

Experimental condition In an experiment, the group that is changed in some way. A particular variable is present in the experimental condition that is absent in the control condition.

Experimental method Research method in which researchers systematically manipulate the independent variable to determine the effects of the independent variable on the dependent variable.

Experimental psychologists Psychologists who conduct research on topics such as perception, learning, memory, thinking, language, motivation, and emotion.

Experimenter bias Researchers' biases and expectations that can influence the results of a study.

Expressed emotion High expressed emotion means that a family member shows highly critical or overinvolved attitudes toward another family member.

Extinction In classical conditioning, the gradual weakening and disappearance of a conditioned response; it occurs when a conditioned stimulus is no longer predictive of an unconditioned stimulus.

Extravert Individual who tends to be outgoing and more oriented toward other people and events than an introvert.

Extrinsic motivation Desire to perform an activity because of external rewards.

Facial feedback hypothesis Theory of emotion stating that changes in facial expression can cause changes in a person's emotional state.

Family consultation Supportive family counseling for families of the mentally ill to relieve their anxieties and help make them more effective in providing for their disabled family member.

Family therapy Psychotherapy that considers the entire family—not just one family member—to be the client. According to the family therapy approach, many problems involve disturbed interactions among several family members, rather than just one person.

Fat cells Cells that store fat. Fat cells may shrink in size when an overweight person diets, but the number remains constant. Shriveled fat cells may send hunger messages to the brain, causing dieters to feel that they are continually hungry.

Fear hierarchy In systematic desensitization, a hierarchy with the least anxiety-provoking items at the bottom and the most terrifying items at the top.

Fear of success Worry that success in competitive achievement situations will lead to unpleasant consequences such as unpopularity.

Feature detectors Cells in the visual cortex that respond to very specific features (e.g., a horizontal line) located in a more complex stimulus.

Feminist A woman or a man whose beliefs, values, and attitudes reflect a high regard for women as human beings.

Feminist approach to therapy Approach to psychotherapy emphasizing that men and women should be valued equally, that women's inferior status in society is often responsible for psychological problems, and that gender-stereotyped behavior is harmful for both women and men.

Fetal alcohol syndrome Condition of children born to women who drank alcohol heavily during pregnancy. These children are likely to be short, with small heads. They have the characteristic facial features of widely spaced eyes, narrow eye slits, and flattened nose, and are likely to be mentally retarded.

Fetal period The developing human from 2 months after conception until the baby is born about 7 months later.

Figure-ground relationship In shape perception, when two areas share a common boundary, the figure is the distinct shape with clearly defined edges. The ground is the part that forms the background in the scene.

Fixation In psychoanalytic theory, becoming permanently locked in conflict about a particular erogenous zone.

Fixed-interval schedule In operant learning, situations in which reinforcement is given for the first correct response made after the specified period of time has passed.

Fixed-ratio schedule In operant learning, situations in which reinforcement is given after a fixed number of responses have been made.

Flashbulb memory Phenomenon whereby people often have very vivid memories of a situation in which they first learned of a surprising and emotionally arousing event.

Flat affect Little sign of either positive or negative emotion, often characteristic of schizophrenics. In flat affect, the voice is a monotone, and the face has no expression.

Flavor Experience of taste, smell, touch, pressure, and pain associated with substances in the mouth.

Fluid intelligence Ability to solve new problems. Fluid intelligence reaches a peak in the late teens and then declines slowly throughout adulthood.

Focused attention Complicated kind of search that requires processing objects one at a time and focusing attention to identify each object.

Foot-in-the-door technique Two-step compliance technique in which an influencer achieves compliance with a small request before making a larger request. People who have said "yes" to the small favor are more likely to say "yes" to the larger favor, in contrast to those who were only asked about the larger favor.

Forebrain The largest part of the brain in humans, consisting of the following structures: cerebral cortex, thalamus, hypothalamus, pituitary gland, and limbic system.

Formal operational period One of Piaget's four stages of human development in which teenagers and

adults can think scientifically and systematically, solve problems without the help of concrete representation, contemplate complex ideas, and think flexibly about a variety of problems.

Fovea In the eye, the tiny region of the retina in which vision is sharpest.

Fraternal twins Twins who came from two separate eggs and are thus no more genetically similar than two siblings.

Free association Psychoanalytic technique in which clients relax and express their thoughts and emotions freely and without censorship.

Free-running Natural tendency for humans to adopt a 25-hour cycle when deprived of zeitgebers.

Frequency Number of cycles a sound wave completes in 1 second.

Frequency distribution Summary of data that shows how often each score occurs. To construct a frequency distribution, divide the entire range of scores into equal intervals and tally the number of scores that fall in each interval.

Frequency theory Theory of auditory processing proposing that the entire basilar membrane vibrates at a frequency that matches the frequency of a tone.

Frontal lobe Part of the cerebral cortex that includes the motor cortex, which controls voluntary movement.

Fugue (*fewg*) Psychological disorder characterized by (1) sudden, unplanned travel away from a familiar location; (2) assumption of a new identity; and (3) inability to recall one's earlier identity.

Functional fixedness Barrier to problem solving in which the function we assign to an object tends to remain fixed or stable.

Functionalism Approach to psychology proposing that psychological processes are adaptive; they allow us to survive and to adapt successfully to our surroundings.

Fundamental attribution error Tendency to overestimate the role of internal causes and underestimate the role of external causes in explaining the behavior of other people.

Ganglion cells In the eye, cells that collect visual information from the bipolar cells of the retina and bring it further toward the brain.

Gate-control theory Theory proposing that pain messages ordinarily pass through a gate in the spinal cord on

their route to the brain. When the gate is open, people experience pain. However, the brain can send messages to the spinal cord, indicating that the gate should be closed, thereby blocking pain messages from reaching the brain. As a consequence, people feel no pain.

Gay person One who is attracted to people of the same gender. In general, the terms *gay* and *lesbian* are preferred to *homosexual* because the word *homosexual* focuses too narrowly on the sexuality of a relationship, rather than the broader psychological and emotional attachments that gay people feel for each other.

Gaze-contingent paradigm Method for measuring the perceptual span by which the reader's eyes are tracked as he or she reads material displayed on a screen; the text display is carefully altered as the person continues reading. The goal of the gaze-contingent paradigm is to determine how many letters can be replaced without altering a person's reading pattern.

Gender constancy Concept that a person's gender stays the same in spite of changes in outward physical appearance.

Gender roles Set of expectations about appropriate activities for females and males.

Gender-schema theory Theory proposing that children use gender as a schema to structure and guide their view of the world.

General adaptation syndrome (GAS) Model of stress, developed by Hans Selye, consisting of three stages of response to stressful situations: (1) the alarm phase, (2) the resistance phase, and (3) the exhaustion phase.

General Problem Solver (GPS) Computer program whose basic strategy is means-ends analysis. The goal is not simply to solve problems in the most efficient way, but to mimic the processes that normal humans use when they tackle these problems.

Generalized anxiety disorders Disorders characterized by continuous, long-lasting uneasiness and tension. People with these disorders cannot identify a specific cause of their anxiety. They also have physical symptoms such as nausea, dizziness, and muscle tension.

Generic masculine Use of masculine pronouns and nouns to refer to all human beings—both males and females—instead of males alone.

Genes Basic units of genetics. In humans, the genes are located on 23 pairs of chromosomes in virtually every cell of the body.

Genital herpes Viral sexually transmitted disease that causes bumps and sores in the genital area.

Genital stage Final stage of psychosexual development in which, during puberty, sexual urges reappear and the genitals once again become an erogenous zone. Freud argues that genital pleasure during the genital stage arises from sexual relationships with others.

Gestalt approach (geh-*shtahlt*) Approach to perception that emphasizes that we perceive objects as well-organized, whole structures rather than as separated, isolated parts.

Gestalt therapy Psychotherapy whose goal is for clients to become aware of what they are doing and how they can change themselves, while also learning to accept and value themselves. It emphasizes getting in touch with present feelings and encourages clients to take responsibility for their own feelings.

Gestures Hand movements that accompany speech.

Gifted Based on the definition of school districts with special programs for the gifted, individuals with IQs over 130, roughly the top 2%. In addition, some argue that people who have exceptional creativity, leadership skills, or artistic abilities should also be called gifted.

Glucose Simple sugar nutrient that provides energy.

Glucostats Neurons that are sensitive to glucose levels.

Gonads Sex glands, including the testes in males and the ovaries in females. The gonads produce a variety of hormones that are crucial in sexual development and reproduction.

Gonorrhea Bacterial sexually transmitted disease that infects the genital membranes.

Goodness-of-fit In developmental psychology, the situation in which the infant's personality matches the opportunities, expectations, and demands of important people in the child's life.

GRIT (Graduated and Reciprocated Initiatives in Tension Reduction) Conflict resolution technique, especially useful in international peacemaking, that consists of a series of steps in which a party announces a step it will take to reduce tension, the party actually takes the step, and then the party states its expectation for some kind of reciprocation. If the other party reciprocates, the first party starts another round of these initiatives.

Group Two or more people interacting with each other.

Group polarization Phenomenon in which discussion among the group members produces a more extreme position on the particular issue; that is, the whole group adopts a more extreme position after discussion.

Group therapy Psychotherapy conducted in a group setting of people who have something in common. The therapist usually does not actively direct the conversation, but lets it unfold naturally. The group is encouraged to use its own resources and to develop a sense of belonging and common goals.

Groupthink Situation in which group harmony becomes more important than wise decision making. When a group is tightly knit and harmonious, the members seem to adopt an unspoken heuristic of preserving group harmony by going along uncritically with whatever consensus seems to be emerging.

Hair cells In the ear, the receptors for hearing, which are embedded in a part of the cochlea called the basilar membrane.

Halfway house Intermediate care facility in which people with similar problems who have recently been discharged from a hospital live together in a home (with trained staff) and learn the skills necessary to live independently.

Hallucinations Strong mental images that seem like they truly occurred. The most common hallucinations are auditory, such as voices coming from outside one's head, but they may also include visions, smells, tastes, and skin-sense hallucinations.

Hallucinogens Chemical substances that alter people's perceptions of reality and may cause vivid hallucinations. Hallucinogens include several synthetic drugs, such as LSD and PCP, as well as substances extracted from plants, such as marijuana.

Health psychology Area of psychology that studies behaviors which promote and damage people's health, using psychological methods.

Heritability In the nature-nurture question, the extent to which the variation in some characteristic can be traced to differences in heredity as opposed to differences in environment. The heritability index can vary between zero (little of the variation can be traced to heredity) and 1.0 (almost all of the variation can be traced to heredity).

Heuristics Rules-of-thumb that are generally accurate.

Hidden-observer phenomenon Hypnotic phenomenon in which the two parts of consciousness are separate from each other, with one part apparently hypnotized and the other, hidden part being more rational.

Hierarchy System in which items are arranged in a series of classes, from the most general to the most specific.

Hindbrain Structure located in the bottom portion of the brain and consisting of the medulla, pons, cerebellum, and reticular formation.

Histogram Graph in which the data are arranged so that they show the frequency of each score.

Homophobia Irrational, persistent fear of and contempt for gay people.

Hormones Chemicals released by the endocrine system. Hormones circulate through all parts of the bloodstream, yet they influence only specific target organs.

Hospices Special organizations in which staff and volunteers aid terminally ill patients and allow them to die with dignity.

Hue Color of a visual stimulus, determined in part by the wavelength of light.

Human immunodeficiency virus (HIV) Virus with the potential to destroy part of the immune system through invasion of white blood cells called T-helper lymphocytes.

Humanistic approach Approach stressing that humans have enormous potential for personal growth. They have the ability to care deeply for other people and to establish meaningful, productive lives for themselves.

Humanistic therapy Psychotherapy designed to remove the blocks to personal growth and to help people appreciate their true selves. Examples include Carl Rogers's person-centered therapy and Gestalt therapy.

Hypnosis Social interaction in which one person—the subject—responds to suggestions offered by another person—the hypnotist; these responses may include alterations in perception, memory, and action.

Hypochondriasis (high-poe-konn-*drie*-uh-siss) Psychological disorder involving persistent anxiety about having a serious disease—one that could even be deadly. Hypochondriasis is typically characterized by numerous physical complaints and a wide variety of problems.

Hypothalamus   That part of the brain lying just below the thalamus and controlling the autonomic nervous systems. Several distinct clusters of neurons regulate different kinds of motivated behavior such as eating, drinking, sexual behavior, aggression, and activity level.

Hypothesis   Tentative explanation, a statement of what you expect to happen if certain conditions are true. A hypothesis tells us what relationship we expect to find between an independent variable and a dependent variable.

Iconic memory   (eye-*conn*-ick) Visual sensory memory, which is so fragile that it usually fades before we can recall all of it.

Id   In psychoanalytic theory, the component of personality that consists of the basic drives, providing both the power and the energy for all human behavior. The id lacks moral judgment and it is unconscious.

Identical twins   Twins who came from a single fertilized egg and are genetically identical.

Illusion   An incorrect perception.

Illustrator   Gesture that accompanies speech and quite literally provides an illustration.

Imagery   Mental representations of objects.

Immune system   System that protects the body from bacteria, viruses, cancer cells, and other dangers.

Impression formation   Integration of various pieces of information about a person.

Incentive theory   Motivation theory that emphasizes how external goals motivate organisms to respond and to act. We therefore engage in a particular activity so that we can receive a specific reward, and we do not engage in other activities because we wish to avoid an undesirable outcome.

Independent variable   In an experiment, the variable that the experimenters manipulate.

In-depth interview   Research method that requires the interviewer to gather answers to open-ended questions, often over a period of many hours or days.

Individual fanning out   Increased variability during aging; the fact that individual differences increase as people grow older. For example, 60-year-olds are more different from one another than 10-year-olds are.

Industrial/organizational psychologists   Psychologists who focus on human behavior in business and industry. Some help organizations hire and train employees, others study the work setting, and others measure consumer attitudes.

Infancy   Period that extends from birth through the first year or year and a half of life.

Inferential statistics   Statistics used when researchers want to draw conclusions based on evidence. Inferential statistics provide a formal procedure for using data to test for statistical significance.

Information-processing approach   Approach to human thinking that describes how information is selected, combined with previous information, and rearranged in various ways. In this approach, the human brain operates like a very sophisticated computer.

Ingroup favoritism   Tendency, influenced by stereotypes, to evaluate members of another group more negatively than our own group.

Inhibitory synapse   In the nervous system, a synapse triggered by an action potential that releases a neurotransmitter which inhibits the receptor neuron on the other side of the synaptic cleft.

Insecure attachment   Negative attachment experience in which babies tend to avoid their caregivers or feel ambivalence toward them. They may also show extreme fear of strangers and become upset when mother leaves the room.

Insight   In psychoanalysis, the client's awareness of the unconscious conflicts causing his or her psychological problems. Insight grows gradually during the course of psychoanalysis as the therapist pieces together evidence from free association, dream analysis, transference, and resistance.

Insomnia   Difficulty in falling asleep and/or remaining asleep.

Instinctive drift principle   Principle indicating that when an animal is engaged in operant conditioning, its behavior will drift in the direction of instinctive behaviors related to the task it is learning.

Instincts   Inborn, internal forces that make us behave in predictable ways.

Instrumental conditioning   The type of conditioning that involves learning to make a response because it leads to a rewarding effect and learning not to make a response because it leads to punishment. Also known as operant conditioning.

Insulin   Hormone secreted by the pancreas that helps convert blood glucose into stored fat.

Intelligence   Capacity to acquire and use knowledge. Intelligence therefore uses a wide range of cognitive skills, including perception, learning, memory, problem solving, and reasoning.

Intelligence quotient (IQ)   Performance on intelligence tests can be scored and transformed into an intelligence quotient, which is currently computed by assigning a score of 100 to a person whose performance is average for a particular age group. Higher and lower IQ scores are then based on where a person's score falls in comparison to the average.

Interest-related friendships   Friendships based on similar lifestyles and interests.

Interference   Theory stating that forgetting occurs because other items get in the way of the information a person wants to remember.

Intimacy   Close, connected feeling of warmth in loving relationships. Some aspects of intimacy include (1) wanting to promote the welfare of the loved one, (2) experiencing happiness with the loved one, (3) having high regard for the loved one, (4) giving and receiving emotional support from the loved one, and (5) valuing the loved one as part of your life.

Intrinsic motivation   Desire to perform an activity for its own sake. We are likely to do something—and to do it well—when we find it inherently enjoyable.

Intrinsic punishment   Internalized sense of dissatisfaction for poor performance.

Intrinsic reinforcement   Internalized sense of satisfaction at performing well.

Introspection   Observation of one's own psychological reactions.

Introvert   Individual who tends to be shy and withdrawn, more oriented toward his or her own internal experience than an extravert.

Iris   In the eye, just behind the cornea, a ring of muscles that gives the eyes a color ranging from pale blue to dark brown. The tiny muscles within the iris contract and dilate to change the amount of light that enters the eye.

Issues proliferation Tendency for parties in a conflict to increase the number of controversial topics, thus increasing the areas of conflict.

Izard's theory Theory of emotion suggesting that two different kinds of emotion activations are responsible for our feelings. Cognition is not necessary for the first kind of emotional experience, but it is for the second kind.

James-Lange theory Theory of emotion proposing that physiological changes are the source of emotional feelings.

Jet lag Disturbances in body rhythm caused by lengthy journeys involving time zone changes.

Jigsaw classroom Method of encouraging equal status in an interracial classroom in which all children must work together to ensure good grades.

Just-noticeable difference (jnd) Smallest change needed in a physical stimulus in order for the observer to notice the change.

Key-word method In memory improvement, method using visual imagery to link a key word with another word.

Latency period One of the stages of psychosexual development during which children's sexual feelings remain in the repressed state in which they were left at the end of the phallic stage. According to Freud, children are presumably ashamed and disgusted about sexual issues, and so they tend to avoid members of the other gender.

Latent content Unconscious, underlying aspects of a dream.

Lateral hypothalamus (LH) The "start eating" center of the brain, located at the side of the hypothalamus.

Lateralization Brain hemispheric specialization (with the left hemisphere being more competent on language tasks and the right hemisphere being more competent on spatial tasks).

Law of closure In shape perception, the law stating that a figure with a gap will be perceived as a closed, intact figure.

Law of good continuation In shape perception, the law stating that people tend to perceive smooth, continuous lines, rather than discontinuous fragments.

Law of proximity In shape perception, the law stating that objects near each other tend to be perceived as a unit.

Law of similarity In shape perception, the law stating that objects similar to each other tend to be seen as a unit.

Learning Relatively permanent change in behavior or knowledge, due to experience.

Lens In the eye, the structure directly behind the iris and the pupil that changes shape to focus on objects that are nearby or far away. The lens helps bend the light rays so that they gather in focus at a point on or near the retina.

Lesion A wound or disruption of the brain. Lesions can be produced in laboratory animals to confirm some suspicions about the functions of brain structure.

Life review Special kind of reminiscing about the past in which an older person recalls past experiences and tries to work through them to understand them more thoroughly.

Lightness constancy Phenomenon by which an object seems to stay the same lightness in spite of changes in the amount of light falling on it.

Limbic system In the brain, several related structures, such as the hippocampus and the amygdala, that help regulate the emotions and are critical in some aspects of memory and thought.

Linearization problem Dilemma involving speech production, in which people may have a general thought they want to express, or a mental image that needs to be conveyed verbally. These ideas need to be translated into a statement that is linear, with one word following after another in a line.

Linguistic determinism Hypothesis stating that the structure of language influences the structure of thought. Also known as the Whorfian hypothesis.

Lithium Chemical that is useful in treating bipolar disorder.

Localization The ability to determine the direction from which a sound is coming.

Longitudinal method Research method used by developmental psychologists in which researchers select one group of individuals who are the same age and retest them periodically.

Long-term memory (LTM) A relatively permanent kind of memory, which has an enormous capacity. LTM stores memories that are decades old, as well as memories that arrived a few minutes ago.

Lose-lose approach Approach to conflict in which both parties will suffer a net loss. War is an example of the lose-lose approach.

Loudness Psychological reaction that corresponds roughly to a tone's amplitude.

Lucid dreaming Type of dreaming in which dreamers know they are dreaming and have the sense that they are conscious. Consciousness seems divided into a dreaming component and a more detached observational component. Lucid dreamers can modify the content of their dreams more readily than other people.

Magnetic resonance imaging (MRI) Imaging technique used to provide a picture of the living human brain by passing a strong (but harmless) magnetic field through a patient's head. The MRI scanner picks up radiation from hydrogen molecules, providing a picture of a "slice" of the human brain.

Major depression Mood disorder characterized by frequent episodes of intense hopelessness and lowered self-esteem.

Male climacteric (klie-*mack*-terr-ick) Change experienced by men during middle age that includes decreased fertility and decreased frequency of orgasm.

Mania Mood disorder characterized by an abnormally positive, over-excited state, accompanied by high self-esteem.

Manifest content The conscious, remembered story line of a dream.

Maslow's hierarchy of needs Theory stating that there are five levels of needs, from the most basic level of physiological needs, to safety needs, belongingness and love needs, esteem needs, and self-actualization needs at the top of the hierarchy. Each lower need must be satisfied before the next level of need can be addressed.

Masochistic (mass-uh-*kiss*-tick) Deriving pleasure from being mistreated.

Matrix Chart that represents all possible combinations. In problem solving, a matrix is an excellent way to keep track of items, particularly when the problem is complex.

Mean In statistics, a measure of central tendency that is the simple average of all scores, obtained by adding all the scores together and dividing by the number of scores.

Meaning-making   Children's active attempts to make sense out of their world and their experiences. They try to construct general concepts based on these experiences.

Means-ends analysis   In problem solving, the problem solver divides the problem into a number of subproblems, or smaller problems. Each of these subproblems is solved by assessing the difference between the original situation and the goal, and then reducing that difference.

Median   In statistics, a measure of central tendency that is the score which falls precisely in the middle of a distribution of scores. To calculate a median, arrange the scores in order from highest to lowest and identify the score in the middle, with half the scores above and half the scores below.

Meditation   Techniques that attempt to focus attention and to avoid rambling or worried thoughts. Some meditation techniques focus on body movement; others emphasize that the meditator should be motionless and passive. Some meditation techniques encourage people to focus their concentration on an external object.

Medulla   That part of the brain found just above the spinal cord and important in several basic functions, such as controlling breathing and heart rate.

Memory   Storing of information over time, involving acquisition, storage, and retrieval.

Menarche   (*men*-ar-kee) The first menstrual period.

Menopause   Time when menstrual periods have stopped for at least a year.

Mental imagery   Mental representations of things that are not physically present. Unlike a perceptual image, a mental image is not produced by stimulating the sensory receptors.

Mental retardation   Features include (1) intellectual functioning that is significantly below average, (2) difficulty functioning in normal settings, and (3) onset prior to age 18.

Mental set   Barrier to problem solving. Problem solvers keep using the same solution they have used in previous problems, even though there may be easier ways of approaching the problem.

Mere exposure effect   Tendency to prefer items (objects, ideas, and people) with which we have had repeated contact.

Meta-analysis   Systematic, statistical method for synthesizing the results from numerous studies on a given topic, yielding a single number that indicates whether a particular factor has an overall effect on behavior.

Metacognition   Knowledge about a person's own cognitive processes.

Metamemory   Knowledge and awareness of a person's own memory.

Method of loci   In memory improvement, method that instructs people to associate items to be learned with a series of physical locations.

Midbrain   The part of the brain that continues upward from the pons portion of the hindbrain. All the signals that pass between the spinal cord and the forebrain—as well as visual information—must pass through this structure.

Minnesota Multiphasic Personality Inventory (MMPI)   Objective personality test that assesses personality traits, using about 550 personality items.

Mnemonics   Use of a strategy to help memory.

Mode   In statistics, a measure of central tendency that is the score which occurs most often in a group of scores. The mode can be established by inspecting the data and noting which number appears most frequently.

Modeling   Learning new behaviors by watching and imitating the behavior of others (models). Also known as observational learning and social learning.

Monocular   In depth perception, factors seen with one eye that can provide information about distance.

Mood disorders   Psychological disorders characterized by persistent, extreme disturbances of mood or emotional state. Examples include major depression and bipolar disorder.

Morpheme   Smallest language unit that has meaning.

Motherese   Language style of adults to their children; it has simple vocabulary, well-formed sentences, many repetitions, a focus on the here and now, and a slow rate of speech.

Motivated forgetting   Phenomenon by which people forget unpleasant memories.

Motivation   Process of activating behavior, sustaining it, and directing it toward a particular goal. Motivation moves us to act and accomplish.

Multiple-jeopardy hypothesis   Hypothesis stating that Black elderly people are particularly handicapped because they experience both prejudice against Blacks and prejudice against elderly persons.

Multiple personality disorders   Psychological disorders in which a person has two or more distinct, well-developed personalities. Typically the personalities are dramatically different from each other, and there is a distinct unawareness of the other personalities.

Myelin sheath   Insulating material that coats the larger axons in the nervous system.

Natural concepts   Concepts encountered in everyday life, such as bread, fruits, and vehicles. Natural concepts are organized according to prototypes, or best examples of a concept.

Naturalistic observation   Research method involving systematic observing and recording in a natural setting. Researchers often use naturalistic observation as a first step in a research project, to identify variables that would be worthwhile studying with one of the other research techniques.

Nature   In the nature-nurture question, nature refers to differences between people determined by the genes they inherited from their parents.

Nature-nurture question   Can development be primarily explained by nature or by genetics? Alternatively, is development primarily determined by nurture, that is, by learning and experience? The appropriate answer is that development is determined by both nature and nurture.

Negative correlation   In correlational research, the situation in which people who receive a high number on Variable A receive a *low* number on Variable B; people with a low number on Variable A receive a *high* number on Variable B. A strong negative correlation coefficient will be close to -1.00.

Negative hallucinations   Hypnotic phenomenon in which subjects can be encouraged *not* to see objects that are present.

Negative reinforcement   In operant conditioning, something negative that is taken away or avoided after the correct response has been made.

Negative symptoms Situation in schizophrenia in which a normal human characteristic is missing; negative symptoms include social withdrawal, impoverished speech, and apathy.

Negativity bias Effect predicting that impression formation is more strongly influenced by a person's negative traits than by his or her positive traits.

Neodissociation theory Theory of hypnosis, proposed by Ernest Hilgard, stressing that hypnosis produces a dissociation or division in consciousness, so that behaviors, thoughts, and feelings operate independently—as if there are two different channels.

Neonatal period First 4 weeks after birth.

Nerve deafness Type of deafness that involves problems either in the cochlea or in the auditory nerve.

Network model Theory of meaning proposing that concepts are organized in memory in a netlike pattern, with many interconnections. The meaning of a particular concept, such as *apple*, depends on the concepts to which it is connected.

Neuromodulators In the nervous system, chemical substances acting at the synapse to modify neuronal activity, either increasing or decreasing it. They operate more slowly and indirectly than neurotransmitters.

Neuron In the nervous system, the cell that is specialized to process, store, and transmit information throughout the body.

Neuroscience Interdisciplinary field that combines the efforts of psychologists, biologists, biochemists, and medical researchers to examine the structure and function of the nervous system.

Neurotransmitters In the nervous system, chemical substances stored in many tiny vesicles (containers) in the terminal button and released when electrical signals arrive. Each vesicle deposits the entire contents of its pouch into the synaptic cleft, and these chemicals spread across the channel to the receptor neurons.

Nightmare Dream that occurs during REM sleep, in which a series of events produces anxiety. Nightmares usually occur during the end of the sleep period.

Nonverbal communication All human communications that do not involve words, including tone of voice, hand movements, posture, rate of speaking, and facial expression.

Norms In testing, established standards of performance on the test. An individual's score on the test becomes meaningful by comparing the score with those standards.

Nurture In the nature-nurture question, nurture refers to differences between people determined by the way they were reared; that is, by their environment.

Obedience Social pressure in which a specific command from an authority forces us to change our behavior.

Object permanence The knowledge that an object exists even if it is temporarily out of sight.

Observational learning Learning of new behaviors by watching and imitating the behavior of others. Also known as modeling and social learning.

Obsessions Persistent, unwanted thoughts that are unreasonable. Typical obsessions include worry over germs or illness and excessive concerns about others.

Obsessive-compulsive disorders Type of relatively rare, disabling anxiety disorder that involves recurrent, time-consuming obsessions and/or compulsions.

Occipital lobe That part of the cerebral cortex at the back of the head. The most important part of this region of the brain is the visual cortex.

Operant conditioning Type of conditioning that involves learning to make a response because it leads to a rewarding effect and learning not to make a response because it leads to punishment.

Operational definition A precise definition that specifies exactly how a concept is to be measured.

Opiates Class of depressants that includes drugs such as morphine and heroin. These psychoactive drugs relieve pain and create a blissful feeling and a decrease in anxiety.

Opponent-process theory In color perception, a theory specifying that a ganglion cell responds by increasing its activity when one color is present and decreasing its activity when another is present.

Opponent-process theory In motivation, a theory arguing that one emotional state will trigger an opposite emotional state that lasts long after the original emotion has disappeared.

Optic chiasm Location at which the two optic nerves come together.

Optic nerve In the eye, the collection of ganglion-cell axons that travels out of the eye and onward to higher levels of visual processing.

Oral stage One of the stages of psychosexual development during which the mouth experiences the most tension. According to Freud, the id tries to reduce this tension by encouraging the child to suck on nipples, thumbs, and pacifiers.

Organic retardation Mental retardation caused by a genetic disorder (such as Down syndrome) or physical damage to the brain caused by an infectious disease or medical complications from a premature delivery.

Orgasmic phase Phase in the sexual response cycle during which the muscles in the pelvic region and the genitals contract rhythmically, producing a pleasurable feeling of sexual release. In addition, the man ejaculates, expelling a milky fluid rich in sperm.

Outcome research Controlled experiments on the effectiveness of psychotherapy.

Outgroup homogeneity Perception influenced by stereotypes that all members of another group are similar, whereas members of one's own group are perceived as diverse and heterogeneous.

Outgroup negativity Tendency, influenced by stereotypes, to evaluate members of another group more negatively than one's own group.

Overextension Use of a word to refer to other objects in addition to the appropriate object.

Oxytocin Hormone released from the pituitary gland that influences the cells in the breast ducts where milk is stored, releasing the flow of milk.

Panic disorders Type of anxiety disorder marked by recurrent panic attacks of overwhelming anxiety that occur suddenly and unexpectedly. Someone in the midst of a panic attack may feel smothering sensations, severe chest pains, and a fear of dying.

Paralanguage The use of vocal cues other than the words themselves, such as voice tone, pitch, pauses, and inflection of the voice.

Parasympathetic system   Part of the autonomic nervous system that slows down body functions and conserves energy.

Parietal lobe   Part of the cerebral cortex, upward from the occipital lobe. The front portion of the parietal lobe is the somatosensory cortex, the portion of the cortex that handles the skin senses.

Parkinson's disease   Disease with symptoms including tremors of the hands and difficulty walking, caused by a deterioration in the neurons in the part of the brain that releases dopamine.

Partial reinforcement   In operant conditioning, situations in which the subject is reinforced only part of the time. Also known as intermittent reinforcement.

Partial-report technique   Method for estimating the true capacity of iconic memory that requires participants to report only a specified portion of the display.

Passion   Drives that lead to physical attraction, romance, and sexual relationships. It often creates intense physiological arousal.

Passive mode of consciousness   The kind of waking consciousness that includes a less focused awareness of the environment, being a receiver of an artistic experience rather than the performer, and daydreaming.

Passive touch   Touch perception in which an object is placed on the skin of a passive person.

Perceived common ground   In a conflict situation, the likelihood of finding an alternative that satisfies both parties' wishes.

Percentile score   In standardized testing, the percentage of people who received scores below one's own score. Useful because it indicates where a score falls relative to other scores.

Perception   Interpretation of basic sensations; perception involves organization and meaning.

Perceptual span   Region seen when the eye pauses after a saccadic movement.

Peripheral nervous system   Everything in the nervous system except the brain and spinal cord. The peripheral nervous system transmits messages from the sensory receptors to the central nervous system, and back out from the central nervous system to the muscles and glands.

Permastore   A relatively permanent, very long-term form of memory.

Permissive parents   Parenting style in which parents make few demands on their children, allowing them to make their own decisions. Children from permissive families tend to be immature; they have little self-control, and they explore less than children from authoritarian and authoritative families.

Person attribution   Type of attribution indicating that we believe an internal trait or characteristic was responsible for the behavior, in contrast to situation attribution.

Person-centered therapy
Psychotherapy developed by Carl Rogers that attempts to focus on the person's own point of view, instead of the therapist's interpretations. Rogers proposed three conditions that are likely to encourage growth in person-centered therapy: congruence, unconditional positive regard, and empathic understanding.

Person perception   Area within social cognition that examines both impression formation (integrating various pieces of information about a person) and attribution (the explanations we create about the reasons for our own behavior and the behavior of others).

Person schema   Generalized idea about a person that consists of selected bits of information organized into a coherent picture.

Personal unconscious   According to Jung, the first layer of the unconscious that stores material which has been forgotten or repressed.

Personality   Pattern of characteristic feelings, thoughts, and behaviors that persists across time and situations; personality distinguishes one person from another.

Personality disorders   Psychological disorder in which personality traits become inflexible and maladaptive. These disorders may prevent normal social interactions, but they do not create the extensive break with reality that happens in schizophrenia.

Personality psychologists   Psychologists who investigate how people are influenced by relatively stable inner factors, focusing on individual differences.

Phallic stage   One of the stages of psychosexual development during which the erogenous zone shifts to the sex organs, and the child presumably finds pleasure in masturbation. Freud proposed that boys in the phallic stage experience an Oedipus complex and girls an Electra complex.

Phobic disorder   Type of anxiety disorder involving excessive fear of a specific object, activity, or situation. This fear is out of proportion to the true danger, and it cannot be eliminated by rational thought.

Phoneme   Basic unit of speech, such as the sounds *th*, *a*, and *t* in the word *that*.

Phonemic restoration   Situation in which people think that they hear a phoneme, even though the correct sound vibrations never reach their ears.

Physiological approach   Approach proposing that each behavior, emotion, and thought corresponds to a physical event in the brain or other parts of the nervous system.

Physiological measures   In a research study, measurements that are objective recordings of physiological states, assessed for example by heart rate, breathing rate, perspiration rate, and recordings of brain activity.

Pitch   Psychological reaction that corresponds to the frequency of a tone.

Pituitary gland   Hormone-producing gland attached by a stalk to the bottom part of the hypothalamus and regulated by the hypothalamus. The pituitary gland manufactures its own hormones and also regulates the other hormonal glands in the body.

Place theory   Theory of auditory processing proposing that each frequency of vibration causes a particular place on the basilar membrane to vibrate.

Placebo   (pluh-*see*-bow) Inactive substance such as a sugar pill that the patient believes is a medication. In research on psychotherapy, a placebo may be given to a control group instead of a medication; the clients may show some spontaneous remission in this condition and may also show improvement because they interact with a supportive psychiatrist.

Plasticity   When one region of the brain is damaged, another region may eventually take over some of the functions originally performed by the damaged portion. Furthermore, a person who has experienced brain damage can sometimes learn to make better use of skills that were impaired but not completely destroyed.

Plateau phase   Phase of the sexual response cycle during which breathing, heart rate, and muscle tension increase further. In the man, the penis reaches a full erection, and fluid may appear at the tip of the penis. In the woman, the lower one third of the vaginal wall becomes engorged with blood, and the clitoris becomes extremely sensitive.

Polygraph examination Lie detector test that measures physiological changes such as heart rate, breathing, and electrodermal response while a person is asked a structured set of questions. The examiner notes the pattern of autonomic-nervous-system arousal in order to decide whether the person being tested is innocent or guilty.

Pons Bulging structure in the brain, located above the medulla. Functions as a bridge, connecting the lower brain regions with the higher brain regions, and also helps regulate facial expression.

Positive correlation In correlational research, the situation in which people who receive a high number on Variable A also receive a high number on Variable B; people who receive a low number on Variable A also receive a low number on Variable B. A strong positive correlation coefficient will be close to +1.00.

Positive hallucinations Hypnotic phenomenon in which subjects can be encouraged to perceive objects that are not present.

Positive reinforcement In operant conditioning, something positive that is added to the situation after the correct response has been made.

Positive symptoms Situation in schizophrenia in which certain characteristics are either too strong or bizarre; positive symptoms include hallucinations, delusions, and bizarre behavior.

Positron emission tomography (PET scan) Imaging technique used to provide a picture of the living human brain by tracing the chemical activity of various parts of the living brain. A tiny amount of a radioactive chemical is injected into the brain, and the active cells in the brain temporarily accumulate this chemical. A machine similar to a CAT scanner then passes beams of X rays through the head.

Posthypnotic amnesia During hypnosis, instructions given to the subject by the hypnotist that the subject will not recall anything about the hypnosis session after leaving the hypnotic state.

Posthypnotic suggestion During hypnosis, instructions given to the

subject by the hypnotist that are to be carried out after the subject returns to the conscious waking state.

Practical significance In a research study, results having some important, practical implications for the real world.

Pragmatics Social aspects of language, including listeners' background knowledge, conversational interactions, and politeness.

Preattentive processing In attention, the automatic registration of the features in a display of objects.

Preconscious In psychoanalytic theory, the preconscious holds material just slightly below the surface of awareness; this material can be easily retrieved.

Prejudice Negative attitude toward a group of people.

Premenstrual syndrome (PMS) Variety of symptoms that may occur a few days before menstruation, including headaches, bloating, and a variety of psychological reactions such as depression and irritability.

Prenatal period Prebirth development.

Preoperational period One of Piaget's four major periods of human development, during which language develops. The child can now use symbols and words, instead of simple physical actions, to represent thought.

Primacy effect Tendency for early information to be considered more important than later information.

Primary reinforcer Reinforcer that can satisfy a basic biological need, most likely food or water.

Proactive interference Phenomenon by which old memories work in a forward direction to interfere with new memories.

Problem-focused coping Method of coping with stress that includes strategies used to solve problems as well as strategies that change a person's own thoughts. These strategies focus on changing the problem that is creating the stress.

Problem solving Mental activity used when we want to reach a certain goal and that goal is not readily available.

Projection Defense mechanisms that involve attributing your own unacceptable feelings to another person.

Projective tests Psychological tests that ask people to respond to a standard set of stimuli that are vague and ambiguous. These stimuli presumably evoke a person's feelings, needs, and personality characteristics.

The two most common projective tests are the Rorschach and the TAT.

Propositional viewpoint View of mental images that people store information in terms of abstract descriptions. These descriptions can then be used to generate a mental image.

Prosocial behavior Action that benefits another person, including comforting, cooperation, generosity, sympathizing, and rescuing.

Prospective memory Remembering to do things at a later time.

Prototype-matching theory In pattern perception, the theory indicating that people store abstract, idealized patterns or prototypes in memory. When people see a particular object, they compare it with this prototype. If it matches, they recognize and identify the pattern.

Prototypes In pattern perception, the abstract, idealized patterns stored in memory. These patterns are then compared with particular objects that are seen. If a match occurs, people recognize and identify the pattern.

Prototypes Pertaining to concepts, natural concepts are organized according to prototypes, the best examples of a concept.

Proximodistal principle Principle of motor development stating that the parts near the center of the infant's body develop before the more distant parts.

Psychiatrists Professionals who receive training in medicine, rather than psychology, with an orientation toward treating certain disorders with medication.

Psychoactive drugs Chemical substances that influence the brain, altering consciousness and producing psychological changes. Psychoactive drugs usually work via the neurotransmitters.

Psychoanalysis Therapy technique developed by Sigmund Freud that attempts to resolve problems by making people aware of the conflicts buried in their unconscious, which often developed during childhood.

Psychoanalytic approach Approach developed by Sigmund Freud that emphasizes three central points: (1) childhood experiences determine adult personality; (2) unconscious mental processes influence everyday behavior; and (3) conflict underlies most human behavior.

Psychodynamic approaches Variety of approaches descended from Freudian theories, which focus on unconscious mental forces.

Psychological test Objective, standardized measure of a sample of behavior.

Psychology Scientific study of behavior and mental processes.

Psychophysics Area of psychology that examines the relationship between physical stimuli and people's psychological reactions to those stimuli.

Psychotherapy Treatment of psychological disorders involving verbal interactions between a person with a psychological disorder and someone who has been trained to help correct that disorder.

Puberty Period of development in which a young person becomes physically capable of sexual reproduction.

Punishment In operant conditioning, something negative that is added or something positive that is taken away following an inappropriate response. Punishment tends to decrease the probability of the response that it follows; however, it does not automatically increase the frequency of the appropriate behavior.

Pupil In the eye, the opening in the center of the iris.

Quasi-experiment Research study resembling an experiment but in which researchers cannot randomly assign participants to different groups. Instead, they locate a situation in which groups already exist that differ substantially from each other.

Racism Bias toward certain racial groups; the bias can be revealed in stereotypes, prejudice, or discrimination. Racism occurs when individuals and institutions use power against a racial group considered to be inferior.

Random assignment In an experiment, the process by which people are assigned to experimental groups using a system—such as a coin toss—ensuring that everybody has an equal chance of being assigned to every group. If the number of participants in the study is sufficiently large, then random assignment usually guarantees that the groups will be similar with respect to important characteristics.

Random sample In a research study, a sample in which every member of the population has an equal chance of being chosen. When a sample is

random, the characteristics of the sample are likely to be similar to the characteristics of the population.

Range In statistics, a measure of variability that is the difference between the highest and the lowest scores.

Rape Sexual intercourse that is forcibly committed, without consent.

Rational-Emotive Therapy (RET) Cognitive therapy, developed by Albert Ellis, that encourages people to examine their beliefs carefully and rationally, to make positive statements about themselves, and to solve problems effectively.

Rationalization Defense mechanism that involves creating false but believable excuses to justify inappropriate behavior.

Reaction formation Defense mechanism that involves replacing an anxiety-producing feeling with its exact opposite, typically going overboard.

Reality monitoring Mental processes we use when we try to determine whether the source of events is real or imagined.

Recall Test of retrieval accuracy that asks us to reproduce the information that we learned earlier.

Reciprocal influences Principle stating that initial individual differences become even stronger because three factors—personal/cognitive, behavior, and environment—all influence each other.

Recognition Test of retrieval accuracy that asks us to select the correct answer from several alternatives.

Reflection In person-centered therapy, the technique by which the therapist summarizes the content and emotion of a client's statements, communicating this summary back to the client.

Reflex arc In the nervous system, the neuronal message traveling between a sensory neuron and a motor neuron.

Regression Defense mechanism that involves acting in ways characteristic of earlier life stages.

Rehearsal In memory, the repetition of items to be remembered.

Reliability In testing, the consistency of a person's scores. This consistency is established by reexamining the test takers with the same test on two different occasions, or by some other method of measuring the stability of the scores.

REM sleep Rapid eye movement sleep, associated with dreaming, during which the EEG shows long

sections with rapid brainwaves, similar to the waves in stage 1 sleep.

Replications Studies in which a phenomenon is tested several times, often under different conditions.

Representativeness heuristic Rule-of-thumb used when people decide whether the sample they are judging matches the appropriate prototype. For example, tossing a coin five times and getting five heads would violate the representativeness heuristic.

Repression Defense mechanism that involves pushing back unacceptable thoughts into the unconscious.

Resistance In psychoanalysis, the process consisting of all the conscious and unconscious forces that work against the treatment process. It is stressful to recall unpleasant memories that had previously been unconscious, and this stress provokes resistance.

Resistance phase Second phase of the general adaptation syndrome (response to stress) during which the organism tries to cope with the stressor by releasing stress hormones. In addition, blood pressure, heart rate, respiration, and body temperature all increase.

Resolution phase Final phase of the sexual response cycle during which breathing, heart rate, and muscle tension return to normal. Genitals also gradually return to the size they were prior to excitement.

Reticular formation That part of the brain running up from the hindbrain through to the midbrain with axons reaching upward into the cerebral cortex at the top of the brain. Important in attention and in sleep, as well as simple learning tasks.

Retina In the eye, the structure that absorbs light rays and converts them into a form which can be transmitted by the neurons.

Retinotopic arrangement Correspondence between the pattern of information on the retina (the receptors at the rear inner surface of the eyeball) and the pattern of information on part of the visual cortex.

Retrieval Pertaining to memory, the third stage of remembering in which we successfully locate the item and use it.

Retrieval failure Theory specifying that memory failures occur when the proper retrieval cues are not available.

Retroactive interference Phenomenon by which new memories work in a backward direction to interfere with old memories.

Retrospective memory   Recall for previously learned information.

Rods   Photoreceptors used for black-and-white vision under poorly lit conditions.

Role   Set of rules describing how people in a particular social position ought to behave.

Rorschach Inkblot Test   Projective test in which people respond to ambiguous inkblots, and the responses are analyzed for recurring themes, emphasis, and emotional characteristics.

Rotation heuristic   Rule-of-thumb stating that figures which are slightly tilted will be remembered as being either more vertical or horizontal than they really are.

Saccadic movement   (suh-*kaad*-dick) Rapid movement of the eye from one location to the next, necessary to bring the fovea into position over the object we want to see clearly.

Sample   Participants for a research study selected from the population to be studied, with the intention of discovering something about the population from which the sample was drawn.

Scapegoat theory   Theory stating that people who are frustrated and unhappy about something will choose a relatively powerless group to take the blame for a situation that is not the group's fault.

Schachter-Singer theory   Theory of emotion stating that an emotion-arousing event causes physiological arousal and people examine the external environment to help interpret that event.

Schema   (*skee*-muh) In observational learning, a generalized idea that captures the important components, but not every exact detail. Pertaining to memory and person perception, a generalized idea about objects, people, and events that are encountered frequently.

Schizophrenia   Psychological disorder that involves severely disordered thoughts; perceptual, emotional, and social processes may also be disturbed. Schizophrenics experience a splitting or disorganization of normal thought processes. In some cases, this disorganization is so extensive that individuals lose contact with reality.

Scientific method   Basis for psychology research, consisting of four basic steps: (1) identification of the research problem; (2) design and conducting of a study; (3) examination of the data; (4) communication of the results.

Secondary reinforcer   Reinforcer that does not satisfy a basic biological need but acquires its rewarding power by association with another established reinforcer.

Secondary trait   In Allport's theory, a characteristic seen only in certain situations, such as "uncomfortable in large crowds" and "likes to drive sports cars."

Secure attachment   Positive attachment experience in which an infant tends to use the caregiver as a secure base. The infant may wander away from the caregiver for a while to explore the surroundings, usually glancing back from time to time and returning frequently.

Selective attention   Focusing attention on one of several simultaneous messages, disregarding the others.

Self-actualization   In humanistic psychology, humans' natural tendency to fulfill their true potential.

Self-concept   Schema of thoughts and feelings about oneself as an individual.

Self-efficacy   Feeling people have that they are competent and effective.

Self-fulfilling prophecy   Situation in which your expectations about someone lead him or her to act in ways that confirm your original expectation.

Self-perception theory   Theory in social psychology proposing that humans are not driven by some need within themselves to be consistent. Instead, we come to know our attitudes by noticing our own observable behaviors.

Self-reference effect   In memory, the deepest, most effective way of processing stimuli, which is in terms of our own experience.

Self-report   Research method for assessing psychological processes in which participants report their own thoughts, emotions, behaviors, or intentions. Self-reports are commonly measured with a rating scale.

Self-report tests   Psychological tests that instruct people to answer questions about their behaviors, beliefs, and feelings. An example is the Minnesota Multiphasic Personality Inventory (MMPI).

Self-statement modification   Therapeutic technique in which people are encouraged to replace negative statements about themselves with more positive statements.

Sensation   Immediate, basic experiences that simple stimuli generate.

Sensorimotor period   One of Piaget's four major periods of human development, in which the infant's major cognitive tasks include sensory activities (such as seeing, hearing, touching, smelling, and tasting) and motor activities (such as kicking, sucking, and reaching).

Sensory memory   Storage system that records information from the senses with reasonable accuracy as the information first enters the memory. The capacity of sensory memory is relatively large, but its duration is less than 2 seconds.

Separation anxiety   Response of an infant (crying or whining) to parents' leaving the room, which develops when the infant has the perceptual and cognitive abilities to discriminate between people.

Set point   Mechanism that seems to keep people at roughly the same weight throughout their adult lives.

Seville Statement   A document, drafted by scientists from 12 countries, stating that it is scientifically incorrect to say we have an inborn, genetic tendency to be aggressive or that evolution has favored aggressive members of our species.

Sex chromosomes   One of the 23 pairs of chromosomes that determine whether someone is male or female. Females have a pair of sex chromosomes called X chromosomes (XX); males have one sex chromosome called X and one called Y (XY).

Sexism   Bias toward people on the basis of their sex, which can be revealed in stereotypes, prejudice, and discrimination.

Sexual coercion   Forcing someone to have sex against her (or his) will. The most extreme example of sexual coercion is rape.

Sexual harassment   Unwelcome sexual advance, request for sexual favors, or other verbal or physical conduct of a sexual nature.

Shape constancy   Phenomenon by which an object seems to stay the same shape, despite changes in the orientation toward the viewer.

Shaping   In operant conditioning, the systematic reinforcement of gradual improvements in the desired behavior.

Shift schedules   Work schedules in which people must work during the normal sleeping hours. As a consequence, these workers sleep fewer hours, and they wake up more often during sleep.

Short-term memory (STM)   Memory that contains only the small amount of material we are currently using. Memories in STM are fragile, and they can be lost from memory within 30 seconds unless they are somehow repeated or rehearsed.

Side effects   Undesirable medical or psychological problems due to the use of medication.

Signal detection theory   In contrast to the classical psychophysics approach, signal detection theory stresses the importance of the observer's criterion when the observer is uncertain about whether the stimulus has been presented. Expectations and prior knowledge influence the probability of the observer's recognition.

Single-cell recording technique   Method for obtaining precise recordings of brain activity by inserting a tiny electrode next to or into a single neuron.

Situation attribution   Type of attribution indicating that we believe that the specific situation was responsible for the behavior, in contrast to person attribution.

Size constancy   Phenomenon by which an object seems to stay the same size despite changes in the distance between the viewer and the object.

Sleep   State of unresponsiveness from which we can be aroused relatively easily. Body movement is greatly reduced during sleep, but the neuron activity of the brain continues.

Slip of the tongue   Error in which sounds, morphemes, or words are rearranged between two or more different words.

Social cognition   How we think about other people and ourselves.

Social cognitive approach   Approach to personality that emphasizes observational learning and the contribution of cognitive factors.

Social facilitation   Tendency to do better on easy tasks and worse on difficult tasks when another person is present.

Social identity theory   Theory stating that we enhance our self-esteem by favoring the groups to which we belong.

Social learning   Learning new behaviors by watching and imitating the behavior of others in a social situation. Also known as observational learning and modeling.

Social-learning theory   Theory of gender development explaining that girls learn to act "feminine" and boys learn to act "masculine" through two major mechanisms: (1) they receive rewards and punishments for their own behavior, and (2) they watch and imitate the behavior of others.

Social psychology   Approach to psychology focusing on the way that other people influence our thoughts, feelings, and behaviors.

Social role theory   Theory of hypnosis, proposed by Theodore Barber, stressing that the hypnotized subject is simply acting out a social role consistent with the social situation.

Socialization   Acquisition of motives, values, knowledge, and behavior needed to function adequately in adult society.

Sociology   Scientific discipline that examines how groups and institutions function in society.

Somatic division   In the nervous system, the sensory and motor neurons that control the voluntary muscles.

Somatoform disorders   Anxiety-based problems in which the individual complains about physical illnesses and problems, yet no organic explanation can be found. The distinctive feature of these disorders is a concern about one's body.

Sound   Perception of successive air pressure changes.

Sound waves   Tiny disturbances in air pressure that cause sound.

Spinal cord   Column of neurons that runs from the base of the brain, down the center of the back, and is protected by a series of bones; one of the components of the central nervous system.

Split-half reliability   Method for measuring the reliability of a test in which everybody takes just one test, but the items are split into two halves (often the even-numbered versus the odd-numbered questions). The split-half reliability is high if each person's score is similar on the two halves.

Spontaneous recovery   In classical conditioning, the reappearance of the conditioned response after previous extinction.

Spontaneous remission   Recovery from a psychological disorder, without any therapy.

Stability-change question   Do people maintain their personal characteristics as they mature from infants into adults (stability)? Alternatively, do infants acquire new characteristics that bear little resemblance to those they had in infancy (change)? There is some stability as infants mature into children, but it is far from complete.

Stage 1 sleep   Stage of light sleep during which the EEG records small, irregular brain waves. A person can be readily awakened from stage 1 sleep.

Stage 2 sleep   Stage of sleep during which the EEG shows very rapid bursts of activity known as sleep spindles.

Stage 3 sleep   Stage of sleep during which the EEG begins to show a few delta waves. Breathing slows substantially, and muscles are completely relaxed.

Stage 4 sleep   Stage of deep sleep during which the EEG shows almost exclusively delta waves.

Standard deviation   Measure of variability; the extent to which scores differ from each other and deviate from the mean.

Standardization   In testing, the process of determining norms on a group of people who have taken a test under uniform conditions.

Statistical significance   In inferential statistics, the situation in which the findings are likely to be due to a real difference between two groups, rather than due to chance alone.

Stereotype   Structured set of beliefs about the way a group of people think and act. Similar to person schemas, except that a schema applies to an individual person and a stereotype applies to a group.

Stimulants   Chemicals that increase central nervous system functioning by increasing the release of neurotransmitters such as dopamine in the cortex and the reticular activating system. Stimulants include caffeine, nicotine, the amphetamines, and cocaine.

Stimulus discrimination   Process whereby organisms learn to tell the difference between similar stimuli.

Stimulus generalization   In classical conditioning, the tendency for stimuli other than the original conditioned stimulus to produce the conditioned response.

Storage   Pertaining to memory, the second stage of remembering, in which we hold the information in memory for later use.

Stress The result of an interaction between a person and the environment, in which the person believes the situation to be overwhelming and dangerous to his or her well-being.

Stressor Unpleasant situation that produces stress.

Stroke Disorder in which a blood clot closes an artery and prevents the artery from supplying oxygen to an area of the brain.

Structuralism Approach to psychology that involves the examination of the structure of the mind and the organization of the basic elements of sensations, feelings, and images.

Subjective well-being Person's current level of happiness or life satisfaction.

Sublimation Defense mechanism that involves redirecting forbidden impulses toward a socially desirable goal.

Superego In psychoanalytic theory, the component of the personality that includes a person's conscience and ideals. The superego acquires its principles from society.

Surface structure Pertaining to sentence structure, the structure that is represented by the words which are actually spoken or written.

Survey method Research method in which a researcher selects a large group of people and asks them questions about their behaviors or thoughts. Typically, the researchers also collect demographic information about such characteristics as gender, age, marital status, race, and education.

Symbolic racism Racial bias reflecting the feeling among some Whites that Blacks are making inappropriate demands for change.

Sympathetic system Part of the autonomic nervous system that prepares the body for action through the secretion of adrenaline.

Synapse In the nervous system, the location at which the axon of one neuron connects with the dendrite of a neighboring neuron.

Synaptic cleft In the synapse, a narrow space between adjacent neurons in the nervous system.

Syntax In grammar, the organizational rules for determining word order, sentence organization, and relationships between words.

Systematic desensitization Behaviorist approach to reducing fear or anxiety by substituting a response that is incompatible with anxiety (i.e., relaxation).

Tardive dyskinesia Condition caused by side effects from using antipsychotic drugs, characterized by involuntary body movements and abnormal gait in walking. This disorder can often be irreversible.

Target effects Improvement of the major symptoms of a disorder through the use of medication.

Taste Perceptions that result when substances make contact with the special receptors in the mouth.

Taste aversion Development of an intense dislike for a food through classical conditioning.

Telegraphic speech Characteristic of children's early sentences that include nouns and verbs but leave out the extra words such as prepositions and articles that only serve a grammatical function.

Temperament Person's characteristic mood and activity level.

Temporal lobes Part of the cerebral cortex that is located on the sides of the head. The temporal lobes contain the auditory cortex, which processes information about sounds, speech, and music.

Terminal buttons In the nervous system, the knobs located at the far end of the axon.

Test-retest reliability Method of measuring the reliability of a test in which the same identical test is administered on two occasions, usually 1 day to several weeks apart. The test-retest reliability is high if each person's score is similar on the two tests.

Thalamus The part of the brain that looks like two eggs resting side by side. Nearly all the information from the senses passes through the thalamus on its route from the sensory receptors to the cerebral cortex and is organized and transformed there.

Thematic Apperception Test (TAT) Projective test that consists of a series of ambiguous scenes, which the test taker is invited to describe, telling what is happening now, what happened in the past, and what will occur in the future.

Theory of cognitive dissonance Theory proposed by Leon Festinger stating that a discrepancy between two inconsistent cognitions produces psychological distress; people will be motivated to reduce this discrepancy or dissonance by changing one of the cognitions.

Theory of learned helplessness Theory proposing that we learn to be helpless when we think that the responses we make are not related to the rewards and punishments we receive. This helplessness leads to depression.

Theory of misapplied constancy Theory of illusions proposing that observers interpret certain cues in an illusion as cues for maintaining size constancy.

Theory of multiple intelligences Theory by Howard Gardner that proposes seven different components of intelligence: language ability, logical-mathematical thinking, spatial thinking, musical thinking, bodily kinesthetic thinking, interpersonal thinking, and intrapersonal thinking.

Thinking Manipulation of mental representations to reach a conclusion. Includes mental imagery, concepts, problem solving, and decision making.

Thyroid gland Gland that regulates the body's metabolism through production of a hormone.

Timbre (*tam*-burr) Sound quality of a tone.

Tip-of-the-nose phenomenon Ability to recognize an odorant as familiar, although its name cannot be recovered.

Tip-of-the-tongue experience People's sensation of being confident that they know the word for which they are searching, yet cannot recall it.

Token economy Tool in behavior modification in which good behavior is reinforced by a token or symbol; the tokens can be accumulated and exchanged for a reinforcer.

Tolerance Condition produced by frequent use of a psychoactive drug that requires increasing amounts of the drug to produce the same effect.

Top-down processing In perception, processing that emphasizes the importance of the observers' concepts, expectations, and prior knowledge—the kind of information stored at the top (or highest level) of perception.

Total time hypothesis Principle stating that the amount a person learns depends on the total amount of time he or she practices.

Trait Specific, stable personality characteristic; a relatively stable way in which individuals differ from one another.

Trait approach Approach to personality proposing that human personality should be described in terms of specific, stable personality characteristics, such as shyness or aggressiveness.

Transduction   In the eye, the process by which cones and rods convert light into electrical activity at the cell membrane.

Transference   In psychoanalysis, the process by which the client transfers both positive and negative emotional reactions associated with childhood authority figures, directing them toward the therapist.

Triangular theory of love   Theory by Robert Sternberg stating that love consists of three components: intimacy, passion, and decision/commitment.

Triarchic theory of intelligence   (try-*are*-kick) According to Sternberg, the theory specifying three important parts of intelligence: (1) componential intelligence, (2) experiential intelligence, and (3) contextual intelligence.

Trichromatic theory   Theory of color vision that points out there are three kinds of cones, each sensitive to light from a different portion of the spectrum.

Twin studies   Research that compares identical and fraternal twins.

Type A behavior pattern (TABP) Personality type with such characteristics as ambitiousness, aggressiveness, competitiveness, and impatience. Type A people speak rapidly and work quickly, and they are likely to respond to hassles with irritation and hostility.

Unconditional positive regard According to Carl Rogers, total, genuine love without special conditions or strings attached. In person-centered therapy, therapist's positive, nonjudgmental attitude toward the client.

Unconditioned response   In classical conditioning, an unlearned response to a stimulus.

Unconditioned stimulus   In classical conditioning, the stimulus that elicits an unlearned response.

Unconscious   In psychoanalytic theory, psychic processes—thoughts

and desires—that are far below the level of conscious awareness.

Validity   In testing, a test's accuracy in measuring what it is supposed to measure.

Variability   In statistics, the measures that indicate the extent to which the scores are spread out, that is, how much the scores differ from one another. The standard deviation is a measure of variability.

Variable-interval schedule   In operant learning, situations in which reinforcement is given for the first response made after a varying period of time has passed.

Variable-ratio schedule   In operant learning, situations in which reinforcement is given after a varying number of responses have been made.

Ventromedial hypothalamus (VMH)   The "stop eating" center of the brain, located toward the center of the hypothalamus.

Vicarious punishment   In observational learning, punishment of the learner that occurs when the model receives punishment.

Vicarious reinforcement   In observational learning, reinforcement of the learner that occurs when the model receives reinforcement.

Visual acuity   Ability to see precise details in a scene.

Visual cortex   Outer part of the brain that is concerned with vision, located at the back of the brain just above the neck.

Wavelength   Distance between two peaks of light, which travels in waves. This distance is measured in nanometers (nm). Wavelength is a characteristic of light that helps to determine the hue or color of a visual stimulus.

Weber's law   (*Vay*-bur) ($\Delta I/I = k$) Weber's law says that if we take the change in intensity and divide it by the original intensity, we obtain a constant number (k).

Well-controlled study   Experiment in which researchers use a technique such as random assignment to eliminate confounding variables. With

a well-controlled study, researchers can feel more confident about drawing cause-and-effect conclusions.

Whorfian hypothesis   Hypothesis stating that the structure of language influences the structure of thought. Also known as linguistic determinism.

Win-lose approach   Approach to conflict in which one player's win is balanced by the other player's loss. Most competitive situations in business involve a win-lose situation.

Win-win approach   Approach to conflict in which both parties gain by cooperating. A win-win approach favors successful conflict resolution.

Withdrawal symptoms   Undesirable effects of discontinued use of a psychoactive drug that include nausea, vomiting, abdominal cramps, and muscle spasms.

Word-superiority effect   In pattern recognition, the phenomenon by which people perceive letters better when they appear in words than when they appear in strings of unrelated letters.

Working memory   Short-term memory is sometimes called working memory because it handles the material we are currently working with, rather than items not attended to in sensory memory or items stored in long-term memory.

Working self-concept   Self-concept at a particular moment, consisting of all accessible self-knowledge.

Working through   In psychotherapy, the development of new behaviors and emotions following insight. After understanding the source of the conflict, clients work through their problems by giving up their maladaptive defenses and relating to people in a more mature fashion.

Zeitgebers   (*tsite*-gay-burs) Clues that help people adopt a 24-hour cycle, such as clocks and watches, the position of the sun, outdoor temperature, and mealtimes.

Zero correlation   In correlational research, a correlation that indicates no substantial relationship between the two variables.

Abelson, R. F. (1988). Conviction. *American Psychologist, 43*, 267–275.

Abramson, L. Y., Metalsky, G. I., & Alloy, L. B. (1989). Hopelessness-depression: A theory-based subtype of depression. *Psychological Review, 9*, 358–372.

Acitelli, L. K., & Duck, S. (1987). Postscript: Intimacy as the proverbial elephant. In D. Perlman & S. Duck (Eds.), *Intimate relationships* (pp. 297–308). Beverly Hills, CA: Sage.

Adams, D. (1990). The Seville Statement on Violence. *American Psychologist, 45*, 1167–1168.

Adams, P. R., & Adams, G. R. (1984). Mount Saint Helens's ashfall: Evidence for a disaster stress reaction. *American Psychologist, 39*, 252–260.

Adelson, E. H. (1978). Iconic storage: The role of rods. *Science, 201*, 544–546.

Adler, A. (1924). *The practice and theory of individual psychology.* New York: Harcourt, Brace.

Adler, T. (1989, February). Two new AIDS drugs may improve cognition. *APA Monitor,* p. 8.

Adler, T. (1989, November). Revision brings test 'to the 21st century.' *APA Monitor,* pp. 1, 6.

Adler, T. (1990, April). Does the 'new' MMPI beat the 'classic'? *APA Monitor,* pp. 18–19.

Agbayewa, M. O. (1986). EEG and CT scan in Alzheimer's disease. *Journal of Clinical Psychiatry, 47*, 217–218.

Aiken, L. R. (1987). *Assessment of intellectual functioning.* Boston: Allyn & Bacon.

Aiken, L. R. (1989). *Assessment of personality.* Boston: Allyn & Bacon.

Ainsworth, M. D. S. (1979). Infant-mother attachment. *American Psychologist, 34*, 932–937.

Ainsworth, M. D. S. (1989). Attachments beyond infancy. *American Psychologist, 44*, 709–716.

Aizenberg, R., & Treas, J. (1985). The family in late life: Psychosocial and demographic considerations. In J. E. Birren & K. W. Schaie (Eds.), *Handbook of the psychology of aging* (2nd ed., pp. 169–189). New York: Van Nostrand Reinhold.

Ajzen, I. (1988). *Attitudes, personality, and behavior.* Chicago: Dorsey.

Albee, G. W. (1982). Preventing psychopathology and promoting human potential. *American Psychologist, 37*, 1043–1050.

Albee, G. W. (1986). Toward a just society: Lessons from observations on the primary prevention of psychopathology. *American Psychologist, 41*, 891–898.

Albee, G. W. (1987). Powerlessness, politics, and prevention. The community mental health approach. In F. Hurrelmann, F. X. Kaufmann, & F. Lösel (Eds.), *Social intervention: Potential and constraints* (pp. 37–52). Berlin: Walter de Gruyter.

Albee, G. W., & Gullotta, T. P. (1986). Facts and fallacies about primary prevention. *Journal of Primary Prevention, 6*, 207–218.

Allen, M. (1983). Models of hemispheric specialization. *Psychological Bulletin, 93*, 73–104.

Allgeier, E. R. (1987). Coercive versus consensual sexual interactions. In V. P. Makosky (Ed.), *The G. Stanley Hall lecture series* (Vol. 7, pp. 7–63). Washington, DC: American Psychological Association.

Allison, J., Blatt, S. J., & Zimet, C. N. (1988). *The interpretation of psychological tests.* Washington, DC: Hemisphere.

Alloy, L. B. (1988). *Cognitive processes in depression.* New York: Guilford Press.

Allport, G. W. (1937). *Personality: A psychological interpretation.* New York: Holt, Rinehart and Winston.

Allport, G. W. (1961). *Pattern and growth in personality.* New York: Holt, Rinehart and Winston.

Allport, G. W. (1967). Gordon W. Allport. In E. G. Boring & G. Lindzey (Eds.), *A history of psychology in autobiography* (Vol. V). New York: Appleton-Century-Crofts.

Allport, G. W., & Odbert, H. S. (1936). Trait-names: A psycho-texical study. *Psychological Monographs, 47*, (Whole No. 211).

Alperstein, G., & Arnstein, E. (1988). Homeless children—a challenge for pediatricians. *The Pediatric Clinics of North America, 35*, 1413–1425.

Alpert, J. L. (1986). Epilogue. In J. L. Alpert (Ed.), *Psychoanalysis and women: Contemporary reappraisals* (pp. 317–323). Hillsdale, NJ: Analytic Press.

Alvarez, C. (1987). El hilo que nos une: Becoming a Puerto Rican woman. In R. Benmayor, A. Juarbe, C. Alvarez, & B. Vázquez (Eds.), *Stories to live by: Continuity and change in three generations of Puerto Rican women* (pp. 24–42). New York: Centro de Estudios Puertorriqueños (Hunter College).

Amabile, T. M. (1983). *The social psychology of creativity.* New York: Springer-Verlag.

American Association for Protecting Children. (1987, October 23). *National estimates of child abuse and neglect reports, 1976–1986.* Denver: American Humane Association.

American Psychiatric Association. (1980). *Diagnostic and statistical manual of mental disorders* (3rd ed.). Washington, DC: American Psychological Association.

American Psychiatric Association. (1987). *Diagnostic and statistical manual of mental disorders* (3rd ed.-Rev.). Washington, DC: American Psychiatric Association.

American Psychological Association. (1973). *Ethical principles in the conduct of research with human participants.* Washington, DC: Author.

American Psychological Association. (1975). Report of the task force on sex bias and sex-role stereotyping in psychotherapeutic practice. *American Psychologist, 30*, 1169–1175.

American Psychological Association. (1982). *Ethical principles in the conduct of research with human participants.* Washington, DC: Author.

American Psychological Association. (1983). *Publication manual of the American Psychological Association* (3rd ed.). Washington, DC: Author.

American Psychological Association, American Educational Research Association, & National Council on Measurement in Education. (1985). *Standards for educational testing.* Washington, DC: American Psychological Association.

Anastasi, A. (1985). Psychological testing: Basic concepts and common misconceptions. In A. M. Rogers & C. J. Scheirer (Eds.), *The G. Stanley Hall lecture* series (Vol. 5, pp. 91–120). Washington, DC: American Psychological Association.

Anastasi, A. (1986). Evolving concepts of test validation. *Annual Review of Psychology, 37*, 1–15.

Anastasi, A. (1988). *Psychological testing* (6th ed.). New York: Macmillan.

Anastasi, A., & Drake, J. (1984). An empirical comparison of certain techniques for estimating the reliability of speeded tests. *Education and Psychological Measurement, 14*, 529–540.

Anch, A. M., Browman, C. P., Milter, M. M., & Walsh, J. K. (1988). *Sleep: A scientific perspective.* Englewood Cliffs, NJ: Prentice Hall.

Anderson, J. R., & Reder, L. (1979). An elaborative processing explanation of depth of processing. In L. S. Cermak & F. I. M. Craik (Eds.), *Levels of processing in human memory.* Hillsdale, NJ: Erlbaum.

Anderson, N. H. (1981). *Foundations of information integration theory.* New York: Academic Press.

Anderson, R. E. (1984). Did I do it or did I only imagine doing it? *Journal of Experimental Psychology: General, 113*, 594–613.

Andreasen, N. C. (1982). Negative versus positive schizophrenia: Definition and validation. *Archives of General Psychiatry, 39*, 789–794.

Andreasen, N. C. (1984). *The broken brain: The biological revolution in psychiatry.* New York: Harper & Row.

Andreasen, N. C. (1988). Brain imaging: Applications in psychiatry. *Science, 239*, 1381–1388.

Angoff, W. H. (1988). The nature-nurture debate, aptitudes, and group differences. *American Psychologist, 43*, 713–720.

Angoff, W. H., & Johnson, E. G. (1988). *A study of the differential impact of curriculum on aptitude test scores.* Princeton, NJ: Educational Testing Service.

Anisfeld, M. (1984). *Language development from birth to three.* Hillsdale, NJ: Erlbaum.

Anschutz, L., Camp, C. J., Markley, R. P., & Kramer, J. J. (1985). Maintenance and generalization of mnemonics for grocery shopping by older adults. *Experimental Aging Research, 11*, 157–160.

Antill, J. K. (1983). Sex role complementarity versus similarity in married couples. *Journal of Personality and Social Psychology, 45*, 145–155.

Antrobus, J. (1987). Cortical hemisphere asymmetry and sleep mentation. *Psychological Review, 94*, 359–368.

Archer, D. (1982). Biochemical findings and medical management of the menopause. In A. M. Voda, M. Dinnerstein, & S. R. O'Donnell (Eds.), *Changing perspectives on menopause* (pp. 39–48). Austin: University of Texas Press.

Argyle, M. (1988). *Bodily communication* (2nd ed.). London: Methuen.

Arlow, J. A. (1989). Psychoanalysis. In R. J. Corsini & D. Wedding (Eds.), *Current psychotherapies* (4th ed., pp. 19–62). Itasca, IL: Peacock.

Arnheim, R. (1986, January–February). The artistry of psychotics. *American Scientist, 74,* 48–54.

Aron, A., & Aron, E. N. (1989). *The heart of social psychology: A backstage view of a passionate science* (2nd ed.). Lexington, MA: Heath.

Aronson, E. (1987). Teaching students what they think they already know about prejudice and desegregation. In V. P. Makosky (Ed.), *The G. Stanley Hall lecture series* (Vol. 7, pp. 69–84). Washington, DC: American Psychological Association.

Aronson, E. (1988a). *The social animal* (5th ed.). New York: Freeman.

Aronson, E. (Ed.). (1988b). *Readings about the social animal* (5th ed.). New York: Freeman.

Aronson, E., & Osherow, N. (1980). Cooperation, prosocial behavior, and academic performance: Experiments in the desegregated classroom. In L. Bickman (Ed.), *Applied social psychology annual* (Vol. 1, pp. 163–196). Beverly Hills, CA: Sage.

Asarnow, J. R., & Goldstein, M. J. (1986). Schizophrenia during adolescence and early adulthood: A developmental perspective on risk research. *Annual Psychology Review, 6,* 211–235.

Asch, S. E. (1952). *Social psychology.* Englewood Cliffs, NJ: Prentice-Hall.

Asch, S. E. (1955). Opinions and social pressures. *Scientific American, 193* (5), 31–35.

Ashmore, R. D., & DelBoca, F. K. (1979). Sex stereotypes and implicit personality theory: Toward a cognitive-social psychological conceptualization. *Sex Roles, 5,* 219–248.

Aslin, R. N. (1988, April). *Visual perception in human infants: The eyes have it.* Paper presented at the convention of the Eastern Psychological Association, Buffalo, NY.

Aslin, R. N., & Smith, L. B. (1988). Perceptual development. *Annual Review of Psychology, 39,* 435–473.

Asso, D. (1983). *The real menstrual cycle.* Chichester, England: Wiley.

Association for Women in Psychology Ad Hoc Committee on Sexist Language. (1975, November). Help stamp out sexism: Change the language! *APA Monitor,* p. 16.

Astin, A. W. (1988). *The American freshmen: National norms for Fall, 1988.* Los Angeles: Higher Education Research Institute.

Atkin, C. K. (1983). Effects of realistic TV violence vs. fictional violence on aggression. *Journalism Quarterly, 60,* 615–621.

Atkinson, D. R. (1985). Research on cross-cultural counseling and psychotherapy: A review and update of reviews. In P. Pedersen (Ed.), *Handbook of cross-cultural counseling and therapy* (pp. 191–197). Westport, CT: Greenwood.

Atkinson, J. W., & Raynor, J. O. (Eds.). (1974). *Motivation and achievement.* Washington, DC: Winston.

Atkinson, K. (1989, September). Mama Nancy. *Toronto Life,* pp. 31–32, 37.

Atkinson, R. C., & Shiffrin, R. M. (1968). Human memory: A proposed system and its control processes. In K. W. Spence & J. T. Spence (Eds.), *The psychology of learning and motivation: Advances in research and theory* (Vol. 2). New York: Academic Press.

Axelrod, S. (1983). Introduction. In S. Axelrod & J. Apsche (Eds.), *The effects of punishment on human behavior* (pp. 1–11). New York: Plenum.

Axsom, D., Yates, S., & Chaiken, S. (1987). Audience response as a heuristic cue in persuasion. *Journal of Personality and Social Psychology, 53,* 30–40.

Ayllon, T., & Azrin, N. H. (1968). *The token economy: A motivational system for therapy and rehabilitation.* New York: Appleton-Century-Crofts.

Baars, B. J. (1986). *The cognitive revolution in psychology.* New York: Guilford Press.

Backer, T. E., Batchelor, W. F., Jones, J. M., & Mays, V. M. (Eds.). (1988). Psychology and AIDS [Special issue]. *American Psychologist, 43*(11).

Backer, T. E., & Richardson, D. (1989). Building bridges: Psychologists and families of the mentally ill. *American Psychologist, 44,* 546–550.

Baddeley, A. D. (1982). *Your memory: A user's guide.* New York: Macmillan.

Baddeley, A. D. (1986). *Working memory.* Oxford, England: Oxford University Press.

Baer, L., & Jenike, M. A. (1986). Introduction. In M. A. Jenike, L. Baer, & W. E. Minichiello (Eds.), *Obsessive-compulsive disorders* (pp. 1–9). Littleton, MA: PSG.

Bahrick, H. P. (1984). Semantic memory content in permastore: Fifty years of memory for Spanish learned in school. *Journal of Experimental Psychology: General, 113,* 1–35.

Bahrick, H. P., & Hall, L. K. (1991). Lifetime maintenance of high school mathematics content. *Journal of Experimental Psychology: General, 120,* 20–33.

Bailey, I. L. (1986). The optometric examination of the elderly patient. In A. A. Rosenbloom & M. W. Morgan (Eds.), *Vision and aging* (pp. 189–209). New York: Professional Press Books.

Bailey, R. E., & Bailey, M. B. (1980). A view from outside the Skinner box. *American Psychologist, 35,* 942–946.

Baker, E. L. (1985). Psychoanalysis and psychoanalytic therapy. In S. J. Lynn & J. P. Garske (Eds.), *Contemporary psychotherapies: Models and methods.* Columbus, OH: Merrill.

Baker, F. M. (1988). Afro-Americans. In L. Comas-Díaz & E. Griffith (Eds.), *Clinical guidelines in cross-cultural mental health* (pp. 151–181). New York: Wiley.

Baldessarini, R. J., & Cole, J. O. (1988). Chemotherapy. In A. M. Nicholi, Jr. (Ed.), *The new Harvard guide to psychiatry* (pp. 481–533). Cambridge, MA: Harvard University Press.

Bales, J. (1988, August). Legalized drugs: Idea flawed, debate healthy. *APA Monitor,* p. 22.

Balota, D. A., Pollatsek, A., & Rayner, K. (1985). The interaction of contextual constraints and parafoveal visual information in reading. *Cognitive Psychology, 17,* 364–390.

Baltes, P. B. (1973). Prototypical paradigms and questions in life-span research on development and aging. *The Gerontologist, 113,* 458–467.

Baltes, P. B., & Kliegl, R. (1989). On the dynamics between growth and decline in the aging of intelligence and memory. In K. Poeck (Ed.), *Proceedings of the XIIIth World Congress of Neurology.* Heidelberg: Springer.

Balthazard, C. G., & Woody, E. Z. (1985). The "stuff" of hypnotic performance: A review of psychometric approaches. *Psychological Bulletin, 98,* 283–296.

Banaji, M. R., & Crowder, R. G. (1989). The bankruptcy of everyday memory. *American Psychologist, 44,* 1185–1193.

Bandura, A. (1963, October 22). What TV violence can do to your child. *Look,* pp. 46–52.

Bandura, A. (1982a). The psychology of chance encounters and life paths. *American Psychologist, 37,* 747–755.

Bandura, A. (1982b). Self-efficacy mechanisms in human agency. *American Psychologist, 37,* 122–147.

Bandura, A. (1986). *Social foundations of thought and action: A social cognitive theory.* Englewood Cliffs, NJ: Prentice-Hall.

Bandura, A., Ross, D., & Ross, S. A. (1961). Transmission of aggression through imitation of aggressive models. *Journal of Abnormal and Social Psychology, 63,* 575–582.

Bandura, A., Ross, D., & Ross, S. A. (1963). Imitation of film-mediated aggressive models. *Journal of Abnormal and Social Psychology, 63,* 311–318.

Banks, W. P., & Barber, G. (1977). Color information in iconic memory. *Psychological Review, 84,* 536–546.

Barber, T. X. (1979). Suggested ("hypnotic") behavior. The trance paradigm versus an alternative paradigm. In E. Fromm & R. E. Shor (Eds.), *Hypnosis: Developments in research and new perspectives* (pp. 217–274). Chicago: Aldine.

Barber, T. X. (1986). Realities of stage hypnosis. In B. Zilbergeld, M. G. Edelstien, & D. L. Araoz (Eds.), *Hypnosis: Questions and answers* (pp. 22–27). New York: Norton.

Barclay, C. R. (1986). Schematization of autobiographical memory. In D. C. Rubin (Ed.), *Autobiographical memory* (pp. 82–99). New York: Cambridge University Press.

Barcus, F. E. (1983). *Images of life on children's television.* New York: Praeger.

Bard, P. A. (1928). A diencephalic mechanism for the expression of rage with special reference to the sympathetic nervous system. *American Journal of Physiology, 84,* 490–515.

Bardwell, J. R., Cochran, S. W., & Walker, S. (1986). Relationship of parental education, race, and gender to sex role stereotyping in five-year-old kindergartners. *Sex Roles, 15,* 275–281.

Barefoot, J. C., Dahlstrom, W. G., & Williams, R. B., Jr. (1983). Hostility, CHD incidence, and total mortality. A 25-year follow-up study of 255 physicians. *Psychosomatic Medicine, 45,* 59–63.

Barlow, D. H. (1988). *Anxiety and its disorders.* New York: Guilford Press.

Barnett, P. A., & Gotlib, I. H. (1988). Psychosocial functioning and depression: Distinguishing among antecedents, concomitants, and consequences. *Psychological Bulletin, 104,* 97–126.

Baron, A. (Ed.). (1981). *Chicano psychology.* New York: Praeger.

Baron, J. (1984). Criteria and explanations. *Behavioral and Brain Sciences, 7,* 287–288.

Barrera, M., & Maurer, D. (1981). Recognition of mother's photographed face by the three-month-old infant. *Child Development, 52,* 714–716.

Barsalou, L. W. (1983). Ad hoc categories. *Memory & Cognition, 11,* 211–227.

Barton, E. J. (1986). Modification of children's prosocial behavior. In P. S. Strain, M. J. Guralnick, & H. M. Walker (Eds.), *Children's social be-*

havior (pp. 331–372). Orlando, FL: Academic Press.

Bartoshuk, L. M. (1971). The chemical senses: I. Taste. In J. W. Kling & L. A. Riggs (Eds.), *Woodworth & Schlosberg's experimental psychology* (3rd ed.). New York: Holt, Rinehart, & Winston.

Bassuk, E. L., Rubin, L., & Lauriat, A. (1984). Is homelessness a mental health problem? *American Journal of Psychiatry, 141,* 1546–1550.

Batchelor, W. F. (1988). AIDS 1988: The science and the limits of science. *American Psychologist, 43,* 853–858.

Batson, C. D. (1987). Prosocial motivation: Is it ever truly altruistic? *Advances in Experimental Social Psychology, 20,* 65–122.

Batson, C. D. (1990). How social an animal? The human capacity for caring. *American Psychologist, 45,* 336–346.

Batson, C. D., Duncan, B. D., Ackerman, P., Buckley, T., & Birch, K. (1981). Is empathic emotion a source of altruistic motivation? *Journal of Personality and Social Psychology, 40,* 290–302.

Baumeister, R. F. (1984). Choking under pressure: Self-consciousness and paradoxical effects of incentives on skillful performance. *Journal of Personality and Social Psychology, 46,* 610–620.

Baumrind, D. (1964). Some thoughts on ethics of research: After reading Milgram's "Behavioral study of obedience." *American Psychologist, 19,* 421–423.

Baumrind, D. (1971). Current patterns of parental authority. *Developmental Psychology Monographs, 4* (1, Pt. 2).

Baumrind, D. (1975). Early socialization and adolescent competence. In S. E. Dragestin & G. H. Elder (Eds.), *Adolescence in the life cycle.* New York: Wiley.

Bayles, K. A., Kaszniak, A. W., & Tomoeda, C. K. (1987). *Communication and cognition in normal aging and dementia.* Boston: Little, Brown.

Bazar, J. (1990, February). Psychologist's death breaks a critical link. *APA Monitor,* p. 30.

Beattie, G. (1983). *Talk: An analysis of speech and nonverbal behaviour in conversation.* Milton Keynes, England: Open University Press.

Beck, A. T. (1976). *Cognitive therapy and the emotional disorders.* New York: International Universities Press.

Beck, A. T. (1982). *Depression: Clinical, experimental, and theoretical aspects.* New York: Harper & Row.

Beck, A. T., Emery, G., & Greenberg, R. L. (1985). *Anxiety disorders and phobias: A cognitive perspective.* New York: Basic.

Beck, A. T., & Greenberg, R. L. (1974). Cognitive therapy with depressed women. In V. Franks & V. Burtle (Eds.), *Women in therapy* (pp. 113–131). New York: Brunner/Mazel.

Becker, B. J. (1986). Influence again: An examination of reviews and studies of gender differences in social influence. In J. S. Hyde & M. C. Linn (Eds.), *The psychology of gender: Advances through meta-analysis* (pp. 178–209). Baltimore: Johns Hopkins University Press.

Bedeian, A. G., Mossholder, K. W., & Touliatos, J. (1990). Type A status and selected work experiences among male and female accountants. *Journal of Social Behavior and Personality, 5,* 291–305.

Bee, H. L. (1987). *The journey of adulthood.* New York: Macmillan.

Bee, H. L. (1989). *The developing child* (5th ed.). New York: Harper & Row.

Begg, I., & White, P. (1985). Encoding specificity in interpersonal communication. *Canadian Journal of Psychology, 39,* 70–87.

Belenky, M. F., Clinchy, B. M., Goldberger, N. R., & Tarule, J. M. (1986). *Women's ways of knowing: The development of self, voice, and mind.* New York: Basic.

Bell, A. P., & Weinberg, M. S. (1978). *Homosexualities.* New York: Simon & Schuster.

Bell, I. P. (1989). The double standard: Age. In J. Freeman (Ed.), *Women: A feminist perspective* (4th ed., pp. 236–244). Mountain View, CA: Mayfield.

Bell, R. (1980). *Changing bodies, changing lives.* New York: Random House.

Belsher, G., & Costello, C. G. (1988). Relapse after recovery from unipolar depression: A critical review. *Psychological Bulletin, 104,* 84–96.

Belsky, J., & Rovine, M. J. (1988). Nonmaternal care in the first year of life and the security of infant-parent attachment. *Child Development, 59,* 157–167.

Bem, D. J. (1972). Self-perception theory. *Advances in Experimental Social Psychology, 6,* 1–62.

Bem, D. J., & Allen, A. (1974). On predicting some of the people some of the time: The search for cross-situational consistency in behavior. *Psychological Review, 81,* 506–520.

Bem, S. L. (1981). Gender schema theory: A cognitive account of sex typing. *Psychological Review, 88,* 354–364.

Bem, S. L. (1985). Androgyny and gender schema theory: A conceptual and empirical integration. In T. B. Sonderegger (Ed.), *Nebraska symposium on motivation, 1984: Psychology and gender* (pp. 179–226). Lincoln: University of Nebraska Press.

Bemis, K. M. (1978). Current approaches to the etiology and treatment of anorexia nervosa. *Psychological Bulletin, 85,* 593–617.

Benbow, C. P. (1988). Sex differences in mathematical reasoning ability in intellectually talented preadolescents: Their nature, effects, and possible causes. *Behavioral and Brain Sciences, 11,* 169–232.

Benbow, C. P., & Stanley, J. C. (1980). Sex differences in mathematical ability: Fact or artifact? *Science, 210,* 1262–1264.

Bengston, V. L., Reedy, M. N., & Gordon, C. (1985). Aging and self-conceptions: Personality processes and social contexts. In J. E. Birren & K. W. Schaie (Eds.), *Handbook of the psychology of aging* (pp. 544–593). New York: Van Nostrand Reinhold.

Benmayor, R. (1987). "For every story there is another story which stands before it." In R. Benmayor, A. Juarbe, C. Alvarez, & B. Vázquez (Eds.), *Stories to live by: Continuity and change in three generations of Puerto Rican women* (pp. 1–13). New York: Centro de Estudios Puertorriqueños (Hunter College).

Bensman, J., & Lilienfeld, R. (1979, October). Friendship and alienation. *Psychology Today,* pp. 56–66.

Benson, H. (1975). *The relaxation response.* New York: Morrow.

Berkowitz, L. (1984). Some effects of thoughts on anti- and prosocial influences of media events: A cognitive-neoassociation analysis. *Psychological Bulletin, 95,* 410–427.

Berkowitz, L. (1989). Frustration-aggression hypothesis: Examination and reformulation.

Psychological Bulletin, 106, 59–73.

Berman, R. F. (1986). Studies of memory processes using electrical brain stimulation. In J. L. Martinez & R. P. Kesner (Eds.), *Learning and memory: A biological view* (pp. 341–376). San Diego: Academic Press.

Bernard, L. I. (1924). *Instinct.* New York: Holt.

Bernheim, K. F. (1989). Psychologists and families of the severely mentally ill: The role of family consultation. *American Psychologist, 44,* 561–564.

Bernheim, K. F., & Lehman, A. F. (1985). *Working with families of the mentally ill.* New York: Norton.

Bernheim, K. F., & Lewine, R. R. J. (1979). *Schizophrenia.* New York: Norton.

Bernheim, K. F., Lewine, R. R. J., & Beale, C. T. (1982). *The caring family: Living with chronic mental illness.* New York: Random House.

Bernstein, I. L. (1978). Learned taste aversions in children receiving chemotherapy. *Science, 200,* 1302–1303.

Best, J. B. (1989). *Cognitive psychology* (2nd ed.). St. Paul, MN: West.

Betz, N. E., & Fitzgerald, L. F. (1987). *The career psychology of women.* New York: Academic Press.

Beyth-Maron, R., & Dekel, S. (1985). *An elementary approach to thinking under uncertainty.* Hillsdale, NJ: Erlbaum.

Bianchini, J. C. (1976, May). *Achievement tests and differentiated norms.* Paper presented at the U.S. Office of Education invitational conference on achievement testing of disadvantaged and minority students for educational program evaluation, Reston, VA.

Biener, L., Abrams, D. B., Emmons, K., & Follick, M. J. (1989). Evaluating worksite smoking policies: Methodologic issues. *New York State Journal of Medicine, 89,* 5–10.

Bierly, M. M. (1985). Prejudice toward contemporary out-groups as a generalized attitude. *Journal of Applied Social Psychology, 15,* 189–199.

Birchler, G. R., Weiss, R. L., & Vincent, J. P. (1975). Multimethod analysis of social reinforcement exchange between maritally distressed and nondistressed spouse and stranger dyads. *Journal of Personality and Social Psychology, 31,* 349–360.

Birren, J. E., Cunningham, W. R., & Yamamoto, K. (1983). Psychology of adult development and aging. *Annual Review of Psychology, 34,* 543–575.

Blackburn, C. (1988, April). Matters of taste. *Piedmont Airlines,* pp. 24–27.

Blakemore, C. (1985). The nature of explanation in the study of the mind. In C. W. Coen (Ed.), *Functions of the brain* (pp. 181–200). Oxford, England: Clarendon.

Blau, F. D., & Winkler, A. E. (1989). Women in the labor force: An overview. In J. Freeman (Ed.), *Women: A feminist perspective* (4th ed., pp. 265–286). Mountain View, CA: Mayfield.

Bleuler, E. (1950). *Dementia praecox or the group of schizophrenias.* New York: International Universities Press. (Original work published 1911)

Blumenthal, A. L. (1975). A reappraisal of Wilhelm Wundt. *American Psychologist, 30,* 1081–1088.

Bock, J. K. (1987). Co-ordinating words and syntax in speech plans. In A. W. Ellis (Ed.), *Progress in the psychology of language* (Vol. 3, pp. 337–390). London: Erlbaum.

Boddé, T. (1988). *Why is my child gay?* Washington, DC: Parents FLAG.

Bodenhausen, G., & Wyer, R. (1985). Effects of stereotypes on decision making and information-processing strategies. *Journal of Personality and Social Psychology, 48,* 267–282.

Bond, C. F., Jr., & Titus, L. J. (1983). Social facilitation: A meta-analysis of 241 studies. *Psychological Bulletin, 94,* 265–292.

Booth-Kewley, S., & Friedman, H. S. (1987). Psychological predictors of heart disease: A quantitative review. *Psychological Bulletin, 101,* 343–362.

Bornstein, R. F. (1989). Exposure and affect: Overview and meta-analysis of research, 1968–1987. *Psychological Bulletin, 106,* 265–289.

Boswell, P. C., & Murray, E. J. (1979). Effects of meditation on psychological and physiological measures of anxiety. *Journal of Consulting and Clinical Psychology, 47,* 606–607.

Bouchard, T. J., & McGee, M. (1981). Familial studies of intelligence: A review. *Science, 212,* 1055–1059.

Boulton, M. G. (1983). *On being a mother.* London: Tavistock.

Bowden, S. C. (1990). Separating cognitive impairment in neurologically asymptomatic alcoholism from Wernicke-Korsakoff syndrome: Is the neuropsychological distinction justified? *Psychological Bulletin, 107,* 355–366.

Bower, G. H. (1970). Analysis of a mnemonic device. *American Scientist, 58,* 496–510.

Bower, G. H., Clark, M. C., Lesgold, A. M., & Winzenz, D. (1969). Hierarchical retrieval schemes in recall of categorized word lists. *Journal of Verbal Learning and Verbal Behavior, 8,* 323–343.

Bower, G. H., & Winzenz, G. (1970). Comparison of associative learning strategies. *Psychonomic Science, 20,* 119–120.

Bowers, K. S. (1976). *Hypnosis for the seriously curious.* Monterey, CA: Brooks/Cole.

Bowers, K. S. (1984). Hypnosis. In N. E. Endler & J. M. Hunt (Eds.), *Personality and the behavioral disorders* (2nd ed., Vol. 1, pp. 439–475). New York: Wiley.

Bowman, P. J., & Howard, C. (1985). Race-related socialization, motivation, and academic achievement: A study of black youths in three-generation families. *Journal of the American Academy of Child Psychiatry, 24,* 134–141.

Boyd, J. H., & Weissman, M. M. (1981). Epidemiology of affective disorders. *Archives of General Psychiatry, 38,* 1039–1046.

Boyer, J. L., & Guthrie, L. (1985). Assessment and treatment of the suicidal patient. In E. E. Beckham & W. R. Leber (Eds.), *Handbook of depression* (pp. 606–633). Homewood, IL: Dorsey.

Boykin, A. W. (1986). The triple quandary and the schooling of Afro-American children. In U. Neisser (Ed.), *The school achievement of minority children* (pp. 57–92). Hillsdale, NJ: Erlbaum.

Boykin, A. W., & Toms, F. D. (1985). Black child socialization: A conceptual framework. In H. P. McAdoo & J. L. McAdoo (Eds.), *Black children* (pp. 33–51). Beverly Hills, CA: Sage.

Bradway, K. P., Thompson, C. W., & Cravens, R. B. (1958). Preschool IQ's after twenty-five years. *Journal of Educational Psychology, 52,* 74–79.

Brady, J. (1982, November). Perfume. *Signature,* pp. 77–89.

Braine, M. D. S. (1987). Acquiring and processing first and second languages. In P. Homel, M. Palij, & D. Aaronson (Eds.), *Childhood bilingualism: Aspects of linguistic, cognitive, and social development* (pp. 121–128). Hillsdale, NJ: Erlbaum.

Branden, N. (1988). A vision of romantic love. In R. J. Sternberg & M. L. Barnes (Eds.), *The psychology of love* (pp. 218–231). New Haven, CT: Yale University Press.

Bransford, J. D., & Franks, J. J. (1971). Abstraction of linguistic ideas. *Cognitive Psychology, 2,* 331–350.

Brehm, S. S. (1985). *Intimate relationships.* New York: Random House.

Brehm, S. S., & Kassin, S. M. (1990). *Social psychology.* Boston: Houghton Mifflin.

Breland, K., & Breland, M. (1961). The misbehavior of organisms. *American Psychologist, 16,* 681–684.

Bretherton, I. (1985). Attachment theory: Retrospect and prospect. *Monographs of the Society for Research in Child Development, 50* (1), 3–35.

Brewer, M. B., & Lui, L. (1984). Categorization of the elderly by the elderly: Effects of perceiver's category membership. *Personality and Social Psychology Bulletin, 10,* 585–595.

Brewer, W. F., & Treyens, J. C. (1981). Role of schemata in memory for places. *Cognitive Psychology, 13,* 207–230.

Brewin, C. R. (1989). Cognitive change processes in psychotherapy. *Psychological Review, 96,* 379–394.

Brickman, P., Coates, D., & Janoff-Bulman, R. J. (1978). Lottery winners and accident victims: Is happiness relative? *Journal of Personality and Social Psychology, 36,* 917–927.

Bridgeman, B. (1988). *The biology of behavior and mind.* New York: Wiley.

Briere, J., & Lanktree, C. (1983). Sex-role related effects of sex bias in language. *Sex Roles, 9,* 625–632.

Broberg, D. J., & Bernstein, I. L. (1987). Candy as a scapegoat in the prevention of food aversions in children receiving chemotherapy. *Cancer, 60,* 2344–2347.

Broca, P. (1861). Remarques sur le siège de la faculté du langage articulé, suivies d'une observation d'aphémie. *Bulletin de la Société anatomique* (Paris), 2nd series 6, 398–407.

Bromley, D. B. (1986). *The case-study method in psychology and related disciplines.* Chichester, England: Wiley.

Bronfenbrenner, U. (1961). The mirror image in Soviet-American relations: A social psychologist's report. *Journal of Social Issues, 17,* 45–56.

Bronstein, P. A., & Paludi, M. (1988). The introductory psychology course from a broader human perspective. In P. A. Bronstein & K. Quina (Eds.), *Teaching a psychology of people* (pp. 21–36). Washington, DC: American Psychological Association.

Brooks-Gunn, J. (1988). Pubertal processes and the early adolescent transition. In W. Damon (Ed.), *Child development today and tomorrow.* San Francisco: Jossey-Bass.

Brooks-Gunn, J. (1989). Adolescents as daughters and as mothers: A developmental perspective. In I. Sigel & G. Brody (Eds.), *Family research.* Hillsdale, NJ: Erlbaum.

Brothers, L. (1989, November). Empathy: Therapeutic and biological views. *The Harvard Medical School Mental Health Letter, 6*(5), 4–6.

Brown, H. C. (1980). From little acorns to tall oaks: From boranes through organoboranes. *Science, 210,* 485–492.

Brown, J. A. (1958). Some tests of the decay theory of immediate memory. *Quarterly Journal of Experimental Psychology, 10,* 12–21.

Brown, P. (1984). *The transfer of care: Psychiatric deinstitutionalization and its aftermath.* Boston: Routledge & Kegan Paul.

Brown, P., & Funk, S. C. (1986). Tardive dyskinesia: Barriers to the professional recognition of an iatrogenic disease. *Journal of Health and Social Behavior, 27,* 116–132.

Brown, P., & Levinson, S. C. (1987). *Politeness: Some universals of language usage.* Cambridge, England: Cambridge University Press.

Brown, R. (1988). More than P's and Q's [Review of *Politeness: Some universals of language usage*]. *Contemporary Psychology, 33,* 749–750.

Brown, R., Cazden, C., & Bellugi-Klima, U. (1968). The child's grammar from I to III. In J. P. Hill (Ed.), *Minnesota Symposium on Child Development* (Vol. 2, pp. 28–73). Minneapolis: University of Minnesota Press.

Brown, R., & Kulik, J. (1977). Flashbulb memories. *Cognition, 5,* 73–99.

Brown, R., & Lenneberg, E. H. (1954). A study in language and cognition. *Journal of Abnormal and Social Psychology, 49,* 454–462.

Brown, R., & McNeill, D. (1966). The "tip of the tongue" phenomenon. *Journal of Verbal Learning and Verbal Behavior, 5,* 325–377.

Brownmiller, S. (1975). *Against our will: Men, women and rape.* New York: Bantam.

Bruce, D. (1985). The how and why of ecological memory. *Journal of Experimental Psychology: General, 114,* 78–90.

Bruch, H. (1978). *The golden cage: The enigma of anorexia nervosa.* Cambridge, MA: Harvard University Press.

Brugge, J. F., & Reale, R. A. (1985). Auditory cortex. In A. Peters & E. G. Jones (Eds.), *Cerebral cortex* (Vol. 4, pp. 229–271). New York: Plenum.

Buchholz, D. (1988). Sleep disorders. *Treatment Trends, 3,* 1–9.

Buck, R. (1988). *Human motivation and emotion* (2nd ed.). New York: Wiley.

Buie, J. (1988, July). Menopause-depression link appears unfounded. *APA Monitor,* p. 47.

Bundesen, C., & Pedersen, L. F. (1983). Color segregation and visual search. *Perception & Psychophysics, 33,* 487–493.

Burchill, S. A. L., & Stiles, W. B. (1988). Interactions of depressed college students with their roommates: Not necessarily negative. *Journal of Personality and Social Psychology, 55,* 410–419.

Burden-Patmon, D. (1989, December). Stand and deliver: Achieving against the odds. *Wheelock Bulletin,* pp. 2, 15.

Bureau of the Census (1984a). *We, the Asian and Pacific Islander Americans.* Washington, DC: U.S. Government Printing Office.

Bureau of the Census (1984b). *We, the Americans.* Washington, DC: U.S. Government Printing Office.

Burgess, A. W., & Holmstrom, L. L. (1980). Rape typology and the coping behavior of rape victims. In S. L. McCombie (Ed.), *The rape crisis intervention handbook* (pp. 27–40). New York: Plenum.

Burgoon, J. K. (1985). Nonverbal signals. In M. L. Knapp & G. R. Miller (Eds.), *Handbook of interpersonal communication* (pp. 344–390). Beverly Hills, CA: Sage.

Bushnell, I. W. R. (1982). Discrimination of faces by young infants. *Journal of Experimental Psychology, 33*, 298–308.

Buss, D. M. (1985, January–February). Human mate selection. *American Scientist*, pp. 47–51.

Buss, D. M., & Barnes, M. (1986). Preferences in human mate selection. *Journal of Personality and Social Psychology, 50*, 559–570.

Butcher, J. N., & Finn, S. (1983). Objective personality assessment in clinical settings. In M. Hersen, A. Kazdin, & A. S. Bellack (Eds.), *The clinical psychology handbook* (pp. 329–344). New York: Pergamon.

Butler, R. N. (1963). The life review: An interpretation of reminiscence in the aged. *Psychiatry, 26*, 65–76.

Butler, R. N. (1975). *Why survive? Being old in America*. New York: Harper & Row.

Byrne, D. (1982). Predicting human sexual behavior. In A. G. Kraut (Ed.), *The G. Stanley Hall lecture series* (Vol. 2). Washington, DC: American Psychological Association.

Byrne, D., Clore, G. I., & Smeaton, G. (1986). The attraction hypothesis: Do similar attitudes affect anything? *Journal of Personality and Social Psychology, 51*, 1167–1170.

Byrne, D., & Murnen, S. K. (1988). Maintaining loving relationships. In R. J. Sternberg & M. L. Barnes (Eds.), *The psychology of love* (pp. 293–310). New Haven, CT: Yale University Press.

Cain, W. S. (1987). Indoor air as a source of annoyance. In H. S. Koelega (Ed.), *Environmental annoyance: Characterization, measurement, and control* (pp. 189–198). Amsterdam: Elsevier.

Cain, W. S. (1988). Olfaction. In R. C. Atkinson, R. J. Herrnstein, G. Lindzey, & R. D. Luce (Eds.), *Stevens' handbook of experimental psychology* (2nd ed., Vol. 1, pp. 409–459). New York: Wiley.

Cain, W. S., Leaderer, B. P., Cannon, L., Tosun, T., & Ismail, H. (1987b). Odorization of inert gas for occupational safety: Psychophysical considerations. *American Industrial Hygiene Association Journal, 48*, 47–55.

Cain, W. S., Tosun, T., See, L., & Leaderer, B. (1987a). Environmental tobacco smoke: Sensory reactions of occupants. *Atmospheric Environment, 21*, 347–353.

Cain, W. S., & Turk, A. (1985). Smell of danger: An analysis of LP-gas odorization. *American Industrial Hygiene Association Journal, 46*, 115–126.

Campione, J. C., Brown, A. L., & Ferrara, R. A. (1982). Mental retardation and intelligence. In R. J. Sternberg (Ed.), *Handbook of human intelligence* (pp. 392–490). New York: Cambridge University Press.

Campos, J. J., Langer, A., & Krowitz, A. (1970). Cardiac responses on the visual cliff in prelocomotor human infants. *Science, 170*, 196–197.

Cannon, L. W., Higginbotham, E., & Leung, M. L. A. (1988). Race and class bias in qualitative research on women. *Gender & Society, 2*, 449–462.

Cannon, W. B. (1927). The James-Lange theory of emotion: A critical examination and an alternative theory. *American Journal of Psychology, 39*, 106–124.

Cantor, N., & Kihlstrom, J. F. (1987). *Personality and social intelligence*. Englewood Cliffs, NJ: Prentice-Hall.

Caplan, P. J. (1984). The myth of women's masochism. *American Psychologist, 39*, 130–139.

Caplan, P. J., MacPherson, G. M., & Tobin, P. (1985). Do sex-related differences in spatial abilities exist? *American Psychologist, 40*, 786–799.

Cappella, J. N. (1985). The management of conversations. In M. L. Knapp & G. R. Miller (Eds.), *Handbook of interpersonal communication* (pp. 393–438). Beverly Hills, CA: Sage.

Cargan, L., & Melko, M. (1985). Being single on Noah's ark. In L. Cargan (Ed.), *Marriage and family: Coping with change*. Belmont, CA: Wadsworth.

Carlson, N. R. (1986). *Physiology of behavior* (3rd ed.). Boston: Allyn & Bacon.

Carney, J. (1989, January 16). Can a driver be too old? *Time*, p. 28.

Caron, R. F., Caron, A. J., & Myers, R. S. (1982). Abstraction of invariant face expressions in infancy. *Child Development, 53*, 1008–1015.

Carroll, D. (1988). How accurate is polygraph lie detection? In A. Gale (Ed.), *The polygraph test* (pp. 19–28). London: Sage.

Carroll, D. W. (1986). *Psychology of language*. Monterey, CA: Brooks/Cole.

Carson, R. C. (1988). *On the biologicalization of human adaptational failure*. Paper presented at the convention of the Western Psychological Association, San Francisco.

Carson, R. C. (1989). Personality. *Annual Review of Psychology, 40*, 227–248.

Carson, R. C., Butcher, J. N., & Coleman, J. C. (1988). *Abnormal psychology and modern life* (8th ed.). Glenview, IL: Scott, Foresman.

Case, R. (1987). The structure and process of intellectual development. *International Journal of Psychology, 22*, 571–607.

Cautela, J. R. (1971). Covert conditioning. In A. Jacobs & J. B. Sachs (Eds.), *The psychology of private events: Perspective on covert response systems*. New York: Academic Press.

Ceci, S. J., Peters, D., & Plotkin, J. (1985). Human subjects review, personal values, and the regulations of social science research. *American Psychologist, 40*, 994–1002.

Centers for Disease Control. (1989). *AIDS/HIV Record, 3*, 7.

Cernoch, J. M., & Porter, R. H. (1985). Recognition of maternal axillary odors by infants. *Child Development, 56*, 1593–1598.

Chaika, E. (1985, August). Crazy talk. *Psychology Today*, pp. 30–35.

Chaiken, S. (1987). The heuristic model of persuasion. In M. P. Zanna, J. M. Olson, & C. P. Herman (Eds.), *Social influence: The Ontario symposium* (Vol. 5, pp. 3–39). Hillsdale, NJ: Erlbaum.

Chambless, D. L., & Goldstein, A. J. (1980). Anxieties: Agoraphobia and hysteria. In A. M. Brodsky & R. T. Hare-Mustin (Eds.), *Women and psychotherapy* (pp. 113–134). New York: Guilford Press.

Chance, P. (1988). *Learning and behavior* (2nd ed.). Belmont, CA: Wadsworth.

Chang, H. H., Murphy, D., Diferdinando, G. T., & Morse, D. L. (1990). Assessment of AIDS knowledge in selected New York state sexually transmitted disease clinics. *New York State Journal of Medicine, 90*, 126–128.

Chastain, G. (1986). Word-to-letter inhibition: Word-inferiority and other interference effects. *Memory & Cognition, 14*, 361–368.

Check, J. V. P. (1984). *The effects of violent and nonviolent pornography*. Ottawa, Ontario: Canadian Department of Justice.

Check, J. V. P., & Malamuth, N. M. (1986). Pornography and social aggression: A social learning theory analysis. In M. L. McLaughlin (Ed.), *Communication yearbook* (Vol. 9, pp. 181–213). Beverly Hills, CA: Sage.

Chehrazi, S. (1986). Female psychology. *Journal of the American Psychoanalytical Association, 34*, 111–162.

Chemers, M. M., Hays, R. B., Rhodewalt, F., & Wysocki, J. (1985). A person-environment analysis of job stress: A contingency model explanation. *Journal of Personality and Social Psychology, 49*, 628–635.

Chen, Y. P. (1985). Economic status of the aging. In R. Binstock & E. Shanas (Eds.), *Handbook of aging and the social sciences* (pp. 641–665). New York: Van Nostrand Reinhold.

Cherry, E. C. (1953). Some experiments on the recognition of speech with one and with two ears. *Journal of Acoustical Society of America, 25*, 975–979.

Cherry, F., & Deaux, K. (1978). Fear of success versus fear of gender-inappropriate behavior. *Sex Roles, 4*, 97–102.

Chess, S., & Thomas, A. (1986). *Temperament in clinical practice*. New York: Guilford Press.

Children's Defense Fund. (1988). *A vision for America's future*. Washington, DC: Children's Defense Fund.

Chiles, J. A., Carlin, A. S., & Beitman, B. D. (1984). A physician, a nonmedical psychotherapist, and a patient: The pharmacotherapy-psychotherapy triangle. In B. D. Beitman & G. L. Klerman (Eds.), *Combining psychotherapy and drug therapy in clinical practice* (pp. 89–101). Jamaica, NY: Spectrum.

Chomsky, N. (1957). *Syntactic structures*. The Hague: Mouton.

Chomsky, N. (1965). *Aspects of the theory of syntax*. Cambridge, MA: MIT Press.

Chomsky, N. (1988). *Language and problems of knowledge: The Managua lectures*. Cambridge, MA: MIT Press.

Chrisler, J. C., & Levy, K. B. (1989, March). *The media construct a menstrual monster: A content analysis of PMS articles in the popular press*. Paper presented at the meeting of the Association for Women in Psychology, Newport, RI.

Cialdini, R. B. (1986). Interpersonal influence: Being ethical and effective. In S. Oskamp & S. Spacapan (Eds.), *Interpersonal processes* (pp. 148–165). Newbury Park, CA: Sage.

Cialdini, R. B. (1988). *Influence: Science and practice* (2nd ed.). Glenview, IL: Scott, Foresman.

Cialdini, R. B., Vincent, J. E., Lewis, S. K., Catalan, J., Wheeler, D., & Darby, B. L. (1975). Reciprocal concessions procedure for inducing compliance: The door-in-the-face technique. *Journal of Personality and Social Psychology, 31*, 206–215.

Clark, H. H. (1985). Language use and language users. In G. Lindzey & E. Aronson (Eds.), *Handbook of social psychology* (2nd ed., Vol. 2, pp. 179–231). New York: Random House.

Clark, H. H., & Clark, E. V. (1977). *Psychology and language: An introduction to psycholinguistics*. New York: Harcourt, Brace, Jovanovich.

Clark, H. H., & Wilkes-Gibbs, D. (1986). Referring as a collaborative process. *Cognition, 22,* 1–39.

Clark, M. S., & Reis, H. T. (1988). Interpersonal processes in close relationships. *Annual Review of Psychology, 39,* 609–672.

Clarke-Stewart, A. (1989). Infant day care: Maligned or malignant. *American Psychologist, 44,* 266–273.

Clarke-Stewart, A., & Fein, G. G. (1983). Early childhood programs. In P. H. Mussen, M. Haith, & J. Campos (Eds.), *Handbook of child psychology* (Vol. 2, pp. 917–1000). New York: Wiley.

Cleary, P. D. (1987). Gender differences in stress-related disorders. In R. C. Barnett, L. Biener, & G. K. Baruch (Eds.), *Gender and stress* (pp. 39–72). New York: Free Press.

Coen, C. W. (1985). Introduction. In C. W. Coen (Ed.), *Functions of the brain* (pp. ix–xiv). Oxford: Clarendon.

Cohen, C. E. (1981). Person categories and social perception: Testing some boundaries of the processing effects of prior knowledge. *Journal of Personality and Social Psychology, 40,* 441–452.

Cohen, G. (1989). *Memory in the real world.* Hillsdale, NJ: Erlbaum.

Cohen, G., Eysenck, M. W., & LeVoi, M. E. (1986). *Memory: A cognitive approach.* Milton Keynes, England: Open University Press.

Cohen, S., Lichtenstein, E., Prochaska, J. O., Rossi, J. S., Gritz, E. R., Carr, C. R., Orleans, C. T., Schoenbach, V. J., Biener, L., Abrams, D., DiClemente, C., Curry, S., Marlatt, G. A., Cummings, K. M., Emont, S. L., Giovino, G., & Ossip-Klein, D. (1989). Debunking myths about self-quitting: Evidence from 10 prospective studies of persons who attempt to quit smoking by themselves. *American Psychologist, 44,* 1355–1365.

Cohen, S., & Wills, T. A. (1985). Stress, social support, and the buffering hypothesis. *Psychological Bulletin, 98,* 310–357.

Coile, D. C., & Miller, N. E. (1984). How radical animal activists try to mislead humane people. *American Psychologist, 39,* 700–701.

Colby, A., & Kohlberg, L. (1987). *The measurement of moral judgment, Vol. I: Theoretical foundations and research validation.* Cambridge, England: Cambridge University Press.

Colby, A., Kohlberg, L., Gibbs, J., & Lieberman, M. (1983). A longitudinal study of moral judgment. *Monographs of the Society for Child Development* (Serial No. 201).

Cole, M., Frankel, F., & Sharp, D. (1971). Development of free recall learning in children. *Developmental Psychology, 4,* 109–123.

Cole, R. A., & Jakimik, J. (1980). A model of speech perception. *Psychological Review, 81,* 348–374.

Coleman, R. M. (1986). *Wide awake at 3:00 a.m.* New York: Freeman.

College Marketing Group. (1988, Fall). *Mailing list catalog.* Winchester, MA: College Marketing Group.

College Marketing Group. (1989, Fall). *Mailing list catalog.* Winchester, MA: College Marketing Group.

Collins, A. M., & Loftus, E. F. (1975). A spreading-activation theory of semantic memory. *Psychological Review, 82,* 407–428.

Comas-Díaz, L. (1988). Cross-cultural mental health treatment. In L. Comas-Díaz & E. Grif-fith (Eds.), *Clinical guidelines in cross-cultural mental health* (pp. 337–361). New York: Wiley.

Comas-Díaz, L., & Griffith, E. (1988). Introduction: On culture and psychotherapeutic care. In L. Comas-Díaz & E. Griffith (Eds.), *Clinical guidelines in cross-cultural mental health* (pp. 1–32). New York: Wiley.

The Commission on the Prevention of Mental-Emotional Disabilities. (1987a). A framework for prevention. *The Journal of Primary Prevention, 7,* 199–203.

The Commission on the Prevention of Mental-Emotional Disabilities. (1987b). Adulthood. *The Journal of Primary Prevention, 7,* 215–218.

The Commission on the Prevention of Mental-Emotional Disabilities. (1987c). Agenda for action. *The Journal of Primary Prevention, 7,* 224–234.

Compas, B. E. (1987). Coping with stress during childhood and adolescence. *Psychological Bulletin, 101,* 393–403.

Condry, J. C., & Condry, S. (1976). Sex differences: A study of the eye of the beholder. *Child Development, 47,* 812–819.

Cook, A. S., & Oltjenbruns, K. A. (1989). *Dying and grieving: Lifespan & family perspectives.* New York: Holt, Rinehart and Winston.

Cook, M. (1988). Person perception. In G. M. Breakwell, H. Foot, & R. Gilmour (Eds.), *Doing social psychology* (pp. 185–201). Cambridge, England: Cambridge University Press.

Cook, M., Mineka, S., Wolkenstein, B., & Laitsch, K. (1985). Observational conditioning of snake fears in unrelated rhesus monkeys. *Journal of Abnormal Psychology, 95,* 195–207.

Cooper, E. R., Pelton, S. I., & LeMay, M. (1988). Acquired immunodeficiency syndrome: A new population of children at risk. *The Pediatric Clinics of North America, 35,* 1365–1387.

Cooper, J., & Fazio, R. H. (1984). A new look at dissonance theory. *Advances in Experimental Social Psychology, 17,* 229–266.

Cooper, J. D., Heron, T. E., & Heward, W. L. (1987). *Applied behavior analysis.* Columbus, OH: Merrill.

Cooper, L. A., & Shepard, R. N. (1984). Turning something over in the mind. *Scientific American, 251*(6), 106–114.

Cooper, W. E., Tye-Murray, N., & Eady, S. J. (1985). Acoustical cues to the reconstruction of missing words in speech perception. *Perception & Psychophysics, 38,* 30–40.

Corballis, M. C. (1983). *Human laterality.* New York: Academic Press.

Corballis, M. C. (1988). Recognition of disoriented shapes. *Psychological Review, 95,* 115–123.

Corder, J., & Stephan, C. W. (1984). Females' combinations of work and family roles: Adolescents' aspirations. *Journal of Marriage and the Family, 46,* 391–402.

Coren, S. (1981). The interaction between eye movements and visual illusions. In D. F. Fisher, R. A. Monty, & J. W. Senders (Eds.), *Eye movements: Cognition and visual perception.* Hillsdale, NJ: Erlbaum.

Coren, S., & Girgus, J. S. (1978). *Seeing is deceiving: The psychology of visual illusions.* Hillsdale, NJ: Erlbaum.

Coren, S., & Porac, C. (1987). Individual differences in visual-geometric illusions: Predictions from measures of spatial cognitive abilities. *Perception & Psychophysics, 41,* 211–219.

Coren, S., & Ward, L. M. (1989). *Sensation & perception* (3rd ed.). San Diego: Harcourt Brace Jovanovich.

Corsini, R. J. (1984). Eysenck, Hans J. In R. J. Corsini (Ed.), *Encyclopedia of psychology* (Vol. 1, p. 481). New York: Wiley.

Corsini, R. J. (1989). Introduction. In R. J. Corsini & D. Wedding (Eds.), *Current psychotherapies* (4th ed., pp. 1–16). Itasca, IL: Peacock.

Corso, J. F. (1981). *Aging sensory systems and perception.* New York: Praeger.

Costantino, G., Malgady, R. G., & Rogler, L. H. (1986). Cuento therapy: A culturally sensitive modality for Puerto Rican children. *Journal of Consulting and Clinical Psychology, 54,* 639–645.

Cotman, C. W., & Nieto-Sampedro, M. (1982). Brain function, synapse renewal, and plasticity. *Annual Review of Psychology, 33,* 371–401.

Covello, E. (1984). Lucid dreaming: A review and experiential study of waking intrusions during stage REM sleep. *The Journal of Mind and Behavior, 5,* 81–98.

Coverman, S. (1989). Women's work is never done: The division of domestic labor. In J. Freeman (Ed.), *Women: A feminist perspective* (4th ed., pp. 356–368). Mountain View, CA: Mayfield.

Cowan, G., & Hoffman, C. D. (1986). Gender stereotyping in young children: Evidence to support a concept-learning approach. *Sex Roles, 14,* 11–224.

Cowan, M. L., & Stewart, B. J. (1977). A methodological study of sex stereotypes. *Sex Roles, 3,* 205–216.

Cowan, N. (1988). Evolving conceptions of memory storage, selective attention, and their mutual constraints within the human information-processing system. *Psychological Bulletin, 104,* 163–191.

Coyne, J. C., Kahn, J., & Gotlib, I. H. (1987). Depression. In T. Jacob (Ed.), *Family interaction and psychopathology* (pp. 509–533). New York: Plenum.

Coyne, J. C., Kessler, R. C., Tal, M., Turnbull, J., Wortman, C. B., & Greden, J. F. (1987). Living with a depressed person. *Journal of Consulting and Clinical Psychology, 55,* 347–352.

Craig, K. D. (1978). Social modeling influences on pain. In R. A. Sternbach (Ed.), *The psychology of pain.* New York: Raven.

Craik, F. I. M. (1977). Depth of processing in recall and recognition. In S. Dornic (Ed.), *Attention and performance.* (Vol. 6). Hillsdale, NJ: Erlbaum.

Craik, F. I. M., Byrd, M., & Swanson, J. M. (1987). Patterns of memory loss in three elderly samples. *Psychology and Aging, 2,* 79–86.

Craik, F. I. M., & Lockhart, R. S. (1972). Levels of processing: A framework for memory research. *Journal of Verbal Learning and Verbal Behavior, 11,* 671–684.

Craik, F. I. M., & Lockhart, R. S. (1986). CHARM is not enough: Comments on Eich's model of cued recall. *Psychological Review, 93,* 360–364.

Cramer, D. (1986). Gay parents and their children: A review of research and practical implications. *Journal of Counseling and Development, 64,* 504–507.

Crandall, C. S. (1984). The overcitation of examples of poor performance: Fad, fashion, or fun? *American Psychologist, 39,* 1499.

Critelli, J. W., & Neumann, K. F. (1984). The placebo: Conceptual analysis of a construct in transition. *American Psychologist, 39*, 32–39.

Crocker, J., Thompson, L. L., McGraw, K. M., & Ingerman, C. (1987). Downward comparison, prejudice, and evaluation of others: Effects of self-esteem and threat. *Journal of Personality and Social Psychology, 52*, 907–916.

Crocker, L., & Algina, J. (1986). *Introduction to classical and modern test theory.* New York: Holt, Rinehart and Winston.

Cronbach, L. J. (1975). Five decades of public controversy over mental testing. *American Psychologist, 30*, 1–14.

Crovitz, H. F., & Daniel, W. F. (1984). Measurements of everyday memory: Toward the prevention of forgetting. *Bulletin of the Psychonomic Society, 22*, 413–414.

Crow, T. J. (1985). The two-syndrome concept: Origins and current status. *Schizophrenia Bulletin, 11*, 471–486.

Crowder, R. G. (1982). Decay of auditory memory in vowel discrimination. *Journal of Experimental Psychology: Learning, Memory, and Cognition, 8*, 153–162.

Crowe, R. R. (1984). Electroconvulsive therapy—A current perspective. *New England Journal of Medicine, 311*, 163–167.

Croyle, R. T., & Cooper, J. (1983). Dissonance arousal: Physiological evidence. *Journal of Personality and Social Psychology, 45*, 782–791.

The cult of death. (1978, December 4). *Newsweek*, pp. 38–60.

Cummings, E. M., Hollenbeck, B., Iannotti, R., Radke-Yarrow, M., & Zahn-Waxler, C. (1986). In C. Zahn-Waxler, E. M. Cummings, & R. Iannotti (Eds.), *Altruism and aggression* (pp. 165–188). Cambridge, England: Cambridge University Press.

Cummins, J. (1987). Bilingualism, language proficiency, and metalinguistic development. In P. Homel, M. Palij, & D. Aaronson (Eds.), *Childhood bilingualism: Aspects of linguistic, cognitive, and social development* (pp. 57–73). Hillsdale, NJ: Erlbaum.

Curran, J. P., & Cirelli, V. A. (1988). The role of psychosocial factors in the etiology, course and outcome of schizophrenia. In M. T. Tsuang & J. C. Simpson (Eds.), *Handbook of schizophrenia* (Vol. 3, pp. 275–297). Amsterdam: Elsevier.

Curtiss, S. (1977). *Genie: A psycholinguistic study of a modern-day "wild child."* New York: Academic Press.

Cutler, A. (1987). Speaking for listening. In A. Allport, D. MacKay, W. Prinz, & E. Scheerer (Eds.), *Language perception and production* (pp. 24–40). London: Academic Press.

Cutting, J. E. (1983). Perceiving and recovering structure from events. In SIGGRAPH/SIGART Interdisciplinary Workshop (Ed.), *Motion: Representation and perception.* New York: Association for Computing Machinery.

Dakof, G. A., & Mendelsohn, G. A. (1986). Parkinson's disease: The psychological aspects of a chronic disease. *Psychological Bulletin, 99*, 375–387.

Daniel, W. F., Crovitz, H. F., & Weiner, R. D. (1987). Neuropsychological aspects of disorientation. *Cortex, 23*, 169–187.

Darley, J. M., & Batson, C. D. (1973). From Jerusalem to Jericho: A study of situational and dispositional variables in helping behavior. *Journal of Personality and Social Psychology, 27*, 269–275.

Darley, J. M., & Gross, P. H. (1983). A hypothesis-confirming bias in labeling effects. *Journal of Personality and Social Psychology, 44*, 20–33.

Dartnall, H. J. A., Bowmaker, J. J., & Mollon, J. D. (1983). Microspectrophotometry of human photoreceptors. In J. D. Mollon & L. T. Sharpe (Eds.), *Color vision* (pp. 69–80). London: Academic Press.

Darwin, C. (1965). *The expression of the emotions in man and animals.* Chicago: University of Chicago Press. (Original work published 1872)

Darwin, C. J. (1976). The perception of speech. In E. C. Carterette & M. P. Friedman (Eds.), *Handbook of perception* (Vol. 7, pp. 175–226). New York: Academic Press.

Darwin, C. J., Turvey, M. T., & Crowder, R. G. (1972). An auditory analogue of the Sperling partial report procedure: Evidence for brief auditory storage. *Cognitive Psychology, 3*, 255–267.

Datan, N., Rodeheaver, D., & Hughes, F. (1987). Adult development and aging. *Annual Review of Psychology, 38*, 153–180.

Davidson, A. R., Yantis, S., Norwood, M., & Montano, D. E. (1985). Amount of information about the attitude object and attitude-behavior consistency. *Journal of Personality and Social Psychology, 49*, 1184–1198.

Davis, P., & Schwartz, G. (1987). Repression and the inaccessibility of affective memories. *Journal of Personality and Social Psychology, 52*, 155–162.

Davis, P. W., & Solomon, E. P. (1986). *The world of biology* (3rd ed.). Philadelphia: Saunders.

Davis, R. H., & Davis, J. A. (1985). *TV's image of the elderly.* Lexington, MA: Lexington.

Davis, R. M. (1987). Current trends in cigarette advertising and marketing. *New England Journal of Medicine, 316*, 725–745.

Davison, G. C., & Neale, J. M. (1986). *Abnormal psychology* (4th ed.). New York: Wiley.

Day, R. H. (1987). Visual size constancy in infancy. In B. E. McKenzie & R. H. Day (Eds.), *Perceptual development in early infancy* (pp. 67–91). London: Erlbaum.

DeAngelis, T. (1988, July). Cognitive therapy still evolving. *APA Monitor*, p. 30.

Deaux, K. (1985). Sex and gender. *Annual Review of Psychology, 36*, 49–81.

Deaux, K., & Major, B. (1987). Putting gender into context: An interactive model of gender-related behavior. *Psychological Review, 94*, 369–389.

Deaux, K., & Wrightsman, L. S. (1988). *Social psychology* (5th ed.). Pacific Grove, CA: Brooks/Cole.

DeBakey, M., & Gotto, A. (1977). *The living heart.* New York: Charter.

DeBono, K. G., & Harnish, R. J. (1988). Source expertise, source attractiveness, and the processing of persuasive information: A functional approach. *Journal of Personality and Social Psychology, 55*, 541–546.

DeCasper, A. J., & Spence, M. J. (1986). Prenatal maternal speech influences newborns' perception of speech sounds. *Infant Behavior and Development, 9*, 133–150.

deCharms, R., & Carpenter, V. (1968). Measuring motivation in culturally disadvantaged school children. In H. J. Klausmeirer & G. T. O'Hearn (Eds.), *Research and development toward the improvement of education.* Madison, WI: Educational Research Services.

Deci, E. L. (1971). Effects of externally mediated rewards on intrinsic motivation. *Journal of Personality and Social Psychology, 18*, 105–115.

Deci, E. L., & Ryan, R. M. (1985). *Intrinsic motivation and self-determination in human behavior.* New York: Plenum.

Deci, E. L., & Ryan, R. M. (1987). The support of autonomy and the control of behavior. *Journal of Personality and Social Psychology, 53*, 1024–1037.

DeFries, J. C., Plomin, R., & LaBuda, M. C. (1987). Genetic stability of cognitive development from childhood to adulthood. *Developmental Psychology, 23*, 4–12.

Deikman, A. J. (1966). Deautomatization and the mystic experience. *Psychiatry, 29*, 324–338.

Delay, J., & Deniker, P. (1952). *Trente-huit cas de psychoses traitées par la cure prolongée et continuée de 4560 RP.* Paris: Masson et Cie.

DelGiudice, G. T. (1986). The relationship between sibling jealousy and presence at a sibling's birth. *Birth, 13*, 250–254.

Dell, G. S. (1986). A spreading-activation theory of retrieval in sentence production. *Psychological Review, 93*, 283–321.

DeLongis, A., Coyne, J. C., Dakof, G., Folkman, S., & Lazarus, R. S. (1982). Relationship of daily hassles, uplifts, and major life events to health status. *Health Psychology, 1*, 119–136.

DeLongis, A., Folkman, S., & Lazarus, R. S. (1988). The impact of daily stress on health and mood: Psychological and social resources as mediators. *Journal of Personality and Social Psychology, 54*, 486–495.

Dembroski, T. M., & MacDougall, J. M. (1985). Beyond global Type A: Relationships of paralinguistic attributes, hostility, and anger-in to coronary heart disease. In T. M. Fields, P. M. McCabe, & N. Schneiderman (Eds.), *Stress and coping* (pp. 223–242). Hillsdale, NJ: Erlbaum.

Dement, W. C. (1986). Normal sleep, disturbed sleep, transient and persistent insomnia. *Acta Psychiatrica Scandinavica, 74*, 41–46.

Demos, V., & Jache, A. (1981). When you care enough: An analysis of attitudes toward aging in humorous birthday cards. *Gerontologist, 21*, 209–215.

DeMott, D. W. (1987). *Peacebuilding: A textbook* (2nd ed.). Geneseo, NY: High Falls Publications.

Dempster, F. N. (1981). Memory span: Sources of individual and developmental differences. *Psychological Bulletin, 89*, 63–100.

Denmark, F., Russo, N. F., Frieze, I. H., & Sechzer, J. A. (1988). Guidelines for avoiding sexism in psychological research: A report of the Ad Hoc Committee on Nonsexist Research. *American Psychologist, 43*, 582–585.

Depue, R. A., & Monroe, S. M. (1986). Conceptualization and measurement of human disorder in life stress research: The problem of chronic disturbance. *Psychological Bulletin, 99*, 36–51.

Des Jarlais, D. C., & Friedman, S. R. (1988). The psychology of preventing AIDS among intravenous drug users: A social learning conceptualization. *American Psychologist, 43*, 865–870.

Desor, J. A., & Beauchamp, G. K. (1974). The human capacity to transmit olfactory information. *Perception & Psychophysics, 16,* 551–556.

Desor, J. A., Maller, O., & Greene, L. S. (1977). Preference for sweet in humans: Infants, children and adults. In J. M. Weiffenbach (Ed.), *Taste and development: The genesis of sweet preference.* Bethesda, MD: U.S. Department of Health, Education and Welfare.

DeSpelder, L. A., & Strickland, A. L. (1987). *The last dance: Encountering death and dying* (2nd ed.). Palo Alto, CA: Mayfield.

Detre, K. M., Feinleib, M., Matthews K. A., & Kerr, B. W. (1987). The federal women's study. In E. Eaker, B. Packard, & N. Wenger (Eds.), *Coronary heart disease in women* (pp. 78–82). New York: Haymarket Doyma.

Deutsch, M. (1983). The prevention of World War III: A psychological perspective. *Political Psychology, 4,* 3–31.

Deutsch, M., & Collins, M. E. (1951). *Interracial housing: A psychological evaluation of a social experiment.* Minneapolis: University of Minnesota Press.

Deutsch, M., & Shichman, S. (1986). Conflict: A social psychological perspective. In M. Hermann (Ed.), *Political psychology* (pp. 219–250). San Francisco: Jossey-Bass.

de Villiers, J. G., & de Villiers, P. A. (1985). The acquisition of English. In D. I. Slobin (Ed.), *The crosslinguistic study of language acquisition* (Vol. 1, pp. 27–139). Hillsdale, NJ: Erlbaum.

Devine, P. G. (1989). Stereotypes and prejudice: Their automatic and controlled components. *Journal of Personality and Social Psychology, 56,* 5–18.

Diaz, R. M. (1983). Thought and two languages: The impact of bilingualism on cognitive development. In E. W. Gordon (Ed.), *Review of research in education* (Vol. 10, pp. 23–54). Washington, DC: American Educational Research Association.

Diener, E. (1984). Subjective well-being. *Psychological Bulletin, 95,* 542–575.

Digman, J. M., & Inouye, J. (1986). Specification of the five robust factors of personality. *Journal of Personality and Social Psychology, 50,* 116–123.

DiMatteo, M. R. (1985). Physician-patient communication: Promoting a positive health care setting. In J. C. Rosen & L. J. Solomon (Eds.), *Prevention in health psychology* (pp. 328–365). Hanover, NH: University Press of New England.

Dion, K. K. (1986). Stereotyping based on physical attractiveness: Issues and conceptual perspectives. In C. P. Herman, M. P. Zanna, & E. T. Higgins (Eds.), *Physical appearance, stigma, and social behavior: The Ontario Symposium* (Vol. 3, pp. 7–21). Hillsdale, NJ: Erlbaum.

Dion, K. K., Berscheid, E., & Walster, E. (1972). What is beautiful is good. *Journal of Personality and Social Psychology, 24,* 207–213.

Dittmann, A. T. (1987). The role of body movement in communication. In A. W. Siegman & S. Feldstein (Eds.), *Nonverbal behavior and communication* (2nd ed., pp. 37–64). Hillsdale, NJ: Erlbaum.

Dobelle, W. H., Mladejovsky, M. G., & Girvin, J. P. (1974). Artificial vision for the blind: Electrical stimulation of visual cortex offers hope for a functional prosthesis. *Science, 183,* 440–444.

Dodge, S. (1989, December 13). Rutgers panel outlines ways to fight homophobia. *The Chronicle of Higher Education,* p. A51.

Dohrenwend, B. P., & Dohrenwend, B. S. (1974). Social and cultural influences on psychopathology. *Annual Review of Psychology, 25,* 417–452.

Doll, L., Darrow, W. W., Jaffe, H., Curran, L., O'Malley, P., Bodecker, T., Campbell, J., & Franks, D. (1987, June). *Self-reported changes in sexual behaviors in gay and bisexual men from the San Francisco City Clinic cohort.* Paper presented at the Third International Conference on AIDS, Washington, DC.

Dollard, J., Doob, L. W., Miller, N. E., Mowrer, O. H., & Sears, R. R. (1939). *Frustration and aggression.* New Haven, CT: Yale University Press.

Domjan, M. (1987). Animal learning comes of age. *American Psychologist, 42,* 556–564.

Domjan, M., & Burkhard, B. (1986). *The principles of learning and behavior* (2nd ed.). Pacific Grove, CA: Brooks/Cole.

Donnerstein, E., & Linz, D. (1984, January). Sexual violence in the media: A warning. *Psychology Today,* pp. 14–15.

Donnerstein, E., Linz, D., & Penrod, S. (1987). *The question of pornography.* New York: Free Press.

Doren, D. M. (1987). *Understanding and treating the psychopath.* New York: Wiley.

Dovidio, J. F. (1984). Helping behavior and altruism: An empirical and conceptual overview. *Advances in experimental social psychology 17,* 362–427.

Dowd, M. (1984, March 12). Twenty years after the murder of Kitty Genovese, the question remains: Why? *New York Times,* pp. B1, B4.

Dowrick, P. W., & Jesdale, D. C. (1990). Effets de la retransmission vidéo structurée sur l'émotion: Implications thérapeutiques [Effects on emotion of structured video replay: Implications for therapy]. *Bulletin de Psychologie, 42,* 512–517.

Dryden, W., & Ellis, A. (1987). Rational-Emotive Therapy (RET). In W. Dryden & W. L. Golden (Eds.), *Cognitive-behavioural approaches to psychotherapy* (pp. 129–168). Cambridge, England: Hemisphere.

Dryden, W., & Golden, W. L. (Eds.). (1987). *Cognitive-behavioural approaches to psychotherapy.* Cambridge, England: Hemisphere.

Duara, R., Crady, C., Haxby, J., Sundaram, M., Cutler, N. R., Heston, L., Moore, A., Schlageter, N., Larson, S., & Rapoport, S. I. (1986). Positron emission tomography in Alzheimer's disease. *Neurology, 36,* 879–887.

Duck, S., & Miell, D. (1986). Charting the development of personal relationships. In R. Gilmour & S. Duck (Eds.), *The emerging field of personal relationships* (pp. 133–143). Hillsdale, NJ: Erlbaum.

Dudycha, G. J. (1936). An objective study of punctuality in relation to personality and achievement. *Archives of Psychology, 204,* 1–319.

Duke, M. P., & Nowicki, S., Jr. (1986). *Abnormal psychology: A new look.* New York: Holt, Rinehart and Winston.

Duncan, S., Jr., & Fiske, D. W. (1977). *Face-to-face interaction.* Hillsdale, NJ: Erlbaum.

Duncker, K. (1945). On problem solving. *Psychological Monographs, 58* (Whole No. 270).

Dunn, J., & Shatz, M. (1989). Becoming a conversationalist despite (or because of) having an older sibling. *Child Development, 60,* 399–410.

Dusek, D. E., & Girdano, D. A. (1987). *Drugs: A factual account* (4th ed.). New York: Random House.

Dush, D. M., Hirt, M. L., & Schroeder, H. (1983). Self-statement modification with adults: A meta-analysis. *Psychological Bulletin, 94,* 408–422.

Dwyan, J., & Bowers, K. (1983). The use of hypnosis to enhance recall. *Science, 222,* 184–185.

Dziech, B. W., & Weiner, L. (1984). *The lecherous professor: Sexual harassment.* Boston: Beacon.

Eagly, A. H. (1987). *Sex differences in social behavior: A social-role interpretation.* Hillsdale, NJ: Erlbaum.

Eagly, A. H., & Carli, L. L. (1981). Sex of researchers and sex-typed communications as determinants of sex differences in influencability: A meta-analysis of social influence studies. *Psychological Bulletin, 90,* 1–20.

Eagly, A. H., & Crowley, M. (1986). Gender and helping behavior: A meta-analytic review of the social psychological literature. *Psychological Bulletin, 100,* 283–308.

Eagly, A. H., & Steffen, V. J. (1986). Gender and aggressive behavior: A meta-analytic review of the social psychological literature. *Psychological Bulletin, 100,* 309–330.

Eaves, G., & Rush, A. J. (1984). Cognitive patterns in symptomatic and remitted unipolar depression. *Journal of Abnormal Psychology, 93,* 31–40.

Eckenrode, J. (1984). Impact of chronic and acute stressors on daily reports of mood. *Journal of Personality and Social Psychology, 46,* 907–918.

Egeland, J. A., Gerhard, D. S., Pauls, D. L., Sussex, J. N., Kidd, K. K., Allen, C. R., Hostetter, A. M., & Housman, D. E. (1987). Bipolar affective disorders linked to DNA markers on chromosome 11. *Nature, 325,* 783–787.

Eich, E. (1985). Context, memory, and integrated item/context imagery. *Journal of Experimental Psychology: Learning, Memory, and Cognition, 11,* 764–770.

Eiger, M. S., & Olds, S. W. (1987). *The complete book of breastfeeding* (2nd ed.). New York: Workman.

Eimas, P. D., Siqueland, E. R., Jusczyk, R., & Vigorito, J. (1971). Speech perception in infants. *Science, 171,* 303–306.

Eisenberg, N. (1986). *Altruistic emotion, cognition, and behavior.* Hillsdale, NJ: Erlbaum.

Eisenberg, N. (1987). Book review of C. Zahn-Waxler, E. M. Cummings & R. Iannotti's *Altruism and aggression. Science, 236,* 728.

Eisenberg, N., & Lennon, R. (1983). Sex differences in empathy and related capacities. *Psychological Bulletin, 94,* 100–131.

Eisenberg, N., & Miller, P. A. (1987). The relation of empathy in prosocial and related behaviors. *Psychological Bulletin, 101,* 91–119.

Ekman, P. (1973). Cross-cultural studies of facial expression. In P. Ekman (Ed.), *Darwin and facial expression* (pp. 169–222). New York: Academic Press.

Ekman, P. (1976, Summer). Nonverbal communication/movements with precise meaning. *Journal of Communication, 26,* 13–26.

Ekman, P. (1984). Expression and the nature of emotion. In K. R. Scherer & P. Ekman (Eds.),

Approaches to emotion (pp. 319–343). Hillsdale, NJ: Erlbaum.

Ekman, P., & Friesen, W. V. (1969). The repertoire of nonverbal behavior: Categories, origins, usage, and coding. *Semiotica, 1,* 49–98.

Ekman, P., & Friesen, W. V. (1971). Constants across cultures in the face and emotion. *Journal of Personality and Social Psychology, 17,* 124–129.

Ekman, P., Friesen, W. V., O'Sullivan, M., Chan, A., Diacoyanni-Tarlatzis, I., Heider, K., Krause, R., LeCompte, W. A., Pitcairn, T., Ricci-Bitti, P. E., Scherer, K., Tomita, M., & Tzavaras, A. (1987). Universals and cultural differences in the judgments of facial expressions of emotion. *Journal of Personality and Social Psychology, 53,* 712–717.

Ekman, P., Levenson, R. W., & Friesen, W. V. (1983). Autonomic nervous system activity distinguishes among emotions. *Science, 221,* 1208–1210.

Elkin, I., Parloff, M. B., Hadley, S. W., & Autry, J. H. (1985). NIMH Treatment of Depression Research Program: Background and research plan. *Archives of General Psychiatry, 42,* 305–316.

Elkin, I., Shea, T., Watkins, J. T., Imber, S. D., Sotsky, S. M., Collins, J. F., Glass, D. R., Pilkonis, P. A., Leber, W. R., Docherty, J. P., Fiester, S. J., & Parloff, M. B. (1989). National Institute of Mental Health Treatment of Depression Collaborative Research Program: General effectiveness of treatments. *Archives of General Psychiatry, 46,* 971–982.

Elkind, D. (1981). *The hurried child: Growing up too fast too soon.* Reading, MA: Addison-Wesley.

Ellis, A. (1979). The practice of rational-emotive therapy. In A. Ellis & J. M. Whiteley (Eds.), *Theoretical and empirical foundations of rational-emotive therapy.* Monterey, CA: Brooks/Cole.

Ellis, A. (1986). Rational-Emotive Therapy. In I. L. Kutash & A. Wolf (Eds.), *Psychotherapist's casebook* (pp. 277–287). San Francisco: Jossey-Bass.

Ellis, A., & Harper, R. A. (1975). *A new guide to rational living.* North Hollywood, CA: Wilshire.

Ellis, H. C. (1987). Recent developments in human memory. In V. P. Makosky (Ed.), *The G. Stanley Hall lecture series* (Vol. 7, pp. 161–206). Washington, DC: American Psychological Association.

Emler, N., Renwick, S., & Malone, B. (1983). The relationship between moral reasoning and political orientation. *Journal of Personality and Social Psychology, 45,* 1073–1080.

Emmelkamp, P. M. G., & Kwee, K. G. (1977). Obsessional ruminations: A comparison between thought stopping and prolonged exposure in imagination. *Behavioral Research and Therapy, 15,* 441–444.

Engen, T. (1971). Psychophysics: I. Discrimination and detection. In J. W. Kling & L. A. Riggs (Eds.), *Woodworth & Schlosberg's experimental psychology* (3rd ed., pp. 11–46). New York: Holt, Rinehart and Winston.

Englander-Golden, P., Sonleitner, F. J., Whitmore, M. R., & Corbley, G. J. M. (1986). Social and menstrual cycles: Methodological and substantive findings. In V. L. Olesen & N. F. Woods (Eds.), *Culture, society and menstruation* (pp. 77–96). Washington, DC: Hemisphere.

Engle, R. W., Fidler, D. S., & Reynolds, L. H.

(1981). Does echoic memory develop? *Journal of Experimental Child Psychology, 32,* 459–473.

Enns, C. Z. (1989). Toward teaching inclusive personality theories. *Teaching of Psychology, 16,* 111–117.

Epstein, H. T. (1979). Correlated brain and intelligence development in humans. In M. E. Hahn, C. Jensen, & B. C. Dullek (Eds.), *Development and evolution of brain size: Behavioral implications.* New York: Academic Press.

Epstein, S. (1983). Aggregation and beyond: Some basic issues on the prediction of behavior. *Journal of Personality, 51,* 360–392.

Epstein, S., & O'Brien, E. J. (1985). The person-situation debate in historical and current perspective. *Psychological Bulletin, 98,* 513–537.

Equal Employment Opportunity Commission. (1980). Guidelines on discrimination because of sex. *Federal Register, 45,* 74676–74677.

Erber, J. T. (1982). Memory and age. In T. M. Field, A. Huston, H. C. Quay, L. Troll, & G. E. Finley (Eds.), *Review of human development* (pp. 569–586). New York: Wiley.

Erdelyi, M. H. (1985). *Psychoanalysis: Freud's cognitive psychology.* New York: Freeman.

Erens, P. B. (1987–1988). The stepfather. *Film Quarterly, 41*(2), 48–54.

Ericsson, K. A., & Chase, W. G. (1982). Exceptional memory. *American Scientist, 70,* 607–615.

Ericsson, K. A., Chase, W. G., & Faloon, S. (1980). Acquisition of a memory skill. *Science, 208,* 1181–1182.

Eriksen, C. W., & Schultz, D. W. (1979). Information processing in visual search: A continuous flow conception and experimental results. *Perception & Psychophysics, 25,* 249–263.

Erikson, E. H. (1950). *Childhood and society.* New York: Norton.

Erikson, E. H. (1968). *Identity: Youth and crisis.* New York: Norton.

Erikson, E. H., Erikson, J. M., & Kivnick, H. Q. (1986). *Vital involvement in old age.* New York: Norton.

Erkinjuntti, T., Ketonen, L., Sulkava, R., Sipponen, J., Vuorialho, M., & Iivanainen, M. (1987). Do white matter changes on MRI and CT differentiate vascular dementia from Alzheimer's disease? *Journal of Neurology, Neurosurgery, and Psychiatry, 50,* 37–42.

Eron, L. D., & Huesmann, L. R. (1987). Television as a source of maltreatment of children. *School Psychology Review, 16,* 195–202.

Etaugh, C., & Malstrom, J. (1981). The effect of marital status on person perception. *Journal of Marriage and the Family, 43,* 801–805.

Evans, C. (1983). *Landscapes of the night.* New York: Viking.

Evans, E. F. (1982). Basic physics and psychophysics of sound. In H. B. Barlow & J. D. Mollon (Eds.), *The senses* (pp. 239–250). Cambridge, England: Cambridge University Press.

Evans, F. J., Cook, M. R., Cohen, H. D., Orne, E. C., & Orne, M. T. (1977). Appetitive and replacement naps: EEG and behavior. *Science, 197,* 687–689.

Evans, J. St. B. T. (1983). Introduction. In J. St. B. T. Evans (Ed.), *Thinking and reasoning: Psychological approaches* (pp. 1–15). London: Routledge & Kegan Paul.

Evans, R. I., Rozelle, R. M., Maxwell, S. E., Raines, B. E., Dill, C. A., Guthrie, T. J., Henderson,

A. H., & Hill, P. C. (1981). Social modeling films to deter smoking in adolescents: Results of a three-year field investigation. *Journal of Applied Psychology, 66,* 399–414.

Everly, G. S., Jr. (1989). *A clinical guide to the treatment of the human stress response.* New York: Plenum.

Ewin, D. M. (1986). Hypnosis and pain management. In B. Zilbergelt, M. G. Edelstien, & D. L. Araoz (Eds.), *Hypnosis: Questions and answers* (pp. 282–288). New York: Norton.

Eysenck, H. J. (1952). The effects of psychotherapy: An evaluation. *Journal of Consulting Psychology, 16,* 319–324.

Eysenck, H. J. (1953). *The structure of human personality.* New York: Wiley.

Eysenck, H. J. (1970). *Readings in extraversion-introversion: Bearings on basic psychological processes* (Vol. 3). New York: Wiley.

Eysenck, H. J. (1975). *The inequality of man.* San Diego, CA: EDITS.

Eysenck, H. J., Wakefield, J. A., & Friedman, A. F. (1983). Diagnosis and clinical assessment: The DSM-III. *Annual Review of Psychology, 34,* 167–193.

Faden, R. R., Beauchamp, T. L., & King, N. M. P. (1986). *A history and theory of informed consent.* New York: Oxford University Press.

Fancher, R. E. (1985). *The intelligence men: Makers of the IQ controversy.* New York: Norton.

Fantini, A. E. (1985). *Language acquisition of a bilingual child: A sociolinguistic perspective.* San Diego, CA: College-Hill Press.

Fantz, R. E. (1961). The origin of form perception. *Scientific American, 204*(5), 66–72.

Faraone, S. V., & Tsuang, M. T. (1985). Quantitative models of the genetic transmission of schizophrenia. *Psychological Bulletin, 98,* 41–66.

Farberow, N. L. (1974). *Suicide.* Morristown, NJ: General Learning Press.

Farmer, H. S. (1988). Predicting who our future scientists and mathematicians will be. *Behavioral and Brain Sciences, 11,* 190–191.

Fazio, R. H., Zanna, M. P., & Cooper, J. (1977). Dissonance and self-perception: An integrative view of each theory's proper domain of application. *Journal of Experimental Social Psychology, 13,* 464–479.

Feather, N. T., & Simon, J. G. (1975). Reactions to male and female success and failure in sex-linked occupations: Impressions of personality, causal attributions, and perceived likelihood of different consequences. *Journal of Personality and Social Psychology, 31,* 20–31.

Feder, H. H. (1984). Hormones and sexual behavior. *Annual Review of Psychology, 35,* 165–200.

Feeney, D. M. (1987). Human rights and animal welfare. *American Psychologist, 42,* 593–599.

Feingold, A. (1988a). Cognitive gender differences are disappearing. *American Psychologist, 43,* 95–103.

Feingold, A. (1988b). Matching for attractiveness in romantic partners and same-sex friends: A meta-analysis and theoretical critique. *Psychological Bulletin, 104,* 226–235.

Feist, J. (1990). *Theories of personality* (2nd ed.). Fort Worth: Holt, Rinehart and Winston.

Fenichel, O. (1945). *The psychoanalytic theory of neurosis.* New York: Norton.

Festinger, L. (1957). *A theory of cognitive dissonance.* Stanford, CA: Stanford University Press.

Festinger, L., & Carlsmith, J. M. (1959). Cognitive consequences of forced compliance. *Journal of Abnormal and Social Psychology, 58*, 203–210.

Festinger, L., Schachter, S., & Back, K. (1950). *Social pressures in informal groups: A study of human factors in housing.* New York: Harper.

Feuerstein, M., Labbé, E. E., & Kuczmierczyk, A. R. (1986). *Health psychology.* New York: Plenum.

Fielding, J. (1985a). Smoking: Health effects and control, Part I. *New England Journal of Medicine, 313*, 491–498.

Fielding, J. (1985b). Smoking: Health effects and control, Part II. *New England Journal of Medicine, 313*, 555–561.

Finkelstein, N. W., & Haskins, R. (1983). Kindergarten children prefer same-color peers. *Child Development, 54*, 502–508.

Fiore, M. C., Novotny, T. E., Pierce, J. P., Hatziandreu, E. J., Patel, K. M., & Davis, R. M. (1989). Trends in cigarette smoking in the United States: The changing influence of gender and race. *Journal of the American Medical Association, 261*, 49–55.

Fischer, G. W., & Johnson, E. J. (1986). Behavioral decision theory and political decision making. In R. R. Lau & D. O. Sears (Eds.), *Political cognition* (pp. 55–65). Hillsdale, NJ: Erlbaum.

Fischer, K. W., & Silvern, L. (1985). Stages and individual differences in cognitive development. *Annual Review of Psychology, 36*, 613–648.

Fisher, R. P., & Craik, F. I. M. (1977). Interaction between encoding and retrieval operations in cued recall. *Journal of Experimental Psychology: Human Learning and Memory, 3*, 701–711.

Fisher, S., & Greenberg, R. P. (1977). *The scientific credibility of Freud's theories and therapy.* New York: Basic.

Fisher, S., Raskin, A., & Uhlenhuth, E. H. (1987). *Cocaine: Clinical and biobehavioral aspects.* New York: Oxford University Press.

Fiske, S. T. (1989). *Interdependence and stereotyping: From the laboratory to the Supreme Court (and back).* Paper presented at the American Psychological Association, New Orleans.

Fiske, S. T., Pratto, F., & Pavelchak, M. A. (1983). Citizens' images of nuclear war: Content and consequences. *Journal of Social Issues, 39*, 41–65.

Fiske, S. T., & Taylor, S. E. (1984). *Social cognition.* New York: Random House.

Fiske, S. T., & Taylor, S. E. (1991). *Social cognition* (2nd ed.). New York: Random House.

Fitzpatrick, M. A. (1988). *Between husbands & wives: Communication in marriage.* Beverly Hills, CA: Sage.

Flaherty, C. F. (1985). *Animal learning and cognition.* New York: Knopf.

Flavell, J. H. (1985). *Cognitive development* (2nd ed.). Englewood Cliffs, NJ: Prentice-Hall.

Flavell, J. H., Beach, D. R., & Chinsky, J. M. (1966). Spontaneous verbal rehearsal in a memory task as a function of age. *Child Development, 37*, 283–299.

Flynn, J. (1987). Race and IQ: Jensen's case refuted. In S. Modgil & C. Modgil (Eds.), *Arthur Jensen: Consensus and controversy* (pp. 221–235). New York: Falmer Press.

Fodor, I. G. (1982). Gender and phobia. In I. Al-Issa (Ed.), *Gender and psychopathology* (pp. 179–197). New York: Academic Press.

Fogel, A. (1984). *Infancy: Infant in family and society.* St. Paul, MN: West.

Fogelman, E., & Wiener, V. L. (1985, August). The few, the brave, the noble. *Psychology Today*, pp. 60–65.

Foley, J. M. (1980). Binocular distance perception. *Psychological Review, 87*, 411–434.

Foley, J. M. (1985). Binocular distance perception: Egocentric distance tasks. *Journal of Experimental Psychology: Human Perception and Performance, 11*, 132–149.

Foley, M. A., & Johnson, M. K. (1985). Confusion between memories for performed and imagined actions. *Child Development, 56*, 1145–1155.

Folstein, M., Anthony, J. C., Parhad, I., Duffy, B., & Gruenberg, E. M. (1985). The meaning of cognitive impairment in the elderly. *Journal of the American Geriatrics Society, 33*, 228–235.

Foss, D. J. (1988). Experimental psycholinguistics. *Annual Review of Psychology, 39*, 301–348.

Fösterling, F. (1985). Attributional retraining: A review. *Psychological Bulletin, 98*, 495–512.

Foulkes, D. (1962). Dream reports from different stages of sleep. *Journal of Abnormal and Social Psychology, 65*, 14–25.

Foulkes, D. (1990). Reflective consciousness and dreaming [Review of *Conscious mind, sleeping brain: Perspectives on lucid dreaming*]. *Contemporary Psychology, 35*, 120–121.

Fouts, D. H. (1987, Winter). Signing interactions between mother and infant chimpanzees. *Friends of Washoe, 6*, 4–8.

Fox, L. H., Tobin, D., & Brody, L. (1979). Sex-role socialization and achievement in mathematics. In M. A. Wittig & A. C. Petersen (Eds.), *Sex-related differences in cognitive functioning* (pp. 303–332). New York: Academic Press.

Fox, M., Gibbs, M., & Auerback, D. (1985). Age and gender dimensions of friendship. *Psychology of Women Quarterly, 9*, 489–501.

Frankenburg, W. K., & Dodds, J. B. (1967). The Denver development screening test. *Journal of Pediatrics, 71*, 181–191.

Fredrickson, P. A. (1987). The relevance of sleep disorders medicine to psychiatric practice. *Psychiatric Annals, 17*, 91–100.

Freedman, J. L. (1984). Effect of television violence on aggressiveness. *Psychological Bulletin, 96*, 227–246.

Freedman, J. L. (1986). Television violence and aggression: A rejoinder. *Psychological Bulletin, 100*, 372–378.

Freedman, J. L., & Fraser, S. C. (1966). Compliance without pressure: The foot-in-the-door technique. *Journal of Personality and Social Psychology, 4*, 195–203.

Freedman, R. (1986). *Beauty bound.* Lexington, MA: Heath.

Freedman, R. R., & Sattler, H. L. (1982). Physiological and psychological factors in sleep-onset insomnia. *Journal of Abnormal Psychology, 91*, 380–389.

Freeman, J. (1985). Emotional aspects of giftedness. In J. Freeman (Ed.), *The psychology of gifted children* (pp. 247–264). Chichester, England: Wiley.

French, E. G., & Thomas, F. H. (1958). The relationship of achievement motivation to problem-solving effectiveness. *Journal of Abnormal and Social Psychology, 56*, 45–48.

Frese, F. J., III. (1989). *A psychologist/consumer's view of mental health services.* Paper presented at the Fifth National Mental Health Consumer/Expatient Conference, Columbia, SC.

Freud, S. (1909). Analysis of a phobia in a five-year-old boy. In J. Strachey (Ed. and Trans.), *The standard edition of the complete psychological works of Sigmund Freud.* London: Hogarth Press.

Freud, S. (1953). *The interpretation of dreams.* London: Hogarth Press. (Original work published 1900)

Freud, S. (1963). Civilization and its discontents. In J. Strachey (Ed. and Trans.), *The standard edition of the complete psychological works of Sigmund Freud.* New York: Norton. (Original work published 1930)

Freud, S. (1964). New introductory lectures on psychoanalysis. In J. Strachey (Ed. and Trans.), *The standard edition of the complete psychological works of Sigmund Freud* (Vol. 23). London: Hogarth Press. (Original work published 1933)

Freud, S. (1976). Some physical consequences of the anatomical distinction between the sexes. In J. Strachey (Ed. and Trans.), *The standard edition of the complete psychological works of Sigmund Freud* (Vol. 19). New York: Norton. (Original work published 1925)

Frey, D. L., & Gaertner, S. I. (1986). Helping and the avoidance of inappropriate interracial behavior: A strategy that perpetuates a nonprejudiced self-image. *Journal of Personality and Social Psychology, 50*, 1083–1090.

Frick, R. W. (1988). Issues of representation and limited capacity in the auditory short-term store. *British Journal of Psychology, 79*, 213–240.

Friedman, M., & Rosenman, R. (1974). *Type A behavior pattern and your heart.* New York: Knopf.

Friedman, W. J., Robinson, A. B., & Friedman, B. L. (1987). Sex differences in moral judgments? A test of Gilligan's theory. *Psychology of Women Quarterly, 11*, 21–46.

Friedrich-Cofer, L., & Huston, A. C. (1986). Television violence and aggression: The debate continues. *Psychological Bulletin, 100*, 364–371.

Frieze, I., Whitley, B. E., Jr., Hanusa, B. H., & McHugh, M. C. (1982). Assessing the theoretical models for sex differences in causal attributions for success and failure. *Sex Roles, 8*, 333–343.

Frodi, A., Macaulay, J., & Thome, P. R. (1977). Are women always less aggressive than men? A review of the experimental literature. *Psychological Bulletin, 84*, 634–660.

Fuchs, A., & Binder, M. D. (1983). Fatigue resistance of human extraocular muscles. *Journal of Neurophysiology, 49*, 28–34.

Funder, D. C. (1987). Errors and mistakes: Evaluating the accuracy of social judgment. *Psychological Bulletin, 101*, 75–90.

Gackenbach, J., & LaBerge, S. (Eds.). (1988). *Conscious mind, sleeping brain: Perspectives on lucid dreaming.* New York: Plenum.

Gaddis, A., & Brooks-Gunn, J. (1985). The male experience of pubertal change. *Journal of Youth and Adolescence, 14*, 61–69.

Gaeddert, W. P. (1987). The relationship of gender, gender-related traits, and achievement orientation to achievement attributions: A study of subject-selected accomplishments. *Journal of Personality, 55*, 687–710.

Gaertner, S. L., & Dovidio, J. F. (1986). The aversive form of racism. In J. F. Dovidio & S. L. Gaertner (Eds.), *Prejudice, discrimination, and racism* (pp. 61–89). New York: Academic Press.

Galanter, E. (1962). Contemporary psychophysics. In R. Brown, E. Galanter, E. H. Hess, & G. Mandler (Eds.), *New directions in psychology*. New York: Holt, Rinehart and Winston.

Gallant, D. M. (1987). *Alcoholism*. New York: Norton.

Galvin, R. M. (1982, August). Control of dreams may be possible for a resolute few. *Smithsonian*, pp. 110–117.

Garcia, J. (1984). Evolution of learning mechanisms. In B. L. Hammond (Ed.), *Psychology and learning*. Washington, DC: American Psychological Association.

Garcia, J., & Koelling, R. (1966). Relation of cue to consequence in avoidance learning. *Psychonomic Science, 4*, 123–124.

Garcia, J., McGowan, G. K., & Green, K. F. (1972). Biological constraints on conditioning. In A. H. Black & W. F. Prokasy (Eds.), *Classical conditioning II: Current research and theory*. New York: Appleton-Century-Crofts.

Garcia, J. M., & Montgomery, P. A. (1990). *The Hispanic population in the United States: March 1990*. Washington, DC: U.S. Government Printing Office.

Gardner, B. T., & Gardner, R. A. (1975). Evidence for sentence constituents in the early utterances of child and chimpanzee. *Journal of Experimental Psychology: General, 104*, 244–267.

Gardner, H. (1983). *Frames of mind: The theory of multiple intelligences*. New York: Basic.

Gardner, H. (1985). *The mind's new science: A history of the cognitive revolution*. New York: Basic.

Gardner, H. (1986). The waning of intelligence tests. In R. J. Sternberg & Douglas K. Detterman (Eds.), *What is intelligence?* (pp. 73–76). Norwood, NJ: Ablex.

Gardner, H. (1988, Summer). Multiple intelligences in today's schools. *Human Intelligence Newsletter, 9*(2), 1–2.

Gardner, H. (1988, August). *Scientific psychology: Should we bury it or praise it?* Paper presented at the annual meeting of the American Psychological Association, Atlanta, GA.

Garfield, S. L., & Bergin, A. E. (Eds.). (1986). *Handbook of psychotherapy and behavior change* (3rd ed.). New York: Wiley.

Gärling, T., Böök, A., & Lindberg, E. (1985). Adults' memory representations of the spatial properties of their everyday physical environment. In R. Cohen (Ed.), *The development of spatial cognition* (pp. 141–184). Hillsdale, NJ: Erlbaum.

Garnham, A. (1985). *Psycholinguistics: Central topics*. London: Methuen.

Garrity, T. F., & Marx, M. B. (1979). Critical life events and coronary disease. In W. D. Gentry & R. B. Williams (Eds.), *Psychological aspects of myocardial infarction and coronary care* (2nd ed., pp. 31–49). St. Louis, MO: Mosby.

Garvey, C. (1984). *Children's talk*. Cambridge, MA: Harvard University Press.

Gaskell, J. (1985). Course enrollment in the high school: The perspective of working-class girls. *Sociology of Education, 58*, 48–59.

Gazzaniga, M. S. (1983). Right hemisphere language following brain bisection. *American Psychologist, 38*, 525–537.

Gazzaniga, M. S. (1986). Introduction. In G. Lynch (Ed.), *Synapses, circuits, and the beginnings of memory* (pp. vii–x). Cambridge, MA: Bradford.

Gazzaniga, M. S., & LeDoux, J. E. (1978). *The integrated mind*. New York: Plenum.

Geen, R. (1984). Human motivation: New perspectives on old problems. In A. M. Rogers & C. J. Scheirer (Eds.), *The G. Stanley Hall lecture series* (Vol. 4, pp. 5–57). Washington, DC: American Psychological Association.

Geffen, G., & Quinn, K. (1984). Hemispheric specialization and ear advantages in processing speech. *Psychological Bulletin, 96*, 273–291.

Geiselman, R. E., Fisher, R. P., MacKinnon, D. P., & Holland, H. L. (1985). Eyewitness memory enhancement in the police interview: Cognitive retrieval mnemonics versus hypnosis. *Journal of Applied Psychology, 70*, 401–412.

Geiwitz, J., & Moursund, J. (1979). *Approaches to personality: An introduction to people*. Monterey, CA: Brooks/Cole.

Geller, J. D. (1988). Racial bias in the evaluation of patients for psychotherapy. In L. Comas-Díaz & E. Griffith (Eds.), *Clinical guidelines in cross-cultural mental health* (pp. 112–134). New York: Wiley.

Gelman, R. (1969). Conservation acquisition: A problem of learning to attend to relevant attributes. *Journal of Experimental Child Psychology, 7*, 67–87.

Gelman, R. (1979). Preschool thought. *American Psychologist, 34*, 900–905.

Gelman, R. (1983). Recent trends in cognitive development. In C. J. Scheirer & A. M. Rogers (Eds.), *The G. Stanley Hall lecture series* (Vol. 3, pp. 141–175). Washington, DC: American Psychological Association.

Gentry, W. D. (1985). Relationship of anger-coping styles and blood pressure among Black Americans. In M. Chesney & R. H. Rosenman (Eds.), *Anger and hostility in cardiovascular and behavioral disorders* (pp. 139–147). Washington, DC: Hemisphere.

George, L. K. (1988). Social participation in later life: Black-white differences. In J. S. Jackson (Ed.), *The black American elderly: Research on physical and psychosocial health* (pp. 99–126). New York: Springer.

Gerbner, G., Gross, L., Signorielli, N., & Morgan, M. (1986). *Television's mean world: Violence profile no. 14–15*. Philadelphia: University of Pennsylvania, Annenberg School of Communications.

Gergen, M. M. (1988, September). Building a feminist methodology. *Contemporary Social Psychology, 13*(2), 47–53.

Gerson, M. J. (1986). The prospect of parenthood for women and men. *Psychology of Women Quarterly, 10*, 49–62.

Gescheider, G. A. (1985). *Psychophysics: Method and theory*. Hillsdale, NJ: Erlbaum.

Geschwind, N. (1985). Brain disease and the mechanisms of mind. In C. W. Coen (Ed.), *Functions of the brain* (pp. 160–180). Oxford, England: Clarendon.

Gesteland, R. C. (1978). The neural code: Integrative neural mechanisms. In E. C. Carterette & M. P. Friedman (Eds.), *Handbook of perception* (Vol. 6A). New York: Academic Press.

Giambra, L. M. (1982). Daydreaming: A black-white comparison for 17–34-year-olds. *Journal of Personality and Social Psychology, 42*, 1146–1156.

Gibbs, N. R. (1988, June 27). The sweet smell of success? *Time*, p. 54.

Gibson, E. J. (1969). *Principles of perceptual learning and development*. Englewood Cliffs, NJ: Prentice-Hall.

Gibson, E. J. (1988). Exploratory behavior in the development of perceiving, acting, and the acquiring of knowledge. *Annual Review of Psychology, 39*, 1–41.

Gibson, E. J., & Spelke, E. S. (1983). The development of perception. In P. H. Mussen (Ed.), *Handbook of child psychology* (Vol. III, pp. 1–76). New York: Wiley.

Gibson, E. J., & Walk, R. D. (1960). The "visual cliff." *Scientific American, 202*(4), 64–71.

Gibson, J. J. (1959). Perception as a function of stimulation. In S. Koch (Ed.), *Psychology: A study of a science* (Vol. 1). New York: McGraw-Hill.

Gibson, J. J. (1962). Observations on active touch. *Psychological Review, 69*, 477–491.

Gibson, J. J. (1979). *The ecological approach to visual perception*. Boston: Houghton Mifflin.

Giesen, C. B., & Datan, N. (1980). The competent older woman. In N. Datan & N. Lohman (Eds.), *Transitions of aging* (pp. 57–72). New York: Academic Press.

Gigy, L. L. (1980). Self-concept of single women. *Psychology of Women Quarterly, 5*, 321–340.

Gilbert, D. T., & Jones, E. E. (1986). Perceiver-induced constraint: Interpretations of self-generated reality. *Journal of Personality and Social Psychology, 50*, 269–280.

Gilhooly, K. J. (1982). *Thinking: Directed, undirected, and creative*. London: Academic Press.

Gillam, B. (1980). Geometric illusions. *Scientific American, 242*, 102–111.

Gilligan, C. (1982). *In a different voice*. Cambridge, MA: Harvard University Press.

Gilliland, B. E., James, R. K., Roberts, G. T., & Bowman, J. T. (1984). *Theories and strategies in counseling and psychotherapy*. Englewood Cliffs, NJ: Prentice-Hall.

Ginsburg, H. P., & Koslowski, B. (1976). Cognitive development. *Annual Review of Psychology, 27*, 29–61.

Ginsburg, H. P., & Opper, S. (1988). *Piaget's theory of intellectual development* (3rd ed.). Englewood Cliffs, NJ: Prentice-Hall.

Gjerde, P. F. (1983). Attentional capacity dysfunction and arousal in schizophrenia. *Psychological Bulletin, 93*, 57–72.

Glenn, E. N., & Feldberg, R. L. (1989). Clerical work: The female occupation. In J. Freeman (Ed.), *Women: A feminist perspective* (4th ed., pp. 287–311). Mountain View, CA: Mayfield.

Glick, P., Zion, C., & Nelson, C. (1988). What mediates sex discrimination in hiring decisions? *Journal of Personality and Social Psychology, 55*, 178–186.

Gogel, W. C. (1977). The metric of visual space. In W. Epstein (Ed.), *Stability and constancy in visual perception: Mechanisms and processes*. New York: Wiley.

Goldberg, M. E., & Bruce, C. J. (1986). The role of the arcuate frontal eye fields in the generation of saccadic eye movements. In H. J. Freund, U. Buttner, B. Cohen, & J. Noth (Eds.), *Progress in brain research* (Vol. 64, pp. 143–174). Amsterdam: Elsevier.

Goldberger, L. (1983). The concept and mechanisms of denial: A selective overview. In S. Berznitz (Ed.), *The denial of stress* (pp. 83–95). New York: International Universities Press.

Golden, W. L., & Dryden, W. (1987). Cognitive-behavioural therapies: Commonalities, divergences and future developments. In W. Dryden & W. L. Golden (Eds.), *Cognitive-behavioural approaches to psychotherapy* (pp. 356–378). Cambridge, England: Hemisphere.

Goldman, H. H. (1982). Mental illness and family burden: A public health perspective. *Hospital and Community Psychiatry, 33*, 557–560.

Goldsmith, H. H., Buss, A. H., Plomin, R., Rothbart, M. K., Thomas, A., Chess, S., Hinde, R. A., & McCall, R. B. (1987). Roundtable: What is temperament? Four approaches. *Child Development, 58*, 505–529.

Goldstein, A. P., & Krasner, L. (1987). *Modern applied psychology.* New York: Pergamon.

Goldstein, E. B. (1989). *Sensation and perception* (3rd ed.). Belmont, CA: Wadsworth.

Goldstein, J. H. (1989). Beliefs about human aggression. In J. Groebel & R. A. Hinde (Eds.), *Aggression and war: Their biological and social bases* (pp. 10–24). Cambridge, England: Cambridge University Press.

Goldstein, M. (1984). *Family factors that antedate the onset of schizophrenia and related disorders: The results of a fifteen-year prospective longitudinal study.* Paper presented at the Regional Symposium of the World Psychiatric Association Meeting, Helsinki, Finland.

Golub, S. (1983). Menarche: The beginning of menstrual life. In S. Golub (Ed.), *Lifting the curse of menstruation* (pp. 17–36). New York: Haworth Press.

Gonzales, H. M., Davis, J. M., Loney, G. L., Lokens, C. K., & Junghans, C. M. (1983). Interactional approach to interpersonal attraction. *Journal of Personality and Social Psychology, 44*, 1192–1197.

Gordon, W. C. (1989). *Learning and memory.* Pacific Grove, CA: Brooks/Cole.

Gorenstein, E. E. (1984). Debating mental illness: Implications for science, medicine, and social policy. *American Psychologist, 39*, 50–56.

Gorman, C. (1989, January 23). Honestly, can we trust you? *Time*, p. 44.

Gorman, J. M. (1987). Generalized anxiety disorders. In D. F. Klein (Ed.), *Modern problems of pharmacopsychiatry* (Vol. 22, pp. 127–140). Basel, Switzerland: Karger.

Gottesman, I. I., & Shields, J. (1982). *Schizophrenia: The epigenetic puzzle.* Cambridge, England: Cambridge University Press.

Gould, B. B., Moon, S., & Van Hoorn, J. (Eds.). (1986). *Growing up scared? The psychological effect of the nuclear threat on children.* Berkeley, CA: Open Books.

Gould, J. L., & Marler, P. (1987). Learning by instinct. *Scientific American, 256*(1), 74–85.

Gould, R. L. (1978). *Transformations: Growth and change in adult life.* New York: Simon & Schuster.

Gove, W. R. (1980). Mental illness and psychiatric treatment among women. *Psychology of Women Quarterly, 4*, 345–362.

Graef, R., Csikszentmihalyi, M., & Gianinno, S. M. (1983). Measuring intrinsic motivation in everyday life. *Leisure Studies, 2*, 155–168.

Graham, J. A., & Heywood, S. (1975). The effects of elimination of hand gestures and verbal coding on speech performance. *European Journal of Social Psychology, 5*, 189–195.

Green, B. F., & Hall, J. A. (1984). Quantitative methods for literature reviews. *Annual Review of Psychology, 35*, 37–53.

Green, D. G., & Powers, M. K. (1982). Mechanisms of light adaptation in rat retina. *Vision Research, 22*, 209–216.

Green, D. M. (1976). *An introduction to hearing.* Hillsdale, NJ: Erlbaum.

Greene, E. (1985). Form light, form bright. . . . *Neuropsychology Foundation Monographs, 1*, 2–11.

Greene, J. (1982, September). The gambling trap. *Psychology Today*, pp. 50–55.

Greene, M. G., Hoffman, S., Charon, R., & Adelman, R. (1987). Psychosocial concerns in the medical encounter: A comparison of the interactions of doctors with their old and young patients. *Gerontologist, 27*, 164–168.

Greeno, C. G., & Maccoby, E. E. (1986). How different is the "different voice"? *Signs, 11*, 310–316.

Greeno, J. G. (1977). Process of understanding in problem solving. In J. J. Castellan, Jr., D. B. Pisoni, & G. R. Potts (Eds.), *Cognitive theory* (Vol. 2, pp. 43–84). Hillsdale, NJ: Erlbaum.

Greenwald, A. G., & Pratkanis, A. R. (1984). The self. In R. S. Wyer & T. K. Srull (Eds.), *Handbook of social cognition* (Vol. 3). Hillsdale, NJ: Erlbaum.

Greenwald, D. S., & Zeitlin, S. J. (1987). *No reason to talk about it: Families confront the nuclear taboo.* New York: Norton.

Gregory, R. L. (1987). *The Oxford companion to the mind.* New York: Oxford University Press.

Groebel, J., & Hinde, R. A. (1989a). A multi-level approach to the problems of aggression and war. In J. Groebel & R. A. Hinde (Eds.), *Aggression and war: Their biological and social bases* (pp. 223–229). Cambridge, England: Cambridge University Press.

Groebel, J., & Hinde, R. A. (Eds.). (1989b). *Aggression and war: Their biological and social bases.* Cambridge, England: Cambridge University Press.

Groninger, L. D. (1971). Mnemonic imagery and forgetting. *Psychonomic Science, 23*, 161–163.

Groninger, L. D., & Groninger, L. K. (1984). Autobiographical memories: Their relation to images, definitions, and word recognition. *Journal of Experimental Psychology: Learning, Memory, and Cognition, 10*, 745–755.

Gross, T. F. (1985). *Cognitive development.* Monterey, CA: Brooks/Cole.

Grossman, B., Wirt, R., & Davids, A. (1985). Self-esteem, ethnic identity and behavioral adjustment among Anglo and Chicano adolescents in West Texas. *Journal of Adolescence, 8*, 57–68.

Grossman, F. K. (1987). Separate and together: Men's autonomy and affiliation in the transition to parenthood. In P. W. Berman & F. A. Pedersen (Eds.), *Men's transitions to parenthood: Longitudinal studies of early family experience* (pp. 89–112). Hillsdale, NJ: Erlbaum.

Grossman, H. J. (1983). *Manual on terminology and classification in mental retardation.* Washington, DC: American Association on Mental Deficiency.

Gudjonsson, G. H. (1988). How to defeat the polygraph tests. In A. Gale (Ed.), *The polygraph test* (pp. 126–136). London: Sage.

Guilford, J. P. (1959). *Personality.* New York: McGraw-Hill.

Guilford, J. P. (1967). *The nature of human intelligence.* New York: McGraw-Hill.

Guilford, J. P. (1985). The structure-of-intellect model. In B. B. Wolman (Ed.), *Handbook of intelligence: Theories, measurements, and applications* (pp. 225–266). New York: Wiley.

Gunter, B. (1986). *Television and sex role stereotyping.* London: John Libbey.

Gurtman, M. B. (1986). Depression and the response of others: Reevaluating the reevaluation. *Journal of Abnormal Psychology, 95*, 99–101.

Guthrie, R. V. (1976). *Even the rat was white: A historical view of psychology.* New York: Harper & Row.

Guttentag, M., & Bray, H. (1977). Teachers as mediators of sex-role standards. In A. G. Sargent (Ed.), *Beyond sex roles* (pp. 395–411). St. Paul, MN: West.

Haber, R. N. (1983). The impending demise of the icon: A critique of the concept of iconic storage in visual information processing. *The Behavioral and Brain Sciences, 6*, 1–11.

Haber, R. N. (1985a) Perception: A one-hundred year perspective. In S. Koch & D. E. Leary (Eds.), *A century of psychology as science* (pp. 250–281). New York: McGraw-Hill.

Haber, R. N. (1985b). An icon can have no worth in the real world: Comments on Loftus, Johnson, and Shimamura's "How much is an icon worth?" *Journal of Experimental Psychology: Human Perception and Performance, 11*, 374–378.

Hagen, M. A. (1985). James J. Gibson's ecological approach to visual perception. In S. Koch & D. E. Leary (Eds.), *A century of psychology as science* (pp. 231–249). New York: McGraw-Hill.

Hakuta, K. (1986). *Mirror of language: The debate on bilingualism.* New York: Basic.

Hakuta, K. (1987). The second-language learner in the context of the study of language acquisition. In P. Homel, M. Palij, & D. Aaronson (Eds.), *Childhood bilingualism: Aspects of linguistic, cognitive, and social development* (pp. 31–55). Hillsdale, NJ: Erlbaum.

Hall, C. S., Domhoff, W., Blick, K. A., & Weesner, K. E. (1982). The dreams of college men and women in 1950 and 1980: A comparison of dream contents and sex differences. *Sleep, 5*, 188–194.

Hall, J. A. (1984). *Nonverbal sex differences: Communication accuracy and expressive style.* Baltimore: Johns Hopkins University Press.

Hall, J. A., Rosenthal, R., Archer, D., DiMatteo, M. R., & Rogers, P. L. (1978, May). Decoding wordless messages. *Human Nature*, pp. 68–75.

Hall, N. R., & Goldstein, A. L. (1986, March/April). Thinking well: The chemical links between emotions and health. *The Sciences*, pp. 34–40.

Hall, N. R. S. (1988). The virology of AIDS. *American Psychologist, 43*, 907–913.

Hall, W. G., & Oppenheim, R. W. (1987). Development. *Annual Review of Psychology, 38*, 91–128.

Hallett, P. E. (1986). Eye movements. In K. R. Boff, L. Kaufman, & J. P. Thomas (Eds.), *Handbook of perception and human performance* (Vol. 1, pp. 10-1–10-112).

Halpern, D. F. (1986). *Sex differences in cognitive abilities.* Hillsdale, NJ: Erlbaum.

Halpern, D. F. (1989). *Thought and knowledge: An introduction to critical thinking* (2nd ed.). Hillsdale, NJ: Erlbaum.

Halpin, J. A., Puff, C. R., Mason, H. F., & Marston, S. P. (1984). Self-reference and incidental recall by children. *Bulletin of the Psychonomic Society, 22,* 87–89.

Hamilton, D. L. (1979). A cognitive-attributional analysis of stereotyping. In L. Berkowitz (Ed.), *Advances in experimental social psychology* (Vol. 12, pp. 53–84). New York: Academic Press.

Hamilton, D. L. (1981). Illusory correlation as a basis for stereotyping. In D. L. Hamilton (Ed.), *Cognitive processes in stereotyping and intergroup behavior* (pp. 115–144). Hillsdale, NJ: Erlbaum.

Hamilton, M. C. (1991). *Preference for sons or daughters and the sex role characteristics of the potential parents.* Paper presented at the meeting of the Association for Women in Psychology, Hartford, CT.

Hamilton, M. K., Gelwick, B. P., & Meade, C. J. (1984). Differential diagnosis: Bulimia, anorexia nervosa, and obesity. In R. C. Wakins, II, W. J. Fremouw, & P. F. Clement (Eds.), *The binge-purge syndrome* (pp. 1–26). New York: Springer.

Hammen, C. L. (1982). Gender and depression. In I. Al-Issa (Ed.), *Gender and psychopathology* (pp. 133–152). New York: Academic Press.

Haney, C., Banks, C., & Zimbardo, P. (1973). Interpersonal dynamics in a simulated prison. *International Journal of Criminology and Penology, 1,* 69–97.

Hannay, H. J. (1986). Some issues and concerns in neuropsychological research. An introduction. In H. J. Hannay (Ed.), *Experimental techniques in human neuropsychology* (pp. 3–14). New York: Oxford University Press.

Härnqvist, K. (1968). Relative changes in intelligence from 13 to 18. *Scandinavian Journal of Psychology, 9,* 50–82.

Harris, B. (1979). Whatever happened to little Albert? *American Psychologist, 34,* 151–160.

Harris, E. L., Noyes, R., Crowe R. R., & Chaudhry, D. R. (1983). Family study of agoraphobia: Report of a pilot study. *Archives of General Psychiatry, 40,* 1061–1064.

Harris, G., Begg, I., & Upfold, D. (1980). On the role of the speaker's expectations in interpersonal communication. *Journal of Verbal Learning and Verbal Behavior, 19,* 597–607.

Harris, J. E. (1980). Memory aids people use: Two interview studies. *Memory & Cognition, 8,* 31–38.

Harris, J. E. (1984). Remembering to do things: A forgotten topic. In J. E. Harris & P. E. Morris (Eds.), *Everyday memory, actions and absent-mindedness* (pp. 71–92). London: Academic Press.

Harris, M., & Coltheart, M. (1986). *Language and processing in children and adults.* London: Routledge & Kegan Paul.

Harris, R. E., Langrod, J., Hebert, J. R., Lowinson, J., Zang, E., & Wynder, E. L. (1990). Changes in AIDS risk behavior among intravenous drug abusers in New York City. *New York State Journal of Medicine, 90,* 123–126.

Hart, J. T. (1965). Memory and the feeling-of-knowing experience. *Journal of Educational Psychology, 56,* 208–216.

Hartman, B. J. (1982). An exploratory study of the effects of disco music on the auditory and vestibular systems. *Journal of Auditory Research, 22,* 271–274.

Hartmann, E. (1981, April). The strangest sleep disorder. *Psychology Today,* pp. 14–18.

Hartup, W. W. (1983). Peer relations. In P. H. Mussen (Ed.), *Handbook of child psychology* (Vol. 4, pp. 103–196). New York: Wiley.

Harvey, P. D. (1985). Reality monitoring in mania and schizophrenia. *Journal of Nervous and Mental Disorders, 173,* 67–73.

Harvey, S. M. (1987). Female sexual behavior: Fluctuations during the menstrual cycle. *Journal of Psychosomatic Research, 31,* 101–110.

Hasher, L., & Zacks, R. T. (1979). Automatic and effortful processes in memory. *Journal of Experimental Psychology: General, 108,* 356–388.

Hasher, L., & Zacks, R. T. (1984). Automatic processing of fundamental information: The case of frequency of occurrence. *American Psychologist, 39,* 1372–1388.

Haskins, R. (1985). Public aggression among children with varying day care experience. *Child Development, 56,* 689–703.

Hatfield, E. (1988). Passionate and companionate love. In R. J. Sternberg & M. L. Barnes (Eds.), *The psychology of love* (pp. 191–217). New Haven, CT: Yale University Press.

Hatfield, E., & Sprecher, S. (1986). *Mirror, mirror . . . The importance of looks in everyday life.* Albany: State University of New York Press.

Hatfield, E., Traupmann, J., & Sprecher, S. (1984). Older women's perceptions of their intimate relationships. *Journal of Social and Clinical Psychology, 2,* 108–124.

Haugeland, J. (1985). *Artificial intelligence: The very idea.* Cambridge, MA: MIT Press.

Hayes, C. (1951). *The ape in our house.* New York: Harper & Row.

Hayes, C. D. (Ed.). (1987). *Risking the future* (Vol. 1). Washington, DC: National Academy Press.

Haynes, D. M. (1982). Course and conduct of normal pregnancy. In D. N. Danforth (Ed.), *Obstetrics and gynecology.* Philadelphia: Harper & Row.

Haynes, S. N. (1983). Behavioral assessment. In M. Hersen, A. E. Kazdin, & A. S. Bellack (Eds.), *The clinical psychology handbook* (pp. 397–425). New York: Pergamon.

Haynes, S., & Feinleib, M. (1980). Women, work, and coronary heart disease: Prospective findings from the Framingham heart study. *American Journal of Public Health, 70,* 133–141.

Hayslip, B., Jr., & Panek, P. E. (1989). *Adult development and aging.* New York: Harper & Row.

Hazelrigg, M. D., Cooper, H. M., & Borduin, C. M. (1987). Evaluating the effectiveness of family therapies: An integrative review and analysis. *Psychological Bulletin, 101,* 428–442.

Hearnshaw, L. S. (1987). *The shaping of modern psychology.* London: Routledge & Kegan Paul.

Hearst, E. (1979). One hundred years: Themes and perspectives. In E. Hearst (Ed.), *The first century of experimental psychology* (pp. 1–38). Hillsdale, NJ: Erlbaum.

Heath, L., Kruttschnitt, C., & Ward, D. (1986). Television and violent criminal behavior: Beyond the Bobo doll. *Victims and Violence, 1,* 177–190.

Heckhausen, H., Schmalt, H. D., & Schneider, K. (1985). *Achievement motivation in perspective.* Orlando, FL: Academic Press.

Heider, E. R. (1972). Universals in color naming and memory. *Journal of Experimental Psychology, 93,* 10–20.

Heilman, K. M., & Valenstein, E. (1985). Introduction. In K. M. Heilman & E. Valenstein (Eds.), *Clinical neuropsychology* (2nd ed., pp. 3–16). New York: Oxford.

Heitler, S. M. (1990). *From conflict to resolution.* New York: Norton.

Heller, M. A. (1984). Active and passive touch: The influence of exploration time on form recognition. *Journal of General Psychology, 110,* 243–249.

Henderson, N. D. (1982). Human behavior genetics. *Annual Review of Psychology, 33,* 403–440.

Hendin, H., Haas, A. P., Singer, P., Ellner, M., & Ulman, R. (1987). *Living high.* New York: Human Sciences.

Hendrick, C., & Hendrick, S. S. (1983). *Liking, loving and relating.* Pacific Grove, CA: Brooks/Cole.

Hendrick, S. S., Hendrick, C., & Adler, N. L. (1988). Romantic relationships: Love, satisfaction, and staying together. *Journal of Personality and Social Psychology, 54,* 980–988.

Henker, F. O. (1981). Male climacteric. In J. G. Howells (Ed.), *Modern perspectives in the psychiatry of middle age.* New York: Brunner/Mazel.

Henley, N. M. (1989). Molehill or mountain? What we know and don't know about sex bias in language. In M. Crawford & M. Gentry (Eds.), *Gender and thought: Psychological perspectives* (pp. 59–78). New York: Springer-Verlag.

Hennessey, B. A., & Amabile, T. M. (1984, April). *The effect of reward and task label on children's verbal creativity.* Paper presented at the meeting of the Eastern Psychological Association, Baltimore.

Hennessey, B. A., & Amabile, T. M. (1988). The conditions of creativity. In R. J. Sternberg (Ed.), *The nature of creativity* (pp. 11–38). Cambridge: Cambridge University Press.

Herek, G. M., & Glunt, E. K. (1988). An epidemic of stigma: Public reactions to AIDS. *American Psychologist, 43,* 886–891.

Hergenhahn, B. R. (1988). *An introduction to theories of learning* (3rd ed.). Englewood Cliffs, NJ: Prentice Hall.

Hernandez, C., Hang, M., & Wagner, N. (1976). *Chicanos: Sociological and psychological perspectives.* St. Louis, MO: Mosby.

Herrmann, D. J. (1991). *Super memory.* Emmaus, PA: Rodale Press.

Herrnstein, R. J. (1984). Objects, categories, and discriminative stimuli. In H. L. Roitblat, T. G. Bever, & H. S. Terrace (Eds.), *Animal cognition* (pp. 233–261). Hillsdale, NJ: Erlbaum.

Herrnstein, R. J., Loveland, D. H., & Cable, D. (1976). Natural concepts in pigeons. *Journal of Experimental Psychology: Animal Behavior Processes, 2,* 285–302.

Hersen, M. (1986). *Pharmacological and behavioral treatment: An integrative approach.* New York: Wiley.

Hess, B., Markson, E. W., & Stein, P. J. (1988). Racial and ethnic minorities: An overview. In P. S. Rothenberg (Ed.), *Racism and sexism* (pp. 88–98). New York: St. Martin's Press.

Hetherington, E. M., & Parke, R. D. (1986). *Child psychology* (3rd ed.). New York: McGraw-Hill.

Heuer, F., & Reisberg, D. (1990). Vivid memories of emotional events: The accuracy of remembered minutiae. *Memory & Cognition, 18,* 496–506.

Hibscher, J. A., & Herman, C. P. (1977). Obesity, dieting, and the expression of "obese" characteristics. *Journal of Comparative and Physiological Psychology, 91*, 374–380.

Hicks, R. A., & Guista, M. (1982). The energy levels of habitual long and short sleepers. *Bulletin of the Psychonomic Society, 19*, 131–132.

Higgins, E. T., & Bargh, J. A. (1987). Social cognition and social perception. *Annual Review of Psychology, 38*, 369–425.

Higgins, S. T., & Morris, E. K. (1984). Generality of free-operant avoidance conditioning to human behavior. *Psychological Bulletin, 96*, 247–272.

Hilberman, E. (1978). The impact of rape. In M. T. Notman & C. C. Nadelson (Eds.), *The woman patient* (Vol. 1, pp. 303–322). New York: Plenum.

Hilgard, E. R. (1965). *Hypnotic susceptibility.* New York: Harcourt, Brace, Jovanovich.

Hilgard, E. R. (1980). Consciousness in contemporary psychology. *Annual Review of Psychology, 31*, 1–26.

Hilgard, E. R. (1986). *Divided consciousness: Multiple controls in human thought and action* (expanded ed.). New York: Wiley.

Hilgard, E. R. (1987). *Psychology in America: A historical survey.* San Diego: Harcourt Brace Jovanovich.

Hilgard, E. R., Morgan, A. H., & Macdonald, H. (1975). Pain and dissociation in the cold pressor test: A study of hypnotic analgesia with "hidden reports" through automatic key-pressing and automatic talking. *Journal of Abnormal Psychology, 84*, 280–289.

Hill, R. D., Evankovich, K. D., Sheikh, J. I., & Yesavage, J. A. (1987). Imagery mnemonic training in a patient with primary degenerative dementia. *Psychology and Aging, 2*, 204–205.

Hinsley, D., Hayes, J. R., & Simon, H. A. (1977). From words to equations: Meaning and representation in algebra word-problems. In P. Carpenter & M. Just (Eds.), *Cognitive processes in comprehension* (pp. 89–108). Hillsdale, NJ: Erlbaum.

Hirschfeld, R. M. A., & Davidson, L. (1988). Risk factors for suicide. In A. J. Frances & R. E. Hales (Eds.), *Review of psychiatry* (Vol. 7). Washington, DC: American Psychiatric Press.

Hirst, W., Spelke, E., Reaves, C. C., Caharack, G., & Neisser, U. (1980). Dividing attention without alternation or automaticity. *Journal of Experimental Psychology: General, 109*, 98–117.

The HIV challenge continues. (1991, February). *Center for Disease Control HIV/AIDS Prevention*, pp. 1–3, 5.

Ho, M. K. (1987). *Family therapy with ethnic minorities.* Newbury Park, CA: Sage.

Hobfoll, S. E. (1988). *The ecology of stress.* New York: Hemisphere.

Hobson, J. A. (1988). *The dreaming brain.* New York: Basic.

Hobson, J. A., & McCarley, R. W. (1977). The brain as a dream state generator: An activation-synthesis hypothesis of the dream process. *American Journal of Psychiatry, 134*, 1335–1348.

Hoch, C., & Reynolds, C. (1986). Sleep disturbances and what to do about them. *Geriatric Nursing, 7*, 24–27.

Hochberg, J. (1988). Visual perception. In R. C. Atkinson, R. J. Herrnstein, G. Lindzey, & R. D. Luce (Eds.), *Stevens' handbook of experimental psychology* (2nd ed., pp. 195–276). New York: Wiley.

Hochschild, A. R. (1973). *The unexpected community.* Englewood Cliffs, NJ: Prentice-Hall.

Hochschild, A. R. (1983). *The managed heart.* Berkeley: University of California Press.

Hoffman, M. L. (1981). The development of empathy. In J. P. Rushton & R. M. Sorrentino (Eds.), *Altruism and helping behavior. Social, personality, and developmental perspectives* (pp. 41–63). Hillsdale, NJ: Erlbaum.

Hogarth, R. (1987). *Judgement and choice* (2nd ed.). Chichester, England: Wiley.

Hogg, J. A., & Deffenbacher, J. L. (1988). A comparison of cognitive and interpersonal-process group therapies in the treatment of depression among college students. *Journal of Counseling Psychology, 35*, 304–310.

Holden, C. (1985). A guarded endorsement for shock therapy. *Science, 228*, 1510–1511.

Hollon, S. D., DeRubeis, R. J., & Evans, M. D. (1987). Causal mediation of change in treatment for depression: Discriminating between nonspecificity and noncausality. *Psychological Bulletin, 102*, 139–149.

Holmes, D. S. (1984a). Meditation and somatic arousal reduction: A review of the experimental evidence. *American Psychologist, 39*, 1–10.

Holmes, D. S. (1984b). Defense mechanisms. In R. Corsini (Ed.), *Encyclopedia of psychology* (Vol. 1, pp. 347–350). New York: Wiley.

Holmes, T. H., & Masuda, M. (1974). Life change and illness susceptibility. In B. S. Dohrenwend & B. P. Dohrenwend (Eds.), *Stressful life events: Their nature and effects* (pp. 45–72). New York: Wiley.

Holmes, T. H., & Rahe, R. H. (1967). The social readjustment rating scale. *Journal of Psychosomatic Research, 11*, 213–218.

Holmes, V. M. (1984). Parsing strategies and discourse context. *Journal of Psycholinguistic Research, 13*, 237–257.

Holtzman, J. M., & Akiyama, H. (1985). What children see: The aged on television in Japan and the United States, *Journal of Gerontology, 25*, 62–68.

Honer, W. G., Geiwirtz, G., & Turey, M. (1987, August 22). Psychosis and violence in cocaine smokers. *Lancet, 8556*, p. 451.

Hood, D. C., & Finkelstein, M. A. (1986). Sensitivity to light. In K. R. Boff, L. Kaufman, & M. P. Thomas (Eds.), *Handbook of perception and human performance* (pp. 5-1–5-66). New York: Wiley.

Hopson, J. L. (1986, June). The unraveling of insomnia. *Psychology Today*, pp. 42–45, 48–49.

Horn, J. L., & Cattell, R. B. (1967). Age differences in fluid and crystallized intelligence. *Acta Psychologica, 26*, 107–129.

Horn, J. L., & Knapp, J. R. (1973). On the subjective character of the empirical base of Guilford's structure-of-intellect model. *Psychological Bulletin, 80*, 33–43.

Horne, J. A. (1988). *Why we sleep: The function of sleep in humans and other mammals.* Oxford, England: Oxford University Press.

Horne, J. A., & Ostberg, O. (1976). A self-assessment questionnaire to determine morningness-eveningness in human circadian rhythms. *International Journal of Chronobiology, 4*, 97–110.

Horner, M. S. (1968). *Sex differences in achievement motivation and performance in competitive and non-competitive situations.* Unpublished doctoral dissertation, University of Michigan.

Horner, M. S. (1972). Toward an understanding of achievement-related conflicts in women. *Journal of Social Issues, 28*, 157–175.

Horney, K. (1945). *Our inner conflicts.* New York: Norton.

Horney, K. (1967). The flight from womanhood. In H. Kelman (Ed.), *Feminine psychology* (pp. 54–70). New York: Norton. (Original work published 1926)

Horowitz, F. D., & O'Brien, M. (1986). Gifted and talented children: State of knowledge and directions for research. *American Psychologist, 41*, 1147–1152.

Horowitz, F. D., & O'Brien, M. (1989a). In the interest of the nation: A reflective essay on the state of our knowledge and the challenges before us. *American Psychologist, 44*, 441–445.

Horowitz, F. D., & O'Brien, M. (Eds.). (1989b). Children and their development: Knowledge base, research agenda, and social policy application [Special issue]. *American Psychologist, 44*(2).

Horowitz, M. J. (1983). Psychological response to serious life events. In S. Breznitz (Ed.), *The denial of stress.* New York: International Universities Press.

Horowitz, M. J., Wilner, N., Kaltreidr, N., & Alvarez, W. (1980). Signs and symptoms of post-traumatic stress disorder. *Archives of General Psychiatry, 37*, 85–92.

Hostetler, A. J. (1988, April). Exploring the 'gatekeeper' of memory. *APA Monitor*, p. 3.

House, J. S., Landis, K. R., & Umberson, D. (1988). Social relationships and health. *Science, 241*, 540–545.

Hoving, K. L., Spencer, T., Robb, K., & Schulte, D. (1978). Developmental changes in visual information processing. In P. A. Ornstein (Ed.), *Memory development in children* (pp. 21–68). Hillsdale, NJ: Erlbaum.

Hovland, C. I., & Weiss, W. (1951). The influence of source credibility on communication effectiveness. *Public Opinion Quarterly, 15*, 635–650.

Howard, A., Pion, G. M., Gottfredson, G. D., Flattau, P. E., Oskamp, S., Pfafflin, S. M., Bray, D. W., & Burstein, A. G. (1986). The changing face of American psychology. *American Psychologist, 41*, 1311–1327.

Howard, D. (1986). Dynamics of feminist therapy. In D. Howard (Ed.), *The dynamics of feminist therapy* (pp. 1–4). New York: Haworth Press.

Howes, C., & Olenick, M. (1986). Family and child care influences on toddlers' compliance. *Child Development, 57*, 202–216.

Howes, M. J., Hokanson, J. E., & Loewenstein, D. A. (1985). Induction of depressive affect after prolonged exposure to a mildly depressed individual. *Journal of Personality and Social Psychology, 49*, 1110–1113.

Hubbell, S. (1988, May 16). Annals of husbandry: The sweet bees. *New Yorker*, pp. 75–94.

Hubel, D. H. (1979, September). The brain. *Scientific American, 242*, 38–47.

Hubel, D. H., & Wiesel, T. N. (1965). Receptive fields of single neurons in two nonstriate visual areas (18 and 19) of the cat. *Journal of Neurophysiology, 28*, 229–289.

Hubel, D. H., & Wiesel, T. N. (1979, March). Brain mechanisms and vision. *Scientific American, 241*, 150–162.

Huber, V. L., Neale, M. A., & Northcraft, G. B. (1987). Decision bias and personnel selection strategies. *Organizational Behavior and Human Decision Processes, 40*, 136–147.

Huesmann, L. R., & Eron, L. D. (Eds.). (1986). *Television and the aggressive child: A cross-national comparison.* Hillsdale, NJ: Erlbaum.

Huesmann, L. R., Eron, L. D., Klein, R., Brice, P., & Fischer, P. (1983). Mitigating the imitation of aggressive behaviors by changing children's attitudes about media violence. *Journal of Personality and Social Psychology, 44*, 899–910.

Hulicka, I. M. (1982). Memory functioning in late adulthood. In F. I. M. Craik & S. Trehub (Eds.), *Aging and cognitive processes* (pp. 331–351). New York: Plenum.

Hull, J. G., & Bond, C. F. (1986). Social and behavioral consequences of alcohol consumption and expectancy: A meta-analysis. *Psychological Bulletin, 99*, 347–360.

Hunter College Women's Studies Collective. (1983). *Women's realities, women's choices.* New York: Oxford University Press.

Hurvich, L. M. (1981). *Color vision.* Sunderland, MA: Sinauer.

Huttenlocher, J., & Goodman, J. (1987). The time to identify spoken words. In A. Allport, D. MacKay, W. Prinz, & E. Scheerer (Eds.), *Language perception and production* (pp. 431–444). London: Academic Press.

Huyck, M. H., & Duchon, J. (1986). Over the miles: Coping, communicating, and commiserating through age-theme greeting cards. In L. Nahemow, K. A. McCluskey-Fawcett, & P. E. McGhee (Eds.), *Humor and aging* (pp. 139–159). Orlando, FL: Academic Press.

Hyde, J. S. (1986a). Introduction: Meta-analysis and the psychology of gender. In J. S. Hyde & M. C. Linn (Eds.), *The psychology of gender: Advances through meta-analysis* (pp. 1–13). Baltimore: Johns Hopkins University Press.

Hyde, J. S. (1986b). Gender differences in aggression. In J. S. Hyde & M. C. Linn (Eds.), *The psychology of gender: Advances through meta-analysis* (pp. 51–66). Baltimore: Johns Hopkins University Press.

Hyde, J. S. (1990). *Understanding human sexuality* (4th ed.). New York: McGraw-Hill.

Hyde, J. S., Fennema, E., & Lamon, S. J. (1990). Gender differences in mathematics performance: A meta-analysis. *Psychological Bulletin, 107*, 139–155.

Hyde, J. S., & Linn, M. C. (1988). Gender differences in verbal ability: A meta-analysis. *Psychological Bulletin, 104*, 53–69.

Iacono, W. G. (1988). Psychotherapy for psychopaths? [Review of *Understanding and treating the psychopath*]. *Contemporary Psychology, 33*, 116–117.

Imperato, P. J., & Mitchell, G. (1986). Cigarette smoking: A "chosen" risk. *New York State Journal of Medicine, 86*, 485–489.

Intelligence and its measurement: A symposium. (1921). *Journal of Educational Psychology, 12*, 123–147, 195–216, 271–275.

Intons-Peterson, M. J. (1988). *Children's concepts of gender.* Norwood, NJ: Ablex.

Intons-Peterson, M. J., & Fournier, J. (1986). External and internal memory aids: When and how often do we use them? *Journal of Experimental Psychology: General, 115*, 267–280.

Intons-Peterson, M. J., & Reddel, M. (1984). What do people ask about a neonate? *Developmental Psychology, 20*, 358–359.

Iosub, S., Bamji, M., Stone, R. K., Gromisch, D. S., & Wasserman, E. (1987). More on human immune deficiency virus embryopathy. *Pediatrics, 80*, 512–516.

Isen, A. M. (1987). Positive affect, cognitive processes, and social behavior. *Advances in Experimental Social Psychology, 20*, 203–253.

Isen, A. M., & Daubman, K. A. (1984). The influence of affect on categorization. *Journal of Personality and Social Psychology, 47*, 1206–1217.

Isen, A. M., Daubman, K. A., & Gorgoglione, J. M. (1987). The influence of positive affect on cognitive organization: Implications for education. In R. E. Snow & M. J. Farr (Eds.), *Aptitude, learning, and instruction* (Vol. 3, pp. 143–164). Hillsdale, NJ: Erlbaum.

Isen, A. M., Daubman, K. A., & Nowicki, G. P. (1987). *Journal of Personality and Social Psychology, 52*, 1122–1131.

Isen, A. M., Johnson, M. M. S., Mertz, E., & Robinson, G. F. (1985). The influence of positive affect on the unusualness of word associations. *Journal of Personality and Social Psychology, 48*, 1413–1426.

Isen, A. M., & Simonds, S. F. (1978). The effect of feeling good on a helping task that is incompatible with good mood. *Social Psychology, 41*, 346–349.

Itzin, C. (1986). Media images of women: The social construction of ageism and sexism. In S. Wilkinson (Ed.), *Feminist social psychology* (pp. 119–134). Milton Keynes, England: Open University Press.

Izard, C. E. (1989). The structure and functions of emotions: Implications for cognition, motivation, and personality. In I. S. Cohen (Ed.), *The G. Stanley Hall lecture series* (Vol. 9, pp. 37–73). Washington, DC: American Psychological Association.

Izard, C. E., Hembree, E. A., Dougherty, L. M., & Spizzirri, C. C. (1983). Changes in facial expressions of 2- and 19-month-old infants following acute pain. *Developmental Psychology, 19*, 418–426.

Jack, D. (1987a). Silencing the self: The power of social imperatives in female depression. In R. Formanek & A. Gurian (Eds.), *Women and depression: A lifespan perspective* (pp. 161–181). New York: Springer.

Jack, D. (1987b). Self-in-relation theory. In R. Formanek & A. Gurian (Eds.), *Women and depression: A lifespan perspective* (pp. 41–45). New York: Springer.

Jack, D. C. (1988, August). *Combining the strengths of qualitative with quantitative research methods.* Paper presented at the American Psychological Association, Atlanta, GA.

Jacklin, C. N. (1989). Female and male: Issues of gender. *American Psychologist, 44*, 127–133.

Jackson, J. J. (1985). Race, national origin, ethnicity, and aging. In R. Binstock & E. Shanas (Eds.), *Handbook of aging and the social sciences* (pp. 264–303). New York: Van Nostrand Reinhold.

Jackson, N. E., & Butterfield, E. C. (1986). A conception of giftedness designed to promote research. In R. J. Sternberg & J. E. Davidson (Eds.), *Conceptions of giftedness* (pp. 151–181). New York: Cambridge University Press.

Jacobs, S. (1985). Language. In M. L. Knapp & G. R. Miller (Eds.), *Handbook of interpersonal communication* (pp. 313–343). Beverly Hills, CA: Sage.

Jacobson, H. G. (1988). Positive emission tomography—A new approach to brain chemistry. *Journal of the American Medical Association, 260*, 2704–2715.

Jacobson, N. S., & Anderson, E. A. (1982). Interpersonal skill and depression in college students: An analysis of the timing of self-disclosures. *Behavior Therapy, 13*, 271–282.

Jacobson, S. W. (1987, September 1). Between two worlds. *Rochester Times-Union,* pp. 1C, 4C.

Jafek, B. W., Esses, B. A., & Moran, D. T. (1988, January). When your patient says, "I can't smell anything." *Journal of Respiratory Diseases,* pp. 79–88.

James, W. (1890). *The principles of psychology.* New York: Henry Holt.

James, W. (1892). *Psychology: The briefer course.* New York: Henry Holt.

Janicak, P. G., Davis, J. M., Gibbons, R. D., Eriksen, S., Chang, S., & Gallagher, P. (1985). Efficacy of ECT: A meta-analysis. *American Journal of Psychiatry, 142*, 297–302.

Janis, I. L. (1982). *Groupthink: Psychological studies of policy decisions and fiascoes.* Boston: Houghton Mifflin.

Janis, I. L. (1989). *Crucial decisions: Leadership in policymaking and crisis management.* New York: Free Press.

Janoff-Bulman, R., & Timko, C. (1987). Coping with traumatic life events: The role of denial in light of people's assumptive worlds. In C. R. Snyder & C. E. Ford (Eds.), *Coping with negative life events* (pp. 135–159). New York: Plenum.

Janowsky, D. S. (1986). Psychopharmacologic therapy. In I. L. Kutash & A. Wolf (Eds.), *Psychotherapist's casebook* (pp. 312–331). San Francisco: Jossey-Bass.

Jeffery, R. W. (1989). Risk behaviors and health: Contrasting individual and population perspectives. *American Psychologist, 44*, 1194–1202.

Jemmott, J. B., Borysenko, M., McClelland, D. C., Chapman, R., Meyer, D., & Benson, H. (1983). Academic stress, power motivation, and decrease in salivary secretory immunoglobulin: A secretion rate. *Lancet,* pp. 1400–1402.

Jemmott, J. B., & Locke, S. E. (1984). Psychosocial factors, immunologic mediation, and human susceptibility to infectious diseases: How much do we know? *Psychological Bulletin, 95*, 52–77.

Jenkins, J. J. (1974). Remember that old theory of memory? Well, forget it. *American Psychologist, 29*, 785–795.

Jensen, A. R. (1969). How much can we boost IQ and scholastic achievement? *Harvard Educational Review, 39*, 1–123.

Johansson, G. (1975). Visual motion perception. *Scientific American, 232*, 76–88.

Johansson, G. (1985). About visual event perception. In W. H. Warren, Jr., & R. W. Shaw (Eds.), *Persistence and change: Proceedings of the First International Conference on Event Perception* (pp. 29–54). Hillsdale, NJ: Erlbaum.

Johansson, G., von Hofsten, C., & Jansson, G. (1980). Event perception. *Annual Review of Psychology, 31*, 27–63.

Johnson, B. T., & Eagly, A. H. (1989). Effects of involvement on persuasion: A meta-analysis.

Psychological Bulletin, 106, 290–314.

Johnson, C. M., Bradley-Johnson, S., McCarthy, R., & Jamie, M. (1984). Token reinforcement during WISC-R administration. *Applied Research on Mental Retardation, 5,* 43–52.

Johnson, J. S., & Newport, E. L. (1989). Critical period effects in second language learning: The influence of maturational state on the acquisition of English as a second language. *Cognitive Psychology, 21,* 60–99.

Johnson, M. H., & Magaro, P. A. (1987). Effects of mood and severity on memory processes in depression and mania. *Psychological Bulletin, 101,* 28–40.

Johnson, M. K., & Foley, M. A. (1984). Differentiating fact from fantasy: The reliability of children's memory. *Journal of Social Issues, 40,* 33–50.

Johnson, M. K., & Hasher, L. (1987). Human learning and memory. *Annual Review of Psychology, 38,* 631–668.

Johnson, M. K., Kahan, T. L., & Raye, C. L. (1984). Dreams and reality monitoring. *Journal of Experimental Psychology: General, 113,* 329–344.

Johnson, M. K., & Raye, C. L. (1981). Reality monitoring. *Psychological Review, 88,* 67–85.

Johnson-Laird, P. N., & Wason, P. C. (1977). Introduction to conceptual thinking. In P. N. Johnson-Laird & P. C. Wason (Eds.), *Thinking: Readings in cognitive science.* Cambridge, England: Cambridge University Press.

Johnston, L. D., O'Malley, P. M., & Bachman, J. G. (1988). Illicit drug use, smoking, and drinking by American high school students, college students, and young adults. Rockville, MD: National Institute on Drug Abuse.

Johnston, W. A., & Dark, V. J. (1986). Selective attention. *Annual Review of Psychology, 37,* 43–75.

Jonas, H. S., & Etzel, S. I. (1988). Graduate medical education. *Journal of the American Medical Association, 260,* 1063–1071.

Jones, B. E., Gray, B. A., & Parson, E. B. (1981). Manic-depressive illness among poor urban Blacks. *American Journal of Psychiatry, 138,* 654–657.

Jones, J. M. (1986). Racism: A cultural analysis of the problem. In J. F. Dovidio & S. L. Gaertner (Eds.), *Prejudice, discrimination, and racism* (pp. 279–314). Orlando, FL: Academic Press.

Jones, L. V. (1983, November). *White-black achievement differences: The narrowing gap.* Invited address presented at the meeting of the Federation of Behavioral, Psychological, and Cognitive Sciences, Washington, DC.

Jordan, N. (1989, June). Spare the rod, spare the child. *Psychology Today,* p. 16.

Joy, L. A., Kimball, M. M., & Zabrack, M. L. (1986). Television and children's aggressive behavior. In T. M. Williams (Ed.), *The impact of television: A natural experiment in three communities* (pp. 303–360). Orlando, FL: Academic Press.

Judd, C. M., & Park, B. (1988). Out-group homogeneity: Judgments of variability at the individual and group levels. *Journal of Personality and Social Psychology, 54,* 778–788.

Jung, C. G. (1953). On the psychology of the unconscious. In H. Read, M. Fordham, & G. Adler (Eds.), *Collected works of C. G. Jung* (Vol. 7). Princeton, NJ: Princeton University Press. (Original work published 1917)

Jussim, L. (1986). Self-fulfilling prophecies: A theoretical and integrative review. *Psychological Review, 93,* 429–445.

Just, M. A., & Carpenter, P. A. (1985). Cognitive coordinate systems: Accounts of mental rotation and individual differences in spatial ability. *Psychological Review, 92,* 137–172.

Kaas, J. H. (1987). The organization of neocortex in mammals: Implications for theories of brain function. *Annual Review of Psychology, 38,* 129–151.

Kagan, J. (1989). Temperamental contributions to social behavior. *American Psychologist, 44,* 668–674.

Kahana, E., & Kiyak, H. (1984). Attitudes and behavior of staff in facilities for the aged. *Research on Aging, 6,* 395–416.

Kahneman, D., & Tversky, A. (1972). Subjective probability: A judgment of representativeness. *Cognitive Psychology, 3,* 430–454.

Kahneman, D., & Tversky, A. (1973). On the psychology of prediction. *Psychological Review, 80,* 237–251.

Kahneman, D., & Tversky, A. (1984). Choices, values, and frames. *American Psychologist, 39,* 341–350.

Kail, R. V., Jr. (1984). *The development of memory in children* (2nd ed.). New York: Freeman.

Kail, R. V., Jr., & Pellegrino, J. W. (1985). *Human intelligence: Perspectives and prospects.* New York: Freeman.

Kaiser, S. B., & Chandler, J. L. (1988). Audience responses to appearance codes: Old-age imagery in the media. *The Gerontologist, 28,* 692–699.

Kalat, J. W. (1988). *Biological psychology* (3rd ed.). Belmont, CA: Wadsworth.

Kamerow, D. B., Pincus, H. A., & Macdonald, D. I. (1986). Alcohol abuse, other drug abuse, and mental disorders in medical practice. *Journal of the American Medical Association, 225,* 2054–2057.

Kamin, L. J. (1969). Predictability, surprise, attention, and conditioning. In B. Campbell & R. Church (Eds.), *Punishment and aversive behavior* (pp. 279–298). New York: Appleton-Century-Crofts.

Kanin, E. J. (1985). Date rapists: Differential sexual socialization and relative deprivation. *Archives of Sexual Behavior, 14,* 129–231.

Kanner, A. D., Coyne, J. C., Schaefer, C., & Lazarus, R. S. (1981). Comparison of two modes of stress measurement: Daily hassles and uplifts versus major life events. *Journal of Behavioral Medicine, 4,* 1–39.

Kantowitz, B. (1987, February 16). Kids and contraceptives. *Newsweek,* pp. 54–65.

Kaplan, R. M. (1982). Nadar's raid on the testing industry: Is it in the best interest of the consumer? *American Psychologist, 37,* 15–23.

Kaplan, R. M. (1985). The controversy related to the use of psychological tests. In B. B. Wolman (Ed.), *Handbook of intelligence* (pp. 465–504). New York: Wiley.

Katz, P. A., & Boswell, S. (1986). Flexibility and traditionality in children's gender roles. *Genetic, Social, and General Psychology Monographs, 112,* 103–147.

Katz, P. A., & Taylor, D. A. (1988a). Introduction. In P. A. Katz & D. A. Taylor (Eds.), *Eliminating racism: Profiles in controversy* (pp. 1–16). New York: Plenum.

Katz, P. A., & Taylor, D. A. (Eds.). (1988b). *Eliminating racism: Profiles in controversy.* New York: Plenum.

Katz, S., & Mazur, M. A. (1979). *Understanding the rape victim.* New York: Wiley.

Katzman, R. (1986). Alzheimer's disease. *New England Journal of Medicine, 314,* 964–973.

Katzman, R. (1987). Alzheimer's disease: Advances and opportunities. *Journal of the American Geriatrics Society, 35,* 69–73.

Kaufert, P. A. (1986). Menstruation and menstrual change: Women in midlife. In V. L. Olesen & N. F. Woods (Eds.), *Culture, society and menstruation* (pp. 63–77). Washington, DC: Hemisphere.

Kaufman, D. R. (1989). Professional women: How real are the recent gains? In J. Freeman (Ed.), *Women: A feminist perspective* (4th ed., pp. 329–346). Mountain View, CA: Mayfield.

Kazdin, A. E. (1982). The token economy: A decade later. *Journal of Applied Behavior Analysis, 15,* 431–445.

Keen, S. (1986). *Faces of the enemy: Reflections of the hostile imagination.* San Francisco: Harper & Row.

Keesey, R. E., & Powley, T. L. (1986). The regulation of body weight. *Annual Review of Psychology, 37,* 109–133.

Keith-Spiegel, P., & Koocher, G. P. (1985). *Ethics in psychology.* Hillsdale, NJ: Erlbaum.

Kelley, H. H. (1967). Attribution theory in social psychology. In D. Levine (Ed.), *Nebraska Symposium on Motivation* (pp. 192–238). Lincoln: University of Nebraska Press.

Kelley, H. H. (1986). Toward a taxonomy of interpersonal conflict processes. In S. Oskamp & S. Spacapan (Eds.), *Interpersonal processes* (pp. 122–147). Newbury Park, CA: Sage.

Kellner, R. (1985). Functional somatic symptoms and hypochondriasis: A survey of empirical studies. *Archives of General Psychiatry, 42,* 821–833.

Kelly, J. A., & St. Lawrence, J. S. (1988). *The AIDS health crisis.* New York: Plenum.

Kelly, M. H., Bock, J. K., & Keil, F. C. (1986). Prototypicality in a linguistic context: Effects on sentence structure. *Journal of Memory and Language, 25,* 59–74.

Kendler, K. S., & Robinette, C. D. (1983). Schizophrenia in the National Academy of Sciences—National Research Council twin registry: A 16-year update. *American Journal of Psychiatry, 140,* 1551–1563.

Kenrick, D. T., & Funder, D. C. (1988). Profiting from controversy: Lessons from the person-situation debate. *American Psychologist, 43,* 23–34.

Kent, D. (1990, May). A conversation with Claude Steele. *APS Observer,* pp. 11–17.

Kessler, R. C., Price, R. H., & Wortman, C. B. (1985) Social factors in psychopathology: Stress, social support and coping processes. *Annual Review of Psychology, 36,* 531–572.

Kiang, N. Y., & Peake, W. T. (1988). Physics and physiology of hearing. In R. C. Atkinson, R. J. Herrnstein, G. Lindzey, & R. D. Luce (Eds.), *Stevens' handbook of experimental psychology* (2nd ed., Vol. I, pp. 277–326). New York: Wiley.

Kidder, L. H., & Judd, C. M. (1986). *Research methods in social relations* (5th ed.). New York: Holt, Rinehart and Winston.

Kiernat, J. M. (1984). Retrospection as a life span

concept. *Physical & Occupational Therapy in Geriatrics, 3,* 35–48.

Kiesler, C. A., & Sibulkin, A. E. (1987). *Mental hospitalization: Myths and facts about a national crisis.* Newbury Park, CA: Sage.

Kihlstrom, J. F. (1985). Hypnosis. *Annual Review of Psychology, 36,* 385–418.

Kimball, J. P. (1973). Seven principles of surface structure parsing in natural language. *Cognition, 2,* 15–47.

Kimball, M. M. (1989). A new perspective on women's math achievement. *Psychological Bulletin, 105,* 198–214.

Kimble, D. P. (1988). *Biological psychology.* New York: Holt, Rinehart and Wisnton.

King, N. J., Hamilton, D. I., & Ollendick, T. H. (1988). *Children's phobias: A behavioural perspective.* Chichester, England: Wiley.

King, P. A. (1985). Formal reasoning in adults: A review and critique. In R. A. Mines & K. S. Kitchener (Eds.), *Adult cognitive development* (pp. 1–21). New York: Praeger.

Kirkley, B. G., Schneider, J. A., Agras, W. S., & Bachman, J. A. (1985). Comparison of two group treatments for bulimia. *Journal of Consulting and Clinical Psychology, 53,* 43–48.

Kite, M. E., & Johnson, B. T. (1988). Attitudes toward older and younger adults: A meta-analysis. *Psychology and Aging, 3,* 233–244.

Kitzinger, C. (1987). *The social construction of lesbianism.* London: Sage.

Klein, S. B., & Kihlstrom, J. F. (1986). Elaboration, organization, and the self-reference effect in memory. *Journal of Experimental Psychology: General, 115,* 26–38.

Kleinke, C. L. (1984). Two models for conceptualizing the attitude-behavior relationship. *Human Relations, 37,* 333–350.

Kleinmuntz, B. (1975). *Personality measurement: An introduction.* Huntington, NY: Krieger.

Kleinmuntz, B., & Szucko, J. J. (1984, March 29). A field study of the fallibility of polygraphic lie detection. *Nature,* pp. 449–450.

Klerman, G. L. (1983). The efficacy of psychotherapy as the basis for public policy. *American Psychologist, 38,* 929–934.

Kline, D. W., & Schieber, F. (1981). What are the age differences in visual sensory memory? *Journal of Gerontology, 36,* 86–89.

Klinger, E. (1987, October). The power of daydreams. *Psychology Today,* pp. 36–44.

Kluft, R. P. (1987). An update on multiple personality disorder. *Hospital and Community Psychiatry, 38,* 363–373.

Knapp, M. L., & Miller, G. R. (Eds.). (1985). *Handbook of interpersonal communication.* Beverly Hills, CA: Sage.

Knox, V. J., Gekoski, W. L., & Johnson, E. A. (1986). Contact with and perceptions of the elderly. *The Gerontologist, 26,* 309–313.

Kohlberg, L. (1964). The development of moral character and moral ideology. In M. Hoffman & L. Hoffman (Eds.), *Review of child development research* (Vol. 1). New York: Russell Sage Foundation.

Kohlberg, L. (1966). A cognitive-developmental analysis of children's sex-role concepts and attitudes. In E. E. Maccoby (Ed.), *The development of sex differences* (pp. 82–173). Stanford, CA: Stanford University Press.

Kohlberg, L. (1969). Stage and sequence: The cognitive-developmental approach to socializa-

tion. In D. A. Goslin (Ed.), *Handbook of socialization theory and research.* Chicago: Rand McNally.

Kohlberg, L. (1984). Essays on moral development: Vol. 2: *The psychology of moral development.* San Francisco: Freeman.

Kohlberg, L., & Ullian, D. Z. (1974). Stages in the development of psychosexual concepts and attitudes. In R. C. Friedman, R. M. Richart, & R. I. Van de Wiele (Eds.), *Sex differences in behavior* (pp. 209–222). New York: Wiley.

Kohn, A. (1988, April). You know what they say. . . . *Psychology Today,* pp. 36–41.

Kohout, J. (1990). *Personal communication from Office of Demographic, Employment and Educational Research, American Psychological Association.*

Kokotovic, A., & Tracey, T. (1990). Working alliance in the early phase of counseling. *Journal of Counseling Psychology, 37,* 16–21.

Kolb, B., & Whishaw, I. Q. (1985). *Fundamentals of human neuropsychology* (2nd ed.). New York: Freeman.

Korchin, S. J., & Schuldberg, D. (1981). The future of clinical assessment. *American Psychologist, 10,* 1147–1158.

Koretz, J. F., & Handelman, G. H. (1988). How the human eye focuses. *Scientific American, 259*(1), 92–99.

Koss, M. P., & Oros, C. J. (1982). Sexual experiences survey: A research instrument investigating sexual aggression and victimization. *Journal of Consulting and Clinical Psychology, 50,* 455–457.

Kosslyn, S. M. (1975). Information representation in visual images. *Cognitive Psychology, 7,* 341–370.

Kosslyn, S. M. (1980). *Image and mind.* Cambridge, MA: Harvard University Press.

Kosslyn, S. M. (1983). *Ghosts in the mind's machine: Creating and using images in the brain.* New York: Norton.

Krantz, D. S., Grunberg, N. E., & Baum, A. (1985). Health psychology. *Annual Review of Psychology, 36,* 349–383.

Kraut, A. M. (1990). Healers and strangers: Immigrant attitudes toward the physician in America—a relationship in historical perspective. *Journal of the American Medical Association. 263,* 1807–1811.

Kravetz, D. (1987). Benefits of consciousness-raising groups for women. In C. M. Brody (Ed.), *Women's therapy groups: Paradigms of feminist treatment* (pp. 55–66). New York: Springer.

Kreipe, R. E., Churchill, B. H., & Strauss, J. (1989). Long-term outcome of adolescents with anorexia nervosa. *American Journal of Diseases of Children, 143,* 1322–1327.

Kroll, N. E. A., Schepeler, E. M., & Angin, K. T. (1986). Bizarre imagery: The misremembered mnemonic. *Journal of Experimental Psychology: Learning, Memory, and Cognition, 12,* 42–53.

Kryter, K. D. (1985). *The effects of noise on man* (2nd ed.). Orlando, FL: Academic Press.

Kübler-Ross, E. (1969). *On death and dying* (2nd ed.). New York: Macmillan.

Kuehnel, J. M., & Liberman, R. P. (1986). Behavior modification. In I. L. Kutash & A. Wolf (Eds.), *Psychotherapist's casebook* (pp. 240–262). San Francisco: Jossey-Bass.

Kuhn, D. (1984). Cognitive development. In M. H. Bornstein & M. E. Lamb (Eds.), *Developmental

psychology: An advanced textbook* (pp. 133–180). Hillsdale, NJ: Erlbaum.

Kunzendorf, R., Brown, C., & McKee, D. (1983). Hypnotizability: Correlations with daydreaming and sleeping. *Psychological Reports, 53,* 406.

Kurdek, L. A., & Schmitt, J. P. (1986). Relationship quality of partners in heterosexual married, heterosexual cohabiting, and gay and lesbian relationships. *Journal of Personality and Social Psychology, 51,* 711–720.

Kutash, I. L., & Wolf, A. (Eds.). (1986). *Psychotherapist's casebook.* San Francisco: Jossey-Bass.

Kutash, S. B. (1976). Modified psychoanalytic therapies. In B. B. Wolman (Ed.), *The therapist's handbook: Treatment methods of mental disorders.* New York: Van Nostrand Reinhold.

Lachman, J. L., & Lachman, R. (1980). Age and the actualization of world knowledge. In L. W. Poon, J. L. Fozard, L. S. Cermak, D. Arenberg, & L. W. Thompson (Eds.), *New directions in memory and aging* (pp. 285–312). Hillsdale, NJ: Erlbaum.

Lachman, R., Lachman, J. L., & Butterfield, E. C. (1979). *Cognitive psychology and information processing: An introduction.* Hillsdale, NJ: Erlbaum.

Ladd, G. W., & Mize, J. (1983). A cognitive-social learning model of social-skill training. *Psychological Review, 90,* 127–137.

LaFromboise, T. D. (1988). American Indian mental health policy. *American Psychologist, 43,* 388–397.

Laird, J. D. (1984). Facial response and emotion. *Journal of Personality and Social Psychology, 47,* 909–917.

Lamb, M. E. (1987). Introduction: The emergent American father. In M. E. Lamb (Ed.), *The father's role: Cross-cultural perspectives* (pp. 3–25). Hillsdale, NJ: Erlbaum.

Lamb, M. E., & Bornstein, M. H. (1987). *Development in infancy: An introduction* (2nd ed.). New York: Random House.

Lambert, M. J., Shapiro, D. A., & Bergin, A. E. (1986). The effectiveness of psychotherapy. In S. L. Garfield & A. E. Bergin (Eds.), *Handbook of psychotherapy and behavior change* (pp. 157–211). New York: Wiley.

Landers, S. (1988, March). Public interest. *APA Monitor,* (pp. 22–23).

Landers, S. (1990, April). Sex, condom use up among teenage boys. *APA Monitor,* p. 25.

Lange, C. (1887). *Uber Gemutsbewegungen: Eine psycho-physiologische Studie.* Leipzig: Thomas.

Langer, E. J. (1989). *Mindfulness.* Reading, MA: Addison-Wesley.

Langer, E. J., & Rodin, J. (1976). The effects of choice and enhanced personal responsibility for the aged: A field experiment in an institutional setting. *Journal of Personality and Social Psychology, 34,* 191–198.

LaPiere, R. T. (1934). Attitudes vs. actions. *Social Forces, 13,* 230–237.

Lappin, J. S., & Preble, L. D. (1975). A demonstration of shape constancy. *Perception & Psychophysics, 25,* 180–184.

Larson, R., Mannell, R., & Zuzanek, J. (1986). Daily well-being of older adults with friends and family. *Psychology and Aging, 1,* 117–126.

Latané, B., & Darley, J. M. (1970). *The unresponsive bystander: Why doesn't he help?* New York: Appleton.

Latané, B., & Nida, S. (1981). Ten years of research on group size and helping. *Psychological Bulletin, 89,* 308–324.

Lauer, J. C., & Lauer, R. H. (1985, June). Marriages made to last. *Psychology Today,* pp. 22–26.

Lavie, P., & Hobson, J. A. (1986). Origin of dreams: Anticipation of modern theories in the philosophy and physiology of the eighteenth and nineteenth centuries. *Psychological Bulletin, 100,* 229–240.

Lawless, H. T., & Engen, T. (1977). Associations to odors: Interference, memories, and verbal labeling. *Journal of Experimental Psychology: Human Learning and Memory, 3,* 52–59.

Lazarus, A. A., & Fay, A. (1984). Behavior therapy. In T. B. Karasu (Ed.), *The psychiatric therapies* (pp. 483–538). Washington, DC: American Psychiatric Association.

Lazarus, J. H. (1986). *Endocrine and metabolic effects of lithium.* New York. Plenum Press.

Lazarus, R. S. (1984). Puzzles in the study of daily hassles. *Journal of Behavioral Medicine, 7,* 375–389.

Lazarus, R. S., & Folkman, S. (1984). *Stress, appraisal, and coping.* New York: Springer.

Leahey, T. H., & Harris, R. J. (1985). *Human learning.* Englewood Cliffs, NJ: Prentice-Hall.

Lebow, J. (1982). Consumer satisfaction with mental health treatment. *Psychological Bulletin, 91,* 244–259.

Lee, C. (1985). Successful rural black adolescents. A psychological profile. *Adolescence, 77,* 131–141.

Lefcourt, H. M., & Martin, R. A. (1986). *Humor and life stress.* New York: Springer-Verlag.

Leff, J., & Vaughan, C. (1985). *Expressed emotion in families.* New York: Guilford Press.

Lefley, H. P. (1989). Family burden and family stigma in major mental illness. *American Psychologist, 44,* 556–560.

Lender, M. E., & Martin, J. K. (1982). *Drinking in America: A history.* New York: Free Press.

Lennie, P. (1980). Parallel visual pathways: A review. *Vision Review, 20,* 561–594.

Leo, J. (1984, October 8). The ups and downs of creativity. *Time,* p. 76.

Leo, J. (1985, February 18). Salvaging victims of torture. *Time,* p. 86.

Lerman, H. (1986a). From Freud to feminist personality theory: Getting here from there. *Psychology of Women Quarterly, 10,* 1–18.

Lerman, H. (1986b). *A mote in Freud's eye: From psychoanalysis to the psychology of women.* New York: Springer.

Lesgold, A. (1988). Problem solving. In R. J. Sternberg & E. E. Smith (Eds.), *The psychology of human thought.* Cambridge: Cambridge University Press.

Leventhal, H., Glynn, K., & Fleming, R. (1987). Is the smoking decision an "informed choice"? Effects of smoking risk factors on smoking beliefs. *Journal of the American Medical Association, 257,* 3373–3376.

Levin, D., Bertelson, A. D., & Lacks, P. (1984). MMPI differences among mild and severe insomniacs and good sleepers. *Journal of Personality Assessment, 48,* 126–129.

Levine, M. (1988). *Effective problem solving.* Englewood Cliffs, NJ: Prentice-Hall.

Levinson, D. J., Darrow, C. M., Klein, E. B., Levinson, M. H., & McKee, B. (1978). *The seasons of a man's life.* New York: Knopf.

Levy, J. (1983). Language, cognition, and the right hemisphere. *American Psychologist, 38,* 538–541.

Levy, J. (1985, May). Right brain, left brain: Fact and fiction. *Psychology Today,* pp. 38–44.

Lewinsohn, P. H. (1984). A behavioral approach to depression. In R. J. Friedman & M. M. Katz (Eds.), *The psychology of depression: Contemporary theory and research.* Washington, DC: Winston-Wiley.

Lewinsohn, P. M., Biglan, A., & Zeiss, A. M. (1976). Behavioral treatment of depression. In P. O. Davidson (Ed.), *The behavioral management of anxiety, depression and pain.* New York: Brunner/Mazel.

Lewis, C. E., Robins, L., & Rice, J. (1985). Association of alcoholism with antisocial personality in urban men. *Journal of Nervous and Mental Disorders, 173,* 166–174.

Lewis, E. R., Everhart, T. E., & Zeevi, Y. Y. (1969). Study of neural organization in Aplysia with the scanning electron microscope. *Science, 165,* 1140–1143.

Lewis, J. W., Terman, G. W., Shavit, Y., Nelson, L. R., & Liebeskind, J. C. (1984). Neural, neurochemical, and hormonal bases of stress-induced analgesia. In L. Kruger & J. C. Liebeskind (Eds.), *Neural mechanisms of pain* (pp. 277–288). New York: Raven.

Lewis, M. (1985). Older women and health: An overview. In S. Golub & R. J. Freedman (Eds.), *Health needs of women as they age* (pp. 1–16). New York: Haworth Press.

Lewis, M., & Brooks, J. (1978). Self-knowledge in emotional development. In M. Lewis & L. Rosenblum (Eds.), *The development of affect* (pp. 205–226). New York: Plenum.

Liben, L. S., & Signorella, M. L. (Eds.). (1987). *Children's gender schemata.* San Francisco: Jossey-Bass.

Lidke, K. (1988, Spring). Cutting through the fog of silence. *University of Michigan Medical Center Advance,* pp. 2–17.

Liebert, R. M., & Sprafkin, J. (1988). *The early window* (3rd ed.). Elmsford, NY: Pergamon.

Lifton, R. J. (1967). *Death in Life: Survivors of Hiroshima.* New York: Simon & Schuster.

Light, L. L., & Anderson, P. A. (1985). Working-memory capacity, age, and memory for discourse. *Journal of Gerontology, 40,* 737–747.

Lindsay, D. S., & Johnson, M. K. (1987). Reality monitoring and suggestibility. In S. J. Ceci, M. P. Toglia, & D. F. Ross (Eds.), *Children's eyewitness memory* (pp. 92–121). New York: Springer-Verlag.

Lindsey, K. P., & Paul, G. L. (1989). Involuntary commitments to public mental institutions: Issues involving the overrepresentation of blacks and assessment of relevant functioning. *Psychological Bulletin, 106,* 171–183.

Lindskold, S. (1978). Trust development, the GRIT proposal, and the effects of conciliatory acts on conflict and cooperation. *Psychological Bulletin, 85,* 772–793.

Lindskold, S. (1985). GRIT: Reducing distrust through carefully introduced conciliation. In S. Worchel & W. G. Austin (Eds.), *Psychology of intergroup relations* (2nd ed., pp. 305–322). Chicago: Nelson-Hall.

Lindsley, J. R. (1975). Producing simple utterances: How far ahead do we plan? *Cognitive Psychology, 7,* 1–19.

Lindy, J. D. (1988). *Vietnam: A casebook.* New York: Brunner/Mazel.

Linn, M. C. (1986). Meta-analysis of studies of gender differences: Implications and future directions. In J. S. Hyde & M. C. Linn (Eds.), *The psychology of gender: Advances through meta-analysis* (pp. 210–231). Baltimore: Johns Hopkins University Press.

Linn, M. C., & Petersen, A. C. (1986). A meta-analysis of gender differences in spatial ability: Implications for mathematics and science achievement. In J. S. Hyde & M. C. Linn (Eds.), *The psychology of gender: Advances through meta-analysis* (pp. 67–101). Baltimore: Johns Hopkins University Press.

Linn, R. I. (1982). Admissions testing on trial. *American Psychologist, 37,* 279–291.

Linville, P. W. (1982). The complexity-extremity effect and age-based stereotyping. *Journal of Personality and Social Psychology, 42,* 193–211.

Linville P. W., & Jones, E. E. (1980). Polarized appraisals of outgroup members. *Journal of Personality and Social Psychology, 38,* 689–703.

Linville, P. W., Salovey, P., & Fischer, G. W. (1986). Stereotyping and perceived distributions of social characteristics: An application to ingroup-outgroup perception. In J. F. Dovidio & S. L. Gaertner (Eds.), *Prejudice, discrimination, and racism* (pp. 165–208). New York: Academic Press.

Liu, S. S. (1971). Differential conditioning and stimulus generalization of the rabbit's nictitating membrane response. *Journal of Comparative and Physiological Psychology, 77,* 136–142.

Locke, E. A. (Ed.). (1986). *Generalizing from laboratory to field settings.* Lexington, MA: Lexington.

Loehlin, J. C., Willerman, L., & Horn, J. M. (1988). Human behavior genetics. *Annual Review of Psychology, 39,* 101–133.

Loftus, E. F. (1986). Ten years in the life of an expert witness. *Law and Human Behavior, 10,* 241–263.

Loftus, E. F., Fienberg, S. E., & Tanur, J. M. (1985). Cognitive psychology meets the national survey. *American Psychologist, 40,* 175–180.

Loftus, E. F., Miller, D. G., & Burns, H. J. (1978). Semantic integration of verbal information into a visual memory. *Journal of Experimental Psychology, 4,* 19–31.

Loftus, G. R. (1985). On worthwhile icons: Reply to DiLollo and Haber. *Journal of Experimental Psychology: Human Perception and Performance, 11,* 384–388.

Logue, A. W. (1986). *The psychology of eating and drinking.* New York: Freeman.

London, P. (1986). Eclectic psychotherapy gets "uppity" [Review of *Casebook of eclectic psychotherapy*]. *Contemporary Psychology, 33,* 697–698.

Long, G. M. (1980). Iconic memory: A review and critique of the study of short-term visual storage. *Psychological Bulletin, 88,* 785–820.

Long, G. M., & Beaton, R. J. (1982). The case for peripheral persistence: Effects of target and background luminance on a partial-report task. *Journal of Experimental Psychology: Human Perception and Performance, 8,* 383–391.

Long, S. (1988). The six group therapies compared. In S. Long (Ed.), *Six group therapies* (pp. 327–338). New York: Plenum.

Lonky, E., Kaus, C. R., & Roodin, P. A. (1984). Life experience and mode of coping: Relation to moral judgment in adulthood. *Developmental Psychology, 20,* 1159–1167.

López, S. R. (1989). Patient variable biases in clinical judgment: Conceptual overview and methodological considerations. *Psychological Bulletin, 106,* 184–203.

Lorenz, K. (1974). *The eight deadly sins of civilized man.* New York: Harcourt Brace Jovanovich.

Lott, B. (1985). The devaluation of women's competence. *Journal of Social Issues, 41,* 43–60.

Lovelace, E. A., & Marsh, G. R. (1985). Prediction and evaluation of memory performance by young and old adults. *Journal of Gerontology, 40,* 192–197.

Lovelace, E. A., & Twohig, P. (1984, August). *Perceptions of memory function by older adults.* Paper presented at the meeting of the American Psychological Association, Toronto.

Lubin, B., Larsen, R. M., & Matarazzo, J. D. (1984). Patterns of psychological test usage in the United States: 1935–1982. *American Psychologist, 39,* 451–454.

Lubomudrov, S. (1987). Congressional perceptions of the elderly: The use of stereotypes in the legislative process. *The Gerontologist, 27,* 77–81.

Luce, R. D., & Krumhansl, C. L. (1988). Measurement, scaling, and psychophysics. In R. C. Atkinson, R. J. Herrnstein, G. Lindzey, & R. D. Luce (Eds.), *Stevens' handbook of experimental psychology* (2nd ed., pp. 3–74). New York: Wiley.

Luchins, A. S. (1957). Primacy-recency in impression formation. In C. I. Hovland (Ed.), *The order of presentation in persuasion* (pp. 33–61). New Haven, CT: Yale University Press.

Luepnitz, D. A. (1988). *The family interpreted: Feminist theory in clinical practice.* New York: Basic.

Lundin, R. W. (1984). Maslow, Abraham H. In R. J. Corsini (Ed.), *Encyclopedia of psychology* (Vol. 2, pp. 342–343). New York: Wiley.

Lynch, G. (1986). *Synapses, circuits, and the beginnings of memory.* Cambridge, MA: MIT Press.

Lynch, G., & Baudry, M. (1984). The biochemistry of memory: A new and specific hypothesis. *Science, 224,* 1057–1064.

Lyons, W. (1986). *The disappearance of introspection.* Cambridge, MA: MIT Press.

Maccoby, E. E. (1984). Socialization and developmental change. *Child Development, 55,* 317–328.

Maccoby, E. E. (1986). Social groupings in childhood: Their relationship to prosocial and antisocial behavior in boys and girls. In D. Olweus, J. Block, & M. Radke-Yarrow (Eds.), *Development of antisocial and prosocial behavior* (pp. 263–284). Orlando, FL: Academic Press.

Maccoby, E. E. (1990, June). Gender differentiation: Explanatory viewpoints. Paper presented at the convention of American Psychological Society, Dallas, TX.

MacGregor, J. N. (1987). Short-term memory capacity: Limitations or optimization? *Psychological Review, 94,* 107–108.

Mackenzie, B. (1984). Explaining race differences in IQ: The logic, the methodology, and the evidence. *American Psychologist, 39,* 1214–1233.

Maddi, S. R., Barton, P. T., & Puccetti, M. C. (1987). Stressful events are indeed a factor in physical illness: Reply to Schroeder and Costa (1984). *Journal of Personality and Social Psychology, 52,* 833–843.

Maddux, J. E., & Stanley, M. A. (1986). Self-efficacy theory in contemporary psychology: An overview. *Journal of Social and Clinical Psychology, 4,* 249–255.

Mailer, N. (1984). *Tough guys don't dance.* New York: Random House.

Maki, R. H., & Berry, S. L. (1984). Metacomprehension of text material. *Journal of Experimental Psychology: Learning, Memory, and Cognition, 10,* 663–679.

Malamuth, N. M. (1987). Do sexually violent media indirectly contribute to antisocial behavior? In M. R. Roth (Ed.), *The psychology of women: Ongoing debates* (pp. 441–459). New Haven, CT: Yale University Press.

Malamuth, N. M., & Check, J. V. P. (1981). The effects of mass media exposure on acceptance of violence against women: A field experiment. *Journal of Research in Personality, 15,* 436–446.

Malamuth, N. M., & Check, J. V. P. (1984). Debriefing effectiveness following exposure to pornographic rape depictions. *The Journal of Sex Research, 20,* 1–13.

Malamuth, N. M., & Check, J. V. P. (1985). The effects of aggressive pornography on beliefs in rape myths: Individual differences. *Journal of Research in Personality, 19,* 299–320.

Maldonado, D., Jr., & Applewhite-Lozano, S. (1986). *The Hispanic elderly: Empowerment through training.* Arlington, TX: Center for Chicano Aged.

Malgady, R. G., Rogler, L. H., & Costantino, G. (1987). Ethnocultural and linguistic bias in mental health evaluation of Hispanics. *American Psychologist, 42,* 228–234.

Malott, R. W. (1986). Self-management, rule-governed behavior, and everyday life. In H. W. Reese & L. J. Parrott (Eds.), *Behavioral science: philosophical, methodological, and empirical advances* (pp. 207–228). Hillsdale, NJ: Erlbaum.

Malson, M. R. (1983). Black women's sex roles: The social context for a new ideology. *Journal of Social Issues, 39,* 101–114.

Mandersheid, R. W., Witkin, M. J., Rosenstein, M. J., Milazzo-Sayre, L. J., Bethel, H. E., & MacAskill, R. L. (1985). Specialty mental health services: System and patient characteristics—United States. In C. A. Taube & S. A. Barrett (Eds.), *Mental Health, United States, 1985.* Washington, DC: National Institute of Mental Health, U.S. Government Printing Office.

Mansfield, T. S., & Busse, T. V. (1981). *The psychology of creativity and discovery.* Chicago: Nelson-Hall.

Marcus, R. F. (1986). Naturalistic observation of cooperation, helping, and sharing and their associations with empathy and affect. In C. Zahn-Waxler, E. M. Cummings, & R. Iannotti (Eds.), *Altruism and aggression* (pp. 256–279). Cambridge, England: Cambridge University Press.

Margolin, L., & White, L. (1987). The continuing role of physical attractiveness in marriage. *Journal of Marriage and the Family, 49,* 21–27.

Markides, K. S. (1983). Minority aging. In M. W. Riley, B. B. Hess, & K. Bond (Eds.), *Aging in society: Selected reviews of recent research* (pp. 115–137). Hillsdale, NJ: Erlbaum.

Marks, I. M. (1987). *Fears, phobias, and rituals.* New York: Oxford University Press.

Markus, H., & Kunda, Z. (1986). Stability and malleability of the self-concept. *Journal of Personality and Social Psychology, 51,* 858–866.

Markus, H., & Wurf, E. (1987). The dynamic self-concept: A social psychological perspective. *Annual Review of Psychology, 38,* 299–337.

Marshall, G. D., & Zimbardo, P. G. (1979). Affective consequences of inadequately explained physiological arousal. *Journal of Personality and Social Psychology, 37,* 970–988.

Marshall, J. F. (1984). Brain function: Neural adaptations and recovery from injury. *Annual Review of Psychology, 35,* 277–308.

Martin, C. L. (1987). A ratio measure of sex stereotyping. *Journal of Personality and Social Psychology, 52,* 489–499.

Martin, D. W. (1977). *Doing psychology experiments.* Monterey, CA: Brooks/Cole.

Martin, G., & Pear, J. (1983). *Behavior modification: What it is and how to use it.* Englewood Cliffs, NJ: Prentice-Hall.

Martin, P., & Bateson, P. (1986). *Measuring behavior.* Cambridge, England: Cambridge University Press.

Martinez, C. (1986). Hispanics: Psychiatric issues. In C. B. Wilkinson (Ed.), *Ethnic psychiatry* (pp. 61–88). New York: Plenum.

Martinez, J. L., Jr., & Mendoza, R. H. (Eds.). (1984). *Chicano psychology* (2nd ed.). New York: Academic Press.

Martinsen, E. W. (1987). The role of aerobic exercise in the treatment of depression. *Stress Medicine, 3,* 93–100.

Martyna, W. (1980). Beyond the "He/Man" approach: The case for nonsexist language. *Signs, 5,* 482–493.

Marx, J. L. (1980). Ape-language controversy flares up. *Science, 207,* 1330–1333.

Maslach, C. (1979). Negative emotional biasing of unexplained arousal. *Journal of Personality and Social Psychology, 37,* 953–969.

Maslow, A. H. (1962). *Toward a psychology of being.* Princeton, NJ: Van Nostrand.

Maslow, A. H. (1968). *Toward a psychology of being* (2nd ed.). Princeton, NJ: Van Nostrand.

Maslow, A. H. (1970). *Motivation and personality* (2nd ed). New York: Harper & Row.

Maslow, A. H. (1971). *The farther reaches of human nature.* New York: Viking.

Massaro, D. W. (1987). *Speech perception by ear and eye.* Hillsdale, NJ: Erlbaum.

Masters, W. H., & Johnson, V. E. (1966). *Human sexual response.* Boston: Little, Brown.

Matas, L., Arend, R. A., & Sroufe, L. A. (1978). Continuity in adaptation: Quality of attachment and later competence. *Child Development, 49,* 547–556.

Matlin, M. W. (1985). Current issues in psycholinguistics. In T. M. Shlechter & M. P. Toglia (Eds.), *New directions in cognitive science* (pp. 217–241). Norwood, NJ: Ablex.

Matlin, M. W. (1987). *Psychology of women.* New York: Holt, Rinehart and Winston.

Matlin, M. W. (1988). *Sensation and perception* (2nd ed.). Boston, MA: Allyn & Bacon.

Matlin, M. W. (1989). *Cognition* (2nd ed.). New York: Holt, Rinehart and Winston.

Matlin, M. W., & Foley, H. (1992). *Sensation and perception* (3rd ed.). Boston, MA: Allyn & Bacon.

Matlin, M. W., & Stang, D. J. (1978). *The Pollyanna principle: Selectivity in language, memory, and thought.* Cambridge, MA: Schenkman.

Matlin, M. W., & Zajonc, R. B. (1968). Social facilitation of word associations. *Journal of Personality and Social Psychology, 10,* 455–461.

Matsumoto, D. (1987). The role of facial response

in the experience of emotion: More methodological problems and a meta-analysis. *Journal of Personality and Social Psychology, 52,* 769–774.

Matthews, K. A. (1988). CHD and Type A behaviors: Update on and alternatives to the Booth-Kewley and Friedman quantitative review. *Psychological Bulletin, 104,* 373–380.

May, R. (1986). The problem of evil. In R. May, C. Rogers, & A. Maslow (Eds.), *Politics and innocence* (pp. 12–23). Dallas: Saybrook.

Mayer, R. E. (1982). The psychology of mathematical problem solving. In F. K. Lester & J. Garofalo (Eds.), *Mathematical problem solving: Issues in research* (pp. 1–13). Philadelphia: The Franklin Institute.

Mayer, R. E. (1985). Implications of cognitive psychology for instruction in mathematical problem solving. In E. A. Silver (Ed.), *Teaching and learning mathematical problem solving* (pp. 123–138). Hillsdale, NJ: Erlbaum.

Mayer, R. E. (1988, August). *Teaching for thinking: Research on the teachability of thinking skills.* Paper presented at the Convention of the American Psychological Association, Atlanta, GA.

McAlister, A., Perry, C., Killen, J., Slinkard, L. A., & Maccoby, N. (1980). Pilot study of smoking, alcohol and drug abuse prevention. *American Journal of Public Health, 70,* 719–721.

McArthur, L. A. (1972). The how and what of why: Some determinants and consequences of casual attribution. *Journal of Personality and Social Psychology, 22,* 171–193.

McCann, I. L., & Holmes, D. S. (1984). Influence of aerobic exercise on depression. *Journal of Personality and Social Psychology, 46,* 1142–1147.

McCauley, C. R., & Segal, M. E. (1987). Social psychology of terrorist groups. In C. Hendrick (Ed.), *Review of personality and social psychology: Group processes and intergroup relations* (Vol. 9, pp. 231–256). Beverly Hills, CA: Sage.

McClelland, D. C. (1985). *Human motivation.* Glenview, IL: Scott, Foresman.

McConkie, G. W., & Zola, D. (1984). Eye movement control during reading. The effect of word units. In W. Prinz & A. F. Sanders (Eds.), *Cognition and motor processes* (pp. 63–74). Berlin: Springer-Verlag.

McCormick, D. A., & Thompson, R. F. (1984). Cerebellum: Essential involvement in the classically conditioned eyelid response. *Science, 223,* 296–299.

McCrae, R. R., & Costa, P. T., Jr. (1985). Updating Norman's "adequate taxonomy": Intelligence and personality dimensions in natural language and in questionnaires. *Journal of Personality and Social Psychology, 49,* 710–721.

McCrae, R. R., & Costa, P. T., Jr. (1986). Clinical assessment can benefit from recent advances in personality psychology. *American Psychologist, 41,* 1001–1003.

McCrae, R. R., & Costa, P. T., Jr. (1987). Validation of the five-factor model of personality across instruments and observers. *Journal of Personality and Social Psychology, 52,* 81–90.

McCurry, C. (1989, July). The business of truth. *APS Observer,* pp. 14–15.

McDougall, W. (1908). *Social psychology.* New York: Putnam.

McFarlane, J., Martin, C. L., & Williams, T. M. (1988). Mood fluctuations: Women versus men and menstrual versus other cycles. *Psychology of Women Quarterly, 12,* 201–223.

McGinnies, E., & Ward, C. D. (1980). Better liked than right: Trustworthiness and expertise as factors in credibility. *Personality and Social Psychology Bulletin, 6,* 467–472.

McGinty, D., & Szymusiak, R. (1988). Neuronal unit activity patterns in behaving animals: Brainstem and limbic system. *Annual Review of Psychology, 39,* 135–168.

McGuinness, D. M. (1985). Sensorimotor biases in cognitive development. In R. L. Hall (Ed.), *Male-female differences: A biocultural perspective* (pp. 57–126). New York: Praeger.

McHugh, M. C., Koeske, R. D., & Frieze, I. H. (1986). Issues to consider in conducting nonsexist psychological research: A guide for researchers. *American Psychologist, 41,* 879–890.

McIntyre, J. J., & Teevan, J. J., Jr. (1972). Television violence and deviant behavior. In G. A. Comstock & E. A. Rubinstein (Eds.), *Television and social behavior: Vol. III. Television and adolescent aggressiveness* (pp. 383–435). Washington, DC: U.S. Government Printing Office.

McKellar, P. (1972). Imagery from the standpoint of introspection. In P. W. Sheehan (Ed.), *The function and nature of imagery* (pp. 36–63). New York: Academic.

McKim, W. A. (1986). *Drugs and behavior.* Englewood Cliffs, NJ: Prentice-Hall.

McKinlay, J. B., McKinlay, S. M., & Brambilla, D. (1987a). Health status and utilization behavior associated with menopause. *American Journal of Epidemiology, 125,* 110–121.

McKinlay, J. B., McKinlay, S. M., & Brambilla, D. (1987b). The relative contributions of endocrine changes and social circumstances to depression in mid-aged women. *Journal of Health and Social Behavior, 28,* 345–363.

McLeod, J. M., Atkin, C. K., & Chaffee, S. H. (1972). Adolescents, parents and television use: Adolescent self-report measures from Maryland and Wisconsin samples. In G. A. Comstock & E. A. Rubinstein (Eds.), *Television and social behavior: Vol. III. Television and adolescent aggressiveness* (pp. 239–313). Washington, DC: U.S. Government Printing Office.

McNeal, E. T., & Cimbolic, P. (1986). Antidepressants and biochemical theories of depression. *Psychological Bulletin, 99,* 361–374.

McNeil, B. J., Pauker, S. G., Sox, H. C., & Tversky, A. (1982). On the elicitation of preferences for alternative therapies. *New England Journal of Medicine, 306,* 1259–1262.

McNeill, D. (1985). So you think gestures are nonverbal? *Psychological Review, 92,* 350–371.

McReynolds, P. (1989). Diagnosis and clinical assessment: Current status and major issues. *Annual Review of Psychology, 40,* 83–108.

McTear, M. F. (1985). *Children's conversations.* Oxford, England: Basil Blackwell.

Meacham, J. A. (1982). A note on remembering to execute planned actions. *Journal of Applied Developmental Psychology, 3,* 121–133.

Meacham, J. A., & Leiman, B. (1982). Remembering to perform future actions. In U. Neisser (Ed.), *Memory observed: Remembering in natural contexts* (pp. 327–336). San Francisco: Freeman.

Mead, M. (1975). Review of Darwin and facial expression. *Journal of Communication, 25,* 209–213.

Meddis, R. (1982). Cognitive dysfunction following loss of sleep. In A. Burton (Ed.), *The pathology and psychology of cognition* (pp. 225–252). London: Methuen.

Meddis, R., Pearson, A., & Langford, G. (1973). An extreme case of healthy insomnia. *Electroencephalography and Clinical Neurophysiology, 35,* 213–214.

Meissner, W. W. (1988). The psychotherapies: Individual, family, and group. In A. M. Nicholi, Jr. (Ed.), *The new Harvard guide to psychiatry* (pp. 449–480). Cambridge, MA: Harvard University Press.

Melamed, B. G., & Siegel, L. J. (1975). Reduction of anxiety in children facing hospitalization and surgery by use of filmed modeling. *Journal of Consulting and Clinical Psychology, 43,* 511–521.

Melzack, R. (1986). Neurophysiological foundations of pain. In R. A. Sternbach (Ed.), *The psychology of pain* (pp. 1–24). New York: Raven Press.

Melzack, R., & Wall, P. D. (1965). Pain mechanisms: A new theory. *Science, 150,* 971–979.

Mendelson, W. B. (1987). *Human sleep: Research and clinical care.* New York: Plenum.

Mensink, G., & Raaijmakers, J. G. W. (1988). A model for interference and forgetting. *Psychological Review, 95,* 434–455.

Merluzzi, T. V., Rudy, T. E., & Krejci, M. J. (1986). Social skill and anxiety: Information processing perspectives. In R. E. Ingram (Ed.), *Information processing approaches to clinical psychology* (pp. 109–129). Orlando, FL: Academic.

Mervis, C. B., Catlin, J., & Rosch, E. (1976). Relationships among goodness-of-example, category norms, and word frequency. *Bulletin of the Psychonomic Society, 7,* 283–284.

Messer, S. B. (1986). Behavioral and psychoanalytic perspectives at therapeutic choice points. *American Psychologist, 41,* 1261–1272.

Messick, S. (1980). *The effectiveness of coaching for the SAT: Review and reanalysis of research from the fifties to the FTC.* Princeton, NJ: Educational Testing Service.

Michael, J. (1985). Fundamental research and behaviour modification. In C. F. Lowe, M. Richelle, D. E. Blackman, & C. M. Bradshaw (Eds.), *Behaviour analysis and contemporary psychology* (pp. 159–170). London: Erlbaum.

Michaels, M., & Willwerth, J. (1989, April 24). How America has run out of time. *Time,* pp. 58–67.

Midkiff, E. E., & Bernstein, I. L. (1985). Targets of learned food aversions in humans. *Physiology & Behavior, 34,* 839–841.

Milgram, S. (1963). Behavioral studies of obedience. *Journal of Abnormal and Social Psychology, 67,* 371–378.

Milgram, S. (1964). Issues in the study of obedience: A reply to Baumrind. *American Psychologist, 19,* 848–852.

Milgram, S. (1965). Some conditions of obedience and disobedience to authority. *Human Relations, 18,* 57–76.

Milgram, S. (1974). *Obedience to authority.* New York: Harper & Row.

Milgram, S., Bickman, L., & Berkowitz, L. (1969). Note on the drawing power of crowds of different size. *Journal of Personality and Social Psychology, 13,* 79–82.

Miller, A. G. (1986). *The obedience experiments.* New York: Praeger.

Miller, E., Cradock-Watson, J. E., & Pollock, T. M. (1982, October 9). Consequences of confirmed maternal rubella at successive stages of pregnancy. *Lancet,* pp. 781–784.

Miller, G. A. (1956). The magical number seven,

plus or minus two: Some limits on our capacity for processing information. *Psychological Review, 63,* 81–97.

Miller, G. A. (1962). *Psychology: The science of mental life.* New York: Harper & Row.

Miller, G. A. (1981). *Language and speech.* San Francisco: Freeman.

Miller, G. A., & Gildea, P. M. (1987). How children learn words. *Scientific American, 257,* 94–99.

Miller, L. L., & Branconnier, R. J. (1983). Cannabis: Effects on memory and the cholinergic limbic system. *Psychological Bulletin, 93,* 441–456.

Miller, N. B. (1982). Social work services to urban Indians. In J. W. Green (Ed.), *Cultural awareness in the human services* (pp. 30). Englewood Cliffs, NJ: Prentice-Hall.

Miller, N. E. (1985). The value of behavioral research on animals. *American Psychologist, 40,* 423–440.

Miller, R. J., Hennessy, R. T., & Leibowitz, H. W. (1973). The effect of hypnotic ablation of the background on the magnitude of the Ponzo perspective illusion. *International Journal of Clinical and Experimental Hypnosis, 21,* 180–191.

Millon, T. (1981). *Disorders of personality.* New York: Wiley.

Milner, B. R. (1970). Memory and medial temporal regions of the brain. In K. H. Pribram & D. E. Broadbent (Eds.), *Biology of memory* (pp. 29–50). Orlando, FL: Academic.

Milner, B. R., Corkin, S., & Teuber, H. L. (1968). Further analysis of the hippocampal amnesic syndrome: 14-year follow-up study of H. M. *Neuropsychologia, 6,* 215–234.

Milner, D. (1983). *Children & race.* Beverly Hills, CA: Sage.

Mineka, S. (1986). The frightful complexity of the origins of fears. In J. B. Overmier & F. R. Brush (Eds.), *Affect, conditioning, and cognition: Essays on the determinants of behavior.* Hillsdale, NJ: Erlbaum.

Mineka, S., Davidson, M., Cook, M., & Keir, R. (1984). Observational conditioning of snake fear in rhesus monkeys. *Journal of Abnormal Psychology, 93,* 355–372.

Minkler, M., & Stone, R. (1985). The feminization of poverty and older women. *Gerontologist, 25,* 351–357.

Mirsky, A. F., & Duncan, C. C. (1986). Etiology and expression of schizophrenia: Neurobiological and psychosocial factors. *Annual Review of Psychology, 37,* 291–319.

Mischel, W. (1966). A social-learning view of sex differences in behavior. In E. Maccoby (Ed.), *The development of sex differences* (pp. 56–81). Stanford: Stanford University Press.

Mischel, W. (1968). *Personality and assessment.* New York: Wiley.

Mischel, W. (1979). On the interface of cognition and personality: Beyond the person-situation debate. *American Psychologist, 34,* 740–754.

Mischel, W. (1986). *Introduction to personality: A new look* (4th ed.). New York: Holt, Rinehart and Winston.

Mishkin, M., & Appenzeller, T. (1987). The anatomy of memory. *Scientific American, 256*(6), 80–89.

Mishler, E. G. (1986). *Research interviewing.* Cambridge, MA: Harvard University Press.

Mistretta, C. M. (1981). Neurophysiological and anatomical aspects of taste development. In R. N. Aslin, J. R. Alberts, & M. P. Petersen (Eds.), *Development of perception* (Vol. 1, pp. 433–455). New York: Academic Press.

Mita, T. H., Dermer, M., & Knight, J. (1977). Reversed facial images and the mere-exposure hypothesis. *Journal of Personality and Social Psychology, 35,* 597–601

Mitchell, J., Wilson, K., Revicki, D., & Parker, L. (1985). *The Gerontologist, 25,* 182–187.

Moar, I., & Bower, G. H. (1983). Inconsistency in spatial knowledge. *Memory & Cognition, 11,* 107–113.

Mobilization for Animals. (1984, February). *Direct Action Program 1984.* Columbus, OH: Mobilization for Animals.

Moely, B. E., Olson, F. A., Halwes, T. G., & Flavell, J. H. (1969). Production deficiency in young children's clustered recall. *Developmental Psychology, 1,* 26–34.

Moll, L. (1991, January). Pediatric AIDS: Hitting closer to home. *Pediatric Management,* pp. 38–41.

Monahan, L., Kuhn, D., & Shaver, P. (1974). Intrapsychic versus cultural explanations of the "fear of success" motive. *Journal of Personality and Social Psychology, 29,* 60–64.

Mönks, F. J., & Van Boxtel, H. W. (1985). Gifted adolescents: A developmental perspective. In J. Freeman (Ed.), *The psychology of gifted children* (pp. 275–295). Chichester, England: Wiley.

Monmaney, T. (1987, September). Are we led by the nose? *Discover,* pp. 48–56.

Monte, C. F. (1987). *Beneath the mask: An introduction to theories of personality* (3rd ed.). New York: Holt, Rinehart and Winston.

Mook, D. G. (1987). *Motivation: The organization of action.* New York: Norton.

Moorcroft, W. H. (1987). An overview of sleep. In J. Gackenback (Ed.), *Sleep and dreams* (pp. 3–29). New York: Garland.

Moorcroft, W. H. (1989). *Sleep, dreaming, and sleep disorders.* Lanham, MD: University Press of America.

Moore, B. C. J. (1977). *Introduction to the psychology of hearing.* Baltimore: University Park Press.

Moore, L. M., Nielsen, C. R., & Mistretta, C. M. (1982). Sucrose taste thresholds: Age-related differences. *Journal of Gerontology, 37,* 64–69.

Morin, S. F. (1988). AIDS: The challenge to psychology. *American Psychologist, 43,* 838–842.

Morris, N. M., & Udry, J. R. (1978). Pheromonal influences on human sexual behavior: An experimental search. *Journal of Biosocial Science, 10,* 147–157.

Morrison, D. M. (1985). Adolescent contraceptive behavior: A review. *Psychological Bulletin, 98,* 538–568.

Moses, S. (1989, October). Therapist touts a blend of techniques. *APA Monitor,* p. 25.

Moskowitz, B. A. (1978). The acquisition of language. *Scientific American, 239,* 92–108.

Moskowitz, H. R. (1978). Odors in the environment: Hedonics, perfumery, and odor abatement. In E. C. Carterette & M. P. Friedman (Eds.), *Handbook of perception* (Vol. 10). New York: Academic Press.

Moulton, J., Robinson, G. M., & Elias, C. (1978). Sex bias in language use: "Neutral pronouns that aren't." *American Psychologist, 33,* 1032–1036.

Moyer, R. S. (1985). *Teaching psychology courses about the nuclear arms race.* Paper presented at the Massachusetts Psychological Association.

Mullen, B. (1987). Introduction: The study of group behavior. In B. Mullen & G. R. Goethals (Eds.), *Theories of group behavior* (pp. 1–19). New York: Springer-Verlag.

Mumford, M. D., & Gustafson, S. B. (1988). Creativity syndrome: Integration, application, and innovation. *Psychological Bulletin, 103,* 27–43.

Mussen, P., & Eisenberg-Berg, N. (1977). *Roots of caring, sharing and helping: The development of prosocial behavior.* San Francisco: Freeman.

My Lai: An American tragedy. (1969, December 5). *Time,* pp. 23–34.

Myers, D. G. (1990). *Social psychology* (3rd ed.). New York: McGraw-Hill.

Myers, D. G., & Bishop, G. D. (1970). Discussion effects on racial attitudes. *Science, 169,* 778–779.

Myers, G. C. (1985). Aging and worldwide population change. In R. Binstock & E. Shanas (Eds.), *Handbook of aging and the social sciences* (pp. 173–198). New York: Van Nostrand Reinhold.

Myers, N. A., & Perlmutter, M. (1978). Memory in the years from two to five. In P. A. Ornstein (Ed.), *Memory development in children* (pp. 191–218). Hillsdale, NJ: Erlbaum.

Namir, S., Wolcott, D. L., Fawzy, F. I., & Alumbaugh, M. J. (1987). Coping with AIDS: Psychological and health implications. *Journal of Applied Social Psychology, 17,* 309–328.

Nash, M. (1987). What, if anything, is regressed about hypnotic age regression? A review of the empirical literature. *Psychological Bulletin, 102,* 42–52.

National Commission on Working Women. (1989, Winter). Women, work and the future. *Women at Work,* p. 5.

National Institute of Mental Health. (1985). *Mental health, United States, 1985.* Washington, DC: U.S. Government Printing Office.

Neisser, U., & Becklen, R. (1975). Selective looking: Attending to visually specified events. *Cognitive Psychology, 7,* 480–494.

Nelson, T. O., Leonesio, R. J., Landwehr, R., & Narens, L. (1986). A comparison of three predictors of an individual's memory performance: The individual's feeling of knowing versus the normative feeling of knowing versus base-rate item difficulty. *Journal of Experimental Psychology: Learning, Memory, and Cognition, 12,* 279–287.

Nemeth, C. J. (1986). Differential contributions of majority and minority influence. *Psychological Review, 93,* 23–32.

Nemeth, C. J., & Chiles, C. (1988). Modeling courage: The role of dissent in fostering independence. *European Journal of Social Psychology, 18,* 275–280.

Nemeth, C. J., & Staw, B. M. (1989). The tradeoffs of social control and innovation in groups and organizations. *Advances in Experimental Social Psychology, 22,* 175–210.

Neugarten, B. L. (1982, August). *Successful aging.* Paper presented at the meeting of the American Psychological Association, Washington, DC.

Nevid, J. S. (1984). Sex differences in factors of romantic attraction. *Sex Roles, 11,* 401–411.

Newell, A., & Simon, H. A. (1972). *Human problem solving.* Englewood Cliffs, NJ: Prentice-Hall.

Newman, J. P., Widom, C. S., & Nathan, S. (1985). Passive avoidance in syndromes of disinhibition: Psychopathy and extraversion. *Journal of*

Personality and Social Psychology, 48, 1316–1327.

Newport, E. L., Gleitman, H., & Gleitman, L. R. (1977). I'd rather do it myself: Some effects and non-effects of maternal speech style. In C. E. Snow & C. A. Fergusson (Eds.), *Talking to children.* Cambridge, England: Cambridge University Press.

Newsom, C., Favell, J. E., & Rincover, A. (1983). Side effects of punishment. In S. Axelrod & J. Apsche (Eds.), *The effects of punishment on human behavior* (pp. 285–316). New York: Academic Press.

Nezu, A. M., Nezu, C. M., & Blissett, S. E. (1988). Sense of humor as a moderator of the relation between stressful events and psychological distress: A prospective analysis. *Journal of Personality and Social Psychology, 54,* 520–525.

Nicholi, A. M., Jr. (Ed.). (1988). *The new Harvard guide to psychiatry.* Cambridge, MA: Harvard University Press.

Nickerson, R. S., & Adams, M. J. (1979). Long-term memory for a common object. *Cognitive Psychology, 11,* 287–307.

Nickerson, R. S., Perkins, D. N., & Smith, E. E. (1985). *The teaching of thinking.* Hillsdale, NJ: Erlbaum.

Nieburg, P., Marks, J. S., McLaren, N. M., & Remington, P. L. (1985). The fetal tobacco syndrome. *Journal of the American Medical Association, 253,* 2998–2999.

Nielsen, L. (1987). *Adolescent psychology.* New York: Holt, Rinehart and Winston.

Nielsen, L. L., & Sarason, I. G. (1981). Emotion, personality, and selective attention. *Journal of Personality and Social Psychology, 41,* 945–960.

Nilsen, A. P., Bosmajian, H., Gershuny, H. L., & Stanley, J. P. (1977). *Sexism and language.* Urbana, IL: National Council of Teachers of English.

Nisbett, R. E., Caputo, C., Legant, P., & Maracek, J. (1973). Behavior as seen by the actor and as seen by the observer. *Journal of Personality and Social Psychology, 27,* 154–164.

Nisbett, R. E., Krantz, D. H., Jepson, C., & Kunda, Z. (1983). The use of statistical heuristics in everyday inductive reasoning. *Psychological Review, 90,* 339–363.

Nisbett, R. E., & Ross, L. (1980). *Human inference: Strategies and shortcomings of social judgment.* Englewood Cliffs, NJ: Prentice-Hall.

Nisbett, R. E., & Wilson, T. D. (1977). Telling more than we can know: Verbal reports on mental processes. *Psychological Review, 84,* 231–259.

Nolen-Hoeksema, S. (1987). Sex differences in unipolar depression: Evidence and theory. *Psychological Bulletin, 101,* 259–282.

Nolen-Hoeksema, S. (1990). *Sex differences in depression.* Stanford, CA: Stanford University Press.

Noller, P., Law, H., & Comrey, A. L. (1987). Cattell, Comrey, and Eysenck personality factors compared: More evidence for the five robust factors? *Journal of Personality and Social Psychology, 53,* 775–782.

Norcross, J. C. (1987). Eclectic psychotherapy: An introduction and overview. In J. C. Norcross (Ed.), *Casebook and eclectic psychotherapy* (pp. 3–24). New York: Brunner/Mazel.

Norman, W. H., Johnson, B. A., & Miller, I. W., III. (1984). Depression: A behavioral-cognitive approach. In E. A. Blechman (Ed.), *Behavior*

modification with women (pp. 275–307). New York: Guilford Press.

Nurnberger, J. I., & Gershon, E. S. (1982). Genetics. In E. S. Paykel (Ed.), *Handbook of affective disorders.* New York: Guilford Press.

Oakland, T., & Parmelee, R. (1985). Mental measurement of minority-group children. In B. B. Wolman (Ed.), *Handbook of intelligence* (pp. 699–736). New York: Wiley.

O'Connell, A., & Russo, N. F. (Eds.). (1983). *Models of achievement: Reflections of eminent women in psychology.* New York: Columbia University Press.

O'Donnell, J. M. (1985). *The origins of behaviorism: American psychology, 1870–1920.* New York: New York University Press.

Offer, D., Ostrov, E., & Howard, K. (1981). *The adolescent: A self-portrait.* New York: Basic.

O'Keeffe, M. K., Nesselhof-Kendall, S., & Baum, A. (1990). Behavior and prevention of AIDS: Bases of research and intervention. *Personality and Social Psychology Bulletin, 16,* 166–180.

Oldfield, S. R., & Parker, S. P. A. (1986). Acuity of sound localisation: A topography of auditory space: III. Monaural hearing conditions. *Perception, 15,* 67–81.

Olds, D. L. (1988). The prenatal/early infancy project. In E. H. Price, E. L. Cowen, R. P. Lorion, & J. Ramos-McKay (Eds.), *Fourteen ounces of prevention* (pp. 9–23). Washington, DC: American Psychological Association.

Olds, D. L., Henderson, C. R., Chamberlin, R., & Tatelbaum, R. (1986). Preventing child abuse and neglect: A randomized trial of nurse home visitation. *Pediatrics, 78,* 65–78.

Oliner, S. P., & Oliner, P. M. (1988). *The altruistic personality.* New York: Free Press.

Olson, J. M. & Cal, A. V. (1984). Source credibility, attitudes, and the recall of past behaviours. *European Journal of Social Psychology, 14,* 203–210.

Oltmanns, T. F., Neale, J. M., & Davison, G. C. (1986). *Case studies in abnormal psychology* (2nd ed.). New York: Wiley.

Olzak, L. A., & Thomas, J. P. (1986). Seeing spatial patterns. In K. R. Boff, L. Kaufman, & J. P. Thomas (Eds.), *Handbook of perception and human performance* (pp. 7-1–7-56). New York: Wiley.

Operation Friendship. (1989, December). *Operation Friendship's friendly focus.* Rochester, NY: Author.

Orford, J. (1985). *Excessive appetites: A psychological view of addictions.* New York: Wiley.

Orne, M. T. (1951). The mechanisms of hypnotic age regression: An experimental study. *Journal of Abnormal Psychology, 46,* 213–225.

Orne, M. T. (1962). On the social psychology of the psychological experiment: With particular reference to demand characteristics and their implications. *American Psychologist, 17,* 776–783.

Orne, M. T. (1986). The validity of memories retrieved in hypnosis. In B. Zilbergeld, M. G. Edelstien, & D. L. Araoz (Eds.), *Hypnosis: Questions and answers* (pp. 45–46). New York: Norton.

Ornstein, R., & Thompson, R. F. (1984). *The amazing brain.* Boston: Houghton Mifflin.

Ortony, A., Clore, G. L., & Collins, A. (1988). *The cognitive structure of emotions.* Cambridge, England: Cambridge University Press.

Ortony, A., & Turner, T. J. (1990). What's basic

about basic emotions? *Psychological Review, 97,* 315–331.

Osgood, C. E. (1962). *An alternative to war or surrender.* Urbana: University of Illinois Press.

Osherow, N. (1988). Making sense of the nonsensical: An analysis of Jonestown. In E. Aronson (Ed.), *Readings about the social animal* (5th ed., pp. 68–86). New York: Freeman.

O'Sullivan, C. S., & Durso, F. T. (1984). Effect of schema-incongruent information on memory for stereotypical attributes. *Journal of Personality and Social Psychology, 47,* 55–70.

Oswald, I. (1987a). Sleep. In R. L. Gregory (Ed.), *The Oxford companion to the mind* (pp. 718–719). New York: Oxford University Press.

Oswald, I. (1987b). Dreaming. In R. L. Gregory (Ed.), *The Oxford companion to the mind* (pp. 201–203). New York: Oxford University Press.

Owens, R. E., Jr. (1988). *Language development: An introduction* (2nd ed.). Columbus, OH: Merrill.

Padawer, W. J., & Goldfried, M. R. (1984). Anxiety-related disorders, fears, and phobias. In E. A. Blechman (Ed.), *Behavior modification with women* (pp. 341–372). New York: Guilford Press.

Paivio, A. (1978). Comparisons of mental clocks. *Journal of Experimental Psychology: Human Perception and Performance, 4,* 61–71.

Palij, M., & Homel, P. (1987). The relationship of bilingualism to cognitive development: Historical, methodological and theoretical considerations. In P. Homel, M. Palij, & D. Aaronson (Eds.), *Childhood bilingualism: Aspects of linguistic, cognitive, and social development* (pp. 131–148). Hillsdale, NJ: Erlbaum.

Pallak, S. R. (1983). Salience of a communicator's physical attractiveness and persuasion: A heuristic versus systematic processing interpretation. *Social Cognition, 2,* 156–168.

Pallak, S. R., Murroni, E., & Koch, J. (1983). Communicator attractiveness and expertise, emotional versus rational appeals, and persuasion: A heuristic versus systematic processing interpretation. *Social Cognition, 2,* 122–141.

Palmore, E. B. (1981). *Social patterns in normal aging: Findings from the Duke Longitudinal Study.* Durham, NC: Duke University Press.

Paludi, M. A. (1984). Psychometric properties and underlying assumptions of four objective measures of fear of success. *Sex Roles, 10,* 765–781.

Palys, P. S. (1986). Testing and common wisdom: The social content of video pornography. *Canadian Psychology, 27,* 22–35.

Panksepp, J. (1986). The neurochemistry of behavior. *Annual Review of Psychology, 37,* 77–107.

Paradise, L. V., & Wall, S. M. (1986). Children's perceptions of male and female principals and teachers. *Sex Roles, 14,* 1–7.

Parker, K. C. H., Hanson, R. K., & Hunsley, J. (1988). MMPI, Rorschach, and WAIS: A meta-analytic comparison of reliability, stability, and validity. *Psychological Bulletin, 103,* 367–373.

Parloff, M. B. (1987, February). Psychotherapy: An import from Japan. *Psychology Today,* pp. 74–75.

Parloff, M. B. London, P., & Wolfe, B. (1986). Individual psychotherapy and behavior change. *Annual Review of Psychology, 37,* 321–349.

Passuth, P. M., & Cook, F. L. (1985). Effects of television viewing on knowledge and attitudes about older adults: A critical reexamination. *The Gerontologist, 25,* 69–77.

Pastalan, L. A. (1982). Environmental design and adaptation to the visual environment of the elderly. In R. Sekuler, D. Kline, & K. Dismukes (Eds.), *Handbook of perception* (Vol. 4). New York: Academic Press.

Paterson, R. J., & Neufeld, R. W. J. (1987). Clear danger: Situational determinants of the appraisal of threat. *Psychological Bulletin. 101,* 404–416.

Patterson, M. L. (1983). *Nonverbal behavior: A functional perspective.* New York: Springer-Verlag.

Pattison, E. M. (1978). The living-dying process. In C. A. Garfield (Ed.), *Psychosocial care of the dying patient* (pp. 133–168). New York: McGraw-Hill.

Pavlov, I. P. (1927). *Conditioned reflexes.* London: Oxford University Press.

Payne, J. W. (1985). Psychology of risky decisions. In G. Wright (Ed.), *Behavioral decision making* (pp. 3–23). New York: Plenum.

Pearce, J. M. (1987). A model for stimulus generalization in Pavlovian conditioning. *Psychological Review, 94,* 61–73.

Pearson, K. (1914). *The life, letters and labours of Francis Galton* (Vol. 1). Cambridge, England: The University Press.

Pedro-Carroll, J. L., & Cowen, E. L. (1985). The children of divorce interaction program: An investigation of the efficacy of a school-based prevention program. *Journal of Consulting and Clinical Psychology, 53,* 603–611.

Pelletier-Stiefel, J., Pepler, D., Crozier, K., Stanhope, L., Corter, C., & Abramovitch, R. (1986). Nurturance in the home: A longitudinal study of sibling interaction. In A. Fogel & G. F. Melson (Eds.), *Origins of nurturance* (pp. 3–24). Hillsdale, NJ: Erlbaum.

Pelosi, N. (1988). Aids and public policy: A legislative view. *American Psychologist, 43,* 843–845.

Penfield, W., & Jasper, H. (1954). *Epilepsy and the functional anatomy of the human brain.* Boston: Little, Brown.

Penfield, W., & Rasmussen, T. (1950). *The cerebral cortex of man.* New York: Macmillan.

Pennebaker, J. W. (1990). *Opening up: The healing power of confiding in others.* New York: Morrow.

Pennebaker, J. W., Kiecolt-Glaser, J., & Glaser, R. (1988). Disclosure of traumas and immune function: Health implications for psychotherapy. *Journal of Consulting and Clinical Psychology, 56,* 239–245.

Pennington, S. B. (1987). Children of lesbian mothers. In F. W. Bozett (Ed.), *Gay and lesbian parents* (pp. 58–74). New York: Praeger.

Peplau, L. A. (1988, July). *Research on lesbian and gay relationships: A decade review.* Paper presented at the International Conference on Personal Relationships, University of British Columbia, Vancouver, Canada.

Peplau, L. A., Padesky, C., & Hamilton, M. (1982). Satisfaction in lesbian relationships. *Journal of Homosexuality, 8,* 23–35.

Perkins, D. N. (1981). *The mind's best work.* Cambridge, MA: Harvard University Press.

Perkins, D. N. (1988). Creativity and the quest for mechanism. In R. J. Sternberg & E. E. Smith (Eds.), *The psychology of human thought* (pp. 309–336). Cambridge, England: Cambridge University Press.

Perlmutter, E., & Bart, P. B. (1982). Changing views of "The change": A critical review and suggestions for an attributional approach. In A. M. Voda, M. Dinnerstein, & S. R. O'Donnell (Eds.), *Changing perspectives on menopause* (pp. 187–199). Austin: University of Texas Press.

Petersen, A. C. (1988). Adolescent development. *Annual Review of Psychology, 39,* 583–607.

Peterson, C., & Seligman, M. E. P. (1985). The learned helplessness model of depression: Current status of theory and research. In E. E. Beckham & W. R. Leber (Eds.), *Handbook of depression* (pp. 914–939). Homewood, IL: Dorsey.

Peterson, C., & Seligman, M. E. P. (1987). Explanatory style and illness. *Journal of Personality, 55,* 237–265.

Peterson, C., Seligman, M. E. P., & Vaillant, G. (1988). Pessimistic explanatory style is a risk factor for physical illness: A thirty-five-year longitudinal study. *Journal of Personality and Social Psychology, 55,* 23–27.

Peterson, C., Semmel, A., von Bayer, C., Abramson, L. Y., Metalsky, G. I., & Seligman, M. E. P. (1982). The Attributional Style Questionnaire. *Cognitive Therapy and Research, 6,* 287–299.

Peterson, C., & Villanova, P. (1988). An expanded attributional style questionnaire. *Journal of Abnormal Psychology, 97,* 87–89.

Peterson, C. C., & Peterson, J. L. (1973). Preference for sex of offspring as a measure of change in sex attitudes. *Psychology, 10,* 3–5.

Peterson, G. C. (1980). Organic mental disorders associated with brain trauma. In H. I. Kaplan, A. M. Freedman, & B. J. Sadlock (Eds.), *Comprehensive textbook of psychiatry* (3rd ed., Vol. 3, pp. 1422–1437). Baltimore: Williams & Wilkins.

Peterson, L. R., & Peterson, M. (1959). Short-term retention of individual verbal items. *Journal of Experimental Psychology, 58,* 193–198.

Petri, H. L. (1986). *Motivation: Theory and research.* Belmont, CA: Wadsworth.

Pettigrew, T. F., & Martin, J. (1987). Shaping the organizational context for black American inclusion. *Journal of Social Issues, 43,* 41–78.

Pettit, R., Holtzman, R. E., & Wollman, N. (1985). Using conflict constructively. In N. Wollman (Ed.), *Working for peace* (pp. 111–119). San Luis Obispo, CA: Impact.

Petty, R. E., & Cacioppo, J. T. (1986a). The elaboration likelihood model of persuasion. *Advances in Experimental Social Psychology, 19,* 123–205.

Petty, R. E., & Cacioppo, J. T. (1986b). *Communication and persuasion.* New York: Springer-Verlag.

Phares, E. J. (1988). *Introduction to personality* (2nd ed.). Glenview, IL: Scott, Foresman.

Phillips, D., McCartney, K., & Scarr, S. (1987). Child-care quality and children's social development. *Developmental Psychology, 23,* 537–543.

Phillips, D. P., & Brugge, J. F. (1985). Progress in neurophysiology of sound localization. *Annual Review of Psychology, 36,* 245–274.

Phillips, V. (1981). *The abilities and achievements of Orientals in North America.* Beverly Hills, CA: Sage.

Piaget, J. (1983). Piaget's theory. In P. H. Mussen (Ed.), *Handbook of child psychology* (4th ed., Vol. 1, pp. 103–128). New York: Wiley.

Pickar, D., Labarca, R., Linnoila, M., Roy, A.,

Hommer, D., Everett, D., & Paul, S. M. (1984). Neuroleptic-induced decrease in plasma homovanillic acid and antipsychotic activity in schizophrenic patients. *Science, 225,* 954–957.

Pierce, C. M. (1984). Television and violence: Social psychiatric perspectives. *American Journal of Social Psychiatry, 3,* 41–44.

Pierce, J. P., Fiore, M. C., Novotny, T. E. Hatziandreu, E. J., & Davis, R. M. (1989). Trends in cigarette smoking in the United States. *Journal of the American Medical Association, 261,* 56–65.

Pietromonaco, P. R., & Markus, H. (1985). The nature of negative thoughts in depression. *Journal of Personality and Social Psychology, 48,* 799–807.

Pietromonaco, P. R., & Rook, K. S. (1987). Decision style in depression: The contribution of perceived risks versus benefits. *Journal of Personality and Social Psychology, 52,* 399–408.

Piliavin, J. A., Callero, P. L., & Evans, D. E. (1982). Addiction to altruism? Opponent-process theory and habitual blood donation. *Journal of Personality and Social Psychology, 43,* 1200–1213.

Pillemer, D. B. (1984). Flashbulb memories of the assassination attempt on President Reagan. *Cognition, 16,* 63–80.

Pinker, S. (1985). Visual cognition: An introduction. In S. Pinker (Ed.), *Visual cognition* (pp. 1–63). Cambridge, MA: MIT Press.

Pinker, S., & Birdsong, D. (1979). Speakers' sensitivity to rules of frozen word order. *Journal of Verbal Learning and Verbal Behavior, 18,* 497–508.

Pitz, G. F., & Sachs, N. J. (1984). Judgment and decision: Theory and application. *Annual Review of Psychology, 35,* 139–163.

Plath, S. (1971). *The bell jar.* New York: Harper & Row.

Pleck, J. H. (1985). *Working wives/working husbands.* Beverly Hills, CA: Sage.

Plomin, R. (1989). Environment and genes: Determinants of behavior. *American Psychologist, 44,* 105–111.

Plomin, R. (1990). The role of inheritance in behavior. *Science, 248,* 183–188.

Plomin, R., & DeFries, J. C. (1985). *Origins of individual differences in infancy: The Colorado Adoption Project.* New York: Academic Press.

Plous, S. (1985). Perceptual illusions and military realities: A social-psychological analysis of the nuclear arms race. *Journal of Conflict Resolution, 29,* 363–389.

Plutchik, R. (1980a). *Emotion: A psycho-evolutionary synthesis.* New York: Harper & Row.

Plutchik, R. (1980b, February). A language for the emotions. *Psychology Today,* pp. 68–78.

Polefrone, J. M., & Manuck, S. B. (1987). Gender differences in cardiovascular and neuroendocrine response to stressors. In R. C. Barnett, L. Biener, & G. K. Baruch (Eds.), *Gender and stress* (pp. 13–38). New York: Free Press.

Polivy, J., & Herman, C. P. (1985). Dieting and binging: A causal analysis. *American Psychologist, 40,* 193–201.

Pollatsek, A., Bolozky, S., Well, A. D., & Rayner, K. (1981). Asymmetries in the perceptual span for Israeli readers. *Brain and Language, 14,* 174–180.

Pomerleau, O. F., & Rodin, J. (1986). Behavioral medicine and health psychology. In S. L. Garfield & A. E. Bergin (Eds.), *Handbook of psychotherapy and behavior change* (3rd ed., pp. 483–522). New York: Wiley.

Pope, K. S., Tabachnick, B. G., & Keith-Spiegel, P. (1987). Ethics of practice: The beliefs and behaviors of psychologists as therapists. *American Psychologist, 42,* 993–1006.

Porter, R. H., Cernoch, J. M., & McLaughlin, F. J. (1983). Maternal recognition of neonates through olfactory cues. *Physiology & Behavior, 30,* 151–154.

Porter, R. H., & Moore, J. D. (1981). Human kin recognition by olfactory cues. *Physiology & Behavior, 27,* 493–495.

Posner, M. I. (1988). Structures and functions of selective attention. In T. Boll & B. Bryant (Eds.), *Clinical neuropsychology and brain function* (pp. 169–202). Washington, DC: American Psychological Association.

Posner, M. I., & Keele, S. W. (1967). Decay of visual information from a single letter. *Science, 158,* 137–139.

Potts, R., Huston, A. C., & Wright, J. C. (1986). The effects of television form and violent content on boys' attention and social behavior. *Journal of Experimental Child Psychology, 41,* 1–17.

Premack, D. (1983). Animal cognition. *Annual Review of Psychology, 34,* 351–362.

Price, S. J., & McKenry, P. C. (1988). *Divorce.* Beverly Hills, CA: Sage.

Prideaux, G. D. (1985). *Psycholinguistics.* New York: Guilford Press.

Pruitt, D. G., & Rubin, J. Z. (1986). *Social conflict.* New York: Random House.

Pugh, E. N., Jr. (1988). Vision: Physics and retinal physiology. In R. C. Atkinson, R. J. Herrnstein, G. Lindzey, & R. D. Luce (Eds.), *Stevens' handbook of experimental psychology* (2nd ed., Vol. 1, pp. 75–163). New York: Wiley.

Pylyshyn, Z. W. (1978). Imagery and artificial intelligence. In C. W. Savage (Ed.), *Perception and cognition issues in the foundations of psychology* (Minnesota studies in the philosophy of science, Vol. 9, pp. 19–56). Minneapolis: University of Minnesota Press.

Pylyshyn, Z. W. (1984). *Computation and cognition.* Cambridge, MA: MIT Press.

Quattrone, G. A. (1986). On the perception of a group's variability. In S. Worchel & W. Austin (Eds.), *Psychology of intergroup relations* (Vol. 2, pp. 25–48). Chicago: Nelson-Hall.

Quattrone, G. A., & Jones, E. E. (1980). The perception of variability within ingroups and outgroups: Implications for the law of small numbers. *Journal of Personality and Social Psychology, 38,* 141–152.

Rabin, M. D., & Cain, W. S. (1986). Determinants of measured olfactory sensitivity. *Perception & Psychophysics, 39,* 281–286.

Radecki, T. E. (1990, April–June). Cartoon monitoring. *National Coalition on Television Violence News,* p. 9.

Radke-Yarrow, M., Zahn-Waxler, C., & Chapman, M. (1983). Children's prosocial dispositions and behavior. In P. H. Mussen (Ed.), *Handbook of child psychology* (Vol. 4, pp. 446–545). New York: Wiley.

Radloff, L. S. (1975). Sex differences in depression: The effects of occupation and marital status. *Sex Roles, 1,* 249–265.

Rados, R., & Cartwright, R. D. (1982). Where do dreams come from? *Journal of Abnormal Psychology, 91,* 433–436.

Rainey, L. C. (1988). The experience of dying. In H. Wass, F. M. Berardo, & R. A. Neimeyer (Eds.), *Dying: Facing the facts* (2nd ed., pp. 137–157). Washington, DC: Hemisphere.

Rango, N. A., & Rampolla, M. (1990). Expanding the focus of human immunodeficiency virus prevention in the 1990s. *New York State Journal of Medicine, 90,* 116–119.

Raskin, P. A., & Israel, A. C. (1981). Sex-role imitation in children: Effects of sex of child, sex of model, and sex-role appropriateness of modeled behavior. *Sex Roles, 7,* 1067–1076.

Rattan, A. I., & Rattan, G. (1987). A historical perspective on the nature of intelligence. In R. S. Dean (Ed.), *Introduction to assessing human intelligence* (pp. 5–28). Springfield, IL: Thomas.

Raw, M. (1986). Smoking cessation strategies. In W. R. Miller & N. Heather (Eds.), *Treating addictive behaviors* (pp. 279–287). New York: Plenum.

Ray, D. C., McKinney, K. A., & Ford, C. V. (1987). Differences in psychologists' ratings of older and younger clients. *The Gerontologist, 27,* 82–86.

Raybon, P. (1989, October 2). A case of 'severe bias.' *Newsweek,* p. 11.

Rayner, K. (1978). Eye movements in reading and information processing. *Psychological Bulletin, 85,* 618–660.

Reason, J. (1984). Absent-mindedness and cognitive control. In J. E. Harris & P. E. Morris (Eds.), *Everyday memory, actions and absent-mindedness* (pp. 113–132). London: Academic Press.

Reason, J., & Mycielska, K. (1982). *Absent-minded? The psychology of mental lapses and everyday errors.* Englewood Cliffs, NJ: Prentice-Hall.

Rebok, G. W. (1987). *Life-span cognitive development.* New York: Holt, Rinehart and Winston.

Reed, G. F. (1985). *Obsessional experience and compulsive behaviour: A cognitive-structural approach.* Orlando, FL: Academic Press.

Reed, S. K., Dempster, A., & Ettinger, M. (1985). Usefulness of analogous solutions for solving algebra word problems. *Journal of Experimental Psychology: Learning, Memory, and Cognition, 11,* 106–125.

Reeder, G. D., McCormick, C. B., & Esselman, E. D. (1987). Self-referent processing and recall of prose. *Journal of Educational Psychology, 79,* 243–248.

Reese, E. P. (1986). Learning about teaching from teaching about learning: Presenting behavioral analysis in an introductory survey course. In V. P. Makosky (Ed.), *The G. Stanley Hall lecture series* (Vol. 6, pp. 65–127). Washington, DC: American Psychological Association.

Reicher, G. M. (1969). Perceptual recognition as a function of meaningfulness of stimulus materials. *Journal of Experimental Psychology, 81,* 275–280.

Reid, P. T. (1988). Racism and sexism: Comparisons and conflicts. In P. A. Katz & D. A. Taylor (Eds.), *Eliminating racism: Profiles in controversy* (pp. 203–221). New York: Plenum.

Reisenzein, R. (1983). The Schachter theory of emotion: Two decades later. *Psychological Bulletin, 94,* 239–264.

Reitman, J. S. (1974). Without surreptitious rehearsal, information in short-term memory decays. *Journal of Verbal Learning and Verbal Behavior, 13,* 365–377.

Renzulli, J. S. (1986). The three-ring conception of giftedness: A developmental model for creative productivity. In R. J. Sternberg & J. E. Davidson (Eds.), *Conceptions of giftedness* (pp. 53–92). New York: Cambridge University Press.

Rescorla, R. A. (1968). Probability of shock in the presence and absence of CS in fear conditioning. *Journal of Comparative and Physiological Psychology, 66,* 1–5.

Rescorla, R. A. (1987). A Pavlovian analysis of goal-directed behavior. *American Psychologist, 42,* 119–129.

Rescorla, R. A. (1988). Pavlovian conditioning: It's not what you think it is. *American Psychologist, 43,* 151–160.

Rescorla, R. A., & Holland, P. C. (1982). Behavioral studies of associative learning in animals. *Annual Review of Psychology, 33,* 265–308.

Revusky, S. H. (1971). The role of interference in association over a delay. In W. K. Honig & P. H. R. James (Eds.), *Animal memory* (pp. 155–213). New York: Academic Press.

Reynolds, C. F. (1986, Spring). Sleep problems. *Generations,* pp. 24–27.

Reynolds, W. M., & Coats, K. I. (1986). A comparison of cognitive-behavioral therapy and relaxation training for the treatment of depression in adolescents. *Journal of Consulting and Clinical Psychology, 54,* 653–660.

Rheingold, H. L., & Emery, G. N. (1986). The nurturant acts of very young children. In D. Olweus, J. Block, & M. Radke-Yarrow (Eds.), *Development of antisocial and prosocial behavior* (pp. 75–96). Orlando, FL: Academic Press.

Rhyne, D. (1981). Bases of marital satisfaction among men and women. *Journal of Marriage and the Family, 43,* 941–955.

Rice, M. L. (1989). Children's language acquisition. *American Psychologist, 44,* 149–156.

Rice, P. L. (1987). *Stress and health.* Monterey, CA: Brooks/Cole.

Rivlin, R., & Gravelle, K. (1984). *Deciphering the senses.* New York: Simon & Schuster.

Robinson, J. (1987, September 12). Senators told of family's plight with AIDS. *Boston Globe,* p. 1.

Rock, I. (1983). *The logic of perception.* Cambridge, MA: MIT Press.

Rodgers, J. E. (1982). The malleable memory of eyewitnesses. *Science Digest, 3,* 32–35.

Rodgers, W. L., & Herzog, A. R. (1987). Interviewing older adults: The accuracy of factual information. *Journal of Gerontology, 42,* 387–394.

Rodin, J. (1981). Current status of the internal-external hypothesis for obesity: What went wrong. *American Psychologist, 36,* 361–372.

Rodin, J. (1985). Insulin levels, hunger, and food intake: An example of feedback loops in body weight regulation. *Health Psychology, 4,* 1–24.

Rodin, J. (1986). Aging and health: Effects of the sense of control. *Science, 233,* 1271–1276.

Rodin, J., & Langer, E. J. (1977). Long-term effects of a control-relevant intervention with the institutionalized aged. *Journal of Personality and Social Psychology, 35,* 897–902.

Rodin, J., & Salovey, P. (1989). Health psychology. *Annual Review of Psychology, 40,* 533–579.

Roffwarg, H. P., Muzio, J. N., & Dement, W. C. (1966). Ontogenetic development of the human sleep-dream cycle. *Science, 37,* 604–619.

Rogers, C. R. (1959). A theory of therapy, personality, and interpersonal relationships, as developed in the client-centered framework. In

S. Koch (Ed.), *Psychology: A study of a science* (Vol. 3). New York: McGraw-Hill.

Rogers, C. R. (1961). *On becoming a person: A therapist's view of psychotherapy.* Boston: Houghton Mifflin.

Rogers, C. R. (1963). Actualizing tendency in relation to "motives" and to consciousness. In M. R. Jones (Ed.), *Nebraska symposium on motivation* (pp. 1–24). Lincoln: University of Nebraska Press.

Rogers, C. R. (1980). *A way of being.* Boston: Houghton Mifflin.

Rogers, C. R. (1985). Toward a more human science of the person. *Journal of Humanistic Psychology, 25,* 7–24.

Rogers, C. R. (1986). Client-centered therapy. In I. L. Kutash & A. Wolf (Eds.), *Psychotherapist's casebook* (pp. 197–208). San Francisco: Jossey-Bass.

Rogers, C. R. (1987). A silent young man. In G. S. Belkin (Ed.), *Contemporary psychotherapies* (2nd. ed., pp. 199–209). Monterey, CA: Brooks/Cole.

Rogers, T. B. (1983). Emotion, imagery, and verbal codes: A closer look at an increasingly complex interaction. In J. Yuille (Ed.), *Imagery, memory, and cognition* (pp. 285–305). Hillsdale, NJ: Erlbaum.

Rogers, T. B., Kuiper, N. A., & Kirker, W. S. (1977). Self-reference and the encoding of personal information. *Journal of Personality and Social Psychology, 35,* 677–688.

Roitblat, H. L. (1987). *Introduction to comparative cognition.* New York: Freeman.

Rolls, B. J., Rowe, E. T., & Rolls, E. T. (1982). How sensory properties of food affect human feeding behavior. *Physiology and Behavior, 29,* 409–417.

Romaniuk, M. (1981). Reminiscence and the second half of life. *Experimental Aging Research, 7,* 315–336.

Rosch, E. E. (1973). Natural categories. *Cognitive Psychology, 4,* 328–350.

Rosch, E. H. (1977). Human categorization. In N. Warren (Ed.), *Advances in cross-cultural psychology* (Vol. 1). London: Academic Press.

Rosch, E. H. (1978). Principles of categorization. In E. H. Rosch & B. Lloyd (Eds.), *Cognition and categorization.* Hillsdale, NJ: Erlbaum.

Rosch, E. H., & Mervis, C. B. (1975). Family resemblances: Studies in the internal structure of categories. *Cognitive Psychology, 7,* 573–605.

Rose, S. M., & Black, B. L. (1985). *Advocacy and empowerment: Mental health care in the community.* London: Routledge & Kegan Paul.

Rosekrans, M., & Hartup, W. (1967). Imitative influences of consistent and inconsistent response consequences to a model on aggressive behavior in children. *Journal of Personality and Social Psychology, 7,* 429–434.

Rosen, C. M. (1987, September). The eerie world of reunited twins. *Discover,* pp. 36–46.

Rosenbaum, M. (1986). The repulsion hypothesis: On the nondevelopment of relationships. *Journal of Personality and Social Psychology, 51,* 1156–1166.

Rosenhan, D. L. (1973). On being sane in insane places. *Science, 179,* 250–258.

Rosenman, R. H. (1990). Type A behavior pattern: A personal overview. *Journal of Social Behavior and Personality, 5,* 1–24.

Rosenthal, R. (1968, September). Self-fulfilling prophecy. *Psychology Today,* pp. 44–51.

Rosenthal, R. (1973, September). The pygmalion effect lives. *Psychology Today,* pp. 56–63

Rosenthal, R. (1974). *On the social psychology of the self-fulfilling prophecy: Further evidence for Pygmalion effects and their mediating mechanisms.* New York: MSS Modular Publications.

Rosenthal, R. (1976). *Experimenter effects in behavioral research* (enlarged ed.). New York: Halstead Press.

Rosenthal, R., & Fode, K. L. (1963). Psychology of the scientist: V. Three experiments in experimenter bias. *Psychological Reports, 12,* 491–511.

Ross, A. O. (1987). *Personality: The scientific study of complex human behavior.* New York: Holt, Rinehart and Winston.

Ross, L. D. (1988). Situationist perspectives on the obedience experiments. [Review of A. G. Miller's *The obedience experiments: A case study of controversy in social science.*] *Contemporary Psychology, 33,* 101–104.

Rosser, P. (1989, May/June). SATs no gauge of students' abilities. *New Directions for Women,* pp. 1, 7.

Rosser, R. A., & Nicholson, G. I. (1984). *Educational psychology: Principles in practice.* Boston: Little, Brown.

Roşu, D., & Natanson, K. (1987, April). Out of the mouths of babes. *Michigan Today,* p. 5.

Rothenberg, P. S. (1988). *Racism and sexism: An integrated study.* New York: St. Martin's Press.

Rotton, J., & Kelly, I. W. (1985). Much ado about the full moon: A meta-analysis of lunar-lunacy research. *Psychological Bulletin, 97,* 286–306.

Rovee-Collier, C. K. (1987, April). *Infant memory.* Paper presented at the annual meeting of the Eastern Psychological Association, Crystal City, VA.

Rovee-Collier, C. K., Griesler, P. C., & Early, L. A. (1985). Contextual determinants of retrieval in three-month-old infants. *Learning and Motivation, 16,* 139–157.

Rovee-Collier, C. K., & Hayne, H. (1987). Reactivation of infant memory: Implications for cognitive development. *Advances in Child Development and Behavior, 20,* 185–238.

Rozin, P., Millman, L., & Nemeroff, C. (1986). Operation of the laws of sympathetic magic in disgust and other domains. *Journal of Personality and Social Psychology, 50,* 703–712.

Rubin, D. C., & Kontis, T. C. (1983). A schema for common cents. *Memory & Cognition, 11,* 335–341.

Rubin, D. H., Krasilnikoff, P. A., Leventhal, J. M., Weile, B., & Berget, A. (1986, August 23). Effect of passive smoking on birth-weight. *Lancet,* pp. 415–417.

Rubin, E. (1958). Synoplevede Figurer. Copenhagen: Cyldendalske. Abridged translation by M. Wertheimer: Figure and ground. In D. C. Beardsley & M. Wertheimer (Eds.), *Readings in perception.* Princeton, NJ: Van Nostrand. (Original work published 1915)

Rubin, Z., Peplau, L. A., & Hill, C. T. (1981). Loving and leaving: Sex differences in romantic attachments. *Sex Roles, 7,* 821–835.

Rubinstein, B. (1986, October 20). Making the private-school grade. *New York,* pp. 54–57.

Ruder, A. M., Flam, R., Flatto, D., & Curran, A. S. (1990). AIDS education: Evaluation of school and worksite-based presentations. *New York State Journal of Medicine, 90,* 129–133.

Rumbaugh, D. M. (1988, August). *Comparative psychology and the great apes: Their competence in learning, language, and numbers.* Paper presented at the convention of the American Psychological Association, Atlanta, GA.

Runeson, S., & Frykholm, G. (1983). Kinematic specifications of dynamics as an informational basis for person-and-action perception: Expectation, gender-recognition, and deceptive intension. *Journal of Experimental Psychology: General, 112,* 585–615.

Rushton, J. P., & Campbell, A. C. (1977). Modeling, vicarious reinforcement and extraversion on blood donating in adults: Immediate and long-term effects. *European Journal of Social Psychology, 7,* 297–306.

Rushton, J. P., Chrisjohn, R. D., & Fekken, G. C. (1981). The altruistic personality and the self-report altruism scale. *Personality and Individual Differences, 2,* 293–302.

Rushton, W. A. H. (1958). Kinetics of cone pigments measured objectively in the living human fovea. *Annals of the New York Academy of Science, 74,* 291–304.

Russell, D. (1975). *The politics of rape.* New York: Stein & Day.

Russell, M. J. (1976). Human olfactory communication. *Nature, 260,* 520–522.

Russo, N. F. (1983). Psychology's foremothers: Their achievements in context. In A. N. O'Connell & N. F. Russo (Eds.), *Models of achievement* (pp. 9–24). New York: Columbia University Press.

Ryan, R. M. (1984). An appropriate, original look at appropriate originality [Review of *The social psychology of creativity*]. *Contemporary Psychology, 29,* 533–535.

Rychlak, J. F. (1981a). *Instructor's manual to Introduction to personality and psychotherapy* (2nd ed.). Boston: Houghton Mifflin.

Rychlak, J. F. (1981b). *Introduction to personality and psychotherapy* (2nd ed.). Boston: Houghton Mifflin.

Sabini, J. (1986). Obituary: Stanley Milgram (1933–1984). *American Psychologist, 41,* 1378–1379.

Safire, W. (1979, May 27). "I led the pigeons to the flag." *New York Times Magazine,* pp. 9–10.

Sakitt, B. (1976). Iconic memory. *Psychological Review, 83,* 257–276.

Salamé, P., & Baddeley, A. (1982). Disruption of short-term memory by unattended speech: Implications for the structure of working memory. *Journal of Verbal Learning and Verbal Behavior, 21,* 150–164.

Salinger, K. (1988a). The future of behavior analysis in psychopathology. *Behavior Analysis, 23,* 53–60.

Salinger, K. (1988b, August). *How a radical behaviorist worked in abnormal psychology and found behavior.* Paper presented at the convention of the American Psychological Association, Atlanta, GA.

Salisbury, S. (1990, March–April). Alcoholism: In the genes? *State University of New York Research,* pp. 8–10.

Salthouse, T. A. (1987). Age, experience and compensation. In C. Schooler, & K. W. Schaie (Eds.), *Cognitive functioning and social structure over the life course* (pp. 142–157). Norwood, NJ: Ablex.

Samelson, F. (1987). Was early mental testing (a) racist inspired, (b) objective science, (c) a technology for democracy, (d) the origin of multiple-choice exams, (e) none of the above?

(Mark the RIGHT answer). In M. M. Sokal (Ed.), *Psychological testing and American society 1890–1930* (pp. 113–127). New Brunswick, NJ: Rutgers University Press.

Samuel, A. G., & Ressler, W. H. (1986). Attention within auditory word perception: Insights from the phonemic restoration illusion. *Journal of Experimental Psychology: Human Perception and Performance, 12*, 70–79.

Sande, G. N., Goethals, G. R., & Radloff, C. E. (1988). Perceiving one's own traits and others': The multifaceted self. *Journal of Personality and Social Psychology, 54*, 13–20.

Sanders, R. (1986). Eye to eye. *UCSF Magazine*, pp. 2–15.

Santrock, J. W., & Yussen, S. R. (1989). *Child development* (4th ed.). Dubuque, IA: Wm. C. Brown.

Sarason, I. G. (1984). Stress, anxiety, and cognitive interference: Reactions to tests. *Journal of Personality and Social Psychology, 46*, 929–938.

Savage, E. S., & Rumbaugh, D. M. (1977). Language learning by a chimp. In D. M. Rumbaugh (Ed.), *Language learning by a chimpanzee* (pp. 287–309). New York: Academic Press.

Savage-Rumbaugh, E. S. (1986). *Ape lamguage.* New York: Columbia University Press.

Saxe, L., Dougherty, D., & Cross, T. (1985). The validity of polygraph testing: Scientific analysis and public controversy. *American Psychologist, 40*, 355–366.

Scarborough, E., & Furumoto, L. (1987). *Untold lives: The first generation of American women psychologists.* New York: Columbia University Press.

Scarf, M. (1979, November). The more sorrowful sex. *Psychology Today*, pp. 45–52, 89–90.

Scarr, S. (1984). Intelligence: What an introductory psychology student might want to know. In A. M. Rogers & C. J. Scheirer (Eds.), *The G. Stanley Hall lecture series* (Vol. 4, pp. 61–99). Washington, DC: American Psychological Association.

Scarr, S., Pakstis, A. J., Katz, S. H., & Barker, W. B. (1977). The absence of a relationship between degree of white ancestry and intellectual skills within a black population. *Human Genetics, 39*, 69–86.

Scarr, S., & Weinberg, R. A. (1976). IQ test performance of black children adopted by white families. *American Psychologist, 31*, 726–739.

Schachter, S., & Singer, J. E. (1962). Cognitive, social, and physiological determinants of emotional state. *Psychological Review, 69*, 379–399.

Schaefer, E. S., & Burnett, C. K. (1987). Stability and predictability of quality of women's marital relationships and demoralization. *Journal of Personality and Social Psychology, 53*, 1129–1136.

Schaie, K. W. (1965). A general model for the study of developmental problems. *Psychological Bulletin, 64*, 92–107.

Scharf, M. B., & Brown, L. (1986). Hypnotic drugs: Use and abuse. *Clinical Psychology Review, 6*, 39–50.

Scheier, M. F., & Carver, C. S. (1987). Dispositional optimism and physical well-being: The influence of generalized outcome expectancies on health. *Journal of Personality, 55*, 169–210.

Scheier, M. F., Weintraub, J. K., & Carver, C. S. (1986). Coping with stress: Divergent strategies of optimists and pessimists. *Journal of Personality and Social Psychology, 51*, 1257–1264.

Schelling, T. C. (1989, April). *Behavioral responses to risk: The case of cigarette smoking.* Paper presented at the convention of the Eastern Psychological Association, Boston.

Scherer, K. R. (1986). Studying emotion empirically: Issues and a paradigm for research. In K. R. Scherer, H. G. Wallbott, & A. B. Summerfield (Eds.), *Experiencing emotion.* Cambridge, England: Cambridge University Press.

Schleifer, S. J., Keller, S. E., Camerino, M., Thornton, J. C., & Stein, M. (1983). Suppression of lymphocyte stimulation following bereavement. *Journal of the American Medical Association, 250*, 374–377.

Schlesier-Stropp, B. (1984). Bulimia: A review of the literature. *Psychological Bulletin, 95*, 247–257.

Schlesinger, K. (1985). A brief introduction to a history of psychology. In G. A. Kimble & K. Schlesinger (Eds.), *Topics in the history of psychology* (Vol. 1, pp. 1–20). Hillsdale, NJ: Erlbaum.

Schlossberg, N. K. (1984). Exploring the adult years. In A. M. Rogers & C. James Scheirer (Eds.), *The G. Stanley Hall lecture series* (Vol. 4, pp. 105–154). Washington, DC: American Psychological Association.

Schmidt, G., & Sigusch, V. (1970). Sex differences in response to psychosexual stimulation by films and slides. *Journal of Sex Research, 6*, 268–283.

Schnaitter, R. (1987). American practicality and America's psychology [Review of *The origins of behaviorism: American psychology, 1870–1920*]. *Contemporary Psychology, 32*, 736–737.

Schneider, A. M., & Tarshis, B. (1986). *Introduction to physiological psychology* (3rd ed.). New York: Random House.

Schneider, B. H. (1987). *The gifted child in peer group perspective.* New York: Springer-Verlag.

Schneider, J. W., & Hacker, S. L. (1973). Sex role imagery and the use of the generic "man" in introductory texts: A case in the sociology of sociology. *American Sociologist, 8*, 12–18.

Schneidman, E. S. (1980). Suicide. In E. S. Schneidman (Ed.), *Death: Current perspectives* (2nd ed., pp. 416–434). Palo Alto, CA: Mayfield.

Schoeneman, T. J., & Rubanowitz, D. E. (1985). Attributions in the advice columns: Actors and observers, causes and reasons. *Personality and Social Psychology Bulletin, 11*, 315–325.

Schooler, C. (1987). Cognitive effects of complex environments during the life span: A review and theory. In C. Schooler & K. W. Schaie (Eds.), *Cognitive functioning and social structure over the life course* (pp. 24–49). Norwood, NJ: Ablex.

Schroeder, D. H., & Costa, P. T. (1984). Influence of life event stress on physical illness: Substantive effects or methodological flaws? *Journal of Personality and Social Psychology, 46*, 853–863.

Schulz, R., & Decker, S. (1985). Long-term adjustment to physical disability: The role of social support, perceived control, and self-blame. *Journal of Personality and Social Psychology, 48*, 1162–1172.

Schutte, N. S., Kenrick, D. T., & Sadalla, E. K. (1985). The search for predictable settings: Situational prototypes, constraint, and behavioral variation. *Journal of Personality and Social Psychology, 49*, 121–128.

Schwartz, B. (1984). *Psychology of learning and behavior* (2nd ed.). New York: Norton.

Schwartz, B. (1989). *Psychology of learning and behavior* (3rd ed.). New York: Norton.

Schwartz, H. J. (1987). Bulimia: Dynamic considerations. In H. L. Field & B. B. Domangue (Eds.), *Eating disorders throughout the life span* (pp. 59–68). New York: Praeger.

Schwartz, R., & Hartstein, N. (1986). Group psychotherapy with gay men. In T. S. Stein & C. J. Cohen (Eds.), *Contemporary perspectives on psychotherapy with lesbians and gay men* (pp. 157–177). New York: Plenum.

Schwartz, S. H. (1971). Modes of representation and problem solving: Well evolved is half solved. *Journal of Experimental Psychology, 91*, 347–350.

Scott, K. P. (1986). Effects of sex-fair reading materials on pupils' attitudes, comprehension, and interest. *American Educational Research Journal, 23*, 105–116.

Scoville, W. B., Milner, B. (1957). Loss of recent memory after bilateral hippocampal lesions. *Journal of Neurology, Neurosurgery, and psychiatry, 20*, 11–21.

Scruggs, T. E., Mastropieri, M. A., Jorgensen, C., & Monson, J. (1986). Effective mnemonic strategies for gifted learners. *Journal of the Education of the Gifted, 9*, 105–121.

Searleman, A. (1988). From swampland to prime real estate: The right hemisphere [Review of *Language, aphasia, and the right hemisphere*]. *Contemporary Psychology, 33*, 663–664.

Sears, D. O. (1988). Symbolic racism. In P. A. Katz & D. A. Taylor (Eds.), *Eliminating racism: Profiles in controversy* (pp. 53–84). New York: Plenum.

Segal, S. J., & Fusela, V. (1970). Influence of imaged pictures and sounds on detection of visual and auditory signals. *Journal of Experimental Psychology, 83*, 458–464.

Segal, Z. V. (1988). Appraisal of the self-schema construct in cognitive models of depression. *Psychological Bulletin, 103*, 147–162.

Seligman, M. E. P. (1974). Depression and learned helplessness. In R. J. Friedman & M. M. Katz (Eds.), *The psychology of depression: Contemporary theory and research* (pp. 83–113). Washington, DC: Winston-Wiley.

Seligman, M. E. P. (1989). Research in clinical psychology: Why is there so much depression today? In I. S. Cohen (Ed.), *The G. Stanley Hall lecture series* (Vol. 9, pp. 75–96). Washington, DC: American Psychological Association.

Selkoe, D. J. (1986). Altered structural proteins in plaques and tangles: What do they tell us about the biology of Alzheimer's disease? *Neurobiology of Aging, 7*, 425–432.

Selye, H. (1956). *The stress of life.* New York: McGraw-Hill.

Serbin, L. A., & O'Leary, K. D. (1975, December). How nursery schools teach girls to shut up. *Psychology Today*, pp. 57–58, 102–103.

Sexton, M., & Hebel, R. (1984). A clinical trial of change in maternal smoking and its effect on birth weight. *Journal of the American Medical Association, 251*, 911–915.

Shaffer, D. R. (1989). *Developmental psychology: Childhood and adolescence* (2nd ed.). Pacific Grove, CA: Brooks/Cole.

Shaffer, L. H. (1975). Multiple attention in continuous verbal tasks. In P. M. Rabbitt & S. Dornic (Eds.), *Attention and performance* (Vol. 5). London: Academic Press.

Shapiro, C. M. (1982). Energy expenditure and restorative sleep. *Biological Psychology, 15,* 229–239.

Shapiro, D. A., & Shapiro, D. (1982a). Meta-analysis of comparative therapy outcome studies: A replication and refinement. *Psychological Bulletin, 92,* 581–604.

Shapiro, D. A., & Shapiro, D. (1982b). Meta-analysis of comparative therapy outcome research: A critical appraisal. *Behavior Psychotherapy, 10,* 4–25.

Shapiro, D. A., & Shapiro, D. (1983). Comparative therapy outcome research: Methodological implications of meta-analysis. *Journal of Consulting and Clinical Psychology, 51,* 42–53.

Shapiro, D. H. (1984). Overview: Clinical and physiological comparison of meditation with other self-control strategies. In D. H. Shapiro & R. N. Walsh (Eds.), *Meditation: Classic and contemporary perspectives* (pp. 5–11). New York: Aldine.

Shatz, M., & Gelman, R. (1973). The development of communication skills. Modifications in the speech of young children as a function of listener. *Monographs of the Society for Research in Child Development, 38* (2, Serial No. 152).

Shaughnessy, J. J., & Zechmeister, E. B. (1990). *Research methods in psychology* (2nd ed.). New York: McGraw-Hill.

Shaver, K. G. (1987). *Principles of social psychology* (3rd ed.). Hillsdale, NJ: Erlbaum.

Shear, M. (1989, March/April). Murder evokes rage. *New Directions for Women,* p. 6.

Sheehan, S. (1982). *Is there no place on earth for me?* Boston: Houghton Mifflin.

Shepard, R. N. (1978). Externalization of mental images and the act of creation. In B. S. Randhawa & W. E. Coffman (Eds.), *Visual learning, thinking, and communication* (pp. 133–190). New York: Academic Press.

Shepard, R. N., & Chipman, S. (1970). Second-order isomorphism of internal representation: Shape of states. *Cognitive Psychology, 1,* 1–17.

Shepard, R. N., & Metzler, J. (1971). Mental rotation of three-dimensional objects. *Science, 171,* 701–703.

Sheppard, A. (1981). Responses to cartoons and attitudes toward aging. *Journal of Gerontology, 36,* 122–126.

Sherrill, R. E. (1986). Gestalt therapy and Gestalt psychology. *The Gestalt Journal, 9,* 53–66.

Sherrod, L. R., & Brim, O. G., Jr. (1986). Epilogue: Retrospective and prospective views of life-course research on human development. In A. B. Sørensen, F. E. Weinert, & L. R. Sherrod (Eds.), *Human development and the life course: Multidisciplinary perspectives* (pp. 557–580). Hillsdale, NJ: Erlbaum.

Shirley, M. N. (1931). *The first two years.* Minneapolis: University of Minnesota Press.

Shneidman, E. S. (1980). *Voices of death.* New York: Harper & Row.

Shneidman, E. S. (1985). *Definition of suicide.* New York: Wiley.

Sholevar, G. P. (1987). Anorexia nervosa and bulimia. In H. L. Field & B. B. Domangue (Eds.), *Eating disorders throughout the life span* (pp. 31–47). New York: Praeger.

Sidorowicz, L. S., & Lunney, G. S. (1980). Baby X revisited. *Sex Roles, 6,* 67–73.

Siegel, S. (1984). Pavlovian conditioning and heroin overdose: Reports by overdose victims. *Bulletin of the Psychonomic Society, 22,* 428–430.

Silberman, E. K. (1987). Medication and psychotherapy: What we know about combining them [Review of *Combining psychotherapy and drug therapy in clinical practice*]. *Contemporary Psychology, 32,* 40–41.

Silver, R. L., Boon, C., & Stones, M. H. (1983). Searching for meaning in misfortune: Making sense of incest. *Journal of Social Issues, 39,* 81–102.

Silverstein, B. (1989). Enemy images: The psychology of U.S. attitudes and cognitions regarding the Soviet Union. *American Psychologist, 44,* 903–913.

Silvis, G. L., & Perry, C. L. (1987). Understanding and deterring tobacco use among adolescents. *Chemical Dependency, 34,* 363–379.

Simkin, J. S., Simkin, A. N., Brien, L., & Sheldon, C. (1986). Gestalt therapy. In I. L. Kutash & A. Wolf (Eds.), *Psychotherapist's casebook* (pp. 209–221). San Francisco: Jossey-Bass.

Simon, B. L. (1987). *Never married women.* Philadelphia: Temple University Press.

Singer, J. L., & Singer, D. G. (1981). *Television, imagination, and aggression: A study of preschoolers.* Hillsdale, NJ: Erlbaum.

Singer, J. L., Singer, D. G., & Rapaczynski, W. (1984, Spring). Family patterns and television viewing as predictors of children's beliefs and aggression. *Journal of Communication, 34,* 73–89.

Sinnott, J. D. (1986). Prospective/intentional and incidental everyday memory: Effects of age and passage of time. *Psychology and Aging, 1,* 110–116.

Sjostrom, L. (1980). Fat cells and bodyweight. In A. J. Stunkard (Ed.), *Obesity.* Philadelphia: Saunders.

Skinner, B. F. (1948). Superstitious behavior in the pigeon. *Journal of Experimental Psychology, 38,* 168–172.

Skinner, B. F. (1953). *Science and human behavior.* New York: Macmillan.

Skinner, B. F. (1957). *Verbal behavior.* Englewood Cliffs, NJ: Prentice-Hall.

Skinner, B. F. (1971). *Beyond freedom and dignity.* New York: Knopf.

Skinner, B. F. (1974). *About behaviorism.* New York: Knopf.

Skinner, B. F. (1987). *Upon further reflection.* Englewood Cliffs, NJ: Prentice-Hall.

Skinner, B. F. (1988a, June). Skinner joins aversives debate. *APA Monitor,* pp. 22–23.

Skinner, B. F. (1988b, August). *The school of the future.* Paper presented at the convention of the American Psychological Association, Atlanta, GA.

Skowronski, J. R., & Carlston, D. E. (1989a). Negativity and extremity biases in impression formation: A review of explanations. *Psychological Bulletin, 105,* 1–12.

Skowronski, J. J., & Carlston, D. E. (1989b). Social judgment and social memory: The role of cue diagnosticity in negativity, positivity, and extremity biases. *Psychological Bulletin, 105,* 131–142.

Slobin, D. I. (1985). *The cross-linguistic study of language acquisition* (Vols. 1 & 2). Hillsdale, NJ: Erlbaum.

Slovic, P., Fischhoff, B., & Lichtenstein, S. (1982). Facts versus fears: Understanding perceived risk. In D. Kahneman, P. Slovic, & A. Tversky (Eds.), *Judgment under uncertainty: Heuristics and bias* (pp. 463–489). New York: Cambridge University Press.

Slovic, P., Kunreuther, H., & White, G. F. (1974). Decision processes, rationality and adjustment to natural hazards. In G. F. White (Ed.), *Natural hazards, local, national and global.* New York: Oxford University Press.

Smetana, J. G. (1986). Pre-school children's conceptions of sex-role transgressions. *Child Development, 57,* 862–871.

Smith, G. J. (1985). Facial and full-length ratings of attractiveness related to the social interactions of young children. *Sex Roles, 12,* 287–293.

Smith, M. C. (1983). Hypnotic memory enhancement of witnesses: Does it work? *Psychological Bulletin, 94,* 387–407.

Smith, M. L., & Glass, G. V. (1977). Meta-analysis of psychotherapy outcome studies. *American Psychologist, 32,* 752–760.

Smith, M. L., Glass, G. V., & Miller, T. I. (1980). *The benefits of psychotherapy.* Baltimore: Johns Hopkins University Press.

Smith, P. B., & Pederson, D. R. (1987, April). *Maternal sensitivity and patterns of infant-mother attachment.* Paper presented at the biennial meeting of the Society for Research in Child Development, Baltimore.

Smith, S. M., Glenberg, A., & Bjork, R. A. (1978). Environmental context and human memory. *Memory & Cognition, 6,* 342–353.

Smollar, J., & Youniss, J. (1982). Social development. In K. Rubin & H. Ross (Eds.), *Peer relationships and social skills in childhood* (pp. 279–298). New York: Springer-Verlag.

Snarey, J. R. (1985). Cross-cultural universality of social-moral development: A critical review of Kohlbergian research. *Psychological Bulletin, 97,* 202–232.

Snodgrass, J. G., Levy-Berger, G., & Haydon, M. (1985). *Human experimental psychology.* New York: Oxford University Press.

Snow, C. W. (1989). *Infant development.* Englewood Cliffs, NJ: Prentice-Hall.

Snyder, C. R., Higgins, R. L., & Stucby, R. J. (1983). *Excuses: Masquerades in search of grace.* New York: Wiley.

Snyder, M., Tanke, E. D., & Berscheid, E. (1977). Social perception and interpersonal behavior: On the self-fulfilling nature of social stereotypes. *Journal of Personality and Social Psychology, 35,* 656–666.

Snyder, M. (1984, November). Medicated minds. *Science 84,* pp. 141–142.

Snyder, S. H. (1985, October). The molecular basis of communication between cells. *Scientific American, 253,* 132–141.

Snyderman, M., & Rothman, S. (1988). *The IQ controversy, the media and public policy.* New Brunswick, NJ: Transaction.

Sohn, D. (1982). Sex differences in achievement self-attributions: An effect-size analysis. *Sex Roles, 8,* 345–357.

Sokal, R. R. (1977). Classification: Purposes, principles, progress, prospects. In P. N. Johnson-Laird & P. C. Wason (Eds.), *Thinking: Readings in cognitive science.* Cambridge, England: Cambridge University Press.

Solomon, R. L. (1980). The opponent-process theory of acquired motivation. *American Psychologist, 35*, 691–712.

Solso, R. L. (1991). *Cognitive psychology* (3rd ed.). Boston: Allyn & Bacon.

Sommer, B. (1983). How does menstruation affect cognitive competence and psychophysiological response? In S. Golub (Ed.), *Lifting the curse of menstruation* (pp. 53–90). New York: Haworth Press.

Sontag, S. (1979). The double standard of aging. In J. Williams (Ed.), *Psychology of women: Selected readings* (pp. 462–478). New York: Norton.

Soper, B., & Rosenthal, G. (1988). The number of neurons in the brain: How we report what we do not know. *Teaching of Psychology, 15*, 153–156.

Spanos, N. P., Gwynn, M. I., & Stam, H. J. (1983). Instructional demands and ratings of overt and hidden pain during hypnotic analgesia. *Journal of Abnormal Psychology, 92*, 479–488.

Spearman, C. (1904). "General intelligence" objectively determined and measured. *American Journal of Psychology, 15*, 201–293.

Spearman, C. (1923). *The nature of "intelligence" and the principles of cognition.* London: Macmillan.

Spelke, H. W., Hirst, W., & Neisser, U. (1976). Skills of divided attention. *Cognition, 4*, 215–230.

Spencer, G. (1988). *Projections of the United States, by age, sex, and race: 1988 to 2080.* Washington, DC: Bureau of the Census.

Sperling, G. (1960). The information available in brief visual presentations. *Psychological Monographs, 74*, 1–29.

Sperry, R. W. (1982). Some effects of disconnecting the cerebral hemispheres. *Science, 217*, 1223–1226.

Spitz, H. H. (1986). *The raising of intelligence.* Hillsdale, NJ: Erlbaum.

Spitzer, R. L. (1975). On pseudoscience in science, logic in remission, and psychiatric diagnosis: A critique of D. L. Rosenhan's "On being sane in insane places." *Journal of Abnormal Psychology, 84*, 442–452.

Sprafkin, J., Gadow, K. D., & Grayson, P. (1987). Effects of viewing aggressive cartoons on the behavior of learning disabled children. *Journal of Child Psychology and Psychiatry and Allied Disciplines, 28*, 387–398.

Springer, S. P., & Deutsch, G. (1985). *Left brain, right brain.* San Francisco: Freeman.

Squire, L. R. (1986). Mechanisms of memory. *Science, 232*, 1612–1619.

Squire, L. R. (1987). *Memory and brain.* New York: Oxford University Press.

Sroufe, L. A., & Cooper, R. G. (1988). *Child development.* New York: Knopf.

Stachnik, T. J., & Stoffelmayr, B. E. (1983). Worksite smoking cessation programs: A potential for national impact. *American Journal of Public Health, 73*, 1395–1396.

Staddon, J. E. R., & Simmelhag, V. L. (1971). The "superstition" experiment: A reexamination of its implications for the principles of adaptive behavior. *Psychological Review, 78*, 3–43.

Stanley, B., Sieber, J. E., & Melton, G. B. (1987). Empirical studies of ethical issues in research: A research agenda. *American Psychologist, 42*, 735–741.

Starker, S. (1985). Daydreams, nightmares, and insomnia: The relation of waking fantasy to sleep disturbances. *Imagination, Cognition and Personality, 4*, 237–248.

Steblay, N. M. (1987). Helping behavior in rural and urban environments: A meta-analysis. *Psychological Bulletin, 102*, 346–356.

Stein, J. F. (1985). The control of movement. In C. W. Coen (Ed.), *Functions of the brain* (pp. 67–97). Oxford, England: Clarendon.

Steinberg, D. D. (1982). *Psycholinguistics: Language, mind, and world.* London: Longman.

Stellar, E. (1954). The physiology of motivation. *Psychological Review, 61*, 5–22.

Stendhal [Beyle, M. H.]. (1927). *On love.* New York: Honi & Liveright.

Stephan, C. W., & Langlois, J. H. (1984). Baby beautiful: Adult attributions of infant competence as a function of infant attractiveness. *Child Development, 55*, 576–585.

Stern, D. (1985). *The interpersonal world of the infant.* New York: Basic.

Sternbach, R. A. (1968). *Pain: A psychophysiological analysis.* New York: Academic Press.

Sternbach, R. A. (1978). Psychological dimensions and perceptual analyses, including pathologies of pain. In E. C. Carterette & M. P. Friedman (Eds.), *Handbook of perception* (Vol. 6B). New York: Academic Press.

Sternberg, R. J. (1984a). Toward a triarchic theory of human intelligence. *Behavioral and Brain Sciences, 7*, 269–315.

Sternberg, R. J. (1984b). If at first you don't believe, try "tri" again. *Behavioral and Brain Sciences, 7*, 304–315.

Sternberg, R. J. (1985a). Human intelligence: The model is the message. *Science, 230*, 1111–1118.

Sternberg, R. J. (1985b). *Beyond IQ: A triarchic theory of human intelligence.* New York: Cambridge University Press.

Sternberg, R. J. (1986a). *Intelligence applied.* San Diego: Harcourt Brace Jovanovich.

Sternberg, R. J. (1986b). A triangular theory of love. *Psychological Review, 93*, 119–135.

Sternberg, R. J. (1988a). A three-facet model of creativity. In R. J. Sternberg (Ed.), *The nature of creativity* (pp. 125–147). Cambridge, England: Cambridge University Press.

Sternberg, R. J. (1988b). *The triarchic mind: A new theory of human intelligence.* New York: Viking.

Sternberg, R. J. (1988c). Triangulating love. In R. J. Sternberg & M. L. Barnes (Eds.), *The psychology of love* (pp. 119–138). New Haven, CT: Yale University Press.

Sternberg, R. J., & Barnes, M. L. (Eds.). (1988). *The psychology of love.* New Haven, CT: Yale University Press.

Sternberg, R. J., Conway, B. E., Ketron, J. L., & Bernstein, M. (1981). People's conceptions of intelligence. *Journal of Personality and Social Psychology, 41*, 37–55.

Sternberg, R. J., & Davidson, J. E. (1982, June). The mind of the puzzler. *Psychology Today*, pp. 37–44.

Sternberg, R. J., & Grajek, S. (1984). The nature of love. *Journal of Personality and Social Psychology, 47*, 312–329.

Sternberg, R. J., & Powell, J. S. (1983). Comprehending verbal comprehension. *American Psychologist, 38*, 878–893.

Stevens, A., & Coupe, P. (1978). Distortions in judged spatial relations. *Cognitive Psychology, 10*, 422–437.

Stevens, J. C., & Cain, W. S. (1987). Old-age deficits in the sense of smell as gauged by thresholds, magnitude matching, and odor identification. *Psychology and Aging, 2*, 36–42.

Stinnett, N., Walters, J., & Kaye, E. (1984). *Relationships in marriage and the family* (2nd ed.). New York: Macmillan.

Stoltzman, S. M. (1986). Menstrual attitudes, beliefs, and symptom experiences of adolescent females, their peers, and their mothers. In V. L. Olesen & N. F. Woods (Eds.), *Culture, society, and menstruation* (pp. 97–114). Washington, DC: Hemisphere.

Stone, A. A. (1984). Presidential address: Conceptual ambiguity and morality in modern psychiatry. In P. P. Rieker & E. Carmen (Eds.), *The gender gap in psychotherapy* (pp. 5–14). New York: Plenum.

Stone, A. A., & Neale, J. M. (1984). New measures of daily coping: Development and preliminary results. *Journal of Personality and Social Psychology, 46*, 892–906.

Stone, M. (1989, August 14). What really happened in Central Park. *New York*, pp. 30–43.

Stone, W. F., & Schaffner, P. E. (1988). *The psychology of politics* (2nd ed.). New York: Springer-Verlag.

Strack, F., Martin, L. L., & Stepper, S. (1988). Inhibiting and facilitating conditions of facial expressions: A non-obtrusive test of the facial feedback hypothesis. *Journal of Personality and Social Psychology, 54*, 768–777.

Strack, S., & Coyne, J. C. (1983). Social confirmation of dysphoria: Shared and private reactions to depression. *Journal of Personality and Social Psychology, 44*, 798–806.

Strasburger, V. C. (1985, May). When parents ask about . . . the influence of TV on their kids. *Contemporary Pediatrics*, pp. 18–30.

Straus, M. A. & Gelles, R. J. (1980). *Behind closed doors.* New York: Anchor/Doubleday.

Straus, M. A., Gelles, R. J., & Steinmetz, S. K. (1980). *Behind closed doors: Violence in the American family.* Garden City, NY: Anchor.

Streissguth, A. P., Martin, D. C., Barr, H. M., Sandman, B. M., Kirchner, G. L., & Darby, D. L. (1984). Intrauterine alcohol and nicotine exposure: Attention and reaction time in 4-year-old children. *Developmental Psychology, 20*, 533–541.

Strongman, K. T. (1987). *The psychology of emotion* (3rd ed.). New York: Wiley.

Strube, M. J. (Ed.). (1990). Type A behavior [Special issue]. *Journal of Social Behavior and Personality, 5*(1).

Strupp, H. H. (1986). Psychotherapy: Research, practice, and public policy (how to avoid dead ends). *American Psychologist, 41*, 120–130.

Stubbs, N., & Harrison, J. F. (1982). *Digest of education statistics 1982.* Washington, DC: National Center for Education Statistics.

Stunkard, A. J., Sørensen, T. I. A., Hanis, C., Teasdale, T. W., Chakraborty, R., Schull, W. J., & Schulsinger, F. (1986). An adoption study of human obesity. *The New England Journal of Medicine, 314*, 193–198.

Stuss, D. T., & Benson, D. F. (1984). Neuropsychological studies of the frontal lobe. *Psychological Bulletin, 95*, 3–28.

Suarez, M. G. (1983). *Implications of Spanish-English bilingualism on the TAT stories.* Unpublished doctoral dissertation, University of Connecticut.

Suddath, R. L., Casanova, M. F., Goldberg, T. E., Daniel, D. G., Kelsoe, J. R., & Weinberger, D. R. (1989). Temporal lobe pathology in schizophrenia: A quantitative magnetic resonance imaging study. *American Journal of Psychiatry, 146,* 464–472.

Sudman, S., & Bradburn, N. M. (1982). *Asking questions: A practical guide to questionnaire design.* San Francisco: Jossey-Bass.

Sue, D. W. (Ed.). (1981). *Counseling the culturally different.* New York: Wiley.

Sue, D. W., & Sue, D. (1985). Asian-Americans and Pacific Islanders. In P. Pedersen (Ed.), *Handbook of cross-cultural counseling and therapy* (pp. 141–155). Westport, CT: Greenwood Press.

Sue, D. W., Sue, D., & Sue, S. (1986). *Understanding abnormal behavior* (2nd ed.). Boston: Houghton Mifflin.

Sullivan-Bolyai, J., Hull, H. F., Wilson, C., & Corey, L. (1983). Neonatal herpes simplex virus infection in King County, Washington. *Journal of the American Medical Association, 250,* 3059–3062.

Suls, J., & Fletcher, B. (1985). The relative efficacy of avoidant and nonavoidant coping strategies: A meta-analysis. *Health Psychology, 4,* 249–288.

Summers, W. L., Majovski, V., Marsh, G. M., Tachiki, K., & Kling, A. (1986). Oral tetrahydroaminoacridine in long-term treatment of senile dementia, Alzheimer type. *New England Journal of Medicine, 315,* 1241–1245.

Sundberg, N. D. (1990). *Assessment of persons* (2nd ed.). Englewood Cliffs, NJ: Prentice-Hall.

Surgeon General. (1988). *The health consequences of smoking: Nicotine addiction.* Rockville, MD: U.S. Department of Health and Human Services.

Swann, W. B., Jr. (1984). Quest for accuracy in person perception: A matter of pragmatics. *Psychological Review, 91,* 457–477.

Swann, W. B., Jr., & Ely, R. J. (1984). A battle of wills: Self-verification versus behavioral confirmation. *Journal of Personality and Social Psychology, 46,* 1287–1302.

Sweeney, P. D., Anderson, K., & Bailey, S. (1986). Attributional style in depression: A meta-analytic review. *Journal of Personality and Social Psychology, 50,* 974–991.

Tajfel, H. (Ed.). (1982). *Social identity and intergroup relations.* London: Cambridge University Press.

Tajfel, H., & Turner, J. C. (1986). The social identity theory of intergroup behavior. In S. Worchel & W. G. Austin (Eds.), *The psychology of intergroup relations* (2nd ed., pp. 7–24). Chicago: Nelson-Hall.

Talk of the Town. (1989, February 27). *The New Yorker,* pp. 25–27.

Tanzi, R. E., Gusella, J. F., Watkins, P. C., Bruns, G. A. P., St. George-Hyslop, P. H., Van Keuren, M. L., Patterson, D., Pagan, S., Kurnit, D. M., & Neve, R. L. (1987). Amyloid protein gene: cDNA, mRNA distribution, and genetic linkage near the Alzheimer's locus. *Science, 235,* 880–884.

Tardif, T. Z., & Sternberg, R. J. (1988). What do we know about creativity? In R. J. Sternberg (Ed.), *The nature of creativity* (pp. 429–440). Cambridge, England: Cambridge University Press.

Tartter, V. C. (1986). *Language processes.* New York: Holt, Rinehart and Winston.

Tauber, R. T. (1988). Overcoming misunderstanding about the concept of negative reinforcement. *Teaching of Psychology, 15,* 152–153.

Tavris, C., & Offir, C. (1977). *The longest war: Sex differences in perspective.* New York: Harcourt Brace Jovanovich.

Taylor, C. B., & Arnow, B. (1988). *The nature and treatment of anxiety disorders.* New York: Free Press.

Taylor, I., & Taylor, M. M. (1983). *The psychology of reading.* New York: Academic Press.

Taylor, J. K. (1986). Family therapy. In I. L Kutash & A. Wolf (Eds.), *Psychotherapist's casebook* (pp. 439–459). San Francisco: Jossey-Bass.

Taylor, S. E. (1986). *Health psychology.* New York: Random House.

Taylor, S. E. (1989). *Positive illusions.* New York: Basic.

Taylor, S. E. (1991a). *Self-evaluation, stress and coping.* Paper presented at the meeting of the Eastern Psychological Association, New York, NY.

Taylor, S. E. (1991b). *Health psychology* (2nd ed.). New York: McGraw-Hill.

Taylor, S. E., & Brown, J. D. (1988). Illusion and well-being: A social psychological perspective on mental health. *Psychological Bulletin, 103,* 193–210.

Teghtsoonian, M. (1983). Olfaction: Perception's Cinderella. *Contemporary Psychology, 28,* 763–764.

Teitelbaum, P. H., & Epstein, A. N. (1962). The lateral hypothalamic syndrome: Recovery of feeding and drinking after lateral hypothalamic lesions. *Psychological Review, 69,* 74–90.

Terrace, H. S. (1979). *Nim: A chimpanzee who learned sign language.* New York: Knopf.

Terrace, H. S. (1981). A report to an academy, 1980. *Annals of the New York Academy of Sciences, 364,* 115–129.

Tesser, A., & Shaffer, D. R. (1990). Attitudes and attitude change. *Annual Review of Psychology, 41,* 479–523.

Thaler, R. (1980). Toward a positive theory of consumer choice. *Journal of Economic Behavior and Organization, 1,* 39–60.

Thomas, A., & Chess, S. (1977). *Temperament and development.* New York: Brunner/Mazel.

Thomas, A., & Chess, S. (1985). The behavioral study of temperament. In J. Strelau, F. Farleu, & A. Gale (Eds.), *The biological basis of personality and behavior* (Vol. 1, pp. 213–225). Washington, DC: Hemisphere.

Thomas, A., & Chess, S. (1986). The New York Longitudinal Study: From infancy to early adult life. In R. Plomin & J. Dunn (Eds.), *The study of temperament: Changes, continuities and challenges* (pp. 39–52). Hillsdale, NJ: Erlbaum.

Thomas, A., Chess, S., & Birch, H. G. (1968). *Temperament and behavior disorders in children.* New York: New York University Press.

Thomas, J. C. (1974). An analysis of behavior in the Hobbits-Orcs program. *Cognitive Psychology, 6,* 257–269.

Thompson, G. E. (1980, May). Hypertension: Implications of comparisons among blacks and whites. *Urban Health,* pp. 31–33.

Thompson, R. F. (1985). *The brain: An introduction to neuroscience.* New York: Freeman.

Thompson, S. K. (1975). Gender labels and early sex-role development. *Child Development, 46,* 339–347.

Thomson, J. R., & Chapman, R. S. (1977). Who is "Daddy" revisited: The status of two-year-olds' overextended words in use and comprehension. *Journal of Child Language, 4,* 359–375.

Thoreau, H. D. (1971). *Walden.* Princeton, NJ: Princeton University Press. (Original work published 1854)

Thoresen, C. E., & Low, K. G. (1990). Women and the type A behavior pattern: Review and commentary. *Journal of Social Behavior and Personality, 5,* 117–133.

Thorndike, E. L. (1898). Animal intelligence: An experimental study of the associative processes in animals. *Psychological Monographs, 2* (Whole no. 8).

Thorndike, R. L., Hagen, E. P., & Sattler, J. M. (1986). *The Stanford-Binet Intelligence Scale: Fourth Edition, Guide for administering and scoring.* Chicago: Riverside.

Thurstone, L. L. (1955). *The differential growth of mental abilities* (Psychometric Laboratory Rep. No. 14). Chapel Hill: University of North Carolina Press.

Tomlinson-Keasey, C. (1985). *Child development.* Homewood, IL: Dorsey.

Torrey, E. F. (1988). *Nowhere to go: The tragic odyssey of the homeless mentally ill.* New York: Harper & Row.

Torrey, E. F. (1988). *Surviving schizophrenia.* New York: Harper & Row.

Toufexis, A. (1989, January 23). A not-so-happy anniversary. *Time,* p. 54.

Travis, C. B. (1988). *Women and health psychology.* Hillsdale, NJ: Erlbaum.

Treisman, A. M. (1986, November). Features and objects in visual processing. *Scientific American, 255*(5), 114B–125.

Treisman, A. M., & Gelade, G. (1980). A feature-integration theory of attention. *Cognitive Psychology, 12,* 97–136.

Treisman, A., & Gormican, S. (1988). Feature analysis in early vision: Evidence from search asymmetries. *Psychological Review, 95,* 15–48.

Trepanier, M. L., & Romatowski, J. A. (1985). Attributes and roles assigned to characters in children's writing: Sex differences and sex-role perceptions. *Sex Roles, 13,* 263–272.

Tresemer, D. (1977). *Fear of success.* New York: Plenum.

Trevarthen, C. (1987). Split-brain and the mind. In R. L. Gregory (Ed.), *The Oxford companion to the mind* (pp. 740–746). New York: Oxford University Press.

Trimble, J. E., & LaFromboise, T. (1985). American Indians and the counseling process: Culture, adaptation, and style. In P. Pedersen (Ed.), *Handbook of cross-cultural counseling and therapy* (pp. 127–140). Westport, CT: Greenwood.

Trinder, J. (1988). Subjective insomnia without objective findings: A pseudo diagnostic classification? *Psychological Bulletin, 103,* 87–94.

Triplett, N. (1897–1898). The dynamogenic factors in pacemaking and competition. *American Journal of Psychology, 9,* 507–533.

Trope, Y. (1986). Identification and inferential processes in dispositional attribution. *Psychological Review, 93,* 239–257.

Tsai, M., & Uemura, A. (1988). Asian Americans: The struggles, the conflicts, and the successes. In P. A. Bronstein & K. Quina (Eds.), *Teaching a psychology of people* (pp. 125–133). Washington, DC: American Psychological Association.

Tucker, D. M., & Williamson, P. A. (1984). Asymmetric neural control systems in human self-regulation. *Psychological Review, 91,* 185–215.

Tulving, E. (1983). *Elements of episodic memory.* New York: Oxford University Press.

Turner, B. F. (1981). Sex-related differences in aging. In B. Wolman & G. Stricker (Eds.), *Handbook of developmental psychology.* Englewood Cliffs, NJ: Prentice-Hall.

Turner, B. F., & Turner, C. B. (1982). Mental health in the adult years. In T. M. Field, A. Huston, H. C. Quay, L. Troll, & G. E. Finley (Eds.), *Review of Human Development* (pp. 456–484). New York: Wiley.

Turner, J. S., & Helms, D. B. (1989). *Contemporary adulthood* (4th ed.). New York: Holt, Rinehart & Winston.

Turner, S. M., Beidel, D. C., & Nathan, R. S. (1985). Biological factors in obsessive-compulsive disorders. *Psychological Bulletin, 97,* 430–450.

Turner, S. M., McCann, B. S., Beidel, D. C., & Mezzich, J. E. (1986). DSM-III classification of the anxiety disorders: A psychometric study. *Journal of Abnormal Psychology, 95,* 168–172.

Tversky, A., & Kahneman, D. (1973). Availability: A heuristic for judging frequency and probability. *Cognitive Psychology, 5,* 207–232.

Tversky, A., & Kahneman, D. (1974). Judgments under uncertainty: Heuristics and biases. *Science, 185,* 1124–1131.

Tversky, A., & Kahneman, D. (1982). Judgment under uncertainty: Heuristics and biases. In D. Kahneman, P. Slovic, & A. Tversky (Eds.), *Judgment under uncertainty: Heuristics and biases* (pp. 3–20). New York: Cambridge University Press.

Tversky, A., & Kahneman, D. (1983). Extensional versus intuitive reasoning: The conjunction fallacy in probability judgment. *Psychological Review, 90,* 293–315.

Tversky, B. (1981). Distortions in memory for maps. *Cognitive Psychology, 13,* 407–433.

Tversky, B. (1990). Distortions in memory for visual displays. In S. R. Ellis, M. Kaisin, & A. Grunewald (Ed.), *Spatial instruments and spatial displays.* Hillsdale, NJ: Erlbaum.

Tyler, L. E. (1984). Some possible implications of Sternberg's triarchic theory of intelligence. *Behavioral and Brain Sciences, 7,* 301–302.

Ullman, S. (1983). The measurement of visual motion. *Trends in NeuroSciences, 6,* 177–179.

Underwood, R. N., & McConkie, G. W. (1985). Perceptual span for letter distinctions during reading. *Reading Research Quarterly, 20,* 153–162.

Unger, R. K. (1979). Toward a redefinition of sex and gender. *American Psychologist, 34,* 1085–1094.

U.S. Congress, Office of Technology Assessment. (1987). *Losing a million minds: Confronting the tragedy of Alzheimer's disease and other dementias.* Washington, DC: U.S. Government Printing Office.

U.S Department of Labor. (1980). *Perspectives on working women: A databook.* Washington, DC: U.S. Government Printing Office.

Valliant, G. (1977). *Adaptation to life.* Boston: Little, Brown.

Vaillant, G. E., & Milofsky, E. S. (1977). The etiology of alcoholism: A prospective viewpoint. *American Psychologist, 37,* 494–503.

Valenstein, A. F. (1985). Working through and resistance to change: Insight and the action system. In H. P. Blum (Ed.), *Defense and resistance* (pp. 353–373). New York: International Universities Press.

Valian, V. V., & Wales, R. J. (1976). What's what: Talkers help listeners hear and understand by clarifying sentential relations. *Cognition, 4,* 115–176.

Vance, E. B., & Wagner, N. N. (1977). Written descriptions of orgasm: A study of sex differences. In D. Byrne & L. A. Byrne (Eds.), *Exploring human sexuality* (pp. 201–212). New York: Crowell.

Van der Heijden, A. H. C. (1981). *Short-term visual information forgetting.* London: Routledge & Kegan Paul.

Van Houten, R., & Doleys, D. M. (1983). Are social reprimands effective? In S. Axelrod & J. Apsche (Eds.), *The effects of punishment on human behavior* (pp. 45–70). New York: Academic Press.

Vasquez, M. J. T., & Barón, A., Jr. (1988). The psychology of the Chicano experience: A sample course structure. In P. A. Bronstein & K. Quina (Eds.), *Teaching a psychology of people* (pp. 147–155). Washington, DC: American Psychological Association.

Vaughan, D., & Asbury, T. (1986). *General ophthalmology* (11th ed.). Los Altos, CA: Lange.

Venn, J. (1986). Hypnosis and the Lamaze method: A reply to Wideman and Singer. *American Psychologist, 41,* 475–476.

Verbrugge, L. M. (1985). Gender and health: An update on hypotheses and evidence. *Journal of Health and Social Behavior, 26,* 156–182.

Vernon, P. E. (1984). Intelligence: Some neglected topics. *Behavioral and Brain Sciences, 7,* 302–303.

von Baeyer, C. L., Sherk, D. L., & Zanna, M. P. (1981). Impression management in the job interview: When the female applicant meets the male "chauvinist" interviewer. *Personality and Social Psychology Bulletin, 7,* 45–51.

Vonnegut, M. (1975). *The Eden express: A personal account of schizophrenia.* New York: Praeger.

Vorhees, C. V., & Mollnow, E. (1987). Behavioral teratogenesis: Long-term influences on behavior from early exposure to environmental agents. In J. D. Osofsky (Ed.), *Handbook of infant development* (2nd ed., pp. 913–971). New York: Wiley.

Wagstaff, G. F. (1983). Attitudes to poverty, the Protestant ethic, and political affiliation: A preliminary investigation. *Social Behavior and Personality, 11,* 45–47.

Waldrop, M. M. (1988). Toward a unified theory of cognition. *Science, 241,* 296–298.

Walker, L. J. (1984). Sex differences in the development of moral reasoning: A critical review. *Child Development, 55,* 667–691.

Walker, L. J., de Vries, B., & Richard, S. L. (1984). The hierarchical nature of stages of moral development. *Development Psychology, 20,* 960–966.

Walker-Andrews, A. S. (1986). Intermodal perception of expressive behaviors: Relation of eye and voice? *Developmental Psychology, 22,* 373–377.

Wallach, M. A., & Kogan, N. (1959). Sex differences in judgment. *Journal of Personality, 27,* 555–564.

Wallach, M. A., & Wallach, L. (1983). *Psychology's sanction for selfishness.* San Francisco: Freeman.

Wallis, C. (1984, July 11). Unlocking pain's secrets. *Time,* pp. 58–66.

Walsh, W. B., & Betz, N. E. (1990). *Tests and assessment* (2nd ed.). Englewood Cliffs, NJ: Prentice Hall.

Walster, E., Aronson, V., Abrahams, D., & Rottmann, L. (1966). Importance of physical attractiveness in dating behavior. *Journal of Personality and Social Psychology, 4,* 508–516.

Wangensteen, O. H., & Carlson, A. J. (1931). Hunger sensation after total gastrectomy. *Proceedings of the Society for Experimental Biology, 28,* 545–547.

Wardman, W. (1985). The experience of agoraphobia. In J. C. Clarke & W. Wardman (Eds.), *Agoraphobia: A clinical and personal account* (pp. 29–43). Sydney, Australia: Pergamon.

Warga, C. (1988, September). You are what you think. *Psychology Today,* pp. 54–58.

Warr, P., & Parry, G. (1982). Paid employment and women's psychological well-being. *Psychological Bulletin, 91,* 498–516.

Warren, L. W., & McEachren, L. (1983). Psychosocial correlates of depressive symptomatology in adult women. *Journal of Abnormal Psychology, 92,* 151–160.

Warren, M. P. (1983). Physical and biological aspects of puberty. In J. Brooks-Gunn & A. C. Petersen (Eds.), *Girls at puberty* (pp. 3–28). New York: Plenum.

Warren, R. M. (1984). Perceptual restoration of obliterated sounds. *Psychological Bulletin, 96,* 371–383.

Warren, R. M., & Warren, R. P. (1970). Auditory illusions and confusions. *Scientific American, 223*(6), 30–36.

Warwick, D. P. (1975, February). Deceptive research: Social scientists ought to stop lying. *Psychology Today,* pp. 38–40; 105–106.

Washton, A. M., & Gold, M. S. (1987). *Cocaine.* New York: Guilford Press.

Wass, H., Berardo, F. M., & Neimeyer, R. A. (Eds.). (1988). *Dying: Facing the facts.* New York: Hemisphere.

Watson, J. B. (1913). Psychology as the behaviorist views it. *Psychological Review, 20,* 158–177.

Watson, J. B., & Rayner, R. (1920). Conditioned emotional reactions. *Journal of Experimental Psychology, 3,* 1–14.

Weaver, J. B., Masland, J. L., & Zillman, D. (1984). Effect of erotica on young men's aesthetic perception of their female sexual partners. *Perceptual and Motor Skills, 58,* 929–930.

Webb, M. (1989, January 16). The great white hope: Mr. G. and his Brownsville dreamers. *New York,* pp. 50–53.

Webb, W. B. (1982). Sleep and biological rhythms. In W. B. Webb (Ed.), *Biological rhythms, sleep, and performance* (pp. 87–110). New York: Wiley.

Webb, W. B. (1985). A further analysis of age and sleep deprivation effects. *Psychophysiology, 22,* 156–161.

Webb, W. B. (1988). An objective behavioral model of sleep. *Sleep, 11,* 488–496.

Webbink, P. (1986). *The power of the eyes.* New York: Springer.

Wegman, M. E. (1989). Special article: Annual summary of vital statistics—1988. *Pediatrics, 84,* 943–956.

Wehr, G. (1987). *Jung: A biography.* Boston: Shambala.

Weick, K. E. (1985). Systematic observational methods. In G. Lindzey & E. Aronson (Eds.), *Handbook of social psychology* (Vol. 1, pp. 567–634). New York: Random House.

Weigel, R. H., & Howes, P. W. (1985). Conceptions of racial prejudice: Symbolic racism reconsidered. *Journal of Social Issues, 41,* 117–138.

Weiner, B. (1985a). An attributional theory of achievement motivation and emotion. *Psychological Review, 92,* 548–573.

Weiner, B. (1985b). "Spontaneous" causal thinking. *Psychological Bulletin, 97,* 74–84.

Weiner, B., Graham, S., & Chandler, C. (1982). Causal antecedents of pity, anger and guilt. *Personality and Social Psychology Bulletin, 8,* 226–232.

Weiner, R. D. (1984). Does electroconvulsive therapy cause brain damage? *The Behavioral and Brain Sciences, 7,* 1–53.

Weingarten, H. P. (1982). Diet palability modulates sham feeding in VMH-lesioned and normal rats: Implications for finickiness and evaluation of sham-feeding data. *Journal of Comparative and Physiological Psychology, 96,* 223–233.

Weinstein, N. D. (1989). Effects of personal experience on self-protective behavior. *Psychological Bulletin, 105,* 31–50.

Weinstein, S. (1968). Intensive and extensive aspects of tactile sensitivity as a function of body part, sex, and laterality. In D. R. Kenshalo (Ed.), *The skin senses.* Springfield, IL: Thomas.

Weisberg, R. W., & Suls, J. M. (1973). An information-processing model of Duncker's candle problem. *Cognitive Psychology, 4,* 255–276.

Weishaar, M. E., & Beck, A. T. (1987). Cognitive therapy. In W. Dryden & W. L. Golden (Eds.), *Cognitive-behavioural approaches to psychotherapy* (pp. 61–91). Cambridge, England: Hemisphere.

Weiss, B., Weisz, J. R., & Bromfield, R. (1986). Performance of retarded and nonretarded persons on information-processing tasks: Further tests of the similar structure hypothesis. *Psychological Bulletin, 100,* 157–175.

Weissman, M. M. (1980). Depression. In A. M. Brodsky & R. T. Hare-Mustin (Eds.), *Women and psychotherapy* (pp. 97–112). New York: Guilford Press.

Weissman, M. M., & Klerman, G. L. (1979). *Sex differences and the epidemiology of depression* (pp. 381–425). New York: Brunner/Mazel.

Weitzman, M., & Adair, R. (1988). Divorce and children. *The Pediatric Clinics of North America, 35,* 1313–1323.

Wellman, H. M. (1985). A child's theory of mind: The development of conceptions of cognition. In S. R. Yussen (Ed.), *The growth of reflection in children* (pp. 169–203). New York: Academic Press.

Wells, G. L., & Loftus, E. F. (Eds.). (1984). *Eyewitness testimony.* New York: Cambridge University Press.

Wender, P. H., Kety, S. S., Rosenthal, D., Schulsinger, F., Ortmann, J., & Lunde, I. (1986). Psychiatric disorders in the biological and adoptive families of adopted individuals with affective disorders. *Archives of General Psychiatry, 43,* 923–929.

Werker, J. F., & Tees, R. C. (1984). Cross-language speech perception: Evidence for perceptual reorganization during the first year of life. *Infant Behavior and Development, 7,* 49–63.

Wertheimer, M. (1987). *A brief history of psychology* (3rd ed.). New York: Holt, Rinehart and Winston.

Wessells, M. G. (1982). *Cognitive psychology.* New York: Harper & Row.

West, M. O., & Prinz, R. J. (1987). Parental alcoholism and childhood psychopathology. *Psychological Bulletin, 102,* 204–218.

Wester, W. C. (1986). The relationship between hypnosis and other activities such as sleep. In B. Zilbergeld, M. G. Edelstien, & D. L. Araoz (Eds.), *Hypnosis: Questions and answers* (pp. 5–8). New York: Norton.

Westheimer, G. (1988). Vision: Space and movement. In R. C. Atkinson, R. J. Herrnstein, G. Lindzey, & R. D. Luce (Eds.), *Stevens' handbook of experimental psychology* (2nd ed., Vol. I, pp. 165–193). New York: Wiley.

Weston, C. (1985, November). Pop quiz: Are you a worrywart? *Seventeen,* p. 48.

Weston, D., & Main, M. (1980, April). *Infant responses to the crying of an adult actor in the laboratory: Stability and correlates of "concerned attention."* Paper presented at the meeting of the International Conference of Infant Studies, New Haven, CT.

Whitbourne, S. K. (1985). *The aging body: Physiological changes and psychological consequences.* New York: Springer-Verlag.

Whitbourne, S. K. (1986a). *Adult development* (2nd ed.). New York: Praeger.

Whitbourne, S. K. (1986b). *The me I know: A study of adult identity.* New York: Springer-Verlag.

White, R. K. (1988). Specifics in a positive approach to peace. *Journal of Social Issues, 44*(2), 191–202.

White, R. W. (1959). Motivation reconsidered: The concept of competence. *Psychological Review, 66,* 297–333.

Whorf, B. L. (1956). Science and linguistics. In J. B. Carroll (Ed.), *Language, thought, and reality: Selected writings of Benjamin Lee Whorf.* Cambridge, MA: MIT Press.

Wickelgren, W. A. (1965). Acoustic similarity and intrusion errors in short-term memory. *Journal of Experimental Psychology, 70,* 102–108.

Wickens, D. D., Dalezman, R. E., & Eggemeier, F. T. (1976). Multiple encoding of word attributes in memory. *Memory & Cognition, 4,* 307–310.

Widom, C. S. (1989). Does violence beget violence? A critical examination of the literature. *Psychological Bulletin, 106,* 3–28.

Wiener, D. (1988). *Albert Ellis: Passionate skeptic.* New York: Praeger.

Wilder, D. A. (1978). Reduction of intergroup discrimination through individuation of the outgroup. *Journal of Personality and Social Psychology, 36,* 1361–1374.

Williams, G. D., & Williams, A. M. (1982). Sexual behavior and the menstrual cycle. In R. C. Friedman (Ed.), *Behavior and the menstrual cycle* (pp. 155–176). New York: Marcel Dekker.

Williams, J. E., & Bennett, S. M. (1975). The definition of sex stereotypes via the adjective check list. *Sex Roles, 1,* 327–337.

Williams, J. M. G., Watts, F. N., MacLeod, C., & Mathews, A. (1988). *Cognitive psychology and emotional disorders.* Chichester, England: Wiley.

Williams, R. B., Jr., Barefoot, J. C., & Shekelle, R. B. (1985). The health consequences of hostility. In M. A. Chesney & R. H. Rosenman (Eds.), *Anger and hostility in cardiovascular and behavioral disorders* (pp. 173–185). Washington, DC: Hemisphere.

Williams, R. J., & Karacan, I. (1985). Recent developments in the diagnosis and treatment of sleep disorders. *Hospital and Community Psychiatry, 36,* 951–957.

Willner, P. (1985). Antidepressants and serotonergic neurotransmission: An integrative review. *Psychopharmacology, 85,* 387–404.

Wilson, B. A. (1984). Memory therapy in practice. In B. A. Wilson & N. Moffat (Eds.), *Clinical management of memory problems* (pp. 89–111). Rockville, MD: Aspen.

Wilson, B. A. (1987). *Rehabilitation of memory.* New York: Guilford Press.

Wise, P. H., & Meyers, A. (1988). Poverty and child health. *The Pediatric Clinics of North America, 35,* 1169–1186.

Women's Programs Office. (1988). *Women in the American Psychological Association 1988.* Washington, DC: American Psychological Association.

Wong, D. F., Wagner, H. N., Tune, L. E., Dannals, R. F., Pearlson, G. D., Links, J. M., Tamminga, C. A., Broussolle, E. P., Ravert, H. T., Wilson, A. A., Toung, J. K. T., Malat, J., Williams, J. A., O'Tuama, L. A., Snyder, S. H., Kuhar, M. J., & Gjedde, A. (1986). Positron emission tomography reveals elevated D_2 dopamine receptors in drug-naive schizophrenics. *Science, 234,* 1558–1563.

Wood, G. (1984). Research methodology: A decision-making perspective. In A. M. Rogers & C. J. Scheirer (Eds.), *The G. Stanley Hall lecture series* (Vol. 4, pp. 191–217). Washington, DC: American Psychological Association.

Woodford, J. (1989, February). The transformation of Benjamin Carson. *Michigan Today,* pp. 6–7.

Woods, N. F. (1986). Socialization and social context: Influence on perimenstrual symptoms, disability, and menstrual attitudes. In V. L. Olesen & N. F. Woods (Eds.), *Culture, society and menstruation* (pp. 115–129). Washington, DC: Hemisphere.

Woods, P. J. (1987). *Is psychology the major for you? Planning for your undergraduate years.* Washington, DC: American Psychological Association.

Wooley, S., Wooley, O. W., & Dyrenforth, S. (1979). Theoretical, practical, and social issues in behavioral treatments of obesity. *Journal of Applied Behavior Analysis, 12,* 3–25.

Word, C. H., Zanna, M. P., & Cooper, J. (1974). The nonverbal mediation of self-fulfilling prophecies in intersocial interaction. *Journal of Experimental Social Psychology, 10,* 109–120.

Wright, B. A. (1988). Attitudes and the fundamental negative bias: Conditions and corrections. In H. E. Yuker (Ed.), *Attitudes toward persons with disabilities* (pp. 3–21). New York: Springer.

Wundt, W. (1973). *An introduction to psychology* (R. Pintner, Trans.). London: George Allen. Reproduced by Arno Press, New York. (Original work published 1912)

Wurtman, R. J. (1984, January) Alzheimer's disease. *Scientific American, 252,* 62–74.

Yamamoto, J. (1986). Therapy for Asian Americans and Pacific Islanders. In C. B. Wilkinson (Ed.), *Ethnic psychiatry* (pp. 89–142). New York: Plenum.

Yarkin, K. L., Town, J. P., & Wallston, B. S. (1982). Blacks and women must try harder: Stimulus persons' race and sex attributions of causality. *Personality and Social Psychology Bulletin, 8,* 21–24.

Yellott, J. I. (1981). Binocular depth inversion. *Scientific American, 245*(1), 148–159.

Yontef, G. M., & Simkin, J. S. (1989). Gestalt therapy. In R. J. Corsini & D. Wedding (Eds.), *Current psychotherapies* (4th ed., pp. 323–361). Itasca, IL: Peacock.

Yu, B., Zhang, W., Jing, Q., Peng, R., Zhang, G., & Simon, H. A. (1985). STM capacity for Chinese and English language materials. *Memory & Cognition, 13,* 202–207.

Yussen, S. R. (1984). A triarchic reaction to a triarchic theory of intelligence. *Behavioral and Brain Sciences, 7,* 303.

Yussen, S. R., & Levy, V. M. (1975). Developmental changes in predicting one's own span of short-term memory. *Journal of Experimental Child Psychology, 19,* 502–508.

Zahn-Waxler, C., Cummings, E. M., & Iannotti, R. (1986). Altruism and aggression: Problems and progress in research. In C. Zahn-Waxler, E. M. Cummings, & R. Iannotti (Eds.), *Altruism and aggression* (pp. 1–15). Cambridge, England: Cambridge University Press.

Zajonc, R. B. (1965). Social facilitation. *Science, 149,* 269–275.

Zajonc, R. B. (1968). Attitudinal effects of mere exposure. *Journal of Personality and Social Psychology Monograph, 9* (1–29, Pt. 2).

Zajonc, R. B. (1980). Feeling and thinking: Preferences need no inferences. *American Psychologist, 35,* 151–175.

Zajonc, R. B. (1984). On the primacy of affect. *American Psychologist, 39,* 117–123.

Zajonc, R. B., Murphy, S. T., & Inglehart, M. (1989). Feeling and facial efference: Implications of the vascular theory of emotion. *Psychological Review, 96,* 395–416.

Zamansky, H. S., & Bartis, S. P. (1985). The dissociation of an experience: The hidden observer observed. *Journal of Abnormal Psychology, 94,* 243–248.

Zaragoza, M., McCloskey, M., & Jamis, M. (1987). Misleading postevent information and recall of the original event: Further evidence against the memory impairment hypothesis. *Journal of Experimental Psychology: Learning, Memory, and Cognition, 13,* 36–44.

Zechmeister, E. B., Rusch, K. M., & Markell, K. A. (1986). Training college students to assess accurately what they know and don't know. *Human Learning, 5,* 3–19.

Zelinski, E. M., Light, L. L., & Gilewski, M. J. (1984). Adult age differences in memory for prose: The question of sensitivity to passage structure. *Developmental Psychology, 20,* 1181–1192.

Zhang, G., & Simon, H. A. (1985). STM capacity for Chinese words and idioms: Chunking and acoustical loop hypothesis. *Memory & Cognition, 13,* 193–210.

Zigler, E., & Balla, D. A. (1982). *Mental retardation: The developmental-difference controversy.* Hillsdale, NJ: Erlbaum.

Zigler, E., & Glick, M. (1986). *A developmental approach to adult psychopathology.* New York: Wiley.

Zigler, E. F. (1987). Formal schooling for four-year-olds? No. *American Psychologist, 42,* 254–260.

Zilbergeld, B., & Ellison, C. R. (1980). Desire discrepancies and arousal problems in sex therapy. In S. R. Leiblum & L. A. Pervin (Eds.), *Principles and practice of sex therapy.* New York: Guilford Press.

Zimbardo, P. G. (1971, October 25). *The psychological power and pathology of imprisonment.* A statement prepared for the U.S. House of Representatives Committee on the Judiciary, Subcommittee No. 3: Hearings on Prison Reform, San Francisco.

Zimbardo, P. G., Haney, C., & Banks, W. C. (1973, April 8). A Pirandellian prison. *New York Times Magazine,* pp. 38–60.

Zimbardo, P. G., Haney, C., Banks, W. C., & Jaffe, D. (1972). *The psychology of imprisonment: Privation, power and pathology.* Unpublished manuscript, Stanford University.

PHOTO CREDITS

Chapter 1 Chapter opening, David Roth; p. 4, The Bettmann Archive; p. 5, Archives of the History of American Psychology, Akron, Ohio; p. 6 (top, left to right), Archives of the History of American Psychology, The Bettmann Archive, Archives of the History of American Psychology, Courtesy of Wellesley College Archives; p. 6 (bottom, left to right), Department of Manuscripts and University Archives Cornell University Library, Archives of the History of American Psychology, Archives of the History of American Psychology, Culver Pictures; p. 8, The Bettmann Archive; p. 11 (top), The Bettmann Archive; p. 11 (bottom), Courtesy of the Center for Studies of the Person; p. 12 (top), William Carter; p. 12 (bottom), Yoav Levy/Phototake; p. 13 (top), Courtesy of Dr. George Rebok; p. 13 (middle), John P. Fox/Beaver College; p. 13 (bottom), Courtesy of Dr. Lynn Offermann; p. 14 (both), Robert V. Guthrie Collection; p. 15, Robert E. Daemmrich/TSW—Click/Chicago, Ltd.

Chapter 2 Page 20, Andre Gallanto/The Image Bank; p. 25, Comstock; p. 39 (top), Custom Medical Stock Photography, Inc.; p. 39 (bottom), @ 1987 Robert Houser/Comstock; p. 42, Ron Pretzer/LUXE; p. 45 (top), Custom Medical Stock Photography, Inc.; p. 45 (bottom), Janeart, Ltd./The Image Bank.

Chapter 3 Page 56, Phototake; p. 59 (top), Biological Photo Service; p. 59 (bottom), Dr. E. R. Lewis/University of California at Berkeley; p. 65, Dan McCoy/Rainbow; p. 67, Dr. William Feindel/Montreal Neurological Institute; p. 68 (top), @ S.I.U./Visuals Unlimited; p. 68 (bottom), Courtesy of Drs. Michael E. Phelps and John C. Mazziotta, UCLA School of Medicine; p. 70, Bonnie Kamin; p. 73, Lester V. Bergman and Associates, Inc.; p. 80, Ron Pretzer/LUXE; p. 81, Will McIntyre/Science Source/Photo Researchers; p. 82, Dr. Marshall Folstein/Johns Hopkins Hospital; p. 83 (top), Office of Technology Assessment, U.S. Congress; p. 83 (bottom), Dr. Dennis Dickson, Albert Einstein College of Medicine/Peter Arnold, Inc.; p. 85, Peter Chapman; p. 87, Dan McCoy/Rainbow; p. 87 (bottom), Dan McCoy/Rainbow; p. 88 (left), Wide World Photos, David Toy, Lake Graphics; p. 88 (right).

Chapter 4 Page 92, Jake Rajs/The Image Bank; p. 95, Elinore Matlin; p. 96, The Image Bank; p. 101, Courtesy of Dr. E. R. Lewis, University of California at Berkeley; p. 108, Elinore Matlin; p. 111, @ 1990 M. C. Escher Heirs/Cordon Art/Baarn, Holland; p. 112, Ron Pretzer/LUXE; p. 113, Sverker Runeson/Uppsala Universitet; p. 114, Stanford University Photographic Services; p. 115, Kunio Owaki/The Stock Market; p. 116, Ron Pretzer/LUXE; p. 122, Dr. G. Bredberg/Science Photo Library/Photo Researchers, Inc.; p. 127, @ Steve Leonard TSW—Click/Chicago, Ltd.; p. 129, Ron Pretzer/LUXE; p. 130, Courtesy of A. K. Das.

Chapter 5 Page 136, Eddie Hironaka/The Image Bank; p. 142, Owen Franken/Stock Boston; p. 145, Michel Heron/Woodfin Camp and Associates; p. 150 (left), National Gallery of Art/Art Resource; p. 150 (right), Bildarchiv Foto Marburg/Art Resource; p. 153, @ 1982 Pier Angelo Simon; p. 155, @ Martin A. Levick, Scarsdale, NY; p. 158, Sandoz Pharmaceuticals, A. G.; p. 160 (top), @ David Parker/Photo Researchers, Inc.; p. 160 (bottom), Mary Evans Picture Library/Photo Researchers, Inc.; p. 166 (left), Ian Berry/Magnum Photos; p. 166 (right), Michael P. Gadomski/Photo Researchers, Inc.

Chapter 6 Page 170, Hank Morgan/Science Source/Photo Researchers, Inc.; p. 178 (left), Gabe Palmer/The Stock Market; p. 178 (right), @ 1987 David Lawrence/The Stock Market; p. 181, Tom Ulrich/TSW—Click/Chicago, Ltd.; p. 183, @ Lawrence Migdale/Stock Boston; p. 185, R. Epstein; p. 188, R. Epstein; p. 189 (top), David Austen/Stock Boston; p. 189 (bottom), Bob Daemmrich/Stock Boston; p. 193 (top), Courtesy Dr. R. J. Herrnstein, Harvard University; p. 193 (bottom), @ Breck P. Kent/Animals, Animals; p. 194, @ Cathlyn Melloan/TSW—Click/Chicago, Ltd.; p. 195, Bob Daemmrich/Stock Boston; p. 196, Lawrence Migdale/Stock Boston; p. 202, Martin A. Levick, Scarsdale, NY.

Chapter 7 Page 206, David Roth; p. 210 (top), Piotr Kapa/The Stock Market; p. 210 (bottom), Ron Pretzer/LUXE; p. 212, Ron Pretzer/LUXE; p. 221, Comstock; p. 223, The Bettmann Archive; p. 226, Ron Pretzer/LUXE; p. 228, Academic Press; p. 241, Ron Pretzer/LUXE.

Chapter 8 Page 244, Romilly Lockyer/The Image Bank; p. 250, @ 1984 Martin Rogers/Stock Boston; p. 254, Ron Pretzer/LUXE/Courtesy of Rochester Telephone; p. 255, Jerry Cooke/Animals, Animals; p. 261, Ron Pretzer/LUXE; p. 262 (bottom), P and G Bowater/The Image Bank; p. 267, Ron Pretzer/LUXE; p. 273, Ron Pretzer/LUXE.

Chapter 9 Page 274, J. R. Williams/Earth Scenes; p. 285, R. Michael Stuckey/Comstock; p. 288, Bob Daemmrich/Stock Boston; p. 289, Courtesy of New England Telephone; p. 290, David Woods/The Stock Market; p. 292 (top left), @ 1985 Richard Pasley/Stock Boston; p. 292 (top right), Myrleen Ferguson/PhotoEdit; p. 292 (bottom), Dr. R. Allen Gardner/University of Nevada at Reno; p. 294, Jack Elness/Comstock; p. 296, Ron Pretzer/LUXE; p. 297, Ron Pretzer/LUXE.

Chapter 10 Page 300, Kirkendall-Spring Photographers; p. 303 (top), Bill Binzen/The Stock Market; p. 303 (bottom), Per Sundstrom/Gamma-Liason; p. 304, Petit Format/Nestle/Science Source, Photo Researchers, Inc.; p. 305, University of Washington; p. 306, American Cancer Society; p. 309, Elizabeth Robbins/Courtesy of Dr. Richard D. Walk; p. 310, @ Barbara Filet/Tony Stone Worldwide; p. 311, Dr. Carolyn Rovee-Collier/Rutgers University; p. 312, Louise Wadsworth; p. 314 (both), Louise Wadsworth; p. 315, Ron Pretzer/LUXE; p. 317, Quesada/Burke Photography, New York; p. 319, Julie Houck/Stock Boston; p. 323 (top left), Michael A. Keller/The Stock Market; p. 323 (top right), Joan Trasdale/The Stock Market; p. 323 (bottom), Steven Burr Williams/The Image Bank; p. 326, Philip Jon Bailey/Stock Boston; p. 328, Margaret Matlin; p. 329, Dan McCoy/Rainbow; p. 332, Louise Wadsworth; p. 337, @ John Chaisson/Gamma-Liason; p. 338, Tony Freeman/PhotoEdit.

Chapter 11 Page 342, Freeman Patterson/Masterfile; p. 345, Bob Daemmrich/The Image Works; p. 348, Dr. Leon A. Pastalan/University of Michigan; p. 349, Jeffrey Mark Dunn/Stock Boston; p. 357, @ Spence Grant/Photo Researchers, Inc.; p. 358, Bettye Lane; p. 360, David Sutherland/TSW—Click/Chicago, Ltd.; p. 361, Sobel/Klonsky/The Image Bank; p. 365, Ernie Medina/Andrews University; p. 367, Elinore Matlin; p. 370, Gabe Palmer/The Stock Market; p. 371, John Moss/Photo Researchers, Inc.; p. 372, Tom Killips; p. 373 (left), David Lindsey/West Graphics; p. 373 (right), Ron Pretzer/LUXE.

Chapter 12 Page 378, Jay Dickman/Art Rep, Inc.; p. 381, Courtesy of Ashrita Furman; p. 383, Richard Howard; p. 385, Rich Chisholm/The Stock Market; p. 386, Holt, Rinehart and Winston Library; p. 388, Charles Gupton/Stock Boston; p. 392, Bernard Gaini/Vandystad/Photo Researchers, Inc.; p. 395, Michael Philip Manheim/The Stock Market; p. 396, Richard Hutchins/InfoEdit; p. 399, Peter Lamberti/Tony Stone Worldwide; p. 400, Tony Freeman/PhotoEdit; p. 403, Nubar Alexanian/Stock Boston; p. 404, Howard Frank Archives; p. 406, Human Interaction Laboratory; p. 407, Comstock; p. 408, Michael Greco/Stock Boston; p. 411, @ Tim Davis; p. 414, Ron Pretzer/LUXE; p. 416, Alan Oddie/PhotoEdit.

Chapter 13 Page 420, Cotten Alston; p. 424, Mary Evans Picture Library, London; p. 425, Louise Wadsworth; p. 428 (top), Scala/Art Resource; p. 428 (bottom), Margaret Matlin; p. 430, Elyse Lewin/The Image Bank; p. 431 (left), Collection of the Newark Museum of Art; p. 431 (right), Princeton University Press; p. 435, Mark Reinstein/TSW—Click/Chicago, Ltd.; p. 438, Martin A. Levick; p. 444, Arnold H. Matlin, M.D.; p. 448, Joseph Sohn/Stock Boston; p. 451, Margot Granitsas/Photo Researchers, Inc.; p. 452, @ J. Barry O'Rourke/The Stock Market; p. 453, Jane Addams Memorial Collection, University of Illinois at Chicago.

Chapter 14 Page 458, Charles C. Place/The Image Back; p. 461, Jim Harrison/Stock Boston; p. 468, @ 1986 Riverside Publishing Company; p. 469, Judith A. Sedwick/The Picture Cube; p. 472, Alan Carey/The Image Works; p. 473, Ron Pretzer/LUXE; p. 477, Comstock; p. 479, Focus on Sports, Inc.; p. 482, Courtesy of Louise Slaughter.

Chapter 15 Page 492, Jay Dickman/Art Rep, Inc.; p. 495, Joe Wrinn/Harvard University; p. 497, J. Barry O'Rourke/The Stock Market; p. 499, David York/The Stock Shop; p. 500, Superstock Four by Five; p. 501, Ron Pretzer/LUXE; p. 502, The Bettmann Archive; p. 509, Myrleen Ferguson/PhotoEdit; p. 514, Billy Barnes/Stock Boston; p. 515, Giraudon/Art Resource; p. 516, Superstock Four by Five; p. 518 (top), Barbara J. Feigles/Stock Boston; p. 518 (bottom), Ray Scioscia/Habitat for Humanity, Inc.; p. 522, The Prinzhorn Collection/University of Heidelberg, p. 523 (top), Superstock Four by Five; p. 523 (bottom), Courtesy of Dr. Frederick Frese; p. 525, University of California at Irvine; p. 527, Bettmann Newsphotos.

Chapter 16 Page 532, Richard Moore; p. 534, Chip Clark; p. 538, Rick Friedman/Black Star; p. 539, @ S.I.U./Visuals Unlimited; p. 546 (top), Kay Chernush/The Image Bank; p. 546 (bottom), Dr. Rose K. Gantner/Comstock; p. 549, Courtesy of Joan Nobiling; p. 550, @ Will McIntyre/Science Source/Photo Researchers; p. 555, Courtesy of Dr. Irene Elkin; p. 556, Hazel Hankin/Stock Boston; p. 559 (both), Fordham University/Lutheran Medical Center; p. 563 (top), M. Dwyer/Stock Boston; p. 563 (bottom), Courtesy of Operation Friendship.

Chapter 17 Page 566, Nick Nicholson/The Image Bank; p. 571, Ron Pretzer/LUXE; p. 574, Bettmann Newsphotos; p. 577, Courtesy of Canali USA, Inc.; p. 579, Chip Hires/Gamma-Liason; p. 581, Myrleen Ferguson/PhotoEdit; p. 583, Thomas Ives/The Stock Market; p. 588, Shirley Nakao; p. 589, Library of Congress; p. 590, Jack Iwata/National Japanese-American Historical Society; p. 593, Comstock; p. 594, Stacy Pick/Stock Boston; p. 598, Ron Pretzer/LUXE; p. 601 (left), Comstock; p. 601 (right), @ 1989 Arvind Garg/Photo Researchers, Inc.; p. 604, Courtesy of the author.

Chapter 18 Page 608, Janeart, Ltd./The Image Bank; p. 613, Dr. Philip Zimbardo/Stanford University; p. 615, The Bettmann Archive; p. 621, The Bettmann Archive; p. 622, Rhoda Sydney/PhotoEdit; p. 625, Matthew Naythons/Gamma-Liason; p. 627, Roswell Angier/Stock Boston; p. 631, The National Archive; p. 635, The Stock Market; p. 636 (top), @ 1988 Louie Psihoyos/Matrix; p. 636 (bottom), Arnold H. Matlin, M.D.; p. 639, Alan Oddie/PhotoEdit.

Chapter 19 Page 644, Kent Kirkley/Art Rep, Inc.; p. 647. Tom Brod; p. 651, Arnold H. Matlin, M.D.; p. 653, Bonnie Kamin/Comstock; p. 654, The Image Works; p. 657, Grant Le Duc/Monkmeyer Press; p. 661, National Baseball Hall of Fame and Museum, Inc.; p. 663, Eric Lars Bakke; p. 666, New York City Board of Health; p. 667, @ 1983 Alan Reininger/Contact Press Images; p. 668, New York State Department of Health; p. 671, Michael Greco/Stock Boston; p. 673, American Cancer Society.

COPYRIGHT ACKNOWLEDGMENTS

NAME INDEX